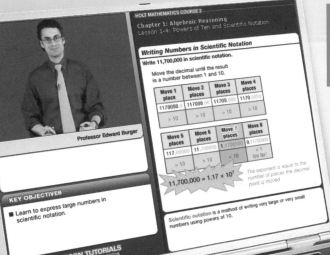

HOLT

GEORGIA

Mathematics
Course 2

Jennie M. Bennett

Edward B. Burger

David J. Chard

Audrey L. Jackson

Paul A. Kennedy

Freddie L. Renfro

Janet K. Scheer

Bert K. Waits

HOLT, RINEHART AND WINSTON

A Harcourt Education Company

Orlando • **Austin** • New York • San Diego • London

Course 2 Contents in Brief

Student Handbook

ISBN 0-03-092020-5

7 8 9 10 073 12 11 10 09 08

Cover photo: The Stata Center at MIT, Boston, Massachusetts, USA.
© Scott Gilchrist/Masterfile

AUTHORS

Jennie M. Bennett, Ph.D. is a mathematics teacher at Hartman Middle School in Houston, Texas. Jennie is past president of the Benjamin Banneker Association, the Second Vice-President of NCSM, and a former board member of NCTM.

Paul A. Kennedy, Ph.D. is a professor in the Department of Mathematics at Colorado State University. Dr. Kennedy is a leader in mathematics education. His research focuses on developing algebraic thinking by using multiple representations and technology. He is the author of numerous publications.

Edward B. Burger, Ph.D. is Professor of Mathematics and Chair at Williams College and is the author of numerous articles, books, and videos. He has won several of the most prestigious writing and teaching awards offered by the Mathematical Association of America. Dr. Burger has appeared on NBC TV, National Public Radio, and has given innumerable mathematical performances around the world.

Freddie L. Renfro, MA, has 35 years of experience in Texas education as a classroom teacher and director/coordinator of Mathematics PreK-12 for school districts in the Houston area. She has served as TEA TAAS/TAKS reviewer, team trainer for Texas Math Institutes, TEKS Algebra Institute writer, and presenter at math workshops.

David J. Chard, Ph.D., is an Associate Dean of Curriculum and Academic Programs at the University of Oregon. He is the President of the Division for Research at the Council for Exceptional Children, is a member of the International Academy for Research on Learning Disabilities, and is the Principal Investigator on two major research projects for the U.S. Department of Education.

Janet K. Scheer, Ph.D., Executive Director of Create A Vision™, is a motivational speaker and provides customized K-12 math staff development. She has taught internationally and domestically at all grade levels.

Audrey L. Jackson, M. Ed., is on the Board of Directors for NCTM. She is the Program Coordinator for Leadership Development with the St. Louis, public schools and is a former school administrator for the Parkway School District.

Bert K. Waits, Ph.D., is a Professor Emeritus of Mathematics at The Ohio State University and co-founder of T³ (Teachers Teaching with Technology), a national professional development program.

CONTRIBUTING AUTHORS

Linda Antinone
Fort Worth, TX

Ms. Antinone teaches mathematics at R. L. Paschal High School in Fort Worth, Texas. She has received the Presidential Award for Excellence in Teaching Mathematics and the National Radio Shack Teacher award. She has coauthored several books for Texas Instruments on the use of technology in mathematics.

Carmen Whitman
Pflugerville, TX

Ms. Whitman travels nationally helping districts improve mathematics education. She has been a program coordinator on the mathematics team at the Charles A. Dana Center, and has served as a secondary math specialist for the Austin Independent School District.

REVIEWERS

Thomas J. Altonjy
Assistant Principal
Robert R. Lazar Middle School
Montville, NJ

Jane Bash, M.A.
Math Education
Eisenhower Middle School
San Antonio, TX

Charlie Bialowas
District Math Coordinator
Anaheim Union High School District
Anaheim, CA

Lynn Bodet
Math Teacher
Eisenhower Middle School
San Antonio, TX

Debbie Brown
Mathematics Teacher
Eanes ISD
Austin, TX

Louis D'Angelo, Jr.
Math Teacher
Archmere Academy
Claymont, DE

Troy Deckebach
Math Teacher
Tredyffrin-Easttown Middle School
Berwyn, PA

Mary Gorman
Math Teacher
Sarasota, FL

Brian Griffith
Supervisor of Mathematics, K–12
Mechanicsburg Area School District
Mechanicsburg, PA

Ruth Harbin-Miles
District Math Coordinator
Instructional Resource Center
Olathe, KS

Anastasia Hay-Shelton
Mathematics Department Chair
San Antonio ISD
San Antonio, TX

Kim Hayden
Math Teacher
Milford Jr. High School
Milford, OH

Emily Hodges
Mathematics Teacher
Austin ISD
Austin, TX

Susan Howe
Math Teacher
Lime Kiln Middle School
Fulton, MD

Paula Jenniges
Austin, TX

Martha Krauss
Mathematics Teacher
Round Rock ISD
Round Rock, TX

Ronald J. Labrocca
District Mathematics Coordinator
Manhasset Public Schools
Manhasset, NY

Brenda Law
Mathematics Department Chair
Corpus Christi ISD
Corpus Christi, TX

PREPARING FOR CRCT

Holt Mathematics provides many opportunities
for you to prepare for the CRCT.

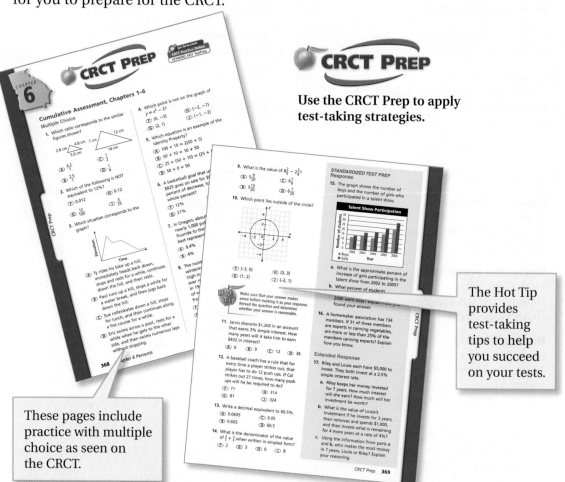

CRCT PREP

Use the CRCT Prep to apply
test-taking strategies.

The Hot Tip
provides
test-taking
tips to help
you succeed
on your tests.

These pages include
practice with multiple
choice as seen on
the CRCT.

Countdown to CRCT

Use the Countdown to CRCT to practice for your state test every day.

There are 24 pages of practice for your state test. Each page is designed to be used in a week so that all practice will be completed before your state test is given.

Each week's page has five practice test items, one for each day of the week.

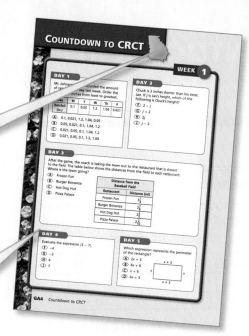

TEST TACKLER

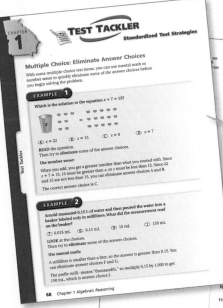

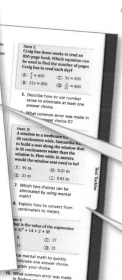

Use the Test Tackler to become familiar with and practice test-taking strategies.

The first page of this feature explains and shows an example of a test-taking strategy.

The second page guides you through applications of the test-taking strategy.

Test-Taking Tips

☑ Get plenty of sleep the night before the test. A rested mind thinks more clearly and you won't feel like falling asleep while taking the test.

☑ Draw a figure when one is not provided with the problem. If a figure is given, write any details from the problem on the figure.

☑ Read each problem carefully. As you finish each problem, read it again to make sure your answer is reasonable.

☑ Review the formula sheet that will be supplied with the test. Make sure you know when to use each formula.

☑ First answer problems that you know how to solve. If you do not know how to solve a problem, skip it and come back to it when you have finished the others.

☑ Use other test-taking strategies that can be found throughout this book, such as working backward and eliminating answer choices.

COUNTDOWN TO CRCT

DAY 1

Mr. Johnson's class recorded the amount of rainfall each day last week. Order the number of inches from least to greatest.

Day	M	T	W	Th	F
Rainfall (in.)	0.1	0.05	1.2	1.04	0.021

- (A) 0.1, 0.021, 1.2, 1.04, 0.05
- (B) 0.05, 0.021, 0.1, 1.04, 1.2
- (C) 0.021, 0.05, 0.1, 1.04, 1.2
- (D) 0.021, 0.05, 0.1, 1.2, 1.04

DAY 2

Chuck is 2 inches shorter than his sister, Jan. If j is Jan's height, which of the following is Chuck's height?

- (F) $2 - j$
- (G) $j + 2$
- (H) $2j$
- (J) $j - 2$

DAY 3

After the game, the coach is taking the team out to the restaurant that is closest to the field. The table below shows the distances from the field to each restaurant. Where is the team going?

- (A) Frozen Fun
- (B) Burger Bonanza
- (C) Hot Dog Hut
- (D) Pizza Palace

Distance from the Baseball Field	
Restaurant	Distance (mi)
Frozen Fun	$3\frac{1}{4}$
Burger Bonanza	$2\frac{7}{8}$
Hot Dog Hut	$2\frac{3}{5}$
Pizza Palace	$2\frac{2}{10}$

DAY 4

Evaluate the expression $|3 - 7|$.

- (F) -4
- (G) -3
- (H) 4
- (J) 7

DAY 5

Which expression represents the perimeter of the rectangle?

- (A) $2x + 3$
- (B) $4x + 6$
- (C) $x + 6$
- (D) $4x + 3$

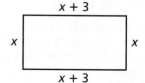

DAY 1

What point is located at (3, 5) on this coordinate plane?

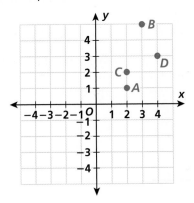

- (A) A
- (B) B
- (C) C
- (D) D

DAY 2

Use the table of Andrea's chores. How much time does it take Andrea to complete all three chores?

Andrea's Chores	
Chore	Time (hours)
Mow lawn	1.35
Do dishes	0.25
Clean room	0.9

- (F) 1.6 hours
- (G) 1.7 hours
- (H) 2.5 hours
- (J) 2.6 hours

DAY 3

When Kit woke up, it was −15°C outside. By that afternoon, the temperature had risen 20 degrees. What was the afternoon temperature?

- (A) −5°C
- (B) 5°C
- (C) 20°C
- (D) 35°C

DAY 4

Admission to Fun Zone costs $5. Each ride costs $3. Yvonne visits Fun Zone and goes on x rides. Which expression gives her total cost?

- (F) $3x + 5$
- (G) $8x$
- (H) $5x + 3$
- (J) $5 + 8x$

DAY 5

Which of the following expressions is equivalent to $3(m - 4)$?

- (A) $3m - 4$
- (B) $3(4 - m)$
- (C) $3m - 12$
- (D) $3 + m - 4$

DAY 1

Sue needed $3\frac{2}{7}$ yards of fringe to trim each drape. If she had 8 drapes to trim, how much fringe did she need?

- (A) $4\frac{6}{7}$ yards
- (B) $11\frac{2}{7}$ yards
- (C) $24\frac{3}{7}$ yards
- (D) $26\frac{2}{7}$ yards

DAY 2

Which of the following is equal to 3?

- (F) $|-2 - 1|$
- (G) $|-2 + 1|$
- (H) $|1 - 2|$
- (J) $|-1 + 2|$

DAY 3

Which point is described by the ordered pair $(2, -2)$?

- (A) B
- (B) D
- (C) E
- (D) F

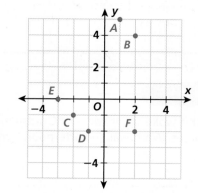

DAY 4

Find the sum of $3x - 4$ and $x + 7$.

- (F) $3x + 7$
- (G) $4x + 11$
- (H) $4x + 3$
- (J) $4x - 11$

DAY 5

Sam is growing a tomato plant in his garden. Last week, Sam picked one tomato that had a mass of 213.5 grams and another tomato that has a mass of 190.62 grams. What is the difference in mass of the two tomatoes?

- (A) 22.43 grams
- (B) 22.88 grams
- (C) 23.05 grams
- (D) 23.12 grams

DAY 1

What is the rule for the pattern in the table below?

x	1	2	3	4
y	1	4	7	10

- (A) $y = 2x + 2$
- (B) $y = 3x - 2$
- (C) $y = \frac{x}{2} \cdot 5$
- (D) $y = 2x + 1$

DAY 2

Miguel has 3 times as many stamps in his collection as Robert. Robert has s stamps in his collection. Which expression represents the number of stamps in Miguel's collection?

- (F) $\frac{s}{3}$
- (G) $s + 3$
- (H) $3s$
- (J) $3 - s$

DAY 3

Mark is researching the effects of diet on mice. The table below shows the percent change in weight of each mouse studied. If the mice weighed the same at the start of the experiment, which mouse lost the most weight?

- (A) 1
- (B) 2
- (C) 3
- (D) 4

Mouse	% Change in Weight
1	−9.2
2	3.25
3	−9.05
4	−9.095

DAY 4

Which point is at $(-5, -\frac{1}{2})$?

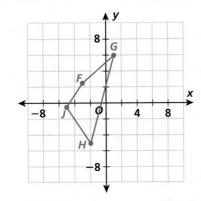

- (F) F
- (G) G
- (H) H
- (J) J

DAY 5

What is the product of 3.2 and −4.5?

- (A) −14.4
- (B) −1.3
- (C) 1.3
- (D) 14.4

DAY 1

A manufacturer of doll clothes produces more white dresses than blue dresses by a factor of 3.5. Given b, the number of blue dresses produced, which equation shows w, the number of white dresses produced?

- (A) $w = b \div 3.5$
- (B) $w = \frac{3.5}{b}$
- (C) $w = 3.5b$
- (D) $w = 3.5 + b$

DAY 2

If these two figures are similar, what is the missing length of figure B?

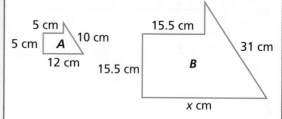

- (F) 3.1 centimeters
- (G) 22.5 centimeters
- (H) 25.2 centimeters
- (J) 37.2 centimeters

DAY 3

Mrs. Robbins is knitting a scarf for her niece. She knitted $1\frac{7}{8}$ feet yesterday and $1\frac{2}{3}$ feet today. How many feet did Mrs. Robbins knit in both days?

- (A) $\frac{5}{24}$ foot
- (C) $2\frac{9}{11}$ feet
- (B) $1\frac{3}{4}$ feet
- (D) $3\frac{13}{24}$ feet

DAY 4

Evaluate the expression $|2 - 9|$.

- (F) −11
- (G) −7
- (H) 7
- (J) 11

DAY 5

What is the price of the most expensive TV?

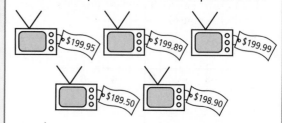

- (A) $199.89
- (C) $189.50
- (B) $199.99
- (D) $198.90

DAY 1

Find the sum of $5m - 11$ and $2m + 3$.

- (A) $7m - 14$
- (B) $3m - 14$
- (C) $7m - 8$
- (D) $3m + 8$

DAY 2

What is the solution of the equation $x - 2.5 = 6.1$?

- (F) $x = 3.6$
- (G) $x = 4.1$
- (H) $x = 6.1$
- (J) $x = 8.6$

DAY 3

Which two of the figures below are similar?

Figure A

10 ft

5 ft

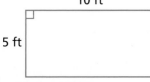

Figure B

4 ft

4 ft

Figure C

6 ft

3 ft

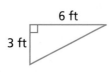

Figure D

4 ft

2 ft

- (A) Figures A and D
- (B) Figures A and B
- (C) Figures B and D
- (D) Figures B and C

DAY 4

Which point lies in Quadrant II of the coordinate plane?

- (F) $(3, 5)$
- (G) $(-4, -1)$
- (H) $(-6, 2)$
- (J) $(4, -4)$

DAY 5

Ryan is making $7\frac{1}{2}$ cups of rice to serve at dinner with his friends. If he wants to give $\frac{3}{4}$ cup of rice to each guest, how many people will the rice serve?

- (A) 8
- (B) 10
- (C) 12
- (D) 14

DAY 1

Which pair of triangles are similar?

Ⓐ

Ⓑ

Ⓒ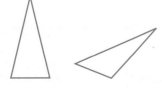

Ⓓ

DAY 2

Which point is described by the ordered pair (−1, −1)?

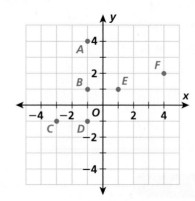

Ⓕ B

Ⓖ D

Ⓗ E

Ⓙ F

DAY 3

The Gordon family is driving to the Grand Canyon from Lubbock, Texas. If they drive an average of 55 miles per hour for h hours, which equation shows d, the distance they traveled?

Ⓐ $d = 55h$

Ⓒ $d = \frac{h}{55}$

Ⓑ $d = 55 \div h$

Ⓓ $d = 55 + h$

DAY 4

The expression $2.5n + 7$ gives the cost in dollars of printing n posters at Copy Magic. How much does it cost to print 8 posters?

Ⓕ $17.50

Ⓖ $20

Ⓗ $27

Ⓙ $37.50

DAY 5

Find the quotient: $8.4 \div (-2)$

Ⓐ −6.4

Ⓑ −4.2

Ⓒ 4.2

Ⓓ 6.4

DAY 1

Which pair contains similar figures?

Ⓐ

Ⓑ

Ⓒ

Ⓓ

DAY 2

Which equation is shown in the graph?

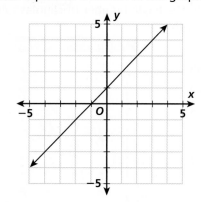

Ⓕ $y = x$ Ⓗ $y = 2x$

Ⓖ $y = x - 1$ Ⓙ $y = x + 1$

DAY 3

A computer's hard drive spins at 5400 revolutions per minute. If the hard drive has been running for m minutes, which equation shows r, the total number of revolutions?

Ⓐ $r = m + 5400$

Ⓑ $r = 5400 \cdot m$

Ⓒ $r = m \div 5400$

Ⓓ $r = \frac{5400}{m}$

DAY 4

Frank received the following test scores: 90, 82, 90, 93, 85. What is the range of his scores?

Ⓕ 5

Ⓖ 82

Ⓗ 11

Ⓙ 90

DAY 5

Which of the following is greater than 5?

Ⓐ $|-3|$

Ⓑ $|3|$

Ⓒ $|-6|$

Ⓓ $|5|$

DAY 1

What is the mean number of candles sold per month?

Ⓐ 25
Ⓑ 35
Ⓒ 40
Ⓓ 45

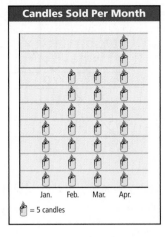

Candles Sold Per Month

Jan. Feb. Mar. Apr.

🕯 = 5 candles

DAY 2

Which equation represents the relationship in the table?

x	6	8	11	12
y	3	5	8	9

Ⓕ $y = x - 3$
Ⓖ $y = 3 - x$
Ⓗ $y = \frac{x}{2}$
Ⓙ $y = x + 3$

DAY 3

What is the solution of the equation $m + 4.5 = 2$?

Ⓐ $m = -6.5$
Ⓑ $m = -2.5$
Ⓒ $m = 2.5$
Ⓓ $m = 6.5$

DAY 4

Which expression gives the perimeter of the triangle?

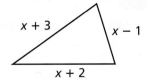

$x + 3$
$x - 1$
$x + 2$

Ⓕ $x + 6$
Ⓖ $x + 4$
Ⓗ $3x + 6$
Ⓙ $3x + 4$

DAY 5

Louis received the following scores on his English quizzes this semester: 95, 95, 80, 70, 60. Which description of this data set would make Louis' results look best?

Ⓐ the mean of his scores
Ⓑ the median of his scores
Ⓒ the mode of his scores
Ⓓ the range of his scores

DAY 1

Naomi surveyed a group of people about their favorite movie genre: comedy, drama, action, musical, or science-fiction. Which of the following would be the best way for Naomi to display her results?

- **A** line graph
- **B** line plot
- **C** circle graph
- **D** scatter plot

DAY 2

The expression $150m + 40$ gives the number of granola bars produced in m minutes at a factory. The expression $200m - 30$ gives the number of raisin clusters produced in m minutes at the factory. Which expression gives the total number of snacks produced in m minutes?

- **F** $50m + 70$
- **G** $350m + 10$
- **H** $150m - 10$
- **J** $350m - 70$

DAY 3

Which equation is shown in the graph?

- **A** $y = -x$
- **B** $y = x$
- **C** $y = x - 1$
- **D** $y = -x + 1$

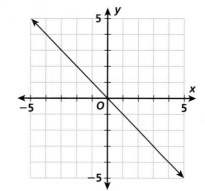

DAY 4

The data set shows the number of hours that several students spent studying for an exam. What is the range for this data set?

$$3.5, 1.5, 2, 4, 3.5, 2, 2.5, 3.5$$

- **F** 0.5
- **G** 1.5
- **H** 2.5
- **J** 3.5

DAY 5

Which of the following statements is NOT true?

- **A** If two figures are congruent, then they have the same size.
- **B** If two figures are congruent, then they are also similar.
- **C** If two figures are similar, then they are also congruent.
- **D** If two figures are similar, then they have the same shape.

DAY 1

What is the mode of this set of data?

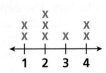

(A) 1   (C) 3

(B) 2   (D) 4

DAY 2

Dante recorded the following information about a seedling's growth for science class. How many inches did the seedling grow in three weeks?

Week	1	2	3
Inches Grown	$\frac{7}{8}$	$\frac{5}{6}$	$\frac{7}{24}$

(F) $1\frac{1}{6}$ inches   (H) 2 inches

(G) $1\frac{17}{24}$ inches   (J) 48 inches

DAY 3

The two rectangles are similar. Which of the following could be the value of x?

(A) 2.8

(B) 3.6

(C) 4.8

(D) 5.4

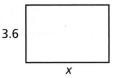

2.4   3.6

3.6 x

DAY 4

Tamara records the high temperature for each day this month. Which would be the most appropriate way for Tamara to display the data if she wants to see the change in temperature over time?

(F) circle graph   (H) line graph

(G) line plot   (J) scatter plot

DAY 5

What is the solution of the equation $15 = -3x$?

(A) $x = 18$

(B) $x = -12$

(C) $x = -5$

(D) $x = 5$

DAY 1

If figure *FGHJ* is reflected across the *x*-axis, what will the new coordinates of *J* be?

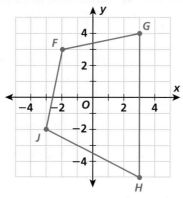

- **A** (−3, 2)
- **B** (3, −2)
- **C** (−3, −2)
- **D** (2, −3)

DAY 2

The frequency table shows the number of days of rain in each month for one year. Which of the following is the most appropriate way to represent this data?

Days of Rain	0–2	3–5	6–8	9–11
Frequency	4	6	2	0

- **F** histogram
- **G** bar graph
- **H** circle graph
- **J** line plot

DAY 3

Rebecca is 5 years older than twice Maria's age. If Maria's age is *m*, which expression gives Rebecca's age?

- **A** 2(*m* + 5)
- **B** 5 − 2*m*
- **C** 2*m* + 5
- **D** 5*m* + 2

DAY 4

Carlos is driving at 55 mi/h. The equation $d = 55t$ gives the distance in miles, *d*, that he drives in *t* hours. As the value of the variable *t* increases, what happens to the value of the variable *d*?

- **F** It decreases.
- **G** It remains the same.
- **H** It gets closer and closer to 0.
- **J** It increases.

DAY 5

Ravi is studying fruit flies. What is the length of the smallest fly?

2.605 mm   2.456 mm   2.508 mm   2.6 mm

- **A** 2.605 mm
- **B** 2.501 mm
- **C** 2.6 mm
- **D** 2.456 mm

DAY 1

Which transformation was used to transform Figure 1 into Figure 2?

Figure 1   **Figure 2**

A translation

B rotation

C reflection

D dilation

DAY 2

If figure ABCDE is reflected across the x-axis, what will the new coordinates of E be?

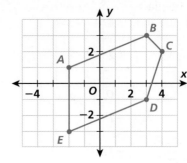

F (−2, 3)   H (−3, 2)

G (2, 3)   J (2, −3)

DAY 3

The figure shows the beginning of a compass and straightedge construction. Which construction is it?

A copy a line segment

B bisect an angle

C copy an angle

D bisect a line segment

DAY 4

What is the sum of $3b − 4$ and $-2b + 7$?

F $b + 3$

G $5b − 11$

H $-b + 3$

J $-5b − 3$

DAY 5

What is the mean of this set of data?

90, 108, 67, 84, 90, 82, 73, 90

A 41   C 87

B 85.5   D 90

DAY 1

Alex is using a compass and straightedge to bisect ∠ABC. He has already completed the work shown in the figure. Where should he place the point of his compass to continue the construction?

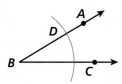

Ⓐ Point A

Ⓑ Point B

Ⓒ Point C

Ⓓ Point D

DAY 2

Gena used software to draw Figure 1. Then she used a transformation to create Figure 2. Which transformation did she use?

Figure 1   **Figure 2**

Ⓕ reflection

Ⓖ rotation

Ⓗ dilation

Ⓙ translation

DAY 3

The line plot shows the daily low temperatures during one week. What is the mean low temperature for the entire week?

Ⓐ 60°F   Ⓒ 62°F

Ⓑ 61°F   Ⓓ 63°F

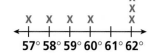

DAY 4

Apples cost c dollars per pound. Alison has $10 to spend on apples for holiday pies. The equation $n = \frac{10}{c}$ gives the number of pounds of apples, n, that Alison can buy. As the cost, c, increases, what happens to the value of the variable n?

Ⓕ It decreases.

Ⓖ It increases.

Ⓗ It does not change.

Ⓙ It increases, then decreases.

DAY 5

What is the interquartile range for this set of data?

1, 3, 3, 4, 5, 8, 9

Ⓐ 3

Ⓑ 4

Ⓒ 5

Ⓓ 8

DAY 1

Figures A and B are similar. If the area of Figure A is 218.75 square centimeters, which expression could you use to determine the area of Figure B?

Figure A

17.5 cm | 218.75 cm² | **Figure B** ? | 3.5 cm

Ⓐ 17.5 ÷ 3.5

Ⓑ 218.75 ÷ 25

Ⓒ 5 · 218.75

Ⓓ 3.5 · 17.5

DAY 2

In which of the following is Figure 2 a translation of Figure 1?

Ⓕ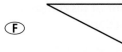

Figure 1   Figure 2

Ⓖ

Figure 1   Figure 2

Ⓗ

Figure 1   Figure 2

Ⓙ

Figure 1   Figure 2

DAY 3

It costs $6 to join a DVD club. After joining, each DVD costs $12. Which equation shows the total cost, c, of joining the club and buying n DVDs?

Ⓐ $c = 12 + 6n$

Ⓑ $c = 6 + 12n$

Ⓒ $c = 18n$

Ⓓ $c = 12n - 6$

DAY 4

The data set shows Ashley's scores on her history exams. What is the interquartile range of the data set?

79, 82, 82, 84, 88, 92, 97, 97, 97, 99, 100

Ⓕ 5

Ⓖ 10

Ⓗ 15

Ⓙ 21

DAY 5

Which expression is equivalent to $-2(x + 3)$?

Ⓐ $-2x - 6$

Ⓑ $-2x + 3$

Ⓒ $-2x + 1$

Ⓓ $-2x - 5$

DAY 1

Which conclusion can you draw based on the data in this scatter plot?

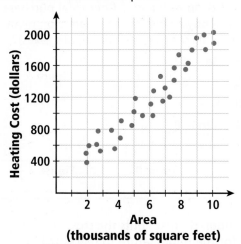

(A) The smaller the area, the more expensive the heating costs.

(B) Heating costs remain constant.

(C) The scatter plot does not show a trend.

(D) The larger the area, the greater the heating costs.

DAY 2

If figure ABCD is reflected across the y-axis, what will the new coordinates of D be?

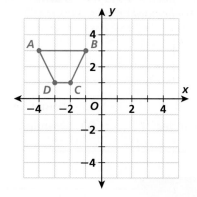

(F) (3, 1)

(G) (2, 2)

(H) (−3, −1)

(J) (−3, 1)

DAY 3

Triangle ABC is similar to triangle DEF. What is the length of side $\overline{DE}$?

(A) 6 in.   (C) 9 in.

(B) 8 in.   (D) 10 in.

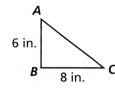

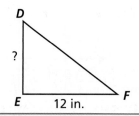

DAY 4

Chris bought $\frac{3}{4}$ pound of peanuts and ate $\frac{1}{2}$ pound. How many pounds of peanuts remain?

(F) $\frac{1}{8}$ pound   (H) $\frac{1}{2}$ pound

(G) $\frac{1}{4}$ pound   (J) $1\frac{1}{4}$ pounds

DAY 5

Kyle is recording the speed of cars as they pass by his house. Which of the following is the most appropriate way for Kyle to display his data?

(A) bar graph   (C) line graph

(B) histogram   (D) scatter plot

DAY 1

The rectangle in the figure is rotated through space around line 1. Which three-dimensional figure is formed?

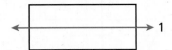

- **A** cone
- **B** cylinder
- **C** prism
- **D** pyramid

DAY 2

At Monster Music, all CDs cost $12. Lara has a coupon for $8 off her total purchase. If Lara buys n CDs, which expression gives her total cost (not including sales taxes)?

- **F** $8n - 12$
- **G** $12 - 8n$
- **H** $8 - 12n$
- **J** $12n - 8$

DAY 3

Steve's wood-burning stove can heat his house 6°F an hour. He first lights the stove at 6:00 AM when it is 52°F. How many hours will it take for the temperature to reach 82°F?

- **A** 3
- **B** 4
- **C** 5
- **D** 6

Hour	0	1	2	3	4
Temperature (°F)	52	58	64		

DAY 4

Figure *ABCD* is dilated by a scale factor of $\frac{3}{2}$. What are the coordinates of *C* after the dilation?

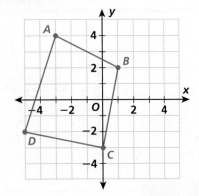

- **F** $(2, -4)$
- **G** $(0, -4\frac{1}{2})$
- **H** $(0, -1\frac{1}{2})$
- **J** $(0, -2)$

DAY 5

Which conclusion can you draw about worker productivity based on the scatter plot?

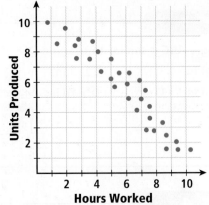

- **A** Productivity increases during the work day.
- **B** There is no trend for productivity in the scatter plot.
- **C** As the work day progresses, productivity declines.
- **D** Productivity remains constant during the work day.

DAY 1

What kind of correlation would you expect to find in a scatter plot comparing people's ages and favorite colors?

(A) negative

(B) no correlation

(C) positive

(D) There is not enough information to answer the question.

DAY 2

A cone is cut by a plane that is parallel to the base of the cone. What shape is the cross section?

(F) oval

(G) circle

(H) triangle

(J) square

DAY 3

The triangle in the figure is rotated through space around line *m*. Which three-dimensional figure is formed?

(A) pyramid

(B) cylinder

(C) prism

(D) cone

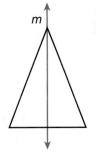

DAY 4

Keiko drew Figure 1. Then she used a transformation to make Figure 2. Which transformation did she use?

Figure 1   **Figure 2**

(F) rotation

(G) dilation

(H) translation

(J) none of the above

DAY 5

The expression $8n + 15$ gives the cost in dollars of printing *n* custom t-shirts. The expression $3.5 + 2n$ gives the cost of folding and shipping *n* t-shirts. Which expression gives the total cost of printing, folding, and shipping *n* t-shirts?

(A) $11.5n + 17$

(B) $10n + 18.5$

(C) $17 + 11.5n$

(D) $15 + 10n$

DAY 1

What is the interquartile range of the data set shown in the line plot?

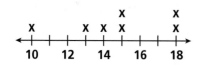

Ⓐ 3

Ⓑ 4

Ⓒ 5

Ⓓ 8

DAY 2

You conduct a survey to see if the number of hours of sleep that people need is related to their age. Which type of graph should you use to help you analyze your data?

Ⓕ line plot

Ⓖ circle graph

Ⓗ bar graph

Ⓙ scatter plot

DAY 3

Which two figures appear to be similar?

Ⓐ Figure 1 and Figure 2

Ⓑ Figure 2 and Figure 3

Ⓒ Figure 1 and Figure 4

Ⓓ Figure 3 and Figure 4

Figure 1

Figure 2

Figure 3

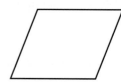

Figure 4

DAY 4

A cylinder is cut by a plane that is perpendicular to the bases of the cylinder. What shape is the cross section?

Ⓕ rectangle

Ⓖ circle

Ⓗ triangle

Ⓙ parallelogram

DAY 5

The point (3, −2) is translated 4 units right and 3 units up. What are the new coordinates of the point?

Ⓐ (−1, 1)

Ⓑ (7, 1)

Ⓒ (0, −6)

Ⓓ (6, 2)

DAY 1

Which statement about the graph of the equation $y = 6x$ is NOT true?

Ⓐ The graph is a straight line.

Ⓑ The graph passes through the origin.

Ⓒ Part of the graph lies in Quadrant II.

Ⓓ The graph includes the point (2, 12).

DAY 2

Victor bought a book for $7. He also bought several CDs for $9 each. He spent a total of $43. Which equation could you solve to find the number of CDs Victor bought?

Ⓕ $43 = 9x - 7$

Ⓖ $43 = 7 + 9x$

Ⓗ $43 = 9 + 7x$

Ⓙ $43 = 7 \cdot 9x$

DAY 3

The circle in the figure is rotated through space around line m. Which three-dimensional figure is formed?

Ⓐ cone

Ⓑ cylinder

Ⓒ hemisphere

Ⓓ sphere

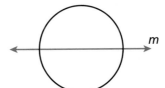

DAY 4

What is the solution of the equation $4m - 6 = 18$?

Ⓕ $m = 2$

Ⓖ $m = 3$

Ⓗ $m = 6$

Ⓙ $m = 12$

DAY 5

Jorge recorded the following information while studying the effects of sunlight on plant growth. Which plant grew the most?

Plant	1	2	3	4
Change in Height (in.)	$\frac{1}{2}$	$-\frac{3}{8}$	$-\frac{1}{4}$	$\frac{7}{16}$

Ⓐ 1   Ⓒ 3

Ⓑ 2   Ⓓ 4

DAY 1

Emily wants to use a compass and straightedge to bisect ∠ABC. Which figure shows the mark she should make for her first step?

(A)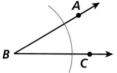

(B)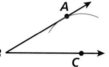

(C)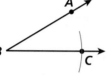

(D)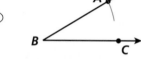

DAY 2

Tyler drew Figure 1 and then used a transformation to make Figure 2. Which transformation did he use?

Figure 1   Figure 2

(F) dilation

(G) rotation

(H) reflection

(J) translation

DAY 3

The table shows how much different numbers of tickets to a hockey game cost. How many dollars would 10 tickets cost?

(A) $21.60

(B) $24.00

(C) $29.20

(D) $32.00

Tickets	2	3	5	8
Cost ($)	4.80	7.20	12.00	19.20

DAY 4

Liu is researching the speeds of some of the fastest animals on Earth. Which of the following graphs is the best choice for displaying the data on animals and their top speeds?

(F) scatter plot

(G) line graph

(H) circle graph

(J) bar graph

DAY 5

Bruno surveys his classmates about their favoriet pet. What is the best measure of central tendency of this data?

(A) mode

(B) range

(C) mean

(D) median

DAY 1

What kind of correlation would you expect to find in a scatter plot that compares people's heights and shoe sizes?

- (A) positive correlation
- (B) negative correlation
- (C) no correlation
- (D) There is not enough information to answer the question.

DAY 2

What is the value of the expression $|6 - 15|$?

- (F) -15
- (G) -9
- (H) 9
- (J) 21

DAY 3

Parallelogram *PQRS* is similar to parallelogram *TUVW*. What is the value of *x*?

- (A) 60
- (B) 120
- (C) 135
- (D) 180

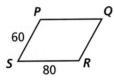

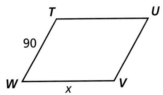

DAY 4

Mrs. Weyland is making 7 cups of juice for her children's friends. If she wants to serve each guest $\frac{3}{4}$ cup of juice, how many children will the juice serve?

- (F) 8
- (G) 9
- (H) 10
- (J) 11

DAY 5

Casey wants to solve the equation $6x - 5 = 40$. What should she do as her first step?

- (A) Divide both sides by 5.
- (B) Add 5 to both sides.
- (C) Subtract 5 from both sides.
- (D) Subtract 40 from both sides.

DAY 1

If figure *LMNO* is reflected across the x-axis, which point(s) will **not** change locations?

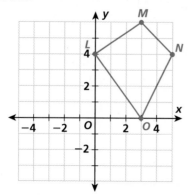

- **A** L and O
- **B** L
- **C** O
- **D** L and N

DAY 2

If figure *PQRS* is dilated by a scale factor of $\frac{1}{2}$, which point will be located at $\left(2, -1\frac{1}{2}\right)$?

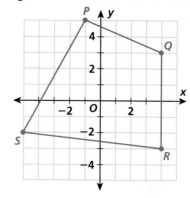

- **F** P
- **G** Q
- **H** R
- **J** S

DAY 3

A cone is cut by a plane that passes through the cone's vertex and is perpendicular to the base. What shape is the cross section?

- **A** circle
- **B** triangle
- **C** oval
- **D** rectangle

DAY 4

Which of the following is a true statement about the graph of the equation $y = \frac{5}{x}$?

- **F** The graph passes through the origin.
- **G** The graph lies in Quadrant II of the coordinate plane.
- **H** The graph is a straight line.
- **J** The graph includes the point (5, 1).

DAY 5

At dinner, Mr. and Mrs. Brandt decide to leave a 20% tip for their server. Which is the best estimate of their tip if their meals total $63.20?

- **A** $1.20
- **B** $12.00
- **C** $14.00
- **D** $120.00

DAY 1

If these two figures are similar, what is the missing measure in figure B?

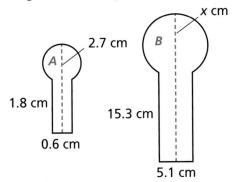

- (A) 18 centimeters
- (B) 20.4 centimeters
- (C) 22.95 centimeters
- (D) 30.6 centimeters

DAY 2

Beth is using a compass and straightedge to construct the perpendicular bisector of $\overline{AB}$. She has already completed the steps shown in the figure. What should she do next?

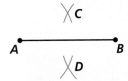

- (F) Place the point of the compass on point A.
- (G) Place the point of the compass on point C.
- (H) Use the straightedge to draw a line through points A and C.
- (J) Use the straightedge to draw a line through points C and D.

DAY 3

Jamal is solving the equation $16 = 4x + 2.5$. What should he do as his first step?

- (A) Subtract 16 from both sides of the equation.
- (B) Subtract 2.5 from both sides of the equation.
- (C) Add 2.5 to both sides of the equation.
- (D) Add 4x to both sides of the equation.

DAY 4

Which equation has a graph that is NOT a straight line?

- (F) $y = 3x$
- (G) $y = x + 3$
- (H) $y = \frac{3}{x}$
- (J) $y = \frac{x}{3}$

DAY 5

Which value does NOT make the following statement true?

$$0.028 < \boxed{} < 0.064$$

- (A) 0.027
- (B) 0.029
- (C) 0.043
- (D) 0.062

Georgia
The Peach State

The State Capitol in Atlanta

Peach Tree Blossoms

Turner Field

GA28

Georgia Mathematics Performance Standards Grade 7

By the end of grade seven, students will understand and use rational numbers, including signed numbers; solve linear equations in one variable; sketch and construct plane figures; demonstrate understanding of transformations; use and apply properties of similarity; examine properties of geometric shapes in space; describe and sketch solid figures, including their cross-sections; represent and describe relationships between variables in tables, graphs, and formulas; analyze the characteristics of linear relationships; and represent and analyze data using graphical displays, measures of central tendency, and measures of variation.

Instruction and assessment should include the appropriate use of manipulatives and technology. Topics should be represented in multiple ways, such as concrete/pictorial, verbal/written, numeric/data-based, graphical, and symbolic. Concepts should be introduced and used, where appropriate, in the context of realistic phenomena.

Concepts/Skills to Maintain

Operations with positive rational numbers, including mixed numbers
Line and rotational symmetry
Surface area and volume
Ratio as a representation of quantitative relationships

NUMBERS AND OPERATIONS

Students will further develop their understanding of the concept of rational numbers and apply them to real world situations.

M7N1. Students will understand the meaning of positive and negative rational numbers and use them in computation.

a Find the absolute value of a number and understand it as the distance from zero on a number line.

b Compare and order rational numbers, including repeating decimals.

c Add, subtract, multiply, and divide positive and negative rational numbers.

d Solve problems using rational numbers.

GEOMETRY

Students will further develop and apply their understanding of plane and solid geometric figures through the use of constructions and transformations. Students will explore the properties of similarity and further develop their understanding of 3-dimensional figures.

M7G1. Students will construct plane figures that meet given conditions.

a Perform basic constructions using both compass and straight edge, and appropriate technology. Constructions should include copying a segment; copying an angle; bisecting a segment; bisecting an angle; constructing perpendicular lines, including the perpendicular bisector of a line segment; and constructing a line parallel to a given line through a point not on the line.

Stone Mountain Park carving

b Recognize that many constructions are based on the creation of congruent triangles.

M7G2. Students will demonstrate understanding of transformations.

a Demonstrate understanding of translations, dilations, rotations, reflections, and relate symmetry to appropriate transformations.

b Given a figure in the coordinate plane, determine the coordinates resulting from a translation, dilation, rotation, or reflection.

M7G3. Students will use the properties of similarity and apply these concepts to geometric figures.

a Understand the meaning of similarity, visually compare geometric figures for similarity, and describe similarities by listing corresponding parts.

b Understand the relationships among scale factors, length ratios, and area ratios between similar figures. Use scale factors, length ratios, and area ratios to determine side lengths and areas of similar geometric figures.

c Understand congruence of geometric figures as a special case of similarity: The figures have the same size and shape.

M7G4. Students will further develop their understanding of three-dimensional figures.

a Describe three-dimensional figures formed by translations and rotations of plane figures through space.

b Sketch, model, and describe cross-sections of cones, cylinders, pyramids, and prisms.

Field of flowers, Georgia

ALGEBRA

Students will demonstrate an understanding of linear relations and fundamental algebraic concepts.

M7A1. Students will represent and evaluate quantities using algebraic expressions.

a Translate verbal phrases to algebraic expressions.

b Simplify and evaluate algebraic expressions, using commutative, associative, and distributive properties as appropriate.

c Add and subtract linear expressions.

M7A2. Students will understand and apply linear equations in one variable.

a Given a problem, define a variable, write an equation, solve the equation, and interpret the solution.

b Use the addition and multiplication properties of equality to solve one- and two-step linear equations.

M7A3. Students will understand relationships between two variables.

a Plot points on a coordinate plane.

b Represent, describe, and analyze relations from tables, graphs, and formulas.

c Describe how change in one variable affects the other variable.

d Describe patterns in the graphs of proportional relationships, both direct $(y = kx)$ and inverse $(y = k/x)$.

Chattahoochee National Forest

DATA ANALYSIS AND PROBABILITY

Students will demonstrate understanding of data analysis by posing questions, collecting data, analyzing the data using measures of central tendency and variation, and using the data to answer the questions posed. Students will understand the role of probability in sampling.

M7D1. Students will pose questions, collect data, represent and analyze the data, and interpret results.

a Formulate questions and collect data from a census of at least 30 objects and from samples of varying sizes.

b Construct frequency distributions.

c Analyze data using measures of central tendency (mean, median, and mode), including recognition of outliers.

d Analyze data with respect to measures of variation (range, quartiles, interquartile range).

e Compare measures of central tendency and variation from samples to those from a census. Observe that sample statistics are more likely to approximate the population parameters as sample size increases.

f Analyze data using appropriate graphs, including pictographs, histograms, bar graphs, line graphs, circle graphs, and line plots introduced earlier, and using box-and-whisker plots and scatter plots.

g Analyze and draw conclusions about data, including a description of the relationship between two variables.

PROCESS STANDARDS

The following process standards are essential to mastering each of the mathematics content standards. They emphasize critical dimensions of the mathematical proficiency that all students need.

M7P1. Students will solve problems (using appropriate technology).

a Build new mathematical knowledge through problem solving.

b Solve problems that arise in mathematics and in other contexts.

c Apply and adapt a variety of appropriate strategies to solve problems.

d Monitor and reflect on the process of mathematical problem solving.

Terms/Symbols: natural number, whole number, sign, integer, opposite, negative, positive, absolute value, term, variable, commutative property, associative property, distributive property, algebraic expression, linear equation, direct and indirect proportions, constant of proportionality ($y = kx$), variation, polyhedron, translation, rotation, reflection, dilation, symmetry, bisector, parallel lines, perpendicular lines, cross-section, similar, congruent, point, line, plane, line segment, endpoints, intersection, ray, parallel lines, perpendicular lines, similar, similarity, rate, scale drawings, corresponding sides, corresponding angles, congruent, diagonal, algebraic expression, commutative property, associative property, distributive property, direct variation, inverse variation, inversely proportional, mean, median, mode, range, quartile, interquartile range, outlier, histogram, scatter plot, line plot, box-and-whisker plot, $\cong, \sim, \approx, \|, \perp, \angle$

Centennial Park, Atlanta

GA33

M7P2. Students will reason and evaluate mathematical arguments.

a Recognize reasoning and proof as fundamental aspects of mathematics.

b Make and investigate mathematical conjectures.

c Develop and evaluate mathematical arguments and proofs.

d Select and use various types of reasoning and methods of proof.

M7P3. Students will communicate mathematically.

a Organize and consolidate their mathematical thinking through communication.

b Communicate their mathematical thinking coherently and clearly to peers, teachers, and others.

c Analyze and evaluate the mathematical thinking and strategies of others.

d Use the language of mathematics to express mathematical ideas precisely.

M7P4. Students will make connections among mathematical ideas and to other disciplines.

a Recognize and use connections among mathematical ideas.

b Understand how mathematical ideas interconnect and build on one another to produce a coherent whole.

c Recognize and apply mathematics in contexts outside of mathematics.

boats at sunset, Georgia

M7P5. Students will represent mathematics in multiple ways.

a Create and use representations to organize, record, and communicate mathematical ideas.

b Select, apply, and translate among mathematical representations to solve problems.

c Use representations to model and interpret physical, social, and mathematical phenomena.

Melon Bluff Nature Center

Algebraic Reasoning

go.hrw.com
Online Resources
KEYWORD: MS7 TOC

Career:
Cosmologist

Tools for Success

Reading Math 5, 10, 15, 46

Writing Math 9, 13, 17, 19, 21, 26, 31, 37, 41, 45, 49, 55, 59

Vocabulary 10, 18, 23, 28, 34, 42, 46, 52, 56

Know-It Notebook Chapter 1

Homework Help Online 8, 12, 16, 20, 25, 30, 36, 40, 44, 48, 54, 58

Student Help 18, 43, 56

CRCT Prep, GPS Support, and Spiral Review 9, 13, 17, 21, 26, 31, 37, 41, 45, 49, 55, 59

Multi-Step Test Prep 61

Test Tackler 68

CRCT Prep 70

Integers and Rational Numbers

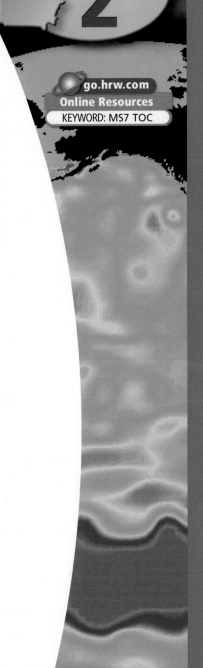

Table of Contents

Career: Oceanographer

Tools for Success

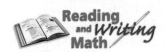

Reading Math 77, 125

Writing Math 75, 79, 85, 97, 103, 106, 109, 113, 117, 123, 127, 131

Vocabulary 76, 106, 110, 114, 120, 124, 128

Know-It Notebook Chapter 2

Homework Help Online 78, 84, 90, 96, 102, 108, 112, 116, 122, 130

Student Help 76, 94, 121, 129, 134

CRCT Prep, GPS Support, and Spiral Review 79, 85, 91, 97, 103, 109, 113, 117, 123, 127, 131

Multi-Step Test Prep 133

CRCT Prep 142

CHAPTER 3
Applying Rational Numbers

go.hrw.com
Online Resources
KEYWORD: MS7 TOC

Career: Chef

Tools for Success

Writing Math 153, 157, 163, 169, 177, 183, 189, 193, 199, 203, 207

Vocabulary 150, 200

Know-It Notebook Chapter 3

Study Strategy 149

Homework Help Online 152, 156, 162, 168, 172, 176, 182, 188, 192, 198, 202, 206

Student Help 150, 151, 155, 166, 167, 174, 191, 196, 205

CRCT Prep, GPS Support, and Spiral Review 153, 157, 163, 169, 173, 177, 183, 189, 193, 199, 203, 207

Multi-Step Test Prep 209

Test Tackler 216

CRCT Prep 218

Patterns and Functions

go.hrw.com
Online Resources
KEYWORD: MS7 TOC

Career: Roller Coaster Designer

Tools for Success

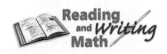

Reading and Writing Math

Writing Math 223, 227, 231, 235, 241, 251

Vocabulary 224, 238, 242, 248, 254

Study Skills

Know-It Notebook Chapter 4

Homework Help Online 226, 230, 234, 240, 244, 250

Student Help 239

TEST PREP

CRCT Prep, GPS Support, and Spiral Review 227, 231, 235, 241, 245, 251

Multi-Step Test Prep 253

CRCT Prep 262

go.hrw.com
Online Resources
KEYWORD: MS7 TOC

Proportional Relationships

Career: Model Builder

Reading and Writing Math

Study Skills

TEST PREP

Percents

go.hrw.com
Online Resources
KEYWORD: MS7 TOC

Career: Urban Archaeologist

Tools for Success

Reading Math 330

Writing Math 332, 335, 339, 345, 349, 359

Vocabulary 330, 352, 356

Know-It Notebook Chapter 6

Study Strategy 329

Homework Help Online 331, 334, 338, 344, 348, 354, 358

Student Help 333, 336

CRCT Prep, GPS Support, and Spiral Review 332, 335, 339, 345, 349, 355, 359

Multi-Step Test Prep 361

CRCT Prep 368

Collecting, Displaying, and Analyzing Data

go.hrw.com
Online Resources
KEYWORD: MS7 TOC

Career: Field Biologist

Tools for Success

Reading Math 375

Writing Math 380, 385, 389, 393, 397, 405, 411, 415, 425

Vocabulary 376, 381, 386, 390, 394, 402, 412, 416

Know-It Notebook Chapter 7

Homework Help Online 378, 384, 388, 392, 396, 404, 410, 414, 418, 424

Student Help 383, 394, 413

CRCT Prep, GPS Support, and Spiral Review 380, 385, 389, 393, 397, 405, 411, 415, 419, 425

Multi-Step Test Prep 427

Test Tackler 434

CRCT Prep 436

Geometric Figures

Career: Bridge Designer

Tools for Success

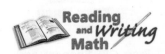

Reading Math 443, 449, 452, 453, 460, 485, 489

Writing Math 441, 445, 448, 455, 463, 473, 477, 481, 487, 492, 497

Vocabulary 442, 448, 452, 460, 466, 474, 488, 494, 502

Know-It Notebook Chapter 8

Homework Help Online 444, 454, 462, 468, 472, 476, 480, 486, 490, 496

Student Help 449, 467, 502

CRCT Prep, GPS Support, and Spiral Review 445, 450, 455, 463, 469, 473, 477, 481, 487, 492, 497

Multi-Step Test Prep 501

CRCT Prep 510

Measurement: Two-Dimensional Figures

Tools for Success

Reading Math 517, 535

Writing Math 527, 533, 537, 541, 545, 553, 559

Vocabulary 518, 524, 530, 556, 562

Know-It Notebook Chapter 9

Homework Help Online 520, 526, 532, 536, 540, 544, 552, 558

Student Help 538, 562

CRCT Prep, GPS Support, and Spiral Review 521, 527, 533, 537, 541, 545, 553, 559

Multi-Step Test Prep 561

Test Tackler 570

CRCT Prep 572

Measurement: Three-Dimensional Figures

Career:
Archaeological
Architect

Tools for Success

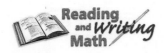

Reading Math 586
Writing Math 593, 601
Vocabulary 580, 586, 597, 612

Know-It Notebook Chapter 10
Study Strategy 577
Homework Help Online 582, 588, 592, 600, 607
Student Help 580, 604, 605

CRCT Prep, GPS Support, and Spiral Review 583, 589, 593, 601, 608

Multi-Step Test Prep 611

CRCT Prep 620

Probability

go.hrw.com
Online Resources
KEYWORD: MS7 TOC

Career:
Demographer

Tools for Success

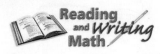
Reading Math 627
Writing Math 632, 639, 643, 651
Vocabulary 628, 632, 636, 640, 648, 652, 656

Know-It Notebook Chapter 11
Homework Help Online 630, 634, 638, 642, 650, 654, 658
Student Help 641, 657

CRCT Prep, GPS Support, and Spiral Review 641, 645, 649, 655, 661, 665
Multi-Step Test Prep 661
Test Tackler 668
CRCT Prep 670

Multi-Step Equations and Inequalities

GPS

go.hrw.com
Online Resources
KEYWORD: MS7 TOC

Career: Satellite Engineer

Tools for Success

Reading Math 693
Writing Math 685, 689, 693, 699, 702, 707
Vocabulary 692

Know-It Notebook Chapter 12
Study Strategy 675
Homework Help Online 680, 684, 688, 694, 698, 702, 706
Student Help 678, 682, 697, 704

CRCT Prep, GPS Support, and Spiral Review 681, 685, 689, 694, 699, 702, 707
Multi-Step Test Prep 709
CRCT Prep 718

INTERDISCIPLINARY CONNECTIONS

Many fields of study require knowledge of the mathematical skills and concepts taught in *Holt Mathematics Course 2*. Examples and exercises throughout the book highlight the math you will need to understand in order to study other subjects, such as Earth science or art, or to pursue a career in fields such as the environment or economics.

Fitness Four friends had a competition to see how far they could walk while spinning a hoop around their waists. The table shows how far each friend walked. Use the table for Exercises 51–53.

Person	Distance (mi)
Rosalyn	$\frac{1}{8}$
Cai	$\frac{3}{4}$
Lauren	$\frac{2}{3}$
Janna	$\frac{7}{10}$

51. How much farther did Lauren walk than Rosalyn?

52. What is the combined distance that Cai and Rosalyn walked?

53. Who walked farther, Janna or Cai?

54. **Measurement** A shrew weighs $\frac{3}{16}$ lb. A hamster weighs $\frac{1}{4}$ lb.
   a. How many more pounds does a hamster weigh than a shrew?
   b. There are 16 oz in 1 lb. How many more ounces does the hamster weigh than the shrew?

55. **Multi-Step** To make $\frac{3}{4}$ lb of mixed nuts, how many pounds of cashews would you add to $\frac{1}{8}$ lb of almonds and $\frac{1}{4}$ lb of peanuts?

56. **Write a Problem** Use facts you find in a newspaper or magazine to write a problem that can be solved using addition or subtraction of fractions.

57. **Write About It** Explain the steps you use to add or subtract fractions that have different denominators.

58. **Challenge** The sum of two fractions is 1. If one fraction is $\frac{3}{8}$ greater than the other, what are the two fractions?

Science

Astronomy 19, 20, 91, 153, 187
Chemistry 290
Computer Science 245
Earth Science 11, 12, 21, 49, 78, 95, 96, 97, 130, 161, 173, 206, 251, 290, 294, 307, 345, 391, 405, 480, 553, 631, 635, 695, 707
Ecology 131, 285
Environment 251
Life Science 12, 13, 17, 41, 131, 183, 207, 284, 286, 290, 380, 390, 405, 411, 415, 497, 589, 631, 699
Measurement 17, 180, 189, 190, 199, 305, 309, 397, 539, 540
Physical Science 20, 36, 37, 54, 103, 157, 177, 199, 205, 241, 273, 345, 541, 685, 699, 710, 711
Weather 157, 162, 206, 227, 241, 633, 697, 698

Language Arts

Literature 294, 652, 659

Health and Fitness

Fitness 189, 630, 679
Health 9, 57, 231, 349, 384, 521, 639, 659, 681
Nutrition 41, 169, 332, 345, 411

Recreation 79, 85, 103, 115, 116, 163, 169, 182, 193, 589, 637, 639, 643, 689, 703
Sports 31, 53, 79, 84, 91, 102, 125, 126, 153, 192, 276, 277, 339, 385, 397, 632, 659

Social Studies

Agriculture 193, 282, 295, 527, 592, 701
Geography 343, 393, 451, 527, 535
History 20, 207, 311, 349, 559, 583, 608
Social Studies 9, 13, 79, 117, 123, 153, 177, 201, 277, 389, 422, 477, 492, 494, 539, 703

Economics

Business 45, 59, 78, 101, 102, 109, 182, 231, 339, 353, 354, 425, 651, 706
Consumer Math 25, 26, 58, 152, 168, 176, 275, 276, 336, 337, 338, 344, 348, 680, 684, 685, 687, 688, 698, 707
Economics 127, 355
Finance 84, 97, 122, 358

Fine and Performing Arts

Architecture 30, 207, 473
Art 16, 113, 307, 309, 359, 445, 469, 497, 533, 655
Industrial Arts 203, 525, 531
Music 349, 656

WHY LEARN MATHEMATICS?

Throughout the text, links to interesting application topics, such as architecture, music, and sports, will help you see how math is used in the real world. Some of the links have additional information and activities at go.hrw.com. For a complete list of all real-world problems in **Holt Mathematics Course 2,** see page 834 in the Index.

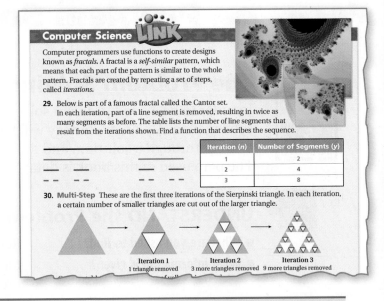

Computer Science LINK

Computer programmers use functions to create designs known as *fractals*. A fractal is a *self-similar* pattern, which means that each part of the pattern is similar to the whole pattern. Fractals are created by repeating a set of steps, called *iterations*.

29. Below is part of a famous fractal called the Cantor set. In each iteration, part of a line segment is removed, resulting in twice as many segments as before. The table lists the number of line segments that result from the iterations shown. Find a function that describes the sequence.

Iteration (n)	Number of Segments (y)
1	2
2	4
3	8

30. **Multi-Step** These are the first three iterations of the Sierpinski triangle. In each iteration, a certain number of smaller triangles are cut out of the larger triangle.

Iteration 1
1 triangle removed

Iteration 2
3 more triangles removed

Iteration 3
9 more triangles removed

Real-World LINKS

Georgia LINK

Art

The Savannah College of Art and Design was named the "Hottest School for the Study of Art" in 2006 edition of Newsweek-Kaplan's "America's 25 Hottest Schools."

go.hrw.com
Web Extra!
KEYWORD: MS7 Reserve

Georgia LINK

Health

Health and fitness advocate Aimee Mullins set Paralympic records in the 100-meter dash and long jump at the 1996 Paralympics in Atlanta, Georgia.

LINK

Weather

When the wind speed of a tropical storm reaches 74 mi/h, it is classified as a hurricane.

Focus on Problem Solving

The Problem Solving Plan

In order to be a good problem solver, you first need a good problem-solving plan. A plan or strategy will help you to understand the problem, to work through a solution, and to check that your answer makes sense. The plan used in this book is detailed below.

UNDERSTAND the Problem

- **What are you asked to find?** — Restate the problem in your own words.
- **What information is given?** — Identify the important facts in the problem.
- **What information do you need?** — Determine which facts are needed to solve the problem.
- **Is all the information given?** — Determine whether all the facts are given.

Make a PLAN

- **Have you ever solved a similar problem?** — Think about other problems like this that you successfully solved.
- **What strategy or strategies can you use?** — Determine a strategy that you can use and how you will use it.

SOLVE

- **Follow your plan.** — Show the steps in your solution. Write your answer as a complete sentence.

LOOK BACK

- **Have you answered the question?** — Be sure that you answered the question that is being asked.
- **Is your answer reasonable?** — Your answer should make sense in the context of the problem.
- **Is there another strategy you could use?** — Solving the problem using another strategy is a good way to check your work.
- **Did you learn anything while solving this problem that could help you solve similar problems in the future?** — Try to remember the problems you have solved and the strategies you used to solve them.

Using the Problem Solving Plan

During summer vacation, Ricardo will go to space camp and then to visit his relatives. He will be gone for 5 weeks and 4 days and will spend 11 more days with his relatives than at space camp. How long will Ricardo stay at each place?

UNDERSTAND the Problem

List the important information.

- Ricardo will be gone for 5 weeks and 4 days.
- He will spend 11 more days with his relatives than at space camp.

The answer will be how long Ricardo stays at each place.

Make a PLAN

You can **draw a diagram** to show how long he will stay at each place. Use boxes for the length of each stay. The length of each box will represent the length of each stay.

SOLVE

Think: There are 7 days in a week, so 5 weeks and 4 days is a total of 39 days. Your diagram might look like this:

Relatives

? days	11 days

Space camp

? days

} = 39 days

$39 - 11 = 28$ Subtract 11 days from the total number of days.
$28 \div 2 = 14$ Divide this number by 2 for the 2 places he visits.

Relatives

| 14 days | 11 days | = 25 days
|---|---|

Space camp

| 14 days | = 14 days
|---|

So Ricardo will stay with his relatives for 25 days and at space camp for 14 days.

LOOK BACK

Twenty-five days is 11 days longer than 14 days. The total length of the two stays is $25 + 14 = 39$ days, or 5 weeks and 4 days. This solution fits the information given in the problem.

USING YOUR BOOK FOR SUCCESS

This book has many features designed to help you learn and study math. Becoming familiar with these features will prepare you for greater success on your exams.

Learn

Preview new **vocabulary** terms listed at the beginning of every lesson.

Look for the **Student Help** for hints and reminders.

Study the **examples** to learn new math ideas and skills. The examples include step-by-step solutions.

Practice

Look back at examples from the lesson to solve the **Guided Practice** exercises.

If you get stuck, use the internet for **Homework Help Online**.

Review

Study and review **vocabulary** from the entire chapter.

Test yourself with **practice problems** from every lesson in the chapter.

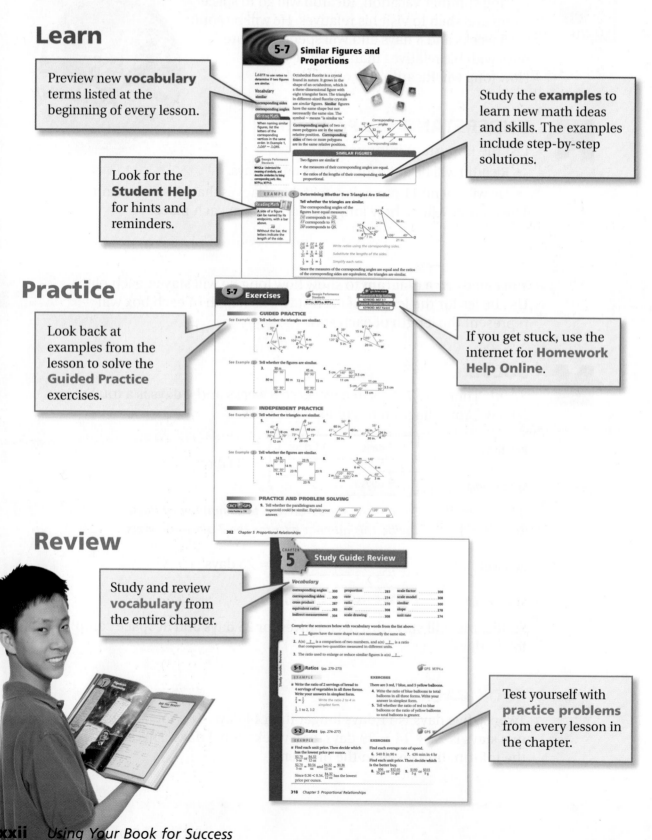

Scavenger Hunt

Holt Mathematics is your resource to help you succeed. Use this scavenger hunt to discover some of the many tools Holt provides to help you be an independent learner.

On a separate sheet of paper, fill in the blanks to answer each question below. In each answer, one letter will be in a yellow box. When you have answered every question, use the letters to fill in the blank at the bottom of the page.

1. What is the first key **vocabulary** term in the Study Guide: Preview for chapter 8?

■■■■■

2. What is the last key **vocabulary** term in the Study Guide: Review for chapter 7?

■■■■■ ■■■■■■■

3. What game is featured in chapter 2 **Game Time**?

■■■■■ ■■■■■■■

4. What keyword should you enter for **Parent Resources Online** on page 338?

■■■ ■■■■■■

5. What project is outlined in chapter 7 **It's in the Bag**?

■■■■■ ■■■■■

6. What **career** is spotlighted on page 438?

■■■■■■ ■■■■■■■

7. What scenic structures are featured in chapter 2 **Problem Solving on Location**?

■■■■■■■ ■■■■■■■

8. The chapter 5 **Test Tackler** gives strategies for what kind of standardized test item?

■■■■■■■■ ■■■■■■■

Math Humor

Why did the chicken add its opposite to itself? To get to the other side of the...

■■■■■■■

CHAPTER 1

Algebraic Reasoning

CRCT PREP

go.hrw.com
Chapter Project Online
KEYWORD: MS7 Ch1

Astronomical Distances	
Object	Distance from the Sun (km)*
Mercury	5.80×10^7
Venus	1.082×10^8
Earth	1.495×10^8
Mars	2.279×10^8
Jupiter	7.780×10^8
Saturn	1.43×10^9
Uranus	2.90×10^9
Neptune	4.40×10^9
Pluto	5.80×10^9
Nearest star	3.973×10^{13}

*Distances of planets from the Sun are average distances.

Career Cosmologist

Dr. Stephen Hawking is a cosmologist. Cosmologists study the universe as a whole. They are interested in the origins, the structure, and the interaction of space and time.

The invention of the telescope has extended the vision of scientists far beyond nearby stars and planets. It has enabled them to view distant galaxies and structures that at one time were only theorized by astrophysicists such as Dr. Hawking. Astronomical distances are so great that we use scientific notation to represent them.

ARE YOU READY?

✓ Vocabulary

Choose the best term from the list to complete each sentence.

1. The operation that gives the quotient of two numbers is ___?___.

2. The ___?___ of the digit 3 in 4,903,672 is thousands.

3. The operation that gives the product of two numbers is ___?___.

4. In the equation 15 ÷ 3 = 5, the ___?___ is 5.

division

multiplication

place value

product

quotient

Complete these exercises to review skills you will need for this chapter.

✓ Find Place Value

Give the place value of the digit 4 in each number.

5. 4,092
6. 608,241
7. 7,040,000
8. 4,556,890,100
9. 3,408,289
10. 34,506,123
11. 500,986,402
12. 3,540,277,009

✓ Use Repeated Multiplication

Find each product.

13. $2 \cdot 2 \cdot 2$
14. $9 \cdot 9 \cdot 9 \cdot 9$
15. $14 \cdot 14 \cdot 14$
16. $10 \cdot 10 \cdot 10 \cdot 10$
17. $3 \cdot 3 \cdot 5 \cdot 5$
18. $2 \cdot 2 \cdot 5 \cdot 7$
19. $3 \cdot 3 \cdot 11 \cdot 11$
20. $5 \cdot 10 \cdot 10 \cdot 10$

✓ Division Facts

Find each quotient.

21. $49 \div 7$
22. $54 \div 9$
23. $96 \div 12$
24. $88 \div 8$
25. $42 \div 6$
26. $65 \div 5$
27. $39 \div 3$
28. $121 \div 11$

✓ Whole Number Operations

Add, subtract, multiply, or divide.

29. $\begin{array}{r} 425 \\ + 12 \\ \hline \end{array}$
30. $\begin{array}{r} 619 \\ + 254 \\ \hline \end{array}$
31. $\begin{array}{r} 62 \\ - 47 \\ \hline \end{array}$
32. $\begin{array}{r} 373 \\ + 86 \\ \hline \end{array}$
33. $\begin{array}{r} 62 \\ \times 42 \\ \hline \end{array}$
34. $\begin{array}{r} 122 \\ \times 15 \\ \hline \end{array}$
35. $7)\overline{623}$
36. $24)\overline{149}$

Study Guide: Preview

Where You've Been

Previously, you

- converted between metric units of measurement.

- applied the properties of rational numbers to numerical expressions.

In This Chapter

You will study

- using conversions in the metric system to make comparisons.

- applying the order of operations and properties of rational numbers.

- identifying and extending number and geometric patterns.

- writing and simplifying numbers in exponential form.

- writing and solving algebraic expressions and equations.

Where You're Going

You can use the skills learned in this chapter

- to express distances and sizes of objects in scientific fields such as astronomy and biology.

- to solve problems in math and science classes such as Algebra and Physics.

Key Vocabulary/Vocabulario

algebraic expression	expresión algebraica
Associative Property	propiedad asociativa
Commutative Property	propiedad conmutativa
Distributive Property	propiedad distributiva
equation	ecuación
exponent	exponente
numerical expression	expresión numérica
order of operations	orden de las operaciones
term	termino
variable	variable

Vocabulary Connections

To become familiar with some of the vocabulary terms in the chapter, consider the following. You may refer to the chapter, the glossary, or a dictionary if you like.

1. The words *equation, equal,* and *equator* all begin with the Latin root *equa-,* meaning "level." How can the Latin root word help you define **equation**?

2. The word *numerical* means "of numbers." How might a **numerical expression** differ from an expression such as "the sum of two and five"?

3. When something is *variable,* it has the ability to change. In mathematics, a **variable** is an algebraic symbol. What special property do you think this type of symbol has?

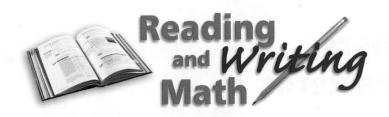

Reading and Writing Math

Reading Strategy: Use Your Book for Success

Understanding how your textbook is organized will help you locate and use helpful information.

As you read through an example problem, pay attention to the **margin notes**, such as Helpful Hints, Reading Math notes, and Caution notes. These notes will help you understand concepts and avoid common mistakes.

Reading Math

Read -4^3 as "-4 to the 3rd power or -4 cubed".

Writing Math

A repeating decimal can be written with a bar over the digits that repeat. So...

Helpful Hint

In Example 1A, parentheses are not needed because multiplication is...

Caution!

An open circle means that the corresponding value not a solution. A sol...

The **glossary** is found in the back of your textbook. Use it to find definitions and examples of unfamiliar words or properties.

The **index** is located at the end of your textbook. Use it to find the page where a particular concept is taught.

The **Skills Bank** is found in the back of your textbook. These pages review concepts from previous math courses.

Glossary/Glos

B _____

bar graph A graph that uses vertical or horizontal bars to display data. (p. 284)

Index

A

Abacus, 7
Absolute value, 451
Acute angles, 326

Skills Bank

Place Value—Hu
Hundred-thousa

You can use a place-value ch

Try This

Use your textbook for the following problems.

1. Use the index to find the page where *exponent* is defined.

2. In Lesson 1-9, what does the Remember box, located in the margin of page 43, remind you about the perimeter of a figure?

3. Use the glossary to find the definition of each term: *order of operations, numerical expression, equation.*

4. Where can you review how to multiply whole numbers?

1-1 Numbers and Patterns

Learn to identify and extend patterns.

Georgia Performance Standards

M7P5.a Create and use representations to organize, record, and communicate mathematical ideas. Also, M7P2.c, M7P2.d, M7P5.b.

Each year, football teams battle for the state championship. The table shows the number of teams in each round of a division's football playoffs. You can look for a pattern to find out how many teams are in rounds 5 and 6.

Football Playoffs						
Round	1	2	3	4	5	6
Number of Teams	64	32	16	8	▓	▓

EXAMPLE 1 **Identifying and Extending Number Patterns**

Identify a possible pattern. Use the pattern to write the next three numbers.

Ⓐ 64, 32, 16, 8, ▓, ▓, ▓, . . .

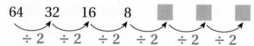

A pattern is to divide each number by 2 to get the next number.

$8 \div 2 = 4$ $\qquad$ $4 \div 2 = 2$ $\qquad$ $2 \div 2 = 1$

The next three numbers will be 4, 2, and 1.

Ⓑ 51, 44, 37, 30, ▓, ▓, ▓, . . .

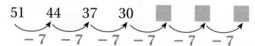

A pattern is to subtract 7 from each number to get the next number.

$30 - 7 = 23$ $\qquad$ $23 - 7 = 16$ $\qquad$ $16 - 7 = 9$

The next three numbers will be 23, 16, and 9.

Ⓒ 2, 3, 5, 8, 12, ▓, ▓, ▓, . . .

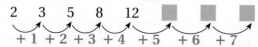

A pattern is to add one more than you did the time before.

$12 + 5 = 17$ $\qquad$ $17 + 6 = 23$ $\qquad$ $23 + 7 = 30$

The next three numbers will be 17, 23, and 30.

EXAMPLE 2 **Identifying and Extending Geometric Patterns**

Identify a possible pattern. Use the pattern to draw the next three figures.

A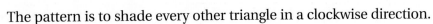

The pattern is alternating squares and circles with triangles between them.

The next three figures will be   .

B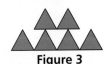

The pattern is to shade every other triangle in a clockwise direction.

The next three figures will be   .

EXAMPLE 3 **Using Tables to Identify and Extend Patterns**

Make a table that shows the number of triangles in each figure. Then tell how many triangles are in the fifth figure of the pattern. Use drawings to justify your answer.

Figure 1   Figure 2   Figure 3

The table shows the number of triangles in each figure.

Figure	1	2	3	4	5
Number of Triangles	2	4	6	8	10

+2 +2 +2 +2

The pattern is to add 2 triangles each time.

Figure 4 has 6 + 2 = 8 triangles.   Figure 5 has 8 + 2 = 10 triangles.

Figure 4

Figure 5

Think and Discuss   GPS M7P1.d, M7P2.d

1. **Describe** two different number patterns that begin with 3, 6, . . .

2. **Tell** when it would be useful to make a table to help you identify and extend a pattern.

Georgia Performance Standards

M7P2.d, M7P3.a, M7P3.c

go.hrw.com
Homework Help Online
KEYWORD: MS7 1-1
Parent Resources Online
KEYWORD: MS7 Parent

GUIDED PRACTICE

See Example 1   **Identify a possible pattern. Use the pattern to write the next three numbers.**

1. 6, 14, 22, 30, ▨, ▨, ▨, . . .

2. 1, 3, 9, 27, ▨, ▨, ▨, . . .

3. 59, 50, 41, 32, ▨, ▨, ▨, . . .

4. 8, 9, 11, 14, ▨, ▨, ▨, . . .

See Example 2   **Identify a possible pattern. Use the pattern to draw the next three figures.**

5.

6.

See Example 3   **7.** Make a table that shows the number of green triangles in each figure. Then tell how many green triangles are in the fifth figure of the pattern. Use drawings to justify your answer.

Figure 1   Figure 2   Figure 3

INDEPENDENT PRACTICE

See Example 1   **Identify a possible pattern. Use the pattern to write the next three numbers.**

8. 27, 24, 21, 18, ▨, ▨, ▨, . . .

9. 4,096, 1,024, 256, 64, ▨, ▨, ▨, . . .

10. 1, 3, 7, 13, 21, ▨, ▨, ▨, . . .

11. 14, 37, 60, 83, ▨, ▨, ▨, . . .

See Example 2   **Identify a possible pattern. Use the pattern to draw the next three figures.**

12.

13.

See Example 3   **14.** Make a table that shows the number of dots in each figure. Then tell how many dots are in the sixth figure of the pattern. Use drawings to justify your answer.

Figure 1   Figure 2   Figure 3   Figure 4

PRACTICE AND PROBLEM SOLVING

CRCT GPS

Extra Practice p. 724

Use the rule to write the first five numbers in each pattern.

15. Start with 7; add 16 to each number to get the next number.

16. Start with 96; divide each number by 2 to get the next number.

17. Start with 50; subtract 2, then 4, then 6, and so on, to get the next number.

18. Critical Thinking Suppose the pattern 3, 6, 9, 12, 15 . . . is continued forever. Will the number 100 appear in the pattern? Why or why not?

Identify a possible pattern. Use the pattern to find the missing numbers.

19. 3, 12, ▨, 192, 768, ▨, ▨, ...

20. 61, 55, ▨, 43, ▨, ▨, 25, ...

21. ▨, ▨, 19, 27, 35, ▨, 51, ...

22. 2, ▨, 8, ▨, 32, 64, ▨, ...

23. Health The table shows the target heart rate during exercise for athletes of different ages. Assuming the pattern continues, what is the target heart rate for a 40-year-old athlete? a 65-year-old athlete?

Target Heart Rate	
Age	Heart Rate (beats per minute)
20	150
25	146
30	142
35	138

Draw the next three figures in each pattern.

24. ▷1 , △5 , ◁9 , ▽13 , ▷17 , △21 , ...

25. ●4 , ■5 , △7 , ●10 , ■14 , △19 , ●25 , ...

26. Social Studies In the ancient Mayan civilization, people used a number system based on bars and dots. Several numbers are shown below. Look for a pattern and write the number 18 in the Mayan system.

$$\overset{\bullet\bullet\bullet}{} \quad \overline{} \quad \overset{\bullet\bullet\bullet}{\overline{}} \quad \overset{}{\overline{\overline{}}} \quad \overset{\bullet\bullet\bullet}{\overline{\overline{}}} \quad \overline{\overline{\overline{}}}$$

    3   5   8   10   13   15

27. What's the Error? A student was asked to write the next three numbers in the pattern 96, 48, 24, 12, ... The student's response was 6, 2, 1. Describe and correct the student's error.

28. Write About It A school chess club meets every Tuesday during the month of March. March 1 falls on a Sunday. Explain how to use a number pattern to find all the dates when the club meets.

29. Challenge Find the 83rd number in the pattern 5, 10, 15, 20, 25, ...

CRCT Prep • GPS Support • Spiral Review

30. Multiple Choice Which is the missing number in the pattern 2, 6, ▨, 54, 162, ... ?

  Ⓐ 10   Ⓑ 18   Ⓒ 30   Ⓓ 48

31. Gridded Response Find the next number in the pattern 9, 11, 15, 21, 29, 39, ...

Round each number to the nearest ten. (Previous course)

32. 61   **33.** 88   **34.** 105   **35.** 2,019   **36.** 11,403

Round each number to the nearest hundred. (Previous course)

37. 91   **38.** 543   **39.** 952   **40.** 4,050   **41.** 23,093

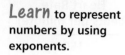

1-2 Exponents

Learn to represent numbers by using exponents.

Vocabulary

power

exponent

base

Georgia Performance Standards

M7P1.b Solve problems that arise in mathematics and other contexts. Also, M7P4.c.

Reading Math

Read 2^4 as "the fourth power of 2" or "2 to the fourth power."

A DNA molecule makes a copy of itself by splitting in half. Each half becomes a molecule that is identical to the original. The molecules continue to split so that the two become four, the four become eight, and so on.

Each time DNA copies itself, the number of molecules doubles. After four copies, the number of molecules is $2 \cdot 2 \cdot 2 \cdot 2 = 16$.

This multiplication can also be written as a **power**, using a base and an *exponent*. The **exponent** tells how many times to use the **base** as a factor.

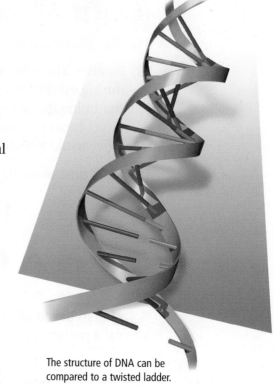

The structure of DNA can be compared to a twisted ladder.

$$2 \cdot 2 \cdot 2 \cdot 2 = 2^4 = 16$$

Exponent

Base

EXAMPLE 1 Evaluating Powers

Find each value.

A 5^2

$5^2 = 5 \cdot 5$ *Use 5 as a factor 2 times.*

$\quad = 25$

B 2^6

$2^6 = 2 \cdot 2 \cdot 2 \cdot 2 \cdot 2 \cdot 2$ *Use 2 as a factor 6 times.*

$\quad = 64$

C 25^1

$25^1 = 25$ *Any number to the first power is equal to that number.*

Any number to the zero power, except zero, is equal to 1.

$6^0 = 1$ $10^0 = 1$ $19^0 = 1$

Zero to the zero power is *undefined,* meaning that it does not exist.

To express a whole number as a power, write the number as the product of equal factors. Then write the product using the base and an exponent. For example, $10,000 = 10 \cdot 10 \cdot 10 \cdot 10 = 10^4$.

EXAMPLE 2 **Expressing Whole Numbers as Powers**

Write each number using an exponent and the given base.

A **49, base 7**

$49 = 7 \cdot 7$ *7 is used as a factor 2 times.*

$\quad = 7^2$

B **81, base 3**

$81 = 3 \cdot 3 \cdot 3 \cdot 3$ *3 is used as a factor 4 times.*

$\quad = 3^4$

EXAMPLE 3 *Earth Science Application*

Georgia LINK
Earth Science

In 1886, an earthquake caused a crack in the six-feet-thick walls of the Tybee Island Lighthouse.

The Richter scale measures an earthquake's strength, or magnitude. Each category in the table is 10 times stronger than the next lower category. For example, a large earthquake is 10 times stronger than a moderate earthquake. How many times stronger is a great earthquake than a moderate one?

Earthquake Strength	
Category	**Magnitude**
Moderate	5
Large	6
Major	7
Great	8

An earthquake with a magnitude of 6 is 10 times stronger than one with a magnitude of 5.

An earthquake with a magnitude of 7 is 10 times stronger than one with a magnitude of 6.

An earthquake with a magnitude of 8 is 10 times stronger than one with a magnitude of 7.

$$10 \cdot 10 \cdot 10 = 10^3 = 1,000$$

A great earthquake is 1,000 times stronger than a moderate one.

Think and Discuss  GPS M7P2.c, M7P3.b

1. **Describe** a relationship between 3^5 and 3^6.

2. **Tell** which power of 8 is equal to 2^6. Explain.

3. **Explain** why any number to the first power is equal to that number.

Georgia Performance Standards

M7P2.c, M7P2.d, M7P3.c, M7P4.c

go.hrw.com
Homework Help Online
KEYWORD: MS7 1-2
Parent Resources Online
KEYWORD: MS7 Parent

GUIDED PRACTICE

See Example **1** Find each value.

1. 2^5 **2.** 3^3 **3.** 6^2 **4.** 9^1 **5.** 10^6

See Example **2** Write each number using an exponent and the given base.

6. 25, base 5   **7.** 16, base 4   **8.** 27, base 3   **9.** 100, base 10

See Example **3** **10. Earth Science** On the Richter scale, a great earthquake is 10 times stronger than a major one, and a major one is 10 times stronger than a large one. How many times stronger is a great earthquake than a large one?

INDEPENDENT PRACTICE

See Example **1** Find each value.

11. 11^2 **12.** 3^5 **13.** 8^3 **14.** 4^3 **15.** 3^4

16. 2^5 **17.** 5^1 **18.** 2^3 **19.** 5^3 **20.** 30^1

See Example **2** Write each number using an exponent and the given base.

21. 81, base 9   **22.** 4, base 4   **23.** 64, base 4

24. 1, base 7   **25.** 32, base 2   **26.** 128, base 2

27. 1,600, base 40   **28.** 2,500, base 50   **29.** 100,000, base 10

See Example **3** **30.** In a game, a contestant had a starting score of one point. He tripled his score every turn for four turns. Write his score after four turns as a power. Then find his score.

PRACTICE AND PROBLEM SOLVING

Extra Practice p. 724

Give two ways to represent each number using powers.

31. 81   **32.** 16   **33.** 64   **34.** 729   **35.** 625

Compare. Write <, >, or =.

36. 4^2 ▮ 15   **37.** 2^3 ▮ 3^2 **38.** 64 ▮ 4^3 **39.** 8^3 ▮ 7^4

40. 10,000 ▮ 10^5 **41.** 6^5 ▮ 3,000   **42.** 9^3 ▮ 3^6 **43.** 5^4 ▮ 7^3

44. To find the volume of a cube, find the third power of the length of an edge of the cube. What is the volume of a cube that is 6 inches long on an edge?

45. Patterns Domingo decided to save $0.03 the first day and to triple the amount he saves each day. How much will he save on the seventh day?

46. Life Science A newborn panda cub weighs an average of 4 ounces. How many ounces might a one-year-old panda weigh if its weight increases by the power of 5 in one year?

47. Social Studies If the populations of the cities in the table double every 10 years, what will their populations be in 2034?

City	Population (2004)
Yuma, AZ	86,070
Phoenix, AZ	1,421,298

48. Critical Thinking Explain why $6^3 \neq 3^6$.

49. Hobbies Malia is making a quilt with a pattern of rings. In the center ring, she uses four stars. In each of the next three rings, she uses three times as many stars as in the one before. How many stars does she use in the fourth ring? Write the answer using a power and find its value.

Order each set of numbers from least to greatest.

50. $29, 2^3, 6^2, 16, 3^5$

51. $4^3, 33, 6^2, 5^3, 10^1$

52. $7^2, 2^4, 80, 10^2, 1^8$

53. $2, 1^8, 3^4, 16^1, 0$

54. $5^2, 21, 11^2, 13^1, 1^9$

55. $2^5, 3^3, 9, 5^2, 8^1$

56. Life Science The cells of some kinds of bacteria divide every 30 minutes. If you begin with a single cell, how many cells will there be after 1 hour? 2 hours? 3 hours?

 57. What's the Error? A student wrote 64 as $8 \cdot 2$. How did the student apply exponents incorrectly?

 58. Write About It Is 2^5 greater than or less than 3^3? Explain your answer.

59. Challenge What is the length of the edge of a cube if its volume is 1,000 cubic meters?

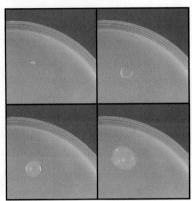

Bacteria divide by pinching in two. This process is called binary fission.

CRCT Prep • GPS Support • Spiral Review

60. Multiple Choice What is the value of 4^6?

(A) 24 (B) 1,024 (C) 4,096 (D) 16,384

61. Multiple Choice Which of the following is NOT equal to 64?

(F) 6^4 (G) 4^3 (H) 2^6 (J) 8^2

62. Gridded Response Simplify $2^3 + 3^2$.

Simplify. (Previous course)

63. $15 + 27 + 5 + 3 + 11 + 16 + 7 + 4$

64. $2 + 6 + 5 + 7 + 100 + 1 + 75$

65. $2 + 9 + 8 + 12 + 6 + 8 + 5 + 6 + 7$

66. $9 + 30 + 4 + 1 + 4 + 1 + 7 + 5$

Identify a possible pattern. Use the pattern to write the next three numbers. (Lesson 1-1)

67. 100, 91, 82, 73, 64, . . .

68. 17, 19, 22, 26, 31, . . .

69. 2, 6, 18, 54, 162, . . .

1-3 Metric Measurements

Learn to identify, convert, and compare metric units.

Georgia Performance Standards

M7P4.c Recognize and apply mathematics in contexts outside of mathematics. Also, M7P1.b, M7P4.a, M7P4.b.

The Micro Flying Robot II is the world's lightest helicopter. Produced in Japan in 2004, the robot is 85 millimeters tall and has a mass of 8.6 grams.

You can use the following benchmarks to help you understand millimeters, grams, and other metric units.

	Metric Unit	Benchmark
Length	Millimeter (mm)	Thickness of a dime
	Centimeter (cm)	Width of your little finger
	Meter (m)	Width of a doorway
	Kilometer (km)	Length of 10 football fields
Mass	Milligram (mg)	Mass of a grain of sand
	Gram (g)	Mass of a small paperclip
	Kilogram (kg)	Mass of a textbook
Capacity	Milliliter (mL)	Amount of liquid in an eyedropper
	Liter (L)	Amount of water in a large water bottle
	Kiloliter (kL)	Capacity of 2 large refrigerators

EXAMPLE 1 Choosing the Appropriate Metric Unit

Choose the most appropriate metric unit for each measurement. Justify your answer.

A The length of a car

Meters—the length of a car is similar to the width of several doorways.

B The mass of a skateboard

Kilograms—the mass of a skateboard is similar to the mass of several textbooks.

C The recommended dose of a cough syrup

Milliliters—one dose of cough syrup is similar to the amount of liquid in several eyedroppers.

The prefixes of metric units correlate to place values in the base-10 number system. The table shows how metric units are based on powers of 10.

1,000	100	10	1	0.1	0.01	0.001
Thousands	Hundreds	Tens	Ones	Tenths	Hundredths	Thousandths
Kilo-	Hecto-	Deca-	Base unit	Deci-	Centi-	Milli-

You can convert units within the metric system by multiplying or dividing by powers of 10. To convert to a smaller unit, you must multiply. To convert to a larger unit, you must divide.

EXAMPLE 2 Converting Metric Units

Convert each measure.

A 510 cm to meters

510 cm = (510 ÷ 100) m   *100 cm = 1 m, so divide by 100.*

= 5.1 m   *Move the decimal point 2 places left: 5.10.*

B 2.3 L to milliliters

2.3 L = (2.3 × 1,000) mL   *1 L = 1,000 mL, so multiply by 1,000.*

= 2,300 mL   *Move the decimal point 3 places right: 2.300.*

EXAMPLE 3 Using Unit Conversion to Make Comparisons

Mai and Brian are measuring the mass of rocks in their earth science class. Mai's rock has a mass of 480 g. Brian's rock has a mass of 0.05 kg. Whose rock has the greater mass?

You can convert the mass of Mai's rock to kilograms.

480 g = (480 ÷ 1,000) kg   *1,000 g = 1 kg, so divide by 1,000.*

= 0.48 kg   *Move the decimal point 3 places left: 480.*

Since 0.48 kg > 0.05 kg, Mai's rock has the greater mass.

Check

Use number sense. There are 1,000 grams in a kilogram, so the mass of Mai's rock is about half a kilogram, or 0.5 kg. This is much greater than 0.05 kg, the mass of Brian's rock, so the answer is reasonable.

Think and Discuss   GPS M7P1.d, M7P4.a

1. Tell how the metric system relates to the base-10 number system.

2. Explain why it makes sense to multiply when you convert to a smaller unit.

Georgia Performance
Standards

M7P3.a, M7P3.c

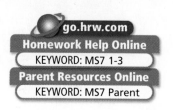

go.hrw.com
Homework Help Online
KEYWORD: MS7 1-3
Parent Resources Online
KEYWORD: MS7 Parent

GUIDED PRACTICE

See Example **1** Choose the most appropriate metric unit for each measurement.
Justify your answer.

1. The mass of a pumpkin

2. The amount of water in a pond

3. The length of an eagle's beak

4. The mass of a penny

See Example **2** Convert each measure.

5. 12 kg to grams

6. 4.3 m to centimeters

7. 0.7 mm to centimeters

8. 3,200 mL to liters

See Example **3** **9.** On Sunday, Li ran 0.8 km. On Monday, she ran 7,200 m. On which day did Li run farther? Use estimation to explain why your answer makes sense.

INDEPENDENT PRACTICE

See Example **1** Choose the most appropriate metric unit for each measurement.
Justify your answer.

10. The capacity of a teacup

11. The mass of 10 grains of salt

12. The height of a palm tree

13. The distance between your eyes

See Example **2** Convert each measure.

14. 0.067 L to milliliters

15. 1.4 m to kilometers

16. 900 mg to grams

17. 355 cm to millimeters

See Example **3** **18.** Carmen pours 75 mL of water into a beaker. Nick pours 0.75 L of water into a different beaker. Who has the greater amount of water? Use estimation to explain why your answer makes sense.

PRACTICE AND PROBLEM SOLVING

Extra Practice p. 724

Convert each measure.

19. 1.995 m = ▊ cm

20. 0.00004 kg = ▊ g

21. 2,050 kL = ▊ L

22. 0.002 mL = ▊ L

23. 3.7 mm = ▊ cm

24. 61.8 g = ▊ mg

Compare. Write <, >, or =.

25. 0.1 cm ▊ 1 mm

26. 25 g ▊ 3,000 mg

27. 340 mg ▊ 0.4 g

28. 0.05 kL ▊ 5 L

29. 0.3 mL ▊ 0.005 L

30. 1.3 kg ▊ 1,300 g

31. Art The *Mona Lisa* by Leonardo da Vinci is 77 cm tall. *Starry Night* by Vincent Van Gogh is 0.73 m tall. Which is the taller painting? How much taller is it?

Write each set of measures in order from least to greatest.

32. 0.005 kL; 4.1 L; 6,300 mL

33. 1.5 m; 1,200 mm; 130 cm

34. 4,000 mg; 50 kg; 70 g

35. 9.03 g; 0.0008 kg; 1,000 mg

36. Measurement Use a ruler to measure the line segment at right in centimeters. Then give the length of the segment in millimeters and meters.

Life Science The table gives information about several species of Vesper, or Evening, bats. Use the table for Exercises 37 and 38.

37. Which bat has the greatest mass?

38. Which bat has a longer wingspread, the Red Bat or the Big Brown Bat? How much longer is its wingspread?

U.S. Vesper Bats		
Name	Wingspread	Mass
Red Bat	0.3 m	10.9 g
Silver-Haired Bat	28.7 cm	8,500 mg
Big Brown Bat	317 mm	0.01 kg

39. Critical Thinking One milliliter of water has a mass of 1 gram. What is the mass of a liter of water?

 40. What's the Error? A student converted 45 grams to milligrams as shown below. Explain the student's error.

$$45 \text{ g} = (45 \div 1{,}000) \text{ mg} = 0.045 \text{ mg}$$

 41. Write About It Explain how to decide whether milligrams, grams, or kilograms are the most appropriate unit for measuring the mass of an object.

 42. Challenge A decimeter is $\frac{1}{10}$ of a meter. Explain how to convert millimeters to decimeters.

CRCT PREP • GPS SUPPORT • SPIRAL REVIEW

43. Multiple Choice Which of these is the same as 0.4 grams?

(A) 0.0004 mg   (B) 0.004 mg   (C) 400 mg   (D) 4,000 mg

44. Short Response Which has a greater capacity, a measuring cup that holds 250 mL or a measuring cup that holds 0.5 L? Justify your answer.

Identify a possible pattern. Use the pattern to write the next three numbers. (Lesson 1-1)

45. 19, 16, 13, 10, ▨, ▨, ▨, . . .

46. 5, 15, 45, 135, ▨, ▨, ▨, . . .

47. 5, 6, 8, 11, 15, ▨, ▨, ▨, . . .

48. 256, 128, 64, 32, ▨, ▨, ▨, . . .

Find each value. (Lesson 1-2)

49. 9^2 **50.** 12^1 **51.** 2^7 **52.** 7^3 **53.** 3^4

1-4 Applying Exponents

 **Learn** to multiply by powers of ten and express large numbers in scientific notation.

Vocabulary

scientific notation

Georgia Performance Standards

M7P4.a Recognize and use connections among mathematical ideas. Also, M7P4.b, M7P4.c.

The distance from Venus to the Sun is greater than 100,000,000 kilometers. You can write this number as a power of ten by using a base of ten and an exponent.

$$10 \cdot 10 \cdot 10 \cdot 10 \cdot 10 \cdot 10 \cdot 10 \cdot 10 = 10^8$$

Power of ten ⟶

The table shows several powers of ten.

Power of 10	Meaning	Value
10^1	10	10
10^2	$10 \cdot 10$	100
10^3	$10 \cdot 10 \cdot 10$	1,000
10^4	$10 \cdot 10 \cdot 10 \cdot 10$	10,000

Astronomers estimate that there are 100 billion billion, or 10^{20}, stars in the universe.

You can find the product of a number and a power of ten by multiplying or by moving the decimal point of the number. For powers of ten with positive exponents, move the decimal point to the right.

EXAMPLE 1 Multiplying by Powers of Ten

Multiply $137 \cdot 10^3$.

A Method 1: Evaluate the power.

$137 \cdot 10^3 = 137 \cdot (10 \cdot 10 \cdot 10)$ *Multiply 10 by itself 3 times.*

$= 137 \cdot 1,000$ *Multiply.*

$= 137,000$

B Method 2: Use mental math.

$137 \cdot 10^3 = 137.000$ *Move the decimal point 3 places.*

$= 137,000$ ⟵ 3 places   *(You will need to add 3 zeros.)*

Remember!

A factor is a number that is multiplied by another number to get a product.

Scientific notation is a kind of shorthand that can be used to write large numbers. Numbers expressed in scientific notation are written as the product of two *factors*.

In scientific notation, 17,900,000 is written as

Writing Math

In scientific notation, it is customary to use a multiplication cross (×) instead of a dot.

A number greater than or equal to 1 but less than 10 →

1.79×10^7

← A power of 10

EXAMPLE 2 Writing Numbers in Scientific Notation

Write 9,580,000 in scientific notation.

$9{,}580{,}000 = 9{,}580{,}000.$ *Move the decimal point to get a number between 1 and 10.*

$= 9.58 \times 10^6$ *The exponent is equal to the number of places the decimal point is moved.*

EXAMPLE 3 Writing Numbers in Standard Form

Pluto is about 3.7×10^9 miles from the Sun. Write this distance in standard form.

$3.7 \times 10^9 = 3.700000000$ *Since the exponent is 9, move the decimal point 9 places to the right.*

$= 3{,}700{,}000{,}000$

Pluto is about 3,700,000,000 miles from the Sun.

EXAMPLE 4 Comparing Numbers in Scientific Notation

Mercury is 9.17×10^7 kilometers from Earth. Jupiter is 6.287×10^8 kilometers from Earth. Which planet is closer to Earth?

To compare numbers written in scientific notation, first compare the exponents. If the exponents are equal, then compare the decimal portion of the numbers.

Mercury: 9.17×10^7 km

Jupiter: 6.287×10^8 km   *Compare the exponents.*

Notice that $7 < 8$. So $9.17 \times 10^7 < 6.287 \times 10^8$.

Mercury is closer to Earth than Jupiter.

Think and Discuss   GPS M7P2.c, M7P3.b

1. **Tell** whether 15×10^9 is in scientific notation. Explain.

2. **Compare** 4×10^3 and 3×10^4. Explain how you know which is greater.

Georgia Performance
Standards

M7P1.b, M7P3.a, M7P4.c

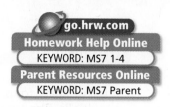

go.hrw.com
Homework Help Online
KEYWORD: MS7 1-4
Parent Resources Online
KEYWORD: MS7 Parent

GUIDED PRACTICE

See Example **Multiply.**

1. $15 \cdot 10^2$ **2.** $12 \cdot 10^4$ **3.** $208 \cdot 10^3$ **4.** $113 \cdot 10^7$

See Example **Write each number in scientific notation.**

5. 3,600,000 **6.** 214,000 **7.** 8,000,000,000 **8.** 42,000

See Example ③ **9.** A drop of water contains about 2.0×10^{21} molecules. Write this number in standard form.

See Example ④ **10. Astronomy** The diameter of Neptune is 4.9528×10^7 meters. The diameter of Mars is 6.7868×10^6 meters. Which planet has the larger diameter?

INDEPENDENT PRACTICE

See Example ① **Multiply.**

11. $21 \cdot 10^2$ **12.** $8 \cdot 10^4$ **13.** $25 \cdot 10^5$ **14.** $40 \cdot 10^4$

15. $268 \cdot 10^3$ **16.** $550 \cdot 10^7$ **17.** $2,115 \cdot 10^5$ **18.** $70,030 \cdot 10^1$

See Example **Write each number in scientific notation.**

19. 428,000 **20.** 1,610,000 **21.** 3,000,000,000 **22.** 60,100

23. 52.000 **24.** $29.8 \cdot 10^7$ **25.** 8,900,000 **26.** $500 \cdot 10^3$

See Example **27. History** Ancient Egyptians hammered gold into sheets so thin that it took 3.67×10^5 sheets to make a pile 2.5 centimeters high. Write the number of sheets in standard form.

See Example **28. Astronomy** Mars is 7.83×10^7 kilometers from Earth. Venus is 4.14×10^7 kilometers from Earth. Which planet is closer to Earth?

PRACTICE AND PROBLEM SOLVING

Extra Practice p. 725

Find the missing number or numbers.

29. $24,500 = 2.45 \times 10^{\blacksquare}$ **30.** $16,800 = \blacksquare \times 10^4$ **31.** $\blacksquare = 3.40 \times 10^2$

32. $280,000 = 2.8 \times 10^{\blacksquare}$ **33.** $5.4 \times 10^8 = \blacksquare$ **34.** $60,000,000 = \blacksquare \times 10^{\blacksquare}$

Tell whether each number is written in scientific notation. Then order the numbers from least to greatest.

35. 43.7×10^6 **36.** 1×10^7 **37.** 2.9×10^7 **38.** 305×10^6

39. Physical Science In a vacuum, light travels at a speed of about nine hundred and eighty million feet per second. Write this speed in scientific notation.

40. The earliest rocks native to Earth formed during the Archean eon. Calculate the length of this eon. Write your answer in scientific notation.

41. Dinosaurs lived during the Mesozoic era. Calculate the length of the Mesozoic era. Write your answer in scientific notation.

42. Tropites were prehistoric marine animals whose fossil remains can be used to date the rock formations in which they are found. Such fossils are known as *index fossils*. Tropites lived between 2.08×10^8 and 2.30×10^8 years ago. During what geologic time period did they live?

43. ✏ **Write About It** Explain why scientific notation is especially useful in earth science.

44. ⭐ **Challenge** We live in the Holocene epoch. Write the age of this epoch in scientific notation.

Geologic Time Scale		
Eon	**Era**	**Period**
Phanerozoic (540 mya*–present)	**Cenozoic** (65 mya–present)	**Quaternary** (1.8 mya–present) Holocene epoch (11,000 yrs ago–present) Pleistocene epoch (1.8 mya–11,000 yrs ago) **Tertiary** (65 mya–1.8 mya) Pliocene epoch (5.3 mya–1.8 mya) Miocene epoch (23.8 mya–5.3 mya) Oligocene epoch (33.7 mya–23.8 mya) Eocene epoch (54.8 mya–33.7 mya) Paleocene epoch (65 mya–54.8 mya)
	Mesozoic (248 mya–65 mya)	Cretaceous (144 mya–65 mya) Jurassic (206 mya–144 mya) Triassic (248 mya–206 mya)
	Paleozoic (540 mya–248 mya)	Permian (290 mya–248 mya) Pennsylvanian (323 mya–290 mya) Mississippian (354 mya–323 mya) Devonian (417 mya–354 mya) Silurian (443 mya–417 mya) Ordovician (490 mya–443 mya) Cambrian (540 mya–490 mya)
Proterozoic (2,500 mya–540 mya)		
Archean (3,800 mya–2,500 mya)		
Hadean (4,600 mya–3,800 mya)		

*mya = million years ago

CRCT Prep • GPS Support • Spiral Review

45. Multiple Choice Kaylee wrote in her dinosaur report that the Jurassic period was 1.75×10^8 years ago. According to Kaylee's report, how many years ago was the Jurassic period?

  Ⓐ 1,750,000   Ⓑ 17,500,000   Ⓒ 175,000,000   Ⓓ 17,500,000,000

46. Multiple Choice What is 2,430,000 in scientific notation?

  Ⓕ 243×10^4 Ⓖ 24.3×10^5 Ⓗ 2.43×10^5 Ⓙ 2.43×10^6

Write each number using an exponent and the given base. (Lesson 1-2)

47. 625, base 5   **48.** 512, base 8   **49.** 512, base 2

Convert each measure. (Lesson 1-3)

50. 2.87 kg to grams   **51.** 1,700 m to kilometers   **52.** 8 L to milliliters

Technology LAB 1-4

Scientific Notation with a Calculator

Use with Lesson 1-4

Georgia Performance Standards

M7P1.a, M7P1.c

go.hrw.com
Lab Resources Online
KEYWORD: MS7 Lab1

Scientists often have to work with very large numbers. For example, the Andromeda Galaxy contains over 200,000,000,000 stars. Scientific notation is a compact way of expressing large numbers such as this.

Activity

① Show 200,000,000,000 in scientific notation.

Enter 200,000,000,000 on your graphing calculator. Then press ENTER .

2 E 11 on the calculator display means 2×10^{11}, which is 200,000,000,000 in scientific notation. Your calculator automatically puts very large numbers into scientific notation.

You can use the **EE** function to enter 2×10^{11} directly into the calculator. Enter 2×10^{11} by pressing 2 2nd , 11 ENTER .

② Simplify $2.31 \times 10^4 \div 525$.

Enter 2.31×10^4 into your calculator in scientific notation, and then divide by 525. To do this, press 2.31 2nd , 4 ÷ 525 ENTER . Your answer should be 44.

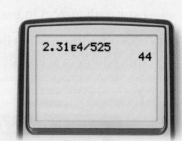

Think and Discuss

1. Explain how scientific notation and calculator notation are similar. What could the "E" possibly stand for in calculator notation?

Try This

Use the calculator to write each number in scientific notation.

1. 6,500,000
2. 15,000,000
3. 360,000,000,000

Simplify each expression, and express your answer in scientific notation.

4. $8.4 \times 10^6 \div 300$
5. $9 \times 10^3 - 900$
6. $2.5 \times 10^9 \times 10$
7. $3 \times 10^2 + 6000$
8. $2.85 \times 10^8 \div 95$
9. $1.5 \times 10^7 \div 150$

1-5 Order of Operations

**Learn** to use the order of operations to simplify numerical expressions.

Vocabulary

numerical expression

order of operations

Georgia Performance Standards

M7P1.b Solve problems that arise in mathematics and in other contexts. Also, M7P4.c.

When you get ready for school, you put on your socks *before* you put on your shoes. In mathematics, as in life, some tasks must be done in a certain order.

A **numerical expression** is made up of numbers and operations. When simplifying a numerical expression, rules must be followed so that everyone gets the same answer. That is why mathematicians have agreed upon the **order of operations**.

ORDER OF OPERATIONS

1. Perform operations within grouping symbols.
2. Evaluate powers.
3. Multiply and divide in order from left to right.
4. Add and subtract in order from left to right.

EXAMPLE 1 Using the Order of Operations

Simplify each expression.

A $27 - 18 \div 6$

$27 - 18 \div 6$	*Divide.*
$27 - 3$	*Subtract.*
24	

B $36 - 18 \div 2 \cdot 3 + 8$

$36 - 18 \div 2 \cdot 3 + 8$	*Divide and multiply from left to right.*
$36 - 9 \cdot 3 + 8$	
$36 - 27 + 8$	*Subtract and add from left to right.*
$9 + 8$	
17	

C $5 + 6^2 \cdot 10$

$5 + 6^2 \cdot 10$	*Evaluate the power.*
$5 + 36 \cdot 10$	*Multiply.*
$5 + 360$	*Add.*
365	

EXAMPLE **2** **Using the Order of Operations with Grouping Symbols**

Simplify each expression.

A $36 - (2 \cdot 6) \div 3$

$36 - (2 \cdot 6) \div 3$ *Perform the operation in parentheses.*

$36 - 12 \div 3$ *Divide.*

$36 - 4$ *Subtract.*

32

Helpful Hint

When an expression has a set of grouping symbols within a second set of grouping symbols, begin with the innermost set.

B $[(4 + 12 \div 4) - 2]^3$

$[(4 + 12 \div 4) - 2]^3$ *The parentheses are inside the brackets,*

$[(4 + 3) - 2]^3$ *so perform the operations inside the*

$[7 - 2]^3$ *parentheses first.*

5^3

125

EXAMPLE **3** *Career Application*

Maria works part-time in a law office, where she earns $20 per hour. The table shows the number of hours she worked last week. Simplify the expression $(6 + 5 \cdot 3) \cdot 20$ to find out how much money Maria earned last week.

Day	Hours
Monday	6
Tuesday	5
Wednesday	5
Thursday	5

$(6 + 5 \cdot 3) \cdot 20$ *Perform the operations in parentheses.*

$(6 + 15) \cdot 20$ *Add.*

$21 \cdot 20$ *Multiply.*

420

Maria earned $420 last week.

Think and Discuss 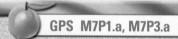 GPS M7P1.a, M7P3.a

1. **Apply** the order of operations to determine if the expressions $3 + 4^2$ and $(3 + 4)^2$ have the same value.

2. **Give** the correct order of operations for simplifying $(5 + 3 \cdot 20) \div 13 + 3^2$.

3. **Determine** where grouping symbols should be inserted in the expression $3 + 9 - 4 \cdot 2$ so that its value is 13.

1-5 **Exercises**

Georgia Performance Standards

M7P1.c, M7P3.a, M7P4.c

go.hrw.com
Homework Help Online
KEYWORD: MS7 1-5
Parent Resources Online
KEYWORD: MS7 Parent

GUIDED PRACTICE

See Example ① Simplify each expression.

1. $43 + 16 \div 4$

2. $28 - 4 \cdot 3 \div 6 + 4$

3. $25 - 4^2 \div 8$

See Example ② **4.** $26 - (7 \cdot 3) + 2$

5. $(3^2 + 11) \div 5$

6. $32 + 6(4 - 2^2) + 8$

See Example ③ **7.** **Career** Caleb earns $10 per hour. He worked 4 hours on Monday, Wednesday, and Friday. He worked 8 hours on Tuesday and Thursday. Simplify the expression $(3 \cdot 4 + 2 \cdot 8) \cdot 10$ to find out how much Caleb earned in all.

INDEPENDENT PRACTICE

See Example ① Simplify each expression.

8. $3 + 7 \cdot 5 - 1$

9. $5 \cdot 9 - 3$

10. $3 - 2 + 6 \cdot 2^2$

See Example ② **11.** $(3 \cdot 3 - 3)^2 \div 3 + 3$

12. $2^5 - (4 \cdot 5 + 3)$

13. $(3 \div 3) + 3 \cdot (3^3 - 3)$

14. $4^3 \div 8 - 2$

15. $(8 - 2)^2 \cdot (8 - 1)^2 \div 3$

16. $9{,}234 \div [3 \cdot 3(1 + 8^3)]$

See Example ③ **17.** **Consumer Math** Maki paid a $14 basic fee plus $25 a day to rent a car. Simplify the expression $14 + 5 \cdot 25$ to find out how much it cost her to rent the car for 5 days.

18. **Consumer Math** Enrico spent $20 per square yard for carpet and $35 for a carpet pad. Simplify the expression $35 + 20(12^2 \div 9)$ to find out how much Enrico spent to carpet a 12 ft by 12 ft room.

PRACTICE AND PROBLEM SOLVING

Extra Practice p. 725

Simplify each expression.

19. $90 - 36 \times 2$

20. $16 + 14 \div 2 - 7$

21. $64 \div 2^2 + 4$

22. $10 \times (18 - 2) + 7$

23. $(9 - 4)^2 - 12 \times 2$

24. $[1 + (2 + 5)^2] \times 2$

Compare. Write <, >, or =.

25. $8 \cdot 3 - 2 \;\blacksquare\; 8 \cdot (3 - 2)$

26. $(6 + 10) \div 2 \;\blacksquare\; 6 + 10 \div 2$

27. $12 \div 3 \cdot 4 \;\blacksquare\; 12 \div (3 \cdot 4)$

28. $18 + 6 - 2 \;\blacksquare\; 18 + (6 - 2)$

29. $[6(8 - 3) + 2] \;\blacksquare\; 6(8 - 3) + 2$

30. $(18 - 14) \div (2 + 2) \;\blacksquare\; 18 - 14 \div 2 + 2$

Critical Thinking Insert grouping symbols to make each statement true.

31. $4 \cdot 8 - 3 = 20$

32. $5 + 9 - 3 \div 2 = 8$

33. $12 - 2^2 \div 5 = 20$

34. $4 \cdot 2 + 6 = 32$

35. $4 + 6 - 3 \div 7 = 1$

36. $9 \cdot 8 - 6 \div 3 = 6$

37. Bertha earned $8.00 per hour for 4 hours babysitting and $10.00 per hour for 5 hours painting a room. Simplify the expression $8 \cdot 4 + 10 \cdot 5$ to find out how much Bertha earned in all.

38. Consumer Math Mike bought a painting for $512. He sold it at an antique auction for 4 times the amount that he paid for it, and then he purchased another painting with half of the profit that he made. Simplify the expression $(512 \cdot 4 - 512) \div 2$ to find how much Mike paid for the second painting.

39. Multi-Step Anelise bought four shirts and two pairs of jeans. She paid $6 in sales tax.

   a. Write an expression that shows how much she spent on shirts.

   b. Write an expression that shows how much she spent on jeans.

   c. Write and evaluate an expression to show how much she spent on clothes, including sales tax.

 40. Choose a Strategy There are four children in a family. The sum of the squares of the ages of the three youngest children equals the square of the age of the oldest child. How old are the children?

   (A) 1, 4, 8, 9   (B) 1, 3, 6, 12   (C) 4, 5, 8, 10   (D) 2, 3, 8, 16

 41. Write About It Describe the order in which you would perform the operations to find the correct value of $[(2 + 4)^2 - 2 \cdot 3] \div 6$.

 42. Challenge Use the numbers 3, 5, 6, 2, 54, and 5 in that order to write an expression that has a value of 100.

CRCT PREP • GPS SUPPORT • SPIRAL REVIEW

43. Multiple Choice Which operation should be performed first to simplify the expression $18 - 1 \cdot 9 \div 3 + 8$?

   (A) Addition   (B) Subtraction   (C) Multiplication   (D) Division

44. Multiple Choice Which expression does NOT simplify to 81?

   (F) $9 \cdot (4 + 5)$ (G) $7 + 16 \cdot 4 + 10$ (H) $3 \cdot 25 + 2$ (J) $10^2 - 4 \cdot 5 + 1$

45. Multiple Choice Quinton bought 2 pairs of jeans for $30 each and 3 pairs of socks for $5 each. Which expression can be simplified to determine the total amount Quinton paid for the jeans and socks?

   (A) $2 \cdot 3(30 + 5)$ (B) $(2 + 3) \cdot (30 + 5)$ (C) $2 \cdot (30 + 5) \cdot 3$ (D) $2 \cdot 30 + 3 \cdot 5$

Find each value. (Lesson 1-2)

46. 8^6 **47.** 9^3 **48.** 4^5 **49.** 3^3 **50.** 7^1

Multiply. (Lesson 1-4)

51. $612 \cdot 10^3$ **52.** $43.8 \cdot 10^6$ **53.** $590 \cdot 10^5$ **54.** $3.1 \cdot 10^7$ **55.** $1.91 \cdot 10^2$

Explore Order of Operations

Georgia Performance Standards
M7P1.c, M7P2.c

go.hrw.com
Lab Resources Online
KEYWORD: MS7 Lab1

REMEMBER

The order of operations
1. Perform operations within grouping symbols.
2. Evaluate powers.
3. Multiply and divide in order from left to right.
4. Add and subtract in order from left to right.

Many calculators have an x^2 key that allows you to find the square of a number. On calculators that do not have this key, or to use exponents other than 2, you can use the caret key, ∧ .

For example, to evaluate 3^5, press 3 ∧ 5, and then press ENTER .

Activity

1 Simplify $4 \cdot 2^3$ using paper and pencil. Then check your answer with a calculator.

First simplify the expression using paper and pencil:
$4 \cdot 2^3 = 4 \cdot 8 = 32$.

Then simplify $4 \cdot 2^3$ using your calculator.

Notice that the calculator automatically evaluates the power first. If you want to perform the multiplication first, you must put that operation inside parentheses.

2 Use a calculator to simplify $\frac{(2 + 5 \cdot 4)^3}{4^2}$.

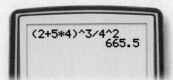

Think and Discuss

1. Is $2 + 5 \cdot 4^3 + 4^2$ equivalent to $(2 + 5 \cdot 4^3) + 4^2$? Explain.

Try This

Simplify each expression with pencil and paper. Check your answers with a calculator.

1. $3 \cdot 2^3 + 5$ 2. $3 \cdot (2^3 + 5)$ 3. $(3 \cdot 2)^2$ 4. $3 \cdot 2^2$ 5. $2^{(3 \cdot 2)}$

Use a calculator to simplify each expression. Round your answers to the nearest hundredth.

6. $(2.1 + 5.6 \cdot 4^3) \div 6^4$ 7. $[(2.1 + 5.6) \cdot 4^3] \div 6^4$ 8. $[(8.6 - 1.5) \div 2^3] \div 5^2$

1-6 Properties

Learn how to identify properties of rational numbers and use them to simplify numerical expressions.

Vocabulary

Commutative Property

Associative Property

Identity Property

Distributive Property

Georgia Performance Standards

M7P1.c Adapt and apply a variety of appropriate strategies to solve problems. Also, M7P4.a.

In Lesson 1-5 you learned how to use the order of operations to simplify numerical expressions. The following properties of rational numbers are also useful when you simplify expressions.

Commutative Property		
Words	**Numbers**	**Algebra**
You can add numbers in any order and multiply numbers in any order.	$3 + 8 = 8 + 3$ $5 \cdot 7 = 7 \cdot 5$	$a + b = b + a$ $ab = ba$

Associative Property		
Words	**Numbers**	**Algebra**
When you add or multiply, you can group the numbers together in any combination.	$(4 + 5) + 1 = 4 + (5 + 1)$ $(9 \cdot 2) \cdot 6 = 9 \cdot (2 \cdot 6)$	$(a + b) + c = a + (b + c)$ $(a \cdot b) \cdot c = a \cdot (b \cdot c)$

Identity Property		
Words	**Numbers**	**Algebra**
The sum of 0 and any number is the number. The product of 1 and any number is the number.	$4 + 0 = 4$ $8 \cdot 1 = 8$	$a + 0 = a$ $a \cdot 1 = a$

EXAMPLE 1 Identifying Properties of Addition and Multiplication

Tell which property is represented.

A $2 + (7 + 8) = (2 + 7) + 8$

$2 + (7 + 8) = (2 + 7) + 8$ *The numbers are regrouped.*

Associative Property

B $25 \cdot 1 = 25$

$25 \cdot 1 = 25$ *One of the factors is 1.*

Identity Property

C $xy = yx$

$xy = yx$ *The order of the variables is switched.*

Commutative Property

You can use properties and mental math to rearrange or regroup numbers into combinations that are easier to work with.

EXAMPLE 2 **Using Properties to Simplify Expressions**

Simplify each expression. Justify each step.

A $12 + 19 + 18$

$12 + 19 + 18 = 19 + 12 + 18$	*Commutative Property*
$= 19 + (12 + 18)$	*Associative Property*
$= 19 + 30$	*Add.*
$= 49$	

B $25 \cdot 13 \cdot 4$

$25 \cdot 13 \cdot 4 = 25 \cdot 4 \cdot 13$	*Commutative Property*
$= (25 \cdot 4) \cdot 13$	*Associative Property*
$= 100 \cdot 13$	*Multiply.*
$= 1,300$	

You can use the Distributive Property to multiply numbers mentally by breaking apart one of the numbers and writing it as a sum or difference.

Distributive Property		
Numbers	$6 \cdot (9 + 14) = 6 \cdot 9 + 6 \cdot 14$	$8 \cdot (5 - 2) = 8 \cdot 5 - 8 \cdot 2$
Algebra	$a \cdot (b + c) = ab + ac$	$a \cdot (b - c) = ab - ac$

EXAMPLE 3 **Using the Distributive Property to Multiply Mentally**

Use the Distributive Property to find 7(29).

Method 1		Method 2
$7(29) = 7(20 + 9)$	*Rewrite 29.*	$7(29) = 7(30 - 1)$
$= (7 \cdot 20) + (7 \cdot 9)$	*Use the Distributive Property.*	$= (7 \cdot 30) - (7 \cdot 1)$
$= 140 + 63$	*Multiply.*	$= 210 - 7$
$= 203$	*Simplify.*	$= 203$

Think and Discuss  GPS M7P3.a, M7P3.b

1. Describe two different ways to simplify the expression $7 \cdot (3 + 9)$.

2. Explain how the Distributive Property can help you find $6 \cdot 102$ using mental math.

Georgia Performance Standards

M7P3.a, M7P3.c, M7P4.c

go.hrw.com
Homework Help Online
KEYWORD: MS7 1-6
Parent Resources Online
KEYWORD: MS7 Parent

GUIDED PRACTICE

See Example 1 **Tell which property is represented.**

1. $1 + (6 + 7) = (1 + 6) + 7$ **2.** $1 \cdot 10 = 10$ **3.** $3 \cdot 5 = 5 \cdot 3$

4. $6 + 0 = 6$ **5.** $4 \cdot (4 \cdot 2) = (4 \cdot 4) \cdot 2$ **6.** $x + y = y + x$

See Example 2 **Simplify each expression. Justify each step.**

7. $8 + 23 + 2$ **8.** $2 \cdot (17 \cdot 5)$ **9.** $(25 \cdot 11) \cdot 4$

10. $17 + 29 + 3$ **11.** $16 + (17 + 14)$ **12.** $5 \cdot 19 \cdot 20$

See Example 3 **Use the Distributive Property to find each product.**

13. $2(19)$ **14.** $5(31)$ **15.** $(22)2$

16. $(13)6$ **17.** $8(26)$ **18.** $(34)6$

INDEPENDENT PRACTICE

See Example 1 **Tell which property is represented.**

19. $1 + 0 = 1$ **20.** $xyz = x \cdot (yz)$ **21.** $9 + (9 + 0) = (9 + 9) + 0$

22. $11 + 25 = 25 + 11$ **23.** $7 \cdot 1 = 7$ **24.** $16 \cdot 4 = 4 \cdot 16$

See Example 2 **Simplify each expression. Justify each step.**

25. $50 \cdot 16 \cdot 2$ **26.** $9 + 34 + 1$ **27.** $4 \cdot (25 \cdot 9)$

28. $27 + 28 + 3$ **29.** $20 + (63 + 80)$ **30.** $25 + 17 + 75$

See Example 3 **Use the Distributive Property to find each product.**

31. $9(15)$ **32.** $(14)5$ **33.** $3(58)$

34. $10(42)$ **35.** $(23)4$ **36.** $(16)5$

PRACTICE AND PROBLEM SOLVING

Extra Practice p. 725

Write an example of each property using whole numbers.

37. Commutative Property **38.** Identity Property

39. Associative Property **40.** Distributive Property

41. Architecture The figure shows the floor plan for a studio loft. To find the area of the loft, the architect multiplies the length and the width: $(14 + 8) \cdot 10$. Use the Distributive Property to find the area of the loft.

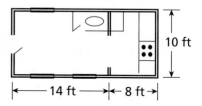

10 ft

14 ft 8 ft

Simplify each expression. Justify each step.

42. $32 + 26 + 43$ **43.** $50 \cdot 45 \cdot 4$ **44.** $5 + 16 + 25$ **45.** $35 \cdot 25 \cdot 20$

Complete each equation. Then tell which property is represented.

46. $5 + 16 = 16 +$ ▨

47. $15 \cdot 1 =$ ▨

48. ▨ $\cdot (4 + 7) = 3 \cdot 4 + 3 \cdot 7$

49. $20 +$ ▨ $= 20$

50. $2 \cdot$ ▨ $\cdot 9 = (2 \cdot 13) \cdot 9$

51. $8 + ($ ▨ $+ 4) = (8 + 8) + 4$

52. $2 \cdot (6 + 1) = 2 \cdot$ ▨ $+ 2 \cdot 1$

53. $(12 - 9) \cdot$ ▨ $= 12 \cdot 2 - 9 \cdot 2$

54. **Sports** Janice wants to know the total number of games won by the Denver Nuggets basketball team over the three seasons shown in the table. What expression should she simplify? Explain how she can use mental math and the properties of this lesson to simplify the expression.

Denver Nuggets		
Season	Won	Lost
2001–02	27	55
2002–03	17	65
2003–04	43	39

55. **What's the Error?** A student simplified the expression $6 \cdot (9 + 12)$ as shown. What is the student's error?

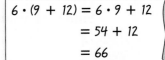
$6 \cdot (9 + 12) = 6 \cdot 9 + 12$
$= 54 + 12$
$= 66$

56. **Write About It** Do you think there is a Commutative Property of Subtraction? Give an example to justify your answer.

57. **Challenge** Use the Distributive Property to simplify $\frac{1}{6} \cdot (36 + \frac{1}{2})$.

---

58. **Multiple Choice** Which is an example of the Associative Property?

Ⓐ $4 + 0 = 4$

Ⓒ $5 + 7 = 7 + 5$

Ⓑ $9 + 8 + 2 = 9 + (8 + 2)$

Ⓓ $5 \cdot (12 + 3) = 5 \cdot 12 + 5 \cdot 3$

59. **Multiple Choice** Which property is $2 \cdot (3 + 7) = (2 \cdot 3) + (2 \cdot 7)$ an example of?

Ⓕ Associative   Ⓖ Commutative   Ⓗ Distributive   Ⓙ Identity

60. **Short Response** Show how to use the Distributive Property to simplify the expression $8(27)$.

Write each number using an exponent and the given base. (Lesson 1-2)

61. 36, base 6

62. 64, base 2

63. 9, base 3

64. 1,000, base 10

Simplify each expression. (Lesson 1-5)

65. $25 + 5 - (6^2 - 7)$

66. $3^3 - (6 + 3)$

67. $(4^2 + 5) \div 7$

68. $(5 - 3)^2 \div (3^2 - 7)$

READY TO GO ON?

Quiz for Lessons 1-1 Through 1-6

1-1 Numbers and Patterns

Identify a possible pattern. Use the pattern to write the next three numbers or figures.

1. 8, 15, 22, 29, . . .   **2.** 79, 66, 53, 40, . . .

3.

1-2 Exponents

Find each value.

4. 8^4 **5.** 7^3 **6.** 4^5 **7.** 6^2

8. The number of bacteria in a sample doubles every hour. How many bacteria cells will there be after 8 hours if there is one cell at the beginning? Write your answer as a power.

1-3 Metric Measurements

Convert each measure.

9. 17.3 kg to grams   **10.** 540 mL to liters   **11.** 0.46 cm to millimeters

12. Cat ran in the 400-meter dash and the 800-meter run. Hilo ran in the 2-kilometer cross-country race. All together, who ran the farthest, Cat or Hilo?

1-4 Applying Exponents

Multiply.

13. $456 \cdot 10^5$ **14.** $9.3 \cdot 10^2$ **15.** $0.36 \cdot 10^8$

Write each number in scientific notation.

16. 8,400,000   **17.** 521,000,000   **18.** 29,000

19. In May 2005, the world's population was over 6,446,000,000 and was increasing by 140 people each minute! Write this population in scientific notation.

1-5 Order of Operations

Simplify each expression.

20. $8 - 14 \div (9 - 2)$ **21.** $54 - 6 \cdot 3 + 4^2$ **22.** $4 - 24 \div 2^3$ **23.** $4(3 + 2)^2 - 9$

1-6 Properties

Simplify each expression. Justify each step.

24. $29 + 50 + 21$ **25.** $5 \cdot 18 \cdot 20$ **26.** $34 + 62 + 36$ **27.** $3 \cdot 11 \cdot 20$

Focus on Problem Solving

 Solve

• **Choose an operation: multiplication or division**

To solve a word problem, you must determine which mathematical operation you can use to find the answer. One way of doing this is to determine the action the problem is asking you to take. If you are putting equal parts together, then you need to multiply. If you are separating something into equal parts, then you need to divide.

 Decide what action each problem is asking you to take, and tell whether you must multiply or divide. Then explain your decision.

1 Judy plays the flute in the band. She practices for 3 hours every week. Judy practices only half as long as Angie, who plays the clarinet. How long does Angie practice playing the clarinet each week?

2 Each year, members of the band and choir are invited to join the bell ensemble for the winter performance. There are 18 bells in the bell ensemble. This year, each student has 3 bells to play. How many students are in the bell ensemble this year?

3 For every percussion instrument in the band, there are 4 wind instruments. If there are 48 wind instruments in the band, how many percussion instruments are there?

4 A group of 4 people singing together in harmony is called a quartet. At a state competition for high school choir students, 7 quartets from different schools competed. How many students competed in the quartet competition?

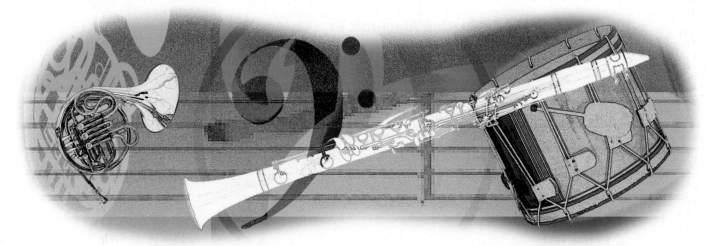

1-7 Variables and Algebraic Expressions

Learn to evaluate algebraic expressions.

Vocabulary

variable

constant

algebraic expression

evaluate

Georgia Performance Standards

M7A1.b Evaluate algebraic expressions, using commutative, associative, and distributive properties as appropriate. Also, M7P5.a.

Ron Howard was born in 1954. You can find out what year Ron turned 16 by adding 16 to the year he was born.

$$1954 + 16$$

In algebra, letters are often used to represent numbers. You can use a letter such as *a* to represent Ron Howard's age. When he turns *a* years old, the year will be

$$1954 + a.$$

The letter *a* has a value that can change, or vary. When a letter represents a number that can vary, it is called a **variable**. The year 1954 is a **constant** because the number cannot change.

An **algebraic expression** consists of one or more variables. It usually contains constants and operations. For example, 1954 + *a* is an algebraic expression for the year Ron Howard turns a certain age.

Age	Year born + age = year at age	
16	1954 + 16	1970
18	1954 + 18	1972
21	1954 + 21	1975
36	1954 + 36	1990
a	1954 + *a*	

To **evaluate** an algebraic expression, substitute a number for the variable.

EXAMPLE 1 **Evaluating Algebraic Expressions**

Evaluate *n* + 7 for each value of *n*.

A *n* = 3   *n* + 7

           3 + 7   *Substitute 3 for n.*

           10   *Add.*

B *n* = 5   *n* + 7

           5 + 7   *Substitute 5 for n.*

           12   *Add.*

Multiplication and division of variables can be written in several ways, as shown in the table.

When evaluating expressions, use the order of operations.

Multiplication		Division	
$7t$	$7 \cdot t$	$\dfrac{q}{2}$	$q/2$
$7(t)$	$7 \times t$	$q \div 2$	
ab	$a \cdot b$	$\dfrac{s}{r}$	s/r
$a(b)$	$a \times b$	$s \div r$	

EXAMPLE 2 **Evaluating Algebraic Expressions Involving Order of Operations**

Evaluate each expression for the given value of the variable.

A $3x - 2$ for $x = 5$

$3(5) - 2$	*Substitute 5 for x.*
$15 - 2$	*Multiply.*
13	*Subtract*

B $n \div 2 + n$ for $n = 4$

$4 \div 2 + 4$	*Substitute 4 for n.*
$2 + 4$	*Divide.*
6	*Add.*

C $6y^2 + 2y$ for $y = 2$

$6(2)^2 + 2(2)$	*Substitute 2 for y.*
$6(4) + 2(2)$	*Evaluate the power.*
$24 + 4$	*Multiply.*
28	*Add.*

EXAMPLE 3 **Evaluating Algebraic Expressions with Two Variables**

Evaluate $\dfrac{3}{n} + 2m$ for $n = 3$ and $m = 4$.

$\dfrac{3}{n} + 2m$	
$\dfrac{3}{3} + 2(4)$	*Substitute 3 for n and 4 for m.*
$1 + 8$	*Divide and multiply from left to right.*
9	*Add.*

Think and Discuss
GPS M7P3.a, M7P3.d

1. Write each expression another way.   **a.** $12x$ **b.** $\dfrac{4}{y}$ **c.** $\dfrac{3xy}{2}$

2. Explain the difference between a variable and a constant.

1-7 Exercises

Georgia Performance Standards

M7P1.b, M7P3.c, M7P3.d

go.hrw.com
Homework Help Online
KEYWORD: MS7 1-7
Parent Resources Online
KEYWORD: MS7 Parent

GUIDED PRACTICE

See Example **1** Evaluate $n + 9$ for each value of n.

    1. $n = 3$ **2.** $n = 2$ **3.** $n = 11$

See Example **2** Evaluate each expression for the given value of the variable.

    4. $2x - 3$ for $x = 4$ **5.** $n \div 3 + n$ for $n = 6$ **6.** $5y^2 + 3y$ for $y = 2$

See Example **3** Evaluate each expression for the given values of the variables.

    7. $\dfrac{8}{n} + 3m$ for $n = 2$ and $m = 5$ **8.** $5a - 3b + 5$ for $a = 4$ and $b = 3$

INDEPENDENT PRACTICE

See Example **1** Evaluate $n + 5$ for each value of n.

    9. $n = 17$ **10.** $n = 9$ **11.** $n = 0$

See Example **2** Evaluate each expression for the given value of the variable.

    12. $5y - 1$ for $y = 3$ **13.** $10b - 9$ for $b = 2$ **14.** $p \div 7 + p$ for $p = 14$

    15. $n \div 5 + n$ for $n = 20$ **16.** $3x^2 + 2x$ for $x = 10$ **17.** $3c^2 - 5c$ for $c = 3$

See Example **3** Evaluate each expression for the given values of the variables.

    18. $\dfrac{12}{n} + 7m$ for $n = 6$ and $m = 4$ **19.** $7p - 2t + 3$ for $p = 6$ and $t = 2$

    20. $9 - \dfrac{3x}{4} + 20y$ for $x = 4$ and $y = 5$ **21.** $r^2 + 15k$ for $r = 15$ and $k = 5$

PRACTICE AND PROBLEM SOLVING

Extra Practice p. 725

Evaluate each expression for the given values of the variables.

22. $20x - 10$ for $x = 4$ **23.** $4d^2 - 3d$ for $d = 2$

24. $22p \div 11 + p$ for $p = 3$ **25.** $q + q^2 + q \div 2$ for $q = 4$

26. $\dfrac{16}{k} + 7h$ for $k = 8$ and $h = 2$ **27.** $f \div 3 + f$ for $f = 18$

28. $3t \div 3 + t$ for $t = 13$ **29.** $9 + 3p - 5t + 3$ for $p = 2$ and $t = 1$

30. $108 - 12j + j$ for $j = 9$ **31.** $3m^3 + \dfrac{y}{5}$ for $m = 2$ and $y = 35$

32. The expression $60m$ gives the number of seconds in m minutes. Evaluate $60m$ for $m = 7$. How many seconds are there in 7 minutes?

33. **Money** Betsy has n quarters. You can use the expression $0.25n$ to find the total value of her coins in dollars. What is the value of 18 quarters?

34. **Physical Science** A color TV has a power rating of 200 watts. The expression $200t$ gives the power used by t color TV sets. Evaluate $200t$ for $t = 13$. How much power is used by 13 TV sets?

35. Physical Science The expression $1.8c + 32$ can be used to convert a temperature in degrees Celsius c to degrees Fahrenheit. What is the temperature in degrees Fahrenheit if the temperature is 30°C?

36. Physical Science The graph shows the changes of state for water.

    a. What is the boiling point of water in degrees Celsius?

    b. Use the expression $1.8c + 32$ to find the boiling point of water in degrees Fahrenheit.

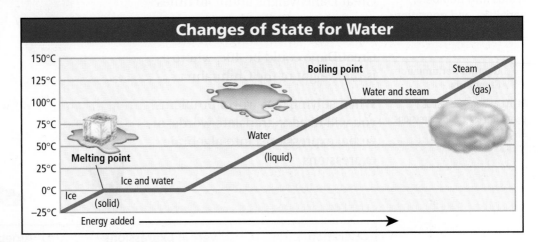

37. What's the Error? A student was asked to identify the variable in the expression $72x + 8$. The student answered $72x$. What was the student's error?

38. Write About It Explain why letters such as x, p, and n used in algebraic expressions are called variables. Use examples to illustrate your response.

39. Challenge Evaluate the expression $\dfrac{x + y}{y - x}$ for $x = 6$ and $y = 8$.

40. Multiple Choice Which expression does NOT equal 15?

    (A) $3t$ for $t = 5$ (B) $3 + t$ for $t = 12$ (C) $t \div 3$ for $t = 60$ (D) $t - 10$ for $t = 25$

41. Multiple Choice A group of 11 students go rock climbing at a local gym. It costs $12 per student plus $4 for each shoe rental. If only 8 students rent shoes, what is the total cost for the group to go climbing? Use the expression $12x + 4y$, where x represents the total number of students and y represents the number of students who rent shoes.

    (F) $132   (G) $140   (H) $164   (J) $176

Write each number in scientific notation. (Lesson 1-4)

42. 102.45   **43.** 62,100,000   **44.** 769,000   **45.** 800,000

Use the Distributive Property to find each product. (Lesson 1-6)

46. 5(16)   **47.** (17)4   **48.** 7(23)   **49.** (29)3

 **Translate Words into Math**

 Problem Solving Skill

 **to translate words into numbers, variables, and operations.**

Georgia Performance Standards

M7A1.a Translate verbal phrases to algebraic expressions. Also, M7P4.c, M7P5.b.

Although they are closely related, a Great Dane weighs about 40 times as much as a Chihuahua. An expression for the weight of the Great Dane could be 40*c*, where *c* is the weight of the Chihuahua.

When solving real-world problems, you will need to translate words, or verbal expressions, into algebraic expressions.

Operation	Verbal Expressions	Algebraic Expression
+	• add 3 to a number • a number plus 3 • the sum of a number and 3 • 3 more than a number • a number increased by 3	$n + 3$
−	• subtract 12 from a number • a number minus 12 • the difference of a number and 12 • 12 less than a number • a number decreased by 12 • take away 12 from a number • a number less 12	$x - 12$
✕	• 2 times a number • 2 multiplied by a number • the product of 2 and a number	$2m$ or $2 \cdot m$
÷	• 6 divided into a number • a number divided by 6 • the quotient of a number and 6	$a \div 6$ or $\frac{a}{6}$

EXAMPLE 1 Translating Verbal Expressions into Algebraic Expressions

Write each phrase as an algebraic expression.

A the product of 20 and *t*

product means "multiply"

$20t$

B 24 less than a number

less than means "subtract from"

$n - 24$

Write each phrase as an algebraic expression.

C 4 times the sum of a number and 2

4 times the sum of a number and 2

$$4 \quad \cdot \qquad\qquad n + 2$$

$$4(n + 2)$$

D the sum of 4 times a number and 2

the sum of 4 times a number and 2

$$4 \quad \cdot \quad n \qquad\qquad + 2$$

$$4n + 2$$

When solving real-world problems, you may need to determine the action to know which operation to use.

Action	Operation
Put parts together	Add
Put equal parts together	Multiply
Find how much more or less	Subtract
Separate into equal parts	Divide

EXAMPLE 2 Translating Real-World Problems into Algebraic Expressions

A Jed reads p pages each day of a 200-page book. Write an algebraic expression for how many days it will take Jed to read the book.

You need to *separate* the total number of pages *into equal parts*. This involves division.

$$\frac{\text{total number of pages}}{\text{pages read each day}} \quad = \quad \frac{200}{p}$$

B To rent a certain car for a day costs $84 plus $0.29 for every mile the car is driven. Write an algebraic expression to show how much it costs to rent the car for a day.

The cost includes $0.29 per mile. Use m for the number of miles.

Multiply to *put equal parts together:* $\qquad$ $0.29m$

In addition to the fee per mile, the cost includes a flat fee of $84.

Add to *put parts together:* $\qquad$ $84 + 0.29m$

Think and Discuss  GPS M7P3.b, M7P5.b

1. **Write** three different verbal expressions that can be represented by $2 - y$.

2. **Explain** how you would determine which operation to use to find the number of chairs in 6 rows of 100 chairs each.

Georgia Performance Standards

M7P1.b, M7P3.a, M7P5.b

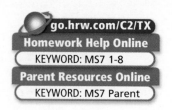

go.hrw.com/C2/TX
Homework Help Online
KEYWORD: MS7 1-8
Parent Resources Online
KEYWORD: MS7 Parent

GUIDED PRACTICE

See Example **1** **Write each phrase as an algebraic expression.**

1. the product of 7 and p

2. 3 less than a number

3. 12 divided into a number

4. 3 times the sum of a number and 5

See Example **2** **5.** Carly spends $5 for n notebooks. Write an algebraic expression to represent the cost of one notebook.

6. A company charges $46 for cable TV installation and $21 per month for basic cable service. Write an algebraic expression to represent the total cost of m months of basic cable service, including installation.

INDEPENDENT PRACTICE

See Example **1** **Write each phrase as an algebraic expression.**

7. the sum of 5 and a number

8. 2 less than a number

9. the quotient of a number and 8

10. 9 times a number

11. 10 less than the product of a number and 3

See Example **2** **12.** Video Express sells used tapes. Marta bought v tapes for $45. Write an algebraic expression for the average cost of each tape.

13. A 5-foot pine tree was planted and grew 2 feet each year. Write an algebraic expression for the height of the tree after t years.

PRACTICE AND PROBLEM SOLVING

CRCT GPS

Extra Practice p. 726

Write each phrase as an algebraic expression.

14. m plus the product of 6 and n

15. the quotient of 23 and u minus t

16. 14 less than the quantity k times 6

17. 2 times the sum of y and 5

18. the quotient of 100 and the quantity 6 plus w

19. 35 multiplied by the quantity r less 45

20. **Multi-Step** An ice machine can produce 17 pounds of ice in one hour.

   a. Write an algebraic expression to describe the number of pounds of ice produced in n hours.

   b. How many pounds of ice can the machine produce in 4 hours?

21. **Career** Karen earns $65,000 a year as an optometrist. She received a bonus of b dollars last year and expects to get double that amount as a bonus this year. Write an algebraic expression to show the total amount Karen expects to earn this year.

Up to 25 follicle mite nymphs can hatch in a single hair follicle.

Write a verbal expression for each algebraic expression.

22. $h + 3$ **23.** $90 \div y$ **24.** $s - 405$ **25.** $16t$

26. $5(a - 8)$ **27.** $4p - 10$ **28.** $(r + 1) \div 14$ **29.** $\frac{m}{15} + 3$

30. **Life Science** Tiny and harmless, follicle mites live in our eyebrows and eyelashes. They are relatives of spiders and like spiders, they have eight legs. Write an algebraic expression for the number of legs in m mites.

Nutrition The table shows the estimated number of grams of carbohydrates commonly found in various types of foods.

31. Write an algebraic expression for the number of grams of carbohydrates in y pieces of fruit and 1 cup of skim milk.

32. How many grams of carbohydrates are in a sandwich made from t ounces of lean meat and 2 slices of bread?

Food	Carbohydrates
1 c skim milk	12 g
1 piece of fruit	15 g
1 slice of bread	15 g
1 oz lean meat	0 g

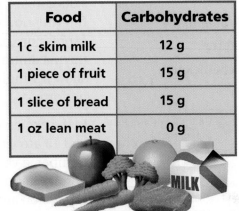

33. **What's the Question?** Al has twice as many baseball cards as Frank and four times as many football cards as Joe. The expression $2x + 4y$ can be used to show the total number of baseball and football cards Al has. If the answer is y, then what is the question?

34. **Write About It** If you are asked to compare two numbers, what two operations might you use? Why?

35. **Challenge** In 1996, one U.S. dollar was equivalent, on average, to $1.363 in Canadian money. Write an algebraic expression for the number of U.S. dollars you could get for n Canadian dollars.

CRCT Prep • GPS Support • Spiral Review

36. **Multiple Choice** Which verbal expression does NOT represent $9 - x$?

  Ⓐ x less than nine   Ⓒ subtract x from nine

  Ⓑ x decreased by nine   Ⓓ the difference of nine and x

37. **Short Response** A room at the Oak Creek Inn costs $104 per night for two people. There is a $19 charge for each extra person. Write an algebraic expression that shows the cost per night for a family of four staying at the inn. Then evaluate your expression for 3 nights.

Simplify each expression. (Lesson 1-5)

38. $6 + 4 \div 2$ **39.** $9 \cdot 1 - 4$ **40.** $5^2 - 3$ **41.** $24 \div 3 + 3^3$

42. Evaluate $b - a^2$ for $a = 2$ and $b = 9$. (Lesson 1-7)

1-9 Simplifying Algebraic Expressions

Learn to simplify algebraic expressions.

Vocabulary

term

coefficient

Georgia Performance Standards

M7A1.b Simplify and evaluate algebraic expressions, using commutative, associative, and distributive properties as appropriate. Also, M7A1.a, M7A1.c, M7P5.c.

Caution!

A variable by itself, such as y, has a coefficient of 1. So $y = 1y$.

Individual skits at the talent show can last up to x minutes each, and group skits can last up to y minutes each. Intermission will be 15 minutes. The expression $7x + 9y + 15$ represents the maximum length of the talent show if 7 individuals and 9 groups perform.

In the expression $7x + 9y + 15$, $7x$, $9y$, and 15 are *terms*. A **term** can be a number, a variable, or a product of numbers and variables. Terms in an expression are separated by plus or minus signs.

In the term $7x$, 7 is called the *coefficient*. A **coefficient** is a number that is multiplied by a variable in an algebraic expression.

Coefficient   Variable

Like terms are terms with the same variable raised to the same power. The coefficients do not have to be the same. Constants, like 5, $\frac{1}{2}$, and 3.2, are also like terms.

Like Terms	$3x$ and $2x$	w and $\frac{w}{7}$	5 and 1.8
Unlike Terms	$5x^2$ and $2x$ *The exponents are different.*	$6a$ and $6b$ *The variables are different.*	3.2 and n *Only one term contains a variable.*

EXAMPLE 1 Identifying Like Terms

Identify like terms in the list.

$$5a \quad \frac{t}{2} \quad 3y^2 \quad 7t \quad x^2 \quad 4z \quad k \quad 4.5y^2 \quad 2t \quad \frac{2}{3}a$$

Look for like variables with like powers.

Helpful Hint

Use different shapes or colors to indicate sets of like terms.

$5a$ $\frac{t}{2}$ $3y^2$ $7t$ x^2 $4z$ k $4.5y^2$ $2t$ $\frac{2}{3}a$

Like terms: $5a$ and $\frac{2}{3}a$ $\frac{t}{2}$, $7t$, and $2t$ $3y^2$ and $4.5y^2$

To simplify an algebraic expression that contains like terms, combine the terms. Combining like terms is like grouping similar objects.

$$4x \quad + \quad 5x \quad = \quad 9x$$

To combine like terms that have variables, add or subtract the coefficients.

EXAMPLE 2 **Simplifying Algebraic Expressions**

Simplify. Justify your steps using the Commutative, Associative, and Distributive Properties when necessary.

A $7x + 2x$

$7x + 2x$	*7x and 2x are like terms.*
$9x$	*Add the coefficients.*

B $5x^3 + 3y + 7x^3 - 2y - 4x^2$

$5x^3 + 3y + 7x^3 - 2y - 4x^2$	*Identify like terms.*
$5x^3 + 7x^3 + 3y - 2y - 4x^2$	*Commutative Property*
$(5x^3 + 7x^3) + (3y - 2y) - 4x^2$	*Associative Property*
$12x^3 + y - 4x^2$	*Add or subtract the coefficients.*

C $2(a + 2a^2) + 2b$

$2(a + 2a^2) + 2b$	
$2a + 4a^2 + 2b$	*Distributive Property*

There are no like terms to combine.

EXAMPLE 3 *Geometry Application*

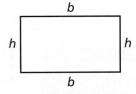

Write an expression for the perimeter of the rectangle. Then simplify the expression.

$b + h + b + h$	*Write an expression using the side lengths.*
$(b + b) + (h + h)$	*Identify and group like terms.*
$2b + 2h$	*Add the coefficients.*

Remember!

To find the perimeter of a figure, add the lengths of the sides.

Think and Discuss GPS M7P1.d, M7P3.b

1. Explain whether $5x$, $5x^2$, and $5x^3$ are like terms.

2. Explain how you know when an expression cannot be simplified.

Georgia Performance
Standards

M7P3.a, M7P4.c

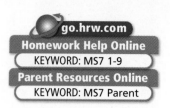

go.hrw.com
Homework Help Online
KEYWORD: MS7 1-9
Parent Resources Online
KEYWORD: MS7 Parent

GUIDED PRACTICE

See Example **1** Identify like terms in each list.

1. $6b$ $5x^2$ $4x^3$ $\frac{b}{2}$ x^2 $2e$ **2.** $12a^2$ $4x^3$ b $4a^2$ $3.5x^3$ $\frac{5}{6}b$

See Example **2** Simplify. Justify your steps using the Commutative, Associative, and Distributive Properties when necessary.

3. $5x + 3x$ **4.** $6a^2 - a^2 + 16$ **5.** $4a^2 + 5a + 14b$

See Example **3** **6. Geometry** Write an expression for the perimeter of the rectangle. Then simplify the expression.

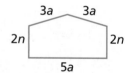

$5n$

$6b$ $6b$

$5n$

INDEPENDENT PRACTICE

See Example **1** Identify like terms in each list.

7. $2b$ b^6 b x^4 $3b^6$ $2x^2$ **8.** 6 $2n$ $3n^2$ $6m^2$ $\frac{n}{4}$ 7

9. $10k^2$ m 3^3 $\frac{p}{6}$ $2m$ 2 **10.** 6^3 y^3 $3y^2$ 6^2 y $5y^3$

See Example **2** Simplify. Justify your steps using the Commutative, Associative, and Distributive Properties when necessary.

11. $3a + 2b + 5a$ **12.** $5b + 7b + 10$ **13.** $a + 2b + 2a + b + 2c$

14. $y + 4 + 2x + 3y$ **15.** $q^2 + 2q + 2q^2$ **16.** $18 + 2d^3 + d + 3d$

See Example **3** **17. Geometry** Write an expression for the perimeter of the given figure. Then simplify the expression.

$3a$ $3a$

$2n$ $2n$

$5a$

PRACTICE AND PROBLEM SOLVING

Extra Practice p. 726

Simplify each expression.

18. $4x + 5x$ **19.** $32y - 5y$ **20.** $4c^2 + 5c + 2c$

21. $5d^2 - 3d^2 + d$ **22.** $5f^2 + 2f + f^2$ **23.** $7x + 8x^2 - 3y$

24. $p + 9q + 9 + 14p$ **25.** $6b + 6b^2 + 4b^3$ **26.** $a^2 + 2b + 2a^2 + b + 2c$

27. Geometry Write an expression for the perimeter of the given triangle. Then evaluate the perimeter when n is 1, 2, 3, 4, and 5.

n		1	2	3	4	5
Perimeter						

$4n$ $6n$

$5n$

Business

The winner of each year's National Best Bagger Competition gets a bag-shaped trophy and a cash prize.

28. Critical Thinking Determine whether the expression $9m^2 + k$ is equal to $7m^2 + 2(2k - m^2) + 5k$. Use properties to justify your answer.

29. Multi-Step Brad makes d dollars per hour as a cook at a deli. The table shows the number of hours he worked each week in June.

Hours Brad Worked	
Week	Hours
1	21.5
2	23
3	15.5
4	19

  a. Write and simplify an expression for the amount of money Brad earned in June.

  b. Evaluate your expression from part **a** for $d = \$9.50$.

  c. What does your answer to part **b** represent?

30. Business Ashley earns $8 per hour working at a grocery store. Last week she worked h hours bagging groceries and twice as many hours stocking shelves. Write and simplify an expression for the amount Ashley earned.

31. Critical Thinking The terms $3x$, $23x^2$, $6y^2$, $2x$, y^2 and one other term can be written in an expression which, when simplified, equals $5x + 7y^2$. Identify the term missing from the list and write the expression.

32. What's the Question? At one store, a pair of jeans costs $29 and a shirt costs $25. At another store, the same kind of jeans costs $26 and the same kind of shirt costs $20. The answer is $29j - 26j + 25s - 20s = 3j + 5s$. What is the question?

33. Write About It Describe the steps for simplifying the expression $2x + 3 + 5x - 15$.

34. Challenge A rectangle has a width of $x + 2$ and a length of $3x + 1$. Write and simplify an expression for the perimeter of the rectangle.

CRCT Prep • GPS Support • Spiral Review

35. Multiple Choice Translate "six times the sum of x and y" and "five less than y." Which algebraic expression represents the sum of these two verbal expressions?

    Ⓐ $6x + 5$ Ⓑ $6x + 2y - 5$ Ⓒ $6x + 5y + 5$ Ⓓ $6x + 7y - 5$

36. Multiple Choice The side length of a square is $2x + 3$. Which expression represents the perimeter of the square?

    Ⓕ $2x + 12$ Ⓖ $4x + 6$ Ⓗ $6x + 7$ Ⓙ $8x + 12$

Compare. Write <, >, or =. (Lesson 1-3)

37. 2.3 mm ▧ 23 cm   **38.** 6 km ▧ 600 m   **39.** 449 mg ▧ 0.5 g

Evaluate the expression $9y - 3$ for each given value of the variable. (Lesson 1-7)

40. $y = 2$ **41.** $y = 6$ **42.** $y = 10$ **43.** $y = 18$

1-10 Equations and Their Solutions

 **Learn** to determine whether a number is a solution of an equation.

Vocabulary

equation

solution

Ella has 22 CDs. This is 9 more than Kay has.

This situation can be written as an *equation*. An **equation** is a mathematical statement that two expressions are equal in value.

An equation is like a balanced scale.

 **Georgia Performance Standards**

M7A1.a Translate verbal phrases to algebraic expressions. Also, M7A1.b, M7P5.b, M7P5.c.

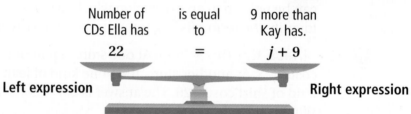

Number of CDs Ella has	is equal to	9 more than Kay has.
22	=	$j + 9$

Left expression   **Right expression**

Just as the weights on both sides of a balanced scale are exactly the same, the expressions on both sides of an equation represent exactly the same value.

When an equation contains a variable, a value of the variable that makes the statement true is called a **solution** of the equation.

Reading Math

The symbol ≠ means "is not equal to."

$22 = j + 9$ $j = 13$ is a solution because $22 = 13 + 9$.

$22 = j + 9$ $j = 15$ is not a solution because $22 \neq 15 + 9$.

EXAMPLE 1   **Determining Whether a Number Is a Solution of an Equation**

Determine whether the given value of the variable is a solution.

A $18 = s - 7; s = 11$

$18 = s - 7$

$18 \stackrel{?}{=} 11 - 7$ *Substitute 11 for s.*

$18 \stackrel{?}{=} 4$ ✗

11 is not a solution of $18 = s - 7$.

B $w + 17 = 23; w = 6$

$w + 17 = 23$

$6 + 17 \stackrel{?}{=} 23$ *Substitute 6 for w.*

$23 \stackrel{?}{=} 23$ ✔

6 is a solution of $w + 17 = 23$.

EXAMPLE 2 Writing an Equation to Determine Whether a Number Is a Solution

Tyler wants to buy a new skateboard. He has $57, which is $38 less than he needs. Does the skateboard cost $90 or $95?

You can write an equation to find the price of the skateboard. If s represents the price of the skateboard, then $s - 38 = 57$.

$90

$$s - 38 = 57$$
$$90 - 38 \overset{?}{=} 57 \qquad \textit{Substitute 90 for s.}$$
$$52 \overset{?}{=} 57 \; ✗$$

$95

$$s - 38 = 57$$
$$95 - 38 \overset{?}{=} 57 \qquad \textit{Substitute 95 for s.}$$
$$57 \overset{?}{=} 57 \; ✔$$

The skateboard costs $95.

EXAMPLE 3 Deriving a Real-World Situation from an Equation

Which problem situation best matches the equation $3x + 4 = 22$?

Situation A:

Harvey spent $22 at the gas station. He paid $4 per gallon for gas and $3 for snacks. How many gallons of gas did Harvey buy?

The variable x represents the number of gallons of gas that Harvey bought.

$$\$4 \text{ per gallon} \longrightarrow 4x$$

Since $4x$ is not a term in the given equation, Situation A does not match the equation.

Situation B:

Harvey spent $22 at the gas station. He paid $3 per gallon for gas and $4 for snacks. How many gallons of gas did Harvey buy?

$$\$3 \text{ per gallon} \longrightarrow 3x$$
$$\$4 \text{ on snacks} \longrightarrow + 4$$

Harvey spent $22 in all, so $3x + 4 = 22$. Situation B matches the equation.

Think and Discuss

GPS M7P3.b, M7P3.d

1. Compare equations with expressions.

2. Give an example of an equation whose solution is 5.

Georgia Performance Standards

M7P3.a, M7P4.c

go.hrw.com

Homework Help Online
KEYWORD: MS7 1-10

Parent Resources Online
KEYWORD: MS7 Parent

GUIDED PRACTICE

See Example **Determine whether the given value of the variable is a solution.**

1. $19 = x + 4$; $x = 23$ **2.** $6n = 78$; $n = 13$ **3.** $k \div 3 = 14$; $k = 42$

See Example **4.** Mavis wants to buy a book. She has $25, which is $9 less than she needs. Does the book cost $34 or $38?

See Example **5.** Which problem situation best matches the equation $10 + 2x = 16$?

Situation A: Angie bought peaches for $2 per pound and laundry detergent for $10. She spent a total of $16. How many pounds of peaches did Angie buy?

Situation B: Angie bought peaches for $10 per pound and laundry detergent for $2. She spent a total of $16. How many pounds of peaches did Angie buy?

INDEPENDENT PRACTICE

See Example 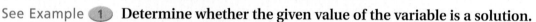 **Determine whether the given value of the variable is a solution.**

6. $r - 12 = 25$; $r = 37$ **7.** $39 \div x = 13$; $x = 4$ **8.** $21 = m + 9$; $m = 11$

9. $\frac{a}{18} = 7$; $a = 126$ **10.** $16f = 48$; $f = 3$ **11.** $71 - y = 26$; $y = 47$

See Example **12.** Curtis wants to buy a new snowboard. He has $119, which is $56 less than he needs. Does the snowboard cost $165 or $175?

See Example **13.** Which problem situation best matches the equation $2m + 10 = 18$?

Situation A: A taxi service charges a $2 fee, plus $18 per mile. Jeremy paid the driver $10. How many miles did Jeremy ride in the taxi?

Situation B: A taxi service charges a $10 fee, plus $2 per mile. Jeremy paid the driver $18. How many miles did Jeremy ride in the taxi?

PRACTICE AND PROBLEM SOLVING

CRCT GPS

Extra Practice p. 726

Determine whether the given value of the variable is a solution.

14. $j = 6$ for $15 - j = 21$ **15.** $x = 36$ for $48 = x + 12$

16. $m = 18$ for $16 = 34 - m$ **17.** $k = 23$ for $17 + k = 40$

18. $y = 8$ for $9y + 2 = 74$ **19.** $c = 12$ for $100 - 2c = 86$

20. $q = 13$ for $5q + 7 - q = 51$ **21.** $w = 15$ for $13w - 2 - 6w = 103$

22. $t = 12$ for $3(50 - t) - 10t = 104$ **23.** $r = 21$ for $4r - 8 + 9r - 1 = 264$

24. Hobbies Monique has a collection of stamps from 6 different countries. Jeremy has stamps from 3 fewer countries than Monique does. Write an equation showing this, using j as the number of countries from which Jeremy has stamps.

25. The diagram shows approximate elevations for different climate zones in the Colorado Rockies. Use the diagram to write an equation that shows the vertical distance d from the summit of Mount Evans (14,264 ft) to the tree line, which marks the beginning of the alpine tundra zone.

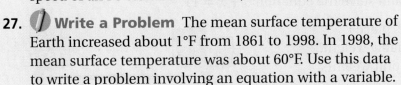

West ← | East →

Tree line

Piñon-Juniper, 7,000–9,000 ft
Semidesert, 5,500–7,000 ft

Alpine tundra, above 10,500 ft
Subalpine, 9,000–10,500 ft
Montane forest, 7,500–9,000 ft
Foothills, 5,500–7,500 ft
Great Plains, 3,000–5,500 ft

Source: Colorado Mall

26. The top wind speed of an F5 tornado, the strongest known kind of tornado, is 246 mi/h faster than the top wind speed of an F1 tornado, the weakest kind of tornado. The top wind speed of an F1 tornado is 72 mi/h. Is the top wind speed of an F5 tornado 174 mi/h, 218 mi/h, or 318 mi/h?

27. **✏ Write a Problem** The mean surface temperature of Earth increased about 1°F from 1861 to 1998. In 1998, the mean surface temperature was about 60°F. Use this data to write a problem involving an equation with a variable.

28. **★ Challenge** In the 1980s, about 9.3×10^4 acres of tropical forests were destroyed each year due to deforestation. About how many acres of tropical forests were destroyed during the 1980s?

Maroon Bells in the Colorado Rockies

CRCT Prep • GPS Support • Spiral Review

29. Multiple Choice Jack's rectangular bedroom has a length of 10 feet. He used the formula $A = 10w$ to find the area of his room. He found that his bedroom had an area of 150 square feet. What was the width of his bedroom?

   Ⓐ 15 feet   Ⓑ 25 feet   Ⓒ 30 feet   Ⓓ 15,000 feet

30. Multiple Choice The number of seventh-graders at Pecos Middle School is 316. This is 27 more than the number of eighth-graders. How many eighth-graders are enrolled?

   Ⓕ 289   Ⓖ 291   Ⓗ 299   Ⓙ 343

Write each number in scientific notation. (Lesson 1-4)

31. 10,850,000   **32.** 627,000   **33.** 9,040,000

Tell which property is represented. (Lesson 1-6)

34. $(7 + 5) + 3 = 7 + (5 + 3)$ **35.** $181 + 0 = 181$ **36.** $bc = cb$

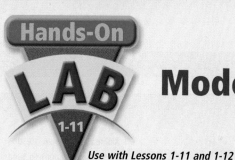
Model Solving Equations

Use with Lessons 1-11 and 1-12

go.hrw.com
Lab Resources Online
KEYWORD: MS7 Lab1

Georgia Performance Standards

M7A2.b, M7P5.a, M7P5.b, M7P5.c

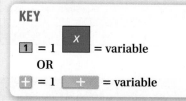

KEY

$\boxed{1}$ = 1 $\boxed{x}$ = variable

OR

$\boxplus$ = 1 $\boxed{+}$ = variable

REMEMBER

- In an equation, the expressions on both sides of the equal sign are equivalent.
- A variable can have any value that makes the equation true.

You can use balance scales and algebra tiles to model and solve equations.

Activity

1 Use a balance scale to model and solve the equation $3 + x = 11$.

a. On the left side of the scale, place 3 unit weights and one variable weight. On the right side, place 11 unit weights. This models $3 + x = 11$.

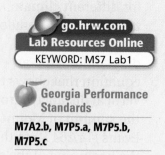

$$3 + x = 11$$

b. Remove 3 of the unit weights from each side of the scale to leave the variable weight by itself on one side.

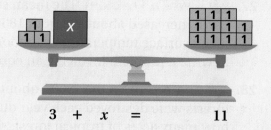

$$\begin{array}{ccc} 3 + x & = & 11 \\ -3 & & -3 \end{array}$$

c. Count the remaining unit weights on the right side of the scale. This number represents the solution of the equation.

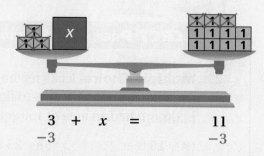

$$x = 8$$

The model shows that if $3 + x = 11$, then $x = 8$.

2 Use algebra tiles to model and solve the equation $3y = 15$.

a. On the left side of the mat, place 3 variable tiles. On the right side, place 15 unit tiles. This models $3y = 15$.

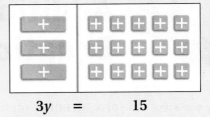

$$3y \quad = \quad 15$$

b. Since there are 3 variable tiles, divide the tiles on each side of the mat into 3 equal groups.

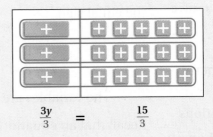

$$\frac{3y}{3} \quad = \quad \frac{15}{3}$$

c. Count the number of unit tiles in one of the groups. This number represents the solution of the equation.

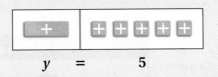

$$y \quad = \quad 5$$

The model shows that if $3y = 15$, then $y = 5$.

To check your solutions, substitute the variable in each equation with your solution. If the resulting equation is true, your solution is correct.

$3 + x = 11$

$3 + 8 \stackrel{?}{=} 11$

$11 \stackrel{?}{=} 11$ ✔

$3y = 15$

$3 \cdot 5 \stackrel{?}{=} 15$

$15 \stackrel{?}{=} 15$ ✔

Think and Discuss

1. What operation did you use to solve the equation $3 + x = 11$ in **1**? What operation did you use to solve $3y = 15$ in **2**?

2. Compare using a balance scale and weights with using a mat and algebra tiles. Which method of modeling equations is more helpful to you? Explain.

Try This

Use a balance scale or algebra tiles to model and solve each equation.

1. $4x = 16$
2. $3 + 5 = n$
3. $5r = 15$
4. $n + 7 = 12$
5. $y + 6 = 13$
6. $8 = 2r$
7. $9 = 7 + w$
8. $18 = 6p$

1-11 Addition and Subtraction Equations

Learn to solve one-step equations by using addition or subtraction.

Vocabulary

Addition Property of Equality

inverse operations

Subtraction Property of Equality

Georgia Performance Standards

M7A2.b Use the addition property of equality to solve one-step linear equations. Also, M7A2.a, M7P.5b, M7P5.c.

To solve an equation means to find a solution to the equation. To do this, isolate the variable—that is, get the variable alone on one side of the equal sign.

$x = 8 - 5$
$7 - 3 = y$

The variables are isolated.

$x + 5 = 8$
$7 = 3 + y$

The variables are *not* isolated.

Recall that an equation is like a balanced scale. If you increase or decrease the weights by the same amount on both sides, the scale will remain balanced.

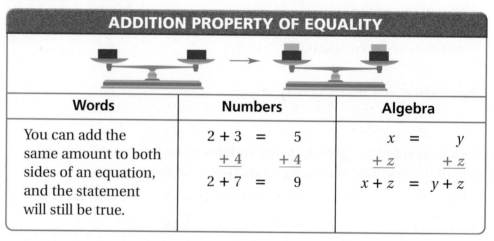

	ADDITION PROPERTY OF EQUALITY	
Words	**Numbers**	**Algebra**
You can add the same amount to both sides of an equation, and the statement will still be true.	$2 + 3 = 5$ $+ 4 \quad\quad + 4$ $2 + 7 = 9$	$x = y$ $+ z \quad\quad + z$ $x + z = y + z$

Use *inverse operations* when isolating a variable. Addition and subtraction are **inverse operations**, which means that they "undo" each other.

$$2 \boxed{+5} = 7 \longleftrightarrow 7 \boxed{-5} = 2$$

EXAMPLE 1 Solving an Equation by Addition

Solve the equation $x - 8 = 17$. Check your answer.

$\begin{aligned} x - 8 &= 17 \\ +8 \quad &+ 8 \\ x &= 25 \end{aligned}$

Think: 8 is subtracted from x, so add 8 to both sides to isolate x.

Check

$\begin{aligned} x - 8 &= 17 \\ 25 - 8 &\stackrel{?}{=} 17 \\ 17 &\stackrel{?}{=} 17 \checkmark \end{aligned}$

Substitute 25 for x.

25 is a solution.

SUBTRACTION PROPERTY OF EQUALITY

Words	Numbers	Algebra
You can subtract the same amount from both sides of an equation, and the statement will still be true.	$\begin{aligned} 4 + 7 &= 11 \\ -3 \quad &-3 \\ 4 + 4 &= 8 \end{aligned}$	$\begin{aligned} x &= y \\ -z \quad &-z \\ x - z &= y - z \end{aligned}$

EXAMPLE 2 · Solving an Equation by Subtraction

Solve the equation $a + 5 = 11$. Check your answer.

$$a + 5 = 11$$
$$\underline{\;-5 \quad -5\;}$$
$$a \quad = 6$$

*Think: 5 is **added** to a, so **subtract** 5 from both sides to isolate a.*

Check

$$a + 5 = 11$$
$$6 + 5 \overset{?}{=} 11 \qquad \textit{Substitute 6 for a.}$$
$$11 \overset{?}{=} 11 \; ✔ \qquad \textit{6 is a solution.}$$

EXAMPLE 3 · *Sports Application*

Michael Jordan's highest point total for a single game was 69. The entire team scored 117 points in that game. How many points did his teammates score?

Let p represent the points scored by the rest of the team.

Jordan's points	+	Teammates' points	=	Final score
69	+	p	=	117

$$69 + p = 117$$
$$\underline{-69 \qquad -69} \qquad \textit{Subtract 69 from both sides to isolate p.}$$
$$p = 48$$

His teammates scored 48 points.

Think and Discuss   GPS M7P1.d, M7P3.b

1. **Explain** how to decide which operation to use in order to isolate the variable in an equation.

2. **Describe** what would happen if a number were added or subtracted on one side of an equation but not on the other side.

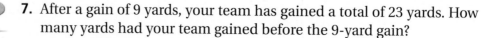

Georgia Performance Standards

M7P3.a, M7P3.c, M7P4.c

go.hrw.com
Homework Help Online
KEYWORD: MS7 1-11
Parent Resources Online
KEYWORD: MS7 Parent

GUIDED PRACTICE

See Example 1   **Solve each equation. Check your answer.**

1. $r - 77 = 99$ **2.** $102 = v - 66$ **3.** $x - 22 = 66$

See Example 2   **4.** $d + 83 = 92$ **5.** $45 = 36 + f$ **6.** $987 = 16 + m$

See Example 3   **7.** After a gain of 9 yards, your team has gained a total of 23 yards. How many yards had your team gained before the 9-yard gain?

INDEPENDENT PRACTICE

See Example 1   **Solve each equation. Check your answer.**

8. $n - 36 = 17$ **9.** $t - 28 = 54$ **10.** $p - 56 = 12$

11. $b - 41 = 26$ **12.** $m - 51 = 23$ **13.** $k - 22 = 101$

See Example 2   **14.** $x + 15 = 43$ **15.** $w + 19 = 62$ **16.** $a + 14 = 38$

17. $110 = s + 65$ **18.** $x + 47 = 82$ **19.** $18 + j = 94$

20. $97 = t + 45$ **21.** $q + 13 = 112$ **22.** $44 = 16 + n$

See Example 3   **23.** Hank is on a field trip. He has to travel 56 miles to reach his destination. He has traveled 18 miles so far. How much farther does he have to travel?

24. Sandy read 8 books in April. If her book club requires her to read 6 books each month, how many more books did she read than what was required?

PRACTICE AND PROBLEM SOLVING

Extra Practice p. 726

Solve each equation. Check your answer.

25. $p - 7 = 3$ **26.** $n + 17 = 98$ **27.** $23 + b = 75$

28. $356 = y - 219$ **29.** $105 = a + 60$ **30.** $g - 720 = 159$

31. $651 + c = 800$ **32.** $f - 63 = 937$ **33.** $59 + m = 258$

34. $16 = h - 125$ **35.** $s + 841 = 1,000$ **36.** $711 = q - 800$

37. $63 + x = 902$ **38.** $z - 712 = 54$ **39.** $120 = w + 41$

40. Physical Science An object weighs less when it is in water. This is because water exerts a buoyant force on the object. The weight of an object out of water is equal to the object's weight in water plus the buoyant force of the water. Suppose an object weighs 103 pounds out of water and 55 pounds in water. Write and solve an equation to find the buoyant force of the water.

41. Banking After Lana deposited a check for $65, her new account balance was $315. Write and solve an equation to find the amount that was in Lana's account before the deposit.

42. Music Jason wants to buy the trumpet advertised in the classified ads. He has saved $156. Using the information from the ad, write and solve an equation to find how much more money he needs to buy the trumpet.

 43. What's the Error? Describe and correct the error.
$x = 50$ for $(8 + 4)2 + x = 26$

 44. Write About It Explain how you know whether to add or subtract to solve an equation.

 45. Challenge Kwan keeps a record of his football team's gains and losses on each play of the game. The record is shown in the table. Find the missing information by writing and solving an equation.

Play	Play Gain/Loss	Overall Gain/Loss
1st down	Gain of 2 yards	Gain of 2 yards
2nd down	Loss of 5 yards	Loss of 3 yards
3rd down	Gain of 7 yards	Gain of 4 yards
4th down		Loss of 7 yards

46. Gridded Response Morgan has read 78 pages of *Treasure Island*. The book has 203 pages. How many pages of the book does Morgan have left to read?

47. Multiple Choice Which problem situation best represents the equation $42 - x = 7$?

Ⓐ Craig is 42 years old. His brother is 7 years older than he is. How old is Craig's brother?

Ⓑ Dylan has 42 days to finish his science fair project. How many weeks does he have left to finish his project?

Ⓒ The total lunch bill for a group of 7 friends is $42. If the friends split the cost of the meal evenly, how much should each person pay?

Ⓓ Each student in the Anderson Junior High Spanish Club has paid for a club T-shirt. If there are 42 students in the club and only 7 shirts are left to be picked up, how many students have already picked up their shirts?

Write each phrase as an algebraic expression. (Lesson 1-8)

48. the product of 16 and n **49.** 17 decreased by k **50.** 8 times the sum of x and 4

Simplify each expression. (Lesson 1-9)

51. $6(2 + 2n) + 3n$ **52.** $4x - 7y + x$ **53.** $8 + 3t + 2(4t)$

1-12 Multiplication and Division Equations

Learn to solve one-step equations by using multiplication or division.

Like addition and subtraction, multiplication and division are inverse operations. They "undo" each other.

$$2 \cdot 5 = 10$$
$$10 \div 5 = 2$$

Vocabulary

Multiplication Property of Equality

Division Property of Equality

Georgia Performance Standards

M7A2.b Use the multiplication property of equality to solve one-step linear equations. Also, M7A2.a, M7P4.c, M7P5.b.

MULTIPLICATION PROPERTY OF EQUALITY		
Words	**Numbers**	**Algebra**
You can multiply both sides of an equation by the same number, and the statement will still be true.	$3 \cdot 4 = 12$ $2 \cdot 3 \cdot 4 = 2 \cdot 12$ $6 \cdot 4 = 24$	$x = y$ $zx = zy$

If a variable is divided by a number, you can often use multiplication to isolate the variable. Multiply both sides of the equation by the number.

EXAMPLE 1 **Solving an Equation by Multiplication**

Solve the equation $\frac{x}{7} = 20$. Check your answer.

$$\frac{x}{7} = 20$$

$$(7)\frac{x}{7} = 20(7) \qquad \textit{Think: x is \textbf{divided} by 7, so \textbf{multiply} both sides by 7 to isolate x.}$$

$$x = 140$$

Check

$$\frac{x}{7} = 20$$

$$\frac{140}{7} \overset{?}{=} 20 \qquad \textit{Substitute 140 for x.}$$

$$20 \overset{?}{=} 20 \checkmark \qquad \textit{140 is a solution.}$$

Remember!

You cannot divide by 0.

DIVISION PROPERTY OF EQUALITY		
Words	**Numbers**	**Algebra**
You can divide both sides of an equation by the same nonzero number, and the statement will still be true.	$5 \cdot 6 = 30$ $\frac{5 \cdot 6}{3} = \frac{30}{3}$ $5 \cdot \frac{6}{3} = 10$ $5 \cdot 2 = 10$	$x = y$ $\frac{x}{z} = \frac{y}{z}$ $z \neq 0$

If a variable is multiplied by a number, you can often use division to isolate the variable. Divide both sides of the equation by the number.

EXAMPLE 2 **Solving an Equation by Division**

Solve the equation 240 = 4z. Check your answer.

$240 = 4z$ *Think: z is **multiplied** by 4, so*

$\dfrac{240}{4} = \dfrac{4z}{4}$ ***divide** both sides by 4 to isolate z.*

$60 = z$

Check

$240 = 4z$

$240 \overset{?}{=} 4(60)$ *Substitute 60 for z.*

$240 \overset{?}{=} 240$ ✔   *60 is a solution.*

EXAMPLE 3 *Health Application*

If you count your heartbeats for 10 seconds and multiply that number by 6, you can find your heart rate in beats per minute. Lance Armstrong, who won the Tour de France seven years in a row, from 1999 to 2005, has a resting heart rate of 30 beats per minute. How many times does his heart beat in 10 seconds?

Use the given information to write an equation, where b is the number of heartbeats in 10 seconds.

Beats in 10 s	.	6	=	beats per minute
b	.	6	=	30

$6b = 30$ *Think: b is **multiplied** by 6, so*

$\dfrac{6b}{6} = \dfrac{30}{6}$ ***divide** both sides by 6 to isolate b.*

$b = 5$

Lance Armstrong's heart beats 5 times in 10 seconds.

Health

In 2005, Lance Armstrong won his seventh consecutive Tour de France. He is the first person to win the 2,051-mile bicycle race more than five years in a row.

go.hrw.com
Web Extra!
KEYWORD: MS7 Lance

Think and Discuss

GPS M7P1.d, M7P2.c, M7P3.b

1. Explain how to check your solution to an equation.

2. Describe how to solve $13x = 91$.

3. When you solve $5p = 35$, will p be greater than 35 or less than 35? **Explain** your answer.

4. When you solve $\dfrac{p}{5} = 35$, will p be greater than 35 or less than 35? **Explain** your answer.

1-12 **Exercises**

Georgia Performance
Standards

M7P1.b, M7P3.a, M7P3.c

go.hrw.com
Homework Help Online
KEYWORD: MS7 1-12
Parent Resources Online
KEYWORD: MS7 Parent

GUIDED PRACTICE

See Example **1** Solve each equation. Check your answer.

1. $\frac{s}{77} = 11$ **2.** $b \div 25 = 4$ **3.** $y \div 8 = 5$

See Example **2** **4.** $72 = 8x$ **5.** $3c = 96$ **6.** $x \cdot 18 = 18$

See Example **3** **7.** On Friday nights, a local bowling alley charges \$5 per person to bowl all night. If Carol and her friends paid a total of \$45 to bowl, how many people were in their group?

INDEPENDENT PRACTICE

See Example **1** Solve each equation. Check your answer.

8. $12 = s \div 4$ **9.** $\frac{k}{18} = 72$ **10.** $13 = \frac{z}{5}$

11. $\frac{c}{5} = 35$ **12.** $\frac{w}{11} = 22$ **13.** $17 = n \div 18$

See Example **2** **14.** $17x = 85$ **15.** $63 = 3p$ **16.** $6u = 222$

17. $97a = 194$ **18.** $9q = 108$ **19.** $495 = 11d$

See Example **3** **20.** It costs \$6 per ticket for groups of ten or more people to see a minor league baseball game. If Albert's group paid a total of \$162 for game tickets, how many people were in the group?

PRACTICE AND PROBLEM SOLVING

CRCT GPS

Extra Practice p. 726

Solve each equation. Check your answer.

21. $9 = g \div 3$ **22.** $150 = 3j$ **23.** $68 = m - 42$

24. $7r = 84$ **25.** $5x = 35$ **26.** $9 = \frac{s}{38}$

27. $b + 33 = 95$ **28.** $\frac{p}{15} = 6$ **29.** $12f = 240$

30. $504 = c - 212$ **31.** $8a = 288$ **32.** $157 + q = 269$

33. $21 = d \div 2$ **34.** $\frac{h}{20} = 83$ **35.** $r - 92 = 215$

Multi-Step Translate each sentence into an equation. Then solve the equation.

36. A number d divided by 4 equals 3.

37. The sum of 7 and a number n is 15.

38. The product of a number b and 5 is 250.

39. Twelve is the difference of a number q and 8.

40. **Consumer Math** Nine weeks from now Susan hopes to buy a bicycle that costs \$180. How much money must she save per week?

41. School A school club is collecting toys for a children's charity. There are 18 students in the club. The goal is to collect 216 toys. Each member will collect the same number of toys. How many toys should each member collect?

42. Travel Lissa drove from Los Angeles to New York City and averaged 45 miles per hour. Her driving time totaled 62 hours. Write and solve an equation to find the distance Lissa traveled.

43. Business A store rents space in a building at a cost of $19 per square foot. If the store is 700 square feet, how much is the rent?

44. What's the Error? For the equation $7x = 56$, a student found the value of x to be 392. What was the student's error?

45. Write About It How do you know whether to use multiplication or division to solve an equation?

46. Challenge The graph shows the results of a survey about electronic equipment used by 8,690,000 college students. If you multiply the number of students who use portable CD players by 5 and then divide by 3, you get the total number of students represented by the survey. Write and solve an equation to find the number of students who use portable CD players.

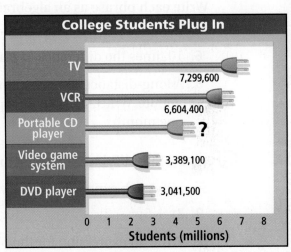

College Students Plug In

TV — 7,299,600
VCR — 6,604,400
Portable CD player — **?**
Video game system — 3,389,100
DVD player — 3,041,500

0 1 2 3 4 5 6 7 8
Students (millions)

CRCT PREP • GPS SUPPORT • SPIRAL REVIEW

47. Multiple Choice Mr. Tomkins borrowed $1,200 to buy a computer. He wants to repay the loan in 8 equal payments. How much will each payment be?

   (A) $80   (B) $100   (C) $150   (D) $200

48. Multiple Choice Solve the equation $16x = 208$.

   (F) $x = 11$ (G) $x = 12$ (H) $x = 13$ (J) $x = 14$

49. Extended Response It costs $18 per ticket for groups of 20 or more people to enter an amusement park. If Celia's group paid a total of $414 to enter, how many people were in her group?

Determine whether the given value of the variable is a solution. (Lesson 1-10)

50. $x + 34 = 48; x = 14$ **51.** $d - 87 = 77; d = 10$

Solve each equation. (Lesson 1-11)

52. $76 + n = 115$ **53.** $j - 97 = 145$ **54.** $t - 123 = 455$ **55.** $a + 39 = 86$

READY TO GO ON?

Quiz for Lessons 1-7 Through 1-12

✓ 1-7 Variables and Algebraic Expressions

Evaluate each expression for the given values of the variable.

1. $7(x + 4)$ for $x = 5$ **2.** $11 - n \div 3$ for $n = 6$ **3.** $p + 6t^2$ for $p = 11$ and $t = 3$

✓ 1-8 Translate Words into Math

Write each phrase as an algebraic expression.

4. the quotient of a number and 15 **5.** a number decreased by 13

6. 10 times the difference of p and 2 **7.** 3 plus the product of a number and 8

8. A long-distance phone company charges a $2.95 monthly fee plus $0.14 for each minute. Write an algebraic expression to show the cost of calling for t minutes in one month.

✓ 1-9 Simplifying Algebraic Expressions

Simplify each expression. Justify your steps.

9. $2y + 5y^2 - 2y^2$ **10.** $x + 4 + 7x + 9$ **11.** $10 + 9b - 6a - b$

12. Write an expression for the perimeter of the given figure. Then simplify the expression.

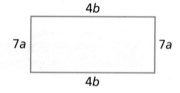

✓ 1-10 Equations and Their Solutions

Determine whether the given value of the variable is a solution.

13. $22 - x = 7$; $x = 15$ **14.** $\frac{56}{r} = 8$; $r = 9$ **15.** $m + 19 = 47$; $m = 28$

16. Last month Sue spent $147 on groceries. This month she spent $29 more on groceries than last month. Did Sue spend $118 or $176 on groceries this month?

✓ 1-11 Addition and Subtraction Equations

Solve each equation.

17. $g - 4 = 13$ **18.** $20 = 7 + p$ **19.** $t - 18 = 6$ **20.** $m + 34 = 53$

✓ 1-12 Multiplication and Division Equations

Solve each equation.

21. $\frac{k}{8} = 7$ **22.** $3b = 39$ **23.** $n \div 16 = 7$ **24.** $330 = 22x$

25. A water jug holds 128 fluid ounces. How many 8-ounce servings of water does the jug hold?

Ready to Go On?

MULTI-STEP TEST PREP

Have a Heart Chuck's family decides to begin a fitness program. Their doctor encourages each family member to determine his or her maximum heart rate and then exercise at a lower rate.

1. The table shows the recommended maximum heart rate for people of various ages. Describe the pattern in the table. Then find the maximum heart rate for Chuck's father, who is 45 years old.

2. There is another way to find a person's maximum heart rate. The sum of the maximum heart rate, h, and the person's age, a, should be 220. Write an equation that relates h and a.

3. Chuck's mother used the equation from problem 2 to determine that her maximum heart rate is 174 beats per minute. How old is Chuck's mother?

Maximum Heart Rate	
Age	Rate (beats per minute)
10	210
15	205
20	200
25	195
30	190
35	185

4. Chuck's mother counts the number of heartbeats in 10 seconds and multiplies by 6 to find her heart rate. Write and solve an equation to find the number of times her heart beats in 10 seconds when she is at her maximum heart rate.

5. The family doctor recommends warming up before exercise. The expression $110 - a \div 2$ gives a warm-up heart rate based on a person's age, a. Find the warm-up heart rate for Chuck's mother.

Multi-Step Test Prep

Game Time

Jumping Beans

You will need a grid that is 4 squares by 6 squares. Each square must be large enough to contain a bean. Mark off a 3-square by 3-square section of the grid. Place nine beans in the nine spaces, as shown below.

You must move all nine beans to the nine marked-off squares in the fewest number of moves.

Follow the rules below to move the beans.

❶ You may move to any empty square in any direction.

❷ You may jump over another bean in any direction to an empty square.

❸ You may jump over other beans as many times as you like.

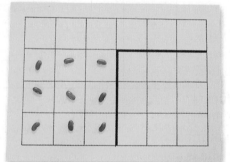 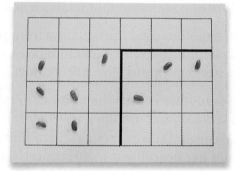

Moving all the beans in ten moves is not too difficult, but can you do it in nine moves?

Trading Spaces

The purpose of the game is to replace the red counters with the yellow counters, and the yellow counters with the red counters, in the fewest moves possible. The counters must be moved one at a time in an L-shape. No two counters may occupy the same square.

A complete copy of the rules and a game board are available online.

go.hrw.com
Game Time Extra
KEYWORD: MS7 Games

Materials
- 1 full sheet of decorative paper
- 3 smaller pieces of decorative paper
- stapler
- scissors
- markers
- pencil

It's in the Bag!

PROJECT **Step-by-Step Algebra**

This "step book" is a great place to record sample algebra problems.

Directions

1. Lay the $11\frac{1}{2}$-by-$7\frac{3}{4}$-inch sheet of paper in front of you. Fold it down $2\frac{1}{2}$ inches from the top and make a crease. **Figure A**

2. Slide the $7\frac{1}{4}$-by-$7\frac{3}{4}$-inch sheet of paper under the flap of the first piece. Do the same with the $5\frac{1}{2}$-by-$7\frac{3}{4}$-inch and $3\frac{3}{4}$-by-$7\frac{3}{4}$-inch sheets of paper to make a step book. Staple all of the sheets together at the top. **Figure B**

3. Use a pencil to divide the three middle sheets into thirds. Then cut up from the bottom along the lines you drew to make slits in these three sheets. **Figure C**

4. On the top step of your booklet, write the number and title of the chapter.

Taking Note of the Math

Label each of the steps in your booklet with important concepts from the chapter: "Using Exponents," "Expressing Numbers in Scientific Notation," and so on. On the bottom sheet, write "Solving Equations." Write sample problems from the chapter on the appropriate steps.

A

B

C

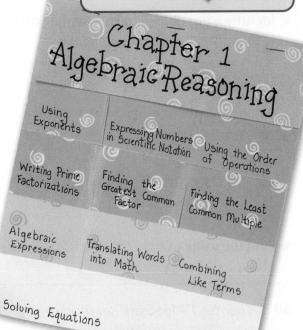

Chapter 1
Algebraic Reasoning

Using Exponents

Expressing Numbers in Scientific Notation

Using the Order of Operations

Writing Prime Factorizations

Finding the Greatest Common Factor

Finding the Least Common Multiple

Algebraic Expressions

Translating Words into Math

Combining Like Terms

Solving Equations

Study Guide: Review

Vocabulary

Complete the sentences below with vocabulary words from the list above.

1. The ___?___ tells how many times to use the ___?___ as a factor.

2. A(n) ___?___ is a mathematical phrase made up of numbers and operations.

3. A(n) ___?___ is a mathematical statement that two expressions are equal in value.

4. A(n) ___?___ consists of constants, variables, and operations.

1-1 Numbers and Patterns (pp. 6–9)

GPS M7P5.a

EXAMPLE

■ Identify a possible pattern. Use the pattern to write the next three numbers.

2, 8, 14, 20, . . .

$2 + 6 = 8$ $8 + 6 = 14$ $14 + 6 = 20$

A possible pattern is to add 6 each time.

$20 + 6 = 26$ $26 + 6 = 32$ $32 + 6 = 38$

EXERCISES

Identify a possible pattern. Use the pattern to write the next three numbers.

5. 6, 10, 14, 18, . . .   **6.** 15, 35, 55, 75, . . .

7. 7, 14, 21, 28, . . .   **8.** 8, 40, 200, 1,000, . . .

9. 41, 37, 33, 29, . . . **10.** 68, 61, 54, 47, . . .

1-2 Exponents (pp. 10–13)

GPS M7P1.b

EXAMPLE

■ Find the value of 4^3.

$4^3 = 4 \cdot 4 \cdot 4 = 64$

EXERCISES

Find each value.

11. 9^2 **12.** 10^1 **13.** 2^7 **14.** 1^7 **15.** 11^2

1-3 Metric Measurements (pp. 14–17)

 GPS M7P4.c

EXAMPLE

- Convert 63 m to centimeters.

  $63\text{ m} = (63 \times 100)\text{ cm}$ *100 cm = 1 m*

        $= 6,300\text{ cm}$

EXERCISES

Convert each measure.

16. 18 L to mL   **17.** 720 mg to g

18. 5.3 km to m   **19.** 0.6 cm to mm

1-4 Applying Exponents (pp. 18–21)

 GPS M7P4.a

EXAMPLE

- Multiply $157 \cdot 10^4$.

  $157 \cdot 10^4 = 1570000$

        $= 1,570,000$

EXERCISES

Multiply.

20. $144 \cdot 10^2$ **21.** $1.32 \cdot 10^3$ **22.** $22 \cdot 10^7$

Write each number in scientific notation.

23. 48,000   **24.** 7,020,000   **25.** 149,000

1-5 Order of Operations (pp. 23–26)

 GPS M7P1.b

EXAMPLE

- Simplify $(18 + 6) \cdot 5$.

  $(18 + 6) \cdot 5 = 24 \cdot 5 = 120$

EXERCISES

Simplify each expression.

26. $2 + (9 - 6) \div 3$ **27.** $12 \cdot 3^2 - 5$

28. $11 + 2 \cdot 5 - (9 + 7)$ **29.** $75 \div 5^2 + 8^2$

1-6 Properties (pp. 28–31)

 GPS M7P1.c

EXAMPLE

- Tell which property is represented.

  $(10 \cdot 13) \cdot 28 = 10 \cdot (13 \cdot 28)$

  Associative Property

EXERCISES

Tell which property is represented.

30. $42 + 17 = 17 + 42$

31. $m + 0 = m$

32. $6 \cdot (x - 5) = 6 \cdot x - 6 \cdot 5$

1-7 Variables and Algebraic Expressions (pp. 34–37)

GPS M7A1.b

EXAMPLE

- Evaluate $5a - 6b + 7$ for $a = 4$ and $b = 3$.

  $5a - 6b + 7$

  $5(4) - 6(3) + 7$

  $20 - 18 + 7$

  9

EXERCISES

Evaluate each expression for the given values of the variables.

33. $4x - 5$ for $x = 6$

34. $8y^3 + 3y$ for $y = 4$

35. $\dfrac{n}{5} + 6m - 3$ for $n = 5$ and $m = 2$

1-8 Translate Words into Math (pp. 38–41)

 GPS M7A1.a

EXAMPLE

■ Write as an algebraic expression.

5 times the sum of a number and 6
$5(n + 6)$

EXERCISES

Write as an algebraic expression.

36. 4 divided by the sum of a number and 12

37. 2 times the difference of t and 11

1-9 Simplifying Algebraic Expressions (pp. 42–45)

 GPS M7A1.a, M7A1.b, M7A1.c

EXAMPLE

■ Simplify the expression.

$4x^3 + 5y + 8x^3 - 4y - 5x^2$
$4x^3 + 5y + 8x^3 - 4y - 5x^2$
$12x^3 + y - 5x^2$

EXERCISES

Simplify each expression.

38. $7b^2 + 8 + 3b^2$

39. $12a^2 + 4 + 3a^2 - 2$

40. $x^2 + x^3 + x^4 + 5x^2$

1-10 Equations and Their Solutions (pp. 46–49)

 GPS M7A1.a, M7A1.b

EXAMPLE

■ Determine whether 22 is a solution.

$24 \stackrel{?}{=} s - 13$
$24 \stackrel{?}{=} 22 - 13$
$24 \stackrel{?}{=} 9$ ✗   *22 is not a solution.*

EXERCISES

Determine whether the given value of the variable is a solution.

41. $36 = n - 12$; $n = 48$

42. $9x = 117$; $x = 12$

1-11 Addition and Subtraction Equations (pp. 52–55)

 GPS M7A2.a, M7A2.b

EXAMPLE

■ Solve the equation. Then check.

$$b + 12 = 16$$
$$\underline{-12 \quad -12}$$
$$b = 4$$

$b + 12 \stackrel{?}{=} 16$
$4 + 12 \stackrel{?}{=} 16$
$16 \stackrel{?}{=} 16$ ✔

EXERCISES

Solve each equation. Then check.

43. $8 + b = 16$

44. $20 = n - 12$

45. $27 + c = 45$

46. $t - 68 = 44$

1-12 Multiplication and Division Equations (pp. 56–59)

GPS M7A2.a, M7A2.b

EXAMPLE

■ Solve the equation. Then check.

$$2r = 12$$
$$\frac{2r}{2} = \frac{12}{2}$$
$$r = 6$$

$2r = 12$
$2(6) \stackrel{?}{=} 12$
$12 \stackrel{?}{=} 12$ ✔

EXERCISES

Solve each equation. Then check.

47. $n \div 12 = 6$

48. $3p = 27$

49. $\frac{d}{14} = 7$

50. $6x = 78$

51. Lee charges $8 per hour to baby-sit. Last month she earned $136. How many hours did Lee baby-sit last month?

Identify a possible pattern. Use the pattern to write the next three numbers.

1. 24, 32, 40, 48, . . . **2.** 6, 18, 54, 162, . . . **3.** 64, 58, 52, 46, . . . **4.** 13, 30, 47, 64, . . .

Find each value.

5. 6^2 **6.** 7^5 **7.** 8^6 **8.** 3^5

Convert each measure.

9. 180 mL to liters **10.** 7.8 m to centimeters **11.** 23.4 kg to grams

12. Jesse is 1,460 millimeters tall. Her sister is 168 centimeters tall, and her brother is 1.56 meters tall. Who is the tallest?

Multiply.

13. $148 \cdot 10^2$ **14.** $56.3 \cdot 10^3$ **15.** $6.89 \cdot 10^4$ **16.** $7.5 \cdot 10^4$

Write each number in scientific notation.

17. 406,000,000 **18.** 1,905,000 **19.** 22,400 **20.** 500,000

Simplify each expression.

21. $18 \cdot 3 \div 3^3$ **22.** $36 + 16 - 50$ **23.** $149 - (2^8 - 200)$ **24.** $(4 \div 2) \cdot 9 + 11$

Tell which property is represented.

25. $0 + 45 = 45$ **26.** $(r + s) + t = r + (s + t)$ **27.** $84 \cdot 3 = 3 \cdot 84$

Evaluate each expression for the given values of the variables.

28. $4a + 6b + 7$ for $a = 2$ and $b = 3$ **29.** $7y^2 + 7y$ for $y = 3$

Write each phrase as an algebraic expression.

30. a number increased by 12 **31.** the quotient of a number and 7

32. 5 less than the product of 7 and s **33.** the difference between 3 times x and 4

Simplify each expression. Justify your steps.

34. $b + 2 + 5b$ **35.** $16 + 5b + 3b + 9$ **36.** $5a + 6t + 9 + 2a$

Solve each equation.

37. $x + 9 = 19$ **38.** $21 = y - 20$ **39.** $m - 54 = 72$ **40.** $136 = y + 114$

41. $16 = \dfrac{y}{3}$ **42.** $102 = 17y$ **43.** $\dfrac{r}{7} = 1,400$ **44.** $6x = 42$

45. A caterer charged $15 per person to prepare a meal for a banquet. If the total catering charge for the banquet was $1,530, how many people attended?

TEST TACKLER

Standardized Test Strategies

Multiple Choice: Eliminate Answer Choices

With some multiple-choice test items, you can use mental math or number sense to quickly eliminate some of the answer choices before you begin solving the problem.

EXAMPLE **1**

Which is the solution to the equation $x + 7 = 15$?

A $x = 22$ **B** $x = 15$ **C** $x = 8$ **D** $x = 7$

READ the question.
Then try to **eliminate** some of the answer choices.

Use number sense:

When you add, you get a greater number than what you started with. Since $x + 7 = 15$, 15 must be greater than x, or x must be less than 15. Since 22 and 15 are not less than 15, you can eliminate answer choices A and B.

The correct answer choice is C.

EXAMPLE **2**

Arnold measured 0.15 L of water and then poured the water into a beaker labeled only in milliliters. What did the measurement read on the beaker?

F 0.015 mL **G** 0.15 mL **H** 15 mL **J** 150 mL

LOOK at the choices.
Then try to **eliminate** some of the answer choices.

Use mental math:

A milliliter is smaller than a liter, so the answer is greater than 0.15. You can eliminate answer choices F and G.

The prefix *milli-* means "thousandth," so multiply 0.15 by 1,000 to get 150 mL, which is answer choice J.

Test Tackler

Before you work a test question, use mental math to help you decide if there are answer choices that you can eliminate right away.

Read each test item and answer the questions that follow.

Item A
During the August back-to-school sale, 2 pairs of shoes cost $34, a shirt costs $15, and a pair of pants costs $27. Janet bought 2 pairs of shoes, 4 shirts, and 4 pairs of pants and then paid an additional $7 for tax. Which expression shows the total that Janet spent?

(A) $34 + 4(15 + 27)$

(B) $34 + 4(15 + 27) + 7$

(C) $4(34 + 15 + 27) + 7$

(D) $34 + 15 + 4 \cdot 27$

1. Can any of the answer choices be eliminated immediately? If so, which choices and why?

2. Describe how you can determine the correct answer from the remaining choices.

Item B
Anthony saved $1 from his first paycheck, $2 from his second paycheck, then $4, $8, and so on. How much money did Anthony save from his tenth paycheck?

(F) $10   (H) $512

(G) $16   (J) $1,023

3. Are there any answer choices you can eliminate immediately? If so, which choices and why?

4. What common error was made in finding answer choice F?

Item C
Craig has three weeks to read an 850-page book. Which equation can be used to find the number of pages Craig has to read each day?

(A) $\frac{x}{3} = 850$ (C) $3x = 850$

(B) $21x = 850$ (D) $\frac{x}{21} = 850$

5. Describe how to use number sense to eliminate at least one answer choice.

6. What common error was made in finding answer choice D?

Item D
A window in a treehouse measures 56 centimeters wide. Samantha wants to build a seat along the window that is 35 centimeters wider than the window is. How wide, in meters, would the window seat need to be?

(F) 91 m   (H) 0.21 m

(G) 21 m   (J) 0.91 m

7. Which two choices can be eliminated by using mental math?

8. Explain how to convert from centimeters to meters.

Item E
What is the value of the expression $(1 + 2)^2 + 14 \div 2 + 5$?

(A) 0   (C) 17

(B) 11   (D) 21

9. Use mental math to quickly eliminate one answer choice. Explain your choice.

10. What common error was made in finding answer choice B?

11. What common error was made in finding answer choice C?

Cumulative Assessment, Chapter 1

Multiple Choice

1. Which expression has a value of 74 when $x = 10$, $y = 8$, and $z = 12$?

   Ⓐ $4xyz$ Ⓒ $2xz - 3y$

   Ⓑ $x + 5y + 2z$ Ⓓ $6xyz + 8$

2. What is the next number in the pattern?

   $3, 3^2, 27, 3^4, 3^5, \ldots$

   Ⓕ 729   Ⓗ 243

   Ⓖ 3^7 Ⓙ 3^8

3. A contractor charges $22 to install one miniblind. How much does the contractor charge to install m miniblinds?

   Ⓐ $22m$ Ⓒ $22 + m$

   Ⓑ $\frac{m}{22}$ Ⓓ $\frac{22}{m}$

4. Which of the following is an example of the Commutative Property?

   Ⓕ $20 + 10 = 2(10 + 5)$

   Ⓖ $20 + 10 = 10 + 20$

   Ⓗ $5 + (20 + 10) = (5 + 20) + 10$

   Ⓙ $20 + 0 = 20$

5. Which expression simplifies to $9x + 3$ when you combine like terms?

   Ⓐ $10x^2 - x^2 - 3$

   Ⓑ $3x + 7 - 4 + 3x$

   Ⓒ $18 + 4x - 15 + 5x$

   Ⓓ $7x^2 + 2x + 6 - 3$

6. What is the solution to the equation $810 = x - 625$?

   Ⓕ $x = 185$ Ⓗ $x = 845$

   Ⓖ $x = 215$ Ⓙ $x = 1,435$

7. Tia maps out her jogging route as shown in the table. How many kilometers does Tia plan to jog?

Tia's Jogging Route	
Street	**Meters**
1st to Park	428
Park to Windsor	112
Windsor to East	506
East to Manor	814
Manor to Vane	660
Vane to 1st	480

   Ⓐ 3,000 km   Ⓒ 30 km

   Ⓑ 300 km   Ⓓ 3 km

8. To make a beaded necklace, Kris needs 88 beads. If Kris has 1,056 beads, how many necklaces can she make?

   Ⓕ 968   Ⓗ 264

   Ⓖ 12   Ⓙ 8

9. What are the next two numbers in the pattern?

   $75, 70, 60, 55, 45, 40, \ldots$

   Ⓐ 35, 30

   Ⓑ 30, 20

   Ⓒ 30, 25

   Ⓓ 35, 25

10. Marc spends $78 for n shirts. Which expression can be used to represent the cost of one shirt?

   Ⓕ $\frac{n}{78}$ Ⓗ $\frac{78}{n}$

   Ⓖ $78n$ Ⓙ $78 + n$

CRCT Prep

70   *Chapter 1 Algebraic Reasoning*

11. Which situation best matches the expression $0.29x + 2$?

  Ⓐ A taxi company charges a $2.00 flat fee plus $0.29 for every mile.

  Ⓑ Jimmy ran 0.29 miles, stopped to rest, and then ran 2 more miles.

  Ⓒ There are 0.29 grams of calcium in 2 servings of Hearty Health Cereal.

  Ⓓ Amy bought 2 pieces of gum for $0.29 each.

12. Which of the following should be performed first to simplify this expression?

   $$16 \cdot 2 + (20 \div 5) - 3^2 \div 3 + 1$$

  Ⓕ $3^2 \div 3$

  Ⓖ $20 \div 5$

  Ⓗ $16 \cdot 2$

  Ⓙ $3 + 1$

 When you read a word problem, cross out any information that is not needed to solve the problem.

13. If $x = 15$ and $y = 5$, what is the value of $\frac{2x}{y} + 3y$?

  Ⓐ 17   Ⓒ 21

  Ⓑ 18   Ⓓ 51

14. An airplane has seats for 198 passengers. If each row seats 6 people, how many rows are on the plane?

  Ⓕ 32   Ⓗ 38

  Ⓖ 33   Ⓙ 40

15. What is the value of the expression $3^2 \times (2 + 3 \times 4) - 5$?

  Ⓐ −5   Ⓒ 15

  Ⓑ 121   Ⓓ 224

16. What is the solution to the equation $10 + s = 42$?

  Ⓕ 32   Ⓗ 40

  Ⓖ 38   Ⓙ 52

Short Response

17. Luke can swim 25 laps in one hour. Write an algebraic expression to show how many laps Luke can swim in h hours. How many hours will it take Luke to swim 100 laps?

18. An aerobics instructor teaches a 45-minute class at 9:30 A.M., three times a week. She dedicates 12 minutes during each class to stretching. The rest of the class consists of aerobic dance. How many minutes of each class does the instructor spend teaching aerobic dance? Write and solve an equation to explain how you found your answer.

19. Ike and Joe ran the same distance but took different routes. Ike ran 3 blocks east and 7 blocks south. Joe ran 4 blocks west and then turned north. How far north did Joe run? Show your work.

Extended Response

20. The Raiders and the Hornets are buying new uniforms for their baseball teams. Each team member will receive a new cap, a jersey, and a pair of pants.

Uniform Costs		
	Raiders	Hornets
Cap	$15	$15
Jersey	$75	$70
Pants	$60	$70

  a. Let r represent the number of Raiders team members, and let h represent the number of Hornets team members. For each team, write an expression that gives the total cost of the team's uniforms.

  b. If the Raiders and the Hornets both have 12 team members, how much will each team spend on uniforms? Which team will spend the most, and by how much? Show your work.

CRCT Prep

Integers and Rational Numbers

CRCT PREP

go.hrw.com
Chapter Project Online
KEYWORD: MS7 Ch2

Speed of Sound Through Different Materials	
Material	**Speed (m/s)**
Air at 20°C	344
Water at 20°C	1,500
Wood (oak) at 20°C	3,850
Glass at 20°C	4,540
Steel at 20°C	5,200

Career *Oceanographer*

Is Earth warming? Or is it cooling? The temperature of the oceans is a very important factor in answering these questions. Oceanographers have been studying the temperature of the Pacific Ocean by measuring the speed of sound waves in the water.

How does this work? The speed of sound is affected by the temperature of the material through which the sound travels. In air, for example, the speed of sound increases about 0.6 meter per second for every degree Celsius that the temperature rises. By measuring the speed of sound in water, scientists can tell the water's temperature.

ARE YOU READY?

✓ Vocabulary

Choose the best term from the list to complete each sentence.

1. To __?__ a number on a number line, mark and label the point that corresponds to that number.

2. The expression $1 < 3 < 5$ tells the __?__ of these three numbers on a number line.

3. A(n) __?__ is a mathematical statement showing two things are equal.

4. Each number in the set 0, 1, 2, 3, 4, 5, 6, 7, ... is a(n) __?__.

5. To __?__ an equation, find a value that makes it true.

whole number

expression

graph

solve

equation

order

Complete these exercises to review skills you will need for this chapter.

✓ Order of Operations

Simplify.

6. $7 + 9 - 5 \cdot 2$

7. $12 \cdot 3 - 4 \cdot 5$

8. $115 - 15 \cdot 3 + 9(8 - 2)$

9. $20 \cdot 5 \cdot 2(7 + 1) \div 4$

10. $300 + 6(5 - 3) - 11$

11. $14 - 13 + 9 \cdot 2$

✓ Find Multiples

Find the first five multiples of each number.

12. 2

13. 9

14. 15

15. 1

16. 101

17. 54

18. 326

19. 1,024

✓ Find Factors

List all the factors of each number.

20. 8

21. 22

22. 36

23. 50

24. 108

25. 84

26. 256

27. 630

✓ Use Inverse Operations to Solve Equations

Solve.

28. $n + 3 = 10$

29. $x - 4 = 16$

30. $9p = 63$

31. $\frac{t}{5} = 80$

32. $x - 3 = 14$

33. $\frac{q}{3} = 21$

34. $9 + r = 91$

35. $15p = 45$

Study Guide: Preview

Where You've Been

Previously, you

- used order of operations to simplify whole number expressions without exponents.
- used multiplication and division to solve problems involving whole numbers.
- converted measures within the same measurement system.
- wrote large numbers in standard form.

In This Chapter

You will study

- simplifying numerical expressions involving order of operations and exponents.
- using concrete models to solve equations.
- finding solutions to application problems involving related measurement units.
- writing large numbers in scientific notation.

Where You're Going

You can use the skills learned in this chapter

- to express negative numbers related to scientific fields such as marine biology or meteorology.
- to find equivalent measures.

Key Vocabulary/Vocabulario

equivalent fraction	fracción equivalente
greatest common factor (GCF)	máximo común divisor (MCD)
improper fraction	fracción impropia
integer	entero
least common multiple (LCM)	mínimo común múltiplo (mcm)
mixed number	número mixto
prime factorization	factorización prima
rational number	número racional
repeating decimal	decimal periódico
terminating decimal	decimal cerrado

Vocabulary Connections

To become familiar with some of the vocabulary terms in the chapter, consider the following. You may refer to the chapter, the glossary, or a dictionary if you like.

1. The word *common* means "belonging to or shared by two things." How can you use this definition to explain what the **least common multiple** of two numbers is?

2. Rational numbers come in many forms, including whole numbers and fractions. *Mixed* means "made up of more than one kind." What do you think a **mixed number** might be?

3. A decimal is a number that has digits to the right of the decimal point. What might you predict about those digits in a **repeating decimal**?

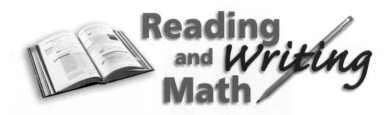

Reading and Writing Math

Writing Strategy: Translate Between Words and Math

As you read a real-world math problem, look for key words to help you translate between the words and the math.

Example

At FunZone the cost to play laser tag is $8 per game. The cost to play miniature golf is $5 per game. The one-time admission fee to the park is $3. Jonna wants to play both laser tag and miniature golf. Write an algebraic expression to find the total amount Jonna would pay to play ℓ laser tag games and m golf games at FunZone.

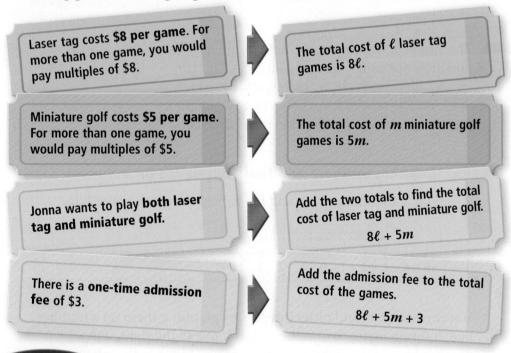

Laser tag costs **$8 per game**. For more than one game, you would pay multiples of $8.

The total cost of ℓ laser tag games is 8ℓ.

Miniature golf costs **$5 per game**. For more than one game, you would pay multiples of $5.

The total cost of m miniature golf games is $5m$.

Jonna wants to play **both laser tag and miniature golf.**

Add the two totals to find the total cost of laser tag and miniature golf.
$8\ell + 5m$

There is a **one-time admission fee of $3.**

Add the admission fee to the total cost of the games.
$8\ell + 5m + 3$

Try This

Write an algebraic expression that describes the situation. Explain why you chose each operation in the expression.

1. School supplies are half-price at Bargain Mart this week. The original prices were $2 per package of pens and $4 per notebook. Cally buys 1 package of pens and n notebooks. How much does Cally spend?

2. Fred has f cookies, and Gary has g cookies. Fred and Gary each eat 3 cookies. How many total cookies are left?

Reading and Writing Math

2-1 Integers

Learn to compare and order integers and to determine absolute value.

Vocabulary
opposite
integer
absolute value

The **opposite** of a number is the same distance from 0 on a number line as the original number, but on the other side of 0. Zero is its own opposite.

Dr. Sylvia Earle holds the world record for the deepest solo dive.

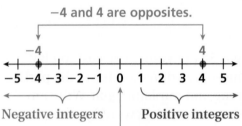
−4 and 4 are opposites.

−4   4

Negative integers   Positive integers

0 is neither positive nor negative.

> **Remember!**
> The whole numbers are the counting numbers and zero: 0, 1, 2, 3, ...

The **integers** are the set of whole numbers and their opposites. By using integers, you can express elevations above, below, and at sea level. Sea level has an elevation of 0 feet. Sylvia Earle's record dive was to an elevation of −1,250 feet.

EXAMPLE 1 Graphing Integers and Their Opposites on a Number Line

Graph the integer −3 and its opposite on a number line.

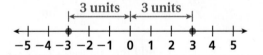
3 units   3 units
−5 −4 −3 −2 −1 0 1 2 3 4 5

The opposite of −3 is 3.

Georgia Performance Standards

M7N1.a Find the absolute value of a number and understand it as the distance from zero on a number line. Also, M7P5.a, M7P5.b, M7P5.c.

You can compare and order integers by graphing them on a number line. Integers increase in value as you move to the right along a number line. They decrease in value as you move to the left.

EXAMPLE 2 Comparing Integers Using a Number Line

Compare the integers. Use < or >.

> **Remember!**
> The symbol < means "is less than," and the symbol > means "is greater than."

Ⓐ 2 ☐ −2

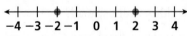
−4 −3 −2 −1 0 1 2 3 4

2 is farther to the right than −2, so 2 > −2.

Compare the integers. Use < or >.

B −10 [ ] −7

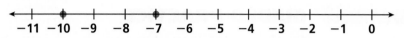

−10 is farther to the left than −7, so −10 < −7.

EXAMPLE 3 **Ordering Integers Using a Number Line**

Use a number line to order the integers −2, 5, −4, 1, −1, and 0 from least to greatest.

Graph the integers on a number line. Then read them from left to right.

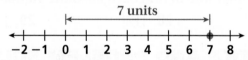

The numbers in order from least to greatest are −4, −2, −1, 0, 1, and 5.

A number's **absolute value** is its distance from 0 on a number line. Since distance can never be negative, absolute values are never negative. They are always positive or zero.

EXAMPLE 4 **Finding Absolute Value**

Use a number line to find each absolute value.

Reading Math

The symbol | | is read as "the absolute value of." For example, |−3| means "the absolute value of −3."

A |7|

7 units

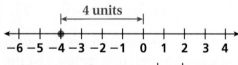

7 is 7 units from 0, so |7| = 7.

B |−4|

4 units

−4 is 4 units from 0, so |−4| = 4.

Think and Discuss   GPS M7P3.b, M7P3.d

1. Tell which number is greater: −4,500 or −10,000.

2. Name the greatest negative integer and the least nonnegative integer. Then compare the absolute values of these integers.

2-1 **Exercises**

Georgia Performance Standards
M7P3.c, M7P4.c, M7P5.b

go.hrw.com
Homework Help Online
KEYWORD: MS7 2-1
Parent Resources Online
KEYWORD: MS7 Parent

GUIDED PRACTICE

See Example ① Graph each integer and its opposite on a number line.

1. 2   **2.** −9   **3.** −1   **4.** 6

See Example ② Compare the integers. Use < or >.

5. 5 ▉ −5   **6.** −9 ▉ −18   **7.** −21 ▉ −17   **8.** −12 ▉ 12

See Example ③ Use a number line to order the integers from least to greatest.

9. 6, −3, −1, −5, 4   **10.** 8, −2, 7, 1, −8   **11.** −6, −4, 3, 0, 1

See Example ④ Use a number line to find each absolute value.

12. |−2| **13.** |8| **14.** |−7| **15.** |−10|

INDEPENDENT PRACTICE

See Example ① Graph each integer and its opposite on a number line.

16. −4   **17.** 10   **18.** −12   **19.** 7

See Example ② Compare the integers. Use < or >.

20. −14 ▉ −7   **21.** 9 ▉ −9   **22.** −12 ▉ 12   **23.** −31 ▉ −27

See Example ③ Use a number line to order the integers from least to greatest.

24. −3, 2, −5, −6, 5   **25.** −7, −9, −2, 0, −5   **26.** 3, −6, 9, −1, −2

See Example ④ Use a number line to find each absolute value.

27. |−16| **28.** |12| **29.** |−20| **30.** |15|

PRACTICE AND PROBLEM SOLVING

Extra Practice p. 727

Compare. Write <, >, or =.

31. −25 ▉ 25   **32.** 18 ▉ −55   **33.** |−21| ▉ 21   **34.** −9 ▉ −27

35. 34 ▉ |34| **36.** 64 ▉ |−75| **37.** |−3| ▉ |3| **38.** −100 ▉ −82

39. Earth Science The table shows the average temperatures in Vostok, Antarctica from March to October. List the months in order from coldest to warmest.

Month	Mar	Apr	May	Jun	Jul	Aug	Sep	Oct
Temperature (°F)	−72	−84	−86	−85	−88	−90	−87	−71

40. What is the opposite of |32|?   **41.** What is the opposite of |−29|?

42. Business A company reported a net loss of $2,000,000 during its first year. In its second year it reported a profit of $5,000,000. Write each amount as an integer.

43. Critical Thinking Give an example in which a negative number has a greater absolute value than a positive number.

44. Social Studies Lines of latitude are imaginary lines that circle the globe in an east-west direction. They measure distances north and south of the equator. The equator represents 0° latitude.

  a. What latitude is opposite of 30° north latitude?

  b. How do these latitudes' distances from the equator compare?

Sports The graph shows how participation in several sports changed between 1999 and 2000 in the United States.

45. By about what percent did participation in racquetball increase or decrease?

46. By about what percent did participation in wall climbing increase or decrease?

 47. What's the Error? At 9 A.M. the outside temperature was −3°F. By noon, the temperature was −12°F. A newscaster said that it was getting warmer outside. Why is this incorrect?

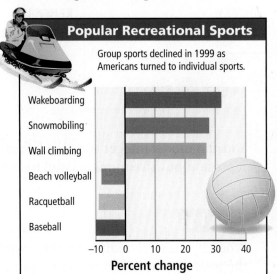

Source: *USA Today*, July 6, 2001

 48. Write About It Explain how to compare two integers.

49. Challenge What values can x have if $|x| = 11$?

CRCT PREP • GPS SUPPORT • SPIRAL REVIEW

50. Multiple Choice Which list shows the integers in order from least to greatest?

  (A) −5, −6, −7, 2, 3   (B) 2, 3, −5, −6, −7   (C) −7, −6, −5, 2, 3   (D) 3, 2, −7, −6, −5

51. Multiple Choice The table shows the average temperatures in Barrow, Alaska, for several months. In which month is the average temperature lowest?

  (F) January   (H) May

  (G) March   (J) July

Monthly Temperatures	
January	−12°F
March	−13°F
May	20°F
July	40°F

Convert each measure. (Lesson 1-3)

52. 3.2 kg to g   **53.** 167 cm to m   **54.** 18 cm to mm   **55.** 10.3 L to mL

Use the Distributive Property to find each product. (Lesson 1-6)

56. 3(12)   **57.** 2(56)   **58.** (27)6   **59.** (34)5

Model Integer Addition

Use with Lesson 2-2

go.hrw.com
Lab Resources Online
KEYWORD: MS7 Lab2

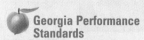
Georgia Performance Standards

M7P2.c, M7P5.a, M7P5.b, M7P5.c

KEY	REMEMBER
= 1	• Adding or subtracting zero does not change the value of an expression.

You can model integer addition by using integer chips. Yellow chips represent positive numbers and red chips represent negative numbers.

Activity

When you model adding numbers with the same sign, you can count the total number of chips to find the sum.

   *The total number of positive chips is 7.*

$3 + 4 = 7$

   *The total number of negative chips is 7.*

$-3 + (-4) = -7$

1 Use integer chips to find each sum.

a. $2 + 4$ **b.** $-2 + (-4)$ **c.** $6 + 3$ **d.** $-5 + (-4)$

When you model adding numbers with different signs, you cannot count the chips to find their sum.

⬤ + ⬤ = 2 and ⬤ + ⬤ = −2

but ⬤ + ⬤ = 0   *A red chip and a yellow chip make a neutral pair.*

When you model adding a positive and a negative number, you need to remove all of the neutral pairs that you can find—that is, all pairs of 1 red chip and 1 yellow chip. These pairs have a value of zero, so they do not affect the sum.

You cannot just count the colored chips to find their sum.

$3 + (-4) = \blacksquare$

Before you count the chips, you need to remove all of the zero pairs.

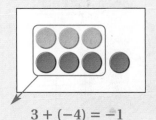

When you remove the zero pairs, there is one red chip left. So the sum of the chips is -1.

$3 + (-4) = -1$

2 Use integer chips to find each sum.

a. $4 + (-6)$ **b.** $-5 + 2$ **c.** $7 + (-3)$ **d.** $-6 + 3$

Think and Discuss

1. Will $8 + (-3)$ and $-3 + 8$ give the same answer? Why or why not?

2. If you have more red chips than yellow chips in a group, is the sum of the chips positive or negative?

3. If you have more yellow chips than red chips in a group, is the sum of the chips positive or negative?

4. Make a rule for the sign of the answer when negative and positive integers are added. Give examples.

Try This

Use integer chips to find each sum.

1. $4 + (-7)$ **2.** $-5 + (-4)$ **3.** $-5 + 1$ **4.** $6 + (-4)$

Write the addition problems modeled below.

5.

6.

7.

8.

Learn to add integers.

Georgia Performance Standards

M7A1.b Evaluate algebraic expressions. Also, M7P5.a, M7P5.b, M7P5.c.

The Debate Club wanted to raise money for a trip to Washington, D.C. They began by estimating their income and expenses.

Income items are positive, and expenses are negative. By adding all your income and expenses, you can find your total earnings or losses.

One way to add integers is by using a number line.

Club Ledger

Estimated Income and Expenses

Description	Amount
Car wash supplies	–$25.00
Car wash earnings	$300.00
Bake sale supplies	–$50.00
Bake sale earnings	$250.00

E X A M P L E **1** **Modeling Integer Addition**

Use a number line to find each sum.

A $-3 + (-6)$

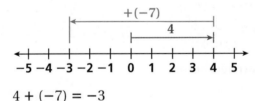

Start at 0. Move left 3 units. Then move left 6 more units.

$-3 + (-6) = -9$

B $4 + (-7)$

Start at 0. Move right 4 units. Then move left 7 units.

$4 + (-7) = -3$

You can also use absolute value to add integers.

Adding Integers

To add two integers with the same sign, find the sum of their absolute values. Use the sign of the two integers.

To add two integers with different signs, find the difference of their absolute values. Use the sign of the integer with the greater absolute value.

EXAMPLE 2 **Adding Integers Using Absolute Values**

Find each sum.

A $-7 + (-4)$

The signs are the **same**. Find the **sum** of the absolute values.

$-7 + (-4)$ *Think: 7 + 4 = 11.*

-11 *Use the sign of the two integers.*

B $-8 + 6$

The signs are **different**. Find the **difference** of the absolute values.

$-8 + 6$ *Think: 8 − 6 = 2.*

-2 *Use the sign of the integer with the greater absolute value.*

EXAMPLE 3 **Evaluating Expressions with Integers**

Helpful Hint

When adding integers, think: If the signs are the *same,* find the *sum.* If the signs are *different,* find the *difference.*

Evaluate $a + b$ for $a = 6$ and $b = -10$.

$a + b$

$6 + (-10)$ *Substitute 6 for **a** and −10 for **b**. The signs are **different**. Think: 10 − 6 = 4.*

-4 *Use the sign of the integer with the greater absolute value (**negative**).*

EXAMPLE 4 *Banking Application*

The Debate Club's income from a car wash was $300, including tips. Supply expenses were $25. Use integer addition to find the club's total profit or loss.

$300 + (-25)$ *Use negative for the expenses.*

$300 - 25$ *Find the difference of the absolute values.*

275 *The answer is positive.*

The club earned $275.

Think and Discuss  GPS M7P1.a, M7P2.c

1. **Explain** whether $-7 + 2$ is the same as $7 + (-2)$.

2. **Use** the Commutative Property to write an expression that is equivalent to $3 + (-5)$.

Georgia Performance
Standards
M7P1.b, M7P3.a, M7P5.b

go.hrw.com
Homework Help Online
KEYWORD: MS7 2-2
Parent Resources Online
KEYWORD: MS7 Parent

GUIDED PRACTICE

See Example **Use a number line to find each sum.**

1. $9 + 3$ **2.** $-4 + (-2)$ **3.** $7 + (-9)$ **4.** $-3 + 6$

See Example **Find each sum.**

5. $7 + 8$ **6.** $-1 + (-12)$ **7.** $-25 + 10$ **8.** $31 + (-20)$

See Example **Evaluate $a + b$ for the given values.**

9. $a = 5, b = -17$ **10.** $a = 8, b = -8$ **11.** $a = -4, b = -16$

See Example **12. Sports** A football team gains 8 yards on one play and then loses 13 yards on the next. Use integer addition to find the team's total yardage.

INDEPENDENT PRACTICE

See Example **Use a number line to find each sum.**

13. $-16 + 7$ **14.** $-5 + (-1)$ **15.** $4 + 9$ **16.** $-7 + 8$

17. $10 + (-3)$ **18.** $-20 + 2$ **19.** $-12 + (-5)$ **20.** $-9 + 6$

See Example **Find each sum.**

21. $-13 + (-6)$ **22.** $14 + 25$ **23.** $-22 + 6$ **24.** $35 + (-50)$

25. $-81 + (-7)$ **26.** $28 + (-3)$ **27.** $-70 + 15$ **28.** $-18 + (-62)$

See Example **Evaluate $c + d$ for the given values.**

29. $c = 6, d = -20$ **30.** $c = -8, d = -21$ **31.** $c = -45, d = 32$

See Example **32.** The temperature dropped 17°F in 6 hours. The final temperature was -3°F. Use integer addition to find the starting temperature.

PRACTICE AND PROBLEM SOLVING

CRCT GPS

Extra Practice p. 727

Find each sum.

33. $-8 + (-5)$ **34.** $14 + (-7)$ **35.** $-41 + 15$

36. $-22 + (-18) + 22$ **37.** $27 + (-29) + 16$ **38.** $-30 + 71 + (-70)$

Compare. Write <, >, or =.

39. $-23 + 18 \, \blacksquare \, -41$ **40.** $59 + (-59) \, \blacksquare \, 0$ **41.** $31 + (-20) \, \blacksquare \, 9$

42. $-24 + (-24) \, \blacksquare \, 48$ **43.** $25 + (-70) \, \blacksquare \, -95$ **44.** $16 + (-40) \, \blacksquare \, -24$

45. Personal Finance Cody made deposits of $45, $18, and $27 into his checking account. He then wrote checks for $21 and $93. Write an expression to show the change in Cody's account. Then simplify the expression.

Evaluate each expression for $w = -12$, $x = 10$, **and** $y = -7$.

46. $7 + y$ **47.** $-4 + w$ **48.** $w + y$ **49.** $x + y$ **50.** $w + x$

51. Recreation Hikers along the Appalachian Trail camped overnight at Horns Pond, at an elevation of 3,100 ft. Then they hiked along the ridge of the Bigelow Mountains to West Peak, which is one of Maine's highest peaks. Use the diagram to determine the elevation of West Peak.

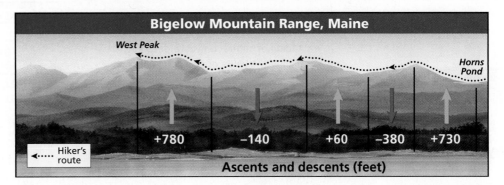

Bigelow Mountain Range, Maine

West Peak   Horns Pond

+780   −140   +60   −380   +730

Hiker's route

Ascents and descents (feet)

52. Multi-Step Hector and Luis are playing a game. In the game, each player starts with 0 points, and the player with the most points at the end wins. Hector gains 5 points, loses 3, loses 2, and then gains 3. Luis loses 5 points, gains 1, gains 5, and then loses 3. Determine the final scores by modeling the problem on a number line. Then tell who wins the game and by how much.

53. What's the Question? The temperature was −8°F at 6 A.M. and rose 15°F by 9 A.M. The answer is 7°F. What is the question?

54. Write About It Compare the method used to add integers with the same sign and the method used to add integers with different signs.

55. Challenge A business had losses of $225 million, $75 million, and $375 million and profits of $15 million and $125 million. How much was its overall profit or loss?

CRCT Prep • GPS Support • Spiral Review

56. Multiple Choice Which expression is represented by the model?

(A) $-4 + (-1)$ (C) $-4 + 3$

(B) $-4 + 0$ (D) $-4 + 4$

+ 3
−4
−5 −4 −3 −2 −1 0

57. Multiple Choice Which expression has the greatest value?

(F) $-4 + 8$ (G) $-2 + (-3)$ (H) $1 + 2$ (J) $4 + (-6)$

Simplify each expression. (Lesson 1-5)

58. $2 + 5 \cdot 2 - 3$ **59.** $3^3 - (6 \cdot 4) + 1$ **60.** $30 - 5 \cdot (3 + 2)$ **61.** $15 - 3 \cdot 2^2 + 1$

Compare. Write $<$, $>$, **or** $=$. (Lesson 2-1)

62. -14 ▓ -12 **63.** $\Omega-4\Omega$ ▓ 3 **64.** $\Omega-6\Omega$ ▓ 6 **65.** -9 ▓ -11

Hands-On LAB 2-3

Use with Lesson 2-3

Model Integer Subtraction

go.hrw.com
Lab Resources Online
KEYWORD: MS7 Lab2

Georgia Performance Standards

M7P2.c, M7P5.a, M7P5.b, M7P5.c

KEY

= 1

= –1

+ = 0

REMEMBER

- Adding or subtracting zero does not change the value of an expression.

You can model integer subtraction by using integer chips.

Activity

These groups of chips show three different ways of modeling 2.

1 Show two other ways of modeling 2.

These groups of chips show two different ways of modeling −2.

 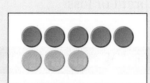

2 Show two other ways of modeling −2.

You can model subtraction problems involving two integers with the same sign by taking away chips.

$$8 - 3 = 5$$

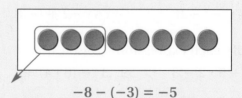

$$-8 - (-3) = -5$$

3 Use integer chips to find each difference.

a. $6 - 5$ **b.** $-6 - (-5)$ **c.** $10 - 7$ **d.** $-7 - (-4)$

To model subtraction problems involving two integers with different signs, such as −6 − 3, you will need to add zero pairs before you can take chips away.

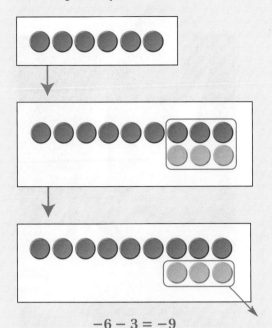

Use 6 red chips to represent −6.

Since you cannot take away 3 yellow chips, add 3 yellow chips paired with 3 red chips.

Now you can take away 3 yellow chips.

$$-6 - 3 = -9$$

4 Use integer chips to find each difference.

a. −6 − 5   **b.** 5 − (−6)   **c.** 4 − 7   **d.** −2 − (−3)

Think and Discuss

1. How could you model the expression 0 − 5?

2. When you add zero pairs to model subtraction using chips, does it matter how many zero pairs you add?

3. Would 2 − 3 have the same answer as 3 − 2? Why or why not?

4. Make a rule for the sign of the answer when a positive integer is subtracted from a negative integer. Give examples.

Try This

Use integer chips to find each difference.

1. 4 − 2   2. −4 − (−2)   3. −2 − (−3)

4. 3 − 4   5. 2 − 3   6. 0 − 3

7. 5 − 3   8. −3 − (−5)   9. 6 − (−4)

2-3 Subtracting Integers

Learn to subtract integers.

Georgia Performance Standards

M7A1.b Evaluate algebraic expressions. Also, M7P5.a, M7P5.b, M7P5.c.

During flight, the space shuttle may be exposed to temperatures as low as −250°F and as high as 3,000°F.

To find the difference in these temperatures, you need to know how to subtract integers with different signs.

You can model the difference between two integers using a number line. When you subtract a positive number, the difference is *less* than the original number, so you move to the *left*. To subtract a negative number, move to the *right*.

EXAMPLE 1 **Modeling Integer Subtraction**

Use a number line to find each difference.

A 3 − 8

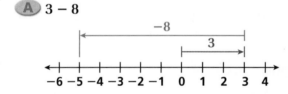

$3 - 8 = -5$

Start at 0.
Move right 3 units.
To subtract 8,
move to the left.

Helpful Hint

If the number being subtracted is less than the number it is subtracted from, the answer will be positive. If the number being subtracted is greater, the answer will be negative.

B −4 − 2

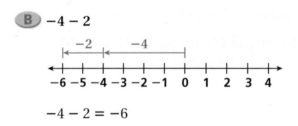

$-4 - 2 = -6$

Start at 0.
Move left 4 units.
To subtract 2,
move to the left.

C 2 − (−3)

$2 - (-3) = 5$

Start at 0.
Move right 2 units.
To subtract −3,
move to the right.

Addition and subtraction are inverse operations—they "undo" each other. Instead of subtracting a number, you can *add its opposite*.

EXAMPLE 2 **Subtracting Integers by Adding the Opposite**

Find each difference.

A $5 - 9$

$5 - 9 = 5 + (-9)$ *Add the opposite of 9.*

$\quad\quad = -4$

B $-9 - (-2)$

$-9 - (-2) = -9 + 2$ *Add the opposite of −2.*

$\quad\quad\quad = -7$

C $-4 - 3$

$-4 - 3 = -4 + (-3)$ *Add the opposite of 3.*

$\quad\quad\quad = -7$

EXAMPLE 3 **Evaluating Expressions with Integers**

Evaluate $a - b$ for each set of values.

A $a = -6, b = 7$

$a - b$

$-6 - 7 = -6 + (-7)$ *Substitute for a and b. Add the opposite*

$\quad\quad\quad = -13$ *of 7.*

B $a = 14, b = -9$

$a - b$

$14 - (-9) = 14 + 9$ *Substitute for a and b. Add the opposite*

$\quad\quad\quad = 23$ *of −9.*

EXAMPLE 4 *Temperature Application*

Find the difference between 3,000°F and −250°F, the temperatures the space shuttle must endure.

$3,000 - (-250)$

$3,000 + 250 = 3,250$ *Add the opposite of −250.*

The difference in temperatures the shuttle must endure is 3,250°F.

Think and Discuss  GPS M7P1.a, M7P2.c

1. **Suppose** you subtract one negative integer from another. Will your answer be greater than or less than the number you started with?

2. **Tell** whether you can reverse the order of integers when subtracting and still get the same answer. Why or why not?

Georgia Performance
Standards
M7P4.c, M7P5.a, M7P5.b

go.hrw.com
Homework Help Online
KEYWORD: MS7 2-3
Parent Resources Online
KEYWORD: MS7 Parent

GUIDED PRACTICE

See Example ① **Use a number line to find each difference.**

1. $4 - 7$ **2.** $-6 - 5$ **3.** $2 - (-4)$ **4.** $-8 - (-2)$

See Example ② **Find each difference.**

5. $6 - 10$ **6.** $-3 - (-8)$ **7.** $-1 - 9$ **8.** $-12 - (-2)$

See Example ③ **Evaluate $a - b$ for each set of values.**

9. $a = 5, b = -2$ **10.** $a = -8, b = 6$ **11.** $a = 4, b = 18$

See Example ④ **12.** In 1980, in Great Falls, Montana, the temperature rose from $-32°F$ to $15°F$ in seven minutes. How much did the temperature increase?

INDEPENDENT PRACTICE

See Example ① **Use a number line to find each difference.**

13. $7 - 12$ **14.** $-5 - (-9)$ **15.** $2 - (-6)$ **16.** $7 - (-8)$

17. $9 - (-3)$ **18.** $-4 - 10$ **19.** $8 - (-8)$ **20.** $-3 - (-3)$

See Example ② **Find each difference.**

21. $-22 - (-5)$ **22.** $-4 - 21$ **23.** $27 - 19$ **24.** $-10 - (-7)$

25. $30 - (-20)$ **26.** $-15 - 15$ **27.** $12 - (-6)$ **28.** $-31 - 15$

See Example ③ **Evaluate $a - b$ for each set of values.**

29. $a = 9, b = -7$ **30.** $a = -11, b = 2$ **31.** $a = -2, b = 3$

32. $a = 8, b = 19$ **33.** $a = -10, b = 10$ **34.** $a = -4, b = -15$

See Example ④ **35.** In 1918, in Granville, North Dakota, the temperature rose from $-33°F$ to $50°F$ in 12 hours. How much did the temperature increase?

PRACTICE AND PROBLEM SOLVING

Extra Practice p. 727

Simplify.

36. $2 - 8$ **37.** $-5 - 9$ **38.** $15 - 12 - 8$

39. $6 + (-5) - 3$ **40.** $1 - 8 + (-6)$ **41.** $4 - (-7) - 9$

42. $(2 - 3) - (5 - 6)$ **43.** $5 - (-8) - (-3)$ **44.** $10 - 12 + 2$

Evaluate each expression for $m = -5, n = 8,$ and $p = -14$.

45. $m - n + p$ **46.** $n - m - p$ **47.** $p - m - n$ **48.** $m + n - p$

49. Patterns Find the next three numbers in the pattern $7, 3, -1, -5, -9 \ldots$. Then describe the pattern.

50. The temperature of Mercury, the planet closest to the Sun, can be as high as 873°F. The temperature of the dwarf planet Pluto is about −393°F. What is the difference between these temperatures?

51. One side of Mercury always faces the Sun. The temperature on this side can reach 873°F. The temperature on the other side can be as low as −361°F. What is the difference between the two temperatures?

Maat Mons volcano on Venus
Source: NASA (computer-generated from the *Magellan* probe)

52. Earth's moon rotates relative to the Sun about once a month. The side facing the Sun at a given time can be as hot as 224°F. The side away from the Sun can be as cold as −307°F. What is the difference between these temperatures?

53. The highest recorded temperature on Earth is 136°F. The lowest is −129°F. What is the difference between these temperatures?

Use the graph for Exercises 54 and 55.

54. How much deeper is the deepest canyon on Mars than the deepest canyon on Venus?

55. ⭐ **Challenge** What is the difference between Earth's highest mountain and its deepest ocean canyon? What is the difference between Mars' highest mountain and its deepest canyon? Which difference is greater? How much greater is it?

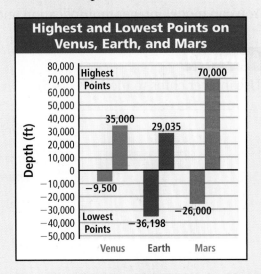

Highest and Lowest Points on Venus, Earth, and Mars

CRCT PREP • GPS SUPPORT • SPIRAL REVIEW

56. Multiple Choice Which expression does NOT have a value of −3?

Ⓐ −2 − 1　　　Ⓑ 10 − 13　　　Ⓒ 5 − (−8)　　　Ⓓ −4 − (−1)

57. Extended Response If $m = -2$ and $n = 4$, which expression has the least absolute value: $m + n$, $n - m$, or $m - n$? Explain your answer.

Evaluate each expression for the given values of the variables. (Lesson 1-7)

58. $3x - 5$ for $x = 2$　　　**59.** $2n^2 + n$ for $n = 1$　　　**60.** $4y^2 - 3y$ for $y = 2$

61. $4a + 7$ for $a = 3$　　　**62.** $x^2 + 9$ for $x = 1$　　　**63.** $5z + z^2$ for $z = 3$

64. Sports In three plays, a football team gained 10 yards, lost 22 yards, and gained 15 yards. Use integer addition to find the team's total yardage for the three plays. (Lesson 2-2)

Hands-On LAB 2-4

Model Integer Multiplication and Division

Use with Lesson 2-4

go.hrw.com
Lab Resources Online
KEYWORD: MS7 Lab2

Georgia Performance Standards

M7P1.a, M7P5.a, M7P5.b, M7P5.c

KEY

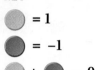

● = 1

● = −1

● + ● = 0

REMEMBER
- The Commutative Property states that two numbers can be multiplied in any order without changing the product.
- Multiplication is repeated addition.
- Multiplication and division are inverse operations.

You can model integer multiplication and division by using integer chips.

Activity 1

Use integer chips to model $3 \cdot (-5)$.

Think: $3 \cdot (-5)$ means 3 groups of −5.

Arrange 3 groups of 5 red chips.
There are a total of 15 red chips.

$3 \cdot (-5) = -15$

1 Use integer chips to find each product.

   a. $2 \cdot (-2)$ **b.** $3 \cdot (-6)$ **c.** $5 \cdot (-4)$ **d.** $6 \cdot (-3)$

Use integer chips to model $-4 \cdot 2$.

Using the Commutative Property, you can write $-4 \cdot 2$ as $2 \cdot (-4)$.

Think: $2 \cdot (-4)$ means 2 groups of −4.

Arrange 2 groups of 4 red chips.
There are a total of 8 red chips.

$-4 \cdot 2 = -8$

2 Use integer chips to find each product.

   a. $-6 \cdot 5$ **b.** $-4 \cdot 6$ **c.** $-3 \cdot 4$ **d.** $-2 \cdot 3$

1. What is the sign of the product when you multiply two positive numbers? a negative and a positive number? two negative numbers?

2. If 12 were the answer to a multiplication problem, list all of the possible factors that are integers.

Try This

Use integer chips to find each product.

1. $4 \cdot (-5)$ **2.** $-3 \cdot 2$ **3.** $1 \cdot (-6)$ **4.** $-5 \cdot 2$

5. On days that Kathy has swimming lessons, she spends $2.00 of her allowance on snacks. Last week, Kathy had swimming lessons on Monday, Wednesday, and Friday. How much of her allowance did Kathy spend on snacks last week? Use integer chips to model the situation and solve the problem.

Activity 2

Use integer chips to model $-15 \div 3$.

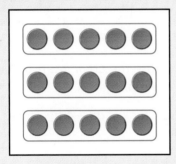

Think: −15 is separated into 3 equal groups.

Arrange 15 red chips into 3 equal groups.

There are 5 red chips in each group.

$$-15 \div 3 = -5$$

1 Use integer chips to find each quotient.

a. $-20 \div 5$ **b.** $-18 \div 6$ **c.** $-12 \div 4$ **d.** $-24 \div 8$

Think and Discuss

1. What is the sign of the answer when you divide two negative integers? a negative integer by a positive integer? a positive integer by a negative integer?

2. How are multiplication and division of integers related?

Try This

Use integer chips to find each quotient.

1. $-21 \div 7$ **2.** $-12 \div 4$ **3.** $-8 \div 2$ **4.** $-10 \div 5$

5. Ty spent $18 of his allowance at the arcade. He hit baseballs, played pinball, and played video games. Each of these activities cost the same amount at the arcade. How much did each activity cost? Use integer chips to model the situation and solve the problem.

2-4 Multiplying and Dividing Integers

Learn to multiply and divide integers.

You can think of multiplication as repeated addition.

$$3 \cdot 2 = 2 + 2 + 2 = 6 \text{ and } 3 \cdot (-2) = (-2) + (-2) + (-2) = -6$$

EXAMPLE 1 **Multiplying Integers Using Repeated Addition**

Use a number line to find each product.

A $3 \cdot (-3)$

$+(-3)$ $+(-3)$ -3

−10 −9 −8 −7 −6 −5 −4 −3 −2 −1   0   1

Think: Add −3 three times.

$3 \cdot (-3) = -9$

B $-4 \cdot 2$

$-4 \cdot 2 = 2 \cdot (-4)$ *Use the Commutative Property.*

$+(-4)$ $+(-4)$

−10 −9 −8 −7 −6 −5 −4 −3 −2 −1   0   1

Think: Add −4 two times.

$-4 \cdot 2 = -8$

Georgia Performance Standards

M7P5.b Select, apply, and translate among mathematical representations to solve problems. Also, M7P4.c, M7P5.a, M7P5.c.

Remember!

Multiplication and division are inverse operations. They "undo" each other. Notice how these operations undo each other in the patterns shown.

The patterns below suggest that when the signs of two integers are different, their product or quotient is negative. The patterns also suggest that the product or quotient of two negative integers is positive.

$-3 \cdot \quad 2 = -6$	$-6 \div (-3) = \quad 2$
$-3 \cdot \quad 1 = -3$	$-3 \div (-3) = \quad 1$
$-3 \cdot \quad 0 = \quad 0$	$0 \div (-3) = \quad 0$
$-3 \cdot (-1) = \quad 3$	$3 \div (-3) = -1$
$-3 \cdot (-2) = \quad 6$	$6 \div (-3) = -2$

Multiplying and Dividing Integers

If the signs are:	Your answer will be:
the same $\longrightarrow$	positive
different $\longrightarrow$	negative

EXAMPLE 2 **Multiplying Integers**

Find each product.

A $-4 \cdot (-2)$

$-4 \cdot (-2)$ *Both signs are*
       negative, so the
     8   *product is positive.*

B $-3 \cdot 6$

$-3 \cdot 6$ *The signs are*
       different, so the
   -18 *product is negative.*

EXAMPLE 3 **Dividing Integers**

Find each quotient.

A $72 \div (-9)$

$72 \div (-9)$ *Think: 72 ÷ 9 = 8.*

   -8 *The signs are different, so the quotient is negative.*

B $-144 \div 12$

$-144 \div 12$ *Think: 144 ÷ 12 = 12.*

   -12 *The signs are different, so the quotient is negative.*

C $-100 \div (-5)$

$-100 \div (-5)$ *Think: 100 ÷ 5 = 20.*

    20   *The signs are the same, so the quotient is positive.*

EXAMPLE 4 *Earth Science Application*

Jonie recorded the temperature change every hour for 4 hours as a cold front approached. The temperature dropped steadily a total of 24°F over the 4-hour period. What was the change in temperature during the first hour?

The temperature dropped 24°F. You can write this as -24.

$-24 \div 4 = -6$ *Divide the total drop in temperature*
                by the total recording time.

The temperature change during the first hour was $-6°F$.

Earth Science

Each year there are about 16 million thunderstorms around the globe. Thunderstorms develop when moist air rises and encounters cooler air.

Think and Discuss

GPS **M7P1.a, M7P3.b**

1. List at least four different multiplication examples that have 24 as their product. Use both positive and negative integers.

2. Explain how the signs of two integers affect their products and quotients.

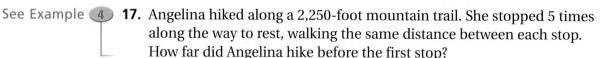

Georgia Performance Standards
M7P1.b, M7P3.a, M7P3.c, M7P5.b

go.hrw.com
Homework Help Online
KEYWORD: MS7 2-4
Parent Resources Online
KEYWORD: MS7 Parent

GUIDED PRACTICE

See Example **1** Use a number line to find each product.

1. $5 \cdot (-3)$ **2.** $5 \cdot (-2)$ **3.** $-3 \cdot 5$ **4.** $-4 \cdot 6$

See Example **2** Find each product.

5. $-5 \cdot (-3)$ **6.** $-2 \cdot 5$ **7.** $3 \cdot (-5)$ **8.** $-7 \cdot (-4)$

See Example **3** Find each quotient.

9. $32 \div (-4)$ **10.** $-18 \div 3$ **11.** $-20 \div (-5)$ **12.** $49 \div (-7)$

13. $-63 \div (-9)$ **14.** $-50 \div 10$ **15.** $63 \div (-9)$ **16.** $-45 \div (-5)$

See Example **4** **17.** Angelina hiked along a 2,250-foot mountain trail. She stopped 5 times along the way to rest, walking the same distance between each stop. How far did Angelina hike before the first stop?

INDEPENDENT PRACTICE

See Example **1** Use a number line to find each product.

18. $2 \cdot (-1)$ **19.** $-5 \cdot 2$ **20.** $-4 \cdot 2$ **21.** $3 \cdot (-4)$

See Example **2** Find each product.

22. $4 \cdot (-6)$ **23.** $-6 \cdot (-8)$ **24.** $-8 \cdot 4$ **25.** $-5 \cdot (-7)$

See Example **3** Find each quotient.

26. $48 \div (-6)$ **27.** $-35 \div (-5)$ **28.** $-16 \div 4$ **29.** $-64 \div 8$

30. $-42 \div (-7)$ **31.** $81 \div (-9)$ **32.** $-77 \div 11$ **33.** $27 \div (-3)$

See Example **4** **34.** A scuba diver descended below the ocean's surface in 35-foot intervals as he examined a coral reef. He dove to a total depth of 140 feet. In how many intervals did the diver make his descent?

PRACTICE AND PROBLEM SOLVING

CRCT GPS

Extra Practice p. 727

Find each product or quotient.

35. $-4 \cdot 10$ **36.** $-3 \cdot (-9)$ **37.** $-45 \div 15$ **38.** $-3 \cdot 4 \cdot (-1)$

39. $-500 \div (-10)$ **40.** $5 \cdot (-4) \cdot (-2)$ **41.** $225 \div (-75)$ **42.** $-2 \cdot (-5) \cdot 9$

Evaluate each expression for $a = -5$, $b = 6$, and $c = -12$.

43. $-2c + b$ **44.** $4a - b$ **45.** $ab + c$ **46.** $ac \div b$

47. **Earth Science** A scuba diver is swimming at a depth of -12 feet in the Flower Garden Banks National Marine Sanctuary. She dives down to a coral reef that is at five times this depth. What is the depth of the coral reef?

Simplify each expression. Justify your steps using the Commutative, Associative, and Distributive Properties when necessary.

48. $(-3)^2$ **49.** $-(-2 + 1)$ **50.** $8 + (-5)^3 + 7$ **51.** $(-1)^5 \cdot (9 + 3)$

52. $29 - (-7) - 3$ **53.** $-4 \cdot 14 \cdot (-25)$ **54.** $25 - (-2) \cdot 4^2$ **55.** $8 - (6 \div (-2))$

56. Earth Science The table shows the depths of major caves in the United States. Approximately how many times deeper is Jewel Cave than Kartchner Caverns?

Depths of Major U.S. Caves	
Cave	**Depth (ft)**
Carlsbad Caverns	−1,022
Caverns of Sonora	−150
Ellison's Cave	−1,000
Jewel Cave	−696
Kartchner Caverns	−137
Mammoth Cave	−379

Source: NSS U.S.A. Long Cave List, Caves over one mile long as of 10/18/2001

Personal Finance Does each person end up with more or less money than he started with? By how much?

57. Kevin spends $24 a day for 3 days.

58. Devin earns $15 a day for 5 days.

59. Evan spends $20 a day for 3 days. Then he earns $18 a day for 4 days.

60. What's the Error? A student writes, "The quotient of an integer divided by an integer of the opposite sign has the sign of the integer with the greater absolute value." What is the student's error?

61. Write About It Explain how to find the product and the quotient of two integers.

62. Challenge Use > or < to compare $-2 \cdot (-1) \cdot 4 \cdot 2 \cdot (-3)$ and $-1 + (-2) + 4 + (-25) + (-10)$.

CRCT PREP • GPS SUPPORT • SPIRAL REVIEW

63. Multiple Choice Which of the expressions are equal to −20?

I $-2 \cdot 10$ **II** $-40 \div (-2)$ **III** $-5 \cdot (-2)^2$ **IV** $-4 \cdot 2 - 12$

ⓐ I only   ⓑ I and II   ⓒ I, III, and IV   ⓓ I, II, III, IV

64. Multiple Choice Which expression has a value that is greater than the value of $-25 \div (-5)$?

ⓕ $36 \div (-6)$ ⓖ $-100 \div 10$ ⓗ $-50 \div (-10)$ ⓙ $-45 \div (-5)$

Write each phrase as an algebraic expression. (Lesson 1-8)

65. the sum of a number and 6

66. the product of −3 and a number

67. 4 less than twice a number

68. 5 more than a number divided by 3

Find each difference. (Lesson 2-3)

69. $3 - (-2)$ **70.** $-5 - 6$ **71.** $6 - 8$ **72.** $2 - (-7)$

Hands-On LAB 2-5

Model Integer Equations

Use with Lesson 2-5

go.hrw.com
Lab Resources Online
KEYWORD: MS7 Lab2

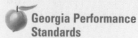

Georgia Performance Standards

M7A2.b, M7P2.c, M7P5.b, M7P5.c

KEY	REMEMBER
➕ = 1 ➖ = –1 ➕ + ➖ = 0 ▮ = x	• Adding or subtracting zero does not change the value of an expression.

You can use algebra tiles to model and solve equations.

Activity

To solve the equation $x + 2 = 3$, you need to get x alone on one side of the equal sign. You can add or remove tiles as long as you add the same amount or remove the same amount on both sides.

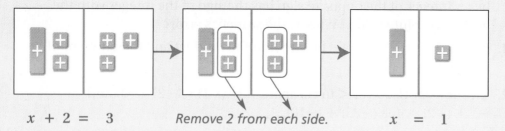

$x + 2 = 3$ *Remove 2 from each side.* $x = 1$

1 Use algebra tiles to model and solve each equation.

a. $x + 3 = 5$ **b.** $x + 4 = 9$ **c.** $x + 5 = 8$ **d.** $x + 6 = 6$

The equation $x + 6 = 4$ is more difficult to model because there are not enough tiles on the right side of the mat to remove 6 from each side.

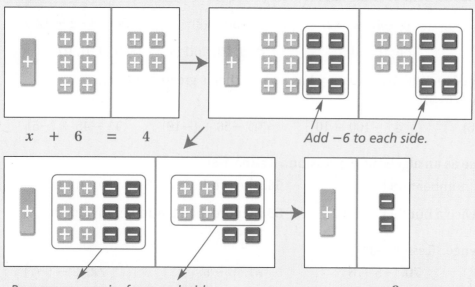

$x + 6 = 4$ *Add −6 to each side.*

Remove zero pairs from each side. $x = -2$

2 Use algebra tiles to model and solve each equation.

    a. $x + 5 = 3$ **b.** $x + 4 = 2$ **c.** $x + 7 = -3$ **d.** $x + 6 = -2$

When modeling an equation that involves subtraction, such as $x - 6 = 2$, you must first rewrite the equation as an addition equation. For example, the equation $x - 6 = 2$ can be rewritten as $x + (-6) = 2$.

Modeling equations that involve addition of negative numbers is similar to modeling equations that involve addition of positive numbers.

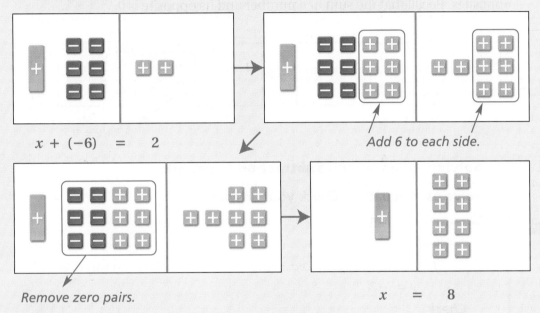

$x + (-6) = 2$ *Add 6 to each side.*

Remove zero pairs. $x = 8$

3 Use algebra tiles to model and solve each equation.

    a. $x - 4 = 3$ **b.** $x - 2 = 8$ **c.** $x - 5 = -5$ **d.** $x - 7 = 0$

Think and Discuss

1. When you remove tiles, what operation are you modeling? When you add tiles, what operation are you modeling?

2. How can you use the original model to check your solution?

3. To model $x - 6 = 2$, you must rewrite the equation as $x + (-6) = 2$. Why are you allowed to do this?

Try This

Use algebra tiles to model and solve each equation.

  1. $x + 7 = 10$ **2.** $x - 5 = -8$ **3.** $x + (-5) = -4$ **4.** $x - 2 = 1$

  5. $x + 4 = 8$ **6.** $x + 3 = -2$ **7.** $x + (-1) = 9$ **8.** $x - 7 = -6$

2-5 Solving Equations Containing Integers

Learn to solve one-step equations with integers.

To solve integer equations such as $x - 2 = -3$ you must isolate the variable on one side of the equation. One way to isolate the variable is to add opposites. Recall that the sum of a number and its opposite is 0.

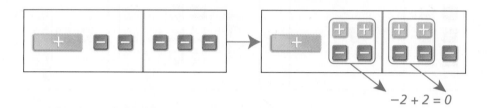

$$-2 + 2 = 0$$

EXAMPLE 1 Solving Addition and Subtraction Equations

Helpful Hint

$3 + (-3) = 0$
3 is the opposite of -3.

Georgia Performance Standards

M7A2.a Given a problem, define a variable, write an equation, solve the equation, and interpret the solution. Also, M7A1.a, M7A2.b, M7P4.c.

Solve each equation. Check your answer.

A $-3 + y = -5$

$$-3 + y = -5$$
$$\underline{+3 \qquad +3}$$ Add 3 to both sides to isolate the variable.
$$y = -2$$

Check

$$-3 + y = -5$$
$$-3 + (-2) \overset{?}{=} -5$$ Substitute −2 for y in the original equation.
$$-5 \overset{?}{=} -5 ✔$$ True. −2 is the solution to $-3 + y = -5$.

B $n + 3 = -10$

$$n + 3 = \quad -10$$
$$\underline{+(-3) \quad +(-3)}$$ Add −3 to both sides to isolate the variable.
$$n = \quad -13$$

Check

$$n + 3 = -10$$
$$-13 + 3 \overset{?}{=} -10$$ Substitute −13 for n in the original equation.
$$-10 \overset{?}{=} -10 ✔$$ True. −13 is the solution to $n + 3 = -10$.

C $x - 8 = -32$

$$x - 8 = -32$$
$$\underline{+8 \qquad +8}$$ Add 8 to both sides to isolate the variable.
$$x = -24$$

Check

$$x - 8 = -32$$
$$-24 - 8 \overset{?}{=} -32$$ Substitute −24 for x in the original equation.
$$-32 \overset{?}{=} -32 ✔$$ True. −24 is the solution to $x - 8 = -32$.

EXAMPLE 2 — Solving Multiplication and Division Equations

Solve each equation. Check your answer.

A $\dfrac{a}{-3} = 9$

$$\dfrac{a}{-3} = 9$$

$$(-3)\left(\dfrac{a}{-3}\right) = (-3)9 \qquad \text{Multiply both sides by } -3 \text{ to isolate the variable.}$$

$$a = -27$$

Check $\quad \dfrac{a}{-3} = 9$

$$\dfrac{-27}{-3} \overset{?}{=} 9 \qquad \text{Substitute } -27 \text{ for } a.$$

$$9 \overset{?}{=} 9 \checkmark \qquad \text{True. } -27 \text{ is the solution.}$$

B $-120 = 6x$

$$-120 = 6x$$

$$\dfrac{-120}{6} = \dfrac{6x}{6} \qquad \text{Divide both sides by 6 to isolate the variable.}$$

$$-20 = x$$

Check $\quad -120 = 6x$

$$-120 \overset{?}{=} 6(-20) \qquad \text{Substitute } -20 \text{ for } x.$$

$$-120 \overset{?}{=} -120 \checkmark \qquad \text{True. } -20 \text{ is the solution.}$$

EXAMPLE 3 — *Business Application*

A shoe manufacturer made a profit of $800 million. This amount is $200 million more than last year's profit. What was last year's profit?

Let p represent last year's profit (in millions of dollars).

This year's profit	is	$200 million	more than	last year's profit.
800	=	200	+	p

$$800 = 200 + p$$
$$\underline{-\,200 \quad -\,200}$$
$$600 = p \qquad \text{Last year's profit was \$600 million.}$$

Think and Discuss

GPS M7P1.d, M7P2.c

1. Tell what value of n makes $-n + 32$ equal to zero.

2. Explain why you would or would not multiply both sides of an equation by 0 to solve it.

Georgia Performance Standards

M7P1.c, M7P3.a, M7P4.c

go.hrw.com
Homework Help Online
KEYWORD: MS7 2-5
Parent Resources Online
KEYWORD: MS7 Parent

GUIDED PRACTICE

See Example 1 Solve each equation. Check your answer.

1. $w - 6 = -2$

2. $x + 5 = -7$

3. $k = -18 + 11$

See Example 2 **4.** $\dfrac{n}{-4} = 2$

5. $-240 = 8y$

6. $-5a = 300$

See Example 3 **7. Business** Last year, a chain of electronics stores had a loss of $45 million. This year the loss is $12 million more than last year's loss. What is this year's loss?

INDEPENDENT PRACTICE

See Example 1 Solve each equation. Check your answer.

8. $b - 7 = -16$

9. $k + 6 = 3$

10. $s + 2 = -4$

11. $v + 14 = 10$

12. $c + 8 = -20$

13. $a - 25 = -5$

See Example 2 **14.** $9c = -99$

15. $\dfrac{t}{8} = -4$

16. $-16 = 2z$

17. $\dfrac{n}{-5} = -30$

18. $200 = -25p$

19. $\dfrac{l}{-12} = 12$

See Example 3 **20.** The temperature in Nome, Alaska, was $-50°F$. This was $18°F$ less than the temperature in Anchorage, Alaska, on the same day. What was the temperature in Anchorage?

PRACTICE AND PROBLEM SOLVING

Extra Practice p. 728

Solve each equation. Check your answer.

21. $9y = 900$

22. $d - 15 = 45$

23. $j + 56 = -7$

24. $\dfrac{s}{-20} = 7$

25. $-85 = -5c$

26. $v - 39 = -16$

27. $11y = -121$

28. $\dfrac{n}{36} = 9$

29. $w + 41 = 0$

30. $\dfrac{r}{238} = 8$

31. $-23 = x + 35$

32. $0 = -15m$

33. $4x = 2 + 14$

34. $c + c + c = 6$

35. $t - 3 = 4 + 2$

36. Geometry The three angles of a triangle have equal measures. The sum of their measures is $180°$. What is the measure of each angle?

37. Sports Herb has 42 days to prepare for a cross-country race. During his training, he will run a total of 126 miles. If Herb runs the same distance every day, how many miles will he run each day?

38. Multi-Step Jared bought one share of stock for $225.
 a. He sold the stock for a profit of $55. What was the selling price of the stock?
 b. The price of the stock dropped $40 the day after Jared sold it. At what price would Jared have sold it if he had waited until then?

Translate each sentence into an equation. Then solve the equation.

39. The sum of -13 and a number p is 8.

40. A number x divided by 4 is -7.

41. 9 less than a number t is -22.

42. Physical Science On the Kelvin temperature scale, pure water boils at 373 K. The difference between the boiling point and the freezing point of water on this scale is 100 K. What is the freezing point of water?

Recreation The graph shows the most popular travel destinations over the 2001 Labor Day weekend. Use the graph for Exercises 43 and 44.

43. Which destination was 5 times more popular than theme or amusement parks?

44. According to the graph, the mountains were as popular as state or national parks and what other destination combined?

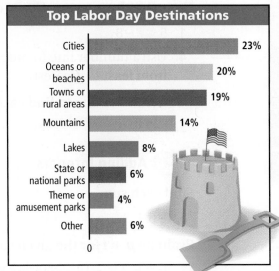

Top Labor Day Destinations

- Cities — 23%
- Oceans or beaches — 20%
- Towns or rural areas — 19%
- Mountains — 14%
- Lakes — 8%
- State or national parks — 6%
- Theme or amusement parks — 4%
- Other — 6%

Source: AAA

 45. Choose a Strategy Matthew (M) earns $23 less a week than his sister Allie (A). Their combined salaries are $93. How much does each of them earn per week?

    Ⓐ *A*: $35; *M*: $12   Ⓑ *A*: $35; *M*: $58   Ⓒ *A*: $58; *M*: $35

 46. Write About It Explain how to isolate a variable in an equation.

 47. Challenge Write an equation that includes the variable p and the numbers 5, 3, and 31 so that the solution is $p = 16$.

CRCT PREP • GPS SUPPORT • SPIRAL REVIEW

48. Multiple Choice Solve $-15m = 60$.

    Ⓐ $m = -4$ Ⓑ $m = 5$ Ⓒ $m = 45$ Ⓓ $m = 75$

49. Multiple Choice For which equation does $x = 2$?

    Ⓕ $-3x = 6$ Ⓖ $x + 3 = -5$ Ⓗ $x + x = 4$ Ⓙ $\frac{x}{4} = -8$

Identify a possible pattern. Use the pattern to write the next three numbers. (Lesson 1-1)

50. 26, 21, 16, 11, 6, . . .   **51.** 1, 2, 4, 8, 16, . . .   **52.** 1, 4, 3, 6, 5, . . .

Compare. Write <, >, or =. (Lessons 2-1, 2-2, and 2-3)

53. -5 ▨ -8 **54.** 4 ▨ $|-4|$ **55.** $|-7|$ ▨ $|-9|$

56. -10 ▨ $|-10|$ **57.** $-7 - 8$ ▨ -15 **58.** -12 ▨ $10 + (-12)$

READY TO GO ON?

Quiz for Lessons 2-1 Through 2-5

2-1 Integers

Compare the integers. Use < or >.

1. 5 ▨ −8

2. −2 ▨ −6

3. −4 ▨ 3

4. Use a number line to order the integers −7, 3, 6, −1, 0, 5, −4, and 7 from least to greatest.

Use a number line to find each absolute value.

5. $|-23|$

6. $|17|$

7. $|-10|$

2-2 Adding Integers

Find each sum.

8. −6 + 3

9. 5 + (−9)

10. −7 + (−11)

Evaluate $p + t$ for the given values.

11. $p = 5, t = -18$

12. $p = -4, t = -13$

13. $p = -37, t = 39$

2-3 Subtracting Integers

Find each difference.

14. −21 − (−7)

15. 9 − (−11)

16. 6 − 17

17. When Cai traveled from New Orleans, Louisiana, to the Ozark Mountains in Arkansas, the elevation changed from 7 ft below sea level to 2,314 ft above sea level. How much did the elevation increase?

2-4 Multiplying and Dividing Integers

Find each product or quotient.

18. $-7 \cdot 3$

19. $30 \div (-15)$

20. $-5 \cdot (-9)$

21. After reaching the top of a cliff, a rock climber descended the rock face using a 65 ft rope. The distance to the base of the cliff was 585 ft. How many rope lengths did it take the climber to complete her descent?

2-5 Solving Equations Containing Integers

Solve each equation. Check your answer.

22. $3x = 30$

23. $k - 25 = 50$

24. $y + 16 = -8$

25. This year, 72 students completed projects for the science fair. This was 23 more students than last year. How many students completed projects for the science fair last year?

Focus on Problem Solving

 Make a Plan

- **Choose a method of computation**

When you know the operation you must use and you know exactly which numbers to use, a calculator might be the easiest way to solve a problem. Sometimes, such as when the numbers are small or are multiples of 10, it may be quicker to use mental math.

Sometimes, you have to write the numbers to see how they relate in an equation. When you are working an equation, using a pencil and paper is the simplest method to use because you can see each step as you go.

For each problem, tell whether you would use a calculator, mental math, or pencil and paper to solve it. Explain your answer. Then solve the problem.

1. A scouting troop is collecting aluminum cans to raise money for charity. Their goal is to collect 3,000 cans in 6 months. If they set a goal to collect an equal number of cans each month, how many cans can they expect to collect each month?

2. The Grand Canyon is 29,000 meters wide at its widest point. The Empire State Building, located in New York City, is 381 meters tall. Laid end to end, how many Empire State Buildings would fit across the Grand Canyon at its widest point?

3. On a piano keyboard, all but one of the black keys are arranged in groups so that there are 7 groups with 2 black keys each and 7 groups with 3 black keys each. How many black keys are there on a piano?

4. Some wind chimes are made of rods. The rods are usually of different lengths, producing different sounds. The frequency (which determines the pitch) of the sound is measured in hertz (Hz). If one rod on a chime has a frequency of 55 Hz and another rod has a frequency that is twice that of the first rod's, what is the frequency of the second rod?

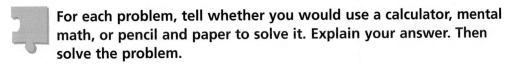

 **Learn** to find the prime factorizations of composite numbers.

Vocabulary

prime number

composite number

prime factorization

Nayan Hajratwala received a $50,000 award for discovering a new prime number.

Georgia Performance Standards

M7P5.b Select, apply, and translate among mathematical representations to solve problems. Also, M7P5.a, M7P5.c.

In June 1999, Nayan Hajratwala discovered the first known *prime number* with more than one million digits. The new prime number, $2^{6,972,593} - 1$, has 2,098,960 digits.

A **prime number** is a whole number greater than 1 that has exactly two factors, 1 and itself. Three is a prime number because its only factors are 1 and 3.

A **composite number** is a whole number that has more than two factors. Six is a composite number because it has more than two factors—1, 2, 3, and 6. The number 1 has exactly one factor and is neither prime nor composite.

EXAMPLE 1 **Identifying Prime and Composite Numbers**

Tell whether each number is prime or composite.

A 19

The factors of 19 are 1 and 19.

So 19 is prime.

B 20

The factors of 20 are 1, 2, 4, 5, 10, and 20.

So 20 is composite.

A composite number can be written as the product of its prime factors. This is called the **prime factorization** of the number. You can use a factor tree to find the prime factors of a composite number.

EXAMPLE 2 **Using a Factor Tree to Find Prime Factorization**

Write the prime factorization of each number.

Writing Math

You can write prime factorizations by using exponents. The exponent tells how many times to use the base as a factor.

A 36

```
        36
       /  \
      4  ·  9
     / \   / \
    2 · 2 · 3 · 3
```

Write 36 as the product of two factors.

Continue factoring until all factors are prime.

The prime factorization of 36 is $2 \cdot 2 \cdot 3 \cdot 3$, or $2^2 \cdot 3^2$.

Write the prime factorization of each number.

(B) 280

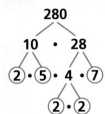

Write 280 as the product of two factors.

Continue factoring until all factors are prime.

The prime factorization of 280 is $2 \cdot 2 \cdot 2 \cdot 5 \cdot 7$, or $2^3 \cdot 5 \cdot 7$.

You can also use a step diagram to find the prime factorization of a number. At each step, divide by a prime factor. Continue dividing until the quotient is 1.

EXAMPLE 3 Using a Step Diagram to Find Prime Factorization

Write the prime factorization of each number.

(A) 252

```
2 | 252        Divide 252 by 2. Write the quotient below 252.
2 | 126        Keep dividing by a prime factor.
  3 | 63
    3 | 21
      7 | 7
        1      Stop when the quotient is 1.
```

The prime factorization of 252 is $2 \cdot 2 \cdot 3 \cdot 3 \cdot 7$, or $2^2 \cdot 3^2 \cdot 7$.

(B) 495

```
3 | 495        Divide 495 by 3.
  3 | 165      Keep dividing by a prime factor.
    5 | 55
     11 | 11
         1     Stop when the quotient is 1.
```

The prime factorization of 495 is $3 \cdot 3 \cdot 5 \cdot 11$, or $3^2 \cdot 5 \cdot 11$.

There is only one prime factorization for any given composite number. Example 3B began by dividing 495 by 3, the smallest prime factor of 495. Beginning with any prime factor of 495 gives the same result.

```
 5 | 495       11 | 495
 3 | 99         3 | 45
 3 | 33         5 | 15
11 | 11         3 | 3
      1             1
```

Think and Discuss   GPS M7P3.a, M7P3.b

1. **Explain** how to decide whether 47 is prime.

2. **Compare** prime numbers and composite numbers.

Georgia Performance
Standards

M7P1.b, M7P3.a, M7P4.c

go.hrw.com
Homework Help Online
KEYWORD: MS7 2-6
Parent Resources Online
KEYWORD: MS7 Parent

GUIDED PRACTICE

See Example **1**   Tell whether each number is prime or composite.

1. 7   **2.** 15   **3.** 49   **4.** 12

See Example **2**   Write the prime factorization of each number.

5. 16   **6.** 54   **7.** 81   **8.** 105

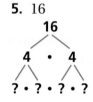

9. 18   **10.** 26   **11.** 45   **12.** 80

See Example **3**   **13.** 250   **14.** 190   **15.** 100   **16.** 360

17. 639   **18.** 414   **19.** 1,000   **20.** 140

INDEPENDENT PRACTICE

See Example **1**   Tell whether each number is prime or composite.

21. 31   **22.** 18   **23.** 67   **24.** 8

25. 77   **26.** 5   **27.** 9   **28.** 113

See Example **2**   Write the prime factorization of each number.

29. 68   **30.** 75   **31.** 120   **32.** 150

33. 135   **34.** 48   **35.** 154   **36.** 210

37. 800   **38.** 310   **39.** 625   **40.** 2,000

See Example **3**   **41.** 315   **42.** 728   **43.** 189   **44.** 396

45. 242   **46.** 700   **47.** 187   **48.** 884

49. 1,225   **50.** 288   **51.** 360   **52.** 1,152

PRACTICE AND PROBLEM SOLVING

CRCT GPS

Extra Practice p. 728

Complete the prime factorization for each composite number.

53. $180 = 2^2 \cdot \blacksquare \cdot 5$ **54.** $462 = 2 \cdot 3 \cdot 7 \cdot \blacksquare$ **55.** $1{,}575 = 3^2 \cdot \blacksquare \cdot 7$

56. $117 = 3^2 \cdot \blacksquare$ **57.** $144 = \blacksquare \cdot 3^2$ **58.** $13{,}000 = 2^3 \cdot \blacksquare \cdot 13$

59. Critical Thinking One way to factor 64 is $1 \cdot 64$.

  a. What other ways can 64 be written as the product of two factors?

  b. How many prime factorizations of 64 are there?

60. Critical Thinking If the prime factors of a number are all the prime numbers less than 10 and no factor is repeated, what is the number?

61. Critical Thinking A number n is a prime factor of 28 and 63. What is the number?

62. A rectangular area on a farm has side lengths that are factors of 308. One of the side lengths is a prime number. Which of the areas in the diagram have the correct dimensions?

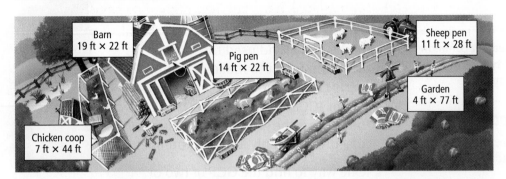

Barn
19 ft × 22 ft

Pig pen
14 ft × 22 ft

Sheep pen
11 ft × 28 ft

Garden
4 ft × 77 ft

Chicken coop
7 ft × 44 ft

63. Business Eric is catering a party for 152 people. He wants to seat the same number of people at each table. He also wants more than 2 people but fewer than 10 people at a table. How many people can he seat at each table?

64. Write a Problem Using the information in the table, write a problem using prime factorization that includes the number of calories per serving of the melons.

65. Write About It Describe how to use factor trees to find the prime factorization of a number.

66. Challenge Find the smallest number that is divisible by 2, 3, 4, 5, 6, 7, 8, 9, and 10.

Fruit	Calories per Serving
Cantaloupe	66
Watermelon	15
Honeydew	42

67. Multiple Choice Which is the prime factorization of 75?

Ⓐ $3^2 \cdot 5$　　　Ⓑ $3 \cdot 5^2$　　　Ⓒ $3^2 \cdot 5^2$　　　Ⓓ $3 \cdot 5^3$

68. Multiple Choice Write the composite number for $2 \cdot 3^3 \cdot 5^2$.

Ⓕ 84　　　Ⓖ 180　　　Ⓗ 450　　　Ⓙ 1,350

69. Short Response Create two different factor trees for 120. Then write the prime factorization for 120.

Multiply. (Lesson 1-4)

70. $2.45 \cdot 10^3$　　　**71.** $58.7 \cdot 10^1$　　　**72.** $200 \cdot 10^2$　　　**73.** $1,480 \cdot 10^4$

Solve each equation. Check your answer. (Lesson 2-5)

74. $3x = -6$　　　**75.** $y - 4 = -3$　　　**76.** $z + 4 = 3 - 5$　　　**77.** $0 = -4x$

2-7 Greatest Common Factor

Learn to find the greatest common factor of two or more whole numbers.

Vocabulary

greatest common factor (GCF)

When getting ready for the Fall Festival, Sasha and David used the greatest common factor to make matching party favors. The **greatest common factor (GCF)** of two or more whole numbers is the greatest whole number that divides evenly into each number.

One way to find the GCF of two or more numbers is to list all the factors of each number. The GCF is the greatest factor that appears in all the lists.

Georgia Performance Standards

M7P4.a Recognize and use connections among mathematical ideas. Also, M7P1.c, M7P1.d, M7P4.b.

EXAMPLE 1 Using a List to Find the GCF

Find the greatest common factor (GCF) of 24, 36, and 48.

Factors of 24: 1, 2, 3, 4, 6, 8, ⑫, 24
Factors of 36: 1, 2, 3, 4, 6, 9, ⑫, 18, 36
Factors of 48: 1, 2, 3, 4, 6, 8, ⑫, 16, 24, 48

The GCF is 12.

List all the factors of each number.

Circle the greatest factor that is in all the lists.

A second way to find the GCF is to use prime factorization.

EXAMPLE 2 Using Prime Factorization to Find the GCF

Find the greatest common factor (GCF).

Ⓐ 60, 45

$60 = 2 \cdot 2 \cdot ③ \cdot ⑤$
$45 = ③ \cdot 3 \cdot ⑤$

Write the prime factorization of each number and circle the common prime factors.

$3 \cdot 5 = 15$

Multiply the common prime factors.

The GCF is 15.

Ⓑ 504, 132, 96, 60

$504 = ②\cdot②\cdot 2 \cdot ③\cdot 3 \cdot 7$
$132 = ②\cdot②\cdot③\cdot 11$
$\;96 = ②\cdot②\cdot 2 \cdot 2 \cdot 2 \cdot③$
$\;60 = ②\cdot②\cdot③\cdot 5$

Write the prime factorization of each number and circle the common prime factors.

$2 \cdot 2 \cdot 3 = 12$

Multiply the common prime factors.

The GCF is 12.

EXAMPLE 3

PROBLEM SOLVING

PROBLEM SOLVING APPLICATION

Sasha and David are making centerpieces for the Fall Festival. They have 50 small pumpkins and 30 ears of corn. What is the greatest number of matching centerpieces they can make using all of the pumpkins and corn?

1 Understand the Problem

Rewrite the question as a statement.
- Find the greatest number of centerpieces they can make.

List the **important information:**
- There are 50 pumpkins.
- There are 30 ears of corn.
- Each centerpiece must have the same number of pumpkins and the same number of ears of corn.

The **answer** will be the GCF of 50 and 30.

2 Make a Plan

You can write the prime factorizations of 50 and 30 to find the GCF.

3 Solve

$$50 = ②\cdot⑤\cdot 5$$
$$30 = ②\cdot 3 \cdot⑤ \quad \textit{Multiply the prime factors that are}$$
$$2 \cdot 5 = 10 \quad \textit{common to both 50 and 30.}$$

Sasha and David can make 10 centerpieces.

4 Look Back

If Sasha and David make 10 centerpieces, each one will have 5 pumpkins and 3 ears of corn, with nothing left over.

Think and Discuss   GPS M7P2.b, M7P2.c, M7P3.d

1. **Tell** what the letters GCF stand for and explain what the GCF of two numbers is.

2. **Discuss** whether the GCF of two numbers could be a prime number.

3. **Explain** whether every factor of the GCF of two numbers is also a factor of each number. Give an example.

Georgia Performance
Standards
M7P3.a, M7P3.c, M7P4.c

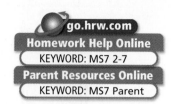

go.hrw.com
Homework Help Online
KEYWORD: MS7 2-7
Parent Resources Online
KEYWORD: MS7 Parent

GUIDED PRACTICE

See Example 1 **Find the greatest common factor (GCF).**

1. 30, 42   **2.** 36, 45   **3.** 24, 36, 60, 84

See Example 2   **4.** 60, 231   **5.** 12, 28   **6.** 20, 40, 50, 120

See Example 3   **7.** The Math Club members are preparing identical welcome kits for the sixth-graders. They have 60 pencils and 48 memo pads. What is the greatest number of kits they can prepare using all of the pencils and memo pads?

INDEPENDENT PRACTICE

See Example 1 **Find the greatest common factor (GCF).**

8. 60, 126   **9.** 12, 36   **10.** 75, 90

11. 22, 121   **12.** 28, 42   **13.** 38, 76

See Example 2 **14.** 28, 60   **15.** 54, 80   **16.** 30, 45, 60, 105

17. 26, 52   **18.** 11, 44, 77 **19.** 18, 27, 36, 48

See Example 3 **20.** Hetty is making identical gift baskets for the Senior Citizens Center. She has 39 small soap bars and 26 small bottles of lotion. What is the greatest number of baskets she can make using all of the soap bars and bottles of lotion?

PRACTICE AND PROBLEM SOLVING

Extra Practice p. 728

Find the greatest common factor (GCF).

21. 5, 7   **22.** 12, 15   **23.** 4, 6

24. 9, 11   **25.** 22, 44, 66 **26.** 77, 121

27. 80, 120   **28.** 20, 28   **29.** 2, 3, 4, 5, 7

30. 4, 6, 10, 22   **31.** 14, 21, 35, 70   **32.** 6, 10, 11, 14

33. 6, 15, 33, 48 **34.** 18, 45, 63, 81   **35.** 13, 39, 52, 78

36. Critical Thinking Which pair of numbers has a GCF that is a prime number, 48 and 90 or 105 and 56?

37. Museum employees are preparing an exhibit of ancient coins. They have 49 copper coins and 35 silver coins to arrange on shelves. Each shelf will have the same number of copper coins and the same number of silver coins. How many shelves will the employees need for this exhibit?

38. Multi-Step Todd and Elizabeth are making treat bags for the hospital volunteers. They have baked 56 shortbread cookies and 84 lemon bars. What is the greatest number of bags they can make if all volunteers receive identical treat bags? How many cookies and how many lemon bars will each bag contain?

Georgia LINK

Art

This sculpture called "Coca-Cola Bottle, #38,348" by Howard Finster is part of the permanent collection of the High Museum of Art in Atlanta.

39. School Some of the students in the Math Club signed up to bring food and drinks to a party.

   a. If each club member gets the same amount of each item at the party, how many students are in the Math Club?

   b. How many cookies, pizza slices, cans of juice, and apples can each club member have at the party?

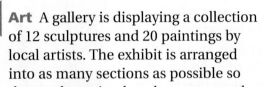
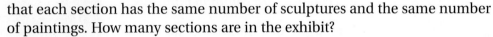

Food and Drink Sign-up Sheet

Student	Item	Amount
Erica	Apples	14
Alejandro	Pizza	21 slices
Michael	Juice	7 cans
Jennifer	Gingerbread Cookies	35

40. Art A gallery is displaying a collection of 12 sculptures and 20 paintings by local artists. The exhibit is arranged into as many sections as possible so that each section has the same number of sculptures and the same number of paintings. How many sections are in the exhibit?

41. What's the Error? A student used these factor trees to find the GCF of 50 and 70. The student decided that the GCF is 5. Explain the student's error and give the correct GCF.

42. Write About It The GCF of 1,274 and 1,365 is 91, or 7 · 13. Are 7, 13, and 91 factors of both 1,274 and 1,365? Explain.

43. Challenge Find three *composite* numbers that have a GCF of 1.

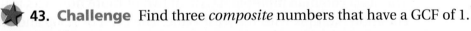

CRCT PREP • GPS SUPPORT • SPIRAL REVIEW

44. Gridded Response What is the greatest common factor of 28 and 91?

45. Multiple Choice Which pair of numbers has a greatest common factor that is NOT a prime number?

  Ⓐ 15, 20   Ⓑ 18, 30   Ⓒ 24, 75   Ⓓ 6, 10

Find each value. (Lesson 1-2)

46. 10^3 **47.** 13^1 **48.** 6^3 **49.** 3^4

Use a number line to find each sum or difference. (Lessons 2-2 and 2-3)

50. $-5 + (-3)$ **51.** $2 - 7$ **52.** $4 + (-8)$ **53.** $-3 - (-5)$

Complete the prime factorization for each composite number. (Lesson 2-6)

54. $100 = \blacksquare \cdot 5^2$ **55.** $147 = 3 \cdot \blacksquare$ **56.** $270 = 2 \cdot 3^3 \cdot \blacksquare$ **57.** $140 = \blacksquare \cdot 5 \cdot 7$

2-8 Least Common Multiple

Learn to find the least common multiple of two or more whole numbers.

Vocabulary

multiple

least common multiple (LCM)

Georgia Performance Standards

M7P1.c Apply and adapt a variety of appropriate strategies to solve problems. Also, M7P4.a, M7P4.b, M7P4.c.

The maintenance schedule on Kendra's pickup truck shows that the tires should be rotated every 7,500 miles and that the oil filter should be replaced every 5,000 miles. What is the lowest mileage at which both services are due at the same time? To find the answer, you can use *least common multiples.*

A **multiple** of a number is the product of that number and a nonzero whole number. Some multiples of 7,500 and 5,000 are as follows:

7,500: 7,500, **15,000**, 22,500, **30,000**, 37,500, 45,000, . . .
5,000: 5,000, 10,000, **15,000**, 20,000, 25,000, **30,000**, . . .

A common multiple of two or more numbers is a number that is a multiple of each of the given numbers. So **15,000** and **30,000** are common multiples of 7,500 and 5,000.

The **least common multiple (LCM)** of two or more numbers is the common multiple with the least value. The LCM of 7,500 and 5,000 is **15,000**. This is the lowest mileage at which both services are due at the same time.

EXAMPLE 1 **Using a List to Find the LCM**

Find the least common multiple (LCM).

A 3, 5

Multiples of 3: 3, 6, 9, 12, ⑮, 18   *List multiples of each number.*
Multiples of 5: 5, 10, ⑮, 20, 25   *Find the least value that is in both lists.*

The LCM is 15.

B 4, 6, 12

Multiples of 4: 4, 8, ⑫, 16, 20, 24, 28   *List multiples of each number.*
Multiples of 6: 6, ⑫, 18, 24, 30   *Find the least value that is in all the lists.*
Multiples of 12: ⑫, 24, 36, 48

The LCM is 12.

Sometimes, listing the multiples of numbers is not the easiest way to find the LCM. For example, the LCM of 78 and 110 is 4,290. You would have to list 55 multiples of 78 and 39 multiples of 110 to reach 4,290!

EXAMPLE **Using Prime Factorization to Find the LCM**

Find the least common multiple (LCM).

A **78, 110**

$78 = \boxed{2} \cdot 3 \cdot 13$ *Write the prime factorization of each number.*
$110 = \boxed{2} \cdot 5 \cdot 11$ *Circle the common prime factors.*

②, 3, 13, 5, 11   *List the prime factors of the numbers, using the circled factors only once.*

$2 \cdot 3 \cdot 13 \cdot 5 \cdot 11$ *Multiply the factors in the list.*

The LCM is 4,290.

B **9, 27, 45**

$9 = \boxed{3} \cdot \boxed{3}$ *Write the prime factorization of each number.*
$27 = \boxed{3} \cdot \boxed{3} \cdot 3$ *Circle the common prime factors.*
$45 = \boxed{3} \cdot \boxed{3} \cdot 5$

③, ③, 3, 5   *List the prime factors of the numbers, using the circled factors only once.*

$3 \cdot 3 \cdot 3 \cdot 5$ *Multiply the factors in the list.*

The LCM is 135.

EXAMPLE **Recreation Application**

Charla and her little brother are walking laps on a track. Charla walks one lap every 4 minutes, and her brother walks one lap every 6 minutes. They start together. In how many minutes will they be together at the starting line again?

Find the LCM of 4 and 6.

$4 = \boxed{2} \cdot 2$
$6 = \boxed{2} \cdot 3$

The LCM is ② $\cdot \, 2 \cdot 3 = 12$.

They will be together at the starting line in 12 minutes.

GPS M7P1.d, M7P3.a, M7P3.b

Think and Discuss

1. Tell what the letters LCM stand for and explain what the LCM of two numbers is.

2. Describe a way to remember the difference between GCF and LCM.

3. List four common multiples of 6 and 9 that are not the LCM.

2-8 **Exercises**

Georgia Performance
Standards

M7P1.a, M7P1.b, M7P3.a

go.hrw.com
Homework Help Online
KEYWORD: MS7 2-8
Parent Resources Online
KEYWORD: MS7 Parent

GUIDED PRACTICE

See Example Find the least common multiple (LCM).

1. 4, 7
2. 14, 21, 28
3. 4, 8, 12, 16

See Example **4.** 30, 48
5. 3, 9, 15
6. 10, 40, 50

See Example **7.** Jerry and his dad are walking around the track. Jerry completes one lap every 8 minutes. His dad completes one lap every 6 minutes. They start together. In how many minutes will they be together at the starting line again?

INDEPENDENT PRACTICE

See Example Find the least common multiple (LCM).

8. 6, 9
9. 8, 12
10. 15, 20

11. 6, 14
12. 18, 27
13. 8, 10, 12

See Example **14.** 6, 27
15. 16, 20
16. 12, 15, 22

17. 10, 15, 18, 20
18. 11, 22, 44
19. 8, 12, 18, 20

See Example **20.** **Recreation** On her bicycle, Anna circles the block every 4 minutes. Her brother, on his scooter, circles the block every 10 minutes. They start out together. In how many minutes will they meet again at the starting point?

21. Rod helped his mom plant a vegetable garden. Rod planted a row every 30 minutes, and his mom planted a row every 20 minutes. If they started together, how long will it be before they both finish a row at the same time?

PRACTICE AND PROBLEM SOLVING

Extra Practice p. 729

Find the least common multiple (LCM).

22. 3, 7
23. 4, 6
24. 9, 12

25. 22, 44, 66
26. 80, 120
27. 10, 18

28. 3, 5, 7
29. 3, 6, 12
30. 5, 7, 9

31. 24, 36, 48
32. 2, 3, 4, 5
33. 14, 21, 35, 70

34. Jack mows the lawn every three weeks and washes the car every two weeks. If he does both today, how many days will pass before he does them both on the same day again?

35. **Critical Thinking** Is it possible for two numbers to have the same LCM and GCF? Explain.

36. **Multi-Step** Milli jogs every day, bikes every 3 days, and swims once a week. She does all three activities on October 3. On what date will she next perform all three activities?

The Mayan, the Chinese, and the standard western calendar are all based on cycles.

37. The Mayan ceremonial calendar, or *tzolkin*, was 260 days long. It was composed of two independent cycles, a 13-day cycle and a 20-day cycle. At the beginning of the calendar, both cycles are at day 1. Will both cycles be at day 1 at the same time again before the 260 days are over? If so, when?

38. The Chinese calendar has 12 months of 30 days each and 6-day weeks. The Chinese New Year begins on the first day of a month and the first day of a week. Will the first day of a month and the first day of a week occur again at the same time before the 360-day year is over? If so, when? Explain your answer.

39. **Write About It** The Julian Date calendar assigns each day a unique number. It begins on day 0 and adds 1 for each new day. So JD 2266296, or October 12, 1492, is 2,266,296 days from the beginning of the calendar. What are some advantages of using the Julian Date calendar? What are some advantages of using calendars that are based on cycles?

40. **Challenge** The Mayan Long Count calendar used the naming system at right. Assuming the calendar began on JD 584285, express JD 2266296 in terms of the Mayan Long Count calendar. Start by finding the number of pictun that had passed up to that date.

Mayan Long Count Calendar
1 Pictun = 20 Baktun = 2,880,000 days
1 Baktun = 20 Katun = 144,000 days
1 Katun = 20 Tun = 7,200 days
1 Tun = 18 Winal = 360 days
1 Winal = 20 Kin = 20 days
1 Kin = 1 day

CRCT PREP • GPS SUPPORT • SPIRAL REVIEW

41. Multiple Choice Which is the least common multiple of 4 and 10?

   (A) 2   (B) 10   (C) 20   (D) 40

42. Multiple Choice Which pair of numbers has a least common multiple of 150?

   (F) 10, 15   (G) 150, 300   (H) 2, 300   (J) 15, 50

Simplify each expression. (Lesson 1-9)

43. $3c + 2c - 2$ **44.** $5x + 3x^2 - 2x$ **45.** $7u + 3v - 4$ **46.** $m + 1 - 6m$

Find the greatest common factor (GCF). (Lesson 2-7)

47. 12, 28   **48.** 16, 24   **49.** 15, 75   **50.** 28, 70

READY TO GO ON?

Quiz for Lessons 2-6 Through 2-8

2-6 Prime Factorization

Complete each factor tree to find the prime factorization.

1. 24
6 · 4
? · ? · ? · ?

2. 140
14 · 10
? · ? · ? · ?

3. 45
3 · ?
3 · ? · ?

4. 42
? · ?
3 · 7 · ?

Write the prime factorization of each number.

5. 96
6. 125
7. 99
8. 105
9. 324
10. 500

2-7 Greatest Common Factor

Find the greatest common factor (GCF).

11. 66, 96
12. 18, 27, 45
13. 16, 28, 44
14. 14, 28, 56
15. 85, 102
16. 76, 95
17. 52, 91, 104
18. 30, 75, 90
19. 118, 116

20. Yasmin and Jon have volunteered to prepare snacks for the first-grade field trip. They have 63 carrot sticks and 105 strawberries. What is the greatest number of identical snacks they can prepare using all of the carrot sticks and strawberries?

2-8 Least Common Multiple

Find the least common multiple (LCM).

21. 35, 40
22. 8, 25
23. 64, 72
24. 12, 20
25. 21, 33
26. 6, 30
27. 20, 42
28. 9, 13
29. 14, 18

30. Eddie goes jogging every other day, lifts weights every third day, and swims every fourth day. If Eddie begins all three activities on Monday, how many days will it be before he does all three activities on the same day again?

31. Sean and his mom start running around a 1-mile track at the same time. Sean runs 1 mile every 8 minutes. His mom runs 1 mile every 10 minutes. In how many minutes will they be together at the starting line again?

Focus on Problem Solving

Look Back

• **Check that your answer is reasonable**

In some situations, such as when you are looking for an estimate or completing a multiple-choice question, check to see whether a solution or answer is reasonably accurate. One way to do this is by rounding the numbers to the nearest multiple of 10 or 100, depending on how large the numbers are. Sometimes it is useful to round one number up and another down.

Read each problem, and determine whether the given solution is too high, is too low, or appears to be correct. Explain your answer.

1 The cheerleading team is preparing to host a spaghetti dinner as a fund-raising project. They have set up and decorated 54 tables in the gymnasium. Each table can seat 8 people. How many people can be seated at the spaghetti dinner?

Solution: 432 people

2 The cheerleaders need to raise $4,260 to attend a cheerleader camp. How much money must they charge each person if they are expecting 400 people at the spaghetti dinner?

Solution: $4

3 To help out the fund-raising project, local restaurants have offered $25 gift certificates to give as door prizes. One gift certificate will be given for each door prize, and there will be six door prizes in all. What is the total value of all of the gift certificates given by the restaurants?

Solution: $250

4 The total cost of hosting the spaghetti dinner will be about $270. If the cheerleaders make $3,280 in ticket sales, how much money will they have after paying for the spaghetti dinner?

Solution: $3,000

5 Eighteen cheerleaders and two coaches plan to attend the camp. If each person will have an equal share of the $4,260 expense money, how much money will each person have?

Solution: $562

2-9 Equivalent Fractions and Mixed Numbers

Learn to identify, write, and convert between equivalent fractions and mixed numbers.

Vocabulary
equivalent fractions

improper fraction

mixed number

Georgia Performance Standards

M7N1.d Solve problems using rational numbers. Also, M7P4.a, M7P4.b, M7P5.c.

In some recipes the amounts of ingredients are given as fractions, and sometimes those amounts don't equal the fractions on a measuring cup. Knowing how fractions relate to each other can be very helpful.

Different fractions can name the same number.

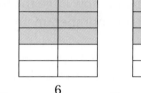

$$\frac{3}{5} = \frac{6}{10} = \frac{15}{25}$$

In the diagram, $\frac{3}{5} = \frac{6}{10} = \frac{15}{25}$. These are called **equivalent fractions** because they are different expressions for the same nonzero number.

To create fractions equivalent to a given fraction, multiply or divide the numerator and denominator by the same number.

EXAMPLE 1 **Finding Equivalent Fractions**

Find two fractions equivalent to $\frac{14}{16}$.

$\frac{14}{16} = \frac{14 \cdot 2}{16 \cdot 2} = \frac{28}{32}$ *Multiply the numerator and denominator by 2.*

$\frac{14}{16} = \frac{14 \div 2}{16 \div 2} = \frac{7}{8}$ *Divide the numerator and denominator by 2.*

The fractions $\frac{7}{8}$, $\frac{14}{16}$, and $\frac{28}{32}$ in Example 1 are equivalent, but only $\frac{7}{8}$ is in simplest form. A fraction is in simplest form when the greatest common factor of its numerator and denominator is 1.

EXAMPLE 2 **Writing Fractions in Simplest Form**

Write the fraction $\frac{24}{36}$ in simplest form.

Find the GCF of 24 and 36.

$24 = 2 \cdot 2 \cdot 2 \cdot 3$ *The GCF is $12 = 2 \cdot 2 \cdot 3$.*

$36 = 2 \cdot 2 \cdot 3 \cdot 3$

$\frac{24}{36} = \frac{24 \div 12}{36 \div 12} = \frac{2}{3}$ *Divide the numerator and denominator by 12.*

To determine if two fractions are equivalent, find a common denominator and compare the numerators.

EXAMPLE 3 Determining Whether Fractions Are Equivalent

Determine whether the fractions in each pair are equivalent.

A $\frac{6}{8}$ and $\frac{9}{12}$

Both fractions can be written with a denominator of 4.

$$\frac{6}{8} = \frac{6 \div 2}{8 \div 2} = \frac{3}{4} \qquad\qquad \frac{9}{12} = \frac{9 \div 3}{12 \div 3} = \frac{3}{4}$$

The numerators are equal, so the fractions are equivalent.

B $\frac{18}{15}$ and $\frac{25}{20}$

Both fractions can be written with a denominator of 60.

$$\frac{18}{15} = \frac{18 \cdot 4}{15 \cdot 4} = \frac{72}{60} \qquad\qquad \frac{25}{20} = \frac{25 \cdot 3}{20 \cdot 3} = \frac{75}{60}$$

The numerators are *not* equal, so the fractions are *not* equivalent.

$\frac{8}{5}$ is an **improper fraction**. Its numerator is greater than its denominator.

$$\frac{8}{5} = 1\frac{3}{5}$$

$1\frac{3}{5}$ is a **mixed number**. It contains both a whole number and a fraction.

EXAMPLE 4 Converting Between Improper Fractions and Mixed Numbers

Remember!

$$\begin{array}{r} \text{Quotient} \longrightarrow 5 \\ 4)\overline{21} \\ -20 \\ \hline \text{Remainder} \longrightarrow 1 \end{array}$$

A Write $\frac{21}{4}$ as a mixed number.

First divide the numerator by the denominator.

$$\frac{21}{4} = 5\frac{1}{4} \quad \textit{Use the quotient and remainder to write the mixed number.}$$

B Write $4\frac{2}{3}$ as an improper fraction.

First multiply the denominator and whole number, and then add the numerator.

 $4\frac{2}{3} = \frac{3 \cdot 4 + 2}{3} = \frac{14}{3}$ *Use the result to write the improper fraction.*

Think and Discuss    GPS M7P3.a, M7P3.b

1. Explain a process for finding common denominators.

2. Describe how to convert between improper fractions and mixed numbers.

2-9 Exercises

Georgia Performance
Standards
M7P1.b, M7P3.a, M7P4.c

go.hrw.com
Homework Help Online
KEYWORD: MS7 2-9
Parent Resources Online
KEYWORD: MS7 Parent

GUIDED PRACTICE

See Example 1 **Find two fractions equivalent to the given fraction.**

1. $\frac{21}{42}$ **2.** $\frac{33}{55}$ **3.** $\frac{10}{12}$ **4.** $\frac{15}{40}$

See Example 2 **Write each fraction in simplest form.**

5. $\frac{13}{26}$ **6.** $\frac{54}{72}$ **7.** $\frac{12}{15}$ **8.** $\frac{36}{42}$

See Example 3 **Determine whether the fractions in each pair are equivalent.**

9. $\frac{3}{9}$ and $\frac{6}{8}$ **10.** $\frac{10}{12}$ and $\frac{20}{24}$ **11.** $\frac{8}{6}$ and $\frac{20}{15}$ **12.** $\frac{15}{8}$ and $\frac{19}{12}$

See Example 4 **Write each as a mixed number.**

13. $\frac{15}{4}$ **14.** $\frac{22}{5}$ **15.** $\frac{17}{13}$ **16.** $\frac{14}{3}$

Write each as an improper fraction.

17. $6\frac{1}{5}$ **18.** $1\frac{11}{12}$ **19.** $7\frac{3}{5}$ **20.** $2\frac{7}{16}$

INDEPENDENT PRACTICE

See Example 1 **Find two fractions equivalent to the given fraction.**

21. $\frac{18}{20}$ **22.** $\frac{25}{50}$ **23.** $\frac{9}{15}$ **24.** $\frac{42}{70}$

See Example 2 **Write each fraction in simplest form.**

25. $\frac{63}{81}$ **26.** $\frac{14}{21}$ **27.** $\frac{34}{48}$ **28.** $\frac{100}{250}$

See Example 3 **Determine whether the fractions in each pair are equivalent.**

29. $\frac{5}{10}$ and $\frac{14}{28}$ **30.** $\frac{15}{20}$ and $\frac{20}{24}$ **31.** $\frac{125}{100}$ and $\frac{40}{32}$ **32.** $\frac{10}{5}$ and $\frac{18}{8}$

33. $\frac{2}{3}$ and $\frac{12}{18}$ **34.** $\frac{8}{12}$ and $\frac{24}{36}$ **35.** $\frac{54}{99}$ and $\frac{84}{132}$ **36.** $\frac{25}{15}$ and $\frac{175}{75}$

See Example 4 **Write each as a mixed number.**

37. $\frac{19}{3}$ **38.** $\frac{13}{9}$ **39.** $\frac{81}{11}$ **40.** $\frac{71}{8}$

Write each as an improper fraction.

41. $25\frac{3}{5}$ **42.** $4\frac{7}{16}$ **43.** $9\frac{2}{3}$ **44.** $4\frac{16}{31}$

PRACTICE AND PROBLEM SOLVING

CRCT GPS

Extra Practice p. 729

45. Personal Finance Every month, Adrian pays for his own long-distance calls made on the family phone. Last month, 15 of the 60 minutes of long-distance charges were Adrian's, and he paid $2.50 of the $12 long-distance bill. Did Adrian pay his fair share?

Write a fraction equivalent to the given number.

46. 8   **47.** $6\frac{1}{2}$ **48.** $2\frac{2}{3}$ **49.** $\frac{8}{21}$ **50.** $9\frac{8}{11}$

51. $\frac{55}{10}$ **52.** 101   **53.** $6\frac{15}{21}$ **54.** $\frac{475}{75}$ **55.** $11\frac{23}{50}$

Find the equivalent pair of fractions in each set.

56. $\frac{6}{15}, \frac{21}{35}, \frac{3}{5}$ **57.** $\frac{7}{12}, \frac{12}{20}, \frac{6}{10}$ **58.** $\frac{2}{3}, \frac{12}{15}, \frac{20}{30}, \frac{15}{24}$ **59.** $\frac{7}{4}, \frac{9}{5}, \frac{32}{20}, \frac{72}{40}$

There are 12 inches in 1 foot. Write a mixed number to represent each measurement in feet. (Example: 14 inches $= 1\frac{2}{12}$ feet or $1\frac{1}{6}$ feet)

60. 25 inches   **61.** 100 inches   **62.** 362 inches   **63.** 42 inches

64. Social Studies A dollar bill is $15\frac{7}{10}$ centimeters long and $6\frac{13}{20}$ centimeters wide. Write each number as an improper fraction.

65. Food A bakery uses $37\frac{1}{2}$ cups of flour to make 25 loaves of bread each day. Write a fraction that shows how many $\frac{1}{4}$ cups of flour are used to make bread each day at the bakery.

66. Write a Problem Cal made the graph at right. Use the graph to write a problem involving fractions.

67. Write About It Draw a diagram to show how you can use division to write $\frac{25}{3}$ as a mixed number. Explain your diagram.

68. Challenge Kenichi spent $\frac{2}{5}$ of his $100 birthday check on clothes. How much did Kenichi's new clothes cost?

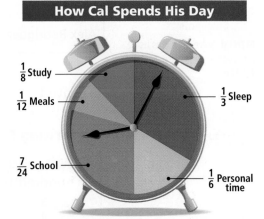

How Cal Spends His Day

$\frac{1}{8}$ Study $\frac{1}{12}$ Meals $\frac{7}{24}$ School $\frac{1}{3}$ Sleep $\frac{1}{6}$ Personal time

---

CRCT PREP • GPS SUPPORT • SPIRAL REVIEW

69. Multiple Choice Which improper fraction is NOT equivalent to $2\frac{1}{2}$?

(A) $\frac{5}{2}$ (B) $\frac{10}{4}$ (C) $\frac{20}{6}$ (D) $\frac{25}{10}$

70. Multiple Choice Which fraction is equivalent to $\frac{5}{6}$?

(F) $\frac{20}{24}$ (G) $\frac{10}{18}$ (H) $\frac{6}{7}$ (J) $\frac{6}{5}$

71. Short Response Maria needs $\frac{4}{3}$ cups of flour, $\frac{11}{4}$ cups of water, and $\frac{3}{2}$ tablespoons of sugar. Write each of these measures as a mixed number.

Solve each equation. Check your answer. (Lessons 1-11 and 1-12)

72. $5b = 25$ **73.** $6 + y = 18$ **74.** $k - 57 = 119$ **75.** $\frac{z}{4} = 20$

Find the least common multiple (LCM). (Lesson 2-8)

76. 2, 3, 4   **77.** 9, 15   **78.** 15, 20   **79.** 3, 7, 8

2-10 Equivalent Fractions and Decimals

Learn to write fractions as decimals, and vice versa, and to determine whether a decimal is terminating or repeating.

Vocabulary

terminating decimal

repeating decimal

Georgia Performance Standards

M7N1.d Solve problems using rational numbers. Also, M7P4.a, M7P4.c.

In baseball, a player's batting average compares the number of hits with the number of times the player has been at bat. The statistics below are for the 2004 Major League Baseball season.

Lance Berkman had 172 hits in the 2004 season.

Player	Hits	At Bats	Hits / At Bats	Batting Average (thousandths)
Lance Berkman	172	544	$\frac{172}{544}$	$172 \div 544 \approx 0.316$
Alex Rodriguez	172	601	$\frac{172}{601}$	$172 \div 601 \approx 0.286$

To convert a fraction to a decimal, divide the numerator by the denominator.

EXAMPLE 1 **Writing Fractions as Decimals**

Write each fraction as a decimal. Round to the nearest hundredth, if necessary.

A $\frac{3}{4}$

$$\begin{array}{r} 0.75 \\ 4\overline{)3.00} \\ -28 \\ \hline 20 \\ -20 \\ \hline 0 \end{array}$$

$\frac{3}{4} = 0.75$

B $\frac{6}{5}$

$$\begin{array}{r} 1.2 \\ 5\overline{)6.0} \\ -5 \\ \hline 10 \\ -10 \\ \hline 0 \end{array}$$

$\frac{6}{5} = 1.2$

C $\frac{1}{3}$

$$\begin{array}{r} 0.333\ldots \\ 3\overline{)1.000} \\ -9 \\ \hline 10 \\ -9 \\ \hline 10 \\ -9 \\ \hline 10 \\ -9 \\ \hline 1 \end{array}$$

$\frac{1}{3} = 0.333\ldots$
≈ 0.33

Helpful Hint

You can use a calculator to check your division:

3 ÷ 4 = 0.75

6 ÷ 5 = 1.2

1 ÷ 3 = 0.333...

The decimals 0.75 and 1.2 in Example 1 are **terminating decimals** because the decimals come to an end. The decimal 0.333... is a **repeating decimal** because the decimal repeats a pattern forever. You can also write a repeating decimal with a bar over the repeating part.

$0.333\ldots = 0.\overline{3}$ $0.8333\ldots = 0.8\overline{3}$ $0.727272\ldots = 0.\overline{72}$

You can use place value to write some fractions as decimals.

EXAMPLE 2   **Using Mental Math to Write Fractions as Decimals**

Write each fraction as a decimal.

A $\dfrac{2}{5}$

$\dfrac{2}{5} \times \dfrac{2}{2} = \dfrac{4}{10}$ *Multiply to get a power of ten in the denominator.*

$= 0.4$

B $\dfrac{7}{25}$

$\dfrac{7}{25} \times \dfrac{4}{4} = \dfrac{28}{100}$ *Multiply to get a power of ten in the denominator.*

$= 0.28$

You can also use place value to write a terminating decimal as a fraction. Use the place value of the last digit to the right of the decimal point as the denominator of the fraction.

EXAMPLE 3   **Writing Decimals as Fractions**

Write each decimal as a fraction in simplest form.

Reading Math

You read the decimal 0.036 as "thirty-six thousandths."

A 0.036

$0.036 = \dfrac{36}{1,000}$ *6 is in the thousandths place.*

$= \dfrac{36 \div 4}{1,000 \div 4}$

$= \dfrac{9}{250}$

B 1.28

$1.28 = \dfrac{128}{100}$ *8 is in the hundredths place.*

$= \dfrac{128 \div 4}{100 \div 4}$

$= \dfrac{32}{25}, \text{ or } 1\dfrac{7}{25}$

EXAMPLE 4   *Sports Application*

During a football game, Albert completed 23 of the 27 passes he attempted. Find his completion rate to the nearest thousandth.

Fraction	What the Calculator Shows	Completion Rate
$\dfrac{23}{27}$	23 ÷ 27 ENTER 0.851851852	0.852

His completion rate is 0.852.

Think and Discuss   GPS M7P1.d, M7P3.b

1. Tell how to write a fraction as a decimal.

2. Explain how to use place value to convert 0.2048 to a fraction.

Georgia Performance
Standards

M7P1.a, M7P2.c, M7P3.a

go.hrw.com
Homework Help Online
KEYWORD: MS7 2-10
Parent Resources Online
KEYWORD: MS7 Parent

GUIDED PRACTICE

See Example **1** **Write each fraction as a decimal. Round to the nearest hundredth, if necessary.**

1. $\frac{4}{7}$ **2.** $\frac{21}{8}$ **3.** $\frac{11}{6}$ **4.** $\frac{7}{9}$

See Example **2** **Write each fraction as a decimal.**

5. $\frac{3}{25}$ **6.** $\frac{7}{10}$ **7.** $\frac{1}{20}$ **8.** $\frac{3}{5}$

See Example **3** **Write each decimal as a fraction in simplest form.**

9. 0.008   **10.** −0.6   **11.** −2.05   **12.** 3.75

See Example **4** **13. Sports** After sweeping the Baltimore Orioles at home in 2001, the Seattle Mariners had a record of 103 wins out of 143 games played. Find the Mariners' winning rate. Write your answer as a decimal rounded to the nearest thousandth.

INDEPENDENT PRACTICE

See Example **1** **Write each fraction as a decimal. Round to the nearest hundredth, if necessary.**

14. $\frac{9}{10}$ **15.** $\frac{32}{5}$ **16.** $\frac{18}{25}$ **17.** $\frac{7}{8}$

18. $\frac{16}{11}$ **19.** $\frac{500}{500}$ **20.** $\frac{17}{3}$ **21.** $\frac{23}{12}$

See Example **2** **Write each fraction as a decimal.**

22. $\frac{5}{4}$ **23.** $\frac{4}{5}$ **24.** $\frac{15}{25}$ **25.** $\frac{11}{20}$

See Example **3** **Write each decimal as a fraction in simplest form.**

26. 0.45   **27.** 0.01   **28.** −0.25   **29.** −0.08

30. 1.8   **31.** 15.25   **32.** 5.09   **33.** 8.375

See Example **4** **34. School** On a test, Caleb answered 73 out of 86 questions correctly. What portion of his answers was correct? Write your answer as a decimal rounded to the nearest thousandth.

PRACTICE AND PROBLEM SOLVING

Extra Practice p. 729

Give two numbers equivalent to each fraction or decimal.

35. $8\frac{3}{4}$ **36.** 0.66   **37.** 5.05   **38.** $\frac{8}{25}$

39. 15.35   **40.** $8\frac{3}{8}$ **41.** $4\frac{3}{1,000}$ **42.** $3\frac{1}{3}$

Determine whether the numbers in each pair are equivalent.

43. $\frac{3}{4}$ and 0.75   **44.** $\frac{7}{20}$ and 0.45   **45.** $\frac{11}{21}$ and 0.55   **46.** 0.8 and $\frac{4}{5}$

47. 0.275 and $\frac{11}{40}$ **48.** $1\frac{21}{25}$ and 1.72   **49.** 0.74 and $\frac{16}{25}$ **50.** 0.35 and $\frac{7}{20}$

Use the table for Exercises 51 and 52.

XYZ Stock Values (October 2001)				
Date	Open	High	Low	Close
Oct 16	17.89	18.05	17.5	17.8
Oct 17	18.01	18.04	17.15	17.95
Oct 18	17.84	18.55	17.81	18.20

51. Write the highest value of stock XYZ for each day as a mixed number in simplest form.

52. On which date did the price of stock XYZ rise by $\frac{9}{25}$ of a dollar between the open and close of the day?

Traders watch the stock prices change from the floor of a stock exchange.

53. ✏ **Write About It** Until recently, prices of stocks were expressed as mixed numbers, such as $24\frac{15}{32}$ dollars. The denominators of such fractions were multiples of 2, such as 2, 4, 6, 8, and so forth. Today, the prices are expressed as decimals to the nearest hundredth, such as 32.35 dollars.

a. What are some advantages of using decimals instead of fractions?

b. The old ticker-tape machine punched stock prices onto a tape. Perhaps because fractions could not be shown using the machine, the prices were punched as decimals. Write some decimal equivalents of fractions that the machine might print.

Before the days of computer technology, ticker-tape machines were used to punch the stock prices onto paper strands.

54. ⭐ **Challenge** Write $\frac{1}{9}$ and $\frac{2}{9}$ as decimals. Use the results to predict the decimal equivalent of $\frac{8}{9}$.

go.hrw.com
Web Extra!
KEYWORD: MS7 Stock

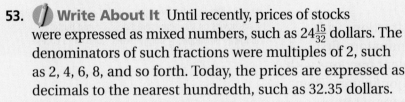

CRCT Prep • GPS Support • Spiral Review

55. **Multiple Choice** Which is NOT equivalent to 0.35?

Ⓐ $\frac{35}{100}$ Ⓑ $\frac{7}{20}$ Ⓒ $\frac{14}{40}$ Ⓓ $\frac{25}{80}$

56. **Gridded Response** Write $\frac{6}{17}$ as a decimal rounded to the nearest hundredth.

Determine whether the given value of the variable is a solution. (Lesson 1-10)

57. $x = 2$ for $3x - 4 = 1$ 58. $x = 3$ for $5x + 4 = 19$ 59. $x = 14$ for $9(4 + x) = 162$

Write each as an improper fraction. (Lesson 2-9)

60. $4\frac{1}{5}$ 61. $3\frac{1}{4}$ 62. $1\frac{2}{3}$ 63. $6\frac{1}{4}$

Comparing and Ordering Rational Numbers

**Learn** to compare and order fractions and decimals.

Vocabulary

rational number

Georgia Performance Standards

M7N1.b Compare and order rational numbers, including repeating decimals. Also, M7N1.d, M7P5.a, M7P5.c.

Which is greater, $\frac{7}{9}$ or $\frac{2}{9}$?

To compare fractions with the same denominator, just compare the numerators.

$\frac{7}{9} > \frac{2}{9}$ because $7 > 2$.

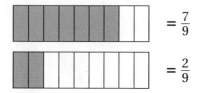

To compare fractions with unlike denominators, first write equivalent fractions with common denominators. Then compare the numerators.

I would like an extra-large pizza with $\frac{1}{2}$ pepperoni, $\frac{4}{5}$ sausage, $\frac{1}{3}$ anchovies on the pepperoni side, $\frac{3}{8}$ peanut butter fudge, $\frac{5}{11}$ pineapple, $\frac{2}{13}$ doggy treats…and extra cheese.

EXAMPLE 1 **Comparing Fractions**

Compare the fractions. Write < or >.

A $\frac{5}{6}$ $\frac{7}{10}$

The LCM of the denominators 6 and 10 is 30.

$\frac{5}{6} = \frac{5 \cdot 5}{6 \cdot 5} = \frac{25}{30}$ *Write equivalent fractions with 30 as the denominator.*

$\frac{7}{10} = \frac{7 \cdot 3}{10 \cdot 3} = \frac{21}{30}$

$\frac{25}{30} > \frac{21}{30}$, and so $\frac{5}{6} > \frac{7}{10}$.   *Compare the numerators.*

B $-\frac{3}{5}$ ■ $-\frac{5}{9}$

Both fractions can be written with a denominator of 45.

$-\frac{3}{5} = \frac{-3 \cdot 9}{5 \cdot 9} = \frac{-27}{45}$ *Write equivalent fractions with 45 as the denominator. Put the negative signs in the numerators.*

$-\frac{5}{9} = \frac{-5 \cdot 5}{9 \cdot 5} = \frac{-25}{45}$

$\frac{-27}{45} < \frac{-25}{45}$, and so $-\frac{3}{5} < -\frac{5}{9}$.

Helpful Hint

A fraction less than 0 can be written as $-\frac{3}{5}$, $\frac{-3}{5}$, or $\frac{3}{-5}$.

To compare decimals, line up the decimal points and compare digits from left to right until you find the place where the digits are different.

EXAMPLE 2 **Comparing Decimals**

Compare the decimals. Write < or >.

A 0.81 ▆ 0.84

0.81

↕

0.84

Line up the decimal points.
The tenths are the same.
Compare the hundredths: 1 < 4.

Since 0.01 < 0.04, 0.81 < 0.84.

B $0.\overline{34}$ ▆ 0.342

$0.\overline{34} = 0.3434\ldots$

↕

0.342

$0.\overline{34}$ is a repeating decimal.
Line up the decimal points.
The tenths and hundredths are the same.
Compare the thousandths: 3 > 2.

Since 0.003 > 0.002, $0.\overline{34}$ > 0.342.

A **rational number** is a number that can be written as a fraction with integers for its numerator and denominator. When rational numbers are written in a variety of forms, you can compare the numbers by writing them all in the same form.

EXAMPLE 3 **Ordering Fractions and Decimals**

Order $\frac{3}{5}$, $0.\overline{77}$, −0.1, and $1\frac{1}{5}$ from least to greatest.

$\frac{3}{5} = 0.60$ $\qquad$ $0.\overline{77} \approx 0.78$

$-0.1 = -0.10$ $\qquad$ $1\frac{1}{5} = 1.20$

Write as decimals with the same number of places.

Graph the numbers on a number line.

> **Remember!**
>
> The values on a number line increase as you move from left to right.

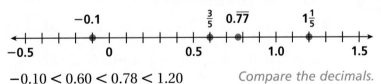

$-0.10 < 0.60 < 0.78 < 1.20$ $\qquad$ *Compare the decimals.*

From least to greatest, the numbers are -0.1, $\frac{3}{5}$, $0.\overline{77}$, and $1\frac{1}{5}$.

Think and Discuss  **GPS M7P2.c, M7P3.b**

1. Tell how to compare two fractions with different denominators.

2. Explain why −0.31 is greater than −0.325 even though 2 > 1.

2-11 Exercises

Georgia Performance
Standards
M7P3.a, M7P3.c, M7P4.c

go.hrw.com
Homework Help Online
KEYWORD: MS7 2-11
Parent Resources Online
KEYWORD: MS7 Parent

GUIDED PRACTICE

See Example 1   Compare the fractions. Write < or >.

1. $\frac{3}{5} \blacksquare \frac{4}{5}$ **2.** $-\frac{5}{8} \blacksquare -\frac{7}{8}$ **3.** $-\frac{2}{3} \blacksquare -\frac{4}{7}$ **4.** $3\frac{4}{5} \blacksquare 3\frac{2}{3}$

See Example 2   Compare the decimals. Write < or >.

5. $0.622 \blacksquare 0.625$ **6.** $0.405 \blacksquare 0.\overline{45}$ **7.** $-3.822 \blacksquare -3.819$

See Example 3   Order the numbers from least to greatest.

8. $0.\overline{55}, \frac{3}{4}, 0.505$ **9.** $2.5, 2.05, -\frac{13}{5}$ **10.** $\frac{5}{8}, -0.875, 0.877$

INDEPENDENT PRACTICE

See Example 1   Compare the fractions. Write < or >.

11. $\frac{6}{11} \blacksquare \frac{7}{11}$ **12.** $-\frac{5}{9} \blacksquare -\frac{6}{9}$ **13.** $-\frac{5}{6} \blacksquare -\frac{8}{9}$ **14.** $10\frac{3}{4} \blacksquare 10\frac{3}{5}$

15. $\frac{5}{7} \blacksquare \frac{2}{7}$ **16.** $-\frac{3}{4} \blacksquare \frac{1}{4}$ **17.** $\frac{7}{4} \blacksquare -\frac{1}{4}$ **18.** $-\frac{2}{3} \blacksquare \frac{4}{3}$

See Example 2   Compare the decimals. Write < or >.

19. $3.8 \blacksquare 3.6$ **20.** $0.088 \blacksquare 0.109$ **21.** $4.\overline{26} \blacksquare 4.266$

22. $-1.902 \blacksquare 0.920$ **23.** $-0.7 \blacksquare -0.07$ **24.** $3.\overline{08} \blacksquare 3.808$

See Example 3   Order the numbers from least to greatest.

25. $0.7, 0.755, \frac{5}{8}$ **26.** $1.82, 1.6, 1\frac{4}{5}$ **27.** $-2.25, 2.05, \frac{21}{10}$

28. $-3.\overline{02}, -3.02, 1\frac{1}{2}$ **29.** $2.88, -2.98, -2\frac{9}{10}$ **30.** $\frac{5}{6}, \frac{4}{5}, 0.82$

PRACTICE AND PROBLEM SOLVING

Extra Practice p. 729

Choose the greater number.

31. $\frac{3}{4}$ or 0.7 **32.** 0.999 or 1.0 **33.** $\frac{7}{8}$ or $\frac{13}{20}$ **34.** -0.93 or 0.2

35. 0.32 or 0.088 **36.** $-\frac{1}{2}$ or -0.05 **37.** $-\frac{9}{10}$ or $-\frac{7}{8}$ **38.** 23.44 or 23

39. Earth Science Density is a measure of the amount of matter in a specific unit of space. The mean densities (measured in grams per cubic centimeter) of the planets of our solar system are given in order of the planets' distance from the Sun. Rearrange the planets from least to most dense.

Planet	Density	Planet	Density	Planet	Density
Mercury	5.43	Mars	3.93	Uranus	1.32
Venus	5.20	Jupiter	1.32	Neptune	1.64
Earth	5.52	Saturn	0.69	Pluto*	2.05

*designated a dwarf planet in 2006

Life Science

An algae that grows in sloths' fur makes them look slightly green. This helps them blend into the trees and stay out of sight from predators.

40. Multi-Step Twenty-four karat gold is considered pure.

    a. Angie's necklace is 22-karat gold. What is its purity as a fraction?

    b. Luke's ring is 0.75 gold. Whose jewelry contains more gold, Angie's or Luke's?

41. Life Science Sloths are tree-dwelling animals that live in South and Central America. They generally sleep about $\frac{3}{4}$ of a 24-hour day. Humans sleep an average of 8 hours each day. Which sleep the most each day, sloths or humans?

42. Ecology Of Beatrice's total household water use, $\frac{5}{9}$ is for bathing, toilet flushing, and laundry. How does her water use for these purposes compare with that shown in the graph?

43. What's the Error? A recipe for a large cake called for $4\frac{1}{2}$ cups of flour. The chef added 10 one-half cupfuls of flour to the mixture. What was the chef's error?

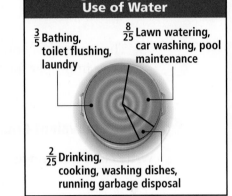

Average Daily Household Use of Water

$\frac{3}{5}$ Bathing, toilet flushing, laundry

$\frac{8}{25}$ Lawn watering, car washing, pool maintenance

$\frac{2}{25}$ Drinking, cooking, washing dishes, running garbage disposal

44. Write About It Explain how to compare a mixed number with a decimal.

45. Challenge Scientists estimate that Earth is approximately 4.6 billion years old. We are currently in what is called the Phanerozoic eon, which has made up about $\frac{7}{60}$ of the time that Earth has existed. The first eon, called the Hadean, made up approximately 0.175 of the time Earth has existed. Which eon represents the most time?

CRCT Prep • GPS Support • Spiral Review

46. Multiple Choice Which number is the greatest?

   Ⓐ 0.71   Ⓑ $\frac{5}{8}$ Ⓒ 0.65   Ⓓ $\frac{5}{7}$

47. Multiple Choice Which shows the order of the animals from fastest to slowest?

   Ⓕ Spider, tortoise, snail, sloth

   Ⓖ Snail, sloth, tortoise, spider

   Ⓗ Tortoise, spider, snail, sloth

   Ⓙ Spider, tortoise, sloth, snail

Maximum Speed (mi/h)				
Animal	Snail	Tortoise	Spider	Sloth
Speed	0.03	0.17	1.17	0.15

Compare. Write <, >, or =. (Lesson 2-1)

48. $|-14|$ ▦ -12 **49.** -7 ▦ -8 **50.** -4 ▦ 0 **51.** 3 ▦ -5

Simplify. (Lessons 2-2 and 2-3)

52. $-13 + 51$ **53.** $142 - (-27)$ **54.** $-118 - (-57)$ **55.** $-27 + 84$

READY TO GO ON?

Quiz for Lessons 2-9 Through 2-11

2-9 **Equivalent Fractions and Mixed Numbers**

Determine whether the fractions in each pair are equivalent.

1. $\frac{3}{4}$ and $\frac{2}{3}$ **2.** $\frac{3}{12}$ and $\frac{4}{16}$ **3.** $\frac{7}{25}$ and $\frac{6}{20}$ **4.** $\frac{5}{9}$ and $\frac{25}{45}$

5. There are $2\frac{54}{100}$ centimeters in an inch. When asked to write this value as an improper fraction, Aimee wrote $\frac{127}{50}$. Was she correct? Explain.

2-10 **Equivalent Fractions and Decimals**

Write each fraction as a decimal. Round to the nearest hundredth, if necessary.

6. $\frac{7}{10}$ **7.** $\frac{5}{8}$ **8.** $\frac{2}{3}$ **9.** $\frac{14}{15}$

Write each decimal as a fraction in simplest form.

10. 0.22   **11.** −0.135   **12.** −4.06   **13.** 0.07

14. In one 30-gram serving of snack crackers, there are 24 grams of carbohydrates. What fraction of a serving is made up of carbohydrates? Write your answer as a fraction and as a decimal.

15. During a softball game, Sara threw 70 pitches. Of those pitches, 29 were strikes. What portion of the pitches that Sara threw were strikes? Write your answer as a decimal rounded to the nearest thousandth.

2-11 **Comparing and Ordering Rational Numbers**

Compare the fractions. Write < or >.

16. $\frac{3}{7}$ ▮ $\frac{2}{4}$ **17.** $-\frac{1}{8}$ ▮ $-\frac{2}{11}$ **18.** $\frac{5}{4}$ ▮ $\frac{4}{5}$ **19.** $-1\frac{2}{3}$ ▮ $\frac{1}{2}$

Compare the decimals. Write < or >.

20. 0.521 ▮ 0.524   **21.** 2.05 ▮ −2.50   **22.** 3.001 ▮ 3.010   **23.** −0.26 ▮ −0.626

Order the numbers from least to greatest.

24. $\frac{3}{7}$, −0.372, −$\frac{2}{3}$, 0.5   **25.** $2\frac{9}{11}$, $\frac{4}{5}$, 2.91, 0.9

26. −5.36, 2.36, −$5\frac{1}{3}$, −$2\frac{3}{6}$ **27.** 8.75, $\frac{7}{8}$, 0.8, $\frac{8}{7}$

28. Rafael measured the rainfall at his house for 3 days. On Sunday, it rained $\frac{2}{5}$ in. On Monday, it rained $\frac{5}{8}$ in. On Wednesday, it rained 0.57 in. List the days in order from the least to the greatest amount of rainfall.

MULTI-STEP TEST PREP

Ups and Downs Plaza Tower is a recently completed skyscraper in the downtown business district. To serve each of its 60-story towers, the building has multiple banks of elevators.

1. Eleven people get on one of the skyscraper's elevators. At the first stop, 5 people get off. At the second stop, 7 people get on. At the third stop, 8 people get off. How many people remain on the elevator? Use a number line to model and solve the problem.

2. On a different trip, the number of people getting on and off the elevator is modeled by $12 + (-5) + (-3) + 4$. How many people remain on the elevator?

3. The tower has two express elevators. One stops at the first floor and at floors that are multiples of 6. The other stops at the first floor and at floors that are multiples of 8. On which floors can you catch both express elevators? Explain.

4. The table shows the times that it takes four of the tower's elevators to travel various distances. The speed of each elevator is the distance divided by the time. Which elevator is fastest? slowest? Explain your reasoning.

	Distance (ft)	Time (s)	Speed (ft/s)
Elevator A	600	29	$\frac{600}{29}$
Elevator B	574	28	$\frac{574}{28}$
Elevator C	207	10	20.7
Elevator D	$20\frac{4}{5}$	1	$20\frac{4}{5}$

Multi-Step Test Prep

Negative Exponents

Learn to evaluate negative exponents and use them to write numbers in scientific notation and in standard form.

When a whole number has a positive exponent, the value of the power is greater than 1. When a whole number has a negative exponent, the value of the power is less than 1. When any number has a zero exponent, the value of the power is equal to 1.

Power	Value
10^2	100
10^1	10
10^0	1
10^{-1}	$\frac{1}{10^1}$ or 0.1
10^{-2}	$\frac{1}{10^2}$ or 0.01
10^{-3}	$\frac{1}{10^3}$ or 0.001

$\div 10$
$\div 10$
$\div 10$
$\div 10$
$\div 10$

Do you see a pattern in the table at right? The negative exponent becomes positive when it is in the denominator of the fraction.

Georgia Performance Standards

M7N1.d Solve problems using rational numbers. Also, M7N1.b.

EXAMPLE 1 **Evaluating Negative Exponents**

Evaluate 10^{-4}.

$10^{-4} = \dfrac{1}{10^4}$ *Write the fraction with a positive exponent in the denominator.*

$= \dfrac{1}{10,000}$ *Evaluate the power.*

$= 0.0001$ *Write the decimal form.*

In Chapter 1, you learned to write large numbers in scientific notation using powers of ten with positive exponents. In the same way, you can write very small numbers in scientific notation using powers of ten with negative exponents.

EXAMPLE 2 **Writing Small Numbers in Scientific Notation**

Write 0.000065 in scientific notation.

$0.000065 = 0.000065$ *Move the decimal point 5 places to the right.*

$= 6.5 \times 0.00001$ *Write as a product of two factors.*

$= 6.5 \times 10^{-5}$ *Write in exponential form. Since the decimal point was moved 5 places, the exponent is −5.*

Remember!

Move the decimal point to get a number that is greater than or equal to 1 and less than 10.

EXAMPLE 3 **Writing Small Numbers in Standard Form**

Write 3.4×10^{-6} in standard form.

$3.4 \times 10^{-6} = 0000003.4$ *Since the exponent is −6, move the decimal point 6 places to the left.*

$= 0.0000034$

When comparing numbers in scientific notation, you may need to compare only the powers of ten to see which value is greater.

EXAMPLE 4 **Comparing Numbers Using Scientific Notation**

Compare. Write <, >, or =.

A 3.7×10^{-8} ▨ 6.1×10^{-12}

$10^{-8} > 10^{-12}$ *Compare the powers of ten.*

Since $10^{-8} > 10^{-12}$, $3.7 \times 10^{-8} > 6.1 \times 10^{-12}$.

B 4.9×10^{-5} ▨ 7.3×10^{-5}

$10^{-5} = 10^{-5}$ *Compare the powers of ten.*

Since the powers of ten are equal, compare the decimals.

$4.9 < 7.3$ *4 is less than 7.*

Since $4.9 < 7.3$, $4.9 \times 10^{-5} < 7.3 \times 10^{-5}$.

EXTENSION

Exercises

Find each value.

1. 10^{-8} **2.** 10^{-6} **3.** 10^{-5} **4.** 10^{-10} **5.** 10^{-7}

Write each number in scientific notation or standard form.

6. 0.00000021   **7.** 0.00086   **8.** 0.0000000066   **9.** 0.007

10. 0.0009   **11.** 0.0453   **12.** 0.0701   **13.** 0.00003021

14. 5.8×10^{-9} **15.** 4.5×10^{-5} **16.** 3.2×10^{-3} **17.** 1.4×10^{-11}

18. 2.77×10^{-1} **19.** 9.06×10^{-2} **20.** 7×10^{-10} **21.** 8×10^{-8}

Compare. Write <, >, or =.

22. 7.6×10^{-1} ▨ 7.7×10^{-1} **23.** 8.2×10^{-7} ▨ 8.1×10^{-6}

24. 2.8×10^{-6} ▨ 2.8×10^{-7} **25.** 5.5×10^{-2} ▨ 2.2×10^{-5}

 26. Write About It Explain the effect that a zero exponent has on a power.

Game Time

Magic Squares

A magic square is a grid with numbers, such that the numbers in each row, column, and diagonal have the same "magic" sum. Test the square at right to see an example of this.

You can use a magic square to do some amazing calculations. Cover a block of four squares (2 × 2) with a piece of paper. There is a way you can find the sum of these squares without looking at them. Try to find it. (*Hint:* What number in the magic square can you subtract from the magic sum to give you the sum of the numbers in the block? Where is that number located?)

Here's the answer: To find the sum of any block of four numbers, take 65 (the magic sum) and subtract from it the number that is diagonally two squares away from a corner of the block.

18	10	22	14	1
12	4	16	8	25
6	23	15	2	19
5	17	9	21	13
24	11	3	20	7

65 − 21 = 44

18	10	22	14	1
12	4	16	8	25
6	23	15	2	19
5	17	9	21	13
24	11	3	20	7

65 − 1 = 64

The number you subtract must fall on an extension of a diagonal of the block. For each block that you choose, there will be only one direction you can go.

Try to create a 3 × 3 magic square with the numbers 1–9.

Modified Tic-Tac-Toe

The board has a row of nine squares numbered 1 through 9. Players take turns selecting squares. The goal of the game is for a player to select squares such that any three of the player's squares add up to 15. The game can also be played with a board numbered 1 through 16 and a sum goal of 34.

A complete copy of the rules and a game board are available online.

go.hrw.com
Game Time Extra
KEYWORD: MS7 Games

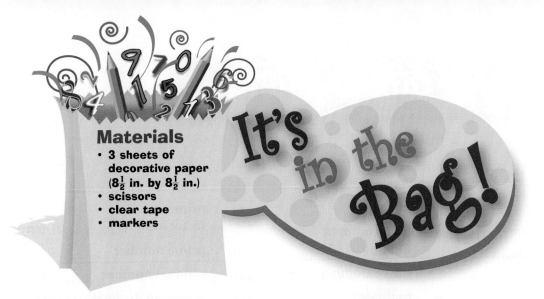

Materials
- **3 sheets of decorative paper** ($8\frac{1}{2}$ in. by $8\frac{1}{2}$ in.)
- **scissors**
- **clear tape**
- **markers**

It's in the Bag!

PROJECT **Flipping Over Integers and Rational Numbers**

Create your own flip-flop-fold book and use it to write definitions, sample problems, and practice exercises.

Directions

1. Stack the sheets of decorative paper. Fold the stack into quarters and then unfold it. Use scissors to make a slit from the edge of the stack to the center of the stack along the left-hand crease. **Figure A**

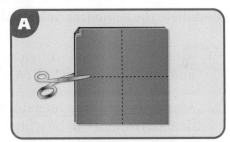

2. Place the stack in front of you with the slit on the left side. Fold the top left square over to the right side of the stack. **Figure B**

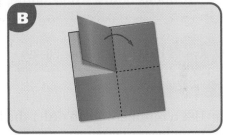

3. Now fold down the top two squares from the top right corner. Along the slit, tape the bottom left square to the top left square. **Figure C**

4. Continue folding around the stack, always in a clockwise direction. When you get to the second layer, tape the slit in the same place as before.

Taking Note of the Math

Unfold your completed booklet. This time, as you flip the pages, add definitions, sample problems, practice exercises, or any other notes you need to help you study the material in the chapter.

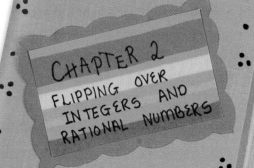

CHAPTER 2
FLIPPING OVER
INTEGERS AND
RATIONAL NUMBERS

Study Guide: Review

Vocabulary

absolute value 77

composite number 106

equivalent fractions ...120

greatest common
factor (GCF) 110

improper fraction 121

integer 76

least common
multiple (LCM) 114

mixed number 121

multiple 114

opposite 76

prime
factorization 106

prime number 106

rational number 129

repeating decimal 124

terminating decimal ...124

Complete the sentences below with vocabulary words from the list above.

1. A(n) ___?___ can be written as the ratio of one ___?___ to another and can be represented by a repeating or ___?___.

2. A(n) ___?___ has a numerator that is greater than its denominator; it can be written as a(n) ___?___, which contains both a whole number and a fraction.

2-1 Integers (pp. 76–79)

 GPS M7N1.a

EXAMPLE

■ Use a number line to order the integers from least to greatest.

3, 4, −2, 1, −3

```
←+―+―+●―+―+●―+●―+●―+●―+→
 −6  −4  −2   0   2   4   6
```

−3, −2, 1, 3, 4

EXERCISES

Compare the integers. Use < or >.

3. −8 ▮ −15   4. −7 ▮ 7

Use a number line to order the integers from least to greatest.

5. −6, 4, 0, −2, 5   6. 8, −3, 2, −8, 1

Use a number line to find each absolute value.

7. |0| 8. |−17| 9. |6|

2-2 Adding Integers (pp. 82–85)

 GPS M7A1.b

EXAMPLE

■ Find the sum.

−7 + (−11)

−7 + (−11)   *The signs are the same.*

   −18

EXERCISES

Find each sum.

10. −8 + 5   11. 7 + (−6)

12. −16 + (−40)   13. −9 + 18

14. −2 + 16   15. 12 + (−18)

2-3 Subtracting Integers (pp. 88–91)

GPS M7A1.b

EXAMPLE

■ Find the difference.

$-5 - (-3)$

$-5 + 3 = -2$ *Add the opposite of −3.*

EXERCISES

Find each difference.

16. $8 - 2$ **17.** $10 - 19$

18. $-6 - (-5)$ **19.** $-5 - 4$

2-4 Multiplying and Dividing Integers (pp. 94–97)

GPS M7P5.b

EXAMPLE

Find each product or quotient.

■ $12 \cdot (-3)$ *The signs are different, so*
  -36 *the product is negative.*

■ $-16 \div (-4)$ *The signs are the same, so*
  4 *the quotient is positive.*

EXERCISES

Find each product or quotient.

20. $5 \cdot (-10)$ **21.** $-27 \div (-9)$

22. $-2 \cdot (-8)$ **23.** $-40 \div 20$

24. $-3 \cdot 4$ **25.** $45 \div (-15)$

2-5 Solving Equations Containing Integers (pp. 100–103)

GPS M7A1.a,
M7A2.a, M7A2.b

EXAMPLE

Solve.

■ $x - 12 = 4$
  $\underline{+12 +12}$ *Add 12 to each side.*
  $x = 16$

■ $-10 = -2f$
  $\dfrac{-10}{-2} = \dfrac{-2f}{-2}$ *Divide each side by −2.*
  $5 = f$

EXERCISES

Solve.

26. $7y = 70$ **27.** $d - 8 = 6$

28. $j + 23 = -3$ **29.** $\frac{n}{36} = 2$

30. $-26 = -2c$ **31.** $28 = -7m$

32. $-15 = \frac{y}{7}$ **33.** $g - 12 = -31$

34. $-13 + p = 8$ **35.** $-8 + f = 8$

2-6 Prime Factorization (pp. 106–109)

GPS M7P5.b

EXAMPLE

■ Write the prime factorization of 56.

$56 = 8 \cdot 7 = 2 \cdot 2 \cdot 2 \cdot 7$, or $2^3 \cdot 7$

EXERCISES

Write the prime factorization.

36. 88   **37.** 27   **38.** 162   **39.** 96

2-7 Greatest Common Factor (pp. 110–113)

GPS M7P4.a

EXAMPLE

■ Find the GCF of 32 and 12.

Factors of 32: 1, 2, ④ 8, 16, 32
Factors of 12: 1, 2, 3, ④ 6, 12
The GCF is 4.

EXERCISES

Find the greatest common factor.

40. 120, 210   **41.** 81, 132

42. 36, 60, 96   **43.** 220, 440, 880

2-8 Least Common Multiple (pp. 114–117)

GPS M7P1.c

EXAMPLE

- Find the LCM of 8 and 10.

  Multiples of 8: 8, 16, 24, 32, ⓐ40
  Multiples of 10: 10, 20, 30, 40
  The LCM is 40.

EXERCISES

Find the least common multiple.

44. 5, 12   **45.** 4, 32   **46.** 3, 27

47. 15, 18   **48.** 6, 12   **49.** 5, 7, 9

2-9 Equivalent Fractions and Mixed Numbers (pp. 120–123)

GPS M7N1.d

EXAMPLE

- Write $5\frac{2}{3}$ as an improper fraction.

  $5\frac{2}{3} = \frac{3 \cdot 5 + 2}{3} = \frac{17}{3}$

- Write $\frac{17}{4}$ as a mixed number.

  $\frac{17}{4} = 4\frac{1}{4}$ *Divide the numerator by the denominator.*

EXERCISES

Write each as an improper fraction.

50. $4\frac{1}{5}$ **51.** $3\frac{1}{6}$ **52.** $10\frac{3}{4}$

Write each as a mixed number.

53. $\frac{10}{3}$ **54.** $\frac{5}{2}$ **55.** $\frac{17}{7}$

Find two fractions equivalent to the given fraction.

56. $\frac{16}{18}$ **57.** $\frac{21}{24}$ **58.** $\frac{48}{63}$

2-10 Equivalent Fractions and Decimals (pp. 124–127)

GPS M7N1.d

EXAMPLE

- Write 0.75 as a fraction in simplest form.

  $0.75 = \frac{75}{100} = \frac{75 \div 25}{100 \div 25} = \frac{3}{4}$

- Write $\frac{5}{4}$ as a decimal.

  $\frac{5}{4} = 5 \div 4 = 1.25$

EXERCISES

Write each decimal as a fraction in simplest form.

59. 0.25   **60.** −0.004   **61.** 0.05

Write each fraction as a decimal.

62. $\frac{7}{2}$ **63.** $\frac{3}{5}$ **64.** $\frac{2}{3}$

2-11 Comparing and Ordering Rational Numbers (pp. 128–131)

GPS M7N1.b, M7N1.d

EXAMPLE

- Compare. Write $<$ or $>$.

  $-\frac{3}{4} \,\blacksquare\, -\frac{2}{3}$

  $-\frac{3}{4} \cdot \frac{3}{3} \,\blacksquare\, -\frac{2}{3} \cdot \frac{4}{4}$ *Write as fractions with common denominators.*

  $-\frac{9}{12} < -\frac{8}{12}$

EXERCISES

Compare. Write $<$ or $>$.

65. $\frac{4}{5} \,\blacksquare\, 0.81$ **66.** $0.22 \,\blacksquare\, \frac{3}{20}$

67. $-\frac{3}{5} \,\blacksquare\, -1.5$ **68.** $1\frac{1}{8} \,\blacksquare\, 1\frac{2}{9}$

69. Order $\frac{6}{13}$, 0.58, −0.55, and $\frac{1}{2}$ from least to greatest.

CHAPTER TEST

Use a number line to order the integers from least to greatest.

1. $-4, 3, -2, 0, 1$

2. $7, -6, 5, -8, -3$

Use a number line to find each absolute value.

3. $|11|$

4. $|-5|$

5. $|-74|$

6. $|-1|$

Find each sum, difference, product, or quotient.

7. $-7 + (-3)$

8. $-6 - 3$

9. $17 - (-9) - 8$

10. $102 + (-97) + 3$

11. $-3 \cdot 20$

12. $-36 \div 12$

13. $-400 \div (-10)$

14. $-5 \cdot (-2) \cdot 9$

Solve.

15. $w - 4 = -6$

16. $x + 5 = -5$

17. $-6a = 60$

18. $\dfrac{n}{-4} = 12$

19. Kathryn's tennis team has won 52 matches. Her team has won 9 more matches than Rebecca's team. How many matches has Rebecca's team won this season?

Write the prime factorization of each number.

20. 30

21. 66

22. 78

23. 110

Find the greatest common factor (GCF).

24. 18, 27, 45

25. 16, 28, 44

26. 14, 28, 56

27. 24, 36, 64

Find the least common multiple (LCM).

28. 24, 36, 64

29. 24, 72, 144

30. 12, 15, 36

31. 9, 16, 25

Determine whether the fractions in each pair are equivalent.

32. $\dfrac{6}{12}$ and $\dfrac{13}{26}$

33. $\dfrac{17}{20}$ and $\dfrac{20}{24}$

34. $\dfrac{30}{24}$ and $\dfrac{35}{28}$

35. $\dfrac{5}{3}$ and $\dfrac{8}{5}$

Write each fraction as a decimal. Write each decimal as a fraction in simplest form.

36. $\dfrac{3}{50}$

37. $\dfrac{25}{10}$

38. 3.15

39. 0.004

40. The Drama Club has 52 members. Of these members, 18 are in the seventh grade. What fraction of the Drama Club is made up of seventh-graders? Write your answer as a fraction and a decimal. Round the decimal to the nearest thousandth.

Compare. Write < or >.

41. $\dfrac{2}{3}$ ▇ 0.62

42. 1.5 ▇ $1\dfrac{6}{20}$

43. $-\dfrac{9}{7}$ ▇ -1

44. $\dfrac{11}{5}$ ▇ $1\dfrac{2}{3}$

Cumulative Assessment, Chapters 1–2

Multiple Choice

1. During a week in January in Cleveland, Ohio, the daily high temperatures were −4°F, −2°F, −12°F, 5°F, 12°F, 16°F, and 20°F. Which expression can be used to find the difference between the highest temperature of the week and the lowest temperature of the week?

   Ⓐ 20 − 2
   Ⓒ 20 − 12
   Ⓑ 20 − (−2)
   Ⓓ 20 − (−12)

2. Find the greatest common factor of 16 and 32.

   Ⓕ 2
   Ⓗ 32
   Ⓖ 16
   Ⓙ 512

3. The fraction $\frac{3}{5}$ is found between which pair of fractions on a number line?

   Ⓐ $\frac{1}{2}$ and $\frac{2}{10}$
   Ⓑ $\frac{1}{2}$ and $\frac{7}{10}$
   Ⓒ $\frac{3}{10}$ and $\frac{5}{15}$
   Ⓓ $\frac{3}{10}$ and $\frac{8}{15}$

4. Maxie earns $210 a week working as a lifeguard. After she gets paid, she gives each of her three sisters $20, and her mom $120 for her car payment. Which equation can be used to find p, the amount of money Maxie has left after she pays her mom and sisters?

   Ⓕ $p = 210 − (3 × 20) − 120$
   Ⓖ $p = 210 − 20 − 120$
   Ⓗ $p = 120 − (3 × 20) − 120$
   Ⓙ $p = 3 × (210 − 20 − 120)$

5. Which expression can be used to represent a pattern in the table?

x	?
−3	4
−5	2
−7	0
−9	−2

   Ⓐ $x + 2$
   Ⓒ $x − (−7)$
   Ⓑ $−2x$
   Ⓓ $x − 7$

6. Which of the following shows a list of numbers in order from least to greatest?

   Ⓕ −1.05, −2.55, −3.05
   Ⓖ −2.75, $2\frac{5}{6}$, 2.50
   Ⓗ −0.05, −0.01, $3\frac{1}{4}$
   Ⓙ $−1\frac{2}{8}$, $−1\frac{4}{8}$, 1.05

7. Which of the following is an example of the Associative Property?

   Ⓐ $5 + (4 + 1) = (5 + 4) + 1$
   Ⓑ $32 + (2 + 11) = 32 + (11 + 2)$
   Ⓒ $(2 × 10) + (2 × 4) = 2 × 14$
   Ⓓ $4(2 × 7) = (4 × 2) + (4 × 7)$

8. There are 100 centimeters in 1 meter. Which mixed number represents 625 centimeters in meters?

   Ⓕ $6\frac{1}{4}$ m
   Ⓗ $6\frac{2}{5}$ m
   Ⓖ $6\frac{2}{4}$ m
   Ⓙ $6\frac{3}{5}$ m

9. An artist is creating a design with 6 stripes. The first stripe is 2 meters long. The second stripe is 4 meters long, the third stripe is 8 meters long, and the fourth stripe is 16 meters long. If the pattern continues, how long is the sixth stripe?

Ⓐ 24 m   Ⓒ 64 m

Ⓑ 32 m   Ⓓ 128 m

10. Simplify the expression $(-5)^2 - 3 \cdot 4$.

Ⓕ −112   Ⓗ 13

Ⓖ −37   Ⓙ 88

11. Evaluate $a - b$ for $a = 25$ and $b = 3$.

Ⓐ −8   Ⓒ 2

Ⓑ −2   Ⓓ 8

Be careful when working problems that involve positive and negative numbers. The answer choices often include the opposite of the correct answer.

12. Evaluate $-t + 3 \cdot 5$ for $t = 10$.

Ⓕ −10   Ⓗ −5

Ⓖ 5   Ⓙ 10

13. What is the solution to the equation $x + 6 = -4$?

Ⓐ −24   Ⓒ 10

Ⓑ −10   Ⓓ 24

14. Garrett dusts his bedroom every four days and sweeps his bedroom every three days. If he does both today, how many days will pass before he does them both on the same day again?

Ⓕ 3   Ⓗ 7

Ⓖ 4   Ⓙ 12

15. What is the power of 10 if you write 5,450,000,000 in scientific notation?

Ⓐ 6   Ⓒ 9

Ⓑ 7   Ⓓ 10

STANDARDIZED TEST PREP
Short Response

16. The sponsors of the marching band provided 128 sandwiches for a picnic. After the picnic, s sandwiches were left.

a. Write an expression that shows how many sandwiches were handed out.

b. Evaluate your expression for $s = 15$. What does your answer represent?

17. Casey said the solution to the equation $x + 42 = 65$ is 107. Identify the error that Casey made. Explain why this answer is unreasonable. Show how to solve this equation correctly. Explain your work.

Extended Response

18. Mary's allowance is based on the amount of time that she spends practicing different activities each week. This week Mary spent 12 hours practicing and earned $12.00.

a. Mary spent the following amounts of time on each activity: $\frac{1}{5}$ practicing flute, $\frac{1}{6}$ studying Spanish, $\frac{1}{3}$ playing soccer, and $\frac{3}{10}$ studying math. Write an equivalent decimal for the amount of time that she spent on each activity. Round to the nearest hundredth, if necessary.

b. For each activity, Mary earned the same fraction of her allowance as the time spent on a particular activity. This week, she was paid $3.60 for math practice. Was this the correct amount? Explain how you know.

c. Order the amount of time that Mary spent practicing each activity from least to greatest.

d. Write a decimal to represent the fraction of time Mary would have spent practicing soccer for 5 hours instead of 4 hours this week.

Problem Solving on Location

GEORGIA

Georgia Performance Standards

M7P1.c, M7P4.c, M7P5.a

⭐ Okefenokee Swamp Park

Located in the southeast corner of the state, Okefenokee Swamp Park is sometimes called Georgia's Natural Wonder. The nickname is fitting because Okefenokee is the largest swamp in North America. Its 700 square miles feature dazzling wildflowers, peaceful canoe trails, and plenty of alligators!

Choose one or more strategies to solve each problem.

1. Boat tours of Okefenokee Swamp cost $12 for adults and $11 for children. A group of visitors pay $93 for a boat tour. How many children are in the group?

For 2 and 3, use the graph.

2. A park ranger prepares posters about the reptiles and amphibians in the swamp. Each reptile and amphibian appears on only one poster. The number of reptiles and amphibians on each poster is the same. The ranger makes the greatest possible number of posters.

   a. How many reptiles and how many amphibians are displayed on each poster?

   b. How many posters are there?

Species at Okefenokee Swamp Park

Number of Species (0, 10, 20, 30, 40, 50, 60, 70)

Mammals — 40
Reptiles — 50
Amphibians — 60
Fish — 34

Class of Animal

3. An information center has photographs of all the mammals in the swamp. The photos are arranged in rows on a wall. Except for the bottom row, there are 7 photos in each row. How many rows are there?

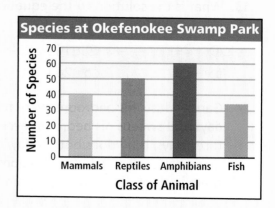

144

Problem Solving Strategies

Draw a Diagram
Make a Model
Guess and Test
Work Backward
Find a Pattern
Make a Table
Solve a Simpler Problem
Use Logical Reasoning
Act It Out
Make an Organized List

⭐ Covered Bridges

Georgia is home to many covered bridges. The oldest of the bridges, at Big Red Oak Creek, was built in the 1840s. The newest, built in 1997, shows that interest in these scenic structures hasn't faded with time.

"W" Style Truss

Choose one or more strategies to solve each problem.

1. Stovall Mill Bridge is about 40 feet long. The bridge's roof is supported by *trusses*. The first and last trusses are 4 ft from either end of the bridge, and there are 4 ft between each truss along the bridge's length. How many trusses are there?

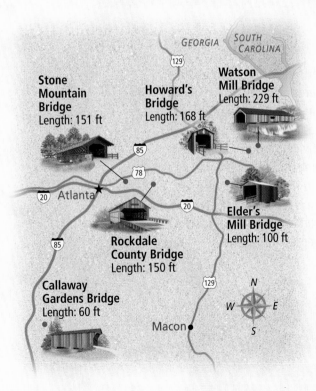

Stone Mountain Bridge
Length: 151 ft

Howard's Bridge
Length: 168 ft

Watson Mill Bridge
Length: 229 ft

GEORGIA SOUTH CAROLINA

Atlanta

Rockdale County Bridge
Length: 150 ft

Elder's Mill Bridge
Length: 100 ft

Callaway Gardens Bridge
Length: 60 ft

Macon

For 2 and 3, use the map.

2. Coheelee Creek Bridge is 62 ft longer than Lula Bridge. Lula Bridge is 195 ft shorter than Watson Mill Bridge. How long is Coheelee Creek Bridge?

3. All of the bridges on the map are at least 100 years old, except for one bridge that was built in 1997. The bridge that was built in 1997 is more than twice the length of Callaway Gardens Bridge. It is also less than 160 ft long. Stone Mountain Bridge was built in 1891. Which bridge was built in 1997?

Applying Rational Numbers

CRCT PREP

go.hrw.com
Chapter Project Online
KEYWORD: MS7 Ch3

Ingredients	10 Waffles	25 Waffles	50 Waffles
Flour	2 c	5 c	10 c
Salt	$\frac{3}{4}$ tsp	$1\frac{7}{8}$ tsp	$3\frac{3}{4}$ tsp
Baking powder	3 tsp	$7\frac{1}{2}$ tsp	15 tsp
Milk	$1\frac{2}{3}$ c	$4\frac{1}{6}$ c	$8\frac{1}{3}$ c
Butter (melted)	$\frac{1}{2}$ c	$1\frac{1}{4}$ c	$2\frac{1}{2}$ c

 **Chef**

Tom Culbertson is a pastry chef. He develops and prepares all of the baked goods for his restaurant. In his work, Tom often uses fractions when measuring ingredients. He must also multiply and divide fractions to increase or decrease the number of servings for a recipe. In addition to the breads and desserts that he creates, Tom is famous for his breakfast waffles. Tom often adds fresh fruits, such as blueberries, strawberries, or bananas, to his waffles.

ARE YOU READY?

✓ Vocabulary

Choose the best term from the list to complete each sentence.

1. A(n) __?__ is a number that is written using the base-ten place value system.

2. An example of a(n) __?__ is $\frac{14}{5}$.

3. A(n) __?__ is a number that represents a part of a whole.

decimal

fraction

improper fraction

mixed number

simplest form

Complete these exercises to review the skills you will need for this chapter.

✓ Simplify Fractions

Write each fraction in simplest form.

4. $\frac{24}{40}$　　5. $\frac{64}{84}$　　6. $\frac{66}{78}$　　7. $\frac{64}{192}$

8. $\frac{21}{35}$　　9. $\frac{11}{99}$　　10. $\frac{16}{36}$　　11. $\frac{20}{30}$

✓ Write Mixed Numbers as Fractions

Write each mixed number as an improper fraction.

12. $7\frac{1}{2}$　　13. $2\frac{5}{6}$　　14. $1\frac{14}{15}$　　15. $3\frac{2}{11}$

16. $3\frac{7}{8}$　　17. $8\frac{4}{9}$　　18. $4\frac{1}{7}$　　19. $5\frac{9}{10}$

✓ Write Fractions as Mixed Numbers

Write each improper fraction as a mixed number.

20. $\frac{23}{6}$　　21. $\frac{17}{3}$　　22. $\frac{29}{7}$　　23. $\frac{39}{4}$

24. $\frac{48}{5}$　　25. $\frac{82}{9}$　　26. $\frac{69}{4}$　　27. $\frac{35}{8}$

✓ Add, Subtract, Multiply, or Divide Integers

Find each sum, difference, product, or quotient.

28. $-11 + (-24)$　　29. $-11 - 7$　　30. $-4 \cdot (-10)$

31. $-22 \div (-11)$　　32. $23 + (-30)$　　33. $-33 - 74$

34. $-62 \cdot (-34)$　　35. $84 \div (-12)$　　36. $-26 - 18$

Study Guide: Preview

Where You've Been

Previously, you

- added, subtracted, multiplied, and divided whole numbers.

- used models to solve equations with whole numbers.

In This Chapter

You will study

- using models to represent multiplication and division situations involving fractions and decimals.

- using addition, subtraction, multiplication, and division to solve problems involving fractions and decimals.

- solving equations with rational numbers.

Where You're Going

You can use the skills learned in this chapter

- to estimate total cost when purchasing several items at the grocery store.

- to find measurements in fields such as carpentry.

Key Vocabulary/Vocabulario

compatible numbers	números compatibles
reciprocal	recíproco

Vocabulary Connections

To become familiar with some of the vocabulary terms in the chapter, consider the following. You may refer to the chapter, the glossary, or a dictionary if you like.

1. When two things are compatible, they make a good match. You can match a fraction with a number that is easier to work with, such as 1, $\frac{1}{2}$, or 0, by rounding up or down. How could you use these **compatible numbers** to estimate the sums and differences of fractions?

2. When fractions are **reciprocals** of each other, they have a special relationship. The fractions $\frac{3}{5}$ and $\frac{5}{3}$ are reciprocals of each other. What do you think the relationship between reciprocals is?

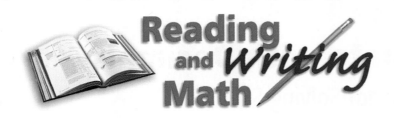

Reading and Writing Math

Study Strategy: Use Your Notes Effectively

Taking notes helps you understand and remember information from your textbook and lessons in class. Listed below are some steps for effectively using your notes before and after class.

Step 1: Before Class
- Read through your notes from the last class.
- Then look ahead to the the next lesson. Write down any questions you have.

Step 2: During Class
- Write down main points that your teacher stresses.
- If you miss something, leave a blank space and keep taking notes.
- Use abbreviations. Make sure you will understand any abbreviations later.
- Draw pictures or diagrams.

Step 3: After Class
- Fill in any information you may have missed.
- Highlight or circle the most important ideas, such as vocabulary, formulas and rules, or steps.
- Use your notes to quiz a friend or yourself.

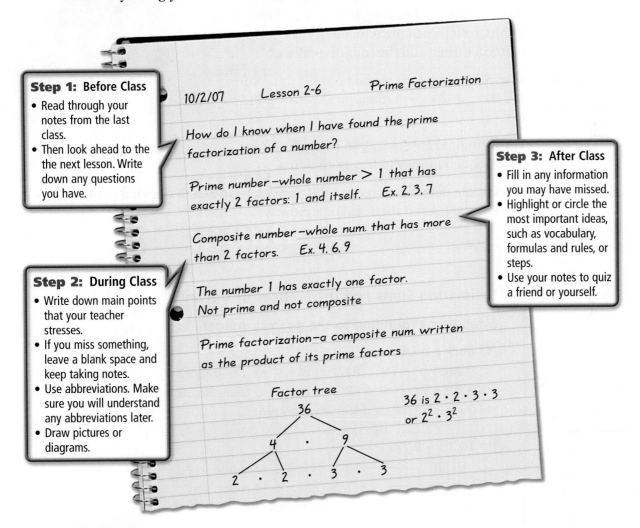

10/2/07   Lesson 2-6   Prime Factorization

How do I know when I have found the prime factorization of a number?

Prime number — whole number > 1 that has exactly 2 factors: 1 and itself.   Ex. 2, 3, 7

Composite number — whole num. that has more than 2 factors.   Ex. 4, 6, 9

The number 1 has exactly one factor. Not prime and not composite

Prime factorization — a composite num. written as the product of its prime factors

Factor tree

36 is $2 \cdot 2 \cdot 3 \cdot 3$ or $2^2 \cdot 3^2$

Try This

1. Look at the next lesson in your textbook. Think about how the new vocabulary terms relate to previous lessons. Write down any questions you have.

2. With a classmate, compare the notes you took during the last class. Are there differences in the main points that you each recorded? Then brainstorm two ways you can improve your note-taking skills.

3-1 Estimate with Decimals

Problem Solving Skill

Learn to estimate decimal sums, differences, products, and quotients.

Vocabulary

compatible numbers

Georgia Performance Standards

M7N1.c Add, subtract, multiply, and divide rational numbers. Also, M7N1.d, M7P1.c, M7P1.d.

Jessie earned $26.00 for baby-sitting. She wants to use the money to buy a ticket to a waterpark for $14.75 and a souvenir T-shirt for $13.20.

To find out if Jessie has enough money to buy both items, you can use estimation. To estimate the total cost of the ticket and the T-shirt, round each price to the nearest dollar, or integer. Then add the rounded values.

$14.75	*7 > 5, so round to $15.*	$15
$13.20	*2 < 5, so round to $13.*	+ $13
		$28

The estimated cost is $28, so Jessie does not have enough money to buy both items.

To estimate decimal sums and differences, round each decimal to the nearest integer and then add or subtract.

EXAMPLE 1 Estimating Sums and Differences of Decimals

Estimate by rounding to the nearest integer.

Remember!

To round to the nearest integer, look at the digit in the tenths place. If it is greater than or equal to 5, round to the next integer. If it is less than 5, keep the same integer.

A $86.9 + 58.4$

86.9	$\longrightarrow$	87	*9 > 5, so round to 87.*
+ 58.4	$\longrightarrow$	+ 58	*4 < 5, so round to 58.*
		145	$\longleftarrow$ *Estimate*

B $10.38 - 6.721$

10.38	$\longrightarrow$	10	*3 < 5, so round to 10.*
− 6.721	$\longrightarrow$	− 7	*7 > 5, so round to 7.*
		3	$\longleftarrow$ *Estimate*

C $-26.3 + 15.195$

−26.3	$\longrightarrow$	−26	*3 < 5, so round to −26.*
+ 15.195	$\longrightarrow$	+ 15	*1 < 5, so round to 15.*
		−11	$\longleftarrow$ *Estimate*

You can use *compatible numbers* when estimating. **Compatible numbers** are numbers that replace the numbers in the problem and are easy to use.

Guidelines for Using Compatible Numbers	
When multiplying . . .	**When dividing . . .**
round numbers to the nearest nonzero integer or to numbers that are easy to multiply.	round numbers so that they divide without leaving a remainder.

EXAMPLE 2 **Estimating Products and Quotients of Decimals**

Use compatible numbers to estimate.

A 32.66 · 7.69

$$32.66 \longrightarrow 30$$ *Round to the nearest multiple of 10.*
$$\times\ 7.69 \longrightarrow \underline{\times\ 8}$$ *6 > 5, so round to 8.*
$$240 \longleftarrow$$ *Estimate*

Remember!

A prime number has exactly two factors, 1 and itself. So the factors of 37 are 1 and 37.

B 36.5 ÷ (−8.241)

$$36.5 \longrightarrow 36$$ *37 is a prime number, so round to 36.*
$$-8.241 \longrightarrow -9$$ *−9 divides into 36 without a remainder.*

$$36 \div (-9) = -4 \longleftarrow$$ *Estimate*

When you solve problems, using an estimate can help you decide whether your answer is reasonable.

EXAMPLE 3 *School Application*

On a math test, a student worked the problem 6.2)‾5‾5‾.‾9‾ and got the answer 0.9. Use estimation to check whether the answer is reasonable.

$$6.2 \longrightarrow 6$$ *2 < 5, so round to 6.*
$$55.9 \longrightarrow 60$$ *6 divides into 60 without a remainder.*
$$60 \div 6 = 10 \longleftarrow$$ *Estimate*

The estimate is more than ten times the student's answer, so 0.9 is not a reasonable answer.

Think and Discuss  GPS M7P1.d, M7P2.c

1. **Explain** whether your estimate will be greater than or less than the actual answer when you round both numbers down in an addition or multiplication problem.

2. **Describe** a situation in which you would want your estimate to be greater than the actual amount.

Georgia Performance
Standards
M7P3.a, M7P4.c, M7P5.a

go.hrw.com
Homework Help Online
KEYWORD: MS7 3-1
Parent Resources Online
KEYWORD: MS7 Parent

GUIDED PRACTICE

See Example **1** **Estimate by rounding to the nearest integer.**

1. $37.2 + 25.83$ **2.** $18.256 - 5.71$ **3.** $-9.916 + 12.4$

See Example **2** **Use compatible numbers to estimate.**

4. $8.09 \cdot 28.32$ **5.** $-3.45 \cdot 73.6$ **6.** $41.9 \div 6.391$

See Example **3** **7. School** A student worked the problem $35.8 \cdot 9.3$. The student's answer was 3,329.4. Use estimation to check whether this answer is reasonable.

INDEPENDENT PRACTICE

See Example **1** **Estimate by rounding to the nearest integer.**

8. $5.982 + 37.1$ **9.** $68.2 + 23.67$ **10.** $-36.8 + 14.217$

11. $15.23 - 6.835$ **12.** $6.88 + (-8.1)$ **13.** $80.38 - 24.592$

See Example **2** **Use compatible numbers to estimate.**

14. $51.38 \cdot 4.33$ **15.** $46.72 \div 9.24$ **16.** $32.91 \cdot 6.28$

17. $-3.45 \cdot 43.91$ **18.** $2.81 \cdot (-79.2)$ **19.** $28.22 \div 3.156$

See Example **3** **20.** Ann has a piece of rope that is 12.35 m long. She wants to cut it into smaller pieces that are each 3.6 m long. She thinks she will get about 3 smaller pieces of rope. Use estimation to check whether her assumption is reasonable.

PRACTICE AND PROBLEM SOLVING

Extra Practice p. 730

Estimate.

21. $5.921 - 13.2$ **22.** $-7.98 - 8.1$ **23.** $-42.25 + (-17.091)$

24. $98.6 + 43.921$ **25.** $4.69 \cdot (-18.33)$ **26.** $62.84 - 35.169$

27. $-48.28 + 11.901$ **28.** $31.53 \div (-4.12)$ **29.** $35.9 - 24.71$

30. $69.7 - 7.81$ **31.** $-6.56 \cdot 14.2$ **32.** $4.513 + 72.45$

33. $-8.9 \cdot (-24.1)$ **34.** $6.92 \cdot (-3.714)$ **35.** $-78.3 \div (-6.25)$

36. Jo needs 10 lb of ground beef for a party. She has packages that weigh 4.23 lb and 5.09 lb. Does she have enough?

37. Consumer Math Ramón saves $8.35 each week. He wants to buy a video game that costs $61.95. For about how many weeks will Ramón have to save his money before he can buy the video game?

38. Multi-Step Tickets at a local movie theater cost $7.50 each. A large bucket of popcorn at the theater costs $4.19, and a large soda costs $3.74. Estimate the amount that 3 friends spent at the theater when they saw one movie, shared one large bucket of popcorn, and had one large soda each.

39. Transportation Kayla stopped for gasoline at a station that was charging $2.719 per gallon. If Kayla had $14.75 in cash, approximately how many gallons of gas could she buy?

40. Social Studies The circle graph shows the languages spoken in Canada.

a. Which language do approximately 60% of Canadians speak?

b. What is the approximate difference between the percent of people who speak English and the percent who speak French?

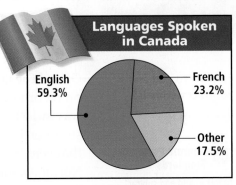

Languages Spoken in Canada

English 59.3%
French 23.2%
Other 17.5%

41. Astronomy Jupiter is 5.20 astronomical units (AU) from the Sun. Neptune is almost 6 times as far from the Sun as Jupiter is. Estimate Neptune's distance from the Sun in astronomical units.

42. Sports Scott must earn a total of 27 points to advance to the final round in an ice-skating competition. He earns scores of 5.9, 5.8, 6.0, 5.8, and 6.0. Scott estimates that his total score will allow him to advance. Is his estimate reasonable? Explain.

43. Write a Problem Write a problem that can be solved by estimating with decimals.

44. Write About It Explain how an estimate helps you decide whether an answer is reasonable.

45. Challenge Estimate. $6.35 - 15.512 + 8.744 - 4.19 - 72.7 + 25.008$

CRCT PREP • GPS SUPPORT • SPIRAL REVIEW

46. Multiple Choice Which is the best estimate for $24.976 \div (-4.893)$?

Ⓐ 20　　　Ⓑ −6　　　Ⓒ −5　　　Ⓓ 2

47. Multiple Choice Steve is saving $10.50 from his allowance each week to buy a printer that costs $150. Which is the best estimate of the number of weeks he will have to save his money until he can buy the printer?

Ⓕ 5 weeks　　　Ⓖ 10 weeks　　　Ⓗ 12 weeks　　　Ⓙ 15 weeks

48. Short Response Joe's restaurant bill was $16.84. He had $20 in his wallet. Explain how to use rounding to estimate whether Joe had enough money to leave a $2.75 tip.

Simplify each expression. (Lessons 2-3 and 2-4)

49. $-5 + 4 - 2$

50. $16 \cdot (-3) + 12$

51. $28 - (-2) \cdot (-3)$

52. $-90 - (-6) \cdot (-8)$

53. $-7 - 3 - 1$

54. $-10 \cdot (-5) + 2$

Adding and Subtracting Decimals

Learn to add and subtract decimals.

Georgia Performance Standards

M7N1.c Add and subtract positive and negative rational numbers. Also, M7N1.d, M7P4.c.

One of the coolest summers on record in the Midwest was in 1992. The average summertime temperature that year was 66.8°F. Normally, the average temperature is 4°F higher than it was in 1992.

To find the normal average summertime temperature in the Midwest, you can add 66.8°F and 4°F.

66.8
+ 4.0 ← *Use zero as a placeholder so that both numbers have the same number of digits after their decimal points.*
‾‾‾‾‾‾
70.8 ← *Add each column just as you would add integers.*
↑
Line up the decimal points.

The normal average summertime temperature in the Midwest is 70.8°F.

EXAMPLE **1** **Adding Decimals**

Add. Estimate to check whether each answer is reasonable.

A 3.62 + 18.57

    3.62   *Line up the decimal points.*
 + 18.57
  ‾‾‾‾‾
  22.19   *Add.*

Estimate
4 + 19 = 23   *22.19 is a reasonable answer.*

B 9 + 3.245

  9.000   *Use zeros as placeholders.*
 + 3.245   *Line up the decimal points.*
 ‾‾‾‾‾
 12.245   *Add.*

Estimate
9 + 3 = 12   *12.245 is a reasonable answer.*

Add. Estimate to check whether each answer is reasonable.

C $-5.78 + (-18.3)$

$-5.78 + (-18.3)$	*Think: 5.78 + 18.3.*
5.78	*Line up the decimal points.*
$\underline{+18.30}$	*Use zero as a placeholder.*
24.08	*Add.*
$-5.78 + (-18.3) = -24.08$	*Use the sign of the two numbers.*

Estimate

$-6 + (-18) = -24$ *−24.08 is a reasonable answer.*

EXAMPLE 2   **Subtracting Decimals**

Subtract.

A $12.49 - 7.25$

12.49	*Line up the decimal points.*
$\underline{-7.25}$	
5.24	*Subtract.*

B $14 - 7.32$

$\overset{13910}{14.\cancel{00}}$	*Use zeros as placeholders.*
$\underline{-7.32}$	*Line up the decimal points.*
6.68	*Subtract.*

EXAMPLE 3   *Transportation Application*

During one month in the United States, 492.23 million commuter trips were taken on buses, and 26.331 million commuter trips were taken on light rail. How many more trips were taken on buses than on light rail? Estimate to check whether your answer is reasonable.

492.230	*Use zero as a placeholder.*
$\underline{-26.331}$	*Line up the decimal points.*
465.899	*Subtract.*

Estimate

$490 - 30 = 460$ *465.899 is a reasonable answer.*

465.899 million more trips were taken on buses than on light rail.

Think and Discuss    GPS M7P1.d, M7P3.c

$$\begin{array}{r} 12.3 \\ +\ 4.68 \\ \hline 5.91 \end{array}$$

1. **Tell** whether the addition is correct. If it is not, explain why not.

2. **Describe** how you can check an answer when adding and subtracting decimals.

Georgia Performance
Standards
M7P1.b, M7P1.c, M7P3.a

go.hrw.com
Homework Help Online
KEYWORD: MS7 3-2
Parent Resources Online
KEYWORD: MS7 Parent

GUIDED PRACTICE

See Example **1** Add. Estimate to check whether each answer is reasonable.

1. $5.37 + 16.45$ **2.** $2.46 + 11.99$ **3.** $7 + 5.826$ **4.** $-5.62 + (-12.9)$

See Example **2** Subtract.

5. $7.89 - 5.91$ **6.** $17 - 4.12$ **7.** $4.97 - 3.2$ **8.** $9 - 1.03$

See Example **3** **9.** In 1990, international visitors to the United States spent $58.3 billion. In 1999, international visitors spent $95.5 billion. By how much did spending by international visitors increase from 1990 to 1999?

INDEPENDENT PRACTICE

See Example **1** Add. Estimate to check whether each answer is reasonable.

10. $7.82 + 31.23$ **11.** $5.98 + 12.99$ **12.** $4.917 + 12$ **13.** $-9.82 + (-15.7)$

14. $6 + 9.33$ **15.** $10.022 + 0.11$ **16.** $8 + 1.071$ **17.** $-3.29 + (-12.6)$

See Example **2** Subtract.

18. $5.45 - 3.21$ **19.** $12.87 - 3.86$ **20.** $15.39 - 2.6$ **21.** $21.04 - 4.99$

22. $5 - 0.53$ **23.** $14 - 8.9$ **24.** $41 - 9.85$ **25.** $33 - 10.23$

See Example **3** **26.** Angela runs her first lap around the track in 4.35 minutes and her second lap in 3.9 minutes. What is her total time for the two laps?

27. A jeweler has 122.83 grams of silver. He uses 45.7 grams of the silver to make a necklace and earrings. How much silver does he have left?

PRACTICE AND PROBLEM SOLVING

Extra Practice p. 730

Add or subtract. Estimate to check whether each answer is reasonable.

28. $-7.238 + 6.9$ **29.** $4.16 - 9.043$ **30.** $-2.09 - 15.271$

31. $5.23 - (-9.1)$ **32.** $-123 - 2.55$ **33.** $5.29 - 3.37$

34. $32.6 - (-15.86)$ **35.** $-32.7 + 62.82$ **36.** $-51 + 81.623$

37. $5.9 - 10 + 2.84$ **38.** $-4.2 + 2.3 - 0.7$ **39.** $-8.3 + 5.38 - 0.537$

40. Multi-Step Students at Hill Middle School plan to run a total of 2,462 mi, which is the distance from Los Angeles to New York City. So far, the sixth grade has run 273.5 mi, the seventh grade has run 275.8 mi, and the eighth grade has run 270.2 mi. How many more miles must the students run to reach their goal?

41. Critical Thinking Why must you line up the decimal points when adding and subtracting decimals?

Physical Science

Egg-drop competitions challenge students to build devices that will protect eggs when they are dropped from as high as 100 ft.

Weather The graph shows the five coolest summers recorded in the Midwest. The average summertime temperature in the Midwest is 70.8°F.

42. How much warmer was the average summertime temperature in 1950 than in 1915?

43. In what year was the temperature 4.4°F cooler than the average summertime temperature in the Midwest?

44. **Physical Science** To float in water, an object must have a density of less than 1 gram per milliliter. The density of a fresh egg is about 1.2 grams per milliliter. If the density of a spoiled egg is about 0.3 grams per milliliter less than that of a fresh egg, what is the density of a spoiled egg? How can you use water to tell whether an egg is spoiled?

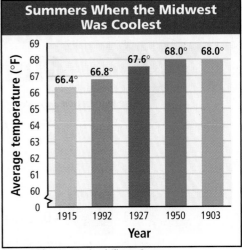

Summers When the Midwest Was Coolest

Source: Midwestern Regional Climate Center

45. **Choose a Strategy** How much larger in area is Agua Fria than Pompeys Pillar?

Ⓐ 6.6 thousand acres

Ⓑ 20.1 thousand acres

Ⓒ 70.59 thousand acres

Ⓓ 71.049 thousand acres

National Monument	Area (thousand acres)
Agua Fria	71.1
Pompeys Pillar	0.051

46. **Write About It** Explain how to find the sum or difference of two decimals.

47. **Challenge** Find the missing number. $5.11 + 6.9 - 15.3 + \boxed{} = 20$

CRCT PREP • GPS SUPPORT • SPIRAL REVIEW

48. Multiple Choice In the 1900 Olympic Games, the 200-meter dash was won in 22.20 seconds. In 2000, the 200-meter dash was won in 20.09 seconds. How many seconds faster was the winning time in the 2000 Olympics?

Ⓐ 1.10 seconds　　Ⓑ 2.11 seconds　　Ⓒ 2.29 seconds　　Ⓓ 4.83 seconds

49. Multiple Choice John left school with $2.38. He found a quarter on his way home and then stopped to buy a banana for $0.89. How much money did he have when he got home?

Ⓕ $1.24　　　Ⓖ $1.74　　　Ⓗ $3.02　　　Ⓙ $3.52

Solve each equation. Check your answer. (Lesson 2-5)

50. $x - 8 = -22$　　**51.** $-3y = -45$　　**52.** $\frac{z}{2} = -8$　　**53.** $29 = -10 + p$

Estimate. (Lesson 3-1)

54. $15.85 \div 4.01$　　**55.** $18.95 + 3.21$　　**56.** $44.217 - 19.876$　　**57.** $21.43 \cdot 1.57$

Model Decimal Multiplication

Use with Lesson 3-3

Georgia Performance Standards

M7N1.c, M7N1.d, M7P5.a, M7P5.b

go.hrw.com
Lab Resources Online
KEYWORD: MS7 Lab3

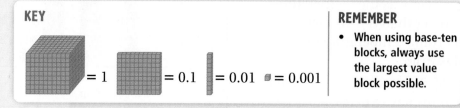

KEY

= 1   = 0.1   = 0.01   = 0.001

REMEMBER
• When using base-ten blocks, always use the largest value block possible.

You can use base-ten blocks to model multiplying decimals by whole numbers.

Activity 1

1 Use base-ten blocks to find 3 · 0.1.

Multiplication is repeated addition, so 3 · 0.1 = 0.1 + 0.1 + 0.1.

3 · 0.1 = 0.3

2 Use base-ten blocks to find 5 · 0.03.

5 · 0.03 = 0.03 + 0.03 + 0.03 + 0.03 + 0.03

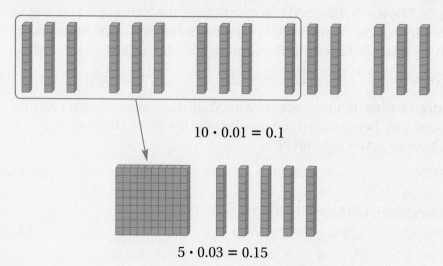

10 · 0.01 = 0.1

5 · 0.03 = 0.15

1. Why can't you use base-ten blocks to model multiplying a decimal by a decimal?

2. Is the product of a whole number and a decimal less than or greater than the whole number? Explain.

Try This

Use base-ten blocks to find each product.

1. 4 · 0.5   **2.** 2 · 0.04   **3.** 3 · 0.16   **4.** 6 · 0.2

5. 3 · 0.33   **6.** 0.25 · 5   **7.** 0.42 · 3   **8.** 1.1 · 4

You can use decimal grids to model multiplying decimals by decimals.

Activity 2

1 Use a decimal grid to find 0.4 · 0.7.

Shade **0.4** horizontally.   Shade **0.7** vertically.   The area where the shaded regions overlap is the answer.

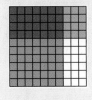

0.4   ×   0.7   =   0.28

Think and Discuss

1. Explain the steps you would take to model 0.5 · 0.5 with a decimal grid.

2. How could you use decimal grids to model multiplying a decimal by a whole number?

Try This

Use decimal grids to find each product.

1. 0.6 · 0.6   **2.** 0.5 · 0.4   **3.** 0.3 · 0.8

4. 0.2 · 0.8   **5.** 3 · 0.3   **6.** 0.8 · 0.8

7. 2 · 0.5   **8.** 0.1 · 0.9   **9.** 0.1 · 0.1

3-3 Multiplying Decimals

Learn to multiply decimals.

Georgia Performance Standards

M7N1.c Multiply positive and negative rational numbers. Also, M7N1.d, M7P1.b, M7P5.c.

You can use decimal grids to model multiplication of decimals. Each large square represents 1. Each row and column represents 0.1. Each small square represents 0.01. The area where the shading overlaps shows the product of the two decimals.

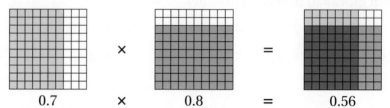

| 0.7 | × | 0.8 | = | 0.56 |

To multiply decimals, multiply as you would with integers. To place the decimal point in the product, count the number of decimal places in each factor. The product should have the same number of decimal places as the sum of the decimal places in the factors.

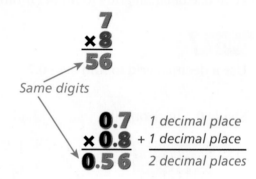

$$\begin{array}{r} 7 \\ \times\, 8 \\ \hline 56 \end{array}$$

Same digits

$$\begin{array}{r} 0.7 \\ \times\, 0.8 \\ \hline 0.56 \end{array}$$
1 decimal place
+ 1 decimal place
2 decimal places

EXAMPLE **1**   **Multiplying Integers by Decimals**

Multiply.

A 6 · 0.1

$$\begin{array}{r} 6 \\ \times\, 0.1 \\ \hline 0.6 \end{array}$$
0 decimal places
1 decimal place
0 + 1 = 1 decimal place

B −2 · 0.04

$$\begin{array}{r} -2 \\ \times\, 0.04 \\ \hline -0.08 \end{array}$$
0 decimal places
2 decimal places
0 + 2 = 2 decimal places. Use zero as a placeholder.

C 1.25 · 23

$$\begin{array}{r} 1.25 \\ \times\, 23 \\ \hline 3\,75 \\ +\, 25\,00 \\ \hline 28.75 \end{array}$$
2 decimal places
0 decimal places

2 + 0 = 2 decimal places

EXAMPLE 2
Multiplying Decimals by Decimals

Multiply. Estimate to check whether each answer is reasonable.

A) 1.2 · 1.6

$$
\begin{array}{r}
1.2 \\
\times\ 1.6 \\
\hline
72 \\
120 \\
\hline
1.92
\end{array}
$$

1 decimal place
1 decimal place

1 + 1 = 2 decimal places

Estimate
1 · 2 = 2   *1.92 is a reasonable answer.*

B) −2.78 · 0.8

$$
\begin{array}{r}
-2.78 \\
\times\ 0.8 \\
\hline
-2.224
\end{array}
$$

2 decimal places
1 decimal place
2 + 1 = 3 decimal places

Estimate
−3 · 1 = −3   *−2.224 is a reasonable answer.*

EXAMPLE 3
Earth Science Application

On average, 0.36 kg of carbon dioxide is added to the atmosphere for each mile a single car is driven. How many kilograms of carbon dioxide are added for each mile the 132 million cars in the United States are driven?

$$
\begin{array}{r}
132 \\
\times\ 0.36 \\
\hline
792 \\
3960 \\
\hline
47.52
\end{array}
$$

0 decimal places
2 decimal places

0 + 2 = 2 decimal places

Estimate
130 · 0.5 = 65   *47.52 is a reasonable answer.*

Approximately 47.52 million (47,520,000) kilograms of carbon dioxide are added to the atmosphere for each mile driven.

Think and Discuss   GPS M7P1.d, M7P3.b

1. Explain whether the multiplication 2.1 · 3.3 = 69.3 is correct.

2. Compare multiplying integers with multiplying decimals.

Georgia Performance Standards

M7P3.a, M7P4.c, M7P5.b

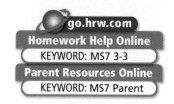

go.hrw.com
Homework Help Online
KEYWORD: MS7 3-3
Parent Resources Online
KEYWORD: MS7 Parent

GUIDED PRACTICE

See Example **1** Multiply.

1. $-9 \cdot 0.4$ **2.** $3 \cdot 0.2$ **3.** $0.06 \cdot 3$ **4.** $-0.5 \cdot 2$

See Example **2** Multiply. Estimate to check whether each answer is reasonable.

5. $1.7 \cdot 1.2$ **6.** $2.6 \cdot 0.4$ **7.** $1.5 \cdot (-0.21)$ **8.** $-0.4 \cdot 1.17$

See Example **3**   **9.** If Carla is able to drive her car 24.03 miles on one gallon of gas, how far could she drive on 13.93 gallons of gas?

INDEPENDENT PRACTICE

See Example **1** Multiply.

10. $8 \cdot 0.6$ **11.** $5 \cdot 0.07$ **12.** $-3 \cdot 2.7$ **13.** $0.8 \cdot 4$

14. $6 \cdot 4.9$ **15.** $1.7 \cdot (-12)$ **16.** $43 \cdot 2.11$ **17.** $-7 \cdot (-1.3)$

See Example **2** Multiply. Estimate to check whether each answer is reasonable.

18. $2.4 \cdot 3.2$ **19.** $2.8 \cdot 1.6$ **20.** $5.3 \cdot 4.6$ **21.** $4.02 \cdot 0.7$

22. $-5.14 \cdot 0.03$ **23.** $1.04 \cdot (-8.9)$ **24.** $4.31 \cdot (-9.5)$ **25.** $-6.1 \cdot (-1.01)$

See Example **3** **26.** Nicholas bicycled 15.8 kilometers each day for 18 days last month. How many kilometers did he bicycle last month?

27. While walking, Lara averaged 3.63 miles per hour. How far did she walk in 1.5 hours?

PRACTICE AND PROBLEM SOLVING

CRCT GPS

Extra Practice p. 730

Multiply. Estimate to check whether each answer is reasonable.

28. $-9.6 \cdot 2.05$ **29.** $0.07 \cdot 0.03$ **30.** $4 \cdot 4.15$

31. $-1.08 \cdot (-0.4)$ **32.** $1.46 \cdot (-0.06)$ **33.** $-3.2 \cdot 0.9$

34. $-325.9 \cdot 1.5$ **35.** $14.7 \cdot 0.13$ **36.** $-28.5 \cdot (-1.07)$

37. $-7.02 \cdot (-0.05)$ **38.** $1.104 \cdot (-0.7)$ **39.** $0.072 \cdot 0.12$

40. Multi-Step Bo earns $8.95 per hour plus commission. Last week, he worked 32.5 hours and earned $28.75 in commission. How much money did Bo earn last week?

41. Weather As a hurricane increases in intensity, the air pressure within its eye decreases. In a Category 5 hurricane, which is the most intense, the air pressure measures approximately 27.16 inches of mercury. In a Category 1 hurricane, which is the least intense, the air pressure is about 1.066 times that of a Category 5 hurricane. What is the air pressure within the eye of a Category 1 hurricane? Round your answer to the nearest hundredth.

Georgia LINK

Sports

Sea kayaking is popular in the coastal waters of Georgia.

42. **Estimation** The graph shows the results of a survey about river recreation activities.

a. A report claimed that about 3 times as many people enjoyed canoeing in 1999–2000 than in 1994–1995. According to the graph, is this claim reasonable?

b. Suppose a future survey shows that 6 times as many people enjoyed kayaking in 2009–2010 than in 1999–2000. About how many people reported that they enjoyed kayaking in 2009–2010?

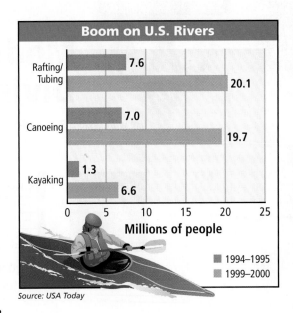

Boom on U.S. Rivers

Rafting/Tubing 7.6, 20.1
Canoeing 7.0, 19.7
Kayaking 1.3, 6.6

Millions of people

■ 1994–1995
■ 1999–2000

Source: USA Today

Multiply. Estimate to check whether each answer is reasonable.

43. $0.3 \cdot 2.8 \cdot (-10.6)$

44. $1.3 \cdot (-4.2) \cdot (-3.94)$

45. $0.6 \cdot (-0.9) \cdot 0.05$

46. $-6.5 \cdot (-1.02) \cdot (-12.6)$

47. $-22.08 \cdot (-5.6) \cdot 9.9$

48. $-63.75 \cdot 13.46 \cdot 7.8$

 49. **What's the Question?** In a collection, each rock sample has a mass of 4.35 kilograms. There are a dozen rocks in the collection. If the answer is 52.2 kilograms, what is the question?

 50. **Write About It** How do the products $4.3 \cdot 0.56$ and $0.43 \cdot 5.6$ compare? Explain.

 51. **Challenge** Evaluate $(0.2)^5$.

CRCT PREP • GPS SUPPORT • SPIRAL REVIEW

52. **Multiple Choice** Which expression is equal to -4.3?

Ⓐ $0.8 \cdot (-5.375)$ Ⓑ $-1.2 \cdot (-3.6)$ Ⓒ $-0.75 \cdot 5.6$ Ⓓ $2.2 \cdot (-1.9)$

53. **Gridded Response** Julia walked 1.8 mi each day from Monday through Friday. On Saturday, she walked 2.3 mi. How many miles did she walk in all?

Write the prime factorization of each number. (Lesson 2-6)

54. 20 **55.** 35 **56.** 120 **57.** 64

Add or subtract. Estimate to check whether each answer is reasonable. (Lesson 3-2)

58. $-4.875 + 3.62$ **59.** $5.83 - (-2.74)$ **60.** $6.32 + (-3.62)$ **61.** $-8.34 - (-4.6)$

62. $9.3 + 5.88$ **63.** $32.08 - 12.37$ **64.** $19 - 6.92$ **65.** $-75.25 + 6.382$

Hands-On LAB 3-4

Model Decimal Division

Use with Lessons 3-4 and 3-5

Georgia Performance Standards

M7N1.c, M7N1.d, M7P5.a, M7P5.b

go.hrw.com
Lab Resources Online
KEYWORD: MS7 Lab3

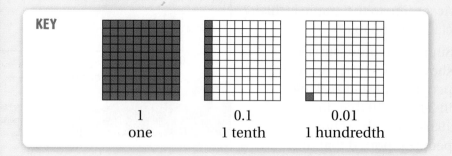

KEY

1
one

0.1
1 tenth

0.01
1 hundredth

You can use decimal grids to model dividing decimals by integers and by decimals.

Activity

1 Use a decimal grid to find 0.6 ÷ 2.

Shade 6 columns to represent 0.6.

Divide the 6 columns into 2 equal groups.

There are 3 columns, or 30 squares, in each group. 3 columns = 0.3

$0.6 ÷ 2 = 0.3$

2 Use decimal grids to find 2.25 ÷ 5.

Shade 2 grids and 25 squares of a third grid to represent 2.25.

Divide the grids and squares into 5 equal groups. Use scissors to cut apart the grids. Think: 225 squares ÷ 5 = 45 squares.

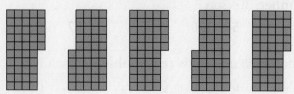

There are 45 squares, or 4.5 columns, in each group. 4.5 columns = 0.45

$2.25 ÷ 5 = 0.45$

3 Use decimal grids to find 0.8 ÷ 0.4.

Shade 8 columns to represent 0.8.

Divide the 8 columns into groups that each contain 0.4 of a decimal grid, or 4 columns.

There are 2 groups that each contain 0.4 of a grid.
0.8 ÷ 0.4 = 2

4 Use decimal grids to find 3.9 ÷ 1.3.

Shade 3 grids and 90 squares of a fourth grid to represent 3.9.

Divide the grids and squares into groups that each contain 1.3 of a decimal grid, or 13 columns.

There are 3 groups that each contain 1.3 grids.
3.9 ÷ 1.3 = 3

Think and Discuss

1. Explain why you think division is or is not commutative.

2. How is dividing a decimal by a whole number different from dividing a decimal by another decimal?

Try This

Use decimal grids to find each quotient.

1. 0.8 ÷ 4   **2.** 0.6 ÷ 4   **3.** 0.9 ÷ 0.3   **4.** 0.6 ÷ 0.4

5. 4.5 ÷ 9   **6.** 1.35 ÷ 3   **7.** 3.6 ÷ 1.2   **8.** 4.2 ÷ 2.1

3-4 Dividing Decimals by Integers

**Learn** to divide decimals by integers.

Georgia Performance Standards

M7N1.c Divide positive and negative rational numbers. Also, M7N1.d, M7P4.c, M7P5.c.

Elena received scores of 6.85, 6.95, 7.2, 7.1, and 6.9 on the balance beam at a gymnastics meet. To find her average score, add her scores and then divide by 5.

$6.85 + 6.95 + 7.2 + 7.1 + 6.9 = 35$

$35 \div 5 = 7$

Elena's average score was 7, or 7.0.

Notice that the sum of Elena's scores is an integer. But what if the sum is not an integer? You can find the average score by dividing a decimal by a whole number.

Remember!

Division can undo multiplication.
$0.2 \cdot 4 = 0.8$ and
$0.8 \div 4 = 0.2$

$0.8 \div 4$ *0.8 divided into 4 equal groups.*

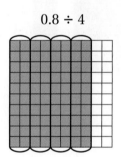

$0.8 \div 4 = 0.2$ *The size of each group is the answer.*
Each group is 2 columns, or 0.2.

EXAMPLE 1 **Dividing Decimals by Integers**

Divide. Estimate to check whether each answer is reasonable.

Remember!

$0.6 \div 3 = 0.2$
Dividend / Quotient
Divisor
0.2
$3)\overline{0.6}$

A **48.78 ÷ 6**

$$
\begin{array}{r}
8.13 \\
6)\overline{48.78} \\
-48 \\
\hline
0\,7 \\
-6 \\
\hline
18 \\
-18 \\
\hline
0
\end{array}
$$

Place the decimal point in the quotient directly above the decimal point in the dividend.

Divide as with whole numbers.

Estimate

$48 \div 6 = 8$ *8.13 is a reasonable answer.*

Divide. Estimate to check whether each answer is reasonable.

B 0.18 ÷ 2

$$\begin{array}{r} 0.09 \\ 2\overline{)0.18} \\ -18 \\ \hline 0 \end{array}$$

Place the decimal point in the quotient directly above the decimal point in the dividend. Add a zero as a placeholder in the quotient.

Estimate

0.2 ÷ 2 = 0.1   *0.09 is a reasonable answer.*

C 71.06 ÷ (−34)

$$\begin{array}{r} 2.09 \\ 34\overline{)71.06} \\ -68 \\ \hline 3\;06 \\ -3\;06 \\ \hline 0 \end{array}$$

The signs are different. Think: 71.06 ÷ 34. Place the decimal point in the quotient directly above the decimal point in the dividend.

71.06 ÷ (−34) = −2.09

Estimate

68 ÷ (−34) = −2   *−2.09 is a reasonable answer.*

EXAMPLE **2** *Money Application*

For Mrs. Deece's birthday, her class bought her a pendant for $76.50 and a card for $2.25. If there are 25 students in the class, what is the average amount each student paid for the gift?

First find the total cost of the gift. Then divide by the number of students.

76.50 + 2.25 = 78.75   *The gift cost a total of $78.75.*

$$\begin{array}{r} 3.15 \\ 25\overline{)78.75} \\ -75 \\ \hline 3\;7 \\ -2\;5 \\ \hline 1\;25 \\ -1\;25 \\ \hline 0 \end{array}$$

Place the decimal point in the quotient directly above the decimal point in the dividend.

Each student paid an average of $3.15 for the gift.

Think and Discuss   **GPS M7P1.d, M7P3.b**

1. Describe how to place the decimal point in the quotient when you divide a decimal by an integer.

2. Explain how to divide a positive decimal by a negative integer.

Georgia Performance
Standards

M7P1.a, M7P1.b, M7P3.a

go.hrw.com
Homework Help Online
KEYWORD: MS7 3-4
Parent Resources Online
KEYWORD: MS7 Parent

GUIDED PRACTICE

See Example 1 **Divide. Estimate to check whether each answer is reasonable.**

1. $42.98 \div 7$ **2.** $24.48 \div 8$ **3.** $64.89 \div (-21)$

4. $-94.72 \div 37$ **5.** $0.136 \div 8$ **6.** $1.404 \div 6$

See Example 2 **7. Hobbies** Members of a reading group order books for $89.10 and bookmarks for $10.62. If there are 18 people in the reading group, how much does each person owe on average?

INDEPENDENT PRACTICE

See Example 1 **Divide. Estimate to check whether each answer is reasonable.**

8. $12.8 \div 4$ **9.** $80.1 \div (-9)$ **10.** $14.58 \div 3$

11. $-62.44 \div 7$ **12.** $7.2 \div 12$ **13.** $33.6 \div (-7)$

14. $0.108 \div 6$ **15.** $65.28 \div 32$ **16.** $-0.152 \div 8$

17. $21.47 \div 19$ **18.** $0.148 \div 4$ **19.** $79.82 \div (-26)$

See Example 2 **20.** Cheryl ran three laps during her physical education class. If her times were 1.23 minutes, 1.04 minutes, and 1.18 minutes, what was her average lap time?

21. Consumer Math Randall spent $61.25 on some CDs and a set of headphones. All of the CDs were on sale for the same price. The set of headphones cost $12.50. If he bought 5 CDs, what was the sale price of each CD?

22. In qualifying for an auto race, one driver had lap speeds of 195.3 mi/h, 190.456 mi/h, 193.557 mi/h, and 192.575 mi/h. What was the driver's average speed for these four laps?

PRACTICE AND PROBLEM SOLVING

CRCT GPS

Extra Practice p. 730

Divide. Estimate to check whether each answer is reasonable.

23. $-9.36 \div (-6)$ **24.** $48.1 \div (-13)$ **25.** $20.95 \div 5$

26. $0.84 \div 12$ **27.** $-39.2 \div 14$ **28.** $9.45 \div (-9)$

29. $47.75 \div (-25)$ **30.** $-94.86 \div (-31)$ **31.** $-0.399 \div 21$

Simplify each expression.

32. $0.29 + 18.6 \div 3$ **33.** $1.1 - 7.28 \div 4 + 0.9$

34. $(19.2 \div 16)^2$ **35.** $-63.93 \cdot (-12.3) \div (-3)$

36. $-2.7 \div 9 \div 12$ **37.** $5 \cdot [-99.25 \div (-5)] \cdot 20$

38. Multi-Step A ticket broker bought two dozen concert tickets for $455.76. To resell the tickets, he will include a service charge of $3.80 for each ticket. What is the resale price of each ticket?

39. Recreation The graph shows the number of visitors to the three most visited U.S. national parks in 2000. What was the average number of visitors to these three parks? Round your answer to the nearest hundredth.

40. Nutrition On average, each American consumed 261.1 lb of red meat and poultry in 2000. How many pounds of red meat and poultry did the average American eat during each month of 2000? Round your answer to the nearest tenth.

41. Critical Thinking Explain why using estimation to check the answer to 56.21457 ÷ 7 is useful.

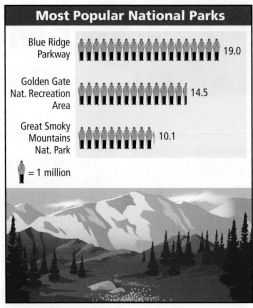

Most Popular National Parks

Blue Ridge Parkway 19.0

Golden Gate Nat. Recreation Area 14.5

Great Smoky Mountains Nat. Park 10.1

= 1 million

Source: USA Today

 42. Write a Problem Find some supermarket advertisements. Use the ads to write a problem that can be solved by dividing a decimal by a whole number.

 43. Write About It Compare dividing integers by integers with dividing decimals by integers.

44. Challenge Use a calculator to simplify the expression $(2^3 \cdot 7.5 + 3.69) \div 48.25 \div [1.04 - (0.08 \cdot 2)]$.

---

45. Multiple Choice Which expression is NOT equal to -1.34?

Ⓐ $-6.7 \div 5$ Ⓑ $16.08 \div (-12)$ Ⓒ $-12.06 \div (-9)$ Ⓓ $-22.78 \div 17$

46. Multiple Choice Simplify $-102.45 \div (-15)$.

Ⓕ -8.25 Ⓖ -7.37 Ⓗ 5.46 Ⓙ 6.83

47. Gridded Response Rujuta spent a total of $49.65 on 5 CDs. What was the average cost in dollars for each CD?

Simplify each expression. (Lesson 1-5)

48. $2 + 6 \cdot 2$

49. $3^2 - 8 \cdot 0$

50. $(2 - 1)^5 + 3 \cdot 2^2$

51. $10 - (5 - 3)^2 + 4 \div 2$

52. $2^5 \div (7 + 1)$

53. $6 - 2 \cdot 3 + 5$

Multiply. Estimate to check whether each answer is reasonable. (Lesson 3-3)

54. $-2.75 \cdot 6.34$

55. $0.2 \cdot (-4.6) \cdot (-2.3)$

56. $1.3 \cdot (-6.7)$

57. $-6.87 \cdot (-2.65)$

58. $9 \cdot 4.26$

59. $7.13 \cdot (-14)$

3-5 Dividing Decimals and Integers by Decimals

Learn to divide decimals and integers by decimals.

Georgia Performance Standards

M7N1.c Divide positive and negative rational numbers. Also, M7N1.d, M7P1.b, M7P5.c.

How many groups of 0.3 are in 0.6?

This problem is equivalent to 0.6 ÷ 0.3. You can use a grid to model this division by circling groups of 0.3 and counting the number of groups.

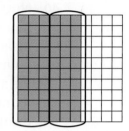

There are 2 groups of 0.3 in 0.6, so 0.6 ÷ 0.3 = 2.

When you divide two numbers, you can multiply *both numbers* by the same power of ten without changing the final answer.

Multiply both 0.6 and 0.3 by 10: 0.6 · **10** = 6 and 0.3 · **10** = 3

$$0.6 \div 0.3 = 2 \quad \text{and} \quad 6 \div 3 = 2$$

By multiplying both numbers by the same power of ten, you can make the divisor an integer. Dividing by an integer is much easier than dividing by a decimal.

E X A M P L E **1** **Dividing Decimals by Decimals**

Divide.

Helpful Hint

Multiply both numbers by the least power of ten that will make the divisor an integer.

A 4.32 ÷ 3.6

4.32 ÷ 3.6 = 43.2 ÷ 36

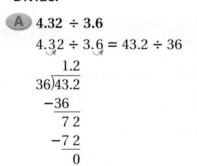

Multiply both numbers by 10 to make the divisor an integer.

Divide as with whole numbers.

B 12.95 ÷ (−1.25)

12.95 ÷ (−1.25) = 1295 ÷ (−125)

```
      10.36
125)1,295.00
   −1 25
      45 0
     −37 5
      7 50
     −7 50
         0
```

12.95 ÷ (−1.25) = −10.36

Multiply both numbers by 100 to make the divisor an integer.

Use zeros as placeholders.

Divide as with whole numbers.

The signs are different.

170 *Chapter 3 Applying Rational Numbers*

EXAMPLE 2 Dividing Integers by Decimals

Divide. Estimate to check whether each answer is reasonable.

A $9 \div 1.25$

$$9.00 \div 1.25 = 900 \div 125$$

Multiply both numbers by 100 to make the divisor an integer.

$$\begin{array}{r} 7.2 \\ 125\overline{)900.0} \\ -875 \\ \hline 25\ 0 \\ -25\ 0 \\ \hline 0 \end{array}$$

Use zero as a placeholder. Divide as with whole numbers.

Estimate $9 \div 1 = 9$

7.2 is a reasonable answer.

B $-12 \div (-1.6)$

$$-12.0 \div (-1.6) = -120 \div (-16)$$

Multiply both numbers by 10 to make the divisor an integer.

$$\begin{array}{r} 7.5 \\ 16\overline{)120.0} \\ -112 \\ \hline 8\ 0 \\ -8\ 0 \\ \hline 0 \end{array}$$

Divide as with whole numbers.

$$-12 \div (-1.6) = 7.5$$

The signs are the same.

Estimate $-12 \div (-2) = 6$

7.5 is a reasonable answer.

EXAMPLE 3 *Transportation Application*

If Sandy used 15.45 gallons of gas to drive her car 370.8 miles, how many miles per gallon did she get?

$$370.80 \div 15.45 = 37{,}080 \div 1{,}545$$

Multiply both numbers by 100 to make the divisor an integer.

$$\begin{array}{r} 24 \\ 1{,}545\overline{)37{,}080} \\ -30\ 90 \\ \hline 6\ 180 \\ -6\ 180 \\ \hline 0 \end{array}$$

Divide as with whole numbers.

Sandy got 24 miles per gallon.

> **Helpful Hint**
>
> To calculate miles per gallon, divide the number of miles driven by the number of gallons of gas used.

Think and Discuss  GPS M7P3.b

1. Explain whether $4.27 \div 0.7$ is the same as $427 \div 7$.

2. Explain how to divide an integer by a decimal.

3-5 Exercises

Georgia Performance Standards

M7P1.a, M7P1.b, M7P4.c

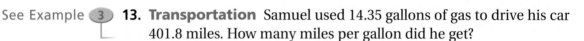

GUIDED PRACTICE

See Example ① **Divide.**

1. $3.78 \div 4.2$

2. $13.3 \div (-0.38)$

3. $14.49 \div 3.15$

4. $1.06 \div 0.2$

5. $-9.76 \div 3.05$

6. $263.16 \div (-21.5)$

See Example ② **Divide. Estimate to check whether each answer is reasonable.**

7. $3 \div 1.2$

8. $84 \div 2.4$

9. $36 \div (-2.25)$

10. $24 \div (-1.2)$

11. $-18 \div 3.75$

12. $189 \div 8.4$

See Example ③ **13. Transportation** Samuel used 14.35 gallons of gas to drive his car 401.8 miles. How many miles per gallon did he get?

INDEPENDENT PRACTICE

See Example ① **Divide.**

14. $81.27 \div 0.03$

15. $-0.408 \div 3.4$

16. $38.5 \div (-5.5)$

17. $-1.12 \div 0.08$

18. $27.82 \div 2.6$

19. $14.7 \div 3.5$

See Example ② **Divide. Estimate to check whether each answer is reasonable.**

20. $35 \div (-2.5)$

21. $361 \div 7.6$

22. $63 \div (-4.2)$

23. $5 \div 1.25$

24. $14 \div 2.5$

25. $-78 \div 1.6$

See Example ③ **26. Transportation** Lonnie used 26.75 gallons of gas to drive his truck 508.25 miles. How many miles per gallon did he get?

27. Mitchell walked 8.5 laps in 20.4 minutes. If he walked each lap at the same pace, how long did it take him to walk one full lap?

PRACTICE AND PROBLEM SOLVING

CRCT GPS

Extra Practice p. 731

Divide. Estimate to check whether each answer is reasonable.

28. $-24 \div 0.32$

29. $153 \div 6.8$

30. $-2.58 \div (-4.3)$

31. $4.12 \div (-10.3)$

32. $-17.85 \div 17$

33. $64 \div 2.56$

Simplify each expression.

34. $-4.2 + (11.5 \div 4.6) - 5.8$

35. $2 \cdot (6.8 \div 3.4) \cdot 5$

36. $(6.4 \div 2.56) - 1.2 - 2.5$

37. $11.7 \div (0.7 + 0.6) \cdot 2$

38. $4 \cdot (0.6 + 0.78) \cdot 0.25$

39. $(1.6 \div 3.2) \cdot (4.2 + 8.6)$

40. Critical Thinking A car loan totaling $13,456.44 is to be paid off in 36 equal monthly payments. Lin Yao can afford no more than $350 per month. Can she afford the loan? Explain.

41. Glaciers form when snow accumulates faster than it melts and thus becomes compacted into ice under the weight of more snow. Once the ice reaches a thickness of about 18 m, it begins to flow. If ice were to accumulate at a rate of 0.0072 m per year, how long would it take to start flowing?

42. An alpine glacier is estimated to be flowing at a rate of 4.75 m per day. At this rate, how long will it take for a marker placed on the glacier by a researcher to move 1,140 m?

A glacier in Col Ferret, a pass in the Swiss Alps

43. If the Muir Glacier in Glacier Bay, Alaska, retreats at an average speed of 0.73 m per year, how long will it take to retreat a total of 7.9 m? Round your answer to the nearest year.

44. **Multi-Step** The table shows the thickness of a glacier as measured at five different points using radar. What is the average thickness of the glacier?

Location	Thickness (m)
A	180.23
B	160.5
C	210.19
D	260
E	200.22

45. The Harvard Glacier in Alaska is advancing at a rate of about 0.055 m per day. At this rate, how long will it take the glacier to advance 20 m? Round your answer to the nearest hundredth.

46. ⭐ **Challenge** Hinman Glacier, on Mount Hinman, in Washington State, had an area of 1.3 km^2 in 1958. The glacier has lost an average of 0.06875 km^2 of area each year. In what year was the total area 0.2 km^2?

47. **Multiple Choice** Simplify $-4.42 \div 2.6 - 4.6$.

  Ⓐ -6.3 Ⓑ -2.9 Ⓒ 1.4 Ⓓ 5.7

48. **Multiple Choice** A deli is selling 5 sandwiches for $5.55, including tax. A school spent $83.25 on roast beef sandwiches for its 25 football players. How many sandwiches did each player get?

  Ⓕ 1 Ⓖ 2 Ⓗ 3 Ⓙ 5

Write each decimal or improper fraction as a mixed number. (Lessons 2-9 and 2-10)

49. $\frac{28}{3}$ 50. 6.29 51. $\frac{17}{5}$ 52. 5.7

Simplify each expression. (Lesson 3-4)

53. $6.3 + (-2.5) \div 2$ 54. $-5.38 \cdot 2.6 \div 4$ 55. $16.2 \div (-6)$ 56. $5.6 - 3.2 \div 2$

3-6 Solving Equations Containing Decimals

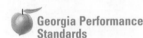 **to solve one-step equations that contain decimals.**

Georgia Performance Standards

M7N1.d Solve problems using rational numbers. Also, M7N1.c, M7A2.a, M7A2.b, M7P1.c, M7P1.d.

Students in a physical education class were running 40-yard dashes as part of a fitness test. The slowest time in the class was 3.84 seconds slower than the fastest time of 7.2 seconds.

You can write an equation to represent this situation. The slowest time s minus 3.84 is equal to the fastest time of 7.2 seconds.

$$s - 3.84 = 7.2$$

EXAMPLE 1 **Solving Equations by Adding or Subtracting**

Solve.

A $s - 3.84 = 7.2$

$$
\begin{array}{rl}
s - 3.84 = & 7.20 \\
+ 3.84 & + 3.84 \\
\hline
s \quad = & 11.04
\end{array}
$$
Add to isolate s.

> **Remember!**
>
> You can solve an equation by performing the same operation on both sides of the equation to isolate the variable.

B $y + 20.51 = 26$

$$
\begin{array}{rl}
y + 20.51 = & 2\overset{5\ 9\ 10}{6.00} \\
- 20.51 & - 20.51 \\
\hline
y \quad = & 5.49
\end{array}
$$
Subtract to isolate y.

EXAMPLE 2 **Solving Equations by Multiplying or Dividing**

Solve.

A $\dfrac{w}{3.9} = 1.2$

$$\frac{w}{3.9} = 1.2$$

$$\frac{w}{3.9} \cdot 3.9 = 1.2 \cdot 3.9$$ *Multiply to isolate w.*

$$w = 4.68$$

B $4 = 1.6c$

$$4 = 1.6c$$

$$\frac{4}{1.6} = \frac{1.6c}{1.6}$$ *Divide to isolate c.*

$$\frac{4}{1.6} = c$$ *Think: 4 ÷ 1.6 = 40 ÷ 16.*

$$2.5 = c$$

Yancey wants to buy a new snowboard that costs $396.00. If she earns $8.25 per hour at work, how many hours must she work to earn enough money to buy the snowboard?

1 Understand the Problem

Rewrite the question as a statement.

- Find the number of hours Yancey must work to earn $396.00.

List the **important information**:

- Yancey earns $8.25 per hour.
- Yancey needs $396.00 to buy a snowboard.

2 Make a Plan

Yancey's pay is equal to her hourly pay times the number of hours she works. Since you know how much money she needs to earn, you can write an equation with h being the number of hours.

$$8.25h = 396$$

3 Solve

$$8.25h = 396$$
$$\frac{8.25h}{8.25} = \frac{396}{8.25} \qquad \text{\textit{Divide to isolate h.}}$$
$$h = 48$$

Yancey must work 48 hours.

4 Look Back

You can round 8.25 to 8 and 396 to 400 to estimate how many hours Yancey needs to work.

$$400 \div 8 = 50$$

So 48 hours is a reasonable answer.

Think and Discuss   GPS M7P1.d, M7P3.b

1. Describe how to solve the equation $-1.25 + x = 1.25$. Then solve.

2. Explain how you can tell if 1.01 is a solution of $10s = -10.1$ without solving the equation.

Exercises

Georgia Performance Standards

M7P3.a, M7P3.c, M7P4.c

go.hrw.com
Homework Help Online
KEYWORD: MS7 3-6
Parent Resources Online
KEYWORD: MS7 Parent

GUIDED PRACTICE

See Example **Solve.**

1. $w - 5.8 = 1.2$

2. $x + 9.15 = 17$

3. $k + 3.91 = 28$

4. $n - 1.35 = 19.9$

See Example 5. $\dfrac{b}{1.4} = 3.6$

6. $\dfrac{x}{0.8} = 7.2$

7. $3.1t = 27.9$

8. $7.5 = 5y$

See Example 9. **Consumer Math** Jeff bought a sandwich and a salad for lunch. His total bill was $7.10. The salad cost $2.85. How much did the sandwich cost?

INDEPENDENT PRACTICE

See Example **Solve.**

10. $v + 0.84 = 6$

11. $c - 32.56 = 12$

12. $d - 14.25 = -23.9$

13. $3.52 + a = 8.6$

14. $w - 9.01 = 12.6$

15. $p + 30.34 = -22.87$

See Example (2) 16. $3.2c = 8$

17. $72 = 4.5z$

18. $21.8x = -124.26$

19. $\dfrac{w}{2.8} = 4.2$

20. $\dfrac{m}{0.19} = 12$

21. $\dfrac{a}{21.23} = -3.5$

See Example (3) 22. At the fair, 25 food tickets cost $31.25. What is the cost of each ticket?

23. To climb the rock wall at the fair, you must have 5 ride tickets. If each ticket costs $1.50, how much does it cost to climb the rock wall?

PRACTICE AND PROBLEM SOLVING

Extra Practice p. 731

Solve.

24. $1.2y = -1.44$

25. $\dfrac{n}{8.2} = -0.6$

26. $w - 4.1 = -5$

27. $r + 0.48 = 1.2$

28. $x - 5.2 = -7.3$

29. $1.05 = -7m$

30. $a + 0.81 = -6.3$

31. $60k = 54$

32. $\dfrac{h}{-7.1} = 0.62$

33. $\dfrac{t}{-0.18} = -5.2$

34. $7.9 = d + 12.7$

35. $-1.8 + v = -3.8$

36. $-k = 287.658$

37. $-n = -12.254$

38. $0.64f = 12.8$

39. $15.217 - j = 4.11$

40. $-2.1 = p + (-9.3)$

41. $\dfrac{27.3}{g} = 54.6$

42. The Drama Club at Smith Valley Middle School is selling cookie dough in order to raise money for costumes. If each tub of cookie dough costs $4.75, how many tubs must members sell to make $570.00?

43. **Consumer Math** Gregory bought a computer desk at a thrift store for $38. The regular price of a similar desk at a furniture store is 4.5 times as much. What is the regular price of the desk at the furniture store?

44. Physical Science Pennies minted, or created, before 1982 are made mostly of copper and have a density of 8.85 g/cm³. Because of an increase in the cost of copper, the density of pennies made after 1982 is 1.71 g/cm³ less. What is the density of pennies minted today?

 45. Social Studies The table shows the most common European ancestral origins of Americans (in millions), according to a Census 2000 supplementary survey. In addition, 19.6 million people stated that their ancestry was "American."

Ancestral Origins of Americans	
European Ancestry	**Number (millions)**
English	28.3
French	9.8
German	46.5
Irish	33.1
Italian	15.9
Polish	9.1
Scottish	5.4

a. How many people claimed ancestry from the countries listed, according to the survey?

b. If the data were placed in order from greatest to least, between which two nationalities would "American" ancestry be placed?

 46. What's the Error? A student's solution to the equation $m + 0.63 = 5$ was $m = 5.63$. What is the error? What is the correct solution?

 47. Write About It Compare the process of solving equations containing integers with the process of solving equations containing decimals.

48. Challenge Solve the equation $-2.8 + (b - 1.7) = -0.6 \cdot 9.4$.

CRCT PREP • GPS SUPPORT • SPIRAL REVIEW

49. Multiple Choice What is the solution to the equation $-4.55 + x = 6.32$?

Ⓐ $x = -1.39$ Ⓑ $x = 1.77$ Ⓒ $x = 10.87$ Ⓓ $x = 28.76$

50. Multiple Choice The pep squad is selling tickets for a raffle. The tickets are $0.25 each or 5 for $1.00. Julie bought a pack of 5 tickets. Which equation can be used to find how much Julie paid per ticket?

Ⓕ $5x = 0.25$ Ⓖ $0.25x = 1.00$ Ⓗ $5x = 1.00$ Ⓙ $1.00x = 0.25$

51. Extended Response Write a word problem that the equation $6.25x = 125$ can be used to solve. Solve the problem and explain what the solution means.

Write each number in scientific notation. (Lesson 1-4)

52. 340,000

53. 6,000,000

54. $32.4 \cdot 10^2$

Simplify each expression. (Lesson 3-5)

55. $6.3 \div 2.1 - 1.5$

56. $4 \cdot 5.1 \div 2 + 3.6$

57. $(1.6 + 3.8) \div 1.8$

58. $(-5.4 + 3.6) \div 0.9$

59. $-4.5 \div 0.6 \cdot (-1.2)$

60. $5.8 + 3.2 \div (-6.4)$

READY TO GO ON?

Quiz for Lessons 3-1 Through 3-6

✓ 3-1 Estimate with Decimals

Estimate.

1. $163.2 \cdot 5.4$ **2.** $37.19 + 100.94$ **3.** $376.82 - 139.28$ **4.** $33.19 \div 8.18$

5. Brad worked the homework problem 119.67 m ÷ 10.43 m. His answer was 11.47 m. Use estimation to check whether this answer is reasonable.

✓ 3-2 Adding and Subtracting Decimals

Add or subtract.

6. $4.73 + 29.68$ **7.** $-6.89 - (-29.4)$ **8.** $23.58 - 8.36$ **9.** $-15 + (-9.44)$

✓ 3-3 Multiplying Decimals

Multiply.

10. $3.4 \cdot 9.6$ **11.** $-2.66 \cdot 0.9$ **12.** $-7 \cdot (-0.06)$ **13.** $6.94 \cdot (-24)$

14. Cami can run 7.02 miles per hour. How many miles can she run in 1.75 hours? Round your answer to the nearest hundredth.

✓ 3-4 Dividing Decimals by Integers

Divide.

15. $10.8 \div (-4)$ **16.** $6.5 \div 2$ **17.** $-45.6 \div 12$ **18.** $-99.36 \div (-4)$

✓ 3-5 Dividing Decimals and Integers by Decimals

Divide.

19. $10.4 \div (-0.8)$ **20.** $18 \div 2.4$ **21.** $-3.3 \div 0.11$ **22.** $-36 \div (-0.9)$

23. Cynthia ran 17.5 laps in 38.5 minutes. If she ran each lap at the same pace, how long did it take her to run one full lap?

✓ 3-6 Solving Equations Containing Decimals

Solve.

24. $3.4 + n = 8$ **25.** $x - 1.75 = -19$ **26.** $-3.5 = -5x$ **27.** $10.1 = \dfrac{s}{8}$

28. Pablo earns $5.50 per hour. His friend Raymond earns 1.2 times as much. How much does Raymond earn per hour?

Focus on Problem Solving

Look Back

Look Back

- **Does your solution answer the question in the problem?**

Sometimes, before you solve a problem, you first need to use the given data to find additional information. Any time you find a solution for a problem, you should ask yourself if your solution answers the question being asked, or if it just gives you the information you need to find the final answer.

Read each problem, and determine whether the given solution answers the question in the problem. Explain your answer.

1 At one store, a new CD costs $15.99. At a second store, the same CD costs 0.75 as much. About how much does the second store charge?

Solution: The second store charges about $12.00.

2 Bobbie is 1.4 feet shorter than her older sister. If Bobbie's sister is 5.5 feet tall, how tall is Bobbie?

Solution:
Bobbie is 4.1 feet tall.

3 Juanita ran the 100-yard dash 1.12 seconds faster than Kellie. Kellie's time was 0.8 seconds faster than Rachel's. If Rachel's time was 15.3 seconds, what was Juanita's time?

Solution: Kellie's time was 14.5 seconds.

4 The playscape at a local park is located in a triangular sandpit. Side A of the sandpit is 2 meters longer than side B. Side B is twice as long as side C. If side C is 6 meters long, how long is side A?

Solution: Side B is 12 meters long.

5 Both Tyrone and Albert walk to and from school every day. Albert has to walk 1.25 miles farther than Tyrone does each way. If Tyrone's house is 0.6 mi from school, how far do the two boys walk altogether?

Solution: Albert lives 1.85 mi from school.

 **Estimate with Fractions**

 Problem Solving Skill

Learn to estimate sums, differences, products, and quotients of fractions and mixed numbers.

One of the largest lobsters ever caught was found off the coast of Nova Scotia, Canada, and weighed $44\frac{3}{8}$ lb. About how much heavier was this than an average lobster, which may weigh $3\frac{1}{4}$ lb?

Georgia Performance Standards

M7N1.c Add, subtract, multiply, and divide positive and negative rational numbers. Also, M7N1.d, M7P4.c, M7P5.c.

Sometimes, when solving problems, you may not need an exact answer. To estimate sums and differences of fractions and mixed numbers, round each fraction to 0, $\frac{1}{2}$, or 1. You can use a number line to help.

$\frac{2}{5}$ is closer to $\frac{1}{2}$ than to 0.

You can also round fractions by comparing numerators with denominators.

Benchmarks for Rounding Fractions		
Round to **0** if the numerator is much smaller than the denominator.	Round to $\frac{1}{2}$ if the numerator is about half the denominator.	Round to **1** if the numerator is nearly equal to the denominator.
Examples: $\frac{1}{9}, \frac{3}{20}, \frac{2}{11}$	Examples: $\frac{2}{5}, \frac{5}{12}, \frac{7}{13}$	Examples: $\frac{8}{9}, \frac{23}{25}, \frac{97}{100}$

EXAMPLE **1** *Measurement Application*

One of the largest lobsters ever caught weighed $44\frac{3}{8}$ lb. Estimate how much more this lobster weighed than an average $3\frac{1}{4}$ lb lobster.

$44\frac{3}{8} - 3\frac{1}{4}$

$44\frac{3}{8} \longrightarrow 44\frac{1}{2}$ $3\frac{1}{4} \longrightarrow 3\frac{1}{2}$ *Round each mixed number.*

$44\frac{1}{2} - 3\frac{1}{2} = 41$ *Subtract.*

The lobster weighed about 41 lb more than an average lobster.

Helpful Hint

Round $\frac{1}{4}$ to $\frac{1}{2}$, round $\frac{1}{3}$ to $\frac{1}{2}$, and round $\frac{3}{4}$ to 1.

EXAMPLE 2
Estimating Sums and Differences

Estimate each sum or difference.

A $\dfrac{4}{7} - \dfrac{13}{16}$

$\dfrac{4}{7} \longrightarrow \dfrac{1}{2}$ $\dfrac{13}{16} \longrightarrow 1$ *Round each fraction.*

$\dfrac{1}{2} - 1 = -\dfrac{1}{2}$ *Subtract.*

B $3\dfrac{3}{8} + 3\dfrac{1}{3}$

$3\dfrac{3}{8} \longrightarrow 3\dfrac{1}{2}$ $3\dfrac{1}{3} \longrightarrow 3\dfrac{1}{2}$ *Round each mixed number.*

$3\dfrac{1}{2} + 3\dfrac{1}{2} = 7$ *Add.*

C $5\dfrac{7}{8} + \left(-\dfrac{2}{5}\right)$

$5\dfrac{7}{8} \longrightarrow 6$ $-\dfrac{2}{5} \longrightarrow -\dfrac{1}{2}$ *Round each number.*

$6 + \left(-\dfrac{1}{2}\right) = 5\dfrac{1}{2}$ *Add.*

Helpful Hint

In the fraction $\dfrac{7}{8}$, the numerator is close in value to the denominator. So round $\dfrac{7}{8}$ to 1.

You can estimate products and quotients of mixed numbers by rounding to the nearest whole number. If the fraction in a mixed number is greater than or equal to $\dfrac{1}{2}$, round the mixed number up to the next whole number. If the fraction is less than $\dfrac{1}{2}$, round down to a whole number by dropping the fraction.

EXAMPLE 3 **Estimating Products and Quotients**

Estimate each product or quotient.

A $4\dfrac{2}{7} \cdot 6\dfrac{9}{10}$

$4\dfrac{2}{7} \longrightarrow 4$ $6\dfrac{9}{10} \longrightarrow 7$ *Round each mixed number to the nearest whole number.*

$4 \cdot 7 = 28$ *Multiply.*

B $11\dfrac{3}{4} \div 2\dfrac{1}{5}$

$11\dfrac{3}{4} \longrightarrow 12$ $2\dfrac{1}{5} \longrightarrow 2$ *Round each mixed number to the nearest whole number.*

$12 \div 2 = 6$ *Divide.*

Think and Discuss GPS M7P2.c, M7P3.b

1. Demonstrate how to round $\dfrac{5}{12}$ and $5\dfrac{1}{5}$.

2. Explain how you know that $25\dfrac{5}{8} \cdot 5\dfrac{1}{10} > 125$.

3-7 Exercises

Georgia Performance Standards

M7P1.b, M7P2.c, M7P3.a

go.hrw.com
Homework Help Online
KEYWORD: MS7 3-7
Parent Resources Online
KEYWORD: MS7 Parent

GUIDED PRACTICE

See Example 1

1. The length of a large SUV is $18\frac{9}{10}$ feet, and the length of a small SUV is $15\frac{1}{8}$ feet. Estimate how much longer the large SUV is than the small SUV.

See Example 2 **Estimate each sum or difference.**

2. $\frac{5}{6} + \frac{5}{12}$

3. $\frac{15}{16} - \frac{4}{5}$

4. $2\frac{1}{6} + 3\frac{6}{11}$

5. $5\frac{2}{7} - 2\frac{7}{9}$

See Example 3 **Estimate each product or quotient.**

6. $1\frac{3}{25} \cdot 9\frac{6}{7}$

7. $21\frac{2}{7} \div 7\frac{1}{3}$

8. $31\frac{7}{8} \div 4\frac{1}{5}$

9. $12\frac{2}{5} \cdot 3\frac{6}{9}$

INDEPENDENT PRACTICE

See Example 1

10. Measurement Sarah's bedroom is $14\frac{5}{6}$ feet long and $12\frac{1}{4}$ feet wide. Estimate the difference between the length and width of Sarah's bedroom.

See Example 2 **Estimate each sum or difference.**

11. $\frac{4}{9} + \frac{3}{5}$

12. $2\frac{5}{9} + 1\frac{7}{8}$

13. $8\frac{3}{4} - 6\frac{2}{5}$

14. $6\frac{1}{3} + \left(-\frac{5}{6}\right)$

15. $\frac{7}{8} - \frac{2}{5}$

16. $15\frac{1}{7} - 10\frac{8}{9}$

17. $8\frac{7}{15} + 2\frac{7}{8}$

18. $\frac{4}{5} + 7\frac{1}{8}$

See Example 3 **Estimate each product or quotient.**

19. $23\frac{5}{7} \div 3\frac{6}{9}$

20. $10\frac{2}{5} \div 4\frac{5}{8}$

21. $2\frac{1}{8} \cdot 14\frac{5}{6}$

22. $7\frac{9}{10} \cdot 11\frac{3}{4}$

23. $5\frac{3}{5} \div 2\frac{2}{3}$

24. $12\frac{4}{6} \cdot 3\frac{2}{7}$

25. $8\frac{1}{4} \div 1\frac{7}{8}$

26. $15\frac{12}{15} \cdot 1\frac{5}{7}$

PRACTICE AND PROBLEM SOLVING

Extra Practice p. 731

Estimate each sum, difference, product, or quotient.

27. $\frac{7}{9} - \frac{3}{8}$

28. $\frac{3}{5} + \frac{6}{7}$

29. $2\frac{5}{7} \cdot 8\frac{3}{11}$

30. $16\frac{7}{20} \div 3\frac{8}{9}$

31. $-1\frac{3}{5} \cdot 4\frac{6}{13}$

32. $5\frac{3}{5} - 4\frac{1}{3}$

33. $3\frac{7}{8} + \frac{2}{15}$

34. $19\frac{5}{7} \div \left(-5\frac{2}{5}\right)$

35. $\frac{3}{8} + 3\frac{5}{7} + 6\frac{7}{8}$

36. $8\frac{4}{5} + 6\frac{1}{12} + 3\frac{2}{5}$

37. $14\frac{2}{3} + 1\frac{7}{9} - 11\frac{14}{29}$

38. Kevin has $3\frac{3}{4}$ pounds of pecans and $6\frac{2}{3}$ pounds of walnuts. About how many more pounds of walnuts than pecans does Kevin have?

39. Business October 19, 1987, is known as Black Monday because the stock market fell 508 points. Xerox stock began the day at $\$70\frac{1}{8}$ and finished at $\$56\frac{1}{4}$. Approximately how far did Xerox's stock price fall during the day?

40. Recreation Monica and Paul hiked $5\frac{3}{8}$ miles on Saturday and $4\frac{9}{10}$ miles on Sunday. Estimate the number of miles Monica and Paul hiked.

41. Critical Thinking If you round a divisor down, is the quotient going to be less than or greater than the actual quotient? Explain.

Life Science The diagram shows the wingspans of different species of birds. Use the diagram for Exercises 42 and 43.

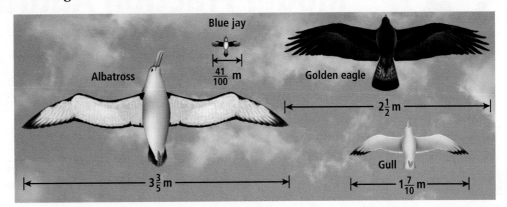

42. Approximately how much longer is the wingspan of an albatross than the wingspan of a gull?

43. Approximately how much longer is the wingspan of a golden eagle than the wingspan of a blue jay?

44. **Write a Problem** Using mixed numbers, write a problem in which an estimate is enough to solve the problem.

45. **Write About It** How is estimating fractions or mixed numbers similar to rounding whole numbers?

46. **Challenge** Suppose you had bought 10 shares of Xerox stock on October 16, 1987, for $73 per share and sold them at the end of the day on October 19, 1987, for $56\frac{1}{4}$ per share. Approximately how much money would you have lost?

CRCT PREP • GPS SUPPORT • SPIRAL REVIEW

47. **Multiple Choice** For which of the following would 2 be the best estimate?

(A) $8\frac{7}{9} \cdot 4\frac{2}{5}$ (B) $4\frac{1}{5} \div 2\frac{5}{9}$ (C) $8\frac{7}{9} \cdot 2\frac{1}{5}$ (D) $8\frac{1}{9} \div 4\frac{2}{5}$

48. **Multiple Choice** The table shows the distance Maria biked each day last week.

Day	Mon	Tue	Wed	Thu	Fri	Sat	Sun
Distance (mi)	$12\frac{3}{8}$	$9\frac{11}{15}$	$3\frac{1}{4}$	$8\frac{1}{2}$	0	$4\frac{3}{4}$	$5\frac{2}{5}$

Which is the best estimate for the total distance Maria biked last week?

(F) 40 mi   (G) 44 mi   (H) 48 mi   (J) 52 mi

Solve each equation. Check your answer. (Lessons 1-11 and 1-12)

49. $x + 16 = 43$ 50. $y - 32 = 14$ 51. $5m = 65$ 52. $\frac{n}{3} = 18$

Solve. (Lesson 3-6)

53. $-7.1x = -46.15$ 54. $8.7 = y + (-4.6)$ 55. $\frac{q}{-5.4} = 3.6$ 56. $r - 4 = -31.2$

Hands-On LAB 3-8

Model Fraction Addition and Subtraction

Use with Lesson 3-8

go.hrw.com
Lab Resources Online
KEYWORD: MS7 Lab3

Georgia Performance Standards
M7N1.c, M7N1.d, M7P5.a, M7P5.b, M7P5.c

Fraction bars can be used to model addition and subtraction of fractions.

Activity

You can use fraction bars to find $\frac{3}{8} + \frac{2}{8}$.

Use fraction bars to represent both fractions. Place the fraction bars side by side.

$\frac{1}{8}$	$\frac{1}{8}$	$\frac{1}{8}$	$\frac{1}{8}$	$\frac{1}{8}$

$$\frac{3}{8} + \frac{2}{8} = \frac{5}{8}$$

1 Use fraction bars to find each sum.

a. $\frac{1}{3} + \frac{1}{3}$ **b.** $\frac{2}{4} + \frac{1}{4}$ **c.** $\frac{3}{12} + \frac{2}{12}$ **d.** $\frac{1}{5} + \frac{2}{5}$

You can use fraction bars to find $\frac{1}{3} + \frac{1}{4}$.

Use fraction bars to represent both fractions. Place the fraction bars side by side. Which kind of fraction bar placed side by side will fit below $\frac{1}{3}$ and $\frac{1}{4}$? (*Hint:* What is the LCM of 3 and 4?)

$\frac{1}{3}$		$\frac{1}{4}$	
$\frac{1}{12}$ $\frac{1}{12}$ $\frac{1}{12}$ $\frac{1}{12}$		$\frac{1}{12}$ $\frac{1}{12}$ $\frac{1}{12}$	

$$\frac{1}{3} + \frac{1}{4} = \frac{7}{12}$$

2 Use fraction bars to find each sum.

a. $\frac{1}{2} + \frac{1}{3}$ **b.** $\frac{1}{2} + \frac{1}{4}$ **c.** $\frac{1}{3} + \frac{1}{6}$ **d.** $\frac{1}{4} + \frac{1}{6}$

You can use fraction bars to find $\frac{1}{3} + \frac{5}{6}$.

Use fraction bars to represent both fractions. Place the fraction bars side by side. Which kind of fraction bar placed side by side will fit below $\frac{1}{3}$ and $\frac{5}{6}$? (*Hint:* What is the LCM of 3 and 6?)

$\frac{1}{3}$		$\frac{1}{6}$	$\frac{1}{6}$	$\frac{1}{6}$	$\frac{1}{6}$	$\frac{1}{6}$
$\frac{1}{6}$	$\frac{1}{6}$	$\frac{1}{6}$	$\frac{1}{6}$	$\frac{1}{6}$	$\frac{1}{6}$	$\frac{1}{6}$

$$\frac{1}{3} + \frac{5}{6} = \frac{7}{6}$$

When the sum is an improper fraction, you can use the 1 bar along with fraction bars to find the mixed-number equivalent.

$$\frac{7}{6} = 1\frac{1}{6}$$

③ Use fraction bars to find each sum.

a. $\frac{3}{4} + \frac{3}{4}$ **b.** $\frac{2}{3} + \frac{1}{2}$ **c.** $\frac{5}{6} + \frac{1}{4}$ **d.** $\frac{3}{8} + \frac{3}{4}$

You can use fraction bars to find $\frac{2}{3} - \frac{1}{2}$.

Place a $\frac{1}{2}$ bar beneath bars that show $\frac{2}{3}$, and find which fraction fills in the remaining space.

$$\frac{2}{3} - \frac{1}{2} = \frac{1}{6}$$

④ Use fraction bars to find each difference.

a. $\frac{2}{3} - \frac{1}{3}$ **b.** $\frac{1}{4} - \frac{1}{6}$ **c.** $\frac{1}{2} - \frac{1}{3}$ **d.** $\frac{3}{4} - \frac{2}{3}$

Think and Discuss

1. Model and solve $\frac{3}{4} - \frac{1}{6}$. Explain your steps.

2. Two students solved $\frac{1}{4} + \frac{1}{3}$ in different ways. One got $\frac{7}{12}$ for the answer, and the other got $\frac{2}{7}$. Use models to show which student is correct.

3. Find three different ways to model $\frac{1}{2} + \frac{1}{4}$.

Try This

Use fraction bars to find each sum or difference.

1. $\frac{1}{2} + \frac{1}{2}$ **2.** $\frac{2}{3} + \frac{1}{6}$ **3.** $\frac{1}{4} + \frac{1}{6}$ **4.** $\frac{1}{3} + \frac{7}{12}$

5. $\frac{5}{12} - \frac{1}{3}$ **6.** $\frac{1}{2} - \frac{1}{4}$ **7.** $\frac{3}{4} - \frac{1}{6}$ **8.** $\frac{2}{3} - \frac{1}{4}$

9. You ate $\frac{1}{4}$ of a pizza for lunch and $\frac{5}{8}$ of the pizza for dinner. How much of the pizza did you eat in all?

10. It is $\frac{5}{6}$ mile from your home to the library. After walking $\frac{3}{4}$ mile, you stop to visit a friend on your way to the library. How much farther must you walk to reach the library?

3-8 Adding and Subtracting Fractions

Learn to add and subtract fractions.

Georgia Performance Standards

M7N1.c Add and subtract positive and negative rational numbers. Also, M7N1.d, M7P1.b.

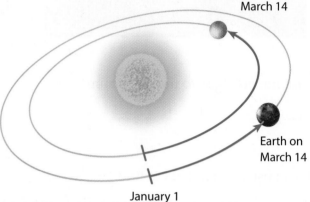

Venus on March 14

Earth on March 14

January 1

From January 1 to March 14 of any given year, Earth completes approximately $\frac{1}{5}$ of its orbit around the Sun, while Venus completes approximately $\frac{1}{3}$ of its orbit. The illustration shows what the positions of the planets would be on March 14 if they started at the same place on January 1 and their orbits were circular. To find out how much more of its orbit Venus completes than Earth, you need to subtract fractions.

EXAMPLE **1** **Adding and Subtracting Fractions with Like Denominators**

Add or subtract. Write each answer in simplest form.

A $\frac{3}{10} + \frac{1}{10}$

$$\frac{3}{10} + \frac{1}{10} = \frac{3+1}{10}$$ *Add the numerators and keep the common denominator.*

$$= \frac{4}{10} = \frac{2}{5}$$ *Simplify.*

B $\frac{7}{9} - \frac{4}{9}$

$$\frac{7}{9} - \frac{4}{9} = \frac{7-4}{9}$$ *Subtract the numerators and keep the common denominator.*

$$= \frac{3}{9} = \frac{1}{3}$$ *Simplify.*

To add or subtract fractions with different denominators, you must rewrite the fractions with a common denominator.

Helpful Hint

The LCM of two denominators is the lowest common denominator (LCD) of the fractions.

Two Ways to Find a Common Denominator
• Find the LCM (least common multiple) of the denominators.
• Multiply the denominators.

EXAMPLE 2

Adding and Subtracting Fractions with Unlike Denominators

Add or subtract. Write each answer in simplest form.

A $\dfrac{3}{8} + \dfrac{5}{12}$

$\dfrac{3}{8} + \dfrac{5}{12} = \dfrac{3 \cdot 3}{8 \cdot 3} + \dfrac{5 \cdot 2}{12 \cdot 2}$ *The LCM of the denominators is 24.*

$= \dfrac{9}{24} + \dfrac{10}{24}$ *Write equivalent fractions using a common denominator.*

$= \dfrac{19}{24}$ *Add.*

B $\dfrac{1}{10} - \dfrac{5}{8}$

$\dfrac{1}{10} - \dfrac{5}{8} = \dfrac{1 \cdot 4}{10 \cdot 4} - \dfrac{5 \cdot 5}{8 \cdot 5}$ *The LCM of the denominators is 40.*

$= \dfrac{4}{40} - \dfrac{25}{40}$ *Write equivalent fractions using a common denominator.*

$= -\dfrac{21}{40}$ *Subtract.*

C $-\dfrac{2}{3} + \dfrac{5}{8}$

$-\dfrac{2}{3} + \dfrac{5}{8} = -\dfrac{2 \cdot 8}{3 \cdot 8} + \dfrac{5 \cdot 3}{8 \cdot 3}$ *Multiply the denominators.*

$= -\dfrac{16}{24} + \dfrac{15}{24}$ *Write equivalent fractions using a common denominator.*

$= -\dfrac{1}{24}$ *Add.*

EXAMPLE 3

Astronomy Application

From January 1 to March 14, Earth completes about $\dfrac{1}{5}$ of its orbit, while Venus completes about $\dfrac{1}{3}$ of its orbit. How much more of its orbit does Venus complete than Earth?

$\dfrac{1}{3} - \dfrac{1}{5} = \dfrac{1 \cdot 5}{3 \cdot 5} - \dfrac{1 \cdot 3}{5 \cdot 3}$ *The LCM of the denominators is 15.*

$= \dfrac{5}{15} - \dfrac{3}{15}$ *Write equivalent fractions.*

$= \dfrac{2}{15}$ *Subtract.*

Venus completes $\dfrac{2}{15}$ more of its orbit than Earth does.

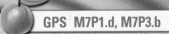

Think and Discuss   GPS M7P1.d, M7P3.b

1. Describe the process for subtracting fractions with different denominators.

2. Explain whether $\dfrac{3}{4} + \dfrac{2}{3} = \dfrac{5}{7}$ is correct.

Georgia Performance
Standards
M7P3.a, M7P4.c, M7P5.a

go.hrw.com
Homework Help Online
KEYWORD: MS7 3-8
Parent Resources Online
KEYWORD: MS7 Parent

GUIDED PRACTICE

See Example **1** Add or subtract. Write each answer in simplest form.

1. $\frac{2}{3} - \frac{1}{3}$

2. $\frac{1}{12} + \frac{1}{12}$

3. $\frac{16}{21} - \frac{7}{21}$

4. $\frac{4}{17} + \frac{11}{17}$

See Example **2** 5. $\frac{1}{6} + \frac{1}{3}$

6. $\frac{9}{10} - \frac{3}{4}$

7. $\frac{2}{3} + \frac{1}{8}$

8. $\frac{5}{8} - \frac{3}{10}$

See Example **3** 9. Parker spends $\frac{1}{4}$ of his earnings on rent and $\frac{1}{6}$ on entertainment. How much more of his earnings does Parker spend on rent than on entertainment?

INDEPENDENT PRACTICE

See Example **1** Add or subtract. Write each answer in simplest form.

10. $\frac{2}{3} + \frac{1}{3}$

11. $\frac{3}{20} + \frac{7}{20}$

12. $\frac{5}{8} + \frac{7}{8}$

13. $\frac{6}{15} + \frac{3}{15}$

14. $\frac{7}{12} - \frac{5}{12}$

15. $\frac{5}{6} - \frac{1}{6}$

16. $\frac{8}{9} - \frac{5}{9}$

17. $\frac{9}{25} - \frac{4}{25}$

See Example **2** 18. $\frac{1}{5} + \frac{2}{3}$

19. $\frac{1}{6} + \frac{1}{12}$

20. $\frac{5}{6} + \frac{3}{4}$

21. $\frac{1}{2} + \frac{2}{8}$

22. $\frac{21}{24} - \frac{1}{2}$

23. $\frac{3}{4} - \frac{11}{12}$

24. $\frac{1}{2} - \frac{2}{7}$

25. $\frac{7}{10} - \frac{1}{6}$

See Example **3** 26. Seana picked $\frac{3}{4}$ quart of blackberries. She ate $\frac{1}{12}$ quart. How much was left?

27. Armando lives $\frac{2}{3}$ mi from his school. If he has walked $\frac{1}{2}$ mi already this morning, how much farther must he walk to get to his school?

PRACTICE AND PROBLEM SOLVING

Extra Practice p. 731

Find each sum or difference. Write your answer in simplest form.

28. $\frac{4}{5} + \frac{6}{7}$

29. $\frac{5}{6} - \frac{1}{9}$

30. $\frac{1}{2} - \frac{3}{4}$

31. $\frac{2}{3} + \frac{2}{15}$

32. $\frac{5}{7} + \frac{1}{3}$

33. $\frac{1}{2} - \frac{7}{12}$

34. $\frac{3}{4} + \frac{2}{5}$

35. $\frac{9}{14} - \frac{1}{7}$

36. $\frac{7}{8} + \frac{2}{3} + \frac{5}{6}$

37. $\frac{3}{5} + \frac{1}{10} - \frac{3}{4}$

38. $\frac{3}{10} + \frac{5}{8} + \frac{1}{5}$

39. $\frac{2}{5} - \frac{1}{6} + \frac{7}{10}$

40. $-\frac{1}{2} + \frac{3}{8} + \frac{2}{7}$

41. $\frac{1}{3} + \frac{3}{7} - \frac{1}{9}$

42. $\frac{2}{9} - \frac{7}{18} + \frac{1}{6}$

43. $\frac{2}{15} + \frac{4}{9} + \frac{1}{3}$

44. $\frac{9}{35} - \frac{4}{7} - \frac{5}{14}$

45. $\frac{1}{3} - \frac{5}{7} + \frac{8}{21}$

46. $-\frac{2}{9} - \frac{1}{12} - \frac{7}{18}$

47. $-\frac{2}{3} + \frac{4}{5} + \frac{5}{8}$

48. **Cooking** One fruit salad recipe calls for $\frac{1}{2}$ cup of sugar. Another recipe calls for 2 tablespoons of sugar. Since 1 tablespoon is $\frac{1}{16}$ cup, how much more sugar does the first recipe require?

49. It took Earl $\frac{1}{2}$ hour to do his science homework and $\frac{1}{3}$ hour to do his math homework. How long did Earl work on homework?

50. **Music** In music written in $\frac{4}{4}$ time, a half note lasts for $\frac{1}{2}$ measure and an eighth note lasts for $\frac{1}{8}$ measure. In terms of a musical measure, what is the difference in the duration of the two notes?

Fitness Four friends had a competition to see how far they could walk while spinning a hoop around their waists. The table shows how far each friend walked. Use the table for Exercises 51–53.

Person	Distance (mi)
Rosalyn	$\frac{1}{8}$
Cai	$\frac{3}{4}$
Lauren	$\frac{2}{3}$
Janna	$\frac{7}{10}$

51. How much farther did Lauren walk than Rosalyn?

52. What is the combined distance that Cai and Rosalyn walked?

53. Who walked farther, Janna or Cai?

54. Measurement A shrew weighs $\frac{3}{16}$ lb. A hamster weighs $\frac{1}{4}$ lb.

   a. How many more pounds does a hamster weigh than a shrew?

   b. There are 16 oz in 1 lb. How many more ounces does the hamster weigh than the shrew?

55. Multi-Step To make $\frac{3}{4}$ lb of mixed nuts, how many pounds of cashews would you add to $\frac{1}{8}$ lb of almonds and $\frac{1}{4}$ lb of peanuts?

56. Write a Problem Use facts you find in a newspaper or magazine to write a problem that can be solved using addition or subtraction of fractions.

57. Write About It Explain the steps you use to add or subtract fractions that have different denominators.

58. Challenge The sum of two fractions is 1. If one fraction is $\frac{3}{8}$ greater than the other, what are the two fractions?

CRCT Prep • GPS Support • Spiral Review

59. Multiple Choice What is the value of the expression $\frac{3}{7} + \frac{1}{5}$?

  Ⓐ $\frac{1}{3}$ Ⓑ $\frac{22}{35}$ Ⓒ $\frac{2}{3}$ Ⓓ $\frac{26}{35}$

60. Short Response Grace has $\frac{1}{2}$ pound of apples. Julie has $\frac{2}{5}$ pound of apples. They want to combine their apples to use in a recipe that calls for 1 pound of apples. How many more pounds of apples do they need? Show your work.

Find the greatest common factor (GCF). (Lesson 2-7)

61. 5, 9   **62.** 6, 54   **63.** 18, 24   **64.** 12, 36, 50

Estimate each sum or difference. (Lesson 3-7)

65. $\frac{4}{7} + \frac{1}{9}$ **66.** $4\frac{2}{3} - 2\frac{3}{5}$ **67.** $7\frac{5}{9} - \left(-3\frac{2}{7}\right)$ **68.** $6\frac{1}{8} + 2\frac{4}{7}$

Adding and Subtracting Mixed Numbers

Learn to add and subtract mixed numbers.

Georgia Performance Standards

M7N1.c Add and subtract positive and negative rational numbers. Also, M7N1.d, M7P4.c.

Beetles can be found all over the world in a fabulous variety of shapes, sizes, and colors. The giraffe beetle from Madagascar can grow about $6\frac{2}{5}$ centimeters longer than the giant green fruit beetle can. The giant green fruit beetle can grow up to $1\frac{1}{5}$ centimeters long. To find the maximum length of the giraffe beetle, you can add $6\frac{2}{5}$ and $1\frac{1}{5}$.

EXAMPLE 1 *Measurement Application*

Helpful Hint

A mixed number is the sum of an integer and a fraction: $3\frac{4}{5} = 3 + \frac{4}{5}$.

The giraffe beetle can grow about $6\frac{2}{5}$ centimeters longer than the giant green fruit beetle can. The giant green fruit beetle can grow up to $1\frac{1}{5}$ centimeters long. What is the maximum length of the giraffe beetle?

$$6\frac{2}{5} + 1\frac{1}{5} = 7 + \frac{3}{5} \qquad \text{\textit{Add the integers, and then add the fractions.}}$$

$$= 7\frac{3}{5} \qquad \text{\textit{Add.}}$$

The maximum length of the giraffe beetle is $7\frac{3}{5}$ centimeters.

EXAMPLE 2 Adding Mixed Numbers

Add. Write each answer in simplest form.

(A) $3\frac{4}{5} + 4\frac{2}{5}$

$$3\frac{4}{5} + 4\frac{2}{5} = 7 + \frac{6}{5} \qquad \text{\textit{Add the integers, and then add the fractions.}}$$

$$= 7 + 1\frac{1}{5} \qquad \text{\textit{Rewrite the improper fraction as a mixed number.}}$$

$$= 8\frac{1}{5} \qquad \text{\textit{Add.}}$$

(B) $1\frac{2}{15} + 7\frac{1}{6}$

$$1\frac{2}{15} + 7\frac{1}{6} = 1\frac{4}{30} + 7\frac{5}{30} \qquad \text{\textit{Find a common denominator.}}$$

$$= 8 + \frac{9}{30} \qquad \text{\textit{Add the integers, and then add the fractions.}}$$

$$= 8\frac{9}{30} = 8\frac{3}{10} \qquad \text{\textit{Add. Then simplify.}}$$

Sometimes, when you subtract mixed numbers, the fraction portion of the first number is less than the fraction portion of the second number. In these cases, you must regroup before subtracting.

REGROUPING MIXED NUMBERS	
Words	**Numbers**
Regroup. Rewrite 1 as a fraction with a common denominator. Add.	$7\frac{1}{8} = 6 + 1 + \frac{1}{8}$ $= 6 + \frac{8}{8} + \frac{1}{8}$ $= 6\frac{9}{8}$

Remember!

Any fraction in which the numerator and denominator are the same is equal to 1.

EXAMPLE **3** **Subtracting Mixed Numbers**

Subtract. Write each answer in simplest form.

A $10\frac{7}{9} - 4\frac{2}{9}$

$10\frac{7}{9} - 4\frac{2}{9} = 6\frac{5}{9}$ *Subtract the integers, and then subtract the fractions.*

B $12\frac{7}{8} - 5\frac{17}{24}$

$12\frac{7}{8} - 5\frac{17}{24} = 12\frac{21}{24} - 5\frac{17}{24}$ *Find a common denominator.*

$= 7\frac{4}{24}$ *Subtract the integers, and then subtract the fractions.*

$= 7\frac{1}{6}$ *Simplify.*

C $72\frac{3}{5} - 63\frac{4}{5}$

$72\frac{3}{5} - 63\frac{4}{5} = 71\frac{8}{5} - 63\frac{4}{5}$ *Regroup. $72\frac{3}{5} = 71 + \frac{5}{5} + \frac{3}{5}$*

$= 8\frac{4}{5}$ *Subtract the integers, and then subtract the fractions.*

Think and Discuss  GPS M7P1.d, M7P3.b, M7P3.c

1. **Describe** the process for subtracting mixed numbers.

2. **Explain** whether $2\frac{3}{5} + 1\frac{3}{5} = 3\frac{6}{5}$ is correct. Is there another way to write the answer?

3. **Demonstrate** how to regroup to simplify $6\frac{2}{5} - 4\frac{3}{5}$.

3-9 Exercises

Georgia Performance Standards

M7P1.b, M7P1.c, M7P3.a

go.hrw.com

Homework Help Online
KEYWORD: MS7 3-9

Parent Resources Online
KEYWORD: MS7 Parent

GUIDED PRACTICE

See Example **1**

1. **Measurement** Chrystelle's mother is $1\frac{2}{3}$ ft taller than Chrystelle. If Chrystelle is $3\frac{1}{2}$ ft tall, how tall is her mother?

See Example **2**

Add. Write each answer in simplest form.

2. $3\frac{2}{5} + 4\frac{1}{5}$ 3. $2\frac{7}{8} + 3\frac{3}{4}$ 4. $1\frac{8}{9} + 4\frac{4}{9}$ 5. $5\frac{1}{2} + 2\frac{1}{4}$

See Example **3**

Subtract. Write each answer in simplest form.

6. $6\frac{2}{3} - 5\frac{1}{3}$ 7. $8\frac{1}{6} - 2\frac{5}{6}$ 8. $3\frac{2}{3} - 2\frac{3}{4}$ 9. $7\frac{5}{8} - 3\frac{2}{5}$

INDEPENDENT PRACTICE

See Example **1**

10. **Sports** The track at Daytona International Speedway is $\frac{24}{25}$ mi longer than the track at Atlanta Motor Speedway. If the track at Atlanta is $1\frac{27}{50}$ mi long, how long is the track at Daytona?

See Example **2**

Add. Write each answer in simplest form.

11. $6\frac{1}{4} + 8\frac{3}{4}$ 12. $3\frac{3}{5} + 7\frac{4}{5}$ 13. $3\frac{5}{6} + 1\frac{5}{6}$ 14. $2\frac{3}{5} + 4\frac{1}{3}$

15. $2\frac{3}{10} + 4\frac{1}{2}$ 16. $6\frac{1}{8} + 8\frac{9}{10}$ 17. $6\frac{1}{6} + 5\frac{3}{10}$ 18. $1\frac{2}{5} + 9\frac{1}{4}$

See Example **3**

Subtract. Write each answer in simplest form.

19. $2\frac{1}{14} - 1\frac{3}{14}$ 20. $4\frac{5}{12} - 1\frac{7}{12}$ 21. $8 - 2\frac{3}{4}$ 22. $7\frac{3}{4} - 5\frac{2}{3}$

23. $8\frac{3}{4} - 6\frac{2}{5}$ 24. $3\frac{1}{3} - 2\frac{5}{8}$ 25. $4\frac{2}{5} - 3\frac{1}{2}$ 26. $11 - 6\frac{5}{9}$

PRACTICE AND PROBLEM SOLVING

Extra Practice p. 732

Add or subtract. Write each answer in simplest form.

27. $7\frac{1}{3} + 8\frac{1}{5}$ 28. $14\frac{3}{5} - 8\frac{1}{2}$ 29. $9\frac{1}{6} + 4\frac{6}{9}$ 30. $21\frac{8}{12} - 3\frac{1}{2}$

31. $3\frac{5}{8} + 2\frac{7}{12}$ 32. $25\frac{1}{3} + 3\frac{5}{6}$ 33. $1\frac{7}{9} - \frac{17}{18}$ 34. $3\frac{1}{2} + 5\frac{1}{4}$

35. $1\frac{7}{15} + 2\frac{7}{10}$ 36. $12\frac{4}{6} - \frac{2}{5}$ 37. $4\frac{2}{3} + 1\frac{7}{8} + 3\frac{1}{2}$ 38. $5\frac{1}{6} + 8\frac{2}{3} - 9\frac{1}{2}$

Compare. Write <, >, or =.

39. $12\frac{1}{4} - 10\frac{3}{4}$ ▇ $5\frac{1}{2} - 3\frac{7}{10}$ 40. $4\frac{1}{2} + 3\frac{4}{5}$ ▇ $4\frac{5}{7} + 3\frac{1}{2}$

41. $13\frac{3}{4} - 2\frac{3}{8}$ ▇ $5\frac{5}{6} + 4\frac{2}{9}$ 42. $4\frac{1}{3} - 2\frac{1}{4}$ ▇ $3\frac{1}{4} - 1\frac{1}{6}$

43. The liquid ingredients in a recipe are water and olive oil. The recipe calls for $3\frac{1}{2}$ cups of water and $1\frac{1}{8}$ cups of olive oil. How many cups of liquid ingredients are included in the recipe?

192 *Chapter 3 Applying Rational Numbers*

Travel The table shows the distances in miles between four cities. To find the distance between two cities, locate the square where the row for one city and the column for the other city intersect.

	Atherton	Baily	Charleston	Dixon
Atherton	✕	$40\frac{2}{3}$	$100\frac{5}{6}$	$16\frac{1}{2}$
Baily	$40\frac{2}{3}$	✕	$210\frac{3}{8}$	$30\frac{2}{3}$
Charleston	$100\frac{5}{6}$	$210\frac{3}{8}$	✕	$98\frac{3}{4}$
Dixon	$16\frac{1}{2}$	$30\frac{2}{3}$	$98\frac{3}{4}$	✕

44. How much farther is it from Charleston to Dixon than from Atherton to Baily?

45. If you drove from Charleston to Atherton and then from Atherton to Dixon, how far would you drive?

Agriculture

The Netherlands produces more than 3 billion tulips each year.

46. Agriculture In 2003, the United States imported $\frac{97}{100}$ of its tulip bulbs from the Netherlands and $\frac{1}{50}$ of its tulip bulbs from New Zealand. What fraction more of tulip imports came from the Netherlands?

47. Recreation Kathy wants to hike to Candle Lake. The waterfall trail is $1\frac{2}{3}$ miles long, and the meadow trail is $1\frac{5}{6}$ miles long. Which route is shorter and by how much?

48. Choose a Strategy Spiro needs to draw a 6-inch-long line. He does not have a ruler, but he has sheets of notebook paper that are $8\frac{1}{2}$ in. wide and 11 in. long. Describe how Spiro can use the notebook paper to measure 6 in.

49. Write About It Explain why it is sometimes necessary to regroup a mixed number when subtracting.

50. Challenge Todd had d pounds of nails. He sold $3\frac{1}{2}$ pounds on Monday and $5\frac{2}{3}$ pounds on Tuesday. Write an expression to show how many pounds he had left and then simplify it.

CRCT PREP • GPS SUPPORT • SPIRAL REVIEW

51. Multiple Choice Which expression is NOT equal to $2\frac{7}{8}$?

(A) $1\frac{1}{2} + 1\frac{3}{8}$
(B) $5\frac{15}{16} - 3\frac{1}{16}$
(C) $6 - 3\frac{1}{8}$
(D) $1\frac{1}{8} + 1\frac{1}{4}$

52. Short Response Where Maddie lives, there is a $5\frac{1}{2}$-cent state sales tax, a $1\frac{3}{4}$-cent county sales tax, and a $\frac{3}{4}$-cent city sales tax. The total sales tax is the sum of the state, county, and city sales taxes. What is the total sales tax where Maddie lives? Show your work.

Find each sum. (Lesson 2-2)

53. $-3 + 9$
54. $6 + (-15)$
55. $-4 + (-8)$
56. $-11 + 5$

Find each sum or difference. Write your answer in simplest form. (Lesson 3-8)

57. $\frac{2}{5} + \frac{7}{20}$
58. $\frac{3}{7} - \frac{1}{3}$
59. $\frac{3}{4} + \frac{7}{18}$
60. $\frac{1}{3} - \frac{4}{5}$

Model Fraction Multiplication and Division

Use with Lessons 3-10 and 3-11

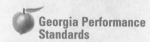
go.hrw.com
Lab Resources Online
KEYWORD: MS7 Lab3

Georgia Performance Standards

M7N1.c, M7N1.d, M7P5.a, M7P5.b, M7P5.c

You can use grids to model fraction multiplication and division.

Activity 1

Use a grid to model $\frac{3}{4} \cdot \frac{1}{2}$.

Think of $\frac{3}{4} \cdot \frac{1}{2}$ as $\frac{3}{4}$ of $\frac{1}{2}$.

Model $\frac{1}{2}$ by shading half of a grid.

The denominator tells you to divide the grid into 2 parts.
The numerator tells you how many parts to shade.

Divide the grid into 4 equal horizontal sections.

Use a different color to shade $\frac{3}{4}$ of the same grid.

The denominator tells you to divide the grid into 4 parts.
The numerator tells you how many parts to shade.

What fraction of $\frac{1}{2}$ is shaded?

To find the numerator, think: How many parts overlap?
To find the denominator, think: How many total parts are there?

$$\frac{3}{4} \cdot \frac{1}{2} = \frac{3}{8}$$

Think and Discuss

1. Are $\frac{2}{3} \cdot \frac{1}{5}$ and $\frac{1}{5} \cdot \frac{2}{3}$ modeled the same way? Explain.

2. When you multiply a positive fraction by a positive fraction, the product is less than either factor. Why?

Use a grid to find each product.

1. $\frac{1}{2} \cdot \frac{1}{2}$

2. $\frac{3}{4} \cdot \frac{2}{3}$

3. $\frac{5}{8} \cdot \frac{1}{3}$

4. $\frac{2}{5} \cdot \frac{5}{6}$

Activity 2

Use grids to model $4\frac{1}{3} \div \frac{2}{3}$.

Divide 5 grids into thirds. Shade 4 grids and $\frac{1}{3}$ of a fifth grid to represent $4\frac{1}{3}$.

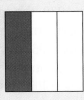

Think: How many groups of $\frac{2}{3}$ are in $4\frac{1}{3}$?

Divide the shaded grids into equal groups of 2.

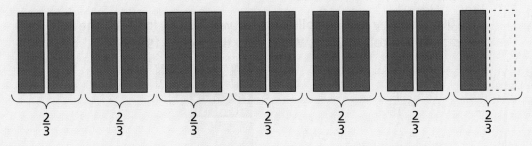

There are 6 groups of $\frac{2}{3}$, with $\frac{1}{3}$ left over. This piece is $\frac{1}{2}$ of a group of $\frac{2}{3}$.

Thus there are $6 + \frac{1}{2}$ groups of $\frac{2}{3}$ in $4\frac{1}{3}$.

$$4\frac{1}{3} \div \frac{2}{3} = 6\frac{1}{2}$$

Think and Discuss

1. Are $\frac{3}{4} \div \frac{1}{6}$ and $\frac{1}{6} \div \frac{3}{4}$ modeled the same way? Explain.

2. When you divide fractions, is the quotient greater than or less than the dividend and the divisor? Explain.

Try This

Use grids to find each quotient.

1. $\frac{7}{12} \div \frac{1}{6}$

2. $\frac{4}{5} \div \frac{3}{10}$

3. $\frac{2}{3} \div \frac{4}{9}$

4. $3\frac{2}{5} \div \frac{3}{5}$

3-10 Multiplying Fractions and Mixed Numbers

Learn to multiply fractions and mixed numbers.

Georgia Performance Standards

M7N1.c Multiply positive and negative rational numbers. Also, M7N1.d, M7P1.b, M7P5.c.

The San Francisco–Oakland Bay Bridge, which opened in 1936, is a toll bridge used by drivers traveling between the two cities. In 1939, the toll for a car crossing the bridge was $\frac{2}{15}$ of the toll in 2005. To find the toll in 1939, you will need to multiply the toll in 2005 by a fraction.

EXAMPLE 1 *Transportation Application*

In 2005, the Bay Bridge toll for a car was $3.00. In 1939, the toll was $\frac{2}{15}$ of the toll in 2005. What was the toll in 1939?

$$3 \cdot \frac{2}{15} = \frac{2}{15} + \frac{2}{15} + \frac{2}{15}$$

$$= \frac{6}{15}$$

$$= \frac{2}{5} \qquad \textit{Simplify.}$$

$$= 0.40 \qquad \textit{Divide 2 by 5 to write the fraction as a decimal.}$$

The Bay Bridge toll for a car was $0.40 in 1939.

To multiply fractions, multiply the numerators to find the product's numerator. Then multiply the denominators to find the product's denominator.

EXAMPLE 2 **Multiplying Fractions**

Multiply. Write each answer in simplest form.

Remember!

You can write any integer as a fraction with a denominator of 1.

(A) $-15 \cdot \frac{2}{3}$

$$-15 \cdot \frac{2}{3} = -\frac{15}{1} \cdot \frac{2}{3} \qquad \textit{Write −15 as a fraction.}$$

$$= -\frac{\overset{5}{\cancel{15}} \cdot 2}{1 \cdot \cancel{3}_1} \qquad \textit{Simplify.}$$

$$= -\frac{10}{1} = -10 \qquad \textit{Multiply numerators. Multiply denominators.}$$

Multiply. Write each answer in simplest form.

B $\frac{1}{4} \cdot \frac{4}{5}$

$$\frac{1}{4} \cdot \frac{4}{5} = \frac{1 \cdot \overset{1}{\cancel{4}}}{\underset{1}{\cancel{4}} \cdot 5}$$ *Simplify.*

$$= \frac{1}{5}$$ *Multiply numerators. Multiply denominators.*

C $\frac{3}{4} \cdot \left(-\frac{1}{2}\right)$

$$\frac{3}{4} \cdot \left(-\frac{1}{2}\right) = -\frac{3 \cdot 1}{4 \cdot 2}$$ *The signs are different, so the answer will be negative.*

$$= -\frac{3}{8}$$ *Multiply numerators. Multiply denominators.*

EXAMPLE 3 Multiplying Mixed Numbers

Multiply. Write each answer in simplest form.

A $8 \cdot 2\frac{3}{4}$

$$8 \cdot 2\frac{3}{4} = \frac{8}{1} \cdot \frac{11}{4}$$ *Write mixed numbers as improper fractions.*

$$= \frac{\overset{2}{\cancel{8}} \cdot 11}{1 \cdot \underset{1}{\cancel{4}}}$$ *Simplify.*

$$= \frac{22}{1} = 22$$ *Multiply numerators. Multiply denominators.*

B $\frac{1}{3} \cdot 4\frac{1}{2}$

$$\frac{1}{3} \cdot 4\frac{1}{2} = \frac{1}{3} \cdot \frac{9}{2}$$ *Write the mixed number as an improper fraction.*

$$= \frac{1 \cdot \overset{3}{\cancel{9}}}{\underset{1}{\cancel{3}} \cdot 2}$$ *Simplify.*

$$= \frac{3}{2} \text{ or } 1\frac{1}{2}$$ *Multiply numerators. Multiply denominators.*

C $3\frac{3}{5} \cdot 1\frac{1}{12}$

$$3\frac{3}{5} \cdot 1\frac{1}{12} = \frac{18}{5} \cdot \frac{13}{12}$$ *Write mixed numbers as improper fractions.*

$$= \frac{\overset{3}{\cancel{18}} \cdot 13}{5 \cdot \underset{2}{\cancel{12}}}$$ *Simplify.*

$$= \frac{39}{10} \text{ or } 3\frac{9}{10}$$ *Multiply numerators. Multiply denominators.*

Think and Discuss  **GPS M7P1.d, M7P3.b, M7P3.c**

1. Describe how to multiply a mixed number and a fraction.

2. Explain why $\frac{1}{2} \cdot \frac{1}{3} \cdot \frac{1}{4} = \frac{1}{24}$ is or is not correct.

3. Explain why you may want to simplify before multiplying $\frac{2}{3} \cdot \frac{3}{4}$. What answer will you get if you don't simplify first?

Georgia Performance
Standards

M7P1.c, M7P3.a, M7P5.a

go.hrw.com
Homework Help Online
KEYWORD: MT7 3-10
Parent Resources Online
KEYWORD: MT7 Parent

GUIDED PRACTICE

See Example **1**

1. On average, people spend $\frac{1}{4}$ of the time they sleep in a dream state. If Maxwell slept 10 hours last night, how much time did he spend dreaming? Write your answer in simplest form.

See Example **2** **Multiply. Write each answer in simplest form.**

2. $-8 \cdot \frac{3}{4}$
3. $\frac{2}{3} \cdot \frac{3}{5}$
4. $\frac{1}{4} \cdot \left(-\frac{2}{3}\right)$
5. $\frac{3}{5} \cdot (-15)$

See Example **3**
6. $4 \cdot 3\frac{1}{2}$
7. $\frac{4}{9} \cdot 5\frac{2}{5}$
8. $1\frac{1}{2} \cdot 1\frac{5}{9}$
9. $2\frac{6}{7} \cdot (-7)$

INDEPENDENT PRACTICE

See Example **1**

10. Sherry spent 4 hours exercising last week. If $\frac{5}{6}$ of the time was spent jogging, how much time did she spend jogging? Write your answer in simplest form.

11. **Measurement** A cookie recipe calls for $\frac{1}{3}$ tsp of salt for 1 batch. Doreen is making cookies for a school bake sale and wants to bake 5 batches. How much salt does she need? Write your answer in simplest form.

See Example **2** **Multiply. Write each answer in simplest form.**

12. $5 \cdot \frac{1}{8}$
13. $4 \cdot \frac{1}{8}$
14. $3 \cdot \frac{5}{8}$
15. $6 \cdot \frac{2}{3}$

16. $\frac{2}{5} \cdot \frac{5}{7}$
17. $\frac{3}{8} \cdot \frac{2}{3}$
18. $\frac{1}{2} \cdot \left(-\frac{4}{9}\right)$
19. $-\frac{5}{6} \cdot \frac{2}{3}$

See Example **3**
20. $7\frac{1}{2} \cdot 2\frac{2}{5}$
21. $6 \cdot 7\frac{2}{5}$
22. $2\frac{4}{7} \cdot \frac{1}{6}$
23. $2\frac{5}{8} \cdot 6\frac{2}{3}$

24. $\frac{2}{3} \cdot 2\frac{1}{4}$
25. $1\frac{1}{2} \cdot 1\frac{5}{9}$
26. $7 \cdot 5\frac{1}{8}$
27. $3\frac{3}{4} \cdot 2\frac{1}{5}$

PRACTICE AND PROBLEM SOLVING

Extra Practice p. 732

Multiply. Write each answer in simplest form.

28. $\frac{5}{8} \cdot \frac{4}{5}$
29. $4\frac{3}{7} \cdot \frac{5}{6}$
30. $-\frac{2}{3} \cdot 6$
31. $2 \cdot \frac{1}{6}$

32. $\frac{1}{8} \cdot 5$
33. $-\frac{3}{4} \cdot \frac{2}{9}$
34. $4\frac{2}{3} \cdot 2\frac{4}{7}$
35. $-\frac{4}{9} \cdot \left(-\frac{3}{16}\right)$

36. $3\frac{1}{2} \cdot 5$
37. $\frac{1}{2} \cdot \frac{2}{3} \cdot \frac{3}{5}$
38. $\frac{6}{7} \cdot 5$
39. $1\frac{1}{2} \cdot \frac{3}{5} \cdot \frac{7}{9}$

40. $-\frac{2}{3} \cdot 1\frac{1}{2} \cdot \frac{2}{3}$
41. $\frac{8}{9} \cdot \frac{3}{11} \cdot \frac{33}{40}$
42. $\frac{1}{6} \cdot 6 \cdot 8\frac{2}{3}$
43. $-\frac{8}{9} \cdot \left(-1\frac{1}{8}\right)$

Complete each multiplication sentence.

44. $\frac{1}{2} \cdot \blacksquare = \frac{3}{16}$
45. $\frac{2}{3} \cdot \blacksquare = \frac{1}{2}$
46. $\blacksquare \cdot \frac{5}{8} = \frac{5}{12}$
47. $\frac{3}{5} \cdot \blacksquare = \frac{3}{7}$

48. $\frac{5}{6} \cdot \frac{3}{\blacksquare} = \frac{1}{4}$
49. $\frac{4}{\blacksquare} \cdot \frac{4}{5} = \frac{8}{15}$
50. $\frac{2}{3} \cdot \frac{9}{\blacksquare} = \frac{3}{11}$
51. $\frac{\blacksquare}{15} \cdot \frac{3}{5} = \frac{1}{25}$

52. **Measurement** A standard paper clip is $1\frac{1}{4}$ in. long. If you laid 75 paper clips end to end, how long would the line of paper clips be?

53. Physical Science The weight of an object on the moon is $\frac{1}{6}$ its weight on Earth. If a bowling ball weighs $12\frac{1}{2}$ pounds on Earth, how much would it weigh on the moon?

54. In a survey, 200 students were asked what most influenced them to buy their latest CD. The results are shown in the circle graph.

   a. How many students said radio most influenced them?

   b. How many more students were influenced by radio than by a music video channel?

   c. How many said a friend or relative influenced them or they heard the CD in a store?

55. The Mississippi River flows at a rate of 2 miles per hour. If Eduardo floats down the river in a boat for $5\frac{2}{3}$ hours, how far will he travel?

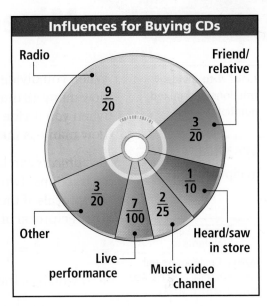

Influences for Buying CDs

Radio $\frac{9}{20}$
Friend/relative $\frac{3}{20}$
$\frac{1}{10}$ Heard/saw in store
$\frac{2}{25}$ Music video channel
$\frac{7}{100}$ Live performance
$\frac{3}{20}$ Other

56. Choose a Strategy What is the product of $\frac{1}{2} \cdot \frac{2}{3} \cdot \frac{3}{4} \cdot \frac{4}{5}$?

   Ⓐ $\frac{1}{5}$ Ⓑ 5 Ⓒ $\frac{1}{20}$ Ⓓ $\frac{3}{5}$

57. Write About It Explain why the product of two positive proper fractions is always less than either fraction.

58. Challenge Write three multiplication problems to show that the product of two fractions can be less than, equal to, or greater than 1.

CRCT Prep • GPS Support • Spiral Review

59. Multiple Choice Which expression is greater than $5\frac{5}{8}$?

   Ⓐ $8 \cdot \frac{9}{16}$ Ⓑ $-\frac{7}{9} \cdot \left(-8\frac{2}{7}\right)$ Ⓒ $3\frac{1}{2} \cdot \frac{5}{7}$ Ⓓ $-\frac{3}{7} \cdot \frac{14}{27}$

60. Multiple Choice The weight of an object on Mars is about $\frac{3}{8}$ its weight on Earth. If Sam weighs 85 pounds on Earth, how much would he weigh on Mars?

   Ⓕ 11 pounds   Ⓖ $31\frac{7}{8}$ pounds   Ⓗ $120\frac{4}{5}$ pounds   Ⓙ $226\frac{2}{3}$ pounds

Use a number line to order the integers from least to greatest. (Lesson 2-1)

61. $-7, 5, -3, 0, 4$ **62.** $-5, -10, -15, -20, 0$ **63.** $9, -9, -4, 1, -1$

Add or subtract. Write each answer in simplest form. (Lesson 3-9)

64. $4\frac{3}{5} + 2\frac{1}{5}$ **65.** $2\frac{3}{4} - 1\frac{1}{3}$ **66.** $5\frac{1}{7} + 3\frac{5}{14}$ **67.** $4\frac{5}{6} + 2\frac{5}{8}$

3-11 **Dividing Fractions and Mixed Numbers**

Learn to divide fractions and mixed numbers.

Vocabulary

reciprocal

Georgia Performance Standards

M7N1.c Divide positive and negative rational numbers. Also, M7N1.d, M7P4.c, M7P5.c.

When you divide 8 by 4, you find how many 4's there are in 8. Similarly, when you divide 2 by $\frac{1}{3}$, you find how many $\frac{1}{3}$'s there are in 2.

Reciprocals can help you divide by fractions. Two numbers are **reciprocals** if their product is 1. The reciprocal of $\frac{1}{3}$ is 3 because

$$\frac{1}{3} \cdot 3 = \frac{1}{3} \cdot \frac{3}{1} = \frac{3}{3} = 1.$$

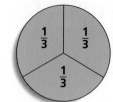

There are six $\frac{1}{3}$'s in 2.

To divide by a fraction, find its reciprocal and then multiply.

$$2 \div \frac{1}{3} = 2 \cdot 3 = 6$$

EXAMPLE **1** **Dividing Fractions**

Divide. Write each answer in simplest form.

A $\frac{2}{3} \div \frac{1}{5}$

$$\frac{2}{3} \div \frac{1}{5} = \frac{2}{3} \cdot \frac{5}{1} \qquad \text{\textit{Multiply by the reciprocal of } } \frac{1}{5}.$$

$$= \frac{2 \cdot 5}{3 \cdot 1}$$

$$= \frac{10}{3} \text{ or } 3\frac{1}{3}$$

B $\frac{3}{5} \div 6$

$$\frac{3}{5} \div 6 = \frac{3}{5} \cdot \frac{1}{6} \qquad \text{\textit{Multiply by the reciprocal of 6.}}$$

$$= \frac{{}^1\cancel{3} \cdot 1}{5 \cdot \cancel{6}_2} \qquad \text{\textit{Simplify.}}$$

$$= \frac{1}{10}$$

EXAMPLE **2** **Dividing Mixed Numbers**

Divide. Write each answer in simplest form.

A $4\frac{1}{3} \div 2\frac{1}{2}$

$$4\frac{1}{3} \div 2\frac{1}{2} = \frac{13}{3} \div \frac{5}{2} \qquad \text{\textit{Write mixed numbers as improper fractions.}}$$

$$= \frac{13}{3} \cdot \frac{2}{5} \qquad \text{\textit{Multiply by the reciprocal of } } \frac{5}{2}.$$

$$= \frac{26}{15} \text{ or } 1\frac{11}{15}$$

Divide. Write each answer in simplest form.

B $\dfrac{5}{6} \div 7\dfrac{1}{7}$

$\dfrac{5}{6} \div 7\dfrac{1}{7} = \dfrac{5}{6} \div \dfrac{50}{7}$ *Write $7\dfrac{1}{7}$ as an improper fraction.*

$= \dfrac{5}{6} \cdot \dfrac{7}{50}$ *Multiply by the reciprocal of $\dfrac{50}{7}$.*

$= \dfrac{\overset{1}{\cancel{5}} \cdot 7}{6 \cdot \underset{10}{\cancel{50}}}$ *Simplify.*

$= \dfrac{7}{60}$

C $4\dfrac{4}{5} \div \dfrac{6}{7}$

$4\dfrac{4}{5} \div \dfrac{6}{7} = \dfrac{24}{5} \div \dfrac{6}{7}$ *Write $4\dfrac{4}{5}$ as an improper fraction.*

$= \dfrac{24}{5} \cdot \dfrac{7}{6}$ *Multiply by the reciprocal of $\dfrac{6}{7}$.*

$= \dfrac{\overset{4}{} 24 \cdot 7}{5 \cdot \underset{1}{\cancel{6}}}$ *Simplify.*

$= \dfrac{28}{5}$ or $5\dfrac{3}{5}$

EXAMPLE  **3**

Social Studies Application

Use the bar graph to determine how many times longer a $100 bill is expected to stay in circulation than a $1 bill.

The life span of a $1 bill is $1\dfrac{1}{2}$ years. The life span of a $100 bill is 9 years.

Think: How many $1\dfrac{1}{2}$'s are there in 9?

$9 \div 1\dfrac{1}{2} = \dfrac{9}{1} \div \dfrac{3}{2}$ *Write both numbers as improper fractions.*

$= \dfrac{9}{1} \cdot \dfrac{2}{3}$ *Multiply by the reciprocal of $\dfrac{3}{2}$.*

$= \dfrac{\overset{3}{\cancel{9}} \cdot 2}{1 \cdot \underset{1}{\cancel{3}}}$ *Simplify.*

$= \dfrac{6}{1}$ or 6

A $100 bill is expected to stay in circulation 6 times longer than a $1 bill.

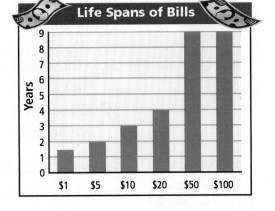

Life Spans of Bills

Social Studies

The German monetary unit, the mark, plummeted in value following World War I. By November 1923, a single loaf of bread cost 2,000,000,000 marks. People used the worthless paper money for many unusual purposes, such as building kites.

Think and Discuss   GPS M7P3.b, M7P3.d

1. Explain whether $\dfrac{1}{2} \div \dfrac{2}{3}$ is the same as $2 \cdot \dfrac{2}{3}$.

2. Compare the steps used in multiplying mixed numbers with those used in dividing mixed numbers.

Georgia Performance Standards

M7P1.a, M7P1.b, M7P4.c

go.hrw.com
Homework Help Online
KEYWORD: MS7 3-11
Parent Resources Online
KEYWORD: MS7 Parent

GUIDED PRACTICE

See Example 1 · **Divide. Write each answer in simplest form.**

1. $6 \div \frac{1}{3}$ **2.** $\frac{3}{5} \div \frac{3}{4}$ **3.** $\frac{3}{4} \div 8$ **4.** $-\frac{5}{9} \div \frac{2}{5}$

See Example 2 **5.** $\frac{5}{6} \div 3\frac{1}{3}$ **6.** $5\frac{5}{8} \div 4\frac{1}{2}$ **7.** $10\frac{4}{5} \div 5\frac{2}{5}$ **8.** $2\frac{1}{10} \div \frac{3}{5}$

See Example 3 · **9.** Kareem has $12\frac{1}{2}$ yards of material. A cape for a play takes $3\frac{5}{6}$ yards. How many capes can Kareem make with the material?

INDEPENDENT PRACTICE

See Example 1 · **Divide. Write each answer in simplest form.**

10. $2 \div \frac{7}{8}$ **11.** $10 \div \frac{5}{9}$ **12.** $\frac{3}{4} \div \frac{6}{7}$ **13.** $\frac{7}{8} \div \frac{1}{5}$

14. $\frac{8}{9} \div \frac{1}{4}$ **15.** $\frac{4}{9} \div 12$ **16.** $\frac{9}{10} \div 6$ **17.** $-16 \div \frac{2}{5}$

See Example 2 **18.** $\frac{7}{11} \div 4\frac{1}{5}$ **19.** $\frac{3}{4} \div 2\frac{1}{10}$ **20.** $22\frac{1}{2} \div 4\frac{2}{7}$ **21.** $-10\frac{1}{2} \div \frac{3}{4}$

22. $3\frac{5}{7} \div 9\frac{1}{7}$ **23.** $14\frac{2}{3} \div 1\frac{1}{6}$ **24.** $7\frac{7}{10} \div 2\frac{2}{5}$ **25.** $8\frac{2}{5} \div \frac{7}{8}$

See Example 3 **26.** A juicer holds $43\frac{3}{4}$ pints of juice. How many $2\frac{1}{2}$-pint bottles can be filled with that much juice?

27. Measurement How many $24\frac{1}{2}$ in. pieces of ribbon can be cut from a roll of ribbon that is 147 in. long?

PRACTICE AND PROBLEM SOLVING

Extra Practice p. 732

Evaluate. Write each answer in simplest form.

28. $6\frac{2}{3} \div \frac{7}{9}$ **29.** $9 \div 1\frac{2}{3}$ **30.** $\frac{2}{3} \div \frac{8}{9}$ **31.** $-1\frac{7}{11} \div \left(-\frac{9}{11}\right)$

32. $\frac{1}{2} \div 4\frac{3}{4}$ **33.** $\frac{4}{21} \div 3\frac{1}{2}$ **34.** $4\frac{1}{2} \div 3\frac{1}{2}$ **35.** $-1\frac{3}{5} \div 2\frac{1}{2}$

36. $\frac{7}{8} \div 2\frac{1}{10}$ **37.** $1\frac{3}{5} \div \left(2\frac{2}{9}\right)$ **38.** $\left(\frac{1}{2} + \frac{2}{3}\right) \div 1\frac{1}{2}$ **39.** $\left(2\frac{3}{4} + 3\frac{2}{3}\right) \div \frac{11}{18}$

40. $2\frac{2}{3} \div \left(\frac{1}{5} \cdot \frac{2}{3}\right)$ **41.** $\frac{4}{5} \cdot \frac{3}{8} \div \frac{9}{10}$ **42.** $-\frac{12}{13} \cdot \frac{13}{18} \div 1\frac{1}{2}$ **43.** $\frac{3}{7} \div \frac{15}{28} \div \left(-\frac{4}{5}\right)$

44. Multi-Step Three friends will be driving to an amusement park that is $226\frac{4}{5}$ mi from their town.

 a. If each friend drives the same distance, how far will each drive?

 b. Since the first driver will be in rush hour traffic, the friends agree the first driver will drive only $\frac{1}{3}$ of the distance found in part **a**. How far will the first driver drive?

45. Multi-Step How many $\frac{1}{4}$ lb hamburger patties can be made from a $10\frac{1}{4}$ lb package and an $11\frac{1}{2}$ lb package of ground meat?

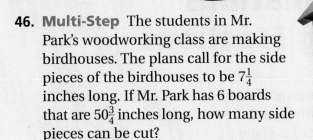

46. Multi-Step The students in Mr. Park's woodworking class are making birdhouses. The plans call for the side pieces of the birdhouses to be $7\frac{1}{4}$ inches long. If Mr. Park has 6 boards that are $50\frac{3}{4}$ inches long, how many side pieces can be cut?

47. For his drafting class, Manuel is drawing plans for a bookcase. Because he wants his drawing to be $\frac{1}{4}$ the actual size of the bookcase, Manuel must divide each measurement of the bookcase by 4. If the bookcase will be $3\frac{2}{3}$ feet wide, how wide will Manuel's drawing be?

48. The table shows the total number of hours that the students in each of Mrs. Anwar's 5 industrial arts classes took to complete their final projects. If the third-period class has 17 students, how many hours did each student in that class work on average?

Period	Hours
1st	$200\frac{1}{2}$
2nd	$179\frac{2}{5}$
3rd	$199\frac{3}{4}$
5th	$190\frac{3}{4}$
6th	$180\frac{1}{4}$

49. Critical Thinking Brandy is stamping circles from a strip of aluminum. If each circle is $1\frac{1}{4}$ inches tall, how many circles can she get from an $8\frac{3}{4}$-inch by $1\frac{1}{4}$-inch strip of aluminum?

50. ⭐ **Challenge** Alexandra is cutting wood stencils to spell her first name with capital letters. Her first step is to cut a square of wood that is $3\frac{1}{2}$ in. long on a side for each letter in her name. Will Alexandra be able to make all of the letters of her name from a single piece of wood that is $7\frac{1}{2}$ in. wide and 18 in. long? Explain your answer.

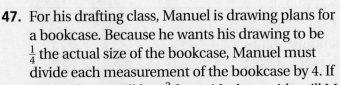

CRCT Prep • GPS Support • Spiral Review

51. Multiple Choice Which expression is NOT equivalent to $2\frac{2}{3} \div 1\frac{5}{8}$?

Ⓐ $\frac{8}{3} \cdot \frac{8}{13}$ Ⓑ $2\frac{2}{3} \div \frac{13}{8}$ Ⓒ $\frac{8}{3} \div \frac{13}{8}$ Ⓓ $\frac{8}{3} \cdot 1\frac{5}{8}$

52. Multiple Choice What is the value of the expression $\frac{3}{5} \cdot \frac{1}{6} \div \frac{2}{5}$?

Ⓕ $\frac{1}{25}$ Ⓖ $\frac{1}{4}$ Ⓗ $\frac{15}{22}$ Ⓙ 25

53. Gridded Response Each cat at the animal shelter gets $\frac{3}{4}$ c of food every day. If Alysse has $16\frac{1}{2}$ c of cat food, how many cats can she feed?

Find the least common multiple (LCM). (Lesson 2-8)

54. 2, 15 **55.** 6, 8 **56.** 4, 6, 18 **57.** 3, 4, 8

Multiply. Write each answer in simplest form. (Lesson 3-10)

58. $-\frac{2}{15} \cdot \frac{5}{8}$ **59.** $1\frac{7}{20} \cdot 6$ **60.** $1\frac{2}{7} \cdot 2\frac{3}{4}$ **61.** $\frac{1}{8} \cdot 6 \cdot 2\frac{5}{9}$

3-12 Solving Equations Containing Fractions

 **Learn** to solve one-step equations that contain fractions.

 **Georgia Performance Standards**

M7N1.d Solve problems using rational numbers. Also, M7N1.c, M7A2.a, M7A2.b.

Gold classified as 24 karat is pure gold, while gold classified as 18 karat is only $\frac{3}{4}$ pure. The remaining $\frac{1}{4}$ of 18-karat gold is made up of one or more different metals, such as silver, copper, or zinc. The color of gold varies, depending on the type and amount of each metal added to the pure gold.

Equations can help you determine the amounts of metals in different kinds of gold. The goal when solving equations that contain fractions is the same as when working with other kinds of numbers—*to isolate the variable* on one side of the equation.

EXAMPLE 1 **Solving Equations by Adding or Subtracting**

Solve. Write each answer in simplest form.

A $x - \frac{1}{5} = \frac{3}{5}$

$$x - \frac{1}{5} = \frac{3}{5}$$

$$x - \frac{1}{5} + \frac{1}{5} = \frac{3}{5} + \frac{1}{5} \qquad \textit{Add to isolate x.}$$

$$x = \frac{4}{5} \qquad \textit{Add.}$$

Helpful Hint

You can also isolate the variable y by adding the opposite of $\frac{5}{12}$, $-\frac{5}{12}$, to both sides.

B $\frac{5}{12} + y = \frac{2}{3}$

$$\frac{5}{12} + y = \frac{2}{3}$$

$$\frac{5}{12} + y - \frac{5}{12} = \frac{2}{3} - \frac{5}{12} \qquad \textit{Subtract to isolate y.}$$

$$y = \frac{8}{12} - \frac{5}{12} \qquad \textit{Find a common denominator.}$$

$$y = \frac{3}{12} = \frac{1}{4} \qquad \textit{Subtract. Then simplify.}$$

C $\frac{7}{18} + u = -\frac{14}{27}$

$$\frac{7}{18} + u = -\frac{14}{27}$$

$$\frac{7}{18} + u - \frac{7}{18} = -\frac{14}{27} - \frac{7}{18} \qquad \textit{Subtract to isolate u.}$$

$$u = -\frac{28}{54} - \frac{21}{54} \qquad \textit{Find a common denominator.}$$

$$u = -\frac{49}{54} \qquad \textit{Subtract.}$$

EXAMPLE 2 **Solving Equations by Multiplying**

Solve. Write each answer in simplest form.

A $\frac{2}{3}x = \frac{4}{5}$

$$\frac{2}{3}x = \frac{4}{5}$$

$$\frac{2}{3}x \cdot \frac{3}{2} = \frac{\overset{2}{\cancel{4}}}{5} \cdot \frac{3}{\underset{1}{\cancel{2}}}$$ *Multiply by the reciprocal of $\frac{2}{3}$. Then simplify.*

$$x = \frac{6}{5} \text{ or } 1\frac{1}{5}$$

B $3y = \frac{6}{7}$

$$3y = \frac{6}{7}$$

$$3y \cdot \frac{1}{3} = \frac{\overset{2}{\cancel{6}}}{7} \cdot \frac{1}{\underset{1}{\cancel{3}}}$$ *Multiply by the reciprocal of 3. Then simplify.*

$$y = \frac{2}{7}$$

> **Caution!**
>
> To undo multiplying by $\frac{2}{3}$, you must divide by $\frac{2}{3}$ or multiply by its reciprocal, $\frac{3}{2}$.

EXAMPLE 3 *Physical Science Application*

Pink gold is made of pure gold, silver, and copper. There is $\frac{11}{20}$ more pure gold than copper in pink gold. If pink gold is $\frac{3}{4}$ pure gold, what portion of pink gold is copper?

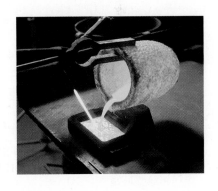

Let c represent the amount of copper in pink gold.

$$c + \frac{11}{20} = \frac{3}{4}$$ *Write an equation.*

$$c + \frac{11}{20} - \frac{11}{20} = \frac{3}{4} - \frac{11}{20}$$ *Subtract to isolate c.*

$$c = \frac{15}{20} - \frac{11}{20}$$ *Find a common denominator.*

$$c = \frac{4}{20}$$ *Subtract.*

$$c = \frac{1}{5}$$ *Simplify.*

Pink gold is $\frac{1}{5}$ copper.

Think and Discuss   GPS M7P1.d, M7P2.c, M7P3.b

1. Show the first step you would use to solve $m + 3\frac{5}{8} = 12\frac{1}{2}$.

2. Describe how to decide whether $\frac{2}{3}$ is a solution of $\frac{7}{8}y = \frac{3}{5}$.

3. Explain why solving $\frac{2}{5}c = \frac{8}{9}$ by multiplying both sides by $\frac{5}{2}$ is the same as solving it by dividing both sides by $\frac{2}{5}$.

Georgia Performance Standards

M7P3.a, M7P3.c, M7P5.a

go.hrw.com
Homework Help Online
KEYWORD: MS7 3-12
Parent Resources Online
KEYWORD: MS7Parent

GUIDED PRACTICE

See Example **1** Solve. Write each answer in simplest form.

1. $a - \frac{1}{2} = \frac{1}{4}$ **2.** $m + \frac{1}{6} = \frac{5}{6}$ **3.** $p - \frac{2}{3} = \frac{5}{6}$

See Example **2** **4.** $\frac{1}{5}x = 8$ **5.** $\frac{2}{3}r = \frac{3}{5}$ **6.** $3w = \frac{3}{7}$

See Example **3** **7.** Kara has $\frac{3}{8}$ cup less oatmeal than she needs for a cookie recipe. If she has $\frac{3}{4}$ cup of oatmeal, how much oatmeal does she need?

INDEPENDENT PRACTICE

See Example **1** Solve. Write each answer in simplest form.

8. $n - \frac{1}{5} = \frac{3}{5}$ **9.** $t - \frac{3}{8} = \frac{1}{4}$ **10.** $s - \frac{7}{24} = \frac{1}{3}$

11. $x + \frac{2}{3} = 2\frac{7}{8}$ **12.** $h + \frac{7}{10} = \frac{7}{10}$ **13.** $y + \frac{5}{6} = \frac{19}{20}$

See Example **2** **14.** $\frac{1}{5}x = 4$ **15.** $\frac{1}{4}w = \frac{1}{8}$ **16.** $5y = \frac{3}{10}$

17. $6z = \frac{1}{2}$ **18.** $\frac{5}{8}x = \frac{2}{5}$ **19.** $\frac{5}{8}n = 1\frac{1}{5}$

See Example **3** **20.** **Earth Science** Carbon-14 has a half-life of 5,730 years. After 17,190 years, $\frac{1}{8}$ of the carbon-14 in a sample will be left. If 5 grams of carbon-14 are left after 17,190 years, how much was in the original sample?

PRACTICE AND PROBLEM SOLVING

Extra Practice p. 732

Solve. Write each answer in simplest form.

21. $\frac{4}{5}t = \frac{1}{5}$ **22.** $m - \frac{1}{2} = \frac{2}{3}$ **23.** $\frac{1}{8}w = \frac{3}{4}$

24. $\frac{8}{9} + t = \frac{17}{18}$ **25.** $\frac{5}{3}x = 1$ **26.** $j + \frac{5}{8} = \frac{11}{16}$

27. $\frac{4}{3}n = 3\frac{1}{5}$ **28.** $z + \frac{1}{6} = 3\frac{9}{15}$ **29.** $\frac{3}{4}y = \frac{3}{8}$

30. $-\frac{5}{26} + m = -\frac{7}{13}$ **31.** $-\frac{8}{77} + r = -\frac{1}{11}$ **32.** $y - \frac{3}{4} = -\frac{9}{20}$

33. $h - \frac{3}{8} = -\frac{11}{24}$ **34.** $-\frac{5}{36}t = -\frac{5}{16}$ **35.** $-\frac{8}{13}v = -\frac{6}{13}$

36. $4\frac{6}{7} + p = 5\frac{1}{4}$ **37.** $d - 5\frac{1}{8} = 9\frac{3}{10}$ **38.** $6\frac{8}{21}k = 13\frac{1}{3}$

39. **Food** Each person in Finland drinks an average of $24\frac{1}{4}$ lb of coffee per year. This is $13\frac{1}{16}$ lb more than the average person in Italy consumes. On average, how much coffee does an Italian drink each year?

40. **Weather** Yuma, Arizona, receives $102\frac{1}{100}$ fewer inches of rain each year than Quillayute, Washington, which receives $105\frac{9}{50}$ inches per year. (*Source: National Weather Service*). How much rain does Yuma get in one year?

41. Life Science Scientists have discovered $1\frac{1}{2}$ million species of animals. This is estimated to be $\frac{1}{10}$ the total number of species thought to exist. About how many species do scientists think exist?

42. History The circle graph shows the birthplaces of the United States' presidents who were in office between 1789 and 1845.

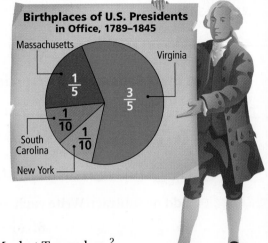

Birthplaces of U.S. Presidents in Office, 1789–1845

Massachusetts $\frac{1}{5}$

Virginia $\frac{3}{5}$

$\frac{1}{10}$

South Carolina

$\frac{1}{10}$

New York

a. If six of the presidents represented in the graph were born in Virginia, how many presidents are represented in the graph?

b. Based on your answer to **a**, how many of the presidents were born in Massachusetts?

43. Architecture In Indianapolis, the Market Tower has $\frac{2}{3}$ as many stories as the Bank One Tower. If the Market Tower has 32 stories, how many stories does the Bank One Tower have?

44. Multi-Step Each week, Jennifer saves $\frac{1}{5}$ of her allowance and spends some of the rest on lunches. This week, she had $\frac{2}{15}$ of her allowance left after buying her lunch each day. What fraction of her allowance did she spend on lunches?

45. What's the Error? A student solved $\frac{3}{5}x = \frac{2}{3}$ and got $x = \frac{2}{5}$. Find the error.

46. Write About It Solve $3\frac{1}{3}z = 1\frac{1}{2}$. Explain why you need to write mixed numbers as improper fractions when multiplying and dividing.

47. Challenge Solve $\frac{3}{5}w = 0.9$. Write your answer as a fraction and as a decimal.

48. Multiple Choice Which value of y is the solution to the equation $y - \frac{7}{8} = \frac{3}{5}$?

Ⓐ $y = -\frac{11}{40}$ Ⓑ $y = \frac{10}{13}$ Ⓒ $y = 1\frac{19}{40}$ Ⓓ $y = 2$

49. Multiple Choice Which equation has the solution $x = -\frac{2}{5}$?

Ⓕ $\frac{2}{5}x = -1$ Ⓖ $-\frac{3}{4}x = \frac{6}{20}$ Ⓗ $-\frac{4}{7} + x = \frac{2}{3}$ Ⓙ $x - 3\frac{5}{7} = 3\frac{1}{2}$

Order the numbers from least to greatest. (Lesson 2-11)

50. $-0.61, -\frac{3}{5}, -\frac{4}{3}, -1.25$ **51.** $3.25, 3\frac{2}{10}, 3, 3.02$ **52.** $\frac{1}{2}, -0.2, -\frac{7}{10}, 0.04$

Estimate. (Lesson 3-1)

53. $5.87 - 7.01$ **54.** $4.0387 + (-2.13)$ **55.** $6.785 \cdot 3.01$

READY TO GO ON?

Quiz for Lessons 3-7 Through 3-12

3-7 Estimate with Fractions

Estimate each sum, difference, product, or quotient.

1. $\frac{3}{4} - \frac{2}{9}$ **2.** $-\frac{2}{7} + 5\frac{6}{11}$ **3.** $4\frac{9}{15} \cdot 3\frac{1}{4}$ **4.** $9\frac{7}{9} \div 4\frac{3}{5}$

3-8 Adding and Subtracting Fractions

Add or subtract. Write each answer in simplest form.

5. $\frac{5}{8} + \frac{1}{8}$ **6.** $\frac{14}{15} - \frac{11}{15}$ **7.** $-\frac{1}{3} + \frac{6}{9}$ **8.** $\frac{5}{8} - \frac{2}{3}$

3-9 Adding and Subtracting Mixed Numbers

Add or subtract. Write each answer in simplest form.

9. $6\frac{1}{9} + 2\frac{2}{9}$ **10.** $1\frac{3}{6} + 7\frac{2}{3}$ **11.** $5\frac{5}{8} - 3\frac{1}{8}$ **12.** $8\frac{1}{12} - 3\frac{1}{4}$

13. A mother giraffe is $13\frac{7}{10}$ ft tall. She is $5\frac{1}{2}$ ft taller than her young giraffe. How tall is the young giraffe?

3-10 Multiplying Fractions and Mixed Numbers

Multiply. Write each answer in simplest form.

14. $-12 \cdot \frac{5}{6}$ **15.** $\frac{5}{14} \cdot \frac{7}{10}$ **16.** $8\frac{4}{5} \cdot \frac{10}{11}$ **17.** $10\frac{5}{12} \cdot 1\frac{3}{5}$

18. A recipe calls for $1\frac{1}{3}$ cups flour. Tom is making $2\frac{1}{2}$ times the recipe for his family reunion. How much flour does he need? Write your answer in simplest form.

3-11 Dividing Fractions and Mixed Numbers

Divide. Write each answer in simplest form.

19. $\frac{1}{6} \div \frac{5}{6}$ **20.** $\frac{2}{3} \div 4$ **21.** $5\frac{3}{5} \div \frac{4}{5}$ **22.** $4\frac{2}{7} \div 1\frac{1}{5}$

23. Nina has $9\frac{3}{7}$ yards of material. She needs $1\frac{4}{7}$ yards to make a pillow case. How many pillow cases can Nina make with the material?

3-12 Solving Equations Containing Fractions

Solve. Write each answer in simplest form.

24. $x - \frac{2}{3} = \frac{2}{15}$ **25.** $\frac{4}{9} = -2q$ **26.** $\frac{1}{6}m = \frac{1}{9}$ **27.** $\frac{3}{8} + p = -\frac{1}{6}$

28. A recipe for Uncle Frank's homemade hush puppies calls for $\frac{1}{8}$ teaspoon of cayenne pepper. The recipe calls for 6 times as much salt as it does cayenne pepper. How much salt does Uncle Frank's recipe require?

MULTI-STEP TEST PREP

Heading South The Estrada family is planning to vacation at the beach in Corpus Christi, Texas. The Estradas live in Fort Worth and are considering different ways to make the trip. Corpus Christi is 372 miles south of Fort Worth.

1. A roundtrip airfare is available on the Internet for $139.55. How much would it cost all four family members to fly to Corpus Christi?

2. Gasoline costs $2.31 per gallon, and the family's car gets 21 miles to the gallon. How much does it cost the family to drive 1 mile?

3. How much would the family pay to drive roundtrip to Corpus Christi? Explain.

4. How much money can the family save by driving instead of flying?

5. The Estradas decide to drive and stop for a break in Waco. What fraction of the trip will be completed when they reach Waco?

6. The distance from Waco to San Antonio is $\frac{9}{20}$ of the trip. What fraction of the trip will be completed when the family reaches San Antonio?

7. The Estradas extend their trip to Raymondville, which is $1\frac{1}{4}$ times farther from Fort Worth than Corpus Christi is. How far is Raymondville from Fort Worth?

TEXAS

Fort Worth

93 mi

N

Waco

35

Austin

San Antonio

37

Corpus Christi

Raymondville

Game Time

Number Patterns

The numbers one through ten form the pattern below. Each arrow indicates some kind of relationship between the two numbers. Four relates to itself. Can you figure out what the pattern is?

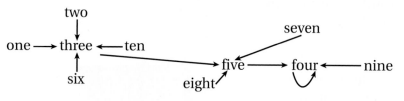

The Spanish numbers *uno* through *diez* form a similar pattern. In this case, *cinco* relates to itself.

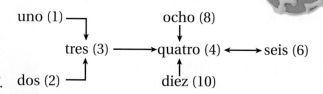

Other interesting number patterns involve cyclic numbers. Cyclic numbers sometimes occur when a fraction converts to a repeating nonterminating decimal. One of the most interesting cyclic numbers is produced by converting the fraction $\frac{1}{7}$ to a decimal.

$$\frac{1}{7} = 0.142857142857142\ldots$$

Multiplying 142857 by the numbers 1–6 produces the same digits in a different order.

$1 \cdot 142857 = 142857$ $3 \cdot 142857 = 428571$ $5 \cdot 142857 = 714285$

$2 \cdot 142857 = 285714$ $4 \cdot 142857 = 571428$ $6 \cdot 142857 = 857142$

Fraction Action

Roll four number cubes and use the numbers to form two fractions. Add the fractions and try to get a sum as close to 1 as possible. To determine your score on each turn, find the difference between the sum of your fractions and 1. Keep a running total of your score as you play. The winner is the player with the lowest score at the end of the game.

go.hrw.com
Game Time Extra
KEYWORD: MS7 Games

A complete copy of the rules are available online.

Materials
- file folder
- ruler
- pencil
- scissors
- markers

It's in the Bag!

PROJECT ▶ **Operation Slide Through**

Slide notes through the frame to review key concepts about operations with rational numbers.

Directions

1 Keep the file folder closed throughout the project. Cut off a $3\frac{1}{2}$-inch strip from the bottom of the folder. Trim the remaining folder so that is has no tabs and measures 8 inches by 8 inches. **Figure A**

2 Cut out a thin notch about 4 inches long along the middle of the folded edge. **Figure B**

3 Cut a $3\frac{3}{4}$-inch slit about 2 inches to the right of the notch. Make another slit, also $3\frac{3}{4}$ inches long, about 3 inches to the right of the first slit. **Figure C**

4 Weave the $3\frac{1}{2}$-inch strip of the folder into the notch, through the first slit, and into the second slit. **Figure D**

Taking Note of the Math

As you pull the strip through the frame, divide the strip into several sections. Use each section to record vocabulary and practice problems from the chapter.

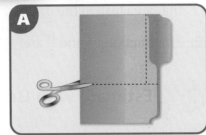
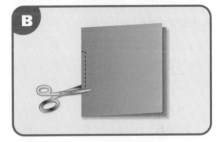
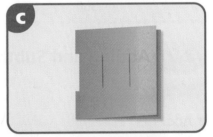
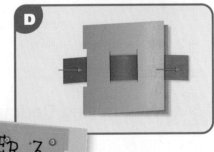

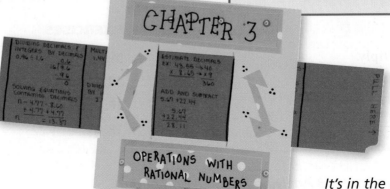

Study Guide: Review

Vocabulary

compatible numbers 150   reciprocal 200

Complete the sentences below with vocabulary words from the list above.

1. When estimating products or quotients, you can use ___?___ that are close to the original numbers and easy to use.

2. The fractions $\frac{3}{8}$ and $\frac{8}{3}$ are ___?___ because they multiply to give 1.

3-1 Estimate with Decimals (pp. 150–153)

 GPS M7N1.c, M7N1.d

EXAMPLE

- Estimate.

      63.28 ⟶   63   *Round each decimal to*
    + 16.52 ⟶ + 17   *the nearest integer.*
    ─────────   ──
                 80

      43.55 ⟶   40   *Use compatible*
    × 8.65 ⟶   × 9   *numbers.*
    ─────────   ───
                360

EXERCISES

Estimate.

3. $54.4 + 55.99$ 4. $11.48 - 5.6$

5. $24.77 \cdot 3.45$ 6. $37.8 \div 9.3$

7. Helen saves $7.85 each week. She wants to buy a TV that costs $163.15. For about how many weeks will Helen have to save her money before she can buy the TV?

3-2 Adding and Subtracting Decimals (pp. 154–157)

 GPS M7N1.c, M7N1.d

EXAMPLE

- Add.

    5.67 + 22.44
       5.67   *Line up the decimal points.*
    + 22.44
    ────────
      28.11   *Add.*

EXERCISES

Add or subtract.

8. $4.99 + 22.89$ 9. $-6.7 + (-44.5)$

10. $18.09 - 11.87$ 11. $47 + 5.902$

12. $23 - 8.905$ 13. $4.68 + 31.2$

3-3 Multiplying Decimals (pp. 160–163)

 GPS M7N1.c, M7N1.d

EXAMPLE

- Multiply.

    1.44 · 0.6
      1.44   *2 decimal places*
    × 0.6   *1 decimal place*
    ──────
    0.864   *2 + 1 = 3 decimal places*

EXERCISES

Multiply.

14. $7 \cdot 0.5$ 15. $-4.3 \cdot 9$

16. $4.55 \cdot 8.9$ 17. $7.88 \cdot 7.65$

18. $63.4 \cdot 1.22$ 19. $-9.9 \cdot 1.9$

3-4 Dividing Decimals by Integers (pp. 166–169)

 GPS M7N1.c, M7N1.d

EXAMPLE

■ Divide.

$2.8 \div 7$

$$\begin{array}{r} 0.4 \\ 7\overline{)2.8} \\ -2\ 8 \\ \hline 0 \end{array}$$

Place the decimal point in the quotient directly above the decimal point in the dividend.

EXERCISES

Divide.

20. $16.1 \div 7$

21. $102.9 \div (-21)$

22. $0.48 \div 6$

23. $17.4 \div (-3)$

24. $8.25 \div (-5)$

25. $81.6 \div 24$

3-5 Dividing Decimals and Integers by Decimals (pp. 170–173)

EXAMPLE

 GPS M7N1.c, M7N1.d

■ Divide.

$0.96 \div 1.6$

$$\begin{array}{r} 0.6 \\ 16\overline{)9.6} \\ -9\ 6 \\ \hline 0 \end{array}$$

Multiply both numbers by 10 to make the divisor an integer.

EXERCISES

Divide.

26. $7.65 \div 1.7$

27. $9.483 \div (-8.7)$

28. $126.28 \div (-8.2)$

29. $2.5 \div (-0.005)$

30. $9 \div 4.5$

31. $13 \div 3.25$

3-6 Solving Equations Containing Decimals (pp. 174–177)

EXAMPLE

GPS M7N1.c, M7N1.d, M7A2.a, M7A2.b

■ Solve.

$$\begin{array}{rl} n - 4.77 = & 8.60 \\ + 4.77 & + 4.77 \\ \hline n \quad = & 13.37 \end{array}$$

Add to isolate n.

EXERCISES

Solve.

32. $x + 40.44 = 30$

33. $\frac{s}{1.07} = 100$

34. $0.8n = 0.0056$

35. $k - 8 = 0.64$

36. $3.65 + e = -1.4$

37. $\frac{w}{-0.2} = 15.4$

3-7 Estimate with Fractions (pp. 180–183)

EXAMPLE

GPS M7N1.c, M7N1.d

■ Estimate.

$7\frac{3}{4} - 4\frac{1}{3}$

$7\frac{3}{4} \longrightarrow 8 \qquad 4\frac{1}{3} \longrightarrow 4\frac{1}{2}$

$8 - 4\frac{1}{2} = 3\frac{1}{2}$

$11\frac{7}{12} \div 3\frac{2}{5}$

$11\frac{7}{12} \longrightarrow 12 \quad 3\frac{2}{5} \longrightarrow 3$

$12 \div 3 = 4$

EXERCISES

Estimate each sum, difference, product, or quotient.

38. $11\frac{1}{7} + 12\frac{3}{4}$

39. $5\frac{5}{7} - 13\frac{10}{17}$

40. $9\frac{7}{8} + \left(-7\frac{1}{13}\right)$

41. $11\frac{8}{9} - 11\frac{1}{20}$

42. $5\frac{13}{20} \cdot 4\frac{1}{2}$

43. $-6\frac{1}{4} \div \left(-1\frac{5}{8}\right)$

44. Sara ran $2\frac{1}{3}$ laps on Monday and $7\frac{3}{4}$ laps on Friday. About how many more laps did Sara run on Friday?

3-8 Adding and Subtracting Fractions (pp. 186–189)

GPS M7N1.c, M7N1.d

EXAMPLE

■ Add.

$$\frac{1}{3} + \frac{2}{5} = \frac{5}{15} + \frac{6}{15}$$

$$= \frac{11}{15}$$

Write equivalent fractions using a common denominator.

EXERCISES

Add or subtract. Write each answer in simplest form.

45. $\frac{3}{4} - \frac{1}{3}$ **46.** $\frac{1}{4} + \frac{3}{5}$

47. $\frac{4}{11} + \frac{4}{44}$ **48.** $\frac{4}{9} - \frac{1}{3}$

3-9 Adding and Subtracting Mixed Numbers (pp. 190–193)

GPS M7N1.c, M7N1.d

EXAMPLE

■ Add.

$$1\frac{1}{3} + 2\frac{1}{2} = 1\frac{2}{6} + 2\frac{3}{6}$$

$$= 3 + \frac{5}{6}$$

$$= 3\frac{5}{6}$$

Add the integers, and then add the fractions.

EXERCISES

Add or subtract. Write each answer in simplest form.

49. $3\frac{7}{8} + 2\frac{1}{3}$ **50.** $2\frac{1}{4} + 1\frac{1}{12}$

51. $8\frac{1}{2} - 2\frac{1}{4}$ **52.** $11\frac{3}{4} - 10\frac{1}{3}$

3-10 Multiplying Fractions and Mixed Numbers (pp. 196–199)

GPS M7N1.c, M7N1.d

EXAMPLE

■ Multiply. Write the answer in simplest form.

$$4\frac{1}{2} \cdot 5\frac{3}{4} = \frac{9}{2} \cdot \frac{23}{4}$$

$$= \frac{207}{8} \text{ or } 25\frac{7}{8}$$

EXERCISES

Multiply. Write each answer in simplest form.

53. $1\frac{2}{3} \cdot 4\frac{1}{2}$ **54.** $\frac{4}{5} \cdot 2\frac{3}{10}$

55. $4\frac{6}{7} \cdot 3\frac{5}{9}$ **56.** $3\frac{4}{7} \cdot 1\frac{3}{4}$

3-11 Dividing Fractions and Mixed Numbers (pp. 200–203)

GPS M7N1.c, M7N1.d

EXAMPLE

■ Divide.

$$\frac{3}{4} \div \frac{2}{5} = \frac{3}{4} \cdot \frac{5}{2}$$

$$= \frac{15}{8} \text{ or } 1\frac{7}{8}$$

Multiply by the reciprocal of $\frac{2}{5}$.

EXERCISES

Divide. Write each answer in simplest form.

57. $\frac{1}{3} \div 6\frac{1}{4}$ **58.** $\frac{1}{2} \div 3\frac{3}{4}$

59. $\frac{11}{13} \div \frac{11}{13}$ **60.** $2\frac{7}{8} \div 1\frac{1}{2}$

3-12 Solving Equations Containing Fractions (pp. 204–207)

 GPS M7N1.c, M7N1.d, M7A2.a, M7A2.b

EXAMPLE

■ Solve. Write the answer in simplest form.

$$\frac{1}{4}x = \frac{1}{6}$$

$$\frac{4}{1} \cdot \frac{1}{4}x = \frac{1}{6} \cdot \frac{4}{1}$$

$$x = \frac{4}{6} = \frac{2}{3}$$

Multiply by the reciprocal of $\frac{1}{4}$.

EXERCISES

Solve. Write each answer in simplest form.

61. $\frac{1}{5}x = \frac{1}{3}$ **62.** $\frac{1}{3} + y = \frac{2}{5}$

63. $\frac{1}{6}x = \frac{2}{7}$ **64.** $\frac{2}{7} + x = \frac{3}{4}$

Estimate.

1. $19.95 + 21.36$ **2.** $49.17 - 5.88$ **3.** $3.21 \cdot 16.78$ **4.** $49.1 \div 5.6$

Add or subtract.

5. $3.086 + 6.152$ **6.** $5.91 + 12.8$ **7.** $3.1 - 2.076$ **8.** $14.75 - 6.926$

Multiply or divide.

9. $3.25 \cdot 24$ **10.** $-3.79 \cdot 0.9$ **11.** $3.2 \div 16$ **12.** $3.57 \div (-0.7)$

Solve.

13. $w - 5.3 = 7.6$ **14.** $4.9 = c + 3.7$ **15.** $b \div 1.8 = 2.1$ **16.** $4.3h = 81.7$

Estimate each sum, difference, product, or quotient.

17. $\frac{3}{4} + \frac{3}{8}$ **18.** $5\frac{7}{8} - 3\frac{1}{4}$ **19.** $6\frac{5}{7} \cdot 2\frac{2}{9}$ **20.** $8\frac{1}{5} \div 3\frac{9}{10}$

Add or subtract. Write each answer in simplest form.

21. $\frac{3}{10} + \frac{2}{5}$ **22.** $\frac{11}{16} - \frac{7}{8}$ **23.** $7\frac{1}{3} + 5\frac{11}{12}$ **24.** $9 - 3\frac{2}{5}$

Multiply or divide. Write each answer in simplest form.

25. $5 \cdot 4\frac{1}{3}$ **26.** $2\frac{7}{10} \cdot 2\frac{2}{3}$ **27.** $\frac{3}{10} \div \frac{4}{5}$ **28.** $2\frac{1}{5} \div 1\frac{5}{6}$

29. A recipe calls for $4\frac{4}{5}$ tbsp of butter. Nasim is making $3\frac{1}{3}$ times the recipe for his soccer team. How much butter does he need? Write your answer in simplest form.

30. Brianna has $11\frac{2}{3}$ cups of milk. She needs $1\frac{1}{6}$ cups of milk to make a pot of hot cocoa. How many pots of hot cocoa can Brianna make?

Solve. Write each answer in simplest form.

31. $\frac{1}{5}a = \frac{1}{8}$ **32.** $\frac{1}{4}c = 980$ **33.** $-\frac{7}{9} + w = \frac{2}{3}$ **34.** $z - \frac{5}{13} = \frac{6}{7}$

35. Alan finished his homework in $1\frac{1}{2}$ hours. It took Jimmy $\frac{3}{4}$ of an hour longer than Alan to finish his homework. How long did it take Jimmy to finish his homework?

36. Mya played in two softball games one afternoon. The first game lasted 42 min. The second game lasted $1\frac{2}{3}$ times longer than the first game. How long did Mya's second game last?

Chapter Test

TEST TACKLER

Gridded Response: Write Gridded Responses

When responding to a test item that requires you to place your answer in a grid, you must fill in the grid on your answer sheet correctly, or the item will be marked as incorrect.

EXAMPLE 1

Gridded Response: Solve the equation $0.23 + r = 1.42$.

$$
\begin{array}{rcr}
0.23 + r = & 1.42 \\
- 0.23 & - 0.23 \\
\hline
r = & 1.19
\end{array}
$$

- Using a pencil, write your answer in the answer boxes at the top of the grid. Put the first digit of your answer in the leftmost box, or put the last digit of your answer in the rightmost box. On some grids, the fraction bar and the decimal point have a designated box.

- Put only one digit or symbol in each box. Do not leave a blank box in the middle of an answer.

- Shade the bubble for each digit or symbol in the same column as in the answer box.

EXAMPLE 2

Gridded Response: Divide. $3 \div 1\frac{4}{5}$

$$3 \div 1\frac{4}{5} = \frac{3}{1} \div \frac{9}{5}$$

$$= \frac{3}{1} \cdot \frac{5}{9}$$

$$= \frac{15}{9} = \frac{5}{3} = 1\frac{2}{3} = 1.\overline{6}$$

The answer simplifies to $\frac{5}{3}$, $1\frac{2}{3}$, or $1.\overline{6}$.

- Mixed numbers and repeating decimals cannot be gridded, so you must grid the answer as $\frac{5}{3}$.

- Write your answer in the answer boxes at the top of the grid.

- Put only one digit or symbol in each box. Do not leave a blank box in the middle of an answer.

- Shade the bubble for each digit or symbol in the same column as in the answer box.

If you get a negative answer to a gridded response item, rework the problem carefully. Response grids do not include negative signs, so if you get a negative answer, you probably made a math error.

Read each statement, and then answer the questions that follow.

Sample A
A student correctly solved an equation for x and got 42 as a result. Then the student filled in the grid as shown.

1. What error did the student make when filling in the grid?

2. Explain a second method of filling in the answer correctly.

Sample B
A student correctly multiplied 0.16 and 0.07. Then the student filled in the grid as shown.

3. What error did the student make when filling in the grid?

4. Explain how to fill in the answer correctly.

Sample C
A student subtracted -12 from 5 and got an answer of -17. Then the student filled in the grid as shown.

5. What error did the student make when finding the answer?

6. Explain why you cannot fill in a negative number on a grid.

7. Explain how to fill in the answer to $5 - (-12)$ correctly.

Sample D
A student correctly simplified $\frac{5}{6} + \frac{11}{12}$ and got $1\frac{9}{12}$ as a result. Then the student filled in the grid as shown.

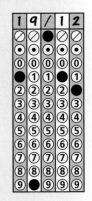

8. What answer is shown in the grid?

9. Explain why you cannot show a mixed number in a grid.

10. Write two equivalent forms of the answer $1\frac{9}{12}$ that could be filled in the grid correctly.

Cumulative Assessment, Chapters 1–3

Multiple Choice

1. A cell phone company charges $0.05 per text message. Which expression represents the cost of t text messages?

  Ⓐ $0.05t$ Ⓒ $0.05 - t$

  Ⓑ $0.05 + t$ Ⓓ $0.05 \div t$

2. Ahmed had $7.50 in his bank account on Sunday. The table shows his account activity for each day last week. What was the balance in Ahmed's account on Friday?

Day	Deposit	Withdrawal
Monday	$25.25	none
Tuesday	none	−$108.13
Wednesday	$65.25	none
Thursday	$32.17	none
Friday	none	−$101.50

  Ⓕ −$86.96   Ⓗ $0

  Ⓖ −$79.46   Ⓙ $96.46

3. Natasha is designing a doghouse. She wants the front of the doghouse to be $3\frac{1}{2}$ feet wide, and she wants the side of the doghouse to be $2\frac{3}{4}$ feet wider than the front. Which equation can be used to find x, the length of the side of the doghouse?

  Ⓐ $3\frac{1}{2} + 2\frac{3}{4} = x$ Ⓒ $3\frac{1}{2} \cdot 2\frac{3}{4} = x$

  Ⓑ $3\frac{1}{2} - 2\frac{3}{4} = x$ Ⓓ $3\frac{1}{2} \div 2\frac{3}{4} = x$

4. What is the value of $5\frac{2}{3} \div \frac{3}{9}$?

  Ⓕ 17   Ⓗ 10

  Ⓖ $\frac{17}{9}$ Ⓙ $5\frac{1}{3}$

5. Mrs. Herold has $5\frac{1}{4}$ yards of material to make two dresses. The larger dress requires $3\frac{3}{4}$ yards of material. Which equation can be used to find t, the number of yards of material remaining to make the smaller dress?

  Ⓐ $3\frac{3}{4} - t = 5\frac{1}{4}$ Ⓒ $3\frac{3}{4} \div t = 5\frac{1}{4}$

  Ⓑ $3\frac{3}{4} \cdot t = 5\frac{1}{4}$ Ⓓ $3\frac{3}{4} + t = 5\frac{1}{4}$

6. Carl is building a picket fence. The first picket in the fence is 1 m long, the second picket is $1\frac{1}{4}$ m long, and the third picket is $1\frac{1}{2}$ m long. If the pattern continues, how long is the seventh picket?

  Ⓕ $1\frac{3}{4}$ m   Ⓗ $2\frac{1}{4}$ m

  Ⓖ 2 m   Ⓙ $2\frac{1}{2}$ m

7. Daisy the bulldog weighs $45\frac{13}{16}$ pounds. Henry the beagle weighs $21\frac{3}{4}$ pounds. How many more pounds does Daisy weigh than Henry?

  Ⓐ $23\frac{15}{16}$ pounds   Ⓒ $24\frac{1}{16}$ pounds

  Ⓑ $24\frac{5}{6}$ pounds   Ⓓ $67\frac{9}{16}$ pounds

8. What is the prime factorization of 110?

  Ⓕ $55 \cdot 2$ Ⓗ $11 \cdot 5 \cdot 2$

  Ⓖ $22 \cdot 5 \cdot 2$ Ⓙ $110 \cdot 1$

9. Joel threw a shot put $24\frac{2}{9}$ yards. Jamil threw the shot put $33\frac{10}{11}$ yards. Estimate how much farther Jamil threw the shot put than Joel did.

  Ⓐ 8 yards   Ⓒ 12 yards

  Ⓑ 10 yards   Ⓓ 15 yards

When possible, use logic to eliminate at least two answer choices.

10. Which model best represents the expression $\frac{6}{8} \times \frac{1}{2}$?

11. The table shows the different types of pets owned by the 15 students in Mrs. Sizer's Spanish class. What fraction of the students listed own a dog?

Type of Pet	Number of Students
Cat	5
Dog	9
Hamster	1

Ⓐ $\frac{3}{5}$ Ⓒ $\frac{1}{15}$

Ⓑ $\frac{1}{5}$ Ⓓ $\frac{1}{9}$

12. Solve the equation $\frac{5}{12}x = \frac{1}{4}$ for x.

Ⓕ $\frac{5}{48}$ Ⓗ $\frac{5}{12}$

Ⓖ $\frac{1}{4}$ Ⓙ $\frac{3}{5}$

13. What is the value of the expression $2(3.1) + 1.02(-4) - 8 + 3^2$?

Ⓐ −2.88   Ⓒ 5.28

Ⓑ 3.12   Ⓓ 11.28

Short Response

14. Louise is staying on the 22nd floor of a hotel. Her mother is staying on the 43rd floor. Louise wants to visit her mother, but the elevator is temporarily out of service. Write and solve an equation to find the number of floors that Louise must climb if she takes the stairs.

15. Mari bought 3 packages of colored paper. She used $\frac{3}{4}$ of a package to make greeting cards and used $1\frac{1}{6}$ packages for an art project. She gave $\frac{2}{3}$ of a package to her brother. How much colored paper does Mari have left? Show the steps you used to find the answer.

16. A building proposal calls for 6 acres of land to be divided into $\frac{3}{4}$-acre lots. How many lots can be made? Explain your answer.

Extended Response

17. A high school is hosting a triple-jump competition. In this event, athletes make three leaps in a row to try to cover the greatest distance.

a. Tony's first two jumps were $11\frac{2}{3}$ ft and $11\frac{1}{2}$ ft. His total distance was 44 ft. Write and solve an equation to find the length of his final jump.

b. Candice's three jumps were all the same length. Her total distance was 38 ft. What was the length of each of her jumps?

c. The lengths of Davis's jumps were 11.6 ft, $11\frac{1}{4}$ ft, and $11\frac{2}{3}$ ft. Plot these lengths on a number line. What was the farthest distance he jumped? How much farther was this distance than the shortest distance Davis jumped?

CRCT Prep

Patterns and Functions

CRCT PREP

go.hrw.com
Chapter Project Online
KEYWORD: MS7 Ch4

Fastest U.S. Roller Coasters	
Roller Coaster	**Speed (mi/h)**
Superman the Escape	100
Millennium Force	92
Goliath	85
Titan	85

Career *Roller Coaster Designer*

Traditional roller-coaster designs rely on gravity for a coaster to gain speed. Some of these designs include loops and turns to make rides more exciting.

Jim Seay is a roller-coaster designer who uses high-tech methods to create exhilarating rides. His designs include a system that can propel a coaster from 0 to 70 miles per hour in less than four seconds!

ARE YOU READY?

✓ Vocabulary

Choose the best term from the list to complete each sentence.

1. A(n) __?__ states that two expressions are equivalent.

2. To __?__ an expression is to substitute a number for the variable and simplify.

3. A value of the variable in an equation that makes the statement true is a(n) __?__ of the equation.

4. A(n) __?__ is a number that can be written as a ratio of two integers.

equation

evaluate

irrational number

rational number

solution

Complete these exercises to review skills you will need for this chapter.

✓ Evaluate Expressions

Evaluate each expression.

5. $x + 5$ for $x = -18$

6. $-9y$ for $y = 13$

7. $\frac{z}{-6}$ for $z = 96$

8. $w - 9$ for $w = -13$

9. $-3z + 1$ for $z = 4$

10. $3w + 9$ for $w = 7$

11. $5 - \frac{y}{3}$ for $y = -3$

12. $x^2 + 1$ for $x = -2$

✓ Solve Equations

Solve each equation.

13. $y + 14 = -3$

14. $-4y = -72$

15. $y - 6 = 39$

16. $\frac{y}{3} = -9$

17. $56 = 8y$

18. $26 = y + 2$

19. $25 - y = 7$

20. $\frac{121}{y} = 11$

21. $-72 = 3y$

22. $25 = \frac{150}{y}$

23. $15 + y = 4$

24. $-120 = -2y$

✓ Number Patterns

Find the next three numbers in the pattern.

25. 95, 112, 129, 146, . . .

26. 85, 65, 60, 40, 35, . . .

27. 20, 20, 100, 100, 500, . . .

28. 12, 14, 17, 21, 26, . . .

29. 1, 3, 5, 7, . . .

30. $-19, -12, -5, 2, . . .$

31. $5, -10, 20, -40, 80, . . .$

32. $0, -10, -5, -15, -10, . . .$

Study Guide: Preview

Where You've Been

Previously, you

- graphed ordered pairs of non-negative rational numbers on a coordinate plane.

- used tables to generate formulas representing relationships.

- formulated equations from problem situations.

In This Chapter

You will study

- plotting and identifying ordered pairs of integers on a coordinate plane.

- graphing to demonstrate relationships between data sets.

- describing the relationship between the terms in a sequence and their positions in a sequence.

- formulating problem situations when given a simple equation.

Where You're Going

You can use the skills learned in this chapter

- to sketch or interpret a graph that shows how a measurement such as distance, speed, cost, or temperature changes over time.

- to interpret patterns and make predictions in science, business, and personal finance.

Key Vocabulary/Vocabulario

coordinate plane	plano cartesiano
function	función
linear equation	ecuación lineal
linear function	función lineal
ordered pair	par ordenado
origin	origen
quadrant	cuadrante
sequence	sucesión
x-axis	eje x
y-axis	eje y

Vocabulary Connections

To become familiar with some of the vocabulary terms in the chapter, consider the following. You may refer to the chapter, the glossary, or a dictionary if you like.

1. A **sequence** is an ordered list of numbers, such as 2, 4, 6, and 8. Can you make up a sequence with a pattern and describe the pattern?

2. The word "linear" comes from the word *line*. What do you think the graph of a **linear equation** looks like?

3. An *origin* is the point at which something begins. Can you describe where to begin when you plot a point on a coordinate plane? Can you guess why the point where the x-axis and y-axis cross is called the **origin**?

4. *Quadrupeds* are animals with four feet, and a *quadrilateral* is a four-sided figure. A coordinate plane has sections called **quadrants**. What does this word imply about the number of sections in a coordinate plane?

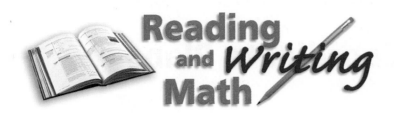 **Reading** and **Writing Math**

Writing Strategy:
Write a Convincing Argument

A convincing argument or explanation should include the following:

• The problem restated in your own words

• A short response

• Evidence to support the response

• A summary statement

 **Example**

✏ **Write About It**
Explain how to find the next three integers in the pattern −43, −40, −37, −34, ...

Step 1 **Identify the goal.**

Explain how to find the next three integers in the pattern
−43, −40, −37, −34, ...

Step 2 **Provide a short response.**

As the pattern continues, the integers increase in value. Find the amount of increase from one integer to the next. Then add that amount to the last integer in the pattern. Follow this step two more times to get the next three integers in the pattern.

Step 3 **Provide evidence to support your response.**

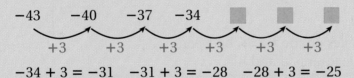

Find the amount of increase from one integer to the next.

−34 + 3 = −31   −31 + 3 = −28   −28 + 3 = −25

The next three integers are −31, −28, and −25.

The pattern is to add 3 to each integer to get the next integer.

Step 4 **Summarize your argument.**

To find the next three integers in the pattern −43, −40, −37, −34, . . . , find the amount that is added to each integer to get the next integer in the pattern.

Try This

Write a convincing argument using the method above.

1. Explain how to find the next three integers in the pattern 0, −2, −4, −6, ...

2. Explain how to find the seventh integer in the pattern −18, −13, −8, −3, ...

4-1 The Coordinate Plane

Learn to plot and identify ordered pairs on a coordinate plane.

Vocabulary

coordinate plane

x-axis

y-axis

origin

quadrant

ordered pair

A **coordinate plane** is a plane containing a horizontal number line, the **x-axis**, and a vertical number line, the **y-axis**. The intersection of these axes is called the **origin**.

The axes divide the coordinate plane into four regions called **quadrants**, which are numbered I, II, III, and IV.

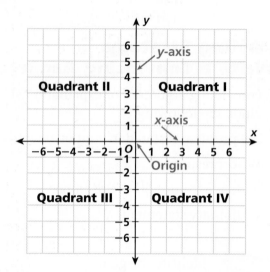

EXAMPLE 1 Identifying Quadrants on a Coordinate Plane

Identify the quadrant that contains each point.

A *P*

P lies in Quadrant II.

B *Q*

Q lies in Quadrant IV.

C *R*

R lies on the *x*-axis, between Quadrants II and III.

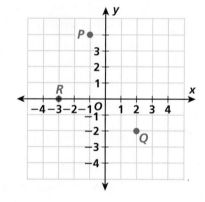

An **ordered pair** is a pair of numbers that can be used to locate a point on a coordinate plane. The two numbers that form the ordered pair are called coordinates. The origin is identified by the ordered pair (0, 0).

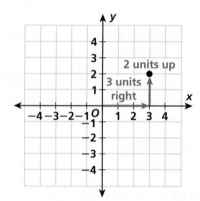

Ordered pair

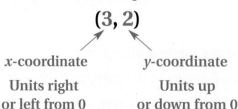

224 *Chapter 4 Patterns and Functions*

EXAMPLE 2 **Plotting Points on a Coordinate Plane**

Plot each point on a coordinate plane.

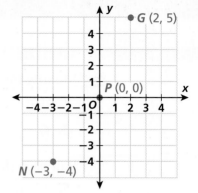

A $G\,(2, 5)$

Start at the origin. Move 2 units right and 5 units up.

B $N\,(-3, -4)$

Start at the origin. Move 3 units left and 4 units down.

C $P\,(0, 0)$

Point P is at the origin.

EXAMPLE 3 **Identifying Points on a Coordinate Plane**

Give the coordinates of each point.

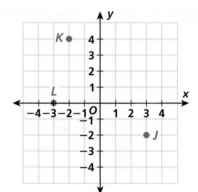

A J

Start at the origin. Point J is 3 units right and 2 units down.

The coordinates of J are $(3, -2)$.

B K

Start at the origin. Point K is 2 units left and 4 units up.

The coordinates of K are $(-2, 4)$.

C L

Start at the origin. Point L is 3 units left on the x-axis.

The coordinates of L are $(-3, 0)$.

Think and Discuss   GPS M7P3.a, M7P3.b

1. **Explain** whether point $(4, 5)$ is the same as point $(5, 4)$.

2. **Name** the x-coordinate of a point on the y-axis. Name the y-coordinate of a point on the x-axis.

3. **Suppose** the equator represents the x-axis on a map of Earth and a line called the *prime meridian*, which passes through England, represents the y-axis. Starting at the origin, which of these directions —east, west, north, and south—are positive? Which are negative?

Georgia Performance Standards

M7P3.a, M7P3.c, M7P4.c

go.hrw.com
Homework Help Online
KEYWORD: MS7 4-1
Parent Resources Online
KEYWORD: MS7 Parent

GUIDED PRACTICE

See Example 1   **Identify the quadrant that contains each point.**

1. A **2.** B

3. C **4.** D

See Example 2   **Plot each point on a coordinate plane.**

5. $E(-1, 2)$ **6.** $N(2, -4)$

7. $H(-3, -4)$ **8.** $T(5, 0)$

See Example 3   **Give the coordinates of each point.**

9. J **10.** P

11. S **12.** M

INDEPENDENT PRACTICE

See Example 1   **Identify the quadrant that contains each point.**

13. F **14.** J

15. K **16.** E

See Example 2   **Plot each point on a coordinate plane.**

17. $A(-1, 1)$ **18.** $M(2, -2)$

19. $W(-5, -5)$ **20.** $G(0, -3)$

See Example 3   **Give the coordinates of each point.**

21. Q **22.** V **23.** R

24. P **25.** S **26.** L

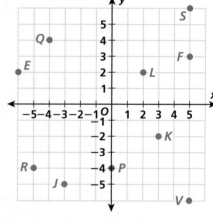

PRACTICE AND PROBLEM SOLVING

CRCT GPS

Extra Practice p. 733

For Exercises 27 and 28, use graph paper to graph the ordered pairs. Use a different coordinate plane for each exercise.

27. $(-8, 1)$; $(4, 3)$; $(-3, 6)$ **28.** $(-8, -2)$; $(-1, -2)$; $(-1, 3)$; $(-8, 3)$

29. Geometry Connect the points in Exercise 27. Identify the figure and the quadrants in which it is located.

30. Geometry Connect the points in Exercise 28 in the order listed. Identify the figure and the quadrants in which it is located.

Identify the quadrant of each point described below.

31. The x-coordinate and the y-coordinate are both negative.

32. The x-coordinate is negative and the y-coordinate is positive.

33. What point is 9 units right and 3 units up from point (3, 4)?

34. **Critical Thinking** After being moved 6 units right and 4 units down, a point is located at (6, 1). What were the original coordinates of the point?

35. **Weather** The map shows the path of Hurricane Andrew. Estimate to the nearest integer the coordinates of the storm for each of the times below.

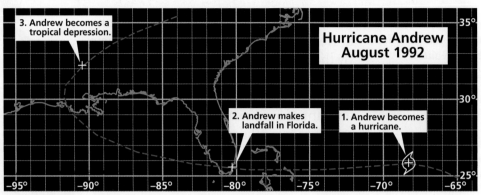

a. when Andrew first became a hurricane

b. when Andrew made landfall in Florida

c. when Andrew weakened to a tropical depression

36. **What's the Error?** To plot (−12, 1), a student started at (0, 0) and moved 12 units right and 1 unit down. What did the student do wrong?

37. **Write About It** Why is order important when graphing an ordered pair on a coordinate plane?

38. **Challenge** Armand and Kayla started jogging from the same point. Armand jogged 4 miles south and 6 miles east. Kayla jogged west and 4 miles south. If they were 11 miles apart when they stopped, how far west did Kayla jog?

CRCT Prep • GPS Support • Spiral Review

39. **Multiple Choice** Which of the following points lie within the circle graphed at right?

   Ⓐ (2, 6)   Ⓑ (−4, 4)   Ⓒ (0, −4)   Ⓓ (−6, 6)

40. **Multiple Choice** Which point on the *x*-axis is the same distance from the origin as (0, −3)?

   Ⓕ (0, 3)   Ⓖ (3, 0)   Ⓗ (3, −3)   Ⓙ (−3, 3)

Find each sum. (Lesson 2-2)

41. −17 + 11   **42.** 29 + 8   **43.** 40 + (−64)   **44.** −55 + (−32)

Divide. Write each answer in simplest form. (Lesson 3-11)

45. $8 \div 1\frac{1}{4}$ **46.** $\frac{3}{5} \div \frac{6}{15}$ **47.** $2\frac{1}{3} \div 1\frac{2}{3}$ **48.** $\frac{5}{8} \div \frac{3}{4}$

4-2 Tables and Graphs

Learn to identify and graph ordered pairs from a table of values.

In October 2004, five lion cubs were born at Henry Vilas Zoo in Madison, Wisconsin. By the time the cubs were three months old, they were each eating $2\frac{1}{2}$ pounds of food per day. The table shows the amount of food needed to feed one cub over several days.

Georgia Performance Standards

M7A3.b Represent, describe, and analyze relations from tables, graphs, and formulas. Also, M7A3.a, M7P4.a, M7P4.b, M7P5.c.

EXAMPLE 1 **Identifying Ordered Pairs from a Table of Values**

Write the ordered pairs from the table.

x	y
5	6
7	7
9	7
11	9

→

(x, y)
(5, 6)
(7, 7)
(9, 7)
(11, 9)

The ordered pairs are (5, 6), (7, 7), (9, 7), and (11, 9).

EXAMPLE 2 **Graphing Ordered Pairs from a Table of Values**

Write and graph the ordered pairs from the table.

x	−3	−1	1	3
y	4	1	−2	−5

The ordered pairs are (−3, 4), (−1, 1), (1, −2), and (3, −5).

Plot the points on a coordinate plane.

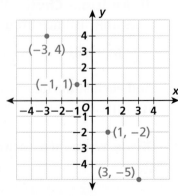

228 *Chapter 4 Patterns and Functions*

EXAMPLE 3 *Life Science Application*

The zookeepers at Henry Vilas Zoo are buying food for the lion cubs. The table shows the amount of food needed to feed one cub for 4 days. Graph the data. What appears to be the relationship between the number of days and the amount of food?

Number of Days	1	2	3	4
Amount of Food (lb)	2.5	5	7.5	10

Write the ordered pairs from the table.

Number of Days	1	2	3	4
Amount of Food (lb)	2.5	5	7.5	10
(x, y)	(1, 2.5)	(2, 5)	(3, 7.5)	(4, 10)

The ordered pairs are (1, 2.5), (2, 5), (3, 7.5), and (4, 10).

Now plot the points on a coordinate plane. Label the axes.

The graph shows that for each additional day, $2\frac{1}{2}$ additional pounds of food are needed for one lion cub.

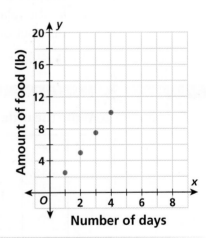

Think and Discuss   GPS M7P1.d

1. **Give an example** of a table that includes the origin as one of its ordered pairs.

2. **Explain** whether you could use the graph in Example 3 to find the amount of food needed to feed one cub for 14 days.

3. **Describe** a real-world situation that could be represented by a graph that has distinct points.

🍎 **Georgia Performance Standards**

M7P1.b, M7P3.a, M7P5.b

go.hrw.com
Homework Help Online
KEYWORD: MS7 4-2
Parent Resources Online
KEYWORD: MS7 Parent

GUIDED PRACTICE

See Example **Write the ordered pairs from each table.**

1.

x	y
1	1
2	1
3	1
4	1

2.

x	y
8	4
10	5
12	6
14	7

3.

x	y
−2	0
−1	9
0	18
1	27

See Example **Graph the ordered pairs from each table.**

4.

x	1	2	3	4
y	−2	−1	0	1

5.

x	−5	−3	−1	1
y	4	2	0	−2

See Example **6.** The table shows the total cost of buying different numbers of drinks. Graph the data. What appears to be the relationship between the number of drinks and the total cost?

Number of Drinks	1	2	3	4
Total Cost ($)	1.50	3.00	4.50	6.00

INDEPENDENT PRACTICE

See Example **Write the ordered pairs from each table.**

7.

x	y
−15	15
−10	10
−5	5
0	0

8.

x	y
−2	0
0	−1
4	−2
6	−3

9.

x	y
−11	−6
−9	−5
−7	−4
−5	−3

See Example **Graph the ordered pairs from each table.**

10.

x	0	2	4	6
y	−1	1	3	5

11.

x	−3	−1	1	3
y	3	1	1	3

See Example **12.** The table shows the total cost of an international phone call for different numbers of minutes. Graph the data. What appears to be the relationship between the number of minutes and the cost of a phone call?

Number of Minutes	2	4	6	8
Total Cost ($)	2	3	4	5

PRACTICE AND PROBLEM SOLVING

13. **Business** An accountant uses 3.5 gallons of gas each day driving to and from her office.

   a. Make a table showing the total number of gallons of gas she uses for each of 5 days.

   b. Graph the data from your answer to **a**.

14. **Crafts** Candle makers calculate the burn time for a candle by lighting the candle and recording the amount of wax remaining at various times. The table shows data for a 6-ounce candle.

   a. Make a graph of the data.

   b. Explain how you can use the graph to find the amount of wax remaining after 35 hours.

Elapsed Time (hr)	Wax Remaining (oz)
0	6
7	5
14	4
21	3

 15. **Write a Problem** Create a table of data representing the number of hours of homework you do for each of 5 days. Graph the data from your table.

 16. **Write About It** A table of data shows the number of times a whale's heart beats in 3, 4, 5, and 6 minutes. Describe how to make a graph to show the relationship between the number of minutes and the number of heartbeats.

 17. **Challenge** A table of data has the ordered pairs $(-2, 5)$, $(1, 4)$, and $(4, 3)$. Kim plots the points and connects them with a straight line. At what point does the line cross the x-axis?

CRCT PREP • GPS SUPPORT • SPIRAL REVIEW

18. **Multiple Choice** Miguel plotted the ordered pairs $(-3, -5)$, $(-2, -1)$, $(-1, 3)$, and $(0, 7)$. How many points did he plot in Quadrant III?

   (A) 0   (B) 1   (C) 2   (D) 3

19. **Short Response** The table shows the perimeters and areas of several rectangles. Make a graph of the data.

Perimeter (in.)	6	10	14	18
Area (in²)	2	6	12	20

Divide. Estimate to check whether each answer is reasonable. (Lesson 3-4)

20. $48.6 \div 6$ **21.** $31.5 \div (-5)$ **22.** $-8.32 \div 4$ **23.** $-74.1 \div 6$

Add. Write each answer in simplest form. (Lesson 3-9)

24. $1\frac{1}{5} + 3\frac{3}{5}$ **25.** $7\frac{2}{3} + 8\frac{2}{3}$ **26.** $9\frac{1}{4} + 6\frac{2}{3}$ **27.** $4\frac{7}{10} + 3\frac{1}{8}$

Plot each point on a coordinate plane. (Lesson 4-1)

28. $A(-4, 1)$ **29.** $B(0, 3)$ **30.** $C(2, -2)$ **31.** $D(1, 5)$

4-3 Interpreting Graphs

Learn to relate graphs to situations.

Georgia Performance Standards

M7A3.b Represent, describe, and analyze relations from graphs. Also, M7A3.c, M7P1.c, M7P1.d.

You can use a graph to show the relationship between speed and time, time and distance, or speed and distance.

The graph at right shows the varying speeds at which Emma exercises her horse. The horse walks at a constant speed for the first 10 minutes. Its speed increases over the next 7 minutes, and then it gallops at a constant rate for 20 minutes. Then it slows down over the next 3 minutes and then walks at a constant pace for 10 minutes.

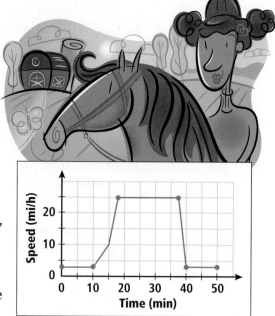

EXAMPLE **1** Relating Graphs to Situations

Jenny leaves home and drives to the beach. She stays at the beach all day before driving back home. Which graph best shows the situation?

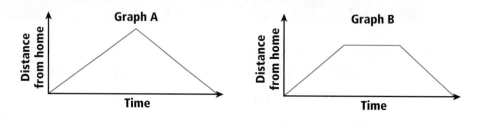

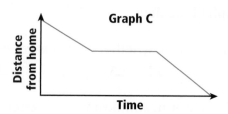

As Jenny drives to the beach, her distance from home *increases*. While she is at the beach, her distance from home is *constant*. As she drives home, her distance from home *decreases*. The answer is graph b.

Maili and Katrina traveled 10 miles from Maili's house to the movie theater. They watched a movie, and then they traveled 5 miles farther to a restaurant to eat lunch. After eating they returned to Maili's house. Sketch a graph to show the distance that the two friends traveled compared to time. Use your graph to find the total distance traveled.

1 Understand the Problem

The answer will be the total distance that Katrina and Maili traveled.

List the **important information:**

- The friends traveled 10 miles from Maili's house to the theater.
- They traveled an additional 5 miles and then ate lunch.
- They returned to Maili's house.

2 Make a Plan

Sketch a graph that represents the situation. Then use the graph to find the total distance Katrina and Maili traveled.

3 Solve

The distance from Maili's house increases from 0 to 10 miles when the friends travel to the theater. The distance increases from 10 to 15 miles when they go to the restaurant. The distance does not change while the friends watch the movie and eat lunch. The distance decreases from 15 to 0 miles when they return home.

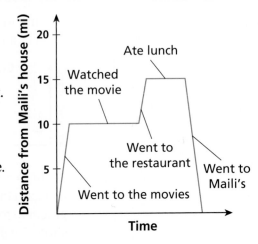

Maili and Katrina traveled a total of 30 miles.

4 Look Back

The theater is 10 miles away, so the friends must have traveled twice that distance just to go to the theater and return. The answer, 30 miles, is reasonable since it is greater than 20 miles.

Think and Discuss  GPS M7P3.b

1. **Explain** the meaning of a horizontal segment on a graph that compares distance to time.

2. **Describe** a real-world situation that could be represented by a graph that has connected lines or curves.

Georgia Performance Standards

M7P1.c, M7P3.a, M7P5.c

go.hrw.com
Homework Help Online
KEYWORD: MS7 4-3
Parent Resources Online
KEYWORD: MS7 Parent

GUIDED PRACTICE

See Example **1.** The temperature of an ice cube increases until it starts to melt. While it melts, its temperature stays constant. Which graph best shows the situation?

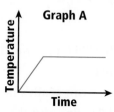

See Example **2** **2.** Mike and Claudia rode a bus 15 miles to a wildlife park. They waited in line to ride a train, which took them on a 3-mile ride around the park. After the train ride, they ate lunch, and then they rode the bus home. Sketch a graph to show the distance Mike and Claudia traveled compared to time. Use your graph to find the total distance traveled.

INDEPENDENT PRACTICE

See Example **3.** The ink in a printer is used until the ink cartridge is empty. The cartridge is refilled, and the ink is used up again. Which graph best shows the situation?

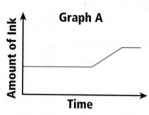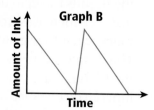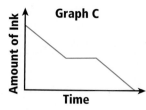

See Example **4.** On her way from home to the grocery store, a 6-mile trip, Veronica stopped at a gas station to buy gas. After filling her tank, she continued to the grocery store. She then returned home after shopping. Sketch a graph to show the distance Veronica traveled compared to time. Use your graph to find the total distance traveled.

PRACTICE AND PROBLEM SOLVING

CRCT GPS

Extra Practice p. 733

5. Describe a situation that fits the graph at right.

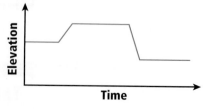

6. Lynn jogged for 2.5 miles. Then she walked a little while before stopping to stretch. Sketch a graph to show Lynn's speed compared to time.

7. On his way to the library, Jeff runs two blocks and then walks three more blocks. Sketch a graph to show the distance Jeff travels compared to time.

8. **Critical Thinking** The graph at right shows high school enrollment, including future projections.

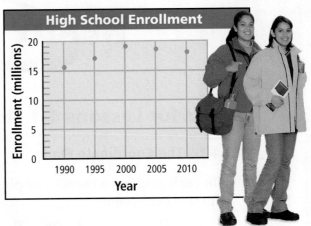

High School Enrollment

a. Describe what is happening in the graph.

b. Does it make sense to connect the points in the graph? Explain.

9. **Choose a Strategy** Three bananas were given to two mothers who were with their daughters. Each person had a banana to eat. How is that possible?

10. **Write About It** A driver sets his car's cruise control to 55 mi/h. Describe a graph that shows the car's speed compared to time. Then describe a second graph that shows the distance traveled compared to time.

11. **Challenge** The graph at right shows the temperature of an oven after the oven is turned on. Explain what the graph shows.

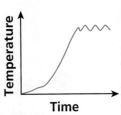

CRCT PREP • GPS SUPPORT • SPIRAL REVIEW

12. **Multiple Choice** How does speed compare to time in the graph at right?

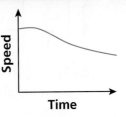

Ⓐ It increases.

Ⓑ It decreases.

Ⓒ It stays the same.

Ⓓ It fluctuates.

13. **Short Response** Keisha takes a big drink from a bottle of water. She sets the bottle down to tie her shoe and then picks up the bottle to take a small sip of water. Sketch a graph to show the amount of water in the bottle over time.

Find each absolute value. (Lesson 2-1)

14. $|9|$ 15. $|-3|$ 16. $|-15|$ 17. $|0|$ 18. $|5|$

Find the greatest common factor. (Lesson 2-7)

19. 12, 45   20. 33, 110   21. 6, 81   22. 24, 36

Write the ordered pairs from each table. (Lesson 4-2)

23.
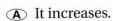

x	1	3	5	7
y	4	6	8	10

24.
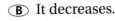

x	−6	0	6	12
y	0	6	−12	18

4-3 Interpreting Graphs **235**

READY TO GO ON?

Quiz for Lessons 4-1 Through 4-3

4-1 The Coordinate Plane

Plot each point on a coordinate plane. Then identify the quadrant that contains each point.

1. $W(1, 5)$ **2.** $X(5, -3)$ **3.** $Y(-1, -5)$ **4.** $Z(-8, 2)$

Give the coordinates of each point.

5. A **6.** B

7. C **8.** D

9. E **10.** F

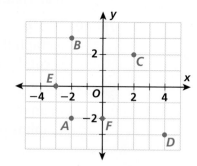

4-2 Tables and Graphs

Write and graph the ordered pairs from each table.

11.

x	y
1	5
-3	0
2	-5

12.

x	y
7	4
0	0
-4	3

13.

x	y
0	2
-6	6
-1	-2

14. The table shows the number of quarts there are in each number of gallons. Graph the data. What appears to be the relationship between the number of quarts and the number of gallons?

Quarts	8	12	16
Gallons	2	3	4

4-3 Interpreting Graphs

15. Raj climbs to the top of a cliff. He descends a little bit to another cliff, and then he begins to climb again. Which graph best shows the situation?

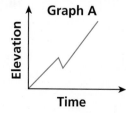

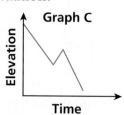

16. Ty walks 1 mile to the mall. An hour later, he walks $\frac{1}{2}$ mile farther to a park and eats lunch. Then he walks home. Sketch a graph to show the distance Ty traveled compared to time. Use your graph to find the total distance traveled.

Focus on Problem Solving

Understand the Problem

• **Sequence and prioritize information**

When you are reading a math problem, putting events in order, or in *sequence,* can help you understand the problem better. It helps to *prioritize* the information when you put it in order. To prioritize, you decide which of the information in your list is most important. The most important information has highest priority.

Use the information in the list or table to answer each question.

① The list at right shows all of the things that Roderick has to do on Saturday. He starts the day without any money.

a. Which two activities on Roderick's list must be done before any of the other activities? Do these two activities have higher or lower priority?

b. Is there more than one way that he can order his activities? Explain.

c. List the order in which Roderick's activities could occur on Saturday.

Saturday Activities
- Attend birthday party at 4 P.M.
- Buy gift - either a CD for $18 or a computer game for $25.
- Get haircut at 2 P.M.; pay $16.
- Mow Mrs. Mayberry's lawn before 10 A.M.; earn $15.
- Mow Mr. Boyar's lawn and trim hedge anytime after 10 A.M.; earn $25.

② Tara and her family will visit Ocean World Park from 9:30 to 4:00. They want to see the waterskiing show at 10:00. Each show in the park is 50 minutes long. The time they choose to eat lunch will depend on the schedule they choose for seeing the shows.

a. Which of the information given in the paragraph above has the highest priority? Which has the lowest priority?

b. List the order in which they can see all of the shows, including the time they will see each.

c. At what time should they plan to have lunch?

Show Times at Ocean World Park	
9:00, 12:00	Underwater acrobats
9:00, 3:00	Whale acts
10:00, 2:00	Dolphin acts
10:00, 1:00	Waterskiing
11:00, 4:00	Aquarium tour

 **4-4** **Functions, Tables, and Graphs**

Learn to use function tables to generate and graph ordered pairs.

Vocabulary

function

input

output

 Georgia Performance Standards

M7A3.b Represent, describe, and analyze relations from tables, graphs, and formulas. Also, M7A1.b, M7A3.a, M7P4.a, M7P4.b.

Rube Goldberg, a famous cartoonist, invented machines that perform ordinary tasks in extraordinary ways. Each machine operates according to a rule, or a set of steps, to produce a particular *output*.

In mathematics, a **function** operates according to a rule to produce exactly one output value for each input value. The **input** is the value substituted into the function. The **output** is the value that results from the substitution of a given input into the function.

A function can be represented by a rule written in words, such as **"double the number and then add nine to the result,"** or by an equation with two variables. One variable represents the input, and the other represents the output.

As you raise spoon of soup (A) to your mouth, it pulls string (B), thereby jerking ladle (C), which throws cracker (D) past parrot (E). Parrot jumps after cracker, and perch (F) tilts, upsetting seeds (G) into pail (H). Extra weight in pail pulls cord (I), which opens and lights automatic cigar lighter (J), setting off sky rocket (K), which causes sickle (L) to cut string (M) and allow pendulum with attached napkin to swing back and forth, thereby wiping off your chin.

Function Rule

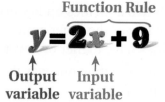

$$y = 2x + 9$$

Output variable   Input variable

You can use a table to organize and display the input and output values of a function.

EXAMPLE **1** **Completing a Function Table**

Find the output for each input.

A $y = 4x - 2$

Input	Rule	Output
x	4*x* − 2	*y*
−1	4(−1) − 2	−6
0	4(0) − 2	−2
3	4(3) − 2	10

Substitute −1 for x. Then simplify.

Substitute 0 for x. Then simplify.

Substitute 3 for x. Then simplify.

Find the output for each input.

B $y = 6x^2$

Input	Rule	Output
x	$6x^2$	y
-5	$6(-5)^2$	150
0	$6(0)^2$	0
5	$6(5)^2$	150

Substitute -5 for x. Then simplify.
Substitute 0 for x. Then simplify.
Substitute 5 for x. Then simplify.

Remember!

An ordered pair is a pair of numbers that represents a point on a graph.

You can also use a graph to represent a function. The corresponding input and output values together form unique ordered pairs.

EXAMPLE 2 **Graphing Functions Using Ordered Pairs**

Make a function table, and graph the resulting ordered pairs.

A $y = 2x$

Helpful Hint

When writing an ordered pair, write the input value first and then the output value.

Input	Rule	Output	Ordered Pair
x	$2x$	y	(x, y)
-2	$2(-2)$	-4	$(-2, -4)$
-1	$2(-1)$	-2	$(-1, -2)$
0	$2(0)$	0	$(0, 0)$
1	$2(1)$	2	$(1, 2)$
2	$2(2)$	4	$(2, 4)$

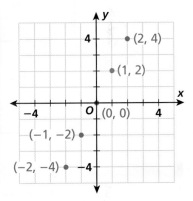

B $y = x^2$

Input	Rule	Output	Ordered Pair
x	x^2	y	(x, y)
-2	$(-2)^2$	4	$(-2, 4)$
-1	$(-1)^2$	1	$(-1, 1)$
0	$(0)^2$	0	$(0, 0)$
1	$(1)^2$	1	$(1, 1)$
2	$(2)^2$	4	$(2, 4)$

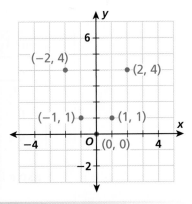

Think and Discuss GPS M7P3.b

1. **Describe** how a function works like a machine.

2. **Give an example** of a rule that takes an input value of 4 and produces an output value of 10.

Georgia Performance
Standards

M7P3.a, M7P3.c, M7P5.b

GUIDED PRACTICE

See Example ① **Find the output for each input.**

1. $y = 2x + 1$

Input	Rule	Output
x	2x + 1	y
−3		
0		
1		

2. $y = -x + 3$

Input	Rule	Output
x	−x + 3	y
−2		
0		
2		

3. $y = 2x^2$

Input	Rule	Output
x	2x²	y
−5		
1		
3		

See Example ② **Make a function table, and graph the resulting ordered pairs.**

4. $y = 3x - 2$

Input	Rule	Output	Ordered Pair
x	3x − 2	y	(x, y)
−1			
0			
1			
2			

5. $y = x^2 + 2$

Input	Rule	Output	Ordered Pair
x	x² + 2	y	(x, y)
−1			
0			
1			
2			

INDEPENDENT PRACTICE

See Example ① **Find the output for each input.**

6. $y = -2x$

Input	Rule	Output
x	−2x	y
−2		
0		
4		

7. $y = 3x + 2$

Input	Rule	Output
x	3x + 2	y
−3		
−1		
2		

8. $y = 3x^2$

Input	Rule	Output
x	3x²	y
−10		
−6		
−2		

See Example ② **Make a function table, and graph the resulting ordered pairs.**

9. $y = x \div 2$

Input	Rule	Output	Ordered Pair
x	x ÷ 2	y	(x, y)
−1			
0			
1			
2			

10. $y = x^2 - 4$

Input	Rule	Output	Ordered Pair
x	x² − 4	y	(x, y)
−1			
0			
1			
2			

PRACTICE AND PROBLEM SOLVING

11. **Weather** The Northeast gets an average of 11.66 inches of rain in the summer.

    a. Write an equation that can be used to find y, the difference in rainfall between the average amount of summer rainfall and x, a given year's summer rainfall.

    b. Make a function table using each year's summer rainfall data.

12. **Physical Science** The equation $F = \frac{9}{5}C + 32$ gives the Fahrenheit temperature F for a given Celsius temperature C. Make a function table for the values $C = -20°, -5°, 0°, 20°$, and $100°$.

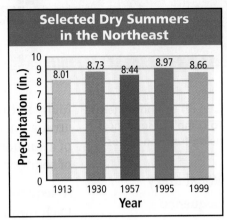

Selected Dry Summers in the Northeast

Source: USA Today, August 17, 2001

 13. **What's the Error?** What is the error in the function table at right?

 14. **Write About It** Explain how to make a function table for $y = 2x + 11$.

 15. **Challenge** Mountain Rental charges a $25 deposit plus $10 per hour to rent a bicycle. Write an equation that gives the cost y to rent a bike for x hours. Then write the ordered pairs for $x = \frac{1}{2}$, 5, and $8\frac{1}{2}$.

x	$y = -x - 5$	y
−2	$y = -(-2) - 5$	−7
−1	$y = -(-1) - 5$	−6
0	$y = -(0) - 5$	−5
1	$y = -(1) - 5$	−6
2	$y = -(2) - 5$	−7

CRCT Prep • GPS Support • Spiral Review

16. **Multiple Choice** Which table shows correct input and output values for the function $y = -2x + 3$?

Ⓐ
x	y
−1	−1
0	0

Ⓑ
x	y
−3	−2
−2	−1

Ⓒ
x	y
−5	−7
−1	1

Ⓓ
x	y
−3	9
−1	5

17. **Multiple Choice** Which function matches the function table?

    Ⓕ $y = x + 3$ Ⓗ $y = 5x + 1$

    Ⓖ $y = x^2 + 7$ Ⓙ $y = x^3 + 3$

x	0	1	2
y	3	4	11

Simplify. (Lesson 2-3)

18. $43 - (-18)$

19. $3 - (-2) - (5 + 1)$

20. $-4 - 8 - (-3)$

Solve. Write each answer in simplest form. (Lesson 3-12)

21. $\frac{1}{7}x = \frac{6}{7}$

22. $4z = \frac{4}{5}$

23. $\frac{6}{9}y = 3$

24. $\frac{1}{10}x = \frac{7}{8}$

Find a Pattern in Sequences

Problem Solving Skill

 **Learn** to find patterns to complete sequences using function tables.

Vocabulary

sequence

term

arithmetic sequence

geometric sequence

Georgia Performance Standards

M7A1.a Translate verbal phrases to algebraic expressions. Also, M7A1.b, M7A3.b, M7A3.c.

Many natural things, such as the arrangement of seeds in the head of a sunflower, follow the pattern of sequences.

A **sequence** is an ordered list of numbers. Each number in a sequence is called a **term**. When the sequence follows a pattern, the terms in the sequence are the output values of a function, and the value of each term depends on its position in the sequence.

You can use a variable, such as *n*, to represent a number's position in a sequence.

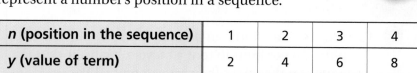

n (position in the sequence)	1	2	3	4
y (value of term)	2	4	6	8

In an **arithmetic sequence**, the same amount is added each time to get the next term in the sequence. In a **geometric sequence**, each term is multiplied by the same amount to get the next term in the sequence.

E X A M P L E 1 Identifying Patterns in Sequences

Tell whether each sequence of *y*-values is arithmetic or geometric. Then find *y* when *n* = 5.

A

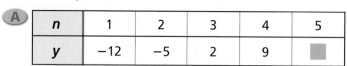

n	1	2	3	4	5
y	−12	−5	2	9	▪

In the sequence −12, −5, 2, 9, ▪, . . . , 7 is added to each term.

9 + 7 = 16   *Add 7 to the fourth term.*

The sequence is arithmetic. When *n* = 5, *y* = 16.

B

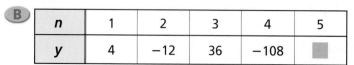

n	1	2	3	4	5
y	4	−12	36	−108	▪

In the sequence 4, −12, 36, −108, ▪, . . . , each term is multiplied by −3.

−108 · (−3) = 324   *Multiply the fourth term by −3.*

The sequence is geometric. When *n* = 5, *y* = 324.

EXAMPLE 2 **Identifying Functions in Sequences**

Write a function that describes each sequence.

A 2, 4, 6, 8, . . .

Make a function table.

n	Rule	y
1	1 · 2	2
2	2 · 2	4
3	3 · 2	6
4	4 · 2	8

Multiply n by 2.

The function $y = 2n$ describes this sequence.

B 4, 5, 6, 7, . . .

Make a function table.

n	Rule	y
1	1 + 3	4
2	2 + 3	5
3	3 + 3	6
4	4 + 3	7

Add 3 to n.

The function $y = n + 3$ describes this sequence.

EXAMPLE 3 **Using Functions to Extend Sequences**

Sara has one week to read a book. She plans to increase the number of chapters that she reads each day. Her plan is to read 3 chapters on Sunday, 5 on Monday, 7 on Tuesday, and 9 on Wednesday. Write a function that describes the sequence. Then use the function to predict how many chapters Sara will read on Saturday.

Write the number of chapters she reads each day: 3, 5, 7, 9, . . .
Make a function table.

n	Rule	y
1	1 · 2 + 1	3
2	2 · 2 + 1	5
3	3 · 2 + 1	7
4	4 · 2 + 1	9

Multiply n by 2. Then add 1.

$y = 2n + 1$.*Write the function.*

Saturday corresponds to $n = 7$. When $n = 7$, $y = 2 · 7 + 1 = 15$.
Sara plans to read 15 chapters on Saturday.

GPS M7P1.d, M7P3.b

Think and Discuss

1. **Give an example** of a sequence involving addition, and give the rule you used.

2. **Describe** how to find a pattern in the sequence 1, 4, 16, 64, ...

Georgia Performance
Standards

M7P1.b, M7P5.b, M7P5.c

go.hrw.com
Homework Help Online
KEYWORD: MS7 4-5
Parent Resources Online
KEYWORD: MS7 Parent

GUIDED PRACTICE

See Example **1** Tell whether each sequence of y-values is arithmetic or geometric. Then find
y when $n = 5$.

1.

n	1	2	3	4	5
y	−4	9	22	35	

2.

n	1	2	3	4	5
y	8	4	2	1	

See Example **2** Write a function that describes each sequence.

3. 3, 6, 9, 12, . . .   **4.** 3, 4, 5, 6, . . .   **5.** 0, 1, 2, 3, . . .   **6.** 5, 10, 15, 20, . . .

See Example **3** **7.** In March, WaterWorks recorded $195 in swimsuit sales. The store
recorded $390 in sales in April, $585 in May, and $780 in June. Write a
function that describes the sequence. Then use the function to predict
the store's swimsuit sales in July.

INDEPENDENT PRACTICE

See Example **1** Tell whether each sequence of y-values is arithmetic or geometric. Then find
y when $n = 5$.

8.

n	1	2	3	4	5
y	13	26	52	104	

9.

n	1	2	3	4	5
y	14	30	46	62	

See Example **2** Write a function that describes each sequence.

10. 5, 6, 7, 8, . . .   **11.** 7, 14, 21, 28, . . .   **12.** −2, −1, 0, 1, . . .

13. 20, 40, 60, 80, . . .   **14.** $\frac{1}{2}$, 1, $\frac{3}{2}$, 2, . . .   **15.** 1.5, 2.5, 3.5, 4.5, . . .

See Example **3** **16.** The number of seats in the first row of a concert hall is 6. The second row
has 9 seats, the third row has 12 seats, and the fourth row has 15 seats.
Write a function to describe the sequence. Then use the function to
predict the number of seats in the eighth row.

PRACTICE AND PROBLEM SOLVING

Extra Practice p. 734

Write a rule for each sequence in words. Then find the next three terms.

17. 35, 70, 105, 140, . . .   **18.** 0.7, 1.7, 2.7, 3.7, . . .   **19.** $\frac{3}{2}$, $\frac{5}{2}$, $\frac{7}{2}$, $\frac{9}{2}$, . . .

20. −1, 0, 1, 2, . . .   **21.** $\frac{1}{3}$, $\frac{2}{3}$, 1, $\frac{4}{3}$, . . .   **22.** 6, 11, 16, 21, . . .

Write a function that describes each sequence. Use the function to find the
tenth term in the sequence.

23. 0.5, 1.5, 2.5, 3.5, . . .   **24.** 0, 2, 4, 6, . . .   **25.** 5, 8, 11, 14, . . .

26. 3, 8, 13, 18, . . .   **27.** 1, 3, 5, 7, . . .   **28.** 6, 10, 14, 18, . . .

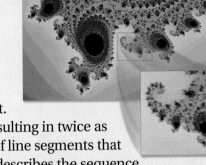

Computer programmers use functions to create designs known as *fractals*. A fractal is a *self-similar* pattern, which means that each part of the pattern is similar to the whole pattern. Fractals are created by repeating a set of steps, called *iterations*.

29. Below is part of a famous fractal called the Cantor set. In each iteration, part of a line segment is removed, resulting in twice as many segments as before. The table lists the number of line segments that result from the iterations shown. Find a function that describes the sequence.

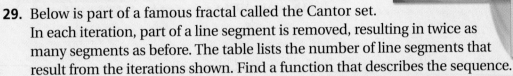

Iteration (n)	Number of Segments (y)
1	2
2	4
3	8

30. **Multi-Step** These are the first three iterations of the Sierpinski triangle. In each iteration, a certain number of smaller triangles are cut out of the larger triangle.

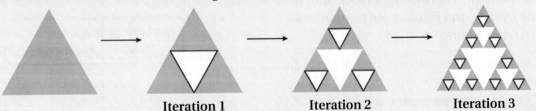

Iteration 1
1 triangle removed

Iteration 2
3 more triangles removed

Iteration 3
9 more triangles removed

Create a table to list the number of yellow triangles that exist after each iteration. Then find a function that describes the sequence.

31. ⭐ **Challenge** Find a function that describes the number of triangles removed in each iteration of the Sierpinski triangle.

go.hrw.com
Web Extra!
KEYWORD: MS7 Fractals

CRCT PREP • GPS SUPPORT • SPIRAL REVIEW

32. **Multiple Choice** Which function describes the sequence 1, 4, 7, 10, . . . ?

Ⓐ $y = 3n$　　Ⓑ $y = n + 3$　　Ⓒ $y = 3n - 2$　　Ⓓ $y = 2n$

33. **Extended Response** Create a sequence, and then write a function that describes it. Use the function to find the ninth term in the sequence.

Find each value. (Lesson 1-2)

34. 15^2　　**35.** 10^7　　**36.** 7^4　　**37.** 9^3

Find each product. (Lesson 2-4)

38. $-16 \cdot 2$　　**39.** $-40 \cdot (-5)$　　**40.** $4 \cdot (-11)$　　**41.** $-5 \cdot (-21)$

Explore Linear Functions

Hands-On LAB 4-6

Use with Lesson 4-6

Georgia Performance Standards

M7A3.b, M7A3.c, M7P5.a

go.hrw.com
Lab Resources Online
KEYWORD: MS7 Lab4

When the graph of a function is a line or a set of points that lie on a line, the function is *linear*. You can use patterns to explore linear functions.

Activity

1 The perimeter of a 1-inch-long square tile is 4 inches. Place 2 tiles together side by side. The perimeter of this figure is 6 inches.

a. Complete the table at right by adding tiles side by side and finding the perimeter of each new figure.

b. If *x* equals the number of tiles, what is the difference between consecutive *x*-values? If *y* equals the perimeter, what is the difference between consecutive *y*-values? How do these differences compare?

c. Graph the ordered pairs from your table on a coordinate plane. Is the graph linear? What does the table indicate about this function?

Number of Tiles	Perimeter (in.)
1	4
2	6
3	
4	
5	

2 Draw the pattern at right and complete the next two sets of dots in the pattern.

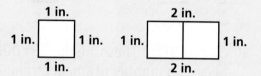

a. Complete the table at right. Let *x* equal the number of dots in the top row of each set. Let *y* equal the total number of dots in the set.

b. What is the difference between consecutive *x*-values? What is the difference between consecutive *y*-values? How do these differences compare?

c. Graph the ordered pairs on a coordinate plane. Is the graph linear? What does the table indicate about this function?

x	*y*
2	3
3	
4	
5	
6	

3 Use square tiles to model rectangles with the following dimensions: 2 × 1, 2 × 2, 2 × 3, 2 × 4, and 2 × 5. The first three rectangles are shown.

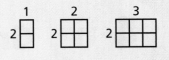

a. Find the perimeter and area of each rectangle. Complete the table at right. Let x equal perimeter and y equal area. (To find the area of a rectangle, multiply its length by its width. The areas of the first two rectangles are shown in the table.)

b. What is the difference between consecutive x-values? What is the difference between consecutive y-values? How do these differences compare?

c. Using what you have observed in **1** and **2**, tell whether the relationship between x and y in the table is linear.

d. Graph the ordered pairs from your table on a coordinate plane. Does the shape of your graph agree with your answer to **c**?

Rectangle	Perimeter x	Area y
2 × 1	■	2
2 × 2	■	4
2 × 3	■	■
2 × 4	■	■
2 × 5	■	■

Think and Discuss

1. How can you tell by looking at a function table whether the graph of the function is a line?

2. Is $y = x^2$ a linear function? Explain your answer.

Try This

1. Use square tiles to model each of the patterns shown below.

2. Model the next two sets in each pattern using square tiles.

3. Complete each table.

4. Graph the ordered pairs in each table, and then tell whether the function is linear.

Pattern 1

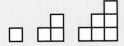

Number of Tiles x	Perimeter y
■	4
■	8
■	12
■	■
■	■

Pattern 2

Perimeter x	Area y
8	■
12	■
16	■
■	■
■	■

Pattern 3

Perimeter x	Area y
4	■
6	■
8	■
■	■
■	■

4-6 Graphing Linear Functions

Learn to identify and graph linear equations.

Vocabulary

linear equation

linear function

Georgia Performance Standards

M7A1.b Simplify and evaluate algebraic expressions, using commutative, associative, and distributive properties as appropriate. Also, M7A1.a, M7A3.a, M7A3.b.

The graph below shows how far an inner tube travels down a river if the current flows 2 miles per hour. The graph is linear because all of the points fall on a line. It is part of the graph of a *linear equation*.

A **linear equation** is an equation whose graph is a line. The solutions of a linear equation are the points that make up its graph. Linear equations and linear graphs can be different representations of *linear functions*. A **linear function** is a function whose graph is a nonvertical line.

Only two points are needed to draw the graph of a linear function. However, graphing a third point serves as a check. You can use a function table to find each ordered pair.

EXAMPLE 1 **Graphing Linear Functions**

Graph the linear function $y = 2x + 1$.

Input	Rule	Output	Ordered Pair
x	$2x + 1$	y	(x, y)
-1	$2(-1) + 1$	-1	$(-1, -1)$
0	$2(0) + 1$	1	$(0, 1)$
1	$2(1) + 1$	3	$(1, 3)$

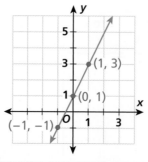

Place each ordered pair on the coordinate grid. Then connect the points to form a line.

EXAMPLE 2 *Physical Science Application*

For every degree that temperature increases on the Celsius scale, the temperature increases by 1.8 degrees on the Fahrenheit scale. When the temperature is 0°C, it is 32°F. Write a linear function that describes the relationship between the Celsius and Fahrenheit scales. Then make a graph to show the relationship.

Let x represent the input, which is the temperature in degrees Celsius. Let y represent the output, which is the temperature in degrees Fahrenheit.

The function is $y = 1.8x + 32$.

Make a function table. Include a column for the rule.

Input	Rule	Output
x	$1.8x + 32$	y
0	$1.8(0) + 32$	32
15	$1.8(15) + 32$	59
30	$1.8(30) + 32$	86

Multiply the input by 1.8 and then add 32.

Graph the ordered pairs (0, 32), (15, 59), and (30, 86) from your table. Connect the points to form a line.

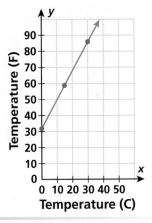

Since each output y depends on the input x, y is called the *dependent variable* and x is called the *independent variable*.

Think and Discuss  GPS M7P1.d, M7P3.b

1. **Describe** how a linear equation is related to a linear graph.

2. **Explain** how to use a graph to find the output value of a linear function for a given input value.

Georgia Performance Standards

M7P3.a, M7P5.a, M7P5.b

go.hrw.com
Homework Help Online
KEYWORD: MS7 4-6
Parent Resources Online
KEYWORD: MS7 Parent

GUIDED PRACTICE

See Example **Graph each linear function.**

1. $y = x + 3$

Input	Rule	Output	Ordered Pair
x	$x + 3$	y	(x, y)
-2			
0			
2			

2. $y = 2x - 2$

Input	Rule	Output	Ordered Pair
x	$2x - 2$	y	(x, y)
-1			
0			
1			

See Example **3.** A water tanker is used to fill a community pool. The tanker pumps 750 gallons of water per hour. Write a linear function that describes the amount of water in the pool over time. Then make a graph to show the amount of water in the pool over the first 6 hours.

INDEPENDENT PRACTICE

See Example ① **Graph each linear function.**

4. $y = -x - 2$

Input	Rule	Output	Ordered Pair
x	$-x - 2$	y	(x, y)
0			
1			
2			

5. $y = x - 1$

Input	Rule	Output	Ordered Pair
x	$x - 1$	y	(x, y)
3			
4			
5			

6. $y = 3x - 1$

Input	Rule	Output	Ordered Pair
x	$3x - 1$	y	(x, y)
-4			
0			
4			

7. $y = 2x + 3$

Input	Rule	Output	Ordered Pair
x	$2x + 3$	y	(x, y)
-2			
-1			
0			

See Example **8. Physical Science** The temperature of a liquid is increasing at the rate of 3°C per hour. When Joe begins measuring the temperature, it is 40°C. Write a linear function that describes the temperature of the liquid over time. Then make a graph to show the temperature over the first 12 hours.

PRACTICE AND PROBLEM SOLVING

9. Earth Science The water level in a well is 100 m. Water is seeping into the well and raising the water level by 10 cm per year. Water is also draining out of the well at a rate of 2 m per year. What will the water level be in 10 years?

10. Multi-Step Graph the function $y = -2x + 1$. If the ordered pair $(x, -5)$ lies on the graph of the function, what is the value of x? Use your graph to find the answer.

11. Environment The graph shows the amount of carbon dioxide in the atmosphere from 1958 to 1994.

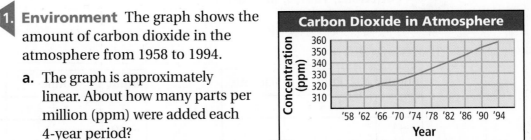

a. The graph is approximately linear. About how many parts per million (ppm) were added each 4-year period?

b. Given the parts per million in 1994 shown on the graph, about how many parts per million do you predict there will be after four more 4-year periods, or in 2010?

12. What's the Question Tron used the equation $y = 100 + 25x$ to track his savings y after x months. If the answer is $250, what is the question?

 13. Write About It Explain how to graph $y = 2x - 5$.

14. Challenge Certain bacteria divide every 30 minutes. You can use the function $y = 2^x$ to find the number of bacteria after each half-hour period, where x is the number of half-hour periods. Make a table of values for $x = 1, 2, 3, 4,$ and 5. Graph the points. How does the graph differ from those you have seen so far in this lesson?

CRCT PREP • GPS SUPPORT • SPIRAL REVIEW

15. Multiple Choice The graph of which linear function passes through the origin?

   Ⓐ $y = x + 2$ Ⓑ $y = 3x$ Ⓒ $y = x - 1$ Ⓓ $y = 2x + 4$

16. Short Response Simon graphed the linear function $y = -x + 3$ at right. Explain his error, and graph $y = -x + 3$ correctly on a coordinate grid.

17. Tell a story that fits the graph. (Lesson 4-3)

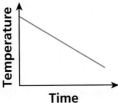

Write a function that describes each sequence. (Lesson 4-5)

18. $15, 10, 5, 0, \ldots$ **19.** $-4, -2, 0, 2, \ldots$ **20.** $0.2, 1.2, 2.2, 3.2, \ldots$

READY TO GO ON?

Quiz for Lessons 4-4 Through 4-6

✓ 4-4 Functions, Tables, and Graphs

Find the output for each input.

1. $y = -3x + 2$

Input	Rule	Output
x	$-3x + 2$	y
-1		
0		
1		

2. $y = x \div 2$

Input	Rule	Output
x	$x \div 2$	y
-10		
2		
6		

Make a function table, and graph the resulting ordered pairs.

3. $y = -6x$ **4.** $y = 4x - 3$ **5.** $y = 4x^2$

✓ 4-5 Find a Pattern in Sequences

Tell whether the sequence of y-values is arithmetic or geometric. Then find y when $n = 5$.

6.

n	1	2	3	4	5
y	-2	7	16	25	■

7.

n	1	2	3	4	5
y	30	60	120	240	■

8.

n	1	2	3	4	5
y	16	9	2	-5	■

9.

n	1	2	3	4	5
y	-5	15	-45	135	■

Write a function that describes each sequence. Use the function to find the eleventh term in the sequence.

10. $1, 2, 3, 4, \ldots$ **11.** $4, 8, 12, 16, \ldots$ **12.** $11, 21, 31, 41, \ldots$ **13.** $1, 4, 9, 16, \ldots$

✓ 4-6 Graphing Linear Functions

Graph each linear function.

14. $y = x - 4$ **15.** $y = 2x - 5$ **16.** $y = -x + 7$ **17.** $y = -2x + 1$

18. A freight train travels 50 miles per hour. Write a linear function that describes the distance the train travels over time. Then make a graph to show the distance the train travels over the first 9 hours.

Going for a Ride Shauna and her family are planning to spend a day at a local amusement park. The park charges an admission fee and sells tickets for the rides.

1. The table at right can be used to determine how much Shauna and her family could spend in a day at the park. Complete the table.

Number of Rides	Rule	Cost
0	▨	$8
1	8 + 3(1)	$11
2	▨	$14
3	8 + 3(3)	▨
4	▨	$20
6	8 + 3(6)	▨
8	▨	$32
12	▨	▨

2. What is the park's admission fee? How much does it cost to go on each ride?

3. Suppose x represents the number of rides and y represents the cost. Write a function that describes the data in the table.

4. Use the function you wrote in Problem 3 to find the cost of 14 rides.

5. Make a graph that shows the cost as a function of the number of rides.

6. The park offers a flat-rate "ride all day" pass for $38. Explain when this is a better deal than paying for each individual ride.

7. Shauna and her brother each plan to go on 15 rides. Her parents will each go on 6 rides. Find the cost for the family to go to the park. Explain your answer.

Multi-Step Test Prep

Nonlinear Functions

Learn to identify nonlinear functions.

Vocabulary

nonlinear function

Georgia Performance Standards

M7A3.c Describe how change in one variable affects the other variable. Also, M7A3.b, M7P5.a, M7P5.b.

As you inflate a balloon, its volume increases. The table at right shows the increase in volume of a round balloon as its radius changes. Do you think a graph of the data would or would not be a straight line? You can make a graph to find out.

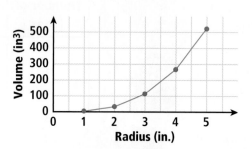

Radius (in.)	Volume (in³)
1	4.19
2	33.52
3	113.13
4	268.16
5	523.75

A **nonlinear function** is a function whose graph is not a straight line.

EXAMPLE **Identifying Graphs of Nonlinear Functions**

Tell whether the graph is linear or nonlinear.

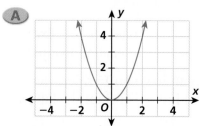

The graph is not a straight line, so it is nonlinear.

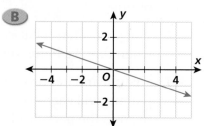

The graph is a straight line, so it is linear.

You can use a function table to determine whether ordered pairs describe a linear or a nonlinear relationship.

For a function that has a linear relationship, when the difference between each successive input value is constant, the difference between each corresponding output value is *constant*.

For a function that has a nonlinear relationship, when the difference between each successive input value is constant, the difference between each corresponding output value *varies*.

EXAMPLE **Identifying Nonlinear Relationships in Function Tables**

Tell whether the function represented in each table has a linear or nonlinear relationship.

A

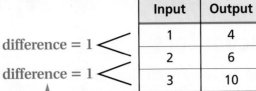

difference = 1

difference = 1

difference = 2

difference = 4

The difference is constant.   *The difference varies.*

The function represented in the table has a nonlinear relationship.

B

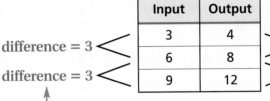

difference = 3

difference = 3

difference = 4

difference = 4

The difference is constant.   *The difference is constant.*

The function represented in the table has a linear relationship.

EXTENSION

Exercises

Tell whether the graph is linear or nonlinear.

1.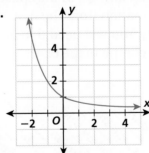

2.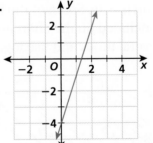

3.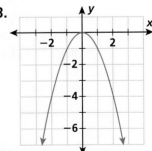

Tell whether the function represented in each table has a linear or nonlinear relationship.

4.

Input	Output
2	5
4	7
6	9

5.

Input	Output
1	6
2	9
3	14

6.

Input	Output
4	25
8	36
12	49

Game Time

Clothes Encounters

Five students from the same math class met to study for an upcoming test. They sat around a circular table with seat 1 and seat 5 next to each other. No two students were wearing the same color of shirt or the same type of shoes. From the clues provided, determine where each student sat, each student's shirt color, and what type of shoes each student was wearing.

❶ The girls' shoes were sandals, flip-flops, and boots.

❷ Robin, wearing a blue shirt, was sitting next to the person wearing the green shirt. She was not sitting next to the person wearing the orange shirt.

❸ Lila was sitting between the person wearing sandals and the person in the yellow shirt.

❹ The boy who was wearing the tennis shoes was wearing the orange shirt.

❺ April had on flip-flops and was sitting between Lila and Charles.

❻ Glenn was wearing loafers, but his shirt was not brown.

❼ Robin sat in seat 1.

You can use a chart like the one below to organize the information given. Put *X*'s in the spaces where the information is false and *O*'s in the spaces where the information is true. Some of the information from the first two clues has been included on the chart already. You will need to read through the clues several times and use logic to complete the chart.

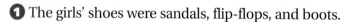

	Seat 1	Seat 2	Seat 3	Seat 4	Seat 5	Blue shirt	Green shirt	Orange shirt	Yellow shirt	Brown shirt	Sandals	Flip-flops	Boots	Tennis shoes	Loafers
Lila					X									X	X
Robin					O	X	X	X	X					X	X
April					X									X	X
Charles					X										
Glenn					X										

Materials
- 6 sheets of unlined paper
- scissors
- markers

It's in the Bag!

PROJECT — **Patterns and Functions Fold-A-Books**

These handy books will store your notes from each lesson of the chapter.

Directions

1 Fold a sheet of paper in half down the middle. Then open the paper and lay it flat so it forms a peak. **Figure A**

2 Fold the left and right edges to the crease in the middle. When you're done, the paper will be folded into four sections, accordion-style. **Figure B**

3 Pinch the middle sections together. Use scissors to cut a slit down the center of these sections, stopping when you get to the folds. **Figure C**

4 Hold the paper on either side of the slit. As you open the slit, the paper will form a four-page book. **Figure D**

5 Crease the top edges and fold the book closed. Repeat all the steps to make five more books.

Taking Note of the Math

On the cover of each book, write the number and name of a lesson from the chapter. Use the remaining pages to take notes on the lesson.

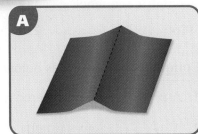

A

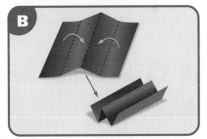

B

C

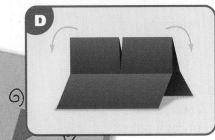

D

CHAPTER 4
PATTERNS & FUNCTIONS

It's in the Bag! **257**

Study Guide: Review

Vocabulary

arithmetic sequence 242
coordinate plane 224
function 238
geometric sequence 242
input 238

linear equation 248
linear function 248
ordered pair 224
origin 224
output 238

quadrant 224
sequence 242
term 242
x-axis 224
y-axis 224

Complete the sentences below with vocabulary words from the list above.

1. A(n) ___?___ is an ordered list of numbers.

2. A(n) ___?___ gives exactly one output for every input.

3. A(n) ___?___ is a function whose graph is a nonvertical line.

4-1 The Coordinate Plane (pp. 224–227)

 GPS M7A3.a

EXAMPLE

Plot each point on a coordinate plane.

- **M(−3, 1)**
  Start at the
  origin. Move
  3 units left
  and 1 unit up.

- **R(3, −4)**
  Start at the
  origin. Move
  3 units right and
  4 units down.

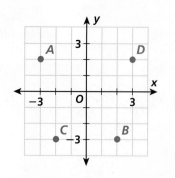

- **Give the
  coordinates
  of each point
  and tell which
  quadrant
  contains it.**
  A(−3, 2); II
  B(2, −3); IV
  C(−2, −3); III
  D(3, 2); I

EXERCISES

Plot each point on a coordinate plane.

4. A(4, 2)   **5.** B(−4, −2)

6. C(−2, 4)   **7.** D(2, −4)

Give the coordinates of each point and tell which quadrant contains it.

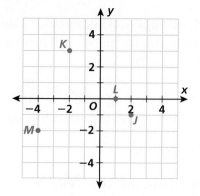

8. J   **9.** K

10. L   **11.** M

4-2 Tables and Graphs (pp. 228–231)

 GPS M7A3.a, M7A3.b

EXAMPLE

■ Write the ordered pairs from the table.

x	y
3	1
2	4
5	7

The ordered pairs are (3, 1), (2, 4), and (5, 7).

EXERCISES

Write and graph the ordered pairs from each table.

12.

x	y
−2	0
1	1
3	−4

13.

x	y
5	2
−2	−6
0	3

4-3 Interpreting Graphs (pp. 232–235)

GPS M7A3.b, M7A3.c

EXAMPLE

■ Ari visits his grandmother, who lives 45 miles away. After the visit, he returns home, stopping for gas along the way. Sketch a graph to show the distance Ari traveled compared to time. Use your graph to find the total distance traveled.

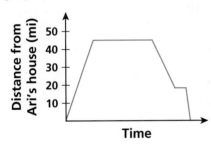

The graph increases from 0 to 45 miles and then decreases from 45 to 0 miles. The distance does not change while Ari visits his grandmother and stops for gas. Ari traveled a total of 90 miles.

EXERCISES

14. Amanda walks 1.5 miles to school in the morning. After school, she walks 0.5 mile to the public library. After she has chosen her books, she walks 2 miles home. Sketch a graph to show the distance Amanda traveled compared to time. Use your graph to find the total distance traveled.

15. Joel rides his bike to the park, 12 miles away, to meet his friends. He then rides an additional 6 miles to the grocery store and then 18 miles back home. Sketch a graph to show the distance Joel traveled compared to time. Use your graph to find the total distance traveled.

4-4 Functions, Tables, and Graphs (pp. 238–241)

 GPS M7A1.b, M7A3.a, M7A3.b

EXAMPLE

■ Find the output for each input.

$y = 3x + 4$

Input	Rule	Output
x	3x + 4	y
−1	3(−1) + 4	1
0	3(0) + 4	4
2	3(2) + 4	10

EXERCISES

Find the output for each input.

16. $y = x^2 - 1$

Input	Rule	Output
x	$x^2 - 1$	y
−2		
3		
5		

Study Guide: Review

4-5 Find a Pattern in Sequences (pp. 242–245)

GPS M7A1.a, M7A1.b, M7A3.b, M7A3.c

EXAMPLE

■ Tell whether the sequence of
  y-values is arithmetic or geometric.
  Then find y when $n = 5$.

n	1	2	3	4	5
y	−1	3	7	11	▨

In the sequence, 4 is added to each term.

$11 + 4 = 15$ *Add 4 to the fourth term.*

The sequence is arithmetic.
When $n = 5$, $y = 15$.

■ Write a function that describes the
  sequence. Use the function to find
  the eighth term in the sequence.

3, 6, 9, 12, . . .

n	Rule	y
1	1 · 3	3
2	2 · 3	6
3	3 · 3	9
4	4 · 3	12

Function: $y = 3n$
When $n = 8$, $y = 24$.

EXERCISES

Tell whether each sequence of
y-values is arithmetic or geometric.
Then find y when $n = 5$.

17.

n	1	2	3	4	5
y	3	9	27	81	▨

18.

n	1	2	3	4	5
y	14	3	−8	−19	▨

Write a function that describes each
sequence. Use the function to find the
eighth term in the sequence.

19. 25, 50, 75, 100, . . .

20. −3, −2, −1, 0, . . .

21. −4, −1, 2, 5, . . .

22. 4, 6, 8, 10, . . .

4-6 Graphing Linear Functions (pp. 248–251)

GPS M7A1.a, M7A1.b, M7A3.a, M7A3.b

EXAMPLE

■ Graph the linear function $y = -x + 2$.

Input	Rule	Output	Ordered Pair
x	$-x + 2$	y	(x, y)
−1	−(−1) + 2	3	(−1, 3)
0	−(0) + 2	2	(0, 2)
2	−(2) + 2	0	(2, 0)

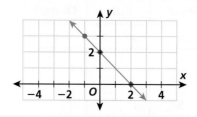

EXERCISES

Graph each linear function.

23. $y = 2x - 1$

24. $y = -3x$

25. $y = x - 3$

26. $y = 2x + 4$

27. $y = x - 6$

28. $y = 3x - 9$

CHAPTER TEST

Plot each point on a coordinate plane. Then identify the quadrant that contains each point.

1. $L(4, -3)$ **2.** $M(-5, 2)$ **3.** $N(7, 1)$ **4.** $O(-7, -2)$

Give the coordinates of each point.

5. A **6.** B **7.** C

8. D **9.** E **10.** F

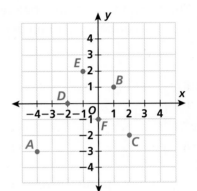

Write and graph the ordered pairs from each table.

11.

x	y
1	5
-3	0
2	-5

12.

x	y
0	2
-6	6
-1	-2

13. Ian jogs 4 miles to the lake and then rests for 30 min before jogging home. Sketch a graph to show the distance Ian traveled compared to time. Use your graph to find the total distance traveled.

Find the output for each input.

14. $y = -2x + 5$

Input	Rule	Output
x	-2x + 5	y
-1		
0		
1		

15. $y = x \div 4$

Input	Rule	Output
x	x ÷ 4	y
-8		
0		
4		

Tell whether each sequence of y-values is arithmetic or geometric. Then find y when $n = 5$.

16.

n	1	2	3	4	5
y	-2	8	-32	128	■

17.

n	1	2	3	4	5
y	-27	-16	-5	6	■

Write a function that describes each sequence. Use the function to find the eleventh term in the sequence.

18. 1, 3, 5, 7 . . . **19.** 11, 21, 31, 41 . . . **20.** 0, 3, 8, 15 . . .

Graph each linear function.

21. $y = 3x - 4$ **22.** $y = x - 8$ **23.** $y = 2x + 7$

Cumulative Assessment, Chapters 1–4

Multiple Choice

CRCT Prep

1. The fraction $\frac{7}{12}$ is found between which pair of numbers on a number line?

Ⓐ $\frac{5}{12}$ and $\frac{1}{2}$

Ⓑ $\frac{13}{24}$ and $\frac{3}{4}$

Ⓒ $\frac{1}{3}$ and $\frac{11}{24}$

Ⓓ $\frac{2}{3}$ and $\frac{5}{6}$

2. Which description shows the relationship between a term and n, its position in the sequence?

Position	Value of Term
1	1.25
2	3.25
3	5.25
4	7.25
n	

Ⓕ Add 1.25 to n.

Ⓖ Add 1 to n and multiply by 2.

Ⓗ Multiply n by 1 and add 1.25.

Ⓙ Multiply n by 2 and subtract 0.75.

3. For which equation is $x = -10$ the solution?

Ⓐ $2x - 20 = 0$

Ⓑ $\frac{1}{5}x + 2 = 0$

Ⓒ $\frac{1}{5}x - 2 = 0$

Ⓓ $-2x + 20 = 0$

4. What is the least common multiple of 10, 25, and 30?

Ⓕ 5

Ⓖ 50

Ⓗ 150

Ⓙ 200

5. Which problem situation matches the equation below?

$$x + 55 = 92$$

Ⓐ Liam has 55 tiles but needs a total of 92 to complete a project. How many more tiles does Liam need?

Ⓑ Cher spent $55 at the market and has only $92 left. How much did Cher start with?

Ⓒ Byron drove 55 miles each day for 92 days. How many total miles did he drive?

Ⓓ For every 55 students who buy "spirit wear," the boosters donate $92. How many students have bought spirit wear so far?

6. A recipe that makes 2 cups of guacamole dip calls for $1\frac{3}{4}$ cups of mashed avocados. How much avocado is needed to make 4 cups of dip with this recipe?

Ⓕ 3.25 cups

Ⓖ 3.5 cups

Ⓗ 3.75 cups

Ⓙ 4 cups

7. Which ordered pair is located on the x-axis?

Ⓐ $(0, -5)$

Ⓑ $(5, -5)$

Ⓒ $(-5, 0)$

Ⓓ $(1, -5)$

8. Which ordered pair is NOT a solution of $y = 5x - 4$?

Ⓕ $(2, 6)$

Ⓖ $(0, -4)$

Ⓗ $(1, 0)$

Ⓙ $(-1, -9)$

9. Carolyn makes between $5.75 and $9.50 per hour baby-sitting. Which is the best estimate of the total amount she makes for 9 hours of baby-sitting?

   Ⓐ From $30 to $55

   Ⓑ From $55 to $80

   Ⓒ From $80 to $105

   Ⓓ From $105 to $130

10. Patrick is going to spend the next 28 days preparing for a weight-lifting competition. He plans to spend a total of 119 hours at the gym. If Patrick is at the gym for the same amount of time every day, how many hours will he be at the gym each day?

    Ⓕ $\frac{4}{17}$ Ⓗ $\frac{17}{4}$

    Ⓖ $\frac{1}{4}$ Ⓙ 4

11. Solve the equation $-4.3x = -0.215$ for x.

    Ⓐ -20 Ⓒ 0.05

    Ⓑ -0.05 Ⓓ 20

12. Determine the y-coordinate of the point.

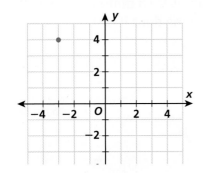

    Ⓕ -4 Ⓗ 3

    Ⓖ -3 Ⓙ 4

Short Response

13. A teacher discussed 112 of the 164 pages of the textbook. What portion of the pages did the teacher discuss? Write your answer as a decimal rounded to the nearest thousandth and as a fraction in simplest form.

14. A bag of nickels and quarters contains four times as many nickels as quarters. The total value of the coins in the bag is $1.35.

    a. How many nickels are in the bag?

    b. How many quarters are in the bag?

15. Describe in what order you would perform the operations to find the value of $(4 \cdot 4 - 6)^2 + (5 \cdot 7)$.

16. A recipe calls for $\frac{3}{4}$ cup flour and $\frac{2}{3}$ cup butter. Does the recipe require more flour or butter? Is this still true if the recipe is doubled? Explain how you determined your answer.

Extended Response

17. A bus travels at an average rate of 50 miles per hour from Nashville, Tennessee, to El Paso, Texas. To find the distance y traveled in x hours, use the equation $y = 50x$.

    a. Make a table of ordered pairs using the domain $x = 1, 2, 3, 4,$ and 5.

    b. Graph the solutions from the table of ordered pairs on a coordinate plane.

    c. Brett leaves Nashville by bus at 6:00 A.M. He needs to be in El Paso by 5:00 A.M. the following day. If Nashville is 1,100 miles from El Paso, will Brett make it on time? Explain how you determined your answer.

Problem Solving on Location

GEORGIA

— Atlanta

🍑 **Georgia Performance Standards**

M7P1.c, M7P4.c, M7P5.a

⭐ The Silver Comet Trail

Built on an abandoned railroad line, the Silver Comet Trail offers walkers, joggers, and bikers a continuous, 60-mile pathway. The scenic trail begins just west of Atlanta in Smyrna and continues west all the way to the Alabama border.

Choose one or more strategies to solve each problem.

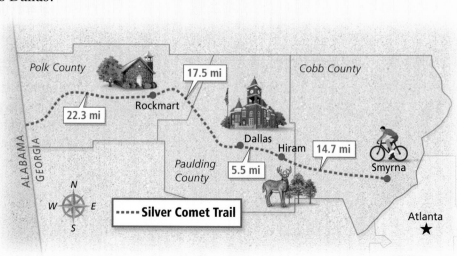

1. Along the trail, the distance from Carter Rd. to Sailor's Parkway is half the distance from Concord Rd. to Floyd Rd. The total length of these two sections of the trail is 2.4 miles. What is the distance from Carter Rd. to Sailor's Parkway?

For Problems 2 and 3, use the map.

2. A hiker walks from Hiram to Dallas. He covers 0.5 miles every 8 minutes and he stops for a 5-minute rest after every mile. How long does it take him to walk from Hiram to Dallas?

3. Heading west on the trail from Dallas to Rockmart, bikers pass the town of Rambo and then Coots Lake. The distance from Dallas to Coots Lake is 13.3 miles. The distance from Rambo to Rockmart is 15.5 miles. What is the distance from Rambo to Coots Lake?

Polk County

17.5 mi

Cobb County

Rockmart

22.3 mi

ALABAMA

GEORGIA

Dallas

Hiram 14.7 mi

Smyrna

Paulding County

5.5 mi

N
W   E
S

----- Silver Comet Trail

Atlanta
★

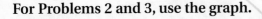

⭐ MARTA

MARTA (Metropolitan Atlanta Rapid Transit Authority) is one of the nation's largest and busiest transit systems, with 691 buses and 350 rail cars. Since its rail service began in 1979, the system has carried more than 3.5 billion people.

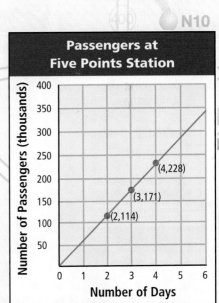

Problem Solving Strategies

Draw a Diagram
Make a Model
Guess and Test
Work Backward
Find a Pattern
Make a Table
Solve a Simpler Problem
Use Logical Reasoning
Act It Out
Make an Organized List

Choose one or more strategies to solve each problem.

1. MARTA provides shuttle service to Atlanta Braves baseball games. The shuttles start 90 minutes before each game and run throughout the game. The shuttles stop one hour after the game ends. If a shuttle departs every 15 minutes, how many shuttle runs are there for a Braves game that lasts 3 hours?

For Problems 2 and 3, use the graph.

2. Five Points Station is MARTA's busiest station. The graph shows the number of passengers served by MARTA at Five Points. How many passengers use MARTA at this station over the course of 7 days?

3. How many days does it take for the total number of passengers at Five Points Station to exceed 600,000?

Passengers at Five Points Station

Number of Passengers (thousands) vs. Number of Days

Points shown: (2, 114), (3, 171), (4, 228)

Proportional Relationships

CRCT PREP

go.hrw.com
Chapter Project Online
KEYWORD: MS7 Ch5

Lengths of Ships and Their Models			
Ship	Length of Ship (m)	Scale	Length of Model (mm)
Santa Maria	36.4	$\frac{1}{65}$	560
Golden Hind	25.9	$\frac{1}{72}$	360
HMS Bounty	47.0	$\frac{1}{48}$	980
Mayflower	38.7	$\frac{1}{64}$	605

Career Model Builder

When creating models of historical ships, model builders are careful to build their models to scale and with as much detail as possible. Model ships that are built for movies are much smaller than the original ships, while those built for display are often the same size as the original ships.

In the table, the scales show how the sizes of some models compare with the sizes of the original ships.

ARE YOU READY?

✓ Vocabulary

Choose the best term from the list to complete each sentence.

1. A(n) __?__ is a number that represents a part of a whole.

2. A closed figure with three sides is called a(n) __?__.

3. Two fractions are __?__ if they represent the same number.

4. One way to compare two fractions is to first find a(n) __?__.

common
  denominator

equivalent

fraction

quadrilateral

triangle

Complete these exercises to review skills you will need for this chapter.

✓ Write Equivalent Fractions

Find two fractions that are equivalent to each fraction.

5. $\frac{2}{5}$ 6. $\frac{7}{11}$ 7. $\frac{25}{100}$ 8. $\frac{4}{6}$

9. $\frac{5}{17}$ 10. $\frac{15}{23}$ 11. $\frac{24}{78}$ 12. $\frac{150}{325}$

✓ Compare Fractions

Compare. Write < or >.

13. $\frac{5}{6}$ ▨ $\frac{2}{3}$ 14. $\frac{3}{8}$ ▨ $\frac{2}{5}$ 15. $\frac{6}{11}$ ▨ $\frac{1}{4}$ 16. $\frac{5}{8}$ ▨ $\frac{11}{12}$

17. $\frac{8}{9}$ ▨ $\frac{12}{13}$ 18. $\frac{5}{11}$ ▨ $\frac{7}{21}$ 19. $\frac{4}{10}$ ▨ $\frac{3}{7}$ 20. $\frac{3}{4}$ ▨ $\frac{2}{9}$

✓ Solve Multiplication Equations

Solve each equation.

21. $3x = 12$ 22. $15t = 75$ 23. $2y = 14$ 24. $7m = 84$

25. $25c = 125$ 26. $16f = 320$ 27. $11n = 121$ 28. $53y = 318$

✓ Multiply Fractions

Solve. Write each answer in simplest form.

29. $\frac{2}{3} \cdot \frac{5}{7}$ 30. $\frac{12}{16} \cdot \frac{3}{9}$ 31. $\frac{4}{9} \cdot \frac{18}{24}$ 32. $\frac{1}{56} \cdot \frac{50}{200}$

33. $\frac{1}{5} \cdot \frac{5}{9}$ 34. $\frac{7}{8} \cdot \frac{4}{3}$ 35. $\frac{25}{100} \cdot \frac{30}{90}$ 36. $\frac{46}{91} \cdot \frac{3}{6}$

Study Guide: Preview

Where You've Been

Previously, you

- used ratios to describe proportional situations.
- used ratios to make predictions in proportional situations.
- used tables to describe proportional relationships involving conversions.

In This Chapter

You will study

- using division to find unit rates and ratios in proportional relationships.
- estimating and finding solutions to application problems involving proportional relationships.
- generating formulas involving unit conversions.
- using critical attributes to define similarity.
- using ratios and proportions in scale drawings and scale models.

Where You're Going

You can use the skills learned in this chapter

- to read and interpret maps.
- to find heights of objects that are too tall to measure.

Key Vocabulary/Vocabulario

corresponding angles	ángulos correspondientes
corresponding sides	lados correspondientes
equivalent ratios	razones equivalentes
proportion	proporción
rate	tasa
ratio	razón
scale	escala
scale drawing	dibujo a escala
scale model	modelo a escala
similar	semejante
slope	pendiente

Vocabulary Connections

To become familiar with some of the vocabulary terms in the chapter, consider the following. You may refer to the chapter, the glossary, or a dictionary if you like.

1. "Miles per hour," "students per class," and "Calories per serving" are all examples of *rates*. What other rates can you think of? How would you describe a **rate** to someone if you couldn't use examples in your explanation?

2. *Similar* means "having characteristics in common." If two triangles are **similar**, what might they have in common?

3. The *slope* of a mountain trail describes the steepness of a climb. What might the **slope** of a line describe?

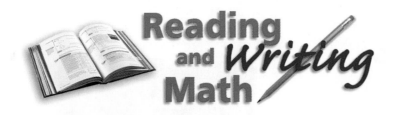

Writing Strategy: Use Your Own Words

Using your own words to explain a concept can help you understand the concept. For example, learning how to solve equations might seem difficult if the textbook does not explain solving equations in the same way that you would.

As you work through each lesson:

- Identify the important ideas from the explanation in the book.

- Use your own words to explain these ideas.

What Sara Reads

An **equation** is a mathematical statement that two expressions are equal in value.

When an equation contains a variable, a value of the variable that makes the statement true is called a **solution** of the equation.

If a variable is multiplied by a number, you can often use division to isolate the variable. Divide both sides of the equation by the number.

What Sara Writes

An _equation_ has an equal sign to show that two expressions are equal to each other.

The _solution_ of an equation that has a variable in it is the number that the variable is equal to.

When the variable is multiplied by a number, you can undo the multiplication and get the variable alone by dividing both sides of the equation by the number.

Rewrite each sentence in your own words.

1. When solving addition equations involving integers, isolate the variable by adding opposites.

2. When you solve equations that have one operation, you use an inverse operation to isolate the variable.

5-1 Ratios

**Learn** to identify, write, and compare ratios.

Vocabulary

ratio

Georgia Performance Standards

M7P4.a Recognize and use connections among mathematical ideas. Also, M7P1.b, M7P4.b, M7P4.c.

In basketball practice, Kathlene made 17 baskets in 25 attempts. She compared the number of baskets she made to the total number of attempts she made by using the *ratio* $\frac{17}{25}$. A **ratio** is a comparison of two quantities by division.

Kathlene can write her ratio of baskets made to attempts in three different ways.

$$\frac{17}{25} \qquad 17 \text{ to } 25 \qquad 17{:}25$$

EXAMPLE 1 Writing Ratios

A basket of fruit contains 6 apples, 4 bananas, and 3 oranges. Write each ratio in all three forms.

A bananas to apples

$$\frac{\text{number of bananas}}{\text{number of apples}} = \frac{4}{6} \qquad \textit{There are 4 bananas and 6 apples.}$$

The ratio of bananas to apples can be written as $\frac{4}{6}$, 4 to 6, or 4:6.

B bananas and apples to oranges

$$\frac{\text{number of bananas and apples}}{\text{number of oranges}} = \frac{4+6}{3} = \frac{10}{3}$$

The ratio of bananas and apples to oranges can be written as $\frac{10}{3}$, 10 to 3, or 10:3.

C oranges to total pieces of fruit

$$\frac{\text{number of oranges}}{\text{number of total pieces of fruit}} = \frac{3}{6+4+3} = \frac{3}{13}$$

The ratio of oranges to total pieces of fruit can be written as $\frac{3}{13}$, 3 to 13, or 3:13.

270 *Chapter 5 Proportional Relationships*

Sometimes a ratio can be simplified. To simplify a ratio, first write it in fraction form and then simplify the fraction.

EXAMPLE 2 **Writing Ratios in Simplest Form**

Remember!

A fraction is in simplest form when the GCF of the numerator and denominator is 1.

At Franklin Middle School, there are 252 students in the seventh grade and 9 seventh-grade teachers. Write the ratio of students to teachers in simplest form.

$$\frac{\text{students}}{\text{teachers}} = \frac{252}{9}$$ *Write the ratio as a fraction.*

$$= \frac{252 \div 9}{9 \div 9}$$ *Simplify.*

$$= \frac{28}{1}$$ *For every 28 students, there is 1 teacher.*

The ratio of students to teachers is 28 to 1.

To compare ratios, write them as fractions with common denominators. Then compare the numerators.

EXAMPLE 3 **Comparing Ratios**

Tell whether the wallet size photo or the portrait size photo has the greater ratio of width to length.

	Width (in.)	Length (in.)
Wallet	3.5	5
Personal	4	6
Desk	5	7
Portrait	8	10

Wallet: $\dfrac{\text{width (in.)}}{\text{length (in.)}} = \dfrac{3.5}{5}$ *Write the ratios as fractions with common denominators.*

Portrait: $\dfrac{\text{width (in.)}}{\text{length (in.)}} = \dfrac{8}{10} = \dfrac{4}{5}$

Because $4 > 3.5$ and the denominators are the same, the portrait size photo has the greater ratio of width to length.

Think and Discuss   GPS M7P1.d, M7P3.b

1. Explain why you think the ratio $\frac{10}{3}$ in Example 1B is not written as a mixed number.

2. Tell how to simplify a ratio.

3. Explain how to compare two ratios.

Georgia Performance Standards
M7P1.b, M7P4.c, M7P5.b

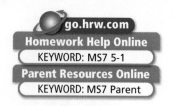
go.hrw.com
Homework Help Online
KEYWORD: MS7 5-1
Parent Resources Online
KEYWORD: MS7 Parent

GUIDED PRACTICE

See Example **Sun-Li has 10 blue marbles, 3 red marbles, and 17 white marbles. Write each ratio in all three forms.**

1. blue marbles to red marbles

2. red marbles to total marbles

See Example **2** **3.** In a 40-gallon aquarium, there are 21 neon tetras and 7 zebra danio fish. Write the ratio of neon tetras to zebra danio fish in simplest form.

See Example **3** **4.** Tell whose DVD collection has the greater ratio of comedy movies to adventure movies.

	Joseph	Yolanda
Comedy	5	7
Adventure	3	5

INDEPENDENT PRACTICE

See Example **A soccer league has 25 sixth-graders, 30 seventh-graders, and 15 eighth-graders. Write each ratio in all three forms.**

5. 6th-graders to 7th-graders

6. 6th-graders to total students

7. 7th-graders to 8th-graders

8. 7th- and 8th-graders to 6th-graders

See Example **9.** Thirty-six people auditioned for a play, and 9 people got roles. Write the ratio in simplest form of the number of people who auditioned to the number of people who got roles.

See Example **10.** Tell whose bag of nut mix has the greater ratio of peanuts to total nuts.

	Dina	Don
Almonds	6	11
Cashews	8	7
Peanuts	10	18

PRACTICE AND PROBLEM SOLVING

Extra Practice p. 735

Use the table for Exercises 11–13.

11. Tell whether group 1 or group 2 has the greater ratio of the number of people for an open-campus lunch to the number of people with no opinion.

Opinions on Open-Campus Lunch			
	Group 1	Group 2	Group 3
For	9	10	12
Against	14	16	16
No Opinion	5	6	8

12. Which group has the least ratio of the number of people against an open-campus lunch to the total number of survey responses?

13. **Estimation** For each group, is the ratio of the number of people for an open-campus lunch to the number of people against it less than or greater than $\frac{1}{2}$?

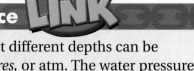
The pressure of water at different depths can be measured in *atmospheres,* or atm. The water pressure on a scuba diver increases as the diver descends below the surface. Use the table for Exercises 14–20.

Write each ratio in all three forms.

14. pressure at −33 ft to pressure at surface

15. pressure at −66 ft to pressure at surface

16. pressure at −99 ft to pressure at surface

17. pressure at −66 ft to pressure at −33 ft

18. pressure at −99 ft to pressure at −66 ft

19. Tell whether the ratio of pressure at −66 ft to pressure at −33 ft is greater than or less than the ratio of pressure at −99 ft to pressure at −66 ft.

20. ⭐ **Challenge** The ratio of the beginning pressure and the new pressure when a scuba diver goes from −33 ft to −66 ft is less than the ratio of pressures when the diver goes from the surface to −33 ft. The ratio of pressures is even less when the diver goes from −66 ft to −99 ft. Explain why this is true.

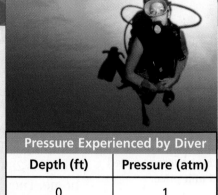

Pressure Experienced by Diver	
Depth (ft)	**Pressure (atm)**
0	1
−33	2
−66	3
−99	4

go.hrw.com
Web Extra!
KEYWORD: MS7 Pressure

CRCT Prep • GPS Support • Spiral Review

21. Multiple Choice Johnson Middle School has 125 sixth-graders, 150 seventh-graders, and 100 eighth-graders. Which statement is NOT true?

Ⓐ The ratio of sixth-graders to seventh-graders is 5 to 6.

Ⓑ The ratio of eighth-graders to seventh-graders is 3:2.

Ⓒ The ratio of sixth-graders to students in all three grades is 1:3.

Ⓓ The ratio of eighth-graders to students in all three grades is 4 to 15.

22. Short Response A pancake recipe calls for 4 cups of pancake mix for every 3 cups of milk. A biscuit recipe calls for 2 cups of biscuit mix for every 1 cup of milk. Which recipe has a greater ratio of mix to milk? Explain.

Solve. (Lesson 3-6)

23. $1.23 + x = -5.47$

24. $3.8y = 27.36$

25. $v - 3.8 = 4.7$

26. Identify the quadrant in which the point $(5, -7)$ lies. (Lesson 4-1)

5-2 Rates

Learn to find and compare unit rates, such as average speed and unit price.

Vocabulary

rate

unit rate

Georgia Performance Standards

M7P1.b Solve problems that arise in mathematics and in other contexts. Also, M7P4.c.

The Lawsons are going camping at Rainbow Falls, which is 288 miles from their home. They would like to reach the campground in 6 hours of driving so that they can set up their campsite while it is still light. What should their average speed be in miles per hour?

A **rate** is a ratio that compares two quantities measured in different units. In order to answer the question above, you need to find the family's rate of travel.

Their rate is $\frac{288 \text{ miles}}{6 \text{ hours}}$.

A **unit rate** is a rate whose denominator is 1. To change a rate to a unit rate, divide both the numerator and denominator by the denominator.

EXAMPLE **1** **Finding Unit Rates**

A During exercise, Sonia's heart beats 675 times in 5 minutes. How many times does it beat per minute?

$\frac{675 \text{ beats}}{5 \text{ minutes}}$ *Write a rate that compares heart beats and time.*

$\frac{675 \text{ beats} \div 5}{5 \text{ minutes} \div 5}$ *Divide the numerator and denominator by 5.*

$\frac{135 \text{ beats}}{1 \text{ minute}}$ *Simplify.*

Sonia's heart beats 135 times per minute.

B To make 4 large pizza pockets, Paul needs 14 cups of broccoli. How much broccoli does he need for 1 large pizza pocket?

$\frac{14 \text{ cups broccoli}}{4 \text{ pizza pockets}}$ *Write a rate that compares cups to pockets.*

$\frac{14 \text{ cups broccoli} \div 4}{4 \text{ pizza pockets} \div 4}$ *Divide the numerator and denominator by 4.*

$\frac{3.5 \text{ cups broccoli}}{1 \text{ pizza pocket}}$ *Simplify.*

Paul needs 3.5 cups of broccoli to make 1 large pizza pocket.

274 *Chapter 5 Proportional Relationships*

An average rate of speed is the ratio of distance traveled to time. The ratio is a rate because the units in the numerator and denominator are different.

EXAMPLE **2** **Finding Average Speed**

The Lawsons want to drive the 288 miles to Rainbow Falls in 6 hours. What should their average speed be in miles per hour?

$$\frac{288 \text{ miles}}{6 \text{ hours}}$$ *Write the rate as a fraction.*

$$\frac{288 \text{ miles} \div 6}{6 \text{ hours} \div 6} = \frac{48 \text{ miles}}{1 \text{ hour}}$$ *Divide the numerator and denominator by the denominator.*

Their average speed should be 48 miles per hour.

A unit price is the price of one unit of an item. The unit used depends on how the item is sold. The table shows some examples.

Type of Item	Examples of Units
Liquid	Fluid ounces, quarts, gallons, liters
Solid	Ounces, pounds, grams, kilograms
Any item	Bottle, container, carton

EXAMPLE **3** *Consumer Math Application*

The Lawsons stop at a roadside farmers' market. The market offers lemonade in three sizes. Which size lemonade has the lowest price per fluid ounce?

Size	Price
12 fl oz	$0.89
18 fl oz	$1.69
24 fl oz	$2.09

Divide the price by the number of fluid ounces (fl oz) to find the unit price of each size.

$$\frac{\$0.89}{12 \text{ fl oz}} \approx \frac{\$0.07}{\text{fl oz}} \qquad \frac{\$1.69}{18 \text{ fl oz}} \approx \frac{\$0.09}{\text{fl oz}} \qquad \frac{\$2.09}{24 \text{ fl oz}} \approx \frac{\$0.09}{\text{fl oz}}$$

Since $0.07 < $0.09, the 12 fl oz lemonade has the lowest price per fluid ounce.

Think and Discuss    GPS M7P3.b

1. **Explain** how can you tell whether an expression represents a unit rate.

2. **Suppose** a store offers cereal with a unit price of $0.15 per ounce. Another store offers cereal with a unit price of $0.18 per ounce. Before determining which is the better buy, what variables must you consider?

Georgia Performance Standards

M7P3.a, M7P4.c, M7P5.c

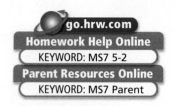
go.hrw.com
Homework Help Online
KEYWORD: MS7 5-2
Parent Resources Online
KEYWORD: MS7 Parent

GUIDED PRACTICE

See Example **1.** A faucet leaks 668 milliliters of water in 8 minutes. How many milliliters of water does the faucet leak per minute?

2. A recipe for 6 muffins calls for 360 grams of oat flakes. How many grams of oat flakes are needed for each muffin?

See Example **3.** An airliner makes a 2,748-mile flight in 6 hours. What is the airliner's average rate of speed in miles per hour?

See Example **4.** **Consumer Math** During a car trip, the Webers buy gasoline at three different stations. At the first station, they pay $18.63 for 9 gallons of gas. At the second, they pay $29.54 for 14 gallons. At the third, they pay $33.44 for 16 gallons. Which station offers the lowest price per gallon?

INDEPENDENT PRACTICE

See Example **5.** An after-school job pays $116.25 for 15 hours of work. How much money does the job pay per hour?

6. It took Samantha 324 minutes to cook a turkey. If the turkey weighed 18 pounds, how many minutes per pound did it take to cook the turkey?

See Example **7.** **Sports** The first Indianapolis 500 auto race took place in 1911. The winning car covered the 500 miles in 6.7 hours. What was the winning car's average rate of speed in miles per hour?

See Example **8.** **Consumer Math** A supermarket sells orange juice in three sizes. The 32 fl oz container costs $1.99, the 64 fl oz container costs $3.69, and the 96 fl oz container costs $5.85. Which size orange juice has the lowest price per fluid ounce?

PRACTICE AND PROBLEM SOLVING

Extra Practice p. 735

Find each unit rate. Round to the nearest hundredth, if necessary.

9. 9 runs in 3 games   **10.** $207,000 for 1,800 ft^2 **11.** $2,010 in 6 mo

12. 52 songs on 4 CDs   **13.** 226 mi on 12 gal   **14.** 324 words in 6 min

15. 12 hr for $69   **16.** 6 lb for $12.96   **17.** 488 mi in 4 trips

18. 220 m in 20 s   **19.** 1.5 mi in 39 min   **20.** 24,000 km in 1.5 hr

21. In Grant Middle School, each class has an equal number of students. There are 38 classes and a total of 1,026 students. Write a rate that describes the distribution of students in the classes at Grant. What is the unit rate?

22. **Estimation** Use estimation to determine which is the better buy: 450 minutes of phone time for $49.99 or 800 minutes for $62.99.

Find each unit price. Then decide which is the better buy.

23. $\dfrac{\$2.52}{42 \text{ oz}}$ or $\dfrac{\$3.64}{52 \text{ oz}}$

24. $\dfrac{\$28.40}{8 \text{ yd}}$ or $\dfrac{\$55.50}{15 \text{ yd}}$

25. $\dfrac{\$8.28}{0.3 \text{ m}}$ or $\dfrac{\$13.00}{0.4 \text{ m}}$

26. **Sports** In the 2004 Summer Olympics, Justin Gatlin won the 100-meter race in 9.85 seconds. Shawn Crawford won the 200-meter race in 19.79 seconds. Which runner ran at a faster average rate?

27. **Social Studies** The population density of a country is the average number of people per unit of area. Write the population densities of the countries in the table as unit rates. Round your answers to the nearest person per square mile. Then rank the countries from least to greatest population density.

Country	Population	Land Area (mi²)
France	60,424,213	210,669
Germany	82,424,609	134,836
Poland	38,626,349	117,555

28. **Write a Problem** A store sells paper towels in packs of 6 and packs of 8. Use this information to write a problem about comparing unit rates.

29. **Write About It** Michael Jordan has the highest scoring average in NBA history. He played in 1,072 games and scored 32,292 points. Explain how to find a unit rate to describe his scoring average. What is the unit rate?

30. **Challenge** Mike fills his car's gas tank with 20 gallons of regular gas at $2.01 per gallon. His car averages 25 miles per gallon. Serena fills her car's tank with 15 gallons of premium gas at $2.29 per gallon. Her car averages 30 miles per gallon. Compare the drivers' unit costs of driving one mile.

CRCT PREP • GPS SUPPORT • SPIRAL REVIEW

31. Multiple Choice What is the unit price of a 16-ounce box of cereal that sells for $2.48?

Ⓐ $0.14　　　Ⓑ $0.15　　　Ⓒ $0.0155　　　Ⓓ $0.155

32. Short Response A carpenter needs 3 minutes to make 5 cuts in a board. If each cut takes the same length of time, at what rate is the carpenter cutting?

Compare. Write <, >, or =. (Lesson 1-3)

33. 600 mL ▮ 5 L

34. 0.009 mg ▮ 8.91 g

35. 254 cm ▮ 25.4 mm

36. Julita's walking stick is $3\frac{2}{3}$ feet long, and Toni's walking stick is $3\frac{3}{8}$ feet long. Whose walking stick is longer and by how much? (Lesson 3-9)

5-3 Slope and Rates of Change

Learn to determine the slope of a line and to recognize constant and variable rates of change.

Vocabulary
slope

Georgia Performance Standards

M7A3.b Represent, describe, and analyze relations from tables, graphs, and formulas. Also, M7A3.a, M7P4.a, M7P4.b.

The steepness of the pyramid steps is measured by dividing the height of each step by its depth. Another way to express the height and depth is with the words *rise* and *run*.

The **slope** of a line is a measure of its steepness and is the ratio of rise to run:

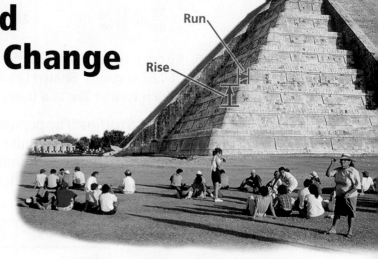

In Chichén Itzá, Mexico, during the spring and fall equinoxes, shadows fall on the pyramid El Castillo, giving the illusion of a snake crawling down the steps.

$$\text{slope} = \frac{\text{rise}}{\text{run}}$$

If a line rises from left to right, its slope is positive. If a line falls from left to right, its slope is negative.

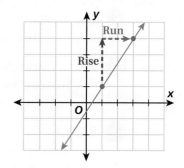

EXAMPLE 1 **Identifying the Slope of the Line**

Tell whether the slope is positive or negative. Then find the slope.

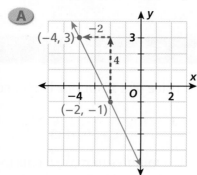

A

The line falls from left to right.
The slope is negative.

$\text{slope} = \dfrac{\text{rise}}{\text{run}}$

$\quad = \dfrac{4}{-2}$ *The rise is 4.*
The run is −2.

$\quad = -2$

B

The line rises from left to right.
The slope is positive.

$\text{slope} = \dfrac{\text{rise}}{\text{run}}$

$\quad = \dfrac{2}{3}$ *The rise is 2.*
The run is 3.

You can graph a line if you know its slope and one of its points.

EXAMPLE 2 **Using Slope and a Point to Graph a Line**

Use the given slope and point to graph each line.

A $-\frac{3}{4}$; $(-3, 2)$

slope $= \frac{\text{rise}}{\text{run}} = \frac{-3}{4}$ or $\frac{3}{-4}$

From point $(-3, 2)$, move 3 units down and 4 units right, or move 3 units up and 4 units left. Mark the point where you end up, and draw a line through the two points.

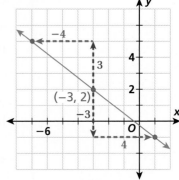

B 3; $(-1, -2)$

$3 = \frac{3}{1}$ *Write the slope as a fraction.*

slope $= \frac{\text{rise}}{\text{run}} = \frac{3}{1}$

From point $(-1, -2)$, move 3 units up and 1 unit right. Mark the point where you end up, and draw a line through the two points.

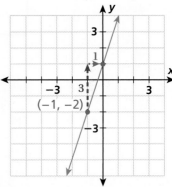

Remember!

You can write an integer as a fraction by putting the integer in the numerator of the fraction and a 1 in the denominator.

The ratio of two quantities that change, such as slope, is a *rate of change*.

A *constant rate of change* describes changes of the same amount during equal intervals. A *variable rate of change* describes changes of a different amount during equal intervals.

The graph of a constant rate of change is a line, and the graph of a variable rate of change is not a line.

EXAMPLE 3 **Identifying Rates of Change in Graphs**

Tell whether each graph shows a constant or variable rate of change.

A

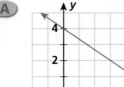
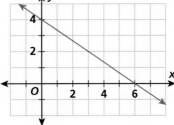

The graph is a line, so the rate of change is constant.

B

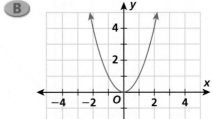

The graph is not a line, so the rate of change is variable.

EXAMPLE 4 Using Rate of Change to Solve Problems

The graph shows the distance a bicyclist travels over time. Does the bicyclist travel at a constant or variable speed? How fast does the bicyclist travel?

The graph is a line, so the bicyclist is traveling at a constant speed.

The amount of distance is the rise, and the amount of time is the run. You can find the speed by finding the slope.

$$\text{slope (speed)} = \frac{\text{rise (distance)}}{\text{run (time)}} = \frac{15}{1}$$

The bicyclist travels at 15 miles per hour.

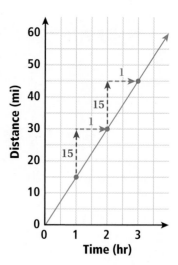

Think and Discuss GPS M7P3.a, M7P3.b

1. Describe a line with a negative slope.

2. Compare constant and variable rates of change.

3. Give an example of a real-world situation involving a rate of change.

5-3 Exercises

Georgia Performance Standards

M7P3.a, M7P3.c, M7P5.a

GUIDED PRACTICE

See Example ① **Tell whether the slope is positive or negative. Then find the slope.**

1.

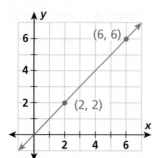

2.

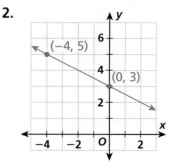

See Example ② **Use the given slope and point to graph each line.**

3. 3; $(4, -2)$ **4.** -2; $(-3, -2)$ **5.** $-\frac{1}{4}$; $(0, 5)$ **6.** $\frac{3}{2}$; $(-1, 1)$

See Example 3 **Tell whether each graph shows a constant or variable rate of change.**

7.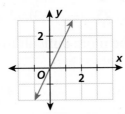

8.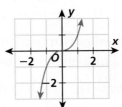

9.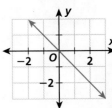

See Example 4 **10.** The graph shows the distance a trout swims over time. Does the trout swim at a constant or variable speed? How fast does the trout swim?

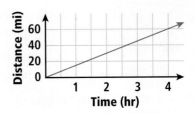

INDEPENDENT PRACTICE

See Example 1 **Tell whether the slope is positive or negative. Then find the slope.**

11.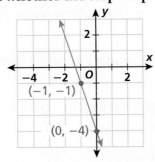

12.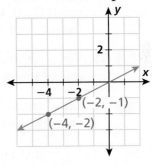

See Example 2 **Use the given slope and point to graph each line.**

13. -1; $(-1, 4)$ **14.** 4; $(-1, -3)$ **15.** $\frac{3}{5}$; $(3, -1)$ **16.** $\frac{2}{3}$; $(0, 5)$

See Example 3 **Tell whether each graph shows a constant or variable rate of change.**

17.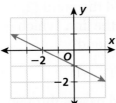

18.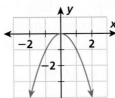

19.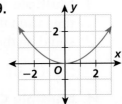

See Example 4 **20.** The graph shows the amount of rain that falls over time. Does the rain fall at a constant or variable rate? How much rain falls per hour?

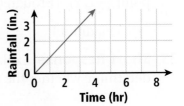

PRACTICE AND PROBLEM SOLVING

21. Multi-Step A line has a slope of 5 and passes through the points $(4, 3)$ and $(2, y)$. What is the value of y?

22. A line passes through the origin and has a slope of $-\frac{3}{2}$. Through which quadrants does the line pass?

Graph the line containing the two points, and then find the slope.

23. $(-2, 13), (1, 4)$ **24.** $(-2, -6), (2, 2)$ **25.** $(-2, -3), (2, 3)$ **26.** $(2, -3), (3, -5)$

27. Explain whether you think it would be more difficult to run up a hill with a slope of $\frac{1}{3}$ or a hill with a slope of $\frac{3}{4}$.

28. Agriculture The graph at right shows the cost per pound of buying peaches.

  a. Is the cost per pound a constant or variable rate?

  b. What is the cost per pound of peaches?

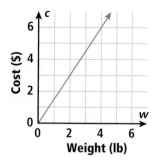

29. Critical Thinking A line has a negative slope. Explain how the y-values of the line change as the x-values increase.

30. What's the Error? Kyle graphed a line, given a slope of $-\frac{4}{3}$ and the point $(2, 3)$. When he used the slope to find the second point, he found $(5, 7)$. What error did Kyle make?

31. Write About It Explain how to graph a line when given the slope and one of the points on the line.

32. Challenge The population of prairie dogs in a park doubles every year. Does this population show a constant or variable rate of change? Explain.

CRCT PREP • GPS SUPPORT • SPIRAL REVIEW

33. Multiple Choice To graph a line, Caelyn plotted the point $(2, 1)$ and then used the slope $-\frac{1}{2}$ to find another point on the line. Which point could be the other point on the line that Caelyn found?

   (A) $(1, 3)$ (B) $(4, 0)$ (C) $(1, -1)$ (D) $(0, 0)$

34. Multiple Choice A line has a positive slope and passes through the point $(-1, 2)$. Through which quadrant can the line NOT pass?

   (F) Quadrant I   (G) Quadrant II   (H) Quadrant III   (J) Quadrant IV

35. Short Response Explain how you can use three points on a graph to determine whether the rate of change is constant or variable.

Find each value. (Lesson 1-2)

36. 3^5 **37.** 5^3 **38.** 4^1 **39.** 10^5

Write a rule for each sequence in words. Then find the next three terms. (Lesson 4-5)

40. $3.7, 3.2, 2.7, 2.2, \ldots$ **41.** $-\frac{3}{2}, 0, \frac{3}{2}, 3, \ldots$ **42.** $3, -1, \frac{1}{3}, -\frac{1}{9}, \ldots$

5-4 Identifying and Writing Proportions

**Learn** to find equivalent ratios and to identify proportions.

Vocabulary

equivalent ratios

proportion

🍎 **Georgia Performance Standards**

M7N1.b Compare and order rational numbers. Also, M7N1.d, M7P1.b, M7P4.c.

Reading Math

Read the proportion $\frac{10}{6} = \frac{25}{15}$ by saying "ten is to six as twenty-five is to fifteen."

Students in Mr. Howell's math class are measuring the width w and the length ℓ of their heads. The ratio of ℓ to w is 10 inches to 6 inches for Jean and 25 centimeters to 15 centimeters for Pat.

These ratios can be written as the fractions $\frac{10}{6}$ and $\frac{25}{15}$. Since both ratios simplify to $\frac{5}{3}$, they are equivalent. **Equivalent ratios** are ratios that name the same comparison.

Calipers have adjustable arms that are used to measure the thickness of objects.

An equation stating that two ratios are equivalent is called a **proportion** . The equation, or proportion, below states that the ratios $\frac{10}{6}$ and $\frac{25}{15}$ are equivalent.

$$\frac{10}{6} = \frac{25}{15}$$

If two ratios are equivalent, they are said to be *proportional* to each other, or *in proportion*.

EXAMPLE 1 **Comparing Ratios in Simplest Form**

Determine whether the ratios are proportional.

A $\frac{2}{7}, \frac{6}{21}$

$\frac{2}{7}$ *$\frac{2}{7}$ is already in simplest form.*

$\frac{6}{21} = \frac{6 \div 3}{21 \div 3} = \frac{2}{7}$ *Simplify $\frac{6}{21}$.*

Since $\frac{2}{7} = \frac{2}{7}$, the ratios are proportional.

B $\frac{8}{24}, \frac{6}{20}$

$\frac{8}{24} = \frac{8 \div 8}{24 \div 8} = \frac{1}{3}$ *Simplify $\frac{8}{24}$.*

$\frac{6}{20} = \frac{6 \div 2}{20 \div 2} = \frac{3}{10}$ *Simplify $\frac{6}{20}$.*

Since $\frac{1}{3} \neq \frac{3}{10}$, the ratios are *not* proportional.

5-4 Identifying and Writing Proportions   **283**

EXAMPLE **2** **Comparing Ratios Using a Common Denominator**

Use the data in the table to determine whether the ratios of oats to water are proportional for both servings of oatmeal.

Servings of Oatmeal	Cups of Oats	Cups of Water
8	2	4
12	3	6

Write the ratios of oats to water for 8 servings and for 12 servings.

Ratio of oats to water, 8 servings: $\frac{2}{4}$ *Write the ratio as a fraction.*

Ratio of oats to water, 12 servings: $\frac{3}{6}$ *Write the ratio as a fraction.*

$\frac{2}{4} = \frac{2 \cdot 6}{4 \cdot 6} = \frac{12}{24}$ *Write the ratios with a common*

$\frac{3}{6} = \frac{3 \cdot 4}{6 \cdot 4} = \frac{12}{24}$ *denominator, such as 24.*

Since both ratios are equal to $\frac{12}{24}$, they are proportional.

You can find an equivalent ratio by multiplying or dividing the numerator and the denominator of a ratio by the same number.

EXAMPLE **3** **Finding Equivalent Ratios and Writing Proportions**

Find a ratio equivalent to each ratio. Then use the ratios to write a proportion.

 $\frac{8}{14}$

$\frac{8}{14} = \frac{8 \cdot 20}{14 \cdot 20} = \frac{160}{280}$ *Multiply both the numerator and denominator by any number, such as 20.*

$\frac{8}{14} = \frac{160}{280}$ *Write a proportion.*

 $\frac{4}{18}$

$\frac{4}{18} = \frac{4 \div 2}{18 \div 2} = \frac{2}{9}$ *Divide both the numerator and denominator by a common factor, such as 2.*

$\frac{4}{18} = \frac{2}{9}$ *Write a proportion.*

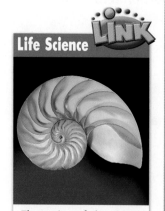

Life Science LINK

The ratios of the sizes of the segments of a nautilus shell are approximately equal to the *golden ratio*, 1.618.... This ratio can be found in many places in nature.

go.hrw.com
Web Extra!
KEYWORD: MS7 Golden

Think and Discuss   GPS M7P1.d, M7P3.b

1. **Explain** why the ratios in Example 1B are not proportional.

2. **Describe** what it means for ratios to be proportional.

3. **Give an example** of a proportion. Then tell how you know it is a proportion.

Georgia Performance
Standards

M7P2.c, M7P3.a, M7P3.c

go.hrw.com
Homework Help Online
KEYWORD: MS7 5-4
Parent Resources Online
KEYWORD: MS7 Parent

GUIDED PRACTICE

See Example ① Determine whether the ratios are proportional.

1. $\frac{2}{3}, \frac{4}{6}$ **2.** $\frac{5}{10}, \frac{8}{18}$ **3.** $\frac{9}{12}, \frac{15}{20}$ **4.** $\frac{3}{4}, \frac{8}{12}$

See Example ② **5.** $\frac{10}{12}, \frac{15}{18}$ **6.** $\frac{6}{9}, \frac{8}{12}$ **7.** $\frac{3}{4}, \frac{5}{6}$ **8.** $\frac{4}{6}, \frac{6}{9}$

See Example ③ Find a ratio equivalent to each ratio. Then use the ratios to write a proportion.

9. $\frac{1}{3}$ **10.** $\frac{9}{21}$ **11.** $\frac{8}{3}$ **12.** $\frac{10}{4}$

INDEPENDENT PRACTICE

See Example ① Determine whether the ratios are proportional.

13. $\frac{5}{8}, \frac{7}{14}$ **14.** $\frac{8}{24}, \frac{10}{30}$ **15.** $\frac{18}{20}, \frac{81}{180}$ **16.** $\frac{15}{20}, \frac{27}{35}$

See Example ② **17.** $\frac{2}{3}, \frac{4}{9}$ **18.** $\frac{18}{12}, \frac{15}{10}$ **19.** $\frac{7}{8}, \frac{14}{24}$ **20.** $\frac{18}{54}, \frac{10}{30}$

See Example ③ Find a ratio equivalent to each ratio. Then use the ratios to write a proportion.

21. $\frac{5}{9}$ **22.** $\frac{27}{60}$ **23.** $\frac{6}{15}$ **24.** $\frac{121}{99}$

25. $\frac{11}{13}$ **26.** $\frac{5}{22}$ **27.** $\frac{78}{104}$ **28.** $\frac{27}{72}$

PRACTICE AND PROBLEM SOLVING

Extra Practice p. 735

Complete each table of equivalent ratios.

29.

angelfish	4	8		20
tiger fish		6	18	

30.

squares	2	4	6	8
circles		16		

Find two ratios equivalent to each given ratio.

31. 3 to 7 **32.** 6:2 **33.** $\frac{5}{12}$ **34.** 8:4

35. 6 to 9 **36.** $\frac{10}{50}$ **37.** 10:4 **38.** 1 to 10

39. Ecology If you recycle one aluminum can, you save enough energy to run a TV for four hours.

   a. Write the ratio of cans to hours.

   b. Marti's class recycled enough aluminum cans to run a TV for 2,080 hours. Did the class recycle 545 cans? Justify your answer using equivalent ratios.

40. Critical Thinking The ratio of girls to boys riding a bus is 15:12. If the driver drops off the same number of girls as boys at the next stop, does the ratio of girls to boys remain 15:12? Explain.

41. Critical Thinking Write all possible proportions using only the numbers 1, 2, and 4.

42. School Last year in Kerry's school, the ratio of students to teachers was 22:1. Write an equivalent ratio to show how many students and teachers there could have been at Kerry's school.

43. Life Science Students in a biology class surveyed four ponds to determine whether salamanders and frogs were inhabiting the area.

Pond	Number of Salamanders	Number of Frogs
Cypress Pond	8	5
Mill Pond	15	10
Clear Pond	3	2
Gill Pond	2	7

a. What was the ratio of salamanders to frogs in Cypress Pond?

b. In which two ponds was the ratio of salamanders to frogs the same?

44. Marcus earned $230 for 40 hours of work. Phillip earned $192 for 32 hours of work. Are these pay rates proportional? Explain.

45. What's the Error? A student wrote the proportion $\frac{13}{20} = \frac{26}{60}$. What did the student do wrong?

46. Write About It Explain two different ways to determine if two ratios are proportional.

47. Challenge A skydiver jumps out of an airplane. After 0.8 second, she has fallen 100 feet. After 3.1 seconds, she has fallen 500 feet. Is the rate (in feet per second) at which she falls the first 100 feet proportional to the rate at which she falls the next 400 feet? Explain.

CRCT PREP • GPS SUPPORT • SPIRAL REVIEW

48. Multiple Choice Which ratio is NOT equivalent to $\frac{32}{48}$?

Ⓐ $\frac{2}{3}$ Ⓑ $\frac{8}{12}$ Ⓒ $\frac{64}{96}$ Ⓓ $\frac{128}{144}$

49. Multiple Choice Which ratio can form a proportion with $\frac{5}{6}$?

Ⓕ $\frac{13}{18}$ Ⓖ $\frac{25}{36}$ Ⓗ $\frac{70}{84}$ Ⓙ $\frac{95}{102}$

Divide. Estimate to check whether each answer is reasonable. (Lesson 3-5)

50. $14.35 \div 0.7$ **51.** $-9 \div 2.4$ **52.** $12.505 \div 3.05$ **53.** $427 \div (-5.6)$

Make a function table. (Lesson 4-4)

54. $y = 2x - 1$ **55.** $y = -x + 3$ **56.** $y = \frac{x}{3} - 2$ **57.** $y = -3x + 4$

5-5 Solving Proportions

Learn to solve proportions by using cross products.

Vocabulary

cross product

Georgia Performance Standards

M7A2.a Given a problem, define a variable, write an equation, solve the equation, and interpret the solution. Also, M7A2.b, M7P1.c, M7P1.d.

Density is a ratio that compares a substance's mass to its volume. If you are given the density of ice, you can find the mass of 3 mL of ice by solving a proportion.

For two ratios, the product of the numerator in one ratio and the denominator in the other is a cross product . If the cross products of the ratios are equal, then the ratios form a proportion.

$$\frac{2}{5} \times \frac{6}{15} \quad \begin{array}{l} 5 \cdot 6 = 30 \\ 2 \cdot 15 = 30 \end{array}$$

Ice floats in water because the density of ice is less than the density of water.

CROSS PRODUCT RULE

In the proportion $\frac{a}{b} = \frac{c}{d}$, where $b \neq 0$ and $d \neq 0$, the cross products, $a \cdot d$ and $b \cdot c$, are equal.

You can use the cross product rule to solve proportions with variables.

EXAMPLE 1 Solving Proportions Using Cross Products

Use cross products to solve the proportion $\frac{p}{6} = \frac{10}{3}$.

$$\frac{p}{6} = \frac{10}{3}$$

$p \cdot 3 = 6 \cdot 10$ *The cross products are equal.*

$3p = 60$ *Multiply.*

$\dfrac{3p}{3} = \dfrac{60}{3}$ *Divide each side by 3 to isolate the variable.*

$p = 20$

When setting up proportions that include different units of measurement, either the units in the numerators must be the same and the units in the denominators must be the same or the units within each ratio must be the same.

$$\frac{16 \text{ mi}}{4 \text{ hr}} = \frac{8 \text{ mi}}{x \text{ hr}} \qquad \frac{16 \text{ mi}}{8 \text{ mi}} = \frac{4 \text{ hr}}{x \text{ hr}}$$

EXAMPLE 2 **PROBLEM SOLVING APPLICATION**

Density is the ratio of a substance's mass to its volume. The density of ice is 0.92 g/mL. What is the mass of 3 mL of ice?

1 Understand the Problem

Rewrite the question as a statement.

- Find the mass, in grams, of 3 mL of ice.

List the **important information:**

- density $= \dfrac{\text{mass (g)}}{\text{volume (mL)}}$

- density of ice $= \dfrac{0.92 \text{ g}}{1 \text{ mL}}$

2 Make a Plan

Set up a proportion using the given information. Let m represent the mass of 3 mL of ice.

$$\frac{0.92 \text{ g}}{1 \text{ mL}} = \frac{m}{3 \text{ mL}} \begin{array}{l} \leftarrow \textit{mass} \\ \leftarrow \textit{volume} \end{array}$$

3 Solve

Solve the proportion.

$$\frac{0.92}{1} = \frac{m}{3} \qquad \textit{Write the proportion.}$$

$$1 \cdot m = 0.92 \cdot 3 \qquad \textit{The cross products are equal.}$$

$$m = 2.76 \qquad \textit{Multiply.}$$

The mass of 3 mL of ice is 2.76 g.

4 Look Back

Since the density of ice is 0.92 g/mL, each milliliter of ice has a mass of a little less than 1 g. So 3 mL of ice should have a mass of a little less than 3 g. Since 2.76 is a little less than 3, the answer is reasonable.

Think and Discuss  GPS M7P3.b, M7P3.c

1. **Explain** how the term *cross product* can help you remember how to solve a proportion.

2. **Describe** the error in these steps: $\frac{2}{3} = \frac{x}{12}$; $2x = 36$; $x = 18$.

3. **Show** how to use cross products to decide whether the ratios 6:45 and 2:15 are proportional.

Georgia Performance
Standards

M7P3.a, M7P4.c, M7P5.a

go.hrw.com
Homework Help Online
KEYWORD: MS7 5-5
Parent Resources Online
KEYWORD: MS7 Parent

GUIDED PRACTICE

See Example 1 Use cross products to solve each proportion.

1. $\dfrac{6}{10} = \dfrac{36}{x}$ 2. $\dfrac{4}{7} = \dfrac{5}{p}$ 3. $\dfrac{12.3}{m} = \dfrac{75}{100}$ 4. $\dfrac{t}{42} = \dfrac{1.5}{3}$

See Example 2 5. A stack of 2,450 one-dollar bills weighs 5 pounds. How much does a stack of 1,470 one-dollar bills weigh?

INDEPENDENT PRACTICE

See Example 1 Use cross products to solve each proportion.

6. $\dfrac{4}{36} = \dfrac{x}{180}$ 7. $\dfrac{7}{84} = \dfrac{12}{h}$ 8. $\dfrac{3}{24} = \dfrac{r}{52}$ 9. $\dfrac{5}{140} = \dfrac{12}{v}$

10. $\dfrac{45}{x} = \dfrac{15}{3}$ 11. $\dfrac{t}{6} = \dfrac{96}{16}$ 12. $\dfrac{2}{5} = \dfrac{s}{12}$ 13. $\dfrac{14}{n} = \dfrac{5}{8}$

See Example 2 14. Euro coins come in eight denominations. One denomination is the one-euro coin, which is worth 100 cents. A stack of 10 one-euro coins is 21.25 millimeters tall. How tall would a stack of 45 one-euro coins be? Round your answer to the nearest hundredth of a millimeter.

15. There are 18.5 ounces of soup in a can. This is equivalent to 524 grams. If Jenna has 8 ounces of soup, how many grams does she have? Round your answer to the nearest whole gram.

PRACTICE AND PROBLEM SOLVING

Extra Practice p. 735

Solve each proportion. Then find another equivalent ratio.

16. $\dfrac{4}{h} = \dfrac{12}{24}$ 17. $\dfrac{x}{15} = \dfrac{12}{90}$ 18. $\dfrac{39}{4} = \dfrac{t}{12}$ 19. $\dfrac{5.5}{6} = \dfrac{16.5}{w}$

20. $\dfrac{1}{3} = \dfrac{y}{25.5}$ 21. $\dfrac{18}{x} = \dfrac{1}{5}$ 22. $\dfrac{m}{4} = \dfrac{175}{20}$ 23. $\dfrac{8.7}{2} = \dfrac{q}{4}$

24. $\dfrac{r}{84} = \dfrac{32.5}{182}$ 25. $\dfrac{76}{304} = \dfrac{81}{k}$ 26. $\dfrac{9}{500} = \dfrac{p}{2,500}$ 27. $\dfrac{5}{j} = \dfrac{6}{19.8}$

28. A certain shade of paint is made by mixing 5 parts blue paint with 2 parts white paint. To get the correct shade, how many quarts of white paint should be mixed with 8.5 quarts of blue paint?

29. **Measurement** If you put an object that has a mass of 8 grams on one side of a balance scale, you would have to put about 20 paper clips on the other side to balance the weight. How many paper clips would balance the weight of a 10-gram object?

30. Sandra drove 126.2 miles in 2 hours at a constant speed. Use a proportion to find how long it would take her to drive 189.3 miles at the same speed.

31. **Multi-Step** In June, a camp has 325 campers and 26 counselors. In July, 265 campers leave and 215 new campers arrive. How many counselors does the camp need in July to keep an equivalent ratio of campers to counselors?

Recreation

The Skidaway Island State Park offers observation towers to help visitors spot wildlife and migrating birds.

Arrange each set of numbers to form a proportion.

32. 10, 6, 30, 18   **33.** 4, 6, 10, 15   **34.** 12, 21, 7, 4

35. 75, 4, 3, 100   **36.** 30, 42, 5, 7   **37.** 5, 90, 108, 6

38. Life Science On Monday a marine biologist took a random sample of 50 fish from a pond and tagged them. On Tuesday she took a new sample of 100 fish. Among them were 4 fish that had been tagged on Monday.

   a. What comparison does the ratio $\frac{4}{100}$ represent?

   b. What ratio represents the number of fish tagged on Monday to n, the estimated total number of fish in the pond?

   c. Use a proportion to estimate the number of fish in the pond.

39. Chemistry The table shows the type and number of atoms in one molecule of citric acid. Use a proportion to find the number of oxygen atoms in 15 molecules of citric acid.

Composition of Citric Acid	
Type of Atom	**Number of Atoms**
Carbon	6
Hydrogen	8
Oxygen	7

40. Earth Science You can find your distance from a thunderstorm by counting the number of seconds between a lightning flash and the thunder. For example, if the time difference is 21 s, then the storm is 7 km away. How far away is a storm if the time difference is 9 s?

 41. What's the Question? There are 20 grams of protein in 3 ounces of sautéed fish. If the answer is 9 ounces, what is the question?

 42. Write About It Give an example from your own life that can be described using a ratio. Then tell how a proportion can give you additional information.

 43. Challenge Use the Multiplication Property of Equality and the proportion $\frac{a}{b} = \frac{c}{d}$ to show that the cross product rule works.

CRCT PREP • GPS SUPPORT • SPIRAL REVIEW

44. Multiple Choice Which proportion is true?

   Ⓐ $\frac{4}{8} = \frac{6}{10}$ Ⓑ $\frac{2}{7} = \frac{10}{15}$ Ⓒ $\frac{7}{14} = \frac{15}{30}$ Ⓓ $\frac{16}{25} = \frac{13}{18}$

45. Gridded Response Find a ratio to complete the proportion $\frac{2}{3} = \frac{?}{?}$ so that the cross products are equal to 12. Grid your answer in the form of a fraction.

Estimate. (Lesson 3-1)

46. 16.21 − 14.87   **47.** 3.82 · (−4.97)   **48.** −8.7 · (−20.1)

Find each unit rate. (Lesson 5-2)

49. 128 miles in 2 hours   **50.** 9 books in 6 weeks   **51.** $114 in 12 hours

Generate Formulas to Convert Units

Hands-On LAB 5-6

Use with Lesson 5-6

Georgia Performance Standards

M7P1.a, M7P4.b, M7P5.a

go.hrw.com
Lab Resources Online
KEYWORD: MS7 Lab5

Activity

Publishers, editors, and graphic designers measure lengths in *picas*. Measure each of the following line segments to the nearest inch, and record your results in the table.

Segment	Length (in.)	Length (picas)	Ratio of Picas to Inches
1		6	
2		12	
3		24	
4		30	
5		36	

1 _____

2 _____

3 _____

4 _____

5 _____

Think and Discuss

1. Make a conjecture about the relationship between picas and inches.

2. Use your conjecture to write a formula relating inches n to picas p.

3. How many picas wide is a sheet of paper that is $8\frac{1}{2}$ in. wide?

Try This

Using inches for *x*-coordinates and picas for *y*-coordinates, write ordered pairs for the data in the table. Then plot the points and draw a graph.

1. What shape is the graph?

2. Use the graph to find the number of picas that is equal to 3 inches.

3. Use the graph to find the number of inches that is equal to 27 picas.

4. A designer is laying out a page in a magazine. The dimensions of a photo are 18 picas by 15 picas. She doubles the dimensions of the photo. What are the new dimensions of the photo in inches?

5-6 Customary Measurements

Georgia Performance Standards

M7A2.a Given a problem, define a variable, write an equation, solve the equation, and interpret the solution. Also, M7A2.b, M7P1.b, M7P5.a.

The king cobra is one of the world's most poisonous snakes. Just 2 fluid ounces of the snake's venom is enough to kill a 2-ton elephant.

You can use the following benchmarks to help you understand fluid ounces, tons, and other customary units of measure.

	Customary Unit	Benchmark
Length	Inch (in.)	Length of a small paper clip
	Foot (ft)	Length of a standard sheet of paper
	Mile (mi)	Length of about 18 football fields
Weight	Ounce (oz)	Weight of a slice of bread
	Pound (lb)	Weight of 3 apples
	Ton	Weight of a buffalo
Capacity	Fluid ounce (fl oz)	Amount of water in 2 tablespoons
	Cup (c)	Capacity of a standard measuring cup
	Gallon (gal)	Capacity of a large milk jug

EXAMPLE 1 Choosing the Appropriate Customary Unit

Choose the most appropriate customary unit for each measurement. Justify your answer.

A the length of a rug

Feet—the length of a rug is similar to the length of several sheets of paper.

B the weight of a magazine

Ounces—the weight of a magazine is similar to the weight of several slices of bread.

C the capacity of an aquarium

Gallons—the capacity of an aquarium is similar to the capacity of several large milk jugs.

The following table shows some common equivalent customary units. You can use equivalent measures to convert units of measure.

Length	Weight	Capacity
12 inches (in.) = 1 foot (ft) 3 feet = 1 yard (yd) 5,280 feet = 1 mile (mi)	16 ounces (oz) = 1 pound (lb) 2,000 pounds = 1 ton	8 fluid ounces (fl oz) = 1 cup (c) 2 cups = 1 pint (pt) 2 pints = 1 quart (qt) 4 quarts = 1 gallon (gal)

EXAMPLE **Converting Customary Units**

Convert 19 c to fluid ounces.

Method 1: Use a proportion.
Write a proportion using a ratio of equivalent measures.

$$\frac{\text{fluid ounces}}{\text{cups}} \longrightarrow \frac{8}{1} = \frac{x}{19}$$

$$8 \cdot 19 = 1 \cdot x$$

$$152 = x$$

Method 2: Multiply by 1.
Multiply by a ratio equal to 1, and cancel the units.

$$19 \text{ c} = \frac{19\cancel{c}}{1} \times \frac{8 \text{ fl oz}}{1 \cancel{c}}$$

$$= \frac{19 \cdot 8 \text{ fl oz}}{1}$$

$$= 152 \text{ fl oz}$$

Nineteen cups is equal to 152 fluid ounces.

EXAMPLE **Adding or Subtracting Mixed Units of Measure**

A carpenter has a wooden post that is 4 ft long. She cuts 17 in. off the end of the post. What is the length of the remaining post?

First convert 4 ft to inches.

$$\frac{\text{inches}}{\text{feet}} \longrightarrow \frac{12}{1} = \frac{x}{4} \qquad \textit{Write a proportion using 1 ft = 12 in.}$$

$$x = 48 \text{ in.}$$

The carpenter cuts off 17 in., so subtract 17 in.

$$4 \text{ ft} - 17 \text{ in.} = 48 \text{ in.} - 17 \text{ in.}$$

$$= 31 \text{ in.}$$

Write the answer in feet and inches.

$$31 \text{ in.} \times \frac{1 \text{ ft}}{12 \text{ in.}} = \frac{31}{12} \text{ ft} \qquad \textit{Multiply by a ratio equal to 1.}$$

$$= 2\frac{7}{12} \text{ ft, or 2 ft 7 in.}$$

Think and Discuss   GPS M7P3.b

1. Describe an object that you would weigh in ounces.

2. Explain how to convert yards to feet and feet to yards.

 **Georgia Performance Standards**

M7P2.c, M7P3.a, M7P3.c

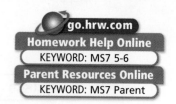 **go.hrw.com**
Homework Help Online
KEYWORD: MS7 5-6
Parent Resources Online
KEYWORD: MS7 Parent

GUIDED PRACTICE

See Example **Choose the most appropriate customary unit for each measurement. Justify your answer.**

1. the width of a sidewalk

2. the amount of water in a pool

3. the weight of a truck

4. the distance across Lake Erie

See Example **2** **Convert each measure.**

5. 12 gal to quarts

6. 8 mi to feet

7. 72 oz to pounds

8. 3.5 c to fluid ounces

See Example **3** **9.** A pitcher contains 4 c of pancake batter. A cook pours out 5 fl oz of the batter to make a pancake. How much batter remains in the pitcher?

INDEPENDENT PRACTICE

See Example **Choose the most appropriate customary unit for each measurement. Justify your answer.**

10. the weight of a watermelon

11. the wingspan of a sparrow

12. the capacity of a soup bowl

13. the height of an office building

See Example **Convert each measure.**

14. 28 pt to quarts

15. 15,840 ft to miles

16. 5.4 tons to pounds

17. $6\frac{1}{4}$ ft to inches

See Example **3** **18.** A sculptor has a 3 lb block of clay. He adds 24 oz of clay to the block in order to make a sculpture. What is the total weight of the clay before he begins sculpting?

PRACTICE AND PROBLEM SOLVING

Extra Practice p. 736

Compare. Write <, >, or =.

19. 6 yd ▉ 12 ft

20. 80 oz ▉ 5 lb

21. 18 in. ▉ 3 ft

22. 5 tons ▉ 12,000 lb

23. 8 gal ▉ 30 qt

24. 6.5 c ▉ 52 fl oz

25. 10,000 ft ▉ 2 mi

26. 20 pt ▉ 40 c

27. 1 gal ▉ 18 c

28. **Literature** The novel *Twenty Thousand Leagues Under the Sea* was written by Jules Verne in 1873. One league is approximately 3.45 miles. How many miles are in 20,000 leagues?

29. **Earth Science** The average depth of the Pacific Ocean is 12,925 feet. How deep is this in miles, rounded to the nearest tenth of a mile?

Order each set of measures from least to greatest.

30. 8 ft; 2 yd; 60 in.

31. 5 qt; 2 gal; 12 pt; 8 c

32. $\frac{1}{2}$ ton; 8,000 oz; 430 lb

33. 2.5 mi; 12,000 ft; 5,000 yd

34. 63 fl oz; 7 c; 1.5 qt

35. 9.5 yd; 32.5 ft; 380 in.

36. Agriculture In one year, the United States produced nearly 895 million pounds of pumpkins. How many ounces were produced by the state with the lowest production shown in the table?

U.S. Pumpkin Production	
State	Pumpkins (million pounds)
California	180
Illinois	364
New York	114
Pennsylvania	109

37. Multi-Step A marathon is a race that is 26 miles 385 yards long. What is the length of a marathon in yards?

38. In 1998, a 2,505-gallon ice cream float was made in Atlanta, Georgia. How many 1-pint servings did the float contain?

39. Critical Thinking Explain why it makes sense to divide when you convert a measurement to a larger unit.

 40. What's the Error? A student converted 480 ft to inches as follows. What did the student do wrong? What is the correct answer?

$$\frac{1 \text{ ft}}{12 \text{ in.}} = \frac{x}{480 \text{ ft}}$$

 41. Write About It Explain how to convert 1.2 tons to ounces.

 42. Challenge A dollar bill is approximately 6 in. long. A radio station gives away a prize consisting of a mile-long string of dollar bills. What is the value of the prize?

CRCT PREP • GPS SUPPORT • SPIRAL REVIEW

43. Multiple Choice Which measure is the same as 32 qt?

Ⓐ 64 pt   Ⓑ 128 gal   Ⓒ 16 c   Ⓓ 512 fl oz

44. Multiple Choice Judy has 3 yards of ribbon. She cuts off 16 inches of the ribbon to wrap a package. How much ribbon does she have left?

Ⓕ 1 ft 8 in.   Ⓖ 4 ft 8 in.   Ⓗ 7 ft 8 in.   Ⓙ 10 ft 4 in.

45. A store sells a television for $486.50. If that price is 3.5 times what the store paid, what was the store's cost? (Lesson 3-6)

Determine whether the ratios are proportional. (Lesson 5-4)

46. $\frac{20}{45}, \frac{8}{18}$

47. $\frac{6}{5}, \frac{5}{6}$

48. $\frac{11}{44}, \frac{7}{28}$

49. $\frac{9}{6}, \frac{27}{20}$

READY TO GO ON?

Quiz for Lessons 5-1 Through 5-6

✓ 5-1 Ratios

1. A concession stand sold 14 strawberry, 18 banana, 8 grape, and 6 orange fruit drinks during a game. Tell whether the ratio of strawberry to orange drinks or the ratio of banana to grape drinks is greater.

✓ 5-2 Rates

2. Shaunti drove 621 miles in 11.5 hours. What was her average speed in miles per hour?

3. A grocery store sells a 7 oz bag of raisins for $1.10 and a 9 oz bag of raisins for $1.46. Which size bag has the lowest price per ounce?

✓ 5-3 Slope and Rates of Change

Tell whether each graph shows a constant or variable rate of change. If constant, find the slope.

4.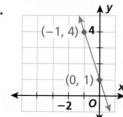

5.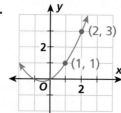

6.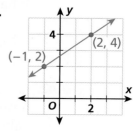

✓ 5-4 Identifying and Writing Proportions

Find a ratio equivalent to each ratio. Then use the ratios to write a proportion.

7. $\frac{10}{16}$ **8.** $\frac{21}{28}$ **9.** $\frac{12}{25}$ **10.** $\frac{40}{48}$

✓ 5-5 Solving Proportions

Use cross products to solve each proportion.

11. $\frac{n}{8} = \frac{15}{4}$ **12.** $\frac{20}{t} = \frac{2.5}{6}$ **13.** $\frac{6}{11} = \frac{0.12}{z}$ **14.** $\frac{15}{24} = \frac{x}{10}$

15. One dog year is said to equal 7 human years. If Cliff's dog is 5.5 years old in dog years, what is his dog's age in human years?

✓ 5-6 Customary Measurements

Convert each measure.

16. 7 lb to ounces   **17.** 15 qt to pints   **18.** 3 mi to feet

19. 20 fl oz to cups   **20.** 39 ft to yards   **21.** 7,000 lb to tons

Focus on Problem Solving

Make a Plan

- **Choose a problem-solving strategy**

The following are strategies that you might choose to help you solve a problem:

- Make a table
- Find a pattern
- Make an organized list
- Work backward
- Act it out

- Draw a diagram
- Guess and test
- Use logical reasoning
- Solve a simpler problem
- Make a model

Tell which strategy from the list above you would use to solve each problem. Explain your choice.

1. A recipe for blueberry muffins calls for 1 cup of milk and 1.5 cups of blueberries. Ashley wants to make more muffins than the recipe yields. In Ashley's muffin batter, there are 4.5 cups of blueberries. If she is using the recipe as a guide, how many cups of milk will she need?

2. The length of a rectangle is 8 cm, and its width is 5 cm less than its length. A larger rectangle with dimensions that are proportional to those of the first has a length of 24 cm. What is the width of the larger rectangle?

3. Jeremy is the oldest of four brothers. Each of the four boys gets an allowance for doing chores at home each week. The amount of money each boy receives depends on his age. Jeremy is 13 years old, and he gets $12.75. His 11-year-old brother gets $11.25, and his 9-year-old brother gets $9.75. How much money does his 7-year-old brother get?

4. According to an article in a medical journal, a healthful diet should include a ratio of 2.5 servings of meat to 4 servings of vegetables. If you eat 7 servings of meat per week, how many servings of vegetables should you eat?

Make Similar Figures

Georgia Performance Standards

M7G3.a, M7P5.a, M7P5.b

go.hrw.com
Lab Resources Online
KEYWORD: MS7 Lab5

Similar figures are figures that have the same shape but not necessarily the same size. You can make similar figures by increasing or decreasing both dimensions of a rectangle while keeping the ratios of the side lengths proportional. Modeling similar figures using square tiles can help you solve proportions.

Activity

A rectangle made of square tiles measures 5 tiles long and 2 tiles wide. What is the length of a similar rectangle whose width is 6 tiles?

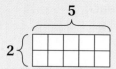

Use tiles to make a 5 × 2 rectangle.

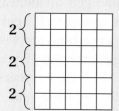

Add tiles to increase the width of the rectangle to 6 tiles.

Notice that there are now 3 sets of 2 tiles along the width of the rectangle because 2 × 3 = 6.

The width of the new rectangle is three times greater than the width of the original rectangle. To keep the ratios of the side measures proportional, the length must also be three times greater than the length of the original rectangle.

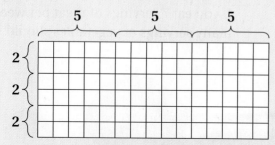

5 × 3 = 15

Add tiles to increase the length of the rectangle to 15 tiles.

The length of the similar rectangle is 15 tiles.

To check your answer, you can use ratios.

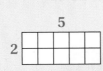
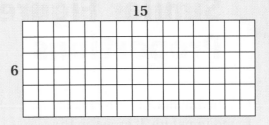

$\frac{2}{6} \stackrel{?}{=} \frac{5}{15}$ *Write ratios using the corresponding side lengths.*

$\frac{1}{3} \stackrel{?}{=} \frac{1}{3}$ ✔   *Simplify each ratio.*

1 Use square tiles to model similar figures with the given dimensions. Then find the missing dimension of each similar rectangle.

a. The original rectangle is 4 tiles wide by 3 tiles long.
The similar rectangle is 8 tiles wide by x tiles long.

b. The original rectangle is 8 tiles wide by 10 tiles long.
The similar rectangle is x tiles wide by 15 tiles long.

c. The original rectangle is 3 tiles wide by 7 tiles long.
The similar rectangle is 9 tiles wide by x tiles long.

Think and Discuss

1. Sarah wants to increase the size of her rectangular backyard patio. Why must she change both dimensions of the patio to create a patio similar to the original?

2. In a backyard, a plot of land that is 5 yd × 8 yd is used to grow tomatoes. The homeowner wants to decrease this plot to 4 yd × 6 yd. Will the new plot be similar to the original? Why or why not?

Try This

1. A rectangle is 3 feet long and 7 feet wide. What is the width of a similar rectangle whose length is 9 feet?

2. A rectangle is 6 feet long and 12 feet wide. What is the length of a similar rectangle whose width is 4 feet?

Use square tiles to model similar rectangles to solve each proportion.

3. $\frac{4}{5} = \frac{8}{x}$ **4.** $\frac{5}{9} = \frac{h}{18}$ **5.** $\frac{2}{y} = \frac{6}{18}$ **6.** $\frac{1}{t} = \frac{4}{16}$

7. $\frac{2}{3} = \frac{8}{m}$ **8.** $\frac{9}{12} = \frac{p}{4}$ **9.** $\frac{6}{r} = \frac{9}{15}$ **10.** $\frac{k}{12} = \frac{7}{6}$

5-7 Similar Figures and Proportions

Learn to use ratios to determine if two figures are similar.

Vocabulary

similar

corresponding sides

corresponding angles

Writing Math

When naming similar figures, list the letters of the corresponding vertices in the same order. In Example 1, $\triangle DEF \sim \triangle QRS$.

Georgia Performance Standards

M7G3.a Understand the meaning of similarity, and describe similarities by listing corresponding parts. Also, M7P4.a, M7P4.b.

Octahedral fluorite is a crystal found in nature. It grows in the shape of an octahedron, which is a three-dimensional figure with eight triangular faces. The triangles in different-sized fluorite crystals are *similar* figures. **Similar** figures have the same shape but not necessarily the same size. The symbol ~ means "is similar to."

Corresponding angles of two or more polygons are in the same relative position. **Corresponding sides** of two or more polygons are in the same relative position.

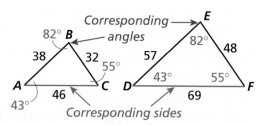

Corresponding angles

Corresponding sides

SIMILAR FIGURES

Two figures are similar if

- the measures of their corresponding angles are equal.
- the ratios of the lengths of their corresponding sides are proportional.

EXAMPLE 1 Determining Whether Two Triangles Are Similar

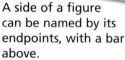

A side of a figure can be named by its endpoints, with a bar above.

$\overline{AB}$

Without the bar, the letters indicate the *length* of the side.

Tell whether the triangles are similar.

The corresponding angles of the figures have equal measures.

$\overline{DE}$ corresponds to $\overline{QR}$.
$\overline{EF}$ corresponds to $\overline{RS}$.
$\overline{DF}$ corresponds to $\overline{QS}$.

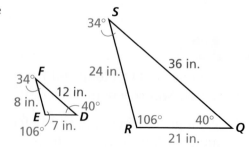

$\dfrac{DE}{QR} \overset{?}{=} \dfrac{EF}{RS} \overset{?}{=} \dfrac{DF}{QS}$ *Write ratios using the corresponding sides.*

$\dfrac{7}{21} \overset{?}{=} \dfrac{8}{24} \overset{?}{=} \dfrac{12}{36}$ *Substitute the lengths of the sides.*

$\dfrac{1}{3} = \dfrac{1}{3} = \dfrac{1}{3}$ *Simplify each ratio.*

Since the measures of the corresponding angles are equal and the ratios of the corresponding sides are equivalent, the triangles are similar.

With triangles, if the corresponding side lengths are all proportional, then the corresponding angles *must* have equal measures. With figures that have four or more sides, if the corresponding side lengths are all proportional, then the corresponding angles *may or may not* have equal angle measures.

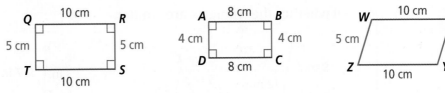

ABCD and QRST
are similar.

ABCD and WXYZ
are not similar.

EXAMPLE 2 **Determining Whether Two Four-Sided Figures Are Similar**

Tell whether the figures are similar.

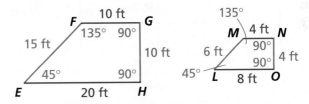

The corresponding angles of the figures have equal measures. Write each set of corresponding sides as a ratio.

$\dfrac{EF}{LM}$ $\overline{EF}$ corresponds to $\overline{LM}$. $\dfrac{FG}{MN}$ $\overline{FG}$ corresponds to $\overline{MN}$.

$\dfrac{GH}{NO}$ $\overline{GH}$ corresponds to $\overline{NO}$. $\dfrac{EH}{LO}$ $\overline{EH}$ corresponds to $\overline{LO}$.

Determine whether the ratios of the lengths of the corresponding sides are proportional.

$\dfrac{EF}{LM} \overset{?}{=} \dfrac{FG}{MN} \overset{?}{=} \dfrac{GH}{NO} \overset{?}{=} \dfrac{EH}{LO}$ *Write ratios using the corresponding sides.*

$\dfrac{15}{6} \overset{?}{=} \dfrac{10}{4} \overset{?}{=} \dfrac{10}{4} \overset{?}{=} \dfrac{20}{8}$ *Substitute the lengths of the sides.*

$\dfrac{5}{2} = \dfrac{5}{2} = \dfrac{5}{2} = \dfrac{5}{2}$ *Write the ratios with common denominators.*

Since the measures of the corresponding angles are equal and the ratios of the corresponding sides are equivalent, $EFGH \sim LMNO$.

Think and Discuss

GPS M7P2.c, M7P3.b

1. Identify the corresponding angles of $\triangle JKL$ and $\triangle UTS$.

2. Explain whether all rectangles are similar. Give specific examples to justify your answer.

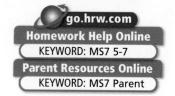

GUIDED PRACTICE

See Example ① **Tell whether the triangles are similar.**

1.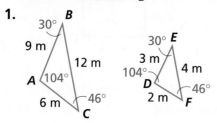

2.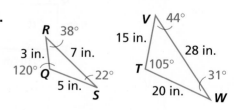

See Example ② **Tell whether the figures are similar.**

3.

4.

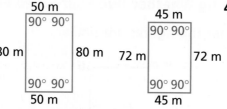

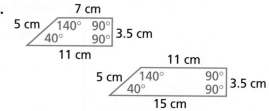

INDEPENDENT PRACTICE

See Example ① **Tell whether the triangles are similar.**

5.

6.

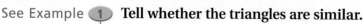

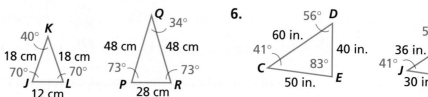

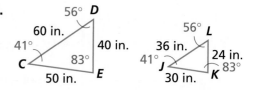

See Example ② **Tell whether the figures are similar.**

7.

8.

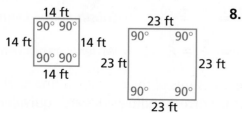

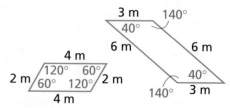

PRACTICE AND PROBLEM SOLVING

Extra Practice p. 736

9. Tell whether the parallelogram and trapezoid could be similar. Explain your answer.

10. Kia wants similar prints in small and large sizes of a favorite photo. The photo lab sells prints in these sizes: 3 in. × 5 in., 4 in. × 6 in., 8 in. × 18 in., 9 in. × 20 in., and 16 in. × 24 in. Which could she order to get similar prints?

Tell whether the triangles are similar.

11.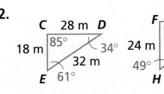

12.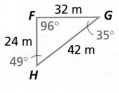

The figure shows a 12 ft by 15 ft rectangle divided into four rectangular parts. Explain whether the rectangles in each pair are similar.

13. rectangle *A* and the original rectangle

14. rectangle *C* and rectangle *B*

15. the original rectangle and rectangle *D*

Critical Thinking For Exercises 16–19, justify your answers using words or drawings.

16. Are all squares similar?

17. Are all parallelograms similar?

18. Are all rectangles similar?

19. Are all right triangles similar?

 20. Choose a Strategy What number gives the same result when multiplied by 6 as it does when 6 is added to it?

 21. Write About It Tell how to decide whether two figures are similar.

 22. Challenge Two triangles are similar. The ratio of the lengths of the corresponding sides is $\frac{5}{4}$. If the length of one side of the larger triangle is 40 feet, what is the length of the corresponding side of the smaller triangle?

CRCT PREP • GPS SUPPORT • SPIRAL REVIEW

23. Multiple Choice Luis wants to make a deck that is similar to one that is 10 feet long and 8 feet wide. If Luis's deck must be 18 feet long, what must its width be?

ⓐ 20 feet   ⓑ 16 feet   ⓒ 14.4 feet   ⓓ 22.5 feet

24. Short Response If a real dollar bill measures 2.61 in. by 6.14 in. and a play dollar bill measures 3.61 in. by 7.14 in., is the play money similar to the real money? Explain your answer.

Multiply. Write each answer in simplest form. (Lesson 3-10)

25. $-\frac{3}{4} \cdot 14$ **26.** $2\frac{1}{8} \cdot (-5)$ **27.** $\frac{1}{4} \cdot 1\frac{7}{8} \cdot 3\frac{1}{5}$

28. Tell whether 5:3 or 12:7 is a greater ratio. (Lesson 5-1)

5-8 Using Similar Figures

Learn to use similar figures to find unknown lengths.

Vocabulary

indirect measurement

Georgia Performance Standards

M7G3.a Understand the meaning of similarity, visually compare geometric figures for similarity, and describe similarities by listing corresponding parts. Also, M7G3.b, M7P1.b, M7P5.a.

Native Americans of the Northwest, such as the Tlingit tribe of Alaska, carved totem poles out of tree trunks. These poles, sometimes painted with bright colors, could stand up to 80 feet tall. Totem poles include carvings of animal figures, such as bears and eagles, which symbolize traits of the family or clan who built them.

Measuring the heights of tall objects, like some totem poles, cannot be done by using a ruler or yardstick. Instead, you can use *indirect measurement*.

Indirect measurement is a method of using proportions to find an unknown length or distance in similar figures.

EXAMPLE **1** **Finding Unknown Lengths in Similar Figures**

$\triangle ABC \sim \triangle JKL$. **Find the unknown length.**

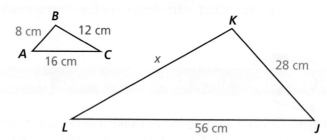

$\dfrac{AB}{JK} = \dfrac{BC}{KL}$ *Write a proportion using corresponding sides.*

$\dfrac{8}{28} = \dfrac{12}{x}$ *Substitute the lengths of the sides.*

$8 \cdot x = 28 \cdot 12$ *Find the cross products.*

$8x = 336$ *Multiply.*

$\dfrac{8x}{8} = \dfrac{336}{8}$ *Divide each side by 8 to isolate the variable.*

$x = 42$

KL is 42 centimeters.

EXAMPLE 2 **Measurement Application**

A volleyball court is a rectangle that is similar in shape to an Olympic-sized pool. Find the width of the pool.

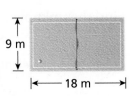

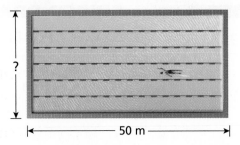

Let w = the width of the pool.

$\dfrac{18}{50} = \dfrac{9}{w}$ *Write a proportion using corresponding side lengths.*

$18 \cdot w = 50 \cdot 9$ *Find the cross products.*

$18w = 450$ *Multiply.*

$\dfrac{18w}{18} = \dfrac{450}{18}$ *Divide each side by 18 to isolate the variable.*

$w = 25$

The pool is 25 meters wide.

EXAMPLE 3 **Estimating with Indirect Measurement**

Estimate the height of the birdhouse in Chantal's yard, shown at right.

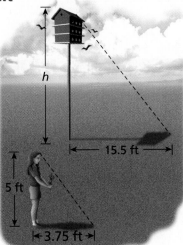

$\dfrac{h}{5} = \dfrac{15.5}{3.75}$ *Write a proportion.*

$\dfrac{h}{5} \approx \dfrac{16}{4}$ *Use compatible numbers to estimate.*

$\dfrac{h}{5} \approx 4$ *Simplify.*

$5 \cdot \dfrac{h}{5} \approx 5 \cdot 4$ *Multiply each side by 5 to isolate the variable.*

$h \approx 20$

The birdhouse is about 20 feet tall.

Think and Discuss   GPS M7P1.c, M7P3.b

1. **Write** another proportion that could be used to find the value of x in Example 1.

2. **Name** two objects that it would make sense to measure using indirect measurement.

Georgia Performance
Standards
M7P3.a, M7P5.a, M7P5.b

go.hrw.com
Homework Help Online
KEYWORD: MS7 5-8
Parent Resources Online
KEYWORD: MS7 Parent

GUIDED PRACTICE

See Example ① △*XYZ* ~ △*PQR* in each pair. Find the unknown lengths.

1.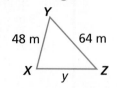

2.

See Example ② **3.** The rectangular gardens at right are similar in shape. How wide is the smaller garden?

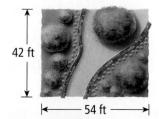 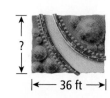

See Example ③ **4.** A water tower casts a shadow that is 21 ft long. A tree casts a shadow that is 8 ft long. Estimate the height of the water tower.

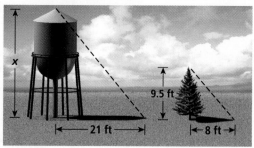

INDEPENDENT PRACTICE

See Example ① △*ABC* ~ △*DEF* in each pair. Find the unknown lengths.

5.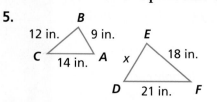

6.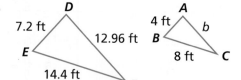

See Example ② **7.** The two rectangular windows at right are similar. What is the height of the bigger window?

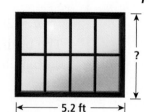 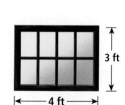

See Example ③ **8.** A cactus casts a shadow that is 14 ft 7 in. long. A gate nearby casts a shadow that is 5 ft long. Estimate the height of the cactus.

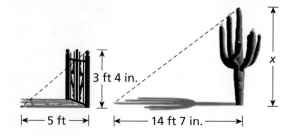

PRACTICE AND PROBLEM SOLVING

9. A building with a height of 14 m casts a shadow that is 16 m long while a taller building casts a 24 m long shadow. What is the height of the taller building?

10. Two common envelope sizes are $3\frac{1}{2}$ in. × $6\frac{1}{2}$ in. and 4 in. × $9\frac{1}{2}$ in. Are these envelopes similar? Explain.

11. **Art** An art class is painting a mural composed of brightly colored geometric shapes. The class has decided that all the right triangles in the design will be similar to the right triangle that will be painted fire red. Find the measures of the right triangles in the table. Round your answers to the nearest tenth.

Triangle Color	Length (in.)	Height (in.)
Fire Red	12	16
Blazing Orange	7	
Grape Purple		4
Dynamite Blue	15	

12. **Write a Problem** Write a problem that can be solved using indirect measurement.

13. **Write About It** Assume you know the side lengths of one triangle and the length of one side of a second similar triangle. Explain how to use the properties of similar figures to find the unknown lengths in the second triangle.

14. **Challenge** $\triangle ABE \sim \triangle ACD$. What is the value of y in the diagram?

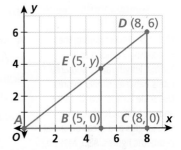

15. **Multiple Choice** Find the unknown length in the similar figures.

    (A) 10 cm   (C) 15 cm

    (B) 12 cm   (D) 18 cm

16. **Gridded Response** A building casts a 16-foot shadow. A 6-foot man standing next to the building casts a 2.5-foot shadow. What is the height, in feet, of the building?

Write each phrase as an algebraic expression. (Lesson 1-8)

17. the product of 18 and y 18. 5 less than a number   19. 12 divided by z

Choose the most appropriate customary unit for each measurement. Justify your answer. (Lesson 5-6)

20. weight of a cell phone   21. height of a cat   22. capacity of a gas tank

5-9 Scale Drawings and Scale Models

Learn to understand ratios and proportions in scale drawings. Learn to use ratios and proportions with scale.

Vocabulary

scale model

scale factor

scale

scale drawing

Georgia Performance Standards

M7G3.b Understanding the relationships among scale factors, length ratios, and area ratios between similar figures. Use scale factors, length ratios, and area ratios to determine side lengths and areas of similar geometric figures. Also, M7P1.b, M7P4.c.

This HO gauge model train is a *scale model* of a historic train. A **scale model** is a proportional three-dimensional model of an object. Its dimensions are related to the dimensions of the actual object by a ratio called the **scale factor**. The HO scale factor is $\frac{1}{87}$. This means that each dimension of the model is $\frac{1}{87}$ of the corresponding dimension of the actual train.

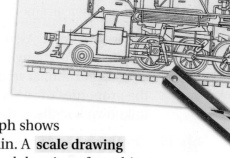

A **scale** is the ratio between two sets of measurements. Scales can use the same units or different units. The photograph shows a *scale drawing* of the model train. A **scale drawing** is a proportional two-dimensional drawing of an object. Both scale drawings and scale models can be smaller or larger than the objects they represent.

EXAMPLE 1 Finding a Scale Factor

Identify the scale factor.

	Race Car	Model
Length (in.)	132	11
Height (in.)	66	5.5

You can use the lengths *or* heights to find the scale factor.

$$\frac{\text{model length}}{\text{race car length}} = \frac{11}{132} = \frac{1}{12} \qquad \textit{Write a ratio. Then simplify.}$$

$$\frac{\text{model height}}{\text{race car height}} = \frac{5.5}{66} = \frac{1}{12}$$

The scale factor is $\frac{1}{12}$. This is reasonable because $\frac{1}{10}$ the length of the race car is 13.2 in. The length of the model is 11 in., which is less than 13.2 in., and $\frac{1}{12}$ is less than $\frac{1}{10}$.

Caution!

A scale factor is always the ratio of the model's dimensions to the actual object's dimensions.

EXAMPLE 2 **Using Scale Factors to Find Unknown Lengths**

A photograph of Vincent van Gogh's painting *Still Life with Irises Against a Yellow Background* has dimensions 6.13 cm and 4.90 cm. The scale factor is $\frac{1}{15}$. Find the size of the actual painting, to the nearest tenth of a centimeter.

Think: $\dfrac{\text{photo}}{\text{painting}} = \dfrac{1}{15}$

$\dfrac{6.13}{\ell} = \dfrac{1}{15}$ *Write a proportion to find the length ℓ.*

$\ell = 6.13 \cdot 15$ *Find the cross products.*

$\ell = 92.0 \text{ cm}$ *Multiply and round to the nearest tenth.*

$\dfrac{4.90}{w} = \dfrac{1}{15}$ *Write a proportion to find the width w.*

$w = 4.90 \cdot 15$ *Find the cross products.*

$w = 73.5 \text{ cm}$ *Multiply and round to the nearest tenth.*

The painting is 92.0 cm long and 73.5 cm wide.

EXAMPLE 3 **Measurement Application**

On a map of Florida, the distance between Hialeah and Tampa is 10.5 cm. What is the actual distance *d* between the cities if the map scale is 3 cm = 80 mi?

Think: $\dfrac{\text{map distance}}{\text{actual distance}} = \dfrac{3}{80}$

$\dfrac{3}{80} = \dfrac{10.5}{d}$ *Write a proportion.*

$3 \cdot d = 80 \cdot 10.5$ *Find the cross products.*

$3d = 840$

$\dfrac{3d}{3} = \dfrac{840}{3}$ *Divide both sides by 3.*

$d = 280 \text{ mi}$

The distance between the cities is 280 miles.

Think and Discuss   GPS M7P2.c, M7P3.b

1. **Explain** how you can tell whether a model with a scale factor of $\frac{5}{3}$ is larger or smaller than the original object.

2. **Describe** how to find the scale factor if an antenna is 60 feet long and a scale drawing shows the length as 1 foot long.

Georgia Performance
Standards

M7P3.a, M7P4.c, M7P5.c

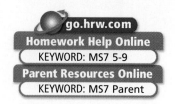
go.hrw.com
Homework Help Online
KEYWORD: MS7 5-9
Parent Resources Online
KEYWORD: MS7 Parent

GUIDED PRACTICE

See Example **1**   **Identify the scale factor.**

1.

	Grizzly Bear	Model
Height (in.)	84	6

2.

	Moray Eel	Model
Length (ft)	5	$1\frac{1}{2}$

See Example **2**   **3.** In a photograph, a sculpture is 4.2 cm tall and 2.5 cm wide. The scale factor is $\frac{1}{16}$. Find the size of the actual sculpture.

See Example **3**   **4.** Ms. Jackson is driving from South Bend to Indianapolis. She measures a distance of 4.3 cm between the cities on her Indiana road map. What is the actual distance between the cities if the map scale is 1 cm = 30 mi?

INDEPENDENT PRACTICE

See Example **1**   **Identify the scale factor.**

5.

	Eagle	Model
Wingspan (in.)	90	6

6.

	Dolphin	Model
Length (cm)	260	13

See Example **2**   **7.** On a scale drawing, a tree is $6\frac{3}{4}$ inches tall. The scale factor is $\frac{1}{20}$. Find the height of the actual tree.

See Example **3**   **8. Measurement** On a road map of Virginia, the distance from Alexandria to Roanoke is 7.6 cm. What is the actual distance between the cities if the map scale is 2 cm = 50 mi?

PRACTICE AND PROBLEM SOLVING

Extra Practice p. 736

The scale factor of each model is 1:12. Find the missing dimensions.

	Item	Actual Dimensions	Model Dimensions
9.	Lamp	Height:	Height: $1\frac{1}{3}$ in.
10.	Couch	Height: 32 in. Length: 69 in.	Height: Length:
11.	Table	Height: Width: Length:	Height: 6.25 cm Width: 11.75 cm Length: 20 cm
12.	Chair	Height: $51\frac{1}{2}$ in.	Height:

13. Critical Thinking A countertop is 18 ft long. How long is it on a scale drawing with the scale 1 in. = 3 yd?

14. Write About It A scale for a scale drawing is 10 cm = 1 mm. Which will be larger, the actual object or the scale drawing? Explain.

Use the map for Exercises 15–16.

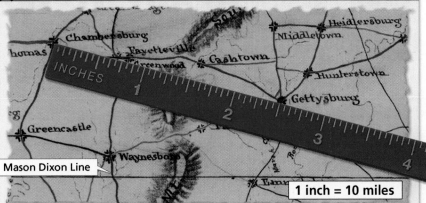

15. In 1863, Confederate troops marched from Chambersburg to Gettysburg in search of badly needed shoes. Use the ruler and the scale of the map to estimate how far the Confederate soldiers, many of whom were barefoot, marched.

1 inch = 10 miles

16. Before the Civil War, the Mason-Dixon Line was considered the dividing line between the North and the South. If Gettysburg is about 8.1 miles north of the Mason-Dixon Line, how far apart in inches are Gettysburg and the Mason-Dixon Line on the map?

17. **Multi-Step** Toby is making a scale model of the battlefield at Fredericksburg. The area he wants to model measures about 11 mi by 7.5 mi. He plans to put the model on a 3.25 ft by 3.25 ft square table. On each side of the model he wants to leave at least 3 in. between the model and the table edges. What is the largest scale he can use?

18. ⭐ **Challenge** A map of Vicksburg, Mississippi, has a scale of "1 mile to the inch." The map has been reduced so that 5 inches on the original map appears as 1.5 inches on the reduced map. If the distance between two points on the reduced map is 1.75 inches, what is the actual distance in miles?

This painting by H.A. Ogden depicts General Robert E. Lee at Fredericksburg in 1862.

CRCT PREP • GPS SUPPORT • SPIRAL REVIEW

19. **Multiple Choice** On a scale model with a scale of $\frac{1}{16}$, the height of a shed is 7 inches. What is the approximate height of the actual shed?

　Ⓐ 2 feet　　　　Ⓑ 9 feet　　　　Ⓒ 58 feet　　　　Ⓓ 112 feet

20. **Gridded Response** On a map, the scale is 3 cm = 75 mi. If the distance between two cities on the map is 6.8 cm, what is the distance between the actual cities in miles?

Order the numbers from least to greatest. (Lesson 2-11)

21. $\frac{4}{7}$, 0.41, 0.054　　　22. $\frac{1}{4}$, 0.2, −1.2　　　23. 0.7, $\frac{7}{9}$, $\frac{7}{11}$　　　24. 0.3, $-\frac{5}{6}$, 0.32

Divide. Estimate to check whether each answer is reasonable. (Lesson 3-4)

25. 0.32 ÷ 5　　　26. 78.57 ÷ 9　　　27. 40.5 ÷ 15　　　28. 29.68 ÷ 28

Quiz for Lessons 5-7 Through 5-9

5-7 Similar Figures and Proportions

1. Tell whether the triangles are similar.

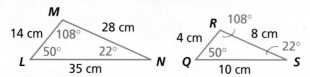

2. Tell whether the figures are similar.

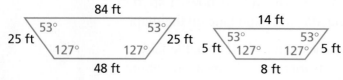

5-8 Using Similar Figures

$\triangle ABC \sim \triangle XYZ$ in each pair. Find the unknown lengths.

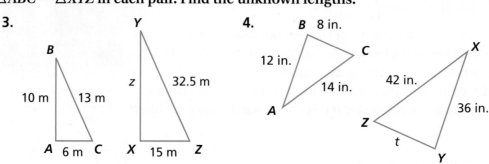

5. Reynaldo drew a rectangular design that was 6 in. wide and 8 in. long. He used a copy machine to enlarge the rectangular design so that the width was 10 in. What was the length of the enlarged design?

6. Redon is 6 ft 2 in. tall, and his shadow is 4 ft 1 in. long. At the same time a building casts a shadow that is 19 ft 10 in. long. Estimate the height of the building.

5-9 Scale Drawings and Scale Models

7. An actor is 6 ft tall. On a billboard for a new movie, the actor's picture is enlarged so that his height is 16.8 ft. What is the scale factor?

8. On a scale drawing, a driveway is 6 in. long. The scale factor is $\frac{1}{24}$. Find the length of the actual driveway.

9. A map of Texas has a scale of 1 in. = 65 mi. If the distance from Dallas to San Antonio is 260 mi, what is the distance in inches between two cities on the map?

MULTI-STEP TEST PREP

Bug Juice When campers get thirsty, out comes the well-known camp beverage bug juice! The recipes show how two camps, Camp Big Sky and Camp Wild Flowers, make their bug juice. Each camp has 180 campers. During a typical day, each camper drinks two 8-ounce cups of bug juice.

1. How many ounces of bug juice are consumed at each camp each day?

2. How much does it cost to make two quarts of bug juice at each camp?

3. Each camp has budgeted $30 per day for bug juice. Is $30 a day enough? How do you know? Show your work.

4. Campers begin to complain. They want their bug juice "buggier." How could each camp change its recipe, continue to serve 180 campers two 8-ounce cups of bug juice daily, and not spend more than $40 per day for bug juice? Explain your reasoning.

Camp Big Sky Bug Juice Recipe

- One 4 oz packet of mix A
- Add tap water to make 2 quarts of bug juice.

Camp Wild Flowers Bug Juice Recipe

- One 0.14 oz packet of mix B
- 4 oz sugar
- Add tap water to make 2 quarts of bug juice.

Prices

4 oz packet of mix A	$0.78
0.14 oz packet of mix B	$0.20
1 lb of sugar	$0.36

EXTENSION

Direct and Inverse Variations

Learn to graph direct and inverse variations.

Vocabulary

direct variation

constant of proportionality

inverse variation

Georgia Performance Standards

M7A3.d Describe patterns in the graphs of proportional relationships, both direct $(y = kx)$ and inverse $\left(y = \frac{k}{x}\right)$. Also, M7A3.a, M7A3.b, M7A3.c.

Sarah and Jonas go on a cycling trip. After 1 hour, they've traveled 5 miles. After 2 hours, they've traveled 10 miles, and so on.

Hours (x)	1	2	2.5	3
Miles (y)	5	10	12.5	15

The relationship between miles and hours can be represented by the linear function $y = 5x$, where y is the number of miles and x is the number of hours.

A relationship that can be represented by a linear function in the form $y = kx$ is called a **direct variation**. When one variable in a direct variation increases, the other variable also increases. The constant k is called the **constant of proportionality** because the ratios of y to x are in proportion:

$$\frac{y}{x} = \frac{5}{1} = \frac{10}{2} = \frac{15}{3} = 5.$$

EXAMPLE 1 Graphing Direct Variations

Alisa and her parents are going on a vacation. The table shows the number of hours they drive and the miles they travel. Graph the data and find the value of k.

Hours (x)	2	2.5	3	4
Miles (y)	120	150	180	240

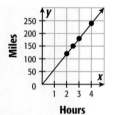

To find k, use one of the data points to calculate the ratio of miles to hours:

$$\frac{\text{miles}}{\text{hours}} = \frac{120}{2} = 60$$

The direct variation equation is $y = 60x$.

Helpful Hint

Direct and inverse variations are sometimes called *direct and inverse proportions.*

The area of a rectangle is given by the formula $A = \ell w$. If the area is constant, then when the width increases, the length decreases. The relationship between length and width is called an **inverse variation**. The graph of an inverse variation is a smooth curve.

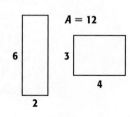

EXAMPLE 2 **Graphing Inverse Variations**

The area of a rectangle is 100 cm². The table shows some of the dimensions the rectangle could have. Find the missing value in the table and draw a graph of the data.

Length (ℓ)	5	10	20	
Width (w)	20	10	5	4

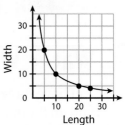

Use the area formula to find the missing value.

$A = \ell w$

$100 = \ell \cdot 4$ *Substitute A = 100 and w = 4.*

$\ell = \dfrac{100}{4} = 25$ *Solve for ℓ.*

Graph each point and then connect them with a smooth curve.

EXTENSION

Exercises

1. Kenji and his mother are driving to visit his aunt and uncle. The table shows the number of hours they drive and the miles they drive. Graph the data and find the value of k.

Hours (x)	1	2	3	4
Miles (y)	45	90	135	180

2. The area of a rectangle is 60 in.². The table shows some of the possible dimensions the rectangle can have. Find the missing value in the table and draw a graph of the data.

Length (ℓ)	5	10	20	30
Width (w)	12		3	2

3. Alyssa and Marcus rent skates to go ice skating. The cost of renting skates is $5.00 for each hour. Write an equation in the form $y = kx$, where x is the number of hours and y is the cost of the rental. Graph the equation.

4. Graph the direct variation equation $y = kx$ for $k = 1, 2,$ and 3. What happens to the graph as the value of k increases?

5. Graph the inverse variation equation $k = xy$ for $k = 30, 20,$ and 10. What happens to the graph as the value of k decreases?

Game Time

Water Works

You have three glasses: a 3-ounce glass, a 5-ounce glass, and an 8-ounce glass. The 8-ounce glass is full of water, and the other two glasses are empty. By pouring water from one glass to another, how can you get exactly 6 ounces of water in one of the glasses? The step-by-step solution is described below.

1 Pour the water from the 8 oz glass into the 5 oz glass.
2 Pour the water from the 5 oz glass into the 3 oz glass.
3 Pour the water from the 3 oz glass into the 8 oz glass.

You now have 6 ounces of water in the 8-ounce glass.

Start again, but this time try to get exactly 4 ounces of water in one glass. (*Hint:* Find a way to get 1 ounce of water. Start by pouring water into the 3-ounce glass.)

Next, using 3-ounce, 8-ounce, and 11-ounce glasses, try to get exactly 9 ounces of water in one glass. Start with the 11-ounce glass full of water. (*Hint:* Start by pouring water into the 8-ounce glass.)

Look at the sizes of the glasses in each problem. The volume of the third glass is the sum of the volumes of the first two glasses: $3 + 5 = 8$ and $3 + 8 = 11$. Using any amounts for the two smaller glasses, and starting with the largest glass full, you can get any multiple of the smaller glass's volume. Try it and see.

Concentration

Each card in a deck of cards has a ratio on one side. Place each card face down. Each player or team takes a turn flipping over two cards. If the ratios on the cards are equivalent, the player or team can keep the pair. If not, the next player or team flips two cards. After every card has been turned over, the player or team with the most pairs wins.

go.hrw.com
Game Time Extra
KEYWORD: MS7 Games

A complete copy of the rules and the game pieces are available online.

Materials
- 2 paper plates
- scissors
- markers

It's in the Bag!

PROJECT **Paper Plate Proportions**

Serve up some proportions on this book made from paper plates.

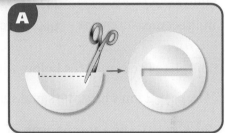

A

1 Fold one of the paper plates in half. Cut out a narrow rectangle along the folded edge. The rectangle should be as long as the diameter of plate's inner circle. When you open the plate, you will have a narrow window in the center. **Figure A**

B

2 Fold the second paper plate in half and then unfold it. Cut slits on both sides of the crease beginning from the edge of the plate to the inner circle. **Figure B**

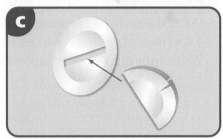

C

3 Roll up the plate with the slits so that the two slits touch each other. Then slide this plate into the narrow window in the other plate. **Figure C**

D

4 When the rolled-up plate is halfway through the window, unroll it so that the slits fit on the sides of the window. **Figure D**

5 Close the book so that all the plates are folded in half.

Taking Note of the Math

Write the number and name of the chapter on the cover of the book. Then review the chapter, using the inside pages to take notes on ratios, rates, proportions, and similar figures

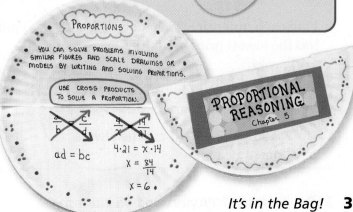

Study Guide: Review

Vocabulary

corresponding angles .. 300
corresponding sides ... 300
cross product 287
equivalent ratios 283
indirect measurement .304

proportion 283
rate 274
ratio 270
scale 308
scale drawing 308

scale factor 308
scale model 308
similar 300
slope 278
unit rate 274

Complete the sentences below with vocabulary words from the list above.

1. __?__ figures have the same shape but not necessarily the same size.

2. A(n) __?__ is a comparison of two numbers, and a(n) __?__ is a ratio that compares two quantities measured in different units.

3. The ratio used to enlarge or reduce similar figures is a(n) __?__ .

5-1 Ratios (pp. 270–273)

 GPS M7P4.a

EXAMPLE

■ Write the ratio of 2 servings of bread to 4 servings of vegetables in all three forms. Write your answers in simplest form.

$\frac{2}{4} = \frac{1}{2}$ *Write the ratio 2 to 4 in simplest form.*

$\frac{1}{2}$, 1 to 2, 1:2

EXERCISES

There are 3 red, 7 blue, and 5 yellow balloons.

4. Write the ratio of blue balloons to total balloons in all three forms. Write your answer in simplest form.

5. Tell whether the ratio of red to blue balloons or the ratio of yellow balloons to total balloons is greater.

5-2 Rates (pp. 274–277)

 GPS M7P1.b

EXAMPLE

■ Find each unit price. Then decide which has the lowest price per ounce.

$\frac{\$2.70}{5 \text{ oz}}$ or $\frac{\$4.32}{12 \text{ oz}}$

$\frac{\$2.70}{5 \text{ oz}} = \frac{\$0.54}{\text{oz}}$ and $\frac{\$4.32}{12 \text{ oz}} = \frac{\$0.36}{\text{oz}}$

Since $0.36 < 0.54$, $\frac{\$4.32}{12 \text{ oz}}$ has the lowest price per ounce.

EXERCISES

Find each average rate of speed.

6. 540 ft in 90 s   7. 436 mi in 4 hr

Find each unit price. Then decide which is the better buy.

8. $\frac{\$56}{25 \text{ gal}}$ or $\frac{\$32.05}{15 \text{ gal}}$ 9. $\frac{\$160}{5 \text{ g}}$ or $\frac{\$315}{9 \text{ g}}$

Study Guide: Review

5-3 Slope and Rates of Change (pp. 278–282)

GPS M7A3.a, M7A3.b

EXAMPLE

■ Tell whether the graph shows a constant or variable rate of change. If constant, find the slope.

The graph is a line, so the rate of change is constant.

slope = $\dfrac{\text{rise}}{\text{run}}$

= $\dfrac{-4}{1}$

= -4

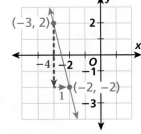

EXERCISES

Tell whether each graph shows a constant or variable rate of change. If constant, find the slope.

10.
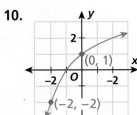

11.
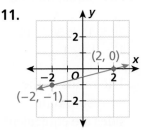

5-4 Identifying and Writing Proportions (pp. 283–286)

GPS M7N1.b, M7N1.d

EXAMPLE

■ Determine if $\dfrac{5}{12}$ and $\dfrac{3}{9}$ are proportional.

$\dfrac{5}{12}$ $\dfrac{5}{12}$ is already in simplest form.

$\dfrac{3}{9} = \dfrac{1}{3}$ Simplify $\dfrac{3}{9}$.

$\dfrac{5}{12} \neq \dfrac{1}{3}$ The ratios are not proportional.

EXERCISES

Determine if the ratios are proportional.

12. $\dfrac{9}{27}, \dfrac{6}{20}$ **13.** $\dfrac{15}{25}, \dfrac{20}{30}$ **14.** $\dfrac{21}{14}, \dfrac{18}{12}$

Find a ratio equivalent to the given ratio. Then use the ratios to write a proportion.

15. $\dfrac{10}{12}$ **16.** $\dfrac{45}{50}$ **17.** $\dfrac{9}{15}$

5-5 Solving Proportions (pp. 287–290)

GPS M7A2.a, M7A2.b

EXAMPLE

■ Use cross products to solve $\dfrac{p}{8} = \dfrac{10}{12}$.

$\dfrac{p}{8} = \dfrac{10}{12}$

$p \cdot 12 = 8 \cdot 10$ *Multiply the cross products.*

$12p = 80$

$\dfrac{12p}{12} = \dfrac{80}{12}$ *Divide each side by 12.*

$p = \dfrac{20}{3}$, or $6\dfrac{2}{3}$

EXERCISES

Use cross products to solve each proportion.

18. $\dfrac{4}{6} = \dfrac{n}{3}$ **19.** $\dfrac{2}{a} = \dfrac{5}{15}$

20. $\dfrac{b}{1.5} = \dfrac{8}{3}$ **21.** $\dfrac{16}{11} = \dfrac{96}{x}$

22. $\dfrac{2}{y} = \dfrac{1}{5}$ **23.** $\dfrac{7}{2} = \dfrac{70}{w}$

5-6 Customary Measurements (pp. 292–295)

GPS M7A2.a, M7A2.b

EXAMPLE

■ Convert 5 mi to feet.

$\dfrac{\text{feet}}{\text{miles}} \longrightarrow \dfrac{5,280}{1} = \dfrac{x}{5}$

$x = 5,280 \cdot 5 = 26,400$ ft

EXERCISES

Convert each measure.

24. 32 fl oz to pints

25. 1.5 tons to pounds

26. 13,200 ft to miles

5-7 Similar Figures and Proportions (pp. 300–303)

EXAMPLE

■ **Tell whether the figures are similar.**

The corresponding angles of the figures have equal measures.

$$\frac{5}{30} \stackrel{?}{=} \frac{3}{18} \stackrel{?}{=} \frac{5}{30} \stackrel{?}{=} \frac{3}{18}$$

$$\frac{1}{6} = \frac{1}{6} = \frac{1}{6} = \frac{1}{6}$$

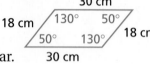

The ratios of the corresponding sides are equivalent. The figures are similar.

EXERCISES

Tell whether the figures are similar.

27.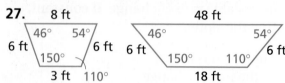

28.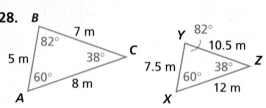

5-8 Using Similar Figures (pp. 304–307)

GPS M7G3.a, M7G3.b

EXAMPLE

■ $\triangle ABC \sim \triangle LMN$. Find the unknown length.

$$\frac{AB}{LM} = \frac{AC}{LN}$$

$$\frac{8}{t} = \frac{11}{44}$$

$$8 \cdot 44 = t \cdot 11$$

$$352 = 11t$$

$$\frac{352}{11} = \frac{11t}{11}$$

$$32 \text{ in.} = t$$

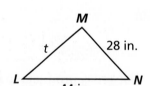

EXERCISES

$\triangle JKL \sim \triangle DEF$. Find the unknown length.

29.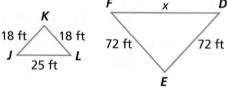

30. A tree casts a $30\frac{1}{2}$ ft shadow at the time of day when a 2 ft stake casts a $7\frac{2}{3}$ ft shadow. Estimate the height of the tree.

5-9 Scale Drawings and Scale Models (pp. 308–311)

EXAMPLE

■ A model boat is 4 inches long. The scale factor is $\frac{1}{24}$. How long is the actual boat?

$$\frac{\text{model}}{\text{boat}} = \frac{1}{24}$$

$$\frac{4}{n} = \frac{1}{24} \qquad \textit{Write a proportion.}$$

$$4 \cdot 24 = n \cdot 1 \qquad \textit{Find the cross products.}$$

$$96 = n \qquad \textit{Solve.}$$

The boat is 96 inches long.

EXERCISES

31. The Wright brothers' *Flyer* had a 484-inch wingspan. Carla bought a model of the plane with a scale factor of $\frac{1}{40}$. What is the model's wingspan?

32. The distance from Austin to Houston on a map is 4.3 inches. The map scale is 1 inch = 38 miles. What is the actual distance?

Study Guide: Review

CHAPTER TEST

1. Stan found 12 pennies, 15 nickels, 7 dimes, and 5 quarters. Tell whether the ratio of pennies to quarters or the ratio of nickels to dimes is greater.

2. Lenny sold 576 tacos in 48 hours. What was Lenny's average rate of taco sales?

3. A store sells a 5 lb box of detergent for $5.25 and a 10 lb box of detergent for $9.75. Which size box has the lowest price per pound?

Tell whether each graph shows a constant or variable rate of change. If constant, find the slope.

4.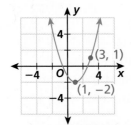

5.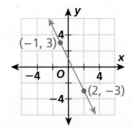

Find a ratio equivalent to each ratio. Then use the ratios to write a proportion.

6. $\dfrac{22}{30}$
7. $\dfrac{7}{9}$
8. $\dfrac{18}{54}$
9. $\dfrac{10}{17}$

Use cross products to solve each proportion.

10. $\dfrac{9}{12} = \dfrac{m}{6}$
11. $\dfrac{x}{2} = \dfrac{18}{6}$
12. $\dfrac{3}{7} = \dfrac{21}{t}$
13. $\dfrac{5}{p} = \dfrac{10}{2}$

Convert each measure.

14. 13,200 ft to miles
15. 3.5 lb to ounces
16. 17 qt to gallons

Tell whether the figures are similar.

17.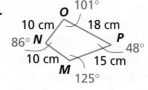

18.

$\triangle WYZ \sim \triangle MNO$ in each pair. Find the unknown lengths.

19.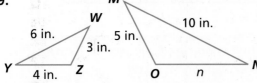

20.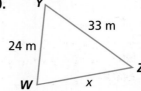

21. A scale model of a building is 8 in. by 12 in. If the scale is 1 in. = 15 ft, what are the dimensions of the actual building?

22. The distance from Portland to Seaside is 75 mi. What is the distance in inches between the two towns on a map if the scale is $1\frac{1}{4}$ in. = 25 mi?

TEST TACKLER

Standardized Test Strategies

Extended Response: Understand the Scores

Extended-response test items usually involve multiple steps and require a detailed explanation. The items are scored using a 4-point rubric. A complete and correct response is worth 4 points, a partial response is worth 2 to 3 points, an incorrect response with no work shown is worth 1 point, and no response at all is worth 0 points.

EXAMPLE

Extended Response A 10-pound bag of apples costs $4. Write and solve a proportion to find how much a 15-pound bag of apples would cost at the same rate. Explain how the increase in weight is related to the increase in cost.

Here are examples of how different responses were scored using the scoring rubric shown.

4-point response:

Let c = the cost of the 15 lb bag.

$$\frac{10 \text{ pounds}}{\$4} = \frac{15 \text{ pounds}}{c}$$

$$10 \cdot c = 4 \cdot 15$$

$$\frac{10c}{10} = \frac{60}{10}$$

$$c = 6$$

The 15 lb bag costs $6.

For every additional 5 pounds, the cost increases by 2 dollars.

3-point response:

Let c = the cost of the 15 lb bag.

$$\frac{10 \text{ pounds}}{\$4} = \frac{15 \text{ pounds}}{c}$$

$$10 \cdot c = 4 \cdot 15$$

$$\frac{10c}{10} = \frac{60}{10}$$

$$c = 6$$

The 15 lb bag costs $6.

For every additional 5 pounds, the cost increases by 6 dollars.

The proportion is set up and solved correctly, and all work is shown, but the explanation is incorrect.

2-point response:

Let c = the cost of the apples.

$$\frac{10 \text{ pounds}}{\$4} = \frac{c}{15 \text{ pounds}}$$

$$10 \cdot 15 = 4 \cdot c$$

$$\frac{150}{4} = \frac{4c}{4}$$

$$37.5 = c$$

The proportion is set up incorrectly, and no explanation is given.

1-point response:

$$37.5 = c$$

The answer is incorrect, no work is shown, and no explanation is given.

After you complete an extended-response test item, double-check that you have answered all parts.

Read each test item and answer the questions that follow using the scoring rubric below.

Scoring Rubric

4 points: The student correctly answers all parts of the question, shows all work, and provides a complete and correct explanation.

3 points: The student answers all parts of the question, shows all work, and provides a complete explanation that demonstrates understanding, but the student makes minor errors in computation.

2 points: The student does not answer all parts of the question but shows all work and provides a complete and correct explanation for the parts answered, or the student correctly answers all parts of the question but does not show all work or does not provide an explanation.

1 point: The student gives incorrect answers and shows little or no work or explanation, or the student does not follow directions.

0 points: The student gives no response.

Item A
Extended Response Alex drew a model of a birdhouse using a scale of 1 inch to 3 inches. On the drawing, the house is 6 inches tall. Define a variable, and then write and solve a proportion to find how many inches tall the actual birdhouse is.

1. Should the response shown receive a score of 4 points? Why or why not?

$$\frac{1 \text{ inch}}{6 \text{ inches}} = \frac{3 \text{ inches}}{h}$$

$$1 \cdot h = 3 \cdot 6$$

$$h = 18$$

The actual birdhouse is 18 inches tall.

Item B
Extended Response Use a table to find a rule that describes the relationship between the first four terms of the sequence 2, 4, 8, 16, . . . and their positions in the sequence. Then find the next three terms in the sequence.

2. What should you add to the response shown, if anything, so that it receives full credit?

n	1	2	3	4
Rule	2^1	2^2	2^3	2^4
y	2	4	8	16

Each term is 2 times as great as the term before it. The rule is 2^n.

Item C
Extended Response The figures are similar. Find the value of x and the sum of the side lengths of one of the figures.

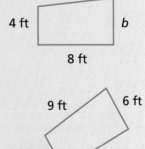

3. What needs to be included in a response that would receive 4 points?

4. Write a response that would receive full credit.

Cumulative Assessment, Chapters 1–5

Multiple Choice

1. What is the unknown length *b* in similar triangles *ABC* and *DEF*?

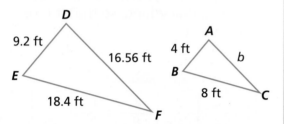

9.2 ft
16.56 ft
18.4 ft
4 ft
8 ft
b

- **A** 7.2 feet
- **C** 4 feet
- **B** 6 feet
- **D** 5.6 feet

2. The total length of the Golden Gate Bridge in San Francisco, California, is 8,981 feet. If a car is traveling at a speed of 45 miles per hour, how many minutes would it take the car to cross the bridge?

- **F** 0.04 minute
- **H** 1.7 minutes
- **G** 1.28 minutes
- **J** 2.27 minutes

3. For which equation is $x = \frac{2}{5}$ the solution?

- **A** $5x - \frac{25}{2} = 0$
- **B** $-\frac{1}{5}x + \frac{2}{25} = 0$
- **C** $\frac{1}{5}x - 2 = 0$
- **D** $-5x + \frac{1}{2} = 0$

4. A hot air balloon descends 38.5 meters in 22 seconds. If the balloon continues to descend at this rate, how long will it take to descend 125 meters?

- **F** 25.25 seconds
- **H** 71.43 seconds
- **G** 86.5 seconds
- **J** 218.75 seconds

5. Which value completes the table of equivalent ratios?

Microphones	3	9	15	36
Karaoke Machines	1	3	?	12

- **A** 5
- **C** 8
- **B** 7
- **D** 9

6. On a baseball field, the distance from home plate to the pitcher's mound is $60\frac{1}{2}$ feet. The distance from home plate to second base is about $127\frac{7}{24}$ feet. What is the difference between the two distances?

- **F** $61\frac{1}{3}$ feet
- **H** $66\frac{19}{24}$ feet
- **G** $66\frac{5}{6}$ feet
- **J** $66\frac{5}{24}$ feet

7. Which word phrase best describes the expression $n - 6$?

- **A** 6 more than a number
- **B** A number less than 6
- **C** 6 minus a number
- **D** A number decreased by 6

8. A football weighs about $\frac{3}{20}$ kilogram. If a coach has 15 footballs in a large bag, which estimate best describes the total weight of the footballs?

- **F** Not quite 3 kilograms
- **G** A little more than 2 kilograms
- **H** Almost 1 kilogram
- **J** Between 1 and 2 kilograms

9. Which point lies on the line $y = 4x + 2$?

 Ⓐ (2, 10) Ⓒ (−4, 2)

 Ⓑ (0, −2) Ⓓ (−2, 6)

10. On a scale drawing, a cell phone tower is 1.25 feet tall. The scale factor is $\frac{1}{150}$. What is the height of the actual cell phone tower?

 Ⓕ 37.5 ft Ⓗ 148 ft

 Ⓖ 120 ft Ⓙ 187.5 ft

 If a diagram or graph is not provided, quickly sketch one to clarify the information provided in the test item.

11. The Liberty Bell weighs 2,080 pounds. How many tons does the Liberty Bell weigh?

 Ⓐ 0.96 Ⓒ 9.6

 Ⓑ 1.04 Ⓓ 10.4

12. Find the quotient of $-51.03 \div (-8.1)$.

 Ⓕ −6.3 Ⓗ 3.6

 Ⓖ −3.6 Ⓙ 6.3

13. What is the slope of the line shown?

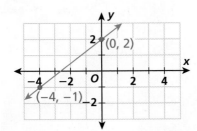

 Ⓐ −4   Ⓒ $\frac{3}{4}$

 Ⓑ $-\frac{1}{4}$ Ⓓ $\frac{4}{3}$

14. A florist is creating flower bouquets using 84 tulips and 56 daisies. Each bouquet has the same number of tulips and daisies. How many bouquets can the florist create?

 Ⓕ 28 Ⓗ 42

 Ⓖ 34 Ⓙ 56

15. Jana began the month with $102.50 in her checking account. During the month, she deposited $8.50 that she earned from baby-sitting, withdrew $9.75 to buy a CD, deposited $5.00 that her aunt gave her, and withdrew $6.50 for a movie ticket. Using compatible numbers, write and evaluate an expression to estimate the balance in Jana's account at the end of the month.

16. A lamppost casts a shadow that is 18 feet long. At the same time of day, Alyce casts a shadow that is 4.2 feet long. Alyce is 5.3 feet tall. Draw a picture of the situation. Set up and solve a proportion to find the height of the lamppost to the nearest foot. Show your work.

Extended Response

17. Riley is drawing a map of the state of Virginia. From east to west, the greatest distance across the state is about 430 miles. From north to south, the greatest distance is about 200 miles.

 a. Riley is using a map scale of 1 inch = 24 miles. Find the length of the map from east to west and the length from north to south. Round your answers to the nearest tenth.

 b. The length between two cities on Riley's map is 9 inches. What is the distance between the cities in miles?

 c. If an airplane travels at a speed of 520 miles per hour, about how many minutes will it take for the plane to fly from east to west across the widest part of Virginia? Show your work.

CRCT Prep

CHAPTER
6

Percents

CRCT PREP

go.hrw.com
Chapter Project Online
KEYWORD: MS7 Ch6

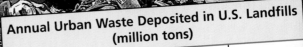

Annual Urban Waste Deposited in U.S. Landfills (million tons)			
Soil	Wood	Concrete	Household Refuse
107.6	87.6	22.5	32.7

Career *Urban Archaeologist*

Have you ever wanted to study the lifestyles of people who lived long ago? If so, becoming an archaeologist might be for you. Archaeologists learn about past civilizations by excavating cities and examining artifacts. They even examine garbage!

From 1973 to 2003, the urban archaeologists of the Garbage Project learned about the habits of present-day societies by excavating landfills and studying the things we throw away. They found that over 80% of urban waste in the United States is deposited in landfills.

ARE YOU READY?

✓ Vocabulary

Choose the best term from the list to complete each sentence.

1. A statement that two ratios are equivalent is called a(n) __?__.

2. To write $\frac{2}{3}$ as a(n) __?__, divide the numerator by the denominator.

3. A(n) __?__ is a comparison by division of two quantities.

4. The __?__ of $\frac{9}{24}$ is $\frac{3}{8}$.

decimal

equation

fraction

proportion

ratio

simplest form

Complete these exercises to review skills you will need for this chapter.

✓ Write Fractions as Decimals

Write each fraction as a decimal.

5. $\frac{8}{10}$ 6. $\frac{53}{100}$ 7. $\frac{739}{1,000}$ 8. $\frac{7}{100}$

9. $\frac{2}{5}$ 10. $\frac{5}{8}$ 11. $\frac{7}{12}$ 12. $\frac{13}{20}$

✓ Write Decimals as Fractions

Write each decimal as a fraction in simplest form.

13. 0.05   14. 0.92   15. 0.013   16. 0.8

17. 0.006   18. 0.305   19. 0.0007   20. 1.04

✓ Solve Multiplication Equations

Solve each equation.

21. $100n = 300$ 22. $38 = 0.4x$ 23. $16p = 1,200$

24. $9 = 72y$ 25. $0.07m = 56$ 26. $25 = 100t$

✓ Solve Proportions

Solve each proportion.

27. $\frac{2}{3} = \frac{x}{12}$ 28. $\frac{x}{20} = \frac{3}{4}$ 29. $\frac{8}{15} = \frac{x}{45}$

30. $\frac{16}{28} = \frac{4}{n}$ 31. $\frac{p}{100} = \frac{12}{36}$ 32. $\frac{42}{12} = \frac{14}{n}$

33. $\frac{8}{y} = \frac{10}{5}$ 34. $\frac{6}{9} = \frac{d}{24}$ 35. $\frac{21}{a} = \frac{7}{5}$

Where You've Been

Previously, you

- modeled percents.

- wrote equivalent fractions, decimals, and percents.

- solved percent problems involving discounts, sales tax, and tips.

In This Chapter

You will study

- modeling and estimating percents.

- writing equivalent fractions, decimals, and percents, including percents less than 1 and greater than 100.

- solving percent problems involving discounts, sales tax, tips, profit, percent of change, and simple interest.

- comparing fractions, decimals, and percents.

Where You're Going

You can use the skills learned in this chapter

- to find or estimate discounts, sales tax, and tips when shopping and eating out.

- to solve problems involving banking.

Key Vocabulary/Vocabulario

interest	interés
percent	porcentaje
percent of change	porcentaje de cambio
percent of decrease	porcentaje de disminución
percent of increase	porcentaje de incremento
principal	capital
simple interest	interés simple

Vocabulary Connections

To become familiar with some of the vocabulary terms in the chapter, consider the following. You may refer to the chapter, the glossary, or a dictionary if you like.

1. The Italian word *cento* and the French term *cent* mean "hundred." What do you think **percent** means?

2. The word *interest* stems from Latin (*inter- + esse*) and means "to be between" and "to make a difference." In business, interest is an amount collected or paid for the use of money. How can you relate the Latin roots and meanings to the business definition of **interest**?

3. *Principal* is the amount of money deposited or borrowed. Interest builds upon the principal. How might common definitions of *principal*, such as "leader of a school" and "a matter of primary importance," help you remember this business meaning of **principal**?

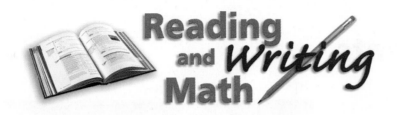 

Study Strategy: Use Multiple Representations

When a new math concept is introduced, the explanation given often presents the topic in more than one way. As you study, pay attention to any models, tables, lists, graphs, diagrams, symbols, and words used to describe a concept.

In this example, the concept of finding equivalent fractions is represented in model, number, and word form.

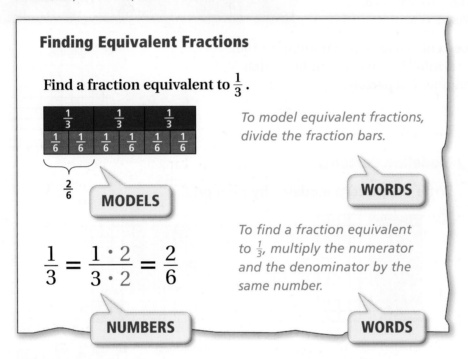

Finding Equivalent Fractions

Find a fraction equivalent to $\frac{1}{3}$.

To model equivalent fractions, divide the fraction bars.

WORDS

MODELS

$$\frac{1}{3} = \frac{1 \cdot 2}{3 \cdot 2} = \frac{2}{6}$$

To find a fraction equivalent to $\frac{1}{3}$, multiply the numerator and the denominator by the same number.

NUMBERS

WORDS

Try This

1. Explain why it could be beneficial to represent a new idea in more than one way when taking notes.

2. Explain how you can use models and numbers to find equivalent fractions. Which method do you prefer? Explain.

6-1 Percents

Learn to model percents and to write percents as equivalent fractions and decimals.

Vocabulary
percent

It is estimated that over half the plant and animal species on Earth live in rain forests. However, rain forests cover less than 6 out of every 100 square miles of Earth's land. You can write this ratio, 6 to 100, as a *percent*, 6%.

Georgia Performance Standards

M7P4.a Recognize and use connections among mathematical ideas. Also, M7P4.b, M7P5.a, M7P5.b, M7P5.c.

A **percent** is a ratio of a number to 100. The symbol % is used to indicate that a number is a percent.

$$\frac{6}{100} = 6\%$$

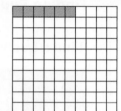

EXAMPLE 1 Modeling Percents

Write the percent modeled by each grid.

The word *percent* means "per hundred." So 6% means "6 out of 100."

A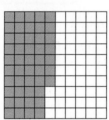

$$\frac{\text{shaded}}{\text{total}} \longrightarrow \frac{47}{100} = 47\%$$

B

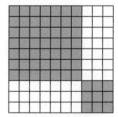

$$\frac{\text{shaded}}{\text{total}} \longrightarrow \frac{49 + 9}{100} = \frac{58}{100} = 58\%$$

You can write percents as fractions or decimals.

EXAMPLE 2 Writing Percents as Fractions

Write 35% as a fraction in simplest form.

$$35\% = \frac{35}{100}$$ *Write the percent as a fraction with a denominator of 100.*

$$= \frac{7}{20}$$ *Simplify.*

So 35% can be written as $\frac{7}{20}$.

EXAMPLE 3 Writing Percents as Decimals

Write 43% as a decimal.

Method 1: Use pencil and paper.

$43\% = \dfrac{43}{100}$ *Write the percent as a fraction.*

$= 0.43$ *Divide 43 by 100.*

Method 2: Use mental math.

$43.\% = 0.43$ *Move the decimal point two places to the left.*

Think and Discuss GPS M7P3.b, M7P5.a

1. Tell in your own words what *percent* means.

2. Explain how to write 5% as a decimal.

6-1 Exercises

 Georgia Performance Standards
M7P1.c, M7P3.a, M7P5.b

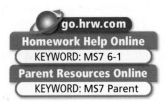 go.hrw.com
Homework Help Online
KEYWORD: MS7 6-1
Parent Resources Online
KEYWORD: MS7 Parent

GUIDED PRACTICE

See Example ① **Write the percent modeled by each grid.**

1.   **2.**   **3.**

See Example ② **Write each percent as a fraction in simplest form.**

4. 65%   **5.** 82%   **6.** 12%   **7.** 38%   **8.** 75%

See Example ③ **Write each percent as a decimal.**

9. 22%   **10.** 51%   **11.** 8.07%   **12.** 1.6%   **13.** 11%

INDEPENDENT PRACTICE

Write the percent modeled by each grid.

See Example ① **14.**   **15.**   **16.**

See Example 2 Write each percent as a fraction in simplest form.

17. 55%   **18.** 34%   **19.** 83%   **20.** 53%   **21.** 81%

See Example 3 Write each percent as a decimal.

22. 48%   **23.** 9.8%   **24.** 30.2%   **25.** 66.3%   **26.** 8.39%

PRACTICE AND PROBLEM SOLVING

Extra Practice p. 737

Write each percent as a fraction in simplest form and as a decimal.

27. 2.70%   **28.** 7.6%   **29.** 44%   **30.** 3.148%   **31.** 10.5%

Compare. Write <, >, or =.

32. $\frac{18}{100}$ ■ 22%   **33.** $\frac{35}{52}$ ■ 72%   **34.** $\frac{10}{50}$ ■ 22%   **35.** $\frac{11}{20}$ ■ 56%

36. 41% ■ $\frac{13}{30}$ **37.** $\frac{17}{20}$ ■ 85%   **38.** $\frac{3}{5}$ ■ 60%   **39.** 15% ■ $\frac{4}{30}$

40. Multi-Step A nutrition label states that one serving of tortilla chips contains 7 grams of fat and 11% of the recommended daily allowance (RDA) of fat.

   a. Write a ratio that represents the percent RDA of fat in one serving of tortilla chips.

   b. Use the ratio from part **a** to write and solve a proportion to determine how many grams of fat are in the recommended daily allowance.

 41. Choose a Strategy During class, Brad finished 63% of his homework, and Liz completed $\frac{5}{7}$ of her homework. Who must finish a greater percent of homework at home?

 42. Write About It Compare ratios and percents. How are they alike? How are they different?

 43. Challenge Write each of the following as a percent: 0.4 and 0.03.

CRCT PREP • GPS SUPPORT • SPIRAL REVIEW

44. Multiple Choice Which inequality is a true statement?

   Ⓐ 24% > $\frac{1}{4}$ Ⓑ 0.76 < 76%   Ⓒ 8% < 0.8   Ⓓ $\frac{1}{5}$ < 5%

45. Short Response Nineteen out of the 25 students on Sean's team sold mugs, and 68% of the students on Chi's team sold caps. Which team had a greater percent of students participate in the fundraiser?

Estimate each sum or difference. (Lesson 3-7)

46. $\frac{7}{8} - \frac{3}{7}$ **47.** $6\frac{1}{10} + 5\frac{7}{9}$ **48.** $5\frac{2}{3} - \left(-\frac{3}{4}\right)$ **49.** $\frac{5}{12} + 2\frac{4}{5}$

Plot each point on a coordinate plane. (Lesson 4-1)

50. $A(2, 3)$ **51.** $B(-1, 4)$ **52.** $C(-2, -6)$ **53.** $D(0, -3)$

6-2 Fractions, Decimals, and Percents

Learn to write decimals and fractions as percents.

Georgia Performance Standards

M7P4.b Understand how mathematical ideas interconnect and build on one another to produce a coherent whole. Also, M7P1.c, M7P1.d, M7P4.a, M7P5.a.

The students at Westview Middle School are collecting cans of food for the local food bank. Their goal is to collect 2,000 cans in one month. After 10 days, they have 800 cans of food.

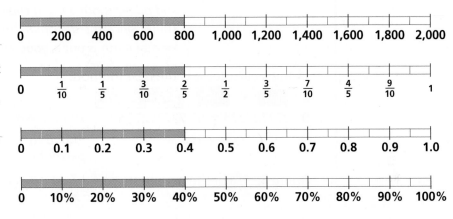

The models show that 800 out of 2,000 can be written as $\frac{800}{2,000}$, $\frac{2}{5}$, 0.4, or 40%. The students have reached 40% of their goal.

EXAMPLE 1 Writing Decimals as Percents

Write 0.2 as a percent.

Method 1: Use pencil and paper.

$0.2 = \frac{2}{10} = \frac{20}{100}$ *Write the decimal as a fraction with a denominator of 100.*

$= 20\%$ *Write the numerator with a percent sign.*

Method 2: Use mental math.

$0.20 = 20.0\%$

$= 20\%$

Move the decimal point two places to the right and add a percent sign.

EXAMPLE 2 Writing Fractions as Percents

Write $\frac{4}{5}$ as a percent.

Remember!

To divide 4 by 5, use long division and place a decimal point followed by a zero after the 4.

$\begin{array}{r} 0.8 \\ 5\overline{)4.0} \end{array}$

Method 1: Use pencil and paper.

$\frac{4}{5} = 4 \div 5$ *Use division to write the fraction as a decimal.*

$= 0.8$

$= 0.80$

$= 80\%$ *Write the decimal as a percent.*

Method 2: Use mental math.

$\frac{4 \cdot 20}{5 \cdot 20} = \frac{80}{100}$ *Write an equivalent fraction with a denominator of 100.*

$= 80\%$ *Write the numerator with a percent sign.*

EXAMPLE 3 **Choosing a Method of Computation**

Decide whether using pencil and paper, mental math, or a calculator is most useful when solving the following problem. Then solve.

In a survey, 55 people were asked whether they prefer cats or dogs. Twenty-nine people said they prefer cats. What percent of the people surveyed said they prefer cats?

$29 \text{ out of } 55 = \dfrac{29}{55}$ *Think: Since 29 ÷ 55 does not divide evenly, pencil and paper is not a good choice.*

Think: Since the denominator is not a factor of 100, mental math is not a good choice.

Using a calculator is the best method.

$0.5272727273 = 52.72727273\%$ *Write the decimal as a percent.*

$\approx 52.7\%$ *Round to the nearest tenth of a percent.*

About 52.7% of the people surveyed said they prefer cats.

 **Think and Discuss** 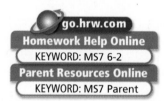 GPS M7P1.d, M7P3.a

1. Describe two methods you could use to write $\frac{3}{4}$ as a percent.

2. Write the ratio 25:100 as a fraction, as a decimal, and as a percent.

6-2 Exercises

Georgia Performance Standards

M7P1.c, M7P3.a, M7P3.c

go.hrw.com
Homework Help Online
KEYWORD: MS7 6-2
Parent Resources Online
KEYWORD: MS7 Parent

GUIDED PRACTICE

 See Example 1 **Write each decimal as a percent.**

  1. 0.6   **2.** 0.32   **3.** 0.544   **4.** 0.06   **5.** 0.087

See Example 2 **Write each fraction as a percent.**

  6. $\frac{1}{4}$ **7.** $\frac{3}{25}$ **8.** $\frac{11}{20}$ **9.** $\frac{7}{40}$ **10.** $\frac{5}{8}$

 See Example 3 **11. Decide** whether using pencil and paper, mental math, or a calculator is most useful when solving the following problem. Then solve.

In a survey, 50 students were asked whether they prefer pepperoni pizza or cheese pizza. Twenty students said they prefer cheese pizza. What percent of the students surveyed said they prefer cheese pizza?

INDEPENDENT PRACTICE

See Example 1 Write each decimal as a percent.

12. 0.15   **13.** 0.83   **14.** 0.325   **15.** 0.081   **16.** 0.42

See Example 2 Write each fraction as a percent.

17. $\frac{3}{4}$ **18.** $\frac{2}{5}$ **19.** $\frac{3}{8}$ **20.** $\frac{3}{16}$ **21.** $\frac{7}{25}$

See Example 3 **22.** Decide whether using pencil and paper, mental math, or a calculator is most useful when solving the following problem. Then solve.

In a theme-park survey, 75 visitors were asked whether they prefer the Ferris wheel or the roller coaster. Thirty visitors prefer the Ferris wheel. What percent of the visitors surveyed said they prefer the Ferris wheel?

PRACTICE AND PROBLEM SOLVING

Extra Practice p. 737

Compare. Write $<$, $>$, or $=$.

23. 45% ▮ $\frac{2}{5}$ **24.** 9% ▮ 0.9   **25.** $\frac{7}{12}$ ▮ 60%   **26.** 0.037 ▮ 37%

27. Multi-Step One-half of the 900 students at Jefferson Middle School are boys. One-tenth of the boys are in the band, and one-fifth of those play the trumpet. What percent of the students at Jefferson are boys who play the trumpet in the band?

28. Life Science Rain forests are home to 90,000 of the 250,000 identified plant species in the world. What percent of the world's identified plant species are found in rain forests?

 29. What's the Error? A student wrote $\frac{2}{5}$ as 0.4%. What was the error?

 30. Write About It Describe two ways to change a fraction to a percent.

 31. Challenge A desert area's average rainfall is 12 inches a year. This year the area received 15 inches of rain. What percent of the average rainfall amount is 15 inches?

CRCT Prep • GPS Support • Spiral Review

32. Multiple Choice Which value is NOT equivalent to 45%?

Ⓐ $\frac{9}{20}$ Ⓑ 0.45   Ⓒ $\frac{45}{100}$ Ⓓ 0.045

33. Short Response Melanie's room measures 10 ft by 12 ft. Her rug covers 90 ft^2. Explain how to determine the percent of floor covered by the rug.

Make a function table for $x = -2, -1, 0, 1,$ and 2. (Lesson 4-4)

34. $y = 5x + 2$ **35.** $y = -2x$ **36.** $y = -\frac{2}{3}x - 4$

37. The actual length of a room is 6 m. The scale factor of a model is 1:15. What is the length of the room in the model? (Lesson 5-9)

6-3 Estimate with Percents

 Problem Solving Skill

 **to estimate percents.**

Georgia Performance Standards

M7P4.c Recognize and apply mathematics in contexts outside of mathematics. Also, M7P1.c, M7P1.d.

A hair dryer at Hair Haven costs $14.99. Carissa's Corner is offering the same hair dryer at 20% off the regular price of $19.99. To find out which store is offering the better deal on the hair dryer, you can use estimation.

The table shows common percents and their fraction equivalents. You can estimate the percent of a number by substituting a fraction that is close to a given percent.

Percent	10%	20%	25%	$33\frac{1}{3}$%	50%	$66\frac{2}{3}$%
Fraction	$\frac{1}{10}$	$\frac{1}{5}$	$\frac{1}{4}$	$\frac{1}{3}$	$\frac{1}{2}$	$\frac{2}{3}$

EXAMPLE 1 **Using Fractions to Estimate Percents**

Use a fraction to estimate 48% of 79.

$$48\% \text{ of } 79 \approx \frac{1}{2} \cdot 79 \qquad \textit{Think: 48\% is about 50\% and } 50\% \textit{ is equivalent to } \frac{1}{2}.$$

$$\approx \frac{1}{2} \cdot 80 \qquad \textit{Change 79 to a compatible number.}$$

$$\approx 40 \qquad \textit{Multiply.}$$

48% of 79 is about 40.

Remember!

Compatible numbers are close to the numbers in a problem and help you use mental math to find a solution.

EXAMPLE 2 *Consumer Math Application*

Carissa's Corner is offering 20% off a hair dryer that costs $19.99. The same hair dryer costs $14.99 at Hair Haven. Which store offers the better deal?

First find the discount on the hair dryer at Carissa's Corner.

$$20\% \text{ of } \$19.99 = \frac{1}{5} \cdot \$19.99 \qquad \textit{Think: 20\% is equivalent to } \frac{1}{5}.$$

$$\approx \frac{1}{5} \cdot \$20 \qquad \textit{Change \$19.99 to a compatible number.}$$

$$\approx \$4 \qquad \textit{Multiply.}$$

The discount is approximately $4. Since $20 − $4 = $16, the $14.99 hair dryer at Hair Haven is the better deal.

Another way to estimate percents is to find 1% or 10% of a number. You can do this by moving the decimal point in the number.

1% of 45 = 45.0
= 0.45

To find 1% of a number, move the decimal point two places to the left.

10% of 45 = 45.0
= 4.5

To find 10% of a number, move the decimal point one place to the left.

EXAMPLE 3 **Estimating with Simple Percents**

Use 1% or 10% to estimate the percent of each number.

A **3% of 59**

59 is about 60, so find 3% of 60.

1% of 60 = 60.0

3% of 60 = 3 · 0.60 = 1.8   *3% equals 3 · 1%.*

3% of 59 is about 1.8.

B **18% of 45**

18% is about 20%, so find 20% of 45.

10% of 45 = 45.0

20% of 45 = 2 · 4.5 = 9.0   *20% equals 2 · 10%.*

18% of 45 is about 9.

EXAMPLE 4 *Consumer Math Application*

Eric and Selena spent $25.85 for their meals at a restaurant. About how much money should they leave for a 15% tip?

Since $25.85 is about $26, find 15% of $26.

15% = 10% + 5%   *Think: 15% is 10% plus 5%.*

10% of $26 = $2.60

5% of $26 = $2.60 ÷ 2 = $1.30   *5% is $\frac{1}{2}$ of 10%, so divide $2.60 by 2.*

$2.60 + $1.30 = $3.90   *Add the 10% and 5% estimates.*

Eric and Selena should leave about $3.90 for a 15% tip.

Think and Discuss   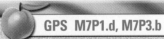 GPS M7P1.d, M7P3.b

1. **Describe** two ways to estimate 51% of 88.

2. **Explain** why you might divide by 7 or multiply by $\frac{1}{7}$ to estimate a 15% tip.

3. **Give an example** of a situation in which an estimate of a percent is sufficient and a situation in which an exact percent is necessary.

 6-3 **Exercises**

 **Georgia Performance Standards**

M7P1.b, M7P3.a, M7P4.c

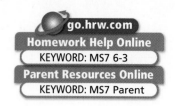 **go.hrw.com**
Homework Help Online
KEYWORD: MS7 6-3
Parent Resources Online
KEYWORD: MS7 Parent

GUIDED PRACTICE

See Example **Use a fraction to estimate the percent of each number.**

1. 30% of 86   **2.** 52% of 83   **3.** 10% of 48   **4.** 27% of 63

See Example 2 **5.** Darden has $35 to spend on a backpack. He finds one on sale for 35% off the regular price of $43.99. Does Darden have enough money to buy the backpack? Explain.

See Example 3 **Use 1% or 10% to estimate the percent of each number.**

6. 5% of 82   **7.** 39% of 19   **8.** 21% of 68   **9.** 7% of 109

See Example 4 **10.** Mrs. Coronado spent $23 on a manicure. About how much money should she leave for a 15% tip?

INDEPENDENT PRACTICE

See Example 1 **Use a fraction to estimate the percent of each number.**

11. 8% of 261   **12.** 34% of 93   **13.** 53% of 142   **14.** 23% of 98

15. 51% of 432   **16.** 18% of 42   **17.** 11% of 132   **18.** 54% of 39

See Example 2 **19. Consumer Math** A pair of shoes at The Value Store costs $20. Fancy Feet has the same shoes on sale for 25% off the regular price of $23.99. Which store offers the better price on the shoes?

See Example 3 **Use 1% or 10% to estimate the percent of each number.**

20. 41% of 16   **21.** 8% of 310   **22.** 83% of 70   **23.** 2% of 634

24. 58% of 81   **25.** 24% of 49   **26.** 11% of 99   **27.** 63% of 39

See Example 4 **28.** Marc's lunch cost $8.92. He wants to leave a 15% tip for the service. About how much should his tip be?

PRACTICE AND PROBLEM SOLVING

 **CRCT GPS**
Extra Practice p. 737

Estimate.

29. 31% of 180   **30.** 18% of 150   **31.** 3% of 96   **32.** 2% of 198

33. 78% of 90   **34.** 52% of 234   **35.** 19% of 75   **36.** 4% of 311

37. The new package of Marti's Snacks contains 20% more snack mix than the old package. There were 22 ounces of snack mix in the old package. About how many ounces are in the new package?

38. Frameworks charges $60.85 for framing. Including the 7% sales tax, about how much will it cost to have a painting framed?

39. Multi-Step Camden's lunch cost $11.67, and he left a $2.00 tip. About how much more than 15% of the bill did Camden leave for the tip?

40. Sports Last season, Ali had a hit 19.3% of the times he came to bat. If Ali batted 82 times last season, about how many hits did he have?

41. Business The table shows the results of a survey about the Internet. The number of people interviewed was 391.

    a. Estimate the number of people willing to give out their e-mail address.

    b. Estimate the number of people not willing to give out their credit card number.

Information People Are Willing to Give Out on the Internet	
Information	**Percent of People**
E-mail address	78
Work phone number	53
Street address	49
Home phone number	35
Credit card number	33
Social Security number	11

42. Multi-Step Sandi earns $43,000 per year. This year, she plans to spend about 27% of her income on rent.

    a. About how much does Sandi plan to spend on rent this year?

    b. About how much does she plan to spend on rent each month?

43. Write a Problem Use information from the table in Exercise 41 to write a problem that can be solved by using estimation of a percent.

44. Write About It Explain why it might be important to know whether your estimate of a percent is too high or too low. Give an example.

45. Challenge Use the table from Exercise 41 to estimate how many more people will give out their work phone number than their Social Security number. Show your work using two different methods.

CRCT PREP • GPS SUPPORT • SPIRAL REVIEW

46. Multiple Choice About 65% of the people answering a survey said that they have read a "blog," or Web log, online. Sixty-six people were surveyed. Which is the best estimate of the number of people surveyed who have read a blog?

    Ⓐ 30   Ⓑ 35   Ⓒ 45   Ⓓ 50

47. Short Response Ryan's dinner bill is $35.00. He wants to leave a 15% tip. Explain how to use mental math to determine how much he should leave as a tip.

Find each product. (Lesson 3-3)

48. $0.8 \cdot 96$ **49.** $30 \cdot 0.04$ **50.** $1.6 \cdot 900$ **51.** $0.005 \cdot 75$

52. Brandi's room was painted in a color that is a blend of 3 parts red paint and 2 parts white paint. How many quarts of white paint does Brandi need to mix with 6 quarts of red paint to match the paint in her room? (Lesson 5-5)

Explore Percents

Use with Lesson 6-4

go.hrw.com
Lab Resources Online
KEYWORD: MS7 Lab6

Georgia Performance Standards

M7P3.b, M7P5.a, M7P5.b

REMEMBER

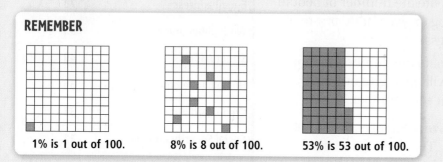

| 1% is 1 out of 100. | 8% is 8 out of 100. | 53% is 53 out of 100. |

You can use 10-by-10 grids to model percents, including those less than 1 or greater than 100.

Activity 1

① Use 10-by-10 grids to model 132%.

Think: 132% means 132 out of 100.

Shade 100 squares plus 32 squares to model 132%.

② Use a 10-by-10 grid to model 0.5%.

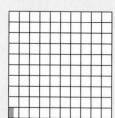

Think: One square equals 1%, so $\frac{1}{2}$ of one square equals 0.5%.

Shade $\frac{1}{2}$ of one square to model 0.5%.

Think and Discuss

1. Explain how to model 36.75% on a 10-by-10 grid.

2. How can you model 0.7%? Explain your answer.

Try This

Use 10-by-10 grids to model each percent.

1. 280%   2. $16\frac{1}{2}\%$ 3. 0.25%   4. 65%   5. 140.75%

You can use a percent bar and a quantity bar to model finding a percent of a number.

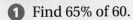

Activity 2

1 Find 65% of 60.

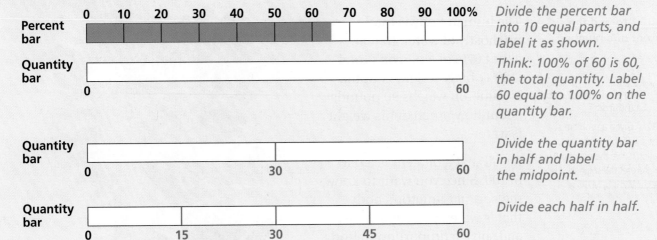

Divide the percent bar into 10 equal parts, and label it as shown.

Think: 100% of 60 is 60, the total quantity. Label 60 equal to 100% on the quantity bar.

Divide the quantity bar in half and label the midpoint.

Divide each half in half.

What point on the quantity bar lines up with 65% on the percent bar?
It appears that 65% of 60 is about 39.   *Check by multiplying: 0.65 · 60 = 39.*

2 Find 125% of 60.   *Think: 125% of a whole is greater than the whole.*
Extend the bars to find 125% of a number.

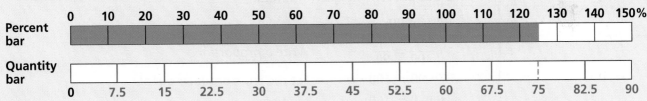

What point on the quantity bar lines up with 125% on the percent bar?
It appears that 125% of 60 is about 75.   *Check by multiplying 1.25 · 60 = 75.*

Think and Discuss

1. Explain how to use a percent bar and a quantity bar to find a percent of a number.

2. Explain how using a percent bar and a quantity bar to model finding a percent of a number involves estimation.

Try This

Use a percent bar and a quantity bar to find the percent of each number. Use a calculator to check your answers.

1. 75% of 36   2. 60% of 15   3. 135% of 40   4. 112% of 25   5. 25% of 75

Percent of a Number

to find the percent of a number.

 Georgia Performance Standards

M7A2.a Given a problem, define a variable, write an equation, solve the equation, and interpret the solution. Also, M7A2.b, M7P1.b, M7P5.a.

The human body is made up mostly of water. In fact, about 67% of a person's total (100%) body weight is water. If Cameron weighs 90 pounds, about how much of his weight is water?

Recall that a percent is a part of 100. Since you want to know the part of Cameron's body that is water, you can set up and solve a proportion to find the answer.

Part → $\dfrac{67}{100} = \dfrac{n}{90}$ ← *Part*
Whole → $\phantom{\dfrac{67}{100}}$ ← *Whole*

EXAMPLE ① **Using Proportions to Find Percents of Numbers**

Find the percent of each number.

Ⓐ **67% of 90**

$\dfrac{67}{100} = \dfrac{n}{90}$ *Write a proportion.*

$67 \cdot 90 = 100 \cdot n$ *Set the cross products equal.*

$6{,}030 = 100n$ *Multiply.*

$\dfrac{6{,}030}{100} = \dfrac{100n}{100}$ *Divide each side by 100 to isolate the variable.*

$60.3 = n$

67% of 90 is 60.3.

Ⓑ **145% of 210**

$\dfrac{145}{100} = \dfrac{n}{210}$ *Write a proportion.*

$145 \cdot 210 = 100 \cdot n$ *Set the cross products equal.*

$30{,}450 = 100n$ *Multiply.*

$\dfrac{30{,}450}{100} = \dfrac{100n}{100}$ *Divide each side by 100 to isolate the variable.*

$304.5 = n$

145% of 210 is 304.5.

Helpful Hint

When solving a problem with a percent greater than 100%, the *part* will be greater than the *whole*.

In addition to using proportions, you can find the percent of a number by using decimal equivalents.

EXAMPLE **2** **Using Decimal Equivalents to Find Percents of Numbers**

Find the percent of each number. Check whether your answer is reasonable.

A **8% of 50**

$$8\% \text{ of } 50 = 0.08 \cdot 50$$ *Write the percent as a decimal.*
$$= 4$$ *Multiply.*

Model

Since 10% of 50 is 5, a reasonable answer for 8% of 50 is 4.

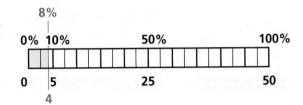

B **0.5% of 36**

$$0.5\% \text{ of } 36 = 0.005 \cdot 36$$ *Write the percent as a decimal.*
$$= 0.18$$ *Multiply.*

Estimate

1% of 36 = 0.36, so 0.5% of 36 is half of 0.36. Thus 0.18 is a reasonable answer.

EXAMPLE **3** **Geography Application**

Earth's total land area is about 57,308,738 mi². The land area of Asia is about 30% of this total. What is the approximate land area of Asia to the nearest square mile?

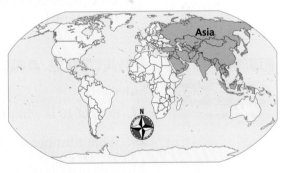

Find 30% of 57,308,738.

0.30 · 57,308,738   *Write the percent as a decimal.*

= 17,192,621.4   *Multiply.*

The land area of Asia is about 17,192,621 mi².

Think and Discuss  GPS M7P1.d, M7P3.b

1. Explain how to set up a proportion to find 150% of a number.

2. Describe a situation in which you might need to find a percent of a number.

 **6-4** **Exercises**

 Georgia Performance Standards

M7P3.a, M7P3.c, M7P5.a

 go.hrw.com
Homework Help Online
KEYWORD: MS7 6-4
Parent Resources Online
KEYWORD: MS7 Parent

GUIDED PRACTICE

See Example **1** Find the percent of each number.

1. 30% of 80   **2.** 38% of 400   **3.** 200% of 10   **4.** 180% of 90

See Example **2** Find the percent of each number. Check whether your answer is reasonable.

5. 16% of 50   **6.** 7% of 200   **7.** 47% of 900   **8.** 40% of 75

See Example **3** **9.** Of the 450 students at Miller Middle School, 38% ride the bus to school. How many students ride the bus to school?

INDEPENDENT PRACTICE

See Example **1** Find the percent of each number.

10. 80% of 35   **11.** 16% of 70   **12.** 150% of 80   **13.** 118% of 3,000

14. 5% of 58   **15.** 1% of 4   **16.** 103% of 50   **17.** 225% of 8

See Example **2** Find the percent of each number. Check whether your answer is reasonable.

18. 9% of 40   **19.** 20% of 65   **20.** 36% of 50   **21.** 2.9% of 60

22. 5% of 12   **23.** 220% of 18   **24.** 0.2% of 160   **25.** 155% of 8

See Example **3** **26.** In 2004, there were 19,396 bulldogs registered by the American Kennel Club. Approximately 86% of this number were registered in 2003. About how many bulldogs were registered in 2003?

PRACTICE AND PROBLEM SOLVING

Extra Practice p. 737

Solve.

27. 60% of 10 is what number?   **28.** What number is 25% of 160?

29. What number is 15% of 30?   **30.** 10% of 84 is what number?

31. 25% of 47 is what number?   **32.** What number is 59% of 20?

33. What number is 125% of 4,100?   **34.** 150% of 150 is what number?

Find the percent of each number. If necessary, round to the nearest tenth.

35. 160% of 50   **36.** 350% of 20   **37.** 480% of 25   **38.** 115% of 200

39. 18% of 3.4   **40.** 0.9% of 43   **41.** 98% of 4.3   **42.** 1.22% of 56

43. **Consumer Math** Fun Tees is offering a 30% discount on all merchandise. Find the amount of discount on a T-shirt that was originally priced at $15.99.

44. **Multi-Step** Shoe Style is discounting everything in the store by 25%. What is the sale price of a pair of flip-flops that was originally priced at $10?

Physical Science

Pure gold is a soft metal that scratches easily. To make the gold in jewelry more durable, it is often combined with other metals, such as copper and nickel.

45. **Nutrition** The United States Department of Agriculture recommends that women should eat 25 g of fiber each day. A granola bar provides 9% of that amount. How many grams of fiber does it contain?

46. **Physical Science** The percent of pure gold in 14-karat gold is about 58.3%. A 14-karat gold ring weighs 5.6 grams. About how many grams of pure gold are in the ring?

47. **Earth Science** The apparent magnitude of the star Mimosa is 1.25. Spica, another star, has an apparent magnitude that is 78.4% of Mimosa's. What is Spica's apparent magnitude?

48. **Multi-Step** Trahn purchased a pair of slacks for $39.95 and a jacket for $64.00. The sales tax rate on his purchases was 5.5%. Find the total cost of Trahn's purchases, including sales tax.

49. The graph shows the results of a student survey about computers. Use the graph to predict how many students in your class have a computer at home.

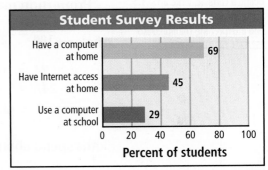

Student Survey Results

Have a computer at home — 69
Have Internet access at home — 45
Use a computer at school — 29

Percent of students

50. **What's the Error?** A student used the proportion $\frac{n}{100} = \frac{5}{26}$ to find 5% of 26. What did the student do wrong?

51. **Write About It** Describe two ways to find 18% of 40.

52. **Challenge** François's starting pay was $6.25 per hour. During his annual review, he received a 5% raise. Find François's pay raise to the nearest cent and the amount he will earn with his raise. Then find 105% of $6.25. What can you conclude?

CRCT PREP • GPS SUPPORT • SPIRAL REVIEW

53. **Multiple Choice** Of the 875 students enrolled at Sycamore Valley Middle School, 48% are boys. How many of the students are boys?

   Ⓐ 250   Ⓑ 310   Ⓒ 420   Ⓓ 440

54. **Gridded Response** A children's multivitamin has 80% of the recommended daily allowance of zinc. The recommended daily allowance is 15 mg. How many milligrams of zinc does the vitamin provide?

Find each unit rate. (Lesson 5-2)

55. Monica buys 3 pounds of peaches for $5.25. What is the cost per pound?

56. Kevin types 295 words in 5 minutes. At what rate does Kevin type?

Write each decimal as a percent. (Lesson 6-2)

57. 0.0125   58. 0.26   59. 0.389   60. 0.099   61. 0.407

6-5 Solving Percent Problems

Learn to solve problems involving percents.

Georgia Performance Standards

M7A2.a Given a problem, define a variable, write an equation, solve the equation, and interpret the solution. Also, M7A2.b, M7P1.c, M7P4.c.

Sloths may seem lazy, but their extremely slow movement helps them seem almost invisible to predators. Sloths sleep an average of 16.5 hours per day. To find out what percent of a 24-hour day 16.5 hours is, you can use a proportion or an equation.

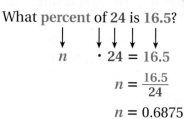

Proportion method

$$\text{Part} \rightarrow \frac{n}{100} = \frac{16.5}{24} \leftarrow \text{Part}$$
$$\text{Whole} \rightarrow \quad\quad\quad\quad \leftarrow \text{Whole}$$

$$n \cdot 24 = 100 \cdot 16.5$$
$$24n = 1{,}650$$
$$n = 68.75$$

Equation method

What **percent** of 24 is 16.5?

$$n \quad \cdot 24 = 16.5$$

$$n = \frac{16.5}{24}$$

$$n = 0.6875$$

Sloths spend about **69%** of the day sleeping!

EXAMPLE 1 Using Proportions to Solve Problems with Percents

Solve.

A What percent of 90 is 45?

$$\frac{n}{100} = \frac{45}{90}$$ *Write a proportion.*

$$n \cdot 90 = 100 \cdot 45$$ *Set the cross products equal.*

$$90n = 4{,}500$$ *Multiply.*

$$\frac{90n}{90} = \frac{4{,}500}{90}$$ *Divide each side by 90 to isolate the variable.*

$$n = 50$$

50% of 90 is 45.

B 12 is 8% of what number?

$$\frac{8}{100} = \frac{12}{n}$$ *Write a proportion.*

$$8 \cdot n = 100 \cdot 12$$ *Set the cross products equal.*

$$8n = 1{,}200$$ *Multiply.*

$$\frac{8n}{8} = \frac{1{,}200}{8}$$ *Divide each side by 8 to isolate the variable.*

$$n = 150$$

12 is 8% of 150.

EXAMPLE 2 Using Equations to Solve Problems with Percents

Solve.

A What percent of 75 is 105?

$$n \cdot 75 = 105$$ *Write an equation.*

$$\frac{n \cdot 75}{75} = \frac{105}{75}$$ *Divide each side by 75 to isolate the variable.*

$$n = 1.4$$

$$n = 140\%$$ *Write the decimal as a percent.*

140% of 75 is 105.

B 48 is 20% of what number?

$$48 = 20\% \cdot n$$ *Write an equation.*

$$48 = 0.2 \cdot n$$ *Write 20% as a decimal.*

$$\frac{48}{0.2} = \frac{0.2 \cdot n}{0.2}$$ *Divide each side by 0.2 to isolate the variable.*

$$240 = n$$

48 is 20% of 240.

EXAMPLE 3 Finding Sales Tax

Helpful Hint

The *sales tax rate* is the percent used to calculate sales tax.

Ravi bought a T-shirt with a retail sales price of $12 and paid $0.99 sales tax. What is the sales tax rate where Ravi bought the T-shirt?

Restate the question: What percent of $12 is $0.99?

$$\frac{n}{100} = \frac{0.99}{12}$$ *Write a proportion.*

$$n \cdot 12 = 100 \cdot 0.99$$ *Set the cross products equal.*

$$12n = 99$$ *Multiply.*

$$\frac{12n}{12} = \frac{99}{12}$$ *Divide each side by 12.*

$$n = 8.25$$

8.25% of $12 is $0.99. The sales tax rate where Ravi bought the T-shirt is 8.25%.

Think and Discuss   GPS M7P1.d, M7P3.b

1. Describe two methods for solving percent problems.

2. Explain whether you prefer to use the proportion method or the equation method when solving percent problems.

3. Tell what the first step is in solving a sales tax problem.

6-5 Exercises

Georgia Performance Standards
M7P1.b, M7P3.a, M7P5.a

go.hrw.com
Homework Help Online
KEYWORD: MS7 6-5
Parent Resources Online
KEYWORD: MS7 Parent

GUIDED PRACTICE

Solve.

See Example 1
1. What percent of 100 is 25?
2. What percent of 5 is 4?
3. 6 is 10% of what number?
4. 8 is 20% of what number?

See Example 2
5. What percent of 50 is 9?
6. What percent of 30 is 27?
7. 7 is 14% of what number?
8. 30 is 15% of what number?

See Example 3
9. The sales tax on a $120 skateboard at Surf 'n' Skate is $9.60. What is the sales tax rate?

INDEPENDENT PRACTICE

Solve.

See Example 1
10. What percent of 60 is 40?
11. What percent of 48 is 16?
12. What percent of 45 is 9?
13. What percent of 6 is 18?
14. 56 is 140% of what number?
15. 45 is 20% of what number?

See Example 2
16. What percent of 80 is 10?
17. What percent of 12.4 is 12.4?
18. 18 is 15% of what number?
19. 9 is 30% of what number?
20. 210% of what number is 147?
21. 8.8 is 40% of what number?

See Example 3
22. A 12-pack of cinnamon-scented pencils sells for $3.00 at a school booster club sale. What is the sales tax rate if the total cost of the pencils is $3.21?

PRACTICE AND PROBLEM SOLVING

Extra Practice p. 738

Solve. Round to the nearest tenth, if necessary.
23. 5 is what percent of 9?
24. What is 45% of 39?
25. 55 is 80% of what number?
26. 12 is what percent of 19?
27. What is 155% of 50?
28. 5.8 is 0.9% of what number?
29. 36% of what number is 57?
30. What percent of 64 is 40?

31. **Multi-Step** The advertised cost of admission to a water park in a nearby city is $25 per student. A student paid $30 for admission and received $3.75 in change. What is the sales tax rate in that city?

32. **Consumer Math** The table shows the cost of sunscreen purchased in Beach City and Desert City with and without sales tax. Which city has a greater sales tax rate? Give the sales tax rate for each city.

	Cost	Cost + Tax
Beach City	$10	$10.83
Desert City	$5	$5.42

33. Critical Thinking What number is always used when you set up a proportion to solve a percent problem? Explain.

34. Health The circle graph shows the approximate distribution of blood types among people in the United States.

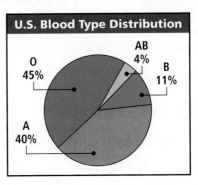

U.S. Blood Type Distribution

O 45%
AB 4%
B 11%
A 40%

    a. In a survey, 126 people had type O blood. Predict how many people were surveyed.

    b. How many of the people surveyed had type AB blood?

35. Music Beethoven wrote 9 trios for the piano, violin, and cello. These trios make up 20% of the chamber music pieces Beethoven wrote. How many pieces of chamber music did he write?

36. History The length of Abraham Lincoln's first inaugural speech was 3,635 words. The length of his second inaugural speech was about 19.3% of the length of his first speech. About how long was Lincoln's second speech?

37. What's the Question? The first lap of an auto race is 2,500 m. This is 10% of the total race distance. The answer is 10. What is the question?

38. Write About It If 35 is 110% of a number, is the number greater than or less than 35? Explain.

39. Challenge Kayleen has been offered two jobs. The first job offers an annual salary of $32,000. The second job offers an annual salary of $10,000 plus 8% commission on all of her sales. How much money per month would Kayleen need to make in sales to earn enough commission to make more money at the second job?

CRCT PREP • GPS SUPPORT • SPIRAL REVIEW

40. Multiple Choice Thirty children from an after-school club went to the matinee. This is 20% of the children in the club. How many children are in the club?

   Ⓐ 6   Ⓑ 67   Ⓒ 150   Ⓓ 600

41. Gridded Response Jason saves 30% of his monthly paycheck for college. He earned $250 last month. How many dollars did he save for college?

Divide. (Lessons 3-4 and 3-5)

42. $-3.92 \div 7$ **43.** $10.68 \div 3$ **44.** $23.2 \div 0.2$ **45.** $19.52 \div 6.1$

Find the percent of each number. If necessary, round to the nearest hundredth.
(Lesson 6-4)

46. 45% of 26   **47.** 22% of 30   **48.** 15% of 17   **49.** 68% of 98

CHAPTER 6

READY TO GO ON?

SECTION 6A

Quiz for Lessons 6-1 Through 6-5

✓ 6-1 Percents

Write each percent as a fraction in simplest form.

1. 9% **2.** 43% **3.** 5% **4.** 18%

Write each percent as a decimal.

5. 22% **6.** 90% **7.** 29% **8.** 5%

✓ 6-2 Fractions, Decimals, and Percents

Write each decimal as a percent.

9. 0.85 **10.** 0.026 **11.** 0.1111 **12.** 0.56

Write each fraction as a percent. Round to the nearest tenth of a percent, if necessary.

13. $\frac{14}{81}$ **14.** $\frac{25}{52}$ **15.** $\frac{55}{78}$ **16.** $\frac{13}{32}$

✓ 6-3 Estimate with Percents

Estimate.

17. 49% of 46 **18.** 9% of 25 **19.** 36% of 150 **20.** 5% of 60

21. 18% of 80 **22.** 26% of 115 **23.** 91% of 300 **24.** 42% of 197

25. Carlton spent $21.85 on lunch for himself and a friend. About how much should he leave for a 15% tip?

✓ 6-4 Percent of a Number

Find the percent of each number.

26. 25% of 84 **27.** 52% of 300 **28.** 0.5% of 40 **29.** 160% of 450

30. 41% of 122 **31.** 178% of 35 **32.** 29% of 88 **33.** 80% of 176

34. Students get a 15% discount off the original prices at the Everything Fluorescent store during its back-to-school sale. Find the amount of discount on fluorescent notebooks originally priced at $7.99.

✓ 6-5 Solving Percent Problems

Solve. Round to the nearest tenth, if necessary.

35. 14 is 44% of what number? **36.** 22 is what percent of 900?

37. 99 is what percent of 396? **38.** 75 is 24% of what number?

39. The sales tax on a $105 digital camera is $7.15. What is the sales tax rate?

Ready to Go On?

Bargain Shopping   Shannon and Mary are training for a triathlon. Mary notices that a local sporting goods store is having a weekend sale on bike helmets. Both girls decide to replace their old helmets.

The girls see two signs when they enter the store on Saturday morning. One sign advertises the weekend sale. A second sign notes an early morning special.

END of WEEK
SALE
40%
off the regular price
of all bike helmets.

EARLY BIRD
SPECIAL!
8:00 A.M. – 11:00 A.M.
*Take an extra $\frac{1}{3}$ off
the END of WEEK SALE
price of all bike helmets!*

1. The helmet Shannon wants has a regular price of $54. What is the cost of this helmet during the weekend sale?

2. How much money will Shannon save off the weekend sale price if she buys her favorite helmet before 11:00 A.M.?

3. The helmet that Mary prefers regularly costs $48. What is the cost of this helmet during the weekend early shopper special?

4. Shannon thinks that with the combined sales the bike helmets are now 70% off the regular price. Mary disagrees. She thinks the total discount is less than 70%. Who has figured the discount correctly, Shannon or Mary? Explain your answer.

Game Time

Lighten Up

On a digital clock, up to seven light bulbs make up each digit on the display. You can label each light bulb as shown below.

If each number were lit up for the same amount of time, you could find out which light bulb is lit the greatest percent of the time. You could also find out which light bulb is lit the least percent of the time.

For each number 0–9, list the letters of the light bulbs that are used when that number is showing. The first few numbers have been done for you.

Once you have determined which bulbs are lit for each number, count how many times each bulb is lit. What percent of the time is each bulb lit? What does this tell you about which bulb will burn out first?

Percent Bingo

Use the bingo cards with numbers and percents provided online. The caller has a collection of percent problems. The caller reads a problem. Then the players solve the problem, and the solution is a number or a percent. If players have the solution on their card, they mark it off. Normal bingo rules apply. You can win with a horizontal, vertical, or diagonal row.

A complete copy of the rules and game pieces is available online.

go.hrw.com
Game Time Extra
KEYWORD: MS7 Games

Materials

- 2 pieces of card stock ($5\frac{1}{4}$ by 12 in.)
- 21 strips of colored paper ($1\frac{1}{2}$ by $5\frac{1}{2}$ in.)
- glue
- markers

It's in the Bag!

PROJECT **Percent Strips**

This colorful booklet holds questions and answers about percents.

Directions

1 Fold one piece of card stock in half. Cut along the crease to make two rectangles that are each $5\frac{1}{4}$ inches by 6 inches. You will use these later as covers for your booklet.

2 On the other piece of card stock, make accordion folds about $\frac{3}{4}$-inch wide. When you are done, there should be 16 panels. These panels will be the pages of your booklet. **Figure A**

3 Fold up the accordion strip. Glue the covers to the top and bottom panels of the strip. **Figure B**

4 Open the front cover. Glue a strip of colored paper to the top and bottom of the first page. **Figure C**

5 Turn the page. Glue a strip of colored paper to the back of the first page between the other two strips. **Figure D**

6 Glue strips to the other pages in the same way.

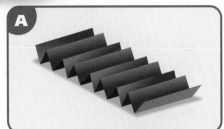

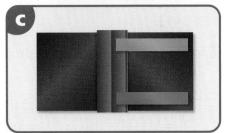

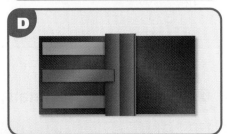

Putting the Math into Action

Write a question about percents on the front of each strip. Write the answer on the back. Trade books with another student and put your knowledge of percents to the test.

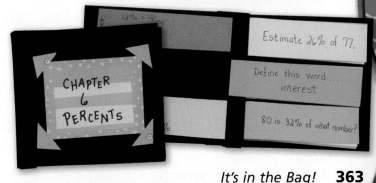

Study Guide: Review

Vocabulary

interest 356

percent 330

percent of change 352

percent of decrease 352

percent of increase 352

principal 356

simple interest 356

Complete the sentences below with vocabulary words from the list above.

1. __?__ is an amount that is collected or paid for the use of money. The equation $I = P \cdot r \cdot t$ is used for calculating __?__. The letter P represents the __?__ and the letter r represents the annual rate.

2. The ratio of an amount of increase to the original amount is the __?__.

3. The ratio of an amount of decrease to the original amount is the __?__.

4. A(n) __?__ is a ratio whose denominator is 100.

6-1 Percents (pp. 330–332)

 GPS M7P4.a

EXAMPLE

■ Write 12% as a fraction in simplest form and as a decimal.

$12\% = \dfrac{12}{100}$ 　　　 $12\% = \dfrac{12}{100}$

$\quad\ = \dfrac{12 \div 4}{100 \div 4}$ 　　 $\quad\ = 0.12$

$\quad\ = \dfrac{3}{25}$

EXERCISES

Write each percent as a fraction in simplest form and as a decimal.

5. 78% 　　　 **6.** 40%

7. 5% 　　　 **8.** 16%

9. 65% 　　　 **10.** 89%

6-2 Fractions, Decimals, and Percents (pp. 333–335)

 GPS M7P4.b

EXAMPLE

Write as a percent.

■ $\dfrac{7}{8}$ 　　　 ■ 0.82

$\dfrac{7}{8} = 7 \div 8$ 　　　 $0.82 = \dfrac{82}{100}$

$\quad\ = 0.875$ 　　　 $\quad\ = 82\%$

$\quad\ = 87.5\%$

EXERCISES

Write as a percent. Round to the nearest tenth of a percent, if necessary.

11. $\dfrac{3}{5}$ 　　　 **12.** $\dfrac{1}{6}$

13. 0.06 　　　 **14.** 0.8

15. $\dfrac{2}{3}$ 　　　 **16.** 0.0056

6-3 Estimate with Percents (pp. 336–339)

 GPS M7P4.c

EXAMPLE

■ **Estimate 26% of 77.**

26% of 77 $\approx \frac{1}{4} \cdot 77$ *26% is about 25% and 25% is equivalent to $\frac{1}{4}$.*

$\approx \frac{1}{4} \cdot 80$ *Change 77 to 80.*

≈ 20 *Multiply.*

26% of 77 is about 20.

EXERCISES

Estimate.

17. 22% of 44   **18.** 74% of 120

19. 43% of 64   **20.** 31% of 97

21. 49% of 82   **22.** 6% of 53

23. Byron and Kate's dinner cost $18.23. About how much money should they leave for a 15% tip?

6-4 Percent of a Number (pp. 342–345)

GPS M7A2.a, M7A2.b

EXAMPLE

■ **Find the percent of the number.**

125% of 610

$\frac{125}{100} = \frac{n}{610}$ *Write a proportion.*

$125 \cdot 610 = 100 \cdot n$

$76{,}250 = 100n$

$\frac{76{,}250}{100} = \frac{100n}{100}$

$762.5 = n$

125% of 610 is 762.5.

EXERCISES

Find the percent of each number.

24. 16% of 425   **25.** 48% of 50

26. 7% of 63   **27.** 96% of 125

28. 130% of 21   **29.** 72% of 75

30. Canyon Middle School has 1,247 students. About 38% of the students are in the seventh grade. About how many seventh-graders currently attend Canyon Middle School?

6-5 Solving Percent Problems (pp. 346–349)

 GPS M7A2.a, M7A2.b

EXAMPLE

■ **Solve.**

80 is 32% of what number?

$80 = 32\% \cdot n$ *Write an equation.*

$80 = 0.32 \cdot n$ *Write 32% as a decimal.*

$\frac{80}{0.32} = \frac{0.32 \cdot n}{0.32}$ *Isolate the variable.*

$250 = n$

80 is 32% of 250.

EXERCISES

Solve.

31. 20% of what number is 25?

32. 4 is what percent of 50?

33. 30 is 250% of what number?

34. What percent of 96 is 36?

35. 6 is 75% of what number?

36. 200 is what percent of 720?

37. The sales tax on a $25 shirt purchased at a store in Oak Park is $1.99. What is the sales tax rate in Oak Park?

6-6 Percent of Change (pp. 352–355)

 GPS M7A2.a, M7A2.b

EXAMPLE

Find each percent of change. Round answers to the nearest tenth, if necessary.

■ **25 is decreased to 16.**

$25 - 16 = 9$

percent of change $= \dfrac{9}{25}$

$= 0.36$

$= 36\%$

The percent of decrease is 36%.

■ **13.5 is increased to 27.**

$27 - 13.5 = 13.5$

percent of change $= \dfrac{13.5}{13.5}$

$= 1$

$= 100\%$

The percent of increase is 100%.

EXERCISES

Find each percent of change. Round answers to the nearest tenth, if necessary.

38. 54 is increased to 81.

39. 14 is decreased to 12.

40. 110 is increased to 143.

41. 90 is decreased to 15.2.

42. 26 is increased to 32.

43. 84 is decreased to 21.

44. The regular price of a new pair of skis is $245. This week the skis are on sale for 15% off. Find the sale price.

45. Bianca makes beaded bracelets. Each bracelet costs $3.25 to make. Bianca sells them at a 140% increase in price. What is the price of each bracelet?

6-7 Simple Interest (pp. 356–359)

 GPS M7A1.b, M7A2.b

EXAMPLE

Find each missing value.

■ $I = \blacksquare$, $P = \$545$, $r = 1.5\%$, $t = 2$ years

$I = P \cdot r \cdot t$

$I = 545 \cdot 0.015 \cdot 2$ *Substitute.*

$I = 16.35$ *Multiply.*

The simple interest is $16.35.

■ $I = \$825$, $P = \blacksquare$, $r = 6\%$, $t = 11$ years

$I = P \cdot r \cdot t$

$825 = P \cdot 0.06 \cdot 11$ *Substitute.*

$825 = P \cdot 0.66$ *Multiply.*

$\dfrac{825}{0.66} = \dfrac{P \cdot 0.66}{0.66}$ *Isolate the variable.*

$1{,}250 = P$

The principal is $1,250.

EXERCISES

Find each missing value.

46. $I = \blacksquare$, $P = \$1{,}000$, $r = 3\%$, $t = 6$ months

47. $I = \$452.16$, $P = \$1{,}256$, $r = 12\%$, $t = \blacksquare$

48. $I = \blacksquare$, $P = \$675$, $r = 4.5\%$, $t = 8$ years

49. $I = \$555.75$, $P = \$950$, $r = \blacksquare$, $t = 15$ years

50. $I = \$172.50$, $P = \blacksquare$, $r = 5\%$, $t = 18$ months

51. Craig deposits $1,000 in a savings account that earns 5% simple interest. How long will it take for the total amount in his account to reach $1,350?

52. Zach deposits $755 in an account that earns 4.2% simple interest. How long will it take for the total amount in the account to reach $1,050?

CHAPTER TEST

Write each percent as a fraction in simplest form and as a decimal.

1. 95% **2.** 37.5% **3.** 4% **4.** 0.01%

Write as a percent. Round to the nearest tenth of a percent, if necessary.

5. 0.75 **6.** 0.06 **7.** 0.8 **8.** 0.0039

9. $\frac{3}{10}$ **10.** $\frac{9}{20}$ **11.** $\frac{5}{16}$ **12.** $\frac{7}{21}$

Estimate.

13. 48% of 8 **14.** 3% of 119 **15.** 26% of 32 **16.** 76% of 280

17. The Pattersons spent $47.89 for a meal at a restaurant. About how much should they leave for a 15% tip?

Find the percent of each number.

18. 90% of 200 **19.** 35% of 210 **20.** 16% of 85

21. 250% of 30 **22.** 38% of 11 **23.** 5% of 145

Solve.

24. 36 is what percent of 150? **25.** What percent of 145 is 29?

26. 51 is what percent of 340? **27.** 36 is 40% of what number?

28. 70 is 14% of what number? **29.** 25 is 20% of what number?

30. Hampton Middle School is expecting 376 seventh-graders next year. This is 40% of the expected school enrollment. How many students are expected to enroll in the school next year?

Find each percent of change. Round answers to the nearest tenth, if necessary.

31. 30 is increased to 45. **32.** 115 is decreased to 46.

33. 116 is increased to 145. **34.** 129 is decreased to 32.

35. A community theater sold 8,500 tickets to performances during its first year. By its tenth year, ticket sales had increased by 34%. How many tickets did the theater sell during its tenth year?

Find each missing value.

36. $I = $ ▮, $P = \$500$, $r = 5\%$, $t = 1$ year **37.** $I = \$702$, $P = \$1,200$, $r = 3.9\%$, $t = $ ▮

38. $I = \$468$, $P = \$900$, $r = $ ▮, $t = 8$ years **39.** $I = \$37.50$, $P = $ ▮, $r = 10\%$, $t = 6$ months

40. Kate invested $3,500 at a 5% simple interest rate. How many years will it take for the original amount to double?

Chapter Test

Cumulative Assessment, Chapters 1–6

Multiple Choice

1. Which ratio corresponds to the similar figures shown?

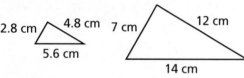

2.8 cm   4.8 cm   7 cm   12 cm

5.6 cm

14 cm

  (A) $\frac{4.2}{1}$ (C) $\frac{1}{2}$

  (B) $\frac{2.5}{1}$ (D) $\frac{1}{4}$

2. Which of the following is NOT equivalent to 12%?

  (F) 0.012   (H) 0.12

  (G) $\frac{12}{100}$ (J) $\frac{3}{25}$

3. Which situation corresponds to the graph?

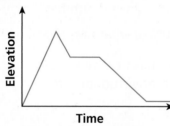

Elevation

Time

  (A) Ty rides his bike up a hill, immediately heads back down, stops and rests for a while, continues down the hill, and then rests.

  (B) Paul runs up a hill, stops a while for a water break, and then jogs back down the hill.

  (C) Sue rollerskates down a hill, stops for lunch, and then continues along a flat course for a while.

  (D) Eric swims across a pool, rests for a while when he gets to the other side, and then swims numerous laps without stopping.

4. Which point is not on the graph of $y = x^2 - 3$?

  (F) $(0, -3)$ (H) $(-2, -7)$

  (G) $(2, 1)$ (J) $(-1, -2)$

5. Which equation is an example of the Identity Property?

  (A) $100 + 10 = 2(50 + 5)$

  (B) $50 + 10 = 10 + 50$

  (C) $25 + (50 + 10) = (25 + 50) + 10$

  (D) $50 + 0 = 50$

6. A basketball goal that usually sells for $825 goes on sale for $650. What is the percent of decrease, to the nearest whole percent?

  (F) 12%   (H) 27%

  (G) 21%   (J) 79%

7. In Oregon, about 40 of the state's nearly 1,000 public water systems add fluoride to their water. What percent best represents this situation?

  (A) 0.4%   (C) 40%

  (B) 4%   (D) 400%

8. The number of whooping cranes wintering in Texas reached an all time high in 2004 at 213. The lowest number ever recorded was 15 whooping cranes in 1941. What is the percent of increase of whooping cranes wintering in Texas from 1941 to 2004?

  (F) 7%   (H) 198%

  (G) 91%   (J) 1,320%

9. What is the value of $8\frac{2}{5} - 2\frac{3}{4}$?

Ⓐ $5\frac{9}{20}$　　　Ⓒ $6\frac{1}{9}$

Ⓑ $5\frac{13}{20}$　　　Ⓓ $6\frac{7}{20}$

10. Which point lies outside of the circle?

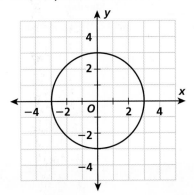

Ⓕ (−3, 0)　　　Ⓗ (3, 3)

Ⓖ (1, 2)　　　Ⓙ (−2, 1)

Make sure that your answer makes sense before marking it as your response. Reread the question and determine whether your answer is reasonable.

11. Jarvis deposits $1,200 in an account that earns 3% simple interest. How many years will it take him to earn $432 in interest?

Ⓐ 6　　Ⓑ 9　　Ⓒ 12　　Ⓓ 36

12. A baseball coach has a rule that for every time a player strikes out, that player has to do 12 push ups. If Cal strikes out 27 times, how many push ups will he be required to do?

Ⓕ 71　　　Ⓗ 314

Ⓖ 81　　　Ⓙ 324

13. Write a decimal equivalent to 60.5%.

Ⓐ 0.0605　　　Ⓒ 6.05

Ⓑ 0.605　　　Ⓓ 60.5

14. What is the denominator of the value of $\frac{3}{2} + \frac{5}{6}$ when written in simplest form?

Ⓕ 2　　Ⓖ 3　　Ⓗ 6　　Ⓙ 8

15. The graph shows the number of boys and the number of girls who participated in a talent show.

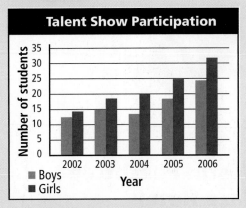

a. What is the approximate percent of increase of girls participating in the talent show from 2002 to 2005?

b. What percent of students participating in the talent show in 2006 were boys? Explain how you found your answer.

16. A homemaker association has 134 members. If 31 of these members are experts in canning vegetables, are more or less than 25% of the members canning experts? Explain how you know.

Extended Response

17. Riley and Louie each have $5,000 to invest. They both invest at a 2.5% simple interest rate.

a. Riley keeps her money invested for 7 years. How much interest will she earn? How much will her investment be worth?

b. What is the value of Louie's investment if he invests for 3 years, then removes and spends $1,000, and then invests what is remaining for 4 more years at a rate of 4%?

c. Using the information from parts a and b, who makes the most money in 7 years, Louie or Riley? Explain your reasoning.

CRCT Prep

Problem Solving on Location

GEORGIA

Atlanta

Georgia Performance Standards

M7P1.c, M7P4.c, M7P5.a

⭐ Westin Peachtree Plaza Hotel

The 73-story Westin Peachtree Plaza is one of the tallest hotels in the world. Soaring more than 720 feet above the streets of downtown Atlanta, the cylindrical building is an unmistakable jewel in the city's skyline.

Choose one or more strategies to solve each problem.

1. The hotel has dozens of conference rooms. The ratio of the capacity of the International conference room to the capacity of the Augusta conference room is 3:4. The two conference rooms have a combined capacity of 140 people. What is the capacity of each conference room?

2. The top floor of the hotel features a revolving restaurant. The restaurant makes $\frac{1}{3}$ of a complete rotation in 10 minutes. How many complete rotations does the restaurant make during the time it is open for dinner, from 6:00 P.M. to 10:00 P.M.?

For 3, use the table.

3. A high-speed elevator takes visitors to the observation deck at the top of the hotel. How long does it take the elevator to travel the 720 feet from the ground floor to the observation deck?

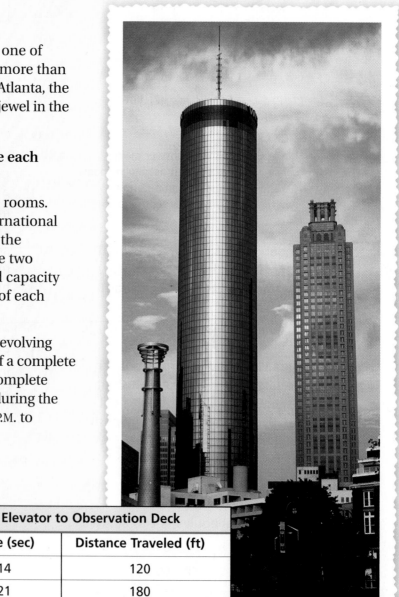

Elevator to Observation Deck	
Time (sec)	Distance Traveled (ft)
14	120
21	180
28	240

Problem Solving Strategies

Draw a Diagram
Make a Model
Guess and Test
Work Backward
Find a Pattern
Make a Table
Solve a Simpler Problem
Use Logical Reasoning
Act It Out
Make an Organized List

⭐ Georgia Peanuts

If you have eaten a peanut butter sandwich recently, you can probably thank a farmer in Georgia. Georgia produces almost half of all the peanuts grown in the United States, and 75% of the state's peanut crop is used to make peanut butter!

Choose one or more strategies to solve each problem.

1. Peanut plants are usually spaced 3 feet apart. A farmer has a square plot that is 30 feet long and 30 feet wide. Assuming plants are placed at the corners and along the edges, how many peanut plants can be grown in the plot?

2. In 2004, peanut production in Marion County was 80% of peanut production in Toombs County. Together, the two counties produced 9 million pounds of peanuts. How many pounds of peanuts were produced in Marion County?

For 3, use the graph.

3. In 2004, peanut production in Colquitt County was 75% of peanut production in Seminole County. Peanut production in Seminole County was 64% of peanut production in Georgia's top-producing county. How many pounds of peanuts were produced in Colquitt County?

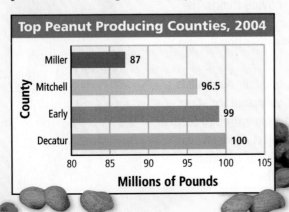

Top Peanut Producing Counties, 2004

County	Millions of Pounds
Miller	87
Mitchell	96.5
Early	99
Decatur	100

Collecting, Displaying, and Analyzing Data

CRCT PREP

go.hrw.com
Chapter Project Online
KEYWORD: MS7 Ch7

Bird	Average Number of Sightings					
	Nov	Dec	Jan	Feb	Mar	Apr
Mourning dove	7.0	8.0	9.0	8.0	6.0	5.0
Red-bellied woodpecker	1.25	1.3	1.3	1.3	1.3	1.5
Carolina chickadee	2.8	2.8	2.8	2.7	2.5	2.4

Career   *Field Biologist*

Field biologists spend time outdoors studying populations of fish, birds, and other living things. The information they collect is often used to determine whether populations are growing or declining.

Sometimes, amateur naturalists help scientists collect information. For example, people with bird feeders can report to Project FeederWatch the number and kinds of birds that they see at their feeders throughout the winter.

ARE YOU READY?

✓ Vocabulary

Choose the best term from the list to complete each sentence.

1. A part of a line consisting of two endpoints and all points between those endpoints is called a(n) __?__.

2. A(n) __?__ is the amount of space between the marked values on the __?__ of a graph.

3. The number of times an item occurs is called its __?__.

circle

frequency

interval

line segment

scale

Complete these exercises to review skills you will need for this chapter.

✓ Order Whole Numbers

Order the numbers from least to greatest.

4. 45, 23, 65, 15, 42, 18

5. 103, 105, 102, 118, 87, 104

6. 56, 65, 24, 19, 76, 33, 82

7. 8, 3, 6, 2, 5, 9, 3, 4, 2

✓ Whole Number Operations

Add or subtract.

8. 18 + 26

9. 23 + 17

10. 75 + 37

11. 98 + 64

12. 133 − 35

13. 54 − 29

14. 200 − 88

15. 1,055 − 899

✓ Locate Points on a Number Line

Copy the number line. Then graph each number.

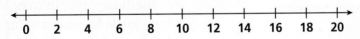

16. 15

17. 2

18. 18

19. 7

✓ Read a Table

Use the data in the table for Exercises 20 and 21.

20. Which animal is the fastest?

21. Which animal is faster, a rabbit or a zebra?

Top Speeds of Some Animals	
Animal	Speed (mi/h)
Elephant	25
Lion	50
Rabbit	35
Zebra	40

Study Guide: Preview

Where You've Been

Previously, you

- collected and organized data in frequency tables.

- found measures of central tendency and described the effects of outliers on them.

- organized data in graphic displays.

In This Chapter

You will study

- finding and selecting appropriate measures of central tendency and describing the effects of outliers on them.

- organizing data and selecting appropriate graphic displays for data.

- interpreting and analyzing data displays, drawing conclusions, and making predictions.

- identifying misleading graphs.

Where You're Going

You can use the skills learned in this chapter

- to analyze trends and make business and marketing decisions.

- to strengthen a persuasive argument by presenting data and trends in visual displays.

Key Vocabulary/Vocabulario

bar graph	gráfica de barras
circle graph	gráfica circular
frequency table	tabla de frecuencia
line graph	gráfica lineal
line plot	diagrama de acumulación
mean	media
median	mediana
mode	moda
scatter plot	diagrama de dispersión
stem-and-leaf plot	diagrama de tallo y hojas

Vocabulary Connections

To become familiar with some of the vocabulary terms in the chapter, consider the following. You may refer to the chapter, the glossary, or a dictionary if you like.

1. The word *median* comes from the Latin word *medius*, meaning "middle." What is the **median** value in a set of data? What other words come from this Latin root?

2. *Scatter* can mean "to spread out" or "to occur at random." What might the data points on a **scatter plot** look like?

3. *Frequency* is a measure of how often an event occurs or the number of like objects that are in a group. What do you think a **frequency table** might show?

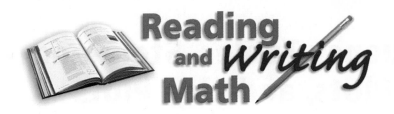 

Reading Strategy: Read a Lesson for Understanding

Before you begin reading a lesson, find out what its main focus, or objective, is. Each lesson is centered on a specific objective, which is located at the top of the first page of the lesson. Reading with the objective in mind will help guide you through the lesson material. You can use the following tips to help you follow the math as you read.

Learn to find the percent of a number.

Identify the objective of the lesson. Then skim through the lesson to get a sense of where the objective is covered.

"How do I find the percent of a number?"

As you read through the lesson, write down any questions, problems, or trouble spots you may have.

Find the percent of each number.

8% of 50

8% of 50 = 0.08 · 50   *Write the percent as a decimal.*

= 4   *Multiply.*

Work through each example, as the examples help demonstrate the objectives.

Think and Discuss

1. **Explain** how to set up a proportion to find 150% of a number.

Check your understanding of the lesson by answering the Think and Discuss questions.

Try This

Use Lesson 6-1 in your textbook to answer each question.

1. What is the objective of the lesson?

2. What new terms are defined in the lesson?

3. What skills are being taught in Example 3 of the lesson?

4. Which parts of the lesson can you use to answer Think and Discuss question 1?

Collecting, Displaying, and Analyzing Data **375**

7-1 Frequency Tables, Stem-and-Leaf Plots, and Line Plots

 **Learn** to organize and interpret data in frequency tables, stem-and-leaf plots, and line plots.

Vocabulary

frequency table

cumulative frequency

stem-and-leaf plot

line plot

Georgia Performance Standards

M7D1.b Construct frequency distributions. Also, M7D1.f, M7P4.c, M7P5.a, M7P5.b.

IMAX® theaters, with their huge screens and powerful sound systems, make viewers feel as if they are in the middle of the action. In 2005, the classic IMAX film *The Dream Is Alive* had total box office receipts of over $149 million.

To see how common it is for an IMAX movie to attract such a large number of viewers, you could use a *frequency table*. A **frequency table** is a way to organize data into categories or groups. By including a **cumulative frequency** column in your table, you can keep a running total of the number of data items.

EXAMPLE 1 Organizing and Interpreting Data in a Frequency Table

The list shows box office receipts in millions of dollars for 20 IMAX films. Make a cumulative frequency table of the data. How many films earned under $40 million?

76, 51, 41, 38, 18, 17, 16, 15, 13, 13, 12, 12, 10, 10, 6, 5, 5, 4, 4, 2

Step 1: Choose a scale that includes all of the data values. Then separate the scale into equal intervals.

Step 2: Find the number of data values in each interval. Write these numbers in the "Frequency" column.

Step 3: Find the cumulative frequency for each row by adding all the frequency values that are above or in that row.

IMAX Films		
Receipts ($ million)	Frequency	Cumulative Frequency
0–19	16	16
20–39	1	17
40–59	2	19
60–79	1	20

The number of films that earned under $40 million is the cumulative frequency of the first two rows: 17.

A **stem-and-leaf plot** uses the digits of each number to organize and display a set of data. Each *leaf* on the plot represents the right-hand digit in a data value, and each *stem* represents the remaining left-hand digits. The key shows the values of the data on the plot.

Stems	Leaves
2	4 7 9
3	0 6

Key: 2|7 means 27

EXAMPLE 2 · Organizing and Interpreting Data in a Stem-and-Leaf Plot

The table shows the number of minutes students spent doing their Spanish homework. Make a stem-and-leaf plot of the data. Then find the number of students who studied longer than 45 minutes.

Minutes Spent Doing Homework

38	48	45	32	29	48
32	45	36	22	21	64
35	45	47	26	43	29

Step 1: Order the data from least to greatest. Since the data values range from 21 to 64, use tens digits for the stems and ones digits for the leaves.

Step 2: List the stems from least to greatest on the plot.

Step 3: List the leaves for each stem from least to greatest.

Step 4: Add a key and title the graph.

Helpful Hint

To represent 5 minutes in the stem-and-leaf plot in Example 2, you would use 0 as the stem and 5 as the leaf.

Minutes Spent Doing Homework

The stems are the tens digits.

Stems	Leaves
2	1 2 6 9 9
3	2 2 5 6 8
4	3 5 5 5 7 8 8
5	
6	4

Key: 3|2 means 32

The leaves are the ones digits.

The entries in the second row represent the data values 32, 32, 35, 36, and 38.

The stem 5 has no leaves, so there are no data values in the 50's.

One student studied for **47** minutes, 2 students studied for **48** minutes, and 1 student studied for **64** minutes.
A total of 4 students studied longer than 45 minutes.

Similar to a stem-and-leaf plot, a **line plot** can be used to show how many times each data value occurs. Line plots use a number line and **X**'s to show frequency. By looking at a line plot, you can quickly see the *distribution*, or spread, of the data.

EXAMPLE 3 **Organizing and Interpreting Data in a Line Plot**

Make a line plot of the data. How many miles per day did Trey run most often?

Number of Miles Trey Ran Each Day During Training								
5	6	5	5	3	5	4	4	6
8	6	3	4	3	2	16	12	12

Step 1: The data values range from 2 to 16. Draw a number line that includes this range.

Step 2: Put an **X** above the number on the number line that corresponds to the number of miles Trey ran each day.

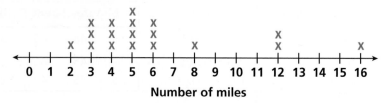

The greatest number of **X**'s appear above the number 5. This means that Trey ran 5 miles most often.

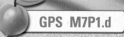

Think and Discuss GPS M7P1.d

1. **Tell** which you would use to determine the number of data values in a set: a cumulative frequency table or a stem-and-leaf plot. Explain.

7-1 Exercises

 **Georgia Performance Standards**

M7P1.a, M7P3.a, M7P5.a, M7P5.b

go.hrw.com
Homework Help Online
KEYWORD: MS7 7-1
Parent Resources Online
KEYWORD: MS7 Parent

GUIDED PRACTICE

Number of Electoral Votes for Select States (2004)											
CA	55	GA	15	IN	11	MI	17	NY	31	PA	21
NJ	15	IL	21	KY	8	NC	15	OH	20	TX	34

See Example 1. Make a cumulative frequency table of the data. How many of the states had fewer than 20 electoral votes in 2004?

See Example 2. Make a stem-and-leaf plot of the data. How many of the states had more than 30 electoral votes in 2004?

See Example 3 3. Make a line plot of the data. For the states shown, what was the most common number of electoral votes in 2004?

INDEPENDENT PRACTICE

The table shows the ages of the first 18 U.S. presidents when they took office.

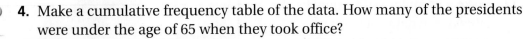

President	Age	President	Age	President	Age
Washington	57	Jackson	61	Fillmore	50
Adams	61	Van Buren	54	Pierce	48
Jefferson	57	Harrison	68	Buchanan	65
Madison	57	Tyler	51	Lincoln	52
Monroe	58	Polk	49	Johnson	56
Adams	57	Taylor	64	Grant	46

See Example ①
4. Make a cumulative frequency table of the data. How many of the presidents were under the age of 65 when they took office?

See Example ②
5. Make a stem-and-leaf plot of the data. How many of the presidents were in their 40s when they took office?

See Example ③
6. Make a line plot of the data. What was the most common age at which the presidents took office?

PRACTICE AND PROBLEM SOLVING

Extra Practice p. 739

Use the stem-and-leaf plot for Exercises 7–9.

7. What is the least data value?
What is the greatest data value?

8. Which data value occurs most often?

9. Critical Thinking Which of the following is most likely the source of the data in the stem-and-leaf plot?

    Ⓐ Shoe sizes of 12 middle school students

    Ⓑ Number of hours 12 adults exercised in one month

    Ⓒ Number of boxes of cereal per household at one time

    Ⓓ Monthly temperatures in degrees Fahrenheit in Chicago, Illinois

Stems	Leaves
0	4 6 6 9
1	2 5 8 8 8
2	0 3
3	1

Key: 1|2 means 12

10. Earth Science The table shows the masses of the largest meteorites found on Earth.

Largest Meteorites			
Meteorite	**Mass (kg)**	**Meteorite**	**Mass (kg)**
Armanty	23.5	Chupaderos	14
Bacubirito	22	Hoba	60
Campo del Cielo	15	Mbosi	16
Cape York (Agpalilik)	20	Mundrabilla	12
Cape York (Ahnighito)	31	Willamette	15

   a. Use the data in the table to make a line plot.

   b. How many of the meteorites have a mass of 15 kilograms or greater?

The map shows the number of critically endangered animal species in each country in South America. A species is critically endangered when it faces a very high risk of extinction in the wild in the near future.

11. Which country has the fewest critically endangered species? Which has the most?

12. Make a cumulative frequency table of the data. How many countries have fewer than 20 critically endangered species?

13. Make a stem-and-leaf plot of the data.

14. **Write About It** Explain how changing the size of the intervals you used in Exercise 12 affects your cumulative frequency table.

15. ★ **Challenge** In a recent year, the number of endangered animal species in the United States was 190. Show how to represent this number on a stem-and-leaf plot.

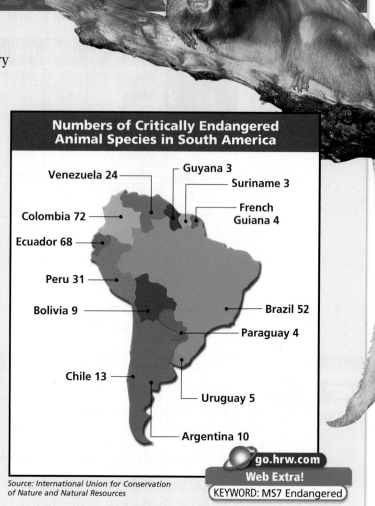

Numbers of Critically Endangered Animal Species in South America

Venezuela 24
Guyana 3
Suriname 3
French Guiana 4
Colombia 72
Ecuador 68
Peru 31
Bolivia 9
Brazil 52
Paraguay 4
Chile 13
Uruguay 5
Argentina 10

go.hrw.com
Web Extra!
KEYWORD: MS7 Endangered

Source: International Union for Conservation of Nature and Natural Resources

---

CRCT PREP • GPS SUPPORT • SPIRAL REVIEW

Use the data for Exercises 16 and 17.

16. **Multiple Choice** How many stems would a stem-and-leaf plot of the data in the table have?

20	30	9	25	28
8	11	12	7	18
33	26	10	9	2

ⓐ 1   ⓒ 3

ⓑ 2   ⓓ 4

17. **Extended Response** Make a stem-and-leaf plot and a line plot of the data in the table. Which data display best shows the distribution of data? Explain.

18. Maria has 18 yards of fabric. A pillowcase takes $1\frac{1}{5}$ yards. How many pillowcases can Maria make with the fabric? (Lesson 3-11)

Find each unit rate. Round to the nearest hundredth if necessary. (Lesson 5-2)

19. 12 hr for $102   20. $2,289 in 7 mo   21. 48 points in 3 games

7-2 Mean, Median, Mode, and Range

 **to find the** mean, median, mode, and range of a data set.

Vocabulary

mean

median

mode

range

outlier

Georgia Performance Standards

M7D1.c Analyze data using measures of central tendency, including recognition of outliers. Also, M7D1.b, M7D1.f, M7D1.g, M7P1.b.

To crack secret messages in code, you can list the number of times each symbol of the code appears in the message. The symbol that appears the most often represents the *mode*, which likely corresponds to the letter *e*.

The mode, along with the *mean* and the *median*, is a measure of *central tendency* used to represent the "middle" of a data set.

Navajo Code Talkers used the Navajo language as the basis of a code in World War II.

- The **mean** is the sum of the data values divided by the number of data items.

- The **median** is the middle value of an odd number of data items arranged in order. For an even number of data items, the median is the mean of the two middle values.

- The **mode** is the value or values that occur most often. When all the data values occur the same number of times, there is no mode.

The **range** of a set of data is the difference between the greatest and least values.

EXAMPLE 1 Finding the Mean, Median, Mode, and Range of a Data Set

Find the mean, median, mode, and range of the data set.

$$2, 1, 8, 0, 2, 4, 3, 4$$

mean:

$2 + 1 + 8 + 0 + 2 + 4 + 3 + 4 = 24$ *Add the values.*

$24 \div 8 = 3$ *Divide the sum by the number of items.*

The mean is 3.

median:

$0, 1, 2, 2, 3, 4, 4, 8$ *Arrange the values in order.*

$\dfrac{2 + 3}{2} = 2.5$ *There are two middle values, so find the mean of these values.*

The median is 2.5.

mode:

$0, 1, 2, 2, 3, 4, 4, 8$ *The values 2 and 4 occur twice.*

The modes are 2 and 4.

range: $8 - 0 = 8$ *Subtract the least value from the greatest value.*

The range is 8.

> **Helpful Hint**
>
> The mean is sometimes called the *average*.

Often one measure of central tendency is more appropriate for describing a set of data than another measure is. Think about what each measure tells you about the data. Then choose the measure that best answers the question being asked.

EXAMPLE 2 **Choosing the Best Measure to Describe a Set of Data**

The line plot shows the number of hours 15 people exercised in one week. Which measure of central tendency best describes these data? Justify your answer.

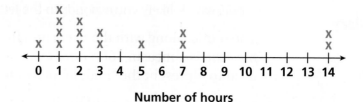

Number of hours

mean:

$$\frac{0 + 1 + 1 + 1 + 1 + 2 + 2 + 2 + 3 + 3 + 5 + 7 + 7 + 14 + 14}{15} = \frac{63}{15} = 4.2$$

The mean is 4.2.

Most of the people exercised fewer than 4 hours, so the mean does not describe the data set best.

median:

0, 1, 1, 1, 1, 2, 2, **2**, 3, 3, 5, 7, 7, 14, 14

The median is 2.

The median best describes the data set because a majority of the data is clustered around the data value 2.

mode:

The greatest number of **X**'s occur above the number 1 on the line plot.

The mode is 1.

The mode represents only 4 of the 15 people. The mode does not describe the entire data set.

In the data set in Example 2, the value **14** is much greater than the other values in the set. An extreme value such as this is called an **outlier** . Outliers can greatly affect the mean of a data set.

Measure	Most Useful When
mean	the data are spread fairly evenly
median	the data set has an outlier
mode	the data involve a subject in which many data points of one value are important, such as election results

EXAMPLE 3 **Exploring the Effects of Outliers on Measures of Central Tendency**

The table shows the number of art pieces created by students in a glass-blowing workshop. Identify the outlier in the data set, and determine how the outlier affects the mean, median, and mode of the data. Then tell which measure of central tendency best describes the data with and without the outlier.

Name	Number of Pieces
Suzanne	5
Glen	1
Charissa	3
Eileen	4
Hermann	14
Tom	2

The outlier is 14.

Without the Outlier

mean:

$$\frac{5 + 1 + 3 + 4 + 2}{5} = 3$$

The mean is 3.
The outlier increases the mean of the data by about 1.8.

median:

1, 2, **3**, 4, 5

The median is 3.
The outlier increases the median of the data by 0.5.

mode:

There is no mode.
The outlier does not change the mode of the data.

With the Outlier

mean:

$$\frac{5 + 1 + 3 + 4 + 14 + 2}{6} \approx 4.8$$

The mean is about 4.8.

median:

1, 2, **3**, **4**, 5, 14

$$\frac{3 + 4}{2} = 3.5$$

The median is 3.5.

mode:

There is no mode.

The median best describes the data with the outlier. The mean and median best describe the data without the outlier.

> **Caution!**
>
> Since all the data values occur the same number of times, the set has no mode.

Think and Discuss  GPS M7P1.d, M7P2.c

1. **Describe** a situation in which the mean would best describe a data set.

2. **Tell** which measure of central tendency must be a data value.

3. **Explain** how an outlier affects the mean, median, and mode of a data set.

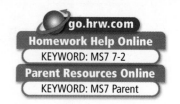
7-2 Exercises

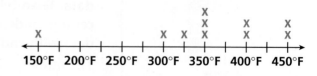
Georgia Performance Standards

M7P3.a, M7P4.c, M7P5.b

GUIDED PRACTICE

See Example **Find the mean, median, mode, and range of each data set.**

1. 5, 30, 35, 20, 5, 25, 20

2. 44, 68, 48, 61, 59, 48, 63, 49

See Example 2 **3.** The line plot shows cooking temperatures required by different recipes. Which measure of central tendency best describes the data? Justify your answer.

See Example **4.** The table shows the number of glasses of water consumed in one day. Identify the outlier in the data set. Then determine how the outlier affects the mean, median, and mode of the data. Then tell which measure of central tendency best describes the data with and without the outlier.

Water Consumption							
Name	Randy	Lori	Anita	Jana	Sonya	Victor	Mark	Jorge
Glasses	4	12	3	1	4	7	5	4

INDEPENDENT PRACTICE

See Example 1 **Find the mean, median, mode, and range of each data set.**

5. 92, 88, 65, 68, 76, 90, 84, 88, 93, 89

6. 23, 43, 5, 3, 4, 14, 24, 15, 15, 13

7. 2.0, 4.4, 6.2, 3.2, 4.4, 6.2, 3.7

8. 13.1, 7.5, 3.9, 4.8, 17.1, 14.6, 8.3, 3.9

See Example 2 **9.** The line plot shows the number of letters in the spellings of the 12 months. Which measure of central tendency best describes the data set? Justify your answer.

See Example **Identify the outlier in each data set. Then determine how the outlier affects the mean, median, and mode of the data. Then tell which measure of central tendency best describes the data with and without the outlier.**

10. 13, 18, 20, 5, 15, 20, 13, 20

11. 45, 48, 63, 85, 151, 47, 88, 44, 68

PRACTICE AND PROBLEM SOLVING

CRCT GPS

Extra Practice p. 739

12. **Health** Based on the data from three annual checkups, Jon's mean height is 62 in. At the first two checkups Jon's height was 58 in. and 61 in. What was his height at the third checkup?

13. Find the mean, median, and mode of the data displayed in the line plot. Then determine how the outlier affects the mean.

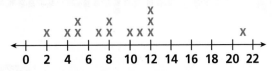

14. Critical Thinking The values in a data set are 95, 93, 91, 95, 100, 99, and 92. What value can be added to the set so that the mean, median, and mode remain the same?

15. Sports The ages of the participants in a mountain bike race are 14, 23, 20, 24, 26, 17, 21, 31, 27, 25, 14, and 28. Which measure of central tendency best represents the ages of the participants? Explain.

16. Estimation The table shows the monthly rainfall in inches for six months. Estimate the mean, median, and range of the data.

Month	Rainfall (in.)
Jan	4.33
Feb	1.62
Mar	2.17
Apr	0.56
May	3.35
Jun	1.14

17. What's the Question? The values in a data set are 10, 7, 9, 5, 13, 10, 7, 14, 8, and 11. What is the question about central tendency that gives the answer 9.5 for the data set?

18. Write About It Which measure of central tendency is most often affected by including an outlier? Explain.

19. Challenge Pick a measure of central tendency that describes each situation. Explain your choice.

a. the number of siblings in a family **b.** the number of days in a month

---

CRCT PREP • GPS SUPPORT • SPIRAL REVIEW

20. Multiple Choice What is the mean of the winning scores shown in the table?

Masters Tournament Winning Scores					
Year	2001	2002	2003	2004	2005
Score	272	276	281	279	276

Ⓐ 276   Ⓒ 282.1

Ⓑ 276.8   Ⓓ 285

21. Multiple Choice In which data set are the mean, median, and mode all the same number?

Ⓕ 6, 2, 5, 4, 3, 4, 1   Ⓗ 2, 3, 7, 3, 8, 3, 2

Ⓖ 4, 2, 2, 1, 3, 2, 3   Ⓙ 4, 3, 4, 3, 4, 6, 4

22. Brett deposits $4,000 in an account that earns 4.5% simple interest. How long will it be before the total amount is $4,800? (Lesson 6-7)

23. Make a stem-and-leaf plot of the following data: 48, 60, 57, 62, 43, 62, 45, and 51. (Lesson 7-1)

Learn to display and analyze data in bar graphs and histograms.

Vocabulary

bar graph

double-bar graph

histogram

Hundreds of different languages are spoken around the world. The graph shows the numbers of native speakers of four languages.

A **bar graph** can be used to display and compare data. The scale of a bar graph should include all the data values and be easily divided into equal intervals.

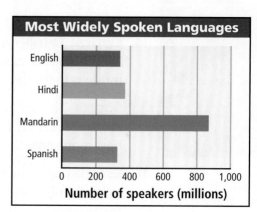
Most Widely Spoken Languages

Number of speakers (millions)

EXAMPLE 1 Interpreting a Bar Graph

Use the bar graph to answer each question.

A Which language has the most native speakers?

The bar for Mandarin is the longest, so Mandarin has the most native speakers.

B About how many more people speak Mandarin than speak Hindi?

About 500 million more people speak Mandarin than speak Hindi.

 Georgia Performance Standards

M7D1.f Analyze data using appropriate graphs. Also, M7D1.g, M7P4.c, M7P5.a, M7P5.b.

You can use a **double-bar graph** to compare two related sets of data.

EXAMPLE 2 Making a Double-Bar Graph

The table shows the life expectancies of people in three Central American countries. Make a double-bar graph of the data.

Country	Male	Female
El Salvador	67	74
Honduras	63	66
Nicaragua	65	70

Step 1: Choose a scale and interval for the vertical axis.

Step 2: Draw a pair of bars for each country's data. Use different colors to show males and females.

Step 3: Label the axes and give the graph a title.

Step 4: Make a key to show what each bar represents.

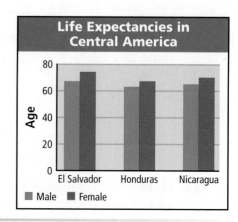
Life Expectancies in Central America

Age

El Salvador   Honduras   Nicaragua

■ Male   ■ Female

A **histogram** is a bar graph that shows the frequency of data within equal intervals. There is no space between the bars in a histogram.

EXAMPLE 3 Making a Histogram

The table below shows survey results about the number of CDs students own. Make a histogram of the data.

Number of CDs									
1	///	5	JHT I	9	JHT I	13	JHT ////	17	JHT ////
2	//	6	///	10	JHT JHT	14	JHT JHT I	18	JHT //
3	JHT	7	JHT ///	11	JHT JHT I	15	JHT JHT I	19	//
4	JHT I	8	JHT //	12	JHT JHT	16	JHT JHT I	20	JHT I

Step 1: Make a frequency table of the data. Be sure to use a scale that includes all of the data values and separate the scale into equal intervals. Use these intervals on the horizontal axis of your histogram.

Number of CDs	Frequency
1–5	22
6–10	34
11–15	52
16–20	35

Step 2: Choose an appropriate scale and interval for the vertical axis. The greatest value on the scale should be at least as great as the greatest frequency.

Step 3: Draw a bar for each interval. The height of the bar is the frequency for that interval. Bars must touch but not overlap.

Step 4: Label the axes and give the graph a title.

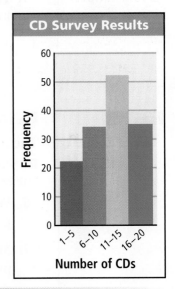

Think and Discuss GPS M7P1.d, M7P3.b

1. Explain how to use the frequency table in Example 3 to find the number of students surveyed.

2. Explain why you might use a double-bar graph instead of two separate bar graphs to display data.

3. Describe the similarities and differences between a bar graph and a histogram.

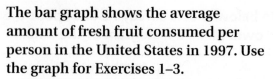

Georgia Performance
Standards

M7P1.a, M7P1.b, M7P5.a,
M7P5.b

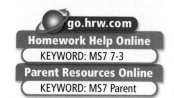
go.hrw.com
Homework Help Online
KEYWORD: MS7 7-3
Parent Resources Online
KEYWORD: MS7 Parent

GUIDED PRACTICE

See Example   The bar graph shows the average amount of fresh fruit consumed per person in the United States in 1997. Use the graph for Exercises 1–3.

1. Which fruit was eaten the least?

2. About how many pounds of apples were eaten per person?

3. About how many more pounds of bananas than pounds of oranges were eaten per person?

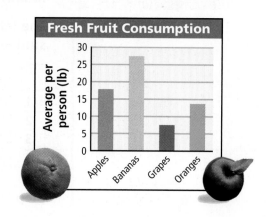

See Example   **4.** The table shows national average SAT scores for three years. Make a double-bar graph of the data.

See Example   **5.** The list below shows the ages of musicians in a local orchestra. Make a histogram of the data.

14, 35, 22, 18, 49, 38, 30, 27, 45, 19, 35, 46, 27, 21, 32, 30

Year	Verbal	Math
1980	502	492
1990	500	501
2000	505	514

INDEPENDENT PRACTICE

See Example   The bar graph shows the maximum precipitation in 24 hours for several states. Use the graph for Exercises 6–8.

6. Which state received the most precipitation in 24 hours?

7. About how many inches of precipitation did Virginia receive?

8. About how many more inches of precipitation did Oklahoma receive than Indiana?

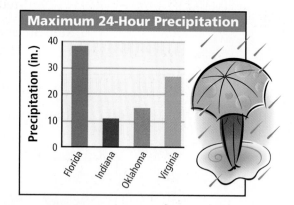

See Example   **9.** The table shows the average annual income per capita for three Chinese cities. Make a double-bar graph of the data.

See Example   **10.** The list below shows the results of a typing test in words per minute. Make a histogram of the data.

Extra Practice p. 739

62, 55, 68, 47, 50, 41, 62, 39, 54, 70, 56, 47, 71, 55, 60, 42

City	1994	2000
Beijing	$614	$1,256
Shanghai	$716	$1,424
Shenzhen	$1,324	$2,626

In 1896 and 1900, William McKinley, a Republican, and William Jennings Bryan, a Democrat, ran for president of the United States. The table shows the number of electoral votes each man received in these elections.

11. Use the data in the table to make a double-bar graph. Label the horizontal axis with the years.

Candidate	1896	1900
McKinley	271	292
Bryan	176	155

William Jennings Bryan

12. Estimation In 1896, about how many more electoral votes did McKinley get than Bryan?

13. The frequency table shows the number of years the first 42 presidents spent in office. Can you tell how many presidents spent exactly six years in office? Explain.

Years in Office	Frequency
0–2	7
3–5	22
6–8	12
9–11	0
12–14	1

14. Use the frequency table to make a histogram.

15. Write About It What does your histogram show you about the number of years the presidents spent in office?

William McKinley

CRCT PREP • GPS SUPPORT • SPIRAL REVIEW

Use the graph for Exercises 16 and 17.

16. Multiple Choice In which year did the Democrats get the fewest number of electoral votes?

   Ⓐ 1988   Ⓒ 2000

   Ⓑ 1996   Ⓓ 2004

Electoral Votes Cast

Number of votes — 1988, 1992, 1996, 2000, 2004 — **Year**

■ Democrats ■ Republicans

17. Multiple Choice In which year was the difference between the number of electoral votes for the Republicans and Democrats the least?

   Ⓕ 1988   Ⓖ 1992   Ⓗ 2000   Ⓙ 2004

Determine whether the ratios are proportional. (Lesson 5-4)

18. $\frac{10}{24}, \frac{15}{36}$ **19.** $\frac{5}{22}, \frac{10}{27}$ **20.** $\frac{2}{20}, \frac{3}{30}$ **21.** $\frac{72}{96}, \frac{9}{12}$

Find the mean, median, mode, and range of each data set. (Lesson 7-2)

22. 42, 29, 49, 32, 19   **23.** 15, 34, 26, 15, 21, 30   **24.** 4, 3, 3, 3, 3, 4, 1

7-4 Reading and Interpreting Circle Graphs

Learn to read and interpret data presented in circle graphs.

Vocabulary

circle graph

sector

🍎 **Georgia Performance Standards**

M7D1.g Analyze and draw conclusions about data. Also, M7D1.f, M7P4.c, M7P5.b.

A **circle graph**, also called a pie chart, shows how a set of data is divided into parts. The entire circle contains 100% of the data. Each **sector**, or slice, of the circle represents one part of the entire data set.

The circle graph compares the number of species in each group of echinoderms. Echinoderms are marine animals that live on the ocean floor. The name *echinoderm* means "spiny-skinned."

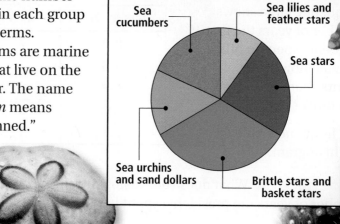

Species of Echinoderms

Sea cucumbers

Sea lilies and feather stars

Sea stars

Sea urchins and sand dollars

Brittle stars and basket stars

E X A M P L E (**1**) **Life Science Application**

Use the circle graph to answer each question.

A Which group of echinoderms includes the greatest number of species?

The sector for brittle stars and basket stars is the largest, so this group includes the greatest number of species.

B Approximately what percent of echinoderm species are sea stars?

The sector for sea stars makes up about one-fourth of the circle. Since the circle shows 100% of the data, about one-fourth of 100%, or 25%, of echinoderm species are sea stars.

C Which group is made up of fewer species—sea cucumbers or sea urchins and sand dollars?

The sector for sea urchins and sand dollars is smaller than the sector for sea cucumbers. This means there are fewer species of sea urchins and sand dollars than species of sea cucumbers.

EXAMPLE 2 Interpreting Circle Graphs

Leon surveyed 30 people about pet ownership. The circle graph shows his results. Use the graph to answer each question.

A **How many people do not own pets?**

The circle graph shows that 50% of the 30 people do not own pets.

$$50\% \text{ of } 30 = 0.5 \cdot 30$$
$$= 15$$

Fifteen people do not own pets.

B **How many people own cats only?**

The circle graph shows that 20% of the 30 people own cats only.

$$20\% \text{ of } 30 = 0.2 \cdot 30$$
$$= 6$$

Six people own cats only.

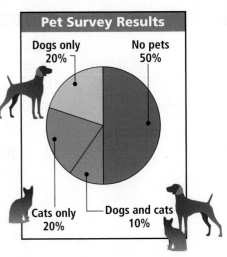

Pet Survey Results

Dogs only 20%
No pets 50%
Cats only 20%
Dogs and cats 10%

EXAMPLE 3 Choosing an Appropriate Graph

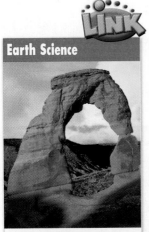

Earth Science

Arches National Park, located in southeastern Utah, covers 73,379 acres. The park is famous for its natural sandstone arches.

Decide whether a bar graph or a circle graph would best display the information. Explain your answer.

A **the percent of a nation's electricity supply generated by each of several fuel sources**

A circle graph is the better choice because it makes it easy to see what part of the nation's electricity comes from each fuel source.

B **the number of participants visitors to Arches National Park in each of the last five years**

A bar graph is the better choice because it makes it easy to see how the number of visitors has changed over the years.

C **the comparison between the time spent in math class and the total time spent in school each day**

A circle graph is the better choice because the sector that represents the time spent in math class could be compared to the entire circle, which represents the total time spent in school.

Think and Discuss  GPS M7P1.d, M7P3.b

1. **Describe** two ways a circle graph can be used to compare data.

2. **Compare** the use of circle graphs with the use of bar graphs to display data.

Georgia Performance Standards
M7P3.a, M7P3.c, M7P4.c, M7P5.b

GUIDED PRACTICE

The circle graph shows the estimated spending on advertising in 2000. Use the graph for Exercises 1–3.

Money Spent on Advertising

Source: USA Today

See Example 1

1. On which type of advertising was the least amount of money spent?

2. Approximately what percent of spending was on radio and magazine advertising?

See Example 2

3. Television and magazine advertising made up about 50% of all advertising spending in 2000. If the total amount spent was $100,000, about how much was spent on television and magazine advertising?

See Example 3

Decide whether a bar graph or a circle graph would best display the information. Explain your answer.

4. the lengths of the five longest rivers in the world

5. the percent of citizens who voted for each candidate in an election

INDEPENDENT PRACTICE

The circle graph shows the results of a survey of 100 teens who were asked about their favorite sports. Use the graph for Exercises 6–8.

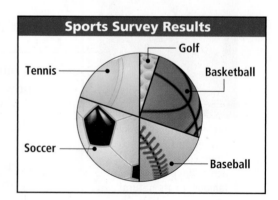

Sports Survey Results

See Example 1

6. Did more teens pick basketball or tennis as their favorite sport?

7. Approximately what percent of teens picked soccer as their favorite sport?

See Example 2

8. According to the survey, 5% of teens chose golf. What is the number of teens who chose golf?

See Example 3

Decide whether a bar graph or a circle graph would best display the information. Explain your answer.

9. the number of calories eaten at breakfast compared with the total number of calories eaten in one day

10. the number of inches of rain that fell each month in Honolulu, Hawaii, during one year

PRACTICE AND PROBLEM SOLVING

CRCT GPS

Extra Practice p. 739

Geography The circle graph shows the percent of Earth's land area covered by each continent. Use the graph for Exercises 11–13.

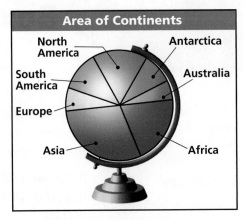

Area of Continents

11. List the continents in order of size, from largest to smallest.

12. Approximately what percent of Earth's total land area is Asia?

13. Approximately what percent of Earth's total land area is North America and South America combined?

14. **Critical Thinking** A group of 200 students were asked how they like to spend their free time. Of the students surveyed, 47% said they like to play on the computer, 59% said they like to go to the mall, 38% said they like to go to the movies, and 41% said they like to play sports. Can you make a circle graph to display this data? Explain.

15. **What's the Error?** The table shows the types of pets owned by a group of students. A circle graph of the data shows that 25% of the students surveyed own a dog. Why is the graph incorrect?

16. **Write About It** What math skills do you use when interpreting information in a circle graph?

Pet	Number of Students
Cat	𝍤𝍤𝍤
Dog	𝍤𝍤 𝍵
Fish	𝍤
Other	𝍤

17. **Challenge** Earth's total land area is approximately 57,900,000 square miles. Antarctica is almost 10% of the total area. What is the approximate land area of Antarctica in square miles?

CRCT PREP • GPS SUPPORT • SPIRAL REVIEW

Use the graph for Exercises 18 and 19.

18. **Multiple Choice** Approximately what percent of the medals won by the United States were gold?

　Ⓐ 25%　　Ⓑ 40%　　Ⓒ 50%　　Ⓓ 75%

19. **Short Response** The United States won a total of 502 medals in the Summer Olympics from 1988 to 2004. About how many of these were bronze medals? Show your work.

U.S. Distribution of Medals Summer Olympics, 1988–2004

Bronze

Gold

Silver

20. José has an American flag that measures 10 inches by 19 inches. He paints a picture of a flag that is 60 inches by 114 inches. Will his painted flag be similar to the American flag? (Lesson 5-7)

Compare. Write <, >, or =. (Lesson 6-2)

21. 0.1 ▨ 0.09　　22. 1.71 ▨ $\frac{24}{11}$　　23. 1.25 ▨ 125%　　24. 32.5 ▨ 69%

Box-and-Whisker Plots

Learn to display and analyze data in box-and-whisker plots.

Vocabulary

box-and-whisker plot

lower quartile

upper quartile

interquartile range

Carson is planning a deep-sea fishing trip. He chooses a fishing charter based on the number of fish caught on different charters.

A **box-and-whisker plot** uses a number line to show the distribution of a set of data.

To make a box-and-whisker plot, first divide the data into four parts using *quartiles*. The median, or *middle quartile*, divides the data into a lower half and an upper half. The median of the lower half is the **lower quartile**, and the median of the upper half is the **upper quartile**.

EXAMPLE 1 Making a Box-and-Whisker Plot

Use the data to make a box-and-whisker plot.

26, 17, 21, 23, 19, 28, 17, 20, 29

Step 1: Order the data from least to greatest. Then find the least and greatest values, the median, and the lower and upper quartiles.

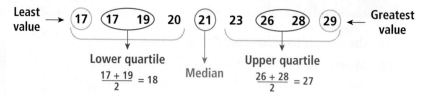

Step 2: Draw a number line. Above the number line, plot a point for each value in Step 1.

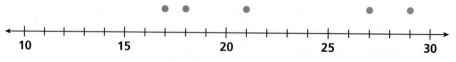

Step 3: Draw a box from the lower to the upper quartile. Inside the box, draw a vertical line through the median. Then draw the "whiskers" from the box to the least and greatest values.

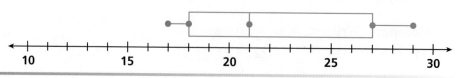

Caution!

To find the median of a data set with an even number of values, find the mean of the two middle values.

Georgia Performance Standards

M7D1.d Analyze data with respect to measures of variation (range, quartiles, interquartile range). Also, M7D1.c, M7D1.f, M7D1.g, M7P5.a.

The **interquartile range** of a data set is the difference between the lower and upper quartiles. It tells how large the spread of data around the median is.

You can use a box-and-whisker plot to analyze how data in a set are distributed. You can also use box-and-whisker plots to help you compare two sets of data.

EXAMPLE 2 **Comparing Box-and-Whisker Plots**

The box-and-whisker plots below show the distribution of the number of fish caught per trip by two fishing charters.

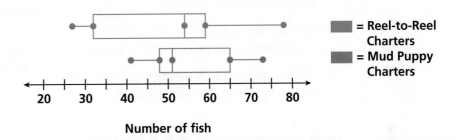

A Which fishing charter has a greater median?

The median number of fish caught on Reel-to-Reel Charters, about 54, is greater than the median number of fish caught on Mud Puppy Charters, about 51.

B Which fishing charter has a greater interquartile range?

The length of the box in a box-and-whisker plot indicates the interquartile range. Reel-to-Reel Charters has a longer box, so it has a greater interquartile range.

C Which fishing charter appears to be more predictable in the number of fish that might be caught on a fishing trip?

The range and interquartile range are smaller for Mud Puppy Charters, which means that there is less variation in the data. So the number of fish caught on Mud Puppy Charters is more predictable.

Think and Discuss

1. **Describe** what you can tell about a data set from a box-and-whisker plot.

2. **Explain** how the range and the interquartile range of a set of data are different. Which measure tells you more about central tendency?

Georgia Performance Standards

M7P1.b, M7P3.a, M7P3.c, M7P5.a

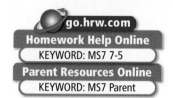

go.hrw.com
Homework Help Online
KEYWORD: MS7 7-5
Parent Resources Online
KEYWORD: MS7 Parent

GUIDED PRACTICE

See Example **1** Use the data to make a box-and-whisker plot.

1. 46   35   46   38   37   33   49   42   35   40   37

See Example **2** Use the box-and-whisker plots of inches flown by two different paper airplanes for Exercises 2–4.

2. Which paper airplane has a greater median flight length?

3. Which paper airplane has a greater interquartile range of flight lengths?

4. Which paper airplane appears to have a more predictable flight length?

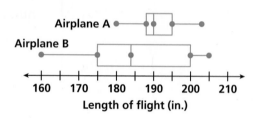

INDEPENDENT PRACTICE

See Example **1** Use the data to make a box-and-whisker plot.

5. 81   73   88   85   81   72   86   72   79   75   76

See Example **2** Use the box-and-whisker plots of apartment rental costs in two different cities for Exercises 6–8.

6. Which city has a greater median apartment rental cost?

7. Which city has a greater interquartile range of apartment rental costs?

8. Which city appears to have a more predictable apartment rental cost?

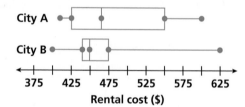

PRACTICE AND PROBLEM SOLVING

CRCT GPS

Extra Practice p. 739

The points scored per game by a basketball player are shown below. Use the data for Exercises 9–11.

12   7   15   23   10   18   39   15   20   8   13

9. Make two box-and-whisker plots of the data on the same number line: one plot with the outlier and one plot without the outlier.

10. How does the outlier affect the interquartile range of the data?

11. Which is affected more by the outlier: the range or the interquartile range?

12. Make a box-and-whisker plot of the data shown in the line plot.

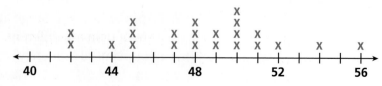

13. **Sports** The table shows the countries that were the top 15 medal winners in the 2004 Olympics.

Country	Medals	Country	Medals	Country	Medals
USA	103	Russia	92	China	63
Australia	49	Germany	48	Japan	37
France	33	Italy	32	Britain	30
Korea	30	Cuba	27	Ukraine	23
Netherlands	22	Romania	19	Spain	19

a. Make a box-and-whisker plot of the data.

b. Describe the distribution of the number of medals won.

14. **Measurement** The stem-and-leaf plot shows the heights in inches of a class of seventh graders.

a. Make a box-and-whisker plot of the data.

b. Three-fourths of the students are taller than what height?

c. Three-fourths of the students are shorter than what height?

Student Heights

Stems	Leaves
5	3 5 6 6 8 8 8 9 9
6	0 0 1 1 1 1 1 2 2 2 4

Key: 5|3 means 53

 15. **What's the Error?** Using the data 2, 9, 5, 14, 8, 13, 7, 5, and 8, a student found the upper quartile to be 9. What did the student do wrong?

 16. **Write About It** Two box-and-whisker plots have the same median and equally long whiskers. If the box of one plot is longer, what can you say about the difference between the two data sets?

17. **Challenge** An outlier is defined to be at least 1.5 times the interquartile range. Name the value that would be considered an outlier in the data set 1, 2, 4, 2, 1, 0, 6, 8, 1, 6, and 2.

CRCT PREP • GPS SUPPORT • SPIRAL REVIEW

Use the graph for Exercises 18 and 19.

18. **Multiple Choice** What is the difference between the interquartile ranges for the two data sets?

Ⓐ 21   Ⓒ 9

Ⓑ 18   Ⓓ 0

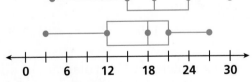

19. **Gridded Response** What is the lower quartile of the box-and-whisker plot with the greater range?

20. A tree casts a 21.25 ft shadow, while a 6 ft tall man casts a 10.5 ft shadow. Estimate the height of the tree. (Lesson 5-8)

21. Mari spent $24.69 on lunch with her mom. About how much should she leave for a 15% tip? (Lesson 6-3)

Use Venn Diagrams to Display Collected Data

Use with Lesson 7-5

Georgia Performance Standards
M7D1.a, M7D1.f, M7P5.a

go.hrw.com
Lab Resources Online
KEYWORD: MS7 Lab7

You can use a Venn diagram to display relationships in data. Use ovals, circles, or other shapes to represent individual data sets.

Activity 1

At Landry Middle School, 127 students play a team sport, 145 play a musical instrument, and 31 do both. Make a Venn diagram to display the relationship in the data.

1 Draw and label two overlapping circles to represent the sets of students who play a team sport and a musical instrument. Label one "Team sport" and the other "Musical instrument."

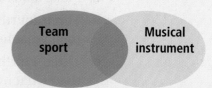

2 Write "31" in the area where the circles overlap. This is the number of students who play a musical instrument and a team sport.

3 To find the number of students who play a team sport *only*, begin with the number of students who play a team sport, 127, and subtract the number of students who do both, 31.

team sport	−	both	=	team sport *only*
127	−	31	=	96

Use the same process to find the number of students who play a musical instrument *only*.

musical instrument	−	both	=	musical instrument *only*
145	−	31	=	114

4 Complete the Venn diagram by adding the number of students who play *only* a team sport and the number of students who play *only* a musical instrument to the diagram.

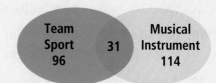

Think and Discuss

1. Explain why some of the numbers that were given in Activity 1, such as 127 and 145, do not appear in the Venn diagram.

2. Describe a Venn diagram that has three individual data sets. How many overlapping areas does it have?

Try This

Responding to a survey about favorite foods, 60 people said they like pasta, 45 said they like chicken, and 70 said they like hot dogs. Also, 15 people said they like both chicken and pasta, 22 said they like both hot dogs and chicken, and 17 said they like both hot dogs and pasta. Only 8 people said they like all 3 foods.

1. How many people like only pasta?

2. How many people like only chicken?

3. How many people like only hot dogs?

4. Make a Venn diagram to show the relationships in the data.

Activity 2

1. Interview your classmates to find out what kinds of movies they like (for example, action, comedy, drama, and horror).

2. Make a Venn diagram to show the relationships in the collected data.

Think and Discuss

1. Tell how many individual sets and how many overlapping areas a Venn diagram of the movie data will have.

2. Describe what a Venn diagram of student ages might look like. Would there be any overlapping sets? Explain.

Try This

1. Interview your classmates to find out what kinds of sports they like to play. Make a Venn diagram to show the relationships in the data.

2. The Venn diagram shows the types of exercise that some students do.

   a. How many students were surveyed?

   b. How many students jog?

   c. How many students like to both bike and walk?

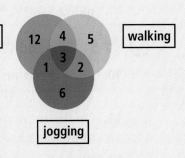

Quiz for Lessons 7-1 Through 7-5

✓ **7-1** **Frequency Tables, Stem-and-Leaf Plots, and Line Plots**

The list shows the top speeds of various land animals.

42 55 62 48 65 51 47 59 67 61 49 54 55 52 44

1. Make a cumulative frequency table of the data.

2. Make a stem-and-leaf plot of the data.

3. Make a line plot of the data.

✓ **7-2** **Mean, Median, Mode, and Range**

The list shows the life spans in years of vampire bats in captivity.

18 22 5 21 19 21 17 3 19 20 29 18 17

4. Find the mean, median, mode, and range of the data. Round your answers to the nearest tenth of a year.

5. Which measure of central tendency best represents the data? Explain.

✓ **7-3** **Bar Graphs and Histograms**

6. The table shows the numbers of students in the sixth and seventh grades who participated in school fairs. Make a double-bar graph of the data.

7. The list below shows the numbers of tracks on a group of CDs. Make a histogram of the data.

13, 7, 10, 8, 15, 17, 22, 9, 11, 10, 16, 12, 9, 20

School Fair Participation		
Fair	Sixth Grade	Seventh Grade
Book	55	76
Health	69	58
Science	74	98

✓ **7-4** **Reading and Interpreting Circle Graphs**

Use the circle graph for problems 8 and 9.

8. Approximately what percent of students picked cheese as their favorite topping?

9. Out of 200 students, 25% picked pepperoni as their favorite pizza topping. How many students picked pepperoni?

Favorite Pizza Toppings

Cheese · Pepperoni · Green peppers · Sausage · Mushrooms

✓ **7-5** **Box-and-Whisker Plots**

10. Make a box-and-whisker plot of the data 14, 8, 13, 20, 15, 17, 1, 12, 18, and 10.

11. On the same number line, make a box-and-whisker plot of the data 3, 8, 5, 12, 6, 18, 14, 8, 15, and 11.

12. Which box-and-whisker plot has a greater interquartile range?

Focus on Problem Solving

 Solve

• **Choose an operation: addition or subtraction**

In order to decide whether to add or subtract to solve a problem, you need to determine what action is taking place in the problem. If you are combining or putting together numbers, you need to add. If you are taking away or finding how far apart two numbers are, you need to subtract.

 Determine the action in each problem. Then determine which operation could be used to solve the problem. Use the table for problems 5 and 6.

1 Betty, Raymond, and Helen ran a three-person relay race. Their individual times were 48 seconds, 55 seconds, and 51 seconds. What was their total time?

2 The Scots pine and the sessile oak are trees native to Northern Ireland. The height of a mature Scots pine is 111 feet, and the height of a mature sessile oak is 90 feet. How much taller is the Scots pine than the sessile oak?

3 Mr. Hutchins has $35.00 to buy supplies for his social studies class. He wants to buy items that cost $19.75, $8.49, and $7.10. Does Mr. Hutchins have enough money to buy all of the supplies?

4 The running time for the 1998 movie *Antz* is 83 minutes. Jordan has watched 25 minutes of the movie. How many minutes does he have left to watch?

Sizes of Marine Mammals	
Mammal	**Weight (kg)**
Killer whale	3,600
Manatee	400
Sea lion	200
Walrus	750

5 The table gives the approximate weights of four marine mammals. How much more does the killer whale weigh than the sea lion?

6 Find the total weight of the manatee, the sea lion, and the walrus. Do these three mammals together weigh more or less than the killer whale?

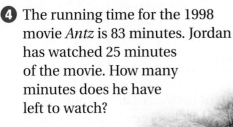

7-6 Line Graphs

Learn to display and analyze data in line graphs.

Vocabulary

line graph

double-line graph

You can use a *line graph* to show how data changes over a period of time. In a **line graph**, line segments are used to connect data points on a coordinate grid. The result is a visual record of change.

Line graphs can be used for a variety of reasons, including showing the growth of a cat over time.

EXAMPLE 1 Making a Line Graph

Make a line graph of the data in the table. Use the graph to determine during which 2-month period the kitten's weight increased the most.

Age (mo)	Weight (lb)
0	0.2
2	1.7
4	3.8
6	5.1
8	6.0
10	6.7
12	7.2

Step 1: Determine the scale and interval for each axis. Place units of time on the horizontal axis.

Helpful Hint

To plot each point, start at zero. Move *right* for the time and *up* for the weight.

Step 2: Plot a point for each pair of values. Connect the points using line segments.

Step 3: Label the axes and give the graph a title.

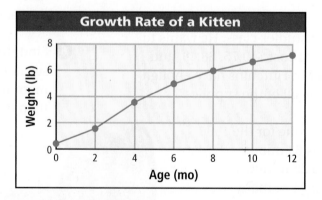

The graph shows the steepest line segment between 2 and 4 months. This means the kitten's weight increased most between 2 and 4 months.

Georgia Performance Standards

M7D1.f Analyze data using appropriate graphs, including line graphs. Also, M7D1.g, M7P5.a, M7P5.b.

You can use a line graph to estimate values between data points.

EXAMPLE 2 Using a Line Graph to Estimate Data

Use the graph to estimate the population of Florida in 1990.

To estimate the population in 1990, find the point on the line between 1980 and 2000 that corresponds to 1990.

The graph shows about 12.5 million. In fact, the population was 12.9 million in 1990.

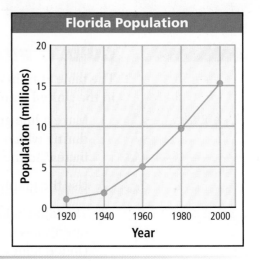

A double-line graph shows change over time for two sets of data.

EXAMPLE 3 Making a Double-Line Graph

The table shows the normal daily temperatures in degrees Fahrenheit in two Alaskan cities. Make a double-line graph of the data.

Month	Nome	Anchorage
Jan	7	15
Feb	4	19
Mar	9	26
Apr	18	36
May	36	47
Jun	46	54

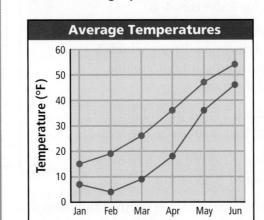

Plot a point for each temperature in Nome and connect the points. Then, using a different color, plot a point for each temperature in Anchorage and connect the points. Make a key to show what each line represents.

Think and Discuss GPS M7P1.d, M7P3.b

1. Describe how a line graph would look for a set of data that increases and then decreases over time.

2. Give an example of a situation that can be described by a double-line graph in which the two sets of data intersect at least once.

Georgia Performance
Standards

**M7P3.a, M7P4.c, M7P5.a,
M7P5.b**

go.hrw.com

Homework Help Online
KEYWORD: MS7 7-6

Parent Resources Online
KEYWORD: MS7 Parent

GUIDED PRACTICE

The table at right shows average movie theater ticket prices in the United States. Use the table for Exercises 1 and 2.

Year	Price ($)
1965	1.01
1970	1.55
1975	2.05
1980	2.69
1985	3.55
1990	4.23
1995	4.35
2000	5.39
2005	6.41

See Example 1   **1.** Make a line graph of the data. Use the graph to determine during which 5-year period the average ticket price increased the least.

See Example 2   **2.** Use the graph to estimate the average ticket price in 1997.

See Example 3   **3.** The table below shows the amount of apple juice and raw apples in pounds consumed per person in the United States. Make a double-line graph of the data.

	2001	2002	2003	2004	2005
Apple Juice	21.4	21.3	21.4	23.1	24.0
Raw Apples	17.5	15.6	16.0	16.9	19.1

INDEPENDENT PRACTICE

The table at right shows the number of teams in the National Basketball Association (NBA). Use the table for Exercises 4–6.

Year	Teams
1965	9
1970	14
1975	18
1980	22
1985	23
1990	27
1995	27
2000	29
2005	30

See Example 1   **4.** Make a line graph of the data. Use the graph to determine during which 5-year period the number of NBA teams increased the most.

5. During which 5-year period did the number of teams increase the least?

See Example 2   **6. Estimation** Use the graph to estimate the number of NBA teams in 1988.

See Example 3   **7.** The table below shows the normal daily temperatures in degrees Fahrenheit in Peoria, Illinois, and Portland, Oregon. Make a double-line graph of the data.

	Jul	Aug	Sept	Oct	Nov	Dec
Peoria	76	73	66	54	41	27
Portland	68	69	63	55	46	40

PRACTICE AND PROBLEM SOLVING

CRCT GPS

Extra Practice p. 740

8. Critical Thinking Explain how the intervals on the vertical axis of a line graph affect the look of the graph.

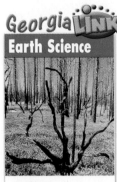

Georgia LINK

Earth Science

In 2004, approximately 634 acres of forest were consumed by wildfires in the Chattahoochee-Oconee National Forest, located in northern and central Georgia.

9. Life Science The table shows the numbers of endangered species of vertebrates for selected years between 1998 and 2004.

	1998	2000	2002	2003	2004
Number of Species (thousands)	3.31	3.51	3.52	3.52	5.19

   a. Make a line graph of the data in the table.

   b. Estimate the number of endangered species of vertebrates in 1999.

10. Earth Science The graph shows the number of acres burned by wildfires in the United States from 1995 to 2000.

   a. During which years did wildfires burn more than 6 million acres?

   b. Explain whether the graph would be useful in predicting future data values.

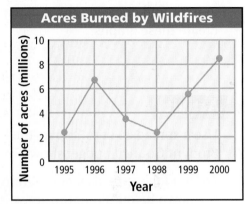

Source: National Interagency Fire Center

11. What's the Error? Denise makes a line plot to display how her town's population has changed over 10 years. Which type of graph would be more appropriate to display this data? Explain.

12. Write About It Explain the benefit of drawing a double-line graph rather than two single-line graphs for related sets of data.

13. Challenge A line graph shows that a town's population was 4,500 in 1980, 5,300 in 1990, and 6,100 in 2000. Assuming the population continues to grow at the same rate, what population will the line graph show in 2010?

CRCT PREP • GPS SUPPORT • SPIRAL REVIEW

Use the graph for Exercises 14 and 15.

14. Multiple Choice During which period did the average cost of a major league baseball ticket increase the most?

   Ⓐ 1991–1993   Ⓒ 1997–2001

   Ⓑ 1993–1997   Ⓓ 2001–2005

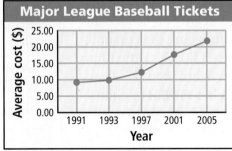

15. Short Response Use the line graph to estimate the average cost of a major league baseball ticket in 2003. Explain.

Write as a percent. Round to the nearest tenth of a percent, if necessary. (Lesson 6-2)

16. 0.15   **17.** 1.36   **18.** $\frac{2}{3}$ **19.** $\frac{11}{20}$

20. Decide whether a bar graph or a circle graph would best display the average temperature for each day of one week. Explain your answer. (Lesson 7-4)

Use Technology to Display Data

Use after Lesson 7-6

go.hrw.com
Lab Resources Online
KEYWORD: MS7 Lab7

There are several ways to display data, including bar graphs, line graphs, and circle graphs. A spreadsheet provides a quick way to create these graphs.

Georgia Performance Standards
M7D1.f, M7P1.c, M7P5.a

Activity

Use a spreadsheet to display the Kennedy Middle School Student Council budget shown in the table at right.

Student Council Budget	
Activity	**Amount ($)**
Assemblies	275
Dances	587
Spring Festival	412
Awards Banquet	384
Other	250

1 Open the spreadsheet program, and enter the data as shown below. Enter the activities in column A and the amount budgeted in column B. Include the column titles in row 1.

	A	B	C
1	Activity	Amount ($)	
2	Assemblies	275	
3	Dances	587	
4	Spring Festival	412	
5	Awards Banquet	384	
6	Other	250	
7			

2 Highlight the data by clicking on cell A1 and dragging the cursor to cell B6. Click the Chart Wizard icon 📊. Then click **FINISH** to choose the first type of column graph.

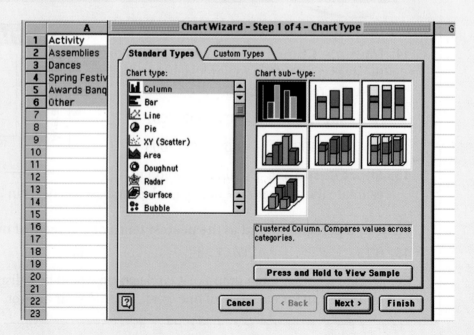

3 The bar graph of the data appears as shown. Resize or reposition the graph, if necessary.

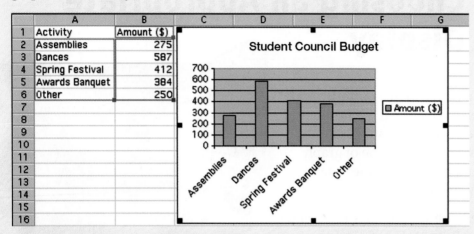

To see a circle graph of the data, select the bar graph (as shown above). Click the Chart Wizard icon and choose "Pie," which is the circle graph. Then click **FINISH** to choose the first type of circle graph.

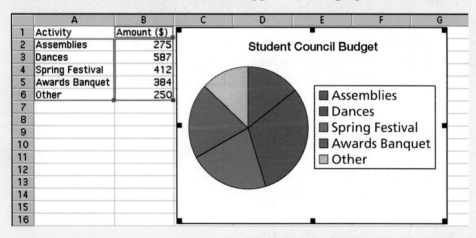

Think and Discuss

1. Which graph best displays the Student Council budget? Why?

2. Would a line graph be an appropriate display of the Student Council budget data? Explain.

Try This

1. The table shows the number of points scored by members of a girls' basketball team in one season. Use a spreadsheet to create a bar graph and a circle graph of the data.

Player	Ana	Angel	Mary	Nia	Tina	Zoe
Points Scored	201	145	89	40	21	8

2. Which type of graph is a better display of the data? Why?

7-7 Choosing an Appropriate Display

Learn to select and use appropriate representations for displaying data.

Georgia Performance Standards

M7D1.f Analyze data using appropriate graphs.
Also, M7P4.c, M7P5.a.

On a field trip to a butterfly park, students recorded the number of species of each butterfly family they saw. Which type of graph would best display the data they collected?

There are several ways to display data. Some types of displays are more appropriate than others, depending on how the data is to be analyzed.

 Use a **bar graph** to display and compare data.

 Use a **circle graph** to show how a set of data is divided into parts.

 Use a **Venn diagram** to show relationships between two or more data sets.

 Use a **line plot** to show the frequency of values.

 Use a **line graph** to show how data change over a period of time.

 Use a **stem-and-leaf plot** to show how often data values occur and how they are distributed.

EXAMPLE 1 Choosing an Appropriate Display

The praying mantis can be seen in Phinzy Swamp Nature Park, near Augusta, Georgia.

A The students want to create a display to show the number of species of each butterfly family they saw. Choose the type of graph that would best represent the data in the table. Explain.

Butterfly Family	Number of Species
Gossamer-wing	7
Skippers	10
Swallowtails	5
Whites and sulphurs	4

There are distinct categories showing the number of species seen in each butterfly family.

A bar graph can be used to display data in categories.

B The students want to create a display to show the population of butterflies in the park for the past few years. Choose the type of graph that would best represent this data. Explain.

A line graph would best represent data that gives population over time.

408 *Chapter 7 Collecting, Displaying, and Analyzing Data*

EXAMPLE 2 Identifying the Most Appropriate Display

The table shows the amount of time the students spent at the different exhibits at the butterfly park. Explain why each display does or does not appropriately represent the data.

Exhibit	Time (min)
Butterflies	60
Insects	45
Invertebrates	30
Birds	15

A

Stems	Leaves
1	5
2	
3	0
4	5
5	
6	0

Key: 2|0 means 20

A stem-and-leaf plot shows how often data values occur and how they are distributed.

There are only four data values, and how often they occur and how they are distributed are not important.

B

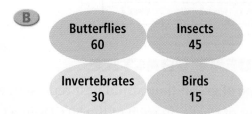

Butterflies 60   Insects 45
Invertebrates 30   Birds 15

A Venn diagram shows the relationship between two or more data sets.

There is no relationship among the times spent at each exhibit.

C

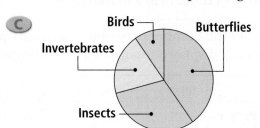

Birds — Butterflies
Invertebrates
Insects

A circle graph shows how a set of data is divided into parts.

This circle graph appropriately shows the proportionate amount of time spent at each exhibit.

D

```
      X        X        X        X
  ┼──┼──┼──┼──┼──┼──┼──┼──┼──┼──┼──┼→
  10 15 20 25 30 35 40 45 50 55 60 65
```

A line plot shows frequency of values.

How often the data values occur is not important.

Think and Discuss   GPS M7P1.d, M7P3.b

1. **Explain** how data displayed in a stem-and-leaf plot and data displayed in a line plot are similar.

2. **Describe** a set of data that could best be displayed in a line graph.

Georgia Performance Standards

M7P1.b, M7P2.c, M7P3.a, M7P5.b

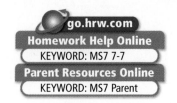

go.hrw.com
Homework Help Online
KEYWORD: MS7 7-7
Parent Resources Online
KEYWORD: MS7 Parent

GUIDED PRACTICE

See Example 1   **Choose the type of graph that would best represent each type of data.**

1. the prices of the five top-selling 42-inch plasma televisions

2. the height of a person from birth to age 21

See Example 2   **The table shows Keiffer's earnings for a month. Explain why each display does or does not appropriately represent the data.**

Week	1	2	3	4
Earnings ($)	20	30	15	25

3.

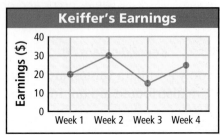

4.

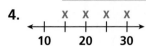

INDEPENDENT PRACTICE

See Example 1   **Choose the type of graph that would best represent each type of data.**

5. the number of tracks on each of the 50 CDs in a CD collection

6. the number of runners in a marathon for the last five years

See Example 2   **The table shows the number of people who participate in various activities. Explain why each display does or does not appropriately represent the data.**

Activity	Biking	Hiking	Skating	Jogging
Number of People	35	20	25	15

7.

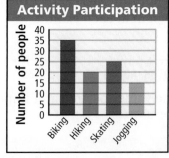

8.

Stems	Leaves
1	5
2	0 5
3	5

Key: 1|5 means 15

PRACTICE AND PROBLEM SOLVING

Extra Practice p. 740

9. The data gives the number of books 25 students read last summer.
7, 10, 8, 6, 0, 5, 3, 8, 12, 7, 2, 5, 9, 10, 15, 8, 3, 1, 0, 4, 7, 10, 8, 2, 11
Make the type of graph that would best represent the data.

10. **Life Science** Komodo Dragons are the world's largest lizard species. The table shows the weights of some adult male Komodo Dragons. Make the type of graph that would best represent the information.

Weight (lb)	Frequency
161–170	4
171–180	8
181–190	12
191–200	11
201–210	7

11. Yoko wants to use a stem-and-leaf plot to show the growth of the sweet peas that she planted last year. She measured how much the vines grew each month. Explain why Yoko's display choice may or may not best represent the data.

12. **Nutrition** The table shows the amount of protein per serving in various foods. Draw two different displays to represent the data. Explain your choices.

Food	Protein (g)
Egg	6
Milk	8
Cheese	24
Roast beef	28

13. **Choose a Strategy** Five friends worked together on a project. Matti, Jerad, and Stu all worked the same length of time. Tisha worked a total of 3 hours, which was equal to the total amount of time that Matti, Jerad, and Stu worked. Pablo and Matti together worked $\frac{1}{2}$ of the total amount of time that the five friends worked. Make the type of graph that would best represent the information.

14. **Write About It** Is a circle graph always appropriate to represent data stated in percents? Explain your answer.

15. **Challenge** The table shows the results of a survey of 50 people about their favorite color. What type of display would you choose to represent the data of those who chose blue, green, or red? Explain.

Color	Blue	Yellow	Green	Red	Other
Number	14	4	6	14	12

CRCT Prep • GPS Support • Spiral Review

16. **Multiple Choice** Which type of display would be most appropriate to compare the monthly rainfall for five cities?

   Ⓐ Line graph   Ⓑ Bar graph   Ⓒ Circle graph   Ⓓ Stem-and-leaf plot

17. **Extended Response** Nathan's family budgets $1,000 a month for expenses. They budget $250 for food, $500 for rent, $150 for transportation, and $100 for utilities. Tell which type of graph would best represent the data, justify your response, and draw the display.

Write each decimal as a percent. (Lesson 6-2)

18. 0.27   **19.** 0.9   **20.** 0.02   **21.** 0.406

22. Of the 75 campers at Happy Trails Summer Camp, 36% are scheduled to go horseback riding on Tuesdays. How many campers are scheduled to go horseback riding on Tuesdays? (Lesson 6-4)

7-8 Populations and Samples

Learn to compare and analyze sampling methods.

Vocabulary

population

sample

random sample

convenience sample

biased sample

In 2002, there were claims that Chronic Wasting Disease (CWD), or Mad Elk Disease, was spreading westward across North America. In order to verify claims such as these, the elk population had to be tested.

When information is gathered about a group, such as all the elk in North America, the entire group is called the **population**. Because testing each member of a large group can be difficult or impossible, researchers often study a part of the population, called a **sample**.

Helpful Hint

A random sample is more likely to be representative of a population than a convenience sample is.

For a **random sample**, members of the population are chosen at random. This gives every member of the population an equal chance of being chosen. A **convenience sample** is based on members of the population that are readily available, such as 30 elk in a wildlife preservation area.

EXAMPLE **1** Analyzing Sampling Methods

Determine which sampling method will better represent the entire population. Justify your answer.

Georgia Performance Standards

M7A2.a Given a problem, define a variable, write an equation, solve the equation, and interpret the solution. Also, M7A2.b, M7P2.c, M7P4.c.

Football Game: Student Attendance	
Sampling Method	**Results of Survey**
Arnie surveys 80 students by randomly choosing names from the school directory.	62% attend football games
Vic surveys 28 students that were sitting near him during lunch.	81% attend football games

Arnie's method produces results that better represent the entire student population because he uses a random sample.

Vic's method produces results that are not as representative of the entire student population because he uses a convenience sample.

A **biased sample** does not fairly represent the population. A study of 50 elk belonging to a breeder could be biased because the breeder's elk might be less likely to have Mad Elk Disease than elk in the wild.

EXAMPLE 2   Identifying Potentially Biased Samples

Determine whether each sample may be biased. Explain.

A The first 50 people exiting a movie are surveyed to find out what type of movie people in the town like to see.

The sample is biased. It is likely that not everyone in the town likes to see the same type of movie that those 50 people just saw.

B A librarian randomly chooses 100 books from the library's database to calculate the average length of a library book.

The sample is not biased. It is a random sample.

Given data about a random sample, you can use proportional reasoning to make predictions or verify claims about the entire population.

EXAMPLE 3   Verifying Claims Based on Statistical Data

A biologist estimates that more than 700 of the 4,500 elk at a wildlife preserve are infected with a parasite. A random sample of 50 elk shows that 8 of them are infected. Determine whether the biologist's estimate is likely to be accurate.

Set up a proportion to predict the total number of infected elk.

$$\frac{\text{infected elk in sample}}{\text{size of sample}} = \frac{\text{infected elk in population}}{\text{size of population}}$$

$$\frac{8}{50} = \frac{x}{4{,}500}$$ *Let x represent the number of infected elk at the preserve.*

$$8 \cdot 4{,}500 = 50 \cdot x$$ *The cross products are equal.*

$$36{,}000 = 50x$$ *Multiply.*

$$\frac{36{,}000}{50} = \frac{50x}{50}$$ *Divide each side by 50 to isolate x.*

$$720 = x$$

Based on the sample, you can predict that there are 720 infected elk at the preserve. The biologist's estimate is likely to be accurate.

Remember!

In the proportion $\frac{a}{b} = \frac{c}{d}$, the cross products, $a \cdot d$ and $b \cdot c$ are equal.

Think and Discuss   GPS M7P1.d, M7P2.c

1. Describe a situation in which you would want to use a sample rather than survey the entire population.

2. Explain why it might be difficult to obtain a truly random sample of a very large population.

7-8 Exercises

Georgia Performance Standards

M7P1.b, M7P2.c, M7P3.a, M7P3.c

go.hrw.com
Homework Help Online
KEYWORD: MS7 7-8
Parent Resources Online
KEYWORD: MS7 Parent

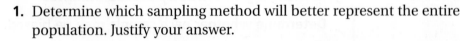

GUIDED PRACTICE

See Example

1. Determine which sampling method will better represent the entire population. Justify your answer.

Lone Star Cars: Customer Satisfaction	
Sampling Method	**Results of Survey**
Nadia surveys 200 customers on the car lot one Saturday morning.	92% are satisfied
Daria mails surveys to 100 randomly-selected customers.	68% are satisfied

See Example **Determine whether each sample may be biased. Explain.**

2. A company randomly selects 500 customers from its computer database and then surveys those customers to find out how they like their service.

3. A city-hall employee surveys 100 customers at a restaurant to learn about the jobs and salaries of city residents.

See Example 3 **4.** A factory produces 150,000 light bulbs per day. The manager of the factory estimates that fewer than 1,000 defective bulbs are produced each day. In a random sample of 250 light bulbs, there are 2 defective bulbs. Determine whether the manager's estimate is likely to be accurate. Explain.

INDEPENDENT PRACTICE

See Example **5.** Determine which sampling method will better represent the entire population. Justify your answer.

Midville Morning News: Subscription Renewals	
Sampling Method	**Results of Survey**
Suzanne surveys 80 subscribers in her neighborhood.	61% intend to renew subscription
Vonetta telephones 150 randomly-selected subscribers.	82% intend to renew subscription

See Example **Determine whether each sample may be biased. Explain.**

6. A disc jockey asks the first 10 listeners who call in if they liked the last song that was played.

7. Members of a polling organization survey 700 registered voters by randomly choosing names from a list of all registered voters.

See Example 3 **8.** A university has 30,600 students. A survey is mailed to a random sample of 240 students, 20 of whom speak three or more languages. Predict the number of students at the university who speak three or more languages.

PRACTICE AND PROBLEM SOLVING

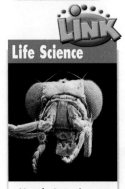

Life Science

North American fruit flies damage cherries, apples, and blueberries. In the Mediterranean, fruit flies are a threat to citrus fruits.

Explain whether you would survey the entire population or use a sample.

9. You want to know the favorite painters of employees at a local art museum.

10. You want to know the types of calculators used by middle school students across the country.

11. You want to know how many hours per week the students in your social studies class spend on their homework.

12. Life Science A biologist chooses a random sample of 50 out of 750 fruit flies. She finds that 2 of them have mutated genes causing deformed wings. The biologist claims that approximately 30 of the 750 fruit flies have deformed wings. Do you agree? Explain.

13. Critical Thinking Explain why surveying 100 people who are listed in the phone book may not be a random sample.

14. What's the Error? The students in Jacy's science class put their names in a hat. Of the 28 names in the hat, Jacy draws 5 names. She finds that 2 of those 5 students say that their favorite subject is science. Jacy predicts that 254 students of the 635 students at her school would say that their favorite subject is science. What is the error in Jacy's prediction?

15. Write About It Suppose you want to know whether the seventh-grade students at your school spend more time watching TV or using a computer. How might you choose a random sample from the population?

16. Challenge A manager at XQJ Software surveyed 200 company employees to find out how many of the employees walk to work. The results are shown in the table. Do you think the manager chose a random sample? Why or why not?

Employees at XQJ Software		
	Total Number	Number Who Walk to Work
Population	9,200	300
Sample	200	40

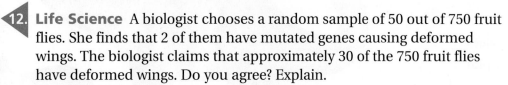

CRCT Prep • GPS Support • Spiral Review

17. Multiple Choice Banneker Middle School has 580 students. Wei surveys a random sample of 30 students and finds that 12 of them have pet dogs. How many students at the school are likely to have pet dogs?

Ⓐ 116   Ⓑ 232   Ⓒ 290   Ⓓ 360

18. Short Response Give an example of a biased sample. Explain why it is biased.

Write each percent as a decimal. (Lesson 6-1)

19. 52%   **20.** 7%   **21.** 110%   **22.** 0.4%

Find the percent of each number. (Lesson 6-4)

23. 11% of 50   **24.** 48% of 600   **25.** 0.5% of 82   **26.** 210% of 16

7-9 Scatter Plots

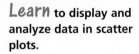

Learn to display and analyze data in scatter plots.

Vocabulary

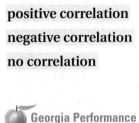

scatter plot

positive correlation

negative correlation

no correlation

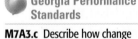

Georgia Performance Standards

M7A3.c Describe how change in one variable affects the other variable. Also, M7A3.a, M7A3.b, M7D1.f, M7D1.g.

The supersaurus, one of the largest known dinosaurs, could weigh as much as 55 tons and grow as long as 100 feet from head to tail. The tyrannosaurus, a large meat-eating dinosaur, was about one-third the length of the supersaurus.

Two sets of data, such as the length and the weight of dinosaurs, may be related. To find out, you can make a *scatter plot* of the data values in each set. A **scatter plot** has two number lines, called *axes*—one for each set of data values. Each point on the scatter plot represents a pair of data values. These points may appear to be scattered or may cluster in the shape of a line or a curve.

EXAMPLE **Making a Scatter Plot**

Use the data to make a scatter plot. Describe the relationship between the data sets.

Step 1: Determine the scale and interval for each axis. Place units of length on the horizontal axis and units of weight on the vertical axis.

Step 2: Plot a point for each pair of values.

Step 3: Label the axes and title the graph.

The scatter plot shows that a dinosaur's weight tends to increase as its length increases.

Name	Length (ft)	Weight (tons)
Triceratops	30	6
Tyrannosaurus	39	7
Euhelopus	50	25
Brachiosaurus	82	50
Supersaurus	100	55

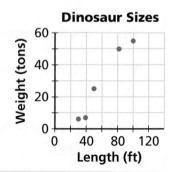

There are three ways to describe data displayed in a scatter plot.

Positive Correlation	Negative Correlation	No Correlation

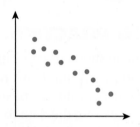 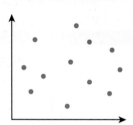

The values in both data sets increase at the same time.

The values in one data set increase as the values in the other set decrease.

The values in both data sets show no pattern.

EXAMPLE 2 **Determining Relationships Between Two Sets of Data**

Write *positive correlation*, *negative correlation*, or *no correlation* to describe each relationship. Explain.

 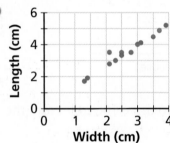

 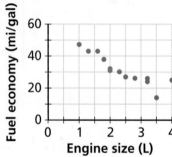

The graph shows that as width increases, length increases. So the graph shows a positive correlation between the data sets.

The graph shows that as engine size increases, fuel economy decreases. So the graph shows a negative correlation between the data sets.

C the ages of people and the number of pets they own

The number of pets a person owns is not related to the person's age. So there seems to be no correlation between the data sets.

Think and Discuss  GPS M7P2.b, M7P3.b

1. **Describe** the type of correlation you would expect between the number of absences in a class and the grades in the class.

2. **Give an example** of a relationship between two sets of data that shows a negative correlation. Then give an example of a positive correlation.

Georgia Performance
Standards

M7P1.a, M7P2.c, M7P4.c,
M7P5.a

go.hrw.com
Homework Help Online
KEYWORD: MS7 7-9
Parent Resources Online
KEYWORD: MS7 Parent

GUIDED PRACTICE

See Example

1. The table shows the typical weights
(in kilograms) and heart rates
(in beats per minute) of several
mammals. Use the data to make
a scatter plot. Describe the
relationship between the data sets.

Mammal	Weight	Heart Rate
Ferret	0.6	360
Human	70	70
Llama	185	75
Red deer	110	80
Rhesus monkey	10	160

See Example Write *positive correlation, negative correlation,* or *no correlation* to describe
each relationship. Explain.

2. **Math Score and Shoe Size**

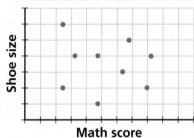

3. **Work Experience**

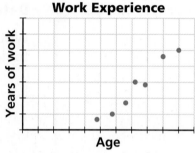

4. the time it takes to drive 100 miles and the driving speed

INDEPENDENT PRACTICE

See Example

5. The table shows solar energy cell
capacity (in megawatts) over several
years. Use the data to make a scatter
plot. Describe the relationship between
the data sets.

Year	Capacity	Year	Capacity
1990	13.8	1993	21.0
1991	14.9	1994	26.1
1992	15.6	1995	31.1

See Example Write *positive correlation, negative correlation,* or *no correlation* to describe
each relationship. Explain.

6. **Sales**

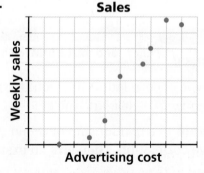

7. **Car's Mileage and Value**

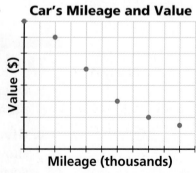

CRCT GPS

Extra Practice p. 740

8. the number of students in a district and the number of buses in the district

Critical Thinking For Exercises 9–11, tell whether you would expect a positive correlation, a negative correlation, or no correlation. Explain your answers.

9. the average temperature of a location and the amount of rainfall it receives each year

10. the latitude of a location and the amount of snow it receives each year

11. the number of hours of daylight and the amount of rainfall in a day

12. The table shows the approximate latitude and average temperature for several locations in the Southern Hemisphere. Construct a scatter plot of the data. What can you conclude from this data?

13. ⭐**Challenge** A location's elevation is negatively correlated to its average temperature and positively correlated to the amount of snow it receives. What kind of correlation would you expect between temperature and the amount of snowfall? Explain.

A scientist launching a weather balloon in Antarctica

Location	Latitude	Temperature
Quito, Ecuador	0° S	55°F
Melbourne, Australia	38° S	43°F
Tucuman, Argentina	27° S	57°F
Tananarive, Madagascar	19° S	60°F
Halley Research Station, Antarctica	76° S	20°F

CRCT PREP • GPS SUPPORT • SPIRAL REVIEW

14. **Multiple Choice** Use the scatter plot to determine which statements are true.

    I The data shows a positive correlation.

    II The data shows a negative correlation.

    III The data shows no correlation.

    IV As the years increase, the prize money increases.

    Ⓐ I only   Ⓑ I and IV   Ⓒ II and IV   Ⓓ III only

Indianapolis 500 Winner's Prize Money

(Scatter plot: Prize money ($) vs. Year, ranging 1900–2020 on x-axis and 0–2,000,000 on y-axis)

15. **Short Response** Give an example of two data sets that you would expect to have a positive correlation. Explain your answer.

Find the percent of each number. If necessary, round to the nearest tenth. (Lesson 6-4)

16. 95% of 80   17. 120% of 63   18. 62% of 14   19. 7% of 50

20. The regular price of a computer monitor at the electronics store is $499. This month the monitor is on sale for 15% off. Find the sale price of the monitor. (Lesson 6-6)

Samples and Lines of Best Fit

Georgia Performance Standards

M7A3.a, M7A3.b, M7A3.c, M7D1.a, M7D1.e

Use after Lesson 7-9

go.hrw.com

Lab Resources Online

KEYWORD: MS7 Lab7

You can use a graphing calculator to display relationships between variables in a scatter plot.

Activity 1

① Survey at least 30 students in your grade to find the following information. Record your data in a table like the one below. (Your table will have at least 30 rows of data.) For **L5**, use numbers for the month. For example, enter "1" for January, "2" for February, etc.

L1 Height (in.)	L2 Age (yr)	L3 Length of Foot (in.)	L4 Length of Forearm (in.)	L5 Month of Birth
66	12	11	10	3
63	13	8	9	10
65	12	10	9.5	7

② Press STAT ENTER to enter all the data into a graphing calculator.

③ Create a scatter plot for height and length of foot.

  a. Press 2nd Y= ENTER for **Plot 1**.

  b. Select ON , and use the arrow keys to select the scatter plot for **Type**.

  c. Use the down arrow to move the cursor to **Xlist**. Press 2nd 1 to select **L1**.

  d. Move the cursor to **Ylist**. Press 2nd 3 to select **L3**.

  e. Press ZOOM and then 9: ZoomStat to view your graph.

Think and Discuss

1. Describe the relationship between height and length of foot that is shown in the scatter plot from Activity 1.

2. What relationships would you expect to see between the other variables in the table?

1. Create a scatter plot of each of the other pairs of variables in your data-collection table. Which variables show a positive correlation? a negative correlation? no correlation?

Activity 2

1 Follow the steps from Activity 1, part 3 to display a scatter plot that shows the relationship between height and length of forearm.

2 Use **TRACE** to move the cursor between points on the graph. Use the coordinates of two points to estimate the slope of a line that would best fit through the data points on the graph.

3 Press **STAT** and then use the right arrow key to select **CALC 4: LinReg (ax + b)**. Then press **2nd** 1 **,** **2nd** 4 **ENTER** to find the equation of the line of best fit.

4 Press **Y=** **VARS** **5: Statistics....** Use the right arrow key to select **EQ 1: RegEQ** and press **ENTER** to put the equation for the line of best fit into the equation editor.

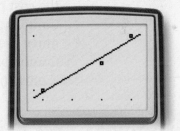

5 Press **GRAPH** to see the line of best fit graphed with the data points on the scatter plot.

Think and Discuss

1. Discuss how estimating the line of best fit gets easier the more data points you have.

2. Explain whether the sample from your class is representative of the population.

Try This

1. **a.** Press **2nd** **STAT** **MATH** **3: mean (** **2nd** 1 **ENTER** to find the mean height of your 30 classmates.

   b. Calculate the mean height of three students from the original survey who sit closest to you. What kind of sample is this? How does the mean height of this sample compare to the mean of the population from part **a**? Explain why they might be different.

   c. Calculate the mean height of 15 students from the original survey. How does this number compare with the mean of the population? Is it closer to the mean than the answer you got in part **b**?

7-10 Misleading Graphs

 **Learn** to identify and analyze misleading graphs.

Georgia Performance Standards

M7D1.f Analyze data using appropriate graphs. Also, M7P2.c, M7P4.c, M7P5.b.

Advertisements and news articles often use data to support a point. Sometimes the data is presented in a way that influences how the data is interpreted. A data display that distorts information in order to persuade can be *misleading*.

An axis in a graph can be "broken" to make the graph easier to read. However, a broken axis can also be misleading. In the graph at right, the cost per minute for service with Company B looks like it is twice as much as the cost for service with Company A. In fact, the difference is only $0.10 per minute.

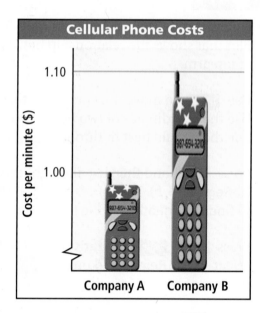

EXAMPLE 1 *Social Studies Application*

Both bar graphs show the percent of people in California, Maryland, Michigan, and Washington who use seat belts. Which graph could be misleading? Why?

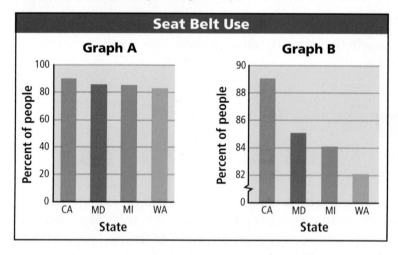

Graph B could be misleading. Because the vertical axis on graph B is broken, it appears that the percent of people in California who wear seat belts is twice as great as the percent in Michigan. In fact, it is only 5% greater. People might conclude from graph B that the percent of people in California who wear seat belts is much greater than the percents in the other states.

EXAMPLE 2 Analyzing Misleading Graphs

Explain why each graph could be misleading.

A
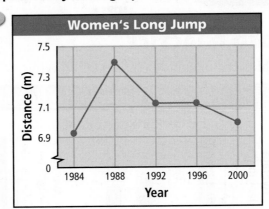

Because the vertical axis is broken, the distance jumped in 1988 appears to be over two times as far as in 1984. In fact, the distance jumped in 1988 is less than 0.5 meter greater than in the other years.

B
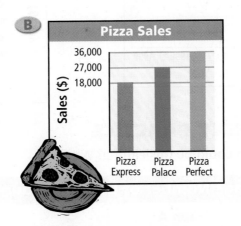

The scale of the graph is wrong. Equal distances on the vertical axis should represent equal intervals of numbers, but in this graph, the first $18,000 in sales is larger than the next $18,000. Because of this, you can't tell from the bars that Pizza Perfect's sales were twice those of Pizza Express.

Think and Discuss GPS M7P2.c, M7P3.b

1. **Explain** how to use the scale of a graph to decide if the graph is misleading.

2. **Describe** what might indicate that a graph is misleading.

3. **Give an example** of a situation in which a misleading graph might be used to persuade readers.

Georgia Performance
Standards

M7P1.b, M7P1.c, M7P2.c,
M7P3.a

go.hrw.com
Homework Help Online
KEYWORD: MS7 7-10
Parent Resources Online
KEYWORD: MS7 Parent

GUIDED PRACTICE

See Example **1**   **1.** Which graph could be misleading? Why?

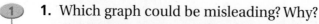

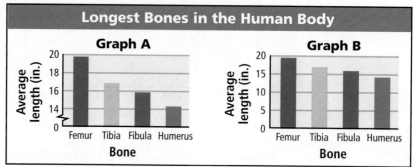

See Example **2**   Explain why each graph could be misleading.

2.

3.

INDEPENDENT PRACTICE

See Example **1**   **4.** Which graph could be misleading? Why?

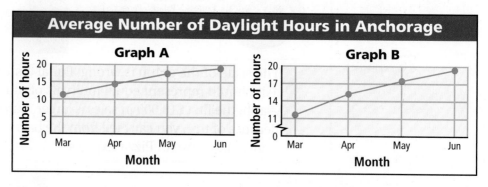

See Example **2**   Explain why each graph could be misleading.

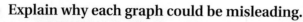

5.

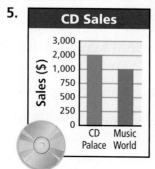

6.

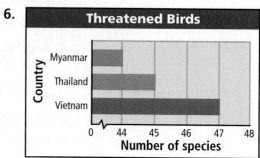

PRACTICE AND PROBLEM SOLVING

7. Business Explain why the graphs below are misleading. Then tell how you can redraw them so that they are not misleading.

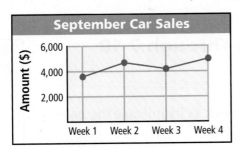

 8. Social Studies The Appalachian Trail is a 2,160-mile footpath that runs from Maine to Georgia. The bar graph shows the number of miles of trail in three states. Redraw the graph so that it is not misleading. Then compare the two graphs.

9. Choose a Strategy Tanya had $1.19 in coins. None of the coins were dollars or 50-cent pieces. Josie asked Tanya for change for a dollar, but she did not have the correct change. Which coins did Tanya have?

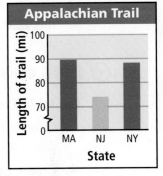

 10. Write About It Why is it important to closely examine graphs in ads?

11. Challenge A company asked 10 people about their favorite brand of toothpaste. Three people chose Sparkle, one chose Smile, and six chose Purely White. An advertisement for Sparkle states, "Three times as many people prefer Sparkle over Smile!" Explain why this statement is misleading.

CRCT PREP • GPS SUPPORT • SPIRAL REVIEW

Use the graph for Exercises 12 and 13.

12. Multiple Choice Which statement is NOT a reason that the graph is misleading?

Ⓐ Broken interval on the vertical axis

Ⓑ The title

Ⓒ Vertical scale is not small enough

Ⓓ Intervals are not equal

13. Short Response Redraw the graph so that it is not misleading.

Solve. Write each answer in simplest form. (Lesson 3-12)

14. $\frac{3}{5}x = \frac{1}{5}$ **15.** $x + \frac{2}{3} = \frac{5}{6}$ **16.** $-\frac{1}{8}x = \frac{3}{4}$ **17.** $x - \frac{3}{8} = -\frac{5}{6}$

Write *positive, negative,* or *no correlation* to describe each relationship. (Lesson 7-9)

18. height and test scores   **19.** speed of a car and time required to travel a distance

READY TO GO ON?

Quiz for Lessons 7-6 Through 7-10

Mileage (thousands)	Value of Truck ($)
0	20,000
20	18,000
40	14,000
60	11,000
80	10,000

✓ 7-6 Line Graphs

The table shows the value of a truck as its mileage increases.

1. Make a line graph of the data.

2. Use the graph to estimate the value of the truck when it has 12,000 miles.

✓ 7-7 Choosing an Appropriate Display

The table shows worldwide earthquake frequency.

3. Choose the type of graph that would best display this data.

4. Create the graph that would best display the data.

Earthquake Frequency	
Category	Annual Frequency
Great	1
Major	18
Strong	120
Moderate	800

✓ 7-8 Populations and Samples

Determine whether each sample may be biased. Explain.

5. Rickie surveys people at an amusement park to find out the average size of people's immediate family.

6. Theo surveys every fourth person entering a grocery store to find out the average number of pets in people's homes.

7. A biologist estimates that there are 1,800 fish in a quarry. To test this estimate, a student caught 150 fish from the quarry, tagged them, and released them. A few days later, the student caught 50 fish and noted that 4 were tagged. Determine whether the biologist's estimate is likely to be accurate.

✓ 7-9 Scatter Plots

8. Use the data to make a scatter plot.

9. Write *positive correlation, negative correlation,* or *no correlation* to describe the relationship between the data sets.

Cost ($)	2	3	4	5
Number of Purchases	12	8	6	3

✓ 7-10 Misleading Graphs

10. Which graph is misleading? Explain.

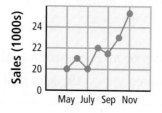

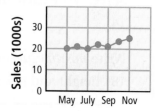

Big Money Prizes A radio station is planning a contest. Each winner will select a money envelope. The station is planning on having 150 winners and giving away $6,000. The table shows the plan for filling the envelopes.

1. The station wants to describe the typical amount of money a winner will receive. What are the mean, median, mode, and range of the amounts won?

2. The sponsors decide to double the amount of money they give away. The station manager wants to do this by doubling the amount of money in each envelope. Make a table showing how much money would be in each envelope.

3. How does the station manager's plan affect the mean, median, mode, and range of the amounts won?

4. The DJs think it would be better to double the number of winners rather than doubling the amount of money in each envelope. They want to double the number of envelopes containing each amount of money. Make a new table that shows their plan.

5. How does the DJs' plan affect the mean, median, mode, and range of the amounts won?

Number of Envelopes	Amount of Money
1	$5,000
2	$250
4	$50
12	$10
6	$5
25	$2
100	$1

Multi-Step Test Prep

Game Time

Code Breaker

A *cryptogram* is a message written in code. One of the most common types of codes is a substitution code, in which each letter of a text is replaced with a different letter. The table shows one way to replace the letters in a text to make a coded message.

Original Letter	A	B	C	D	E	F	G	H	I	J	K	L	M
Code Letter	J	E	O	H	K	A	U	B	L	Y	V	G	P
Original Letter	N	O	P	Q	R	S	T	U	V	W	X	Y	Z
Code Letter	X	N	S	D	Z	Q	M	W	C	R	F	T	I

With this code, the word MATH is written PJMB. You can also use the table as a key to decode messages. Try decoding the following message.

J EJZ UZJSB OJX EK WQKH MN HLQSGJT HJMJ.

Suppose you want to crack a substitution code but are not given the key. You can use letter frequencies to help you. The bar graph below shows the number of times each letter of the English language is likely to appear in a text of 100 letters.

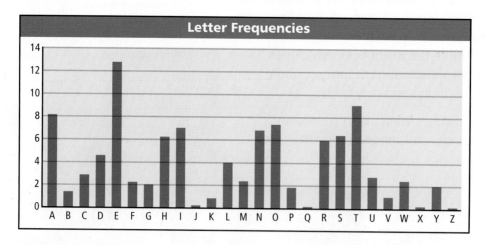

From the graph, you can see that E is the mode. In a coded text, the letter that appears most frequently is likely to represent the letter E. The letter that appears the second most frequently is likely to represent the letter T. Count the number of times each letter appears in the following message. Then use the letter frequencies and a bit of guesswork to decode the message. (*Hint:* In this code, P represents the letter M.)

KSQ PQUR, KSQ PQHGUR, URH KSQ PXHQ KQWW VXE DXPQKSGRT
UCXEK U DQK XZ HUKU.

Materials
- card stock
- scissors
- glue
- colored paper
- magnetic strip
- tape
- empty CD case
- graph paper
- stapler

FOLDNOTES

It's in the Bag!

PROJECT — Graph Match

Use an empty CD case to make a magnetic matching game about different types of graphs.

Directions

1 Trim the card stock to $4\frac{1}{2}$ inches by 5 inches. On the card stock, write "Match the Name and Number" and list the numbers 1 through 5 as shown. Cut small rectangles from the magnetic strip and glue these next to the numbers. **Figure A**

2 Glue colored paper to the rest of the magnetic strip. Write the names of five different types of graphs on the strip. Cut these apart to form magnetic rectangles with the names of the graphs. **Figure B**

3 Put a magnetic name of a graph next to each number on the card stock. Then tape the card stock to the inside back cover of an empty CD case. **Figure C**

4 Cut out five squares of graph paper that are each $4\frac{1}{2}$ inches by $4\frac{1}{2}$ inches. Label the squares 1 through 5. Draw a different type of graph on each square, making sure to match the types that are named on the magnetic rectangles.

5 Staple the graphs together to make a booklet. Insert the booklet into the cover of the CD case.

Putting the Math into Action

Exchange your game with a partner. Can you match each graph with its name?

A

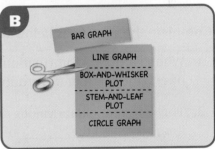

B

C

Vocabulary

Complete the sentences below with vocabulary words from the list above.

1. When gathering information about a(n) ___?___, researchers often study part of the group, called a(n) ___?___.

2. The sum of the data values divided by the number of data items is called the ___?___ of the data.

7-1 Frequency Tables, Stem-and-Leaf Plots, and Line Plots (pp. 376–380)

EXAMPLE

■ Make a line plot of the data.

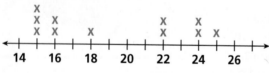

15, 22, 16, 24, 15, 25, 16, 22, 15, 24, 18

EXERCISES

 GPS M7D1.b, M7D1.f

Use the data set 35, 29, 14, 19, 32, 25, 27, 16, and 8 for Exercises 3 through 5.

3. Make a cumulative frequency table.

4. Make a stem-and-leaf plot of the data.

5. Make a line plot of the data.

7-2 Mean, Median, Mode, and Range (pp. 381–385)

 GPS M7D1.b, M7D1.c, M7D1.f, M7D1.g

EXAMPLE

■ Find the mean, median, mode, and range of the data set 3, 7, 10, 2, and 3.

Mean: $3 + 7 + 10 + 2 + 3 = 25$ $\frac{25}{5} = 5$

Median: 2, 3, **3**, 7, 10

Mode: **3**   Range: $10 - 2 = $ **8**

EXERCISES

Find the mean, median, mode, and range of each data set.

6. 324, 233, 324, 399, 233, 299

7. 48, 39, 27, 52, 45, 47, 49, 37

EXAMPLE

- Make a bar graph of the chess club's results: W, L, W, W, L, W, L, L, W, W, W, L, W.

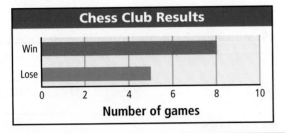

Chess Club Results

EXERCISES

8. Make a double-bar graph of the data.

Favorite Pet	Girls	Boys
Cat	42	31
Dog	36	52
Fish	3	10
Other	19	7

7-4 **Reading and Interpreting Circle Graphs** (pp. 390–393)

GPS M7D1.f, M7D1.g

EXAMPLE

- About what percent of people said yellow was their favorite color?
  about 25%

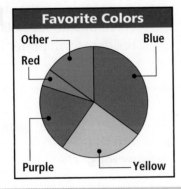

Favorite Colors

EXERCISES

Use the circle graph at left for Exercises 9 and 10.

9. Did more people choose purple or yellow as their favorite color?

10. Out of the 100 people surveyed, 35% chose blue as their favorite color. How many people chose blue?

7-5 **Box-and-Whisker Plots** (pp. 394–397)

GPS M7D1.c, M7D1.d, M7D1.f, M7D1.g

EXAMPLE

- Use the data to make a box-and-whisker plot: 14, 10, 23, 16, 21, 26, 23, 17, and 25.

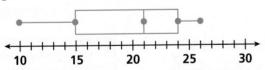

EXERCISES

Use the following data for Exercises 11–12: 33, 38, 43, 30, 29, 40, 51, 27, 42, 23, and 31.

11. Make a box-and-whisker plot.

12. What is the interquartile range?

7-6 **Line Graphs** (pp. 402–405)

GPS M7D1.f, M7D1.g

EXAMPLE

- Make a line graph of the rainfall data: Apr, 5 in.; May, 3 in.; Jun, 4 in.; Jul, 1 in.

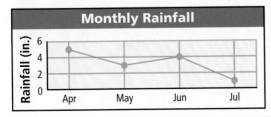

Monthly Rainfall

EXERCISES

13. Make a double-line graph of the data in the table.

U. S. Open Winning Scores					
	1995	1996	1997	1998	1999
Men	280	278	276	280	279
Women	278	272	274	290	272

Study Guide: Review

7-7 Choosing an Appropriate Display (pp. 408–411)

GPS M7D1.f

EXAMPLE

- Choose the type of graph that would best represent the population of a town over a 10-year period.

  Line graph

EXERCISES

Choose the type of graph that would best represent these data.

14. number of dogs in a kennel each day

15. number of exports from different countries

7-8 Populations and Samples (pp. 412–415)

GPS M7A2.a, M7A2.b

EXAMPLE

- In a random sample of 50 pigeons at a park, 4 are found to have a beak deformation. Is it reasonable to claim that about 20 of the pigeon population of 2,000 have this deformation? Explain.

  No; $\frac{4}{50}$ is not closely proportional to $\frac{20}{2,000}$.

EXERCISES

16. Fourteen out of 35 people surveyed prefer Brand X detergent. Is it reasonable for the store manager to claim that about 2,500 of the town's 6,000 residents will prefer Brand X detergent?

7-9 Scatter Plots (pp. 416–419)

GPS M7A3.a, M7A3.b, M7A3.c, M7D1.f, M7D1.g

EXAMPLE

- Write *positive*, *negative*, or *no correlation* to describe the relationship between date of birth and eye color.

  There seems to be no correlation between the data sets.

EXERCISES

17. Use the data to make a scatter plot. Write *positive*, *negative*, or *no correlation*.

Customers	47	56	35	75	25
Sales ($)	495	501	490	520	375

7-10 Misleading Graphs (pp. 422–425)

GPS M7D1.f

EXAMPLE

- Explain why the graph could be misleading.

  The vertical axis is broken, so it appears that A's sales are twice more than B's.

EXERCISES

18. Explain why the graph could be misleading.

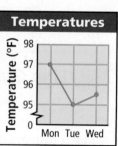

Use the data set 12, 18, 12, 22, 28, 23, 32, 10, 29, and 36 for problems 1–8.

1. Find the mean, median, mode, and range of the data set.

2. How would the outlier 57 affect the measures of central tendency?

3. Make a cumulative frequency table of the data.

4. Make a stem-and-leaf plot of the data.

5. Make a line plot of the data.

6. Make a histogram of the data.

7. Make a box-and-whisker plot of the data.

8. What is the interquartile range?

Use the table for problems 9 and 10.

9. The table shows the weight in pounds of several mammals. Make a double-bar graph of the data.

10. Which mammal shows the greatest weight difference between the male and the female?

Mammal	Male	Female
Gorilla	450	200
Lion	400	300
Tiger	420	300

Use the circle graph for problems 11 and 12.

11. Approximately what percent of the students are seventh graders?

12. If the school population is 1,200 students, are more than 500 students in eighth grade? Explain.

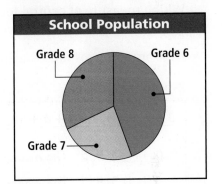

Use the table for problems 13 and 14.

13. The table shows passenger car fuel rates in miles per gallon for several years. Make a line graph of the data. During which 2-year period did the fuel rate decrease?

14. Estimate the fuel rate in 1997.

15. What type of graph would best display student attendance at various sporting events?

Year	1992	1994	1996	1998
Rate	21.0	20.7	21.2	21.6

For problems 16 and 17, write *positive correlation, negative correlation,* or *no correlation* to describe each relationship.

16. size of hand and typing speed

17. height from which an object is dropped and time it takes to hit the ground

18. Explain why the graph at right could be misleading.

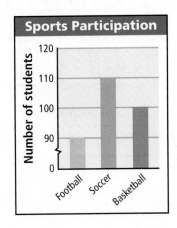

TEST TACKLER

Standardized Test Strategies

Short Response: Write Short Responses

Short-response test items are designed to test your understanding of a math concept. In your response, you usually have to show your work and explain your answer. Scores are based on a 2-point scoring chart called a rubric.

EXAMPLE 1

Short Response The following data represents the number of hours Leann studied each day after school for her history test.

$$0, 1, 0, 1, 5, 3, 4$$

Find the mean, median, and mode for the data set. Which measure of central tendency best represents the data? Explain your answer.

Here are some responses scored using the 2-point rubric.

2-point response:

$\dfrac{0 + 1 + 0 + 1 + 5 + 3 + 4}{7} = 2$ *The mean is 2.*

0 0 1 ① 3 4 5 *The median is 1.*

⓪ ⓪① ① 3 4 5 *The modes are 0 and 1.*

The measure of central tendency that best represents the data is the mean, because it shows the average number of hours that Leann studied before her test.

Scoring Rubric

2 points: The student correctly answers the question, shows all work, and provides a complete and correct explanation.

1 point: The student correctly answers the question but does not show all work or does not provide a complete explanation; or the student makes minor errors resulting in an incorrect solution but shows all work and provides a complete explanation.

0 points: The student gives an incorrect answer and shows no work or explanation, or the student gives no response.

1-point response:

$\dfrac{0 + 1 + 0 + 1 + 5 + 3 + 4}{7} = 2$ *The mean is 2.*

0 0 1 ① 3 4 5 *The median is 1.*

⓪ ⓪① ① 3 4 5 *The modes are 0 and 1.*

Notice that there is no explanation given about the measure of central tendency that best represents the data.

0-point response:

The mean is 2, the median is 2, and the mode is 0.

Notice that the answer is incorrect and there is no explanation.

Test Tackler

HOT TIP! Underline or highlight what you are being asked to do in each question. Be sure to explain how you get your answer in complete sentences.

Read each test item and use the scoring rubric to answer the questions that follow.

Item A
Short Response The box-and-whisker plot shows the height in inches of seventh-grade students. Describe the spread of the data.

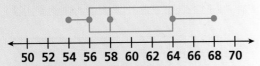

50 52 54 56 58 60 62 64 66 68 70

Student's Answer

> There are more students between 58 and 70 inches tall than there are between 50 and 58 inches tall because the third quartile is farther from the median than the first quartile is.

1. What score should the student's answer receive? Explain your reasoning.

2. What additional information, if any, should the student's answer include in order to receive full credit?

Item B
Short Response Explain the type of graph you would use to represent the number of each type of car sold at a car dealership in May.

Student's Answer

> I would use a bar graph to show how many of each car model was sold during the month.

3. What score should the student's answer receive? Explain your reasoning.

4. What additional information, if any, should the student's answer include in order to receive full credit?

Item C
Short Response Create a scatter plot of the data and describe the correlation between the outside temperature and the number of people at the public pool.

Temperature (°F)	70	75	80	85	90
Number of People	20	22	40	46	67

Student's Answer

> There is a positive correlation between the temperature and the number of people at the public pool because as it gets hotter, more people want to go swimming.

5. What score should the student's answer receive? Explain your reasoning.

6. What additional information, if any, should the student's answer include in order to receive full credit?

Item D
Short Response A survey was conducted to determine which age group attended the most movies in November. Fifteen people at a movie theater were asked their age, and their responses are as follows: 6, 10, 34, 22, 46, 11, 62, 14, 14, 5, 23, 25, 17, 18, and 55. Make a cumulative frequency table of the data. Then explain which group saw the most movies.

Student's Answer

Age Groups	Frequency	Cumulative Frequency
0-13	4	4
14-26	7	11
27-40	1	12
41-54	1	13
55-68	2	15

7. What score should the student's answer receive? Explain your reasoning.

8. What additional information, if any, should the student's answer include in order to receive full credit?

CRCT PREP

Cumulative Assessment, Chapters 1–7

Multiple Choice

1. Which expression is true for the data set?   15, 18, 13, 15, 16, 14

Ⓐ Mean < mode

Ⓑ Median > mean

Ⓒ Median = mean

Ⓓ Median = mode

2. What is the first step to complete in simplifying this expression?

$\frac{2}{5} + [3 - 5(2)] \div 6$

Ⓕ Multiply 5 and 2.

Ⓖ Divide by 6.

Ⓗ Subtract 5 from 3.

Ⓙ Divide 2 by 5.

3. What is the slope of the line shown?

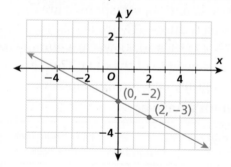

Ⓐ $\frac{1}{2}$ Ⓒ 2

Ⓑ $-\frac{2}{1}$ Ⓓ $-\frac{1}{2}$

4. On Monday the temperature was −13°F. On Tuesday the temperature rose 7°F. What was the temperature on Tuesday?

Ⓕ −20°F   Ⓗ −6°F

Ⓖ −8°F   Ⓙ 7°F

5. Which model best represents the fraction $\frac{5}{8}$?

Ⓐ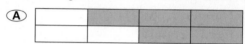

Ⓑ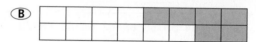

Ⓒ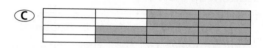

Ⓓ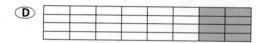

6. Ron eats $\frac{1}{4}$ cup of cereal every day as part of his breakfast. He has had a total of 16 cups of cereal this year. How many days has he eaten cereal?

Ⓕ 4 days   Ⓗ 32 days

Ⓖ 16 days   Ⓙ 64 days

7. A store is offering lip gloss at 25% off its original price. The original price of lip gloss is $7.59. What is the sale price?

Ⓐ $5.69   Ⓒ $3.80

Ⓑ $4.93   Ⓓ $1.90

8. What is the mode of the data given in the stem-and-leaf plot?

Stems	Leaves
6	1 2 2 5 9
7	0 4 6 7 8
8	3 3 3 5 6

Key: 7|0 means 70

Ⓕ 25   Ⓗ 76

Ⓖ 62   Ⓙ 83

9. Solve $8 + 34x = -60$ for x.

(A) $x = -5$ (C) $x = -2$

(B) $x = -0.97$ (D) $x = 2$

10. Which statement is best supported by the data?

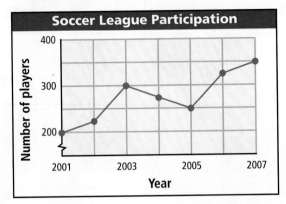

Soccer League Participation

(F) More students played soccer in 2005 than in 2002.

(G) From 2001–2007, soccer participation increased by 100%.

(H) From 2002–2006, soccer participation decreased by 144%.

(J) Participation increased between 2004 and 2005.

Read a graph or diagram as closely as you read the actual test question. These visual aids contain important information.

11. What is the median of the data set?

14, 11, 14, 11, 13, 12, 9, 15, 16

(A) 11   (C) 12.7

(B) 11.5   (D) 13

12. What value represents the upper quartile of the data in the box-and-whisker plot below?

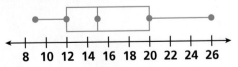

(F) 15   (H) 20

(G) 18   (J) 26

Short Response

13. The graph shows the results of a survey. Aaron read the graph and determined that more than $\frac{1}{5}$ of the students chose drama as their favorite type of movie. Do you agree with Aaron? Why or why not?

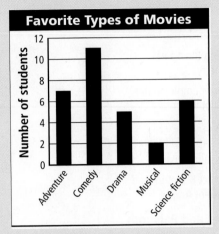

Favorite Types of Movies

14. A land developer purchases 120 acres of land and plans to divide one part into five 5-acre lots, another part into two 10-acre lots, and the rest into $\frac{1}{2}$-acre lots. Each lot will be sold for a future home site. How many total lots can the developer plan to sell?

Extended Response

15. Mr. Parker wants to identify the types of activities in which high school students participate after school, so he surveys the twelfth-graders in his science classes. The table shows the results of the survey.

Activity	Boys	Girls
Play sports	36	24
Talk to friends	6	30
Do homework	15	18
Work	5	4

a. Use the data in the table to construct a double-bar graph.

b. What is the mean number of girls per activity? Show your work.

c. What type of sample is used? Is this sample representative of the population? Explain.

Geometric Figures

CRCT PREP

go.hrw.com
Chapter Project Online
KEYWORD: MS7 Ch8

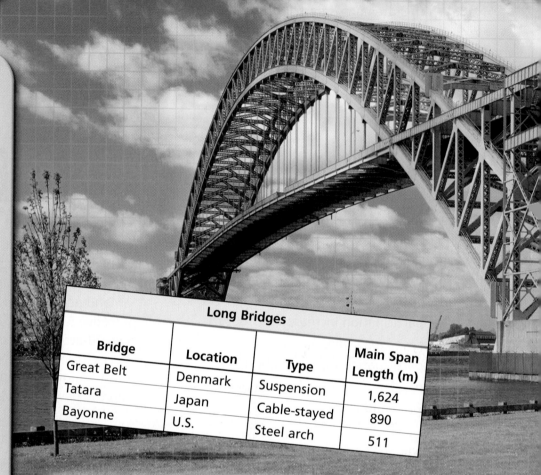

Long Bridges			
Bridge	**Location**	**Type**	**Main Span Length (m)**
Great Belt	Denmark	Suspension	1,624
Tatara	Japan	Cable-stayed	890
Bayonne	U.S.	Steel arch	511

Career Bridge Designer

Many factors influence the way a bridge is constructed. A bridge must be able to withstand winds, snow, and the weight of traffic while supporting its own weight.

Bridge designers also have to consider the distance that a bridge must cross (called the *span*), the nature of the land, and the look of the structure. Bridge designers often combine technological know-how with artistry to create structures that are both functional and beautiful.

ARE YOU READY?

✓ Vocabulary

Choose the best term from the list to complete each sentence.

1. An equation showing that two ratios are equal is a(n) __?__.

2. The coordinates of a point on a grid are written as a(n) __?__.

3. A(n) __?__ is a special ratio that compares a number to 100 and uses the symbol %.

4. The number −3 is a(n) __?__.

decimal

integer

percent

proportion

ordered pair

Complete these exercises to review skills you will need for this chapter.

✓ Percents and Decimals

Write each decimal as a percent.

5. 0.77   **6.** 0.06   **7.** 0.9   **8.** 1.04

Write each percent as a decimal.

9. 42%   **10.** 80%   **11.** 1%   **12.** 131%

✓ Find the Percent of a Number

Solve.

13. What is 10% of 40?   **14.** What is 12% of 100?   **15.** What is 99% of 60?

16. What is 100% of 81?   **17.** What is 45% of 360?   **18.** What is 55% of 1,024?

✓ Inverse Operations

Use the inverse operation to write an equation. Solve.

19. $45 + n = 97$ **20.** $n - 18 = 100$ **21.** $n - 72 = 91$ **22.** $n + 23 = 55$

23. $5 \times t = 105$ **24.** $b \div 13 = 8$ **25.** $k \times 18 = 90$ **26.** $d \div 7 = 8$

✓ Graph Ordered Pairs

Use the coordinate plane at right. Write the ordered pair for each point.

27. point A **28.** point B

29. point C **30.** point D

31. point E **32.** point F

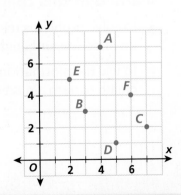

Study Guide: Preview

Where You've Been

Previously, you

- identified relationships involving angles in triangles and quadrilaterals.

- identified similar figures.

- graphed points on a coordinate plane.

In This Chapter

You will study

- classifying pairs of angles as complementary or supplementary.

- classifying triangles and quadrilaterals.

- graphing translations and reflections on a coordinate plane.

- using congruence and similarity to solve problems.

Where You're Going

You can use the skills learned in this chapter

- to solve problems related to architecture and engineering.

- to use transformations to create patterns in art classes.

Key Vocabulary/Vocabulario

angle	ángulo
congruent	congruentes
line symmetry	simetría axial
parallel lines	líneas paralelas
perpendicular lines	líneas perpendiculares
polygon	polígono
quadrilateral	cuadrilátero
rotation	rotación
transformation	transformación
vertex	vértice

Vocabulary Connections

To become familiar with some of the vocabulary terms in the chapter, consider the following. You may refer to the chapter, the glossary, or a dictionary if you like.

1. *Congruent* comes from the Latin word *congruere*, meaning "to agree or correspond." If two figures are **congruent**, do you think they look the same or different?

2. *Polygon* comes from the Greek words *polus*, meaning "many," and *gonia*, meaning "angle." What do you think a shape called a **polygon** includes?

3. *Quadrilateral* comes from the Latin words *quadri*, meaning "four," and *latus*, meaning "sides." How many sides do you think a **quadrilateral** has?

4. *Rotation* can mean "the act of spinning or turning." How do you think a figure is moved when you perform a **rotation** on it?

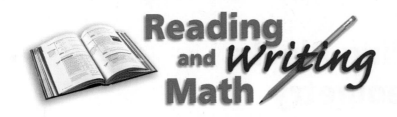

Writing Strategy: Keep a Math Journal

Keeping a math journal can help you improve your writing and reasoning skills and help you make sense of math topics that might be confusing.

You can use your journal to reflect on what you have learned in class or to summarize important concepts and vocabulary. Most important, though, your math journal can help you see your progress throughout the year.

Journal Entry: Read the entry Lydia wrote in her math journal about similar figures.

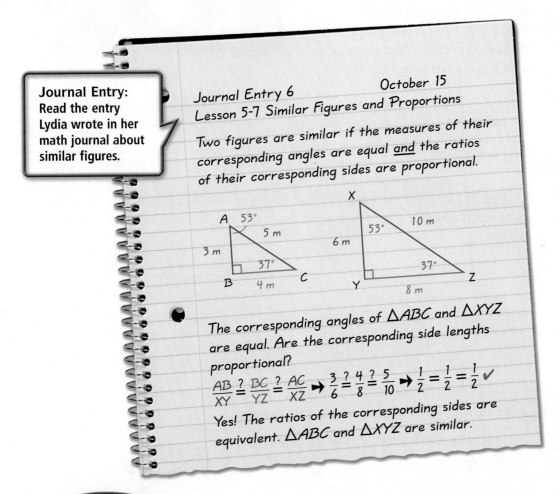

Journal Entry 6   October 15
Lesson 5-7 Similar Figures and Proportions

Two figures are similar if the measures of their corresponding angles are equal <u>and</u> the ratios of their corresponding sides are proportional.

The corresponding angles of △ABC and △XYZ are equal. Are the corresponding side lengths proportional?

$$\frac{AB}{XY} \overset{?}{=} \frac{BC}{YZ} \overset{?}{=} \frac{AC}{XZ} \rightarrow \frac{3}{6} \overset{?}{=} \frac{4}{8} \overset{?}{=} \frac{5}{10} \rightarrow \frac{1}{2} = \frac{1}{2} = \frac{1}{2} \checkmark$$

Yes! The ratios of the corresponding sides are equivalent. △ABC and △XYZ are similar.

Try This

Begin a math journal. Make an entry every day for one week. Use the following ideas to begin your entries. Be sure to date each entry.

- What I already know about this lesson is . . .

- The skills I need to be successful in this lesson are . . .

- What challenges did I have? How did I handle these challenges?

8-1 Building Blocks of Geometry

Learn to identify and describe geometric figures.

Vocabulary

point

line

plane

ray

line segment

congruent

Points, lines, and *planes* are the most basic figures of geometry. Other geometric figures, such as *line segments* and *rays,* are defined in terms of these building blocks.

Artists often use basic geometric figures when creating their works. For example, Wassily Kandinsky used *line segments* in his painting called *Red Circle,* which is shown at right.

Helpful Hint

A number line is an example of a line, and a coordinate plane is an example of a plane.

A **point** is an exact location. It is usually represented as a dot, but it has no size at all.	• A	point *A* *Use a capital letter to name a point.*
A **line** is a straight path that extends without end in opposite directions.	ℓ ← X Y →	$\overleftrightarrow{XY}$, $\overleftrightarrow{YX}$, or ℓ *Use two points on the line or a lowercase letter to name a line.*
A **plane** is a perfectly flat surface that extends infinitely in all directions.	Q• S• R•	plane *QRS* *Use three points in any order, not on the same line, to name a plane.*

EXAMPLE 1 Identifying Points, Lines, and Planes

Identify the figures in the diagram.

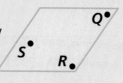

Georgia Performance Standards

M7P3.d Use the language of mathematics to express mathematical ideas precisely. Also, M7P1.b, M7P5.b.

A three points

A, E, and *D*   *Choose any three points.*

B two lines

$\overleftrightarrow{BD}$, $\overleftrightarrow{CE}$ *Choose any two points on a line to name a line.*

C a plane

plane *ABC*   *Choose any three points not on the same line to name a plane.*

A **ray** is a part of a line. It has one endpoint and extends without end in one direction.	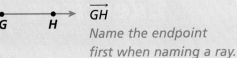	$\overrightarrow{GH}$ *Name the endpoint first when naming a ray.*
A **line segment** is a part of a line or a ray that extends from one endpoint to another.	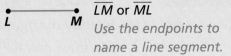	$\overline{LM}$ or $\overline{ML}$ *Use the endpoints to name a line segment.*

EXAMPLE **2** **Identifying Line Segments and Rays**

Identify the figures in the diagram.

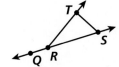

A three rays
$\overrightarrow{RQ}$, $\overrightarrow{RT}$, and $\overrightarrow{SQ}$ *Name the endpoint of a ray first.*

B three line segments
$\overline{RQ}$, $\overline{QS}$, and $\overline{ST}$ *Use the endpoints in any order to name a line segment.*

Figures are **congruent** if they have the same shape and size. Line segments are congruent if they have the same length.

You can use tick marks to indicate congruent line segments. In the triangle at right, line segments *AB* and *BC* are congruent.

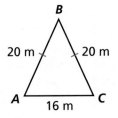

EXAMPLE **3** **Identifying Congruent Line Segments**

Identify the line segments that are congruent in the figure.

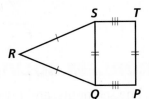

$\overline{QR} \cong \overline{SR}$ *One tick mark*
$\overline{QS} \cong \overline{PT}$ *Two tick marks*
$\overline{QP} \cong \overline{ST}$ *Three tick marks*

Think and Discuss    **GPS M7P1.d, M7P2.c**

1. **Explain** why a line and a plane can be named in more than two ways. How many ways can a line segment be named?

2. **Explain** why it is important to choose three points that are not on the same line when naming a plane.

Georgia Performance Standards

M7P1.a, M7P3.a, M7P3.d, M7P4.c

go.hrw.com
Homework Help Online
KEYWORD: MS7 8-1
Parent Resources Online
KEYWORD: MS7 Parent

GUIDED PRACTICE

See Example 1 **Identify the figures in the diagram.**

1. three points

2. two lines

3. a plane

See Example 2 4. three rays

5. three line segments

See Example 3 6. Identify the line segments that are congruent in the figure.

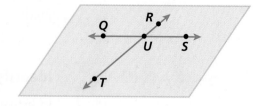

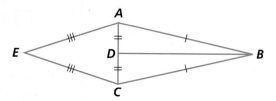

INDEPENDENT PRACTICE

See Example 1 **Identify the figures in the diagram.**

7. three points

8. two lines

9. a plane

See Example 2 10. three rays

11. three line segments

See Example 3 12. Identify the line segments that are congruent in the figure.

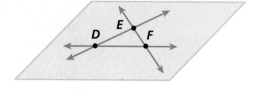

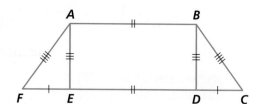

PRACTICE AND PROBLEM SOLVING

Extra Practice p. 741

13. Identify the points, lines, line segments, and rays that are represented in the illustration, and tell what plane each is in. Some figures may be in more than one plane.

14. **Critical Thinking** How many different line segments can be named in the figure below? Name each segment.

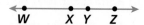

15. Draw a diagram in which a plane, 5 points, 4 rays, and 2 lines can be identified. Then identify these figures.

16. The artwork at right, by Diana Ong, is called *Blocs*.

    a. Copy the line segments in the artwork. Add tick marks to show line segments that appear to be congruent.

    b. Label the endpoints of the segments, including the points of intersection. Then name four pairs of line segments that appear to be congruent.

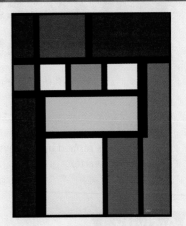

17. Draw a figure that includes at least three sets of congruent line segments. Label the endpoints and use notation to tell which line segments are congruent.

18. **Critical Thinking** Can two endpoints be shared by two different line segments? Make a drawing to illustrate your answer.

19. 🖊 **Write About It** Explain the difference between a line, a line segment, and a ray. Is it possible to estimate the length of any of these figures? If so, tell which ones and why.

20. ⭐ **Challenge** The sandstone sculpture at right, by Georges Vantongerloo, is called *Interrelation of Volumes*. Explain whether two separate faces on the front of the sculpture could be in the same plane.

CRCT PREP • GPS SUPPORT • SPIRAL REVIEW

21. Multiple Choice Identify the line segments that are congruent in the figure.

  I $\overline{AB}, \overline{BC}$ **II** $\overline{AB}, \overline{CD}$

  III $\overline{BC}, \overline{CD}$ **IV** $\overline{BC}, \overline{AD}$

  Ⓐ I only   Ⓑ I and III   Ⓒ II and IV   Ⓓ II only

22. Short Response Draw a plane that contains each of the following: points *A*, *B*, and *C*; line segment *AB*; ray *BC*; and line *AC*.

Find each product or quotient. (Lesson 2-4)

23. $-48 \div (-3)$ **24.** $-2 \cdot (-6)$ **25.** $-56 \div 8$ **26.** $5 \cdot (-13)$

Find each percent of change. Round answers to the nearest tenth of a percent, if necessary. (Lesson 6-6)

27. 85 is decreased to 60.   **28.** 35 is increased to 120.   **29.** 6 is decreased to 1.

Hands-On LAB 8-2

Explore Complementary and Supplementary Angles

Use with Lesson 8-2

go.hrw.com
Lab Resources Online
KEYWORD: MS7 Lab8

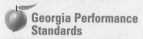

Georgia Performance Standards

M7P2.b, M7P3.b, M7P3.d

REMEMBER

- An angle is formed by two rays with a common endpoint, called the vertex.

Activity 1

You can use a *protractor* to measure angles in units called *degrees*. Find the measure of ∠AVB.

① Place the center point of the protractor on the vertex of the angle.

② Place the protractor so that $\overrightarrow{AV}$ passes through the 0° mark.

③ Using the scale that starts with 0° along $\overrightarrow{AV}$, read the measure where $\overrightarrow{VB}$ crosses the scale. The measure of ∠AVB is 50°.

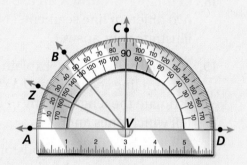

Think and Discuss

1. Explain how to find the measure of ∠BVC without moving the protractor.

Try This

Use the protractor in Activity 1 to find the measure of each angle.

1. ∠AVC   **2.** ∠AVZ   **3.** ∠DVC

Activity 2

Copy and measure each pair of angles.

Type of Angle Pair	Examples	Nonexamples
Complementary	**1.** *A* *B*	**2.** *C* *D*
	3. *E* *F*	**4.** *G* *H*

Type of Angle Pair	Examples	Nonexamples
Supplementary	5. *I J*	6. *K L*
	7. *M* *N*	8. *O* *P*

Think and Discuss

1. For each type of angle pair, complementary and supplementary, write a rule that relates the angle measurements.

Try This

Use a protractor to measure each of the angle pairs below. Tell whether the angle pairs are complementary, supplementary, or neither.

1.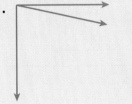

2.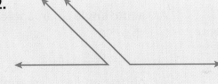

3.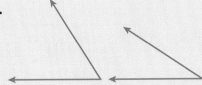

4.

5. How can you tell that the angle pairs in exercise 4 are supplementary without using a protractor?

6. Use a protractor to find all the pairs of complementary and supplementary angles in the figure at right.

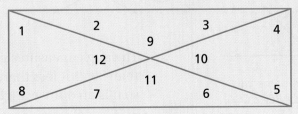

8-2 Classifying Angles

Learn to identify angles and angle pairs.

Vocabulary

angle

vertex

right angle

acute angle

obtuse angle

straight angle

complementary angles

supplementary angles

Georgia Performance Standards

M7A2.a Given a problem, define a variable, write an equation, solve the equation, and interpret the solution. Also, M7A1.a, M7A2.b, M7P3.d.

When riding down a ramp on a skateboard, the speed you gain depends partly on the *angle* that the ramp makes with the ground.

An **angle** is formed by two rays with a common endpoint. The two rays are the sides of the angle. The common endpoint is the **vertex**.

Angles are measured in degrees (°). An angle's measure determines the type of angle it is.

Vertex
30°

A **right angle** is an angle that measures exactly 90°. The symbol ⌐ indicates a right angle.

An **acute angle** is an angle that measures less than 90°.

An **obtuse angle** is an angle that measures more than 90° but less than 180°.

A **straight angle** is an angle that measures exactly 180°.

EXAMPLE 1 Classifying Angles

Tell whether each angle is acute, right, obtuse, or straight.

A

The angle measures greater than 90° but less than 180°, so it is an obtuse angle.

B

The angle measures less than 90°, so it is an acute angle.

Writing Math

You can name this angle ∠ABC, ∠CBA, ∠B, or ∠1.

If the sum of the measures of two angles is 90°, then the angles are **complementary angles**. If the sum of the measures of two angles is 180°, then the angles are **supplementary angles**.

EXAMPLE 2 **Identifying Complementary and Supplementary Angles**

Use the diagram to tell whether the angles are complementary, supplementary, or neither.

Helpful Hint

If the angle you are measuring appears obtuse, then its measure is greater than 90°. If the angle is acute, its measure is less than 90°.

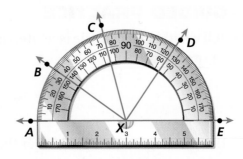

A ∠*DXE* and ∠*AXB*

m∠*DXE* = 55° and m∠*AXB* = 35°

Since 55° + 35° = 90°, ∠*DXE* and ∠*AXB* are complementary.

Reading Math

Read m∠*DXE* as "the measure of angle *DXE*."

B ∠*DXE* and ∠*BXC*

m∠*DXE* = 55°. To find m∠*BXC*, start with the measure that $\overrightarrow{XC}$ crosses, 75°, and subtract the measure that $\overrightarrow{XB}$ crosses, 35°.

m∠*BXC* = 75° − 35° = 40°.

Since 55° + 40° = 95°, ∠*DXE* and ∠*BXC* are neither complementary nor supplementary.

C ∠*AXC* and ∠*CXE*

m∠*AXC* = 75° and m∠*CXE* = 105°

Since 75° + 105° = 180°, ∠*AXC* and ∠*CXE* are supplementary.

EXAMPLE 3 **Finding Angle Measures**

Angles *R* and *V* are supplementary. If m∠*R* is 67°, what is m∠*V*?

Since ∠*R* and ∠*V* are supplementary, m∠*R* + m∠*V* = 180°.

$$m\angle R + m\angle V = 180°$$
$$67° + m\angle V = 180°$$ *Substitute 67° for m∠R.*
$$\underline{-67° \qquad\qquad -67°}$$ *Subtract 67° from both sides*
$$m\angle V = 113°$$ *to isolate m∠V.*

The measure of ∠*V* is 113°.

GPS M7P1.d, M7P3.b

Think and Discuss

1. **Describe** three different ways to classify an angle.

2. **Explain** how to find the measure of ∠*P* if ∠*P* and ∠*Q* are complementary angles and m∠*Q* = 25°.

Georgia Performance Standards

M7P3.a, M7P3.c, M7P3.d, M7P4.c

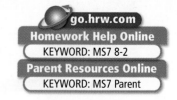
GUIDED PRACTICE

See Example **1** Tell whether each angle is acute, right, obtuse, or straight.

1.

2.

3.

See Example **2** Use the diagram to tell whether the angles are complementary, supplementary, or neither.

4. ∠AXB and ∠BXC   **5.** ∠BXC and ∠DXE

6. ∠DXE and ∠AXD   **7.** ∠CXD and ∠AXB

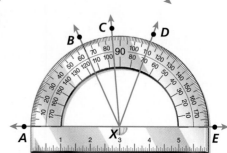

See Example **3** **8.** Angles L and P are complementary. If m∠P is 34°, what is m∠L?

9. Angles B and C are supplementary. If m∠B is 119°, what is m∠C?

INDEPENDENT PRACTICE

See Example **1** Tell whether each angle is acute, right, obtuse, or straight.

10.

11.

12.

See Example **2** Use the diagram to tell whether the angles are complementary, supplementary, or neither.

13. ∠NZO and ∠MZN   **14.** ∠MZN and ∠OZP

15. ∠LZN and ∠NZP   **16.** ∠NZO and ∠LZM

See Example **3** **17.** Angles F and O are supplementary. If m∠F is 85°, what is m∠O?

18. Angles J and K are complementary. If m∠K is 22°, what is m∠J?

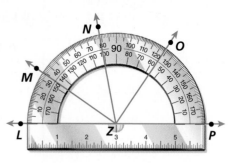

PRACTICE AND PROBLEM SOLVING

CRCT GPS

Extra Practice p. 741

Classify each pair of angles as complementary or supplementary. Then find the missing angle measure.

19.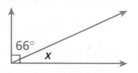

28°   x

20.

66°
x

21.

134°
x

22. Critical Thinking The hands of a clock form an acute angle at 1:00. What type of angle is formed at 6:00? at 3:00? at 5:00?

23. Geography Imaginary curves around Earth show distances in degrees from the equator and Prime Meridian. On a flat map, these curves are displayed as horizontal lines (latitude) and vertical lines (longitude).

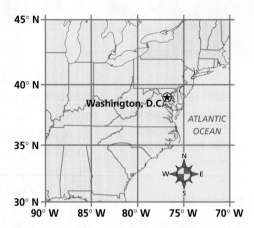

   a. What type of angle is formed where a line of latitude and a line of longitude cross?

   b. Estimate the latitude and longitude of Washington, D.C.

24. What's the Error? A student states that when the sum of two angles equals the measure of a straight angle, the two angles are complementary. Explain why the student is incorrect.

25. Write About It Explain why two obtuse angles cannot be supplementary to one another.

26. Challenge Find m∠*BAC* in the figure.

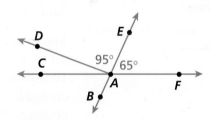

Use the diagram for Exercises 27 and 28.

27. Multiple Choice Which statement is NOT true?

   Ⓐ ∠*BAC* is acute.

   Ⓑ ∠*DAE* is a right angle.

   Ⓒ ∠*FAE* and ∠*EAD* are complementary angles.

   Ⓓ ∠*FAD* and ∠*DAC* are supplementary angles.

28. Multiple Choice What is the measure of ∠*FAD*?

   Ⓕ 30°   Ⓖ 120°   Ⓗ 150°   Ⓙ 180°

Find the mean, median, mode, and range of each data set. (Lesson 7-2)

29. 6, 3, 5, 6, 8   **30.** 14, 18, 10, 20, 23   **31.** 41, 35, 29, 41, 58, 24

32. Identify and name the figure at right. (Lesson 8-1)

Angle Relationships

Learn to identify parallel, perpendicular, and skew lines, and angles formed by a transversal.

Vocabulary

perpendicular lines

parallel lines

skew lines

adjacent angles

vertical angles

transversal

corresponding angles

When lines, segments, or rays intersect, they form angles. If the angles formed by two intersecting lines measure 90°, the lines are **perpendicular lines**. The red and yellow line segments in the photograph are perpendicular.

Some lines in the same plane do not intersect at all. These lines are **parallel lines**. Segments and rays that are parts of parallel lines are also parallel.

Skew lines do not intersect, and yet they are also not parallel. They lie in different planes. The orange line segments in the photograph are skew.

EXAMPLE 1 — Identifying Parallel, Perpendicular, and Skew Lines

Tell whether the lines in the figure appear parallel, perpendicular, or skew.

A $\overleftrightarrow{AB}$ and $\overleftrightarrow{AC}$
$\overleftrightarrow{AB} \perp \overleftrightarrow{AC}$

The lines appear to intersect to form right angles.

B $\overleftrightarrow{CE}$ and $\overleftrightarrow{BD}$
$\overleftrightarrow{CE}$ and $\overleftrightarrow{BD}$ are skew.

The lines are in different planes and do not intersect.

C $\overleftrightarrow{AC}$ and $\overleftrightarrow{BD}$
$\overleftrightarrow{AC} \parallel \overleftrightarrow{BD}$

The lines are in the same plane and do not intersect.

Georgia Performance Standards

M7A2.a Given a problem, define a variable, write an equation, solve the equation, and interpret the solution. Also, M7A2.b, M7P3.d.

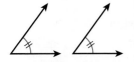

Adjacent angles have a common vertex and a common side, but no common interior points. Angles 2 and 3 in the diagram are adjacent. Adjacent angles formed by two intersecting lines are supplementary.

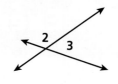

Vertical angles are the opposite angles formed by two intersecting lines. Angles 1 and 3 in the diagram are vertical angles. Vertical angles have the same measure, so they are congruent.

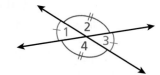

A **transversal** is a line that intersects two or more lines. Line *t* is a transversal. When the lines that are intersected are parallel, four pairs of *corresponding angles* are formed. **Corresponding angles** are on the same side of the transversal and are both above or both below the parallel lines. Angles 1 and 5 are corresponding angles. Corresponding angles are congruent.

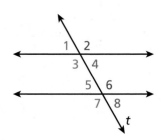

EXAMPLE 2 Using Angle Relationships to Find Angle Measures

Line *n* ∥ line *p*. Find the measure of each angle.

A ∠6

∠6 and the 55° angle are vertical angles. Since vertical angles are congruent, m∠6 = 55°.

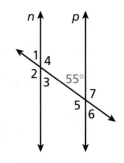

B ∠1

∠1 and the 55° angle are corresponding angles. Since corresponding angles are congruent, m∠1 = 55°.

C ∠7

∠7 and the 55° angle are adjacent, supplementary angles.

$$m\angle 7 + 55° = 180°$$
$$\underline{\quad -55° \quad -55°}$$
$$m\angle 7 \quad = \quad 125°$$

The sum of the measures of supplementary angles is 180°.

Think and Discuss GPS M7P4.c, M7P5.a

1. **Draw** a pair of parallel lines intersected by a transversal. Use tick marks to indicate the congruent angles.

2. **Give** some examples in which parallel, perpendicular, and skew relationships can be seen in the real world.

Georgia Performance Standards

M7P1.c, M7P2.a, M7P2.c, M7P3.a

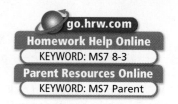

go.hrw.com
Homework Help Online
KEYWORD: MS7 8-3
Parent Resources Online
KEYWORD: MS7 Parent

GUIDED PRACTICE

See Example **Tell whether the lines appear parallel, perpendicular, or skew.**

1. $\overleftrightarrow{JL}$ and $\overleftrightarrow{KM}$

2. $\overleftrightarrow{LM}$ and $\overleftrightarrow{KN}$

3. $\overleftrightarrow{LM}$ and $\overleftrightarrow{KM}$

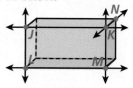

See Example 2 **Line $r \parallel$ line s. Find the measure of each angle.**

4. $\angle 5$

5. $\angle 2$

6. $\angle 7$

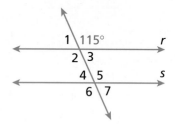

INDEPENDENT PRACTICE

See Example 1 **Tell whether the lines appear parallel, perpendicular, or skew.**

7. $\overleftrightarrow{UX}$ and $\overleftrightarrow{YZ}$

8. $\overleftrightarrow{YZ}$ and $\overleftrightarrow{XY}$

9. $\overleftrightarrow{UX}$ and $\overleftrightarrow{VW}$

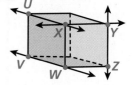

See Example 2 **Line $k \parallel$ line m. Find the measure of each angle.**

10. $\angle 1$

11. $\angle 3$

12. $\angle 6$

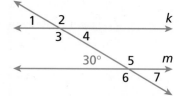

PRACTICE AND PROBLEM SOLVING

CRCT GPS

Extra Practice p. 741

For Exercises 13–16, use the figure to complete each statement.

13. Lines x and y are ___?___.

14. Lines u and x are ___?___.

15. $\angle 3$ and $\angle 4$ are ___?___. They are also ___?___.

16. $\angle 2$ and $\angle 6$ are ___?___. They are also ___?___.

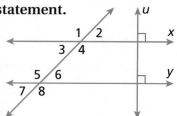

17. **Critical Thinking** A pair of complementary angles are congruent. What is the measure of each angle?

18. **Multi-Step** Two lines intersect to form four angles. The measure of one angle is 27°. Draw a diagram to show the measures of the other three angles. Explain your answer.

Tell whether each statement is always, sometimes, or never true.

19. Adjacent angles are congruent.

20. Intersecting lines are skew.

21. Vertical angles are congruent.

22. Parallel lines intersect.

23. **Construction** In the diagram of the partial wall frame shown, the vertical beams are parallel.

a. Angle *ORT* measures 90°. How are $\overline{OR}$ and $\overline{RS}$ related?

b. $\overline{PT}$ crosses two vertical crossbeams. What word describes $\overline{PT}$?

c. How are ∠1 and ∠2 related?

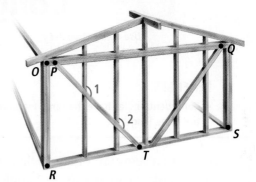

24. **Critical Thinking** Two lines intersect to form congruent adjacent angles. What can you say about the two lines?

25. **Choose a Strategy** Trace the dots in the figure. Draw all the lines that connect three dots. How many pairs of perpendicular lines have you drawn?

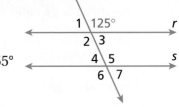

(A) 8   (B) 9   (C) 10   (D) 14

26. **Write About It** Use the definition of a straight angle to explain why adjacent angles formed by two intersecting lines are supplementary.

27. **Challenge** The lines in the parking lot appear to be parallel. How could you check that the lines are parallel?

CRCT Prep • GPS Support • Spiral Review

Use the diagram for Exercises 28 and 29.

28. **Multiple Choice** What is the measure of ∠3?

(A) 125°   (B) 75°   (C) 65°   (D) 55°

29. **Multiple Choice** What is the measure of ∠6?

(F) 125°   (G) 75°   (H) 65°   (J) 55°

Add or subtract. Estimate to check whether each answer is reasonable. (Lesson 3-2)

30. $3.583 - (-2.759)$

31. $-9.43 + 7.68$

32. $-1.03 + (-0.081)$

Classify each pair of angles as complementary or supplementary. Then find the missing angle measure. (Lesson 8-2)

33.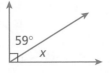

34.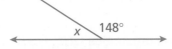

35.

Hands-On LAB 8-3

Construct Bisectors and Congruent Angles

Use with Lesson 8-3

go.hrw.com
Lab Resources Online
KEYWORD: MS7 Lab8

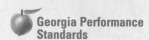
Georgia Performance Standards
M7G1.a, M7P5.a, M7P5.b

REMEMBER
- Congruent angles have the same measure, and congruent segments are the same length.

To bisect a segment or an angle is to divide it into two congruent parts. You can bisect segments and angles, and construct congruent angles without using a protractor or ruler. Instead, you can use a compass and a straightedge.

Activity

1 Bisect a line segment.

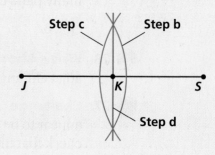

a. Draw a line segment $\overline{JS}$ on a piece of paper.

b. Place your compass on endpoint J and, using an opening that is greater than half the length of $\overline{JS}$, draw an arc that intersects $\overline{JS}$.

c. Place your compass on endpoint S and draw an arc using the same opening as you did in part **b.** The arc should intersect the first arc at both ends.

d. Draw a line to connect the intersections of the arcs. Label the intersection of $\overline{JS}$ and the line point K.

Measure $\overline{JS}$, $\overline{JK}$, and $\overline{KS}$. What do you notice?

The bisector of $\overline{JS}$ is a *perpendicular bisector* because all of the angles it forms with $\overline{JS}$ measure 90°.

2 Bisect an angle.

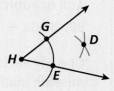

a. Draw an acute angle GHE on a piece of paper. Label the vertex H.

b. Place the point of your compass on H and draw an arc through both sides of the angle. Label points G and E where the arc crosses each side of the angle.

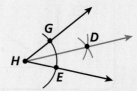

c. Without changing your compass opening, draw intersecting arcs from point G and point E. Label the point of intersection D.

d. Draw $\overrightarrow{HD}$.

Use your protractor to measure angles GHE, GHD, and DHE. What do you notice?

3 Construct congruent angles.

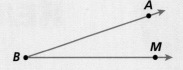

a. Draw angle *ABM* on your paper.

b. To construct an angle congruent to angle *ABM*, begin by drawing a ray, and label its endpoint *C*.

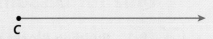

c. With your compass point on *B*, draw an arc through angle *ABM*.

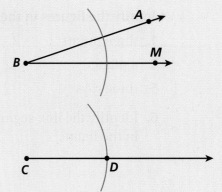

d. With the same compass opening, place the compass point on *C* and draw an arc through the ray. Label point *D* where the arc crosses the ray.

e. With your compass, measure the arc in angle *ABM*.

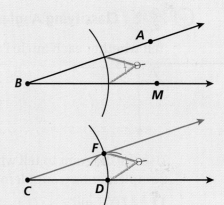

f. With the same opening, place your compass point on *D*, and draw another arc intersecting the first one. Label the intersection *F*. Draw $\overrightarrow{CF}$.

Use your protractor to measure angle *ABM* and angle *FCD*. What do you find?

Think and Discuss

1. How many bisectors would you use to divide an angle into four equal parts?

2. An 88° angle is bisected, and then each of the two angles formed are bisected. What is the measure of each of the smaller angles formed?

Try This

Use a compass and a straightedge to perform each construction.

1. Bisect a line segment.

2. Trace and then bisect angle *GOB*.

3. Draw an angle congruent to angle *GOB*.

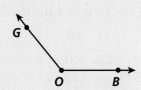

READY TO GO ON?

Quiz for Lessons 8-1 Through 8-3

✓ 8-1 Building Blocks of Geometry

Identify the figures in the diagram.

1. three points
2. three lines
3. a plane
4. three line segments
5. three rays

6. Identify the line segments that are congruent in the figure.

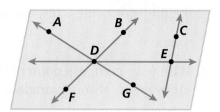

✓ 8-2 Classifying Angles

Tell whether each angle is acute, right, obtuse, or straight.

7.   8.   9.   10.

Use the diagram to tell whether the angles are complementary, supplementary, or neither.

11. ∠DXE and ∠AXD
12. ∠AXB and ∠CXD
13. ∠DXE and ∠AXB
14. ∠BXC and ∠DXE

15. Angles R and S are complementary. If m∠S is 17°, what is m∠R?

16. Angles D and F are supplementary. If m∠D is 45°, what is m∠F?

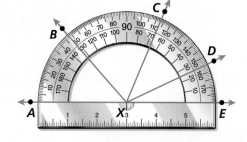

✓ 8-3 Angle Relationships

Tell whether the lines appear parallel, perpendicular, or skew.

17. $\overleftrightarrow{KL}$ and $\overleftrightarrow{MN}$
18. $\overleftrightarrow{JL}$ and $\overleftrightarrow{MN}$
19. $\overleftrightarrow{KL}$ and $\overleftrightarrow{JL}$
20. $\overleftrightarrow{IJ}$ and $\overleftrightarrow{MN}$

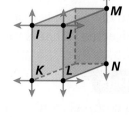

Line a ∥ line b. Find the measure of each angle.

21. ∠3
22. ∠4
23. ∠8
24. ∠6
25. ∠1
26. ∠5

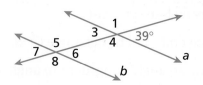

Focus on Problem Solving

Understand the Problem

Understand

• **Restate the problem in your own words**

By writing a problem in your own words, you may understand it better. Before writing the problem, you may need to reread it several times, perhaps aloud, so that you can hear yourself saying the words.

Once you have written the problem in your own words, check to make sure you included all of the necessary information to solve it.

 Write each problem in your own words. Check to make sure you have included all of the information needed to solve the problem.

1 The diagram shows a ray of light being reflected off a mirror. The angle of reflection is congruent to the angle of incidence. Use the diagram to find the measure of the obtuse angle formed by the reflected light.

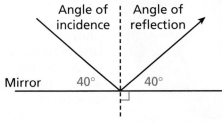

2 At the intersection shown, the turn from northbound Main Street left onto Jefferson Street is dangerous because the turn is too sharp. City planners have decided to change the road to increase the angle of the turn. Explain how the measures of angles 1, 3, and 4 change as the measure of angle 2 increases.

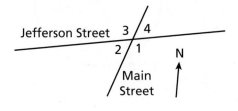

3 Parallel lines s and t are intersected by a transversal r. The obtuse angles formed by lines s and t measure 134°. Find the measure of the acute angles formed by the intersection of lines t and r.

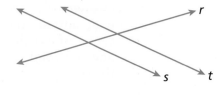

4 Many fashion designers use basic geometric shapes and patterns in their textile designs. In the textile design shown, angles 1 and 2 are formed by two intersecting lines. Find the measures of $\angle 1$ and $\angle 2$ if the angle adjacent to $\angle 2$ measures 88°.

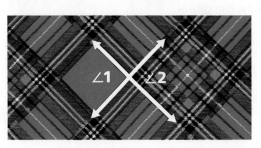

Learn to identify parts of a circle and to find central angle measures.

The wheel is one of the most important inventions of all time. Vehicles with wheels—from ancient chariots to modern bicycles and cars—rely on the idea of a *circle*.

A **circle** is the set of all points in a plane that are the same distance from a given point, called the **center of a circle**.

A circle is named by its center. For example, if point *A* is the center of a circle, then the name of the circle is circle *A*. There are special names for the different parts of a circle.

Vocabulary

circle

center of a circle

arc

radius

diameter

chord

central angle

sector

This relief sculpture was made around 645 C.E., and shows King Ashurbanipal of Nineveh riding on his chariot.

Georgia Performance Standards

M7P3.d Use the language of mathematics to express mathematical ideas precisely. Also, M7P1.c, M7P1.d, M7P4.a, M7P4.b.

Arc
Part of a circle named by its endpoints

Radius
Line segment whose endpoints are the center of a circle and any point on the circle

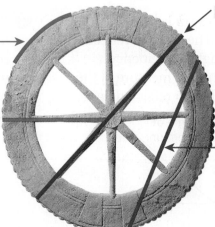

Diameter
Line segment that passes through the center of a circle, and whose endpoints lie on the circle

Chord
Line segment whose endpoints are any two points on a circle

EXAMPLE **1** **Identifying Parts of Circles**

Name the parts of circle *P*.

Reading Math

Radii is the plural form of *radius*.

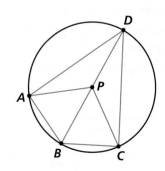

A radii
$\overline{PA}, \overline{PB}, \overline{PC}, \overline{PD}$

B diameter
$\overline{BD}$

C chords
$\overline{AD}, \overline{DC}, \overline{AB}, \overline{BC}, \overline{BD}$

A **central angle** of a circle is an angle formed by two radii. A **sector** of a circle is the part of the circle enclosed by two radii and an arc connecting them.

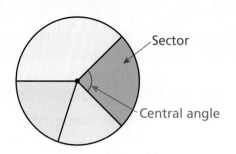

The sum of the measures of all of the nonoverlapping central angles in a circle is 360°. We say that there are 360° in a circle.

EXAMPLE 2

PROBLEM SOLVING

PROBLEM SOLVING APPLICATION

The circle graph shows the results of a survey to determine how people feel about keeping the penny. Find the central angle measure of the sector that shows the percent of people who are against keeping the penny.

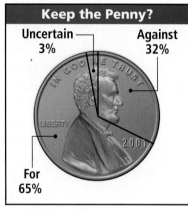

Source: USA Today, 2001

1 Understand the Problem

List the **important information:**
• The percent of people who are against keeping the penny is 32%.

2 Make a Plan

The central angle measure of the sector that represents those people against keeping the penny is 32% of the angle measure of the whole circle. The angle measure of a circle is 360°. Since the sector is 32% of the circle graph, the central angle measure is 32% of 360°.

32% of 360° = 0.32 · 360°

3 Solve

0.32 · 360° = 115.2°   *Multiply.*

The central angle of the sector measures 115.2°.

4 Look Back

The 32% sector is about one-third of the graph, and 120° is one-third of 360°. Since 115.2° is close to 120°, the answer is reasonable.

Think and Discuss    GPS M7P2.c, M7P5.a

1. Explain why a diameter is a chord but a radius is not.

2. Draw a circle with a central angle of 90°.

 **Georgia Performance Standards**

M7P1.b, M7P2.c, M7P3.a, M7P3.d

 go.hrw.com
Homework Help Online
KEYWORD: MS7 8-4
Parent Resources Online
KEYWORD: MS7 Parent

GUIDED PRACTICE

See Example **Name the parts of circle O.**

1. radii

2. diameter

3. chords

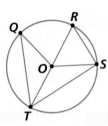

See Example 4. The circle graph shows the results of a survey in which the following question was asked: "If you had to describe your office environment as a type of television show, which would it be?" Find the central angle measure of the sector that shows the percent of people who described their workplace as a courtroom drama.

Describe Your Workplace

Real-life survivors 38%
Soap opera 27%
Medical emergency 18%
Science fiction 7%
Courtroom drama 10%

Source: USA Today

INDEPENDENT PRACTICE

See Example **Name the parts of circle C.**

5. radii

6. diameters

7. chords

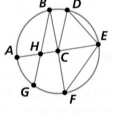

See Example 8. The circle graph shows the areas from which the United States imports bananas. Find the central angle measure of the sector that shows the percent of banana imports from South America.

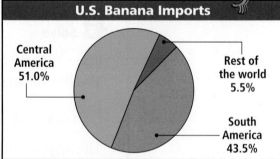

U.S. Banana Imports

Central America 51.0%
Rest of the world 5.5%
South America 43.5%

Source: US Bureau of the Census Trade Data

PRACTICE AND PROBLEM SOLVING

 **CRCT GPS**

Extra Practice p. 742

9. What is the distance between the centers of the circles at right?

10. A circle is divided into five equal sectors. Find the measure of the central angle of each sector.

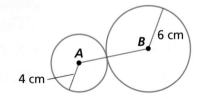

4 cm
6 cm
A
B

Music Citizens of the United States were asked to choose a national song and a national anthem. The circle graph shows the results of the survey. Use the graphs for Exercises 11 and 12.

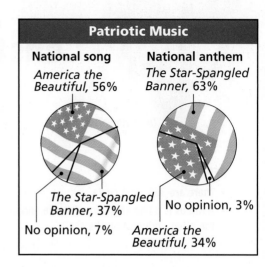

Patriotic Music

National song
America the Beautiful, 56%
The Star-Spangled Banner, 37%
No opinion, 7%

National anthem
The Star-Spangled Banner, 63%
No opinion, 3%
America the Beautiful, 34%

11. Find the central angle measure of the sector that shows the percent of people who chose *The Star-Spangled Banner* as the song they prefer.

12. Find the central angle measure of the sector that shows the percent of people who prefer *America the Beautiful* as the national anthem.

13. If $\overline{AB} \parallel \overline{CD}$ in the circle at right, what is the measure of ∠1? Explain your answer.

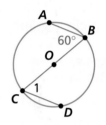

14. Write a Problem Find a circle graph in your science or social studies textbook. Use the graph to write a problem that can be solved by finding the central angle measure of one of the sectors of the circle.

15. Write About It Compare central angles of a circle with sectors of a circle.

16. Challenge Find the angle measure between the minute and hour hands on the clock at right.

CRCT PREP • GPS SUPPORT • SPIRAL REVIEW

Use the figure for Exercises 17 and 18.

17. Multiple Choice Which statement is NOT true about the figure?

Ⓐ $\overline{GI}$ is a diameter of the circle.

Ⓑ $\overline{GI}$ is a chord of the circle.

Ⓒ ∠GIJ is a central angle of the circle.

Ⓓ ∠GFH and ∠HFI are supplementary angles.

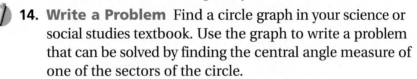

18. Gridded Response The diameter of the circle is perpendicular to chord *HF*. What is the measure of ∠HFI in degrees?

Estimate. (Lesson 6-3)

19. 28% of 150   **20.** 21% of 90   **21.** 2% of 55   **22.** 53% of 72

Use the alphabet at right. (Lesson 8-3)

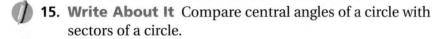

ABCDEFGH
IJKLMN
OPQRST
UVWXYZ

23. Identify the letters that appear to have parallel lines.

24. Identify the letters that appear to have perpendicular lines.

Construct Circle Graphs

Use with Lesson 8-4

go.hrw.com
Lab Resources Online
KEYWORD: MS7 Lab8

Georgia Performance Standards
M7D1.f, M7P1.d, M7P5.a, M7P5.b

REMEMBER
- There are 360° in a circle.
- A radius is a line segment with one endpoint at the center of a circle and the other endpoint on the circle.

A circle graph can be used to compare data that are parts of a whole.

Activity

You can make a circle graph using information from a table.

At Booker Middle School, a survey was conducted to find the percent of students who favor certain types of books. The results are shown in the table below.

To make a circle graph, you need to find the size of each part of your graph. Each part is a *sector*.

To find the size of a sector, you must find the measure of its angle. You do this by finding what percent of the whole circle that sector represents.

Find the size of each sector.

a. Copy the table at right.

b. Find a decimal equivalent for each percent given, and fill in the decimal column of your table.

c. Find the fraction equivalent for each percent given, and fill in the fraction column of your table.

d. Find the angle measure of each sector by multiplying each fraction or decimal by 360°. Fill in the last column of your table.

Students' Favorite Types of Books				
Type of Book	**Percent**	**Decimal**	**Fraction**	**Degrees**
Mysteries	35%			
Science Fiction	25%			
Sports	20%			
Biographies	15%			
Humor	5%			

Follow the steps below to draw a circle graph.

a. Using a compass, draw a circle. Using a straightedge, draw one radius.

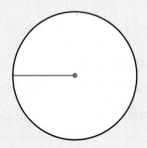

b. Use a protractor to measure the angle of the first sector. Draw the angle.

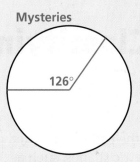

c. Use a protractor to measure the angle of the next sector. Draw the angle.

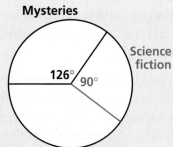

d. Continue until your graph is complete. Label each sector with its name and percent.

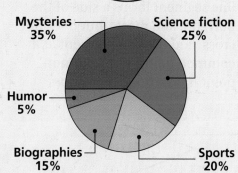

Think and Discuss

1. Total each column in the table from the beginning of the activity. What do you notice?

2. What type of data would you want to display using a circle graph?

3. How does the size of each sector of your circle graph relate to the percent, the decimal, and the fraction in your table?

Try This

1. Complete the table below and use the information to make a circle graph.

On a typical Saturday, Alan divides his leisure time and spends it in the following ways:

Time Spent for Leisure				
Activity	Percent	Decimal	Fraction	Degrees
Reading	30%			
Playing sports	25%			
Working on computer	40%			
Watching TV	5%			

Learn to identify and name polygons.

Vocabulary

polygon

regular polygon

Georgia Performance Standards

M7P2.c Develop and evaluate mathematical arguments. Also, M7P1.b, M7P3.d.

From the earliest recorded time, geometric shapes, such as triangles and rectangles, have been used to decorate buildings and works of art.

Triangles and rectangles are examples of *polygons*. A **polygon** is a closed plane figure formed by three or more line segments. Each line segment forms a side of the polygon, and meets, but does not cross, another line segment at a common point. This common point is a vertex of a polygon.

The Paracas were an ancient native culture of Peru. Among the items that have been excavated from their lands are color tapestries, such as this one.

Reading Math

Vertices is the plural form of *vertex*.

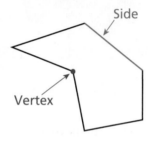

Side

Vertex

The polygon at left has six sides and six vertices.

EXAMPLE **1** **Identifying Polygons**

Determine whether each figure is a polygon. If it is not, explain why not.

The figure is a polygon.
It is a closed figure with 5 sides.

The figure is not a polygon.
It is not a closed figure.

The figure is not a polygon.
Not all of the sides of the figure are line segments.

The figure is not a polygon.
There are line segments in the figure that cross.

Polygons are classified by the number of sides and angles they have.

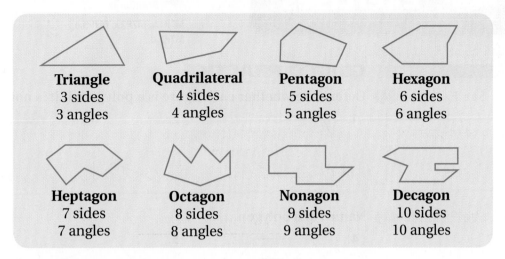

Triangle 3 sides 3 angles	**Quadrilateral** 4 sides 4 angles	**Pentagon** 5 sides 5 angles	**Hexagon** 6 sides 6 angles
Heptagon 7 sides 7 angles	**Octagon** 8 sides 8 angles	**Nonagon** 9 sides 9 angles	**Decagon** 10 sides 10 angles

EXAMPLE 2 Classifying Polygons

Name each polygon.

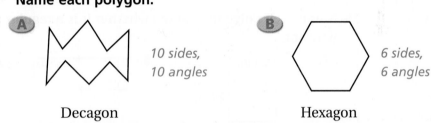

A   10 sides, 10 angles
Decagon

B   6 sides, 6 angles
Hexagon

A **regular polygon** is a polygon in which all sides are congruent and all angles are congruent.

EXAMPLE 3 Identifying and Classifying Regular Polygons

Name each polygon, and tell whether it is a regular polygon. If it is not, explain why not.

Caution!

A polygon with congruent sides is not necessarily a regular polygon. Its angles must also be congruent.

A

The figure has congruent angles and congruent sides. It is a regular triangle.

B   3 m, 3 m, 3 m, 3 m

The figure is a quadrilateral. It is not a regular polygon because not all of the angles are congruent.

GPS M7P2.c, M7P3.b

Think and Discuss

1. Explain why a circle is not a polygon.

2. Name three reasons why a figure would not be a polygon.

Exercises

Georgia Performance Standards
M7P1.a, M7P2.c, M7P3.a, M7P3.d

go.hrw.com
Homework Help Online
KEYWORD: MS7 8-5
Parent Resources Online
KEYWORD: MS7 Parent

GUIDED PRACTICE

See Example ❶ Determine whether each figure is a polygon. If it is not, explain why not.

1.

2.

3.

See Example ❷ Name each polygon.

4.

5.

6.

See Example ❸ Name each polygon, and tell whether it is a regular polygon. If it is not, explain why not.

7.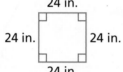

24 in.

24 in.   24 in.

24 in.

8.

9.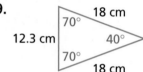

18 cm

70°

12.3 cm   40°

70°

18 cm

INDEPENDENT PRACTICE

See Example ❶ Determine whether each figure is a polygon. If it is not, explain why not.

10.

11.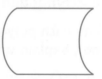

12.

See Example ❷ Name each polygon.

13.

14.

15.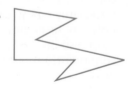

See Example ❸ Name each polygon, and tell whether it is a regular polygon. If it is not, explain why not.

CRCT GPS
Extra Practice p. 742

16.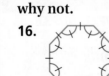

17.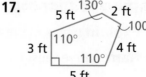

130°
5 ft   2 ft
100°
110°
3 ft
4 ft
110°
5 ft

18.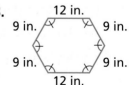

12 in.
9 in.   9 in.
9 in.   9 in.
12 in.

Quilting is an art form that has existed in many countries for hundreds of years. Some cultures record their histories and traditions through the colors and patterns in quilts.

19. The design of the quilt at right is made of triangles.

    a. Name two other polygons in the pattern.

    b. Which of the polygons in the pattern appear to be regular?

Use the photograph of the star quilt for Exercises 20 and 21.

20. The large star in the quilt pattern is made of smaller shapes stitched together. These smaller shapes are all the same type of polygon. What type of polygon are the smaller shapes?

21. A polygon can be named by the number of its sides followed by -*gon*. For example, a polygon with 14 sides is called a 14-gon. What is the name of the large star-shaped polygon on the quilt?

22. ⭐ **Challenge** The quilt at right has a modern design. Find and copy one of each type of polygon, from a triangle up to a decagon, onto your paper from the design. Write the name of each polygon next to its drawing.

CRCT PREP • GPS SUPPORT • SPIRAL REVIEW

23. Multiple Choice What is true about the figure?

    Ⓐ It is a polygon.   Ⓒ It is a quadrilateral.

    Ⓑ It is a regular polygon.   Ⓓ It is a nonagon.

24. Short Response Draw an example of a figure that is NOT a polygon. Explain why it is not a polygon.

Write a function that describes each sequence. (Lesson 4-5)

25. 4, 7, 10, 13,…   **26.** −1, 1, 3, 5,…   **27.** 2.3, 3.3, 4.3, 5.3,…

Solve. Round answers to the nearest tenth, if necessary. (Lesson 6-5)

28. 8 is what percent of 15?   **29.** What is 35% of 58?

30. 63 is 25% of what number?   **31.** 22 is what percent of 85?

8-6 Classifying Triangles

Learn to classify triangles by their side lengths and angle measures.

Vocabulary

scalene triangle

isosceles triangle

equilateral triangle

acute triangle

obtuse triangle

right triangle

Georgia Performance Standards

M7P3.d Use the language of mathematics to express mathematical ideas precisely. Also, M7P1.b.

A harnessed rider uses the triangle-shaped control bar on a hang glider to steer. The framework of most hang gliders is made up of many types of triangles. One way to classify triangles is by the lengths of their sides. Another way is by the measures of their angles.

Triangles classified by sides

A **scalene triangle** has no congruent sides.

An **isosceles triangle** has at least 2 congruent sides.

In an **equilateral triangle**, all of the sides are congruent.

Triangles classified by angles

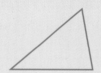

In an **acute triangle**, all of the angles are acute.

An **obtuse triangle** has exactly one obtuse angle.

A **right triangle** has exactly one right angle.

EXAMPLE 1 **Classifying Triangles**

Classify each triangle according to its sides and angles.

Helpful Hint

The base angles of an isosceles triangle are congruent.

A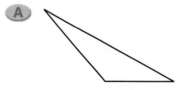

scalene	*No congruent sides*
obtuse	*One obtuse angle*

This is a scalene obtuse triangle.

B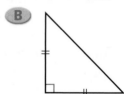

isosceles	*Two congruent sides*
right	*One right angle*

This is an isosceles right triangle.

470 *Chapter 8 Geometric Figures*

Classify each triangle according to its sides and angles.

scalene   *No congruent sides*
right   *One right angle*

This is a scalene right triangle.

isosceles   *Two congruent sides*
obtuse   *One obtuse angle*

This is an isosceles obtuse triangle.

 Identifying Triangles

Identify the different types of triangles in the figure, and determine how many of each there are.

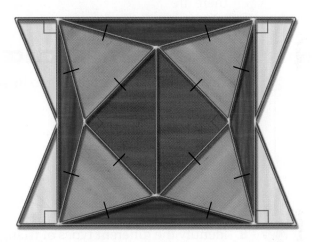

Type	How Many	Colors	Type	How Many	Colors
Scalene	4	Yellow	Right	6	Purple, yellow
Isosceles	10	Green, pink, purple	Obtuse	4	Green
Equilateral	4	Pink	Acute	4	Pink

Think and Discuss   GPS M7P2.c, M7P5.a

1. Draw an isosceles acute triangle and an isosceles obtuse triangle.

2. Draw a triangle that is right and scalene.

3. Explain why any equilateral triangle is also an isosceles triangle, but not all isosceles triangles are equilateral triangles.

Georgia Performance Standards

M7P1.c, M7P2.c, M7P3.d, M7P4.c

go.hrw.com
Homework Help Online
KEYWORD: MS7 8-6
Parent Resources Online
KEYWORD: MS7 Parent

GUIDED PRACTICE

See Example **1** Classify each triangle according to its sides and angles.

1.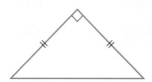

2.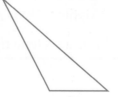

3.

See Example **2** **4.** Identify the different types of triangles in the figure, and determine how many of each there are.

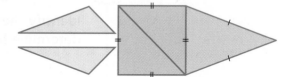

INDEPENDENT PRACTICE

See Example **1** Classify each triangle according to its sides and angles.

5.

6.

7.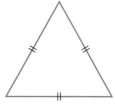

See Example **2** **8.** Identify the different types of triangles in the figure, and determine how many of each there are.

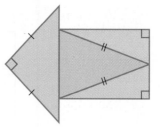

PRACTICE AND PROBLEM SOLVING

Extra Practice p. 742

Classify each triangle according to the lengths of its sides.

9. 6 ft, 9 ft, 12 ft   **10.** 2 in., 2 in., 2 in.   **11.** 7.4 mi, 7.4 mi, 4 mi

Classify each triangle according to the measures of its angles.

12. 105°, 38°, 37°   **13.** 45°, 90°, 45°   **14.** 40°, 60°, 80°

15. **Multi-Step** The sum of the lengths of the sides of triangle ABC is 25 in. The lengths of sides $\overline{AB}$ and $\overline{BC}$ are 9 inches and 8 inches. Find the length of side $\overline{AC}$ and classify the triangle.

16. Draw a square. Divide it into two triangles. Describe the triangles.

472 *Chapter 8 Geometric Figures*

Classify each triangle according to its sides and angles.

17.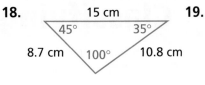
100 ft 62° 100 ft
59° 59°
103 ft

18.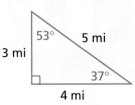
15 cm
45° 35°
8.7 cm 100° 10.8 cm

19.
53° 5 mi
3 mi
37°
4 mi

Geology Each face of a topaz crystal is a triangle whose sides are all different lengths. What kind of triangle is each face of a topaz crystal?

Architecture The Washington Monument is an obelisk, the top of which is a pyramid. The pyramid has four triangular faces. The bottom edge of each face measures 10.5 m. The other edges measure 17.0 m. What kind of triangle is each face of the pyramid?

22. **Critical Thinking** A line segment connects each vertex of a regular octagon to the vertex opposite it. How many triangles are within the octagon? What type of triangles are they?

23. **Choose a Strategy** How many triangles are in the figure?
    Ⓐ 6   Ⓑ 9   Ⓒ 10   Ⓓ 13

    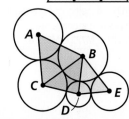

24. **Write About It** Is it possible for an equilateral triangle to be obtuse? Explain your answer.

25. **Challenge** The centers of circles *A*, *B*, *C*, *D*, and *E* are connected by line segments. Classify each triangle in the figure, given that the diameter of circle *D* is 4 and *DE* = 5, *BD* = 6, *CB* = 8, and *AC* = 8.

CRCT PREP • GPS SUPPORT • SPIRAL REVIEW

26. **Multiple Choice** Based on the angle measures given, which triangle is NOT acute?

    Ⓐ 60°, 60°, 60°   Ⓑ 90°, 45°, 45°   Ⓒ 54°, 54°, 72°   Ⓓ 75°, 45°, 60°

27. **Multiple Choice** Which of the following best describes the triangle?
    124° 28° 28°

    Ⓕ Scalene, right triangle   Ⓗ Isosceles, obtuse triangle

    Ⓖ Isosceles, acute triangle   Ⓙ Equilateral, acute triangle

28. Order the numbers $\frac{3}{7}$, −0.4, 2.3, and $1\frac{3}{10}$ from least to greatest. (Lesson 2-11)

Name each polygon, and tell whether it is a regular polygon. If it is not, explain why not. (Lesson 8-5)

29.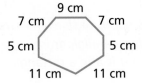
9 cm
7 cm 7 cm
5 cm 5 cm
11 cm 11 cm

30.

31.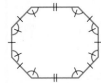

8-7 Classifying Quadrilaterals

Learn to name, identify, and draw types of quadrilaterals.

Vocabulary

parallelogram

rectangle

rhombus

square

trapezoid

Georgia Performance Standards

M7P2.d Select and use various types of reasoning. Also, M7P2.a, M7P2.c, M7P3.d.

College campuses are often built around an open space called a "quad" or "quadrangle." A quadrangle is a four-sided enclosure, or a quadrilateral.

Some quadrilaterals have properties that classify them as *special quadrilaterals*.

The Liberal Arts Quadrangle at the University of Washington, Seattle

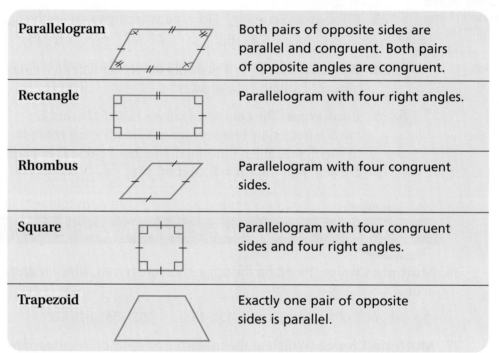

Parallelogram		Both pairs of opposite sides are parallel and congruent. Both pairs of opposite angles are congruent.
Rectangle		Parallelogram with four right angles.
Rhombus		Parallelogram with four congruent sides.
Square		Parallelogram with four congruent sides and four right angles.
Trapezoid		Exactly one pair of opposite sides is parallel.

Quadrilaterals can have more than one name because the special quadrilaterals sometimes share properties.

EXAMPLE 1 Classifying Quadrilaterals

Give all of the names that apply to each quadrilateral. Then give the name that best describes it.

A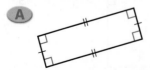

The figure has opposite sides that are parallel, so it is a parallelogram. It has four right angles, so it is also a rectangle.

Rectangle best describes this quadrilateral.

Give all of the names that apply to each quadrilateral. Then give the name that best describes it.

 The figure has exactly one pair of opposite sides that is parallel, so it is a trapezoid.

Trapezoid best describes this quadrilateral.

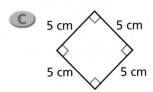 The figure has two pairs of opposite sides that are parallel, so it is a parallelogram. It has four right angles, so it is also a rectangle. It has four congruent sides, so it is also a rhombus and a square.

Square best describes this quadrilateral.

 The figure has two pairs of opposite sides that are parallel, so it is a parallelogram. It has four congruent sides, so it is a rhombus. It does not have four right angles, so it is not a rectangle or a square.

Rhombus best describes this quadrilateral.

EXAMPLE 2 Drawing Quadrilaterals

Draw each figure. If it is not possible to draw, explain why.

A a parallelogram that is not a rhombus

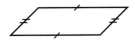 The figure has two pairs of parallel sides, but all sides are not congruent.

B a trapezoid that is also a rectangle

A trapezoid has exactly one pair of opposite sides that is parallel, but a rectangle has two pairs of opposite sides that are parallel. It is not possible to draw this figure.

Think and Discuss GPS M7P2.c, M7P5.a

1. Describe how you can decide whether a rhombus is also a square. Use drawings to justify your answer.

2. Draw a Venn diagram to show how the properties of the five quadrilaterals relate.

Georgia Performance
Standards
M7P2.a, M7P2.c, M7P3.d,
M7P4.c

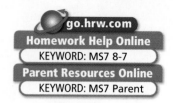

go.hrw.com
Homework Help Online
KEYWORD: MS7 8-7
Parent Resources Online
KEYWORD: MS7 Parent

GUIDED PRACTICE

See Example Give all of the names that apply to each quadrilateral. Then give the name that best describes it.

1.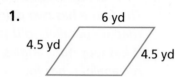

2.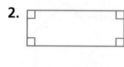

3.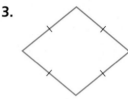

See Example **2** Draw each figure. If it is not possible to draw, explain why.

4. a rectangle that is not a square

5. a parallelogram that is also a trapezoid

INDEPENDENT PRACTICE

See Example **1** Give all of the names that apply to each quadrilateral. Then give the name that best describes it.

6.

7.

8.

9. 7 in.   7 in.
7 in.   7 in.

10.

11. 9m   12m
12m   9m

See Example **2** Draw each figure. If it is not possible to draw, explain why.

12. a parallelogram that is also a rhombus

13. a rhombus that is not a square

PRACTICE AND PROBLEM SOLVING

CRCT GPS

Extra Practice p. 742

Name the types of quadrilaterals that have each property.

14. four right angles

15. two pairs of opposite, parallel sides

16. four congruent sides

17. opposite sides that are congruent

18. Describe how to construct a parallelogram from the figure at right, and then complete the construction.

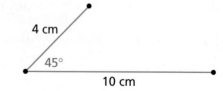

4 cm   45°   10 cm

Tell whether each statement is true or false. Explain your answer.

19. All squares are rhombuses.

20. All rectangles are parallelograms.

21. All squares are rectangles.

22. All rhombuses are rectangles.

23. Some trapezoids are squares.

24. Some rectangles are squares.

25. **Social Studies** Name the polygons made by each color in the flag of the Bahamas. Give the specific names of any quadrilaterals you find.

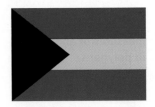

26. Graph the points $A(-2, -2)$, $B(4, 1)$, $C(3, 4)$, and $D(-1, 2)$, and draw line segments to connect the points. What kind of quadrilateral did you draw?

27. Bandon Highway is being built perpendicular to Avenue A and Avenue B, which are parallel. What kinds of polygons could be made by adding a fourth road?

28. **Write a Problem** Draw a design, or find one in a book, and then write a problem about the design that involves identifying quadrilaterals.

29. **Write About It** Quadrilaterals can be found on many college campuses. Describe two special quadrilaterals that you commonly find in the world around you.

30. **Challenge** The coordinates of three vertices of a parallelogram are $(-1, 1)$, $(2, 1)$, and $(0, -4)$. What are the coordinates of the fourth vertex?

CRCT PREP • GPS SUPPORT • SPIRAL REVIEW

31. **Multiple Choice** Which statement is NOT true?

Ⓐ All rhombuses are parallelograms.

Ⓑ All squares are rectangles.

Ⓒ Some trapezoids are rectangles.

Ⓓ Some rhombuses are squares.

32. **Extended Response** Graph the points $A(-1, 5)$, $B(4, 3)$, $C(2, -2)$, and $D(-3, 0)$. Draw segments AB, BC, CD, and AD, and give all of the names that apply to the quadrilateral. Then give the name that best describes it.

Use the data set 43, 28, 33, 49, 18, 44, 57, 34, 40, 57 for Exercises 33 and 34. (Lesson 7-1)

33. Make a stem-and-leaf plot of the data.

34. Make a cumulative frequency table of the data.

Classify each triangle according to the measures of its angles. (Lesson 8-6)

35. 50°, 50°, 80°

36. 40°, 50°, 90°

37. 20°, 30°, 130°

38. 20°, 60°, 100°

Angles in Polygons

Learn to find the measures of angles in polygons.

Georgia Performance Standards

M7A2.a Given a problem, define a variable, write an equation, solve the equation, and interpret the solution. Also, M7A2.b, M7P1.b, M7P5.b.

If you tear off the corners of a triangle and put them together, you will find that they form a straight angle. This suggests that the sum of the measures of the angles in a triangle is 180°.

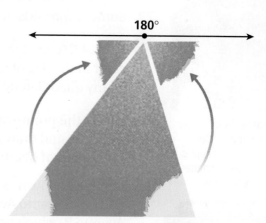

180°

Angles of a Triangle	
The sum of the measures of the angles in a triangle is 180°.	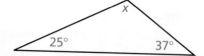 $m\angle 1 + m\angle 2 + m\angle 3 = 180°$

EXAMPLE 1 **Finding an Angle Measure in a Triangle**

Find the unknown angle measure in the triangle.

$$25° + 37° + x = 180°$$

The sum of the angle measures in a triangle is 180°.

$$62° + x = 180°$$

$$\underline{-62 \qquad\quad -62°}$$

$$x = 118°$$

Combine like terms.
Subtract 62° from both sides.

The unknown angle measure is 118°.

The sum of the angle measures in any four-sided figure can be found by dividing the figure into two triangles. Since the sum of the angle measures in each triangle is 180°, the sum of the measures in a four-sided figure is 2 · 180°, or 360°.

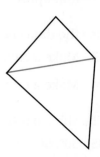

Angles of a Quadrilateral	
The sum of the measures of the angles in a quadrilateral is 360°.	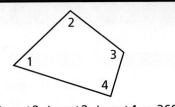 $m\angle 1 + m\angle 2 + m\angle 3 + m\angle 4 = 360°$

EXAMPLE 2 Finding an Angle Measure in a Quadrilateral

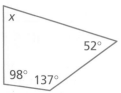

Find the unknown angle measure in the quadrilateral.

$$98° + 137° + 52° + x = 360° \quad \text{\textit{The sum of the angle measures is 360°.}}$$

$$287° + x = 360° \quad \text{\textit{Combine like terms.}}$$

$$\underline{-287° \qquad\quad -287°} \quad \text{\textit{Subtract 287° from both sides.}}$$

$$x = 73°$$

The unknown angle measure is 73°.

By dividing any figure into triangles, you can find the sum of its angle measures.

EXAMPLE 3 Drawing Triangles to Find the Sum of Interior Angles

Divide the polygon into triangles to find the sum of its angle measures.

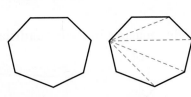

There are 5 triangles.

$5 \cdot 180° = 900°$

The sum of the angle measures of a heptagon is 900°.

Think and Discuss GPS M7P1.d, M7P3.b

1. **Explain** how to find the measure of an angle in a triangle when the measures of the two other angles are known.

2. **Determine** for which polygon the sum of the angle measures is greater, a pentagon or an octagon.

3. **Explain** how the measure of each angle in a regular polygon changes as the number of sides increases.

Georgia Performance
Standards

M7P3.a, M7P3.c, M7P4.c

go.hrw.com
Homework Help Online
KEYWORD: MS7 8-8
Parent Resources Online
KEYWORD: MS7 Parent

GUIDED PRACTICE

See Example 1 Find the unknown angle measure in each triangle.

1.

2.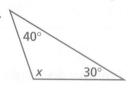

3.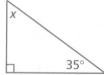

See Example 2 Find the unknown angle measure in each quadrilateral.

4.

5.

6.

See Example 3 Divide each polygon into triangles to find the sum of its angle measures.

7.

8.

9.

INDEPENDENT PRACTICE

See Example 1 Find the unknown angle measure in each triangle.

10.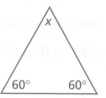

11.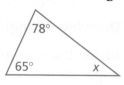

12.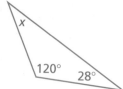

See Example 2 Find the unknown angle measure in each quadrilateral.

13.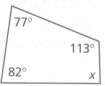

14.

15.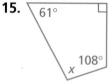

See Example 3 Divide each polygon into triangles to find the sum of its angle measures.

16.

17.

18.

PRACTICE AND PROBLEM SOLVING

Extra Practice p. 742

19. Earth Science A sundial consists of a circular base and a right triangle
mounted upright on the base. One acute angle in the right triangle is 52°.
What is the measure of the other acute angle?

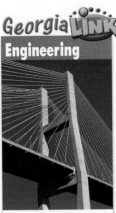

Georgia LINK

Engineering

The Talmadge Memorial Bridge, which crosses the Savannah River, is called a *cable-stayed bridge* because of the cables that help support it.

Find the measure of the third angle in each triangle, given two angle measures. Then classify the triangle.

20. 56°, 101°   **21.** 18°, 63°   **22.** 62°, 58°   **23.** 41°, 49°

24. Multi-Step Each outer wall of the Pentagon in Washington, D.C., measures 921 feet. What is the measure of each angle made by the Pentagon's outer walls?

25. Critical Thinking A truss bridge is supported by triangular frames called trusses. If every truss in a truss bridge is an isosceles right triangle, what is the measure of each angle in one of the trusses? (*Hint:* Two of the angles in each truss are congruent.)

26. What's the Error? A student finds the sum of the angle measures in an octagon by multiplying 7 · 180°. What is the student's error?

27. Write About It Explain how to find the sum of the angle measures in a quadrilateral by dividing the quadrilateral into triangles.

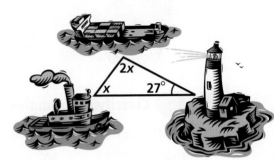

28. Challenge The angle between the lines of sight from a lighthouse to a tugboat and to a cargo ship is 27°. The angle between the lines of sight at the cargo ship is twice the angle between the lines of sight at the tugboat. What are the angles at the tugboat and at the cargo ship?

CRCT PREP • GPS SUPPORT • SPIRAL REVIEW

29. Multiple Choice A triangle has three congruent angles. What is the measure of each angle?

   Ⓐ 50°　　　　Ⓑ 60°　　　　Ⓒ 75°　　　　Ⓓ 100°

30. Gridded Response Two angles of a triangle measure 58° and 42°. What is the measure, in degrees, of the third angle of the triangle?

Solve each proportion. (Lesson 5-5)

31. $\dfrac{x}{3} = \dfrac{30}{18}$　　　**32.** $\dfrac{8}{p} = \dfrac{24}{27}$　　　**33.** $\dfrac{4}{3} = \dfrac{t}{21}$　　　**34.** $\dfrac{0.5}{1.8} = \dfrac{n}{9}$

Name the types of quadrilaterals that have each property. (Lesson 8-7)

35. two pairs of opposite, congruent sides　　　**36.** four congruent sides

READY To Go On?

Quiz for Lessons 8-4 Through 8-8

☑ **8-4** **Properties of Circles**

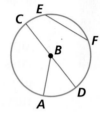

Name the parts of circle *B*.

1. radii **2.** diameter **3.** chords

4. A circle is divided into 6 equal sectors. Find the measure of the central angle of each sector.

☑ **8-5** **Classifying Polygons**

Name each polygon, and tell whether it is a regular polygon. If it is not, explain why not.

5. **6.** **7.**  **8.**

☑ **8-6** **Classifying Triangles**

Classify each triangle according to its sides and angles.

9. **10.** **11.** **12.**

☑ **8-7** **Classifying Quadrilaterals**

Give all of the names that apply to each quadrilateral. Then give the name that best describes it.

13. **14.** **15.** **16.**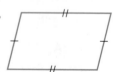

☑ **8-8** **Angles in Polygons**

Find the unknown angle measure in each figure.

17. 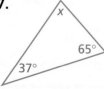 **18.** 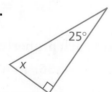 **19.** 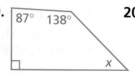 **20.**

Focus on Problem Solving

Understand the Problem

• **Understand the words in the problem**

Words that you do not understand can sometimes make a simple problem seem difficult. Some of those words, such as the names of things or persons, may not even be necessary to solve the problem. If a problem contains an unfamiliar name, or one that you cannot pronounce, you can substitute another word for it. If a word that you don't understand is necessary to solve the problem, look the word up to find its meaning.

Read each problem, and make a list of unusual or unfamiliar words. If a word is not necessary to solve the problem, replace it with a familiar one. If a word is necessary, look up the word and write its meaning.

1 Using a pair of calipers, Mr. Papadimitriou measures the diameter of an ancient Greek amphora to be 17.8 cm at its widest point. What is the radius of the amphora at this point?

2 Joseph wants to plant gloxinia and hydrangeas in two similar rectangular gardens. The length of one garden is 5 ft, and the width is 4 ft. The other garden's length is 20 ft. What is the width of the second garden?

3 Mr. Manityche is sailing his catamaran from Kaua'i to Ni'ihau, a distance of about 12 nautical miles. If his speed averages 10 knots, how long will the trip take him?

4 Aimee's lepidoptera collection includes a butterfly with dots that appear to form a scalene triangle on each wing. What is the sum of the angles of each triangle on the butterfly's wings?

5 Students in a physics class use wire and resistors to build a Wheatstone bridge. Each side of their rhombus-shaped design is 2 cm long. What angle measures would the design have to have for its shape to be a square?

8-9 Congruent Figures

Learn to identify congruent figures and to use congruence to solve problems.

Side-Side-Side Rule

Georgia Performance Standards

M7G3.c Understand congruence of geometric figures as a special case of similarity. Also, M7P2.a, M7P2.c, M7P2.d.

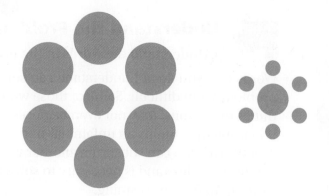

Look at the two patterns. Which center circle do you think is bigger? In spite of appearances, the two center circles are congruent. They are the same size and shape. Their apparent differences are optical illusions. One way to determine whether figures are congruent is to see whether one figure will fit exactly over the other one.

EXAMPLE 1 **Identifying Congruent Figures in the Real World**

Identify any congruent figures.

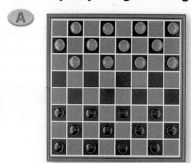

Ⓐ The squares on a checkerboard are congruent. The checkers are also congruent.

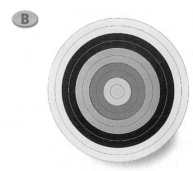

Ⓑ The rings on a target are not congruent. Each ring is larger than the one inside of it.

If all of the corresponding sides and angles of two polygons are congruent, then the polygons are congruent. For triangles in particular, if the corresponding sides are congruent, then the corresponding angles will always be congruent. This is called the **Side-Side-Side Rule**. Because of this rule, when determining whether triangles are congruent, you only need to determine whether the sides are congruent.

EXAMPLE **2** **Identifying Congruent Triangles**

Determine whether the triangles are congruent.

$AC = 3$ m $DF = 3$ m
$AB = 4$ m $DE = 4$ m
$BC = 5$ m $EF = 5$ m

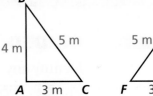
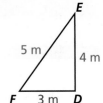

By the Side-Side-Side Rule, △*ABC* is congruent to △*DEF*, or △*ABC* ≅ △*DEF*. If you flip one triangle, it will fit exactly over the other.

For polygons with more than three sides, it is not enough to compare the measures of their sides. For example, the corresponding sides of the figures below are congruent, but the figures are not congruent.

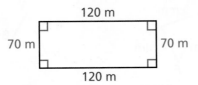
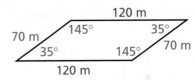

If you know that two figures are congruent, you can find missing measures in the figures.

EXAMPLE 3 **Using Congruence to Find Missing Measures**

Determine the missing measure in each set of congruent polygons.

A

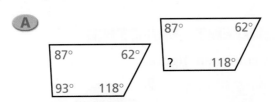

The corresponding angles of congruent polygons are congruent.

The missing angle measure is 93°.

B

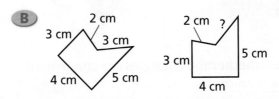

The corresponding sides of congruent polygons are congruent.

The missing side length is 3 cm.

Think and Discuss GPS M7P2.c, M7P2.d

1. Draw an illustration to explain whether an isosceles triangle can be congruent to a right triangle.

2. Explain why congruent figures are always similar figures.

Georgia Performance Standards

M7P2.a, M7P2.c, M7P2.d, M7P4.c

GUIDED PRACTICE

See Example **1** Identify any congruent figures.

1.

2.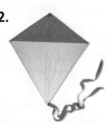

3.

See Example **2** Determine whether the triangles are congruent.

4.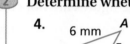

5.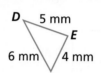

See Example **3** Determine the missing measure in each set of congruent polygons.

6.

7.

INDEPENDENT PRACTICE

See Example **1** Identify any congruent figures.

8.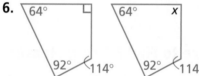

9.

10.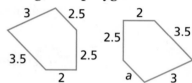

See Example **2** Determine whether the triangles are congruent.

11.

12.

See Example **3** Determine the missing measures in each set of congruent polygons.

13.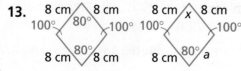

14.

PRACTICE AND PROBLEM SOLVING

Tell the minimum amount of information needed to determine whether the figures are congruent.

15. two triangles   **16.** two squares   **17.** two rectangles   **18.** two pentagons

19. Surveying In the figure, trees *A* and *B* are on opposite sides of the stream. Jamil wants to string a rope from one tree to the other. Triangles *ABC* and *DEC* are congruent. What is the distance between the trees?

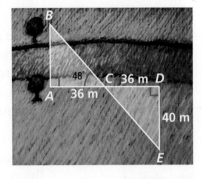

20. Hobbies In the quilt block, which figures appear congruent?

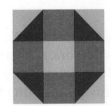

 21. Choose a Strategy Anji and her brother Art walked to school along the routes in the figure. They started at 7:40 A.M. and walked at the same rate. Who arrived first?

    (A) Anji   (B) Art   (C) They arrived at the same time.

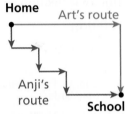

 22. Write About It Explain how you can determine whether two triangles are congruent.

 23. Challenge If all of the angles in two triangles have the same measure, are the triangles necessarily congruent?

CRCT PREP • GPS SUPPORT • SPIRAL REVIEW

24. Multiple Choice Which figures are congruent?

25. Multiple Choice Determine the missing measure in the congruent triangles.

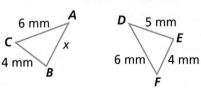

  (F) 4 mm   (H) 6 mm

  (G) 5 mm   (J) Cannot be determined

Plot each point on a coordinate plane. (Lesson 4-1)

26. $A(-4, 3)$ **27.** $B(1, -4)$ **28.** $C(-2, 0)$ **29.** $D(3, 2)$

Find the measure of the third angle in each triangle, given two angle measures. Then classify the triangle. (Lesson 8-8)

30. 25°, 48°   **31.** 125°, 30°   **32.** 60°, 60°   **33.** 72°, 18°

8-10 Translations, Reflections, and Rotations

Learn to recognize, describe, and show transformations.

Vocabulary

transformation

image

translation

reflection

line of reflection

rotation

In the photograph, Michelle Kwan is performing a *layback spin*. She is holding her body in one position while she rotates. This is an example of a *transformation*.

In mathematics, a **transformation** changes the position or orientation of a figure. The resulting figure is the **image** of the original. Images resulting from the transformations described below are congruent to the original figures.

 Georgia Performance Standards

M7G2.b Given a figure in the coordinate plane, determine the coordinates resulting from a translation, rotation, or reflection. Also, M7G2.a, M7P3.d, M7P5.a.

Types of Transformations

Translation	Reflection	Rotation

The figure slides along a straight line without turning.	The figure flips across a **line of reflection**, creating a mirror image.	The figure turns around a fixed point.

EXAMPLE **1** **Identifying Types of Transformations**

Identify each type of transformation.

Helpful Hint

The point that a figure rotates around may be on the figure or away from the figure.

A
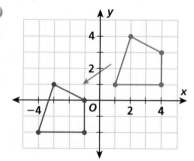

The figure slides along a straight line.

It is a translation.

B
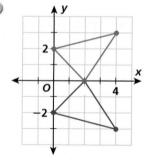

The figure flips across the x-axis.

It is a reflection.

EXAMPLE 2 **Graphing Translations on a Coordinate Plane**

Graph the translation of △ABC 6 units right and 4 units down.

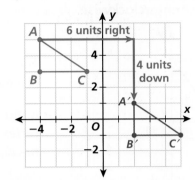

Reading Math

A′ is read "A prime" and is used to represent the point on the image that corresponds to point A of the original figure.

Each vertex is moved 6 units right and 4 units down.

EXAMPLE 3 **Graphing Reflections on a Coordinate Plane**

Graph the reflection of each figure across the indicated axis. Write the coordinates of the vertices of the image.

A *x*-axis

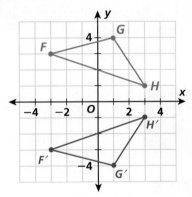

The x-coordinates of the corresponding vertices are the same, and the y-coordinates of the corresponding vertices are opposites.

The coordinates of the vertices of triangle $F'G'H'$ are $F'(-3, -3)$, $G'(1, -4)$, and $H'(3, -1)$.

B *y*-axis

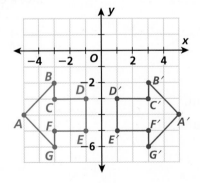

The y-coordinates of the corresponding vertices are the same, and the x-coordinates of the corresponding vertices are opposites.

The coordinates of the vertices of figure $A'B'C'D'E'F'G'$ are $A'(5, -4)$, $B'(3, -2)$, $C'(3, -3)$, $D'(1, -3)$, $E'(1, -5)$, $F'(3, -5)$, and $G'(3, -6)$.

EXAMPLE 4 **Graphing Rotations on a Coordinate Plane**

Triangle *JKL* has vertices *J*(−3, 1), *K*(−3, −2), and *L*(1, −2). Rotate △*JKL* 90° counterclockwise about the vertex *J*.

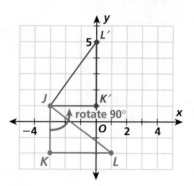

The corresponding sides, $\overline{JK}$ and $\overline{JK'}$, make a 90° angle.

Notice that vertex K is 3 units below vertex J, and vertex K' is 3 units to the right of vertex J.

Think and Discuss

GPS M7P3.b, M7P4.c

1. **Describe** a classroom situation that illustrates a translation.

2. **Explain** how a figure skater might perform a translation and a rotation at the same time.

8-10 Exercises

Georgia Performance Standards

M7P1.a, M7P1.b, M7P3.a, M7P5.a

go.hrw.com
Homework Help Online
KEYWORD: MS7 8-10
Parent Resources Online
KEYWORD: MS7 Parent

GUIDED PRACTICE

See Example 1   **Identify each type of transformation.**

1.

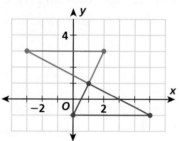

2.

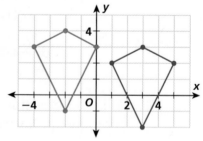

See Example 2   **Graph each translation.**

3. 2 units left and 3 units up

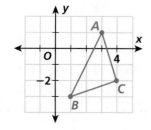

4. 3 units right and 4 units down

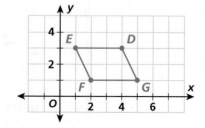

Graph the reflection of each figure across the indicated axis. Write the coordinates of the vertices of the image.

5. *x*-axis

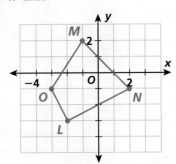

6. *y*-axis

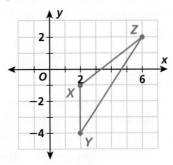

7. Triangle *LMN* has vertices *L*(0, 1), *M*(−3, 0), and *N*(−2, 4). Rotate △*LMN* 180° about the vertex *L*.

INDEPENDENT PRACTICE

Identify each type of transformation.

8.

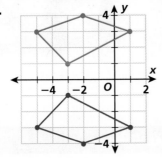

9.

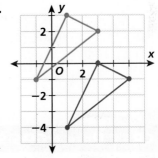

Graph each translation.

10. 5 units right and 1 unit down

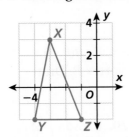

11. 4 units left and 3 units up

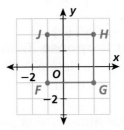

Graph the reflection of each figure across the indicated axis. Write the coordinates of the vertices of the image.

12. *y*-axis

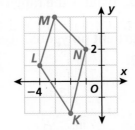

13. *x*-axis

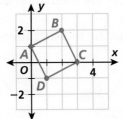

14. Triangle *MNL* has vertices *M*(0, 4), *N*(3, 3), and *L*(0, 0). Rotate △*MNL* 90° counterclockwise about the vertex *L*.

The Native American art pieces in the photos show combinations of transformations. Use the photos for Exercises 15 and 16.

15. ✏️ **Write About It** The Navajo blanket at right has a design based on a sand painting. The two people in the design are standing next to a stalk of corn, which the Native Americans called *maize*. The red, white, and black stripes represent a rainbow. Tell how the design shows reflections. Also explain what parts of the design do not show reflections.

16. ⭐ **Challenge** What part of the bead design in the saddle bag at right can be described as three separate transformations? Draw diagrams to illustrate your answer.

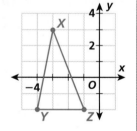

CRCT Prep • GPS Support • Spiral Review

17. **Multiple Choice** What will be the coordinates of point *X* after a translation 2 units down and 3 units to the right?

   Ⓐ (0, 1)   Ⓑ (1, 0)   Ⓒ (−1, 0)   Ⓓ (0, −1)

18. **Short Response** Triangle *ABC* has vertices *A*(−3, 1), *B*(0, 1), and *C*(0, 6). Rotate △*ABC* 90° clockwise around vertex *B*. Draw △*ABC* and its image.

Use the box-and-whisker plot for Exercises 19 and 20. (Lesson 7-5)

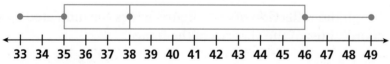

19. What is the median of the data?   20. What is the range of the data?

Determine the missing measure in each set of congruent polygons. (Lesson 8-9)

21.

22.

Technology LAB 8-10

Explore Transformations

Use with Lesson 8-10

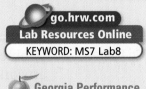

Georgia Performance Standards

M7G2.a, M7P1.c, M7P2.c

You can use geometry software to perform transformations of geometric figures.

Activity

1 Use your dynamic geometry software to construct a 5-sided polygon like the one below. Label the vertices *A, B, C, D,* and *E.* Use the translation tool to translate the polygon 2 units right and $\frac{1}{2}$ unit up.

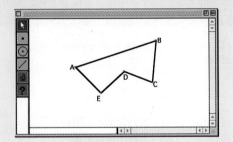
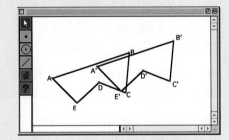

2 Start with the polygon from **1**. Use the rotation tool to rotate the polygon 30° and then 150°, both about the vertex *C.*

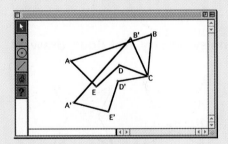
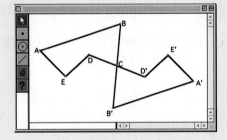

Think and Discuss

1. Rotate a triangle 30° about a point outside the triangle. Can this image be found by combining a vertical translation (slide up or down) and a horizontal translation (slide left or right) of the original triangle?

2. After what angle of rotation will the rotated image of a figure have the same orientation as the original figure?

Try This

1. Construct a quadrilateral *ABCD* using the geometry software.

   a. Translate the figure 2 units right and 1 unit up.

   b. Rotate the figure 30°, 45°, and 60°.

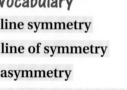

8-11 Symmetry

Learn to identify symmetry in figures.

Vocabulary
line symmetry
line of symmetry
asymmetry
rotational symmetry
center of rotation

Georgia Performance Standards

M7G2.a Demonstrate understanding of transformations and relate symmetry to appropriate transformations. Also, M7P4.c, M7P5.b.

Many architects and artists use symmetry in their buildings and artwork because symmetry is pleasing to the eye.

When you can draw a line through a plane figure so that the two halves are mirror images of each other, the figure has **line symmetry**, or is symmetrical. The line along which the figure is divided is called the **line of symmetry**.

When a figure is not symmetrical, it has **asymmetry**, or is asymmetrical.

The Taj Mahal in Agra, India, is an example of Mughal architecture.

The structure of the Taj Mahal is symmetrical. You can draw a line of symmetry down the center of the building. Also, each window in the building has its own line of symmetry.

EXAMPLE 1 Identifying Line Symmetry

Decide whether each figure has line symmetry. If it does, draw all the lines of symmetry.

 A   B

3 lines of symmetry   4 lines of symmetry

EXAMPLE 2 *Social Studies Application*

Find all the lines of symmetry in each flag.

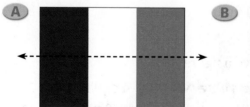

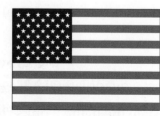

A   There is 1 line of symmetry.   B   There are no lines of symmetry.

A figure has **rotational symmetry** if, when it is rotated less than 360° around a central point, it coincides with itself. The central point is called the **center of rotation**.

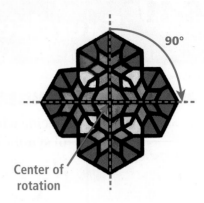

90°

Center of rotation

If the stained glass window at right is rotated 90°, as shown, the image looks the same as the original stained glass window. Therefore the window has rotational symmetry.

EXAMPLE **3** **Identifying Rotational Symmetry**

Tell how many times each figure will show rotational symmetry within one full rotation.

A

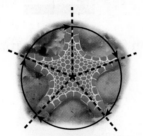

Draw lines from the center of the figure out through identical places in the figure.

The starfish will show rotational symmetry 5 times within a 360° rotation.

Count the number of lines drawn.

B

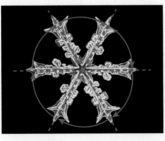

Draw lines from the center of the figure out through identical places in the figure.

The snowflake will show rotational symmetry 6 times within a 360° rotation.

Count the number of lines drawn.

Think and Discuss

GPS M7P3.b, M7P5.a

1. **Draw** a figure that does not have rotational symmetry.

2. **Determine** whether an equilateral triangle has rotational symmetry. If so, tell how many times it shows rotational symmetry within one full rotation.

Georgia Performance
Standards

M7P3.a, M7P4.c, M7P5.b

go.hrw.com
Homework Help Online
KEYWORD: MS7 8-11
Parent Resources Online
KEYWORD: MS7 Parent

GUIDED PRACTICE

See Example 1 **Decide whether each figure has line symmetry. If it does, draw all the lines of symmetry.**

1.

2.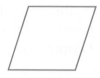

3.

See Example 2 **Find all the lines of symmetry in each flag.**

4.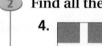

5.

6.

See Example 3 **Tell how many times each figure will show rotational symmetry within one full rotation.**

7.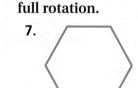

8.

9.

INDEPENDENT PRACTICE

See Example 1 **Decide whether each figure has line symmetry. If it does, draw all the lines of symmetry.**

10.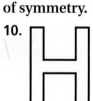

11.

12.

See Example 2 **Find all the lines of symmetry in each flag.**

13.

14.

15.

See Example 3 **Tell how many times each figure will show rotational symmetry within one full rotation.**

16.

17.

18.

PRACTICE AND PROBLEM SOLVING

19. Critical Thinking Which regular polygon shows rotational symmetry 9 times within one full rotation?

20. Life Science How many lines of symmetry does the photo of the moth have?

21. Fold a piece of paper in half vertically and then in half horizontally. Cut or tear a design into one of the folded edges. Then unfold the paper. Does the design have a vertical or horizontal line of symmetry? rotational symmetry? Explain your answer.

22. Art Tell how many times the stained glass image at right shows rotational symmetry in one full rotation if you consider only the shape of the design. Then tell how many times the image shows rotational symmetry if you consider both the shape and the colors in the design.

23. What's the Question? Marla drew a square on the chalkboard. As an answer to Marla's question about symmetry, Rob said "90°." What question did Marla ask?

24. Write About It Explain why an angle of rotation must be less than 360° for a figure to have rotational symmetry.

25. Challenge Print a word in capital letters, using only letters that have horizontal lines of symmetry. Print another word using only capital letters that have vertical lines of symmetry.

CRCT Prep • GPS Support • Spiral Review

26. Multiple Choice How many lines of symmetry does the figure have?

   Ⓐ None   Ⓑ 1   Ⓒ 2   Ⓓ 4

27. Gridded Response How many times will the figure show rotational symmetry within one full rotation?

28. A bridge in an architectural model is 22 cm long. The model scale is 2 cm = 30 m. Find the length of the actual bridge. (Lesson 5-9)

Triangle *JKL* has vertices *J*(−3, −1), *K*(−1, −1), and *L*(−1, −4). Give the coordinates of the vertices of the triangle after each transformation. (Lesson 8-10)

29. Translate the triangle 4 units right and 2 units down.

30. Reflect the triangle across the *y*-axis.

Create Tessellations

Use with Lessons 8-10 and 8-11

Tessellations are patterns of identical shapes that completely cover a plane with no gaps or overlaps. The artist M. C. Escher created many fascinating tessellations.

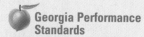

go.hrw.com
Lab Resources Online
KEYWORD: MS7 Lab8

Georgia Performance Standards
M7G2.a, M7P4.a, M7P4.b, M7P5.a

Activity

1 Create a translation tessellation.

The tessellation by M. C. Escher shown at right is an example of a *translation tessellation*. To create your own translation tessellation, follow the steps below.

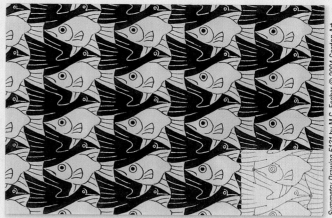

a. Start by drawing a square, rectangle, or other parallelogram. Replace one side of the parallelogram with a curve, as shown.

b. Translate the curve to the opposite side of the parallelogram.

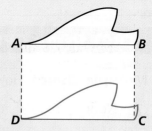

c. Repeat steps **a** and **b** for the other two sides of your parallelogram.

d. The figure can be translated to create an interlocking design, or tessellation. You can add details to your figure or divide it into two or more parts, as shown below.

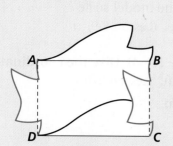

② Create a rotation tessellation.

The tessellation by M. C. Escher shown at right is an example of a *rotation tessellation*. To create your own rotation tessellation, follow the steps below.

a. Start with a regular hexagon. Replace one side of the hexagon with a curve. Rotate the curve about point *B* so that the endpoint at point *A* is moved to point *C*.

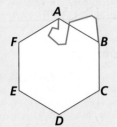
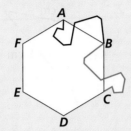

b. Replace side $\overline{CD}$ with a new curve, and rotate it about point *D* to replace side $\overline{DE}$.

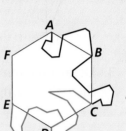

c. Replace side $\overline{EF}$ with a new curve, and rotate it about point *F* to replace side $\overline{FA}$.

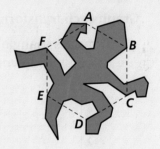

The figure can be rotated and fitted together with copies of itself to create an interlocking design, or tessellation. You can add details to your figure, if desired.

Think and Discuss

1. Explain why the two types of tessellations in this activity are known as translation and rotation tessellations.

Try This

1. Create your own design for a translation or rotation tessellation.

2. Cut out copies of your design from **1** and fit them together to fill a space with your pattern.

READY TO GO ON?

Quiz for Lessons 8-9 Through 8-11

✓ **8-9** **Congruent Figures**

Determine whether the triangles are congruent.

1.

A
10 ft
B
25 ft
20 ft
C

D
10 ft
E
25 ft
20 ft
F

2.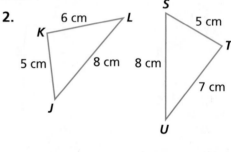

3. Determine the missing measure in the pair of congruent polygons.

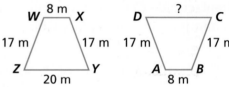

✓ **8-10** **Translations, Reflections, and Rotations**

Graph each transformation. Give the coordinates of the image's vertices.

4. Translate triangle *RST* 5 units down.

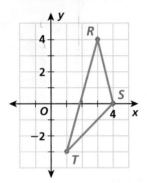

5. Reflect the figure across the *x*-axis.

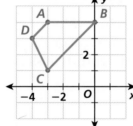

6. Rotate triangle *JKL* 90° clockwise about vertex *L*.

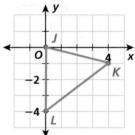

✓ **8-11** **Symmetry**

7. Decide whether the figure has line symmetry. If it does, draw all the lines of symmetry.

8. Tell how many times the figure will show rotational symmetry within one full rotation.

MULTI-STEP TEST PREP

Start Your Engines Several friends are racing remote-controlled cars. They use chalk to lay out the race course shown in the figure. Kendall examines the course beforehand to prepare for the race.

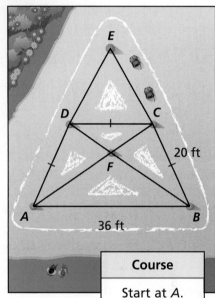

1. Kendall knows that figure *ABCD* is a trapezoid. What can he conclude about $\overline{AB}$ and $\overline{DC}$?

2. Using a protractor, Kendall measures ∠*ADF* as 81° and ∠*DFA* as 66°. He wants to know the angle at which he should turn his car as he goes from *C* to *A* to *D*. Explain how he can find the measure of ∠*CAD* without using a protractor. Then find the angle measure.

3. Triangle *DEC* is equilateral. How long is the section of the course from *E* to *D*?

4. $\overline{AC}$ is congruent to $\overline{DB}$, and $\overline{AC}$ is 33 feet long. What is the total length of the course?

5. Kendall's car moves at about 10 feet per second. Estimate the time it will take his car to complete the course.

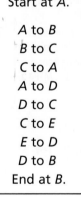

Course
Start at *A*.
A to *B*
B to *C*
C to *A*
A to *D*
D to *C*
C to *E*
E to *D*
D to *B*
End at *B*.

Dilations

Learn to explore similar figures through dilations.

Vocabulary
dilation

You can use computer software to *dilate* an image, such as a photograph. A **dilation** is a transformation that changes the size, but not the shape, of a figure. After a dilation, the image of a figure is similar to the original figure.

Georgia Performance Standards

M7G2.b Given a figure in the coordinate plane, determine the coordinates resulting from a dilation. Also, M7G3.a, M7P4.b, M7P5.b.

EXAMPLE 1 Identifying Dilations

Tell whether each transformation is a dilation.

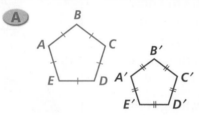

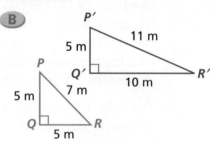

The figures are similar, so the transformation is a dilation.

The figures are not similar, so the transformation is not a dilation.

A dilation enlarges or reduces a figure. The scale factor tells you how much the figure is enlarged or reduced. On a coordinate plane, you can find the image of a figure after a dilation by multiplying the coordinates of the vertices by the scale factor.

EXAMPLE 2 Using a Dilation to Enlarge a Figure

Draw the image of △ABC after a dilation by a scale factor of 2.

Write the coordinates of the vertices of △ABC. Then multiply the coordinates by 2 to find the coordinates of the vertices of △A′B′C′.

$A(1, 3) \rightarrow A'(1 \cdot 2, 3 \cdot 2) = A'(2, 6)$

$B(4, 3) \rightarrow B'(4 \cdot 2, 3 \cdot 2) = B'(8, 6)$

$C(4, 1) \rightarrow C'(4 \cdot 2, 1 \cdot 2) = C'(8, 2)$

Plot A', B', and C' and draw △A′B′C′.

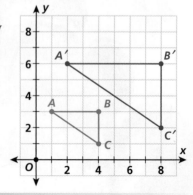

EXAMPLE **3** **Using a Dilation to Reduce a Figure**

Draw the image of △DEF after a dilation by a scale factor of $\frac{1}{3}$.

Write the coordinates of the vertices of △DEF. Then multiply the coordinates by $\frac{1}{3}$ to find the coordinates of the vertices of △D'E'F'.

$D(3, 3) \rightarrow D'(3 \cdot \frac{1}{3}, 3 \cdot \frac{1}{3}) = D'(1, 1)$

$E(9, 6) \rightarrow E'(9 \cdot \frac{1}{3}, 6 \cdot \frac{1}{3}) = E'(3, 2)$

$F(6, 0) \rightarrow F'(6 \cdot \frac{1}{3}, 0 \cdot \frac{1}{3}) = F'(2, 0)$

Plot D', E', and F' and draw △D'E'F'.

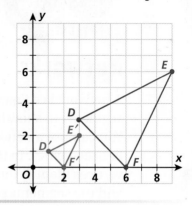

EXTENSION

Exercises

Tell whether each transformation is a dilation.

1.

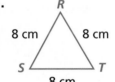

2.

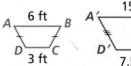

Draw the image of each figure after a dilation by the given scale factor.

3. scale factor 3

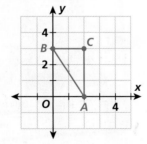

4. scale factor 2

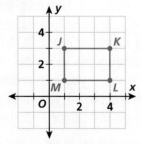

5. scale factor $\frac{1}{2}$

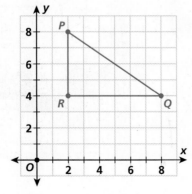

6. scale factor $\frac{1}{3}$

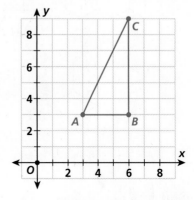

Game Time

Networks

A network is a figure that uses vertices and segments to show how objects are connected. You can use a network to show distances between cities. In the network at right, the vertices identify four cities in North Carolina, and the segments show the distances in miles between the cities.

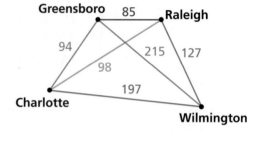

You can use the network to find the shortest route from Charlotte to the other three cities and back to Charlotte. First find all the possible routes. Then find the distance in miles for each route. One route has been identified below.

CGRWC $94 + 85 + 127 + 197 = 503$

Which is the shortest route, and what is the distance?

Color Craze

You can use rhombus-shaped tiles to build a variety of polygons. Each side of a tile is a different color. Build each design by matching the same-colored sides of tiles. Then see if you can create your own designs with the tiles. Try to make designs that have line or rotational symmetry.

A complete set of tiles is available online.

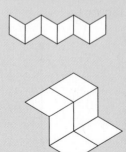

go.hrw.com
Game Time Extra
KEYWORD: MS7 Games

Materials

- 6 sheets of construction paper
- card stock
- scissors
- hole punch
- 4 electrical ties
- white paper
- markers

FOLDNOTES

It's in the Bag!

PROJECT **Brochure Book of Geometric Figures**

Make an organizer to hold brochures that summarize each lesson of the chapter.

Directions

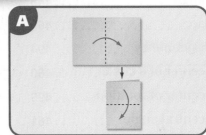

1 Start with sheets of construction paper that are 12 inches by 18 inches. Fold one sheet in half to make it 12 inches by 9 inches and then in half again to make it 6 inches by 9 inches. **Figure A**

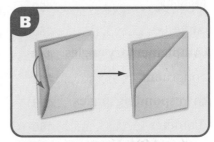

2 Hold the paper with the folds at the bottom and on the right-hand side. Turn the top left-hand corner back and under to form a pocket. **Figure B**

3 Turn the whole thing over and fold the top right-hand corner back and under to form a pocket. Repeat steps 1–3 with the other sheets of construction paper.

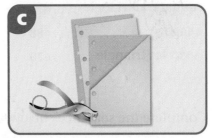

4 Cut out two pieces of card stock that are 6 inches by 9 inches. Punch four equally spaced holes down the length of each piece. Similarly, punch four equally spaced holes on each pocket as shown. **Figure C**

5 Stack the six pockets and put the card stock covers on the front and back of the stack. Insert electrical ties into the holes to hold everything together.

Taking Note of the Math

Fold sheets of plain white paper into thirds like a brochure. Use the brochures to take notes on the lessons of the chapter. Store the brochures in the pockets of your organizer.

Complete the sentences below with vocabulary words from the list above.

1. Every equilateral triangle is also a(n) __?__ triangle.

2. Lines in the same plane that do not intersect are __?__.

3. A line segment whose endpoints are any two points on a circle is a(n) __?__.

8-1 Building Blocks of Geometry (pp. 442–445)

 GPS M7P3.d

EXAMPLE

Identify the figures in the diagram.

- points: *A, B, C*
- lines: $\overrightarrow{AB}$
- planes: *ABC*
- rays: $\overrightarrow{BA}$; $\overrightarrow{AB}$
- line segments: $\overline{AB}$; $\overline{BC}$

EXERCISES

Identify the figures in the diagram.

4. points
5. lines
6. planes
7. rays
8. line segments

8-2 Classifying Angles (pp. 448–451)

 GPS M7A1.a, M7A2.a, M7A2.b

EXAMPLE

- Tell whether the angle is acute, right, obtuse, or straight.

The angle is a right angle.

EXERCISES

Tell whether each angle is acute, right, obtuse, or straight.

9.

10.

8-3 Angle Relationships (pp. 452–455)

 GPS M7A2.a, M7A2.b

EXAMPLE

- Tell whether the lines appear parallel, perpendicular, or skew.

perpendicular

EXERCISES

Tell whether the lines appear parallel, perpendicular, or skew.

11.

12.

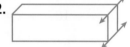

8-4 Properties of Circles (pp. 460–463)

 GPS M7P3.d

EXAMPLE

Name the parts of circle *D*.

- radii: $\overline{DB}, \overline{DC}, \overline{DE}$
- diameter: $\overline{EB}$
- chords: $\overline{AB}, \overline{EB}, \overline{EF}$

EXERCISES

Name the parts of circle *F*.

13. radii
14. diameter
15. chords

8-5 Classifying Polygons (pp. 466–469)

 GPS M7P2.c

EXAMPLE

- Tell whether the figure is a regular polygon. If it is not, explain why not.
  No, all the angles in the polygon are not congruent.

EXERCISES

Tell whether each figure is a regular polygon. If it is not, explain why not.

16.

17.

8-6 Classifying Triangles (pp. 470–473)

 GPS M7P3.d

EXAMPLE

- Classify the triangle according to its sides and angles.

Isosceles right

EXERCISES

Classify each triangle according to its sides and angles.

18.

19.

8-7 **Classifying Quadrilaterals** (pp. 474–477)

 GPS M7P2.d

EXAMPLE

■ Give all of the names that apply to the quadrilateral.

trapezoid

EXERCISES

Give all of the names that apply to each quadrilateral.

20. 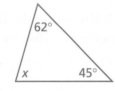   **21.**

 8-8 **Angles in Polygons** (pp. 478–481)

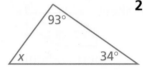 GPS M7A2.a, M7A2.b

EXAMPLE

■ Find the measure of the unknown angle.

$62° + 45° + x = 180°$
$107° + x = 180°$
$x = 73°$

EXERCISES

Find the measure of the unknown angle.

22.   **23.**

8-9 **Congruent Figures** (pp. 484–487)

 GPS M7G3.c

EXAMPLE

■ Determine the missing measure in the set of congruent polygons.

The angle measures 53°.

EXERCISES

24. Determine the missing measure in the set of congruent polygons.

8-10 **Translations, Reflections, and Rotations** (pp. 488–492)

 GPS M7G2.a, M7G2.b

EXAMPLE

■ Graph the translation.

Translate △ABC 1 unit right and 3 units down.

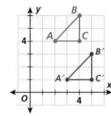

EXERCISES

Graph the translation.

25. Translate △BCD 2 units left and 4 units down.

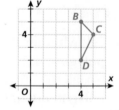

8-11 **Symmetry** (pp. 494–497)

 GPS M7G2.a

EXAMPLE

■ Find all the lines of symmetry in the flag.

The flag has four lines of symmetry.

EXERCISES

26. Find all the lines of symmetry in the flag.

---

508 *Chapter 8 Geometric Figures*

Study Guide: Review

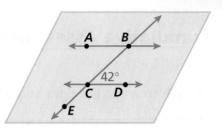

CHAPTER TEST

CHAPTER 8

Identify the figures in the diagram.

1. 4 points   **2.** 3 lines   **3.** a plane

4. 5 line segments   **5.** 6 rays

Line *AB* ∥ line *CD* in the diagram. Find the measure of each angle and tell whether the angle is acute, right, obtuse, or straight.

6. ∠*ABC*   **7.** ∠*BCE*   **8.** ∠*DCE*

Tell whether the lines appear parallel, perpendicular, or skew.

9. $\overleftrightarrow{MN}$ and $\overleftrightarrow{PO}$ **10.** $\overleftrightarrow{LM}$ and $\overleftrightarrow{PO}$ **11.** $\overleftrightarrow{NO}$ and $\overleftrightarrow{MN}$

Name the parts of circle *E*.

12. radii   **13.** chords   **14.** diameter

Tell whether each figure is a regular polygon. If it is not, explain why not.

15.   **16.**   **17.**

Classify each triangle according to its sides and angles.

18.   **19.**   **20.**

Give all the names that apply to each quadrilateral.

21.    **22.**   **23.**

Find the measure of each unknown angle.

24. 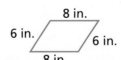   **25.**   **26.**

27. Determine the missing measure in the congruent polygons.

28. The vertices of a triangle have the coordinates *A*(−1, −3), *B*(−4, −1), and *C*(−1, −1). Graph the triangle after a translation 3 units left.

Find all the lines of symmetry in each flag.

29.   **30.**

Chapter Test

Chapter Test **509**

Cumulative Assessment, Chapters 1–8

Multiple Choice

1. Which angle is a right angle?

Ⓐ

Ⓒ

Ⓑ

Ⓓ

2. What is the number 8,330,000,000 written in scientific notation?

Ⓕ 0.83×10^{10}

Ⓗ 83.3×10^{8}

Ⓖ 8.33×10^{9}

Ⓙ 833×10^{7}

3. If point A is translated 5 units left and 2 units up, what will point A's new coordinates be?

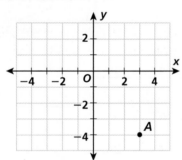

Ⓐ $(-2, -2)$

Ⓒ $(-2, -6)$

Ⓑ $(8, -2)$

Ⓓ $(0, 1)$

4. Nolan spent $\frac{1}{2}$ hour traveling to his orthodontist appointment, $\frac{3}{5}$ hour at his appointment, and $\frac{3}{4}$ hour traveling home. What is the total amount of time Nolan spent for this appointment?

Ⓕ $\frac{7}{11}$ hour

Ⓗ $1\frac{17}{20}$ hours

Ⓖ $\frac{37}{60}$ hour

Ⓙ $\frac{13}{5}$ hours

5. A store sells two dozen rolls of toilet paper for $4.84. What is the unit rate for one roll of toilet paper?

Ⓐ $0.13/roll of toilet paper

Ⓑ $0.20/roll of toilet paper

Ⓒ $0.40/roll of toilet paper

Ⓓ $1.21/roll of toilet paper

6. Which of the following best describes the triangle below?

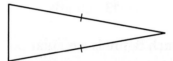

Ⓕ Acute isosceles triangle

Ⓖ Equilateral triangle

Ⓗ Obtuse right triangle

Ⓙ Obtuse scalene triangle

7. Which expression represents "twice the difference of a number and 8"?

Ⓐ $2(x + 8)$

Ⓒ $2(x - 8)$

Ⓑ $2x - 8$

Ⓓ $2x + 8$

8. For which equation is $x = 1$ NOT the solution?

Ⓕ $3x + 8 = 11$

Ⓖ $8 - x = 9$

Ⓗ $-3x + 8 = 5$

Ⓙ $8 + x = 9$

9. Which ratios form a proportion?

Ⓐ $\frac{4}{8}$ and $\frac{3}{6}$

Ⓒ $\frac{4}{10}$ and $\frac{6}{16}$

Ⓑ $\frac{4}{12}$ and $\frac{6}{15}$

Ⓓ $\frac{2}{3}$ and $\frac{5}{8}$

10. The graph shows how Amy spends her earnings each month. Amy earned $100 in May. How much did she spend on transportation and clothing combined?

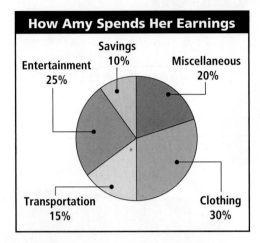

How Amy Spends Her Earnings

- Savings 10%
- Entertainment 25%
- Miscellaneous 20%
- Transportation 15%
- Clothing 30%

F $15   H $45
G $30   J $55

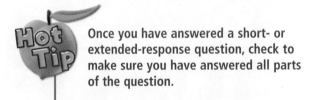
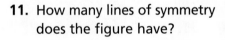

Once you have answered a short- or extended-response question, check to make sure you have answered all parts of the question.

11. How many lines of symmetry does the figure have?

A 0   C 2
B 1   D 4

12. An antiques dealer bought a chair for $85. The dealer sold the chair at her shop for 45% more than what she paid. To the nearest whole dollar, what was the price of the chair?

F 123   H 154
G 130   J 170

13. What is the value of the expression $-4x^2y - y$ for $x = -2$ and $y = -5$?

A −85   C 80
B −75   D 85

STANDARDIZED TEST PREP

14. A figure has vertices $A(-4, -4)$, $B(-3, -2)$, and $C(-3, -6)$. What will the y-coordinate of point A' be after the figure is reflected across the y-axis?

15. How many sets of parallel lines does a rectangle have?

Short Response

16. Triangle ABC, with vertices $A(2, 3)$, $B(4, 0)$, and $C(0, 0)$, is translated 2 units left and 6 units down to form triangle $A'B'C'$.

    a. On a coordinate plane, draw and label triangle ABC and triangle $A'B'C'$.

    b. Give the coordinates of the vertices of triangle $A'B'C'$.

17. Taylor's goal is to spend less than 35% of her allowance each month on cell phone bills. Last month, Taylor spent $45 on cell phone bills. If she gets $120 each month as her allowance, did she achieve her goal? Explain your answer.

18. Consider the sequence 4, 8, 12, 16, 20, ...

    a. Write a rule for the sequence. Use n to represent the position of the term in the sequence.

    b. What is the 8th term in the sequence?

Extended Response

19. Four of the angles in a pentagon measure 74°, 111°, 145°, and 95°.

    a. How many sides and how many angles does a pentagon have?

    b. Is the pentagon a regular pentagon? How do you know?

    c. What is the sum of the angle measures of a pentagon? Include a drawing as part of your answer.

    d. Write and solve an equation to determine the missing angle measure of the pentagon.

CRCT Prep

 Problem Solving on Location

G E O R G I A

Atlanta
Perry

Georgia Performance Standards

M7P1.c, M7P4.c, M7P5.a

 The Georgia National Fair

Since 1990, the Georgia National Fair in Perry has been providing entertainment for the entire family. The annual event features rides, concerts, a circus, a laser show, and an unusual crowd-pleaser: racing pigs!

Choose one or more strategies to solve each problem.

1. The fair attracts exhibitors from many states. Use the following information to find the number of states that sent exhibitors in 2005.
   • More states sent exhibitors to the fair in 2005 than in 2004.
   • The mean number of states that sent exhibitors in 2004 and 2005 was 17.
   • The range of the number of states that sent exhibitors in 2004 and 2005 was 6.

For 2–3, use the graph.

2. The number of people attending the fair has grown steadily in recent years. Assume the total attendance continues to increase as shown in the graph. How many people will attend the fair in 2012?

3. In what year will total attendance hit 500,000 for the first time?

Annual Attendance at the Georgia National Fair

Total Attendance (thousands) vs. Year

360 (2001), 370 (2002), 380 (2003), 390 (2004), 400 (2005)

Problem Solving Strategies

Draw a Diagram
Make a Model
Guess and Test
Work Backward
Find a Pattern
Make a Table
Solve a Simpler Problem
Use Logical Reasoning
Act It Out
Make an Organized List

⭐ Centennial Olympic Park

In 1996, Atlanta hosted the Summer Olympic games. During the games, Centennial Olympic Park was the main gathering place for athletes and sports fans. Since then, the park has hosted hundreds of special events, making it one of Atlanta's most popular destinations.

Choose one or more strategies to solve each problem.

1. The park includes five plazas, each based on a different theme. The themes are nations, Olympic spirit, origins, remembrance, and dreams. In how many different ways can you choose to visit two of the plazas?

2. One of the park's reflecting pools is shaped like a pentagon. Organizers of a special event place poles at the vertices of the pool and hang streamers between all the pairs of poles. How many streamers are needed?

For 3, use the diagram.

3. The park has the world's largest interactive fountain. Water shoots up from five congruent circles that represent the five Olympic rings. The space between the pairs of rings is $3\frac{3}{4}$ feet. What is the diameter of each ring?

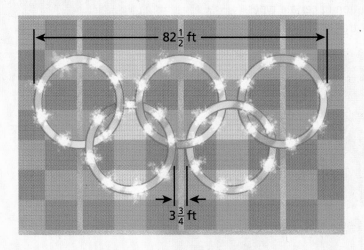

CHAPTER 9

Measurement: Two-Dimensional Figures

CRCT PREP

go.hrw.com
Chapter Project Online
KEYWORD: MS7 Ch9

Florida Tropical Fruit Tree Inventory

Tree Type	Number of Trees	Number of Trees per Acre
Grapefruit	14,751,000	181
Lemon	178,800	173
Lime	502,400	159
Orange	84,200,000	128

Career *Fruit Tree Grower*

Growing fruit trees requires diverse knowledge and skills. A fruit tree grower needs to know how to prepare soil, plant and care for trees, and guard the trees against insects and diseases.

To be successful, a fruit tree grower must also try to maximize the size and quantity of the fruit produced. Growers measure their land to determine the number of trees to plant and where each tree should be planted. The table shows the number and distribution of certain types of fruit trees in Florida.

ARE YOU READY?

✓ Vocabulary

Choose the best term from the list to complete each sentence.

1. A(n) __?__ is a quadrilateral with exactly one pair of parallel sides.

2. A(n) __?__ is a four-sided figure with opposite sides that are congruent and parallel.

3. The __?__ of a circle is one-half the __?__ of the circle.

diameter

parallelogram

radius

right triangle

trapezoid

Complete these exercises to review skills you will need for this chapter.

✓ Round Whole Numbers

Round each number to the nearest ten and nearest hundred.

4. 1,535   5. 294   6. 30,758   7. 497

✓ Round Decimals

Round each number to the nearest whole number and nearest tenth.

8. 6.18   9. 10.50   10. 513.93   11. 29.06

✓ Multiply with Decimals

Multiply.

12. $5.63 \cdot 8$ 13. $9.67 \cdot 4.3$ 14. $8.34 \cdot 16$ 15. $6.08 \cdot 0.56$

16. $0.82 \cdot 21$ 17. $2.74 \cdot 6.6$ 18. $40 \cdot 9.54$ 19. $0.33 \cdot 0.08$

✓ Order of Operations

Simplify each expression.

20. $2 \cdot 9 + 2 \cdot 6$ 21. $2(15 + 8)$ 22. $4 \cdot 6.8 + 7 \cdot 9.3$

23. $14(25.9 + 13.6)$ 24. $(27.3 + 0.7) \div 2^2$ 25. $5 \cdot 3^3 - 8.02$

26. $(63 \div 7) \cdot 4^2$ 27. $1.1 + 3 \cdot 4.3$ 28. $66 \cdot [5 + (3 + 3)^2]$

✓ Identify Polygons

Name each figure.

29.

30.

31.

Study Guide: Preview

Where You've Been

Previously, you

- found the perimeter or circumference of geometric figures.

- explored customary and metric units of measure.

- used proportions to convert measurements within the customary system and within the metric system.

In This Chapter

You will study

- comparing perimeter and circumference with the area of geometric figures.

- finding the area of parallelograms, triangles, trapezoids, and circles.

- finding the area of irregular figures.

- using powers, roots, and the Pythagorean Theorem to find missing measures.

Where You're Going

You can use the skills learned in this chapter

- to create an architectural floor plan.

- to design a building access ramp that meets government regulations.

Key Vocabulary/Vocabulario

area	área
circumference	circunferencia
hypotenuse	hipotenusa
perfect square	cuadrado perfecto
perimeter	perímetro
Pythagorean Theorem	Teorema de Pitágoras
significant digits	dígitos significativos
square root	raíz cuadrada

Vocabulary Connections

To become familiar with some of the vocabulary terms in the chapter, consider the following. You may refer to the chapter, the glossary, or a dictionary if you like.

1. The *square root* of a number is one of the two equal factors of the number. For example, 3 is a square root because $3 \cdot 3 = 9$. How might picturing plant roots help you remember the meaning of **square root**?

2. The word *perimeter* comes from the Greek roots *peri,* meaning "all around," and *metron,* meaning "measure." What do the Greek roots tell you about the **perimeter** of a geometric figure?

3. To *square a number* means "to multiply the number by itself," as in $2 \cdot 2$. Keeping this idea of *square* in mind, what do you think a **perfect square** might be?

4. The word *circumference* comes from the Latin word *circumferre,* meaning "to carry around." How does the Latin meaning help you define the **circumference** of a circle?

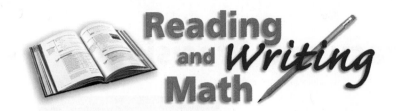

Reading Strategy: Read and Interpret Graphics

Figures, diagrams, tables, and graphs provide important data. Knowing how to read these graphics will help you understand and solve related problems.

Similar Figures

$\triangle ABC$ and $\triangle JKL$ are similar.

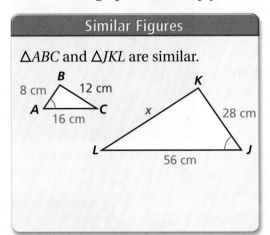

How to Read

Read all labels.
$AB = 8$ cm; $AC = 16$ cm; $BC = 12$ cm; $JK = 28$ cm; $JL = 56$ cm; $KL = x$ cm; $\angle A$ corresponds to $\angle J$.

Be careful about what you assume.
You may think $\overline{AB}$ corresponds to $\overline{LK}$, but this is not so. Since $\angle A$ corresponds to $\angle J$, you know $\overline{AB}$ corresponds to $\overline{JK}$.

Double-Bar Graph

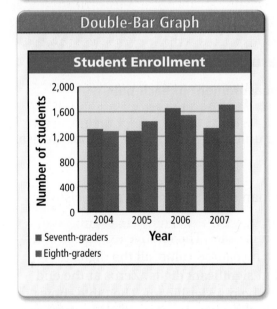

How to Read

Read the title of the graph and any special notes.
Blue indicates seventh-graders.
Purple indicates eighth-graders.

Read each axis label and note the intervals of each scale.
x-axis—year increases by 1.
y-axis—enrollment increases by 400 students.

Determine what information is presented.
student enrollment for seventh- and eighth-graders per year

Try This

Look up each graphic in your textbook and answer the following questions.

1. Lesson 5-7 Exercise 1: Which side of the smaller triangle corresponds to $\overline{BC}$? Which angle corresponds to $\angle EDF$?

2. Lesson 7-3 Example 1: By what interval does the *x*-axis scale increase? About how many people speak Hindi?

Reading and Writing Math

9-1 Accuracy and Precision

Learn to compare the precision of measurements and to determine acceptable levels of accuracy.

Vocabulary

precision

accuracy

significant digits

Georgia Performance Standards

M7P1.c Apply and adapt a variety of appropriate strategies to solve problems. Also, M7P4.c.

Ancient Greeks used measurements taken during lunar eclipses to determine that the Moon was 240,000 miles from Earth. In 1969, the distance was measured as 221,463 miles.

There is a difference between these measurements because modern scientists conducted the measurement with greater *precision*. **Precision** is the level of detail an instrument can measure.

The smaller the unit an instrument can measure, the more precise its measurements will be. For example, a millimeter ruler has greater precision than a centimeter ruler because it can measure smaller units.

At the University of Texas McDonald Observatory, a laser is used to measure the distance from Earth to the Moon.

EXAMPLE 1 **Judging Precision of Measurements**

Choose the more precise measurement in each pair.

A 37 in., 3 ft

Since an inch is a smaller unit than a foot, 37 in. is more precise.

B 5 km, 5.8 km

Since tenths are smaller than ones, 5.8 km is more precise.

In the real world, no measurement is exact. The relative exactness of a measurement is its **accuracy**. In a measured value, all the digits that are known with certainty are called **significant digits**. Zeros at the end of a whole number are assumed to be nonsignificant. The table shows the rules for identifying significant digits.

Rule	Example	Number of Significant Digits
• Nonzero digits	45.7	3 significant digits
• Zeros between significant digits	78,002	5 significant digits
• Zeros after the last nonzero digit and to the right of a decimal point	0.0040	2 significant digits

EXAMPLE 2 Identifying Significant Digits

Determine the number of significant digits in each measurement.

A **120.1 mi**

The digits 1 and 2 are nonzero digits, and 0 is between two nonzero digits.

So 120.1 mi has 4 significant digits.

B **0.0350 kg**

The digits 3 and 5 are nonzero digits, and 0 is to the right of the decimal after the last nonzero digit.

So 0.0350 kg has 3 significant digits.

When you are adding and subtracting measurements, the answer should have the same number of digits to the right of the decimal point as the measurement with the least number of digits to the right of the decimal point.

EXAMPLE 3 Using Significant Digits in Addition or Subtraction

Calculate 45 mi − 0.9 mi. Use the correct number of significant digits in the answer.

$$
\begin{array}{ll}
45 & \textit{0 digits to the right of the decimal point} \\
\underline{-\ 0.9} & \textit{1 digit to the right of the decimal point} \\
44.1 \approx 44 \text{ mi} & \textit{Round the difference so that it has no digits} \\
& \textit{to the right of the decimal point.}
\end{array}
$$

When you are multiplying and dividing measurements, the answer must have the same number of significant digits as the measurement with the least number of significant digits.

EXAMPLE 4 Using Significant Digits in Multiplication or Division

Calculate 32.8 m · 1.5 m. Use the correct number of significant digits in the answer.

$$
\begin{array}{ll}
32.8 & \textit{3 significant digits} \\
\underline{\times\ 1.5} & \textit{2 significant digits} \\
49.2 \approx 49 \text{ m}^2 & \textit{Round the product so that it has 2 significant digits.}
\end{array}
$$

Think and Discuss

GPS M7P2.c, M7P3.b

1. Tell how many significant digits there are in 380.102.

2. Choose the more precise measurement: 18 oz or 1 lb. Explain.

Exercises

Georgia Performance Standards

M7P1.a, M7P1.b, M7P2.c

go.hrw.com

Homework Help Online
KEYWORD: MS7 9-1

Parent Resources Online
KEYWORD: MS7 Parent

GUIDED PRACTICE

See Example **1** Choose the more precise measurement in each pair.

1. 4 ft, 1 yd   **2.** 2 cm, 21 mm   **3.** $5\frac{1}{2}$ in., $5\frac{1}{4}$ in.

See Example **2** Determine the number of significant digits in each measurement.

4. 2.703 g   **5.** 0.02 km   **6.** 28,000 lb

See Example **3** Calculate. Use the correct number of significant digits in each answer.

7. 16 − 3.8   **8.** 3.5 + 0.66   **9.** 11.3 − 4

See Example **4** **10.** 47.9 · 3.8   **11.** 7.0 · 3.6   **12.** 50.2 ÷ 8.0

INDEPENDENT PRACTICE

See Example **1** Choose the more precise measurement in each pair.

13. 11 in., 1 ft   **14.** 7.2 m, 6.2 cm   **15.** 14.2 km, 14 km

16. $4\frac{3}{8}$ in., $4\frac{7}{16}$ in.   **17.** 2.8 m, 3 m   **18.** 37 g, 37.0 g

See Example **2** Determine the number of significant digits in each measurement.

19. 0.00002 kg   **20.** 10,000,000 lb   **21.** 200.060 m

22. 4.003 L   **23.** 0.230 cm   **24.** 940.0 ft

See Example **3** Calculate. Use the correct number of significant digits in each answer.

25. 6.2 + 8.93   **26.** 7.02 + 15   **27.** 8 − 6.6

28. 29.1 − 13.204   **29.** 8.6 + 9.43   **30.** 43.5 + 876.23

See Example **4** **31.** 17 · 104   **32.** 21.8 · 10.9   **33.** 7.0 ÷ 3.11

34. 1,680 ÷ 5.025   **35.** 14.2 ÷ 0.05   **36.** 5.22 · 6.3

PRACTICE AND PROBLEM SOLVING

CRCT GPS

Extra Practice p. 744

Which unit is more precise?

37. foot or mile   **38.** centimeter or millimeter

39. liter or milliliter   **40.** minute or second

Calculate. Use the correct number of significant digits in each answer.

41. 38,000 · 4.8   **42.** 2.879 + 113.6   **43.** 290 − 6.1

44. 5.6 ÷ 0.6   **45.** 40.29 − 18.5   **46.** 24 ÷ 6.02

47. Multi-Step Jay estimates that he walks 15 miles each week. He walks 1.55 miles to school and then 0.4 miles to his aunt's house after school.

     a. Is Jay's estimate reasonable? Explain.

     b. How many miles does Jay walk during a 5-day school week? Use the correct number of significant digits in your answer.

The food labels at right give information about two types of soup: cream of tomato and minestrone. Use the labels for Exercises 48 and 49.

Cream of Tomato

Nutrition Facts
Serving size 1 cup (240mL)
Servings per container about 2

Amount per Serving		
Calories 100	Calories from Fat 20	
		% Daily Value*
Total Fat 2 g		3%
Saturated Fat 1.5 g		6%
Cholesterol 10 mg		3%
Sodium 690 mg		29%
Total Carbohydrate 17 g		6%
Dietary Fiber 4 g		18%
Sugars 11 g		
Protein 2 g		

Vitamin A 20%	—	Vitamin C 20%
Calcium 0%	—	Iron 8%

*Percent daily values are based on a 2,000 calorie diet.

Minestrone

Nutrition Facts
Serving size 1 cup (240mL)
Servings per container about 2

Amount per Serving		
Calories 90	Calories from Fat 10	
		% Daily Value*
Total Fat 1.5 g		2%
Saturated Fat 0 g		0%
Cholesterol 0 mg		0%
Sodium 540 mg		22%
Total Carbohydrate 17 g		6%
Dietary Fiber 3 g		14%
Sugars 5 g		
Protein 3 g		

Vitamin A 30%	—	Vitamin C 10%
Calcium 2%	—	Iron 6%

*Percent daily values are based on a 2,000 calorie diet.

48. Which measurement is more precise, the total amount of fat in cream of tomato soup or the total amount in minestrone? Explain.

49. One serving of cream of tomato soup contains 29% of the recommended daily value of sodium for a 2,000-calorie diet. What is the recommended daily value for sodium, in milligrams? Express your answer with the appropriate number of significant digits.

50. One-half of a medium-sized grapefruit, or 154 grams, counts as one serving of fruit. How many servings of fruit are in 1 kilogram of grapefruit? Express your answer with the appropriate number of significant digits.

51. ⭐ **Challenge** The greatest possible error of any measurement is half of the smallest unit used in the measurement. For example, 1 pt of juice may actually measure between $\frac{1}{2}$ pt and $1\frac{1}{2}$ pt. What is the range of possible actual weights for a watermelon that was weighed at $19\frac{1}{4}$ lb?

CRCT Prep • GPS Support • Spiral Review

52. Multiple Choice Which is the most precise measurement?

Ⓐ 1 mile   Ⓑ 1,758 yards   Ⓒ 5,281 feet   Ⓓ 63,355 inches

53. Multiple Choice Which measurement does NOT have three significant digits?

Ⓕ 63.2 cm   Ⓖ 0.08 ft   Ⓗ 0.00500 m   Ⓙ 4.06 yd

For Exercises 54–56, tell whether you would expect a positive correlation, a negative correlation, or no correlation. (Lesson 7-8)

54. the price of a car and the number of windows it has

55. the speed a car travels and the amount of time it takes to go 100 miles

56. the price per gallon of gasoline and the cost for a tank of gas

Determine whether each figure is a polygon. If it is not, explain why. (Lesson 8-5)

57.   **58.**   **59.**

Explore Perimeter & Circumference

Use with Lesson 9-2

go.hrw.com
Lab Resources Online
KEYWORD: MS7 Lab9

Georgia Performance Standards

M7A3.a, M7A3.b, M7P1.a, M7P5.a

The distance around a figure is its perimeter. You can use a loop of string to explore the dimensions of a rectangle with a perimeter of 18 inches.

Activity 1

1 Cut a piece of string that is slightly longer than 18 inches. Tie the ends together to form an 18-inch loop.

2 Make the loop into a rectangle by placing it around four push pins on a corkboard. Both the length and the width of the rectangle should be a whole number of inches.

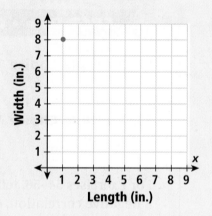

3 Make different rectangles with whole-number lengths and widths. Record the lengths and widths in a table.

Length (in.)	1	2	3					
Width (in.)	8							

4 Graph the data in your table by plotting points on a coordinate plane like the one shown.

Think and Discuss

1. What pattern is made by the points on your graph?

2. How is the sum of the length and width of each rectangle related to the rectangle's perimeter of 18 inches?

3. Suppose a rectangle has length ℓ and width w. Write a rule that you can use to find the rectangle's perimeter.

Try This

Use the rule you discovered to find the perimeter of each rectangle.

1.

4 in.

6 in.

2.

9 ft

3 ft

3.

5 cm

5 cm

The perimeter of a circle is called the *circumference*. You can explore the relationship between a circle's circumference and its diameter by measuring some circles.

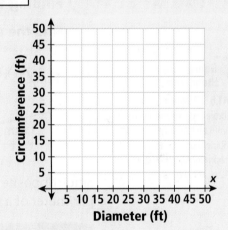

Diameter

Circumference

Activity 2

1 Four students should stand in a circle with their arms outstretched, as shown in the diagram.

2 Another student should find the diameter of the circle by measuring the distance across the middle of the circle with a tape measure.

3 The student should also find the circumference of the circle by measuring the distance around the circle from fingertip to fingertip across the backs of the students.

4 Record the diameter and circumference in a table like the one below.

Diameter (ft)					
Circumference (ft)					

5 Add one or more students to the circle and repeat the process. Record the diameter and circumference for at least five different circles.

6 Graph the data in your table by plotting points on a coordinate plane like the one shown.

Think and Discuss

1. In general, what do you notice about the points on your graph? What shape or pattern do they seem to form?

2. Calculate the ratio of the circumference to the diameter for each of the data points. Then calculate the mean of these ratios. For any circle, the ratio of the circumference to the diameter is a constant, known as *pi* (π). Give an estimate for π based on your findings.

Try This

1. For a circle with circumference C and diameter d, the ratio of the circumference to the diameter is $\frac{C}{d} = \pi$. Use this to write a formula that you can use to find the circumference of a circle when you know its diameter.

2. Use your estimate for the value of π to find the approximate circumference of the circle at right.

$d = 4$ cm

9-2 Perimeter and Circumference

Vocabulary

perimeter

circumference

In volleyball, the player serving must hit the ball over the net but keep it within the court's sidelines and end lines. The two sidelines on a volleyball court are each 18 meters long, and the two end lines are each 9 meters long. Together, the four lines form the *perimeter* of the court.

Perimeter is the distance around a geometric figure. To find the perimeter P of a rectangular volleyball court, you can add the lengths of its sides.

EXAMPLE 1 Finding the Perimeter of a Polygon

Find the perimeter.

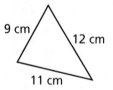

9 cm

12 cm

11 cm

$P = 9 + 12 + 11$ *Use the side lengths.*

$P = 32$ *Add.*

The perimeter of the triangle is 32 cm.

Since opposite sides of a rectangle are equal in length, you can find the perimeter of a rectangle by using a formula.

PERIMETER OF A RECTANGLE		
The perimeter P of a rectangle is the sum of twice its length ℓ and twice its width w.	$P = 2\ell + 2w$	w ℓ

EXAMPLE 2 Using Properties of a Rectangle to Find Perimeter

Find the perimeter.

15 m

32 m

$P = 2\ell + 2w$ *Use the formula.*

$P = (2 \cdot 32) + (2 \cdot 15)$ *Substitute for ℓ and w.*

$P = 64 + 30$ *Multiply.*

$P = 94$ *Add.*

The perimeter of the rectangle is 94 m.

The distance around a circle is called **circumference**. For every circle, the ratio of circumference C to diameter d is the same. This ratio, $\frac{C}{d}$, is represented by the Greek letter π, called *pi*. Pi is approximately equal to 3.14 or $\frac{22}{7}$. By solving the equation $\frac{C}{d} = \pi$ for C, you get the formula for circumference.

CIRCUMFERENCE OF A CIRCLE		
The circumference C of a circle is π times the diameter d, or 2π times the radius r.	$C = \pi d$ or $C = 2\pi r$	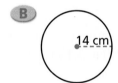 Radius — Diameter — Circumference

EXAMPLE 3 Finding the Circumference of a Circle

Find the circumference of each circle to the nearest tenth, if necessary. Use 3.14 or $\frac{22}{7}$ for π.

A

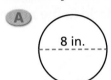

8 in.

$C = \pi d$ *You know the diameter.*

$C \approx 3.14 \cdot 8$ *Substitute 3.14 for π and 8 for d.*

$C \approx 25.12$ *Multiply.*

The circumference of the circle is about 25.1 in.

B

14 cm

$C = 2\pi r$ *You know the radius.*

$C \approx 2 \cdot \frac{22}{7} \cdot 14$ *Substitute $\frac{22}{7}$ for π and 14 for r.*

$C \approx 88$ *Multiply.*

The circumference of the circle is about 88 cm.

EXAMPLE 4 *Design Application*

Lily is drawing plans for a circular fountain. The circumference of the fountain is 63 ft. What is its approximate diameter?

$C = \pi d$ *You know the circumference.*

$63 \approx 3.14 \cdot d$ *Substitute 3.14 for π and 63 for C.*

$\dfrac{63}{3.14} \approx \dfrac{3.14 \cdot d}{3.14}$ *Divide both sides by 3.14 to isolate the variable.*

$20 \approx d$

The diameter of the fountain is about 20 ft.

Think and Discuss   GPS M7P1.d, M7P3.b

1. **Describe** two ways to find the perimeter of a volleyball court.

2. **Explain** how to use the formula $C = \pi d$ to find the circumference of a circle if you know the radius.

Georgia Performance Standards
M7P3.a, M7P4.c

go.hrw.com
Homework Help Online
KEYWORD: MS7 9-2
Parent Resources Online
KEYWORD: MS7 Parent

GUIDED PRACTICE

Find each perimeter.

See Example 1   **1.** 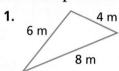   **2.** 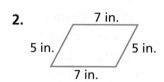   **3.**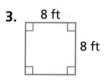

See Example 2   **4.** 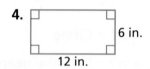   **5.** 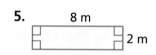   **6.**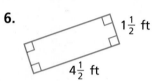

See Example 3   Find the circumference of each circle to the nearest tenth, if necessary. Use 3.14 or $\frac{22}{7}$ for π.

7. 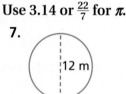   **8.**   **9.**

See Example 4   **10.** A Ferris wheel has a circumference of 440 feet. What is the approximate diameter of the Ferris wheel? Use 3.14 for π.

INDEPENDENT PRACTICE

Find each perimeter.

See Example 1   **11.** 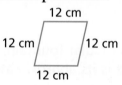   **12.** 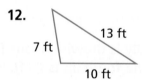   **13.**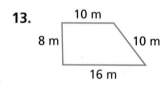

See Example 2   **14.** 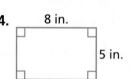   **15.** 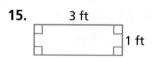   **16.**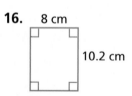

See Example 3   Find the circumference of each circle to the nearest tenth, if necessary. Use 3.14 or $\frac{22}{7}$ for π.

17. 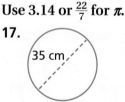   **18.**   **19.**

See Example 4   **20.** The circumference of Kayla's bicycle wheel is 91 inches. What is the approximate diameter of her bicycle wheel? Use 3.14 for π.

PRACTICE AND PROBLEM SOLVING

Find each missing measurement to the nearest tenth. Use 3.14 for π.

21. $r = $ ▨ ; $d = $ ▨ ; $C = 17.8$ m

22. $r = 6.7$ yd; $d = $ ▨ ; $C = $ ▨

23. $r = $ ▨ ; $d = 10.6$ in.; $C = $ ▨

24. $r = $ ▨ ; $d = $ ▨ ; $C = \pi$

Georgia LINK

Architecture

The dome on top of the Georgia State Capitol in Atlanta is covered with two layers of 23 karat gold.

25. Critical Thinking Ben is placing rope lights around the edge of a circular patio with a 24.2 ft diameter. The lights are in lengths of 57 inches. How many strands of lights does he need to surround the patio edge?

26. Geography The map shows the distances in miles between the airports on the Big Island of Hawaii. A pilot flies from Kailua-Kona to Waimea to Hilo and back to Kailua-Kona. How far does he travel?

27. Architecture The Capitol Rotunda connects the House and Senate sides of the U.S. Capitol. The rotunda is 180 feet tall and has a circumference of about 301.5 feet. What is its approximate diameter, to the nearest foot?

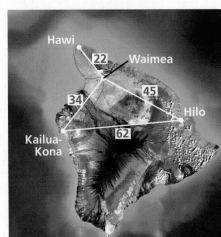

28. Write a Problem Write a problem about finding the perimeter or circumference of an object in your school or classroom.

29. Write About It Explain how to find the width of a rectangle if you know its perimeter and length.

30. Challenge The perimeter of a regular nonagon is $25\frac{1}{2}$ in. What is the length of one side of the nonagon?

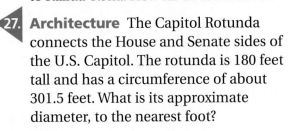

CRCT PREP • GPS SUPPORT • SPIRAL REVIEW

31. Multiple Choice Which is the best estimate for the circumference of a circle with a diameter of 15 inches?

Ⓐ 18.1 inches   Ⓑ 23.6 inches   Ⓒ 32.5 inches   Ⓓ 47.1 inches

32. Multiple Choice John is building a dog pen that is 6 feet by 8 feet. How much fencing material will he need to go all the way around the pen?

Ⓕ 48 feet   Ⓖ 28 feet   Ⓗ 20 feet   Ⓙ 14 feet

Solve. (Lesson 6-5)

33. 18 is 20% of what number?

34. 78% of 65 is what number?

Calculate. Use the correct number of significant digits in each answer. (Lesson 9-1)

35. $5.8 + 3.27$ **36.** $6 - 2.5$ **37.** $22.3 \cdot 6.2$ **38.** $60.6 \div 15$

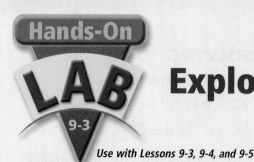

Explore Area of Polygons

Georgia Performance
Standards

M7P1.a, M7P2.d, M7P3.a,
M7P5.b

Use with Lessons 9-3, 9-4, and 9-5

go.hrw.com
Lab Resources Online
KEYWORD: MS7 Lab9

You can use a parallelogram to find the area of a triangle or a trapezoid. To do so, you must first know how to find the area of a parallelogram.

Activity 1

① On a sheet of graph paper, draw a parallelogram with a base of 10 units and a height of 6 units.

② Cut out the parallelogram. Then cut a right triangle off the end of the parallelogram by cutting along the altitude.

③ Move the triangle to the other side of the figure to make a rectangle.

④ How is the area of the parallelogram related to the area of the rectangle?

⑤ What are the length and width of the rectangle? What is the area of the rectangle?

⑥ Find the area of the parallelogram.

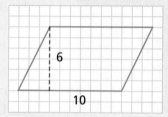

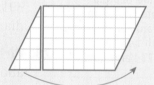

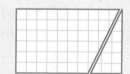

Think and Discuss

1. How are the length and width of the rectangle related to the base and height of the parallelogram?

2. Suppose a parallelogram has base *b* and height *h*. Write a formula for the area of the parallelogram.

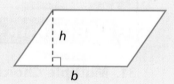

Try This

1. Does your formula work for any parallelogram? If so, show how to use the formula to find the area of the parallelogram at right.

2. Explain what must be true about the areas of the parallelograms below.

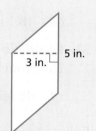

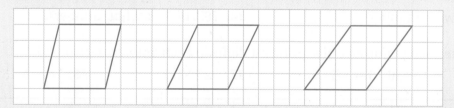

Activity 2

1 On a sheet of graph paper, draw a triangle with a base of 7 units and a height of 4 units.

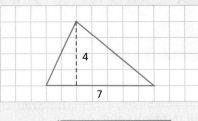

2 Cut out the triangle. Then use the triangle to trace and cut out a second triangle that is congruent to it.

3 Arrange the two triangles to form a parallelogram.

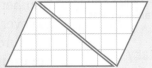

4 How is the area of the triangle related to the area of the parallelogram?

5 Find the areas of the parallelogram and the triangle.

Think and Discuss

1. How are the base and height of the triangle related to the base and height of the parallelogram?

2. Suppose a triangle has base b and height h. Write a formula for the area of the triangle.

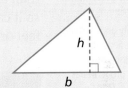

Try This

1. Find the area of a triangle with a base of 10 ft and a height of 5 ft.

Activity 3

1 On a sheet of graph paper, draw a trapezoid with bases 4 units and 8 units long and a height of 3 units.

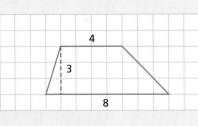

2 Cut out the trapezoid. Then use the trapezoid to trace and cut out a second trapezoid that is congruent to it.

3 Arrange the two trapezoids to form a parallelogram.

4 How is the area of the trapezoid related to the area of the parallelogram?

5 Find the areas of the parallelogram and the trapezoid.

Think and Discuss

1. What is the length of the base of the parallelogram at right? What is the parallelogram's area?

2. What is the area of one of the trapezoids in the figure?

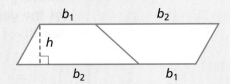

Try This

1. Find the area of a trapezoid with bases 4 in. and 6 in. and a height of 8 in.

Area of Parallelograms

 to find the area of rectangles and other parallelograms.

Vocabulary

area

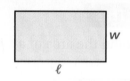 **Georgia Performance Standards**

M7A1.b Simplify and evaluate algebraic expressions, using commutative, associative, and distributive properties as appropriate. Also, M7P4.c, M7P5.b.

The **area** of a figure is the number of unit squares needed to cover the figure. Area is measured in square units. For example, the area of a chessboard can be measured in square inches. The area of a lawn chessboard is much larger than a regular chessboard, so it can be measured in square feet or square yards.

AREA OF A RECTANGLE		
The area A of a rectangle is the product of its length ℓ and its width w.	$A = \ell w$	(rectangle diagram with w and ℓ labels)

EXAMPLE 1 **Finding the Area of a Rectangle**

Find the area of the rectangle.

(rectangle diagram: 7.5 ft height, 10 ft base)

$A = \ell w$ *Use the formula.*

$A = 10 \cdot 7.5$ *Substitute for ℓ and w.*

$A = 75$ *Multiply.*

The area of the rectangle is 75 ft^2.

EXAMPLE 2 **Finding Length or Width of a Rectangle**

Bethany and her dad are planting a rectangular garden. The area of the garden is 1,080 ft^2, and the width is 24 ft. What is the length of the garden?

$A = \ell w$ *Use the formula for the area of a rectangle.*

$1,080 = \ell \cdot 24$ *Substitute 1,080 for A and 24 for w.*

$\dfrac{1,080}{24} = \dfrac{\ell \cdot 24}{24}$ *Divide both sides by 24 to isolate ℓ.*

$45 = \ell$

The length of the garden is 45 ft.

The base of a parallelogram is the length of one side. Its height is the perpendicular distance from the base to the opposite side.

AREA OF A PARALLELOGRAM		
The area A of a parallelogram is the product of its base b and its height h.	$A = bh$	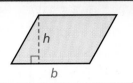

EXAMPLE 3 **Finding the Area of a Parallelogram**

Find the area of the parallelogram.

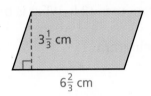

$3\frac{1}{3}$ cm

$6\frac{2}{3}$ cm

$A = bh$ *Use the formula.*

$A = 6\frac{2}{3} \cdot 3\frac{1}{3}$ *Substitute for b and h.*

$A = \frac{20}{3} \cdot \frac{10}{3}$ *Convert to improper fractions.*

$A = \frac{200}{9}$ or $22\frac{2}{9}$ *Multiply.*

The area of the parallelogram is $22\frac{2}{9}$ cm^2.

EXAMPLE 4 *Landscaping Application*

Birgit and Mark are building a rectangular patio measuring 9 yd by 7 yd. How many square feet of tile will they need?

First draw and label a diagram. Look at the units. The patio is measured in yards, but the answer should be in square feet.

$9 \text{ yd} \cdot \dfrac{3 \text{ ft}}{1 \text{ yd}} = 27 \text{ ft}$ *Convert yards to feet by using a unit conversion factor.*

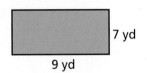

7 yd

9 yd

$7 \text{ yd} \cdot \dfrac{3 \text{ ft}}{1 \text{ yd}} = 21 \text{ ft}$

Now find the area of the patio in square feet.

$A = \ell w$ *Use the formula for the area of a rectangle.*

$A = 27 \cdot 21$ *Substitute 27 for ℓ and 21 for w.*

$A = 567$ *Multiply.*

Birgit and Mark need 567 ft^2 of tile.

Think and Discuss   GPS M7P2.c, M7P3.a

1. Write a formula for the area of a square, using an exponent.

2. Explain why the area of a nonrectangular parallelogram with side lengths 5 in. and 3 in. is not 15 in.^{2}

Exercises

Georgia Performance Standards

M7P1.c, M7P1.d, M7P3.a, M7P5.b

go.hrw.com
Homework Help Online
KEYWORD: MS7 9-3
Parent Resources Online
KEYWORD: MS7 Parent

GUIDED PRACTICE

See Example **1** · **Find the area of each rectangle.**

1.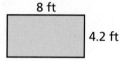
8 ft
4.2 ft

2.
3 m
7 m

3.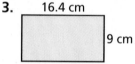
16.4 cm
9 cm

See Example **2** · **4.** Kara wants a rug for her bedroom. She knows the area of her bedroom is 132 ft². The length of her room is 12 ft. What is the width of Kara's bedroom?

See Example **3** · **Find the area of each parallelogram.**

5.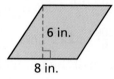
6 in.
8 in.

6.
4 cm
$2\frac{4}{5}$ cm

7.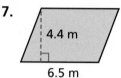
4.4 m
6.5 m

See Example **4** · **8.** Anna is mowing a rectangular field measuring 120 yd by 66 yd. How many square feet will Anna mow?

INDEPENDENT PRACTICE

See Example **1** · **Find the area of each rectangle.**

9.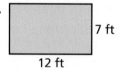
7 ft
12 ft

10.
$15\frac{1}{2}$ in.
$8\frac{1}{2}$ in.

11.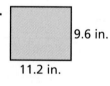
9.6 in.
11.2 in.

See Example **2** · **12.** James and Linda are fencing a rectangular area of the yard for their dog. The width of the dog yard is 4.5 m. Its area is 67.5 m². What is the length of the dog yard?

See Example **3** · **Find the area of each parallelogram.**

13.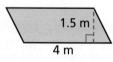
1.5 m
4 m

14.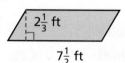
$2\frac{1}{3}$ ft
$7\frac{1}{2}$ ft

15.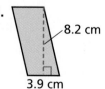
8.2 cm
3.9 cm

See Example **4** · **16.** Abby is painting rectangular blocks on her bathroom walls. Each block is 15 in. by 18 in. What is the area of one block in square feet?

PRACTICE AND PROBLEM SOLVING

Extra Practice p. 744

Find the area of each polygon.

17. rectangle: $\ell = 9$ yd; $w = 8$ yd

18. parallelogram: $b = 7$ m; $h = 4.2$ m

Graph the polygon with the given vertices. Then find the area of the polygon.

19. $(2, 0), (2, -2), (9, 0), (9, -2)$

20. $(4, 1), (4, 7), (8, 4), (8, 10)$

21. Art Without the frame, the painting *Girl of Tehuantepec* by Diego Rivera measures about 23 in. by 31 in. The width of the frame is 3 in.

    a. What is the area of the painting?

    b. What is the perimeter of the painting?

    c. What is the total area covered by the painting and the frame?

22. What is the height of a parallelogram with an area of 66 in² and a base of 11 in.?

Girl of Tehuantepec by Diego Rivera

23. Choose a Strategy The area of a parallelogram is 84 cm². If the base is 5 cm longer than the height, what is the length of the base?

    Ⓐ 5 cm   Ⓑ 7 cm   Ⓒ 12 cm   Ⓓ 14 cm

24. Write About It A rectangle and a parallelogram have sides that measure 3 m, 4 m, 3 m, and 4 m. Do the figures have the same area? Explain.

25. Challenge Two parallelograms have the same base length, but the height of the first is half that of the second. What is the ratio of the area of the first parallelogram to that of the second? What would the ratio be if both the height and the base of the first parallelogram were half those of the second?

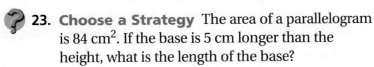

CRCT PREP • GPS SUPPORT • SPIRAL REVIEW

26. Multiple Choice Find the area of the parallelogram.

    Ⓐ 13 in²   Ⓑ 26 in²   Ⓒ 40 in²   Ⓓ 56 in²

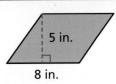

27. Extended Response Kiana is helping her dad build a deck. The plans they have are for a 6-foot-by-8-foot deck, but her dad wants a deck that has twice as much area. He suggests doubling the length of each side of the deck. Will this double the area? If not, suggest another method for doubling the area of the deck.

Tell whether each angle is acute, obtuse, right or straight. (Lesson 8-2)

28.   **29.**   **30.**   **31.**

Find the perimeter of each rectangle, given the dimensions. (Lesson 9-2)

32. 6 in. by 12 in.   **33.** 2 m by 8 m   **34.** 16 cm by 3 cm   **35.** $4\frac{4}{5}$ ft by $1\frac{3}{8}$ ft

9-4 Area of Triangles and Trapezoids

Learn to find the area of triangles and trapezoids.

Georgia Performance Standards

M7A1.b Simplify and evaluate algebraic expressions, using commutative, associative, and distributive properties as appropriate. Also, M7P1.b, M7P5.b, M7P5.c.

The Bermuda Triangle is a triangular region between Bermuda, Florida, and Puerto Rico. To find the area of this region, you could use the formula for the area of a triangle.

The base of a triangle can be any side. The height of a triangle is the perpendicular distance from the base to the opposite vertex.

AREA OF A TRIANGLE		
The area A of a triangle is half the product of its base b and its height h.	$A = \frac{1}{2}bh$	

EXAMPLE 1 Finding the Area of a Triangle

Find the area of each triangle.

A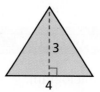

$A = \frac{1}{2}bh$ *Use the formula.*

$A = \frac{1}{2}(4 \cdot 3)$ *Substitute 4 for b and 3 for h.*

$A = 6$

The area of the triangle is 6 square units.

B

$A = \frac{1}{2}bh$ *Use the formula.*

$A = \frac{1}{2}(6 \cdot 5)$ *Substitute 6 for b and 5 for h.*

$A = 15$

The area of the triangle is 15 square units.

The two parallel sides of a trapezoid are its bases, b_1 and b_2. The height of a trapezoid is the perpendicular distance between the bases.

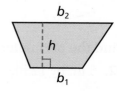

AREA OF A TRAPEZOID

The area of a trapezoid is half its height multiplied by the sum of the lengths of its two bases.	$A = \frac{1}{2}h(b_1 + b_2)$	

EXAMPLE **2** **Finding the Area of a Trapezoid**

Find the area of each trapezoid.

Reading Math

In the term b_1, the number 1 is called a *subscript*. It is read as "*b*-one" or "*b* sub-one."

A

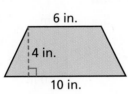

6 in.
4 in.
10 in.

$A = \frac{1}{2}h(b_1 + b_2)$ *Use the formula.*

$A = \frac{1}{2} \cdot 4(10 + 6)$ *Substitute.*

$A = \frac{1}{2} \cdot 4(16)$ *Add.*

$A = 32$ *Multiply.*

The area of the trapezoid is 32 in².

B

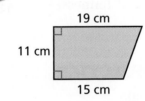

19 cm
11 cm
15 cm

$A = \frac{1}{2}h(b_1 + b_2)$ *Use the formula.*

$A = \frac{1}{2} \cdot 11(15 + 19)$ *Substitute.*

$A = \frac{1}{2} \cdot 11(34)$ *Add.*

$A = 187$ *Multiply.*

The area of the trapezoid is 187 cm².

EXAMPLE **3** **Geography Application**

The state of Nevada is shaped somewhat like a trapezoid. What is the approximate area of Nevada?

320 mi
200 mi
Carson City
NEVADA
475 mi

$A = \frac{1}{2}h(b_1 + b_2)$ *Use the formula.*

$A = \frac{1}{2} \cdot 320(200 + 475)$ *Substitute.*

$A = \frac{1}{2} \cdot 320(675)$ *Add.*

$A = 108{,}000$ *Multiply.*

The area of Nevada is approximately 108,000 square miles.

Think and Discuss   GPS M7P3.b

1. Tell how to use the sides of a right triangle to find its area.

2. Explain how to find the area of a trapezoid.

Georgia Performance Standards

M7P3.a, M7P3.c, M7P4.c

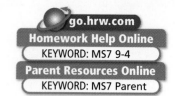
go.hrw.com
Homework Help Online
KEYWORD: MS7 9-4
Parent Resources Online
KEYWORD: MS7 Parent

GUIDED PRACTICE

See Example **Find the area of each triangle.**

1.
7
8

2.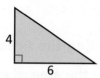
4
6

3.
7
11.2

See Example **Find the area of each trapezoid.**

4.
2.5 cm
2 cm
4 cm

5.
6 m
8 m
10 m

6.
12 ft
6 ft
6 ft

See Example **7.** The state of Tennessee is shaped somewhat like a parallelogram. What is the approximate area of Tennessee?

442 mi
115 mi
Nashville ★
TENNESSEE

INDEPENDENT PRACTICE

See Example **Find the area of each triangle.**

8.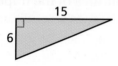
15
6

9.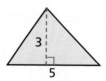
3
5

10.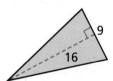
9
16

See Example **Find the area of each trapezoid.**

11.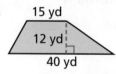
15 yd
12 yd
40 yd

12.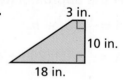
3 in.
10 in.
18 in.

13.
3 cm
10 cm
5 cm

See Example **14.** The state of New Hampshire is shaped somewhat like a right triangle. What is the approximate area of New Hampshire?

NEW HAMPSHIRE
160 mi
★ Concord
← 85 mi →

PRACTICE AND PROBLEM SOLVING

Find the missing measurement of each triangle.

15. $b = 8$ cm
$h = $ ▮
$A = 18$ cm^2

16. $b = 16$ ft
$h = 0.7$ ft
$A = $ ▮

17. $b = $ ▮
$h = 95$ in.
$A = 1,045$ in^2

Graph the polygon with the given vertices. Then find the area of the polygon.

18. $(1, 2), (4, 5), (8, 2), (8, 5)$

19. $(1, -6), (5, -1), (7, -6)$

20. $(2, 3), (2, 10), (7, 6), (7, 8)$

21. $(3, 0), (3, 4), (-3, 0)$

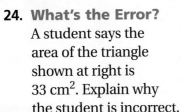

Georgia LINK

Social Studies

The Etowah Indians built large, ceremonial mounds. The sides of this mound are trapezoids.

22. What is the height of a trapezoid with an area of 9 m^2 and bases that measure 2.4 m and 3.6 m?

23. Multi-Step The state of Colorado is somewhat rectangular in shape. Estimate the perimeter and area of Colorado.

24. What's the Error? A student says the area of the triangle shown at right is 33 cm^2. Explain why the student is incorrect.

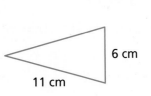

6 cm

11 cm

365 mi

Denver ★

COLORADO

276 mi

 25. Write About It Explain how to use the formulas for the area of a rectangle and the area of a triangle to estimate the area of Nevada.

 26. Challenge The state of North Dakota is trapezoidal in shape and has an area of 70,704 mi^2. If the southern border is 359 mi and the distance between the northern border and the southern border is 210 mi, what is the approximate length of the northern border?

CRCT PREP • GPS SUPPORT • SPIRAL REVIEW

27. Multiple Choice Find the area of the trapezoid.

Ⓐ 8 cm^2

Ⓑ 16 cm^2

Ⓒ 17 cm^2

Ⓓ 30 cm^2

3 cm

2 cm

5 cm

28. Short Response Graph the triangle with vertices $(0, 0)$, $(2, 3)$, and $(6, 0)$. Then find the area of the triangle.

Find the measure of the third angle in each triangle, given two angle measures. (Lesson 8-8)

29. $45°, 45°$

30. $71°, 57°$

31. $103°, 28°$

32. $62°, 19°$

33. Justin is laying a tile floor in a room that measures 5 yd by 6 yd. How many square feet of tile does he need? (Lesson 9-3)

Learn to find the area of circles.

Georgia Performance Standards

M7A1.b Simplify and evaluate algebraic expressions, using commutative, associative, and distributive properties as appropriate. Also, M7P4.c, M7P5.b, M7P5.c.

A circle can be cut into equal-sized sectors and arranged to resemble a parallelogram. The height h of the parallelogram is equal to the radius r of the circle, and the base b of the parallelogram is equal to one-half the circumference C of the circle. So the area of the parallelogram can be written as

$A = bh$, or $A = \frac{1}{2}Cr$.

Since $C = 2\pi r$, $A = \frac{1}{2}(2\pi r)r = \pi r^2$.

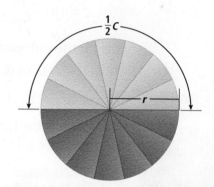

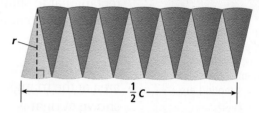

AREA OF A CIRCLE		
The area A of a circle is the product of π and the square of the circle's radius r.	$A = \pi r^2$	

EXAMPLE **1** **Finding the Area of a Circle**

Find the area of each circle to the nearest tenth. Use 3.14 for π.

Remember!

The order of operations calls for evaluating the exponents before multiplying.

A

3 m

$A = \pi r^2$	*Use the formula.*
$A \approx 3.14 \cdot 3^2$	*Substitute. Use 3 for r.*
$A \approx 3.14 \cdot 9$	*Evaluate the power.*
$A \approx 28.26$	*Multiply.*

The area of the circle is about 28.3 m².

B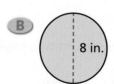

8 in.

$A = \pi r^2$	*Use the formula.*
$A \approx 3.14 \cdot 4^2$	*Substitute. Use 4 for r.*
$A \approx 3.14 \cdot 16$	*Evaluate the power.*
$A \approx 50.24$	*Multiply.*

The area of the circle is about 50.2 in².

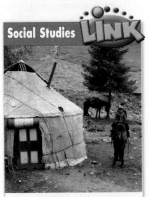
EXAMPLE 2 *Social Studies Application*

A group of historians are building a yurt to display at a local multicultural fair. The yurt has a height of 8 feet 9 inches at its center, and it has a circular floor of radius 7 feet. What is the area of the floor of the yurt? Use $\frac{22}{7}$ for π.

$A = \pi r^2$	*Use the formula for the area of a circle.*
$A \approx \frac{22}{7} \cdot 7^2$	*Substitute. Use 7 for r.*
$A \approx \frac{22}{7_1} \cdot \overset{7}{49}$	*Evaluate the power. Then simplify.*
$A \approx 22 \cdot 7$	
$A \approx 154$	*Multiply.*

The area of the floor of the yurt is about 154 ft².

EXAMPLE 3 *Measurement Application*

Use a centimeter ruler to measure the radius of the circle. Then find the area of the shaded region of the circle. Use 3.14 for π. Round your answer to the nearest tenth.

First measure the radius of the circle: It measures 1.8 cm.

Now find the area of the entire circle.

$A = \pi r^2$	*Use the formula for the area of a circle.*
$A \approx 3.14 \cdot 1.8^2$	*Substitute. Use 1.8 for r and 3.14 for π.*
$A \approx 3.14 \cdot 3.24$	*Evaluate the power.*
$A \approx 10.1736$	*Multiply.*

Since $\frac{1}{4}$ of the circle is shaded, divide the area of the circle by 4.

$10.1736 \div 4 = 2.5434$

The area of the shaded region of the circle is about 2.5 cm².

Helpful Hint

To estimate the area of a circle, you can square the radius and multiply by 3.

Think and Discuss GPS M7P1.d, M7P3.b

1. **Compare** finding the area of a circle when given the radius with finding the area when given the diameter.

2. **Give an example** of a circular object in your classroom. Tell how you could estimate the area of the object, and then estimate.

Georgia Performance Standards

M7P2.c, M7P2.d, M7P3.a

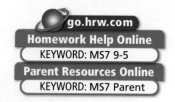

go.hrw.com
Homework Help Online
KEYWORD: MS7 9-5
Parent Resources Online
KEYWORD: MS7 Parent

GUIDED PRACTICE

See Example ① Find the area of each circle to the nearest tenth. Use 3.14 for π.

1.
5 in.

2.
16 cm

3.
20 yd

4.
1.1 m

See Example ② **5.** The most popular pizza at Sam's Pizza is the 14-inch pepperoni pizza. What is the area of a pizza with a diameter of 14 inches? Use $\frac{22}{7}$ for π.

See Example ③ **6.** **Measurement** Use a centimeter ruler to measure the diameter of the circle. Then find the area of the shaded region of the circle. Use 3.14 for π. Round your answer to the nearest tenth.

INDEPENDENT PRACTICE

See Example ① Find the area of each circle to the nearest tenth. Use 3.14 for π.

7.
3 in.

8.
16 ft

9.
6.4 yd

10.
15 cm

See Example ② **11.** A wheel has a radius of 14 centimeters. What is the area of the wheel? Use $\frac{22}{7}$ for π.

See Example ③ **12.** **Measurement** Use a centimeter ruler to measure the radius of the circle. Then find the area of the shaded region of the circle. Use 3.14 for π. Round your answer to the nearest tenth.

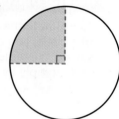

PRACTICE AND PROBLEM SOLVING

CRCT GPS
Extra Practice p. 744

13. A radio station broadcasts a signal over an area with a 75-mile radius. What is the area of the region that receives the radio signal?

14. A circular flower bed in Kay's backyard has a diameter of 8 feet. What is the area of the flower bed? Round your answer to the nearest tenth.

15. A company is manufacturing aluminum lids. The radius of each lid is 3 cm. What is the area of one lid? Round your answer to the nearest tenth.

Given the radius or diameter, find the circumference and area of each circle to the nearest tenth. Use 3.14 for π.

16. $r = 7$ m   **17.** $d = 18$ in.   **18.** $d = 24$ ft   **19.** $r = 6.4$ cm

Given the area, find the radius of each circle. Use 3.14 for π.

20. $A = 113.04$ cm^2 **21.** $A = 3.14$ ft^2 **22.** $A = 28.26$ in^2

23. A hiker was last seen near a fire tower in the Catalina Mountains. Searchers are dispatched to the surrounding area to find the missing hiker.

  a. Assume the hiker could walk in any direction at a rate of 3 miles per hour. How large an area would searchers have to cover if the hiker was last seen 2 hours ago? Use 3.14 for π. Round your answer to the nearest square mile.

  b. How much additional area would the searchers have to cover if the hiker was last seen 3 hours ago?

24. Physical Science The tower of a wind turbine is about the height of a 20-story building. Each turbine can produce 24 megawatt-hours of electricity in one day. Find the area covered by the turbine when it is rotating. Use 3.14 for π. Round your answer to the nearest tenth.

187 ft

25. Critical Thinking Two circles have the same radius. Is the combined area of the two circles the same as the area of a circle with twice the radius?

 26. What's the Question? Chang painted half of a free-throw circle that has a diameter of 12 ft. The answer is 56.52 ft². What is the question?

27. Write About It Describe how to find the area of a circle when given only the circumference of the circle.

28. Challenge How does the area of a circle change if you multiply the radius by a factor of n, where n is a whole number?

CRCT Prep • GPS Support • Spiral Review

29. Multiple Choice The area of a circle is 30 square feet. A second circle has a radius that is 2 feet shorter than that of the first circle. What is the area, to the nearest tenth, of the second circle? Use 3.14 for π.

  (A) 3.7 square feet   (B) 10.0 square feet   (C) 38.0 square feet   (D) 179.2 square feet

30. Short Response A pizza parlor offers a large pizza with a 12-inch diameter. It also offers a "mega" pizza with a 24-inch diameter. The slogan used to advertise the mega pizza is "Twice the pizza of a large, and twice the fun." Is the mega pizza twice as big as the large? If not, how much bigger is it? Explain.

Line a ∥ line b. Use the diagram to find each angle measure. (Lesson 8-3)

31. m∠1   **32.** m∠2   **33.** m∠3

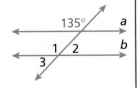

Graph the polygon with the given vertices. Then find the area of the polygon. (Lesson 9-4)

34. $(-1, 1), (0, 4), (4, 1)$ **35.** $(-3, 3), (2, 3), (1, -1), (-1, -1)$

Area of Irregular Figures

Learn to find the area of irregular figures.

You can find the area of an irregular figure by separating it into non-overlapping familiar figures. The sum of the areas of these figures is the area of the irregular figure. You can also estimate the area of an irregular figure by using graph paper.

EXAMPLE 1 Estimating the Area of an Irregular Figure

 **Georgia Performance Standards**

M7A1.b Simplify and evaluate algebraic expressions, using commutative, associative, and distributive properties as appropriate. Also, M7P1.b, M7P1.c, M7P1.d, M7P5.b.

Estimate the area of the figure. Each square represents 1 ft².

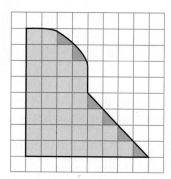

Count the number of filled or almost-filled squares: 35 yellow squares.

Count the number of squares that are about half-filled: 6 blue squares.

Add the number of filled squares plus $\frac{1}{2}$ the number of half-filled squares: $35 + \left(\frac{1}{2} \cdot 6\right) = 35 + 3 = 38$.

The area of the figure is about 38 ft².

EXAMPLE 2 Finding the Area of an Irregular Figure

Find the area of the irregular figure. Use 3.14 for π.

Step 1: Separate the figure into smaller, familiar figures.

Step 2: Find the area of each smaller figure.

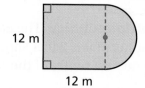

Area of the square:

$A = s^2$ *Use the formula for the area of a square.*

$A = 12^2 = 144$ *Substitute 12 for s. Multiply.*

Area of the semicircle:

$A = \frac{1}{2}(\pi r^2)$ *The area of a semicircle is $\frac{1}{2}$ the area of a circle.*

$A \approx \frac{1}{2}(3.14 \cdot 6^2)$ *Substitute 3.14 for π and 6 for r.*

$A \approx \frac{1}{2}(113.04) \approx 56.52$ *Multiply.*

Step 3: Add the areas to find the total area.

$A \approx 144 + 56.52 = 200.52$

The area of the irregular figure is about 200.52 m².

EXAMPLE 3

PROBLEM SOLVING

PROBLEM SOLVING APPLICATION

Chandra wants to carpet the floor of her closet. A floor plan of the closet is shown at right. How much carpet does she need?

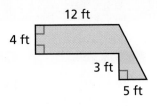

1 Understand the Problem

Rewrite the question as a statement:

• Find the amount of carpet needed to cover the floor of the closet.

List the **important information:**

• The floor of the closet is an irregular figure.

• The amount of carpet needed is equal to the area of the floor.

Helpful Hint

There are often several different ways to separate an irregular figure into familiar figures.

2 Make a Plan

Find the area of the floor by separating the figure into familiar figures: a rectangle and a triangle. Then add the areas of the rectangle and triangle to find the total area.

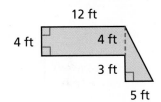

3 Solve

Find the area of each smaller figure.

Area of the rectangle:

$A = \ell w$

$A = 12 \cdot 4$

$A = 48 \text{ ft}^2$

Area of the triangle:

$A = \frac{1}{2}bh$

$A = \frac{1}{2}(5)(3 + 4)$

$A = \frac{1}{2}(35) = 17.5 \text{ ft}^2$

Add the areas to find the total area.

$A = 48 + 17.5 = 65.5$

Chandra needs 65.5 ft^2 of carpet.

4 Look Back

The area of the closet floor must be greater than the area of the rectangle (48 ft^2), so the answer is reasonable.

Think and Discuss

GPS M7P1.d, M7P2.c

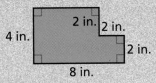

1. Describe two different ways to find the area of the irregular figure at right.

2. Explain why the area of the figure at right must be less than 32 in^2.

Georgia Performance
Standards

M7P1.c, M7P3.a, M7P5.a,
M7P5.b

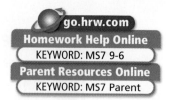

go.hrw.com
Homework Help Online
KEYWORD: MS7 9-6
Parent Resources Online
KEYWORD: MS7 Parent

GUIDED PRACTICE

See Example **1** Estimate the area of each figure. Each square represents 1 ft².

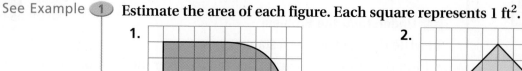

1.

2.

See Example **2** Find the area of each figure. Use 3.14 for π.

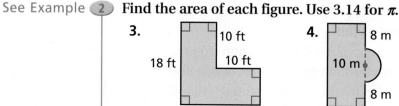 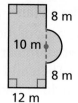 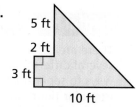

3. 18 ft, 10 ft, 10 ft, 18 ft

4. 8 m, 10 m, 8 m, 12 m

5. 5 ft, 2 ft, 3 ft, 10 ft

See Example **3** **6.** Luis has a model train set. The layout of the
track is shown at right. How much artificial
grass does Luis need in order to fill the
interior of the layout? Use 3.14 for π.

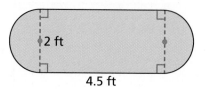

2 ft

4.5 ft

INDEPENDENT PRACTICE

See Example **1** Estimate the area of each figure. Each square represents 1 ft².

7.

8.

See Example **2** Find the area of each figure. Use 3.14 for π.

9.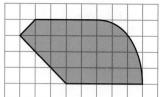
4 m, 4 m, 4 m, 6 m, 4 m

10.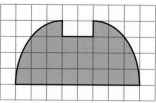
8 ft, 3 ft, 4 ft, 4 ft, 3 ft, 3 ft

11.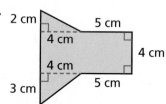
2 cm, 5 cm, 4 cm, 4 cm, 4 cm, 3 cm, 5 cm

See Example **3** **12.** The figure shows the floor plan for a gallery of a
museum. The ceiling of the gallery is to be covered
with soundproofing material. How much material
is needed? Use 3.14 for π.

20 m

6 m

PRACTICE AND PROBLEM SOLVING

Find the area and perimeter of each figure. Use 3.14 for π.

13.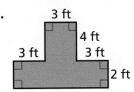

14.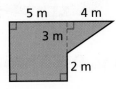

15.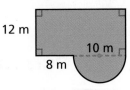

16. Multi-Step A figure has vertices $A(-8, 5)$, $B(-4, 5)$, $C(-4, 2)$, $D(3, 2)$, $E(3, -2)$, $F(6, -2)$, $G(6, -4)$, and $H(-8, -4)$. Graph the figure on a coordinate plane. Then find the area and perimeter of the figure.

17. Critical Thinking The figure at right is made up of an isosceles triangle and a square. The perimeter of the figure is 44 feet. What is the value of x?

18. Choose a Strategy A figure is formed by combining a square and a triangle. Its total area is 32.5 m². The area of the triangle is 7.5 m². What is the length of each side of the square?

Ⓐ 5 m   Ⓑ 15 m   Ⓒ 16.25 m   Ⓓ 25 m

19. Write About It Describe how to find the area of the irregular figure at right.

20. Challenge Find the area and perimeter of the figure at right. Use 3.14 for π.

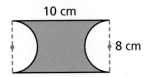

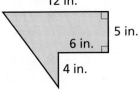

CRCT PREP • GPS SUPPORT • SPIRAL REVIEW

21. Multiple Choice A rectangle is formed by two congruent right triangles. The area of each triangle is 6 in². Each side of the rectangle is a whole number of inches. Which of these CANNOT be the perimeter of the rectangle?

Ⓐ 26 in.   Ⓑ 24 in.   Ⓒ 16 in.   Ⓓ 14 in.

22. Extended Response The shaded area of the garden represents a patch of carrots. Veronica estimates that she will get about 12 carrots from this patch. Veronica is going to plant the rest of her garden with carrots. Estimate the total number of carrots she can expect to grow.

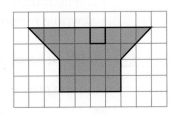

∠1 and ∠2 are complementary angles. Find m∠2. (Lesson 8-2)

23. m∠1 = 33°   **24.** m∠1 = 46°   **25.** m∠1 = 60°   **26.** m∠1 = 25.5°

Given the diameter, find the area of each circle to the nearest tenth. Use 3.14 for π. (Lesson 9-5)

27. $d = 30$ m   **28.** $d = 5.5$ cm   **29.** $d = 18$ in.   **30.** $d = 11$ ft

READY TO GO ON?

Quiz for Lessons 9-1 Through 9-6

9-1 **Accuracy and Precision**

1. Which measurement is more precise—5 in. or 56 ft?

Calculate. Use the correct number of significant digits in each answer.

2. $329 + 640$ 3. $5.6 \cdot 2.59$ 4. $82.5 \div 16$ 5. $27.1 - 4$

9-2 **Perimeter and Circumference**

6. Find the perimeter of the figure at right.

7. If the circumference of a wheel is 94 cm, what is its approximate diameter?

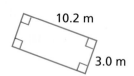

9-3 **Area of Parallelograms**

8. The area of a rectangular courtyard is 1,508 m², and the length is 52 m. What is the width of the courtyard?

9. Jackson's kitchen is 8 yd by 3 yd. What is the area of his kitchen in square feet?

9-4 **Area of Triangles and Trapezoids**

10. Find the area of the trapezoid at right.

11. A triangle has an area of 45 cm² and a base of 12.5 cm. What is the height of the triangle?

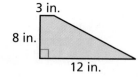

9-5 **Area of Circles**

12. Find the area of the circle to the nearest tenth. Use 3.14 or $\frac{22}{7}$ for π.

13. The radius of a clock face is $8\frac{3}{4}$ in. What is its area to the nearest whole number?

9-6 **Area of Irregular Figures**

Find the area of each figure to the nearest tenth. Use 3.14 for π.

14.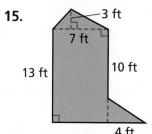

15.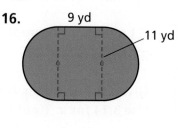

16.

Focus on Problem Solving

Understand the Problem

• **Identify too much or too little information**

Problems involving real-world situations sometimes give too much or too little information. Before solving these types of problems, you must decide what information is necessary and whether you have all the necessary information.

If the problem gives too much information, identify which of the facts are really needed to solve the problem. If the problem gives too little information, determine what additional information is required to solve the problem.

Copy each problem and underline the information you need to solve it. If necessary information is missing, write down what additional information is required.

1 Mrs. Wong wants to put a fence around her garden. One side of her garden measures 8 feet. Another side measures 5 feet. What length of fencing does Mrs. Wong need to enclose her garden?

2 Two sides of a triangle measure 17 inches and 13 inches. The perimeter of the triangle is 45 inches. What is the length in feet of the third side of the triangle? (There are 12 inches in 1 foot.)

3 During swim practice, Peggy swims 2 laps each of freestyle and backstroke. The dimensions of the pool are 25 meters by 50 meters. What is the area of the pool?

4 Each afternoon, Curtis walks his dog two times around the park. The park is a rectangle that is 315 yards long. How far does Curtis walk his dog each afternoon?

5 A trapezoid has bases that measure 12 meters and 18 meters and one side that measures 9 meters. The trapezoid has no right angles. What is the area of the trapezoid?

Explore Square Roots and Perfect Squares

Use with Lesson 9-7

go.hrw.com
Lab Resources Online
KEYWORD: MS7 Lab9

Georgia Performance Standards

M7A3.b, M7P2.c, M7P3.a, M7P5.b

You can use geometric models such as tiles or graph paper to represent squares and square roots.

Activity 1

1. Copy the three square arrangements below on graph paper. Continue the pattern until you have drawn 10 square arrangements.

2. Copy and complete the table below. In the first column, write the number of small squares in each figure you drew. To complete the second column, use a calculator to find the square root.

   (To find the square root of 4, press [2nd] [√x²] 4 [ )] [ENTER] .)

Total Number of Small Squares	Square Root
1	1
4	2
9	3

3. Shade in one column of each square arrangement that you drew in ❶.

Think and Discuss

1. How does the square root relate to the total number of small squares in a figure?

2. How does the square root in the table relate to the shaded portion of each figure?

Try This

Use graph paper to find each square root.

1. 121 **2.** 144 **3.** 196

Activity 2

Follow the steps below to estimate $\sqrt{14}$.

1 On graph paper, use one color to draw the smallest possible square arrangement using at least 14 small squares.

2 On the same arrangement, draw the largest possible square arrangement using less than 14 small squares.

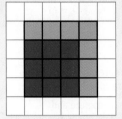

3 Count the number of squares in each arrangement. Notice that 14 is between these numbers.

Number in small arrangement   Number in large arrangement

9 < 14 < 16

4 Use a calculator to find $\sqrt{14}$ to the nearest tenth. $\sqrt{14} = 3.7$. Use inequality symbols to compare the square roots of 9, 14, and 16.

$\sqrt{9} < \sqrt{14} < \sqrt{16}$

$3 < 3.7 < 4$ *The square root of 9 is less than the square root of 14, which is less than the square root of 16.*

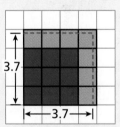

5 Use dashed lines on the figure to sketch a square that is 3.7 units on each side.

Think and Discuss

1. Describe how to use two numbers to estimate the square roots of nonperfect squares without using a calculator.

2. Explain how you can use graph paper to estimate $\sqrt{19}$.

3. Name three numbers that have square roots between 5 and 6.

Try This

Use graph paper to estimate each square root. Then use a calculator to find the square root to the nearest tenth.

1. $\sqrt{19}$ **2.** $\sqrt{10}$ **3.** $\sqrt{28}$ **4.** $\sqrt{35}$

Squares and Square Roots

Learn to find and estimate square roots of numbers.

Vocabulary

perfect square

square root

radical sign

A square with sides that measure 3 units each has an area of $3 \cdot 3$, or 3^2. Notice that the area of the square is represented by a power in which the base is the side length and the exponent is 2. A power in which the exponent is 2 is called a *square*.

Exponent

Base

EXAMPLE 1 **Finding Squares of Numbers**

Georgia Performance Standards

M7P4.a Recognize and use connections among mathematical ideas. Also, M7P1.c, M7P4.b, M7P5.b, M7P5.c.

Find each square.

A 6^2

Method 1: Use a model.

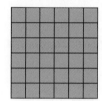

$A = \ell w$

$A = 6 \cdot 6$

$A = 36$

The square of 6 is 36.

B 14^2

Method 2: Use a calculator.

Press 14 [x^2] [ENTER].

$14^2 = 196$

The square of 14 is 196.

A **perfect square** is the square of a whole number. The number 36 is a perfect square because $36 = 6^2$ and 6 is a whole number.

Reading Math

$\sqrt{16} = 4$ is read as "The square root of 16 is 4."

The **square root** of a number is one of the two equal factors of the number. Four is a square root of 16 because $4 \cdot 4 = 16$. The symbol for a square root is $\sqrt{}$, which is called a **radical sign**.

EXAMPLE 2 **Finding Square Roots of Perfect Squares**

Find each square root.

A $\sqrt{64}$

Method 1: Use a model.

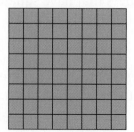

The square root of 64 is 8.

Find each square root.

 $\sqrt{324}$

      Method 2: Use a calculator.   Press 2nd  x^2 324 ENTER .

$$\sqrt{324} = 18$$

    The square root of 324 is 18.

You can use perfect squares to estimate the square roots of nonperfect squares.

EXAMPLE **Estimating Square Roots**

Estimate $\sqrt{30}$ to the nearest whole number. Use a calculator to check your answer.

$1, 4, 9, 16, 25, 36, \ldots$	*List some perfect squares.*
$25 < 30 < 36$	*Find the perfect squares nearest 30.*
$\sqrt{25} < \sqrt{30} < \sqrt{36}$	
$5 < \sqrt{30} < 6$	*Find the square roots of 25 and 36.*
$\sqrt{30} \approx 5$	*30 is closer to 25 than to 36.*

Check

$\sqrt{30} \approx 5.477225575$ *Use a calculator to approximate $\sqrt{30}$.*
                                5 is a reasonable estimate.

EXAMPLE **4** *Recreation Application*

While searching for a lost hiker, a helicopter pilot covers a square area of 150 mi². What is the approximate length of each side of the square area? Round your answer to the nearest mile.

The length of each side of the square is $\sqrt{150}$.

$144 < 150 < 169$	*Find the perfect squares nearest 150.*
$\sqrt{144} < \sqrt{150} < \sqrt{169}$	
$12 < \sqrt{150} < 13$	*Find the square roots of 144 and 169.*
$\sqrt{150} \approx 12$	*150 is closer to 144 than to 169.*

Each side of the search area is about 12 miles long.

Think and Discuss   **GPS M7P1.d, M7P3.b**

1. Explain how to estimate $\sqrt{75}$.

2. Explain how you might find the square root of 3^2.

Georgia Performance
Standards

M7P1.c, M7P2.c, M7P3.a,
M7P4.c

go.hrw.com
Homework Help Online
KEYWORD: MS7 9-7
Parent Resources Online
KEYWORD: MS7 Parent

GUIDED PRACTICE

See Example **1**   Find each square.

1. 4^2 **2.** 17^2 **3.** 9^2 **4.** 15^2

See Example **2**   Find each square root.

5. $\sqrt{400}$ **6.** $\sqrt{9}$ **7.** $\sqrt{144}$ **8.** $\sqrt{529}$

See Example **3**   Estimate each square root to the nearest whole number. Use a calculator to
check your answer.

9. $\sqrt{20}$ **10.** $\sqrt{45}$ **11.** $\sqrt{84}$ **12.** $\sqrt{58}$

See Example **4**   **13.** A Coast Guard ship patrols an area of 125 square miles. The area the ship
patrols is a square. About how long is each side of the area? Round your
answer to the nearest mile.

INDEPENDENT PRACTICE

See Example **1**   Find each square.

14. 3^2 **15.** 16^2 **16.** 8^2 **17.** 11^2

See Example **2**   Find each square root.

18. $\sqrt{361}$ **19.** $\sqrt{16}$ **20.** $\sqrt{169}$ **21.** $\sqrt{441}$

See Example **3**   Estimate each square root to the nearest whole number. Use a calculator to
check your answer.

22. $\sqrt{12}$ **23.** $\sqrt{39}$ **24.** $\sqrt{73}$ **25.** $\sqrt{109}$

See Example **4**   **26.** The area of a square field is 200 ft². What is the approximate length of
each side of the field? Round your answer to the nearest foot.

PRACTICE AND PROBLEM SOLVING

CRCT GPS

Extra Practice p. 745

Estimate each square root to the nearest whole number.

27. $\sqrt{6}$ **28.** $\sqrt{180}$ **29.** $\sqrt{145}$ **30.** $\sqrt{216}$

31. $\sqrt{300}$ **32.** $\sqrt{420}$ **33.** $\sqrt{700}$ **34.** $\sqrt{1,500}$

Use a calculator to find each square root to the nearest tenth.

35. $\sqrt{44}$ **36.** $\sqrt{253}$ **37.** $\sqrt{87}$ **38.** $\sqrt{125}$

39. $\sqrt{380}$ **40.** $\sqrt{94}$ **41.** $\sqrt{202}$ **42.** $\sqrt{571}$

43. Critical Thinking An artist is making two square stained-glass windows.
One window has a perimeter of 48 inches. The other has an area of 110
square inches. Which window is bigger? Explain.

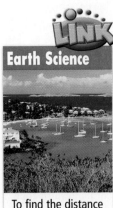

Earth Science

To find the distance at which an object becomes visible, you can use your distance to the horizon and the object's distance to the horizon.

Given the area, find the missing value for each circle. Use 3.14 for π.

44. $A = 706.9 \text{ m}^2$; $r = $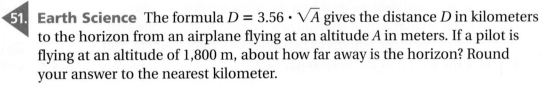

45. $A = 615.44 \text{ yd}^2$; $C = $

46. $A = 28.26 \text{ ft}^2$; $d = $

47. $A = 3.14 \text{ in}^2$; $r = $

Order the numbers from least to greatest.

48. $\sqrt{49}, \frac{17}{3}, 6.5, 8, \frac{25}{4}$

49. $5\frac{2}{3}, \sqrt{25}, 3^2, 7.15, \frac{29}{4}$

50. Find the perimeter of a square whose area is 49 square inches.

51. **Earth Science** The formula $D = 3.56 \cdot \sqrt{A}$ gives the distance D in kilometers to the horizon from an airplane flying at an altitude A in meters. If a pilot is flying at an altitude of 1,800 m, about how far away is the horizon? Round your answer to the nearest kilometer.

52. **Multi-Step** For his new room, Darien's grandmother gave him a handmade quilt. The quilt is made up of 16 squares set in 4 rows of 4. The area of each square is 324 in^2. What are the dimensions of the quilt in inches?

53. **Choose a Strategy** The figure shows how two squares can be formed by drawing only seven lines. Show how two squares can be formed by drawing only six lines.

54. **Write About It** Explain the difference between finding the square of a number and finding the square root of a number. Use models and numbers in your explanation.

55. **Challenge** Find the value of $\sqrt{5^2 + 12^2}$.

CRCT PREP • GPS SUPPORT • SPIRAL REVIEW

56. Multiple Choice Which model represents 5^2?

 (A)   (B) 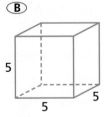   (C) 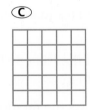   (D)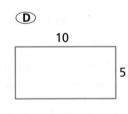

57. Multiple Choice Estimate the value of $\sqrt{87}$ to the nearest whole number.

(F) 9   (G) 10   (H) 11   (J) 12

Classify each triangle according to the lengths of its sides. (Lesson 8-6)

58. 2 in., 3 in., 4 in.

59. 5 cm, 5 cm, 5 cm

60. 8 ft, 6 ft, 8 ft

Given the radius or diameter, find the circumference and area of each circle to the nearest tenth. Use 3.14 for π. (Lesson 9-5)

61. $r = 11$ in.

62. $d = 25$ cm

63. $r = 3$ ft

Hands-On LAB 9-8

Explore the Pythagorean Theorem

Use with Lesson 9-8

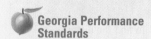

An important and famous relationship in mathematics, known as the Pythagorean Theorem, involves the three sides of a right triangle. Recall that a right triangle is a triangle that has one right angle. If you know the lengths of two sides of a right triangle, you can find the length of the third side.

Activity 1

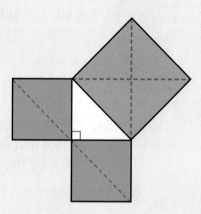

1 The drawing at right shows an isosceles right triangle and three squares. Make your own drawing similar to the one shown. (Recall that an isosceles right triangle has two congruent sides and a right angle.)

Cut out the two smaller squares of your drawing, then cut those squares in half along a diagonal. Fit the pieces of the smaller squares on top of the blue square.

Think and Discuss

1. What can you tell about the relationship between the areas of the squares?

2a. How does the side length of a square relate to the area of the square?

b. How do the side lengths of the triangle in your drawing relate to the areas of the squares around it?

c. Write an equation that shows the relationship between the lengths of the sides of the triangle in your drawing. Use the variables *a* and *b* to represent the lengths of the two shorter sides of your triangle, and *c* to represent the length of the longest side.

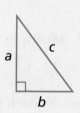

Try This

1. Repeat Activity 1 for other isosceles right triangles. Is the relationship that you found true for the areas of the squares around each triangle?

Activity 2

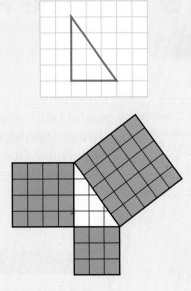

1 On graph paper, draw a segment that is 3 units long. At one end of this segment, draw a perpendicular segment that is 4 units long. Draw a third segment to form a triangle. Cut out the triangle.

Cut out a 3-by-3 square and a 4-by-4 square from the same graph paper. Place the edges of the squares against the corresponding sides of the right triangle.

Cut the two squares into individual squares or strips. Arrange the squares into a large square along the third side of the triangle.

Think and Discuss

1. What is the area of each of the three squares? What relationship is there between the areas of the small squares and the area of the large square?

2. What is the length of the third side of the triangle?

3. Substitute the side lengths of your triangle into the equation you wrote in Think and Discuss Problem **2c** in Activity 1. What do you find?

4. Do you think the relationship is true for triangles that are not right triangles?

Try This

1. Use graph paper to cut out three squares with sides that are 3 units, 4 units, and 6 units long. Fit the squares together to form a triangle as shown at right. Is the relationship between the areas of the red squares and the area of the blue square the same as the relationship shown in Activity 2? Explain.

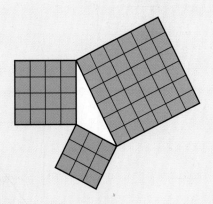

2. If you know the lengths of the two short sides of a right triangle are 9 and 12, can you find the length of the longest side? Show your work.

3. If you know the length of the longest side of a right triangle and the length of one of the shorter sides, how would you find the length of the third side?

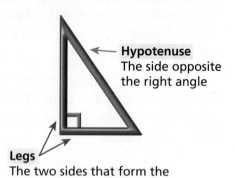

Hypotenuse
The side opposite the right angle

Legs
The two sides that form the right angle in a right triangle

Learn to use the Pythagorean Theorem to find the length of a side of a right triangle.

Vocabulary

leg

hypotenuse

Pythagorean Theorem

One of the first people to recognize the relationship between the sides of a right triangle was the Greek mathematician Pythagoras. This special relationship is called the *Pythagorean Theorem*.

PYTHAGOREAN THEOREM		
In a right triangle, the sum of the squares of the lengths of the legs is equal to the square of the length of the hypotenuse.	$a^2 + b^2 = c^2$	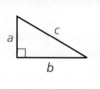

You can use the Pythagorean Theorem to find the length of any side of a right triangle.

EXAMPLE 1 **Calculating the Length of a Side of a Right Triangle**

Use the Pythagorean Theorem to find each missing measure.

A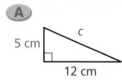

5 cm, c, 12 cm

$a^2 + b^2 = c^2$	Use the Pythagorean Theorem.
$5^2 + 12^2 = c^2$	Substitute for a and b.
$25 + 144 = c^2$	Evaluate the powers.
$169 = c^2$	Add.
$\sqrt{169} = \sqrt{c^2}$	Take the square root of both sides.
$13 = c$	

The length of the hypotenuse is 13 cm.

B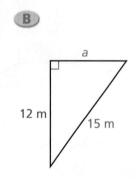

a, 12 m, 15 m

$a^2 + b^2 = c^2$	Use the Pythagorean Theorem.
$a^2 + 12^2 = 15^2$	Substitute for b and c.
$a^2 + 144 = 225$	Evaluate the powers.
$\underline{\quad -144 \quad -144}$	Subtract 144 from both sides.
$a^2 = 81$	
$\sqrt{a^2} = \sqrt{81}$	Take the square root of both sides.
$a = 9$	

The length of the leg is 9 m.

EXAMPLE 2  **PROBLEM SOLVING APPLICATION**

A regulation baseball diamond is a square with sides that measure 90 feet. About how far is it from home plate to second base? Round your answer to the nearest tenth.

1 Understand the Problem

Rewrite the question as a statement.
- Find the distance from home plate to second base.

List the **important information:**
- Drawing a segment between home plate and second base divides the diamond into two right triangles.
- The angle at first base is the right angle, so the segment between home plate and second base is the hypotenuse.
- The base lines are legs, and they are each 90 feet long.

2 Make a Plan

You can use the Pythagorean Theorem to write an equation.

3 Solve

$$a^2 + b^2 = c^2$$ *Use the Pythagorean Theorem.*
$$90^2 + 90^2 = c^2$$ *Substitute for the known variables.*
$$8{,}100 + 8{,}100 = c^2$$ *Evaluate the powers.*
$$16{,}200 = c^2$$ *Add.*
$$127.279 \approx c$$ *Take the square root of both sides.*
$$127.3 \approx c$$ *Round.*

The distance from home plate to second base is about 127.3 ft.

4 Look Back

The hypotenuse is the longest side of a right triangle. Since the distance from home plate to second base is greater than the distance between the bases, the answer is reasonable.

Think and Discuss    GPS M7P2.b, M7P3.b

1. **Explain** whether it is ever possible to use the Pythagorean Theorem to find an unknown side length of a scalene triangle.
2. **Demonstrate** whether a leg of a right triangle can be longer than the hypotenuse.

Georgia Performance Standards

M7P1.a, M7P1.b, M7P2.c, M7P3.a

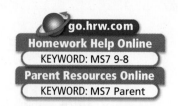
go.hrw.com
Homework Help Online
KEYWORD: MS7 9-8
Parent Resources Online
KEYWORD: MS7 Parent

GUIDED PRACTICE

See Example **1** Use the Pythagorean Theorem to find each missing measure.

1.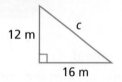

2.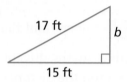

3.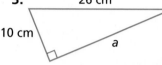

See Example **2**

4. A 10 ft ladder is leaning against a wall. If the ladder is 5 ft from the base of the wall, how far above the ground does the ladder touch the wall? Round your answer to the nearest tenth.

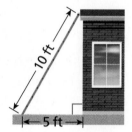

INDEPENDENT PRACTICE

See Example **1** Use the Pythagorean Theorem to find each missing measure.

5.

6.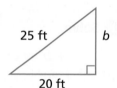

7.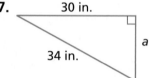

See Example **2**

8. James rides his bike 15 miles west. Then he turns north and rides another 15 miles before he stops to rest. How far is James from his starting point when he stops to rest? Round your answer to the nearest tenth.

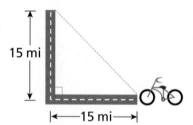

PRACTICE AND PROBLEM SOLVING

CRCT GPS

Extra Practice p. 745

The lengths of two sides of a right triangle are given. Find the length of the third side to the nearest tenth.

9. legs: 5 ft and 8 ft

10. leg: 10 mm; hypotenuse: 15 mm

11. leg: 19 m; hypotenuse: 31 m

12. legs: 21 yd and 20 yd

13. legs: 13.5 in. and 18 in.

14. leg: 13 cm; hypotenuse: 18 cm

15. Critical Thinking The numbers 3, 4, and 5 form a Pythagorean triple because $3^2 + 4^2 = 5^2$. When you double each of these values, does the resulting set of numbers also form a Pythagorean triple? Explain.

16. Ancient Egyptians built pyramids to serve as tombs for their kings. One pyramid, called Menkaure, has a square base with an area of about 12,100 m².

    a. What is the length of each side of the base?

    b. What is the length of a diagonal of the base? Round your answer to the nearest tenth.

17. The photograph shows the Pyramid of Khafre in Egypt. Each side of its square base is about 214 meters long. Each triangular side is an isosceles triangle with a height of about 179 meters. What is the area of one side of the pyramid?

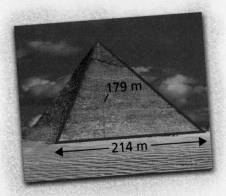
179 m

214 m

18. Use the Pythagorean Theorem to find the distance from one corner of the Pyramid of Khafre to its peak. Round your answer to the nearest tenth.

go.hrw.com
Web Extra!
KEYWORD: MS7 Egypt

19. **Multi-Step** The pyramids were constructed using a unit of measurement called a cubit. There are about 21 inches in 1 cubit. If the height of a pyramid is 471 feet, what is its height in cubits?

20. ✏️ **Write About It** Given a right triangle, explain how you know which values to substitute into the equation $a^2 + b^2 = c^2$.

21. ⭐ **Challenge** The pyramid at right has a square base. Find the height of the pyramid to the nearest tenth.

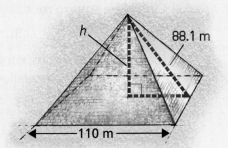
h
88.1 m
110 m

CRCT Prep • GPS Support • Spiral Review

22. **Multiple Choice** Find the missing measure to the nearest tenth.

    Ⓐ 3.6 m   Ⓒ 11.8 m

    Ⓑ 9.2 m   Ⓓ 85 m

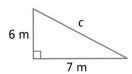
c
6 m
7 m

23. **Gridded Response** A 10-foot ladder is leaning against a wall. The bottom of the ladder is 2 feet away from the bottom of the wall. To the nearest tenth, how many feet up the wall will the ladder reach?

Find the measure of the angle formed by the hour and minute hands of a clock at each time. (Lesson 8-4)

24. 6:00   25. 3:00   26. 5:00   27. 2:00

Estimate each square root to the nearest whole number. (Lesson 9-7)

28. $\sqrt{140}$ 29. $\sqrt{60}$ 30. $\sqrt{200}$ 31. $\sqrt{30}$

READY TO GO ON?

Quiz for Lessons 9-7 Through 9-8

☑ **9-7** **Squares and Square Roots**

Find each square.

1. 21^2 **2.** 7^2 **3.** 12^2 **4.** 13^2

Name the square and the square root represented by each model.

5. 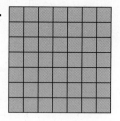 **6.**   **7.**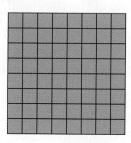

Find each square root.

8. $\sqrt{841}$ **9.** $\sqrt{1,089}$ **10.** $\sqrt{81}$ **11.** $\sqrt{576}$

Estimate each square root to the nearest whole number. Use a calculator to check your answer.

12. $\sqrt{40}$ **13.** $\sqrt{85}$ **14.** $\sqrt{12}$ **15.** $\sqrt{33}$

☑ **9-8** **The Pythagorean Theorem**

Use the Pythagorean Theorem to find each missing measure.

16.   **17.** 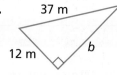 **18.**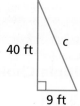

19. Thomas likes to jog at Memorial Park. The running trail he follows is in the shape of a right triangle. He knows one leg of the path is 1.8 miles, and the other leg is 3.2 miles. What is the distance of the third side of the trail to the nearest tenth of a mile?

20. Audrey built a ramp for the set of the new musical at her school. The height of the ramp is 8 feet, and the hypotenuse is 17 feet. What is the length of the ramp's base?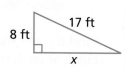

The lengths of two sides of a right triangle are given. Find the length of the third side to the nearest tenth.

21. leg: 14.3 m; hypotenuse: 22 m

22. legs: 10 yd and 24 yd

23. legs: 12.4 in. and 9.0 in.

24. leg: 2.5 cm; hypotenuse: 8 cm

Gabriella's Garden   Gabriella is designing a rectangular garden for her school. As shown in the figure, the garden will be surrounded by a walkway that is 5 feet wide.

1. Gabriella wants to put a fence around the outside of the walkway. How much fencing does she need?

2. Gabriella is going to plant cabbage seedlings around the inside edge of the walkway. The seedlings should be planted 12 inches apart. How many seedlings will she need?

3. The design calls for a circular fountain in the center of the garden. The fountain's diameter will be 10 feet. To the nearest tenth of a foot, what will be the length of the concrete border that forms the edge of the fountain?

4. What is the area of the remaining land that is available for plants? Explain.

5. To help protect and enrich the soil, Gabriella plans to cover the planted part of the garden with mulch. One bag of mulch covers 18 square feet. How many bags should she buy?

6. To celebrate the opening of the garden, Gabriella wants to hang streamers from poles at the outer corners of the walkway, creating an X. How many feet of streamers will Gabriella need?

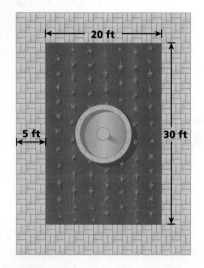

Identifying and Graphing Irrational Numbers

Learn to classify numbers as rational or irrational and graph them on a number line.

Vocabulary

irrational numbers

🍑 **Georgia Performance Standards**

M7P5.b Translate among mathematical representations to solve problems. Also, M7P3.c, M7P5.a, M7P5.c.

Recall from Lesson 2-11 that a rational number can be written as a fraction with integers for its numerator and denominator. When rational numbers are written in decimal form, the decimal may be terminating or nonterminating. If a rational number is nonterminating, then it has a repeating pattern.

A decimal that is nonterminating with no repeating pattern is an **irrational number**.

	Rational		Irrational
Terminating	**Nonterminating, Repeating**		**Nonterminating, Nonrepeating**
$\frac{1}{8} = 0.125$	$\frac{1}{3} = 0.333\ldots$, or $0.\overline{3}$		$\sqrt{2} = 1.414213562\ldots$
$\sqrt{9} = 3$	$\frac{2}{11} = 0.181818\ldots$, or $0.\overline{18}$		$\pi = 3.1415926\ldots$

EXAMPLE 1 Identifying Rational and Irrational Numbers

Identify each number as rational or irrational. Justify your answer.

A $\frac{2}{5}$

$\frac{2}{5} = 0.4$ *Write the number in decimal form.*

Because its decimal form is terminating, $\frac{2}{5}$ is rational.

B $\frac{5}{6}$

$\frac{5}{6} = 0.8333\ldots$, or $0.8\overline{3}$ *Write the number in decimal form.*

Because its decimal form is nonterminating and repeating, $\frac{5}{6}$ is rational.

Remember!

By definition, any ratio of integers is a rational number.

C $\sqrt{16}$

$\sqrt{16} = 4$ *Write the number in decimal form.*

Because its decimal form is terminating, $\sqrt{16}$ is rational.

D $\sqrt{7}$

$\sqrt{7} = 2.645751311\ldots$ *Write the number in decimal form.*

There is no pattern in the decimal form of $\sqrt{7}$. It is a nonterminating, nonrepeating decimal. So $\sqrt{7}$ is irrational.

Every point on the number line corresponds to a real number, either a rational number or an irrational number. Between every two real numbers there is always another real number.

 EXAMPLE 2 **Graphing Rational and Irrational Numbers**

Graph the list of numbers on a number line. Then order the numbers from least to greatest.

$1.4, \sqrt{5}, \frac{3}{8}, \pi, -\frac{2}{3}, \sqrt{4}, \sqrt{16}$

Write all the numbers in decimal form, and then graph them.

$1.4, \sqrt{5} \approx 2.236, \frac{3}{8} = 0.375, \pi \approx 3.14, -\frac{2}{3} = -0.\overline{6}, \sqrt{4} = 2.0, \sqrt{16} = 4.0$

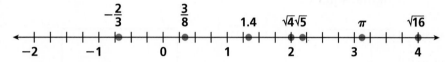

From left to right on the number line, the numbers appear from least to greatest: $-\frac{2}{3} < \frac{3}{8} < 1.4 < \sqrt{4} < \sqrt{5} < \pi < \sqrt{16}$.

EXTENSION

Exercises

Identify each number as rational or irrational. Justify your answer.

1. $\sqrt{8}$
2. $\frac{5}{11}$
3. $\frac{7}{8}$
4. $\sqrt{36}$

5. $\frac{3}{13}$
6. $\sqrt{14}$
7. 2.800
8. $\frac{5}{6}$

9. $\sqrt{5}$
10. $\frac{6}{24}$
11. $\frac{10}{33}$
12. $\sqrt{18}$

Graph each list of numbers on a number line. Then order the numbers from least to greatest.

13. $2.6, 0.5, \sqrt{3}, -\frac{7}{10}, \frac{1}{3}$
14. $\sqrt{12}, \frac{3}{8}, -0.65, \frac{5}{9}, \sqrt{11}$

15. $-1.3, \sqrt{15}, 3.1, -\frac{2}{5}, \sqrt{4}$
16. $-2.1, -\frac{9}{10}, \sqrt{1}, -1.5, \sqrt{9}$

Name the two perfect squares that each square root lies between. Then graph the square root on a number line, and justify its placement.

17. $\sqrt{34}$
18. $\sqrt{46}$
19. $\sqrt{14}$
20. $\sqrt{6}$

21. $\sqrt{99}$
22. $\sqrt{63}$
23. $\sqrt{71}$
24. $\sqrt{13}$

 25. **What's the Error?** A classmate tells you that the square root of any number is irrational. Explain why the classmate is incorrect.

Game Time

Shape Up

Rectangles

The square below has been divided into four rectangles. The areas of two of the rectangles are given. If the length of each of the segments in the diagram is an integer, what is the area of the original square?

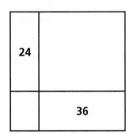

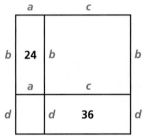

(*Hint:* Remember $a + c = b + d$.)

Use different lengths and a different answer to create your own version of this puzzle.

Circles

What is the maximum number of times that six circles of the same size can intersect? To find the answer, start by drawing two circles that are the same size. What is the greatest number of times they can intersect? Add another circle, and another, and so on.

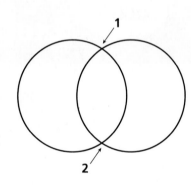

Circles and Squares

Two players start with a sequence of circles and squares. Before beginning the game, each player chooses whether to be a "circle" or a "square." The goal of the game is to have the final remaining shape be the shape you chose to be. Shapes are removed from the sequence according to the following rules: On each move, a player selects two shapes. If the shapes are identical, they are replaced with one square. If the shapes are different, they are replaced with one circle.

go.hrw.com
Game Time Extra
KEYWORD: MS7 Games

A complete copy of the rules and game pieces are available online.

Materials
- lunch bag
- scissors
- tape
- markers
- index cards

FOLDNOTES

It's in the Bag!

PROJECT ## Bag o' Measurement

This bag of index cards will help you organize your notes on measuring two-dimensional figures.

1 Hold the lunch bag with the flap facing you at the top. Cut a thin strip from the flap as shown. **Figure A**

2 Cut along the sides of the flap so you can open it up. Then use your scissors to round off the corners at the top of the flap. **Figure B**

3 Fold up the bottom part of the flap. Then trim this part of the flap by cutting out a trapezoid as shown. **Figure C**

4 Cut another trapezoid from the bottom edge of the bag by cutting through all the layers. Then fold up the bottom of the bag to make two pockets, one below the other. **Figure D**

5 Tape the sides of the bag together to close the pockets. Fold down the flap and label it with the number and title of the chapter.

Taking Note of the Math

Use index cards to record measurement formulas, the Pythagorean Theorem, and other important facts from the chapter. Store the cards in the pockets of the bag.

A

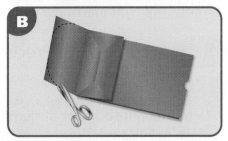

B

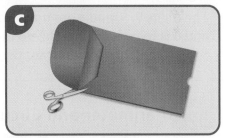

C

D

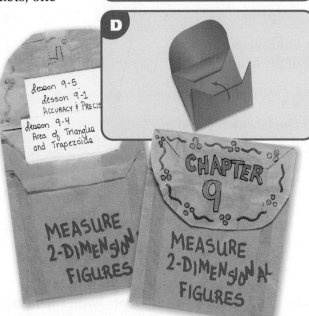

Lesson 9-5
Lesson 9-1
ACCURACY & PRECIS

Lesson 9-4
Area of Triangles
and Trapezoids

MEASURE
2-DIMENSIONAL
FIGURES

CHAPTER
9

MEASURE
2-DIMENSIONAL
FIGURES

Vocabulary

accuracy 518	leg 556	Pythagorean Theorem . 556
area 530	perfect square 550	radical sign 550
circumference 525	perimeter 524	significant digits 518
hypotenuse 556	precision 518	square root 550

Complete the sentences below with vocabulary words from the list above.

1. The longest side of a right triangle is called the ___?___.

2. The ___?___ is the distance around a circle.

3. ___?___ is the level of detail an instrument can measure.

4. A(n) ___?___ is one of the two equal factors of a number.

9-1 Accuracy and Precision (pp. 518–521)

 GPS M7P1.c

EXAMPLE

- Determine the number of significant digits in 705.4 mL.

  The digits 7, 5, and 4 are nonzero digits, and 0 is between two nonzero digits. So 705.4 mL has 4 significant digits.

EXERCISES

Determine the number of significant digits in each measurement.

5. 0.450 kg   **6.** 6,703.0 ft

7. 30,000 lb   **8.** 0.00078 g

9. 900.5 cm   **10.** 1,204 gal

9-2 Perimeter and Circumference (pp. 524–527)

 GPS M7A1.b, M7A2.a, M7A2.b

EXAMPLE

- Find the perimeter of the triangle.

  12 in.
  17 in. 21 in.

  $P = 12 + 17 + 21$
  $P = 50$
  The perimeter is 50 in.

- Find the circumference of the circle. Use 3.14 for π.

  .5 cm

  $C = 2\pi r$
  $C \approx 2 \cdot 3.14 \cdot 5$
  $C \approx 31.4$
  The circumference is about 31.4 cm.

EXERCISES

Find the perimeter of each polygon.

11.
24 m
12 m   15 m
32 m

12.   24.9 cm
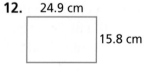
15.8 cm

Find the circumference of each circle to the nearest tenth. Use 3.14 for π.

13.
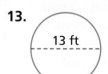
13 ft

14.
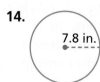
7.8 in.

Study Guide: Review

9-3 Area of Parallelograms (pp. 530–533)

GPS M7A1.b

EXAMPLE

■ Find the area of the rectangle.

14 in.

8.6 in.

$A = \ell w$

$A = 14 \cdot 8.6$

$A = 120.4$

The area of the rectangle is 120.4 in².

EXERCISES

Find the area of each polygon.

15.
8.6 cm

5.9 cm

16.

24.3 yd

34 yd

17. Rose is drawing a portrait for her art class. She is using a sheet of paper that is 6 inches wide and 12 inches long. What is the area of the art paper in square inches?

9-4 Area of Triangles and Trapezoids (pp. 534–537)

GPS M7A1.b

EXAMPLE

■ Find the area of the triangle.

$A = \frac{1}{2}bh$

$A = \frac{1}{2}(4.8 \cdot 2.9)$

$A = \frac{1}{2}(13.92)$

$A = 6.96$

The area of the triangle is 6.96 m².

2.9 m

4.8 m

EXERCISES

Find the area of each polygon.

18.
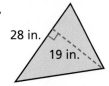
28 in.

19 in.

19.
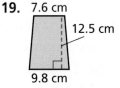
7.6 cm

12.5 cm

9.8 cm

20.
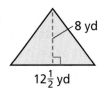
8 yd

$12\frac{1}{2}$ yd

21.

67 in.

42 in.

36 in.

9-5 Area of Circles (pp. 538–541)

GPS M7A1.b

EXAMPLE

■ Find the area of the circle to the nearest tenth. Use 3.14 for π.

5 in.

$A = \pi r^2$

$A \approx 3.14 \cdot 5^2$

$A \approx 3.14 \cdot 25$

$A \approx 78.5$

The area of the circle is about 78.5 in².

EXERCISES

Find the area of each circle to the nearest tenth. Use 3.14 for π.

22.

3.4 m

23.

17 ft

24. The minute hand on a clock is 9 inches long. What is the area of the circle the minute hand covers after one hour? Give your answer in square inches.

9-6 Area of Irregular Figures (pp. 542–545)

GPS M7A1.b

EXAMPLE

■ Find the area of the irregular figure.

Separate the figure into a rectangle and a triangle.

$A = \ell w$

$\quad = 4 \cdot 8 = 32 \text{ m}^2$

$A = \frac{1}{2} bh$

$\quad = \frac{1}{2} (3 \cdot 4) = 6 \text{ m}^2$

$A = 32 + 6 = 38 \text{ m}^2$

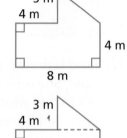

EXERCISES

Find the area of each figure. Use 3.14 for π.

25.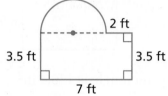

26.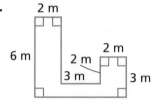

9-7 Squares and Square Roots (pp. 550–553)

GPS M7P4.a

EXAMPLE

■ Estimate $\sqrt{71}$ to the nearest whole number.

$64 < \quad 71 < \quad 81$ *Find the perfect squares nearest 71.*

$\sqrt{64} < \sqrt{71} < \sqrt{81}$

$8 < \sqrt{71} < \quad 9$ *Find the square roots of 64 and 81.*

Since 71 is closer to 64 than to 81, $\sqrt{71} \approx 8$.

EXERCISES

Estimate each square root to the nearest whole number.

27. $\sqrt{29}$ 28. $\sqrt{92}$

29. $\sqrt{106}$ 30. $\sqrt{150}$

31. The area of Rita's square vegetable garden is 265 ft². What is the length of each side of the garden to the nearest foot?

9-8 Pythagorean Theorem (pp. 556–559)

GPS M7A1.a, M7A1.b

EXAMPLE

■ Use the Pythagorean Theorem to find the missing measure.

$a^2 + b^2 = c^2$

$9^2 + 12^2 = c^2$

$81 + 144 = c^2$

$225 = c^2$

$\sqrt{225} = \sqrt{c^2}$

$15 = c$

The hypotenuse is 15 in.

EXERCISES

Use the Pythagorean Theorem to find each missing measure.

32.

33.

34.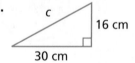

35.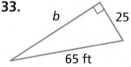

Study Guide: Review

CHAPTER TEST

Choose the more precise measurement in each pair.

1. 80 m, 7.9 cm

2. 18 yd, 5 mi

3. 500 lb, 18 oz

Calculate. Use the correct number of significant digits in each answer.

4. 5.6 lb ÷ 2.59

5. 3.14 · 125 cm

6. 5.882 in. + 5.17 in.

7. Find the perimeter of the trapezoid.

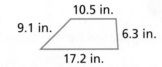

8. The opening of a playscape tunnel has a circumference of 25 ft. What is the radius of the tunnel to the nearest tenth?

Find the area of each figure.

9.

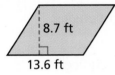

10.

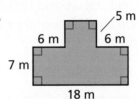

11.

12. The area of a rectangular computer lab is 660 ft², and the width is 22 ft. What is the length of the computer lab?

13. The area of a circular fountain is 66 cm². What is its radius to the nearest tenth?

Use the diagram for Items 14 and 15.

14. Find the circumference of the circle to the nearest tenth.

15. Find the area of the circle to the nearest tenth.

Find each square or square root.

16. 15^2

17. 23^2

18. $\sqrt{1,600}$

19. $\sqrt{961}$

20. The tiles of Sara's new floor are black and white as shown. What is the missing length to the nearest tenth?

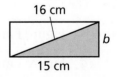

21. Triangle Park has a trail that follows the path of a right triangle. One leg of the trail is 2.1 miles, and the other leg is 3.0 miles. What is the distance of the third side of the trail to the nearest tenth of a mile?

Use the diagram at right for Items 22 and 23.

22. Use the Pythagorean Theorem to find the missing measure.

23. Find the area of the triangle.

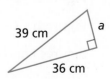

Chapter Test

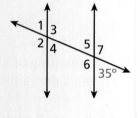

TEST TACKLER

Standardized Test Strategies

Multiple Choice: Context-Based Test Items

Sometimes a multiple-choice test item requires you to use information in the answer choices to determine which choice fits the context of the problem.

EXAMPLE 1

Which statement is supported by the figure?

Ⓐ ∠1 and ∠4 are supplementary.   Ⓒ The measure of ∠7 is 35°.

Ⓑ ∠3 and ∠2 are vertical angles.   Ⓓ ∠5 and ∠6 are congruent.

Read each answer choice to find the best answer.

Choice A: ∠1 and ∠4 are vertical angles and therefore, congruent. Congruent angles are supplementary only if they are right angles. ∠1 and ∠4 measure 35°.

Choice B: ∠3 and ∠2 are vertical angles. This is the correct answer choice.

Choice C: The measure of ∠7 cannot be 35° because ∠7 is supplementary to a 35° angle. Therefore, ∠7 has a measure of 145°.

Choice D: ∠5 and ∠6 are supplementary angles but not right angles. Supplementary angles are congruent only if they are both right angles.

EXAMPLE 2

Which two figures have the same area?

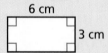

Figure I

Figure II

Figure III

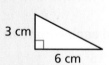

Figure IV

Ⓕ Figure I and Figure II   Ⓗ Figure II and Figure III

Ⓖ Figure I and Figure III   Ⓙ Figure I and Figure IV

Find the areas of all four figures and compare them.

Figure I: $3 \cdot 6 = 18$ cm^2 **Figure III:** $\frac{1}{2} \cdot 4(3 + 6) = 18$ cm^2

Figure II: $3 \cdot 9 = 27$ cm^2 **Figure IV:** $\frac{1}{2} \cdot 6 \cdot 3 = 9$ cm^2

Figures I and III have the same area. Choice G is correct.

Test Tackler

HOT TIP! Do not choose an answer until you have read all of the answer choices.

Read each test item and answer the questions that follow.

Item A
The area of the square is 16 cm². Which of the following is NOT correct about the circle?

(A) $C = 4\pi$ cm

(B) $A = 16\pi$ cm²

(C) $d = 4$ cm

(D) $r = 2$ cm

1. Since only one answer choice has incorrect information, why can you automatically eliminate answer choices C and D?

2. How can you find the side length of the square? What does the side length tell you about the circle?

3. Use your answer to Problem 2 to determine whether answer choice A has correct information.

4. How can you tell that choice B is the correct answer?

Item B
Which figure is an acute isosceles triangle?

 (F)

 (H)

 (G)

 (J)

5. What is an acute triangle?

6. What is an isosceles triangle?

7. Why is choice F incorrect?

Item C
Which graph represents a reflection across the x-axis?

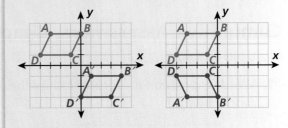

(A) (C)

(B) (D)

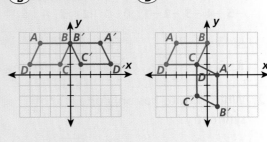

8. Which answer choices do NOT show reflections?

9. What is a reflection across the x-axis?

Item D
The area of the trapezoid is 30 in². Which equation CANNOT be used to find the height of the trapezoid?

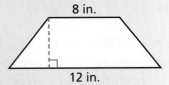

8 in.

12 in.

(F) $30 = \frac{1}{2}(8 + 12)h$

(G) $60 = (8 + 12)h$

(H) $30 = \frac{1}{2}(8 - 12)h$

(J) $\frac{1}{2}(8 + 12)h = 30$

10. What is the formula for the area of a trapezoid?

11. What steps would you take to solve the formula for h?

Cumulative Assessment, Chapters 1–9

Multiple Choice

1. Which expression is represented by the model below?

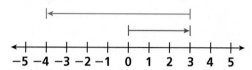

- Ⓐ 3 + (−7)
- Ⓒ −3 + 7
- Ⓑ 3 + 7
- Ⓓ −3 + (−7)

2. Which figure has only one line of symmetry?

3. If $x + 2 = y$ and $y = 4^2$, what is the value of $x + y$?

- Ⓐ 14
- Ⓒ 22
- Ⓑ 16
- Ⓓ 30

4. You invest $200 into a simple interest savings account for 5 years and earn $60 in interest. What interest rate did you earn?

- Ⓕ 1.5%
- Ⓗ 30%
- Ⓖ 6%
- Ⓙ 33.3%

5. A color printer is designed to print 8 pages per minute. How many pages can the printer print in 13 minutes?

- Ⓐ 1.6 pages
- Ⓒ 84 pages
- Ⓑ 21 pages
- Ⓓ 104 pages

6. For which radius r is the area of a circle equal to 153.86 square inches?

- Ⓕ $r = 7$ in.
- Ⓗ $r = 24.5$ in.
- Ⓖ $r = 12.5$ in.
- Ⓙ $r = 49$ in.

7. Which equation describes the graph?

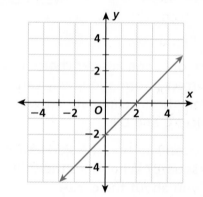

- Ⓐ $y = x − 2$
- Ⓒ $y = 2x + 1$
- Ⓑ $y = x + 2$
- Ⓓ $y = 2x − 2$

8. Seventy percent of historical figures pictured on U.S. currency do not have facial hair. What is the decimal equivalent of this value?

- Ⓕ 0.07
- Ⓗ 7.0
- Ⓖ 0.70
- Ⓙ 70

9. What is the area of the trapezoid?

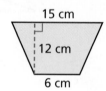

- Ⓐ 81 cm²
- Ⓒ 135 cm²
- Ⓑ 126 cm²
- Ⓓ 252 cm²

10. Paul plans to build a fence around the perimeter of his property. How much fencing does he need?

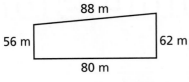

F. 286 m
G. 294 m
H. 4,480 m
J. 5,456 m

11. Gretchen bought six muffins for $3.19, four bottles of juice at $1.25 each, and a bag of apples at $0.89 per pound. She gave the cashier $20. What other information is necessary to find Gretchen's correct change?

A. Cost of one muffin
B. Total cost of the juice
C. Number of pounds of apples bought
D. Reason for buying the food

12. How many significant digits are in the measurement 0.00410 milligrams?

F. 2
G. 3
H. 5
J. 6

13. The diameter of a CD is about 12 cm. What is the circumference of the CD to the nearest tenth of a centimeter? Use 3.14 for π.

A. 226.2
B. 113.1
C. 37.7
D. 18.8

Make a sketch to help solve coordinate grid problems.

14. What is the x-coordinate of the point (−2, 6) after it is translated 5 units right and 7 units down?

F. −1
G. 1
H. 3
J. 5

15. The tennis team had a pizza party at the end of the season. The 17 team members spent a total of $51.95 on pizza and $6.70 on drinks. What is the average amount each team member spent for the party? Show your work.

16. Laurie wants to paste a circular photo onto a rectangular piece of cardboard. The area of the photo is 50.24 in². What are the smallest possible dimensions the piece of cardboard can have and still hold the entire photo? Use 3.14 for π and explain your answer.

17. Find the perimeter and area of a rectangle with length 12 m and width 7 m. Then find the side length of a square that has the same area as the rectangle. Round your answers to the nearest meter, and show your work.

Extended Response

18. Use △ABC and △STU for the following problems.

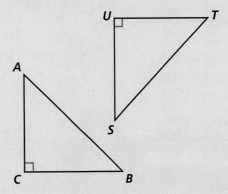

a. If AB = 17 m and AC = 8 m, what theorem can you use to find CB? Find CB, and show your work.

b. If ST = 10 m and △ABC is similar to △STU, what ratio can you use to find SU and UT? Show how to find SU and UT to the nearest tenth of a meter.

c. Find the difference in the areas of the two triangles.

Measurement: Three-Dimensional Figures

CRCT PREP

go.hrw.com
Chapter Project Online
KEYWORD: MS7 Ch10

Pyramid	Location	Height (m)	Base Length (m)
El Castillo	Chichén Itzá, Mexico	55.5	79.0
Tikal	Tikal, Guatemala	30.0	80.0
Pyramid of the Sun	Teotihuácan, Mexico	63.0	225.0

Career *Archaeological Architect*

Did you ever wonder how the pyramids were built? Archaeologists who are also architects combine a love of the past with the skills of a building designer to study the construction of ancient buildings.

In recent years, archaeological architects have built machines like those used in ancient times to demonstrate how the pyramids might have been constructed. The table shows the dimensions of a few famous pyramids.

ARE YOU READY?

☑ Vocabulary

Choose the best term from the list to complete each sentence.

1. A polygon with six sides is called a(n) __?__ .

2. __?__ figures are the same size and shape.

3. A(n) __?__ is a ratio that relates the dimensions of two similar objects.

4. The formula for the __?__ of a circle can be written as πd or $2\pi r$.

5. __?__ figures are the same shape but not necessarily the same size.

6. A polygon with five sides is called a(n) __?__ .

area

circumference

congruent

hexagon

pentagon

scale factor

similar

Complete these exercises to review skills you will need for this chapter.

☑ Area of Squares, Rectangles, Triangles

Find the area of each figure.

7.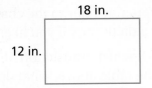
18 in.
12 in.

8.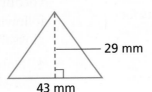
29 mm
43 mm

9.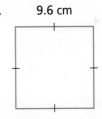
9.6 cm

☑ Area of Circles

Find the area of each circle to the nearest tenth. Use 3.14 for π.

10.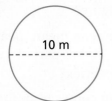
10 m

11.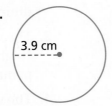
3.9 cm

12.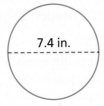
7.4 in.

☑ Find the Cube of a Number

Find each value.

13. 3^3

14. 8^3

15. 2.5^3

16. 6.2^3

17. 10^3

18. 5.9^3

19. 800^3

20. 98^3

Study Guide: Preview

Study Guide: Preview

Where You've Been

Previously, you

- found the area of polygons and irregular figures.

- compared the relationship between a figure's perimeter and its area.

In This Chapter

You will study

- finding the volume of prisms, cylinders, pyramids, and cones.

- using nets to find the surface area of prisms and cylinders.

- finding the volume and surface area of similar three-dimensional figures.

Where You're Going

You can use the skills learned in this chapter

- to determine the amount of materials needed to build a doghouse.

- to convert dimensions of a model to real-world dimensions.

Key Vocabulary/Vocabulario

base	base de una figura tridimensional
edge	arista
face	cara
net	plantilla
polyhedron	poliedro
prism	prisma
surface area	área total
vertex of a polyhedron	vértice de un poliedro
volume	volumen

Vocabulary Connections

To become familiar with some of the vocabulary terms in the chapter, consider the following. You may refer to the chapter, the glossary, or a dictionary if you like.

1. Note the Spanish translation of *surface area* in the table above. What does the term *área total* tell you about the meaning of **surface area**?

2. The word *edge* comes from the Latin word *acer,* meaning "sharp." How does the Latin root help you define an **edge** of a three-dimensional figure?

3. The word *vertex* can mean "peak" or "highest point." What part of a cone or pyramid is the **vertex**?

4. The word *prism* comes from the Greek word *priein,* meaning "to saw." How might you describe a **prism** in terms of something sawn or cut off?

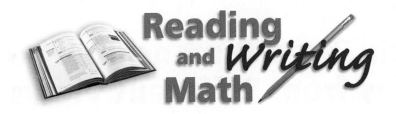

Reading and Writing Math

Study Strategy: Learn and Use Formulas

Throughout this chapter, you will be introduced to many formulas. Although memorizing these formulas is helpful, understanding the concepts on which they are based will help you to re-create the formula if you happen to forget.

One way to memorize a formula is to use flash cards. Write the formula on an index card and review it often. Include a diagram and an example. Add any notes that you choose, such as when to use the formula.

In Lesson 9-3, you learned the formula for area of a rectangle.

Sample Flash Card

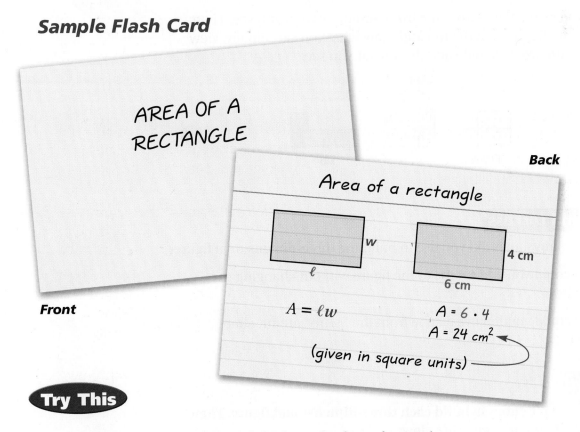

AREA OF A
RECTANGLE

Front

Back

Area of a rectangle

$A = \ell w$

$A = 6 \cdot 4$

$A = 24 \text{ cm}^2$

(given in square units)

Try This

1. Create flash cards for some of the formulas from the previous chapters.

2. Describe a plan to help you memorize the formulas in Chapters 9 and 10.

Hands-On LAB 10-1

Sketch Three-Dimensional Figures from Different Views

Use with Lesson 10-1

go.hrw.com
Lab Resources Online
KEYWORD: MS7 Lab10

Georgia Performance Standards
M7P3.a, M7P5.a, M7P5.b

Three-dimensional figures often look different from different points of view. You can use centimeter cubes to help you visualize and sketch three-dimensional figures.

Activity 1

① Use centimeter cubes to build the three-dimensional figure at right.

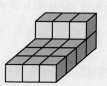

② Now view the figure from the front and draw what you see. Then view the figure from the top and draw what you see. Finally, view the figure from the side and draw what you see.

Front   Top   Side

Think and Discuss

1. How many cubes did you use to build the three-dimensional figure?

2. How could you add a cube to the figure without changing the top view?

3. How could you remove a cube from the figure without changing the side view?

Try This

Use centimeter cubes to build each three-dimensional figure. Then sketch the front, top, and side views.

1.   2.    3. 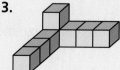   4.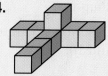

Activity 2

1 Use centimeter cubes to build a figure that has the front, top, and side views shown.

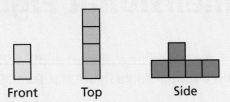

Front   Top   Side

2 You can build the figure by first making a simple figure that matches the front view.

3 Now add cubes so that the figure matches the top view.

4 Finally, remove cubes so that the figure matches the side view. Check that the front and top views are still correct for the figure that you built.

Think and Discuss

1. Discuss whether there is another step-by-step method for building the above figure. If so, is the final result the same?

Try This

The front, top, and side views of a figure are shown. Use centimeter cubes to build the figure. Then sketch the figure.

1.

Front   Top   Side

2.

Front   Top   Side

3. The views below represent a three-dimensional figure that cannot be built from cubes. Determine which three-dimensional figure matches the views.

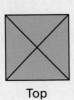

Front   Top   Side

A   B   C   D

10-1 Introduction to Three-Dimensional Figures

Learn to identify various three-dimensional figures.

Vocabulary

face

edge

polyhedron

vertex

base

prism

pyramid

cylinder

cone

Georgia Performance Standards

M7P3.d Use the language of mathematics to express mathematical ideas precisely.

Three-dimensional figures have three dimensions: length, width, and height. A flat surface of a three-dimensional figure is a **face**. An **edge** is where two faces meet.

A **polyhedron** is a three-dimensional figure whose faces are all polygons. A **vertex** of a polyhedron is a point where three or more edges meet. The face that is used to name a polyhedron is called a **base**.

A *prism* has two bases, and a *pyramid* has one base.

Prisms	Pyramids
A **prism** is a polyhedron that has two parallel, congruent bases. The bases can be any polygon. The other faces are parallelograms.	A **pyramid** is a polyhedron that has one base. The base can be any polygon. The other faces are triangles.

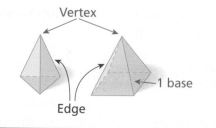

EXAMPLE **1** **Naming Prisms and Pyramids**

Identify the bases and faces of each figure. Then name the figure.

A

There are two rectangular bases.
There are four other rectangular faces.
The figure is a rectangular prism.

B

There is one rectangular base.
There are four triangular faces.
The figure is a rectangular pyramid.

C

There are two triangular bases.
There are three rectangular faces.
The figure is a triangular prism.

D

There is one hexagonal base.
There are six triangular faces.
The figure is a hexagonal pyramid.

Remember!

A polygon with six sides is called a hexagon.

Other three-dimensional figures include *cylinders* and *cones*. These figures are not polyhedrons because they are not made of faces that are all polygons.

Cylinders	Cones
A **cylinder** has two parallel, congruent bases that are circles.	A **cone** has one base that is a circle and a surface that comes to a point called the vertex.

2 bases

Vertex

1 base

You can use properties to classify three-dimensional figures.

EXAMPLE 2 Classifying Three-Dimensional Figures

Classify each figure as a polyhedron or not a polyhedron. Then name the figure.

A
The faces are all polygons, so the figure is a polyhedron.
There is one triangular base.
The figure is a triangular pyramid.

B
The faces are not all polygons, so the figure is not a polyhedron.
There are two circular bases.
The figure is a cylinder.

C
The faces are not all polygons, so the figure is not a polyhedron.
There is one circular base.
The figure is a cone.

Think and Discuss 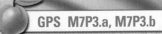 GPS M7P3.a, M7P3.b

1. **Explain** how to identify a prism or a pyramid.

2. **Compare and contrast** cylinders and prisms. How are they alike? How are they different?

3. **Compare and contrast** pyramids and cones. How are they alike? How are they different?

10-1 **Exercises**

Georgia Performance Standards

M7P1.a, M7P3.d, M7P4.c

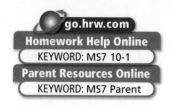

go.hrw.com
Homework Help Online
KEYWORD: MS7 10-1
Parent Resources Online
KEYWORD: MS7 Parent

GUIDED PRACTICE

See Example ① **Identify the bases and faces of each figure. Then name the figure.**

1.   **2.**   **3.**

See Example ② **Classify each figure as a polyhedron or not a polyhedron. Then name the figure.**

4.   **5.**  **6.**

INDEPENDENT PRACTICE

See Example ① **Identify the bases and faces of each figure. Then name the figure.**

7.  **8.** **9.**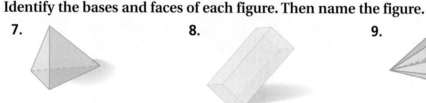

See Example ② **Classify each figure as a polyhedron or not a polyhedron. Then name the figure.**

10.   **11.** 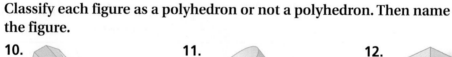 **12.**

PRACTICE AND PROBLEM SOLVING

CRCT GPS

Extra Practice p. 746

Identify the three-dimensional figure described.

13. two parallel, congruent square bases and four other polygonal faces

14. two parallel, congruent circular bases and one curved surface

15. one triangular base and three other triangular faces

16. one circular base and one curved surface

Name two examples of the three-dimensional figure described.

17. two parallel, congruent bases   **18.** one base

19. The structures in the photo at right are tombs of ancient Egyptian kings. No one knows exactly when the tombs were built, but some archaeologists think the first one might have been built around 2780 B.C.E. Name the shape of the ancient Egyptian structures.

20. The Parthenon was built around 440 B.C.E. by the ancient Greeks. Its purpose was to house a statue of Athena, the Greek goddess of wisdom. Describe the three-dimensional shapes you see in the structure.

440 B.C.E.
Parthenon

2600 B.C.E.
Ancient Egyptian structures at Giza

21. The Leaning Tower of Pisa began to lean as it was being built. To keep the tower from falling over, the upper sections (floors) were built slightly off center so that the tower would curve away from the way it was leaning. What shape is each section of the tower?

22. ⭐ **Challenge** The stainless steel structure at right, called the Unisphere, became the symbol of the New York World's Fair of 1964–1965. A sphere is a three-dimensional figure with a surface made up of all the points that are the same distance from a given point. Explain why the structure is not a sphere.

1173
Leaning Tower of Pisa

1964
Unisphere

CRCT PREP • GPS SUPPORT • SPIRAL REVIEW

23. **Multiple Choice** Which figure has six rectangular faces?

　Ⓐ Rectangular prism 　　　Ⓒ Triangular pyramid

　Ⓑ Triangular prism 　　　Ⓓ Rectangular pyramid

24. **Multiple Choice** Which figure does NOT have two congruent bases?

　Ⓕ Cube 　　　Ⓖ Pyramid 　　　Ⓗ Prism 　　　Ⓙ Cylinder

Estimate each sum. (Lesson 3-7)

25. $\frac{2}{5} + \frac{3}{8}$ 　　　26. $\frac{1}{16} + \frac{4}{9}$ 　　　27. $\frac{7}{9} + \frac{11}{12}$ 　　　28. $\frac{1}{10} + \frac{1}{16}$

29. A store sells two sizes of detergent: 300 ounces for $21.63 and 100 ounces for $6.99. Which size detergent has the lowest price per ounce? (Lesson 5-2)

Hands-On LAB 10-2

Explore the Volume of Prisms and Cylinders

Use with Lesson 10-2

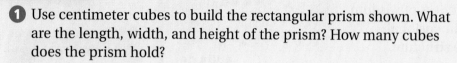
go.hrw.com
Lab Resources Online
KEYWORD: MS7 Lab10

The volume of a three-dimensional figure is the number of cubes that it can hold. One cube represents one cubic unit of volume.

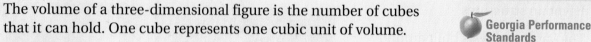

Georgia Performance Standards

M7P2.c, M7P2.d, M7P5.a, M7P5.b

Activity 1

1 Use centimeter cubes to build the rectangular prism shown. What are the length, width, and height of the prism? How many cubes does the prism hold?

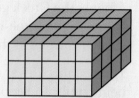

2 You can find out how many cubes the prism holds without counting every cube. First look at the prism from above. How can you find the number of cubes in the top layer without counting every cube?

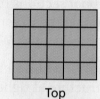

Top

3 Now look at the prism from the side. How many layers does the prism have? How can you use this to find the total number of cubes in the prism?

Side

Think and Discuss

1. Describe a shortcut for finding the number of cubes in a rectangular prism.

2. Suppose you know the area of the base of a prism and the height of the prism. How can you find the prism's volume?

3. Let the area of the base of a prism be B and the height of the prism be h. Write a formula for the prism's volume V.

Try This

Use the formula you discovered to find the volume of each prism.

1.

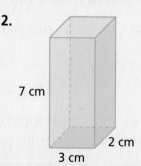

4 cm
6 cm
3 cm

2.

7 cm
3 cm
2 cm

3.

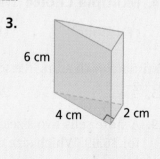

6 cm
4 cm
2 cm

Activity 2

1 You can use a process similar to that in Activity 1 to develop the formula for the volume of a cylinder. You will need an empty soup can or other cylindrical container. Remove one of the bases.

2 Arrange centimeter cubes in a single layer at the bottom of the cylinder. Fit as many cubes into the layer as possible. How many cubes are in this layer?

3 To find how many layers of cubes would fit in the cylinder, make a stack of cubes along the inside of the cylinder. How many layers would fit in the cylinder?

4 How can you use what you know to find the approximate number of cubes that would fit in the cylinder?

Think and Discuss

1. Suppose you know the area of the base of a cylinder and the height of the cylinder. How can you find the cylinder's volume?

2. Let the area of the base of a cylinder be B and the height of the cylinder be h. Write a formula for the cylinder's volume V.

3. The base of a cylinder is a circle with radius r. How can you find the area of the base? How can you use this in your formula for the volume of a cylinder?

Try This

Use the formula you discovered to find the volume of each cylinder. Use 3.14 for π and round to the nearest tenth.

1.

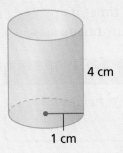

4 cm

1 cm

2.

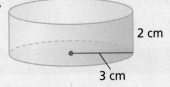

2 cm

3 cm

3.

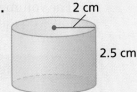

2 cm

2.5 cm

10-2 Volume of Prisms and Cylinders

Learn to find the volume of prisms and cylinders.

Vocabulary

volume

Any three-dimensional figure can be filled completely with congruent cubes and parts of cubes. The **volume** of a three-dimensional figure is the number of cubes it can hold. Each cube represents a unit of measure called a cubic unit.

EXAMPLE 1 Using Cubes to Find the Volume of a Rectangular Prism

Georgia Performance Standards

M7A1.b Simplify and evaluate algebraic expressions using commutative, associative, and distributive properties as appropriate. Also, M7P4.c, M7P5.a, M7P5.b, M7P5.c.

Find how many cubes the prism holds. Then give the prism's volume.

You can find the volume of this prism by counting how many cubes tall, long, and wide the prism is and then multiplying.

$2 \cdot 4 \cdot 2 = 16$

There are 16 cubes in the prism, so the volume is 16 cubic units.

Reading Math

Any unit of measurement with an exponent of 3 is a cubic unit. For example, m^3 means "cubic meter," and in^3 means "cubic inch."

To find a prism's volume, multiply its length by its width by its height.

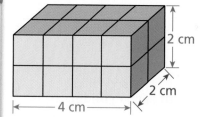

$$4 \text{ cm} \cdot 2 \text{ cm} \cdot 2 \text{ cm} = 16 \text{ cm}^3$$

length · width · height = volume

area of base · height = volume

The volume of a rectangular prism is the area of its base times its height. This formula can be used to find the volume of any prism.

VOLUME OF A PRISM
The volume V of a prism is the area of its base B times its height h. $V = Bh$

EXAMPLE 2 **Using a Formula to Find the Volume of a Prism**

Find the volume of each figure.

A

$V = Bh$ *Use the formula.*
                   The base is a rectangle: $B = 8 \cdot 2 = 16$.

$V = 16 \cdot 12$ *Substitute for B and h.*

$V = 192$ *Multiply.*

The volume of the cereal box is 192 in^3.

B

$V = Bh$ *Use the formula.*

                     The base is a triangle:
                     $B = \frac{1}{2} \cdot 4 \cdot 3 = 6$.

$V = 6 \cdot 15$ *Substitute for B and h.*

$V = 90$ *Multiply.*

The volume of the shipping carton is 90 in^3.

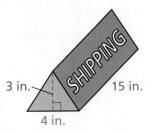

Finding the volume of a cylinder is similar to finding the volume of a prism.

VOLUME OF A CYLINDER

The volume V of a cylinder is the area of its base B times its height h.

$$V = Bh \qquad \text{or} \qquad V = \pi r^2 h, \text{ where } B = \pi r^2$$

EXAMPLE 3 **Using a Formula to Find the Volume of a Cylinder**

A can of shoe polish is shaped like a cylinder. Find its volume to the nearest tenth. Use 3.14 for π.

$V = Bh$ *Use the formula.*

The base is a circle: $B = \pi \cdot 4^2 \approx 50.24 \text{ cm}^2$.

$V \approx 50.24 \cdot 5$ *Substitute for B and h.*

$V \approx 251.2$ *Multiply.*

The volume of the shoe polish can is about 251.2 cm^3.

8 cm

5 cm

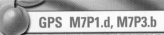

Think and Discuss   GPS M7P1.d, M7P3.b

1. Explain what a cubic unit is. What units would you use for the volume of a figure measured in yards?

2. Compare and contrast the formulas for volume of a prism and volume of a cylinder. How are they alike? How are they different?

Georgia Performance Standards

M7P1.b, M7P3.a, M7P3.c

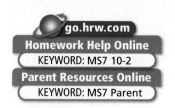

go.hrw.com
Homework Help Online
KEYWORD: MS7 10-2
Parent Resources Online
KEYWORD: MS7 Parent

GUIDED PRACTICE

See Example ① **Find how many cubes each prism holds. Then give the prism's volume.**

1.

2.

3.

See Example ② **Find the volume of each figure.**

4.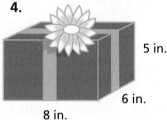
5 in.
6 in.
8 in.

5.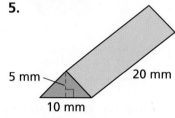
5 mm
20 mm
10 mm

6.
3.5 in.
2.25 in.   0.5 in.

See Example ③ **7.** A can of tomato paste is shaped like a cylinder. It is 4 cm wide and 6 cm tall. Find its volume to the nearest tenth. Use 3.14 for π.

4 cm
TOMATO PASTE   6 cm

INDEPENDENT PRACTICE

See Example ① **Find how many cubes each prism holds. Then give the prism's volume.**

8.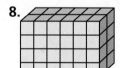

9.

10.

See Example ② **Find the volume of each figure.**

11.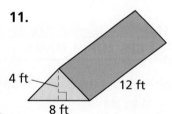
4 ft
12 ft
8 ft

12.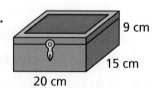
9 cm
15 cm
20 cm

13.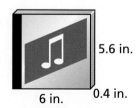
5.6 in.
6 in.   0.4 in.

See Example ③ **14.** A paper towel roll is shaped like a cylinder. It is 4 cm wide and 28 cm tall. Find its volume to the nearest tenth. Use 3.14 for π.

PRACTICE AND PROBLEM SOLVING

15. Multi-Step The base of a triangular prism is a right triangle with hypotenuse 10 m long and one leg 6 m long. If the height of the prism is 12 m, what is the volume of the prism?

16. Life Science An ID tag containing a microchip can be injected into a pet, such as a dog or cat. These microchips are cylindrical and can be as small as 12 mm in length and 2.1 mm in diameter. Use rounding to estimate the volume of one of these microchips. Then find the volume to the nearest tenth. Use 3.14 for π.

17. Recreation The tent shown is in the shape of a triangular prism. How many cubic feet of space are in the tent?

3.5 ft
6 ft
4.5 ft

18. What's the Error? A student said the volume of a cylinder with a 3-inch diameter is two times the volume of a cylinder with the same height and a 1.5-inch radius. What is the error?

19. Write About It Explain the similarities and differences between finding the volume of a cylinder and finding the volume of a triangular prism.

20. Challenge Find the volume, to the nearest tenth, of the material that makes up the pipe shown. Use 3.14 for π.

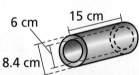

6 cm   15 cm
8.4 cm

CRCT PREP • GPS SUPPORT • SPIRAL REVIEW

21. Multiple Choice What is the volume of a triangular prism that is 10 in. long, 7 in. wide, and 4 in. high?

   (A) 110 in^2 (B) 140 in^2 (C) 205 in^2 (D) 280 in^2

22. Multiple Choice Which figures have the same volume?

  I

3 in.
8 in.
3 in.

  II

3 in.
16 in.
3 in.

  III

7 in.   4 in.

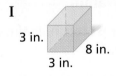 

   (F) I and II   (G) I and III   (H) II and III   (J) I, II, and III

Find the simple interest. (Lesson 6-7)

23. $P = \$3,600$; $r = 5\%$; $t = 1.5$ years

24. $P = \$10,000$; $r = 3.2\%$; $t = 2$ years

25. Students collected data on the number of visitors to an amusement park over a period of 30 days. Choose the type of graph that would best represent the data. (Lesson 7-7)

10-3 Volume of Pyramids and Cones

Learn to find the volume of pyramids and cones.

Georgia Performance Standards

M7A1.b Simplify and evaluate algebraic expressions using commutative, associative, and distributive properties as appropriate. Also, M7P1.b, M7P5.c.

Suppose you have a square-pyramid-shaped container and a square-prism-shaped container, and the bases and heights are the same size. If you pour sand from the pyramid into the prism, it appears that the prism holds three times as much sand as the pyramid.

In fact, the volume of a pyramid is exactly one-third the volume of a prism if they have the same height and same-size base.

The height of a pyramid is the perpendicular distance from the pyramid's base to its vertex.

VOLUME OF A RECTANGULAR PYRAMID

The volume V of a rectangular pyramid is one-third the area of its base B times its height h.

$$V = \frac{1}{3}Bh \quad \text{or} \quad V = \frac{1}{3}\ell wh, \text{ where } B = \ell w$$

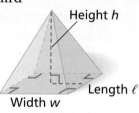

Height h

Length ℓ

Width w

E X A M P L E **1** **Finding the Volume of a Rectangular Pyramid**

Find the volume of the pyramid to the nearest tenth. Estimate to check whether the answer is reasonable.

14 ft

4 ft   8 ft

$V = \frac{1}{3}Bh$ — *Use the formula.*

The base is a rectangle, so $B = 4 \cdot 8 = 32$.

$V = \frac{1}{3} \cdot 32 \cdot 14$ — *Substitute for B and h.*

$V \approx 149.3 \text{ ft}^3$ — *Multiply.*

Estimate $V \approx \frac{1}{3} \cdot 30 \cdot 15$ — *Round the measurements.*

$= 150 \text{ ft}^3$ — *The answer is reasonable.*

Similar to the relationship between volumes of prisms and pyramids, the volume of a cone is one-third the volume of a cylinder with the same height and a congruent base.

The height of a cone is the perpendicular distance from the cone's base to its vertex.

VOLUME OF A CONE

The volume V of a cone is one-third the area of its base B times its height h.

$V = \frac{1}{3}Bh$ or $V = \frac{1}{3}\pi r^2 h$, where $B = \pi r^2$

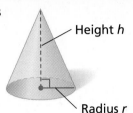

Height h

Radius r

EXAMPLE 2 Finding the Volume of a Cone

Find the volume of each cone to the nearest tenth. Use 3.14 for π. Estimate to check whether the answer is reasonable.

Helpful Hint

To estimate the volume of a cone, round π to 3 so that $\frac{1}{3} \cdot \pi$ becomes $\frac{1}{3} \cdot 3$, which is 1.

A

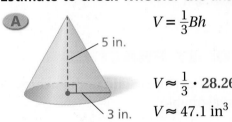

5 in.

3 in.

$V = \frac{1}{3}Bh$ *Use the formula.*

   The base is a circle, so
$B = \pi \cdot r^2 \approx 3.14 \cdot 3^2 \approx \mathbf{28.26}$.

$V \approx \frac{1}{3} \cdot 28.26 \cdot 5$ *Substitute for B and h.*

$V \approx 47.1 \text{ in}^3$ *Multiply.*

Estimate $V = \left(\frac{1}{3} \cdot \pi\right) 3^2 \cdot 5$ $\frac{1}{3} \cdot \pi \approx 1$

     $\approx 45 \text{ in}^3$ *The answer is reasonable.*

B

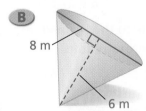

8 m

6 m

$V = \frac{1}{3}Bh$ *Use the formula.*

   The base is a circle, so
$B = \pi \cdot r^2 \approx 3.14 \cdot \left(\frac{8}{2}\right)^2 \approx \mathbf{50.24}$.

$V \approx \frac{1}{3} \cdot 50.24 \cdot 6$ *Substitute for B and h.*

$V \approx 100.5 \text{ m}^3$ *Multiply.*

Estimate $V = \left(\frac{1}{3} \cdot \pi\right) 4^2 \cdot 6$ $\frac{1}{3} \cdot \pi \approx 1$

     $\approx 96 \text{ m}^3$ *The answer is reasonable.*

Think and Discuss      GPS M7P3.a, M7P3.b

1. **Explain** how to find the volume of a cone given the diameter of the base and the height of the cone.

2. **Compare and contrast** the formulas for volume of a pyramid and volume of a cone. How are they alike? How are they different?

Georgia Performance
Standards
M7P2.d, M7P3.a, M7P4.c

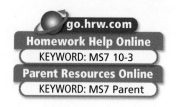

go.hrw.com
Homework Help Online
KEYWORD: MS7 10-3
Parent Resources Online
KEYWORD: MS7 Parent

GUIDED PRACTICE

See Example ① Find the volume of each pyramid to the nearest tenth. Estimate to check whether the answer is reasonable.

1.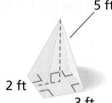
5 ft
2 ft
3 ft

2.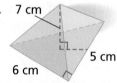
7 cm
5 cm
6 cm

3.
6 m
4 m
4 m

See Example ② Find the volume of each cone to the nearest tenth. Use 3.14 for π. Estimate to check whether the answer is reasonable.

4.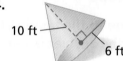
10 ft
6 ft

5.
4 in.
2 in.

6.
5 m
9 m

INDEPENDENT PRACTICE

See Example ① Find the volume of each pyramid to the nearest tenth. Estimate to check whether the answer is reasonable.

7.
8 in.
6 in.
11 in.

8.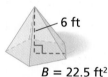
6 ft
B = 22.5 ft²

9.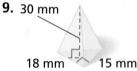
30 mm
18 mm   15 mm

See Example ② Find the volume of each cone to the nearest tenth. Use 3.14 for π. Estimate to check whether the answer is reasonable.

10.
5 in.   3 in.

11.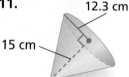
12.3 cm
15 cm

12.
12 m
25 m

PRACTICE AND PROBLEM SOLVING

CRCT ● GPS

Extra Practice p. 746

Find the volume of each figure to the nearest tenth. Use 3.14 for π.

13. a 7 ft tall rectangular pyramid with base 4 ft by 5 ft

14. a cone with radius 8 yd and height 12 yd

15. Multi-Step Find the volume of an 8 in. tall right triangular pyramid with a base hypotenuse of 5 in. and base leg of 3 in.

16. Architecture The steeple on a building is a square pyramid with a base area of 12 square feet and a height of 15 feet. How many cubic feet of concrete was used to make the steeple?

17. Multi-Step A snack bar sells popcorn in the containers shown at right.

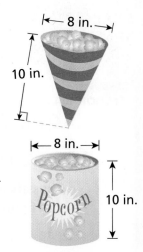

    a. Based on the formulas for volume of a cylinder and a cone, how many times as much popcorn does the larger container hold?

    b. How many cubic inches of popcorn, to the nearest tenth, does the cone-shaped container hold? Use 3.14 for π.

    c. How many cubic inches of popcorn does the cylinder-shaped container hold? Use 3.14 for π.

    d. Do your answers to parts **b** and **c** confirm your answer to part **a**? If not, find the error.

18. Critical Thinking Write a proportion of volumes for the given figures.

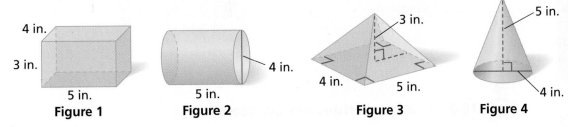

| Figure 1 | Figure 2 | Figure 3 | Figure 4 |

 19. What's the Question? The answer is: The volume of figure A is $\frac{1}{3}$ the volume of figure B. What's the question?

20. Write About It Compare finding the volume of a cylinder with finding the volume of a cone that has the same height and base.

21. Challenge What effect does doubling the radius of a cone's base have on the cone's volume?

CRCT PREP • GPS SUPPORT • SPIRAL REVIEW

22. Multiple Choice Which is the best estimate for the volume of a cone with a radius of 5 cm and a height of 8 cm?

    Ⓐ 40 cm³   Ⓑ 80 cm³   Ⓒ 200 cm³   Ⓓ 800 cm³

23. Short Response A rectangular prism and a square pyramid both have a square base with side lengths of 5 inches and heights of 7 inches. Find the volume of each figure. Then explain the relationship between the volume of the prism and the volume of the pyramid.

Name the types of quadrilaterals that have each property. (Lesson 8-7)

24. four congruent sides

25. two sets of parallel sides

Find the volume of each figure to the nearest tenth. Use 3.14 for π. (Lesson 10-2)

26. cylinder: $d = 6$ m, $h = 8$ m

27. triangular prism: $B = 22$ ft², $h = 5$ ft

READY TO GO ON?

Quiz for Lessons 10-1 Through 10-3

✓ **10-1** **Introduction to Three-Dimensional Figures**

Classify each figure as a polyhedron or not a polyhedron. Then name the figure.

1.

2.

3.

✓ **10-2** **Volume of Prisms and Cylinders**

Find how many cubes each prism holds. Then give the prism's volume.

4.
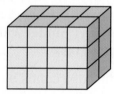

5.
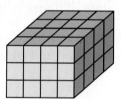

6. A box is shaped like a rectangular prism. It is 6 ft long, 2 ft wide, and 3 ft high. Find its volume.

7. A can is shaped like a cylinder. It is 5.2 cm wide and 2.3 cm tall. Find its volume to the nearest tenth. Use 3.14 for π.

✓ **10-3** **Volume of Pyramids and Cones**

Find the volume of each figure to the nearest tenth. Use 3.14 for π.

8.
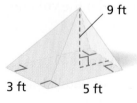
9 ft
3 ft   5 ft

9.
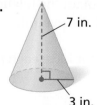
7 in.
3 in.

10.
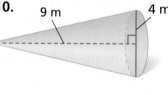
9 m   4 m

11. A cone has a radius of 2.5 cm and a height of 14 cm. What is the volume of the cone to the nearest hundredth? Use 3.14 for π.

Focus on Problem Solving

 Solve

• **Choose an operation**

When choosing an operation to use when solving a problem, you need to decide which action the problem is asking you to take. If you are asked to combine numbers, then you need to add. If you are asked to take away numbers or to find the difference between two numbers, then you need to subtract. You need to use multiplication when you put equal parts together and division when you separate something into equal parts.

 Determine the action in each problem. Then tell which operation should be used to solve the problem. Explain your choice.

1 Jeremy filled a sugar cone completely full of frozen yogurt and then put one scoop of frozen yogurt on top. The volume of Jeremy's cone is about 20.93 in³, and the volume of the scoop that Jeremy used is about 16.75 in³. About how much frozen yogurt, in cubic inches, did Jeremy use?

2 The volume of a cylinder equals the combined volumes of three cones that each have the same height and base size as the cylinder. What is the volume of a cylinder if a cone of the same height and base size has a volume of 45.2 cm³?

3 The biology class at Jefferson High School takes care of a family of turtles that is kept in a glass tank with water, rocks, and plants. The volume of the tank is 2.75 cubic feet. At the end of the year, the baby turtles will have grown and will be moved into a tank that is 6.15 cubic feet. How much greater will the volume of the new tank be than that of the old tank?

4 Brianna is adding a second section to her hamster cage. The two sections will be connected by a tunnel that is made of 4 cylindrical parts, all the same size. If the volume of the tunnel is 56.52 cubic inches, what is the volume of each part of the tunnel?

Hands-On
LAB 10-4

Use Nets to Build Prisms and Cylinders

Use with Lesson 10-4

go.hrw.com
Lab Resources Online
KEYWORD: MS7 Lab10

Georgia Performance Standards
M7P5.a, M7P5.b, M7P5.c

A net is a pattern of two-dimensional figures that can be folded to make a three-dimensional figure. You can use $\frac{1}{4}$-inch graph paper to help you make nets.

Activity

① Use a net to construct a rectangular prism.

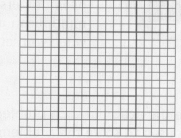

a. Draw the net at right on a piece of graph paper. Each rectangle is 10 squares by 4 squares. The two squares are 4 small squares on each side.

b. Cut out the net. Fold the net along the edges of each rectangle to make a rectangular prism. Tape the edges to hold them in place.

② Use a net to construct a cylinder.

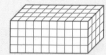

a. Draw the net at right on a piece of graph paper. The rectangle is 25 squares by 8 squares. Use a compass to make the circles. Each circle has a radius of 4 squares.

b. Cut out the net. Fold the net as shown to make a cylinder. Tape the edges to hold them in place.

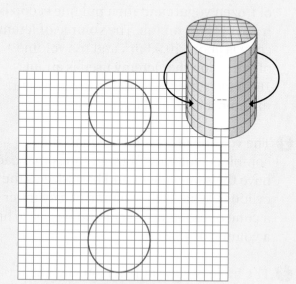

Think and Discuss

1. What are the dimensions, in inches, of the rectangular prism that you built?

2. What is the height, in inches, of the cylinder that you built? What is the cylinder's radius?

Try This

1. Use a net to construct a rectangular prism that is 1 inch by 2 inches by 3 inches.

2. Use a net to construct a cylinder with a height of 1 inch and a radius of $\frac{1}{2}$ in. (*Hint:* The length of the rectangle in the net must match the circumference of the circles, so the length should be $2\pi r = 2\pi\left(\frac{1}{2}\right) \approx 3.14$ inches.)

10-4 Surface Area of Prisms and Cylinders

Learn to find the surface area of prisms and cylinders.

Vocabulary

net

surface area

🍎 **Georgia Performance Standards**

M7A1.b Simplify and evaluate algebraic expressions using commutative, associative, and distributive properties as appropriate. Also, M7P1.c, M7P1.d, M7P5.b, M7P5.c.

If you remove the surface from a three-dimensional figure and lay it out flat, the pattern you make is called a **net** .

Nets allow you to see all the surfaces of a solid at one time. You can use nets to help you find the *surface area* of a three-dimensional figure. **Surface area** is the sum of the areas of all of the surfaces of a figure.

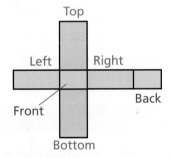

You can use nets to write formulas for the surface area of prisms. The surface area S of a prism is the sum of the areas of the faces of the prism. For the rectangular prism shown:

$$S = \ell w + \ell h + wh + \ell w + \ell h + wh = 2\ell w + 2\ell h + 2wh$$

SURFACE AREA OF A RECTANGULAR PRISM

The surface area of a rectangular prism is the sum of the areas of each face.

$$S = 2\ell w + 2\ell h + 2wh$$

EXAMPLE 1 Finding the Surface Area of a Prism

Find the surface area of the prism formed by the net.

$S = 2\ell w + 2\ell h + 2wh$

$S = (2 \cdot 12 \cdot 8) + (2 \cdot 12 \cdot 6) + (2 \cdot 8 \cdot 6)$ *Substitute.*

$S = 192 + 144 + 96$ *Multiply.*

$S = 432$ *Add.*

The surface area of the prism is 432 in^2.

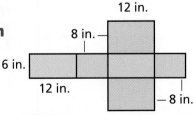

If you could remove the curved surface from a cylinder, like peeling a label from a can, you would see that it has the shape of a rectangle when flattened out.

You can draw a net for a cylinder by drawing the circular bases (like the ends of a can) and the rectangular curved surface as shown below. The length of the rectangle is the circumference, $2\pi r$, of the base of the cylinder. So the area of the curved surface is $2\pi r \cdot h$. The area of each base is πr^2.

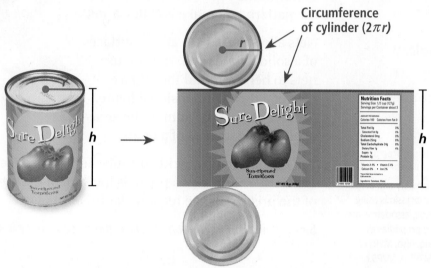

Surface area = area of top + area of bottom + area of curved surface
$$= \pi r^2 + \pi r^2 + (2\pi r)h$$
$$= 2\pi r^2 + 2\pi rh$$

SURFACE AREA OF A CYLINDER

The surface area S of a cylinder is the sum of the areas of its bases, $2\pi r^2$, plus the area of its curved surface, $2\pi rh$.

$$S = 2\pi r^2 + 2\pi rh$$

EXAMPLE 2   **Finding the Surface Area of a Cylinder**

Find the surface area of the cylinder formed by the net to the nearest tenth. Use 3.14 for π.

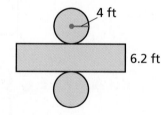

$S = 2\pi r^2 + 2\pi rh$ *Use the formula.*
$S \approx (2 \cdot 3.14 \cdot 4^2) + (2 \cdot 3.14 \cdot 4 \cdot 6.2)$ *Substitute.*
$S \approx 100.48 + 155.744$ *Multiply.*
$S \approx 256.224$ *Add.*
$S \approx 256.2$ *Round.*

The surface area of the cylinder is about 256.2 ft^2.

EXAMPLE 3 **PROBLEM SOLVING APPLICATION**

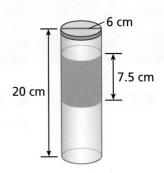

What percent of the total surface area of the tennis ball can is covered by the label? Use 3.14 for π.

1 Understand the Problem

List the **important information:**

- The can is approximately cylinder-shaped.
- The height of the can is 20 cm.
- The diameter of the can is 6 cm.
- The height of the label is 7.5 cm.

2 Make a Plan

Find the surface area of the can and the area of the label. Divide to find the percent of the surface area covered by the label.

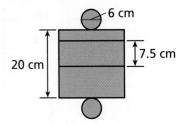

3 Solve

$$S = 2\pi r^2 + 2\pi rh$$
$$\approx 2(3.14)(3)^2 + 2(3.14)(3)(20) \qquad \textit{Substitute for r and h.}$$
$$\approx 433.32 \text{ cm}^2$$

$$A = \ell w$$
$$= (2\pi r)w \qquad \qquad \textit{Substitute } 2\pi r \textit{ for } \ell.$$
$$\approx 2(3.14)(3)(7.5) \qquad \textit{Substitute for r and w.}$$
$$\approx 141.3 \text{ cm}^2$$

Percent of the surface area covered by the label: $\frac{141.3 \text{ cm}^2}{433.32 \text{ cm}^2} \approx 32.6\%$.

About 32.6% of the can's surface area is covered by the label.

4 Look Back

Estimate and compare the areas of the two rectangles in the net.

Label: $2(3)(3)(8) = 144 \text{ cm}^2$ $\frac{144 \text{ cm}^2}{360 \text{ cm}^2} = 40\%$
Can: $2(3)(3)(20) = 360 \text{ cm}^2$

The answer should be less than 40% because you did not consider the area of the two circles. So 32.6% is reasonable.

Think and Discuss  GPS M7P3.a, M7P3.b

1. **Explain** how you would find the surface area of an open-top box that is shaped like a rectangular prism.

2. **Describe** the shapes in a net used to cover a cylinder.

Georgia Performance Standards

M7P1.c, M7P3.a, M7P4.c, M7P5.b

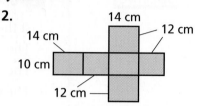

go.hrw.com
Homework Help Online
KEYWORD: MS7 10-4
Parent Resources Online
KEYWORD: MS7 Parent

GUIDED PRACTICE

See Example 1 Find the surface area of the prism formed by each net.

1.

9 ft, 5 ft, 9 ft, 7 ft, 5 ft

2.

14 cm, 14 cm, 12 cm, 10 cm, 12 cm

See Example 2 Find the surface area of the cylinder formed by each net to the nearest tenth. Use 3.14 for π.

3.

3 m, 10 m

4.

5 in., 15 in.

See Example 3 **5.** A travel mug is cylindrical, and its $2\frac{1}{2}$ in. width fits into most drink holders. What percent of the total surface area of the mug is covered by the 2 in. wide grip? Use 3.14 for π.

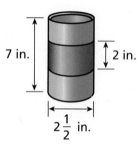

7 in., 2 in., $2\frac{1}{2}$ in.

INDEPENDENT PRACTICE

See Example 1 Find the surface area of the prism formed by each net.

6.

16 in., 20 in., 4 in., 20 in., 4 in.

7.

15 ft, 20 ft, 8 ft, 20 ft, 15 ft, 20 ft

See Example 2 Find the surface area of the cylinder formed by each net to the nearest tenth. Use 3.14 for π.

8.

6 in., 15 in.

9.

1.5 cm, 18.5 cm

See Example 3 **10.** A stack of DVDs sits on a base and is covered by an 11 cm tall cylindrical lid. What percent of the surface area of the lid is covered by the label? Use 3.14 for π. (*Hint:* The lid has no bottom.)

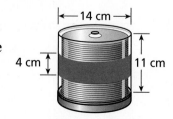

14 cm, 4 cm, 11 cm

PRACTICE AND PROBLEM SOLVING

11. A cannery packs tuna into metal cans like the one shown. Round your answers to the nearest tenth, if necessary. Use 3.14 for π.

|←— 6.8 cm —→|

4.0 cm

a. Draw and label a net for the cylinder.

b. About how many square centimeters of metal are used to make each can?

c. The label for each can goes all the way around the can. About how many square centimeters of paper are needed for each label?

12. The table shows the dimensions of two rectangular prism boxes with equal volumes. Which box requires more material to wrap? Explain.

	Length	Width	Depth
Box 1	20 in.	5 in.	3 in.
Box 2	10 in.	6 in.	5 in.

 13. **Choose a Strategy** A Rubik's Cube® appears to be built of 27 smaller cubes. Only the outside faces are colored. How many of the "cubes" on a Rubik's Cube have exactly 2 colored faces?

 14. **Write About It** Explain how you would find the side lengths of a cube with a surface area of 512 ft^2.

15. **Challenge** Find the surface area of the rectangular prism shown with a rectangular-prism-shaped hole all the way through it.

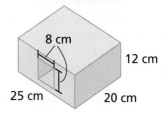

8 cm

12 cm

25 cm   20 cm

CRCT PREP • GPS SUPPORT • SPIRAL REVIEW

16. **Multiple Choice** Find the surface area of the prism formed by the net.

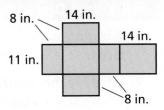

8 in.   14 in.

14 in.

11 in.

8 in.

Ⓐ 286 in^3

Ⓒ 708 in^3

Ⓑ 310 in^3

Ⓓ 1,232 in^3

17. **Gridded Response** Find the number of square centimeters in the surface area of a cylinder with a 5 cm radius and a 15 cm height. Use 3.14 for π.

Find the measure of the third angle in each triangle, given two angle measures. (Lesson 8-8)

18. 83°, 28°

19. 65°, 36°

20. 22°, 102°

Find the volume of each figure to the nearest tenth.

21. a 4 in. tall rectangular prism with base 7 in. by 8 in. (Lesson 10-2)

22. a 9 cm tall square pyramid with base 6 cm by 6 cm (Lesson 10-3)

Hands-On
LAB 10-5

Investigate the Surface Areas of Similar Prisms

Use with Lesson 10-5

go.hrw.com
Lab Resources Online
KEYWORD: MS7 Lab10

Georgia Performance Standards

M7G3.a, M7G3.b, M7P5.a, M7P5.b

Recall that the surface area of a three-dimensional figure is the sum of the areas of all of its surfaces. You can use centimeter cubes to explore the surface areas of prisms.

Activity 1

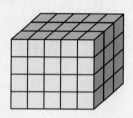

① Use centimeter cubes to build the rectangular prism shown here.

② You can find the surface area of the prism by first finding the areas of its front face, top face, and side face. Look at the prism from each of these views. Count the exposed cube faces to find the area of each face of the prism. Record the areas in the table.

  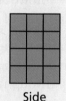

Front   Top   Side

	Front Face	Top Face	Side Face
Area			

③ Find the surface area of the prism as follows:
surface area = 2 · (area of front face) + 2 · (area of top face) + 2 · (area of side face)

Think and Discuss

1. Why do you multiply the areas of the front face, top face, and side face by 2 to find the surface area of the prism?

2. What are the length, width, and height of the prism in centimeters? What surface area do you get when you use the formula $S = 2\ell w + 2\ell h + 2wh$?

Try This

Use centimeter cubes to build each prism. Then find its surface area.

1.

2.

3.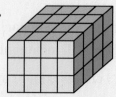

Activity 2

1 Use centimeter cubes to build rectangular prism *A* as shown.

Prism *A*

2 Now use centimeter cubes to build a prism *B* that is similar to prism *A* by a scale factor of 2. Each dimension of the new prism should be 2 times the corresponding dimension of prism *A*.

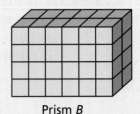

Prism *B*

3 Use the method from Activity 1 to find the areas of the front face, top face, and side face of each prism. Record the areas in the table.

	Area of Front Face	Area of Top Face	Area of Side Face
Prism *A*	▪	▪	▪
Prism *B*	▪	▪	▪

4 Find the surface area of prism *A* and the surface area of prism *B*.

5 Repeat the above process, this time building a prism *C* that is larger than prism *A* by a scale factor of 3. Add a row to your table for prism *C*, and find the areas of the front face, top face, and side face of prism *C*.

Think and Discuss

1. In **4**, how does the surface area of prism *B* compare with the surface area of prism *A*? How is this related to the scale factor?

2. In **5**, how does the surface area of prism *C* compare with the surface area of prism *A*? How is this related to the scale factor?

3. Suppose three-dimensional figure *Y* is similar to three-dimensional figure *X* by a scale factor of *k*. How are the surface areas related?

Try This

1. Find the surface area of prism *R*.

2. Prism *S* is larger than prism *R* by a scale factor of 4. Use what you discovered to find the surface area of prism *S*.

Prism *R*

Learn to find the volume and surface area of similar three-dimensional figures.

Recall that similar figures have proportional side lengths. The surface areas of similar three-dimensional figures are also proportional. To see this relationship, you can compare the areas of corresponding faces of similar rectangular prisms.

Georgia Performance Standards

M7G3.b Understand the relationships between similar figures. Also, M7G3.a, M7P1.b, M7P1.c, M7P1.d.

Remember!

A scale factor is a number that every dimension of a figure is multiplied by to make a similar figure.

Area of front of smaller prism

$\ell \cdot w$
$3 \cdot 5$
15

Area of front of larger prism

$\ell \cdot w$
$6 \cdot 10$
$(3 \cdot 2) \cdot (5 \cdot 2)$ ← Each dimension is
$(3 \cdot 5) \cdot (2 \cdot 2)$ multiplied by a scale
$15 \cdot 2^2$ factor of 2.

The area of the front face of the larger prism is 2^2 times the area of the front face of the smaller prism. This is true for the entire surface area of the prisms.

SURFACE AREA OF SIMILAR FIGURES

If three-dimensional figure B is similar to figure A by a scale factor, then the surface area of B is equal to the surface area of A times the square of the scale factor.

$$\begin{array}{c} \text{surface area of} \\ \text{figure } B \end{array} = \begin{array}{c} \text{surface area of} \\ \text{figure } A \end{array} \cdot (\text{scale factor})^2$$

EXAMPLE 1 **Finding the Surface Area of a Similar Figure**

A The surface area of a box is 27 in². What is the surface area of a similar box that is larger by a scale factor of 5?

$S = 27 \cdot 5^2$ *Multiply by the square of the scale factor.*
$S = 27 \cdot 25$ *Evaluate the power.*
$S = 675 \text{ in}^2$ *Multiply.*

B The surface area of the Great Pyramid was originally 1,160,280 ft². What is the surface area, to the nearest tenth, of a model of the pyramid that is smaller by a scale factor of $\frac{1}{500}$?

$S = 1,160,280 \cdot \left(\frac{1}{500}\right)^2$ *Multiply by the square of the scale factor.*

$S = 1,160,280 \cdot \frac{1}{250,000}$ *Evaluate the power.*

$S = 4.64112$ *Multiply.*

$S \approx 4.6 \text{ ft}^2$

The volumes of similar three-dimensional figures are also related.

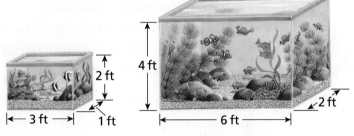

Volume of smaller tank	Volume of larger tank
$\ell \cdot w \cdot h$	$\ell \cdot w \cdot h$
$2 \cdot 3 \cdot 1$	$4 \cdot 6 \cdot 2$
6	$(2 \cdot 2) \cdot (3 \cdot 2) \cdot (1 \cdot 2)$
	$(2 \cdot 3 \cdot 1) \cdot (2 \cdot 2 \cdot 2)$
	$6 \cdot 2^3$

Each dimension has a scale factor of 2.

Remember!

$2 \cdot 2 \cdot 2 = 2^3$

The volume of the larger tank is 2^3 times the volume of the smaller tank.

VOLUME OF SIMILAR FIGURES

If three-dimensional figure *B* is similar to figure *A* by a scale factor, then the volume of *B* is equal to the volume of *A* times the cube of the scale factor.

volume of figure *B* = volume of figure *A* · (scale factor)³

EXAMPLE 2 **Finding Volume Using Similar Figures**

The volume of a bucket is 231 in³. What is the volume of a similar bucket that is larger by a scale factor of 3?

$V = 231 \cdot 3^3$ *Multiply by the cube of the scale factor.*

$V = 231 \cdot 27$ *Evaluate the power.*

$V = 6,237 \text{ in}^3$ *Multiply.*

Estimate $V \approx 230 \cdot 30$ *Round the measurements.*

       $= 6,900 \text{ in}^3$ *The answer is reasonable.*

EXAMPLE 3 **PROBLEM SOLVING APPLICATION**

Elise has a fish tank that measures 10 in. by 23 in. by 5 in. She builds a larger tank by doubling each dimension. There are 231 in³ in 1 gallon. Estimate how many more gallons the larger tank holds.

1 Understand the Problem

Rewrite the question as a statement.

• Compare the capacities of two similar fish tanks, and estimate how much more water the larger tank holds.

List the **important information:**

• The small tank is 10 in. × 23 in. × 5 in.

• The large tank is similar to the small tank by a scale factor of 2.

• 231 in³ = 1 gal

2 Make a Plan

You can write an equation that relates the volume of the large tank to the volume of the small tank. Volume of large tank = Volume of small tank · (scale factor)³. Then convert cubic inches to gallons to compare the capacities of the tanks.

3 Solve

Volume of small tank = 10 × 23 × 5 = **1,150** in³

Volume of large tank = **1,150** · 2³ = 9,200 in³

Convert each volume into gallons:

$1{,}150 \text{ in}^3 \times \frac{1 \text{ gal}}{231 \text{ in}^3} \approx 5 \text{ gal}$ $9{,}200 \text{ in}^3 \times \frac{1 \text{ gal}}{231 \text{ in}^3} \approx 40 \text{ gal}$

Subtract the capacities: 40 gal − 5 gal = 35 gal

The large tank holds about 35 gallons more water than the small tank.

4 Look Back

Double the dimensions of the small tank and find the volume: 20 × 46 × 10 = 9,200 in³. Subtract the volumes of the two tanks: 9,200 − 1,150 = 8,050 in³. Convert this measurement to gallons: $8{,}050 \text{ in}^3 \times \frac{1 \text{ gal}}{231 \text{ in}^3} \approx 35 \text{ gal.}$

Think and Discuss  GPS M7P1.d, M7P3.a

1. **Tell** whether a figure's surface area has increased or decreased if each dimension of the figure is changed by a factor of $\frac{1}{3}$.

2. **Explain** how the surface area of a figure is changed if the dimensions are each multiplied by a factor of 3.

3. **Explain** how the volume of a figure is changed if the dimensions are each multiplied by a factor of 2.

10-5 **Exercises**

Georgia Performance
Standards

M7P1.a, M7P4.c

go.hrw.com
Homework Help Online
KEYWORD: MS7 10-5
Parent Resources Online
KEYWORD: MS7 Parent

GUIDED PRACTICE

1. The surface area of a box is 10.4 cm². What is the surface area of a similar box that is larger by a scale factor of 3?

2. The surface area of a ship's hull is about 11,000 m². What is the surface area, to the nearest tenth, of the hull of a model ship that is smaller by a scale factor of $\frac{1}{150}$?

3. The volume of an ice chest is 2,160 in³. What is the volume of a similar ice chest that is larger by a scale factor of 2.5?

4. A fish tank measures 14 in. by 13 in. by 10 in. A similar fish tank is larger by a scale factor of 3. Estimate how many more gallons the larger tank holds.

INDEPENDENT PRACTICE

5. The surface area of a triangular prism is 13.99 in². What is the surface area of a similar prism that is larger by a scale factor of 4?

6. The surface area of a car frame is about 200 ft². What is the surface area, to the nearest tenth of a square foot, of a model of the car that is smaller by a scale factor of $\frac{1}{12}$?

7. The volume of a cylinder is about 523 cm³. What is the volume, to the nearest tenth, of a similar cylinder that is smaller by a scale factor of $\frac{1}{4}$?

8. A tank measures 27 in. by 9 in. by 12 in. A similar tank is reduced by a scale factor of $\frac{1}{3}$. Estimate how many more gallons the larger tank holds.

PRACTICE AND PROBLEM SOLVING

Extra Practice p. 747

For each figure shown, find the surface area and volume of a similar figure that is larger by a scale factor of 25. Use 3.14 for π.

9.
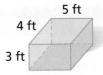
5 ft
4 ft
3 ft

10.
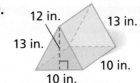
12 in.
13 in.
13 in.
10 in.
10 in.

11.

12 cm
25 cm

12. The surface area of a cylinder is 1,620 m². Its volume is about 1,130 m³. What are the surface area and volume of a similar cylinder that is smaller by a scale factor of $\frac{1}{9}$? Round to the nearest tenth, if necessary.

13. The surface area of a prism is 142 in². Its volume is about 105 in³. What are the surface area and volume of a similar prism that is larger by a scale factor of 6? Round to the nearest tenth, if necessary.

53.3 m

259.8 m

Natalie and Rebecca are making a scale model of the *Titanic* for a history class project. Their model is smaller by a scale factor of $\frac{1}{100}$. For Exercises 14–17, express your answers in both centimeters and meters. Use the conversion chart at right if needed.

METRIC CONVERSIONS	
1 m = 100 cm	1 cm = 0.01 m
1 m² = 10,000 cm²	1 cm² = 0.0001 m²
1 m³ = 1,000,000 cm³	1 cm³ = 0.000001 m³

14. The length and height of the *Titanic* are shown in the drawing above. What are the length and height of the students' scale model?

15. On the students' model, the diameter of the outer propellers is 7.16 cm. What was the diameter of these propellers on the ship?

16. The surface area of the deck of the students' model is 4,156.75 cm². What was the surface area of the deck of the ship?

17. The volume of the students' model is about 127,426 cm³. What was the volume of the ship?

These are propellers from the *Olympic*, the *Titanic*'s sister ship. They are identical to those that were on the *Titanic*.

CRCT PREP • GPS SUPPORT • SPIRAL REVIEW

18. Multiple Choice The surface area of a prism is 144 cm². A similar prism has a scale factor of $\frac{1}{4}$. What is the surface area of the similar prism?

   (A) 36 cm²   (B) 18 cm²   (C) 9 cm²   (D) 2.25 cm²

19. Gridded Response A cube has a volume of 64 in³. A similar cube has a volume of 512 in³. What is the scale factor of the larger cube?

Determine whether the ratios are proportional. (Lesson 5-4)

20. $\frac{7}{56}, \frac{35}{280}$ **21.** $\frac{12}{20}, \frac{60}{140}$ **22.** $\frac{9}{45}, \frac{45}{225}$ **23.** $\frac{5}{82}, \frac{65}{1,054}$

24. Name the polygon that has ten angles and ten sides. (Lesson 8-5)

Technology LAB 10-5

Explore Changes in Dimensions

Use after Lesson 10-5

go.hrw.com
Lab Resources Online
KEYWORD: MS7 Lab10

Georgia Performance Standards
M7P1.c, M7P2.c, M7P5.a

You can use a spreadsheet to explore how changing the dimensions of a rectangular pyramid affects the volume of the pyramid.

Activity

1 On a spreadsheet, enter the following headings:
Base Length in cell A1,
Base Width in cell B1,
Height in cell C1, and
Volume in cell D1.

In row 2, enter the numbers 15, 7, and 22, as shown.

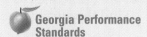

	A	B	C	D
1	Base Length	Base Width	Height	Volume
2	15	7	22	

2 Then enter the formula for the volume of a pyramid in cell D2. To do this, enter **=(1/3)*A2*B2*C2**. Press **ENTER** and notice that the volume is 770.

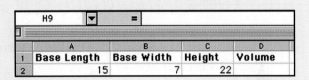

	A	B	C	D	E
1	Base Length	Base Width	Height	Volume	
2	15	7	22	=(1/3)*A2*B2*C2	

3 Enter 30 in cell A2 and 11 in cell C2 to find out what happens to the volume when you double the base length and halve the height.

	A	B	C	D
1	Base Length	Base Width	Height	Volume
2	30	7	11	770

Think and Discuss

1. Explain why doubling the base length and halving the height does not change the volume of the pyramid.

2. What other ways could you change the dimensions of the pyramid without changing its volume?

Try This

1. Use a spreadsheet to compute the volume of each cone. Use 3.14 for π.

   a. radius = 2.75 inches; height = 8.5 inches

   b. radius = 7.5 inches; height = 14.5 inches

2. What would the volumes in problem 1 be if the radii were doubled?

Quiz for Lessons 10-4 Through 10-5

✓ **10-4** Surface Area of Prisms and Cylinders

Find the surface area of the prism formed by each net.

1.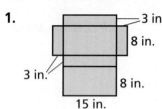

2.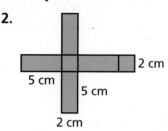

Find the surface area of the cylinder formed by each net to the nearest tenth. Use 3.14 for π.

3.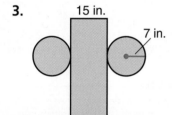

4.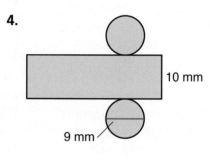

5. The diagram shows a drink can with a drink cooler covering the lower base and part of the curved surface of the can. About how much surface area, in square centimeters, of the drink can is covered by the drink cooler?

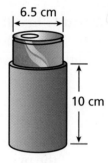

✓ **10-5** Changing Dimensions

6. The surface area of a rectangular prism is 45 ft². What is the surface area of a similar prism that is larger by a scale factor of 3?

7. The surface area of a cylinder is 109 cm². What is the surface area of a similar cylinder that is smaller by a scale factor of $\frac{1}{3}$?

8. The volume of a container is 3,785 in³. A second container is larger by a scale factor of 4. Estimate how many more gallons the larger container holds. (*Hint:* There are 231 in³ in 1 gallon.)

Ready to Go On?

MULTI-STEP TEST PREP

It's a Wrap! Kim and Miguel are raising money for their school track team by running a gift-wrapping service at the mall. Customers can also have their gifts boxed for shipping. Kim and Miguel have rolls of gift wrap, shipping boxes, cardboard, and packing peanuts.

1. A customer wants to wrap and ship a gift that is in the shape of a rectangular prism. The dimensions of the gift are 10 in. by 15 in. by 4 in. How many square inches of wrapping paper are needed to wrap the gift?

2. Kim chooses a shipping box that is 18 in. by 12 in. by 6 in. After the gift is placed inside the box, she will fill the empty space with packing peanuts. How many cubic inches of packing peanuts will Kim need? Explain.

3. Another customer wants to ship a large cone-shaped art piece made out of recycled glass. The figure shows the dimensions of the conic art. Miguel decides to use poster board to make a cylindrical container that is just large enough to hold the art. How much poster board will he need?

4. Once the conic art is placed in the cylindrical container, how many cubic inches of packing peanuts will be needed to fill the empty space?

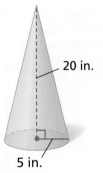

20 in.

5 in.

611

Cross Sections

 Learn to sketch and describe cross sections of three-dimensional figures.

Vocabulary

cross section

When a three-dimensional figure and a plane intersect, the intersection is called a **cross section**. A three-dimensional figure can have many different cross sections. For example, when you cut an orange in half, the cross section that is exposed depends on the direction of the cut.

EXAMPLE 1 Identifying Cross Sections

Identify the cross section that best matches the given figure.

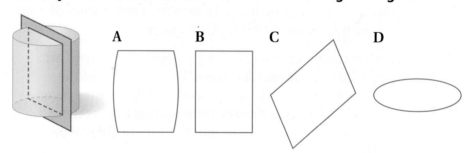

 **Georgia Performance Standards**

M7G4.a Describe three-dimensional figures formed by translations and rotations of plane figures through space. Also, M7G4.b, M7P5.a, M7P5.c.

The bases of the cylinder are parallel, so the cross section must contain a pair of parallel lines. The bases of the cylinder meet the lateral surface at right angles, so the cross section must contain right angles. The best choice is **B**.

EXAMPLE 2 Sketching and Describing Cross Sections

Sketch and describe the cross section of a cone that is cut parallel to its base.

The base of a cone is a circle. Any cross section made by cutting the cone parallel to the base will also be a circle.

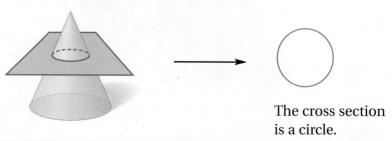

The cross section is a circle.

You can form three-dimensional figures by translating or rotating a cross section through space.

EXAMPLE 3 **Describing Three-Dimensional Figures Formed by Transformations**

Describe the three-dimensional figure formed by rotating an isosceles triangle around its line of symmetry.

Draw an isosceles triangle and its line of symmetry. Visualize rotating the triangle through space around the line. The resulting three-dimensional figure is a cone.

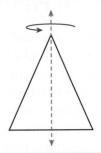 

EXTENSION

Exercises

1. Identify the cross section that best matches the given figure.

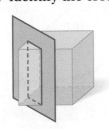   Ⓐ   Ⓑ   Ⓒ   Ⓓ

Sketch and describe each cross section.

2. a cylinder that is cut parallel to its bases

3. a cube that is cut parallel to one of its faces

Describe the three-dimensional figure formed by each transformation.

4. a rectangle that is rotated around a line of symmetry

5. a circle that is translated perpendicularly to the plane in which it lies (*Hint:* Imagine lifting a circle that is lying on a table straight upward.)

6. A sculptor has a block of clay in the shape of a rectangular prism. She uses a piece of wire to cut the clay, and the resulting cross section is a square. Make a sketch showing the prism and how the sculptor may have cut the clay.

Game Time

Blooming Minds

Students in the Agriculture Club at Carter Middle School are designing a flower bed for the front of the school. The flower bed will be in the shape of the letter *C*. After considering the two designs shown below, the students decided to build the flower bed that required the least amount of peat moss. Which design did the students choose? (*Hint:* Find the volume of each flower bed.)

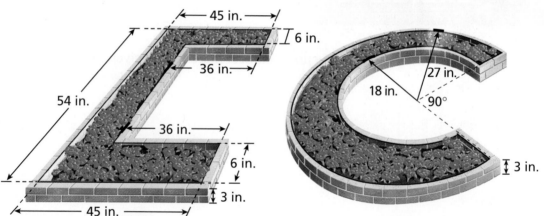

Magic Cubes

Four magic cubes are used in this fun puzzle. A complete set of rules and nets for making the cubes can be found online. Each side of the four cubes has the number 1, 2, 3, or 4 written on it. The object of the game is to stack the cubes so that the numbers along each side of the stack add up to 10. No number can be repeated along any side of the stack.

go.hrw.com
Game Time Extra
KEYWORD: MS7 Games

Materials
- 5 CD envelopes
- hole punch
- chenille stem
- 5 sheets of white paper
- CD
- scissors
- markers

It's in the Bag!

PROJECT **CD 3-D**

Make a set of circular booklets that you can store in CD envelopes.

1 Stack the CD envelopes so that the flap of each envelope is in the back, along the right-hand edge. Punch a hole through the stack in the upper left-hand corner. **Figure A**

2 Insert a chenille stem through the holes, twist to make a loop, and trim the ends. **Figure B**

3 Fold a sheet of white $8\frac{1}{2}$-by-11-inch paper in half to make a sheet that is $8\frac{1}{2}$ inches by $5\frac{1}{2}$ inches. Place the CD on the folded sheet so that it touches the folded edge, and trace around it. **Figure C**

4 Cut out the circular shape that you traced, making sure that the two halves remain hinged together. **Figure D**

5 Repeat the process with the remaining sheets of paper to make a total of five booklets.

Taking Note of the Math

Use each booklet to takes notes on one lesson of the chapter. Be sure to record essential vocabulary, formulas, and sample problems.

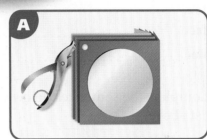

A

B

C

D

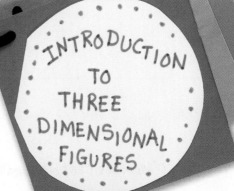

INTRODUCTION TO THREE DIMENSIONAL FIGURES

Vocabulary

Complete the sentences below with vocabulary words from the list above.

1. A(n) ____?____ has two parallel, congruent circular bases connected by a curved surface.

2. The sum of the areas of the surfaces of a three-dimensional figure is called the ____?____.

3. A(n) ____?____ is a three-dimensional figure whose faces are all polygons.

4. A(n) ____?____ has one circular base and a curved surface.

10-1 Introduction to Three-Dimensional Figures (pp. 580–583)

EXAMPLE

EXERCISES

 GPS M7P3.d

■ Name the figure.

There are two bases that are hexagons.

The figure is a hexagonal prism.

Name each figure.

5.

6.

7.

8.

10-2 Volume of Prisms and Cylinders (pp. 586–589)

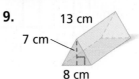
GPS M7A1.b

EXAMPLE

■ Find the volume of the prism.

$V = Bh$
$V = (15 \cdot 4) \cdot 9$
$V = 540$
The volume of the prism is 540 ft³.

4 ft
9 ft
15 ft

■ Find the volume of the cylinder to the nearest tenth. Use 3.14 for π.

$V = \pi r^2 h$
$V \approx 3.14 \cdot 3^2 \cdot 4$
$V \approx 113.04$
The volume is about 113.0 cm³.

3 cm
4 cm

EXERCISES

Find the volume of each prism.

9.
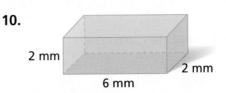
13 cm
7 cm
8 cm

10.
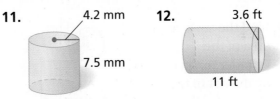
2 mm
2 mm
6 mm

Find the volume of each cylinder to the nearest tenth. Use 3.14 for π.

11.
4.2 mm
7.5 mm

12.
3.6 ft
11 ft

10-3 Volume of Pyramids and Cones (pp. 590–593)

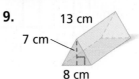
GPS M7A1.b

EXAMPLE

■ Find the volume of the pyramid.

$V = \frac{1}{3} Bh$
$V = \frac{1}{3} \cdot (5 \cdot 6) \cdot 7$
$V = 70$
The volume is 70 m³.

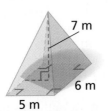
7 m
6 m
5 m

■ Find the volume of the cone to the nearest tenth. Use 3.14 for π.

$V = \frac{1}{3} \pi r^2 h$
$V \approx \frac{1}{3} \cdot 3.14 \cdot 4^2 \cdot 9$
$V \approx 150.72$
The volume is about 150.7 ft³.

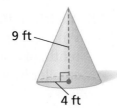
9 ft
4 ft

EXERCISES

Find the volume of the pyramid.

13.
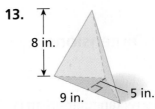
8 in.
9 in.
5 in.

Find the volume of the cone to the nearest tenth. Use 3.14 for π.

14.
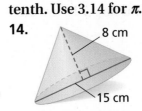
8 cm
15 cm

Study Guide: Review

10-4 Surface Area of Prisms and Cylinders (pp. 597–601)

GPS M7A1.b

EXAMPLE

■ Find the surface area of the rectangular prism formed by the net.

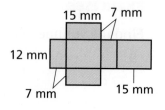

$S = 2\ell w + 2\ell h + 2wh$

$S = (2 \cdot 15 \cdot 7) + (2 \cdot 15 \cdot 12) + (2 \cdot 7 \cdot 12)$

$S = 738$

The surface area is 738 mm².

■ Find the surface area of the cylinder formed by the net to the nearest tenth. Use 3.14 for π.

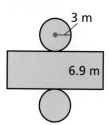

$S = 2\pi r^2 + 2\pi rh$

$S \approx (2 \cdot 3.14 \cdot 3^2) + (2 \cdot 3.14 \cdot 3 \cdot 6.9)$

$S \approx 186.516$

The surface area is about 186.5 m².

EXERCISES

Find the surface area of the rectangular prism formed by each net.

15.

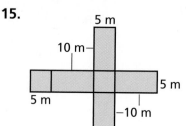

16.

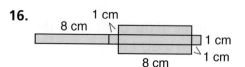

Find the surface area of the cylinder formed by the net to the nearest tenth. Use 3.14 for π.

17.

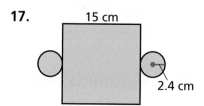

10-5 Changing Dimensions (pp. 604–608)

GPS M7G3.a, M7G3.b

EXAMPLE

■ The surface area of a rectangular prism is 32 m², and its volume is 12 m³. What are the surface area and volume of a similar rectangular prism that is larger by a scale factor of 6?

$S = 32 \cdot 6^2$

$\quad = 1,152$

$V = 12 \cdot 6^3$

$\quad = 2,592$

The surface area of the larger prism is 1,152 m². Its volume is 2,592 m³.

EXERCISES

18. A cylinder has a surface area of 13.2 in². What is the surface area of a similar cylinder that is larger by a scale factor of 15?

19. A refrigerator has a volume of 14 ft³. What is the volume, to the nearest tenth, of a similar refrigerator that is smaller by a scale factor of $\frac{2}{3}$?

Study Guide: Review

Classify each figure as a polyhedron or not a polyhedron. Then name the figure.

1.

2.

3.

4.

5.

6.

Find the volume of each figure to the nearest tenth. Use 3.14 for π.

7.

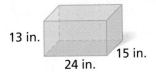

13 in.
15 in.
24 in.

8.

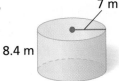

7 m
8.4 m

9.

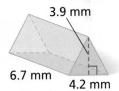

3.9 mm
6.7 mm
4.2 mm

10.

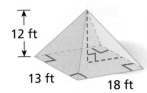

12 ft
13 ft
18 ft

11.

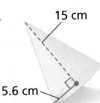

15 cm
5.6 cm

12.

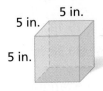

5 in.
5 in.
5 in.

Find the surface area of each figure to the nearest tenth. Use 3.14 for π.

13.

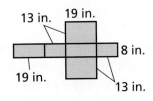

13 in.   19 in.
8 in.
19 in.
13 in.

14.

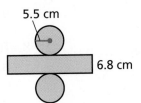

5.5 cm
6.8 cm

15.

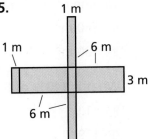

1 m
1 m
6 m
3 m
6 m

16. The surface area of a rectangular prism is 52 ft^2. What is the surface area of a similar prism that is larger by a scale factor of 7?

17. The volume of a cube is 35 mm^3. What is the volume of a similar cube that is larger by a scale factor of 9?

18. The volume of a flowerpot is 7.5 cm^3. What is the volume, to the nearest hundredth, of a similar flowerpot that is smaller by a scale factor of $\frac{1}{2}$?

Cumulative Assessment, Chapters 1–10

Multiple Choice

1. What value represents the median of the data set?

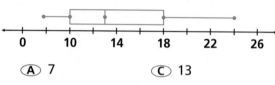

    (A) 7   (C) 13

    (B) 10   (D) 18

2. How much less is the area of the triangle than the area of the rectangle?

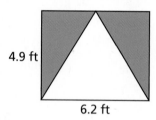

    (F) 15.19 ft²   (H) 9.61 ft²

    (G) 30.38 ft²   (J) Not here

3. A rectangular tank has a height of 9 meters, a width of 5 meters, and a length of 12 meters. What is the volume of the tank?

    (A) 540 m³   (C) 45 m²

    (B) 180 m³   (D) 26 m²

4. What is 140% of 85?

    (F) 11.9   (H) 1,190

    (G) 119   (J) 11,900

5. Clay jumps rope at an average rate of 75 jumps per minute. How long does it take him to make 405 jumps if he does not stop?

    (A) 5 min   (C) $5\frac{2}{5}$ min

    (B) $5\frac{1}{10}$ min   (D) $5\frac{5}{6}$ min

6. A cell-phone company is tracking the sales of a particular model of phone. The sales at one store over six months are shown in the graph. What is the approximate percent increase in sales of Model B phones from October to November?

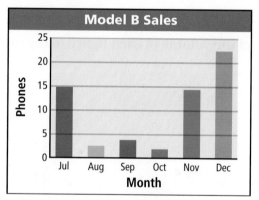

    (F) 40%   (H) 4,000%

    (G) 400%   (J) 4%

7. What is the decimal equivalent of $4\frac{4}{5}$?

    (A) 4.45   (C) 4.8

    (B) 4.54   (D) 24.5

8. The circumference of the given cylinder is 6 in. What additional information is needed to find the volume of the cylinder?

    (F) diameter   (H) height

    (G) area of base   (J) radius

When finding surface area and volume, make sure all the measurements are in the same unit.

9. The straw has a diameter of 0.6 cm. What is the surface area of the straw?

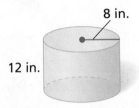

19.5 cm

Ⓐ 11.7 cm²

Ⓑ 5.5 cm²

Ⓒ 37.3 cm²

Ⓓ 36.7 cm²

10. Find the volume of the cylinder to the nearest tenth. Use 3.14 for π.

8 in.

12 in.

Ⓕ 602.9 in³   Ⓗ 1,205.8 in³

Ⓖ 3,215.4 in³   Ⓙ 2,411.5 in³

11. A cone-shaped cup has a radius of 4 in. and a volume of 256 in³. What is the height, in inches, of the cup? Round your answer to the nearest tenth.

Ⓐ 5.1   Ⓒ 20.4

Ⓑ 15.3   Ⓓ 61.1

12. The legs of a right triangle measure 9 units and 12 units. How many units long is the hypotenuse?

Ⓕ $\sqrt{21}$ Ⓗ 21

Ⓖ 15   Ⓙ 225

13. What is the greatest common factor of 180, 16, and 48?

Ⓐ 2   Ⓒ 4

Ⓑ 3   Ⓓ 16

Short Response

14. The surface area of a cylinder is 66 ft².

   a. Find the surface area of a larger similar cylinder with a scale factor of 4.

   b. Explain how the surface area changes when the dimensions are decreased by a factor of $\frac{1}{4}$.

15. A polyhedron has two parallel square bases with edges 9 meters long and a height of 9 meters. Identify the figure and find its volume. Show your work.

16. What is the base length of a parallelogram with a height of 8 in. and an area of 56 in²?

Extended Response

17. Use the figure for the following problems. Round your answers to the nearest hundredth, if necessary. Use 3.14 for π.

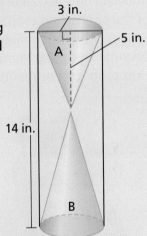

3 in.

5 in.

A

14 in.

B

   a. What three-dimensional shapes make up the sculpture?

   b. What is the combined volume of figures A and B? Show your work.

   c. What is the volume of the space surrounding figures A and B? Show your work and explain your answer.

CRCT Prep

Problem Solving on Location

GEORGIA

— Conyers

Georgia Performance Standards

M7P1.c, M7P4.c, M7P5.a

⭐ Georgia International Horse Park

The Georgia International Horse Park in Conyers is a paradise for anyone who loves horses. The 1,400-acre park was the site of the equestrian events during the 1996 Summer Olympics. Since then, it has become a popular venue for horseback riding, sports competitions, and festivals.

Choose one or more strategies to solve each problem.

1. The horses at the park are fed and cleaned in stalls. Each rectangular stall has an area of 132 ft². The length of the stalls is one foot greater than the width. What are the dimensions of the stalls?

2. One of the park's outdoor arenas is a rectangle measuring approximately 260 ft by 150 ft. The arena is surrounded by a fence that has posts every 10 feet. How many posts are there?

Arenas at the Georgia International Horse Park		
Name	Length (feet)	Width (feet)
Walker Arena	279	115
Warm-Up Ring	430	148
Arena #4	312	148
Arena #6	295	144

For 3, use the table.

3. The park has many different types of arenas. Among the rectangular arenas in the table, two are used for 4-H events. Each of these arenas has a perimeter greater than 800 feet and an area less than 50,000 ft². Which two arenas are used for 4-H events?

Problem Solving Strategies

Draw a Diagram
Make a Model
Guess and Test
Work Backward
Find a Pattern
Make a Table
Solve a Simpler Problem
Use Logical Reasoning
Act It Out
Make an Organized List

⭐ Kudzu

Kudzu is a vine that is native to Asia, but it grows well in the southern United States. Some people would say it grows too well! During the summer months, it is not unusual to see kudzu covering trees and walls alongside Georgia's highways. Entire houses have been known to disappear under the rapidly spreading vines.

Choose one or more strategies to solve each problem.

1. Kudzu is edible and quite nutritious! A 100-gram serving of kudzu contains water, carbohydrates, and protein. There are 26 more grams of carbohydrates than protein, and 42 more grams of water than carbohydrates. How many grams of protein are in 100 grams of kudzu?

For 2–3, use the table.

2. The table shows the rate at which kudzu grows. At the start of the growing season, a kudzu vine is 3 meters long. What is the length of the vine after 30 days? (*Hint:* Recall that 100 cm = 1 m.)

3. Sound walls alongside Georgia freeways are typically 4.5 meters tall. How long would it take a kudzu vine to grow vertically from the bottom of the wall to the top?

Kudzu Growth Rate (During Growing Season)	
Number of Days	**Amount of Growth (cm)**
3	90
5	150
7	210

Probability

CRCT PREP

go.hrw.com
Chapter Project Online
KEYWORD: MS7 Ch11

Career Demographer

Demographers study people: their numbers, how old they are, where they live, with whom they live, where they are moving, and more. They examine how age affects buying habits, which occupations are most popular, how people are affecting the natural environment, and many other behavioral data.

Businesses use demographers to analyze how products are used. The table lists the countries with the highest per capita mobile-phone use. Who might be interested in this kind of demographic information?

Countries with Highest per Capita Mobile-Phone Use	
Country	Mobile Phones per 100 People
Finland	67.8
Norway	62.7
Sweden	59.0
Italy	52.2

ARE YOU READY?

✓ Vocabulary

Choose the best term from the list to complete each sentence.

composite number

even number

odd number

percent

prime number

ratio

1. A(n) __?__ is a comparison of two quantities by division.

2. A(n) __?__ is an integer that is divisible by 2.

3. A(n) __?__ is a ratio that compares a number to 100.

4. A(n) __?__ is a number greater than 1 that has more than two whole number factors.

5. A(n) __?__ is an integer that is not divisible by 2.

Complete these exercises to review skills you will need for this chapter.

✓ Simplify Fractions

Write each fraction in simplest form.

6. $\frac{6}{9}$ 7. $\frac{12}{15}$ 8. $\frac{8}{10}$ 9. $\frac{20}{24}$

10. $\frac{2}{4}$ 11. $\frac{7}{35}$ 12. $\frac{12}{22}$ 13. $\frac{72}{81}$

✓ Write Fractions as Decimals

Write each fraction as a decimal.

14. $\frac{3}{5}$ 15. $\frac{9}{20}$ 16. $\frac{57}{100}$ 17. $\frac{12}{25}$

18. $\frac{3}{25}$ 19. $\frac{1}{2}$ 20. $\frac{7}{10}$ 21. $\frac{9}{5}$

✓ Percents and Decimals

Write each decimal as a percent.

22. 0.14   23. 0.08   24. 0.75   25. 0.38

26. 0.27   27. 1.89   28. 0.234   29. 0.0025

✓ Multiply Fractions

Multiply. Write each answer in simplest form.

30. $\frac{1}{2} \cdot \frac{1}{4}$ 31. $\frac{2}{3} \cdot \frac{3}{5}$ 32. $\frac{3}{10} \cdot \frac{1}{2}$ 33. $\frac{5}{6} \cdot \frac{3}{4}$

34. $\frac{5}{14} \cdot \frac{7}{17}$ 35. $-\frac{1}{8} \cdot \frac{3}{8}$ 36. $-\frac{2}{15} \cdot \left(-\frac{2}{3}\right)$ 37. $\frac{1}{4} \cdot \left(-\frac{1}{6}\right)$

Study Guide: Preview

Where You've Been

Previously, you

- found experimental and theoretical probabilities of compound events.

- used organized lists and tree diagrams to find the sample space of an experiment.

- found the probability that an outcome will not occur.

In This Chapter

You will study

- finding experimental and theoretical probabilities, including those of dependent and independent events.

- using lists and tree diagrams to find combinations and all possible outcomes of an experiment.

- using the Fundamental Counting Principle and factorials to find permutations.

Where You're Going

You can use the skills learned in this chapter

- to determine the effect of chance in games that you play.

- to predict the outcome in situations involving sports and weather.

Key Vocabulary/Vocabulario

combination	combinación
dependent events	sucesos dependientes
event	suceso
experiment	experimento
experimental probability	probabilidad experimental
independent events	sucesos independientes
outcome	resultado
probability	probabilidad
sample space	espacio muestral
theoretical probability	probabilidad teórica

Vocabulary Connections

To become familiar with some of the vocabulary terms in the chapter, consider the following. You may refer to the chapter, the glossary, or a dictionary if you like.

1. An *experiment* is an action done to find out something you do not know. Why can we call flipping a coin, rolling a number cube, or spinning a spinner an **experiment**?

2. Several outcomes, or sometimes just one outcome, make up an *event*. For example, rolling an even number and choosing a challenge card can make up an event in a board game. What is another **event** that can occur when you play board games?

3. The word *depend* comes from the Latin word *dependēre*, meaning "to hang or to be attached." How might the probabilities of **dependent events** be linked?

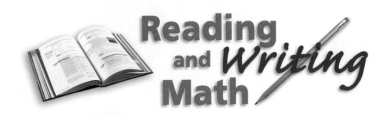 **Reading and Writing Math**

Reading Strategy: Read Problems for Understanding

To best understand a word problem, read it once to note what concept is being reviewed. Then read the problem again, slowly and carefully, to identify what the problem is asking. As you read, highlight the key information. When dealing with a multi-step problem, break the problem into parts and then make a plan to solve it.

> **23. Architecture** The steeple on a building is a square pyramid with base area 12 square feet and height 15 feet. How many cubic feet of concrete was used to make the pyramid?

Step	Question	Answer
Step 1	What concept is being reviewed?	• finding the volume of a pyramid
Step 2	What are you being asked to do?	• Find the number of cubic feet of concrete used to make the steeple.
Step 3	What is the key information needed to solve the problem?	• The steeple is a square pyramid. • The base area of the pyramid is 12 square feet. • The height of the pyramid is 15 feet.
Step 4	What is my plan to solve this multi-part problem?	• Use the formula for finding the volume of a pyramid: $V = \frac{1}{3}Bh$. • Substitute the values for the base area and the height into the formula. • Solve for V.

Try This

For each problem, complete each step in the four-step method described above.

1. Which has a greater volume: a square pyramid with a height of 15 feet and a base with a side length of 3 feet or a cube with a side length of 4 feet?

2. At a party, each child receives the same number of party favors. There are 16 kazoos, 24 snappers, 8 hats, and 32 pieces of gum. What is the greatest number of children that may be at the party?

11-1 Probability

Learn to use informal measures of probability.

Vocabulary

experiment

trial

outcome

event

probability

complement

Georgia Performance Standards

M7N1.d Solve problems using rational numbers. Also, M7P4.c, M7P5.c.

An activity involving chance, such as rolling a number cube, is called an **experiment**. Each repetition or observation of an experiment is a **trial**, and each result is an **outcome**. A set of one or more outcomes is an **event**. For example, rolling a 5 (one outcome) can be an event, or rolling an even number (more than one outcome) can be an event.

The **probability** of an event, written *P*(event), is the measure of how likely the event is to occur. Probability is a measure between 0 and 1, as shown on the number line. You can write probability as a fraction, a decimal, or a percent.

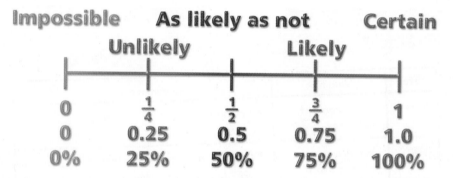

Impossible	Unlikely	As likely as not	Likely	Certain
0	$\frac{1}{4}$	$\frac{1}{2}$	$\frac{3}{4}$	1
0	0.25	0.5	0.75	1.0
0%	25%	50%	75%	100%

EXAMPLE **1** **Determining the Likelihood of an Event**

Determine whether each event is impossible, unlikely, as likely as not, likely, or certain.

A rolling an even number on a number cube

There are 6 possible outcomes:

Even	*Not* Even
2, 4, 6	1, 3, 5

Half of the outcomes are even.

Rolling an even number is as likely as not.

B rolling a 5 on a number cube

There are 6 possible outcomes:

5	*Not* 5
5	1, 2, 3, 4, 6

Only one outcome is a five.

Rolling a 5 is unlikely.

When a number cube is rolled, either a 5 will be rolled or it will not. Rolling a 5 and not rolling a 5 are examples of *complementary events*. The **complement** of an event is the set of all outcomes that are *not* the event.

Because it is certain that either an event or its complement will occur when an activity is performed, the sum of the probabilities is 1.

$$P(\text{event}) + P(\text{complement}) = 1$$

EXAMPLE 2 Using Complements

A bag contains 6 blue marbles, 6 red marbles, 3 green marbles, and 1 yellow marble. The probability of randomly drawing a red marble is $\frac{3}{8}$. What is the probability of not drawing a red marble?

$P(\text{event}) + P(\text{complement}) =$	1	
$P(\text{red}) + P(\text{not red}) =$	1	
$\frac{3}{8} + P(\text{not red}) =$	1	*Substitute $\frac{3}{8}$ for P(red).*
$-\frac{3}{8} \quad\quad\quad\quad = -\frac{3}{8}$		*Subtract $\frac{3}{8}$ from both sides.*
$P(\text{not red}) =$	$\frac{5}{8}$	*Simplify.*

The probability of not drawing a red marble is $\frac{5}{8}$.

EXAMPLE 3 *School Application*

Eric's math teacher almost always gives a pop quiz if the class did not ask many questions during the lesson on the previous class day. If it is Monday and no one asked questions during class on Friday, should Eric expect a pop quiz? Explain.

Since Eric's teacher often gives quizzes on days after few questions were asked, a quiz on Monday is likely.

Think and Discuss  GPS M7P3.b, M7P4.c

1. **Describe** an event that has a probability of 0% and an event that has a probability of 100%.

2. **Give an example** of a real-world event and its complement.

Georgia Performance
Standards

M7P1.b, M7P2.c, M7P3.a

go.hrw.com
Homework Help Online
KEYWORD: MS7 11-1
Parent Resources Online
KEYWORD: MS7 Parent

GUIDED PRACTICE

See Example **1** **Determine whether each event is impossible, unlikely, as likely as not, likely, or certain.**

  1. rolling a number greater than 5 with a number cube

  2. drawing a blue marble from a bag of black and white marbles

See Example **2** **3.** A bag contains 8 purple beads, 2 blue beads, and 2 pink beads. The probability of randomly drawing a pink bead is $\frac{1}{6}$. What is the probability of not drawing a pink bead?

See Example **3** **4.** Natalie almost always sleeps in on Saturday mornings when she does not have to work. If it is Saturday morning and Natalie does not have to work, how likely is it that Natalie will sleep in?

INDEPENDENT PRACTICE

See Example **1** **Determine whether each event is impossible, unlikely, as likely as not, likely, or certain.**

  5. randomly drawing a red or pink card from a deck of red and pink cards

  6. flipping a coin and getting tails

  7. rolling a 6 on a number cube five times in a row

See Example **2** **8.** The probability of rolling a 5 or 6 with a number cube is $\frac{1}{3}$. What is the probability of not rolling a 5 or 6?

  9. The probability of randomly drawing a green marble from a bag of green, red, and blue marbles is $\frac{3}{5}$. What is the probability of randomly drawing a red or blue marble?

See Example **3** **10.** Tim rarely spends more than 30 minutes watching TV in the afternoon. If Tim began watching TV at 4:00 P.M., would you expect that he is still watching TV at 5:00 P.M? Explain.

PRACTICE AND PROBLEM SOLVING

CRCT GPS
Extra Practice p. 748

A bag contains 12 red checkers and 12 black checkers. Determine whether each event is impossible, unlikely, as likely as not, likely, or certain.

11. randomly drawing a red checker

12. randomly drawing a white checker

13. randomly drawing a red or black checker

14. randomly drawing a black checker

15. Exercise Luka almost always jogs in the afternoon when the weather is not cold or rainy. The sky is cloudy and the temperature is 41°F. How likely is it that Luka will jog this afternoon?

16. Life Science A researcher's garden contains 900 sweet pea plants. More than 700 of the plants have purple flowers and about 200 have white flowers. Would you expect that one plant randomly selected from the garden will have purple or white flowers? Explain.

17. Life Science Sharks belong to a class of fishes that have skeletons made of cartilage. Bony fishes, which account for 95% of all species of fish, have skeletons made of bone.

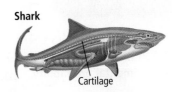

Shark

Cartilage

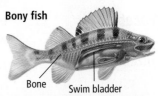

Bony fish

Bone   Swim bladder

  a. How likely is it that a fish you cannot identify at a pet store is a bony fish? Explain.

  b. Only bony fishes have swim bladders, which keep them from sinking. How likely is it that a shark has a swim bladder? Explain.

18. Earth Science The graph shows the carbon dioxide levels in the atmosphere from 1958 to 1994. How likely is it that the level of carbon dioxide fell from 1994 to 2000? Explain.

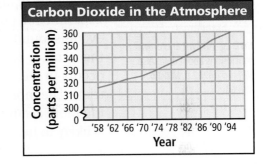

Carbon Dioxide in the Atmosphere

 19. Write a Problem Describe an event that involves rolling a number cube. Determine the likelihood that the event will occur.

 20. Write About It Explain how to tell whether an event is as likely as not.

 21. Challenge A bag contains 10 red marbles and 8 blue marbles, all the same size and weight. Keiko randomly draws 2 red marbles from the bag and does not replace them. Will Keiko be more likely to draw a red marble than a blue marble on her next draw? Explain.

CRCT PREP • GPS SUPPORT • SPIRAL REVIEW

22. Multiple Choice Which percent best shows the probability that Kito will randomly draw an even number from five cards numbered 2, 4, 6, 8, and 10?

Ⓐ 75%   Ⓑ 25%   Ⓒ 50%   Ⓓ 100%

23. Short Response Describe an event that is likely to happen.

24. The sales tax on a $45 DVD player is $3.38. What is the sales tax rate to the nearest tenth of a percent? (Lesson 6-5)

Calculate. Use the correct number of significant digits in each answer. (Lesson 9-1)

25. $8.4 + 2.97$ **26.** $6.53 + 18$ **27.** $7 - 3.6$

28. $12 \cdot 203$ **29.** $14.3 \cdot 10.6$ **30.** $7.0 \div 6.22$

11-2 Experimental Probability

Learn to find experimental probability.

Vocabulary

experimental probability

Georgia Performance Standards

M7D1.g Analyze and draw conclusions about data. Also, M7N1.d, M7A2.b, M7P1.b, M7P5.b.

During hockey practice, Tanya made saves on 15 out of 25 shots. Based on these numbers, you can estimate the probability that Tanya will make a save on the next shot.

Experimental probability is one way of estimating the probability of an event. The **experimental probability** of an event is found by comparing the number of times the event occurs to the total number of trials. The more trials you have, the more accurate the estimate is likely to be.

EXPERIMENTAL PROBABILITY

$$\text{probability} \approx \frac{\text{number of times the event occurs}}{\text{total number of trials}}$$

EXAMPLE 1 Sports Application

Writing Math

"*P*(event)" represents the probability that an event will occur. For example, the probability of a flipped coin landing heads up could be written as "*P*(heads)."

Tanya made saves on 15 out of 25 shots. What is the experimental probability that she will make a save on the next shot? Write your answer as a fraction, as a decimal, and as a percent.

$$P(\text{event}) \approx \frac{\text{number of times the event occurs}}{\text{total number of trials}}$$

$$P(\text{save}) \approx \frac{\text{number of saves made}}{\text{total number of shots attempted}}$$

$$= \frac{15}{25} \qquad \textit{Substitute data from the experiment.}$$

$$= \frac{3}{5} \qquad \textit{Write in simplest form.}$$

$$= 0.6 = 60\% \qquad \textit{Write as a decimal and as a percent.}$$

The experimental probability that Tanya will make a save on the next shot is $\frac{3}{5}$, or 0.6, or 60%.

EXAMPLE 2 *Weather Application*

For the past three weeks, Karl has been recording the daily high temperatures for a science project. His results are shown below.

Week 1	Temp (°F)	Week 2	Temp (°F)	Week 3	Temp (°F)
Sun	76	Sun	72	Sun	78
Mon	74	Mon	79	Mon	76
Tue	79	Tue	78	Tue	77
Wed	80	Wed	79	Wed	75
Thu	77	Thu	77	Thu	79
Fri	76	Fri	74	Fri	77
Sat	75	Sat	73	Sat	75

A **What is the experimental probability that the temperature will be above 75°F on the next day?**

The number of days the temperature was above 75°F is 14.

$$P(\text{above } 75°F) \approx \frac{\text{number of days above } 75°F}{\text{total number of days}}$$

$$= \frac{14}{21} \qquad \textit{Substitute data.}$$

$$= \frac{2}{3} \qquad \textit{Write in simplest form.}$$

The experimental probability that the temperature will be above 75°F on the next day is $\frac{2}{3}$.

B **What is the experimental probability that the temperature will not be above 75°F on the next day?**

$$P(\text{above } 75°F) + P(\text{not above } 75°F) = 1 \qquad \textit{Use the complement.}$$

$$\frac{2}{3} + P(\text{not above } 75°F) = 1 \qquad \textit{Substitute.}$$

$$-\frac{2}{3} \qquad\qquad\qquad = -\frac{2}{3} \qquad \textit{Subtract } \frac{2}{3} \textit{ from both sides.}$$

$$P(\text{not above } 75°F) = \frac{1}{3} \qquad \textit{Simplify.}$$

The experimental probability that the temperature will not be above 75°F on the next day is $\frac{1}{3}$.

Think and Discuss
GPS M7P3.b, M7P4.c

1. Describe a real-world situation in which you could estimate probability using experimental probability.

2. Explain how experimental probability could be used for making predictions.

 **11-2 Exercises**

 **Georgia Performance Standards**

M7P1.a, M7P1.b, M7P5.b

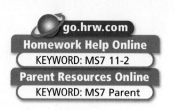
GUIDED PRACTICE

See Example

1. During archery practice, Teri hits the target on 14 out of 20 tries. What is the experimental probability that she will hit the target on her next try? Write your answer as a fraction, as a decimal, and as a percent.

See Example

2. **Government** A reporter surveys 75 people to determine whether they plan to vote for or against a proposed amendment. Of these people, 65 plan to vote for the amendment.

   a. What is the experimental probability that the next person surveyed would say he or she plans to vote for the amendment?

   b. What is the experimental probability that the next person surveyed would say he or she plans to vote against the amendment?

INDEPENDENT PRACTICE

See Example

3. **Sports** Jack hit a baseball on 13 out of 30 tries during practice. What is the experimental probability that he will hit the ball on his next try? Write your answer as a fraction, as a decimal, and as a percent.

4. Cam hit the bull's-eye in darts 8 times out of 15 throws. What is the experimental probability that Cam's next throw will hit the bull's-eye?

See Example

5. For the past two weeks, Benita has been recording the number of people at Eastside Park at lunchtime. During that time, there were 50 or more people at the park 9 out of 14 days.

   a. What is the experimental probability that there will be 50 or more people at the park during lunchtime on the fifteenth day?

   b. What is the experimental probability that there will not be 50 or more people at the park during lunchtime on the fifteenth day?

PRACTICE AND PROBLEM SOLVING

Extra Practice p. 748

6. **Recreation** While bowling with friends, Alexis rolls a strike in 4 out of the 10 frames. What is the experimental probability that Alexis will roll a strike in the first frame of the next game?

7. Jeremiah is greeting customers at a music store. Of the first 25 people he sees enter the store, 16 are wearing jackets and 9 are not. What is the experimental probability that the next person to enter the store will be wearing a jacket?

8. During the month of June, Carmen kept track of the birds she saw in her garden. She saw a blue jay on 12 days of the month. What is the experimental probability that she will see a blue jay on July 1?

9. **Critical Thinking** Claudia finds that the experimental probability of her cat waking her between 5:00 A.M. and 6:00 A.M. is $\frac{8}{11}$. About what percent of the time does Claudia's cat not wake her between 5:00 A.M. and 6:00 A.M.?

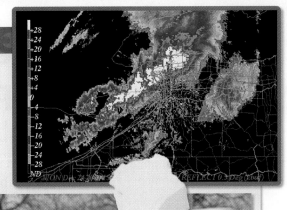

10. **Multi-Step** The stem-and-leaf plot shows the depth of snow in inches recorded in Buffalo, New York, over a 10-day period.

Stems	Leaves
7	9 9
8	
9	1 1 1 1 8 8
10	
11	8
12	
13	0

Key: 7|9 means 7.9

a. What is the median depth of snow for the 10-day period?

b. What is the experimental probability that the snow will be less than 6 in. deep on the eleventh day?

c. What is the experimental probability that the snow will be more than 10 in. deep on the eleventh day?

11. The table shows the high temperatures recorded on July 4 in Orlando, Florida, over an eight-year period.

Year	Temp (°F)	Year	Temp (°F)
1994	86.0	1998	96.8
1995	95.0	1999	89.1
1996	78.8	2000	90.0
1997	98.6	2001	91.0

Source: Old Farmers' Almanac

a. What is the experimental probability that the high temperature on the next July 4 will be below 90°F?

b. What is the experimental probability that the high temperature on the next July 4 will be above 100°F?

12. ⭐ **Challenge** A toy company finds that the experimental probability of manufacturing a defective balance ball is $\frac{3}{50}$. About how many defective balls are likely to be in a batch of 1,800 balls?

CRCT PREP • GPS SUPPORT • SPIRAL REVIEW

13. **Multiple Choice** Darian made 26 of the 32 free throws he attempted. Which percent is closest to the experimental probability that he will make his next free throw?

    Ⓐ 50%   Ⓑ 60%   Ⓒ 70%   Ⓓ 80%

14. **Multiple Choice** Survey results show that cheese is the favorite pizza topping for 18 out of 24 people. Which percent is closest to the experimental probability that a person's favorite pizza topping will NOT be cheese?

    Ⓕ 25%   Ⓖ 33%   Ⓗ 40%   Ⓙ 75%

15. How many days are equal to 360 hours? (Lesson 5-6)

Compare. Write < , > , or =. (Lesson 6-2)

16. $\frac{3}{5}$ ▨ 62%   17. 2.4 ▨ $\frac{12}{5}$ 18. 0.04 ▨ $\frac{3}{10}$ 19. 8.2 ▨ 82%

11-3 Make a List to Find Sample Spaces

 Problem Solving Skill

Learn to use counting methods to determine possible outcomes.

Vocabulary

sample space

Fundamental Counting Principle

Because you can roll the numbers 1, 2, 3, 4, 5, and 6 on a number cube, there are 6 possible outcomes. Together, all the possible outcomes of an experiment make up the **sample space**.

You can make an organized list to show all possible outcomes of an experiment.

Georgia Performance Standards

M7P5.a Create and use representations to organize, record, and communicate mathematical ideas. Also, M7P1.c, M7P1.d, M7P5.c.

EXAMPLE 1 PROBLEM SOLVING APPLICATION

Lucia flips two quarters at the same time. What are all the possible outcomes? How many outcomes are in the sample space?

1. Understand the Problem

Rewrite the question as a statement.

- Find all the possible outcomes of flipping two quarters, and determine the size of the sample space.

List the **important information:**

- There are two quarters.
- Each quarter can land heads up or tails up.

2. Make a Plan

You can make an organized list to show all the possible outcomes.

3. Solve

Quarter 1	Quarter 2
H	H
H	T
T	H
T	T

Let H = heads and T = tails.

Record each possible outcome.

The possible outcomes are HH, HT, TH, and TT. There are four possible outcomes in the sample space.

4. Look Back

Each possible outcome that is recorded in the list is different.

When the number of possible outcomes of an experiment increases, it may be easier to track all the possible outcomes on a tree diagram.

EXAMPLE 2 **Using a Tree Diagram to Find a Sample Space**

Ren spins spinner A and spinner B. What are all the possible outcomes? How many outcomes are in the sample space?

Make a tree diagram to show the sample space. List each color from spinner A. Then for each color, list each number from spinner B.

Spinner A   Spinner B

Red		Blue		Green		
1	2	1	2	1	2	*Spinner A outcomes*
R, 1	R, 2	B, 1	B, 2	G, 1	G, 2	*Spinner B outcomes*
						All possible outcomes

There are six possible outcomes in the sample space.

In Example 1, there are two outcomes for each coin, so there are four total outcomes.

First quarter   Second quarter

In Example 2, there are three outcomes for spinner A and two outcomes for spinner B, so there are six total outcomes.

3 × 2 = 6

Spinner A   Spinner B

The **Fundamental Counting Principle** states that you can find the total number of outcomes for two or more experiments by multiplying the number of outcomes for each separate experiment.

EXAMPLE 3 *Recreation Application*

In a game, each player rolls a number cube and spins a spinner. The spinner is divided into thirds, numbered 1, 2, and 3. How many outcomes are possible during one player's turn?

The number cube has 6 outcomes.   *List the number of outcomes*
The spinner has 3 outcomes.   *for each separate experiment.*

$6 \cdot 3 = 18$ *Use the Fundamental Counting Principle.*

There are 18 possible outcomes during one player's turn.

Think and Discuss  GPS M7P1.d, M7P3.b

1. **Compare** using a tree diagram and using the Fundamental Counting Principle to find a sample space.

2. **Find** the size of the sample space for flipping 5 coins.

 Georgia Performance Standards

M7P1.c, M7P3.a, M7P4.c, M7P5.b

 go.hrw.com

Homework Help Online

KEYWORD: MS7 11-3

Parent Resources Online

KEYWORD: MS7 Parent

GUIDED PRACTICE

 See Example **1**

1. Enrique tosses a coin and spins the spinner at right. What are all the possible outcomes? How many outcomes are in the sample space?

See Example **2**

2. An ice cream stand offers cake cones, waffle cones, or cups to hold ice cream. You can get vanilla, chocolate, strawberry, pistachio, or coffee flavored ice cream. If you order a single scoop, what are all the possible options you have? How many outcomes are in the sample space?

 See Example **3**

3. A game includes a number cube and a spinner divided into 4 equal sectors. Each player rolls the number cube and spins the spinner. How many outcomes are possible?

INDEPENDENT PRACTICE

 See Example **1**

4. At noon, Aretha can watch a football game, a basketball game, or a documentary about horses on TV. At 3:00, she can watch a different football game, a movie, or a concert. What are all the possible outcomes? How many outcomes are in the sample space?

5. A spinner is divided into fourths and numbered 1 through 4. Jory spins the spinner and tosses a coin. What are all the possible outcomes? How many outcomes are in the sample space?

 See Example **2**

6. Berto tosses a coin and spins the spinner at right. What are all the possible outcomes? How many outcomes are in the sample space?

7. For breakfast, Clarissa can choose from oatmeal, cornflakes, or scrambled eggs. She can drink milk, orange juice, apple juice, or hot chocolate. What are all the possible outcomes? How many outcomes are in the sample space?

See Example **3**

8. A pizza shop offers thick crust, thin crust, or stuffed crust. The choices of toppings are pepperoni, cheese, hamburger, Italian sausage, Canadian bacon, onions, bell peppers, mushrooms, and pineapple. How many different one-topping pizzas could you order?

PRACTICE AND PROBLEM SOLVING

 CRCT GPS

Extra Practice p. 748

9. Andie has a blue sweater, a red sweater, and a purple sweater. She has a white shirt and a tan shirt. How many different ways can she wear a sweater and a shirt together?

10. Critical Thinking Suppose you can choose a ball that comes in three colors: blue, red, or green. Make a tree diagram or a list of all the possible ways to choose 2 balls if you are allowed to choose two of the same color.

11. Health For each pair of food groups, give the number of possible outcomes if one item is chosen from each group.

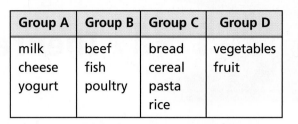

Group A	Group B	Group C	Group D
milk cheese yogurt	beef fish poultry	bread cereal pasta rice	vegetables fruit

    a. group A and group B

    b. group B and group D

    c. group A and group C

12. Health The graph shows the kinds of classes that health club members would like to see offered.

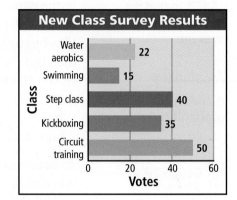

New Class Survey Results

    a. If the health club offers the four most popular classes on one day, how many ways could they be arranged?

    b. If the health club offers each of the five classes on a different weekday, how many ways could they be arranged?

13. Recreation There are 3 trails from the South Canyon trailhead to Lake Solitude. There are 4 trails from Lake Solitude to Hidden Lake. How many possible routes could you take to hike from the South Canyon trailhead to Hidden Lake that pass Lake Solitude?

14. What's the Question? Dan has 4 face cards and 5 number cards. He shuffles the cards separately and places each set in a separate pile. The answer is 20 possible outcomes. What is the question?

15. Write About It Explain how to determine the size of the sample space when you toss three number cubes at the same time.

16. Challenge Suppose you flip a penny, a nickel, and a dime at the same time. What are all the possible outcomes?

Health and fitness advocate Aimee Mullins set Paralympic records in the 100-meter dash and long jump at the 1996 Paralympics in Atlanta, Georgia.

CRCT Prep • GPS Support • Spiral Review

17. Multiple Choice Amber rolls two number cubes. How many outcomes are possible?

   Ⓐ 6   Ⓑ 12   Ⓒ 24   Ⓓ 36

18. Extended Response A sandwich shop offers 3 choices of breads: white, rye, or garlic; 2 choices of cheese: American or Swiss; and 4 choices of meats: beef, turkey, ham, or pork. List the possible choices for a sandwich with 1 bread, 1 cheese, and 1 meat. How many possible choices are there?

Write each fraction as a percent. (Lesson 6-2)

19. $\frac{1}{8}$ **20.** $\frac{3}{4}$ **21.** $\frac{2}{5}$ **22.** $\frac{3}{10}$

23. Find the volume of a cylinder with diameter 8 in. and height 14 in. Use $\frac{22}{7}$ for π. (Lesson 10-2)

11-4 Theoretical Probability

Learn to find the theoretical probability of an event.

Vocabulary

theoretical probability

Georgia Performance Standards

M7N1.d Solve problems using rational numbers. Also, M7A2.b, M7P4.c.

In the game of Scrabble®, players use tiles bearing the letters of the alphabet to form words. Of the 100 tiles used in a Scrabble game, 12 have the letter *E* on them. What is the probability of drawing an *E* from a bag of 100 Scrabble tiles?

To determine the probability of drawing an *E*, you can draw tiles from a bag and record your results to find the experimental probability, or you can calculate the *theoretical probability*. **Theoretical probability** is used to find the probability of an event when all outcomes are equally likely.

THEORETICAL PROBABILITY

$$\text{probability} = \frac{\text{number of ways the event can occur}}{\text{total number of equally likely outcomes}}$$

If each possible outcome of an experiment is equally likely, then the experiment is said to be fair. Experiments involving number cubes and coins are usually assumed to be fair.

EXAMPLE **1** **Finding Theoretical Probability**

Find the probability of each event. Write your answer as a fraction, as a decimal, and as a percent.

A drawing one of the 12 *E*'s from a bag of 100 Scrabble tiles

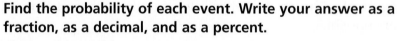

$$P = \frac{\text{number of ways the event can occur}}{\text{total number of equally likely outcomes}}$$

$$P(E) = \frac{\text{number of } E\text{'s}}{\text{total number of tiles}} \quad \textit{Write the ratio.}$$

$$= \frac{12}{100} \quad \textit{Substitute.}$$

$$= \frac{3}{25} \quad \textit{Write in simplest form.}$$

$$= 0.12 = 12\% \quad \textit{Write as a decimal and as a percent.}$$

The theoretical probability of drawing an *E* is $\frac{3}{25}$, 0.12, or 12%.

Find the probability of each event. Write your answer as a fraction, as a decimal, and as a percent.

B rolling a number greater than 2 on a fair number cube

There are four ways the event can occur: 3, 4, 5, and 6.

There are six possible outcomes: 1, 2, 3, 4, 5, and 6.

$$P(\text{greater than 2}) = \frac{\text{number of ways the event can occur}}{\text{total number of equally likely outcomes}}$$

$$= \frac{4}{6} \qquad \text{\textit{Write the ratio.}}$$

$$= \frac{2}{3} \qquad \text{\textit{Write in simplest form.}}$$

$$\approx 0.667 \approx 66.7\% \qquad \text{\textit{Write as a decimal and a percent.}}$$

The theoretical probability of rolling a number greater than 2 is $\frac{2}{3}$, or approximately 0.667, or approximately 66.7%.

EXAMPLE 2 *School Application*

There are 11 boys and 16 girls in Mr. Ashley's class. Mr. Ashley has written the name of each student on a craft stick. He randomly draws one of these sticks to choose a student to answer a question.

A Find the theoretical probability of drawing a boy's name.

$$P(\text{boy}) = \frac{\text{number of boys in class}}{\text{total number of students in class}}$$

$$P(\text{boy}) = \frac{11}{27}$$

B Find the theoretical probability of drawing a girl's name.

$$P(\text{boy}) + P(\text{girl}) = 1 \qquad \text{\textit{Substitute } \frac{11}{27} \text{ for } P(\text{boy}).}$$

$$\frac{11}{27} + P(\text{girl}) = 1$$

$$\underline{-\frac{11}{27} \qquad\qquad = -\frac{11}{27}} \qquad \text{\textit{Subtract } \frac{11}{27} \text{ from both sides.}}$$

$$P(\text{girl}) = \frac{16}{27} \qquad \text{\textit{Simplify.}}$$

> **Remember!**
>
> The sum of the probabilities of an event and its complement is 1.

Think and Discuss  GPS M7P1.d, M7P3.b

1. **Give an example** of an experiment in which all of the outcomes are not equally likely. Explain.

2. **Describe** how the probability in Example 2 can be affected if Mr. Ashley does not draw randomly from the craft sticks.

 Georgia Performance Standards
M7P1.c, M7P3.a, M7P4.c, M7P5.b

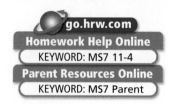 go.hrw.com
Homework Help Online
KEYWORD: MS7 11-4
Parent Resources Online
KEYWORD: MS7 Parent

GUIDED PRACTICE

See Example 1 Find the probability of each event. Write your answer as a fraction, as a decimal, and as a percent.

1. randomly choosing a red marble from a bag of 15 red, 15 blue, 15 green, 15 yellow, 15 black, and 15 white marbles

2. tossing 2 fair coins and both landing heads up

See Example 2 A set of cards includes 15 yellow cards, 10 green cards, and 10 blue cards. Find the probability of each event when a card is chosen at random.

3. yellow
4. green
5. not yellow or green

INDEPENDENT PRACTICE

See Example 1 Find the probability of each event. Write your answer as a fraction, as a decimal, and as a percent.

6. randomly drawing a heart or a club from a shuffled deck of 52 cards with 13-card suits: diamonds, hearts, clubs, and spades

7. randomly drawing a purple disk from a game with 13 red, 13 purple, 13 orange, and 13 white disks of the same size and shape

8. randomly drawing one of the two blank Scrabble tiles from a complete set of 100 Scrabble tiles

See Example 2 Sifu has 6 girls and 8 boys in his karate class. He randomly selects one student to demonstrate a self-defense technique. Find the probability of each event.

9. selecting a girl
10. selecting a boy

PRACTICE AND PROBLEM SOLVING

 Extra Practice p. 748

Find the probability of each event when two fair number cubes are rolled.

11. P(total of 3)
12. P(total of 7)

13. P(total of 4)
14. P(total of 2)

15. P(total of 9)
16. P(total of 13)

17. P(total > 8)
18. P(total ≤ 12)

A spinner is divided equally into 10 sectors. The numbers 1 through 5 are each placed in two different sectors. Find the probability of each event.

19. P(3)
20. P(greater than 3)

21. P(less than 3)
22. P(5)

23. P(8)
24. P(less than 6)

25. P(greater than or equal to 4)
26. P(less than or equal to 2)

Recreation The table shows the approximate number of visitors to five different amusement parks in the United States in one year. Find the probability that a randomly selected visitor to one of the amusement parks visited the parks listed in Exercises 27 and 28. Write each answer as a decimal and as a percent.

Amusement Parks	Number of Visitors
Disney World, FL	15,640,000
Disneyland, CA	13,680,000
SeaWorld, FL	4,900,000
Busch Gardens, FL	4,200,000
SeaWorld, CA	3,700,000

27. Disney World

28. a park in California

Gardening A package of mixed lettuce seeds contains 150 green lettuce seeds and 50 red lettuce seeds. What is the probability that a randomly selected seed will be a red lettuce seed? Write your answer as a percent.

30. Choose a Strategy Francis, Amanda, Raymond, and Albert wore different-colored T-shirts. The colors were tan, orange, purple, and aqua. Neither Raymond nor Amanda ever wears orange, and neither Francis nor Raymond ever wears aqua. Albert wore purple. What color was each person's T-shirt?

31. Write About It Suppose the probability of an event happening is $\frac{3}{8}$. Explain what each number in the ratio represents.

32. Challenge A spinner is divided into three sectors. Half of the spinner is red, $\frac{1}{3}$ is blue, and $\frac{1}{6}$ is green. What is the probability that the spinner will land on either red or green?

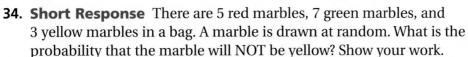
33. Multiple Choice Renae spins the spinner at right. What is the probability that the spinner will land on the number 4?

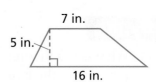

  Ⓐ $\frac{5}{8}$ Ⓒ $\frac{50}{91}$

  Ⓑ $\frac{2}{7}$ Ⓓ $\frac{1}{4}$

34. Short Response There are 5 red marbles, 7 green marbles, and 3 yellow marbles in a bag. A marble is drawn at random. What is the probability that the marble will NOT be yellow? Show your work.

35. Find the area of the trapezoid shown. (Lesson 9-4)

36. Dora is buying one flavor of frozen yogurt. She can choose from two sizes, small and large, and four flavors: berry swirl, vanilla, peach, and lime. How many possible choices are there? (Lesson 11-3)

7 in.

5 in.

16 in.

Experimental and Theoretical Probability

Use with Lesson 11-4

go.hrw.com
Lab Resources Online
KEYWORD: MS7 Lab11

REMEMBER

- The experimental probability of an event is the ratio of the number of times the event occurs to the total number of trials.
- The theoretical probability of an event is the ratio of the number of ways the event can occur to the total number of equally likely outcomes.

Georgia Performance Standards

M7D1.g, M7P1.a, M7P2.c, M7P5.a

Activity 1

① Write the letters *A, B, C,* and *D* on four slips of paper. Fold the slips in half and place them in a bag or other small container.

② You will be choosing these slips of paper without looking. Predict the number of times you expect to choose *A* when you repeat the experiment 12 times.

③ Choose a slip of paper, note the result, and replace the slip. Repeat this 12 times, mixing the slips between trials. Record your results in a table like the one shown.

④ How many times did you choose *A*? How does this number compare to your prediction?

⑤ What is the experimental probability of choosing *A*? What is the theoretical probability of choosing *A*?

⑥ Combine your results with those of your classmates. Find the experimental probability of choosing *A* based on the combined results.

Outcome	Number of Times Chosen
A	//
B	////
C	~~////~~/
D	/

Think and Discuss

1. How is the experimental probability of choosing *A* based on the combined results different from the experimental probability of choosing *A* based on the results of your own experiment?

2. How many times would you expect to choose *A* if you repeat the experiment 500 times?

Try This

1. What is the theoretical probability of choosing *A* from five slips of paper with the letters *A, B, C, D,* and *E*?

2. Predict the number of times you would expect to choose *A* from the five slips in problem 1 if you repeat the experiment 500 times.

Activity 2

1 Write the letters *A*, *B*, *C*, and *D* and the numbers 1, 2, and 3 on slips of paper. Fold the slips in half. Place the slips with the letters in one bag and the slips with the numbers in a different bag.

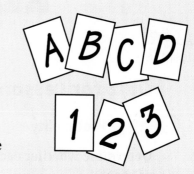

2 In this activity, you will be choosing one slip of paper from each bag without looking. What is the sample space for this experiment? Predict the number of times you expect to choose *A* and 1 (*A*-1) when you repeat the experiment 24 times.

3 Choose a slip of paper from each bag, note the results, and replace the slips. Repeat this 24 times, mixing the slips between trials. Record your results in a table like the one shown.

Outcome	Number of Times Chosen
A-1	/
A-2	⦀⦀
A-3	//
B-1	/

4 How many times did you choose *A*-1? How does this number compare to your prediction?

5 Combine your results with those of your classmates. Find the experimental probability of choosing *A*-1 based on the combined results.

Think and Discuss

1. What do you think is the theoretical probability of choosing *A*-1? Why?

2. How many times would you expect to choose *A*-1 if you repeat the experiment 600 times?

3. Explain the difference between the experimental probability of an event and the theoretical probability of the event.

Try This

1. Suppose you toss a penny and a nickel at the same time.

   a. What is the sample space for this experiment?

   b. Predict the number of times you would expect both coins to land heads up if you repeat the experiment 100 times.

   c. Predict the number of times you would expect one coin to land heads up and one coin to land tails up if you repeat the experiment 1,000 times.

2. You spin the spinner at right and roll a number cube at the same time.

   a. What is the sample space for this experiment?

   b. Describe an experiment you could conduct to find the experimental probability of spinning green and rolling a 4 at the same time.

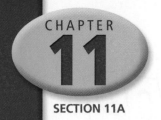

Quiz for Lessons 11-1 Through 11-4

✓ **11-1** **Probability**

Determine whether each event is impossible, unlikely, as likely as not, likely, or certain.

1. rolling 2 number cubes and getting a sum of 2

2. guessing the answer to a true/false question correctly

3. drawing a black marble from a bag containing 2 blue, 3 yellow, and 4 white marbles

4. The probability of Ashur's soccer team winning its next game is $\frac{7}{10}$. What is the probability of Ashur's team not winning the next game?

✓ **11-2** **Experimental Probability**

5. Carl is conducting a survey for the school paper. He finds that 7 students have no pets, 15 have one pet, and 9 have at least two pets. What is the experimental probability that the next student Carl asks will not have a pet?

6. During her ride home from school, Dana sees 15 cars driven by men and 34 cars driven by women. What is the experimental probability that the next car Dana sees will be driven by a man?

✓ **11-3** **Make a List to Find Sample Spaces**

7. Shelly and Anthony are playing a game using a number cube and a nickel. Each player rolls the number cube and flips the coin. What are all the possible outcomes during one turn? How many outcomes are in the sample space?

8. A yogurt shop offers 4 different flavors of yogurt and 3 different fruit toppings. How many different desserts are possible if you can choose one flavor of yogurt and one topping?

✓ **11-4** **Theoretical Probability**

A spinner with 10 equal sectors numbered 1 through 10 is spun. Find the probability of each event. Write your answer as a fraction, as a decimal, and as a percent.

9. $P(5)$ 10. $P(\text{prime number})$

11. $P(\text{even number})$ 12. $P(20)$

13. Sabina has a list of 8 CDs and 5 DVDs that she would like to buy. Her friends randomly select one of the items from the list to give her as a gift. What is the probability Sabina's friends will select a CD? a DVD?

Ready to Go On?

Focus on Problem Solving

 Understand the Problem

• **Identify important details**

When you are solving word problems, you need to identify information that is important to the problem. Read the problem several times to find all the important details. Sometimes it is helpful to read the problem aloud so that you can hear the words. Highlight the facts that are needed to solve the problem. Then list any other information that is necessary.

 Highlight the important information in each problem, and then list any other important details.

① A bag of bubble gum has 25 pink pieces, 20 blue pieces, and 15 green pieces. Lauren selects 1 piece of bubble gum without looking. What is the probability that it is not blue?

② Regina has a bag of marbles that contains 6 red marbles, 3 green marbles, and 4 blue marbles. Regina pulls 1 marble from the bag without looking. What is the probability that the marble is red?

③ Marco is counting the cars he sees on his ride home from school. Of 20 cars, 10 are white, 6 are red, 2 are blue, and 2 are green. What is the experimental probability that the next car Marco sees will be red?

④ Frederica has 8 red socks, 6 blue socks, 10 white socks, and 4 yellow socks in a drawer. What is the probability that she will randomly pull a brown sock from the drawer?

⑤ During the first 20 minutes of lunch, 5 male students, 7 female students, and 3 teachers went through the lunch line. What is the experimental probability that the next person through the line will be a teacher?

11-5 Probability of Independent and Dependent Events

Learn to find the probability of independent and dependent events.

Vocabulary

independent events

dependent events

Georgia Performance Standards

M7N1.d Solve problems using rational numbers. Also, M7P1.b, M7P2.c, M7P3.d.

Raji and Kara must each choose a topic from a list of topics to research for their class. If Raji's choice has no effect on Kara's choice and vice versa, the events are *independent*. For **independent events**, the occurrence of one event has no effect on the probability that a second event will occur.

If once Raji chooses a topic, Kara must choose from the remaining topics, then the events are *dependent*. For **dependent events**, the occurrence of one event *does* have an effect on the probability that a second event will occur.

EXAMPLE 1 Determining Whether Events Are Independent or Dependent

Decide whether each set of events is independent or dependent. Explain your answer.

A **Erika rolls a 3 on one number cube and a 2 on another number cube.**

Since the outcome of rolling one number cube does not affect the outcome of rolling the second number cube, the events are independent.

B **Tomoko chooses a seventh-grader for her team from a group of seventh- and eighth-graders, and then Juan chooses a different seventh-grader from the remaining students.**

Since Juan cannot pick the same student that Tomoko picked, and since there are fewer students for Juan to choose from after Tomoko chooses, the events are dependent.

To find the probability that two independent events will happen, multiply the probabilities of the two events.

Probability of Two Independent Events

$$P(A \text{ and } B) = P(A) \cdot P(B)$$

Probability of both events

Probability of first event

Probability of second event

EXAMPLE 2 **Finding the Probability of Independent Events**

Find the probability of flipping a coin and getting heads and then rolling a 6 on a number cube.

The outcome of flipping the coin does not affect the outcome of rolling the number cube, so the events are independent.

$P(\text{heads and } 6) = P(\text{heads}) \cdot P(6)$

$\qquad = \dfrac{1}{2} \cdot \dfrac{1}{6}$ *There are 2 ways a coin can land and 6 ways a number cube can land.*

$\qquad = \dfrac{1}{12}$ *Multiply.*

The probability of getting heads and a 6 is $\dfrac{1}{12}$.

To find the probability of two dependent events, you must determine the effect that the first event has on the probability of the second event.

Probability of Two Dependent Events

$$P(A \text{ and } B) = P(A) \cdot P(B \text{ after } A)$$

Probability of   Probability of   Probability of second event
both events   first event   given that A has occurred

EXAMPLE 3 **Finding the Probability of Dependent Events**

Mica has five $1 bills, three $10 bills, and two $20 bills in her wallet. She picks two bills at random. What is the probability of her picking the two $20 bills?

The first draw changes the number of bills left, and may change the number of $20 bills left, so the events are dependent.

$P(\text{first } \$20) = \dfrac{2}{10} = \dfrac{1}{5}$ *There are two $20 bills out of ten bills.*

$P(\text{second } \$20) = \dfrac{1}{9}$ *There is one $20 bill left out of nine bills.*

$P(\text{first } \$20, \text{ then second } \$20) = P(A) \cdot P(B \text{ after } A)$

$\qquad\qquad\qquad\qquad = \dfrac{1}{5} \cdot \dfrac{1}{9}$

$\qquad\qquad\qquad\qquad = \dfrac{1}{45}$ *Multiply.*

The probability of Mica picking two $20 bills is $\dfrac{1}{45}$.

Think and Discuss   GPS M7P2.c, M7P3.b

1. **Compare** probabilities of independent and dependent events.

2. **Explain** whether the probability of two events is greater than or less than the probability of each individual event.

Georgia Performance Standards

M7P2.c, M7P3.a, M7P4.c, M7P5.b

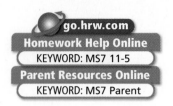
go.hrw.com
Homework Help Online
KEYWORD: MS7 11-5
Parent Resources Online
KEYWORD: MS7 Parent

GUIDED PRACTICE

See Example **Decide whether each set of events is independent or dependent. Explain your answer.**

1. A student flips heads on one coin and tails on a second coin.

2. A student chooses a red marble from a bag of marbles and then chooses another red marble without replacing the first.

See Example **Find the probability of each set of independent events.**

3. a flipped coin landing heads up and rolling a 5 or a 6 on a number cube

4. drawing a 5 from 10 cards numbered 1 through 10 and rolling a 2 on a number cube

See Example 5. Each day, Mr. Samms randomly chooses 2 students from his class to serve as helpers. There are 15 boys and 10 girls in the class. What is the probability that Mr. Samms will choose 2 girls to be helpers?

INDEPENDENT PRACTICE

See Example **Decide whether each set of events is independent or dependent. Explain your answer.**

6. A student chooses a fiction book at random from a list of books and then chooses a second fiction book from those remaining.

7. A woman chooses a lily from one bunch of flowers and then chooses a tulip from a different bunch.

See Example **Find the probability of each set of independent events.**

8. drawing a red marble from a bag of 6 red and 4 blue marbles, replacing it, and then drawing a blue marble

9. rolling an even number on a number cube and rolling an odd number on a second roll of the same cube

See Example 10. Francisco has 7 quarters in his pocket. Of these, 3 depict the state of Delaware, 2 depict Georgia, 1 depicts Connecticut, and 1 depicts Pennsylvania. Francisco removes 1 quarter from his pocket and then removes a second quarter without replacing the first. What is the probability that both will be Delaware quarters?

PRACTICE AND PROBLEM SOLVING

11. An even number is chosen randomly from a set of cards labeled with the numbers 1 through 8. A second even number is chosen without the first card being replaced. Are these independent or dependent events? What is the probability of both events occurring?

12. On a multiple-choice test, each question has five possible answers. A student does not know the answers to two questions, so he guesses. What is the probability that the student will get both answers wrong?

13. **Business** The graph shows the dogs bathed at a dog-grooming business one day. What is the probability that the first two dogs bathed were large dogs?

14. **Write a Problem** Describe two events that are either independent or dependent, and make up a probability problem about them.

15. **Write About It** At the beginning of a game of Scrabble, players take turns drawing 7 tiles. Are drawing A's on the first two tiles dependent or independent events? Explain.

16. **Challenge** Weather forecasters have accurately predicted rain in one community $\frac{4}{5}$ of the time. What is the probability that they will accurately predict rain two days in a row?

CRCT PREP • GPS SUPPORT • SPIRAL REVIEW

17. **Multiple Choice** A bag contains 5 red marbles and 5 purple marbles. What is the probability of drawing a red marble and then a purple marble, without replacing the first marble before drawing the second marble?

   Ⓐ $\frac{2}{9}$ Ⓑ $\frac{5}{18}$ Ⓒ $\frac{1}{3}$ Ⓓ $\frac{1}{2}$

18. **Short Response** José has 3 brown socks, 5 blue socks, and 6 black socks in his sock drawer. He picked one sock and then another sock out of the drawer. Are the events independent or dependent? Explain your answer. What is the probability that he will pick 2 black socks?

19. Fritz jogged $1\frac{3}{4}$ mi on Monday, $2\frac{1}{2}$ mi on Wednesday, and 3 mi on Friday. How many miles did he jog altogether on these days? (Lesson 3-9)

Given the radius or diameter, find the circumference and area of each circle to the nearest tenth. Use 3.14 for π. (Lessons 9-2 and 9-5)

20. $r = 6.5$ in.   21. $d = 15.7$ ft   22. $r = 7$ cm

11-6 Combinations

Learn to find the number of possible combinations.

Vocabulary

combination

Georgia Performance Standards

M7P5.a Create and use representations to organize, and communicate mathematical ideas. Also, M7P1.c, M7P1.d, M7P5.b, M7P5.c.

Mrs. Logan's students have to read any two of the following books.

1. *The Adventures of Tom Sawyer*, by Mark Twain

2. *The Call of the Wild*, by Jack London

3. *A Christmas Carol*, by Charles Dickens

4. *Treasure Island*, by Robert Louis Stevenson

5. *Tuck Everlasting*, by Natalie Babbit

How many possible *combinations* of books could the students choose?

A **combination** is a grouping of objects or events in which the order does not matter. For example, a student can choose books 1 and 2 or books 2 and 1. Since the order does not matter, the two arrangements represent the same combination. One way to find all possible combinations is to make a table.

EXAMPLE **1** **Using a Table to Find Combinations**

How many different combinations of two books are possible from Mrs. Logan's list of five books?

Begin by making a table showing all of the possible groupings of books taken two at a time.

	1	2	3	4	5
1		1, 2	1, 3	1, 4	1, 5
2	2, 1		2, 3	2, 4	2, 5
3	3, 1	3, 2		3, 4	3, 5
4	4, 1	4, 2	4, 3		4, 5
5	5, 1	5, 2	5, 3	5, 4	

Because order does not matter, you can eliminate repeated pairs. For example, 1, 2 is already listed, so 2, 1 can be eliminated.

	1	2	3	4	5
1		1, 2	1, 3	1, 4	1, 5
2	~~2, 1~~		2, 3	2, 4	2, 5
3	~~3, 1~~	~~3, 2~~		3, 4	3, 5
4	~~4, 1~~	~~4, 2~~	~~4, 3~~		4, 5
5	~~5, 1~~	~~5, 2~~	~~5, 3~~	~~5, 4~~	

There are 10 different combinations of two books on Mrs. Logan's list of five books.

You can also use a tree diagram to find possible combinations.

EXAMPLE **2** **PROBLEM SOLVING APPLICATION**

As a caterer, Cuong offers four vegetable choices: broccoli, squash, peas, and carrots. Each person can choose two vegetables. How many different combinations of two vegetables can a person choose?

1 **Understand the Problem**

Rewrite the question as a statement.

• Find the number of possible combinations of two vegetables a person can choose.

List the **important information:**

• There are four vegetable choices in all.

2 **Make a Plan**

You can make a tree diagram to show the possible combinations.

3 **Solve**

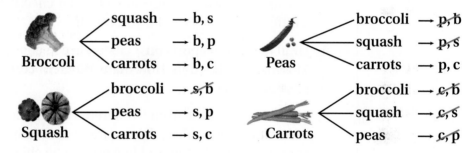

The tree diagram shows 12 possible ways to combine two vegetables, but each combination is listed twice. So there are $12 \div 2 = 6$ possible combinations.

4 **Look Back**

You can check by making a table. The broccoli can be paired with three other vegetables, squash with two, and peas with one. The total number of possible pairs is $3 + 2 + 1 = 6$.

Think and Discuss  GPS M7P1.d, M7P3.b

1. Describe how to use a tree diagram to find the number of combinations in Example 1.

2. Describe how combinations could help you find the probability of an event.

11-6 Exercises

Georgia Performance
Standards
M7P1.a, M7P1.b, M7P5.b

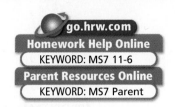

go.hrw.com
Homework Help Online
KEYWORD: MS7 11-6
Parent Resources Online
KEYWORD: MS7 Parent

GUIDED PRACTICE

See Example

1. If you have an apple, a pear, an orange, and a plum, how many combinations of 2 fruits are possible?

2. How many 3-letter combinations are possible from *A, E, I, O,* and *U*?

See Example

3. Robin packs 2 jars of jam in a gift box. She has 5 flavors: blueberry, apricot, grape, peach, and orange marmalade. How many different combinations of 2 jars can she pack in a box?

4. Eduardo has 6 colors of fabric: red, blue, green, yellow, orange, and white. He plans to make flags using 2 colors. How many possible combinations of 2 colors can he choose?

INDEPENDENT PRACTICE

See Example

5. A restaurant allows you to "build your own burger" using a choice of any 2 toppings. The available toppings are bacon, grilled onions, sautéed mushrooms, Swiss cheese, and cheddar cheese. How many burgers with 2 different toppings could you build?

6. Jamil has to do reports on 3 cities. He can choose from Paris, New York, Moscow, and London. How many different combinations of cities are possible?

See Example

7. A florist can choose from 6 different types of flowers to make a bouquet: carnations, roses, lilies, daisies, irises, and tulips. How many different combinations of 2 types of flowers can he choose?

8. How many different 2-member tennis teams can be made from 7 students?

PRACTICE AND PROBLEM SOLVING

Extra Practice p. 749

9. At Camp Allen, campers can choose 2 out of 8 free-time activities. Use the chart to find the number of possible combinations of 2 activities.

10. Rob, Caryn, and Sari are pairing up to play a series of chess matches. In how many different ways can they pair up?

Free-Time Activities	
hiking	volleyball
mosaics	rafting
tennis	pottery
painting	swimming

11. Gary has to write biographies about 2 historical figures. He can choose from Winston Churchill, Dr. Martin Luther King, Jr., and Nelson Mandela. How many different combinations of 2 biographies can Gary write?

12. Trina wants to select 3 of Ansel Adams's 5 "surf sequence" photos to hang on her wall. How many possible combinations are there?

13. Ms. Frennelle is teaching her art history class about famous impressionist painters. She asks her students to choose 2 artists from among Renoir, Monet, Manet, Degas, Pissarro, and Cassatt, and to find information about at least one painting made by each artist. How many possible pairs of artists can be chosen from the six painters?

The White Water Lilies, 1899, by Claude Monet

Woman with a Pearl Necklace in a Loge, 1879, by Mary Cassatt

14. Multi-Step The graph shows the number of paintings by artists of different nationalities displayed in an art book. In how many ways can you combine 4 paintings by Chinese artists?

15. ⭐ **Challenge** A gallery is preparing a show by a new artist. The gallery has enough space to display 7 pieces of art. The artist has prepared 4 paintings and 5 sculptures. How many distinct combinations of the artist's works are possible?

go.hrw.com
Web Extra!
KEYWORD: MS7 Art

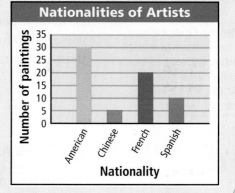

Nationalities of Artists

CRCT Prep • GPS Support • Spiral Review

16. Multiple Choice How many different 2-person teams can be made from 5 people?

    Ⓐ 10   Ⓑ 20   Ⓒ 24   Ⓓ 36

17. Gridded Response How many 2-letter combinations are possible from the letters *A, B, C, D, E,* and *F*?

Estimate each square root to the nearest whole number. (Lesson 9-7)

18. $\sqrt{76}$ **19.** $\sqrt{31}$ **20.** $\sqrt{126}$ **21.** $\sqrt{55}$

Decide whether each set of events is independent or dependent. Explain your answer. (Lesson 11-5)

22. A student is chosen at random from a list. A second student is chosen from the same list.

23. A girl chooses a piece of fruit from one bin. A boy then chooses a piece of fruit from a different bin.

11-7 Permutations

Learn to find the number of possible permutations.

Vocabulary

permutation

factorial

Georgia Performance Standards

M7P5.a Create and use representations to organize, record, and communicate mathematical ideas. Also, M7P1.c, M7P1.d, M7P4.c, M7P5.b.

The conductor of a symphony orchestra is planning a concert titled "An Evening with the Killer B's." The concert will feature music by Bach, Beethoven, Brahms, and Bartok. In how many different orders can the conductor arrange the music of the four composers?

An arrangement of objects or events in which the order is important is called a **permutation**. You can use a list to find the number of permutations of a group of objects.

EXAMPLE 1 Using a List to Find Permutations

In how many different orders can the conductor arrange the music composed by Bach, Beethoven, Brahms, and Bartok?

Use a list to find the possible permutations.

Let 1 = Bach, 2 = Beethoven, 3 = Brahms, and 4 = Bartok.

1-2-3-4	*List all*	2-1-3-4	*List all*
1-2-4-3	*permutations*	2-1-4-3	*permutations*
1-3-2-4	*beginning with 1.*	2-3-1-4	*beginning with 2.*
1-3-4-2		2-3-4-1	
1-4-2-3		2-4-1-3	
1-4-3-2		2-4-3-1	
3-1-2-4	*List all*	4-1-2-3	*List all*
3-1-4-2	*permutations*	4-1-3-2	*permutations*
3-2-1-4	*beginning with 3.*	4-2-1-3	*beginning with 4.*
3-2-4-1		4-2-3-1	
3-4-1-2		4-3-1-2	
3-4-2-1		4-3-2-1	

There are 24 permutations. Therefore, the conductor can arrange the music by the four composers in 24 different orders.

You can use the Fundamental Counting Principle to find the number of permutations.

EXAMPLE 2 **Using the Fundamental Counting Principle to Find the Number of Permutations**

Three students have agreed to serve in leadership positions for the Spanish Club. In how many different ways can the students fill the positions of president, vice-president, and secretary?

Once you fill a position, you have one less choice for the next position.

There are 3 choices for the first position.

There are 2 remaining choices for the second position.

There is 1 remaining choice for the third position.

$3 \cdot 2 \cdot 1 = 6$ *Multiply.*

There are 6 different ways that 3 students can fill the 3 positons.

Remember!

The Fundamental Counting Principle states that you can find the total number of outcomes by multiplying the number of outcomes for each separate experiment.

A **factorial** of a whole number is the product of all the whole numbers except zero that are less than or equal to the number.

"3 factorial" is $3! = 3 \cdot 2 \cdot 1 = 6$

"6 factorial" is $6! = 6 \cdot 5 \cdot 4 \cdot 3 \cdot 2 \cdot 1 = 720$

You can use factorials to find the number of permutations.

EXAMPLE 3 **Using Factorials to Find the Number of Permutations**

There are 9 players in a baseball lineup. How many different batting orders are possible for these 9 players?

Number of permutations $= 9!$

$= 9 \cdot 8 \cdot 7 \cdot 6 \cdot 5 \cdot 4 \cdot 3 \cdot 2 \cdot 1$

$= 362,880$

There are 362,880 different batting orders for 9 players.

Helpful Hint

You can use a calculator to find the factorial of a number. To find 5!, press 5
 PRB 4:!
 .

Think and Discuss  GPS M7P1.d, M7P2.c

1. **Evaluate** how the permutations are listed in Example 1. Why is it important to follow a pattern?

2. **Explain** why 8! gives the number of permutations of 8 objects.

 **11-7 Exercises**

 **Georgia Performance Standards**
M7P1.b, M7P3.a, M7P3.c, M7P5.b

 go.hrw.com
Homework Help Online
KEYWORD: MS7 11-7
Parent Resources Online
KEYWORD: MS7 Parent

GUIDED PRACTICE

 See Example **1**
1. In how many ways can you arrange the numbers 1, 2, 3, and 4 to make a 4-digit number?

 See Example **2**
2. Find the number of permutations of the letters in the word *quiet*.

See Example **3**
3. Sam wants to call 6 friends to invite them to a party. In how many different orders can he make the calls?

4. Seven people are waiting to audition for a play. In how many different orders can the auditions be done?

INDEPENDENT PRACTICE

See Example **1**
5. In how many ways can Eric, Meera, and Roger stand in line?

See Example **2**
6. Find the number of ways you can arrange the letters in the word *art*.

See Example **3**
7. How many permutations of the letters *A* through *J* are there?

8. In how many different ways can 8 riders be matched up with 8 horses?

PRACTICE AND PROBLEM SOLVING

 CRCT GPS
Extra Practice p. 749

Determine whether each problem involves combinations or permutations. Explain your answer.

9. Choose five books to check out from a group of ten.

10. Decide how many ways five people can be assigned to sit in five chairs.

11. Choose a 4-digit PIN using all of the digits 3, 7, 1, and 8.

12. **Sports** Ten golfers on a team are playing in a tournament. How many different lineups can the golf coach make?

13. Carl, Melba, Sean, and Ricki are going to present individual reports in their Spanish class. Their teacher randomly selects which student will speak first. What is the probability that Melba will present her report first?

14. Using the digits 1 through 7, Pima County is assigning new 7-digit numbers to all households. How many possible numbers can the county assign without repeating any of the digits in a number?

15. How many different 5-digit numbers can be made using the digits 6, 3, 5, 0, and 4 without repetitions?

16. In how many different orders can 12 songs on a CD be played?

17. **Multi-Step** If you have 5 items, and you can fit 3 of them on a shelf, how many choices do you have for the first item on the shelf? for the second item? for the third item? How many different orders are possible for the 3 items chosen from 5 items?

18. **Health** A survey was taken to find out how 200 people age 40 and older rate their memory now compared to 10 years ago. In how many different orders could interviews be conducted with people who think their memory is the same?

19. **Literature** The school library has 13 books by Louisa May Alcott. Merina wants to read all 13 of them one after another. Write an expression to show the number of ways she can do that.

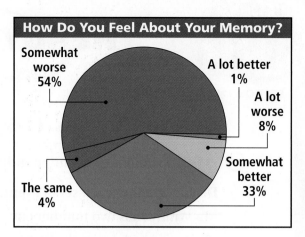

How Do You Feel About Your Memory?

Somewhat worse 54%
A lot better 1%
A lot worse 8%
Somewhat better 33%
The same 4%

20. Use the letters *A, D, E, R*.

   a. How many permutations of the letters are there?

   b. How many arrangements form English words?

21. Josie and Luke have 3 sunflowers and 4 bluebonnets. Josie selects a flower at random. Then Luke chooses a flower at random from the remaining flowers. What is the probability that Josie picks a sunflower and Luke chooses a bluebonnet?

22. **What's the Error?** A student was trying to find 5! and wrote the equation $5 + 4 + 3 + 2 + 1 = 15$. Why is this student incorrect?

23. **Write About It** Explain the difference between combinations of objects and permutations of objects. Give examples of each.

24. **Challenge** Evaluate $\dfrac{11!}{3!(11-3)!}$.

CRCT Prep • GPS Support • Spiral Review

25. **Multiple Choice** Which expression can you use to find the number of 5-digit passwords you can make using the digits 1, 3, 5, 7, and 9, if you do not repeat any of the digits?

   Ⓐ $9 + 7 + 5 + 3 + 1$ Ⓒ $5 + 4 + 3 + 2 + 1$

   Ⓑ $9 \cdot 7 \cdot 5 \cdot 3 \cdot 1$ Ⓓ $5 \cdot 4 \cdot 3 \cdot 2 \cdot 1$

26. **Gridded Response** A school play has seven different characters. In how many different ways can seven students be assigned to the roles?

27. Use the Pythagorean Theorem to find the missing measure in the triangle at right. Round to the nearest tenth. (Lesson 9-8)

c   16 in.

9 in.

28. Margaret is traveling. She can bring two of her 9 favorite books with her. How many different combinations of 2 books can she bring? (Lesson 11-6)

Quiz for Lessons 11-5 Through 11-7

☑ **11-5** **Probability of Independent and Dependent Events**

Decide whether each set of events is independent or dependent. Explain.

1. Winny rolls two number cubes and gets a 5 on one and a 3 on the other.

2. A card with hearts is drawn from a full deck of cards and not replaced. Then a card with clubs is drawn from the same deck.

A bag contains 8 blue and 7 yellow marbles. Use this information for Exercises 3 and 4.

3. Find the probability of randomly drawing a blue marble and then randomly drawing a yellow marble without replacing the first marble.

4. Find the probability of randomly drawing a blue marble and then randomly drawing another blue marble after replacing the first marble.

5. Marcelo has six $1 bills, two $5 bills, and one $10 bill in his pocket. He selects two of the bills at random. What is the probability that Marcelo picks one $5 bill and the $10 bill?

☑ **11-6** **Combinations**

6. Kenny wants the guests to have 2 juice options at his party. There are 8 different juices that he has to choose from. How many different ways can Kenny choose 2 different juices?

7. Find the number of different ways that 2 out of 12 students can volunteer to organize a class party.

8. A restaurant offers entrees with a choice of 2 side dishes. How many combinations of 2 sides are available from a list of 9 side dishes?

☑ **11-7** **Permutations**

9. Four swimmers are chosen to swim in a relay race. How many orders of the 4 swimmers are possible for the relay race?

10. Six students have volunteered to help with the Spring Fest. In how many ways can these six students be assigned the following positions: concession stand, dunking booth, face-painting booth, fishing pond, ring toss, and haystack hunt?

11. Employees on the second floor have been given five 1-digit numbers from which to create a 5-digit passcode to unlock a color copier. From how many different passcodes can they choose if the passcode cannot have repeated numbers?

The Life of the Party Chantal has a party-planning business. She organizes, caters, and runs parties. Chantal sometimes uses probability when planning party activities.

1. Chantal often prepares a Prize Walk for her parties. Guests walk along a circular path with spaces numbered 1 through 24, and Chantal randomly calls out one of the numbers. If someone is standing on that number, he or she wins a prize. What is the probability that someone will win a prize if 8 people are playing? if 10 people are playing?

2. How many people must play the Prize Walk so that the probability of someone winning a prize is at least 0.75?

3. Chantal plans to play two rounds of the Prize Walk at an upcoming party. All 24 guests will participate in both rounds. Chantal is concerned that the same person will win both times. How likely is this? Is the probability greater than or less than 1%? Explain.

4. Chantal will bring six different prizes to the party. How many different combinations of two prizes can be chosen by the Prize Walk winners?

5. Chantal gives away T-shirts at her parties to advertise her business. Use the table to find how many different styles of T-shirts are available.

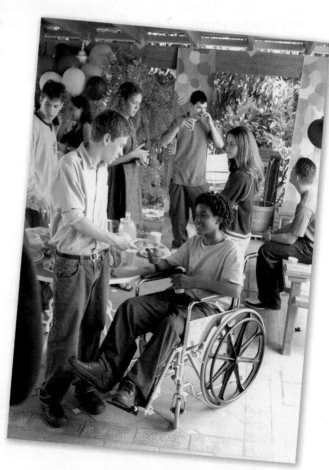

T-Shirt Options	
Sizes	S, M, L, XL
Colors	Blue, white, red
Sleeves	Long, short

GAME TIME

Buffon's Needle

If you drop a needle of a given length onto a wooden floor with evenly spaced cracks, what is the probability that it will land across a crack?

Compte de Buffon (1707–1788) posed this geometric probability problem. To answer his question, Buffon developed a formula using ℓ to represent the length of the needle and d to represent the distance between the cracks.

$$\text{probability} = \frac{2\ell}{\pi d}$$

To re-create this experiment, you need a paper clip and several evenly spaced lines drawn on a piece of paper. Make sure that the distance between the lines is greater than the length of the paper clip. Toss the paper clip onto the piece of paper at least a dozen times. Divide the number of times the paper clip lands across a line by the number of times you toss the paper clip. Compare this quotient to the probability given by the formula.

The other interesting result of Buffon's discovery is that you can use the probability of the needle toss to estimate *pi*.

$$\pi = \frac{2\ell}{\text{probability} \cdot d}$$

Toss the paper clip 20 times to find the experimental probability. Use this probability in the formula above, and compare the result to 3.14.

Pattern Match

This game is for two players. Player A arranges four different pattern blocks in a row out of the view of player B. Player B then tries to guess the arrangement. After each guess, player A reveals how many of the blocks are in the correct position without telling which blocks they are. The round ends when player B correctly guesses the arrangement.

A complete set of game pieces are available online.

go.hrw.com
Game Time Extra
KEYWORD: MS7 Games

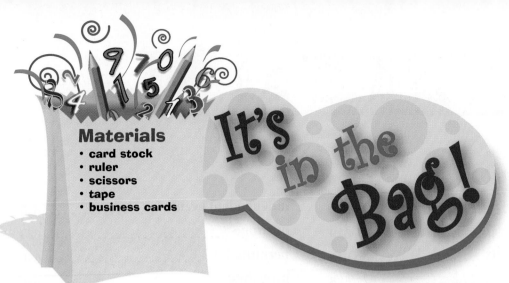

Materials
- card stock
- ruler
- scissors
- tape
- business cards

It's in the Bag!

PROJECT ▶ **The Business of Probability**

Make a holder for business cards. Then use the business cards to take notes on probability.

❶ Cut a piece of card stock to $7\frac{1}{2}$ inches by $4\frac{1}{2}$ inches. Fold the card stock in thirds and then unfold it. **Figure A**

❷ Cut out a trapezoid that is about $\frac{1}{2}$-inch tall from one end of the card stock as shown. **Figure B**

❸ Cut off about $\frac{1}{2}$ inch along the other end of the card stock. Then cut the corners at an angle. **Figure C**

❹ Fold up the bottom section of the card stock and tape the edges closed. **Figure D**

Taking Note of the Math

Use the backs of business cards to take notes on probability. Store the business cards in the holder that you made. Write the name and number of the chapter on the flap of the holder.

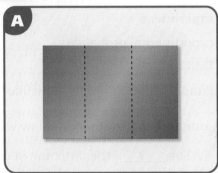

A

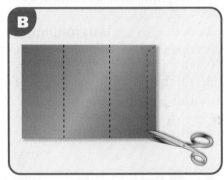

B

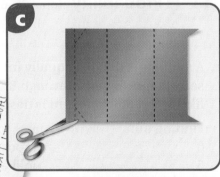

C

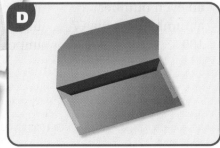

D

Study Guide: Review

Vocabulary

Complete the sentences below with vocabulary words from the list above.

1. For ___?___, the outcome of one event has no effect on the outcome of a second event.

2. A(n) ___?___ is a grouping of objects or events in which order does not matter.

3. All the possible outcomes of an experiment make up the ___?___.

4. A(n) ___?___ is a result of an experiment.

11-1 Probability (pp. 628–631)

 GPS M7N1.d

EXAMPLE

■ A spinner is divided equally into 8 sectors numbered 1 through 8. The likelihood of each event is described.

landing on:

0	impossible
5	unlikely
an even number	as likely as not
a number less than 7	likely
100	impossible

EXERCISES

Determine whether each event is impossible, unlikely, as likely as not, likely, or certain.

5. rolling a sum of 12 with two number cubes

6. rolling a sum of 24 with two number cubes

7. The probability of rain is 20%. What is the probability of no rain?

8. The probability of the football team winning its last game is $\frac{1}{5}$. What is the probability of the team not winning the last game?

11-2 Experimental Probability (pp. 632–635)

 GPS M7N1.d, M7A2.b, M7D1.g

EXAMPLE

■ Of 50 people surveyed, 21 said they liked mysteries better than comedies. What is the probability that the next person surveyed will prefer mysteries?

$$P(\text{mysteries}) = \frac{\text{number who like mysteries}}{\text{total number surveyed}}$$

$$P(\text{mysteries}) = \frac{21}{50}$$

The probability that the next person surveyed will prefer mysteries is $\frac{21}{50}$.

EXERCISES

Sami has been keeping a record of her math grades. Of her first 15 grades, 10 have been above 82.

9. What is the probability that her next grade will be above 82?

10. What is the probability that her next grade will not be above 82?

11-3 Make a List to Find Sample Spaces (pp. 636–639)

 GPS M7P5.a

EXAMPLE

■ Anita tosses a coin and rolls a number cube. How many outcomes are possible?

The coin has 2 outcomes. *List the number* The number cube has 6 *of outcomes.* outcomes.

$2 \cdot 6 = 12$ *Use the Fundamental Counting Principle.*

There are 12 possible outcomes.

EXERCISES

Chen spins each of the spinners once.

11. What are all the possible outcomes?

12. How many outcomes are in the sample space?

11-4 Theoretical Probability (pp. 640–643)

 GPS M7N1.d, M7A2.b

EXAMPLE

■ Find the probability of drawing a 4 from a standard deck of 52 playing cards. Write your answer as a fraction, as a decimal, and as a percent.

$$P(4) = \frac{\text{number of 4's in deck}}{\text{number of cards in deck}}$$

$$= \frac{4}{52}$$

$$= \frac{1}{13}$$

$$\approx 0.077 \approx 7.7\%$$

EXERCISES

Find each probability. Write your answer as a fraction, as a decimal, and as a percent.

13. There are 9 girls and 12 boys on the student council. What is the probability that a girl will be chosen as president?

14. Anita tosses 3 coins. What is the probability that each coin will land tails up?

15. Jefferson chooses a marble from a bag containing 6 blue, 9 white, 3 orange, and 11 green marbles. What is the probability that he will select a green marble?

11-5 Probability of Independent and Dependent Events (pp. 648–651)

GPS M7N1.d

EXAMPLE

■ There are 4 red marbles, 3 green marbles, 6 blue marbles, and 2 black marbles in a bag. What is the probability that Angie will pick a green marble and then a black marble without replacing the first marble?

$P(\text{green marble}) = \frac{3}{15} = \frac{1}{5}$

$P(\text{black after green}) = \frac{2}{14} = \frac{1}{7}$

$P(\text{green, then black}) = \frac{1}{5} \cdot \frac{1}{7} = \frac{1}{35}$

The probability of picking a green marble and then a black marble with no replacement is $\frac{1}{35}$.

EXERCISES

16. There are 40 tags numbered 1 through 40 in a bag. What is the probability that Glenn will randomly pick a multiple of 5 and then a multiple of 9 without replacing the first tag?

17. Each letter of the word *probability* is written on a card and put in a bag. What is the probability of picking a vowel on the first try and again on the second try if the first card is replaced?

11-6 Combinations (pp. 652–655)

GPS M7P5.a

EXAMPLE

■ Tina, Sam, and Jo are trying out for the 2 lead parts in a play. In how many ways can they be chosen for the parts?

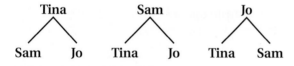

There are 6 possible ways the students can be chosen for the parts.

EXERCISES

18. How many ways can you select 2 pieces of fruit from a basket of 5 pieces?

19. How many 2-person groups can be chosen from 7 people?

20. How many combinations of 2 balloons can be chosen from 9 balloons?

11-7 Permutations (pp. 656–659)

GPS M7P5.a

EXAMPLE

■ How many different four-digit numbers can you make from the numbers 2, 4, 6, and 8 using each just once?

There are 4 choices for the first digit, 3 choices for the second, 2 choices for the third, and 1 for the fourth.

$4 \cdot 3 \cdot 2 \cdot 1 = 24$

There are 24 different four-digit numbers.

EXERCISES

21. How many different batting orders are possible for 10 players on a league softball team?

22. How many different ways can you arrange the letters in the word *number*?

23. In how many ways can Tanya, Rika, Andy, Evan, and Tanisha line up for lunch?

Study Guide: Review

A box contains 3 orange cubes, 2 white cubes, 3 black cubes, and 4 blue cubes. Determine whether each event is impossible, unlikely, as likely as not, likely, or certain.

1. randomly choosing an orange or black cube

2. randomly choosing a white cube

3. randomly choosing a purple cube

4. Simon tosses a coin 20 times. The coin lands heads up 7 times. Based on these results, how many times can Simon expect the coin to land heads up in the next 100 tosses?

5. Emilio spins a spinner that is divided into 8 equal sectors numbered 1 through 8. In his first three spins, the spinner lands on 8. What is the experimental probability that Emilio will spin a 10 on his fourth spin?

6. A brand of jeans comes in 8 different waist sizes: 28, 30, 32, 34, 36, 38, 40, and 42. The jeans also come in three different colors: blue, black, and tan. How many different combinations of waist sizes and colors are possible?

7. Greg is planning his vacation. He can choose from 3 ways to travel—train, bus, or plane—and four different activities—skiing, skating, snowboarding, or hiking. What are all the possible outcomes? How many different vacations can Greg plan?

Rachel spins a spinner that is divided into 10 equal sectors numbered 1 through 10. Find each probability. Write your answer as a fraction, as a decimal, and as a percent.

8. *P*(odd number) 9. *P*(composite number) 10. *P*(number greater than 10)

Find the probability of each event.

11. spinning red on a spinner with equally sized red, blue, yellow, and green sectors, and flipping a coin that lands tails up

12. choosing a card labeled *vanilla* from a group of cards labeled *vanilla, chocolate, strawberry,* and *swirl,* and then choosing a card labeled *chocolate* without replacing the first card

13. How many ways can 2 students be chosen from 10 students?

14. How many ways can you choose 2 different snacks from a menu of raisins, oranges, yogurt, apples, crackers, nuts, and grapes?

15. Timothy wants to arrange his 6 model cars on a shelf. How many ways can he arrange them?

16. How many ways can you choose a 7-letter password from 7 different letters if the letters cannot repeat?

All Types: Use a Diagram

Sometimes drawing a diagram helps you solve a problem. When a diagram is given with a test item, use it as a tool. Get as much information from the drawing as possible. Keep in mind that diagrams are not always drawn to scale and can be misleading.

EXAMPLE 1

Multiple Choice What is the probability of flipping a coin and getting tails, and then rolling an even number on a number cube?

(A) $\frac{1}{2}$

(C) $\frac{1}{6}$

(B) $\frac{1}{4}$

(D) $\frac{1}{12}$

You can create a tree diagram to determine the sample space.

Heads   **Tails**

1 2 3 4 5 6   1 2 3 4 5 6

There are 12 possible outcomes but only 3 ways getting tails and an even number can occur. So the probability is $\frac{3}{12}$, or $\frac{1}{4}$, which is answer choice B.

EXAMPLE 2

Short Response Find the volume and surface area of the cylinder, and round your answers to the nearest tenth. Use 3.14 for π.

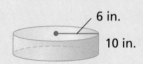

6 in.

10 in.

In the diagram, it appears that the radius is greater than the height. Remember that the scale of a diagram can be misleading. Rely on the information shown, and substitute the given values into each formula.

$V = \pi r^2 h$ $SA = 2\pi r^2 + 2\pi r h$

$V = \pi(6)^2(10)$ $SA = 2\pi(6)^2 + 2\pi(6)(10)$

$V = 360\pi$ $SA = 226.08 + 376.8$

$V \approx 1{,}130.4 \text{ in}^3$ $SA \approx 602.9 \text{ in}^2$

If you are having trouble understanding a test item, draw a diagram to help you answer the question.

Read each test item, and answer the questions that follow.

Item A
Multiple Choice The volume of a box is 6,336 cm³. The width of the box is 16 cm, and the height is 18 cm. What is the length of the box?

Ⓐ 396 cm   Ⓒ 220 cm

Ⓑ 22 cm   Ⓓ 11 cm

---

1. What information about the box is given in the problem statement?

2. Sketch a diagram to help you answer the question. Label each side with the correct dimensions.

3. How does the diagram help you solve the problem?

Item B
Multiple Choice Janet spins two spinners at the same time. One spinner is divided into 3 equal sectors, labeled 1, 2, and 3. The second spinner is divided into 3 equal sectors, labeled A, B, and C. What is the probability that the spinners will land on 1 and A or 1 and C?

Ⓕ $\frac{1}{3}$ Ⓗ $\frac{1}{9}$

Ⓖ $\frac{2}{3}$ Ⓙ $\frac{2}{9}$

---

4. Make a tree diagram to determine the sample space. Then count the ways getting 1 and either A or C can occur.

5. Explain which answer choice is correct.

6. How does the tree diagram help you solve the problem?

Item C
Short Response Which two vats hold the same amount of liquid? Explain.

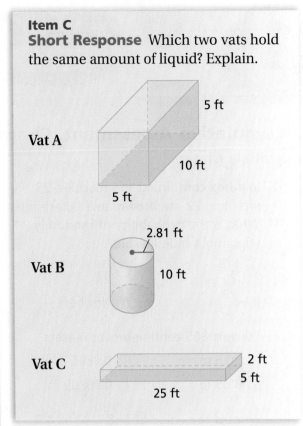

7. Explain why you cannot determine the answer by comparing the scale of each diagram.

8. What formulas do you need to find the answer?

9. Explain which two vats hold the same amount of liquid.

Item D
Gridded Response Determine the surface area in square meters of a rectangular prism that has a length of 13 m, a width of 10 m, and a height of 8 m.

---

10. How do you determine the surface area of a rectangular prism?

11. Create a net for this prism and label it with the correct dimensions.

12. Use the net from problem 11 to find the surface area of the prism.

Cumulative Assessment, Chapters 1–11

Multiple Choice

1. In a box containing 115 marbles, 25 are blue, 22 are brown, and 68 are red. What is the probability of randomly selecting a blue marble?

Ⓐ $\frac{115}{25}$ Ⓒ $\frac{5}{23}$

Ⓑ $\frac{22}{115}$ Ⓓ Not here

2. Convert 805 centimeters to meters.

Ⓕ 80.5 m   Ⓗ 0.0805 m

Ⓖ 8.05 m   Ⓙ 0.00805 m

3. What is the value of $(-8 - 4)^2 + 4^1$?

Ⓐ −143   Ⓒ 145

Ⓑ 0   Ⓓ 148

4. The graph shows a town's high temperatures over a 5-day period. What was the average high temperature over these 5 days?

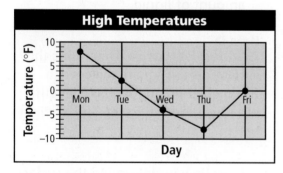

Ⓕ −0.4°F   Ⓗ 0.4°F

Ⓖ 4.4°F   Ⓙ −4.4°F

5. The fraction $\frac{3}{5}$ is found between which pair of fractions on a number line?

Ⓐ $\frac{7}{10}$ and $\frac{3}{4}$ Ⓒ $\frac{2}{5}$ and $\frac{1}{2}$

Ⓑ $\frac{2}{7}$ and $\frac{8}{11}$ Ⓓ $\frac{1}{3}$ and $\frac{5}{13}$

6. Stu wants to leave a 15% tip for his dinner that cost $13.40. About how much tip should Stu leave?

Ⓕ $1.50   Ⓗ $2.00

Ⓖ $1.75   Ⓙ $2.50

7. What is $2\frac{5}{12} \times \frac{12}{7}$?

Ⓐ $\frac{5}{7}$ Ⓒ $2\frac{17}{19}$

Ⓑ $2\frac{5}{7}$ Ⓓ $4\frac{1}{7}$

8. Find the surface area of the rectangular prism.

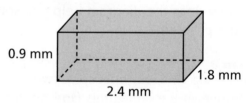

Ⓕ 8.1 mm²   Ⓗ 15.84 mm²

Ⓖ 16.2 mm²   Ⓙ 3.888 mm²

9. A triangle-shaped wheat field has an area of 225 ft². What is the length of the hypotenuse to the nearest tenth?

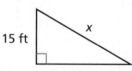

Ⓐ 30 ft   Ⓒ 45 ft

Ⓑ 33.5 ft   Ⓓ 224.5 ft

10. Which number is NOT expressed in scientific notation?

Ⓕ 7×10^5 Ⓗ 0.23×10^9

Ⓖ 1.9×10^1 Ⓙ 9.2×10^{25}

11. Five of the angles in a hexagon measure 155°, 120°, 62°, 65°, and 172°. What is the measure of the sixth angle?

   (A) 115°   (C) 180°

   (B) 146°   (D) 326°

Probability can be expressed as a fraction, decimal, or percent.

Use the following graph for items 12 and 13.

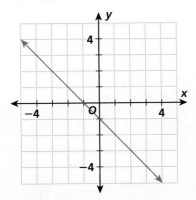

12. Find the *y*-coordinate of the point on the line whose *x*-coordinate is −1.

   (F) −1   (H) 1

   (G) 0   (J) 2

13. Determine the value of *y* when *x* = −6.

   (A) −6   (C) 5

   (B) −5   (D) 6

14. Anji bought 4 shirts for $56.80. She later bought a shirt for $19.20. What was the mean cost of all the shirts in dollars?

   (F) $11.36   (H) $15.20

   (G) $14.20   (J) $38.00

15. What is the value of *x*? $12 = x - \frac{2}{3}$

   (A) $\frac{34}{3}$ (C) 18

   (B) 12   (D) $\frac{38}{3}$

Short Response

16. The diameter of the larger circle is 36 in., and the radius of the smaller circle is 6 in.

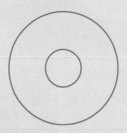

What is the ratio of the smaller circle's area to the larger circle's area written to the nearest whole percent?

17. Rhonda has 3 different-color T-shirts—red, blue, and green—and a pair of blue jeans and a pair of white jeans. She randomly chooses a T-shirt and a pair of jeans. What is the probability that she will pair the red T-shirt with the white jeans? Show how you found your answer.

18. Write $\frac{5}{6}$ and $\frac{3}{4}$ as fractions with a common denominator. Then determine whether the fractions are equivalent. Explain your method.

Extended Response

19. A bag contains 5 blue blocks, 3 red blocks, and 2 yellow blocks.

  a. What is the probability that Tip will draw a red block and then a blue block at random if the first block is replaced before the second is drawn? Show the steps necessary to find your answer.

  b. What is the probability that Tip will draw a red block and then a blue block at random if the first block is not replaced before the second is drawn? Show your work.

  c. Explain how your answers to parts **a** and **b** are affected by whether or not the first block is replaced.

CRCT Prep **671**

Multi-Step Equations and Inequalities

CRCT PREP

go.hrw.com
Chapter Project Online
KEYWORD: MS7 Ch12

Altitudes of Artificial Satellites	
Satellite	Altitude (km)
Sputnik	245
Skylab	270
Mir	390
International Space Station	420

Career *Satellite Engineer*

Artificial satellites were born with the launch of *Sputnik* on October 4, 1957. The 84 kg ball with a 56 cm diameter circled Earth every 35 minutes and signified the beginning of changes in the way people live. Today, there are over 2,500 satellites orbiting Earth.

Satellite engineers work on satellite design, construction, orbit determination, launch, tracking, and orbit adjustment. Satellites can monitor weather, crop growth, and natural resources and communicate this information using television, radio, and other communication signals. Satellites can even directionally guide people who have GPS (Global Positioning System) devices.

ARE YOU READY?

✓ Vocabulary

Choose the best term from the list to complete each sentence.

1. __?__ are mathematical operations that undo each other.

2. To solve an equation you need to __?__.

3. A(n) __?__ is a mathematical statement that two expressions are equivalent.

4. A(n) __?__ is a mathematical statement that two ratios are equivalent.

isolate the variable

equation

proportion

inverse operations

expression

Complete these exercises to review skills you will need for this chapter.

✓ Add Whole Numbers, Decimals, Fractions, and Integers

Add.

5. $24 + 16$

6. $-34 + (-47)$

7. $35 + (-61)$

8. $-12 + (-29) + 53$

9. $2.7 + 3.5$

10. $\frac{2}{3} + \frac{1}{2}$

11. $-5.87 + 10.6$

12. $\frac{8}{9} + \left(-\frac{9}{11}\right)$

✓ Evaluate Expressions

Evaluate each expression for $a = 7$ and $b = -2$.

13. $a - b$

14. $b - a$

15. $\frac{b}{a}$

16. $2a + 3b$

17. $\frac{-4a}{b}$

18. $3a - \frac{8}{b}$

19. $1.2a + 2.3b$

20. $-5a - (-6b)$

✓ Solve Multiplication Equations

Solve.

21. $8x = -72$

22. $-12a = -60$

23. $\frac{2}{3}y = 16$

24. $-12b = 9$

25. $12 = -4x$

26. $13 = \frac{1}{2}c$

27. $-2.4 = -0.8p$

28. $\frac{3}{4} = 6x$

✓ Solve Proportions

Solve.

29. $\frac{3}{4} = \frac{x}{24}$

30. $\frac{8}{9} = \frac{4}{a}$

31. $-\frac{12}{5} = \frac{15}{c}$

32. $\frac{y}{50} = \frac{35}{20}$

33. $\frac{2}{3} = \frac{18}{w}$

34. $\frac{35}{21} = \frac{d}{3}$

35. $\frac{7}{13} = \frac{h}{195}$

36. $\frac{9}{-15} = \frac{-27}{p}$

Study Guide: Preview

Where You've Been

Previously, you

- solved one-step equations.
- read, wrote, and graphed inequalities on a number line.
- solved one-step inequalities.

In This Chapter

You will study

- solving two-step and multi-step equations and equations with variables on both sides.
- reading, writing, and graphing inequalities on a number line.
- solving one-step and two-step inequalities.
- solving equations for a variable.

Where You're Going

You can use the skills learned in this chapter

- to solve problems in the physical sciences that involve comparing speeds, distances, and weights.
- to make decisions when planning events.
- to evaluate options when distributing budget funds.

Key Vocabulary/Vocabulario

algebraic inequality	desigualdad algebraica
compound inequality	desigualdad compuesta
inequality	desigualdad
solution set	conjunto solución

Vocabulary Connections

To become familiar with some of the vocabulary terms in the chapter, consider the following. You may refer to the chapter, the glossary, or a dictionary if you like.

1. What does the word *inequality* mean? How might an **inequality** describe a mathematical relationship? Give an example using numbers.

2. An example of an algebraic equation is $x + 3 = 8$. How do you think $x + 3 = 8$ would change if you were to write it as an **algebraic inequality** instead of as an equation?

3. A compound sentence is made up of two or more independent clauses joined by the words *and* or *or*. What do you think a **compound inequality** might be?

4. A solution of an equation is a value that makes the equation true. For example, $x = 5$ is a solution of $x + 3 = 8$. A set is a group of "items," such as people or numbers, that have a characteristic in common. What do you think a **solution set** might be?

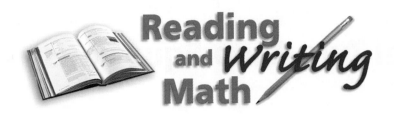 **Reading** and *Writing* **Math**

Study Strategy: Prepare for Your Final Exam

Math is a cumulative subject, so your exam will cover all of the material you have learned from the beginning of the course. Being prepared is the key for you to be successful on your exam.

2 weeks before the final exam

- Review lesson notes and vocabulary.
- Look at previous exams and homework. Rework problems that I answered incorrectly or that I did not complete.
- Make a list of all formulas, rules, and important steps.
- Create a practice exam using problems from the book that are similar to problems from the previous tests.

1 week before the final exam

- Take the practice exam and check it. For each problem I miss, find two or three similar problems and work those.
- Look over each chapter's Study Guide: Review.
- Quiz a friend or myself on the formulas and major points from my list.

1 day before the final exam

- Make sure I have pencils and a calculator. (Check the batteries!)
- Review any problem areas one last time.

 FINAL

Try This

1. Create a timeline that you will use to study for your final exam.

Model Two-Step Equations

Use with Lesson 12-1

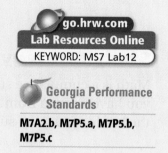

go.hrw.com
Lab Resources Online
KEYWORD: MS7 Lab12

Georgia Performance Standards

M7A2.b, M7P5.a, M7P5.b, M7P5.c

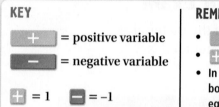

KEY

+ = positive variable

− = negative variable

+ = 1   − = −1

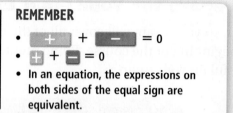

REMEMBER

- + + − = 0
- + + − = 0
- In an equation, the expressions on both sides of the equal sign are equivalent.

In Lab 2-5, you learned how to solve one-step equations using algebra tiles. You can also use algebra tiles to solve two-step equations. When solving a two-step equation, it is easiest to perform addition and subtraction before multiplication and division.

Activity

1 Use algebra tiles to model and solve $2p + 2 = 10$.

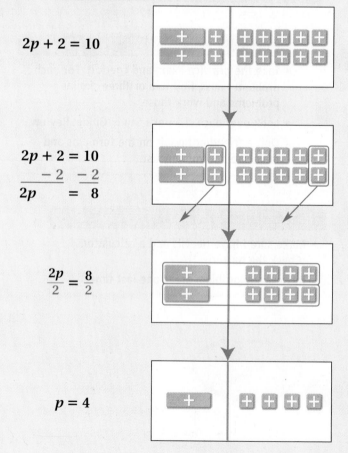

$2p + 2 = 10$ *Model the equation.*

$$\begin{array}{r} 2p + 2 = 10 \\ -2 \quad -2 \\ \hline 2p \quad = 8 \end{array}$$

Remove 2 yellow tiles from each side of the mat.

$$\frac{2p}{2} = \frac{8}{2}$$ *Divide each side into 2 equal groups.*

$p = 4$ *The solution is p = 4.*

2 Use algebra tiles to model and solve $3n + 6 = -15$.

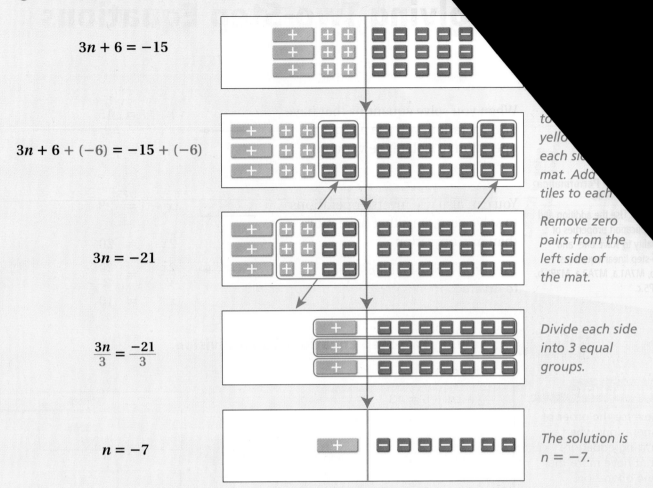

$3n + 6 = -15$

$3n + 6 + (-6) = -15 + (-6)$

to
yello
each si
mat. Add
tiles to each

Remove zero
pairs from the
left side of
the mat.

$3n = -21$

$\dfrac{3n}{3} = \dfrac{-21}{3}$

Divide each side
into 3 equal
groups.

$n = -7$

The solution is
$n = -7$.

Think and Discuss

1. When you add a value to one side of an equation, why do you also have to add the same value to the other side?

2. When you solved $3n + 6 = -15$ in the activity, why were you able to remove six yellow unit tiles and six red unit tiles from the left side of the equation?

3. Model and solve $3x - 5 = 10$. Explain each step.

4. How would you check the solution to $3n + 6 = -15$ using algebra tiles?

Try This

Use algebra tiles to model and solve each equation.

1. $4 + 2x = 20$

2. $3r + 7 = -8$

3. $-4m + 3 = -25$

4. $-2n - 5 = 17$

5. $10 = 2j - 4$

6. $5 + r = 7$

7. $4h + 2h + 3 = 15$

8. $-3g = 9$

9. $5k + (-7) = 13$

Two-Step Equations

Model the
equation.

It is not possible
to remove 6
... tiles from
... side of the
... 6 red
side.

...ns that have
...an inverse
...variable.

$$n + 7 = 15$$
$$\underline{-7 \quad -7}$$
$$n = 8$$

...perations
...ve more

$$2x + 3 = 23$$
$$\underline{-3 \quad -3}$$
$$2x = 20$$

...multiplication
to isolate x.

$$\frac{2x}{2} = \frac{20}{2}$$
$$x = 10$$

EXAMPLE 1 — Solving Two-Step Equations Using Division

Solve.

A $2n + 5 = 13$

Helpful Hint

Reverse the order of
operations when
solving equations
that have more than
one operation.

$$2n + 5 = 13$$
$$\underline{-5 \quad -5}$$
$$2n = 8$$

Subtract 5 from
both sides.

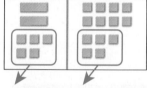

$$\frac{2n}{2} = \frac{8}{2}$$
$$n = 4$$

Divide both
sides by 2.

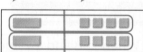

B $19 = -3p - 8$

$$19 = -3p - 8$$
$$\underline{+8 \qquad\quad +8}$$
$$27 = -3p$$

Add 8 to both sides.

$$\frac{27}{-3} = \frac{-3p}{-3}$$

Divide both sides by −3.

$$-9 = p$$

Check

$$19 = -3p - 8$$
$$19 \stackrel{?}{=} -3(-9) - 8 \qquad \text{Substitute −9 for p.}$$
$$19 \stackrel{?}{=} 27 - 8$$
$$19 \stackrel{?}{=} 19 \checkmark \qquad \text{−9 is a solution.}$$

EXAMPLE 2 **Solving Two-Step Equations Using Multiplication**

Solve.

A $8 + \dfrac{m}{4} = 17$

$$\begin{array}{rl} 8 + \dfrac{m}{4} &= 17 \\ -8 \qquad &-8 \end{array}$$ Subtract 8 from both sides.

$$\dfrac{m}{4} = 9$$

$$(4)\dfrac{m}{4} = (4)9$$ Multiply both sides by 4.

$$m = 36$$

B $3 = \dfrac{u}{6} - 12$

$$\begin{array}{rl} 3 &= \dfrac{u}{6} - 12 \\ +12 \qquad &+12 \end{array}$$ Add 12 to both sides.

$$15 = \dfrac{u}{6}$$

$$(6)15 = (6)\dfrac{u}{6}$$ Multiply both sides by 6.

$$90 = u$$

EXAMPLE 3 *Fitness Application*

A new one-year membership at Vista Tennis Center costs $160. A registration fee of $28 is paid up front, and the rest is paid monthly. How much do new members pay each month?

| registration fee | plus | monthly cost | is | $160 |

Let m represent the monthly cost.

| $28 | + | 12$m$ | = | $160 |

$$\begin{array}{rl} 28 + 12m &= 160 \\ -28 \qquad &-28 \end{array}$$ Subtract 28 from both sides.

$$12m = 132$$

$$\dfrac{12m}{12} = \dfrac{132}{12}$$ Divide both sides by 12.

$$m = 11$$

New members pay $11 per month for a one-year membership.

Fitness LINK

Labeled "the sport for a lifetime," tennis is played by people of all ages. Some tennis matches may take just minutes to complete, while others take hours or even days!

Think and Discuss GPS M7P1.d, M7P3.b

1. **Explain** how you decide which inverse operation to use first when solving a two-step equation.

2. **Tell** the steps you would follow to solve $-1 + 2x = 7$.

12-1 Exercises

Georgia Performance Standards

M7P1.a, M7P1.b, M7P5.b

go.hrw.com
Homework Help Online
KEYWORD: MS7 12-1
Parent Resources Online
KEYWORD: MS7 Parent

GUIDED PRACTICE

See Example **Solve.**

1. $3n + 8 = 29$
2. $-4m - 7 = 17$
3. $2 = -6x + 4$

See Example **Solve.**

4. $12 + \frac{b}{6} = 16$
5. $\frac{y}{8} - 15 = 2$
6. $10 = -8 + \frac{n}{4}$

See Example **7.** A coffee shop sells a ceramic refill mug for $8.95. Each refill costs $1.50. Last month Rose spent $26.95 on a mug and refills. How many refills did she buy?

INDEPENDENT PRACTICE

See Example **Solve. Check each answer.**

8. $5x + 6 = 41$
9. $-9p - 15 = 93$
10. $-2m + 14 = 10$

11. $-7 = 7d - 8$
12. $-7 = -3c + 14$
13. $12y - 11 = 49$

See Example **Solve.**

14. $24 + \frac{h}{4} = 10$
15. $\frac{k}{5} - 13 = 4$
16. $-17 + \frac{q}{8} = 13$

17. $24 = \frac{m}{10} + 32$
18. $-9 = 15 + \frac{v}{3}$
19. $\frac{m}{-7} - 14 = 2$

See Example **20.** Each Saturday, a gym holds a 45-minute yoga class. The weekday yoga classes last 30 minutes. The number of weekday classes varies. Last week, the yoga classes totaled 165 minutes. How many weekday yoga classes were held?

PRACTICE AND PROBLEM SOLVING

Extra Practice p. 750

Translate each equation into words, and then solve the equation.

21. $6 + \frac{m}{3} = 18$
22. $3x + 15 = 27$
23. $2 = \frac{n}{5} - 4$

Solve.

24. $18 + \frac{y}{4} = 12$
25. $5x + 30 = 40$
26. $\frac{s}{12} - 7 = 8$

27. $-10 + 6g = 110$
28. $-8 = \frac{z}{7} + 2$
29. $46 = -6w - 8$

30. $15 = -7 + \frac{r}{3}$
31. $-20 = -4p - 12$
32. $\frac{1}{2} + \frac{r}{7} = \frac{5}{14}$

33. Consumer Math A long-distance phone company charges $1.01 for the first 25 minutes of a call, and then $0.09 for each additional minute. A call cost $9.56. How long did it last?

34. The school purchased baseball equipment and uniforms for a total cost of $1,836. The equipment cost $612, and the uniforms were $25.50 each. How many uniforms did the school purchase?

YOUR TOTAL COMES TO $76.41 AND 17,843 CALORIES.

35. If you double the number of calories per day that the U.S. Department of Agriculture recommends for children who are 1 to 3 years old and then subtract 100, you get the number of calories per day recommended for teenage boys. Given that 2,500 calories are recommended for teenage boys, how many calories per day are recommended for children?

36. According to the U.S. Department of Agriculture, children who are 4 to 6 years old need about 1,800 calories per day. This is 700 calories more than half the recommended calories for teenage girls. How many calories per day does a teenage girl need?

As a service to health-conscious customers, many grocery stores have installed scanners that calculate the total number of calories purchased.

37. Hector consumed 2,130 calories from food in one day. Of these, he consumed 350 calories at breakfast and 400 calories having a snack. He also ate 2 portions of one of the items shown in the table for lunch and the same for dinner. What did Hector eat for lunch and dinner?

Calorie Counter		
Food	**Portion**	**Calories**
Stir-fry	1 cup	250
Enchilada	1 whole	310
Pizza	1 slice	345
Tomato soup	1 cup	160

38. ⭐ **Challenge** There are 30 mg of cholesterol in a box of macaroni and cheese. This is 77 mg minus $\frac{1}{10}$ the number of milligrams of sodium it contains. How many milligrams of sodium are in a box of macaroni and cheese?

go.hrw.com
Web Extra!
KEYWORD: MS7 Health

CRCT Prep • GPS Support • Spiral Review

39. Multiple Choice For which equation is $x = -2$ a solution?

   Ⓐ $2x + 5 = 9$　　Ⓑ $8 = 10 - x$　　Ⓒ $\frac{x}{2} + 3 = 2$　　Ⓓ $-16 = -4x - 8$

40. Short Response A taxi cab costs $1.25 for the first mile and $0.25 for each additional mile. Write an equation for the total cost of a taxi ride, where x is the number of miles. How many miles can be traveled in the taxi for $8.00?

Identify the three-dimensional figure described. (Lesson 10-1)

41. 6 rectangular faces

42. 1 hexagonal base and 6 triangular faces

Find the volume of each figure to the nearest tenth. Use 3.14 for π. (Lesson 10-2)

43. cylinder with radius 5 cm and height 7 cm

44. triangular prism with a base with area 18 in² and height 9 in.

12-2 Solving Multi-Step Equations

**Learn** to solve multi-step equations.

Georgia Performance Standards

M7A2.a Given a problem, define a variable, write an equation, solve the equation, and interpret the solution. Also, **M7A2.b, M7P1.b, M7P1.c, M7P1.d.**

Jamal owns twice as many comic books as Levi owns. If you add 6 to the number of comic books Jamal owns and then divide by 7, you get the number of comic books Brooke owns. Brooke owns 30 comic books. How many comic books does Levi own? To answer this question, you need to set up an equation that requires more than two steps to solve.

EXAMPLE 1 **Combining Like Terms to Solve Equations**

Solve $7n - 1 - 2n = 14$.

$$7n - 1 - 2n = 14$$
$$5n - 1 = 14 \qquad \text{Combine like terms.}$$
$$\underline{+1 \qquad +1} \qquad \text{Add 1 to both sides.}$$
$$5n = 15$$
$$\frac{5n}{5} = \frac{15}{5} \qquad \text{Divide both sides by 5.}$$
$$n = 3$$

You may need to use the Distributive Property to solve an equation that has parentheses. Multiply each term inside the parentheses by the factor that is outside the parentheses. Then combine like terms.

EXAMPLE 2 **Using the Distributive Property to Solve Equations**

Remember!

The Distributive Property states that $a(b + c) = ab + ac$. For instance, $2(3 + 5) = 2(3) + 2(5)$.

Solve $3(z - 1) + 8 = 14$.

$$3(z - 1) + 8 = 14$$
$$3(z) - 3(1) + 8 = 14 \qquad \text{Distribute 3 on the left side.}$$
$$3z - 3 + 8 = 14 \qquad \text{Simplify.}$$
$$3z + 5 = 14 \qquad \text{Combine like terms.}$$
$$\underline{-5 \qquad -5} \qquad \text{Add } -5 \text{ to both sides.}$$
$$3z = 9$$
$$\frac{3z}{3} = \frac{9}{3} \qquad \text{Divide both sides by 3.}$$
$$z = 3$$

EXAMPLE 3

PROBLEM SOLVING APPLICATION

Jamal owns twice as many comic books as Levi owns. Adding 6 to the number of comic books Jamal owns and then dividing by 7 gives the number Brooke owns. Brooke owns 30 comic books. How many does Levi own?

PROBLEM SOLVING

1 Understand the Problem

Rewrite the question as a statement.

- Find the number of comic books that Levi owns.

List the **important information:**

- Jamal owns 2 times as many comic books as Levi owns.
- The number of comic books Jamal owns added to 6 and then divided by 7 equals the number Brooke owns.
- Brooke owns 30 comic books.

2 Make a Plan

Let c represent the number of comic books Levi owns. Then $2c$ represents the number Jamal owns, and $\dfrac{2c + 6}{7}$ represents the number Brooke owns, which equals 30. Solve the equation $\dfrac{2c + 6}{7} = 30$ for c.

3 Solve

$$\frac{2c + 6}{7} = 30$$

$$(7)\frac{2c + 6}{7} = (7)30 \qquad \textit{Multiply both sides by 7 to eliminate fractions.}$$

$$2c + 6 = 210$$

$$2c + 6 - 6 = 210 - 6 \qquad \textit{Subtract 6 from both sides.}$$

$$2c = 204$$

$$\frac{2c}{2} = \frac{204}{2} \qquad \textit{Divide both sides by 2.}$$

$$c = 102$$

Levi owns 102 comic books.

4 Look Back

Make sure that your answer makes sense in the original problem. Levi has 102 comic books. Jamal has $2(102) = 204$. Brooke has $\dfrac{204 + 6}{7} = 30$.

Think and Discuss GPS M7P2.c, M7P3.b

1. List the steps required to solve $-n + 5n + 3 = 27$.

2. Describe how to solve the equations $\dfrac{2}{3}x + 7 = 4$ and $\dfrac{2x + 7}{3} = 4$. Are the solutions the same or different? Explain.

12-2 **Exercises**

Georgia Performance Standards

M7P3.a, M7P4.c, M7P5.b

go.hrw.com
Homework Help Online
KEYWORD: MS7 12-2
Parent Resources Online
KEYWORD: MS7 Parent

GUIDED PRACTICE

See Example Solve.

1. $14n + 2 - 7n = 37$ **2.** $10x - 11 - 4x = 43$ **3.** $1 = -3 + 4p - 2p$

See Example **2** **4.** $12 - (x + 3) = 10$ **5.** $15 = 2(q + 4) + 3$ **6.** $5(m - 2) + 36 = -4$

See Example **3** **7.** Keisha read twice as many books this year as Ben read. Subtracting 4 from the number of books Keisha read and dividing by 2 gives the number of books Sheldon read. Sheldon read 10 books. How many books did Ben read?

INDEPENDENT PRACTICE

See Example **1** Solve.

8. $b + 18 + 3b = 74$ **9.** $10x - 3 - 2x = 4$

10. $18w - 10 - 6w = 50$ **11.** $19 = 5n + 7 - 3n$

12. $-27 = -3p + 15 - 3p$ **13.** $-x - 8 + 14x = -34$

See Example **2** **14.** $2(x + 4) + 6 = 22$ **15.** $1 - 3(n + 5) = -8$

16. $4.3 - 1.4(p + 7) = -9.7$ **17.** $1.8 + 6n - 3.2 = 7.6$

18. $0 = 9\left(k - \frac{2}{3}\right) + 33$ **19.** $6(t - 2) - 76 = -142$

See Example **3** **20.** Abby ran 3 times as many laps as Karen. Adding 4 to the number of laps Abby ran and then dividing by 7 gives the number of laps Jill ran. Jill ran 1 lap. How many laps did Karen run?

PRACTICE AND PROBLEM SOLVING

Extra Practice p. 750

Solve.

21. $\frac{0.5x + 7}{8} = 5$ **22.** $4(t - 8) + 20 = 5$ **23.** $63 = 8w + 2.6 - 3.6$

24. $17 = -5(3 + w) + 7$ **25.** $\frac{\frac{1}{4}a - 12}{8} = 4$ **26.** $9 = -(r - 5) + 11$

27. $\frac{2b - 3.4}{0.6} = -29$ **28.** $8.44 = \frac{34.6 + 4h}{5}$ **29.** $5.7 = -2.5x + 18 - 1.6x$

30. Consumer Math Three friends ate dinner at a restaurant. The friends decided to add a 15% tip and then split the bill evenly. Each friend paid $10.35. What was the total bill for dinner before tip?

31. Ann earns 1.5 times her normal hourly pay for each hour that she works over 40 hours in a week. Last week she worked 51 hours and earned $378.55. What is her normal hourly pay?

32. Geometry The base angles of an isosceles triangle are congruent. The measure of each of the base angles is twice the measure of the third angle. Find the measures of all three angles.

33. **Consumer Math** Patrice used a $15 gift certificate when she purchased a pair of sandals. After 8% sales tax was applied to the price of the sandals, the $15 was deducted. Patrice had to pay a total of $12 for the sandals. How much did the sandals cost before tax?

34. **Physical Science** To convert temperatures between degrees Celsius and degrees Fahrenheit, you can use the formula $F = \frac{9}{5}C + 32$. The table shows the melting points of various elements.

    a. What is the melting point in degrees Celsius of gold?

    b. What is the melting point in degrees Celsius of hydrogen?

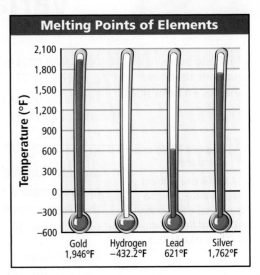

Melting Points of Elements

Gold	Hydrogen	Lead	Silver
1,946°F	−432.2°F	621°F	1,762°F

35. On his first two social studies tests, Billy made an 86 and a 93. What grade must Billy make on the third test to have an average of 90 for all three tests?

 36. **What's the Question?** Three friends shared a taxi ride from the airport to their hotel. After adding a $7.00 tip, the friends divided the cost of the ride evenly. If solving the equation $\frac{c + \$7.00}{3} = \$11.25$ gives the answer, what is the question?

37. **Write About It** Explain why multiplying first in the equation $\frac{2x - 6}{5} = 2$ makes finding the solution easier than adding first does.

38. **Challenge** Are the solutions to the following equations the same? Explain.

$$\frac{3y}{4} + 2 = 4 \text{ and } 3y + 8 = 16$$

CRCT Prep • GPS Support • Spiral Review

39. **Multiple Choice** Solve $\frac{2x - 2}{4} = 7$.

    Ⓐ $x = 15$　　　Ⓑ $x = 18$　　　Ⓒ $x = 20$　　　Ⓓ $x = 21$

40. **Multiple Choice** For which equation(s) is $x = 3$ a solution?

    I $2x - 5 + 3x = 10$　　II $\frac{-x + 7}{2} = 2$　　III $\frac{-4x}{6} = 2$　　IV $6.3x - 2.4 = 16.5$

    Ⓕ I only　　　Ⓖ I and II　　　Ⓗ I, II, and III　　　Ⓙ I, II, and IV

Find the volume of each figure to the nearest tenth. Use 3.14 for π. (Lesson 10-3)

41. a cone with diameter 6 cm and height 4 cm

42. a triangular pyramid with height 7 in. and base area 18 in^2

Solve. (Lesson 12-1)

43. $6x - 4 = 2$　　　44. $7 = -y + 4$　　　45. $5 + \frac{z}{2} = -9$　　　46. $12 - 6d = 54$

12-3 Solving Equations with Variables on Both Sides

Learn to solve equations that have variables on both sides.

 Georgia Performance Standards

M7A2.a Given a problem, define a variable, write an equation, solve the equation, and interpret the solution. Also, M7A2.b, M7P4.c, M7P5.b.

Mari can rent a video game console for $14.49 per week or buy a rebuilt one for $72.45. The cost of renting a game is $7.95 per week. How many weeks would Mari have to rent both the game and the console to pay as much as she would if she had bought the used console and rented the game instead?

Problems such as this require you to solve equations that have the same variable on both sides of the equal sign. To solve this kind of problem, you need to get the terms with variables on one side of the equal sign.

EXAMPLE **1** **Using Inverse Operations to Group Terms with Variables**

Group the terms with variables on one side of the equal sign, and simplify.

A $6m = 4m + 12$

$$6m = 4m + 12$$
$$6m - 4m = 4m - 4m + 12 \qquad \text{\textit{Subtract 4m from both sides.}}$$
$$2m = 12 \qquad \text{\textit{Simplify.}}$$

B $-7x - 198 = 5x$

$$-7x - 198 = 5x$$
$$-7x + 7x - 198 = 5x + 7x \qquad \text{\textit{Add 7x to both sides.}}$$
$$-198 = 12x \qquad \text{\textit{Simplify.}}$$

EXAMPLE **2** **Solving Equations with Variables on Both Sides**

Solve.

A $5n = 3n + 26$

$$5n = 3n + 26$$
$$5n - 3n = 3n - 3n + 26 \qquad \text{\textit{Subtract 3n from both sides.}}$$
$$2n = 26 \qquad \text{\textit{Simplify.}}$$
$$\frac{2n}{2} = \frac{26}{2} \qquad \text{\textit{Divide both sides by 2.}}$$
$$n = 13$$

Solve.

B $19 + 7n = -2n + 37$

$$19 + 7n = -2n + 37$$

$19 + 7n + 2n = -2n + 2n + 37$ *Add 2n to both sides.*

$19 + 9n = 37$ *Simplify.*

$19 + 9n - 19 = 37 - 19$ *Subtract 19 from both sides.*

$9n = 18$ *Simplify.*

$\dfrac{9n}{9} = \dfrac{18}{9}$ *Divide both sides by 9.*

$n = 2$

C $\dfrac{5}{9}x = \dfrac{4}{9}x + 9$

$$\dfrac{5}{9}x = \dfrac{4}{9}x + 9$$

$\dfrac{5}{9}x - \dfrac{4}{9}x = \dfrac{4}{9}x - \dfrac{4}{9}x + 9$ *Subtract $\dfrac{4}{9}x$ from both sides.*

$\dfrac{1}{9}x = 9$ *Simplify.*

$(9)\dfrac{1}{9}x = (9)9$ *Multiply both sides by 9.*

$x = 81$

EXAMPLE 3   *Consumer Math Application*

Mari can buy a video game console for $72.45 and rent a game for $7.95 per week, or she can rent a console and the same game for a total of $22.44 per week. How many weeks would Mari need to rent both the video game and the console to pay as much as she would if she had bought the console and rented the game instead?

Let w represent the number of weeks.

$$22.44w = 72.45 + 7.95w$$

$22.44w - 7.95w = 72.45 + 7.95w - 7.95w$ *Subtract 7.95w from both sides.*

$14.49w = 72.45$ *Simplify.*

$\dfrac{14.49w}{14.49} = \dfrac{72.45}{14.49}$ *Divide both sides by 14.49.*

$w = 5$

Mari would need to rent the video game and the console for 5 weeks to pay as much as she would have if she had bought the console.

Think and Discuss    GPS M7P1.d, M7P3.b

1. **Explain** how you would solve $\frac{1}{2}x + 7 = \frac{2}{3}x - 2$.

2. **Describe** how you would decide which variable term to add or subtract on both sides of the equation $-3x + 7 = 4x - 9$.

12-3 **Exercises**

Georgia Performance Standards
M7P1.b, M7P3.a, M7P3.c

go.hrw.com
Homework Help Online
KEYWORD: MS7 12-3
Parent Resources Online
KEYWORD: MS7 Parent

GUIDED PRACTICE

See Example **Group the terms with variables on one side of the equal sign, and simplify.**

1. $5n = 4n + 32$ **2.** $-6x - 28 = 4x$ **3.** $8w = 32 - 4w$

See Example 2 **Solve.**

4. $4y = 2y + 40$ **5.** $8 + 6a = -2a + 24$ **6.** $\frac{3}{4}d + 4 = \frac{1}{4}d + 18$

See Example 3 **7. Consumer Math** Members at the Star Theater pay $30.00 per month plus $1.95 for each movie. Nonmembers pay the regular $7.95 admission fee. How many movies would both a member and a nonmember have to see in a month to pay the same amount?

INDEPENDENT PRACTICE

See Example 1 **Group the terms with variables on one side of the equal sign, and simplify.**

8. $12h = 9h + 84$ **9.** $-10p - 8 = 2p$ **10.** $6q = 18 - 2q$

11. $-4c - 6 = -2c$ **12.** $-7s + 12 = -9s$ **13.** $6 + \frac{4}{5}a = \frac{9}{10}a$

See Example 2 **Solve.**

14. $9t = 4t + 120$ **15.** $42 + 3b = -4b - 14$ **16.** $\frac{6}{11}x + 4 = \frac{2}{11}x + 16$

17. $1.5a + 6 = 9a + 12$ **18.** $32 - \frac{3}{8}y = \frac{3}{4}y + 5$ **19.** $-6 - 8c = 3c + 16$

See Example 3 **20. Consumer Math** Members at a swim club pay $5 per lesson plus a one-time fee of $60. Nonmembers pay $11 per lesson. How many lessons would both a member and a nonmember have to take to pay the same amount?

PRACTICE AND PROBLEM SOLVING

Extra Practice p. 750

Solve. Check each answer.

21. $3y + 7 = -6y - 56$ **22.** $-\frac{7}{8}x - 6 = -\frac{3}{8}x - 14$

23. $5r + 6 - 2r = 7r - 10$ **24.** $-10p + 8 = 7p + 12$

25. $9 + 5r = -17 - 8r$ **26.** $0.8k + 7 = -0.7k + 1$

27. A choir is singing at a festival. On the first night, 12 choir members were absent, so the choir stood in 5 equal rows. On the second night, only 1 member was absent, so the choir stood in 6 equal rows. The same number of people stood in each row each night. How many members are in the choir?

28. Consumer Math Jaline can purchase tile at a store for $0.99 per tile and rent a tile saw for $24. At another store, she can borrow the tile saw for free if she buys tile there for $1.49 per tile. How many tiles must she buy for the cost to be the same at both stores?

The figures in each pair have the same perimeter. Find the value of each variable.

29.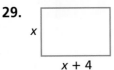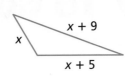

30.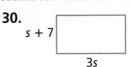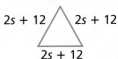

Recreation

Many climbers practice in rock climbing gyms before tackling natural destinations like Tallulah Gorge in Tallulah Falls, Georgia.

31. Recreation A rock-climbing gym charges nonmembers $18 per day to use the wall plus $7 per day for equipment rental. Members pay an annual fee of $400 plus $5 per day for equipment rental. How many days must both a member and a nonmember use the wall in one year so that both pay the same amount?

32. Multi-Step Two families drove from Denver to Cincinnati. After driving 582 miles the first day, the Smiths spread the rest of the trip equally over the next 3 days. The Chows spread their trip equally over 6 days. The distance the Chows drove each day was equal to the distance the Smiths drove each of the three days.

   a. How many miles did the Chows drive each day?

   b. How far is it from Denver to Cincinnati?

 33. What's the Error? To combine terms in the equation $-8a - 4 = 2a + 34$, a student wrote $-6a = 38$. What is the error?

 34. Write About It If the same variable is on both sides of an equation, must it have the same value on each side? Explain your answer.

 35. Challenge Combine terms before solving the equation $12x - 4 - 12 = 4x + 8 + 8x - 24$. Do you think there is just one solution to the equation? Why or why not?

CRCT PREP • GPS SUPPORT • SPIRAL REVIEW

36. Multiple Choice For which equation is $x = 0$ NOT a solution?

   (A) $3x + 2 = 2 - x$ (B) $2.5x + 3 = x$ (C) $-x + 4 = 3x + 4$ (D) $6x + 2 = x + 2$

37. Extended Response One calling plan offers long-distance calls for $0.03 per minute. Another plan costs $2.00 per month but offers long-distance service for $0.01 per minute. Write and solve an equation to find the number of long-distance minutes for which the two plans would cost the same. Write your answer in a complete sentence.

The lengths of two sides of a right triangle are given. Find the length of the third side to the nearest tenth. (Lesson 9-8)

38. legs: 12 cm and 16 cm

39. leg: 11 ft; hypotenuse: 30.5 ft

Solve. (Lesson 12-2)

40. $10x + 4 - 3x = -10$

41. $1.3y + 2.7y - 5 = 3$

42. $5 = \dfrac{4z - 6}{2}$

READY TO GO ON?

Quiz for Lessons 12-1 Through 12-3

✓ 12-1 Solving Two-Step Equations

Solve.

1. $-4x + 6 = 54$

2. $15 + \frac{y}{3} = 6$

3. $\frac{z}{8} - 5 = -3$

4. $-33 = -7a - 5$

5. $-27 = \frac{r}{12} - 19$

6. $-13 = 11 - 2n$

7. $3x + 13 = 37$

8. $\frac{p}{-8} - 7 = 12$

9. $\frac{u}{7} + 45 = -60$

10. A taxi service charges an initial fee of $1.50 plus $1.50 for every mile traveled. A taxi ride costs $21.00. How many miles did the taxi travel?

✓ 12-2 Solving Multi-Step Equations

Solve.

11. $\frac{3x - 4}{5} = 7$

12. $3(3b + 2) = -30$

13. $-12 = \frac{15c + 3}{6}$

14. $\frac{24.6 + 3a}{4} = 9.54$

15. $\frac{2b + 9}{11} = 18$

16. $13 = 2c + 3 + 5c$

17. $\frac{1}{2}(8w - 6) = 17$

18. $\frac{1.2s + 3.69}{0.3} = 47.9$

19. $\frac{1}{2} = \frac{5p - 8}{12}$

20. Peter used a $5.00 gift certificate to help pay for his lunch. After adding a 15% tip to the cost of his meal, Peter still had to pay $2.36 in cash. How much did Peter's meal cost?

21. A group of 10 friends had lunch together at a restaurant. The meal cost a total of $99.50, including a 15% tip. How much was the total bill for lunch before tip?

✓ 12-3 Solving Equations with Variables on Both Sides

Solve.

22. $12m = 3m + 108$

23. $\frac{7}{8}n - 3 = \frac{5}{8}n + 12$

24. $1.2x + 3.7 = 2.2x - 4.5$

25. $-7 - 7p = 3p + 23$

26. $-2.3q + 16 = -5q - 38$

27. $\frac{3}{5}k + \frac{7}{10} = \frac{11}{15}k - \frac{2}{5}$

28. $-19m + 12 = -14m - 8$

29. $\frac{2}{3}v + \frac{1}{6} = \frac{7}{9}v - \frac{5}{6}$

30. $8.9 - 3.3j = -2.2j + 2.3$

31. $4a - 7 = -6a + 12$

32. One shuttle service charges $10 for pickup and $0.10 per mile. Another shuttle service has no pickup fee but charges $0.35 per mile. Find the number of miles for which the cost of the two shuttle services is the same.

Focus on Problem Solving

Solve

• **Write an equation**

When you are asked to solve a problem, be sure to read the entire problem before you begin solving it. Sometimes you will need to perform several steps to solve the problem, and you will need to know all of the information in the problem before you decide which steps to take.

Read each problem and determine what steps are needed to solve it. Then write an equation that can be used to solve the problem.

1 Martin can buy a pair of inline skates and safety equipment for $49.50. At a roller rink, Martin can rent a pair of inline skates for $2.50 per day, but he still needs to buy safety equipment for $19.50. How many days would Martin have to skate in order to pay as much to rent skates and buy safety equipment as he would have to pay to buy both?

2 Christopher draws caricatures at the local mall. He charges $5 for a simple sketch and $15 for a larger drawing. In one day, Christopher earned $175. He drew 20 simple sketches that day. How many larger drawings did he make?

3 Book-club members are required to buy a minimum number of books each year. Leslee bought 3 times the minimum. Denise bought 7 more than the minimum. Together, they bought 23 books. What is the minimum number of books?

4 Coach Willis has won 150 games during his career. This is 10 more than $\frac{1}{2}$ as many games as Coach Gentry has won. How many games has Coach Gentry won?

5 The perimeter of an isosceles triangle is 4 times the length of the shortest side. The longer sides are 4.5 ft longer than the shortest side. What is the length of each side of the triangle?

6 Miss Rankin's class has raised $100.00 for a class trip. The class needs to collect a total of $225.00. How many $0.50 carnations must the class sell to reach its goal?

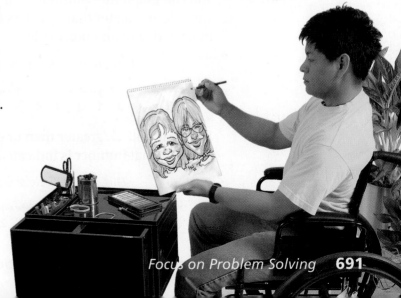

12-4 Inequalities

Learn to read and write inequalities and graph them on a number line.

Vocabulary

inequality

algebraic inequality

solution set

compound inequality

An **inequality** states that two quantities either are not equal or may not be equal. An inequality uses one of the following symbols:

Symbol	Meaning	Word Phrases
<	Is less than	Fewer than, below
>	Is greater than	More than, above
≤	Is less than or equal to	At most, no more than
≥	Is greater than or equal to	At least, no less than

EXAMPLE 1 Writing Inequalities

Georgia Performance Standards

M7A1.a Translate verbal phrases to algebraic expressions. Also, M7P5.a, M7P5.b, M7P5.c.

Write an inequality for each situation.

A There are at least 25 students in the auditorium.

number of students ≥ 25   *"At least" means greater than or equal to.*

B No more than 150 people can occupy the room.

room capacity ≤ 150   *"No more than" means less than or equal to.*

An inequality that contains a variable is an **algebraic inequality**. A value of the variable that makes the inequality true is a solution of the inequality.

An inequality may have more than one solution. Together, all of the solutions are called the **solution set**.

You can graph the solutions of an inequality on a number line. If the variable is "greater than" or "less than" a number, then that number is indicated with an open circle.

This open circle shows that 5 is not a solution.

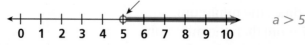

$a > 5$

If the variable is "greater than or equal to" or "less than or equal to" a number, that number is indicated with a closed circle.

This closed circle shows that 3 is a solution.

$b \leq 3$

EXAMPLE 2 Graphing Simple Inequalities

Graph each inequality.

A $x > -2$

Draw an open circle at -2. The solutions are values of x greater than -2, so shade to the right of -2.

B $-1 \geq y$

Draw a closed circle at -1. The solutions are -1 and values of y less than -1, so shade to the left of -1.

Writing Math

The compound inequality $-2 < y$ and $y < 4$ can be written as $-2 < y < 4$.

A **compound inequality** is the result of combining two inequalities. The words *and* and *or* are used to describe how the two parts are related.

$x > 3$ or $x < -1$	$-2 < y$ and $y < 4$
x is either greater than 3 or less than −1.	*y is both greater than −2 and less than 4. y is between −2 and 4.*

EXAMPLE 3 Graphing Compound Inequalities

Graph each compound inequality.

A $s \geq 0$ or $s < -3$

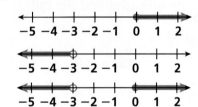

Graph $s \geq 0$.

Graph $s < -3$.

Combine the graphs.

Reading Math

$1 < p$ is the same as $p > 1$.

B $1 < p \leq 5$

Graph $1 < p$.

Graph $p \leq 5$.

Graph the common solutions.

Think and Discuss 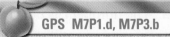 GPS M7P1.d, M7P3.b

1. **Compare** the graphs of the inequalities $y > 2$ and $y \geq 2$.

2. **Explain** how to graph each type of compound inequality.

12-4 **Exercises**

Georgia Performance Standards
M7P1.a, M7P4.c, M7P5.b

go.hrw.com
Homework Help Online
KEYWORD: MS7 12-4
Parent Resources Online
KEYWORD: MS7 Parent

GUIDED PRACTICE

See Example **1** **Write an inequality for each situation.**

1. No more than 18 people are allowed in the gallery at one time.

2. There are fewer than 8 fish in the aquarium.

3. The water level is above 45 inches.

See Example **2** **Graph each inequality.**

4. $x < 3$ **5.** $\frac{1}{2} \geq r$ **6.** $2.8 < w$ **7.** $y \geq -4$

See Example **3** **Graph each compound inequality.**

8. $a > 2$ or $a \leq -1$ **9.** $-4 < p \leq 6$ **10.** $-2 \leq n < 0$

INDEPENDENT PRACTICE

See Example **1** **Write an inequality for each situation.**

11. The temperature is below 40°F.

12. There are at least 24 pictures on the roll of film.

13. No more than 35 tables are in the cafeteria.

14. Fewer than 250 people attended the rally.

See Example **2** **Graph each inequality.**

15. $s \geq -1$ **16.** $y < 0$ **17.** $n \leq -3$

18. $2 < x$ **19.** $-6 \leq b$ **20.** $m < -4$

See Example **3** **Graph each compound inequality.**

21. $p > 3$ or $p < 0$ **22.** $1 \leq x \leq 4$ **23.** $-3 < y < -1$

24. $k > 0$ or $k \leq -2$ **25.** $n \geq 1$ or $n \leq -1$ **26.** $-2 < w \leq 2$

PRACTICE AND PROBLEM SOLVING

CRCT GPS
Extra Practice p. 751

Graph each inequality or compound inequality.

27. $z \leq -5$ **28.** $3 > f$ **29.** $m \geq -2$

30. $3 > y$ or $y \geq 6$ **31.** $-9 < p \leq -3$ **32.** $q > 2$ or $-1 > q$

Write each statement using inequality symbols.

33. The number c is between -2 and 3.   **34.** The number y is greater than -10.

Write an inequality shown by each graph.

35.

36.

Earth Science LINK

The portion of the earth's surface that lies beneath the ocean and consists of continental crust is the continental margin. The continental margin is divided into the continental shelf, the continental slope, and the continental rise.

Continental shelf ▬
Continental slope ▬
Continental rise ▬

Abyssal plain

37. The continental shelf begins at the shoreline and slopes toward the open ocean. The depth of the continental shelf can reach 200 meters. Write a compound inequality for the depth of the continental shelf.

38. The continental slope begins at the edge of the continental shelf and continues down to the flattest part of the ocean floor. The depth of the continental slope ranges from about 200 meters to about 4,000 meters. Write a compound inequality for the depth of the continental slope.

39. The bar graph shows the depth of the ocean in various locations as measured by different research vessels. Write a compound inequality that shows the ranges of depth measured by each vessel.

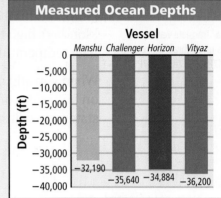

40. ⭐ **Challenge** Water freezes at 32°F and boils at 212°F. Write three inequalities to show the ranges of temperatures for which water is a solid, a liquid, and a gas.

Deep Flight is designed to explore the ocean in underwater flights.

CRCT PREP • GPS SUPPORT • SPIRAL REVIEW

41. **Multiple Choice** Which inequality represents *a number that is greater than −4 and less than 3*?

   Ⓐ $-4 \geq n \geq 3$ Ⓑ $-4 < n < 3$ Ⓒ $-4 > n > 3$ Ⓓ $-4 \leq n \leq 3$

42. **Multiple Choice** Which inequality is shown by the graph?

   Ⓕ $x < -1$ or $x \leq 2$ Ⓖ $x < -1$ or $x \geq 2$ Ⓗ $x \leq -1$ or $x < 2$ Ⓙ $x \leq -1$ or $x > 2$

43. Mateo drove 472 miles in 8 hours. What was his average rate of speed? (Lesson 5-2)

Solve. (Lesson 12-3)

44. $10x + 4 = 6x$ 45. $3y + 8 = 5y - 2$ 46. $1.5z + 3 = 2.7z - 4.2$

12-5 **Solving Inequalities by Adding or Subtracting**

Learn to solve one-step inequalities by adding or subtracting.

Weather conditions can change rapidly. In some areas, people may wear T-shirts and shorts one day and need a warm coat the next day.

Georgia Performance Standards

M7A1.a Translate verbal phrases to algebraic expressions. Also, M7P4.c, M7P5.a, M7P5.b, M7P5.c.

Sunday's high temperature was 72°F. This temperature was at least 40°F higher than Monday's high temperature. To find Monday's high temperature, you can solve an inequality.

When you add or subtract the same number on both sides of an inequality, the resulting statement will still be true.

$$\begin{array}{r} -2 < 5 \\ \underline{+7 \quad +7} \\ 5 < 12 \end{array}$$

You can find solution sets of inequalities the same way you find solutions of equations, by isolating the variable.

EXAMPLE 1 **Solving Inequalities by Adding**

Solve. Then graph each solution set on a number line.

A $x - 12 > 32$

$$\begin{array}{r} x - 12 > 32 \\ \underline{+12 \quad +12} \\ x \quad > \quad 44 \end{array}$$

Add 12 to both sides.

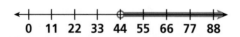

Draw an open circle at 44. Solutions are values of x greater than 44, so shade to the right of 44.

B $-14 \geq y - 8$

$$\begin{array}{r} -14 \geq y - 8 \\ \underline{+8 \quad +8} \\ -6 \geq y \end{array}$$

Add 8 to both sides.

Draw a closed circle at −6. Solutions are −6 and values of y less than −6, so shade to the left of −6.

You can check the solution to an inequality by choosing any number in the solution set and substituting it into the original inequality.

EXAMPLE **2** Solving Inequalities by Subtracting

Solve. Check each answer.

Ⓐ $c + 9 < 20$

$$c + 9 < 20$$
$$\underline{\; - 9 \quad - 9}$$
$$c \qquad < 11$$

Subtract 9 from both sides.

Check

$$c + 9 < 20$$
$$0 + 9 \stackrel{?}{<} 20$$
$$9 \stackrel{?}{<} 20 \;\checkmark$$

0 is less than 11. Substitute 0 for c.

> **Helpful Hint**
>
> When checking your solution, choose a number in the solution set that is easy to work with.

Ⓑ $-2 < x + 16$

$$-2 < x + 16$$
$$\underline{- 16 \qquad - 16}$$
$$-18 < x$$

Subtract 16 from both sides.

Check

$$-2 < x + 16$$
$$-2 \stackrel{?}{<} 0 + 16$$
$$-2 \stackrel{?}{<} 16 \;\checkmark$$

0 is greater than −18. Substitute 0 for x.

EXAMPLE **3** *Weather Application*

Sunday's high temperature of 72°F was at least 40°F higher than Monday's high temperature. What was Monday's high temperature?

Sunday's high	was at least	40°F higher than		Monday's high.
72	≥	40	+	t

$$72 \geq 40 + t$$
$$\underline{- 40 \quad - 40}$$
$$32 \geq t$$
$$t \leq 32$$

Subtract 40 from both sides.
Rewrite the inequality.

Monday's high temperature was at most 32˚F.

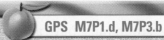

Think and Discuss GPS **M7P1.d, M7P3.b**

1. Compare solving addition and subtraction equations with solving addition and subtraction inequalities.

2. Describe how to check whether −36 is a solution of $s - 5 > 1$.

12-5 **Exercises**

Georgia Performance Standards

M7P1.c, M7P3.a, M7P5.b

go.hrw.com
Homework Help Online
KEYWORD: MS7 12-5
Parent Resources Online
KEYWORD: MS7 Parent

GUIDED PRACTICE

See Example **Solve. Then graph each solution set on a number line.**

1. $x - 9 < 18$ 2. $y - 11 \geq -7$ 3. $4 \geq p - 3$

See Example **Solve. Check each answer.**

4. $n + 5 > 26$ 5. $b + 21 \leq -3$ 6. $9 \leq 12 + k$

See Example 7. **Weather** Yesterday's high temperature was 30°F. Tomorrow's weather forecast includes a high temperature that is no more than 12°F warmer than yesterday's. What high temperatures are forecast for tomorrow?

INDEPENDENT PRACTICE

See Example ① **Solve. Then graph each solution set on a number line.**

8. $s - 2 > 14$ 9. $m - 14 < -3$ 10. $b - 25 > -30$

11. $c - 17 \leq -6$ 12. $-25 > y - 53$ 13. $71 \leq x - 9$

See Example **Solve. Check each answer.**

14. $w + 16 < 4$ 15. $z + 9 > -3$ 16. $p + 21 \leq -4$

17. $26 < f + 32$ 18. $65 > k + 54$ 19. $n + 29 \geq 25$

See Example ③ 20. Clark scored at least 12 points more than Josh scored. Josh scored 15 points. How many points did Clark score?

21. **Life Science** Adriana is helping track bird populations. She counted 8 fewer birds on Tuesday than on Thursday. She counted at most 32 birds on Thursday. How many birds did Adriana count on Tuesday?

PRACTICE AND PROBLEM SOLVING

Extra Practice p. 751

Solve.

22. $k + 3.2 \geq 8$ 23. $a - 1.3 > -1$ 24. $c - 6\frac{1}{2} < -1\frac{1}{4}$

25. $-20 \geq 18 + m$ 26. $4 < x + 7.02$ 27. $g + 3\frac{2}{3} < 10$

28. $-109 > r - 58$ 29. $5.9 + w \leq 21.6$ 30. $n - 21.6 > 26$

31. $-150 \leq t + 92$ 32. $y + 4\frac{3}{4} \geq 1\frac{1}{8}$ 33. $v - 0.9 \leq -1.5$

34. **Consumer Math** To get a group discount for baseball tickets, Marco's group must have at least 20 people. The group needs at least 7 more people to sign up. How many have signed up so far?

35. Mila wants to spend at least $20 on a classified ad in the newspaper. She has $12. How much more does she need?

36. **Transportation** The *shinkansen*, or bullet train, of Japan travels at an average speed of 162.3 miles per hour. It has a top speed of 186 miles per hour. At most, how many more miles per hour can the train travel beyond its average speed before it reaches its maximum speed?

37. **Life Science** The giant spider crab, the world's largest crab, lives off the southeastern coast of Japan. Giant spider crabs can grow as much as 3.6 meters across. A scientist finds one that could still grow another 0.5 m across. How wide is the giant spider crab that he found?

38. The line graph shows the number of miles Amelia rode her bike in each of the last four months. She wants to ride at least 5 miles more in May than she did in April. At least how many miles does Amelia want to ride in May?

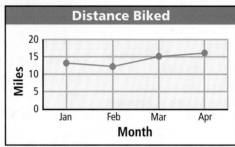

39. **Physical Science** The average human ear can detect sounds that have frequencies between 20 hertz and 20,000 hertz. The average dog ear can detect sounds with frequencies of up to 30,000 hertz greater than those a human ear can detect. Up to how many hertz can a dog hear?

40. **Choose a Strategy** If five days ago was the day after Saturday, what was the day before yesterday?

41. **Write About It** Explain how to solve and check the inequality $n - 9 < -15$.

42. **Challenge** Solve the inequality $x + (4^2 - 2^3)^2 > -1$.

CRCT PREP • GPS SUPPORT • SPIRAL REVIEW

43. **Multiple Choice** Which inequality has the following graphed solution?

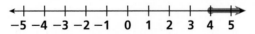

Ⓐ $x - 2 \geq -2$ Ⓑ $x + 3 \geq 7$ Ⓒ $x - 3 \leq 1$ Ⓓ $x + 5 < 9$

44. **Short Response** The highest-paid employee at the movie theater is the manager, who earns $10.25 per hour. The lowest-paid employees earn $3.90 less per hour than the manager. Write and graph a compound inequality to show all the other hourly wages earned at the movie theater.

The surface area of a prism is 16 in^2. Find the surface area of a similar prism that is larger by each scale factor. (Lesson 10-5)

45. scale factor = 3   46. scale factor = 8   47. scale factor = 10

48. Find the probability of flipping a coin and getting tails and then rolling a 2 on a number cube. (Lesson 11-5)

12-6 Solving Inequalities by Multiplying or Dividing

Learn to solve one-step inequalities by multiplying or dividing.

Georgia Performance Standards

M7A1.a Translate verbal phrases to algebraic expressions. Also, M7P1.b.

During the spring, the Schmidt family sells watermelons at a roadside stand for $5 apiece. Mr. Schmidt calculated that it cost $517 to plant, grow, and harvest the melons this year. How many melons must the Schmidts sell in order to make a profit for the year?

Problems like this require you to multiply or divide to solve an inequality.

When you multiply or divide both sides of an inequality by the same positive number, the statement will still be true. However, when you multiply or divide both sides by the same *negative* number, you need to reverse the direction of the inequality symbol for the statement to be true.

$$-4 < 2 \qquad\qquad\qquad -4 < 2$$

$$(3)(-4) \; < \; (3)(2) \qquad\qquad (-3)(-4) \; > \; (-3)(2)$$

$$-12 < 6 \qquad\qquad\qquad 12 > -6$$

EXAMPLE 1 Solving Inequalities by Multiplying

Solve.

Ⓐ $\dfrac{x}{11} < 3$

$$\dfrac{x}{11} < 3$$

$$(11)\dfrac{x}{11} < (11)3 \qquad\text{\textit{Multiply both sides by 11.}}$$

$$x < 33$$

Ⓑ $4.8 \le \dfrac{r}{-6}$

$$4.8 \le \dfrac{r}{-6}$$

$$(-6)4.8 \ge (-6)\dfrac{r}{-6} \qquad\text{\textit{Multiply both sides by -6, and reverse the inequality symbol.}}$$

$$-28.8 \ge r$$

EXAMPLE **2** **Solving Inequalities by Dividing**

Solve. Check each answer.

A $4x > 9$

$$4x > 9$$

$$\frac{4x}{4} > \frac{9}{4}$$ *Divide both sides by 4.*

$$x > \frac{9}{4}, \text{ or } 2\frac{1}{4}$$

Check

$$4x > 9$$

$$4(3) \overset{?}{>} 9$$ *3 is greater than $2\frac{1}{4}$. Substitute 3 for x.*

$$12 \overset{?}{>} 9 ✔$$

B $-60 \geq -12y$

$$-60 \geq -12y$$

$$\frac{-60}{-12} \leq \frac{-12y}{-12}$$ *Divide both sides by -12, and reverse the inequality symbol.*

$$5 \leq y$$

Check

$$-60 \geq -12y$$

$$-60 \overset{?}{\geq} -12(10)$$ *10 is greater than 5. Substitute 10 for y.*

$$-60 \overset{?}{\geq} -120 ✔$$

EXAMPLE **3** *Agriculture Application*

It cost the Schmidts $517 to raise watermelons. How many watermelons must they sell at $5 apiece to make a profit?

To make a profit, the Schmidts need to earn more than $517. Let w represent the number of watermelons they must sell.

$$5w > 517$$ *Write an inequality.*

$$\frac{5w}{5} > \frac{517}{5}$$ *Divide both sides by 5.*

$$w > 103.4$$

The Schmidts cannot sell 0.4 watermelon, so they need to sell at least 104 watermelons to earn a profit.

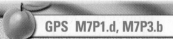

Think and Discuss GPS M7P1.d, M7P3.b

1. **Compare** solving multiplication and division equations with solving multiplication and division inequalities.

2. **Explain** how you would solve the inequality $0.5y > 4.5$.

Georgia Performance
Standards
M7P3.a, M7P4.c, M7P5.b

go.hrw.com
Homework Help Online
KEYWORD: MS7 12-6
Parent Resources Online
KEYWORD: MS7 Parent

GUIDED PRACTICE

See Example **Solve.**

1. $\frac{w}{8} < -4$ **2.** $\frac{z}{-6} \geq 7$ **3.** $-4 < \frac{p}{-12}$

See Example ② **Solve. Check each answer.**

4. $3m > -15$ **5.** $11 > -8y$ **6.** $25c \leq 200$

See Example ③ **7.** It cost Deirdre $212 to make candles. How many candles must she sell at $8 apiece to make a profit?

INDEPENDENT PRACTICE

See Example **Solve.**

8. $\frac{s}{5} > 1.4$ **9.** $\frac{m}{-4} < -13$ **10.** $\frac{b}{6} > -30$

11. $\frac{c}{-10} \leq 12$ **12.** $\frac{y}{9} < 2.5$ **13.** $\frac{x}{1.1} \geq -1$

See Example ② **Solve. Check each answer.**

14. $6w < 4$ **15.** $-5z > -3$ **16.** $15p \leq -45$

17. $-9f > 27$ **18.** $20k < 30$ **19.** $-18n \geq 180$

See Example ③ **20.** Attendance at a museum more than tripled from Monday to Saturday. On Monday, 186 people went to the museum. How many people went to the museum on Saturday?

21. It cost George $678 to make wreaths. How many wreaths must he sell at $15 apiece to make a profit?

PRACTICE AND PROBLEM SOLVING

Extra Practice p. 751

Solve.

22. $\frac{a}{65} \leq -10$ **23.** $0.4p > 1.6$ **24.** $-\frac{m}{5} < -20$

25. $\frac{2}{3}y \geq 12$ **26.** $\frac{x}{-9} \leq \frac{3}{5}$ **27.** $\frac{g}{2.1} > 0.3$

28. $\frac{r}{6} \geq \frac{2}{3}$ **29.** $4w \leq 1\frac{1}{2}$ **30.** $-10n < 10^2$

31. $-1\frac{3}{5}t > -4$ **32.** $-\frac{y}{12} < 3\frac{1}{2}$ **33.** $5.6v \geq -14$

34. A community theater group produced 8 plays over the last two years. The group's goal for the next two years is to produce at least $1\frac{1}{2}$ times as many plays as they did in the two previous years. How many plays does the group want to produce in the next two years?

35. Tammy is going to a family reunion 350 miles away. She plans to travel no faster than 70 miles per hour. What is the least amount of time it will take her to get there?

36. Social Studies Of the total U.S. population, about 874,000 people are Pacific Islanders. The graph shows where most of these Americans live.

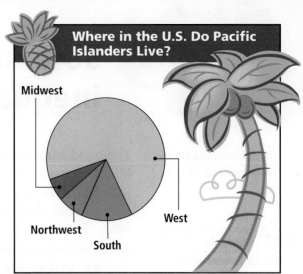

Where in the U.S. Do Pacific Islanders Live?

Midwest

West

Northwest

South

Source: USA Today

   a. According to the graph, less than 10% of Pacific Islanders live in the Midwest. How many Pacific Islanders live in the Midwest?

   b. According to the graph, between 10% and 20% of Pacific Islanders live in the South. How many Pacific Islanders live in the South?

37. Seventh-graders at Mountain Middle School have sold 360 subscriptions to magazines. This is $\frac{3}{4}$ of the number of subscriptions that they need to sell to reach their goal and to beat the eighth grade's sales. How many total subscriptions must they sell to reach their goal?

38. Recreation Malcolm has saved $362 to spend on his vacation. He wants to have at least $35 a day available to spend. How many days of vacation does Malcolm have enough money for?

39. Write a Problem Write a word problem that can be solved using the inequality $\frac{x}{2} \geq 7$. Solve the inequality.

40. Write About It Explain how to solve the inequality $\frac{n}{-8} < -40$.

41. Challenge Use what you have learned about solving multi-step equations to solve the inequality $4x - 5 \leq 7x + 4$.

CRCT PREP • GPS SUPPORT • SPIRAL REVIEW

42. Multiple Choice Solve $\frac{x}{4} > -2$.

  Ⓐ $x > -8$ Ⓑ $x < -8$ Ⓒ $x < 8$ Ⓓ $x > 8$

43. Gridded Response It cost John and Jamie $150 to grow tomatoes. They sell each tomato for $0.50. How many tomatoes must they sell to make a profit?

44. In 16 tries, Sondra made 9 baskets. What is the experimental probability that Sondra will make a basket the next time she tries? (Lesson 11-2)

Solve. (Lesson 12-5)

45. $x - 3 < -2$ **46.** $-6 < y + 4$ **47.** $z - 1 \geq 4$ **48.** $t - 12 \leq 8.4$

12-7 Solving Two-Step Inequalities

Learn to solve simple two-step inequalities.

Georgia Performance Standards

M7A1.a Translate verbal phrases to algebraic expressions. Also, M7P4.c, M7P5.a, M7P5.b, M7P5.c.

The band students at Newman Middle School are trying to raise at least $5,000 to buy new percussion instruments. They already have raised $850. How much should each of the 83 band students still raise, on average, to meet the goal?

When you solve two-step equations, you can use the order of operations in reverse to isolate the variable. You can use the same process when solving two-step inequalities.

EXAMPLE 1 Solving Two-Step Inequalities

Solve. Then graph each solution set on a number line.

Remember!

Draw a closed circle when the inequality includes the point and an open circle when it does not include the point.

A $\dfrac{x}{5} - 15 < 10$

$$\dfrac{x}{5} - 15 < 10$$

$$\underline{ + 15 \qquad + 15} \qquad \text{Add 15 to both sides.}$$

$$\dfrac{x}{5} < 25$$

$$(5)\dfrac{x}{5} < (5)25 \qquad \text{Multiply both sides by 5.}$$

$$x < 125$$

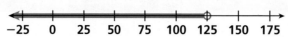

B $42 \le \dfrac{y}{-9} + 30$

$$42 \le \dfrac{y}{-9} + 30$$

$$\underline{-30 - 30} \qquad \text{Subtract 30 from both sides.}$$

$$12 \le \dfrac{y}{-9}$$

$$-9(12) \ge (-9)\dfrac{y}{-9} \qquad \text{Multiply both sides by } -9, \text{ and reverse}$$

$$-108 \ge y \qquad\qquad\qquad \text{the inequality symbol.}$$

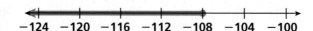

Solve. Then graph each solution set on a number line.

C $3x - 12 \geq 9$

$$3x - 12 \geq 9$$
$$\underline{+12 +12} \qquad \text{\textit{Add 12 to both sides.}}$$
$$3x \geq 21$$

$$\frac{3x}{3} \geq \frac{21}{3} \qquad \text{\textit{Divide both sides by 3.}}$$

$$x \geq 7$$

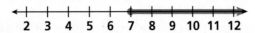

D $10 > -4y + 6$

$$10 > -4y + 6$$
$$\underline{-6 -6} \qquad \text{\textit{Subtract 6 from both sides.}}$$
$$4 > -4y$$

$$\frac{4}{-4} < \frac{-4y}{-4} \qquad \text{\textit{Divide both sides by }-4\text{, and reverse the}}$$
$$-1 < y \qquad \qquad \text{\textit{inequality symbol.}}$$

EXAMPLE 2 *School Application*

The 83 members of the Newman Middle School Band are trying to raise at least \$5,000 to buy new percussion instruments. They have already raised \$850. How much should each student still raise, on average, to meet the goal?

Let d represent the average amount each student should still raise.

$$83d + 850 \geq 5{,}000 \qquad \text{\textit{Write an inequality.}}$$
$$\underline{-850 -850} \qquad \text{\textit{Subtract 850 from both sides.}}$$
$$83d \geq 4{,}150$$

$$\frac{83d}{83} \geq \frac{4{,}150}{83} \qquad \text{\textit{Divide both sides by 83.}}$$

$$d \geq 50$$

On average, each band member should raise at least \$50.

Think and Discuss   GPS M7P1.d, M7P3.b

1. Tell how you would solve the inequality $8x + 5 < 20$.

2. Explain why the *greater than or equal to* symbol was used in the inequality in Example 2.

Georgia Performance
Standards
M7P3.a, M7P3.c, M7P5.b

go.hrw.com
Homework Help Online
KEYWORD: MS7 12-7
Parent Resources Online
KEYWORD: MS7 Parent

GUIDED PRACTICE

See Example 1 **Solve. Then graph each solution set on a number line.**

1. $5x + 3 < 18$

2. $-19 \geq \frac{z}{7} + 23$

3. $3y - 4 \geq 14$

4. $\frac{m}{4} - 2 > -3$

5. $42 \leq -11p - 13$

6. $\frac{n}{-3} - 4 > 4$

See Example 2 **7.** Three students collected more than $93 washing cars. They used $15 to reimburse their parents for cleaning supplies. Then they divided the remaining money equally. How much did each student earn?

INDEPENDENT PRACTICE

See Example 1 **Solve. Then graph each solution set on a number line.**

8. $5s - 7 > -42$

9. $\frac{b}{2} + 3 < 9$

10. $19 \leq -2q + 5$

11. $-8c - 11 \leq 13$

12. $\frac{y}{-4} + 6 > 10$

13. $\frac{x}{9} - 5 \leq -8$

14. $\frac{r}{-2} - 9 > -14$

15. $44 \geq 13j + 18$

16. $\frac{d}{13} - 12 > 27$

See Example 2 **17.** Rico has $5.00. Bagels cost $0.65 each, and a small container of cream cheese costs $1.00. What is the greatest number of bagels Rico can buy if he also buys one small container of cream cheese?

18. The 35 members of a drill team are trying to raise at least $1,200 to cover travel costs to a training camp. They have already raised $500. How much should each member still raise, on average, to meet the goal?

PRACTICE AND PROBLEM SOLVING

Extra Practice p. 751

Solve.

19. $32 \geq -4x + 8$

20. $0.5 + \frac{n}{5} > -0.5$

21. $1.4 + \frac{c}{3} < 2$

22. $-1 < -\frac{3}{4}b - 2.2$

23. $12 + 2w - 8 \leq 20$

24. $5k + 6 - k \geq -14$

25. $\frac{s}{2} + 9 > 12 - 15$

26. $4t - 3 - 10t < 15$

27. $\frac{d}{2} + 1 + \frac{d}{2} \leq 5$

28. Mr. Monroe keeps a bag of small prizes to distribute to his students. He likes to keep at least twice as many prizes in the bag as he has students. The bag currently has 79 prizes in it. Mr. Monroe has 117 students. How many more prizes does he need to buy?

29. Manny needs to buy 5 work shirts that are each the same price. After he uses a $20 gift certificate, he can spend no more than $50. What is the maximum amount that each shirt can cost?

30. Business Darcy earns a salary of $1,400 per month, plus a commission of 4% of her sales. She wants to earn a total of at least $1,600 this month. What is the least amount of sales she needs?

31. Multi-Step The bar graph shows how many students from Warren Middle School participated in a reading challenge each of the past four years. This year, the goal is for at least 10 more students to participate than the average number of participants from the past four years. What is the goal for this year?

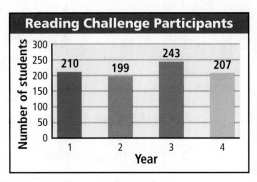

Reading Challenge Participants

32. Consumer Math Michael wants to buy a belt that costs $18. He also wants to buy some shirts that are on sale for $14 each. He has $70. At most, how many shirts can Michael buy together with the belt?

33. Earth Science A granite rock contains the minerals feldspar, quartz, and biotite mica. The rock has $\frac{1}{3}$ as much biotite mica as quartz. The rock is at least 30% quartz. What percent of the rock is feldspar?

Feldspar   Quartz

Biotite mica   Granite

 34. What's the Error? A student's solution to the inequality $\frac{x}{-9} - 5 > 2$ was $x > 63$. What error did the student make in the solution?

 35. Write About It Explain how to solve the inequality $4y + 6 < -2$.

 36. Challenge A student scored 92, 87, and 85 on three tests. She wants her average score for five tests to be at least 90. What is the lowest score the student can get, on average, on her fourth and fifth tests?

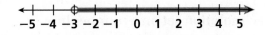

CRCT PREP • GPS SUPPORT • SPIRAL REVIEW

37. Multiple Choice Which inequality has the following graphed solution?

$$-5 \;-4 \;-3 \;-2 \;-1 \;\; 0 \;\; 1 \;\; 2 \;\; 3 \;\; 4 \;\; 5$$

Ⓐ $2x - 5 > 1$ Ⓑ $-x + 3 < 6$ Ⓒ $3x - 12 < -3$ Ⓓ $-5x - 2 > -13$

38. Gridded Response Gretta earns $450 per week plus a 10% commission on book sales. How many dollars of books must she sell to earn at least $650 per week?

39. Jamie flips a coin and rolls a number cube. How many outcomes are possible? (Lesson 11-3)

Solve. (Lesson 12-6)

40. $6x > -24$ **41.** $-4x < -20$ **42.** $-3x \geq 18$ **43.** $\frac{x}{3} + 6 \leq 11$

READY TO GO ON?

Quiz for Lessons 12-4 Through 12-7

✓ **12-4** **Inequalities**

Write an inequality for each situation.

1. Gray has at least 25 blue T-shirts.

2. The room can hold no more than 50 people.

Graph each inequality.

3. $b > -1$ 4. $5 \le t$ 5. $-3 \ge x$

Graph each compound inequality.

6. $5 \ge p$ and $p > -1$ 7. $-8 > g$ or $g \ge -1$ 8. $-4 \le x < 0$

✓ **12-5** **Solving Inequalities by Adding or Subtracting**

Solve. Then graph each solution set on a number line.

9. $28 > m - 4$ 10. $8 + c \ge -13$ 11. $-1 + v < 1$

12. $5 \le p - 3$ 13. $-8 > f + 1$ 14. $-7 - w < 10$

15. A group of climbers are at an altitude of at most 17,500 feet. They are on their way to the top of Mount Everest, which is at an altitude of 29,035 feet. How many more feet do they have left to climb?

✓ **12-6** **Solving Inequalities by Multiplying or Dividing**

Solve. Check each answer.

16. $-8s > 16$ 17. $\dfrac{x}{-2} \le 9$ 18. $-7 \le \dfrac{b}{3}$

19. $\dfrac{c}{-3} \ge -4$ 20. $28 > 7h$ 21. $6y < -2$

✓ **12-7** **Solving Two-Step Inequalities**

Solve. Then graph each solution set on a number line.

22. $2x - 3 > 5$ 23. $3 \ge -2d + 4$ 24. $3g - 2 - 10g > 5$

25. $14 < -4a + 6$ 26. $3.6 + 7.2k < 25.2$ 27. $3z - 2 \le 13$

28. A concert is being held in a gymnasium that can hold no more than 450 people. The bleachers seat 60 people. There will also be 26 rows of chairs set up. At most, how many people can sit in each row?

29. The 23 members of the Westview Journalism Club are trying to raise at least $2,100 to buy new publishing design software. The members have already raised $1,180. How much should each student still raise, on average, to meet the goal?

MULTI-STEP TEST PREP

Classy Music Ricky is learning to play the guitar and is thinking about taking classes at one of the schools listed in the table.

1. Last year, Ricky spent $590 on guitar lessons. If he takes classes at Main Street Music and spends the same amount this year, how many classes can he take?

2. How many classes would Ricky have to take in order for the cost at Main Street Music to be the same as the cost at SoundWorks?

School	Cost of Lessons
Main Street Music	Annual registration fee: $50 $12 per class
SoundWorks	Annual registration fee: $14 $16.50 per class
Town Hall	No annual registration fee $18 per class

3. Ricky plans to buy a new guitar this year. He expects to pay $139 for it. His total budget for the guitar and the classes is $600. Write and solve an inequality to find the maximum number of classes Ricky will be able to take if he goes to Main Street Music and stays within his budget.

4. Write and solve inequalities to find the maximum number of classes Ricky will be able to take with a $600 budget if he goes to the other schools. Assuming the three schools are equal in other respects, which of the schools should he choose? Why?

Multi-Step Test Prep

EXTENSION   Solving for a Variable

Learn to solve formulas with two or more variables for one of the variables.

Georgia Performance Standards

M7P1.b Solve problems that arise in mathmatics and in other contexts. Also, M7P4.c.

The highest recorded speed of a magnetically elevated vehicle was achieved by the MLX01 on the Yamanashi Maglev Test Line in Japan. At its top speed, the MLX01 could travel the 229 miles from Tokyo to Kyoto in less than an hour.

The formula *distance = rate · time* ($d = rt$) tells how far an object travels at a certain rate over a certain time. In an equation or a formula that contains more than one variable, you can isolate one of the variables by using inverse operations. Recall that you cannot divide by a variable if it represents 0.

The MLX01 attained the record speed of 343 miles per hour in January 1998.

EXAMPLE **1**   Solving for Variables in Formulas

Solve $d = rt$ for r.

$$d = rt$$

$$\frac{d}{t} = \frac{rt}{t} \qquad \textit{Divide both sides by t to isolate r.}$$

$$\frac{d}{t} = r$$

EXAMPLE **2**   *Physical Science Application*

How long would it take the MLX01 to travel 1,029 mi if it travels at a speed of 343 mi/h?

First solve the distance formula for t because you want to find the time. Then use the given values to find t.

$$d = rt$$

$$\frac{d}{r} = \frac{rt}{r} \qquad \textit{Divide both sides by r to isolate t.}$$

$$\frac{d}{r} = t$$

$$\frac{1{,}029}{343} = t \qquad \textit{Substitute 1,029 for d and 343 for r.}$$

$$3 = t$$

It would take the MLX01 3 hours to travel 1,029 miles.

Solve each equation for the given variable.

1. $A = bh$ for h

2. $A = bh$ for b

3. $C = \pi d$ for d

4. $P = 4s$ for s

5. $V = Bh$ for B

6. $d = 2r$ for r

7. $xy = k$ for y

8. $A = \ell w$ for w

9. $W = Fd$ for F

10. $I = Prt$ for P

11. $C = 2\pi r$ for r

12. $A = \frac{1}{2}bh$ for h

13. $V = \frac{1}{3}Bh$ for h

14. $K = C + 273$ for C

15. $E = Pt$ for t

16. $D = \frac{m}{v}$ for v

17. $F = ma$ for a

18. $P = VI$ for I

19. $r = \frac{V}{I}$ for V

20. $I = Prt$ for r

21. $P = 2\ell + 2w$ for ℓ

22. $V = \pi r^2 h$ for h

23. **Physical Science** The formula $E = mc^2$ tells the amount of energy an object at rest has. In the equation, E stands for the amount of energy in joules, m stands for the rest mass in kilograms of the object, and c is the speed of light (approximately 300,000,000 meters per second). What is the rest mass of an object that has 90,000,000,000,000 joules of energy?

THE FAR SIDE® BY GARY LARSON

© 1985 FarWorks, Inc. All Rights Reserved/Dist. by Creators Syndicate

The Far Side ® by Gary Larson © 1985 FarWorks, Inc. All Rights Reserved. Used with permission.

"*Now* that desk looks better. Everything's squared away, yessir, squaaaaaared away."

24. **Physical Science** The Kelvin scale is a temperature scale. To convert between the Celsius temperature scale and the Kelvin temperature scale, use the formula $C = K - 273$, where C represents the temperature in degrees Celsius and K represents the temperature in kelvins. Use the formula to convert 38°C to an equivalent Kelvin temperature.

25. **Physical Science** Density is mass per unit volume. The formula for density is $D = \frac{m}{v}$, where D represents density, m represents mass, and v represents volume. Find the mass of a gear with a density of 3.75 g/cm³ and a volume of 20 cm³.

26. What is the height of the cone if its volume is 8,138.88 ft³? Use 3.14 for π.

12 ft

Game Time

Flapjacks

Five pancakes of different sizes are stacked in a random order. How can you get the pancakes in order from largest to smallest by flipping portions of the stack?

To find the answer, stack five disks of different sizes in no particular order. Arrange the disks from largest to smallest in the fewest number of moves possible. Move disks by choosing a disk and flipping over the whole stack from that disk up.

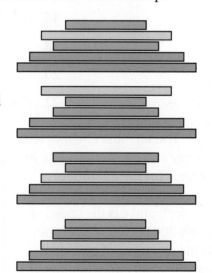

Start with a stack of five.

Flip the stack from the second disk up.

Now flip the stack from the third disk up.

Finally, flip the stack from the second disk up.

At most, it should take $3n - 2$ turns, where n is the number of disks, to arrange the disks from largest to smallest. The five disks above were arranged in three turns, which is less than $3(5) - 2 = 13$. Try it on your own.

Leaping Counters

Remove all but one of the counters from the board by jumping over each counter with another and removing the jumped counter. The game is over when you can no longer jump a counter. A perfect game would result in one counter being left in the center of the board.

A complete copy of the rules and a game board are available online.

go.hrw.com
Game Time Extra
KEYWORD: MS7 Games

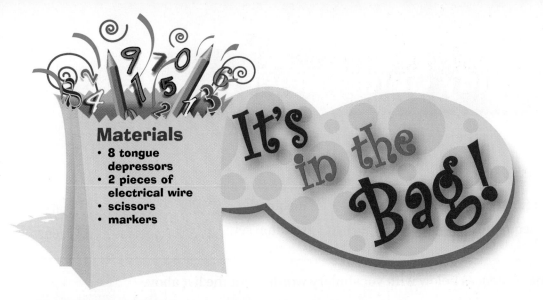

Materials

- 8 tongue depressors
- 2 pieces of electrical wire
- scissors
- markers

It's in the Bag!

PROJECT **Wired for Multi-Step Equations**

These "study sticks" will help you sort out the steps in solving equations.

Directions

❶ Twist a piece of electrical wire around each end of a tongue depressor. Twist the wire tightly so that it holds the tongue depressor securely. **Figure A**

❷ Slide another tongue depressor between the ends of the wires. Slide it down as far as possible and then twist the wires together to hold this tongue depressor securely. **Figure B**

❸ Continue in the same way with the remaining tongue depressors.

❹ Twist the wires together at the top to make a handle. Trim the wires as needed.

Taking Note of the Math

Write the title of the chapter on the top tongue depressor. On each of the remaining tongue depressors, write the steps for solving a sample multi-step equation.

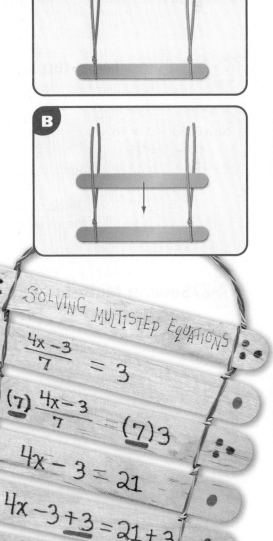

SOLVING MULTISTEP EQUATIONS

$$\frac{4x - 3}{7} = 3$$

$$(7)\frac{4x - 3}{7} = (7)3$$

$$4x - 3 = 21$$

$$4x - 3 + 3 = 21 + 3$$

$$4x = 24$$

$$\frac{4x}{2}$$

713

Vocabulary

algebraic inequality 692   inequality 692

compound inequality 693   solution set 692

Complete the sentences below with vocabulary words from the list above.

1. A(n) __?__ states that two quantities either are not equal or may not be equal.

2. A(n) __?__ is a combination of more than one inequality.

3. Together, the solutions of an inequality are called the __?__.

12-1 Solving Two-Step Equations (pp. 678–681)  GPS M7A1.a, M7A2.a, M7A2.b

EXAMPLE

■ Solve $6a - 3 = 15$.

$6a - 3 = 15$

$6a - 3 + 3 = 15 + 3$ *Add 3 to both sides.*

$6a = 18$

$\dfrac{6a}{6} = \dfrac{18}{6}$ *Divide to isolate the variable.*

$a = 3$

EXERCISES

Solve.

4. $-5y + 6 = -34$

5. $9 + \dfrac{z}{6} = 14$

6. $-8 = \dfrac{w}{-7} + 13$

12-2 Solving Multi-Step Equations (pp. 682–685)  GPS M7A2.a, M7A2.b

EXAMPLE

■ Solve $\dfrac{4x - 3}{7} = 3$.

$\dfrac{4x - 3}{7} = 3$

$(7)\dfrac{4x - 3}{7} = (7)3$ *Multiply.*

$4x - 3 = 21$

$4x - 3 + 3 = 21 + 3$ *Add 3 to both sides.*

$4x = 24$

$\dfrac{4x}{4} = \dfrac{24}{4}$ *Divide both sides by 4.*

$x = 6$

EXERCISES

Solve.

7. $7a + 4 - 13a = 46$ 8. $9 = \dfrac{6j - 18}{4}$

9. $\dfrac{8b - 5}{3} = 9$ 10. $52 = -9 + 16y - 19$

11. Noelle biked twice as many miles as Leila. Adding 2 to the number of miles Noelle biked and dividing by 3 gives the number of miles Dani biked. Dani biked 18 miles. How many miles did Leila bike?

12-3 Solving Equations with Variables on Both Sides (pp. 686–689)

GPS M7A2.a, M7A2.b

EXAMPLE

■ Solve $8a = 3a + 25$.

$$8a = 3a + 25$$
$$8a - 3a = 3a - 3a + 25 \quad \text{Subtract.}$$
$$5a = 25$$
$$\frac{5a}{5} = \frac{25}{5} \quad \text{Divide.}$$
$$a = 5$$

EXERCISES

Solve.

12. $-6b + 9 = 12b$

13. $5 - 7c = -3c - 19$

14. $18m - 14 = 12m + 2$

15. $4 - \frac{2}{5}x = \frac{1}{5}x - 8$

12-4 Inequalities (pp. 692–695)

GPS M7A1.a

EXAMPLE

Write an inequality for each situation.

■ You have to be at least 17 years old to drive a car in New Jersey.
age of driver ≥ 17

■ Graph $x < -1$.

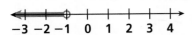

EXERCISES

Write an inequality for each situation.

16. A bridge's load limit is at most 9 tons.

17. The large tree in the park is more than 200 years old.

Graph each inequality.

18. $y \geq 3$

19. $-2 \leq k < -1$

12-5 Solving Inequalities by Adding or Subtracting (pp. 696–699)

GPS M7A1.a

EXAMPLE

Solve. Graph each solution set.

■ $b + 6 > -10$

$$b + 6 > -10$$
$$b + 6 - 6 > -10 - 6$$
$$b > -16$$

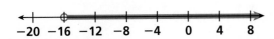

■ $p - 17 \leq 25$

$$p - 17 \leq 25$$
$$p - 17 + 17 \leq 25 + 17$$
$$p \leq 42$$

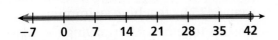

EXERCISES

Solve. Graph each solution set.

20. $r - 16 > 9$

21. $-14 \geq 12 + x$

22. $\frac{3}{4} + g < 8\frac{3}{4}$

23. $\frac{5}{6} > \frac{2}{3} + t$

24. $7.46 > r - 1.54$

25. $u - 57.7 \geq -123.7$

26. The Wildcats scored at least 13 more points than the Stingrays scored. The Stingrays scored 25 points. How many points did the Wildcats score?

27. Gabe saved $113. This amount was at least $19 more than his brother saved. How much money did Gabe's brother save?

Study Guide: Review

12-6 Solving Inequalities by Multiplying or Dividing (pp. 700–703)

EXAMPLE

Solve.

■ $\dfrac{m}{-4} \geq 3.8$

$\dfrac{m}{-4} \geq 3.8$

$(-4)\dfrac{m}{-4} \leq (-4)3.8$ *Multiply and reverse the inequality symbol.*

$m \leq -15.2$

■ $8b < -48$

$8b < -48$

$\dfrac{8b}{8} < \dfrac{-48}{8}$ *Divide both sides by 8.*

$b < -6$

EXERCISES

Solve.

28. $\dfrac{n}{-8} > 6.9$

29. $-18 \leq -3p$

30. $\dfrac{k}{13} < -10$

31. $-5p > -25$

32. $2.3 \leq \dfrac{v}{1.2}$

33. $\dfrac{c}{-11} < -3$

34. It cost Carlita $204 to make beaded purses. How many purses must Carlita sell at $13 apiece to make a profit?

12-7 Solving Two-Step Inequalities (pp. 704–707)

EXAMPLE

Solve. Graph each solution set.

■ $\dfrac{k}{3} - 18 > 24$

$\dfrac{k}{3} - 18 > 24$

$\dfrac{k}{3} - 18 + 18 > 24 + 18$

$\dfrac{k}{3} > 42$

$(3)\dfrac{k}{3} > (3)42$

$k > 126$

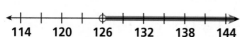

■ $-5b + 11 \leq -4$

$-5b + 11 \leq -4$

$-5b + 11 - 11 \leq -4 - 11$

$-5b \leq -15$

$\dfrac{-5b}{-5} \geq \dfrac{-15}{-5}$

$b \geq 3$

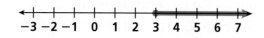

EXERCISES

Solve. Graph each solution set.

35. $-7b - 16 > -2$

36. $3.8 + \dfrac{d}{5} < 2.6$

37. $15 - 4n + 9 \leq 40$

38. $\dfrac{y}{-3} + 18 \geq 12$

39. $\dfrac{c}{3} + 7 > -11$

40. $32 \geq 4x - 8$

41. $18 + \dfrac{h}{6} \geq -8$

42. $14 > -2t - 6$

43. $-3 < \dfrac{w}{-4} + 10$

44. $\dfrac{y}{7} + 3.9 \leq 8.9$

45. Luis has $53.55. T-shirts cost $8.95 each, and a belt costs $16.75. How many T-shirts can Luis buy if he also buys a new belt?

46. Clay, Alberto, and Ciana earned more than $475 by teaching swimming lessons together. After paying the $34 pool fee, they divided their earnings equally. How much money did each teacher earn?

Study Guide: Review

Solve.

1. $3y - 8 = 16$

2. $\frac{x}{3} + 12 = -4$

3. $\frac{a}{6} - 7 = -4$

4. $-7b + 5 = -51$

5. $\frac{5y - 4}{3} = 7$

6. $8r + 7 - 13 = 58$

7. $6 = \frac{12s - 6}{5}$

8. $8.7 = \frac{19.8 - 4t}{3}$

9. $-14q = 4q - 126$

10. $\frac{5}{6}p + 4 = \frac{1}{6}p - 16$

11. $9 - 6k = 3k - 54$

12. $-3.6d = -7d + 34$

13. The bill for the repair of a computer was $179. The cost of the parts was $44, and the labor charge was $45 per hour. How many hours did it take to repair the computer?

14. Members of the choir are baking cookies for a fund-raiser. It costs $2.25 to make a dozen cookies, and the choir's initial expenses were $15.75. They sell the cookies for $4.50 a dozen. How many dozen do they have to sell to cover their costs?

Write an inequality for each situation.

15. You must be more than 4 ft tall to go on the ride.

16. You cannot go more than 65 miles per hour on Route 18.

Graph each inequality.

17. $a < -2$

18. $-5 < d$ and $d \leq 2$

19. $c > -1$ or $c < -5$

20. $b \geq 3$

Solve. Then graph each solution set on a number line.

21. $n + 8 < -9$

22. $n - 124 > -59$

23. $-40 > \frac{x}{32}$

24. $-\frac{3}{4}y \leq -12$

25. Rosa wants to save at least $125 to buy a new skateboard. She has already saved $46. How much more does Rosa need to save?

26. Gasoline costs $2.75 a gallon. At most, how many gallons can be bought for $22.00?

Solve. Then graph each solution set on a number line.

27. $m - 7.8 \leq 23.7$

28. $6z > -2\frac{2}{3}$

29. $\frac{w}{-4.9} \leq 3.4$

30. $-15 < 4a + 9$

31. $2.8 - \frac{c}{4} \geq 7.4$

32. $\frac{d}{5} - 8 > -4$

33. The seventh-grade students at Fulmore Middle School are trying to raise at least $7,500 for the local public library. So far, each of the 198 students has raised an average of $20. How much more money must each seventh-grader collect, on average, to reach the goal?

Cumulative Assessment, Chapters 1–12

Multiple Choice

1. Nolan has 7 red socks, 3 black socks, 10 white socks, and 5 blue socks in a drawer. If Nolan chooses one sock at a time and puts the sock immediately on his foot, what is the probability that he will choose 2 white socks?

Ⓐ $\frac{3}{20}$

Ⓒ $\frac{2}{5}$

Ⓑ $\frac{4}{25}$

Ⓓ $\frac{19}{25}$

2. Of the 10,500 books in the school library, $\frac{2}{5}$ of the books are fiction. Given that 30% of the remaining books are biographies, how many books are biographies?

Ⓕ 4,200

Ⓗ 1,260

Ⓖ 2,940

Ⓙ 1,890

3. There are 126 girls and 104 boys attending a luncheon. Each person at the luncheon writes his or her name on a piece of paper and puts the paper in a barrel. One name is randomly selected from the barrel to win a new MP3 player. What is the probability the person selected is male?

Ⓐ 45.2%

Ⓒ 82.5%

Ⓑ 54.8%

Ⓓ Not here

4. A trapezoid has two bases, b_1 and b_2, and height h. For which values of b_1, b_2, and h is the area of the trapezoid equal to 16 in^2?

Ⓕ $b_1 = 8$ in., $b_2 = 4$ in., $h = 2$ in.

Ⓖ $b_1 = 5$ in., $b_2 = 3$ in., $h = 4$ in.

Ⓗ $b_1 = 2$ in., $b_2 = 8$ in., $h = 6$ in.

Ⓙ $b_1 = 2$ in., $b_2 = 4$ in., $h = 4$ in.

5. Between which two integers does $-\sqrt{32}$ lie?

Ⓐ -2 and -3

Ⓒ 0 and -1

Ⓑ -5 and -6

Ⓓ -7 and -8

6. Two of the angles of this triangle measure 36°. Which of the following descriptions best classifies this triangle?

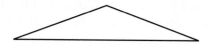

Ⓕ Isosceles, obtuse

Ⓗ Right, acute

Ⓖ Obtuse

Ⓙ Equilateral

7. Martha buys a surfboard that costs $405 for 40% off. How much money does she save?

Ⓐ $243

Ⓒ $24

Ⓑ $162

Ⓓ $17

8. The total number of students in seventh grade at Madison Middle School is expected to increase by 15% from year three to year four. What will enrollment be in year four?

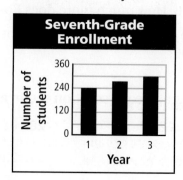

Seventh-Grade Enrollment

Ⓕ 42

Ⓗ 345

Ⓖ 295

Ⓙ 238

9. Calculate 16.0 ft − 9.03 ft. Use the correct number of significant digits in your answer.

Ⓐ 7.0 ft   Ⓒ 6.97 ft

Ⓑ 7 ft   Ⓓ 6 ft

10. Which rational number is greater than $-3\frac{1}{3}$ but less than $-\frac{4}{5}$?

Ⓕ −0.4   Ⓗ −0.19

Ⓖ $-\frac{22}{5}$ Ⓙ $-\frac{9}{7}$

11. Becky tutors third-graders two days after school each week. She saves $\frac{3}{5}$ of her earnings. What percent of her earnings does Becky save?

Ⓐ 35%   Ⓒ 60%

Ⓑ 45%   Ⓓ 70%

Create and use a number line to help you order rational numbers quickly.

12. Fiona has 18 coins, consisting of quarters and dimes, in her pocket. She has 6 more dimes than quarters. How many quarters does she have?

Ⓕ 6   Ⓗ 18

Ⓖ 12   Ⓙ 25

13. Freddy counted the number of bats he saw each night for one week. What is the median of the data set?

Number of Bats Spotted
42, 21, 36, 28, 40, 21, 31

Ⓐ 21   Ⓒ 31

Ⓑ 28   Ⓓ 31.3

14. What is the probability of flipping a coin and getting tails and then rolling a number greater than or equal to 4 on a 6-sided number cube?

Ⓕ 0.25   Ⓗ 0.5

Ⓖ 0.75   Ⓙ 1

15. Solve the inequality $-7y \geq 126$ and then graph the solution set on a number line. Is zero part of the solution set? Explain.

16. Nine less than four times a number is the same as twice the number increased by 11. What is the number?

a. Write the above statement as an equation.

b. Solve the equation.

17. Hallie is baking 5 batches of brownies for the bake sale. Each batch requires $1\frac{2}{3}$ cups of flour. Hallie has $8\frac{1}{4}$ cups of flour. Does she have enough flour to make five batches? Explain your answer.

Extended Response

18. Tim and his crew trim trees. They charge a service fee of $40 for each job, plus an hourly rate.

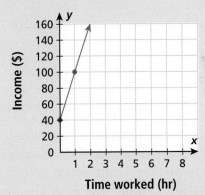

Time worked (hr)

a. Use the graph to determine the crew's hourly rate. Explain how you found your answer.

b. Write an equation to find y, the crew's income for x hours of work.

c. How many hours did Tim's crew work if they earned $490? Show your work.

Problem Solving on Location

GEORGIA

Duluth

Georgia Performance Standards

M7P1.c, M7P4.c, M7P5.a

★ The Southeastern Railway Museum

With more than 90 pieces of retired railroad equipment, the Southeastern Railway Museum in Duluth, Georgia, takes visitors on a ride into the past. Exhibits include steam locomotives, restored cabooses, and the private car that was once used by President Warren G. Harding.

Choose one or more strategies to solve each problem.

1. At the museum, the ratio of baggage cars to cabooses is 2:3. There are a total of 15 baggage cars and cabooses. How many of each type of car is there?

2. Because of the size of the typical railroad car, most cars in the museum's collection are displayed individually. For a special exhibit, the museum staff wants to display a train made up of 5 cars, including passenger cars, one locomotive, and one caboose. The average length of these cars is $56\frac{1}{2}$ feet, and each pair of cars needs $4\frac{1}{2}$ feet of space in between for coupling. How many feet of track would the museum need to display the whole train?

3. A 5-car train must start with a locomotive and end with a caboose. How many different ways can the three passenger cars be arranged?

Problem Solving Strategies

Draw a Diagram
Make a Model
Guess and Test
Work Backward
Find a Pattern
Make a Table
Solve a Simpler Problem
Use Logical Reasoning
Act It Out
Make an Organized List

★ The Peach Packing Industry

Georgia is known around the world for its delicious peaches. For more than a century, the peach-packing industry has provided the link between the tree and the market. Each year, the industry harvests, sorts, and ships more than 130 million pounds of Georgia peaches.

Choose one or more strategies to solve each problem.

1. Workers harvest peaches by placing them into baskets around their necks and then transferring them to bins on a wagon. A basket holds $\frac{1}{36}$ as much as a bin. Each wagon carries 4 bins. A wagon holds 3,600 pounds of peaches. How many pounds of peaches does each basket hold?

For 2 and 3, use the graph.

2. The graph shows the number of bushels of peaches that can be processed at a modern packing facility. How many bushels of peaches can be packed in 11 hours?

3. Working around the clock, how many days would it take to pack 21,600 bushels of peaches?

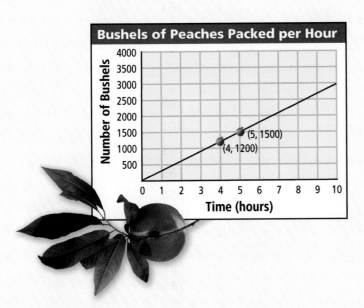

Bushels of Peaches Packed per Hour

(5, 1500)
(4, 1200)

Number of Bushels / Time (hours)

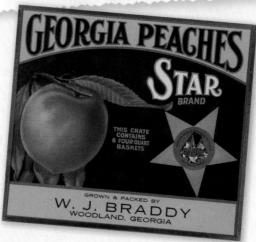

GEORGIA PEACHES
STAR BRAND

THIS CRATE CONTAINS 6 FOUR QUART BASKETS

GROWN & PACKED BY
W. J. BRADDY
WOODLAND, GEORGIA

Student Handbook

LESSON 1-1

Identify a possible pattern. Use the pattern to write the next three numbers.

1. 13, 21, 29, 37, ▪, ▪, ▪, ...

2. 7, 8, 10, 13, ▪, ▪, ▪, ...

3. 165, 156, 147, 138, ▪, ▪, ▪, ...

4. 19, 33, 47, 61, ▪, ▪, ▪, ...

Identify a possible pattern. Use the pattern to draw the next three figures.

5.

6.

7. Make a table that shows the number of dots in each figure. Then tell how many dots are in the fifth figure of the pattern. Use drawings to justify your answer.

Figure 1   Figure 2   Figure 3

LESSON 1-2

Find each value.

8. 5^3

9. 7^3

10. 5^5

11. 6^5

12. 4^1

13. 8^2

14. 12^2

15. 100^3

Write each number using an exponent and the given base.

16. 121, base 11

17. 4,096, base 4

18. 216, base 6

19. 1,296, base 6

20. 256, base 2

21. 8,000, base 20

22. Maria decided to donate $1.00 to her favorite charity the first week of the month and to double the amount she donates each week. How much will she donate the sixth week?

LESSON 1-3

Choose the most appropriate metric unit for each measurement. Justify your answer.

23. The distance from home plate to first base

24. The height of a telephone pole

25. The mass of a marble

26. The capacity of a baby bottle

Convert each measure.

27. 8.9 m to millimeters

28. 56 mg to grams

29. 900 mL to liters

30. 2 L to milliliters

31. 150 m to kilometers

32. 0.002 kg to milligrams

33. Anthony and Melinda are drinking apple juice. Anthony has 300 mL left and Melinda has 0.09L. Who has the greater amount of juice? Use estimation to explain why your answer makes sense.

LESSON 1-4

Multiply.

34. $24 \cdot 10^3$

35. $20 \cdot 10^5$

36. $318 \cdot 10^3$

37. $2{,}180 \cdot 10^4$

38. $2{,}508 \cdot 10^5$

39. $5.555 \cdot 10^6$

Write each number in scientific notation.

40. $387{,}000$

41. $2{,}056{,}000$

42. $65{,}400{,}000$

43. $1{,}560$

44. $7{,}000{,}000{,}000$

45. $206.7 \cdot 10^3$

46. The distance from the Earth to the moon is about 2.48×10^5 miles. Write this distance in standard form.

47. New York City is about 1.0871×10^4 km from Tokyo, Japan. London, England, is about 9.581×10^3 km from Tokyo. Which city is closer to Tokyo?

LESSON 1-5

Simplify each expression.

48. $9 \div 3 + 6 \cdot 5$

49. $16 + (20 \div 5) - 3^2$

50. $(6 - 3)^3 \div 9 + 7$

51. $(4 \cdot 9) - (9 - 3)^2$

52. $5 + 9 \cdot 2^2 \div 6$

53. $6{,}842 - (5^3 \cdot 5 \cdot 10)$

54. Charlotte bought 4 shirts and 3 pairs of pants. She got the pants at a discount. Simplify the expression $4 \cdot 32 + 3 \cdot 25 - (3 \cdot 25) \div 5$ to find out how much she paid for the clothes.

LESSON 1-6

Tell which property is represented.

55. $9 \cdot 2 = 2 \cdot 9$

56. $9 + 0 = 9$

57. $12 \cdot 1 = 1 \cdot 12$

58. $1 \cdot (2 \cdot 3) = (1 \cdot 2) \cdot 3$

59. $xy = yx$

60. $(x + y) + z = x + (y + z)$

Simplify each expression. Justify each step.

61. $5 + 6 + 19$

62. $5 \cdot 10 \cdot 2$

63. $3 \cdot (5 \cdot 9)$

64. $(25 \cdot 8) \cdot 4$

65. $30 + (121 + 39)$

66. $125 \cdot (2 \cdot 3)$

Use the Distributive Property to find each product.

67. $8 \cdot (2 + 10)$

68. $3 \cdot (19 + 4)$

69. $(10 - 2) \cdot 7$

70. $15 \cdot (13 - 8)$

71. $(47 + 88) \cdot 4$

72. $5 \cdot (157 - 45)$

LESSON 1-7

Evaluate each expression for the given value of the variable.

73. $8k - 7$ for $k = 4$

74. $9n + 12$ for $n = 6$

75. $12t - 15$ for $t = 4$

76. $v \div 5 + v$ for $v = 20$

77. $3r - 20 \div r$ for $r = 5$

78. $5x^2 + 3x$ for $x = 3$

LESSON 1-8

Write each phrase as an algebraic expression.

79. 12 less than a number

80. the quotient of a number and 8

81. add 7 to 8 times a number

82. 6 times the sum of 13 and a number

83. A music store sells packages of guitar strings. David bought s strings for $24. Write an algebraic expression for the cost of one string.

LESSON 1-9

Simplify. Justify your steps using the Commutative, Associative, and Distributive Properties when necessary.

84. $5b + 3t + b$

85. $t + 3b + 3t + 3b + x$

86. $8g + 3g + 12$

87. $3u + 6 + 5k + u$

88. $11 + 5t^2 + t + 6t$

89. $y^3 + 3y + 6y^3$

90. Write an expression for the perimeter of the given figure. Then simplify the expression.

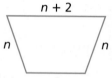

LESSON 1-10

Determine whether each number is a solution of $17 = 45 - j$.

91. 31

92. 28

93. 14

94. 22

Determine whether each number is a solution of $x + 23 = 51$.

95. 42

96. 31

97. 19

98. 28

99. Dano has 87 CDs. This is 12 more than Megan has. The equation $87 = c + 12$ can be used to represent the number of CDs that Megan has. Does Megan have 99, 85, or 75 CDs?

LESSON 1-11

Solve each equation. Check your answer.

100. $n - 22 = 16$

101. $y + 27 = 42$

102. $x - 81 = 14$

103. $t - 32 = 64$

104. $z + 39 = 72$

105. $a + 43 = 61$

106. Raquel is hiking a 9 mile trail in the Grand Canyon. She has already hiked 4 miles. How much farther does she have to hike?

LESSON 1-12

Solve each equation. Check your answer.

107. $20 = s \div 3$

108. $12y = 84$

109. $15 = \frac{n}{9}$

110. $\frac{m}{36} = 12$

111. $144 = 3p$

112. $72j = 360$

113. Adam is saving to buy a computer that costs $400 before school starts. If school starts in 8 weeks, how much will he need to save per week in order to have enough money?

LESSON 2-1

Use a number line to order the integers from least to greatest.

1. $5, -3, -1, 2, 0$

2. $-4, -1, 3, 1, 4$

3. $-5, 0, -3, 2, 4$

Use a number line to find each absolute value.

4. $|-22|$

5. $|9|$

6. $|-13|$

7. $|21|$

LESSON 2-2

Find each sum.

8. $8 + (-4)$

9. $-3 + (-6)$

10. $-5 + 9$

11. $-7 + (-2)$

Evaluate $c + d$ for the given values.

12. $c = 5, d = -9$

13. $c = 12, d = 9$

14. $c = -7, d = -2$

15. $c = -16, d = 8$

16. The temperature in Pierre at 8:00 A.M. was $-33°$F. It rose $20°$F in 9 hours. What was the temperature at 5:00 P.M.?

LESSON 2-3

Find each difference.

17. $6 - (-3)$

18. $-4 - (-8)$

19. $2 - 7$

20. $3 - (-4)$

Evaluate $a - b$ for each set of values.

21. $a = 5, b = -8$

22. $a = -12, b = -6$

23. $a = 6, b = 13$

24. $a = 9, b = -17$

25. The highest mountain in the continental United States is Mount McKinley at about 20,320 feet. Death Valley, California, is the lowest point at about 282 feet below sea level. What is the difference between the highest and lowest points in the United States?

LESSON 2-4

Find each product or quotient.

26. $-9 \div 3$

27. $8 \cdot (-3)$

28. $16 \div 4$

29. $-7 \cdot 3$

30. $-2 \cdot 9$

31. $15 \div (-5)$

32. $6 \cdot 7$

33. $-72 \div (-12)$

34. A submarine descends below the ocean's surface at a rate of 75 feet per minute. How many feet below the ocean's surface will the submarine be in 12 minutes?

LESSON 2-5

Solve each equation. Check your answer.

35. $n - 25 = -18$ **36.** $y + (-13) = 61$ **37.** $21 = \frac{s}{4}$ **38.** $15y = -45$

39. $\frac{k}{-18} = 2$ **40.** $h - (-7) = -42$ **41.** $6 = \frac{z}{9}$ **42.** $68 = 4 + p$

43. Martin deposited \$76 and withdrew \$100 from his bank account. He now has \$202 in his account. How much money did he start with?

LESSON 2-6

Write the prime factorization of each number.

44. 78   **45.** 144   **46.** 96   **47.** 95

48. 176   **49.** 156   **50.** 336   **51.** 675

52. 888   **53.** 2,800   **54.** 780   **55.** 682

LESSON 2-7

Find the greatest common factor (GCF).

56. 6, 15   **57.** 18, 27   **58.** 26, 65   **59.** 60, 25

60. 84, 48   **61.** 90, 34   **62.** 49, 56   **63.** 36, 120

64. 30, 75   **65.** 32, 68   **66.** 81, 75   **67.** 30, 70, 65, 100

68. 21, 77   **69.** 64, 84, 120   **70.** 20, 40, 80, 140   **71.** 49, 98

72. José is making identical gift bags to sell at his concert. He has 51 CDs and 34 copies of his book. What is the greatest number of gift bags José can make using all of the CDs and all of the books?

LESSON 2-8

Find the least common multiple (LCM).

73. 12, 15   **74.** 30, 12   **75.** 16, 32   **76.** 25, 40

77. 30, 75   **78.** 12, 64   **79.** 15, 50   **80.** 15, 30, 50, 100

81. 21, 28   **82.** 15, 22, 30   **83.** 20, 40, 80, 120   **84.** 42, 90

85. Kanisha shoots a basket every 7 seconds. Thomas shoots a basket every 12 seconds. They begin at the same time. How many seconds will have passed when they next shoot a basket at the same time?

LESSON 2-9

Find a fraction equivalent to the given number.

86. $\frac{1}{5}$

87. $7\frac{2}{3}$

88. 96

89. $\frac{50}{13}$

Determine whether the fractions in each pair are equivalent.

90. $\frac{2}{7}$ and $\frac{3}{4}$

91. $\frac{4}{6}$ and $\frac{12}{18}$

92. $\frac{7}{8}$ and $\frac{20}{24}$

93. $\frac{5}{12}$ and $\frac{15}{36}$

Write each improper fraction as a mixed number. Write each mixed number as an improper fraction.

94. $\frac{19}{5}$

95. $\frac{23}{8}$

96. $3\frac{4}{5}$

97. $2\frac{13}{15}$

LESSON 2-10

Write each fraction as a decimal. Round to the nearest hundredth, if necessary.

98. $\frac{4}{5}$

99. $\frac{6}{8}$

100. $\frac{57}{15}$

101. $-\frac{75}{10}$

Write each decimal as a fraction in simplest form.

102. 0.85

103. −0.04

104. 0.875

105. 2.6

106. Brianna sold 84 of the 96 CDs that she brought to sell at her concert. What portion of the CDs did she sell?

107. Jacob used 44 of the 60 pages in his journal. What portion of the pages did he use? Write your answer as a decimal rounded to the nearest hundredth.

LESSON 2-11

Compare the fractions or decimals. Write < or >.

108. $\frac{8}{13}$ ▇ $\frac{5}{13}$

109. 0.82 ▇ 0.88

110. $-\frac{8}{9}$ ▇ $-\frac{11}{12}$

111. −1.024 ▇ 1.007

Order the numbers from least to greatest.

112. 0.5, 0.58, $\frac{6}{13}$

113. 2.7, 2.59, $2\frac{7}{12}$

114. −0.61, −0.55, $-\frac{9}{15}$

CRCT GPS Practice · Chapter 3

LESSON 3-1

Estimate by rounding to the nearest integer.

1. $145.2 \cdot 6.7$
2. $26.23 + 201.86$
3. $438.57 - 129.39$
4. $55.72 \div 7.48$
5. $-5.87 \cdot 7.39$
6. $54.51 + 135.47$
7. $-87.23 - 32.62$
8. $63.38 \div 4.77$

9. Caden has $48.50. He thinks he can buy three CDs for $16.99 each. Use estimation to check whether his assumption is reasonable.

LESSON 3-2

Add or subtract. Estimate to check whether each answer is reasonable.

10. $8.79 + 45.63$
11. $-7.85 - (-34.7)$
12. $43.67 - 14.81$
13. $-18 + (-7.32)$
14. $34.43 + (-62.57)$
15. $-8.26 + 7.4$
16. $-8.75 - 5.43$
17. $-35.4 - (-24.08)$

18. Zoe gets to work in 25.5 minutes and gets home from work in 37.5 minutes. How much time does she spend commuting each day?

LESSON 3-3

Multiply. Estimate to check whether each answer is reasonable.

19. $4.3 \cdot 2.8$
20. $-3.38 \cdot 0.8$
21. $-8 \cdot (-0.07)$
22. $7.59 \cdot (-36)$
23. $-67.4 \cdot (-8.7)$
24. $5.66 \cdot (-16.34)$
25. $-43.9 \cdot (-4.7)$
26. $73.3 \cdot 6.85$

27. Griffin works after school and on weekends. He worked 18.5 hours last week and gets paid $7.90 per hour. How much did he earn last week?

LESSON 3-4

Divide. Estimate to check whether each answer is reasonable.

28. $32.8 \div (-4)$
29. $-10.5 \div 4$
30. $-25.6 \div 8$
31. $-69.6 \div (-6)$
32. $63.5 \div (-2)$
33. $36.6 \div 6$
34. $-62.8 \div 8$
35. $56.05 \div 2$

36. Robert is considering purchasing a bike on the internet. The four bikes he has found are priced $79.15, $101.25, $94.18, and $130.62. What is the average price of these bikes?

CRCT GPS Practice ■ Chapter 3

LESSON 3-5

Divide. Estimate to check whether each answer is reasonable.

37. $16.9 \div (-1.3)$ **38.** $74.25 \div 6.6$ **39.** $-4.8 \div 0.12$ **40.** $-0.63 \div (-0.7)$

41. $-36.04 \div 4.24$ **42.** $34.672 \div (-4.4)$ **43.** $-128.685 \div 37.3$ **44.** $-231.28 \div (-41.3)$

45. The diameter of a northern red oak tree grows an average of 0.4 inches per year. At this rate, how long will it take the tree's diameter to grow to 24.8 inches?

LESSON 3-6

Solve.

46. $4.7 + s = 9$ **47.** $t - 1.35 = -22$ **48.** $-4.8 = -6x$ **49.** $9.6 = \dfrac{v}{8}$

50. $-6.5 + n = 5.9$ **51.** $x - 1.07 = -8.5$ **52.** $-6.2y = -21.08$ **53.** $\dfrac{r}{13} = 3.25$

54. Billy worked 7.5 hours and earned $56.70. What is Billy's hourly wage?

55. A single movie ticket costs $7.25. The Brown family consists of Mr. and Mrs. Brown, Amy, and her two brothers. What does it cost the Brown family to go to the movies together?

56. The same cereal costs $3.99 per box at one store, $3.25 per box at another store, and $3.59 per box at a third store. What is the average price per box of the cereal?

LESSON 3-7

Estimate each sum, difference, product or quotient.

57. $\dfrac{3}{8} + \dfrac{5}{6}$ **58.** $\dfrac{7}{8} - \dfrac{1}{6}$ **59.** $5\dfrac{3}{4} + 2\dfrac{3}{8}$ **60.** $6\dfrac{2}{3} - 2\dfrac{1}{6}$

61. $4\dfrac{7}{12} + 2\dfrac{3}{8}$ **62.** $\dfrac{7}{16} - 2\dfrac{3}{4}$ **63.** $8\dfrac{9}{10} + 1\dfrac{1}{9}$ **64.** $3\dfrac{2}{5} - 1\dfrac{4}{7}$

65. A stock's price in July was $19\dfrac{3}{8}$ and its price in October rose to $27\dfrac{1}{8}$. Estimate the difference between the price in July and the price in October.

LESSON 3-8

Add or subtract. Write each answer in simplest form.

66. $\dfrac{1}{4} + \dfrac{1}{3}$ **67.** $\dfrac{3}{11} - \dfrac{3}{22}$ **68** $-\dfrac{3}{6} + \dfrac{2}{3}$ **69.** $-\dfrac{1}{4} - \dfrac{7}{10}$

70. $\dfrac{3}{7} + \dfrac{5}{9}$ **71.** $\dfrac{7}{8} - \dfrac{2}{3}$ **72.** $\dfrac{7}{12} + \dfrac{5}{6}$ **73.** $\dfrac{4}{5} - \dfrac{9}{10}$

74. Jacob and Julius spent $\dfrac{1}{4}$ hour swimming, $\dfrac{1}{10}$ hour eating a snack, and then $\dfrac{1}{2}$ hour hiking. How long did these activities take Jacob and Julius?

LESSON 3-9

Add or subtract. Write each answer in simplest form.

75. $9\frac{7}{8} - 4\frac{1}{4}$ **76.** $3\frac{1}{2} + 2\frac{3}{4}$ **77.** $9\frac{5}{6} - 6\frac{1}{3}$ **78.** $5\frac{7}{12} + 2\frac{5}{8}$

79. $7\frac{1}{4} - 3\frac{2}{3}$ **80.** $4\frac{2}{3} + 3\frac{7}{8}$ **81.** $8\frac{2}{5} - 3\frac{9}{10}$ **82.** $3\frac{7}{8} + 4\frac{3}{5}$

83. The average male giraffe is about $17\frac{1}{2}$ feet tall. One of the giraffes at the zoo is $18\frac{1}{8}$ feet tall. How much taller is the giraffe at the zoo than the average male giraffe?

LESSON 3-10

Multiply. Write each answer in simplest form.

84. $\frac{2}{3} \cdot 12\frac{3}{4}$ **85.** $3\frac{2}{9} \cdot \frac{1}{2}$ **86.** $\frac{5}{7} \cdot 4\frac{3}{8}$ **87.** $5\frac{2}{3} \cdot \frac{7}{12}$

88. $4\frac{3}{5} \cdot 3\frac{2}{3}$ **89.** $3\frac{1}{3} \cdot 2\frac{5}{6}$ **90.** $2\frac{1}{4} \cdot 3\frac{3}{4}$ **91.** $4\frac{1}{5} \cdot 5\frac{1}{12}$

92. Mary is $2\frac{1}{2}$ times as old as Victor. If Victor is $7\frac{1}{2}$ years old, how old is Mary?

LESSON 3-11

Divide. Write each answer in simplest form.

93. $\frac{7}{8} \div \frac{5}{6}$ **94.** $\frac{7}{12} \div \frac{7}{8}$ **95.** $\frac{2}{3} \div \frac{2}{5}$ **96.** $2\frac{1}{4} \div \frac{1}{2}$

97. $5\frac{7}{8} \div \frac{5}{6}$ **98.** $3\frac{3}{4} \div 1\frac{1}{4}$ **99.** $2\frac{5}{6} \div 4\frac{1}{3}$ **100.** $5\frac{2}{3} \div 2\frac{1}{2}$

101. Each serving of chicken weighs $\frac{1}{3}$ pound. Melanie bought 12 pounds of chicken for a party. How many servings does she have?

LESSON 3-12

Solve. Write each answer in simplest form.

102. $\frac{1}{3} + s = \frac{2}{5}$ **103.** $t - \frac{3}{8} = -\frac{5}{6}$ **104.** $-\frac{5}{6} = -\frac{1}{3}x$ **105.** $\frac{2}{3}w = 240$

106. $-\frac{5}{8} + n = \frac{5}{6}$ **107.** $x - \frac{5}{8} = -\frac{5}{8}$ **108.** $-\frac{2}{3}y = -\frac{3}{4}$ **109.** $\frac{r}{6} = \frac{1}{8}$

110. Jorge owns $1\frac{3}{4}$ acres of land. Juanita, his neighbor, owns $2\frac{2}{3}$ acres. How many acres do they own in all?

111. Kyra uses $2\frac{1}{4}$ feet of ribbon to wrap each of the identical fruit baskets that she sells. How many baskets can she wrap with a 144-foot roll of ribbon?

LESSON 4-1

Plot each point on a coordinate plane. Identify the quadrant that contains each point.

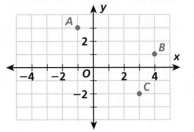

1. $M(-1, 1)$ **2.** $N(4, 4)$ **3.** $Q(3, -1)$

Give the coordinates of each point.

4. A **5.** B **6.** C

LESSON 4-2

Write the ordered pairs from each table.

7.

x	1	2	3	4
y	0	1	2	3

8.

x	5	10	15	20
y	−1	−1	−1	−1

9.

x	2	4	6	8
y	−3	−2	−1	0

Write and graph the ordered pairs from each table.

10.

x	1	2	3	4
y	−3	−2	−1	0

11.

x	0	2	4	6
y	−1	0	1	2

12.

x	−2	−1	0	1
y	3	3	3	3

13. The table shows the total cost of buying different numbers of bottles of water. Graph the data to find the cost of buying 10 bottles of water.

Number of Bottles	1	2	3	4
Total Cost ($)	1.75	3.50	5.25	7.00

LESSON 4-3

14. Abby rode her bike to the park. She had a picnic there with friends before biking home. Which graph best shows the situation?

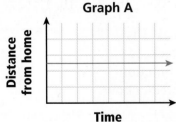

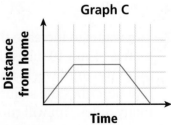

Graph A   Graph B   Graph C

15. Mallory and her sister Jamie walked to a restaurant near their house and had lunch. They then walked to the pool across the street and went for a swim. Their mom picked them up from the pool and drove them home. Sketch a graph to show the distance from home that the two sisters traveled compared to time.

16. Jose is selling tins of popcorn to make money for a school fund-raiser. Each tin of popcorn sells for $12. Draw a graph to show his possible income from sales.

LESSON 4-4

Find the output for each input.

17.

Input	Rule	Output
x	$3x - 1$	y
−2		
0		
2		

18.

Input	Rule	Output
x	$4x^2$	y
1		
3		
5		

Make a function table, and graph the resulting ordered pairs.

19. $y = 2x - 5$

Input	Rule	Output	Ordered Pair
x	$2x - 5$	y	(x, y)
0			
1			
2			

20. $y = x^2 - 1$

Input	Rule	Output	Ordered Pair
x	$x^2 - 1$	y	(x, y)
0			
1			
2			

LESSON 4-5

Tell whether each sequence of y-values is arithmetic or geometric. Then find y when $n = 5$.

21.

n	1	2	3	4	5
y	−4	0	4	8	▧

22.

n	1	2	3	4	5
y	2	4	8	16	▧

Write a function that describes each sequence.

23. $5, 6, 7, 8, \ldots$ **24.** $-4, -3, -2, -1, \ldots$ **25.** $1, 8, 27, 64, \ldots$ **26.** $2, 5, 10, 17, \ldots$

27. Tim wants to increase the number of miles he runs each week. His plan is to run 10 miles the first week, 12 miles the second week, 14 miles the third week, and 16 miles the fourth week. Write a function that describes the sequence, and then use the function to predict how many miles Tim will run during the eighth week.

LESSON 4-6

Graph each linear function.

28. $y = 2x + 2$ **29.** $y = x - 3$ **30.** $y = -x + 2$

31. The outside temperature is increasing at the rate of 6°F per hour. When Reid begins measuring the temperature, it is 52°F. Write a linear function that describes the outside temperature over time. Then make a graph to show the temperature over the first 3 hours.

LESSON 5-1

One day, a veterinarian saw 20 cats and 30 dogs. Write each ratio in all three forms. Make sure each ratio is in simplest form.

1. cats to dogs

2. dogs to cats

3. cats to animals

4. A compact car gets 135 miles per 5 gallons of gas. A midsize car gets 210 miles per 10 gallons of gas. Which car gets more miles per gallon?

LESSON 5-2

5. Jamie's family drives 350 miles to her grandparents' house in 7 hours. What is their average speed in miles per hour?

6. A store sells milk in 3 sizes. The 128 fl oz container costs $4.59, the 64 fl oz container costs $3.29, and the 32 fl oz container costs $1.99. Which size milk has the lowest price per fluid ounce?

LESSON 5-3

Tell whether the slope is positive or negative. Then find the slope.

7.

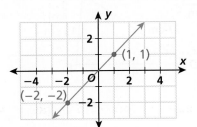

8.

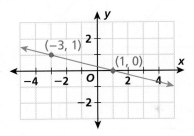

Use the given slope and point to graph each line.

9. $\frac{1}{2}$; $(2, 1)$ **10.** $-\frac{2}{3}$; $(4, 1)$ **11.** $-\frac{4}{5}$; $(-2, -3)$ **12.** 3; $(1, -3)$

LESSON 5-4

Determine whether the ratios are proportional.

13. $\frac{25}{40}, \frac{30}{48}$

14. $\frac{32}{36}, \frac{24}{28}$

15. $\frac{5}{6}, \frac{15}{18}$

16. $\frac{21}{49}, \frac{18}{42}$

Find a ratio equivalent to each ratio. Then use the ratios to write a proportion.

17. $\frac{72}{81}$

18. $\frac{15}{40}$

19. $\frac{24}{32}$

20. $\frac{5}{13}$

LESSON 5-5

Use cross products to solve each proportion.

21. $\frac{8}{n} = \frac{12}{18}$

22. $\frac{4}{7} = \frac{p}{28}$

23. $\frac{u}{14} = -\frac{21}{28}$

24. $\frac{3}{21} = \frac{t}{49}$

25. $\frac{y}{35} = \frac{63}{45}$

26. $-\frac{6}{n} = -\frac{48}{12}$

27. $\frac{32}{x} = \frac{52}{117}$

28. $\frac{56}{80} = \frac{105}{m}$

29. The ratio of a person's weight on Earth to his weight on the Moon is 6 to 1. Rafael weighs 90 pounds on Earth. How much would he weigh on the Moon?

LESSON 5-6

Choose the most appropriate customary unit for each measurement. Justify your answer.

30. the weight of 6 crackers

31. the capacity of a pond

32. the capacity of a baby's bottle

33. the length of a marathon

Convert each measure.

34. 8 pt to cups

35. 5 ft to inches

36. 6.5 lb to ounces

37. The directions on Brant's protein powder say to mix four scoops with 16 ounces of milk to make a protein drink. If Brant has a quart of milk, how many protein drinks can he make?

LESSON 5-7

Use the properties of similarity to determine whether the figures are similar.

38.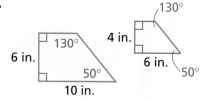

39.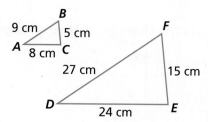

LESSON 5-8

Find the unknown length. $\triangle XYZ \sim \triangle RQS$ **and** $\square ABCD \sim \square KLMN$.

40.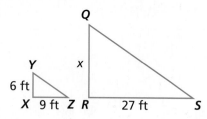

41.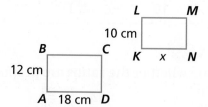

42. A 5-foot-tall girl casts a 7-foot-long shadow. A nearby telephone pole casts a 35-foot-long shadow. What is the height of the telephone pole?

LESSON 5-9

43. A scale model of the Empire State Building is 3.125 feet tall with a scale factor of $\frac{1}{400}$. Find the height of the actual Empire State Building.

44. Kira is drawing a map with a scale of 1 inch = 30 miles. The actual distance from Park City to Gatesville is 80 miles. How far from the dot for Gatesville should Kira draw the dot for Park City?

LESSON 6-1

Write the percent modeled by each grid.

1. 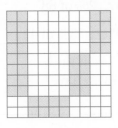   **2.** 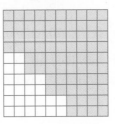   **3.**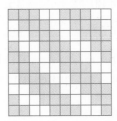

Write each percent as a fraction in simplest form.

4. 14%   **5.** 110%   **6.** 20%   **7.** 9%

Write each percent as a decimal.

8. 27%   **9.** 7%   **10.** 125%   **11.** 0.53%

LESSON 6-2

Write each decimal as a percent.

12. 0.06   **13.** 0.54   **14.** 1.69   **15.** 42.0   **16.** 0.898

Write each fraction as a percent.

17. $\frac{15}{34}$ **18.** $\frac{29}{86}$ **19.** $\frac{33}{44}$ **20.** $\frac{61}{91}$ **21.** $1\frac{2}{5}$

Decide whether using pencil and paper, mental math, or a calculator is most useful when solving the following problem. Then solve.

22. Tyler wants to donate 49% of his 50 stuffed animals to the children's hospital. About how many stuffed animals will he donate?

LESSON 6-3

Use a fraction to estimate the percent of each number.

23. 48% of 200   **24.** 27% of 76   **25.** 65% of 300   **26.** 15% of 15

27. Kel has $25 to spend on a pair of jeans. One pair is on sale for 30% off the regular price of $29.99. Does she have enough money to buy the jeans? Explain.

Use 1% or 10% to estimate the percent of each number.

28. 21% of 88   **29.** 19% of 109   **30.** 2% of 56   **31.** 48% of 200

32. Last year, Maria's retirement fund lost 19%. If the fund was worth $18,000 at the beginning of the year, how much money did she lose?

33. Every year, about 300 movies are made. Only 13% are considered to be hits. About how many movies are considered hits in a year?

CRCT ● GPS Practice

LESSON 6-4

Find the percent of each number. Check whether your answer is reasonable.

34. 35% of 80   **35.** 55% of 256   **36.** 75% of 60   **37.** 2% of 68

38. 17% of 51   **39.** 0.5% of 80   **40.** 1% of 8.5   **41.** 1.25% of 48

42. Ryan bought a new CD holder for his car. He can fit only 60 of his CDs in the holder. This represents 60% of his collection. How many CDs does Ryan have?

LESSON 6-5

Solve.

43. What percent of 150 is 60?   **44.** What percent of 140 is 28?

45. What percent of 120 is 24?   **46.** What percent of 88 is 102?

47. 24 is 60% of what number?   **48.** 9 is 15% of what number?

49. Thomas bought a desk with a retail sales price of $129 and paid $10.32 sales tax. What is the sales tax rate where Thomas bought the desk?

50. The sales tax on a $68 hotel room is $7.48. What is the sales tax rate?

LESSON 6-6

Find each percent of change. Round answers to the nearest tenth of a percent, if necessary.

51. 54 is increased to 68.   **52.** 90 is decreased to 82.   **53.** 60 is increased to 80.

54. 76 is decreased to 55.   **55.** 75 is increased to 120.   **56.** 50 is decreased to 33.

57. Abby's Appliances sells DVD players at 7% above the wholesale cost of $89. How much does the store charge for a DVD player?

58. A market's old parking lot held 48 cars. The new lot holds 37.5% more cars. How many parking spaces are on the new lot?

59. A regular bag of potato chips contains 12 ounces. A jumbo bag of chips contains $166\frac{2}{3}\%$ more chips. How many ounces does the jumbo bag contain?

LESSON 6-7

Find each missing value.

60. $I = \rule{0.5cm}{0.3cm}$, $P = \$500$, $r = 5\%$, $t = 1$ year   **61.** $I = \$30$, $P = \rule{0.5cm}{0.3cm}$, $r = 6\%$, $t = 2$ years

62. $I = \$168$, $P = \$800$, $r = \rule{0.5cm}{0.3cm}$, $t = 3$ years   **63.** $I = \$48$, $P = \$300$, $r = 8\%$, $t = \rule{0.5cm}{0.3cm}$

64. Shane deposits $600 in an account that earns 5.5% simple interest. How long will it be before the total amount is $699?

LESSON 7-1

The table shows the number of points a player scored during the last ten games of the season.

Game Date	Points	Game Date	Points
Feb 7	36	Feb 25	18
Feb 14	34	Feb 27	31
Feb 18	27	Mar 1	43
Feb 20	46	Mar 3	42
Feb 23	32	Mar 4	28

1. Make a cumulative frequency table of the data.

2. Make a stem-and-leaf plot of the data.

3. Make a line plot of the data.

LESSON 7-2

Find the mean, median, mode, and range of each data set.

4. 13, 8, 40, 19, 5, 8

5. 21, 19, 23, 26, 15, 25, 25

Identify the outlier in each data set. Then determine how the outlier affects the mean, median, and mode of the data. Then tell which measure of central tendency best describes the data with and without the outlier.

6. 23, 27, 31, 19, 56, 22, 25, 21

7. 66, 78, 57, 87, 66, 59, 239, 84

LESSON 7-3

8. The table shows the populations of four countries. Make a double-bar graph of the data.

Country	1998 Population (millions)	2001 Population (millions)
Tunisia	9.3	9.7
Syria	15.3	16.7
Turkey	64.5	66.5
Algeria	30.1	31.7

9. The list below shows the scores on a history quiz. Make a histogram of the data.

87, 92, 75, 79, 64, 88, 96, 99, 69, 77, 78, 78, 88, 83, 93, 76

LESSON 7-4

The circle graph shows the results of a survey of 100 people from Iran who were asked about their ethnic backgrounds. Use the graph for Exercises 10–12.

Ethnic Groups of Iran

10. Which ethnic group is the second largest?

11. Approximately what percent of the people are Persian?

12. According to the survey, 3% of the people are Arab. How many of the people surveyed are Arab?

Decide whether a bar graph or a circle graph would best display the information. Explain your answer.

13. the number of guitars sold compared with the number of drum sets sold for the year 2002

14. the average temperature for each day of one week

CRCT ✿ GPS Practice

LESSON 7-5

15. Use the data to make a box-and-whisker plot. 22, 41, 39, 27, 29, 30, 40, 61, 25, 28, 32

LESSON 7-6

The table shows the number of students Karen tutored during certain months. Use the table for Exercises 16 and 17.

Month	Students
Jan	5
Mar	8
May	9
Jul	12
Sep	14
Nov	18

16. Make a line graph of the data. Use the graph to determine during which months the number of students increased the most.

17. Use the graph to estimate the number of students Karen tutored during the month of October.

LESSON 7-7

Choose the type of graph that would best represent each type of data.

18. the number of participants in a hole-in-one contest for the last 10 years

19. the prices of the five top-selling MP3 players

LESSON 7-8

Determine whether each sample may be biased. Explain.

20. A bank asks the first 10 customers that enter in the morning if they are satisfied with the bank's customer service.

21. Members of a polling organization survey 1,000 residents by randomly choosing names from a list of all residents.

LESSON 7-9

22. The table shows the average number of points per game that Michael Jordan scored during each season with the Chicago Bulls. Use the data to make a scatter plot. Describe the relationship between the data sets.

Year	Points	Year	Points
1990	33.6	1994	26.9
1991	31.5	1995	30.4
1992	30.1	1996	29.6
1993	32.6	1997	28.7

LESSON 7-10

Explain why each graph could be misleading.

23.

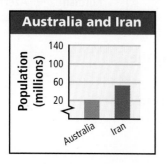

24.

LESSON 8-1

Identify the figures in the diagram.

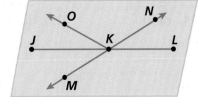

1. three points
2. a line
3. a plane

4. three rays
5. three line segments

6. Identify the line segments that are congruent in the figure.

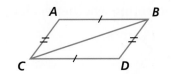

LESSON 8-2

Tell whether each angle is acute, right, obtuse, or straight.

7.
8.
9.
10.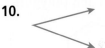

Use the diagram to tell whether the angles are complementary, supplementary, or neither.

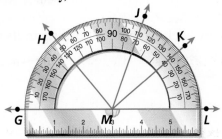

11. ∠GMH and ∠HMJ

12. ∠HMJ and ∠JMK

13. ∠LMK and ∠GMK

14. ∠JMK and ∠KML

15. Angles *Q* and *S* are complementary. If m∠Q is 77°, what is m∠S?

16. Angles *M* and *N* are supplementary. If m∠M is 17°, what is m∠N?

LESSON 8-3

Tell whether the lines appear parallel, perpendicular, or skew.

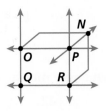

17. $\overleftrightarrow{PN}$ and $\overleftrightarrow{QR}$
18. $\overleftrightarrow{OQ}$ and $\overleftrightarrow{QR}$

19. $\overleftrightarrow{OP}$ and $\overleftrightarrow{QR}$
20. $\overleftrightarrow{PN}$ and $\overleftrightarrow{OQ}$

Line *j* ∥ line *k*. Find the measures of each angle.

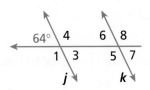

21. ∠1

22. ∠3

23. ∠8

LESSON 8-4

Name the parts of circle *I*.

24. radii   **25.** diameters   **26.** chords

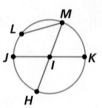

LESSON 8-5

Determine whether each figure is a polygon. If it is not, explain why not.

27.   **28.**   **29.**

Name each polygon.

30.   **31.**    **32.**

LESSON 8-6

Classify each triangle according to its sides and angles.

33.   **34.**   **35.**   **36.**

LESSON 8-7

Give all of the names that apply to each quadrilateral. Then give the name that best describes it.

37.   **38.**   **39.**   **40.**

LESSON 8-8

Find the unknown angle measure in each triangle.

41.   **42.**    **43.** 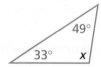   **44.**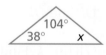

Divide each polygon into triangles to find the sum of its angle measures.

45.    **46.**    **47.**    **48.**

LESSON 8-9

Determine whether the triangles are congruent.

49.

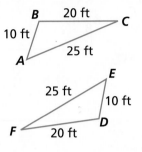

50.

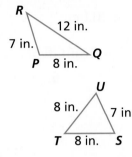

51.

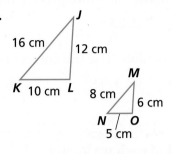

Determine the missing measure(s) in each set of congruent polygons.

52.

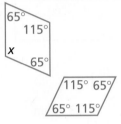

53.

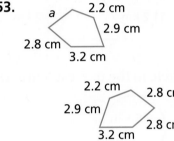

54.

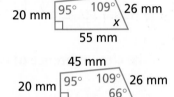

LESSON 8-10

Graph each transformation.

55. Rotate △PQR 90° counter-clockwise about vertex R.

56. Reflect the figure across the y-axis.

57. Translate △RST 3 units right and 3 units down.

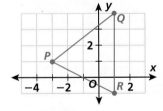

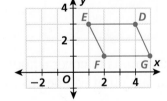

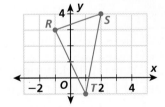

LESSON 8-11

Decide whether each figure has line symmetry. If it does, draw all the lines of symmetry.

58.

59.

60.

Tell how many times each figure will show rotational symmetry within one full rotation.

61.

62.

63.

CRCT 🍑 GPS Practice ▪ Chapter 9

LESSON **9-1**

Choose the more precise measurement in each pair.

1. 2 ft, 23 in.

2. 8.1 m, 811 cm

3. $6\frac{5}{16}$ m, $6\frac{3}{8}$ m

Calculate. Use the correct number of significant digits in each answer.

4. $7.02 + 6.9$

5. $12 - 5.88$

6. $9.20 \div 3.5$

7. $3.6 \cdot 1.8$

LESSON 9-2

Find each perimeter.

8.

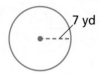

9.

10.

Find the circumference of each circle to the nearest tenth. Use 3.14 or $\frac{22}{7}$ for π.

11.

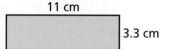

12.

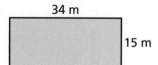

13.

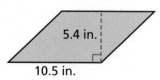

LESSON 9-3

Find the area of each rectangle or parallelogram.

14.

15.

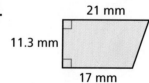

16.

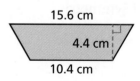

17. Harry is using 16 Japanese tatami mats to cover a floor. Each mat measures 3 feet by 2 feet. What is the total area that will be covered by the mats?

LESSON 9-4

Find the area of each triangle or trapezoid.

18.

19.

20.

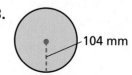

LESSON 9-5

Find the area of each circle to the nearest tenth. Use 3.14 for π.

21.

22.

23.

LESSON 9-6

Estimate the area of each figure. Each square represents 1 ft².

24.
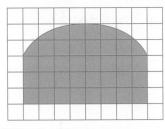

25.
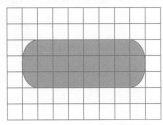

Find the area of each figure. Use 3.14 for *π*.

26.
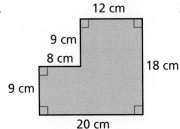

27.
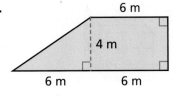

28.
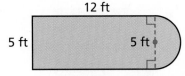

LESSON 9-7

Find each square or square root.

29. 13^2

30. $\sqrt{196}$

31. $\sqrt{625}$

32. 60^2

Estimate each square root to the nearest whole number. Use a calculator to check your answer.

33. $\sqrt{10}$

34. $\sqrt{18}$

35. $\sqrt{53}$

36. $\sqrt{95}$

37. $\sqrt{152}$

38. $\sqrt{221}$

39. $\sqrt{109}$

40. $\sqrt{175}$

41. A square painting has an area of 2,728 square centimeters. About how long is each side of the painting? Round your answer to the nearest centimeter.

LESSON 9-8

Use the Pythagorean Theorem to find each missing measure.

42.
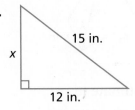

43.
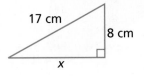

44.
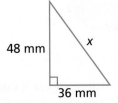

45. Ricky rides his bike 25 miles south and then turns east and rides another 25 miles before he stops to rest. How far is Ricky from his starting point? Round your answer to the nearest tenth.

LESSON 10-1

Identify the bases and faces of each figure. Then name the figure.

1.

2.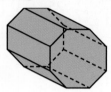

3.

LESSON 10-2

Find how many cubes each prism holds. Then give the prism's volume.

4.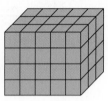

5.

6.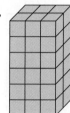

7. The back of a moving van is shaped like a rectangular prism. It is 24 ft long, 7 ft wide, and 8 ft high. Find the volume of the moving van.

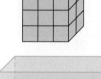
24 ft 7 ft 8 ft

8. A drum is shaped like a cylinder. It is 12.5 in. wide and 8 in. tall. Find its volume. Use 3.14 for π.

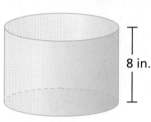
8 in.
12.5 in.

LESSON 10-3

Find the volume of each pyramid to the nearest tenth. Estimate to check whether the answer is reasonable.

9.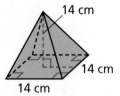
14 cm
14 cm
14 cm

10.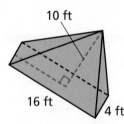
10 ft
16 ft
4 ft

11.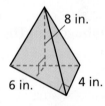
8 in.
6 in.
4 in.

Find the volume of each cone to the nearest tenth. Use 3.14 for π. Estimate to check whether the answer is reasonable.

12.
15 in.
8 in.

13.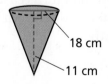
18 cm
11 cm

14.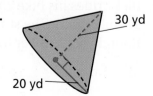
30 yd
20 yd

LESSON 10-4

Find the surface area of the prism formed by each net to the nearest tenth.

15.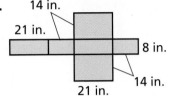

16.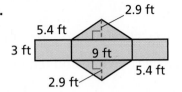

17.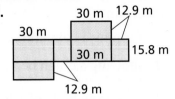

Find the surface area of the cylinder formed by each net to the nearest tenth. Use 3.14 for π.

18.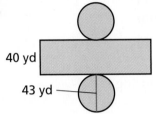

19.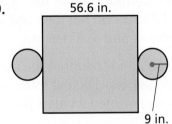

20.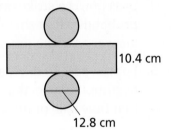

21. An 8 in. tall candle is cylindrical and has a 3 in. wide ribbon around it. What percent of the total surface area of the candle is covered by the 3 in. wide ribbon? Use 3.14 for π. Round your answer to the nearest tenth.

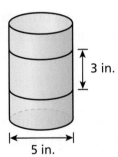

LESSON 10-5

22. The surface area of a cylinder is 49 m². What is the surface area of a similar cylinder that is larger by a scale factor of 6?

23. The surface area of a garden is 36 ft². What is the surface area of a similar garden that is smaller by a scale factor of $\frac{1}{4}$?

24. The surface area of a hexagonal prism is 65 cm². What is the surface area of a similar prism that is larger by a scale factor of 8?

25. The volume of a cube is 50 cm³. What is the volume of a similar cube that is larger by a scale factor of 7?

26. An oil drum has a volume of 513 cm³. What is the volume of a similar oil drum that is smaller by a scale factor of $\frac{1}{3}$?

CRCT GPS Practice ■ Chapter 11

Determine whether each event is impossible, unlikely, as likely as not, likely, or certain.

1. flipping a coin and getting heads twelve times in a row

2. drawing a green bead from a bag of white and red beads

3. The probability of rolling a 2 on a number cube is $\frac{1}{6}$. What is the probability of not rolling a 2?

4. Bess bowls a strike on 6 out of 15 tries. What is the experimental probability that she will bowl a strike on her next try? Write your answer as a fraction, as a decimal, and as a percent.

5. For the past 10 days, a city planner has counted the number of northbound cars that pass through a particular intersection. During that time, 200 or more cars were counted 9 out of 10 days.

   a. What is the experimental probability that there will be 200 or more northbound cars passing through the intersection on the eleventh day?

   b. What is the experimental probability that there will not be 200 or more northbound cars passing through the intersection on the eleventh day?

6. Ronald flips a coin and rolls a number cube at the same time. What are all the possible outcomes? How many outcomes are in the sample space?

7. For lunch, Amy can choose from a salad, a taco, a hamburger, or a fish fillet. She can drink lemonade, milk, juice, or water. What are all the possible outcomes? How many outcomes are in the sample space?

8. A café makes 23 flavors of ice cream. You can get each flavor in a waffle cone, a sugar cone, a cake cone, or a cup. How many outcomes are possible?

Find the probability of each event. Write your answer as a fraction, as a decimal, and as a percent.

9. rolling a number less than 5 on a fair number cube

10. randomly drawing a pink sock out of a drawer of 6 pink, 4 black, 8 white, and 2 blue socks all of the same size

There are 12 boys and 14 girls in Mr. Grimes' class. Each student turns in an essay. Find the theoretical probability of each event when Mr. Grimes randomly selects an essay.

11. selecting a boy's essay

12. selecting a girl's essay

LESSON 11-5

Decide whether each set of events is independent or dependent. Explain your answer.

13. Mr. Fernandez's class contains 14 boys and 16 girls. Mr. Fernandez randomly picks a boy and a girl to represent the class at the school spelling bee.

14. Mrs. Rogers's class received new math books. Mrs. Rogers selects a student to hand out the new books. She also picks a second student to collect the old books.

15. There are 52 playing cards in a standard card deck. Alex draws a card and holds onto it while Suzi draws a card.

Find the probability of each set of independent events.

16. flipping 2 coins at the same time and getting heads on both coins

17. drawing a 3 from 5 cards numbered 1 through 5 and rolling an even number on a number cube

LESSON 11-6

18. Venus has decided to have a 2-color paint job done on her car. There are 6 paint colors from which to choose. How many combinations of 2 colors are possible?

19. Philip has 5 different coins. How many combinations of 3 coins can he make from the 5 coins?

20. A juice bar offers 8 different juices. You and a friend want to each try a different blend. How many different combinations of 2 juices are possible?

LESSON 11-7

21. In how many different ways can Ralph, Randy, and Robert stand in line at the movie theater?

22. Roseanne and Rita join Ralph, Randy, and Robert at the movie theater. In how many different ways could they all stand in line?

23. Doris has a $1 bill, a $2 bill, a $5 bill, a $10 bill, a $20 bill, and a $50 bill. In how many different ways can she arrange them in a stack?

24. In how many different ways can 5 students be matched up with 5 mentors?

CRCT 🍑 GPS Practice ▪ Chapter 12

LESSON 12-1

Solve. Check each answer.

1. $4c - 13 = 15$

2. $3h + 14 = 23$

3. $-5j - 13 = 22$

4. $\frac{e}{7} + 2 = 5$

5. $\frac{m}{6} - 3 = 1$

6. $\frac{x}{3} + 5 = -13$

7. If you multiply the number of DVDs Sarah has by 6 and then add 5, you get 41. How many DVDs does Sarah have?

LESSON 12-2

Solve.

8. $2w - 11 + 4w = 7$

9. $7v + 5 - v = 11$

10. $-7z + 4 - z = -12$

11. $\frac{5x - 7}{3} = 15$

12. $2t - 7 - 5t = 11$

13. $\frac{6t + 8}{5} = 2$

14. $12a - 3 - 8a = -1$

15. $\frac{2.9h - 5.1}{2} = 4.7$

16. $\frac{3s - 14}{4} = 4$

17. $\frac{10 - 4t}{8} = -12$

18. Erika has received scores of 82, 87, 93, 95, 88, and 90 on math quizzes. What score must Erika get on her next quiz to have an average of 90?

LESSON 12-3

Group the terms with variables on one side of the equal sign, and simplify.

19. $6a = 4a - 8$

20. $3d - 5 = 7d - 9$

21. $-2j + 6 = j - 3$

22. $7 + 5m = 2 - m$

Solve.

23. $7y - 9 = -2y$

24. $2c - 13 = 5c + 11$

25. $\frac{2}{5}g + 9 = -6 - \frac{6}{10}g$

26. $7d + 4 = 8 - d$

27. $-3p + 8 = -7p - 12$

28. $1.2k + 2.3 = -0.5k + 7.4$

29. Roberta and Stanley are collecting signatures for a petition. So far, Roberta has twice as many signatures as Stanley. If she collects 30 more signatures, she will have 4 times as many signatures as Stanley currently has. How many signatures has Stanley collected?

30. Gym members pay $3 per workout with a one time membership fee of $98. Nonmembers pay $10 per workout. How many workouts would both a member and a nonmember have to do to pay the same amount?

LESSON 12-4

Write an inequality for each situation.

31. The cafeteria could hold no more than 50 people.

32. There were fewer than 20 boats in the marina.

Graph each inequality.

33. $y < -2$ **34.** $f \geq 3$ **35.** $n \leq -1.5$ **36.** $x > 4$

Graph each compound inequality.

37. $1 < s < 4$ **38.** $-1 \leq v < 2$ **39.** $w < 0$ or $w \geq 5$ **40.** $-3.5 \leq y < -2$

LESSON 12-5

Solve. Then graph each solution set on a number line.

41. $c - 6 > -5$ **42.** $v - 3 \geq 1$ **43.** $w - 6 \leq -7$ **44.** $a - 2 \leq 5$

Solve. Check each answer.

45. $q + 3 \leq 5$ **46.** $m + 1 > 0$ **47.** $p + 7 \leq 4$ **48.** $z + 2 \geq -3$

49. By Saturday night, 3 inches of rain had fallen in Happy Valley. The weekend forecast predicted at least 8 inches of rain. How much more rain must fall on Sunday for this forecast to be correct?

LESSON 12-6

Solve. Check each answer.

50. $\frac{a}{5} \leq 4.5$ **51.** $-\frac{v}{2} > 2$ **52.** $\frac{x}{3.9} \geq -2$ **53.** $-\frac{c}{4} < 2.3$

54. $13y < 39$ **55.** $2t \leq 5$ **56.** $-7r > 56$ **57.** $3s \geq -4.5$

58. The local candy store buys candy in bulk and then sells it by the pound. If the store owner spends $135 on peppermints and then sells them for $3.50 per pound, how many pounds must he sell to make a profit?

LESSON 12-7

Solve. Then graph each solution set on a number line.

59. $\frac{m}{3} - 1 \leq 2$ **60.** $7.2x - 4.8 > 24$ **61.** $-5.5h + 2 < 13$

62. $-1 - \frac{s}{3.5} \geq 1$ **63.** $-\frac{w}{1.5} - 8 \leq -10$ **64.** $4j - 6 > 16$

65. $5 - 2u < 15$ **66.** $\frac{r}{7} - 1 \geq 0$ **67.** $5 - \frac{m}{9} \leq 17$

68. Jill, Serena, and Erin are trying to earn enough money to rent a beach house for a week. They estimate that it will cost at least $1,650. If Jill has already earned $600, how much must each of the others earn?

Draw a Diagram

When problems involve objects, distances, or places, you can **draw a diagram** to make the problem easier to understand. You can use the diagram to look for relationships among the given data and to solve the problem.

Problem Solving Strategies

Draw a Diagram
Make a Model
Guess and Test
Work Backward
Find a Pattern

Make a Table
Solve a Simpler Problem
Use Logical Reasoning
Act It Out
Make an Organized List

A bald eagle has built a nest 18 feet below the top of a 105-foot-tall oak tree. The eagle sits on a limb 72 feet above the ground. What is the vertical distance between the eagle and its nest?

Understand the Problem

Identify the important information.

- The height of the tree is 105 feet.
- The eagle's nest is 18 feet from the top of the tree.
- The eagle is perched 72 feet above the ground.

The answer will be the vertical distance between the eagle and its nest.

Make a Plan

Use the information in the problem to **draw a diagram** showing the height of the tree and the locations of the eagle and its nest.

Solve

To find the height of the nest's location, subtract the distance of the nest from the top of the tree from the height of the tree.

105 feet − 18 feet = 87 feet

To find the vertical distance from the eagle to its nest, subtract the height of the eagle's location from the height of the nest's location.

87 feet − 72 feet = 15 feet

The vertical distance between the eagle and its nest is 15 feet.

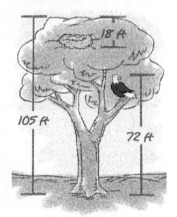

Look Back

Be sure that you have drawn your diagram correctly. Does it match the information given in the problem?

PRACTICE

1. A truck driver travels 17 miles south to drop off his first delivery. Then he drives 19 miles west to drop off a second delivery, and then he drives 17 miles north to drop off another delivery. Finally, he drives 5 miles east for his last delivery. How far is he from his starting point?

2. A table that is standing lengthwise against a wall is 10 feet long and 4 feet wide. Sarah puts balloons 1 foot apart along the three exposed sides, with one balloon at each corner. How many balloons does she use?

Make a Model

When problems involve objects, you can **make a model** using those objects or similar objects. This can help you understand the problem and find the solution.

Problem Solving Strategies

Draw a Diagram	Make a Table
Make a Model	Solve a Simpler Problem
Guess and Test	Use Logical Reasoning
Work Backward	Use a Venn Diagram
Find a Pattern	Make an Organized List

A company packages 6 minipuzzles in a decorated 4 in. cube. They are shipped to the toy store in cartons shaped like rectangular prisms. Twenty cubes fit in each carton. If the height of each carton is 8 in., what are possible dimensions of the carton?

 **Understand the Problem**

Identify the important information.

- Each cube is 4 inches on a side.
- Twenty cubes fit in one carton.
- The height of the carton is 8 inches.

The answer is the dimensions of the carton.

 **Make a Plan**

You can use 20 cubes to **make a model** of cubes packed in a carton. Record possible values for length and width, given a height of 8 in.

 Solve

Begin with a carton that is 8 in., or 2 cubes, high. Use all 20 cubes to make a rectangular prism.

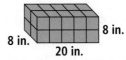

8 in.   8 in.
20 in.

Possible dimensions of the carton are 20 in. × 8 in. × 8 in.

 **Look Back**

The volume of each carton should equal the volume of the 20 cubes.

Volume of cartons: 8 in. × 20 in. × 8 in. = 1,280 in^3

Volume of 1 cube: 4 in. × 4 in. × 4 in. = 64 in^3

Volume of 20 cubes: 20 × 64 = 1,280 in^3

1,280 in^3 = 1,280 in^3 ✔

PRACTICE

1. Give two sets of possible dimensions of a rectangular prism made up of twenty 1-inch cubes.

2. John uses exactly eight 1-inch cubes to form a rectangular prism. Find the length, width, and height of the prism.

Guess and Test

If you do not know how to solve a problem, you can always make a **guess**. Then **test** your guess using the information in the problem. Use what you find out to make a second guess. Continue to **guess and test** until you find the correct answer.

Problem Solving Strategies

Draw a Diagram   Make a Table
Make a Model   Solve a Simpler Problem
Guess and Test   Use Logical Reasoning
Work Backward   Act It Out
Find a Pattern   Make an Organized List

Shannon used equal numbers of quarters and nickels to buy an embossing template that cost $1.50. How many of each coin did she use?

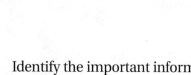

Understand the Problem

Identify the important information.

- Shannon used equal numbers of quarters and nickels.
- The coins she used total $1.50.

The answer will be the number of quarters and the number of nickels Shannon used.

Make a Plan

Start with an educated **guess** in which the numbers of quarters and nickels are the same. Then **test** to see whether the coins total $1.50.

Solve

Make a first guess of 4 quarters and 4 nickels, and find the total value of the coins.

Guess: 4 quarters and 4 nickels
Test: $(4 \times \$0.25) + (4 \times \$0.05) = \$1.00 + \$0.20 = \$1.20$

$1.20 is too low. Increase the number of coins.

Guess: 6 quarters and 6 nickels
Test: $(6 \times \$0.25) + (6 \times \$0.05) = \$1.50 + \$0.30 = \$1.80$

$1.80 is too high. The number of each coin must be between 4 and 6. So Shannon must have used 5 quarters and 5 nickels.

Look Back

Test the answer to see whether the coins add up to $1.50.
$(5 \times \$0.25) + (5 \times \$0.05) = \$1.25 + \$0.25 = \$1.50$ ✓

PRACTICE

1. The sum of Richard's age and his older brother's age is 63. The difference between their ages is 13. How old are Richard and his brother?

2. In the final game of the basketball season, Trinka scored a total of 25 points on 2-point shots and 3-point shots. She made 5 more 2-point shots than 3-point shots. How many of each did she make?

Work Backward

Some problems give you a sequence of information and ask you to find something that happened at the beginning. To solve a problem like this, you may want to start at the end of the problem and **work backward**.

 Problem Solving Strategies

Draw a Diagram	Make a Table
Make a Model	Solve a Simpler Problem
Guess and Test	Use Logical Reasoning
Work Backward	Act It Out
Find a Pattern	Make an Organized List

Tony is selling dried fruit snacks to help raise money for a new school computer. Half of the fruit snacks in the bag are apricots. Of the rest of the fruit snacks, half of them are bananas, and the other 8 are cranberries. How many fruit snacks are in the bag?

 **Understand the Problem**

Identify the important information.

- Half of the fruit snacks are apricots.
- Half of the remaining fruit snacks are bananas.
- The final 8 fruit snacks are cranberries.

The answer will be the total number of fruit snacks in the bag.

Make a Plan

Start with the 8 cranberries, and **work backward** through the information in the problem to the total number of fruit snacks in the bag.

 Solve

There are 8 cranberries.	8
The other half of the remaining fruit snacks are bananas, so there must be 8 bananas.	$8 + 8 = 16$
The other half of the fruit snacks are apricots, so there must be 16 apricots.	$16 + 16 = 32$

There are 32 fruit snacks in the bag.

 **Look Back**

Using the starting amount of 32 fruit snacks, work from the beginning of the problem following the steps.

Start: 32
Half of 32: $32 \div 2 = 16$
Half of 16: $16 \div 2 = 8$
Minus 8: $8 - 8 = 0$ ✓

PRACTICE

1. In a trivia competition, each finalist must answer 4 questions correctly. Each question is worth twice as much as the question before it. The fourth question is worth $1,000. How much is the first question worth?

2. The Ramirez family has 5 children. Sara is 5 years younger than her brother Kenny. Felix is half as old as his sister Sara. Kaitlen, who is 10, is 3 years older than Felix. Kenny and Celia are twins. How old is Celia?

Find a Pattern

In some problems, there is a relationship between different pieces of information. Examine this relationship and try to **find a pattern.** You can then use this pattern to find more information and the solution to the problem.

Problem Solving Strategies

Draw a Diagram	Make a Table
Make a Model	Solve a Simpler Problem
Guess and Test	Use Logical Reasoning
Work Backward	Act It Out
Find a Pattern	Make an Organized List

John made a design using hexagons and triangles. The side lengths of each hexagon and triangle are 1 inch. What is the perimeter of the next figure in his design?

Understand the Problem

Identify the important information.

- The first 5 figures in the design are given.
- The side lengths of each hexagon and triangle are 1 inch.

The answer will be the perimeter of the sixth figure in the design.

Make a Plan

Try to **find a pattern** in the perimeters of the first 5 figures. Use the pattern to find the perimeter of the sixth figure.

Solve

Find the perimeter of the first 5 figures.

Figure	Perimeter (in.)	Pattern
1	6	
2	7	6 + 1 = 7
3	11	7 + 4 = 11
4	12	11 + 1 = 12
5	16	12 + 4 = 16

The pattern appears to be add 1, add 4, add 1, add 4, and so on. So the perimeter of the sixth figure will be 16 + 1, or 17.

Look Back

Use another strategy. **Draw a diagram** of the sixth figure. Then find the perimeter.

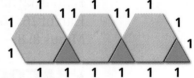

PRACTICE

Describe the pattern, and then find the next number.

1. 1, 5, 9, 13, 17, ...

2. 1, 4, 16, 64, 256, ...

Make a Table

When you are given a lot of information in a problem, it may be helpful to organize that information. One way to organize information is to **make a table**.

Problem Solving Strategies

Draw a Diagram	**Make a Table**
Make a Model	Solve a Simpler Problem
Guess and Test	Use Logical Reasoning
Work Backward	Act It Out
Find a Pattern	Make an Organized List

On November 1, Wendy watered the Gribbles' yard and the Milams' yard. If she waters the Gribbles' yard every 4 days and the Milams' yard every 5 days, when is the next date that Wendy will water both yards?

 **Understand the Problem**

Identify the important information.

- Wendy waters the Gribbles' yard every 4 days and the Milams' yard every 5 days. She watered both yards on November 1.

The answer will be the next date that she waters both yards again.

 **Make a Plan**

Make a table using X's to show the days that Wendy waters each yard. Make one row for the Gribbles and one row for the Milams.

 Solve

Start with an X in both rows for November 1. For the Gribbles, add an X on every fourth day after November 1. For the Milams, add an X every fifth day after November 1.

Date	1	2	3	4	5	6	7	8	9	10	11	12	13	14	15	16	17	18	19	20	21
Gribble	X				X				X				X				X				X
Milam	X					X					X					X					X

November 21 is the next date that Wendy will water both yards.

 **Look Back**

The sum of 1 and five 4's should equal the sum of 1 and four 5's.
$1 + 4 + 4 + 4 + 4 + 4 = 21$ $1 + 5 + 5 + 5 + 5 = 21$ ✔

PRACTICE

1. Jess, Kathy, and Linda work on the math club's newspaper. One is the editor, one is the reporter, and one is the writer. Linda does not participate in sports. Jess and the editor play tennis together. Linda and the reporter are cousins. Find each person's job.

2. A toll booth accepts any combination of coins that total exactly $0.75, but it does not accept pennies or half dollars. In how many different ways can a driver pay the toll?

Solve a Simpler Problem

Problem Solving Strategies

Draw a Diagram	Make a Table
Make a Model	**Solve a Simpler Problem**
Guess and Test	Use Logical Reasoning
Work Backward	Act It Out
Find a Pattern	Make an Organized List

Sometimes a problem may contain large numbers or require many steps to solve. It may appear complicated to solve. Try to **solve a simpler problem** that is similar to the original problem.

Lawrence is making touch pools for a project about sea creatures. The pools are squares that will be arranged side by side. The side of each pool is a 1-meter-long piece of wood. How many meters of wood does Lawrence need to complete 20 square sections of pool?

Understand the Problem

Identify the important information.

- Each square side is a 1-meter-long piece of wood.
- There are 20 square sections set side by side.

The answer will be the total meters of wood needed.

Make a Plan

You could sketch all 20 pools and then count the number of meters of wood. However, it would be easier to first **solve a simpler problem**. Start with 1 square pool, and then move on to 2 and then 3. Then look for a way to solve the problem for 20 pools.

Solve

The first pool requires 4 sides to complete. After that, only 3 sides are needed for each pool.

Notice that 1 pool requires 4 meters of wood, and the 19 other pools require 3 meters of wood each. So $4 + (19 \times 3) = 61$. The pools require 61 meters of wood.

1 square: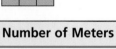

2 squares:

3 squares:

Number of Squares	Number of Meters
1	$4(1) = 4$
2	$4 + (1 \times 3) = 7$
3	$4 + (2 \times 3) = 10$
4	$4 + (3 \times 3) = 13$

Look Back

If the pattern is correct, Lawrence would need 16 meters of wood for 5 pools. Complete the next row of the table to check this answer.

PRACTICE

1. The numbers 11; 444; and 8,888 all contain repeated single digits. How many numbers between 10 and 1,000,000 contain repeated single digits?

2. How many diagonals are there in a dodecagon (a 12-sided polygon)?

Use Logical Reasoning

Sometimes a problem may provide clues and facts that you must use to find a solution. You can **use logical reasoning** to solve this kind of problem.

 Problem Solving Strategies

Draw a Diagram	Make a Table
Make a Model	Solve a Simpler Problem
Guess and Test	**Use Logical Reasoning**
Work Backward	Act It Out
Find a Pattern	Make an Organized List

Jennie, Rachel, and Mia play the oboe, the violin, and the drums. Mia does not like the drums, and she is the sister of the oboe player. Rachel has soccer practice with the person who plays the drums. Which instrument does each person play?

 **Understand the Problem**

Identify the important information.

• There are three people, and each person plays a different instrument.

 **Make a Plan**

Start with clues given in the problem, and **use logical reasoning** to determine which instrument each person plays.

Solve

Make a table. Make a column for each instrument and a row for each person. Work with the clues one at a time. Write "Yes" in a box if the clue reveals that a person plays an instrument. Write "No" in a box if the clue reveals that a person does not play an instrument.

a. Mia does not like the drums, so she does not play the drums.

b. Mia is the sister of the person who plays the oboe, so she does not play the oboe.

	Oboe	Violin	Drums
Jennie			
Rachel			No
Mia	No		No

c. Rachel has soccer practice with the person who plays the drums, so she does not play the drums.

Jennie must play the drums, and Mia must play the violin. So Rachel must play the oboe.

Look Back

Compare your answer to the clues in the problem. Make sure none of your conclusions conflict with the clues.

PRACTICE

1. Kent, Jason, and Newman have a dog, a fish, and a hamster, though not in that order. Kent's pet does not have fur. The owner of the hamster has class with Jason. Match the owners with their pets.

2. Seth, Vess, and Benica are in the sixth, seventh, and eighth grades, though not in that order. Seth is not in seventh grade. The sixth-grader has band with Benica and the same lunchtime as Seth. Match the students with their grades.

Act It Out

Some problems involve actions or processes. To solve these problems, you can **act it out.** Actively modeling the problem can help you find the solution.

Problem Solving Strategies

Draw a Diagram   Make a Table
Make a Model   Solve a Simpler Problem
Guess and Test   Use Logical Reasoning
Work Backward   **Act It Out**
Find a Pattern   Make an Organized List

Ana, Ben, Cleo, and Diego are in a chess club. To choose the president, they write their names on slips of paper and choose one name at random. Then they choose another name to be the vice president. How many different outcomes are possible?

Understand the Problem

Identify the important information.

- There are four students: Ana, Ben, Cleo, and Diego. One student will be the club's president and another will be the club's vice president.

The answer will be the number of different ways students can be chosen to be the president and vice president.

Make a Plan

Act it out to list all the possible outcomes. Then count the number of outcomes.

Solve

Write the students' names on index cards. Choose pairs of index cards to be the president and the vice president. Write down the results and continue the process until all of the possible outcomes have been listed.

Pres.	Ana	Ana	Ana	Ben	Ben	Ben
Vice Pres.	Ben	Cleo	Diego	Ana	Cleo	Diego
Pres.	Cleo	Cleo	Cleo	Diego	Diego	Diego
Vice Pres.	Ana	Ben	Diego	Ana	Ben	Cleo

There are 12 possible different outcomes.

Look Back

Check to see that you have listed all of the possible outcomes and make sure that no outcome is listed more than once.

PRACTICE

1. Joe has five font choices: Times, Arial, Eras, Gigi, and Onyx. How many different ways can he use one font for a Web site and another for a menu?

2. Mike, Jennifer, Ashley, and Kendall stand side-by-side for a photo. How many different ways can the four friends stand next to each other?

Problem Solving Handbook

Make an Organized List

Problem Solving Strategies

Draw a Diagram	Make a Table
Make a Model	Solve a Simpler Problem
Guess and Test	Use Logical Reasoning
Work Backward	Act It Out
Find a Pattern	**Make an Organized List**

In some problems, you will need to find out exactly how many different ways an event can happen. When solving this kind of problem, it is often helpful to **make an organized list**. This will help you count all the possible outcomes.

A spinner has 4 different colors: red, blue, yellow, and white. If you spin the spinner 2 times, how many different color combinations could you get?

 **Understand the Problem**

Identify the important information.

- You spin the spinner 2 times.
- The spinner is divided into 4 different colors.

The answer will be the total number of different color combinations the spinner can land on.

 **Make a Plan**

Make an organized list to determine all the possible different color outcomes. List all the different combinations for each color.

 Solve

First consider the color red. List all the different outcomes for the color red. Then consider blue, adding all the different outcomes, then yellow, and finally white.

Red	Blue	Yellow	White
RR	BB	YY	WW
RB	BY	YW	
RY	BW		
RW			

So there are 10 possible different color combinations.

 **Look Back**

Make sure that all the possible combinations of color are listed and that each set of colors is different.

PRACTICE

1. The Pizza Planet has 5 different choices of pizza toppings: ham, pineapple, pepperoni, olive, and mushroom. You want to order a pizza with 2 different toppings. How many different combinations of toppings can you order?

2. How many ways can you make change for a fifty-cent piece by using a combination of dimes, nickels, and pennies?

Skills Bank   Review Skills

Place Value

You can use a place-value chart to help you read and write numbers.
The number 213,867 is shown.

Hundred Thousands	Ten Thousands	Thousands	Hundreds	Tens	Ones
2	1	3	8	6	7

EXAMPLE

Use the chart to determine the place value of each digit.

A 2
The 2 is in the hundred thousands place.

B 8
The 8 is in the hundreds place.

PRACTICE

Determine the place value of each underlined digit.

1. 543,2<u>0</u>1   **2.** 239,4<u>8</u>7   **3.** 7<u>3</u>0,432   **4.** <u>4</u>,382,121

Compare and Order Whole Numbers

 GPS M7N1.b

You can use place values from left to right to compare and order numbers.

EXAMPLE

Compare and order from least to greatest: 42,810; 142,997; 42,729; 42,638.

Start at the leftmost place value.

There is one number with a digit in the greatest place. It is the greatest of the four numbers.

Compare the remaining three numbers. All values in the next two places, the ten thousands and thousands, are the same.

In the hundreds place, the values are different. Use this digit to order the remaining numbers.

| 42,810 |
| 142,997 |
| 42,729 |
| 42,638 |

42,638; 42,729; 42,810; 142,997

PRACTICE

Compare and order the numbers in each set from least to greatest.

1. 2,564; 2,546; 2,465; 2,654

2. 6,237; 6,372; 6,273; 6,327

3. 132,957; 232,795; 32,975; 31,999

4. 9,614; 29,461; 129,164; 129,146

Read and Write Decimals

When reading and writing a decimal, you need to know the place value of the digit in the last decimal place. Also, when writing a decimal in word form remember the following:

- "and" goes in place of the decimal for numbers greater than one.
- a hyphen is used in two-digit numbers, such as twenty-five.
- a hyphen is used in two-word place values, such as ten-thousandths.

EXAMPLE

Write 728.34 in words.

The 4 is in the hundredths place, so 728.34 is written as "seven hundred twenty-eight and thirty-four hundredths."

PRACTICE

Write each decimal in words.

1. 17.238   **2.** 9.0023   **3.** 534.01972   **4.** 33.00084   **5.** 4,356.67

Rules for Rounding

To round a number to a certain place value, locate the digit with that place value, and look at the digit to the right of it.

- If the digit to the right is 5 or greater, increase the number you are rounding by 1.
- If the digit to the right is 4 or less, leave the number you are rounding as it is.

EXAMPLE

A) Round 765.48201 to the nearest hundredth.

765.4**8**201   *Locate the hundredths place.*

↑

The digit to the right is less than 5, so the digit in the rounding place stays the same.

765.48

B) Round 765.48201 to the nearest tenth.

765.**4**8201   *Locate the tenths place.*

↑

The digit to the right is greater than 5, so the digit in the rounding place increases by 1.

765.5

PRACTICE

Round 203.94587 to the place indicated.

1. hundreds place   **2.** hundredths place   **3.** thousandths place

4. tens place   **5.** ones place   **6.** tenths place

Properties

Addition and multiplication follow certain rules. The tables show basic properties of addition and multiplication.

Addition Properties	
Commutative:	$a + b = b + a$
Associative:	$(a + b) + c = a + (b + c)$
Identity Property of Zero:	$a + 0 = a$
Inverse Property:	$a + (-a) = 0$
Closure Property:	The sum of two real numbers is a real number.

Multiplication Properties	
Commutative:	$a \times b = b \times a$
Associative:	$(a \times b) \times c = a \times (b \times c)$
Identity Property of One:	$a \times 1 = a$
Inverse Property:	$a \times \frac{1}{a} = 1$ if $a \neq 0$
Property of Zero:	$a \times 0 = 0$
Closure Property:	The product of two real numbers is a real number.
Distributive:	$a(b + c) = a \times b + a \times c$

The following properties are true when a, b, and c are real numbers.

Substitution Property: If $a = b$, then a can be substituted for b in any expression.

Transitive Property: If $a = b$ and $b = c$, then $a = c$.

PRACTICE

Name the property represented by each equation.

1. $8 + 0 = 8$

2. $(9 \times 3) \times 7 = 9 \times (3 \times 7)$

3. 3×5 is a real number

4. $7 \times 345 = 345 \times 7$

5. $2(3 + 5) = 2 \times 3 + 2 \times 5$

6. $15 \times \frac{1}{15} = 1$

7. $3.6 + 4.4 = 4.4 + 3.6$

8. $\frac{3}{4} \times \frac{4}{4} = \frac{3}{4}$

9. $18 + (-18) = 0$

10. $(5 + 17) + 23 = 5 + (17 + 23)$

Overestimates and Underestimates

An **overestimate** is an estimate that is greater than the actual answer.
An **underestimate** is an estimate that is less than the actual answer.

EXAMPLE 1

Give an overestimate for each expression.

A $124 + 371$
$$124 + 371 \approx 130 + 380$$
$$\approx 510$$

B $316 \div 12$
$$316 \div 12 \approx 320 \div 10$$
$$\approx 32$$

EXAMPLE 2

Give an underestimate for each expression.

A $64 - 12$
$$64 - 12 \approx 60 - 15$$
$$\approx 45$$

B $28 \cdot 8$
$$28 \cdot 8 \approx 25 \cdot 8$$
$$\approx 200$$

PRACTICE

Give an overestimate and underestimate for each expression.

1. $224 + 545$ **2.** $756 + 142$ **3.** $643 - 104$ **4.** $2{,}456 - 435$

5. 13×17 **6.** 7×85 **7.** $261 \div 9$ **8.** $85 \div 34$

Compatible Numbers

You can use compatible numbers to estimate products and quotients.
Compatible numbers are close to the numbers in the problem and can
help you do math mentally.

EXAMPLE

Estimate each product or quotient.

A $327 \cdot 28$
Compatible numbers
$$327 \cdot 28 \approx 300 \cdot 30$$
$$\approx 9{,}000 \leftarrow Estimate$$

B $637 \div 8$
Compatible numbers
$$637 \div 8 \approx 640 \div 8$$
$$\approx 80 \leftarrow Estimate$$

PRACTICE

Use compatible numbers to estimate each product or quotient.

1. $42 \cdot 7$ **2.** $3{,}957 \div 23$ **3.** $5{,}169 \cdot 21$ **4.** $813 \div 8$ **5.** $78 \cdot 42$

6. $1{,}443 \div 7$ **7.** $98 \cdot 48$ **8.** $3{,}372 \div 415$ **9.** $58 \cdot 9$ **10.** $27{,}657 \div 67$

Multiply and Divide by Powers of Ten

GPS M7N1.c

When you *multiply* by powers of ten, move the decimal point one place to the right for each zero in the power of ten. When you *divide* by powers of ten, move the decimal point one place to the left for each zero in the power of ten.

EXAMPLE

Find each product or quotient.

A 0.37 · 100
$$0.37 \cdot 100 = 0.37$$
$$= 37$$

B 43 · 1,000
$$43 \cdot 1,000 = 43.000$$
$$= 43,000$$

C 0.24 ÷ 10
$$0.24 \div 10 = 0.24$$
$$= 0.024$$

D 1,467 ÷ 100
$$1,467 \div 100 = 1467.$$
$$= 14.67$$

PRACTICE

Find each product or quotient.

1. 10×8.53
2. 0.55×10^4
3. $48.6 \times 1,000$
4. $2.487 \div 1,000$
5. $6.03 \div 10^3$

Multiply Whole Numbers

GPS M7N1.c

When you multiply two whole numbers, think of the second number's expanded form, and multiply by each value.

EXAMPLE

Find the product of 621 · 485.

Step 1: Think of 485 as 4 hundreds, 8 tens, and 5 ones. Multiply 621 by 5 ones.	**Step 2:** Multiply 621 by 8 tens.	**Step 3:** Multiply 621 by 4 hundreds.	**Step 4:** Add the partial products.
621 × 485 3,105 ← 5 × 621	621 × 485 3,105 49,680 ← 80 × 621	621 × 485 3,105 49,680 248,400 ← 400 × 621	621 × 485 3,105 49,680 + 248,400 301,185

621 · 485 = 301,185

PRACTICE

Multiply.

1. 493×37
2. 539×82
3. 134×145
4. 857×662
5. $1,872 \times 43$
6. $5,849 \times 67$
7. $36,735 \times 28$
8. $121,614 \times 58$

Divide Whole Numbers

EXAMPLE

Find the quotient of 5,712 ÷ 28.

Step 1: Write the first number inside the long division symbol, and write the second number to the left of the symbol. Divide by the number outside the symbol. $$\begin{array}{r} 2 \\ 28\overline{)5712} \end{array}$$ *28 cannot go into 5, so try 57.*	**Step 2:** Multiply 28 by 2, and place the product under 57. Subtract and bring down the next digit of the dividend. $$\begin{array}{r} 20 \\ 28\overline{)5712} \\ -56\downarrow \\ \hline 11 \\ -0\downarrow \\ \hline 112 \end{array}$$ *28 cannot go into 11, so put a 0 in the quotient, and bring down the 2.*	**Step 3:** Divide 112 by 28. Multiply 28 by 4 and place the product under 112. Subtract. $$\begin{array}{r} 204 \\ 28\overline{)5712} \\ -56 \\ \hline 11 \\ -0 \\ \hline 112 \\ -112 \\ \hline 0 \end{array}$$

PRACTICE

Divide.

1. 23,148 ÷ 18   **2.** 5,772 ÷ 37   **3.** 56,088 ÷ 41   **4.** 34,540 ÷ 55

5. 68,894 ÷ 74   **6.** 143,296 ÷ 32   **7.** 398,736 ÷ 72   **8.** 566,746 ÷ 79

Divisibility Rules

A number is divisible by another number if the quotient is a whole number with no remainder.

A number is divisible by . . .	Divisible	Not Divisible
2 if the last digit is an even number.	13,776	4,221
3 if the sum of the digits is divisible by 3.	327	97
4 if the last two digits form a number divisible by 4.	3,128	526
5 if the last digit is 0 or 5.	9,415	50,501
6 if the number is divisible by 2 and 3.	762	62
9 if the sum of the digits is divisible by 9.	21,222	96
10 if the last digit is 0.	1,680	8,255

PRACTICE

Determine whether each number is divisible by 2, 3, 4, 5, 6, 9, or 10.

1. 324   **2.** 501   **3.** 200   **4.** 812   **5.** 60

6. 784   **7.** 351   **8.** 3,009   **9.** 2,345   **10.** 555,555

Factors

A **factor** of a number is any number that divides into it without leaving a remainder.

EXAMPLE

List all the factors of 28.

The possible factors are whole numbers from 1 to 28.

$1 \cdot 28 = 28$ *1 and 28 are factors of 28.* $4 \cdot 7 = 28$ *4 and 7 are factors of 28.*

$2 \cdot 14 = 28$ *2 and 14 are factors of 28.* $5 \cdot ? = 28$ *No whole number multiplied by 5 equals 28, so 5 is not a factor of 28.*

$3 \cdot ? = 28$ *No whole number multiplied by 3 equals 28, so 3 is not a factor of 28.*

$6 \cdot ? = 28$ *No whole number multiplied by 6 equals 28, so 6 is not a factor of 28.*

The factors of 28 are 1, 2, 4, 7, 14, and 28.

PRACTICE

List all the factors of each number.

1. 10   **2.** 8   **3.** 18   **4.** 54   **5.** 27   **6.** 36

Roman Numerals

In the Roman numeral system, numbers do not have place values to show what they represent. Instead, numbers are represented by letters.

$I = 1$ $V = 5$ $X = 10$ $L = 50$ $C = 100$ $D = 500$ $M = 1,000$

The values of the letters do not change based on their place in a number.

If a numeral is to the right of an equal or greater numeral, add the two numerals' values. If a numeral is immediately to the left of a greater numeral, subtract the numeral's value from the greater numeral.

EXAMPLE

A **Write CLIV as a decimal number.**

$$CLIV = C + L + (V - I)$$
$$= 100 + 50 + (5 - 1)$$
$$= 154$$

B **Write 1,109 as a Roman numeral.**

$$1,109 = 1,000 + 100 + 9$$
$$= M + C + (X - I)$$
$$= MCIX$$

PRACTICE

Write each decimal number as a Roman numeral and each Roman numeral as a decimal number.

1. XXVI   **2.** 29   **3.** MCMLII   **4.** 224   **5.** DCCCVI

Binary Numbers

Computers use the **binary number system.** In the binary, or base-2, system of numbers, numbers are formed using the digits 0 and 1. Each place in a binary number is associated with a power of 2. Binary numbers are written with the subscript *two* so that they are not confused with numbers in the decimal system.

The binary number 1101_{two} can be thought of as

$(1 \cdot 2^3) + (1 \cdot 2^2) + (0 \cdot 2^1) + (1 \cdot 2^0)$.

Binary Place Value

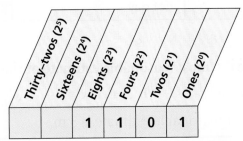

You can use the expanded form of 1101_{two} to find the value of the number as a decimal, or base-10, number.

$$(1 \cdot 2^3) + (1 \cdot 2^2) + (0 \cdot 2^1) + (1 \cdot 2^0) = (1 \cdot 8) + (1 \cdot 4) + (0 \cdot 2) + (1 \cdot 1)$$
$$= 8 + 4 + 0 + 1$$
$$= 13$$

So $1101_{two} = 13_{ten}$.

EXAMPLE

Write each binary number as a decimal number.

A 101110_{two}

$$101110_{two} = (1 \cdot 2^5) + (0 \cdot 2^4) + (1 \cdot 2^3) + (1 \cdot 2^2) + (1 \cdot 2^1) + (0 \cdot 1)$$
$$= 32 + 0 + 8 + 4 + 2 + 0$$
$$= 46$$

B 10001_{two}

$$10001_{two} = (1 \cdot 2^4) + (0 \cdot 2^3) + (0 \cdot 2^2) + (0 \cdot 2^1) + (1 \cdot 1)$$
$$= 16 + 0 + 0 + 0 + 1$$
$$= 17$$

PRACTICE

Write each binary number as a decimal number.

1. 100_{two}
2. 110_{two}
3. 101_{two}
4. 1100_{two}
5. 1011_{two}
6. 11011_{two}
7. 11110_{two}
8. 101010_{two}
9. 111111_{two}
10. 100111_{two}

Estimate Measurements

You can use benchmarks to estimate with metric and customary units.

1 meter (m)	Width of a doorway	1 centimeter (cm)	Width of a large paper clip
1 liter (L)	Water in a 1-quart bottle	1 milliliter (mL)	Water in an eyedropper
1 gram (g)	Mass of a dollar bill	1 kilogram (kg)	Mass of 8 rolls of pennies
30°C (Celsius)	Temperature on a hot day	0°C (Celsius)	Temperature on a freezing day

EXAMPLE 1

Choose the most reasonable estimate of the height of the ceiling in your classroom.

  A 30 cm   **B** 3 m   **C** 30 m   **D** 30,000 cm

The most reasonable estimate is 3 m.

Length	Temperature	Capacity
1 inch (in.)—about the length of a small paper clip **1 foot (ft)**—about the length of a standard sheet of paper **1 yard (yd)**—about the width of a doorway	**32°F (Fahrenheit)**—water freezes **70°F**—air on a comfortably warm day **90°F**—air on a hot day **212°F**—boiling water	**1 fluid ounce (fl oz)**—amount of water in two tablespoons **1 cup (c)**—amount of water held in a standard measuring cup **1 pint (pt), 1 quart (qt), 1 gallon (gal)**—Think about containers of water at a store.

EXAMPLE 2

Choose the most appropriate estimate.

A the length of a classroom
    A 30 in.   **B** 30 ft   **C** 30 yd
    The most appropriate estimate is 30 ft.

B a temperature for wearing a T-shirt
    A 20°F   **B** 40°F   **C** 80°F
    The most appropriate estimate is 80°F.

PRACTICE

Choose the most reasonable estimate.

1. the temperature on a warm day
    A −22°C   **B** 22°C   **C** 68°C

2. the capacity of a kitchen sink
    A 12 mL   **B** 1,200 mL   **C** 12 L

Choose the most appropriate estimate.

3. the capacity of a tall drinking glass
    A 1 pt   **B** 4 qt   **C** $\frac{1}{2}$ gal

4. a temperature for wearing a warm coat
    A 20°F   **B** 60°F   **C** 80°F

5. the temperature of a cup of hot cocoa
    A 32°F   **B** 120°F   **C** 250°F

6. the width of a pizza box
    A 18 in.   **B** 8 ft   **C** 2 yd

Relate Metric Units of Length, Mass, and Capacity

A cube that has a volume of 1 cm³ has a capacity of 1 mL. If the cube were filled with water, the mass of the water would be 1 g.

EXAMPLE

Find the capacity of a 50 cm × 60 cm × 30 cm rectangular box. Then find the mass of the water that would fill the box.

Volume: 50 cm × 60 cm × 30 cm = 90,000 cm³

Capacity: 1 cm³ = 1 mL, so 90,000 cm³ = 90,000 mL, or 90 L.

Mass: 1 mL of water has a mass of 1 g, so 90,000 mL of water has a mass of 90,000 g, or 90 kg.

PRACTICE

Find the capacity of each box. Then find the mass of the water that would fill the box.

1. 2 cm × 5 cm × 8 cm

2. 10 cm × 18 cm × 4 cm

3. 8 cm × 8 cm × 8 cm

4. 10 cm × 10 cm × 10 cm

5. 15 cm × 18 cm × 16 cm

6. 23 cm × 19 cm × 11 cm

Pictographs

Pictographs are graphs that use pictures to display data. Pictographs include a key to tell what each picture represents.

EXAMPLE

How many students chose tacos as their favorite lunch?

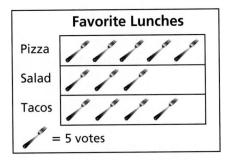

Each 🍴 stands for 5 students.

There are 4 🍴 in the row for tacos.

4 × 5 = 20

So 20 students chose tacos as their favorite lunch.

PRACTICE

Use the pictograph for Exercises 1–3.

1. How many bicycles were rented in May?

2. How many more bicycles were rented in June than in April?

3. How many bicycles were rented altogether from April through June?

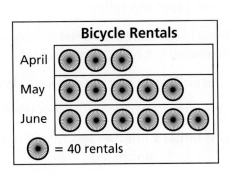

Probability of Two Disjoint Events

In probability, two events are considered to be **disjoint,** or mutually exclusive, if they cannot happen at the same time. Examples of disjoint events are getting a 5 or a 6 on a single roll of a 1–6 number cube. To find the probability that either one or the other of two disjoint events will occur, add the probabilities of each event occurring separately.

EXAMPLE

Find the probability of each set of disjoint events.

Ⓐ **rolling either a 5 or a 6 on a 1–6 number cube**

$$P(5 \text{ or } 6) = P(5) + P(6)$$
$$= \frac{1}{6} + \frac{1}{6}$$
$$= \frac{2}{6}$$
$$= \frac{1}{3}$$

The probability of rolling a 5 or a 6 on a 1–6 number cube is $\frac{1}{3}$.

Ⓑ **choosing either an *A* or an *E* from the letters in the word *mathematics***

$$P(A \text{ or } E) = P(A) + P(E)$$
$$= \frac{2}{11} + \frac{1}{11}$$
$$= \frac{3}{11}$$

The probability of choosing an *A* or an *E* is $\frac{3}{11}$.

PRACTICE

Find the probability of each set of disjoint events.

1. tossing a coin and getting heads or tails

2. spinning red or green on a spinner that has four equal sectors colored red, green, blue, and yellow

3. drawing a black marble or a red marble from a bag that contains 4 white marbles, 3 black marbles, and 2 red marbles

4. choosing either a boy or a girl from a class of 13 boys and 17 girls

5. choosing either *A* or *E* from a list of the five vowels

6. choosing either a number less than 3 or a number greater than 12 from a set of 20 cards numbered 1–20

Inductive and Deductive Reasoning

You use **inductive reasoning** when you look for a pattern in individual cases to draw conclusions. Conclusions drawn using inductive reasoning are sometimes like predictions. They may be proven false.

You use **deductive reasoning** when you use given facts to draw conclusions. A conclusion based on facts must be true.

EXAMPLE

Identify the type of reasoning used. Explain your answers.

A *Statement:* **A number pattern begins with 2, 5, 8, 11, . . .**

   Conclusion: **The next number in the pattern will be 14.**

   This is inductive reasoning. The conclusion is based on the pattern established by the first four terms in the sequence.

B *Statement:* **It has rained for the past three days.**

   Conclusion: **It will rain tomorrow.**

   This is inductive reasoning. The conclusion is based on the weather pattern over the past three days.

C *Statement:* **The measures of two angles of a triangle are 30° and 70°.**

   Conclusion: **The measure of the third angle is 80°.**

   This is deductive reasoning. Since you know that the measures of the angles of a triangle have a sum of 180°, the third angle of this triangle must measure 80° (30° + 70° + 80° = 180°).

PRACTICE

Identify the type of reasoning used. Explain your answers.

1. *Statement:* Shawna has received a score of 100 on the last five math tests.
   Conclusion: Shawna will receive a score of 100 on the next math test.

2. *Statement:* The mail has arrived late every Monday for the past 4 weeks.
   Conclusion: The mail will arrive late next Monday.

3. *Statement:* Three angles of a quadrilateral measure 100°, 90°, and 70°.
   Conclusion: The measure of the fourth angle is 100°.

4. *Statement:* Perpendicular lines *AB* and *CD* intersect at point *E*.
   Conclusion: Angle *AED* is a right angle.

5. *Statement:* A pattern of numbers begins 1, 2, 4, . . .
   Conclusion: The next number in the pattern is 8.

6. *Statement:* Ten of the first ten seventh-grade students surveyed listed soccer as their favorite sport.
   Conclusion: Soccer is the favorite sport of all seventh-graders.

Make Conjectures

Conjecture is another word for conclusion. Conjectures in math are based on observations and in some cases have not yet been proven to be true. To prove that a conjecture is false, you need to find just one case, or *counterexample,* for which the conclusion does not hold true.

EXAMPLE 1

Test each conjecture to decide whether it is true or false. If the conjecture is false, give a counterexample.

A **The sum of two even numbers is always an even number.**

> An even number is divisible by 2. The sum of two even numbers can be written as $2m + 2n = 2(m + n)$, which is divisible by 2, so it is even. The conjecture is true.

B **All prime numbers are odd.**

> The first prime number is 2, which is an even number. The conjecture is false.

EXAMPLE 2

Formulate a conjecture based on the given information. Then test your conjecture.

$$1 \cdot 3 = 3 \qquad 3 \cdot 5 = 15 \qquad 5 \cdot 7 = 35 \qquad 7 \cdot 9 = 63$$

Conjecture: The product of two odd numbers is always an odd number.

An odd number does not have 2 as a factor, so the product of two odd numbers also does not have 2 as a factor. The conjecture is true.

PRACTICE

Test each conjecture to decide whether it is true or false. If the conjecture is false, give a counterexample.

1. The sum of two odd numbers is always an odd number.

2. The product of two even numbers is always an even number.

3. The sum of twice a whole number and 1 is always an odd number.

4. If you subtract a whole number from another whole number, the result will always be a whole number.

5. If you multiply two fractions, the product will always be greater than either fraction.

Formulate a conjecture based on the given information. Then test your conjecture.

6. $12 + 21 = 33$ $13 + 31 = 44$ $23 + 32 = 55$ $17 + 71 = 88$

7. $15 \times 15 = 225$ $25 \times 25 = 625$ $35 \times 35 = 1{,}225$

Trigonometric Ratios

You can use ratios to find information about the sides and angles of a right triangle. These ratios are called *trigonometric ratios*, and they have names, such as **sine** (abbreviated *sin*), **cosine** (abbreviated *cos*), and **tangent** (abbreviated *tan*).

The **sine** of $\angle 1 = \sin \angle 1 = \dfrac{\text{length of side opposite } \angle 1}{\text{length of hypotenuse}} = \dfrac{a}{c}$.

The **cosine** of $\angle 1 = \cos \angle 1 = \dfrac{\text{length of side adjacent to } \angle 1}{\text{length of hypotenuse}} = \dfrac{b}{c}$.

The **tangent** of $\angle 1 = \tan \angle 1 = \dfrac{\text{length of side opposite } \angle 1}{\text{length of side adjacent to } \angle 1} = \dfrac{a}{b}$.

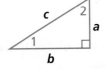

EXAMPLE 1

Find the sine, cosine, and tangent of $\angle J$.

$\sin \angle J = \dfrac{LK}{JK} = \dfrac{3}{5}$

$\cos \angle J = \dfrac{JL}{JK} = \dfrac{4}{5}$

$\tan \angle J = \dfrac{LK}{JL} = \dfrac{3}{4}$

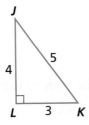

EXAMPLE 2

Use your calculator to find the measure of side $\overline{MN}$ to the nearest tenth.

Side $\overline{MN}$ is adjacent to the 58° angle. The length of the hypotenuse is given. The ratio that uses the lengths of the adjacent side and the hypotenuse is cosine.

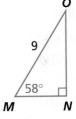

$\cos (58°) = \dfrac{MN}{9}$ *Write the ratio that is equal to the cosine of 58°.*

$9 \cdot \cos (58°) = MN$ *Multiply both sides by 9.*

9 [×] [COS] 58 [ENTER]   *Use your calculator.*

$MN = 4.8$

PRACTICE

Find the sine, cosine, and tangent of each angle.

1. $\angle D$ **2.** $\angle F$

Use your calculator to find the measure of each side, to the nearest tenth.

3. $\overline{QR}$ **4.** $\overline{PR}$

Cube Roots

The volume of the cube at right is $5 \cdot 5 \cdot 5 = 5^3 = 125$. The expression 5^3 is read "5 cubed." Finding a **cube root** is the inverse of cubing a number. The symbol $\sqrt[3]{}$ means "cube root." For example, $\sqrt[3]{125} = 5$. You can use a calculator to estimate cube roots.

EXAMPLE

Use your calculator to find $\sqrt[3]{43}$ to the nearest tenth.

Press **MATH** and select 4: $\sqrt[3]{}$ (from the menu.) Then enter 43 **)** **ENTER** .

$$\sqrt[3]{43} \approx 3.5$$

PRACTICE

Use your calculator to find each cube root to the nearest tenth.

1. $\sqrt[3]{30}$ **2.** $\sqrt[3]{68}$ **3.** $\sqrt[3]{100}$ **4.** $\sqrt[3]{3}$ **5.** $\sqrt[3]{260}$ **6.** $\sqrt[3]{1{,}255}$

Properties of Exponents

Recall that $8^2 = 8 \cdot 8$ and $8^5 = 8 \cdot 8 \cdot 8 \cdot 8 \cdot 8$. Therefore, $8^2 \cdot 8^5 = (8 \cdot 8) \cdot (8 \cdot 8 \cdot 8 \cdot 8 \cdot 8) = 8^7$. Also, $\frac{8^5}{8^2} = \frac{8 \cdot 8 \cdot 8 \cdot 8 \cdot 8}{8 \cdot 8} = 8 \cdot 8 \cdot 8 = 8^3$.
These examples can help you understand the following properties.

- To multiply powers with the same base, keep the base and add the exponents.
- To divide powers with the same base, keep the base and subtract the exponents.

EXAMPLE

Multiply or divide. Write the answer as a power.

A $3^4 \cdot 3^9$

$= 3^{4+9}$ *Add the exponents.*

$= 3^{13}$

B $\dfrac{10^9}{10^5}$

$= 10^{9-5}$ *Subtract the exponents.*

$= 10^4$

PRACTICE

Multiply or divide. Write the answer as a power.

1. $4^8 \cdot 4^2$ **2.** $7^{12} \cdot 7^{12}$ **3.** $5^6 \cdot 5$ **4.** $x^4 \cdot x^5$

5. $\dfrac{5^8}{5^2}$ **6.** $\dfrac{12^{10}}{12^5}$ **7.** $\dfrac{7^{15}}{7^2}$ **8.** $\dfrac{b^{10}}{b^7}$

Absolute Value of Real Numbers

The absolute value of a number is its distance from 0 on the number line. The symbol for absolute value is | |. Note that an absolute value can never be negative.

EXAMPLE

Find the absolute value of each real number.

A 2.7

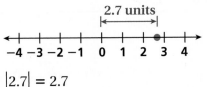

$|2.7| = 2.7$

B $-\pi$

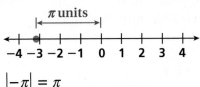

$|-\pi| = \pi$

PRACTICE

Find the absolute value of each real number.

1. $-\dfrac{3}{4}$ **2.** 5.8 **3.** -6.05 **4.** $\sqrt{3}$ **5.** $-\sqrt{10}$ **6.** $3\dfrac{5}{8}$

Polynomials

A **monomial** is a number or a product of numbers and variables with exponents that are whole numbers. The expressions $2n$, x^3, $4a^4b^3$, and 7 are all examples of monomials. The expressions $x^{1.5}$, $2\sqrt{y}$, and $\dfrac{3}{m}$ are not monomials.

A **polynomial** is one monomial or the sum or difference of monomials. Polynomials can be classified by the number of terms. A monomial has one term, a **binomial** has two terms, and a **trinomial** has three terms.

EXAMPLE

Classify each expression as a monomial, a binomial, a trinomial, or not a polynomial.

A $43h + 14b$

binomial   *The expression is a polynomial with 2 terms.*

B $3x^2 - 4xy + \dfrac{3}{x}$

not a polynomial   *There is a variable in a denominator.*

PRACTICE

Classify each expression as a monomial, a binomial, a trinomial, or not a polynomial.

1. $5a^3 + 6a^2 - 3$ **2.** $4xy^2$ **3.** $7b + \dfrac{1}{b^2}$

4. $6c^2d - 4$ **5.** $2x - 3y + 1$ **6.** $-12x^3y^4z^2$

Networks and Paths

A **network** is a set of points and a set of line segments or arcs that connect the points. The points of a network are called **vertices** . The line segments or arcs connecting the vertices are called **edges** .

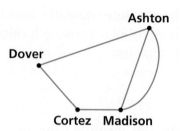

The network at right represents the roads connecting four towns. The network has four vertices and five edges.

A **path** is a way to travel around a network by moving along the edges from one vertex to another. In a simple path, no vertex is visited more than once.

EXAMPLE

Determine the number of simple paths from vertex *A* to vertex *B*.

Make an organized list of the simple paths.

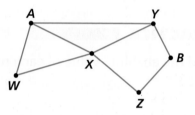

A-Y-B

A-Y-X-Z-B

A-X-Y-B

A-X-Z-B

A-W-X-Y-B

A-W-X-Z-B

There are 6 simple paths.

PRACTICE

Determine the number of simple paths from vertex *A* to vertex *B*.

1.
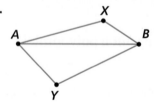

2.
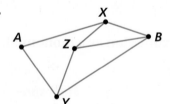

3.
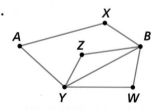

4.
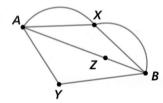

Constructions and Congruent Triangles GPS M7G1.a, M7G1.b

Many constructions are based on congruent triangles. In Lesson 8-9, you learned about the Side-Side-Side Rule for identifying congruent triangles. You can use this rule to find congruent triangles in constructions to see how some constructions work.

EXAMPLE

Find the congruent triangles used to construct congruent angles. Explain why the congruent triangles prove that ∠A ≅ ∠D.

A The first step in constructing an angle congruent to ∠A is to draw an arc across the two rays of the angle.

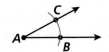

B You use the compass setting to draw a second arc centered on D, so AB = DE.

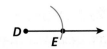

C The next step in the construction is placing your compass point on point B and the pencil on point C. You don't draw $\overline{BC}$ as part of the construction, but $\overline{BC}$ is the third side of △ABC.

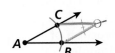

D You use the compass setting from part **c** to draw an arc centered on point E and intersecting the first arc at point F. Because you used the same compass setting from part **c** to draw this, you know that BC = EF.

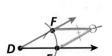

E To complete the construction, you connect points D and F. Because point F is on the first arc you drew, $\overline{DF}$ is the same length as $\overline{AC}$.

You know AB = DE, BC = EF, and DF = AC, so △ABC ≅ △DEF by the Side-Side-Side Rule. That means the corresponding angles of these triangles are congruent, so ∠A ≅ ∠D.

PRACTICE

1. The diagram at right shows the bisection of ∠GHE. Review the steps for this construction and find the pair of congruent triangles that proves ∠GHD ≅ ∠DHE.

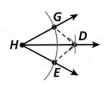

Half-life

Some atoms give off energy by emitting particles from their centers, or nuclei. The ability of these atoms to release nuclear radiation is called *radioactivity*, and the process is called *radioactive decay*.

Half-life is the amount of time it takes for one-half of the nuclei of a radioactive sample to decay. The half-life of an element can range from less than a second to millions of years.

EXAMPLE 1

The half-life of sodium-24 is 15 hours. If a sample of sodium-24 contains $\frac{1}{8}$ of its original amount, how old is the sample?

Every 15 hours, $\frac{1}{2}$ the sample decays.

Fraction of Sample	1	$\frac{1}{2}$	$\frac{1}{4}$	$\frac{1}{8}$
Time	0 hours	15 hours	30 hours	45 hours

The sample is 45 hours old.

EXAMPLE 2

The half-life of phosphorous-24 is 14.3 days. How much of a 6-gram sample will remain after 42.9 days?

Time	0 days	14.3 days	28.6 days	42.9 days
Amount of Sample (g)	6	3	1.5	0.75

After 42.9 days, 0.75 g of phosphorous-24 will remain.

PRACTICE

1. The half-life of cobalt-60 is 5.26 years. If a sample of cobalt-60 contains $\frac{1}{4}$ of its original amount, how old is the sample?

2. The half-life of sodium-24 is 15 hours. How much of a 9.6-gram sample will remain after 60 hours?

3. Iodine-131 has a half-life of 8.07 days. How much of a 4.4 g sample will there be after 40.35 days?

4. A sample of bismuth-212 decayed from 18 g to 1.125 g in 242 minutes. What is the half-life of bismuth-212?

pH Scale

An acid is a compound that produces hydrogen ions in solution. A base is a compound that produces hydroxide ions in solution. Chemists use the **pH scale** to measure how acidic or basic a solution is.

The range of the pH scale for a solution is 0 to 14. A solution with a pH below 7 is acidic. A solution with a pH above 7 is basic. A solution with a pH of 7 is neutral—that is, it has an equal number of hydrogen and hydroxide ions.

The pH numbers are related by powers of 10.

A pH of 6 is 10 times more acidic than a pH of 7.

A pH of 8 is 10 times more basic than a pH of 7.

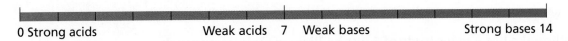

0 Strong acids   Weak acids   7   Weak bases   Strong bases 14

EXAMPLE 1

Solution A and solution B have the same volume. Solution A has a pH of 2, and solution B has a pH of 4. How much more acidic is solution A than solution B?

Since $4 - 2 = 2$ and $10^2 = 100$ solution A is 100 times more acidic than solution B.

EXAMPLE 2

Solution C and solution D have the same volume. Solution C has a pH of 13, and solution D has a pH of 8. How much more basic is solution C than solution D?

Since $13 - 8 = 5$ and $10^5 = 100,000$ solution C is 100,000 times more basic than solution D.

PRACTICE

1. Solution E and solution F have the same volume. Solution E has a pH of 5, and solution F has a pH of 1. How much more basic is solution E than solution F?

2. Solution G and solution H have the same volume. Solution G has a pH of 9, and solution H has a pH of 8. How much more basic is solution G than solution H?

3. Solution K and solution J have the same volume. Solution J has a pH of 7, and solution K has a pH of 5. How much more acidic is solution K than solution J?

4. Solution M and solution L have the same volume. Solution L has a pH of 14, and solution M has a pH of 7. How much more basic is solution L than solution M?

Richter Scale

The magnitude of an earthquake is a measure of the amount of energy the earthquake releases. The **Richter scale** is used to express the magnitude of earthquakes. This scale uses the counting numbers. Each number represents a magnitude that is 10 times stronger than the magnitude represented by the previous number.

You can relate Richter scale numbers to the exponents in powers of 10.

$$10^1 = 10 \qquad 10^2 = 100 \qquad 10^3 = 1{,}000 \qquad 10^4 = 10{,}000 \qquad 10^5 = 100{,}000$$

Just as 10^2 is 10 times 10^1, an earthquake with a magnitude of 2 on the Richter scale is 10 times stronger than an earthquake with a magnitude of 1.

EXAMPLE 1

An earthquake has a magnitude of 5 on the Richter scale. How much stronger is it than an earthquake with a magnitude of 2?

$10^5 = 100{,}000$ and $10^2 = 100$
Since $100{,}000$ is $1{,}000$ times 100, 10^5 is $1{,}000$ times 10^2.

An earthquake with a magnitude of 5 is $1{,}000$ times stronger than an earthquake with a magnitude of 2.

EXAMPLE 2

An earthquake had a magnitude of 3. If the earthquake had been 10,000 times stronger, what would its magnitude have been?

$10^3 = 1{,}000$
$1{,}000 \cdot 10{,}000 = 10{,}000{,}000 = 10^7$

The earthquake would have had a magnitude of 7.

PRACTICE

1. How many times stronger is an earthquake with a magnitude of 3 than an earthquake with a magnitude of 1?

2. How many times stronger is an earthquake with a magnitude of 6 than an earthquake with a magnitude of 3?

3. An earthquake has a magnitude of 2. How many times stronger would the earthquake have to be to have a magnitude of 6?

4. An earthquake has a magnitude of 3. How many times stronger would the earthquake have to be to have a magnitude of 9?

5. An earthquake had a magnitude of 5. If the earthquake had been 1,000 times stronger, what would its magnitude have been?

6. An earthquake had a magnitude of 4. If the earthquake had been 100,000 times stronger, what would its magnitude have been?

Surface Area to Volume Ratios

A surface area to volume ratio is a ratio that compares the surface area and volume of a solid. You can use the surface area to volume ratio of a solid to find the surface area of the solid if you know its volume, or to find the volume of the solid if you know its surface area.

EXAMPLE 1

Find the surface area to volume ratio of the cube.

surface area $= 2\ell w + 2\ell h + 2wh$

$\qquad = (2 \cdot 5 \cdot 5) + (2 \cdot 5 \cdot 5) + (2 \cdot 5 \cdot 5)$

$\qquad = 150$

volume $= \ell wh$

$\qquad = 5 \cdot 5 \cdot 5$

$\qquad = 125$

$\dfrac{\text{surface area}}{\text{volume}} = \dfrac{150}{125}$

$\qquad\qquad = \dfrac{6}{5}$ *Simplify.*

The surface area to volume ratio is $\frac{6}{5}$.

EXAMPLE 2

Find the surface area of a cube that has a volume of 64 cubic units and a surface area to volume ratio of $\frac{3}{2}$.

$\dfrac{3}{2} = \dfrac{\text{surface area}}{64}$ *Write a proportion.*

$2 \cdot \text{surface area} = 3 \cdot 64$ *Find the cross products.*

$2(\text{surface area}) = 192$ *Multiply.*

$\text{surface area} = 96$ *Divide both sides by 2.*

The surface area of the cube is 96 square units.

PRACTICE

Find the surface area to volume ratio of each solid.

1.
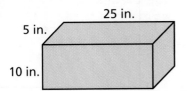

2.
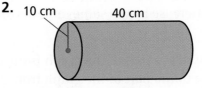

3. Find the surface area of a cylinder that has a volume of 5,001 cubic meters and a surface area to volume ratio of $\frac{1}{3}$.

4. Find the volume of a cylinder that has a surface area of 11,781 square feet and a surface area to volume ratio of $\frac{231}{500}$.

Quadratic Relationships

Quadratic relationships involve one squared value related to another value. An example of a quadratic relationship is shown in the equation $a = x^2 + 5$. If you know the value of one variable, you can substitute for it in the equation and then solve to find the second variable.

EXAMPLE

The distance d in feet that an object falls is related to the amount of time t in seconds that it falls. This relationship is given by the equation $d = 16t^2$.

What distance will an object fall in 3 seconds?

$d = 16t^2$ *Write the equation.*
$d = 16 \cdot (3)^2$ *Substitute 3 for t.*
   $= 144$ *Simplify.*

The object will fall 144 feet in 3 seconds.

PRACTICE

A small rocket is shot vertically upward from the ground. The distance d in feet between the rocket and the ground as the rocket goes up can be found by using the equation $d = 128t - 16t^2$, where t is the amount of time in seconds that the rocket has been flying upward.

1. How far above the ground is the rocket at 1 second and at 2 seconds?

2. Did the rocket's distance change by the same amount in each of the first 2 seconds? Explain.

3. When the rocket is returning to the ground, the distance that the rocket falls is given by the equation $d = 16t^2$. If the rocket hits the ground 4 seconds after it starts to return, how far up did it go?

4. As the rocket falls to the ground, does it fall the same distance each second? Explain.

The graph for $y = x^2$ is shown at right. Use the graph for problems 5–7.

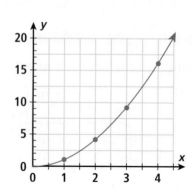

5. Find the value of y for $x = 1, 2, 3, 4,$ and 5.

6. Does y increase by the same amount for each value of x? Explain.

7. How would the part of the graph from $x = 5$ to $x = 6$ compare to the part of the graph from $x = 4$ to $x = 5$?

Selected Answers

Chapter 1

1-1 Exercises

1. Add 8 to get the next number
3. Subtract 9 to get the next number **5.** Equilateral triangles each divided into six congruent triangles with a pair of opposite congruent triangles shaded in two different colors so that the shaded pairs rotate clockwise from each equilateral triangle to the next **7.** 10 green triangles **9.** Divide by 4 to get the next number **11.** Add 23 to get the next number
13. Regular heptagons sliced into 7 triangles with one triangle shaded in each figure. In each successive figure the shaded triangle rotates clockwise 4 triangles. **15.** 7, 23, 39, 55, 71
17. 50, 48, 44, 38, 30 **19.** Multiply by 4 to get the next number
21. Add 8 to get the next number
23. 134 **31.** 51 **33.** 90 **35.** 2,020
37. 100 **39.** 1,000 **41.** 23,100

1-2 Exercises

1. 32 **3.** 36 **5.** 1,000,000 **7.** 4^2
9. 10^2 **11.** 121 **13.** 512 **15.** 81
17. 5 **19.** 125 **21.** 9^2 **23.** 4^3
25. 2^5 **27.** 40^2 **29.** 10^5 **31.** 3^4
33. 8^2 **35.** 5^4 **37.** < **39.** < **41.** >
43. > **45.** $21.87 **47.** Yuma: 688,560; Phoenix: 11,370,384
49. $4 \cdot 3^3 = 108$ stars **51.** 10^1, 33, 6^2, 4^3, 5^3 **53.** 0, 1^8, 2, 16^1, 3^4
55. 8^1, 9, 5^2, 3^3, 2^5 **61.** F
63. 88 **65.** 63 **67.** Subtract 9
69. Multiply by 3

1-3 Exercises

1. kilograms **3.** centimeters
5. 12,000 g **7.** 0.07 cm **9.** Monday
11. milligrams **13.** centimeters
15. 0.0014 km **17.** 3,550 mm
19. 199.5 cm **21.** 2,050,000 L
23. 0.37 cm **25.** = **27.** < **29.** <
31. Mona Lisa **33.** 1,200 mm; 130 cm; 1.5 m **35.** 0.0008 kg; 1,000 mg; 9.03 g **37.** Red Bat
39. 1 kg **43.** C **45.** Subtract 3 to get the next number **47.** Add 1, then 2, then 3, and so on **49.** 81
51. 128 **53.** 81

1-4 Exercises

1. 1,500 **3.** 208,000
5. 3.6×10^6 **7.** 8.0×10^9
9. 2,000,000,000,000,000,000
11. 2,100 **13.** 2,500,000
15. 268,000 **17.** 211,500,000
19. 4.28×10^5 **21.** 3.0×10^9
23. 5.2×10^1 **25.** 8.9×10^6
27. 367,000 **29.** 4 **31.** 340
33. 540,000,000 **35.** no **37.** yes
39. 9.8×10^8 feet per second
41. 1.83×10^8 years **45.** C
47. 5^4 **49.** 2^9 **51.** 1.7 km

1-5 Exercises

1. 47 **3.** 23 **5.** 4 **7.** $280 **9.** 42
11. 15 **13.** 73 **15.** 588 **17.** $139
19. 18 **21.** 20 **23.** 1 **25.** > **27.** >
29. = **31.** $4 \cdot (8 - 5) = 20$
33. $(12 - 2)^2 \div 5 = 20$
35. $(4 + 6 - 3) \div 7 = 1$ **37.** $82
39a. $4 \cdot 15$ **39b.** $2 \cdot 30$
39c. $4 \cdot 15 + 2 \cdot 30 + 6$ **43.** C
45. D **47.** 729 **49.** 27 **51.** 612,000
53. 59,000,000 **55.** 191

1-6 Exercises

1. Assoc. Prop. **3.** Comm. Prop.
5. Assoc. Prop. **7.** 33 **9.** 1,100
11. 47 **13.** 38 **15.** 44 **17.** 208
19. Ident. Prop. **21.** Assoc. Prop.
23. Ident. Prop. **25.** 1,600 **27.** 900

29. 163 **31.** 135 **33.** 174 **35.** 92
41. 220 ft^2 **43.** 9,000 **45.** 17,500
47. 15 **49.** 0 **51.** 8 **53.** 2 **59.** H
61. 6^2 **63.** 3^2 **65.** 1 **67.** 3

1-7 Exercises

1. 12 **3.** 20 **5.** 8 **7.** 19 **9.** 22
11. 5 **13.** 11 **15.** 24 **17.** 12
19. 41 **21.** 300 **23.** 10 **25.** 22
27. 24 **29.** 13 **31.** 31 **33.** $4.50
35. 86°F **41.** H **43.** 6.21×10^7
45. 8×10^5 **47.** 68 **49.** 87

1-8 Exercises

1. $7p$ **3.** $\frac{n}{12}$ **5.** $5 \div n$, or $\frac{5}{n}$
7. $5 + x$ **9.** $n \div 8$ **11.** $3y - 10$
13. $5 + 2t$ **15.** $\frac{23}{u} - t$ **17.** $2(y + 5)$
19. $35(r - 5)$ **21.** $65,000 + 2b$
23. 90 divided by y **25.** 16 multiplied by t **27.** the difference between 4 times p and 10
29. the quotient of m and 15 plus 3
31. $15y + 12$ **37.** $(104 + 19 \cdot 2)x$; $426 **39.** 5 **41.** 35

1-9 Exercises

1. $6b$ and $\frac{b}{2}$ **3.** $8x$ **5.** There are no like terms. **7.** b^6 and $3b^6$
9. m and $2m$ **11.** $8a + 2b$
13. $3a + 3b + 2c$ **15.** $3q^2 + 2q$
17. $2n + 3a + 3a + 2n + 5$
19. $27y$ **21.** $2d^2 + d$ **23.** no like terms **25.** no like terms
27. expression $4n + 5n + 6n = 15n$ **29a.** $21.5d + 23d + 15.5d + 19d$ **b.** $750.50 **c.** the amount Brad earned in June **31.** $23x^2$
35. J **37.** < **39.** < **41.** 51 **43.** 159

1-10 Exercises

1. no **3.** yes **5.** situation A **7.** no
9. yes **11.** no **13.** situation B
15. yes **17.** yes **19.** no **21.** yes
23. yes **25.** $10,500 + d = 14,264$
29. A **31.** 1.085×10^7
33. 9.04×10^6 **35.** Identity Property of Addition

1. $r = 176$ **3.** $x = 88$ **5.** $f = 9$
7. 14 yd **9.** $t = 82$ **11.** $b = 67$
13. $k = 123$ **15.** $w = 43$ **17.** $s = 45$
19. $j = 76$ **21.** $q = 99$ **23.** 38 mi
25. $p = 10$ **27.** $b = 52$ **29.** $a = 45$
31. $c = 149$ **33.** $m = 199$
35. $s = 159$ **37.** $x = 839$
39. $w = 79$ **41.** $x + 65 = 315$; $250
47. D **49.** $17 - k$ **51.** $12 + 5n$
53. $8 + 11t$

1. $s = 847$ **3.** $y = 40$ **5.** $c = 32$
7. 9 people **9.** $k = 1{,}296$
11. $c = 175$ **13.** $n = 306$
15. $p = 21$ **17.** $a = 2$ **19.** $d = 45$
21. $g = 27$ **23.** $m = 110$ **25.** $x = 7$
27. $b = 62$ **29.** $f = 20$ **31.** $a = 36$
33. $d = 42$ **35.** $r = 307$
37. $7 + n = 15$ **39.** $12 = q - 8$
41. 12 toys **43.** $13,300 **47.** C
49. 23 **51.** no **53.** $j = 242$
55. $a = 47$

Chapter 1 Study Guide: Review

1. exponent; base **2.** numerical
expression **3.** equation
4. algebraic expression **5.** Add
4 to get the next number **6.** Add
20 to get the next number
7. Add 7 to get the next number
8. Multiply by 5 to get the next
number **9.** Subtract 4 to get the
next number **10.** Subtract 7 to
get the next number **11.** 81
12. 10 **13.** 128 **14.** 1 **15.** 121
16. 18,000 **17.** 0.72 **18.** 5,300
19. 6 **20.** 14,400 **21.** 1,320
22. 220,000,000 **23.** 4.8×10^4
24. 7.02×10^6 **25.** 1.49×10^5
26. 3 **27.** 103 **28.** 5 **29.** 67
30. Comm. Prop. of Add.
31. Identity Prop. of Add.
32. Distributive Property **33.** 19
34. 524 **35.** 10 **36.** $4 \div (n + 12)$
37. $2(t - 11)$ **38.** $10b^2 + 8$
39. $15a^2 + 2$ **40.** $x^4 + x^3 + 6x^2$
41. yes **42.** no **43.** 8
786 *Selected Answers*

44. 32 **45.** 18 **46.** 112 **47.** 72
48. 9 **49.** 98 **50.** 13 **51.** 17 h

Chapter 2

5. > **7.** < **9.** $-5, -3, -1, 4, 6$
11. $-6, -4, 0, 1, 3$ **13.** 8 **15.** 10
21. > **23.** < **25.** $-9, -7, -5, -2, 0$
27. 16 **29.** 20 **31.** < **33.** = **35.** =
37. = **39.** Aug, Jul, Sep, May, Jun,
Apr, Mar, Oct **41.** -29
45. decreased by about 9% **51.** G
53. 1.67 m **55.** 10,300 mL
57. 112 **59.** 170

1. 12 **3.** -2 **5.** 15 **7.** -15 **9.** -12
11. -20 **13.** -9 **15.** 13 **17.** 7
19. -17 **21.** -19 **23.** -16
25. -88 **27.** -55 **29.** -14
31. -13 **33.** -13 **35.** -26 **37.** 14
39. > **41.** > **43.** > **45.** $45 + 18$
$+ 27 - 21 - 93$; -24; Cody's
account is reduced by $24.
47. -16 **49.** 3 **51.** 4,150 ft **57.** F
59. 4 **61.** 4 **63.** > **65.** >

1. -3 **3.** 6 **5.** -4 **7.** -10 **9.** 7
11. -14 **13.** -5 **15.** 8 **17.** 12
19. 16 **21.** -17 **23.** 8 **25.** 50
27. 18 **29.** 16 **31.** -5 **33.** -20
35. 83°F **37.** -14 **39.** -2 **41.** 2
43. 16 **45.** -27 **47.** -17 **49.** -13,
$-17, -21$ **51.** 1,234°F **53.** 265°F
57. $m + n$ has the least absolute
value **59.** 3 **61.** 19 **63.** 24

1. -15 **3.** -15 **5.** 15 **7.** -15
9. -8 **11.** 4 **13.** 7 **15.** -7
17. 450 feet **19.** -10 **21.** -12
23. 48 **25.** 35 **27.** 7 **29.** -8
31. -9 **33.** -9 **35.** -40 **37.** -3
39. 50 **41.** -3 **43.** 30 **45.** -42
47. -60 ft **49.** 1 **51.** -12
53. 1,400 **55.** 11 **57.** less; $-$72
59. more; $12 **63.** C **65.** $x + 6$
67. $2d - 4$ **69.** 5 **71.** -2

1. $w = 4$ **3.** $k = -7$ **5.** $y = -30$
7. This year's loss is $57 million.
9. $k = -3$ **11.** $v = -4$ **13.** $a = 20$
15. $t = -32$ **17.** $n = 150$
19. $l = -144$ **21.** $y = 100$
23. $j = -63$ **25.** $c = 17$
27. $y = -11$ **29.** $w = -41$
31. $x = -58$ **33.** $x = 4$ **35.** $t = 9$
37. 3 mi **39.** $-13 + p = 8$
41. $t - 9 = -22$ **43.** oceans or
beaches **49.** H **51.** multiply by 2
53. > **55.** < **57.** =

1. prime **3.** composite **5.** 2^4
7. 3^4 **9.** $2 \cdot 3^2$ **11.** $3^2 \cdot 5$
13. $2 \cdot 5^3$ **15.** $2^2 \cdot 5^2$ **17.** $3^2 \cdot 71$
19. $2^3 \cdot 5^3$ **21.** prime **23.** prime
25. composite **27.** composite
29. $2^2 \cdot 17$ **31.** $2^3 \cdot 3 \cdot 5$
33. $3^3 \cdot 5$ **35.** $2 \cdot 7 \cdot 11$ **37.** $2^5 \cdot 5^2$
39. 5^4 **41.** $3^2 \cdot 5 \cdot 7$ **43.** $3^3 \cdot 7$
45. $2 \cdot 11^2$ **47.** $11 \cdot 17$ **49.** $5^2 \cdot 7^2$
51. $2^3 \cdot 3^2 \cdot 5$ **53.** 3^2 **55.** 5^2
57. 2^4 **59a.** $2 \cdot 32$ **b.** one
61. 7 **63.** 4 or 8 people **67.** B
69. $2^3 \cdot 3 \cdot 5$ **71.** 587
73. 14,800,000 **75.** $y = 1$ **77.** $x = 0$

1. 6 **3.** 12 **5.** 4 **7.** 12 kits **9.** 12
11. 11 **13.** 38 **15.** 2 **17.** 26 **19.** 3
21. 1 **23.** 2 **25.** 22 **27.** 40 **29.** 1
31. 7 **33.** 3 **35.** 13 **37.** 7 shelves
39a. 7 students **b.** 5 cookies
45. B **47.** 13 **49.** 81 **51.** -5
53. 2 **55.** 7^2 **57.** 2^2

1. 28 **3.** 48 **5.** 45 **7.** 24 min
9. 24 **11.** 42 **13.** 120 **15.** 80
17. 180 **19.** 360 **21.** 60 min
23. 12 **25.** 132 **27.** 90 **29.** 12
31. 144 **33.** 210 **35.** yes **37.** no
41. C **43.** $5c - 2$ **45.** $7u + 3v - 4$
47. 4 **49.** 15

2-9 Exercises

9. no **11.** yes **13.** $3\frac{3}{4}$ **15.** $1\frac{4}{13}$
17. $\frac{31}{5}$ **19.** $\frac{38}{5}$ **29.** yes **31.** yes
33. yes **35.** no **37.** $6\frac{1}{3}$ **39.** $7\frac{4}{11}$
41. $\frac{128}{5}$ **43.** $\frac{29}{3}$ **45.** No **51.** $\frac{11}{2}$
53. $\frac{141}{21}$ **55.** $\frac{573}{50}$ **57.** $\frac{12}{20}, \frac{6}{10}$
59. $\frac{9}{5}, \frac{72}{40}$ **61.** $8\frac{1}{3}$ ft **63.** $3\frac{1}{2}$ ft
65. $\frac{150}{4}$ **69.** C **71.** $1\frac{1}{3}$ cups of
flour **73.** $y = 12$ **75.** $z = 80$
77. 45 **79.** 168

2-10 Exercises

1. 0.57 **3.** 1.83 **5.** 0.12 **7.** 0.05
9. $\frac{1}{125}$ **11.** $-2\frac{1}{20}$ **13.** 0.720
15. 6.4 **17.** 0.88 **19.** 1 **21.** 1.92
23. 0.8 **25.** 0.55 **27.** $\frac{1}{100}$ **29.** $-\frac{2}{25}$
31. $\frac{61}{4}$ **33.** $8\frac{3}{8}$ **35.** 8.75 **37.** $5\frac{5}{100}$
39. $\frac{307}{20}$ **41.** 4.003 **43.** yes **45.** no
47. yes **49.** no **51.** $18\frac{1}{20}, 18\frac{1}{25},$
$18\frac{11}{20}$ **55.** D **57.** no **59.** yes
61. $\frac{13}{4}$ **63.** $\frac{25}{4}$

2-11 Exercises

1. < **3.** < **5.** < **7.** < **9.** 2.05,
2.5, $\frac{13}{5}$ **11.** < **13.** > **15.** > **17.** >
19. > **21.** < **23.** < **25.** $\frac{5}{8}$, 0.7,
0.755 **27.** -2.25, 2.05, $\frac{21}{10}$
29. $-2.98, -2\frac{9}{10}, 2.88$ **31.** $\frac{3}{4}$
33. $\frac{7}{8}$ **35.** 0.32 **37.** $-\frac{7}{8}$
41. sloths **47.** J **49.** > **51.** >
53. 169 **55.** 57

Chapter 2 Study Guide: Review

1. rational number; integer; terminating decimal
2. improper fraction, mixed number **3.** > **4.** <
5.
$$-6 \quad -2 \quad 0 \quad 4\ 5$$
6.
$$-10 \quad 0 \quad 10$$
$-8 \quad -3 \quad 12 \quad 8$
7. 0 units
$$-1 \quad 0 \quad 1$$
8. 17 units
$$-18 \quad -12 \quad -6 \quad 0$$

9. 6 units
$$-1\ 0\ 1\ 2\ 3\ 4\ 5\ 6$$
10. -3 **11.** 1 **12.** -56 **13.** 9
14. 14 **15.** -6 **16.** 6 **17.** -9
18. -1 **19.** -9 **20.** -50 **21.** 3
22. 16 **23.** -2 **24.** -12 **25.** -3
26. 10 **27.** 14 **28.** -26 **29.** 72
30. 13 **31.** -4 **32.** -105 **33.** -19
34. 21 **35.** 16 **36.** $2^3 \cdot 11$ **37.** 3^3
38. $2 \cdot 3^4$ **39.** $2^5 \cdot 3$ **40.** 30 **41.** 3
42. 12 **43.** 220 **44.** 60 **45.** 32
46. 27 **47.** 90 **48.** 12 **49.** 315
50. $\frac{21}{15}$ **51.** $\frac{19}{6}$ **52.** $\frac{43}{4}$ **53.** $3\frac{1}{3}$
54. $2\frac{1}{2}$ **55.** $2\frac{3}{7}$ **56.** Possible
answer: $\frac{8}{9}, \frac{24}{27}$
57. Possible answer: $\frac{42}{48}, \frac{7}{8}$
58. Possible answer: $\frac{16}{21}, \frac{96}{126}$
59. $\frac{1}{4}$ **60.** $-\frac{1}{250}$ **61.** $\frac{1}{20}$ **62.** 3.5
63. 0.6 **64.** $0.\overline{6}$ **65.** < **66.** >
67. > **68.** < **69.** $-0.55, \frac{6}{13}, \frac{1}{2}, 0.58$

Chapter 3

3-1 Exercises

1. 63 **3.** 2 **5.** -225 **7.** no **9.** 92
11. 8 **13.** 55 **15.** 5 **17.** -120
19. 9 **21.** -7 **23.** -59 **25.** -90
27. -36 **29.** 11 **31.** -98 **33.** 225
35. 13 **37.** about 8 weeks
39. approximately 5 gallons
41. about 30 AU **47.** J **49.** -3
51. 22 **53.** -11

3-2 Exercises

1. 21.82 **3.** 12.826 **5.** 1.98 **7.** 1.77
9. $37.2 billion **11.** 18.97
13. -25.52 **15.** 10.132 **17.** -15.89
19. 9.01 **21.** 16.05 **23.** 5.1
25. 22.77 **27.** 77.13 g **29.** -4.883
31. 14.33 **33.** 1.92 **35.** 30.12
37. -1.26 **39.** -3.457 **41.** You
must keep the place value units
together. **43.** 1915 **49.** G **51.** y
$= 15$ **53.** $p = 39$ **55.** 22 **57.** 42

3-3 Exercises

1. -3.6 **3.** 0.18 **5.** 2.04 **7.** -0.315
9. 334.7379 miles **11.** 0.35 **13.** 3.2
15. -20.4 **17.** 9.1 **19.** 4.48
21. 2.814 **23.** -9.256 **25.** 6.161
27. 5.445 mi **29.** 0.0021 **31.** 0.432
33. -2.88 **35.** 1.911 **37.** 0.351
39. 0.00864 **41.** 28.95 in. of
mercury **43.** -8.904 **45.** -0.027
47. 1,224.1152 **53.** 11.3 mi
55. $5 \cdot 7$ **57.** 2^6 **59.** 8.57 **61.** -3.74
63. 19.71 **65.** -68.868

3-4 Exercises

1. 6.14 **3.** -3.09 **5.** 0.017 **7.** $5.54
9. -8.9 **11.** -8.92 **13.** -4.8
15. 2.04 **17.** 1.13 **19.** -3.07
21. $9.75 **23.** 1.56 **25.** 4.19
27. -2.8 **29.** -1.91 **31.** -0.019
33. 0.18 **35.** -262.113 **37.** 1985
39. 14.53 million people **45.** C
47. $9.93 **49.** 9 **51.** 8 **53.** 5
55. 2.116 **57.** 18.2055

3-5 Exercises

1. 0.9 **3.** 4.6 **5.** -3.2 **7.** 2.5
9. -16 **11.** -4.8 **13.** 28 mi/gal
15. -0.12 **17.** -14 **19.** 4.2
21. 47.5 **23.** 4 **25.** -48.75
27. 2.4 min **29.** 22.5 **31.** -0.4
33. 25 **35.** 20 **37.** 18 **39.** 6.4
41. 2,500 years **43.** 11 years
45. 363.64 days **47.** A **49.** $9\frac{1}{3}$
51. $3\frac{2}{5}$ **53.** 5.05 **55.** -2.7

3-6 Exercises

1. $w = 7$ **3.** $k = 24.09$ **5.** $b = 5.04$
7. $t = 9$ **9.** $4.25 **11.** $c = 44.56$
13. $a = 5.08$ **15.** $p = -53.21$
17. $z = 16$ **19.** $w = 11.76$
21. $a = -74.305$ **23.** $7.50
25. $n = -4.92$ **27.** $r = 0.72$
29. $m = -0.15$ **31.** $k = 0.9$
33. $t = 0.936$ **35.** $v = -2$
37. $n = 12.254$ **39.** $j = 11.107$
41. $g = 0.5$ **43.** $171
45a. 148.1 million **b.** between
English and Italian **49.** C
53. 6.0×10^6 **55.** 1.5
57. 3 **59.** 9

3-7 Exercises

1. about 4 feet **3.** 0 **5.** 2 **7.** 3
9. 48 **11.** 1 **13.** $2\frac{1}{2}$ **15.** $\frac{1}{2}$
17. $11\frac{1}{2}$ **19.** 6 **21.** 30 **23.** 2
25. 4 **27.** $\frac{1}{2}$ **29.** 24 **31.** -8
33. 4 **35.** 11 **37.** 5 **39.** \$14
41. greater **43.** 2 m **47.** D
49. $x = 27$ **51.** $m = 13$ **53.** $x = 6.5$
55. $q = -19.44$

3-8 Exercises

1. $\frac{1}{3}$ **3.** $\frac{3}{7}$ **5.** $\frac{1}{2}$ **7.** $\frac{19}{24}$ **9.** $\frac{1}{12}$ **11.** $\frac{1}{2}$
13. $\frac{3}{5}$ **15.** $\frac{2}{3}$ **17.** $\frac{1}{5}$ **19.** $\frac{1}{4}$ **21.** $\frac{3}{4}$
23. $-\frac{1}{6}$ **25.** $\frac{8}{15}$ **27.** $\frac{1}{6}$ mi **29.** $\frac{13}{18}$
31. $\frac{4}{5}$ **33.** $-\frac{1}{12}$ **35.** $\frac{1}{2}$ **37.** $-\frac{1}{20}$
39. $\frac{14}{15}$ **41.** $\frac{41}{63}$ **43.** $\frac{41}{45}$ **45.** 0
47. $\frac{9}{120}$ **49.** $\frac{5}{6}$ hour **51.** $\frac{13}{24}$ mi
53. Cai **55.** $\frac{3}{8}$ lb of cashews **59.** B
61. 1 **63.** 6 **67.** 11

3-9 Exercises

1. $5\frac{1}{6}$ **3.** $6\frac{5}{8}$ **5.** $7\frac{3}{4}$ **7.** $5\frac{1}{3}$ **9.** $4\frac{9}{40}$
11. 15 **13.** $5\frac{2}{3}$ **15.** $6\frac{4}{5}$ **17.** $11\frac{7}{15}$
19. $\frac{6}{7}$ **21.** $5\frac{1}{4}$ **23.** $2\frac{7}{20}$ **25.** $\frac{9}{10}$
27. $15\frac{8}{15}$ **29.** $13\frac{5}{6}$ **31.** $6\frac{5}{24}$ **33.** $\frac{5}{6}$
35. $4\frac{1}{6}$ **37.** $10\frac{1}{24}$ **39.** < **41.** >
43. $4\frac{5}{8}$ cups **45.** $117\frac{1}{3}$ mi
47. the waterfall trail **51.** D
53. 6 **57.** $\frac{3}{4}$ **59.** $1\frac{5}{36}$

3-10 Exercises

1. $2\frac{1}{2}$ hr **3.** $\frac{2}{5}$ **5.** -9 **7.** $\frac{12}{5}$
9. -20 **11.** $1\frac{2}{3}$ tsp **13.** $\frac{1}{2}$ **15.** 4
17. $\frac{1}{4}$ **19.** $-\frac{5}{9}$ **21.** $\frac{222}{5}$ **23.** $17\frac{1}{2}$
25. $\frac{7}{3}$ **27.** $8\frac{1}{4}$ **29.** $\frac{155}{42}$ **31.** $\frac{1}{3}$
33. $-\frac{1}{6}$ **35.** $\frac{1}{12}$ **37.** $\frac{1}{5}$ **39.** $\frac{7}{10}$
41. $\frac{1}{5}$ **43.** 1 **45.** 3 **47.** 5 **49.** 6
51. 1 **53.** $2\frac{1}{12}$ lb **55.** $11\frac{1}{3}$ mi
59. B **61.** $-7, -3, 0, 4, 5$ **63.** $-9,$
$-4, -1, 1, 9$ **65.** $1\frac{5}{12}$ **67.** $7\frac{11}{24}$

3-11 Exercises

1. 18 **3.** $\frac{3}{32}$ **5.** $\frac{1}{4}$ **7.** 2 **9.** 3 capes
11. 18 **13.** $4\frac{3}{8}$ **15.** $\frac{1}{27}$ **17.** -40
19. $\frac{5}{14}$ **21.** -14 **23.** $\frac{88}{7}$ **25.** $-9\frac{4}{5}$
27. 6 pieces **29.** $5\frac{2}{5}$ **31.** 2

33. $\frac{8}{147}$ **35.** $-\frac{16}{25}$ **37.** $\frac{18}{25}$ **39.** $\frac{21}{2}$
41. $\frac{1}{3}$ **43.** -1 **45.** 87 hamburger
patties **47.** 11 in. **49.** 7 circles
51. D **53.** 22 **55.** 24 **57.** 24
59. $8\frac{1}{10}$ **61.** $1\frac{11}{12}$

3-12 Exercises

1. $a = \frac{3}{4}$ **3.** $p = \frac{3}{2}$ **5.** $r = \frac{9}{10}$
7. $1\frac{1}{8}$ c **9.** $t = \frac{5}{8}$ **11.** $x = \frac{53}{24}$
13. $y = \frac{7}{60}$ **15.** $w = \frac{1}{2}$ **17.** $z = \frac{1}{12}$
19. $n = 1\frac{23}{25}$ **21.** $t = \frac{1}{4}$ **23.** $w = 6$
25. $x = \frac{3}{5}$ **27.** $n = \frac{12}{5}$ **29.** $y = \frac{1}{2}$
31. $r = \frac{1}{77}$ **33.** $h = -\frac{1}{12}$ **35.** $v = \frac{3}{4}$
37. $d = 14\frac{17}{40}$ **39.** $11\frac{3}{16}$
41. 15 million species
43. 48 stories **49.** G
51. $3, 3.02, 3\frac{2}{10}, 3.25$ **53.** -1
55. 21

Chapter 3 Study Guide: Review

1. compatible numbers
2. reciprocals **3.** 110 **4.** 5 **5.** 75
6. 4 **7.** about 20 weeks **8.** 27.88
9. -51.2 **10.** 6.22 **11.** 52.902
12. 14.095 **13.** 35.88 **14.** 3.5
15. -38.7 **16.** 40.495 **17.** 60.282
18. 77.348 **19.** -18.81 **20.** 2.3
21. -4.9 **22.** 0.08 **23.** -5.8
24. -1.65 **25.** 3.4 **26.** 4.5
27. -1.09 **28.** -15.4 **29.** -500
30. 2 **31.** 4 **32.** $x = -10.44$
33. $s = 107$ **34.** $n = 0.007$
35. $k = 8.64$ **36.** $e = -5.05$
37. $w = -3.08$ **38.** 24 **39.** -8
40. 3 **41.** 1 **42.** 30 **43.** 3
44. about $5\frac{1}{2}$ laps **45.** $\frac{5}{12}$ **46.** $\frac{17}{20}$
47. $\frac{5}{11}$ **48.** $\frac{1}{9}$ **49.** $6\frac{5}{24}$ **50.** $3\frac{1}{3}$
51. $6\frac{1}{4}$ **52.** $1\frac{5}{12}$ **53.** $7\frac{1}{2}$ **54.** $1\frac{21}{25}$
55. $17\frac{17}{63}$ **56.** $6\frac{1}{4}$ **57.** $\frac{4}{75}$ **58.** $\frac{2}{15}$
59. 1 **60.** $1\frac{11}{12}$ **61.** $1\frac{2}{3}$ **62.** $\frac{1}{15}$
63. $1\frac{5}{7}$ **64.** $\frac{13}{28}$

Chapter 4

4-1 Exercises

1. II **3.** III
5, 7.

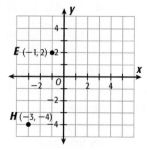

9. $(6, -3)$ **11.** $(-4, 0)$ **13.** I **15.** IV
17, 19.

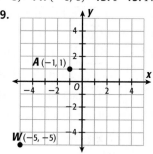

21. $(-4, 4)$ **23.** $(-5, -4)$ **25.** $(5, 6)$
27.

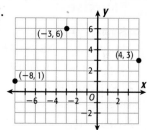

29. triangle; Quadrants I and II
31. III **33.** $(12, 7)$ **39.** B **41.** -6
43. -24 **45.** $6\frac{2}{5}$ **47.** $1\frac{2}{5}$

4-2 Exercises

1. $(1, 1)$ **3.** $(-2, 0)$
5.

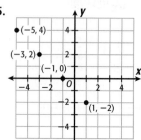

7. $(-15, 15)$, $(-10, 10)$, $(-5, 5)$, $(0, 0)$

9. $(-11, -6)$, $(-9, -5)$, $(-7, -4)$, $(-5, -3)$

11.

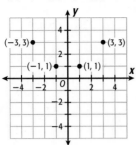

13a.

Days	Gallons of gas
1	3.5
2	7
3	10.5
4	14
5	17.5

21. -6.3 **23.** -12.35 **25.** $16\frac{1}{3}$
27. $7\frac{33}{40}$

4-3 Exercises

1. A   **3.** B   **15.** 3   **17.** 0   **19.** 3
21. 3   **23.** $(1, 4)$

4-4 Exercises

1. $-5, 1, 3$ **3.** $50, 2, 18$
5.

x	−1	0	1	2
y	3	2	3	6

7. $-7, -1, 8$
9.

x	−1	0	1	2
y	$-\frac{1}{2}$	0	$\frac{1}{2}$	1

11a. $y = 11.66 - x$ **17.** J
19. -1 **21.** $x = 6$ **23.** $y = 4\frac{1}{2}$

4-5 Exercises

1. arithmetic   **3.** $y = 3n$
5. $y = n - 1$ **7.** $y = 195n$
9. arithmetic   **11.** $y = 7n$
13. $y = 20n$ **15.** $y = n + 0.5$

17. multiply 35 by n
19. add $\frac{1}{2}$ to n **21.** divide n by 3
23. $y = n - 0.5$ **25.** $y = 3n + 2$
27. $y = 2n - 1$ **29.** $y = 2^n$
35. $10{,}000{,}000$ **37.** 729 **39.** 200
41. 105

4-6 Exercises

1.

Input	Rule	Output	Ordered Pair
x	x + 3	y	(x, y)
−2	−2 + 3	1	(−2, 1)
0	0 + 3	3	(0, 3)
2	2 + 3	5	(2, 5)

3. $y = 750x$
5.

Input	Rule	Output	Ordered Pair
x	x − 1	y	(x, y)
3	3 − 1	2	(3, 2)
4	4 − 1	3	(4, 3)
5	5 − 1	4	(5, 4)

7.

Input	Rule	Output	Ordered Pair
x	2x + 3	y	(x, y)
−2	2 (−2) + 3	−1	(−2, −1)
−1	2 (−1) + 3	1	(−1, 1)
0	2 (0) + 3	3	(0, 3)

9. $8{,}100$ cm
15. B   **19.** $y = 2n - 6$

Chapter 4 Study Guide: Review

1. sequence   **2.** function
3. linear function
4–7.

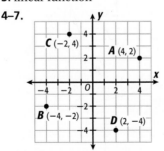

8. $(2, -1)$, IV   **9.** $(-2, 3)$, II
10. $(1, 0)$ **11.** $(-4, -2)$

12.

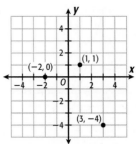

13.

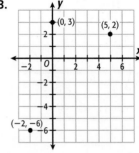

14.

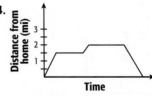

15.

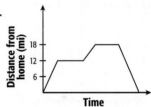

16.

Input	Rule	Output
x	$x^2 - 1$	y
−2	$(-2)^2 - 1$	3
3	$(3)^2 - 1$	8
5	$(5)^2 - 1$	24

17. geometric; 243
18. arithmetic; -30 **19.** $y = 25n$
20. $y = n - 4$ **21.** $y = 3n - 7$
22. $y = 2n + 2$
23.

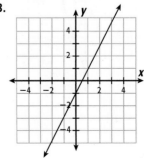

24.

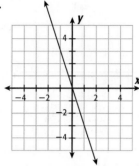

25.

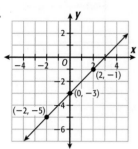

26.

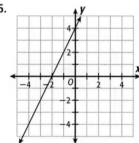

27.

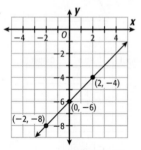

28.

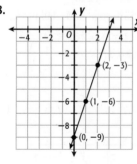

Chapter 5

5-1 Exercises

1. $\frac{10}{3}$, 10 to 3, 10:3 **3.** $\frac{3}{1}$ or 3 to 1
or 3:1 **5.** $\frac{25}{30}$, 25 to 30, 25:30, or $\frac{5}{6}$,
5 to 6, 5:6 **7.** $\frac{30}{15}$, 30 to 15, 30:15,
or $\frac{2}{1}$, 2 to 1, 2:1 **9.** $\frac{4}{1}$ or 4 to 1 or 4:1
11. group 1 **15.** 3:1, $\frac{3}{1}$, 3 to 1
17. 3:2, $\frac{3}{2}$, 3 to 2 **19.** greater than
21. B **23.** $x = -6.7$ **25.** $v = 8.5$

5-2 Exercises

1. 83.5 mL per min **3.** 458 mi/h
5. $7.75 per h **7.** about 74.63 mi/h
9. 3 runs per game **11.** $335
per mo **13.** 18.83 mi per gal
15. $5.75 per h **17.** 122 mi per trip
19. 0.04 mi per min
21. $\frac{1,026 \text{ students}}{38 \text{ classes}}$; 27 students
per class **23.** $0.06, $0.07; $\frac{\$2.52}{42 \text{ oz}}$ is
the better buy **27.** 287, 329, 611
(France, Poland, Germany)
31. D **33.** < **35.** >

5-3 Exercises

1. positive; 1

3.

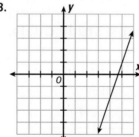

5.

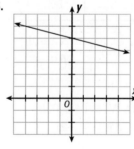

7. constant **9.** constant
11. negative; -3

13.

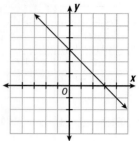

15.

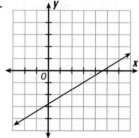

17. constant **19.** variable
21. -7 **23.** -3 **25.** $\frac{3}{2}$
29. The y-value decreased.
33. B **37.** 125 **39.** 100,000
41. add $\frac{3}{2}$ to n; $\frac{9}{2}$, 6, $\frac{15}{2}$

5-4 Exercises

1. yes **3.** yes **5.** yes **7.** no **13.** no
15. no **17.** no **19.** no **29.** 3, 24, 15
39a. $\frac{1 \text{ can}}{4 \text{ hours}}$ **b.** No, 1:4 = x:2,080;
the class recycled 520 cans.
41. 1:2 = 2:4, 2:1 = 4:2, 1:1 = 2:2,
1:1 = 4:4, 2:2 = 4:4 **43a.** 8:5
b. Mill Pond and Clear Pond
49. H **51.** -3.75 **53.** -76.25

55.

Input	Rule	Output	Ordered Pair
x	$-x + 3$	y	(x, y)
-2	$-(-2) + 3$	5	$(-2, 5)$
-1	$-(-1) + 3$	4	$(-1, 4)$
0	$-(0) + 3$	3	$(0, 3)$
1	$-(1) + 3$	2	$(1, 2)$
2	$-(2) + 3$	1	$(2, 1)$

57.

Input	Rule	Output	Ordered Pair
x	$-3x + 4$	y	(x, y)
-2	$-3(-2) + 4$	10	$(-2, 10)$
-1	$-3(-1) + 4$	7	$(-1, 7)$
0	$-3(0) + 4$	4	$(0, 4)$
1	$-3(1) + 4$	1	$(1, 1)$
2	$-3(2) + 4$	-2	$(2, -2)$

5-5 Exercises

1. $x = 60$ **3.** $m = 16.4$ **5.** 3 lb
7. $h = 144$ **9.** $v = 336$ **11.** $t = 36$
13. $n = 22\frac{2}{5}$ **15.** 227 grams
29. 25 paper clips
31. 22 counselors **33.** $\frac{4}{10} = \frac{6}{15}$
35. $\frac{3}{75} = \frac{4}{100}$ **37.** $\frac{5}{6} = \frac{90}{108}$
39. 105 oxygen atoms **45.** $\frac{4}{6}$
47. -20 **49.** 64 mi/h
51. $9.50/h

5-6 Exercises

1. Feet; the width of a sidewalk is similar to the length of several sheets of paper. **3.** Tons; the weight of a truck is similar to the weight of several buffalo. **5.** 48 qt
7. 4.5 lb **9.** 27 fl oz **11.** Inches; the wingspan of a sparrow is similar to the length of several paper clips. **13.** Feet; the height of an office building is similar to the length of many sheets of paper.
15. 3 mi **17.** 75 in. **19.** > **21.** <
23. > **25.** < **27.** < **29.** 2.4 mi
31. 8 c, 5 qt, 12 pt, 2 gal
33. 12,000 ft, 2.5 mi, 5,000 yd
35. 9.5 yd, 380 in., 32.5 ft
37. 46,145 yd **39.** The object that you are measuring will contain fewer of the larger units, so it makes sense to divide to get a smaller value for the measure.
43. A **45.** $139 **47.** no **49.** no

5-7 Exercises

1. similar **3.** similar **5.** not similar
7. similar **9.** no **11.** similar
13. yes **15.** yes **17.** no **19.** no
23. C **25.** $-10\frac{1}{2}$ **27.** $\frac{3}{2}$

5-8 Exercises

1. $a = 22.5$ cm **3.** 28 ft **5.** $x = 13.5$ in. **7.** 3.9 ft **9.** 21 m **15.** B
17. $18 \cdot y$ **19.** $12 \div z$ **21.** inches

5-9 Exercises

1. $\frac{1}{14}$ **3.** 67.2 cm tall, 40 cm wide
5. $\frac{1}{15}$ **7.** 135 in. **9.** 16 in.
11. 75 cm; 141 cm; 240 cm
13. 2 in. **15.** about 25 mi
17. 1 mi = 0.25 ft or 1 ft = 4 mi
19. B **21.** 0.054, 0.41, $\frac{4}{7}$
23. $\frac{7}{11}$, 0.7, $\frac{7}{9}$ **25.** 0.06 **27.** 2.7

Extension

1. $\frac{1\,\text{ft}}{12\,\text{in.}}$ **3.** $\frac{1\,\text{hr}}{60\,\text{min}}$ **5.** 64 oz $\cdot \frac{1\,\text{lb}}{16\,\text{oz}}$ = 4 lb **7.** 3.5 qt $\cdot \frac{2\,\text{pt}}{1\,\text{qt}}$ = 7 pt
9. $\frac{\$1.75}{1\,\text{ft}} \cdot \frac{3\,\text{ft}}{1\,\text{yd}} = \frac{\$5.25}{1\,\text{yd}}$ **11a.** 0.615 Earth years **b.** 4.9 Venus years
13. $225

Chapter 5 Study Guide: Review

1. similar **2.** ratio; unit rate
3. scale factor **4.** $\frac{7}{15}$, 7 to 15, 7:15
5. red to blue **6.** 6 ft per s
7. 109 mi per h **8.** $2.24, about $2.14; $\frac{\$32.05}{15\,\text{gal}}$ **9.** 32 dollars per g, 35 dollars per g; $\frac{\$160}{5g}$ **10.** variable
11. constant; $\frac{1}{4}$ **12.** $\frac{9}{27} \neq \frac{6}{20}$
13. $\frac{15}{25} \neq \frac{20}{30}$ **14.** $\frac{21}{14} = \frac{18}{12}$
15. Possible answer: $\frac{10}{12} = \frac{30}{36}$
16. Possible answer: $\frac{45}{50} = \frac{90}{100}$
17. Possible answer: $\frac{9}{15} = \frac{27}{45}$
18. $n = 2$ **19.** $a = 6$ **20.** $b = 4$
21. $x = 66$ **22.** $y = 10$ **23.** $w = 20$
24. 2 pints **25.** 3,000 pounds
26. 2.5 miles **27.** not similar
28. similar **29.** $x = 100$ ft
30. about 8 ft **31.** 12.1 in.
32. 163.4 mi

Chapter 6

6-1 Exercises

1. 79% **3.** 50% **5.** $\frac{41}{50}$ **7.** $\frac{19}{50}$ **9.** 0.22
11. 0.0807 **13.** 0.11 **15.** 45%
17. $\frac{11}{20}$ **19.** $\frac{83}{100}$ **21.** $\frac{81}{100}$ **23.** 0.098
25. 0.663 **27.** 0.027 **29.** 0.44
31. 0.105 **33.** < **35.** < **41.** Brad
47. 12 **49.** $3\frac{1}{2}$
50–53.

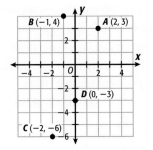

6-2 Exercises

1. 60% **3.** 54.4% **5.** 8.7% **7.** 12%
9. 17.5% **11.** mental math; 40%
13. 83% **15.** 8.1% **17.** 75%
19. 37.5% **21.** 28% **23.** >
25. < **27.** 1%
35.

x	y
-2	4
-1	2
0	0
1	-2
2	-4

37. 0.4 m

6-3 Exercises

5. Yes; 35% of $43.99 is close to $\frac{1}{3}$ of $45, which is $15. Since $45 − $15 = $30, Darden will have enough money. **19.** Fancy Feet
37. about 26 oz **39.** about 2% more **49.** 1.2 **51.** 0.375

6-4 Exercises

1. 24 **3.** 20 **5.** 8 **7.** 423 **9.** 171 students **11.** 11.2 **13.** 3,540
15. 0.04 **17.** 18 **19.** 13 **21.** 1.74
23. 39.6 **25.** 12.4 **27.** 6 **29.** 4.5
31. 11.75 **33.** 5,125 **35.** 80
37. 120 **39.** 0.6 **41.** 4.2

43. $4.80 **45.** 2.25 g **47.** 0.98
53. C **55.** $1.75 per lb **57.** 1.25%
59. 38.9% **61.** 40.7%

6-5 Exercises

1. 25% **3.** 60 **5.** 18% **7.** 50 **9.** 8%
11. $33\frac{1}{3}$% **13.** 300% **15.** 225
17. 100% **19.** 30 **21.** 22 **23.** 55.6%
25. 68.8 **27.** 77.5 **29.** 158.3
31. 5% **33.** You use the number
100 in a proportion to solve a
percent problem. *Percent* means
"per hundred." **35.** 45 pieces
37. How many laps is the race?
39. She needs to make more than
$275,000 per month in sales.
41. 75 **43.** 3.56 **45.** 3.2 **47.** 6.6
49. 66.64

6-6 Exercises

1. 28% **3.** 16.1% **5.** $34.39
7. 37.5% **9.** 22.2% **11.** $55.25
13. 100% **15.** 43.6% **17.** 30
19. 56.25 gal **21.** $48.25
23a. $41,500 **b.** $17,845 **c.** 80.7%
25. about 8,506 trillion Btu **27.** A
29. $\frac{29}{9}$ **31.** $\frac{29}{4}$ **33.** $\frac{73}{3}$ **35.** 3.25 lb

6-7 Exercises

1. I = $24 **3.** P = $400 **5.** just over
4 yr **7.** I = $3,240 **9.** P = $2,200
11. r = 11% **13.** almost 9 yr
15. $5,200 **17.** $212.75 **19.** 20 yr
21. $4 **23.** high yield CD: gain
$606; Dow Jones: loss $684; a
difference of $1,290 **29.** just over
$2\frac{1}{2}$ yr **31.** 29.9% **33.** 93.2%

Chapter 6 Study Guide: Review

1. interest; simple interest;
principal **2.** percent of increase
3. percent of decrease **4.** percent
5. 0.78 **6.** 0.40 **7.** 0.05 **8.** 0.16
9. 0.65 **10.** 0.89 **11.** 60%
12. 16.7% **13.** 6% **14.** 80%
15. 66.7% **16.** 0.56% **17.** Possible
answer: 8 **18.** Possible answer: 90
19. Possible answer: 24

20. Possible answer: 32
21. Possible answer: 40
22. Possible answer: 3
23. Possible answer: $3 **24.** 68
25. 24 **26.** 4.41 **27.** 120 **28.** 27.3
29. 54 **30.** about 474 **31.** 125
32. 8% **33.** 12 **34.** 37.5% **35.** 8
36. 27.8% **37.** 7.96% **38.** 50%
39. 14.3% **40.** 30% **41.** 83.1%
42. 23.1% **43.** 75% **44.** $208.25
45. $7.80 **46.** I = $15
47. t = 3 years **48.** I = $243
49. r = 3.9% **50.** P = $2,300
51. 7 years **52.** 9 years, 3 months

Chapter 7

7-1 Exercises

1. 6 **3.** 15 **5.** 3 **7.** 4; 31 **9.** B
11. Guyana and Suriname;
Colombia **19.** $8.50 per hour
21. 16 points per game

7-2 Exercises

1. 20; 20; 5 and 20; 30 **3.** median
5. 83.3; 88; 88; 28 **9.** mean and
median **11.** 151 **13.** 9; 8; 12
21. J

7-3 Exercises

1. grapes **3.** about 15 pounds
5.

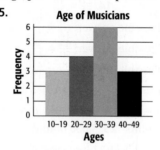
Age of Musicians

7. about 27 inches

9.

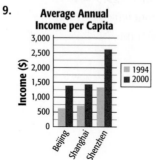
Average Annual Income per Capita

11.

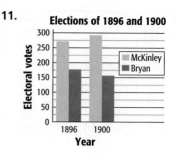
Elections of 1896 and 1900

17. H **19.** no **21.** yes
23. 23.5; 23.5; 15; 19

7-4 Exercises

1. outdoor **3.** $50,000 **5.** circle
graph **7.** 30% **9.** circle graph
11. Asia, Africa, North America,
South America, Antarctica,
Europe, Australia **13.** about 25%
19. about 150 **21.** > **23.** =

7-5 Exercises

1. The range is 16, the interquartile
range is 11, the lower quartile is 35
and the upper quartile is 36.
3. airplane B **5.** The range is 16,
the interquartile is 12, the lower
quartile is 73, and the upper
quartile is 85. **7.** city A **11.** the
range **19.** 15 **21.** $3.75

7-6 Exercises

1. 1990–1995

3.

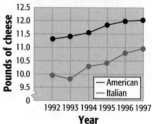
Cheese Consumed per Person in the United States

5. 1990–1995

7.

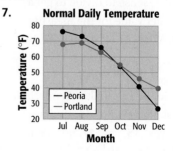
Normal Daily Temperature

9b. about 3,400 **17.** 136%
19. 55%

 Exercises

1. bar graph **3.** line graph
5. line plot or stem-and-leaf plot
19. 90% **21.** 40.6%

7-8 Exercises

1. Daria's method **3.** biased
5. Vonneta's method **7.** not biased
9. entire population **11.** entire
population **17.** B **19.** 0.52 **21.** 1.1
23. 5.5 **25.** 0.41

7-9 Exercises

1. The heart rate decreases as the
weight increases. **3.** positive
correlation **5.** The capacity
increases with time. **7.** negative
correlation **9.** no correlation
11. no correlation **17.** 75.6 **19.** 3.5

7-10 Exercises

1. graph A **3.** The vertical axis
does not begin with zero, so
differences in scales appear
greater. **5.** The scale of the graph
is not divided into equal intervals,
so differences in sales appear less
than they actually are. **7.** The
graphs do not use the same scale,
so it looks as though September
had fewer sales than October,
which is not true; redraw the
graphs using the same scale.
15. $x = \frac{1}{6}$ **17.** $x = -\frac{11}{24}$
19. negative correlation

Chapter 7 Study Guide: Review

1. population; sample **2.** mean
3.

	Frequency	Cumulative Frequency
0–9	1	1
10–19	3	4
20–29	3	7
30–39	2	9

4.

Stems	Leaves
0	8
1	4 6 9
2	5 7 9
3	2 5

Key: 1|4 means 14

5.
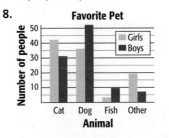

6. 302; 311.5; 233 and 324; 166
7. 43; 46; none; 25
8.

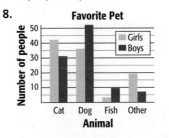

Favorite Pet

9. yellow **10.** 35 people
11.
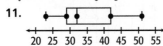

12. 13
13.

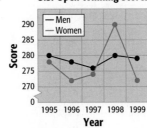

U.S. Open Winning Scores

14. line graph **15.** bar graph
16. 2,500 is a reasonable estimate
based on the data. **17.** positive
correlation **18.** The vertical axis
is broken.

Chapter 8

8-1 Exercises

1. Q, R, S **3.** plane QRS **5.** $\overline{QU}$,
$\overline{RU}, \overline{SU}$ **7.** D, E, F **9.** plane DEF
11. $\overline{DE}, \overline{EF}, \overline{DF}$ **21.** C **23.** 16
25. −7 **27.** 29.4% **29.** 83.3%

8-2 Exercises

1. right angle **3.** straight angle
5. complementary
7. complementary **9.** 61° **11.** right
angle **13.** complementary
15. supplementary **17.** 95°
19. supplementary; 152°
21. supplementary; 46° **23a.** right
angles **b.** about 39°N, 77°W **27.** C
29. 5.6; 6; 6; 5 **31.** 38; 38; 41; 34

8-3 Exercises

1. parallel **3.** perpendicular
5. 115° **7.** skew **9.** parallel
11. 150° **13.** parallel
15. supplementary; adjacent
17. 45° **19.** sometimes **21.** always
23a. They are perpendicular.
b. transversal **c.** They are
corresponding angles. **29.** F
31. −1.75 **33.** complementary;
31° **35.** complementary; 65°

8-4 Exercises

1. $\overline{OQ}, \overline{OR}, \overline{OS}, \overline{OT}$ **3.** $\overline{RT}, \overline{RS}, \overline{ST}$,
$\overline{TQ}$ **5.** $\overline{CA}, \overline{CB}, \overline{CD}, \overline{CE}, \overline{CF}$ **7.** $\overline{GB}$,
$\overline{BF}, \overline{DE}, \overline{FE}, \overline{AE}$ **9.** 10 cm **11.** 133.2°
13. 60° **17.** C **19.** 45 **21.** 1
23. E, F, H, M, N, Z

8-5 Exercises

1. no **3.** no **5.** quadrilateral
7. square **9.** triangle **11.** no
13. pentagon **15.** heptagon
17. pentagon **21.** 16-gon **23.** A
25. $y = 3n + 1$ **27.** $y = n + 1.3$
29. 20.3 **31.** 25.9%

Exercises 8-6

1. isosceles right   **3.** isosceles acute
5. scalene right   **7.** equilateral
acute   **9.** scalene   **11.** isosceles
13. right   **15.** 8 in., isosceles
17. isosceles acute   **19.** scalene
right   **21.** isosceles triangle
23. D   **27.** H   **29.** heptagon
31. octagon

 Exercises 8-7

1. parallelogram   **3.** parallelogram,
rhombus; rhombus   **5.** not
possible   **7.** parallelogram
9. parallelogram; rhombus;
rhombus   **11.** parallelogram,
rectangle; rectangle
13.

15. parallelogram, rectangle,
rhombus, square
17. parallelogram, rhombus,
rectangle, square   **19.** true   **21.** true
23. false   **25.** 1 triangle, 1 pentagon,
and 2 trapezoids   **31.** C

33.

Stems	Leaves
1	8
2	8
3	3, 4
4	0, 3, 4, 9
5	7, 7

35. acute   **37.** obtuse

 Exercises 8-8

1. 77°   **3.** 55°   **5.** 110°   **7.** 720°
9. 360°   **11.** 37°   **13.** 88°   **15.** 101°
17. 1,080°   **19.** 38°   **21.** 99°; obtuse
23. 90°; right   **25.** 45°, 45°, 90°
29. B   **31.** $x = 5$ **33.** $t = 28$
35. parallelogram, rectangle,
rhombus, square

 Exercises 8-9

1. the triangles on the game board
and the holes on the game board
3. the bowling pins   **5.** no   **7.** 2.5
9. the triangles in the kite's design
11. no   **13.** 80°; 8 cm   **15.** the
lengths of all the sides   **17.** the
lengths of adjacent sides in each
rectangle   **19.** 40 m   **25.** G
27, 29.

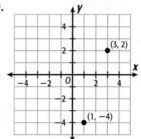

31. 25°; obtuse   **33.** 90°; right

 Exercises 8-10

1. rotation
3.

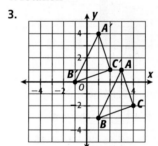

5.

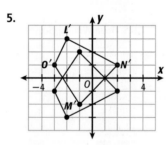

7.

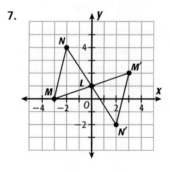

9. translation   **13.** $A'(0, -1)$,
$B'(2, -2)$, $C'(3, 0)$, $D'(1, 1)$ **17.** A
19. 38   **21.** 3 m

 Exercises 8-11

1. The figure has 5 lines of
symmetry.   **3.** The figure has 4 lines
of symmetry.   **5.** none   **7.** 6 times
9. 3 times   **11.** The figure has 6
lines of symmetry.   **13.** none
15. The flag has 2 lines of
symmetry.   **17.** 8 times   **19.** regular
nonagon   **21.** yes; yes   **27.** 8
29. $J'(3, -1)$, $K'(3, 3)$, $L'(3, -6)$

Extension

1. no
3.

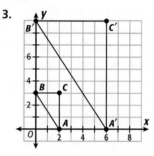

5.

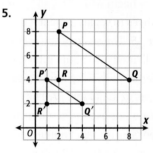

Chapter 8 Study Guide: Review

1. acute or isosceles   2. parallel lines   3. chord   4. D, E, F   5. $\overline{DF}$
6. plane DEF   7. $\overrightarrow{ED}, \overrightarrow{FD}, \overrightarrow{DF}$
8. $\overline{DE}, \overline{DF}, \overline{EF}$ 9. acute
10. straight   11. skew   12. parallel
13. $\overline{HF}, \overline{FI}, \overline{FG}$ 14. $\overline{GI}$
15. $\overline{HI}, \overline{GI}, \overline{GJ}, \overline{JI}$ 16. Yes; it is a square since all sides are congruent and all angles are congruent.
17. No; all sides are not congruent.
18. equilateral acute   19. scalene right   20. parallelogram, rhombus
21. parallelogram, rectangle
22. 53°   23. 101°   24. 133°
25.

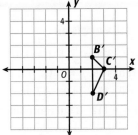

26. 1 vertical line through the center of the flag

Chapter 9

9-1 Exercises

1. 4 ft   3. $5\frac{1}{4}$ in.   5. 1   7. 12   9. 7
11. 25   13. 11 in.   15. 14.2 km
17. 2.8 m   19. 1   21. 6   23. 3
25. 15.1   27. 1   29. 18.0   31. 1,800
33. 2.3   35. 300   37. foot
39. milliliter   41. 180,000   43. 280
45. 21.8   49. 2,400 mg
53. G   55. negative correlation
57. Yes   59. Yes

9-2 Exercises

1. 18 m   3. 32 ft   5. 20 m   7. 37.7 m
9. 132 in.   11. 48 cm   13. 44 m
15. 8 ft   17. 110 cm   19. 32.0 in.
21. 2.8 m; 5.7 m   23. 5.3 in.; 33.3 in.
25. 16 strands   27. 96 ft   31. D
33. 90   35. 9.1   37. 140

9-3 Exercises

1. 33.6 ft²   3. 147.6 cm²   5. 48 in²
7. 28.6 m²   9. 84 ft²   11. 107.52 in²
13. 6 m²   15. 31.98 cm²   17. 72 yd²
19. 14 units²   21a. 713 in²
b. 108 in.   c. 1,073 in²   23. C
29. obtuse   31. right   33. 20 m
35. $12\frac{7}{20}$ ft

9-4 Exercises

1. 28 units²   3. 39.2 units²   5. 64 m²
7. 50,830 mi²   9. 7.5 units²
11. 330 yd²   13. 22.5 cm²
15. 4.5 cm   17. 22 in.
19. 15 units²   21. 12 units²
23. 1,282 mi; 100,740 mi²   27. A
29. 90°   31. 49°   33. 270 ft²

9-5 Exercises

1. 78.5 in²   3. 314 yd²   5. 154 in²
7. 28.3 in²   9. 32.2 yd²   11. 616 cm²
13. 17,662.5 mi²   15. 28.3 cm²
17. 56.5 in.; 254.3 in²   19. 40.2 cm; 128.6 cm²   21. $r = 1$ ft
23a. 113 mi²   b. 141 mi²   29. A
31. 135°   33. 45°   35. 14 units²

9-6 Exercises

1. 28 ft²   3. 224 ft²   5. 38 ft²
7. 25 ft²   9. 84.56 m²   11. 46 cm²
13. 30 ft²; 30 ft   15. 255.25 m²; 65.7 m   17. 10   21. B   23. 57°
25. 30°   27. 706.5 m²   29. 254.3 in²

9-7 Exercises

1. 16   3. 81   5. 20   7. 12   9. 4
11. 9   13. 11 mi   15. 256   17. 121
19. 4   21. 21   23. 6   25. 10   27. 2
29. 12   31. 17   33. 26   35. 6.6
37. 9.3   39. 19.5   41. 14.2
45. 87.92 yd   47. 1 in.   49. $\sqrt{25}$, $5\frac{2}{3}$, 7.15, $\frac{29}{4}$, 3^2 51. 151 km   57. F
47. equilateral   61. 69.1 in; 379.9 in²   63. 18.8 ft; 28.3 ft²

9-8 Exercises

1. 20 m   3. 24 cm   5. 30 yd
7. 16 in.   9. 9.4 ft   11. 24.5 m
13. 22.5 in.   15. yes   17. 19,153 m²

19. 269.1 cubits   21. 68.8 m   23. 9.8
25. 90°   27. 60°   29. 8   31. 5

Extension

1. irrational   3. rational
5. rational   7. rational
9. irrational   11. rational
13.

$$-\frac{7}{10} \quad \frac{1}{3} \quad 0.5 \quad \sqrt{3} \quad 2.6$$
$$-2 \ -1 \ \ 0 \ \ 1 \ \ 2 \ \ 3 \ \ 4$$

15.

$$-1.3 -\frac{2}{5} \quad \sqrt{4} \quad 3.1\sqrt{15}$$
$$-2 \ -1 \ \ 0 \ \ 1 \ \ 2 \ \ 3 \ \ 4$$

17. 5 and 6   19. 3 and 4
21. 9 and 10   23. 8 and 9

Chapter 9 Study Guide: Review

1. hypotenuse   2. circumference
3. precision   4. square root   5. 3 significant digits   6. 5 significant digits   7. 1 significant digit   8. 2 significant digits   9. 4 significant digits   10. 4 significant digits
11. 83 m   12. 81.4 cm   13. 40.8 ft
14. 49.0 in.   15. 50.74 cm²
16. 826.2 yd²   17. 72 in²
18. 266 in²   19. 108.75 cm²
20. 50 yd²   21. 2,163 in²
22. 36.3 m²   23. 226.9 ft²
24. 254.34 in²   25. 34.31 ft²
26. 21 m²   27. 5   28. 10   29. 10
30. 12   31. 16 ft   32. 34 cm
33. 60 ft   34. 2 m   35. 60 mm

Chapter 10

10-1 Exercises

1. pentagon; triangles; pentagonal pyramid   3. triangles; rectangles; triangular prism   5. polyhedron; hexagonal pyramid   7. triangle; triangles; triangular pyramid
9. hexagon; triangles; hexagonal pyramid   11. not polyhedron; cylinder   13. square prism
15. triangular pyramid
19. rectangular pyramid
21. cylinder   23. A   25. 1   27. 2
29. 100 oz for $6.99 is better

1. 24 cubes; 24 cubic units
3. 80 cubes; 80 cubic units
5. 500 mm^3 **7.** 75.4 cm^3
9. 36 cubes; 36 cubic units
11. 192 ft^3 **13.** 13.44 in^3
15. 288 m^3 **17.** 47.25 ft^3 **21.** B
23. $270 **25.** line graph

10-3 **Exercises**

1. 10 ft^3 **3.** 32 m^3 **5.** 16.7 in^3
7. 176 in^3 **9.** 1,350 mm^3
11. 2,375.3 cm^3 **13.** 46.7 ft^3
15. 16 in^3 **17a.** 3 **b.** 167.5 in^3
c. 502.4 in^3 **d.** yes
25. parallelogram **27.** 110 ft^3

10-4 **Exercises**

1. 286 ft^2 **3.** 244.9 cm^2 **5.** about
24.2% **7.** 1,160 ft^2 **9.** 188.4 cm^2
11b. 158.0 cm^2 **c.** 85.4 cm^2
17. 628 **19.** 79° **21.** 224 in^3

10-5 **Exercises**

1. 93.6 cm^2 **3.** 33,750 in^3
5. 223.84 in^2 **7.** 8.2 cm^3
9. 58,750 ft^2; 937,500 ft^3
13. 5,112 in^2; 22,680 in^3
15. 716 cm; 7.16 m
17. 127,426,000,000 cm^3;
127,426 m^3 **19.** 2 **21.** no **23.** no

Extension

1. D **5.** cylinder

Chapter 10 Study Guide: Review

1. cylinder **2.** surface area
3. polyhedron **4.** cone **5.** cylinder
6. rectangular pyramid
7. triangular prism **8.** cone
9. 364 cm^3 **10.** 24 mm^3
11. 415.4 mm^3 **12.** 111.9 ft^3
13. 60 in^3 **14.** 471 cm^3 **15.** 250m^2
16. 34 cm^2 **17.** 262.3 cm^2
18. 2,970 in^2 **19.** 4.1 ft^3

Chapter 11

11-1 **Exercises**

1. unlikely **3.** $\frac{5}{6}$ **5.** certain
7. unlikely **9.** $\frac{2}{5}$ **11.** as likely as not
13. certain **15.** not likely
17a. It is very likely. **b.** It is
impossible. **23.** It is likely that a
test will be given over this chapter.
25. 11.4 **27.** 3 **29.** 152

11-2 **Exercises**

1. 70% **3.** 43% **5a.** $\frac{9}{14}$ **5b.** $\frac{5}{14}$
7. $\frac{16}{25}$ **9.** 27% **11a.** $\frac{3}{8}$ **13.** D
15. 15 days **17.** = **19.** >

11-3 **Exercises**

1. H1, H2, T1, T2; 4 **3.** 24 **5.** 1H,
1T, 2H, 2T, 3H, 3T, 4H, 4T; 8
7. 12 **9.** 6 **11a.** 9 outcomes
b. 6 outcomes **c.** 12 outcomes
13. 12 **17.** D **19.** 12.5% **21.** 40%
23. 704 in^3

11-4 **Exercises**

1. 17% **3.** $\frac{3}{7}$ **5.** $\frac{2}{7}$ **7.** 25% **9.** $\frac{3}{7}$
11. $\frac{1}{18}$ **13.** $\frac{1}{12}$ **15.** $\frac{1}{9}$ **17.** $\frac{5}{18}$ **19.** $\frac{1}{5}$
21. $\frac{2}{5}$ **23.** 0 **25.** $\frac{2}{5}$ **27.** 37%
29. 25% **33.** D **35.** 57.5 in^2

11-5 **Exercises**

1. independent **3.** $\frac{1}{6}$ **5.** $\frac{3}{20}$
7. independent **9.** $\frac{1}{4}$
11. dependent **13.** $\frac{12}{145}$ **17.** B
19. $7\frac{1}{4}$ **21.** 49.3 ft; 193.5 ft^2
22. 44 cm; 153.9 cm^2

11-6 **Exercises**

1. 6 **3.** 10 **5.** 10 **7.** 15 **9.** 28
11. 3 **13.** 15 **17.** 15 **19.** 6 **21.** 7
23. independent

11-7 **Exercises**

1. 24 **3.** 720 **5.** 6 **7.** 3,628,000
9. combinations **11.** permutations
13. $\frac{1}{4}$ **15.** 120 **17.** 5 × 4 × 3 = 60
19. 13! **21.** $\frac{2}{7}$ **25.** D **27.** 18.4 in.

Chapter 11 Study Guide: Review

1. independent events
2. combination **3.** sample space
4. outcome **5.** unlikely
6. impossible **7.** 80% **8.** $\frac{4}{5}$ **9.** $\frac{2}{3}$
10. $\frac{1}{3}$ **11.** R1, R2, R3, R4, W1, W2,
W3, W4, B1, B2, B3, B4 **12.** 12
possible outcomes **13.** 43%
14. 12.5% **15.** 38% **16.** $\frac{4}{195}$
17. $\frac{16}{121}$ **18.** 10 ways **19.** 21
committees **20.** 36 combinations
21. 3,628,800 ways **22.** 720 ways
23. 120 ways

Chapter 12

12-1 **Exercises**

1. $n = 7$ **3.** $x = \frac{1}{3}$ **5.** $y = 136$
7. 12 refills **9.** $p = -12$ **11.** $d = \frac{1}{7}$
13. $y = 5$ **15.** $k = 85$ **17.** $m = -80$
19. $m = -112$ **21.** 6 more than a
number divided by 3 equals 18;
$m = 36$. **23.** 2 equals 4 less than a
number divided by 5; $n = 30$.
25. $x = 2$ **27.** $g = 20$ **29.** $w = -9$
31. $p = 2$ **33.** 120 min **35.** 1,300
calories **37.** 2 slices of pizza for
lunch and again for dinner
39. C **41.** rectangular prism
43. 549.5 cm^3

12-2 **Exercises**

1. $n = 5$ **3.** $p = 2$ **5.** $q = 2$
7. 12 books **9.** $x = \frac{7}{8}$ **11.** $n = 6$
13. $x = -2$ **15.** $n = -2$
17. $n = 1.5$ **19.** $t = -9$ **21.** $x = 66$
23. $w = 8$ **25.** $a = 176$ **27.** $b = -7$
29. $x = 3$ **31.** $6.70 **33.** $25 **35.** 91
39. A **41.** 37.7 cm^3 **43.** $x = 1$
45. $z = -28$

12-3 **Exercises**

1. $n = 32$ **3.** $12w = 32$ **5.** $a = 2$
7. 5 movies **9.** $-8 = 12p$
11. $-6 = 2c$ **13.** $6 = \frac{1}{10}a$
15. $b = -8$ **17.** $a = -0.8$
19. $c = -2$ **21.** $y = -7$ **23.** $r = 4$

25. $r = -2$ **27.** 67 members
29. $x = 6$ **31.** 20 days
37. $0.03m = 2 + 0.01m$; $m = 100$;
100 minutes makes the cost for
long distance from both plans
equal. **39.** 28.4 ft **41.** $y = 2$

12-4 Exercises

1. number of people ≤ 18
3. water level > 45

5.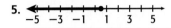
(number line from −5 to 5)

7. (number line from −6 to 4)

9. (number line from −4 to 6)

11. temperature < 40
13. number of tables ≤ 35

15. (number line from −1 to 7)

17. (number line from −5 to 1)

19. (number line from −8 to −2)

21. (number line from −1 to 7)

23. (number line from −4 to 2)

25. (number line from −3 to 3)

27. (number line from −9 to −3)

29. (number line from −4 to 3)

31. (number line from −10 to −2)

33. $-2 < c < 3$ **35.** $-3 < x < 1$
37. $-200 \leq$ depth ≤ 0 **39.** $0 \geq$
Manshu depth measurement $\geq$
$-32{,}190$ ft; $0 \geq$ *Challenger* depth
measurement $\geq -35{,}640$ ft; $0 \geq$
Horizon depth measurement $\geq$
$-34{,}884$ ft; $0 \geq$ *Vityaz* depth
measurement $\geq -36{,}200$ ft **41.** B
43. 59 m/h **45.** $y = 5$

12-5 Exercises

1. $x < 27$ **3.** $p \leq 7$ **5.** $b \leq -24$
7. no more than 42°F **9.** $m < 11$
11. $c \leq 11$ **13.** $x \geq 80$ **15.** $z > -12$

17. $f > -6$ **19.** $n \geq -4$ **21.** at most
24 birds **23.** $a > 0.3$ **25.** $m \leq -38$
27. $g < 6\frac{1}{3}$ **29.** $w \leq 15.7$
31. $t \geq -242$ **33.** $v \leq -0.6$
35. at least $8 **39.** up to 50,000
hertz **43.** B **45.** 144 in^2
47. 1,600 in^2

12-6 Exercises

1. $w < -32$ **3.** $p < 48$ **5.** $y > -\frac{11}{8}$
or $-1\frac{3}{8}$ **7.** at least 27 candles
9. $m > 52$ **11.** $c \geq -120$
13. $x \geq -1.1$ **15.** $z < \frac{3}{5}$
17. $f < -3$ **19.** $n \leq -10$
21. at least 46 wreaths **23.** $p > 4$
25. $y \geq 18$ **27.** $g > 0.63$ **29.** $w \leq \frac{3}{8}$
31. $t < \frac{5}{2}$ **33.** $v \geq -2.5$ **35.** 5 hours
37. at least 480 subscriptions
43. 301 **45.** $x < 1$ **47.** $z \geq 5$

12-7 Exercises

1. $x < 3$ **3.** $y \geq 6$ **5.** $p \leq -5$
7. more than $26 each **9.** $b < 12$
11. $c \geq -3$ **13.** $x \leq -27$ **15.** $j \leq 2$
17. at most 6 bagels **19.** $x \geq -6$
21. $c < 1.8$ **23.** $w \leq 8$ **25.** $s > -24$
27. $d \leq 4$ **29.** $14 **31.** at least 225
students **33.** at most 60% **37.** B
39. 12 **41.** $x > 5$ **43.** $x \leq 15$

Extension

1. $h = \frac{A}{b}$ **3.** $d = \frac{C}{\pi}$ **5.** $B = \frac{V}{h}$
7. $y = \frac{k}{x}$ **9.** $F = \frac{W}{d}$ **11.** $r = \frac{C}{2\pi}$
13. $h = \frac{3V}{B}$ **15.** $t = \frac{E}{P}$ **17.** $a = \frac{F}{m}$
19. $V = rI$ **21.** $\ell = \frac{(P - 2w)}{2}$
23. 0.001 kg **25.** 75 g

Chapter 12 Study Guide: Review

1. inequality **2.** compound
inequality **3.** solution set
4. $y = 8$ **5.** $z = 30$ **6.** $w = 147$
7. $a = -7$ **8.** $j = 9$ **9.** $b = 4$
10. $y = 5$ **11.** 26 mi **12.** $b = \frac{1}{2}$
13. $c = 6$ **14.** $m = \frac{8}{3}$ or $2\frac{2}{3}$
15. $x = 20$ **16.** weight limit $\leq$
9 tons **17.** age > 200

18. (number line from −1 to 5)

19. (number line from −3 to 1)

20. $r > 25$ **21.** $x \leq -26$ **22.** $g < 8$
23. $t \leq \frac{1}{6}$ **24.** $9 > r$ **25.** $u \geq -66$
26. at least 38 points **27.** at most
$94 **28.** $n < -55.2$ **29.** $p \leq 6$
30. $k < -130$ **31.** $p < 5$
32. $v \geq 2.76$ **33.** $c > 33$
34. at least 16 purses **35.** $b < -2$
36. $d < -6$ **37.** $n \geq -4$ **38.** $y \leq$
18 **39.** $c > -54$ **40.** $x \leq 10$
41. $h \geq -156$ **42.** $-10 < t$
43. $52 > w$ **44.** $y \leq 35$ **45.** at most
4 T-shirts **46.** more than $147

Glossary/Glosario

A

ENGLISH	SPANISH	EXAMPLES
absolute value The distance of a number from zero on a number line; shown by ||. (p. 77)	**valor absoluto** Distancia a la que está un número de 0 en una recta numérica. El símbolo del valor absoluto es ||.	$\|5\| = 5$ $\|-5\| = 5$
accuracy The closeness of a given measurement or value to the actual measurement or value. (p. 518)	**exactitud** Cercanía de una medida o un valor a la medida o el valor real.	
acute angle An angle that measures less than 90°. (p. 448)	**ángulo agudo** Ángulo que mide menos de 90°.	
acute triangle A triangle with all angles measuring less than 90°. (p. 470)	**triángulo acutángulo** Triángulo en el que todos los ángulos miden menos de 90°.	
addend A number added to one or more other numbers to form a sum.	**sumando** Número que se suma a uno o más números para formar una suma.	In the expression 4 + 6 + 7, the numbers 4, 6, and 7 are addends.
Addition Property of Equality The property that states that if you add the same number to both sides of an equation, the new equation will have the same solution. (p. 52)	**Propiedad de igualdad de la suma** Propiedad que establece que puedes sumar el mismo número a ambos lados de una ecuación y la nueva ecuación tendrá la misma solución.	$x - 6 = \quad 8$ $\underline{+6 \quad +6}$ $x \quad = \quad 14$
Addition Property of Opposites The property that states that the sum of a number and its opposite equals zero.	**Propiedad de la suma de los opuestos** Propiedad que establece que la suma de un número y su opuesto es cero.	$12 + (-12) = 0$
additive inverse The opposite of a number.	**inverso aditivo** El opuesto de un número.	The additive inverse of 5 is −5.
adjacent angles Two angles in the same plane that have a common vertex and a common side, but no common interior points. (p. 453)	**ángulos adyacentes** Dos ángulos en el mismo plano que comparten un vértice y un lado común pero no comparten puntos internos.	 ∠1 and ∠2 are adjacent angles.
algebraic expression An expression that contains at least one variable. (p. 34)	**expresión algebraica** Expresión que contiene al menos una variable.	$x + 8$ $4(m - b)$

ENGLISH	SPANISH	EXAMPLES
algebraic inequality An inequality that contains at least one variable. (p. 692)	**desigualdad algebraica** Desigualdad que contiene al menos una variable.	$x + 3 > 10$ $5a > b + 3$
angle A figure formed by two rays with a common endpoint called the vertex. (p. 448)	**ángulo** Figura formada por dos rayos con un extremo común llamado vértice.	
arc A part of a circle named by its endpoints. (p. 460)	**arco** Parte de un círculo que se nombra por sus extremos.	
area The number of square units needed to cover a given surface. (p. 530)	**área** El número de unidades cuadradas que se necesitan para cubrir una superficie dada.	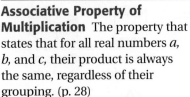The area is 10 square units.
arithmetic sequence A sequence in which the terms change by the same amount each time. (p. 242)	**sucesión aritmética** Una sucesión en la que los términos cambian la misma cantidad cada vez.	The sequence 2, 5, 8, 11, 14 … is an arithmetic sequence.
Associative Property of Addition The property that states that for all real numbers *a, b,* and *c,* the sum is always the same, regardless of their grouping. (p. 28)	**Propiedad asociativa de la suma** Propiedad que establece que para todos los números reales *a, b* y *c,* la suma siempre es la misma sin importar cómo se agrupen.	$2 + 3 + 8 = (2 + 3) + 8 =$ $2 + (3 + 8)$
Associative Property of Multiplication The property that states that for all real numbers *a, b,* and *c,* their product is always the same, regardless of their grouping. (p. 28)	**Propiedad asociativa de la multiplicación** Propiedad que establece que, para todos los números reales *a, b* y *c,* el producto siempre es el mismo sin importar cómo se agrupen.	$2 \cdot 3 \cdot 8 = (2 \cdot 3) \cdot 8 = 2 \cdot (3 \cdot 8)$
asymmetry Not identical on either side of a central line; not symmetrical. (p. 494)	**asimetría** Ocurre cuando dos lados separados por una línea central no son idénticos; falta de simetría.	The quadrilateral has asymmetry.
axes The two perpendicular lines of a coordinate plane that intersect at the origin. (p. 224)	**ejes** Las dos rectas numéricas perpendiculares del plano cartesiano que se intersecan en el origen.	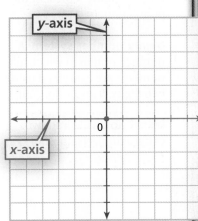

bar graph A graph that uses vertical or horizontal bars to display data. (p. 386)

gráfica de barras Gráfica en la que se usan barras verticales u horizontales para presentar datos.

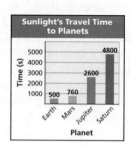

base-10 number system A number system in which all numbers are expressed using the digits 0–9. (p. 15)

sistema de base 10 Sistema de numeración en el que todos los números se expresan con los dígitos 0–9.

base (in numeration) When a number is raised to a power, the number that is used as a factor is the base. (p. 10)

base (en numeración) Cuando un número es elevado a una potencia, el número que se usa como factor es la base.

$3^5 = 3 \cdot 3 \cdot 3 \cdot 3 \cdot 3$; 3 is the base.

base (of a polygon) A side of a polygon.

base (de un polígono) Lado de un polígono.

base (of a three-dimensional figure) A face of a three-dimensional figure by which the figure is measured or classified. (p. 580)

base (de una figura tridimensional) Cara de una figura tridimensional a partir de la cual se mide o se clasifica la figura.

Bases of a cylinder   Bases of a prism

Base of a cone   Base of a pyramid

biased sample A sample that does not fairly represent the population. (p. 413)

muestra no representativa Muestra que no representa adecuadamente la población.

binary number system A number system in which all numbers are expressed using only two digits, 0 and 1. (p. 769)

sistema de números binarios Sistema de numeración en el que todos los números se expresan por medio de dos dígitos, 0 y 1.

bisect To divide into two congruent parts. (p. 456)

trazar una bisectriz Dividir en dos partes congruentes.

$\overrightarrow{JK}$ bisects $\angle LJM$.

ENGLISH	SPANISH	EXAMPLES

box-and-whisker plot A graph that displays the highest and lowest quarters of data as whiskers, the middle two quarters of the data as a box, and the median. (p. 394)

gráfica de mediana y rango Gráfica que muestra los valores máximo y mínimo, los cuartiles superior e inferior, así como la mediana de los datos.

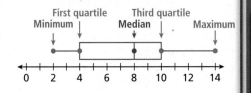

break (graph) A zigzag on a horizontal or vertical scale of a graph that indicates that some of the numbers on the scale have been omitted. (p. 422)

discontinuidad (gráfica) Zig-zag en la escala horizontal o vertical de una gráfica que indica la omisión de algunos de los números de la escala.

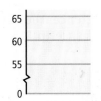

capacity The amount a container can hold when filled.

capacidad Cantidad que cabe en un recipiente cuando se llena.

A large milk container has a capacity of 1 gallon.

Celsius A metric scale for measuring temperature in which 0°C is the freezing point of water and 100°C is the boiling point of water; also called *centigrade*.

Celsius Escala métrica para medir la temperatura, en la que 0° C es el punto de congelación del agua y 100° C es el punto de ebullición. También se llama *centígrado*.

center (of a circle) The point inside a circle that is the same distance from all the points on the circle. (p. 460)

centro (de un círculo) Punto interior de un círculo que se encuentra a la misma distancia de todos los puntos de la circunferencia.

center (of rotation) The point about which a figure is rotated. (p. 495)

centro (de una rotación) Punto alrededor del cual se hace girar una figura.

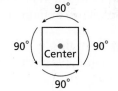

central angle of a circle An angle with its vertex at the center of a circle. (p. 461)

ángulo central de un círculo Ángulo cuyo vértice se encuentra en el centro de un círculo.

certain (probability) Sure to happen; having a probability of 1. (p. 628)

seguro (probabilidad) Que con seguridad sucederá. Representa una probabilidad de 1.

chord A line segment with endpoints on a circle. (p. 460)

cuerda Segmento de recta cuyos extremos forman parte de un círculo.

circle The set of all points in a plane that are the same distance from a given point called the center. (p. 460)

círculo Conjunto de todos los puntos en un plano que se encuentran a la misma distancia de un punto dado llamado centro.

ENGLISH	SPANISH	EXAMPLES
circle graph A graph that uses sectors of a circle to compare parts to the whole and parts to other parts. (p. 390)	**gráfica circular** Gráfica que usa secciones de un círculo para comparar partes con el todo y con otras partes.	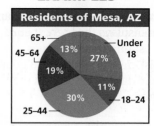
circumference The distance around a circle. (p. 525)	**circunferencia** Distancia alrededor de un círculo.	 Circumference
clockwise A circular movement to the right in the direction shown.	**en el sentido de las manecillas del reloj** Movimiento circular en la dirección que se indica.	
coefficient The number that is multiplied by the variable in an algebraic expression. (p. 42)	**coeficiente** Número que se multiplica por la variable en una expresión algebraica.	5 is the coefficient in 5*b*.
combination An arrangement of items or events in which order does not matter. (p. 652)	**combinación** Agrupación de objetos o sucesos en la cual el orden no es importante.	For objects *A, B, C,* and *D,* there are 6 different combinations of 2 objects: *AB, AC, AD, BC, BD, CD.*
common denominator A denominator that is the same in two or more fractions.	**común denominador** Denominador que es común a dos o más fracciones.	The common denominator of $\frac{5}{8}$ and $\frac{2}{8}$ is 8.
common factor A number that is a factor of two or more numbers.	**factor común** Número que es factor de dos o más números.	8 is a common factor of 16 and 40.
common multiple A number that is a multiple of each of two or more numbers.	**común múltiplo** Número que es múltiplo de dos o más números.	15 is a common multiple of 3 and 5.
Commutative Property of Addition The property that states that two or more numbers can be added in any order without changing the sum. (p. 28)	**Propiedad conmutativa de la suma** Propiedad que establece que sumar dos o más números en cualquier orden no altera la suma.	$8 + 20 = 20 + 8$
Commutative Property of Multiplication The property that states that two or more numbers can be multiplied in any order without changing the product. (p. 28)	**Propiedad conmutativa de la multiplicación** Propiedad que establece que multiplicar dos o más números en cualquier orden no altera el producto.	$6 \cdot 12 = 12 \cdot 6$
compatible numbers Numbers that are close to the given numbers that make estimation or mental calculation easier. (p. 150)	**números compatibles** Números que están cerca de los números dados y hacen más fácil la estimación o el cálculo mental.	To estimate $7{,}957 + 5{,}009$, use the compatible numbers 8,000 and 5,000: $8{,}000 + 5{,}000 = 13{,}000$.

ENGLISH	SPANISH	EXAMPLES
complement All the ways that an event can not happen. (p. 629)	**complemento** Todas las maneras en que no puede ocurrir un suceso.	When rolling a number cube, the complement of rolling a 3 is rolling a 1, 2, 4, 5, or 6.
complementary angles Two angles whose measures add to 90°. (p. 448)	**ángulos complementarios** Dos ángulos cuyas medidas suman 90°.	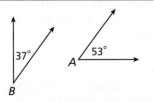
composite number A number greater than 1 that has more than two whole-number factors. (p. 106)	**número compuesto** Número mayor que 1 que tiene más de dos factores que son números cabales.	4, 6, 8, and 9 are composite numbers.
compound event An event made up of two or more simple events.	**suceso compuesto** Suceso que consta de dos o más sucesos simples.	Rolling a 3 on a number cube and spinning a 2 on a spinner is a compound event.
compound inequality A combination of more than one inequality. (p. 693)	**desigualdad compuesta** Combinación de dos o más desigualdades.	$-2 \leq x < 10$
cone A three-dimensional figure with one vertex and one circular base. (p. 581)	**cono** Figura tridimensional con un vértice y una base circular.	
congruent Having the same size and shape. (p. 443)	**congruentes** Que tienen la misma forma y el mismo tamaño.	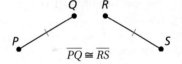 $\overline{PQ} \cong \overline{RS}$
congruent angles Angles that have the same measure. (p. 453)	**ángulos congruentes** Ángulos que tienen la misma medida.	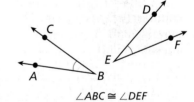 $\angle ABC \cong \angle DEF$
constant A value that does not change. (p. 34)	**constante** Valor que no cambia.	3, 0, π
convenience sample A sample based on members of the population that are readily available. (p. 412)	**muestra de conveniencia** Una muestra basada en miembros de la población que están fácilmente disponibles.	
coordinate One of the numbers of an ordered pair that locate a point on a coordinate graph. (p. 224)	**coordenada** Uno de los números de un par ordenado que ubica un punto en una gráfica de coordenadas.	

coordinate plane (coordinate grid) A plane formed by the intersection of a horizontal number line called the *x*-axis and a vertical number line called the *y*-axis. (p. 224)

plano cartesiano (cuadrícula de coordenadas) Plano formado por la intersección de una recta numérica horizontal llamada eje *x* y otra vertical llamada eje *y*.

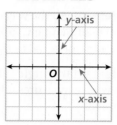

---

correlation The description of the relationship between two data sets. (p. 417)

correlación Descripción de la relación entre dos conjuntos de datos.

---

corresponding angles (for lines) A pair of angles formed by a transversal and two lines. (p. 453)

ángulos correspondientes (en líneas) Par de ángulos formados por una transversal y dos líneas.

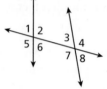

∠1 and ∠3 are corresponding angles.

---

corresponding angles (in polygons) Matching angles of two or more polygons. (p. 300)

ángulos correspondientes (en polígonos) Ángulos que se ubican en la misma posición relativa en dos o más polígonos.

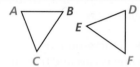

∠*A* and ∠*D* are corresponding angles.

---

corresponding sides Matching sides of two or more polygons. (p. 300)

lados correspondientes Lados que se ubican en la misma posición relativa en dos o más polígonos.

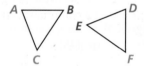

$\overline{AB}$ and $\overline{DE}$ are corresponding sides.

---

counterclockwise A circular movement to the left in the direction shown.

en sentido contrario a las manecillas del reloj Movimiento circular en la dirección que se indica.

---

counterexample An example that shows that a statement is false. (p. 774)

contraejemplo Ejemplo que demuestra que un enunciado es falso.

---

cross product The product of numbers on the diagonal when comparing two ratios. (p. 287)

producto cruzado El producto de los números multiplicados en diagonal cuando se comparan dos razones.

For the proportion $\frac{2}{3} = \frac{4}{6}$, the cross products are $2 \cdot 6 = 12$ and $3 \cdot 4 = 12$.

---

cube (geometric figure) A rectangular prism with six congruent square faces.

cubo (figura geométrica) Prisma rectangular con seis caras cuadradas congruentes.

---

cube (in numeration) A number raised to the third power.

cubo (en numeración) Número elevado a la tercera potencia.

$5^3 = 5 \cdot 5 \cdot 5 = 125$

ENGLISH	SPANISH	EXAMPLES
cumulative frequency The frequency of all data values that are less than or equal to a given value. (p. 376)	**frecuencia acumulativa** La frecuencia de todos los datos que son menores que o iguales a un valor dado.	
customary system of measurement The measurement system often used in the United States. (p. 292)	**sistema usual de medidas** El sistema de medidas que se usa comúnmente en Estados Unidos.	inches, feet, miles, ounces, pounds, tons, cups, quarts, gallons
cylinder A three-dimensional figure with two parallel, congruent circular bases connected by a curved lateral surface. (p. 581)	**cilindro** Figura tridimensional con dos bases circulares paralelas y congruentes, unidas por una superficie lateral curva.	

decagon A polygon with ten sides. (p. 467)	**decágono** Polígono de 10 lados.	
decimal system A base-10 place value system.	**sistema decimal** Sistema de valor posicional de base 10.	
deductive reasoning Using logic to show that a statement is true. (p. 773)	**razonamiento deductivo** Uso de la lógica para demostrar que un enunciado es verdadero.	
degree The unit of measure for angles or temperature. (p. 448)	**grado** Unidad de medida para ángulos y temperaturas.	
denominator The bottom number of a fraction that tells how many equal parts are in the whole.	**denominador** Número de abajo de una fracción que indica en cuántas partes iguales se divide el entero.	$\frac{3}{4}$ ← denominator
dependent events Events for which the outcome of one event affects the probability of the second event. (p. 648)	**sucesos dependientes** Dos sucesos son dependientes si el resultado de uno afecta la probabilidad del otro.	A bag contains 3 red marbles and 2 blue marbles. Drawing a red marble and then drawing a blue marble without replacing the first marble is an example of dependent events.
diameter A line segment that passes through the center of a circle and has endpoints on the circle, or the length of that segment. (p. 460)	**diámetro** Segmento de recta que pasa por el centro de un círculo y tiene sus extremos en la circunferencia, o bien la longitud de ese segmento.	
difference The result when one number is subtracted from another.	**diferencia** El resultado de restar un número de otro.	In $16 - 5 = 11$, 11 is the difference.
dimension The length, width, or height of a figure.	**dimensión** Longitud, ancho o altura de una figura.	

Glossary/Glosario

ENGLISH	SPANISH	EXAMPLES
Distributive Property The property that states if you multiply a sum by a number, you will get the same result if you multiply each addend by that number and then add the products. (p. 29)	**Propiedad distributiva** Propiedad que establece que, si multiplicas una suma por un número, obtendrás el mismo resultado que si multiplicas cada sumando por ese número y luego sumas los productos.	$5(20 + 1) = 5 \cdot 20 + 5 \cdot 1$
dividend The number to be divided in a division problem.	**dividendo** Número que se divide en un problema de división.	In $8 \div 4 = 2$, 8 is the dividend.
divisible Can be divided by a number without leaving a remainder. (p. 767)	**divisible** Que se puede dividir entre un número sin dejar residuo.	18 is divisible by 3.
Division Property of Equality The property that states that if you divide both sides of an equation by the same nonzero number, the new equation will have the same solution. (p. 56)	**Propiedad de igualdad de la división** Propiedad que establece que puedes dividir ambos lados de una ecuación entre el mismo número distinto de cero, y la nueva ecuación tendrá la misma solución.	$4x = 12$ $\frac{4x}{4} = \frac{12}{4}$ $x = 3$
divisor The number you are dividing by in a division problem.	**divisor** El número entre el que se divide en un problema de división.	In $8 \div 4 = 2$, 4 is the divisor.
double-bar graph A bar graph that compares two related sets of data. (p. 386)	**gráfica de doble barra** Gráfica de barras que compara dos conjuntos de datos relacionados.	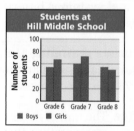
double-line graph A line graph that shows how two related sets of data change over time. (p. 403)	**gráfica de doble línea** Gráfica lineal que muestra cómo cambian con el tiempo dos conjuntos de datos relacionados.	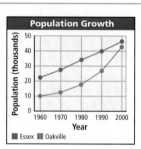

edge The line segment along which two faces of a polyhedron intersect. (p. 580)	**arista** Segmento de recta donde se intersecan dos caras de un poliedro.	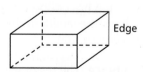
endpoint A point at the end of a line segment or ray.	**extremo** Un punto ubicado al final de un segmento de recta o rayo.	

ENGLISH	SPANISH	EXAMPLES
equally likely outcomes Outcomes that have the same probability. (p. 640)	**resultados igualmente probables** Resultados que tienen la misma probabilidad de ocurrir.	
equation A mathematical sentence that shows that two expressions are equivalent. (p. 46)	**ecuación** Enunciado matemático que indica que dos expresiones son equivalentes.	$x + 4 = 7$ $6 + 1 = 10 - 3$
equilateral triangle A triangle with three congruent sides. (p. 470)	**triángulo equilátero** Triángulo con tres lados congruentes.	
equivalent Having the same value.	**equivalentes** Que tienen el mismo valor.	
equivalent fractions Fractions that name the same amount or part. (p. 120)	**fracciones equivalentes** Fracciones que representan la misma cantidad o parte.	$\frac{1}{2}$ and $\frac{2}{4}$ are equivalent fractions.
equivalent ratios Ratios that name the same comparison. (p. 283)	**razones equivalentes** Razones que representan la misma comparación.	$\frac{1}{2}$ and $\frac{2}{4}$ are equivalent ratios.
estimate (n) An answer that is close to the exact answer and is found by rounding, or other methods.	**estimación (s)** Una solución aproximada a la respuesta exacta que se halla mediante el redondeo u otros métodos.	
estimate (v) To find an answer close to the exact answer by rounding or other methods.	**estimar (v)** Hallar una solución aproximada a la respuesta exacta mediante el redondeo u otros métodos.	
evaluate To find the value of a numerical or algebraic expression. (p. 34)	**evaluar** Hallar el valor de una expresión numérica o algebraica.	Evaluate $2x + 7$ for $x = 3$. $2x + 7$ $2(3) + 7$ $6 + 7$ 13
even number An integer that is divisible by two.	**número par** Número entero divisible entre 2.	2, 4, 6
event An outcome or set of outcomes of an experiment or situation. (p. 628)	**suceso** Un resultado o una serie de resultados de un experimento o una situación.	When rolling a number cube, the event "an odd number" consists of the outcomes 1, 3, and 5.
expanded form A number written as the sum of the values of its digits.	**forma desarrollada** Número escrito como suma de los valores de sus dígitos.	236,536 written in expanded form is 200,000 + 30,000 + 6,000 + 500 + 30 + 6.
experiment In probability, any activity based on chance, such as tossing a coin. (p. 628)	**experimento** En probabilidad, cualquier actividad basada en la posibilidad, como lanzar una moneda.	Tossing a coin 10 times and noting the number of "heads"

ENGLISH	SPANISH	EXAMPLES
experimental probability The ratio of the number of times an event occurs to the total number of trials, or times that the activity is performed. (p. 632)	**probabilidad experimental** Razón del número de veces que ocurre un suceso al número total de pruebas o al número de veces que se realiza el experimento.	Kendra attempted 27 free throws and made 16 of them. Her experimental probability of making a free throw is $\frac{\text{number made}}{\text{number attempted}} = \frac{16}{27} \approx 0.59$.
exponent The number that indicates how many times the base is used as a factor. (p. 10)	**exponente** Número que indica cuántas veces se usa la base como factor.	$2^3 = 2 \cdot 2 \cdot 2 = 8$; 3 is the exponent.
exponential form A number is in exponential form when it is written with a base and an exponent.	**forma exponencial** Se dice que un número está en forma exponencial cuando se escribe con una base y un exponente.	4^2 is the exponential form for $4 \cdot 4$.
expression A mathematical phrase that contains operations, numbers, and/or variables.	**expresión** Enunciado matemático que contiene operaciones, números y/o variables.	$6x + 1$

F

face A flat surface of a polyhedron. (p. 580)	**cara** Superficie plana de un poliedro.	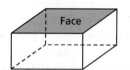
factor A number that is multiplied by another number to get a product. (p. 18)	**factor** Número que se multiplica por otro para hallar un producto.	7 is a factor of 21 since $7 \cdot 3 = 21$.
factor tree A diagram showing how a whole number breaks down into its prime factors. (p. 18)	**árbol de factores** Diagrama que muestra cómo se descompone un número cabal en sus factores primos.	$12 = 3 \cdot 2 \cdot 2$
factorial The product of all whole numbers except zero that are less than or equal to a number. (p. 657)	**factorial** El producto de todos los números cabales, excepto cero que son menores que o iguales a un número.	4 factorial $= 4! = 4 \cdot 3 \cdot 2 \cdot 1$
Fahrenheit A temperature scale in which 32°F is the freezing point of water and 212°F is the boiling point of water.	**Fahrenheit** Escala de temperatura en la que 32° F es el punto de congelación del agua y 212° F es el punto de ebullición.	
fair When all outcomes of an experiment are equally likely, the experiment is said to be fair. (p. 640)	**justo** Se dice de un experimento donde todos los resultados posibles son igualmente probables.	
first quartile The median of the lower half of a set of data; also called *lower quartile*. (p. 394)	**primer cuartil** La mediana de la mitad inferior de un conjunto de datos. También se llama *cuartil inferior*.	

ENGLISH	SPANISH	EXAMPLES
formula A rule showing relationships among quantities.	**fórmula** Regla que muestra relaciones entre cantidades.	$A = \ell w$ is the formula for the area of a rectangle.
fraction A number in the form $\frac{a}{b}$, where $b \neq 0$.	**fracción** Número escrito en la forma $\frac{a}{b}$, donde $b \neq 0$.	

frequency table A table that lists items together according to the number of times, or frequency, that the items occur. (p. 376)

tabla de frecuencia Una tabla en la que se organizan los datos de acuerdo con el número de veces que aparece cada valor (o la frecuencia).

Data set: 1, 1, 2, 2, 3, 4, 5, 5, 5, 6, 6, 6, 6

Frequency table:

Data	1	2	3	4	5	6
Frequency	2	2	1	1	3	4

function An input-output relationship that has exactly one output for each input. (p. 238)

función Relación de entrada-salida en la que a cada valor de entrada corresponde exactamente un valor de salida.

function table A table of ordered pairs that represent solutions of a function. (p. 238)

tabla de función Tabla de pares ordenados que representan soluciones de una función.

x	3	4	5	6
y	7	9	11	13

Fundamental Counting Principle If one event has m possible outcomes and a second event has n possible outcomes after the first event has occurred, then there are $m \cdot n$ total possible outcomes for the two events. (p. 637)

Principio fundamental de conteo Si un suceso tiene m resultados posibles y otro suceso tiene n resultados posibles después de ocurrido el primer suceso, entonces hay $m \cdot n$ resultados posibles en total para los dos sucesos.

There are 4 colors of shirts and 3 colors of pants. There are $4 \cdot 3 = 12$ possible outfits.

G

geometric sequence A sequence in which each term is multiplied by the same value to get the next term. (p. 242)

sucesión geométrica Una sucesión en la que cada término se multiplica por el mismo valor para obtener el siguiente término.

The sequence 2, 4, 8, 16 ... is a geometric sequence.

graph of an equation A graph of the set of ordered pairs that are solutions of the equation. (p. 248)

gráfica de una ecuación Gráfica del conjunto de pares ordenados que son soluciones de la ecuación.

greatest common factor (GCF) The largest common factor of two or more given numbers. (p. 110)

máximo común divisor (MCD) El mayor de los factores comunes compartidos por dos o más números dados.

The GCF of 27 and 45 is 9.

H

height In a pyramid or cone, the perpendicular distance from the base to the opposite vertex. (p. 590)

altura En una pirámide o cono, la distancia perpendicular desde la base al vértice opuesto.

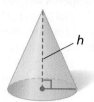

In a triangle or quadrilateral, the perpendicular distance from the base to the opposite vertex or side.

En un triángulo o cuadrilátero, la distancia perpendicular desde la base de la figura al vértice o lado opuesto.

In a prism or cylinder, the perpendicular distance between the bases.

En un prisma o cilindro, la distancia perpendicular entre las bases.

heptagon A seven-sided polygon. (p. 467)

heptágono Polígono de siete lados.

hexagon A six-sided polygon. (p. 467)

hexágono Polígono de seis lados.

histogram A bar graph that shows the frequency of data within equal intervals. (p. 387)

histograma Gráfica de barras que muestra la frecuencia de los datos en intervalos iguales.

hypotenuse In a right triangle, the side opposite the right angle. (p. 556)

hipotenusa En un triángulo rectángulo, el lado opuesto al ángulo recto.

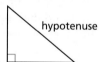

I

Identity Property of One The property that states that the product of 1 and any number is that number. (p. 28)

Propiedad de identidad del uno Propiedad que establece que el producto de 1 y cualquier número es ese número.

$3 \cdot 1 = 3$
$-9 \cdot 1 = -9$

Identity Property of Zero The property that states that the sum of zero and any number is that number. (p. 28)

Propiedad de identidad del cero Propiedad que establece que la suma de cero y cualquier número es ese número.

$5 + 0 = 5$
$-4 + 0 = -4$

image A figure resulting from a transformation. (p. 488)

imagen Figura que resulta de una transformación.

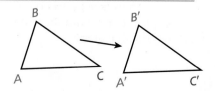

Glossary/Glosario

ENGLISH	SPANISH	EXAMPLES
impossible (probability) Can never happen; having a probability of 0. (p. 628)	**imposible (en probabilidad)** Que no puede ocurrir. Suceso cuya probabilidad de ocurrir es 0.	
improper fraction A fraction in which the numerator is greater than or equal to the denominator. (p. 121)	**fracción impropia** Fracción en la que el numerador es mayor que o igual al denominador.	$\frac{5}{5}$ $\frac{7}{4}$
independent events Events for which the outcome of one event does not affect the probability of the other. (p. 648)	**sucesos independientes** Dos sucesos son independientes si el resultado de uno no afecta la probabilidad del otro.	A bag contains 3 red marbles and 2 blue marbles. Drawing a red marble, replacing it, and then drawing a blue marble is an example of independent events.
indirect measurement The technique of using similar figures and proportions to find a measure. (p. 304)	**medición indirecta** La técnica de usar figuras semejantes y proporciones para hallar una medida.	
inductive reasoning Using a pattern to make a conclusion. (p. 773)	**razonamiento inductivo** Uso de un patrón para sacar una conclusión.	
inequality A mathematical sentence that shows the relationship between quantities that are not equivalent. (p. 692)	**desigualdad** Enunciado matemático que muestra una relación entre cantidades que no son equivalentes.	$5 < 8$ $5x + 2 \geq 12$
input The value substituted into an expression or function. (p. 238)	**valor de entrada** Valor que se usa para sustituir una variable en una expresión o función.	For the function $y = 6x$, the input 4 produces an output of 24.
integers The set of whole numbers and their opposites. (p. 76)	**enteros** Conjunto de todos los números cabales y sus opuestos.	$\ldots -3, -2, -1, 0, 1, 2, 3, \ldots$
interest The amount of money charged for borrowing or using money, or the amount of money earned by saving money. (p. 356)	**interés** Cantidad de dinero que se cobra por el préstamo o uso del dinero, o la cantidad que se gana al ahorrar dinero.	
interquartile range The difference between the upper and lower quartiles in a box-and-whisker plot. (p. 395)	**rango entre cuartiles** La diferencia entre los cuartiles superior e inferior en una gráfica de mediana y rango.	Lower half Upper half 18, (23), 28, 29, (36,) 42 ↑ ↑ Lower Upper quartile quartile Interquartile range: $36 - 23 = 13$
intersecting lines Lines that cross at exactly one point.	**líneas secantes** Líneas que se cruzan en un solo punto.	
interval The space between marked values on a number line or the scale of a graph.	**intervalo** El espacio entre los valores marcados en una recta numérica o en la escala de una gráfica.	

ENGLISH	SPANISH	EXAMPLES
inverse operations Operations that undo each other: addition and subtraction, or multiplication and division. (p. 52)	**operaciones inversas** Operaciones que se cancelan mutuamente: suma y resta, o multiplicación y división.	Addition and subtraction are inverse operations: $5 + 3 = 8$; $8 - 3 = 5$ Multiplication and division are inverse operations: $2 \cdot 3 = 6$; $6 \div 3 = 2$
irrational number A number that cannot be expressed as a ratio of two integers or as a repeating or terminating decimal. (p. 562)	**número irracional** Número que no puede expresarse como una razón de dos enteros ni como un decimal periódico o finito.	$\sqrt{2}$, π
isolate the variable To get a variable alone on one side of an equation or inequality in order to solve the equation or inequality. (p. 52)	**despejar la variable** Dejar sola la variable en un lado de una ecuación o desigualdad para resolverla.	$\begin{aligned} x + 7 &= 22 \\ -7 \quad & -7 \\ \hline x &= 15 \end{aligned}$
isosceles triangle A triangle with at least two congruent sides. (p. 470)	**triángulo isósceles** Triángulo que tiene al menos dos lados congruentes.	

least common denominator (LCD) The least common multiple of two or more denominators.	**mínimo común denominador (mcd)** El mínimo común múltiplo de dos o más denominadores.	The LCD of $\frac{3}{4}$ and $\frac{5}{6}$ is 12.
least common multiple (LCM) The least number, other than zero, that is a multiple of two or more given numbers. (p. 114)	**mínimo común múltiplo (mcm)** El menor de los números, distinto de cero, que es múltiplo de dos o más números.	The LCM of 10 and 18 is 90.
legs In a right triangle, the sides that include the right angle; in an isosceles triangle, the pair of congruent sides. (p. 556)	**catetos** En un triángulo rectángulo, los lados adyacentes al ángulo recto. En un triángulo isósceles, el par de lados congruentes.	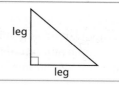
like terms Two or more terms that have the same variable raised to the same power. (p. 42)	**términos semejantes** Dos o más términos que contienen la misma variable elevada a la misma potencia.	In the expression $3a + 5b + 12a$, $3a$ and $12a$ are like terms.
line A straight path that extends without end in opposite directions. (p. 442)	**línea** Trayectoria recta que se extiende de manera indefinida en direcciones opuestas.	$\overleftrightarrow{}\ \ell$
line graph A graph that uses line segments to show how data changes. (p. 402)	**gráfica lineal** Gráfica que muestra cómo cambian los datos mediante segmentos de recta.	

ENGLISH	SPANISH	EXAMPLES
line of reflection A line that a figure is flipped across to create a mirror image of the original figure. (p. 488)	**línea de reflexión** Línea sobre la cual se invierte una figura para crear una imagen reflejada de la figura original.	 Line of reflection
line of symmetry The imaginary "mirror" in line symmetry. (p. 494)	**eje de simetría** El "espejo" imaginario en la simetría axial.	
line plot A number line with marks or dots that show frequency. (p. 377)	**diagrama de acumulación** Recta numérica con marcas o puntos que indican la frecuencia.	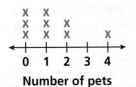 Number of pets
line segment A part of a line between two endpoints. (p. 443)	**segmento de recta** Parte de una línea con dos extremos.	
line symmetry A figure has line symmetry if one-half is a mirror-image of the other half. (p. 494)	**simetría axial** Una figura tiene simetría axial si una de sus mitades es la imagen reflejada de la otra.	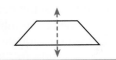
linear equation An equation whose solutions form a straight line on a coordinate plane. (p. 248)	**ecuación lineal** Ecuación cuyas soluciones forman una línea recta en un plano cartesiano.	$y = 2x + 1$
linear function A function whose graph is a straight line. (p. 248)	**función lineal** Función cuya gráfica es una línea recta.	$y = x - 1$ 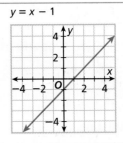
lower quartile The median of the lower half of a set of data. (p. 394)	**cuartil inferior** La mediana de la mitad inferior de un conjunto de datos.	Lower half Upper half 18, (23,) 28, 29, 36, 42 ↑ Lower quartile

 _____

mean The sum of the items in a set of data divided by the number of items in the set; also called average. (p. 381)	**media** La suma de todos los elementos de un conjunto de datos dividida entre el número de elementos del conjunto. También se llama *promedio*.	Data set: 4, 6, 7, 8, 10 Mean: $\frac{4+6+7+8+10}{5} = \frac{35}{5} = 7$
measure of central tendency A measure used to describe the middle of a data set; the mean, median, and mode are measures of central tendency. (p. 381)	**medida de tendencia dominante** Medida que describe la parte media de un conjunto de datos; la media, la mediana y la moda son medidas de tendencia dominante.	

ENGLISH	SPANISH	EXAMPLES
median The middle number, or the mean (average) of the two middle numbers, in an ordered set of data. (p. 381)	**mediana** El número intermedio, o la media (el promedio), de los dos números intermedios en un conjunto ordenado de datos.	Data set: 4, 6, 7, 8, 10 Median: 7
metric system of measurement A decimal system of weights and measures that is used universally in science and commonly throughout the world. (p. 14)	**sistema métrico de medición** Sistema decimal de pesos y medidas empleado universalmente en las ciencias y comúnmente en todo el mundo.	centimeters, meters, kilometers, grams, kilograms, milliliters, liters
midpoint The point that divides a line segment into two congruent line segments.	**punto medio** El punto que divide un segmento de recta en dos segmentos de recta congruentes.	A B C B is the midpoint of $\overline{AC}$.
mixed number A number made up of a whole number that is not zero and a fraction. (p. 121)	**número mixto** Número compuesto por un número cabal distinto de cero y una fracción.	$5\frac{1}{8}$
mode The number or numbers that occur most frequently in a set of data; when all numbers occur with the same frequency, we say there is no mode. (p. 381)	**moda** Número o números más frecuentes en un conjunto de datos; si todos los números aparecen con la misma frecuencia, no hay moda.	Data set: 3, 5, 8, 8, 10 Mode: 8
multiple The product of any number and any nonzero whole number is a multiple of that number. (p. 114)	**múltiplo** El producto de un número y cualquier número cabal distinto de cero es un múltiplo de ese número.	30, 40, and 90 are all multiples of 10.
Multiplication Property of Equality The property that states that if you multiply both sides of an equation by the same number, the new equation will have the same solution. (p. 56)	**Propiedad de igualdad de la multiplicación** Propiedad que establece que puedes multiplicar ambos lados de una ecuación por el mismo número y la nueva ecuación tendrá la misma solución.	$\frac{1}{3}x = 7$ $(3)(\frac{1}{3}x) = (3)(7)$ $x = 21$
Multiplication Property of Zero The property that states that for all real numbers a, $a \times 0 = 0$ and $0 \times a = 0$. (p. 764)	**Propiedad de multiplicación del cero** Propiedad que establece que para todos los números reales a, $a \times 0 = 0$ y $0 \times a = 0$.	$6 \cdot 0 = 0$ $-5 \cdot 0 = 0$
mutually exclusive Two events are mutually exclusive if they cannot occur in the same trial of an experiment. (p. 772)	**mutuamente excluyentes** Dos sucesos son mutuamente excluyentes cuando no pueden ocurrir en la misma prueba de un experimento.	

| **negative correlation** Two data sets have a negative correlation, or relationship, if one set of data values increases while the other decreases. (p. 417) | **correlación negativa** Dos conjuntos de datos tienen correlación, o relación, negativa, si los valores de un conjunto aumentan a medida que los valores del otro conjunto disminuyen. | |

ENGLISH	SPANISH	EXAMPLES
negative integer An integer less than zero. (p. 76)	**entero negativo** Entero menor que cero.	 −2 is a negative integer.
net An arrangement of two-dimensional figures that can be folded to form a polyhedron. (p. 597)	**plantilla** Arreglo de figuras bidimensionales que se doblan para formar un poliedro.	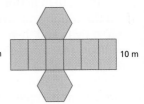 10 m 6 m 10 m 6 m
no correlation Two data sets have no correlation when there is no relationship between their data values. (p. 417)	**sin correlación** Caso en que los valores de dos conjuntos de datos no muestran ninguna relación.	
nonlinear function A function whose graph is not a straight line. (p. 254)	**función no lineal** Función cuya gráfica no es una línea recta.	
nonterminating decimal A decimal that never ends. (p. 562)	**decimal infinito** Decimal que nunca termina.	
numerator The top number of a fraction that tells how many parts of a whole are being considered.	**numerador** El número de arriba de una fracción; indica cuántas partes de un entero se consideran.	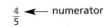 $\frac{4}{5}$ ← numerator
numerical expression An expression that contains only numbers and operations. (p. 23)	**expresión numérica** Expresión que incluye sólo números y operaciones.	$(2 \cdot 3) + 1$

ENGLISH	SPANISH	EXAMPLES
obtuse angle An angle whose measure is greater than 90° but less than 180°. (p. 448)	**ángulo obtuso** Ángulo que mide más de 90° y menos de 180°.	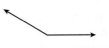
obtuse triangle A triangle containing one obtuse angle. (p. 470)	**triángulo obtusángulo** Triángulo que tiene un ángulo obtuso.	
octagon An eight-sided polygon. (p. 467)	**octágono** Polígono de ocho lados.	
odd number An integer that is not divisible by two.	**número impar** Entero que no es divisible entre 2.	
opposites Two numbers that are an equal distance from zero on a number line; also called *additive inverse*. (p. 76)	**opuestos** Dos números que están a la misma distancia de cero en una recta numérica. También se llaman *inversos aditivos*.	5 and −5 are opposites. 5 units 5 units −6 −5 −4 −3 −2 −1 0 1 2 3 4 5 6

ENGLISH	SPANISH	EXAMPLES
order of operations A rule for evaluating expressions: first perform the operations in parentheses, then compute powers and roots, then perform all multiplication and division from left to right, and then perform all addition and subtraction from left to right. (p. 23)	**orden de las operaciones** Regla para evaluar expresiones: primero se hacen las operaciones entre paréntesis, luego se hallan las potencias y raíces, después todas las multiplicaciones y divisiones de izquierda a derecha y, por último, todas las sumas y restas de izquierda a derecha.	$3^2 - 12 \div 4$ $9 - 12 \div 4$ Evaluate the power. $9 - 3$ Divide. 6 Subtract.
ordered pair A pair of numbers that can be used to locate a point on a coordinate plane. (p. 224)	**par ordenado** Par de números que sirven para ubicar un punto en un plano cartesiano.	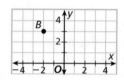 The coordinates of *B* are (−2, 3).
origin The point where the *x*-axis and *y*-axis intersect on the coordinate plane; (0, 0). (p. 224)	**origen** Punto de intersección entre el eje *x* y el eje *y* en un plano cartesiano: (0, 0).	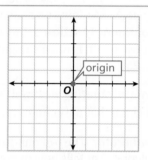
outcome A possible result of a probability experiment. (p. 628)	**resultado** Posible resultado de un experimento de probabilidad.	When rolling a number cube, the possible outcomes are 1, 2, 3, 4, 5, and 6.
outlier A value much greater or much less than the others in a data set. (p. 382)	**valor extremo** Un valor mucho mayor o menor que los demás de un conjunto de datos.	
output The value that results from the substitution of a given input into an expression or function. (p. 238)	**valor de salida** Valor que resulta después de sustituir un valor de entrada determinado en una expresión o función.	For the function $y = 6x$, the input 4 produces an output of 24.
overestimate An estimate that is greater than the exact answer.	**estimación alta** Estimación mayor que la respuesta exacta.	100 is an overestimate for the sum $23 + 24 + 21 + 22$.

P

parallel lines Lines in a plane that do not intersect. (p. 452)	**líneas paralelas** Líneas que se encuentran en el mismo plano pero que nunca se intersecan.	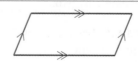
parallelogram A quadrilateral with two pairs of parallel sides. (p. 474)	**paralelogramo** Cuadrilátero con dos pares de lados paralelos.	

ENGLISH	SPANISH	EXAMPLES
pentagon A five-sided polygon. (p. 467)	**pentágono** Polígono de cinco lados.	
percent A ratio comparing a number to 100. (p. 330)	**porcentaje** Razón que compara un número con el número 100.	$45\% = \frac{45}{100}$
percent of change The amount stated as a percent that a number increases or decreases. (p. 352)	**porcentaje de cambio** Cantidad en que un número aumenta o disminuye, expresada como un porcentaje.	
percent of decrease A percent change describing a decrease in a quantity. (p. 352)	**porcentaje de disminución** Porcentaje de cambio en que una cantidad disminuye.	An item that costs $8 is marked down to $6. The amount of the decrease is $2 and the percent of decrease is $\frac{2}{8} = 0.25 = 25\%$.
percent of increase A percent change describing an increase in a quantity. (p. 352)	**porcentaje de incremento** Porcentaje de cambio en que una cantidad aumenta.	The price of an item increases from $8 to $12. The amount of the increase is $4 and the percent of increase is $\frac{4}{8} = 0.5 = 50\%$.
perfect square A square of a whole number. (p. 550)	**cuadrado perfecto** El cuadrado de un número cabal.	$5^2 = 25$, so 25 is a perfect square.
perimeter The distance around a polygon. (p. 524)	**perímetro** Distancia alrededor de un polígono.	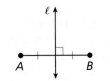 perimeter = 18 + 6 + 18 + 6 = 48 ft
permutation An arrangement of items or events in which order is important. (p. 656)	**permutación** Arreglo de objetos o sucesos en el que el orden es importante.	For objects *A*, *B*, and *C*, there are 6 different permutations, *ABC, ACB, BAC, BCA, CAB, CBA*.
perpendicular bisector A line that intersects a segment at its midpoint and is perpendicular to the segment. (p. 456)	**mediatriz** Línea que cruza un segmento en su punto medio y es perpendicular al segmento.	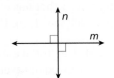
perpendicular lines Lines that intersect to form right angles. (p. 452)	**líneas perpendiculares** Líneas que al intersecarse forman ángulos rectos.	
pi (π) The ratio of the circumference of a circle to the length of its diameter; $\pi \approx 3.14$ or $\frac{22}{7}$. (p. 525)	**pi (π)** Razón de la circunferencia de un círculo a la longitud de su diámetro; $\pi \approx 3.14$ ó $\frac{22}{7}$.	
plane A flat surface that extends forever. (p. 442)	**plano** Superficie plana que se extiende de manera indefinida en todas direcciones.	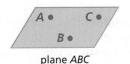 plane *ABC*

ENGLISH	SPANISH	EXAMPLES
point An exact location in space. (p. 442)	**punto** Ubicación exacta en el espacio.	P • point P
polygon A closed plane figure formed by three or more line segments that intersect only at their endpoints (vertices). (p. 466)	**polígono** Figura plana cerrada, formada por tres o más segmentos de recta que se intersecan sólo en sus extremos (vértices).	
polyhedron A three-dimensional figure in which all the surfaces or faces are polygons. (p. 580)	**poliedro** Figura tridimensional cuyas superficies o caras tienen forma de polígonos.	
population The entire group of objects or individuals considered for a survey. (p. 412)	**población** Grupo completo de objetos o individuos que se desea estudiar.	In a survey about the study habits of middle school students, the population is all middle school students.
positive correlation Two data sets have a positive correlation, or relationship, when their data values increase or decrease together. (p. 417)	**correlación positiva** Dos conjuntos de datos tienen una correlación, o relación, positiva cuando los valores de ambos conjuntos aumentan o disminuyen al mismo tiempo.	
positive integer An integer greater than zero. (p. 76)	**entero positivo** Entero mayor que cero.	
power A number produced by raising a base to an exponent. (p. 10)	**potencia** Número que resulta al elevar una base a un exponente.	$2^3 = 8$, so 2 to the 3rd power is 8.
precision The level of detail of a measurement, determined by the unit of measure. (p. 518)	**precisión** Detalle de una medición, determinado por la unidad de medida.	A ruler marked in millimeters has a greater level of precision than a ruler marked in centimeters.
prime factorization A number written as the product of its prime factors. (p. 106)	**factorización prima** Un número escrito como el producto de sus factores primos.	$10 = 2 \cdot 5$ $24 = 2^3 \cdot 3$
prime number A whole number greater than 1 that has exactly two factors, itself and 1. (p. 106)	**número primo** Número cabal mayor que 1 que sólo es divisible entre 1 y él mismo.	5 is prime because its only factors are 5 and 1.
principal The initial amount of money borrowed or saved. (p. 356)	**capital** Cantidad inicial de dinero depositada o recibida en préstamo.	
prism A polyhedron that has two congruent polygon-shaped bases and other faces that are all parallelograms. (p. 580)	**prisma** Poliedro con dos bases congruentes con forma de polígono y caras con forma de paralelogramo.	
probability A number from 0 to 1 (or 0% to 100%) that describes how likely an event is to occur. (p. 628)	**probabilidad** Un número entre 0 y 1 (ó 0% y 100%) que describe qué tan probable es un suceso.	A bag contains 3 red marbles and 4 blue marbles. The probability of randomly choosing a red marble is $\frac{3}{7}$.

ENGLISH	SPANISH	EXAMPLES
product The result when two or more numbers are multiplied.	**producto** Resultado de multiplicar dos o más números.	The product of 4 and 8 is 32.
proper fraction A fraction in which the numerator is less than the denominator.	**fracción propia** Fracción en la que el numerador es menor que el denominador.	$\frac{3}{4}, \frac{1}{13}, \frac{7}{8}$
proportion An equation that states that two ratios are equivalent. (p. 283)	**proporción** Ecuación que establece que dos razones son equivalentes.	$\frac{2}{3} = \frac{4}{6}$
protractor A tool for measuring angles. (p. 446)	**transportador** Instrumento para medir ángulos.	
pyramid A polyhedron with a polygon base and triangular sides that all meet at a common vertex. (p. 580)	**pirámide** Poliedro cuya base es un polígono; tiene caras triangulares que se juntan en un vértice común.	
Pythagorean Theorem In a right triangle, the square of the length of the hypotenuse is equal to the sum of the squares of the lengths of the legs. (p. 556)	**Teorema de Pitágoras** En un triángulo rectángulo, la suma de los cuadrados de los catetos es igual al cuadrado de la hipotenusa.	13 cm 5 cm 12 cm $5^2 + 12^2 = 13^2$ $25 + 144 = 169$

Q

quadrant The x- and y-axes divide the coordinate plane into four regions. Each region is called a quadrant. (p. 224)	**cuadrante** El eje x y el eje y dividen el plano cartesiano en cuatro regiones. Cada región recibe el nombre de cuadrante.	Quadrant II Quadrant I O Quadrant III Quadrant IV
quadratic function A function of the form $y = ax^2 + bx + c$, where $a \neq 0$. (p. 788)	**función cuadrática** Función del tipo $y = ax^2 + bx + c$, donde $a \neq 0$.	$y = 2x^2 - 12x + 10,$ $y = 3x^2$
quadrilateral A four-sided polygon. (p. 467)	**cuadrilátero** Polígono de cuatro lados.	
quartile Three values, one of which is the median, that divide a data set into fourths. See also *first quartile, third quartile*. (p. 394)	**cuartiles** Cada uno de tres valores, uno de los cuales es la mediana, que dividen en cuartos un conjunto de datos. Ver también *primer cuartil, tercer cuartil*.	
quotient The result when one number is divided by another.	**cociente** Resultado de dividir un número entre otro.	In $8 \div 4 = 2$, 2 is the quotient.

R

---

radical sign The symbol $\sqrt{}$ used to represent the nonnegative square root of a number. (p. 550) | **símbolo de radical** El símbolo $\sqrt{}$ con que se representa la raíz cuadrada no negativa de un número. | $\sqrt{36} = 6$

---

radius A line segment with one endpoint at the center of a circle and the other endpoint on the circle, or the length of that segment. (p. 460) | **radio** Segmento de recta con un extremo en el centro de un círculo y el otro en la circunferencia; o bien la longitud de ese segmento.

Radius

---

random sample A sample in which each individual or object in the entire population has an equal chance of being selected. (p. 412) | **muestra aleatoria** Muestra en la que cada individuo u objeto de la población tiene la misma oportunidad de ser elegido. | Mr. Henson chose a random sample of the class by writing each student's name on a slip of paper, mixing up the slips, and drawing five slips without looking.

---

range (in statistics) The difference between the greatest and least values in a data set. (p. 381) | **rango (en estadística)** Diferencia entre los valores máximo y mínimo de un conjunto de datos. | Data set: 3, 5, 7, 7, 12
Range: $12 - 3 = 9$

---

rate A ratio that compares two quantities measured in different units. (p. 274) | **tasa** Una razón que compara dos cantidades medidas en diferentes unidades. | The speed limit is 55 miles per hour, or 55 mi/h.

---

rate of interest The percent charged or earned on an amount of money; see *simple interest*. (p. 356) | **tasa de interés** Porcentaje que se cobra por una cantidad de dinero prestada o que se gana por una cantidad de dinero ahorrada; ver *interés simple*.

---

ratio A comparison of two quantities by division. (p. 270) | **razón** Comparación de dos cantidades mediante una división. | 12 to 25, 12:25, $\frac{12}{25}$

---

rational number Any number that can be expressed as a ratio of two integers. (p. 129) | **número racional** Número que se puede escribir como una razón de dos enteros. | 6 can be expressed as $\frac{6}{1}$.
0.5 can be expressed as $\frac{1}{2}$.

---

ray A part of a line that starts at one endpoint and extends forever. (p. 443) | **rayo** Parte de una línea que comienza en un extremo y se extiende de manera indefinida.
D

---

real number A rational or irrational number. | **número real** Número racional o irracional.

---

reciprocal One of two numbers whose product is 1; also called *multiplicative inverse*. (p. 200) | **recíproco** Uno de dos números cuyo producto es igual a 1. También se llama *inverso multiplicativo*. | The reciprocal of $\frac{2}{3}$ is $\frac{3}{2}$.

---

rectangle A parallelogram with four right angles. (p. 474) | **rectángulo** Paralelogramo con cuatro ángulos rectos.

ENGLISH	SPANISH	EXAMPLES

rectangular prism A polyhedron whose bases are rectangles and whose other faces are parallelograms. (p. 580)

prisma rectangular Poliedro cuyas bases son rectángulos y cuyas caras tienen forma de paralelogramo.

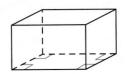

---

reflection A transformation of a figure that flips the figure across a line. (p. 488)

reflexión Transformación que ocurre cuando se invierte una figura sobre una línea.

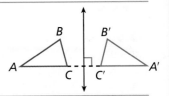

---

regular polygon A polygon with congruent sides and angles. (p. 467)

polígono regular Polígono con lados y ángulos congruentes.

---

repeating decimal A decimal in which one or more digits repeat infinitely. (p. 124)

decimal periódico Decimal en el que uno o más dígitos se repiten infinitamente.

$0.757575\ldots = 0.\overline{75}$

---

rhombus A parallelogram with all sides congruent. (p. 474)

rombo Paralelogramo en el que todos los lados son congruentes.

---

right angle An angle that measures 90°. (p. 448)

ángulo recto Ángulo que mide exactamente 90°.

---

right triangle A triangle containing a right angle. (p. 470)

triángulo rectángulo Triángulo que tiene un ángulo recto.

---

rise The vertical change when the slope of a line is expressed as the ratio $\frac{\text{rise}}{\text{run}}$, or "rise over run." (p. 278)

distancia vertical El cambio vertical cuando la pendiente de una línea se expresa como la razón $\frac{\text{distancia vertical}}{\text{distancia horizontal}}$, o "distancia vertical sobre distancia horizontal".

For the points $(3, -1)$ and $(6, 5)$, the rise is $5 - (-1) = 6$.

---

rotation A transformation in which a figure is turned around a point. (p. 488)

rotación Transformación que ocurre cuando una figura gira alrededor de un punto.

---

rotational symmetry A figure has rotational symmetry if it can be rotated less than 360° around a central point and coincide with the original figure. (p. 495)

simetría de rotación Ocurre cuando una figura gira menos de 360° alrededor de un punto central sin dejar de ser congruente con la figura original.

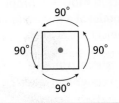

---

rounding Replacing a number with an estimate of that number to a given place value.

redondear Sustituir un número por una estimación de ese número hasta cierto valor posicional.

2,354 rounded to the nearest thousand is 2,000, and 2,354 rounded to the nearest 100 is 2,400.

Glossary/Glosario **821**

ENGLISH	SPANISH	EXAMPLES
run The horizontal change when the slope of a line is expressed as the ratio $\frac{rise}{run}$, or "rise over run." (p. 278)	**distancia horizontal** El cambio horizontal cuando la pendiente de una línea se expresa como la razón $\frac{distancia\ vertical}{distancia\ horizontal}$, o "distancia vertical sobre distancia horizontal".	For the points (3, −1) and (6, 5), the run is 6 − 3 = 3.

ENGLISH	SPANISH	EXAMPLES
sales tax A percent of the cost of an item, which is charged by governments to raise money.	**impuesto sobre la venta** Porcentaje del costo de un artículo que los gobiernos cobran para recaudar fondos.	
sample A part of the population. (p. 412)	**muestra** Una parte de la población.	In a survey about the study habits of middle school students, a sample is a survey of 100 randomly-chosen students.
sample space All possible outcomes of an experiment. (p. 636)	**espacio muestral** Conjunto de todos los resultados posibles de un experimento.	When rolling a number cube, the sample space is 1, 2, 3, 4, 5, 6.
scale The ratio between two sets of measurements. (p. 308)	**escala** La razón entre dos conjuntos de medidas.	1 cm:5 mi
scale drawing A drawing that uses a scale to make an object smaller than or larger than the real object. (p. 308)	**dibujo a escala** Dibujo en el que se usa una escala para que un objeto se vea mayor o menor que el objeto real al que representa.	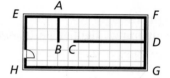 A blueprint is an example of a scale drawing.
scale factor The ratio used to enlarge or reduce similar figures. (p. 308)	**factor de escala** Razón que se usa para agrandar o reducir figuras semejantes.	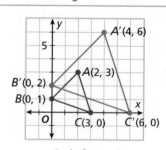 Scale factor: 2
scale model A proportional model of a three-dimensional object. (p. 308)	**modelo a escala** Modelo proporcional de un objeto tridimensional.	
scalene triangle A triangle with no congruent sides. (p. 470)	**triángulo escaleno** Triángulo que no tiene lados congruentes.	

ENGLISH	SPANISH	EXAMPLES

scatter plot A graph with points plotted to show a possible relationship between two sets of data. (p. 416)

diagrama de dispersión Gráfica de puntos que se usa para mostrar una posible relación entre dos conjuntos de datos.

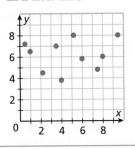

scientific notation A method of writing very large or very small numbers by using powers of 10. (p. 18)

notación científica Método que se usa para escribir números muy grandes o muy pequeños mediante potencias de 10.

$$12{,}560{,}000{,}000{,}000 = 1.256 \times 10^{13}$$

sector A region enclosed by two radii and the arc joining their endpoints. (p. 461)

sector Región encerrada por dos radios y el arco que une sus extremos.

sector (data) A section of a circle graph representing part of the data set. (p. 390)

sector (datos) Sección de una gráfica circular que representa una parte del conjunto de datos.

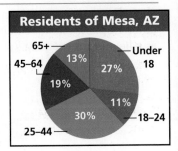

The circle graph has 5 sectors.

segment A part of a line between two endpoints. (p. 442)

segmento Parte de una línea entre dos extremos.

sequence An ordered list of numbers. (p. 242)

sucesión Lista ordenada de números.

2, 4, 6, 8, 10, ...

side A line bounding a geometric figure; one of the faces forming the outside of an object. (p. 466)

lado Línea que delimita las figuras geométricas; una de las caras que forman la parte exterior de un objeto.

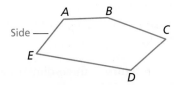

Side-Side-Side (SSS) A rule stating that if three sides of one triangle are congruent to three sides of another triangle, then the triangles are congruent. (p. 484)

Lado-Lado-Lado (LLL) Regla que establece que dos triángulos son congruentes cuando sus tres lados correspondientes son congruentes.

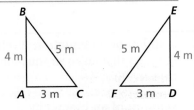

$\triangle ABC \cong \triangle DEF$

significant digits The digits used to express the precision of a measurement. (p. 518)

dígitos significativos Dígitos usados para expresar la precisión de una medida.

0.048 has 2 significant digits.
5.003 has 4 significant digits.

similar Figures with the same shape but not necessarily the same size are similar. (p. 300)

semejantes Figuras que tienen la misma forma, pero no necesariamente el mismo tamaño.

---

simple interest A fixed percent of the principal. It is found using the formula $I = Prt$, where P represents the principal, r the rate of interest, and t the time. (p. 356)

interés simple Un porcentaje fijo del capital. Se calcula con la fórmula $I = Cit$, donde C representa el capital, i, la tasa de interés y t, el tiempo.

$100 is put into an account with a simple interest rate of 5%. After 2 years, the account will have earned
$I = 100 \cdot 0.05 \cdot 2 = \$10$.

---

simplest form A fraction is in simplest form when the numerator and denominator have no common factors other than 1.

mínima expresión Una fracción está en su mínima expresión cuando el numerador y el denominador no tienen más factor común que 1.

Fraction: $\frac{8}{12}$

Simplest form: $\frac{2}{3}$

---

simplify To write a fraction or expression in simplest form.

simplificar Escribir una fracción o expresión numérica en su mínima expresión.

---

skew lines Lines that lie in different planes that are neither parallel nor intersecting. (p. 452)

líneas oblicuas Líneas que se encuentran en planos distintos, por eso no se intersecan ni son paralelas.

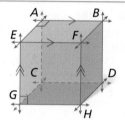

$\overrightarrow{AE}$ and $\overrightarrow{CD}$ are skew lines.

---

slope A measure of the steepness of a line on a graph; the rise divided by the run. (p. 278)

pendiente Medida de la inclinación de una línea en una gráfica. Razón de la distancia vertical a la distancia horizontal.

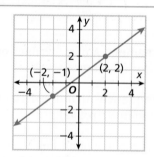

Slope $= \frac{\text{rise}}{\text{run}} = \frac{3}{4}$

---

solid figure A three-dimensional figure. (p. 586)

cuerpo geométrico Figura tridimensional.

---

solution of an equation A value or values that make an equation true. (p. 46)

solución de una ecuación Valor o valores que hacen verdadera una ecuación.

Equation: $x + 2 = 6$
Solution: $x = 4$

---

solution of an inequality A value or values that make an inequality true. (p. 692)

solución de una desigualdad Valor o valores que hacen verdadera una desigualdad.

Inequality: $x + 3 \geq 10$
Solution: $x \geq 7$

---

solution set The set of values that make a statement true. (p. 692)

conjunto solución Conjunto de valores que hacen verdadero un enunciado.

Inequality: $x + 3 \geq 5$
Solution set: $x \geq 2$

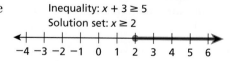

---

solve To find an answer or a solution. (p. 52)

resolver Hallar una respuesta o solución.

---

square (geometry) A rectangle with four congruent sides. (p. 474)

cuadrado (en geometría) Rectángulo con cuatro lados congruentes.

---

square (numeration) A number raised to the second power. (p. 550)

cuadrado (en numeración) Número elevado a la segunda potencia.

In 5^2, the number 5 is squared.

---

square number The product of a number and itself. (p. 550)

cuadrado de un número El producto de un número y sí mismo.

25 is a square number.
$5 \cdot 5 = 25$.

---

square root One of the two equal factors of a number. (p. 550)

raíz cuadrada Uno de los dos factores iguales de un número.

$16 = 4 \cdot 4$ and $16 = -4 \cdot -4$, so 4 and -4 are square roots of 16.

---

standard form (in numeration) A way to write numbers by using digits. (p. 19)

forma estándar (en numeración) Una manera de escribir números por medio de dígitos.

Five thousand, two hundred ten in standard form is 5,210.

---

stem-and-leaf plot A graph used to organize and display data so that the frequencies can be compared. (p. 377)

diagrama de tallo y hojas Gráfica que muestra y ordena los datos, y que sirve para comparar las frecuencias.

Stem	Leaves
3	2 3 4 4 7 9
4	0 1 5 7 7 7 8
5	1 2 2 3

Key: 3|2 means 32

---

straight angle An angle that measures 180°. (p. 448)

ángulo llano Ángulo que mide exactamente 180°.

---

substitute To replace a variable with a number or another expression in an algebraic expression.

sustituir Reemplazar una variable por un número u otra expresión en una expresión algebraica.

Subtraction Property of Equality The property that states that if you subtract the same number from both sides of an equation, the new equation will have the same solution. (p. 53)

Propiedad de igualdad de la resta Propiedad que establece que puedes restar el mismo número de ambos lados de una ecuación y la nueva ecuación tendrá la misma solución.

$$x + 6 = 8$$
$$\underline{-6 \quad -6}$$
$$x = 2$$

---

sum The result when two or more numbers are added.

suma Resultado de sumar dos o más números.

The sum of $6 + 7 + 1$ is 14.

---

supplementary angles Two angles whose measures have a sum of 180°. (p. 448)

ángulos suplementarios Dos ángulos cuyas medidas suman 180°.

30° 150°

---

surface area The sum of the areas of the faces, or surfaces, of a three-dimensional figure. (p. 597)

área total Suma de las áreas de las caras, o superficies, de una figura tridimensional.

12 cm

6 cm

8 cm

Surface area = $2(8)(12) + 2(8)(6) + 2(12)(6) = 432$ cm^2

ENGLISH	SPANISH	EXAMPLES
term (in an expression) The parts of an expression that are added or subtracted. (p. 42)	**término (en una expresión)** Las partes de una expresión que se suman o se restan.	$3x^2$ + $6x$ − 8 ↑ ↑ ↑ Term Term Term
term (in a sequence) An element or number in a sequence. (p. 242)	**término (en una sucesión)** Elemento o número de una sucesión.	5 is the third term in the sequence 1, 3, 5, 7, 9, …
terminating decimal A decimal number that ends or terminates. (p. 124)	**decimal finito** Decimal con un número determinado de posiciones decimales.	6.75
tessellation A repeating pattern of plane figures that completely covers a plane with no gaps or overlaps. (p. 498)	**teselado** Patrón repetido de figuras planas que cubren totalmente un plano sin superponerse ni dejar huecos.	
theoretical probability The ratio of the number of equally likely outcomes in an event to the total number of possible outcomes. (p. 640)	**probabilidad teórica** Razón del número de resultados igualmente probables en un suceso al número total de resultados posibles.	When rolling a number cube, the theoretical probability of rolling a 4 is $\frac{1}{6}$.
third quartile The median of the upper half of a set of data; also called *upper quartile*. (p. 394)	**tercer cuartil** La mediana de la mitad superior de un conjunto de datos. También se llama *cuartil superior*.	
transformation A change in the position or orientation of a figure. (p. 488)	**transformación** Cambio en la posición u orientación de una figura.	
translation A movement (slide) of a figure along a straight line. (p. 488)	**traslación** Desplazamiento de una figura a lo largo de una línea recta.	
transversal A line that intersects two or more lines. (p. 453)	**transversal** Línea que cruza dos o más líneas.	
trapezoid A quadrilateral with exactly one pair of parallel sides. (p. 474)	**trapecio** Cuadrilátero con un par de lados paralelos.	

ENGLISH	SPANISH	EXAMPLES
tree diagram A branching diagram that shows all possible combinations or outcomes of an event. (p. 637)	**diagrama de árbol** Diagrama ramificado que muestra todas las posibles combinaciones o resultados de un suceso.	
trial In probability, a single repetition or observation of an experiment. (p. 628)	**prueba** En probabilidad, una sola repetición u observación de un experimento.	When rolling a number cube, each roll is one trial.
triangle A three-sided polygon. (p. 467)	**triángulo** Polígono de tres lados.	
Triangle Sum Theorem The theorem that states that the measures of the angles in a triangle add to 180°.	**Teorema de la suma del triángulo** Teorema que establece que las medidas de los ángulos de un triángulo suman 180°.	
triangular prism A polyhedron whose bases are triangles and whose other faces are parallelograms. (p. 580)	**prisma triangular** Poliedro cuyas bases son triángulos y cuyas demás caras tienen forma de paralelogramo.	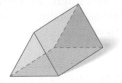

ENGLISH	SPANISH	EXAMPLES
underestimate An estimate that is less than the exact answer.	**estimación baja** Estimación menor que la respuesta exacta.	
unit conversion The process of changing one unit of measure to another. (p. 314)	**conversión de unidades** Proceso que consiste en cambiar una unidad de medida por otra.	
unit conversion factor A fraction used in unit conversion in which the numerator and denominator represent the same amount but are in different units. (p. 314)	**factor de conversión de unidades** Fracción que se usa para la conversión de unidades, donde el numerador y el denominador representan la misma cantidad pero están en unidades distintas.	$\dfrac{60 \text{ min}}{1 \text{ h}}$ or $\dfrac{1 \text{ h}}{60 \text{ min}}$
unit price A unit rate used to compare prices.	**precio unitario** Tasa unitaria que sirve para comparar precios.	
unit rate A rate in which the second quantity in the comparison is one unit. (p. 274)	**tasa unitaria** Una tasa en la que la segunda cantidad de la comparación es la unidad.	10 cm per minute
upper quartile The median of the upper half of a set of data. (p. 394)	**cuartil superior** La mediana de la mitad superior de un conjunto de datos.	Lower half Upper half 18, 23, 28, 29, ⟨36,⟩ 42 ↑ Upper quartile

ENGLISH	SPANISH	EXAMPLES

variable A symbol used to represent a quantity that can change. (p. 34)

variable Símbolo que representa una cantidad que puede cambiar.

In the expression 2x + 3, x is the variable.

Venn diagram A diagram that is used to show relationships between sets.

diagrama de Venn Diagrama que muestra las relaciones entre conjuntos.

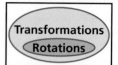

verbal expression A word or phrase. (p. 38)

expresión verbal Palabra o frase.

vertex On an angle or polygon, the point where two sides intersect. (p. 448)

vértice En un ángulo o polígono, el punto de intersección de dos lados.

A is the vertex of ∠CAB.

vertical angles A pair of opposite congruent angles formed by intersecting lines. (p. 453)

ángulos opuestos por el vértice Par de ángulos opuestos congruentes formados por líneas secantes.

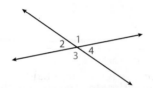

∠1 and ∠3 are vertical angles.
∠2 and ∠4 are vertical angles.

volume The number of cubic units needed to fill a given space. (p. 586)

volumen Número de unidades cúbicas que se necesitan para llenar un espacio.

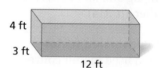

Volume = 3 · 4 · 12 = 144 ft³

x-axis The horizontal axis on a coordinate plane. (p. 224)

eje x El eje horizontal del plano cartesiano.

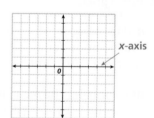

x-axis

ENGLISH	SPANISH	EXAMPLES
x-coordinate The first number in an ordered pair; it tells the distance to move right or left from the origin, (0, 0). (p. 224)	**coordenada x** El primer número en un par ordenado; indica la distancia que debes avanzar hacia la izquierda o hacia la derecha desde el origen, (0, 0).	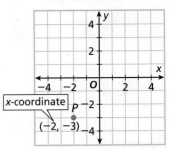

y-axis The vertical axis on a coordinate plane. (p. 224)	**eje y** El eje vertical del plano cartesiano.	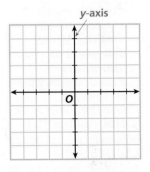
y-coordinate The second number in an ordered pair; it tells the distance to move up or down from the origin, (0, 0). (p. 224)	**coordenada y** El segundo número de un par ordenado; indica la distancia que debes avanzar hacia arriba o hacia abajo desde el origen, (0, 0).	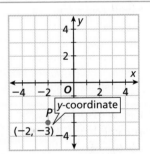

Index

A

Absolute value, 77
Accuracy, 518
  precision and, 518–519
Acute angles, 448
Acute triangles, 470
Act It Out, 760
Addition
  of decimals, 154–155
  of fractions, 186–187
    modeling, 184–185
  of integers, 82–83
    modeling, 80–81
  of mixed numbers, 190–191
  properties, 764
  solving inequalities by, 696–697
Addition equations, 52–53
Addition Property of Equality, 52
Adjacent angles, 453
Agriculture, 193, 282, 295, 701
Alcott, Louisa May, 659
Algebra
The development of algebra skills and concepts is a central focus of this course and is found throughout this book.
  combining like terms, 42–43, 682–683
  equations, 46
    addition, 52–53
    division, 56–57
    integer, *see* Integer equations
    multi-step, *see* Multi-step equations
    multiplication, 56–57
    solutions of, 46–47
    subtraction, 52–53
    two-step, *see* Two-step equations
  expressions, 34–35
  formulas, learning and using, 577
  functions, 238
    linear, 246–249
    nonlinear, 254–255
    patterns and, 220–265
    tables and graphs and, 238–239
  graphs, tables and functions and, 238–239
  inequalities, 692–693
    solving, 696–705
  linear functions, 246–249
  multi-step equations, 682–683
  nonlinear functions, 252–253
  properties, 28–29
    Addition, of Equality, 52
    Associative, 28
    of circles, 460–461
    Commutative, 28
    Distributive, 29, 682
    Division, of Equality, 56
    Identity, 28

Multiplication, of Equality, 56
    Subtraction, of Equality, 53
  proportions, solving, 287–288
  solving equations
    by adding or subtracting, 52–53
    containing decimals, 174–175
    containing fractions, 204–205
    containing integers, 100–101
    modeling, 50–51
    by multiplying or dividing, 56–57
    multi-step, 682–683
    two-step equations, 678–679
    with variables on both sides, 686–687
  solving inequalities
    by adding or subtracting, 696–697
    by multiplying or dividing, 700–701
    two-step, 704–705
  translating between words and math, 75
  translating words into math, 38–39
  variables, 34
    on both sides, solving equations with, 686–687
    dependent, 249
    independent, 249
    isolating, 52
    solving for, 710
Algebra tiles, 50–51, 98–99
Algebraic expressions
  evaluating, 34–35
  simplifying, 42–43
Algebraic inequalities, 692
Amusement parks, 643
Analysis, dimensional, 314
Angles, 446, 448
  acute, 448
  adjacent, 452
  central, 461
  classifying, 448–449
  complementary, *see* Complementary angles
  congruent, *see* Congruent angles
  corresponding, 300
  obtuse, 448
  in polygons, 478–479
  of quadrilaterals, 479
  relationships of, 452–453
  right, 448
  straight, 448
  supplementary, *see* Supplementary angles
  of triangles, 478
  vertical, 453
Answer choices, eliminating, 68–69
Appalachian Trail, 85
Applications
  Agriculture, 193, 282, 295, 701
  Architecture, 30, 207, 473, 527, 592
  Art, 16, 113, 359, 497, 533
  Astronomy, 20, 153, 187
  Banking, 83, 358
  Business, 45, 59, 78, 101, 102, 109, 182, 231, 339, 353, 354, 425, 651, 706
  Career, 24, 25, 40

Chemistry, 290
  Construction, 455
  Consumer Math, 25, 26, 152, 176, 241, 275, 276, 336, 337, 344, 348, 680, 684, 685, 687, 688, 698, 707
  Cooking, 188
  Crafts, 231
  Design, 525
  Earth Science, 11, 12, 78, 95, 96, 97, 130, 161, 206, 251, 290, 295, 307, 313, 345, 405, 481, 553, 631, 707
  Ecology, 131, 285
  Environment, 251
  Exercise, 630
  Finance, 162, 358
  Fitness, 189, 679
  Food, 123, 206
  Gardening, 643
  Geography, 343, 393, 527, 535
  Geology, 473
  Geometry, 43, 44, 102, 449, 684
  Health, 9, 57, 231, 349, 385, 639, 659
  History, 20, 207, 349
  Hobbies, 13, 302, 425, 487
  Landscaping, 531
  Life Science, 13, 17, 41, 131, 183, 207, 286, 390, 405, 411, 415, 497, 589, 631, 699
  Literature, 294, 659
  Measurement, 17, 180, 189, 190, 199, 305, 309, 397, 539, 540
  Money, 36, 167, 313
  Music, 55, 189, 349, 463
  Nutrition, 41, 169, 235, 345, 411
  Patterns, 12, 90
  Personal Finance, 84, 97, 122
  Physical Science, 36, 37, 54, 103, 157, 177, 199, 205, 241, 345, 541, 685, 699, 710, 711
  Recreation, 85, 103, 115, 116, 169, 182, 193, 551, 589, 637, 639, 643, 689, 703
  School, 59, 113, 126, 151, 629, 641, 705
  Social Studies, 9, 13, 79, 123, 153, 177, 201, 422, 477, 494, 539, 703
  Sports, 31, 53, 79, 84, 91, 102, 125, 126, 153, 192, 234, 276, 286, 339, 385, 397, 632, 658
  Surveying, 487
  Temperature, 89
  Transportation, 153, 155, 171, 196
  Travel, 59, 193
  Weather, 157, 162, 206, 227, 241, 633, 697
Appropriate displays, choosing, 408–409
Arc, 460
Arches National Park, 391
Architecture, 30, 207, 473, 527, 592
Are You Ready?, 3, 73, 147, 221, 267, 327, 373, 439, 515, 575, 625, 673
Area, 530
  of circles, 538–539
  of irregular figures, 542–543
  of parallelograms, 530–531
  of polygons, exploring, 528–529

Index

Index

Credits

■ Staff Credits

Bruce Albrecht, Margaret Chalmers, Justin Collins, Lorraine Cooper, Marc Cooper, Jennifer Craycraft, Martize Cross, Nina Degollado, Lydia Doty, Sam Dudgeon, Kelli R. Flanagan, Mary Fraser, Stephanie Friedman, Paul Frisoli, Jeff Galvez, José Garza, Diannia Green, Jennifer Gribble, Liz Huckestein, Jevara Jackson, Kadonna Knape, Cathy Kuhles, Jill M. Lawson, Peter Leighton, Christine MacInnis, Rosalyn K. Mack, Jonathan Martindill, Virginia Messler, Susan Mussey, Kim Nguyen, Matthew Osment, Theresa Reding, Manda Reid, Patrick Ricci, Michael Rinella, Michelle Rumpf-Dike, Beth Sample, Annette Saunders, John Saxe, Kay Selke, Robyn Setzen, Patricia Sinnott, Victoria Smith, Jeannie Taylor, Ken Whiteside, Sherri Whitmarsh, Aimee F. Wiley, Alison Wohlman

■ Photo Credits

Cover: © Scott Gilchrist/Masterfile **Master icons:** Teens (All), Sam Dudgeon/HRW **Author photos:** (All) HRW **Table of Contents:** vi (l), © AFP/Corbis; vii (r), Tom Pantages Photography; viii (l), © Brian Leatart/FoodPix; ix (r), © Kelly-Mooney Photography/Corbis; x (l), Ship model by Jean K. Eckert/Photo Courtesy of ©The Mariners' Museum, Newport News, Virginia; xi (r), © Mark E. Gibson Photography; xii (l), © Sam Fried/Photo Researchers, Inc.; xiii (r), © 2002 Bruno Burklin/Aerial Aesthetics; xiv (l), © Mark E. Gibson c/o MIRA; xv (r), © Arvind Garg/Corbis; xvi (l), © Getty Images/Stone; xvii (r), NASA. **Frontmatter:** xviii (tc), © Gallo Images/Corbis; xvii (tr), G.K. & Vikki Hart/Getty Images; xix (l) Associated Press, AP/Wide World Photos; xix (tr), RO-MA Stock/Index Stock Imagery, Inc.; xix (c), © Ron Kimball Studios; xix (r), © Stock Trek/PhotoDisc/Picture Quest; xxi (tr), Victoria Smith/HRW; xxii (tr), © Gisela Damm/eStock Photography/PictureQuest; xxii (bl), Sam Dudgeon/HRW. **Chapter 1:** 2, (bkgd), © AFP/CORBIS; 2, (br), David Gamble/Sygma; 6 (tr), © Royalty Free Corbis; 11, (cl), © AFP/CORBIS; 13, (tl), Bruce Iverson; 13, (tr), Bruce Iverson; 13, (bl), Bruce Iverson; 13, (br), Bruce Iverson; 14 (tr), Yoshikazu Tsuno/AFP/GettyImages; 17 (cl), National Geographic/GettyImages; 18 (tr), © Bill Frymire/Masterfile 105, (b), Sam Dudgeon/HRW/Sheet music courtesy Martha Dudgeon.; 26 (br), Sam Dudgeon/HRW; 33 (bc), EyeWire - Digital Image copyright © (2004) EyeWire; 34 (t), Everett Collection; 34 (b), Frederic De Lafosse/Sygma; 34 (c), Ulvis Alberts/Motion Picture & Television Photo Archive; 38 © David Allan Brandt/Getty Images/Stone; 41 (l), Photo Researchers, Inc.; 42 (tr), Digital Vision/GettyImages; 45 Courtesy of the National Grocers Association Best Bagger Contest; 46 (tr), Peter Van Steen/HRW; 47 (r), Sam Dudgeon/HRW/Courtesy Fast Forward Skate Shop, Austin, TX; 47 (l), Sam Dudgeon/HRW/Courtesy Fast Forward Skate Shop, Austin, TX; 49 (br), James Urbach/SuperStock; 57 © Reuters NewMedia Inc./CORBIS; 61 (cr), PhotoDisc/GettyImages; 62 (cl), © Jenny Thomas/HRW; 62 (b), © Jenny Thomas/HRW **Chapter 2:** 72 (br), © Jay Ireland & Georgienne E. Bradley; 72 (bkgd), Tom Pantages Photography; 76 (br), Chuck Nicklin/Al Giddings Images, Inc.; 76 (tl), NATALIE B. FORBES National Geographic Image Collection; 79 (l), © Neil Rabinowitz/CORBIS; 82 ©2001 Jay Mallin; 85 (l), Lee Foster; 91 (t), © CORBIS; 95, © Purcell Team; 97 © Ann Purcell; Carl Purcell/Words & Pictures/PictureQuest; 110 (tr), Sam Dudgeon/HRW; 111 (tr), Victoria Smith/HRW; 111 (cr), Victoria Smith/HRW; 113 (l), Collection Walker Art Center, Minneapolis Gift of Fredrick R. Weisman in honor of his parents, William and Mary Weisman, 1988; 117 (t), © D. Donne Bryant/DDB Stock Photo/All Rights Reserved; 117 (b), Erich Lessing/Art Resource, NY; 119 (b), Lisette LeBon/SuperStock; 120 Victoria Smith/HRW; 123 (l), Michael Rosenfeld/Stone/Getty Images; 124 (tr), © Tim Johnson/Reuters/CORBIS; 127 (t), Image Copyright © Digital Vision; 127 (c), © Underwood & Underwood/CORBIS; 131 (l), © Buddy Mays/CORBIS; 136 (br), © Jenny Thomas/HRW; 137 (br), Sam Dudgeon/HRW; 144 (cr), © Farrell Grehan/Corbis; 144 (bl), © Bruce Coleman Inc./Alamy; 145 (t), © Tom Till/Alamy **Chapter 3:** 146 (b), Jenny Thomas/HRW; 146 (bkgd), © Brian Leatart/FoodPix; 150 Richard Nowitz/Photo Researchers, Inc.; 153 (l), © Paul Almasy/CORBIS; 154 © Lynn Stone/Index Stock Imagery/PictureQuest; 157 (l), AP Photo/The Fresno Bee, Richard Darby/Wide World Photos; 166 (tr), Darren Carroll/HRW; 173 © Galen Rowell/CORBIS; 174 (tr), Sam Dudgeon/HRW; 175 Victoria Smith/HRW/Courtesy Oshman's, Austin, TX; 177 (l), © Gail Mooney/CORBIS; 179 (b), Ken Karp/HRW; 180 (r), © Jeffrey L. Rotman/CORBIS; 189 (l), © Gallo Images/CORBIS; 189 (r), G.K. & Vikki Hart/Getty Images; 190 (tr), Dorling Kindersley/GettyImages; 190 (tr), Botanica/GettyImages; 193 (l), © Michael John Kielty/CORBIS; 196 (tr), © Glen Allison/Alamy Photos; 201 (l), Hulton Archive by Getty Images; 203 (r), Victoria Smith/HRW; 203 (tl), Richard Heinzen/SuperStock; 204 Peter Van Steen/HRW/Courtesy Russell Korman Fine Jewelry, Austin, TX; 205 © Charles O'Rear/CORBIS; 209 (tl), PhotoDisc/GettyImages; 209 (cr), © Charles O'Rear/CORBIS; 210 (b), © Jenny Thomas/HRW; 211 (br), Sam Dudgeon/HRW **Chapter 4:** 220 (bkgd), © Kelly-Mooney Photography/CORBIS; 220 (br), Roberto Borea/AP/Wide World Photos; 227 (l), © Stock Trek/PhotoDisc/ Picture Quest; 228 (tr), Anna Zieminski/AFP/GettyImages; 235 (r), John Langford/HRW; 235 (l), John Langford/HRW; 237 (b), © Michael T. Sedam/CORBIS; 238 Stamp Designs © 1994 32À Rube Goldberg's Inventions (Scott # 3000f) United States Postal Service, Displayed with permission. All rights reserved. Written authorization from the Postal Service is required to use, reproduce, post, transmit, distribute, or publicly display these images. © Rube Goldberg, Inc.; 242 (t), © Helen Norman/CORBIS; 242 (bl), © John Kaprielian/Photo Researchers, Inc.; 242 (bc), © John Pointer/Animals Animals/Earth Scenes; 242 (r), © ChromaZone Images/Index Stock Imagery/PictureQuest; 245 (t), RO-MA Stock/Index Stock Imagery, Inc.; 245 (inset), RO-MA Stock/Index Stock Imagery, Inc.; 248 Scott Vallance/VIP Photographic Associates; 251 (l), © Ron Kimball Studios; 253 (b), Digital Vision/ GettyImages; 257 (br), Sam Dudgeon/HRW; 264 (cr), Photo courtesy of the PATH Foundation; 265 (tr), Courtesy of MARTA; 265 (bl), Courtesy of MARTA **Chapter 5:** 266 (bkgd), Ship model by Jean K. Eckert/Photo Courtesy of ©The Mariners' Museum, Newport News, Virginia; 266 (b), Gordon Chibroski/Press Herald/AP/Wide World Photos; 270 (tr), Darren Carrol/HRW; 273 (bc), © Chris Mellor/Lonely Planet Images; 273 (t), © Gavin Anderson/Lonely Planet Images; 283 Victoria Smith/HRW; 284 James L. Amos/SuperStock; 286 (cr), © Lynda Richardson/Corbis; 287 (tr), © Ralph A. Clevenger/CORBIS; 292 (tr), © Copyright Johnér Bildbyrå AB; 297 (b), Sam Dudgeon/HRW; 300 Peter Van Steen/HRW; 304 © Francis E. Caldwell/Affordable Photo Stock; 308 (t), Sam Dudgeon/HRW/Courtesy Chuck and Nan Ellis; 308 Victoria Smith/HRW; 309 Van Gogh Museum, Amsterdam/SuperStock; 311 (t), Library of Congress; 311 (b), Library of Congress; 311 (c), Victoria Smith/HRW; 311 (t-frame), ©1999 Image Farm Inc.; 317 (br), Sam Dudgeon/HRW; 317 (br), Sam Dudgeon/HRW **Chapter 6:** 326 (bkgd), © Mark E. Gibson Photography; 326 (br), Victoria Smith/HRW; 330 (tr), © Louie Psihoyos/Corbis; 345 (cl), © Tim Graham/Alamy; 346 (tr), © Buddy Mays/CORBIS; 352 (tr), Sam Dudgeon/HRW; 361 (tl), © Hemera Technologies/Alamy; 361 (br), Getty Images/Taxi; 363 (br), Sam Dudgeon/HRW; 363 (br), Sam Dudgeon/HRW; 370 (r), © Mark E. Gibson/Corbis; 371 (tr), AP Photo/U.S. Department of Agriculture, Don Schuart, File; 371 (cr), © Michael Barley/Corbis; 371 (bl), Stephanie Friedman/HRW **Chapter 7:** 372 (bkgd), © Sam Fried/Photo Researchers, Inc.; 372 (br), Victoria Smith/HRW; 376 Courtesy IMAX Corporation, Smithsonian Institution and Lockheed Martin Corporation; 381 © CORBIS; 383 (l), © James L. Amos/ CORBIS/Collection of The Corning Museum of Glass, Corning, New York; 385 © Karl Weatherly/CORBIS; 388 (tr), PhotoDisc - Digital Image copyright © 2004 PhotoDisc; 388 (tl), PhotoDisc - Digital Image copyright © 2004 PhotoDisc; 389 (cl), © David J. & Janice L. Frent Collection/CORBIS; 389 (tl), © CORBIS; 389 (cr), © CORBIS; 389 (bl), © David J. & Janice L. Frent Collection/CORBIS; 390 (br), © Kathy deWet-Oleson/Lonely Planet Images; 390 (bl), © Jeffrey L. Rotman/CORBIS; 391 (l), © Ron Sanford/Photo Researchers, Inc.; 392 (t), Sam Dudgeon/HRW; 394 (tr), Image Bank/GettyImages; 401 (b), © Stephen Frink/StephenFrink Collection.com; 402 (c), SuperStock; 402 (l), SuperStock; 402 (r), SuperStock; 405 SuperStock; 408 (tr), © V. Brockhaus/zefa/CORBIS; 412 (b), Victoria Smith/HRW; 412 (tr), © Randy M. Ury/CORBIS; 415 (tl), FlyBase/Dr. F. R. Turner; 419 © Ecoscene/CORBIS; 423 (r), © James A. Sugar/CORBIS; 427 (br), © Richard Hutchings/PhotoEdit; 427 (bc), © Thinkstock/Alamy; 427 (tr), © 2004 Kelly Houle; 429 (br), Sam Dudgeon/HRW **Chapter 8:** 438 (bkgd), © 2002 Bruno Burklin/Aerial Aesthetics; 438 (br), © Stone/Getty Images/Stone; 442 The Art Archive/Private Collection/Harper Collins Publishers/ © 2004 Artists Rights Society (ARS), New York/ADAGP, Paris; 444 Science Kit & Boreal Laboratories; 445 (t), © Diana Ong/Superstock; 445 (b), Copyright Tate Gallery, London, Great Britain/Art Resource, NY/© 2004 Artist Rights Society (ARS), New York/Pro Litteris, Zurich; 452 ©GiselaDamm/eStockPhotography/ PictureQuest; 455 (l), John Burke/SuperStock; 459 (br), © Robert Landau/Corbis; 460 (t), © Archivo Iconografico, S.A./CORBIS; 460 (b), © Archivo Iconografico, S.A./CORBIS; 466 © Gianni Dagh Orti/CORBIS; 469 (t), John Warden/SuperStock; 469 (tc), © Roman Soumar/CORBIS; 469 (b), © Jacqui Hurst/CORBIS; 473 (r), © Craig Aurness/CORBIS; 474 (tr), UW/Mary Levin; 477 (l), © Bob Krist/CORBIS; 481 (t), © CORBIS; 483 (b), © Craig Aurness/CORBIS; 488 (tr), Matthew Stockman/GettyImages; 494 (tr), Steve Vidler/SuperStock; 495 (tr), © Arthur Thévenart/CORBIS; 495 (c), © Karen Gowlett-Holmes; 497 © Nigel J. Dennis/Photo Researchers, Inc.; 497 (b), © William Panzer/Stock

Credits

Table of Measures

METRIC

Length

1 kilometer (km) = 1,000 meters (m)

1 meter = 100 centimeters (cm)

1 centimeter = 10 millimeters (mm)

Capacity

1 liter (L) = 1,000 milliliters (mL)

Mass and Weight

1 kilogram (kg) = 1,000 grams (g)

1 gram = 1,000 milligrams (mg)

CUSTOMARY

Length

1 mile (mi) = 5,280 feet (ft)

1 yard (yd) = 3 feet

1 foot = 12 inches (in.)

Capacity

1 gallon (gal) = 4 quarts (qt)

1 quart = 2 pints (pt)

1 pint = 2 cups (c)

1 cup = 8 fluid ounces (fl oz)

Mass and Weight

1 ton (T) = 2,000 pounds (lb)

1 pound = 16 ounces (oz)

TIME

1 year (yr) = 365 days

1 year = 12 months (mo)

1 year = 52 weeks (wk)

1 week = 7 days

1 day = 24 hours (hr)

1 hour = 60 minutes (min)

1 minute = 60 seconds (s)

Formulas

Perimeter

Square $\qquad P = 4s$

Rectangle $\qquad P = 2\ell + 2w$ or
$P = 2(\ell + w)$

Polygon $\qquad P =$ sum of the lengths of the sides

Circumference

Circle $\qquad C = 2\pi r$ or $C = \pi d$